THE PASHTUN BORDERLAND

Since the Taliban returned to power in Afghanistan in 2021, the need to understand the group's history and ideology has only increased. Jan-Peter Hartung's timely study examines the phenomenon of the Taliban through a topographically, ethnically and geopolitically distinct space: the Pashtun Borderland of today's Afghanistan and Pakistan. Emphasizing the central role of Pashtun ethnicity, Hartung covers approximately 500 years of Pashtun history: from the early modern Mughal Empire to the first Durrani Empire in the eighteenth century and the regional developments during the colonial period in the nineteenth and early twentieth century. Drawing from a wealth of primary source materials in Pashto, Persian, Urdu and Arabic, Hartung moves the discussion of the Taliban beyond the immediacy of journalistic reportage and security-orientated studies, to a nuanced analysis of a wide range of actors and ideologies, refracting Afghanistan's present moment through the lens of its long cultural and religious history.

JAN-PETER HARTUNG has an MA in South and Central Asian Studies and Philosophy, a doctorate in the Study of Religions and a senior doctorate (Habilitation) in the Study of Islam. His special focus is on South Asia and the wider Persianate world from around the eighteenth century to the present.

THE PASHTUN BORDERLAND

A Religious and Cultural History of the Taliban

JAN-PETER HARTUNG

Friedrich-Alexander-Universität Erlangen-Nürnberg, Germany

CAMBRIDGE
UNIVERSITY PRESS

Shaftesbury Road, Cambridge CB2 8EA, United Kingdom

One Liberty Plaza, 20th Floor, New York, NY 10006, USA

477 Williamstown Road, Port Melbourne, VIC 3207, Australia

314–321, 3rd Floor, Plot 3, Splendor Forum, Jasola District Centre, New Delhi – 110025, India

103 Penang Road, #05–06/07, Visioncrest Commercial, Singapore 238467

Cambridge University Press is part of Cambridge University Press & Assessment, a department of the University of Cambridge.

We share the University's mission to contribute to society through the pursuit of education, learning and research at the highest international levels of excellence.

www.cambridge.org
Information on this title: www.cambridge.org/9781009289276

DOI: 10.1017/9781009289245

When citing this work, please include a reference to the DOI 10.1017/9781009289245

First published 2024

A catalogue record for this publication is available from the British Library.

A Cataloging-in-Publication data record for this book is available from the Library of Congress

ISBN 978-1-009-28927-6 Hardback

This publication is part of a project that has received funding from the European Research Council (ERC) under the European Union's Horizon 2020 research and innovation programme (Grant agreement No. 693457).

CONTENTS

MAPS AND FIGURES

ABBREVIATIONS

AIAḤC	*All-India Ahl-i Ḥadīs̱ Conference*
ANP	*Awami National Party*
ART	*al-Rashīd Trust*
ASṢ	*Anjuman-i Sipāh-i Ṣaḥābah* (Ḥaqq Navāz Jhangvī)
DIIA	*Dawlat-i Inqilāb-i Islāmī-yi Afghānistān* (Muḥammad Afẕal)
FATA	*Federally Administered Tribal Areas* (August 1947–May 2018)
FCR	*Frontier Crimes Regulation* (valid since 1901)
ḤII	*Ḥarakat-i Inqilāb-i Islāmī* (Muḥammad Nabī Muḥammadī)
ḤII[N]	*Ḥarakat-i Inqilāb-i Islāmī* (Naṣrallāh Manṣūr)
ḤiI-Ḥ	*Ḥizb-i Islāmī* (Gulbuddīn Ḥikmatyār faction)
ḤiI-Kh	*Ḥizb-i Islāmī* (Muḥammad Yūnus Khāliṣ faction)
ḤM	*Ḥizb al-Mujāhidīn* (Sayyid Ṣalāḥ al-Dīn)
ḤuM	*Ḥarakat al-Mujāhidīn* (Masʿūd Aẓhār)
ḤMDA	*Ḥizb-i Mutaraqqī-yi Dimūkrāt-i Afghānistān*
ḤVIA	*Ḥizb-i Vaḥdat-i Islāmī-yi Afghānistān* (ʿAbd al-ʿAlī Mazārī)
IEA	*Də Afghānistān Islāmī Imārat* (since October 1997)
IIAA	*Ittiḥād-i Islāmī Barā-yi Āzādī-yi Afghānistān* (ʿAbd Rabb al-Rasūl Sayyāf)
IIMA	*Ittiḥād-i Islāmī-yi Mujāhidīn-i Afghānistān* ("Seven-Parties Coalition")
IIUI	*International Islamic University of Islamabad*
IMFF	*Də Afghānistān Islāmī Taḥrīk Fidāʾī Maḥāẕ* (Manṣūr Dādallāh)
IMU	*Özbekiston Islomiy Harakatï* (Jumaboi Khodžaev / Tohir Yol'doshev)
IS	*al-Dawla al-Islāmiyya (fī'l-ʿIrāq wa'l-Shām)*
IUM	*Islamic University of Medina*
IJI	*Islāmī Jumhūrī Ittiḥād*
IJṬ	*Islāmī Jamʿiyyat-i Ṭalabah*
ISI	*Inter-Services Intelligence* Agency
JDN	*Jarayān-i Dimūkrātīk-i Navīn*
JDQS	*Jamāʿat al-Daʿwa ilá 'l-Qurʾān wa'l-Sunna* (Jamīl al-Raḥmān)
JIA	*Jamʿiyyat-i Islāmī-yi Afghānistān* (Burhān al-Dīn Rabbānī)
JiI	*Jamāʿat-i Islāmī*
JIM	*al-Jamāʿa al-Islāmiyya bi-Miṣr*
JITS[a]	*Jamāʿat-i Ishāʿat al-Tawḥīd va 'l-Sunnah* (Muḥammad Ṭāhir Panjpīrī)
JITS[b]	*Jamāʿat-i Ishāʿat al-Tawḥīd va 'l-Sunnah* (ʿInāyatallāh Shāh Bukhārī)

JMIA	*Junbish-i Millī-yi Islāmī-yi Afghānistān* (ʿAbd al-Rashīd Dūstam)
JNM	*Jabhat-i Najāt-i Millī* (Ṣibghatallāh Mujaddidī)
JQSQH	*Jamāʿat Qāʿidat al-Jihād fī Shibh al-Qārra al-Hindiyya*
JUH	*Jamʿiyyat al-ʿUlamāʾ-i Hind* (Ḥusayn Aḥmad Madanī et al.)
JUI	*Jamʿiyyat al-ʿUlamāʾ-i Islām* (Shabbīr Aḥmad ʿUs̱manī et al.)
JUI-F	*Jamʿiyyat al-ʿUlamāʾ-i Islām* (Faẕl al-Raḥmān faction)
JUI-S	*Jamʿiyyat al-ʿUlamāʾ-i Islām* (Samīʿ al-Ḥaqq Akōṛavī faction)
JUS	*Jamʿiyyat al-ʿUlamāʾ-i Sarḥadd* (ʿAbd al-Raḥīm Pōpalzay et al.)
KP	*Khyber Pakhtunkhwa*
LiṬ	*Lashkar-i Ṭayyibah* (Ḥāfiẓ Muḥammad Saʿīd)
LJh̄	*Lashkar-i Jh̄angvī*
MB	*Jamāʿat al-Ikhwān al-Muslimīn* (Society of the Muslim Brethren)
MʿUJM	*Manbaʿ al-ʿUlūm Jihādī Maḥāẕ* (Jalāl al-Dīn Ḥaqqānī; later IEA)
MKh	*Maktab al-Khidamāt al-Mujāhidīn al-ʿArab* (ʿAbdallāh ʿAzzām)
MMA	*Muttaḥidah Majlis-i ʿAmal*
MMIA	*Maḥāẕ-i Millī-yi Islāmī-yi Afghānistān* (Sayyid Aḥmad Gīlānī)
NJBS	*Naw-Javān Bh̄ārat Sabh̄ā* (Bh̄agat Siṅgh̄ et al.)
NWFP	*North-West Frontier Province* (1901–2010)
PATA	*Provincially Administered Tribal Areas* (August 1973–May 2018)
PDPA	*People's Democratic Party of Afghanistan*
PNA	*Pakistan National Assembly*
PSF	*Pakhtun Student Federation* (*Paxtūn Pohānō Ghūnḋ*)
PPP	*Pakistan People's Party* (Ẕ. ʿA. Bh̄uṫṫō et al.)
PTI	*Pākistān Taḥrīk-i Inṣāf* (ʿImrān Khān et al.)
RAI	*Rābiṭat al-ʿĀlam al-Islāmī* (Muslim World League, Mecca)
SJM	*Sāzmān-i Javānān-i Musalmān* (Ghulām Muḥammad Niyāzī)
SJT	*Sāzmān-i Javānān-i Taraqqī*
TBJM	*Tōrah Bōṛah Jihādī Maḥāẕ* (ḤiI-Kh, later IEA)
ṬIT	*Də Ṭālibānō Islāmī Taḥrīk* (1994–7)
TJ	*Tablīghī Jamāʿat*
TJP	*Taḥrīk-i Jaʿfariyyah-yi Pākistān* (Sayyid ʿĀrif Ḥusayn al-Ḥusaynī)
TNFJ	*Taḥrīk-i Nifāẕ-i Fiqh-i Jaʿfariyyah* (Muftī Jaʿfar Ḥusayn)
TNSM	*Taḥrīk-i Nifāẕ-i Sharīʿat-i Muḥammadī* (Ṣūfī Muḥammad)
TṬP	*Taḥrīk-i Ṭālibān-i Pākistān*

FOREWORD

Sometimes, it seems to take almost an entire academic lifetime to finally reach the point that triggered one's academic interest in the first instance. And while, for many of the *éminences grises* in the research on "Afghanistan", this country was inseparably linked with the individual, yet equally collective, effervescent experience of the overland trail to India and Nepal, my growing up behind the Iron Curtain exposed me to that country in quite a different way. I vividly remember the image of Babrak Kārmal (d. 1996) on the title sheet of *Neues Deutschland*, then the official newspaper of the *Socialist Unity Party* (SED), after he had been installed in Kabul as head of state at the behest of the leadership of the Communist Party of the Soviet Union, an act that was accompanied by the invasion of Afghanistan by Soviet military forces in December 1979. Even more clearly, I recall seeing footage of the first press conference of the government of the Islamic State of Afghanistan in April 1992 on television, where the posturing of the newly appointed office-holders appeared to me to already be exposing the illusory nature of the ostensible mutual agreement among them, something that would become ever more manifest during the almost simultaneously erupting civil war.

I visited war-ridden Afghanistan for the first time only two years later, spending some time in Herat and thereabouts. Here, I was surrounded by reports of the perpetually disintegrating situation in heavily contested Kabul and an increasing level of banditry and dacoity in large parts of central Afghanistan recounted by people who had fled from there to the safety that Herat provided at that time, as well as laudatory stories by locals of the wartime heroics of Muḥammad Ismāʿīl Khān (b. 1365/1946), then governor of Herat Province. Less than one year later, the guards at the southern end of the Termiz-Ḥayrātān border crossing turned me away, indicating that a permit by the representatives of the government of the Islamic State of Afghanistan was no good in the northern provinces: the large image of ʿAbd al-Rashīd Dūstam (b. 1373/1954) at the border post, that greeted everyone who entered the country from the north instead of one of then-President Burhān al-Dīn Rabbānī (assassinated 1432/2011), served only as a reminder of the fact that I had been wantonly complacent in assuming that I could navigate Afghanistan, even more so at such a point in time.

It was then, namely, that reports appeared in the international media of a new military force that went by the somewhat elusive name of "Taliban".

Apparently, this entity had set out from southern Afghanistan and contested seemingly successfully the government of the Islamic State of Afghanistan as well as its various adversaries, including Dūstam's *Junbish-i Millī-yi Islāmī-yi Afghānistān* (JMIA). When I probed officials at the Afghan Embassy in Tashkent for their assessment, they waved away even the need to take these "Taliban" into consideration as a serious factor in the delicate power constellations in Afghanistan at that moment. It seems that I was not alone in being complacent: twenty months later, "the Taliban" had taken Kabul; another eight months later, Dūstam was forced to temporarily flee to Uzbekistan and on to Turkey when they finally pushed their way also into Mazār-i Sharīf, where they would maintain a central government until December 2001.[1]

What followed were occasional and sensationalistic reports in the media of the Global North[2] on various excesses in the governance of what had meanwhile become the *Islamic Emirate of Afghanistan*, especially in the few large cities of Afghanistan, first and foremost Kabul. Yet, my own first-hand encounters of political propaganda during the first decades of my life had made me quite sensitive to all sorts of subtle and less refined attempts to influence public opinion for ends which, more often than not, remain unspoken. Additionally, under the same circumstances, I learned that Berlin had hardly ever been representative of the entire German Democratic Republic, which meant that one needs to look away from the metropoles in order to get a more balanced idea. Last but not least, the time I have spent in the Indo-Afghan region over the following decades has exposed me to ever higher levels of complexity and, thus, engendered a sense of humility in the face of the culturally different. As a result, I grew increasingly suspicious of all the scholarship produced in the academia of the Global North, which came across as a little too self-confident for my liking. This whole imbroglio gained ever more momentum when, on 11 September 2001, members of the *al-Qāʿida* organization attacked various targets on the East Coast of the USA that were of high symbolic value, and all the more so for an aspirant Islamicist.[3]

In the following years, I have, therefore, tried to attain an understanding of the inner logic of ideologically sustained Muslim socio-political activism, especially in South Asia, prominently including those developments that could hardly be

[1] For a breakdown of the events around the ascent to power of these Taliban, although spiked with anecdotal evidence and referenced in a nonchalant fashion, see Rashid (2010), 17–80 and 256–62.

[2] Rather than the commonly employed term "the West", and all its grammatical derivatives, the less essentialist notion of the "Global North" has been chosen to denote a hemisphere determined by socio-economic criteria: see Trefzer, Jackson, McKee and Dellinger (2014); Boatcă (2015).

[3] Despite perhaps a little unwieldiness, the popular label "9/11" for these particular *al-Qāʿida* attacks is, nonetheless, consistently avoided in this book, because the allusion to the US-American emergency phone number, of which the majority of users might not be fully aware, somewhat suggests that events in the USA are of global importance, while implying that events in other countries are obviously less significant.

understood through the hermeneutical prism of my own cultural socialization, which, in turn, made me also increasingly suspicious of the grand narrative of Modernity: is there really a singular privileged way to deal with the contingencies of life, or is the global impact of this grand narrative not rather the result of discursive practices, frequently emphasized further by the use of physical force? If this hypothesis carries any currency, then a way forward would surely be to investigate the discourse in historical depth and put the findings in conversation with alternative or counter-discursive narratives. This, in fact, is what I have attempted to do here, and the book in hand is a quite faithful status report of where I currently am on this path.

Without a large and diverse host of friends, colleagues, associates and students, I would not have been able to achieve even this. They are, in fact, so numerous that it is absolutely impossible to thank them all individually and I apologize beforehand to all those whom I cannot mention by name here, because their contributions have been as significant as any. Still, this book would have been impossible to write without the generous companionship of friends at the University of Peshawar over the years: Rauf, Altaf, Aamer, Sami, Ayub Jan, Anoosh, Wajid, Sajjad, Hassan Shah, Muhammad Tariq, Gulzar, … They all went far beyond what *melmah pālənah* might have compelled them to do.

My greatest academic debt, however, is to James Caron, who is much more to me than just a former colleague at the School of Oriental and African Studies (SOAS) of the University of London. Without his works and our many conversations, I would perhaps still be engaging more with the thought of socio-religious elites, rather than having begun to truly appreciate the ideas and actions of those whom Antonio Gramsci had alternately termed "organic intellectuals" (*intellettuali organici*), "embedded historians" (*storici integrali*) or "community writers" (*pensatori collettivi*).[4]

Finally, it is my pleasant duty to acknowledge that my affiliation with the European Research Council (ERC)-funded research project no. 693 457, Private Pieties, Mundane Islam and New Forms of Muslim Religiosity: Impact on Contemporary Social and Political Dynamics, at the Institute of Social Anthropology of the University of Göttingen, Germany (2016–22), has provided me with the means to conduct the bulk of the research that went into the present book and that the ERC shared the financial burden for the copy-editing of the final manuscript with my current academic home, the FAU Research Centre for Islam and Law in Europe (FAU EZIRE) of the University of Erlangen-Nuremberg. My last expression of gratitude goes to Jens Schönstedt (Erlangen) for his expert production of all the maps throughout this book.

4 See Gramsci (1977), II: 1 392 (*Quaderno XI*), III: 1 513 (*Quaderno XII: Appunti e note sparse per un gruppo di saggi sulla storia degli intellettuali*; 1932) and 2 283f. (*Quaderno XXV: Ai margini della storia*; 1934).

NOTE ON TRANSLITERATION, ET CETERA

Whenever multiple languages with their own respective conventions for transliteration need to be navigated, compromises have to be made. Regarding Arabic, Persian and Turkic languages, the American Library Association–Library of Congress (ALA–LC) Romanization tables have been followed throughout; for Urdu the respective table has been slightly modified to avoid possible conflicts with Arabic: the retroflex dentals ٹ / ټ and ڈ / ډ are given as ṫ and ḋ, and ں / ڼ as ṇ, while aspirates are signified by ħ. Also the transliteration of Pashto largely follows the recommendations of the ALA–LC standard; its vocalization, however, follows *The Pashto–English Dictionary* of Zeeya A. Pashtoon (Hyattsville, MD: Dunwoody Press, 2009). The spelling of Nuristani languages, finally, follows the conventions introduced by Richard F. Strand (2016).

For the convenience of the reader, terms lexicalized in English are spelled according to the Oxford English Dictionary (OED), although a single high reversed quotation mark (ʿ) has been added for the Arabic ع, and a closing single quote mark (ʾ) for ء. Similarly, lexicalized place names are spelled according to the OED, while a simplified form is used for others, with a properly transliterated spelling provided in brackets at their first occurrence. This procedure was also adopted for the names of ideational currents and their adherents, while those of distinct institutions and organizations are given in italics. Lastly, the names of major Pashtun tribal communities also follow this pattern; for the transliterations at first mention the spelling in "Syāl" Mōmand (1365sh/1986) has been adopted.

The numbering of *aḥādīth* follows the lauded edition of the *kutub sitta* by the Thesaurus Islamic Foundation, Vaduz, in collaboration with Dār al-Kutub, Cairo (2001).

The positions of locations shown in the maps are geometrically as accurate as possible; the sources on which they are based are duly listed. Still, academic honesty demands that one acknowledge the difficulties in ascertaining the precise course of shifting pre-modern frontiers over a substantial period of time. The image presented in Map 2.1 can therefore only be a rather static and woodcut-like approximation to the actual historial realities. More problematic still is the impression of clearly defined settlement areas of Pashtun tribal communities that is given in Map 2.2, all the more so as they appear to coincide with the administrative demarcations of provinces and their subdivisions in Afghanistan as well as in Pakistan. The image provided is therefore to be considered only a rough estimation of majorities, bearing in mind that there might even be substantial proportions of other communities residing there as well. Lastly, due to large-scale destruction of militant training camps by USA-led military forces in the region, exact locations could not be ascertained for all those that are shown in Map 4.3. Still, I wish to maintain that their geometrical positions are given as accurately as the available and duly listed materials would allow.

1

Introduction

On 15 August 2021, images of heavily armed bearded men behind and around a desk in the Citadel of Kabul were broadcast by media outlets all over the world. They were vividly illustrating the breaking news that the warriors of the *Islamic Emirate of Afghanistan* (*Də Afghānistān Islāmī Imārat*; henceforth IEA), colloquially known as "The Taliban", had taken the Afghan capital for the second time, while President Ashraf Ghanī (b. 1949), having precipitately fled his country to the safety of Tashkent, declared his resignation via Facebook. All of a sudden, it seemed, those who had confidently been declared defeated by a USA-led military invasion in late 2001 in reprisal for the infamous *al-Qāʿida* attacks on 11 September of that year were back in charge. Leading politicians in the Global North were simultaneously left the humiliating task of accounting for a whole decade of military engagement in Afghanistan that had caused over 46 000 civilian and more than 3 500 military casualties, with costs incurred amounting to around 840 billion US$ for the USA alone.[1]

Indeed, "The Taliban" had resurfaced to the attention of a wider international public only almost exactly one and a half years before their second takeover of Kabul, when the US-American top-diplomat Zalmay Khalīlzad and then-IEA negotiator ʿAbd al-Ghanī Barādar signed an "Agreement for Bringing Peace to Afghanistan" in front of a high-profile international audience in Qatar's capital Doha, an agreement that stipulated the gradual withdrawal of the US contingent of troops from Afghanistan. However, the fact that the armed forces of the IEA advanced across the entire country almost in synchronicity with the incremental withdrawal is clear evidence that their ultimate defeat in December 2001 had been little more but wishful thinking. In fact, all that "Operation Enduring Freedom" had ended was the first central government of the IEA, forcing its leadership council to relocate from Kandahar to Quetta, only some 120 miles away and just on the other side of the national borderline with Pakistan, but firmly controlling and effectively governing numerous pockets of Afghanistan, some of them less than 100 miles away from Kabul. Meanwhile, with the USA-led military invasion of Iraq in

[1] See, for example, SIGAR (2022), 44–6.

March 2003 under a similar pretext, the focus of media and, subsequently, public attention shifted there, putting Afghanistan back in its former place of rather marginal public and geopolitical interest. However, ending the thirty-five years of uninterrupted and increasingly oppressive rule of the *Arab Socialist Baʿth Party in Iraq* (*Ḥizb al-Baʿth al-ʿArabī al-Ishtirākī fi'l-ʿIrāq*) plunged the country subsequently into a bloody civil war that ultimately gave rise to *al-Dawla al-Islāmiyya* (*fi'l-ʿIrāq wa'l-Shām*) – often referred to by its Arabic acronym "DĀʿISH" (here, however, henceforth IS) – and its Islamic Caliphate in eastern Syria and north-western Iraq.

Under such circumstances, it seemed easy to forget about those who, under the leadership of the elusive Mullā Muḥammad ʿUmar ibn Ghulām Nabī (d. c. 1434/2013), had initially set out as the *Islamic Movement of the Taliban* (*Də Ṭālibānō Islāmī Taḥrīk*; ṬIT) and who, since October 1997, go formally by the name of its government, the IEA. Surprisingly, however, even the emergence of an IS chapter in the wider region of Afghanistan and adjacent territories, openly declaring itself in stark opposition to the IEA, did not prompt a significant revivification of serious academic investigations into the latter's religious and political underpinnings.[2] Still widely regarded as only one of many militant groups in and around Afghanistan, and, despite this, lacking sound legal foundations,[3] they were conveniently marked up as "unlawful combatants" and "insurgents" against the UN-approved governments of Afghanistan after 2001. Consequently, most scholarship devoted to them since then has belonged to the fields of geopolitics and security studies. As such, it has tacitly affirmed this label when considering "The Taliban", first and foremost, as a significant factor in security risk assessments for the national reconstruction programmes that the nation-states of the Global North were conducting in the aftermath of their military invasion of Afghanistan.[4]

Certainly, the sheer volume of widely noted publications on the matter carrying the word "Taliban" (with a capital initial) in their titles might lead us to assume that we are fairly well informed about what lies behind this label. Starting with investigative journalist Ahmed Rashid's best-selling and

[2] Green (2017), 26, names Nagamine (2015) and Hartung (2016a) as the only two more recent relevant studies on the ideological set-up of the IEA after 2001.

[3] Wolfrum and Philipp (2002), 578–86, demonstrate that this status, stipulated by International Humanitarian Law rooted in the Third Geneva Convention of 1949, is not straightforwardly applicable to a *de facto* political regime, regardless of whether or not it is recognized as such by the governments of other individual nations. Consequently, experts on international law have strongly questioned the legality of the endorsement of the combatant status by the Security Council of the UN in its Resolution 1373, adopted on 28 September 2001, which, in fact, served the US government as a mighty tool in its efforts to legitimize its course of action against the IEA: see Kirgis (2001).

[4] The lopsidedness of the current research landscape in this regard has been analysed in Hartung (2024), 21–7. In fact, the arguments presented there follow from the earlier epistemic criticisms of M. J. Hanifi (2011) and S. M. Hanifi (2016; 2018).

generally quite informative account of the political history of the ṬIT / IEA in 2000 (updated in 2008 and fully revised in 2010), such works range from the *Poetry of the Taliban* to *Decoding the New Taliban*, culminating in the more recent *Taliban Reader*.[5] After all, the textbook-like format of a reader on whatever topic insinuates that the contours of the object of study have been quite firmly established and that the gobbets selected for it are comprehensively representative.

Still, it is my contention here that this would actually be quite a fallacy, one that most probably contributed to the misinterpretation of the situation in Afghanistan in 2021 by so-called "experts" advising various governments in the Global North.[6] In fact, it shall be argued here that, although we know of certain names and public responsibilities within a particular military and governmental organization,[7] such data seem to fall seriously short of telling us more about those to whom the label "*taliban*" is attached either by themselves or from the outside, and what they represent in their distinct respective local contexts. In order to get closer to meaningful answers, we would be well advised to cast our view much wider, way beyond those cadres of the ṬIT / IEA of the past and present that we know by name and office. This, in fact, is what is attempted in this present book, and it is, therefore, reasonable to assume that what is understood as "*taliban*" here goes well beyond the confines of the ṬIT / IEA, and may perhaps not be what the esteemed reader might initially expect.

The "*Taliban*" of the Present Book

The first contention, therefore, is that the *taliban*, in this case deliberately with a lower-case initial letter and italics, have historically been more than the ṬIT-cum-IEA of the late twentieth and twenty-first centuries. The lion's share of publications on the subject, however, is focused explicitly and exclusively on this contemporary and organizational facet, which, in fact, is what security analysts and policymakers – a major target audience of these works – are predominantly interested in.[8] While those works are still valuable and

[5] See Giustozzi (2009); Strick van Linschoten and Kuehn (2012; 2018); also, for example, Schetter and Klusmann (2011).

[6] This matter is well illustrated by the official statement of the then-Foreign Minister of the Federal Republic of Germany, Heiko Maaß: see AA (2021).

[7] See, for example, Yunas (1998), II: 771–5; Rashid (2010), 250–5.

[8] The deep and highly problematic entanglement of academic studies on contemporary Afghanistan and, more pointedly still, those which involve empirical social research, and the military and wider security establishments, especially of the USA, is indeed a matter of serious concern. As careful investigations have unveiled, the at times naïve, at others, deliberately top-down, approach to land and people, going back to the 1960s, has seldom had such a direct and devastating political impact as in the case of Afghanistan: see M. J. Hanifi (2004; 2011); S. M. Hanifi (2016; 2018); Rzehak (2018). In fact, the invasion of the country by USA-led armed forces against the then-central rule of the ṬIT / IEA over

generally useful, they reveal a structural problem: most of the works that bear the term "Taliban" in their title, as well as those that focus on its regional ancillaries, such as the so-called "Ḥaqqānī Network",[9] are greatly lacking in historical depth. As a result, even the ṬIT / IEA has so far, by and large, been presented to us as a solitary group with a definite objective – political rule over Afghanistan and possibly also at least over some parts of Pakistan – bound together by a comprehensible command structure and a singular, distinct ideology.

In fact, all this has already been claimed by Rashid, and, to date, has not been challenged much, thus, equally impacting popular knowledge, political decision-making and academic perspectives. Not least because of its enormous ramifications, it is worth recalling what Rashid had to say on the issue of "The Taliban", or ṬIT / IEA, ideology: according to him, they 'did have an [i.e., a singular uniform] ideological base – *an extreme form of Deobandism*, which was being preached by Pakistani Islamic parties in Afghan refugee camps in Pakistan'.[10] While the role of what, for a number of reasons provided elsewhere, is here preferentially called "Deobandiyyat"[11] is certainly a factor to be taken into account, Rashid's own understanding of "Deobandism", which he presented briefly in the following paragraph, is helpful only to a very limited extent:

> Semi-educated mullahs who were far removed from the original reformist agenda of the Deobandi school [and whose] interpretation of Sharia was heavily influenced by Pashtunwali, the tribal code of the Pashtuns, while funds from Saudi Arabia to *madrassas* [sic] and parties which were sympathetic to the Wahabbi [sic] creed, as the Deobandis were, helped these *madrassas* [sic] turn out young militants who were deeply cynical of those who had fought the jihad against the Soviets.[12]

To reiterate the salient points here: "Deobandism", according to the above, is a conglomeration of an 'original reformist agenda' of the Deoband school and

Afghanistan after September 2001 has only intensified already prevalent tendencies to choose research areas and methodical approaches based on current geostrategic and security interests. Meanwhile, the focus on "the Taliban" so determined has been expanded to the IS in the region, with similar pitfalls regarding the scope, depth and direction of the analysis, as prominently represented by Giustozzi (2018).

9 See Brown and Rassler (2013). Especially because this label has almost instantly been welcomed in the circles of foreign policy and security advisers across the Global North (see, e.g., Giustozzi [2018], 22) and has consequently informed geostrategic and security policy discourse there, it will benefit from a less partial reassessment: see Section 4.3.

10 Rashid (2010), 88 (emphasis added).

11 See Hartung (2016b), 351 and 361.

12 Rashid (2010), 89f. At this point, we should only take note of Rashid's aligning of Deobandis with Wahhabi Islam, the official interpretation in the Kingdom of Saudi Arabia, because this conjecture will be subjected to careful reassessment subsequently in this book.

a Pashtun tribal code, which is financially, if not ideologically, tied to Saudi Arabia. "Deobandism" comes in variant degrees of radicality. The one that, for Rashid, represents "The Taliban", is inseparably tied to only one of those 'madrassas', situated in Pakistan's former North-West Frontier Province (NWFP, officially renamed Khyber-Pakhtunkhwa in 2010), and characterized as an 'extremist breakaway faction' of "the" Deobandi tradition, which Rashid problematically conflated here with the *Jamʿiyyat al-ʿUlamāʾ-i Islām* (JUI).[13] More precarious still is Rashid's rather elitist denigration of local religious functionaries as 'semi-educated'. In fact, it will be argued in the present study that it was exactly such dismissive top-down judgements that have contributed over the centuries to the emergence of strong sentiments of suspicion among Borderland inhabitants against imperial narratives and their underlying agendas, sentiments which more often than not were expressed in a violent fashion.

In fact, a quite similar point had already been made in an article on the ideology of "The Taliban" by Pulitzer laureate Anand Gopal and then-researcher Alex Strick van Linschoten[14] in 2017, although not explicitly directed against some derogatory sentiments towards subaltern religiosity and its practitioners.[15] In this important contribution, the two authors succeeded in redirecting our view from Rashid's earlier narrative on the ideological underpinnings of "The Taliban" to a much more complex one that pivots predominantly on subaltern culture in the rural setting of southern Afghanistan.[16] More importantly still, the two authors place their emphasis on the more informal study circles in the public houses (*ḥujrē*; sg. *ḥujrah*) of the southern Pashtun villages, in contrast to the fixation on a more formal religious education in a *madrasah*, as a formative feature in the *taliban* universe.

13 This imbalance of the image, in fact, points to a methodological problem that occurs more often than not in empirical research on contemporary religio-political dynamics in this region, especially where the information is based mainly on accounts of interlocutors and has not been correlated with other and perhaps less personal archives. In the case at hand, Rashid appears to have bought perhaps all too willingly into the institutional narrative of the leadership of the Deobandi JUI in Pakistan regarding their affiliation to the ṬIT / IEA.

14 According to his personal internet site, Strick van Linschoten appears to have left academia, at least for now, and joined the world of computer software development instead: see www.alexstrick.com/about-alex (accessed 20 April 2022).

15 In the present study, the concept of "subalternity", with all its various grammatical derivatives, is understood as developed by Sardinian Marxist Antonio Gramsci (d. 1937), although without its original ideological implications: as correlational to "dominance", it applies to – economically determined – social groups who are 'always subject to the activity of ruling [or directive social] groups [*gruppi sociale dominante e dirigente*; which, according to Gramsci, are those underpinning the state], even when they rebel or rise up: only "permanent" victory breaks their subordination, [though] not immediately' (Gramsci [1977], III: 2283, first insertion ibid., III: 1589). For an application of this concept to the contemporary Pashtun context, see Hartung (2022a).

16 See Gopal and Strick van Linschoten (2017), 9–15. In fact, the arguments presented in this article also challenge some of the views expressed not that long before by Semple (2014).

However, important as such contemporary observations undoubtedly are, they still call for at least two somewhat interrelated interventions. One is, once again, a lack of historical depth, the other, the fact that, here too, *taliban* are presented as a rather clear-cut entity, pivoting on the high command of the ṬIT / IEA, all of whom share the same regional background.

An interesting alternative is inherent in James Caron's critical remarks on the *Poetry of the Taliban*, a valuable edition of English translations of Pashto poems collected by Strick van Linschoten and his companion Felix Kuehn[17] during their three-year sojourn in Kandahar between 2006 and 2009, from where they were operating the then-nascent research and media-monitoring enterprise *AfghanWire*.[18] Unconvinced by the arguments presented to justify the portrayal of the poems as of ṬIT / IEA provenance, Caron, a profound expert on past and present Pashto literature, suggests viewing this collection more as one of subaltern poetic reflections of 'scattered provenance', dating from a specific period in Afghan history, the 1980s and 1990s.[19] However valid this assessment, the actual point which is intriguing to think further in this direction when considering "The Taliban" is another statement of Caron's in the same book review:

> Instead of documenting "The Taliban," it seems, many of these words simply resonated with individuals who interact with a piecemeal Taliban media infrastructure, and who decided to submit poems, whether their own or other people's, to a Taliban website, just as they might share something with a Facebook group.[20]

What this argument points to is that "*taliban*" frequently actually signifies something that goes well beyond the actual organization of the ṬIT / IEA with which the overwhelming bulk of works that carry the term in their respective titles are primarily concerned.[21] Instead, "*taliban*" appears to designate

[17] See Strick van Linschoten and Kuehn (2012; 2018).

[18] The archive from which these poems have been taken constitutes what the two authors, alongside Anand Gopal and in conjunction with London-based research and advisory firm Thesigers, keep advertising as their *Taliban Sources Project*, currently hosted by the Interdisciplinary Center for Innovative Theory and Empirics at Columbia University in New York (URL: http://incite.columbia.edu/taliban-sources-project; accessed 24 February 2024) and the Norwegian Defence Research Establishment FFI, in collaboration with the University of Oslo (URL: www.hf.uio.no/ikos/english/research/taliban-sources-repository; accessed 24 February 2024). The First Draft Publishing company (www.firstdraft-publishing.com), set up by Strick van Linschoten and Kuehn in 2014 in Berlin, whereby select items from their collection are published in English translation, is also related to this.

[19] Caron (2012b).

[20] Ibid. A similar point is suggested by Edwards (2017), 163–98, esp. 173–7 (section entitled "Talifans").

[21] *Editorial Note*: This is the rationale behind using the abbreviations ṬIT and IEA throughout for all those instances in which the focus is on the religious and political

a distinct discourse, shaped by widespread literary tropes[22] and selective historical references, all of which are prone to shift with time and space.

"Space", in turn, is a category of crucial importance for the case under review here, because it appears to be one, if not the, formative principle underlying the "*taliban* discourse": materially informed by a distinct topography and climate, it informed both the ethnically defined communal environs and the discursive practice of distinct geopolitical placement by larger imperial powers. Because such practices are ultimately tied to language regimes, such hegemonic actors commonly employ terms such as "tribal societies" to indicate territorially determined socio-political otherness and "frontier" to designate the geopolitical placement within the imperial imaginary, a fact that, consequently, will have to be looked at more closely in the conceptual considerations that make up the following chapter.

Now, because any discourse is highly contingent on ever-changing contexts, at times, the "*taliban* discourse" becomes manifest in organizational forms – the ṬIT / IEA and the slightly later *Taḥrīk-i Ṭālibān-i Pākistān* (TṬP) are just recent cases in point. At other times, however, "*taliban*" reflects rather a certain ethos carried by countless local actors with their individual stakes in it, who would unite in action for distinct and usually locally confined purposes, and would disintegrate again, only to form new temporary and purpose-bound entities, thus reflecting very much what in the present book shall be called "Borderland pragmatics".

Consequently, if we wish to understand the "*taliban* phenomenon" in such a broader and historically deeper manner – and we might be well advised to do so – we inevitably must depart from the trajectory of the current body of *taliban*-related research literature, including, by and large, all the studies named above, with their clear focus on the ṬIT / IEA as a matter of security analyses and geopolitical strategies. Instead, the present volume is inspired far more by the much earlier groundbreaking works of Asta Olesen and, if only to an certain extent, those of David B. Edwards on what he calls "Moral Fault Lines on the Afghan Frontier".[23] Both authors show that they are very conscious of the colourful fabric of texts of quite various provenance, as well as of the need for greater historical depth, and their writings thus allow one to understand the ideational background of the events and people which are at

organization of the late twentieth and early twenty-first centuries. The term "taliban", in turn, with a lower-case initial letter and italicized, is employed alternately for a distinct literary trope and as a label for an equally distinct discourse within the "Pashtun Borderland".

22 A vivid example of this would be the very popular love story of Ṭālib Jān and Gul Bashrah: see Nūrī (1387sh/2008); for contextualized analyses, see Caron (2012a); Hartung (2019a), 322f.; (2024), 31.

23 See Olesen (1995); Edwards (1996, 2002); albeit to a much lesser extent, Edwards (2017).

the core of most extant works on "The Taliban" – namely the ṬIT / IEA – from a much wider and deeper perspective.

Still, the angle taken in the present book differs from those of Olesen and Edwards in some significant regards. Olesen's expositions, for one thing, are entirely focused on the nation-state of Afghanistan, which appears, in itself, perfectly fair. The spatial reference in the present book, however, is owed to the acknowledgement that political borders are essentially discursive, as is demonstrated not least by the persistent refusal of successive Afghan governments to recognize the legality of the national border with Pakistan.[24]

Social anthropologist Edwards, in turn, remains confined to the more common methods of his discipline, which results almost inevitably in much less historical depth as well as the omission of a deeper engagement with indigenous literary production, especially that in Pashto.[25] The present book has attempted to close the gap in research that results from this, acknowledging that what one may call "Borderland literature" represents an important historical backdrop against which realities in the here and now are individually and collectively interpreted.

The work perhaps closest to what is attempted in this present work is that which Nile Green seems to have had in mind when quite recently putting together the edited volume *Afghanistan's Islam*.[26] Of course, as is the nature of an edited volume, argumentative coherence between the separate chapters written by different authors can be provided only to a certain degree, and obtaining such coherence remains obviously rather the prerogative of a monograph by a single author. And, while the same can be said regarding the spatial limitations of the content of Green's volume as in the case of Olesen above, the time frame "From Conversion to the Taliban" appears to be cast a little too wide to have sufficient analytical scope.

Already a decade earlier, Sana Haroon, one of the contributors to Green's volume, had, in her *Frontiers of Faith*, been following a somewhat similar idea. Yet, while highly relevant to the present study, there are two issues with this work that this research tries to redress: first of all, while the time frame of Green's volume seems a bit too ambitious, Haroon limited her investigation to the British colonial period, although with an outlook on the period between the early 1970s and the present in the epilogue.[27] This restriction of the period

[24] Right from the inception of Pakistan, Afghan governments have, with one exception, continued to dispute the validity of the national border established in 1893 by a series of treaties between the British Empire and the Emirate of Afghanistan: see Hayat Khan (2000), 185–96; Leake (2017), 120–236. This position was maintained well into the present: see Faizy (2017).

[25] For a comprehensive, although to my taste in a few instances a little too unforgiving, critique of Edwards' work in this regard, see Hanifi (2004).

[26] See Green (2017).

[27] See Haroon (2007), 197–216.

under investigation is reflected consistently in the body of textual references, which is dominated by colonial archives that, in turn, shape the author's own perspective of the period under study and of the actors and events therein. In addition, though, a larger stock of Urdu materials was employed, including, as recognized by Caron, 'well-known *tazkiras*, or biographical dictionaries, some containing primary material by the subjects themselves'.[28] Works in other relevant idioms, however, appear to have been used only sparsely.

In contrast, British colonial archives play a much more subordinate role in the present volume, and, where they do, it has been attempted to deconstruct them as constituents of imperial discursive formations. Very much the same effort is made with materials in the many other relevant languages, predominantly Pashto, Urdu and Farsi, owing to the above insight that both language and literature constitute powerful discursive tools, and that any proposition is directed by individual interests and transindividual paradigms.[29] Moreover, what is attempted in this book, both in contrast to and in conversation with core publications on the matter, such as those critically appraised above, is to analytically identify various threads of religious thought and practice that have emerged in response to particular socio-political circumstances, reaching way back in time, but have survived – sometimes only as faint traces – to impact the "*taliban* discourse". This discourse, in turn, emerges less as a set of the kind of fault lines that Edwards is interested in, but more as something like a braid, plaited from all these various threads of different volume and density, in a rather makeshift fashion. Moreover, it is argued here that these processes coincide with those of Pashtun ethnogenesis, mutually shaping each other well into the present, both within each of the communities concerned and across them, and strongly informed by wider geopolitical constellations.

Consequently, the present book contains two larger main sections. The first (Chapter 3) deals with the historical antecedents of the various ideational, or religious, threads that have informed the "*taliban* discourse". These threads are subsequently investigated in the second main section (Chapter 4). Regarding the first part, a *longue durée* perspective[30] has been adopted for the reconstruction of the diverse religious currents that shape the "*taliban* discourse" at the time when Pashtuns themselves had emerged as imperial competitors to their mighty neighbours to the east, west and north, developing their own imperial aspirations in the course of time. While initially buying into external imperial ascriptions of a homogeneous national identity to Pashtuns, this attitude,

28 Caron (2016b), 331 (italics in the original).

29 The understanding of "paradigm" here follows largely that of Kuhn (1962), insofar as it represents the convention within a certain epistemic framework that informs all practices within a given community by claiming universal validity. The significance of power to enforce such a claimed validity was ultimately highlighted only a few years later by Foucault (1966), 13, who used the term "épistémè" to mark this significant difference.

30 Braudel (1958), esp. 733f., was foundational for this approach.

which had formerly been the privilege of the larger political entities against which the Borderland residents positioned themselves – the Mughals, the Safavids and the Afsharids as their immediate successors, and the various Uzbek Khanates – was embraced by Pashtun Borderland communities themselves. The pivot of this development had been the polity established by the tribal confederation of the Durrani (*də Durrāniyānō ṫōlvākmanī*) in the middle of the eighteenth century, starting out in and around Kandahar, but soon making Kabul their capital, with the other few larger cities under their rule as important imperial nodes.

Yet, not every Pashto-speaking tribal community in the Durrani territories was content with being governed by a single dominant tribal confederation, especially not those in the mountainous areas further to the north and east. It will be argued that, in those places, a critical mass remained highly suspicious of any form of imperial outreach, a fact that made them highly receptive to all kinds of anti-imperialist activism brought to them from outside the Borderland, even more so if those forms of activism were sustained by religious precepts. In Sections 3.2 and 3.3, these historical developments are traced, up to the point when the British parted from their Indian crown colony, highlighting how these waves of originally external religio-political activism resulted in a continuous presence of their underlying ideas and personnel in the Pashtun Borderland. During the period of 150 years that brackets these developments, the inhabitants of the Borderland also had their first exposure to the nation-state ideology, and subsequently appropriated its arguments, leaving them in constant negotiation with the nation-states that Pashtuns found themselves in from the middle of the twentieth century.[31]

The events which unfolded in the early age of the nation-state heightened the tensions between the state's claim of a monopoly on all administrative matters within the now meticulously established and formally documented territorial confines. It consequently set, as will be argued here, the tone for those political and, moreover, ideational developments that would ultimately culminate in the various socio-political manifestations of the "*taliban* discourse" since the 1990s on either side of the intricate national borderline between Afghanistan and Pakistan.

Subsequently, in the second main part of the book (i.e., Chapter 4), four ideational currents at play in the later twentieth and twenty-first centuries are traced in a somewhat ideal-typical fashion. In reality, of course, they frequently overlapped in manifold ways, depending very much on the Borderland

[31] As such, Pashtun communities share a common fate with peoples in similar topographical and geopolitical constellations, for example, with Kurdish ones mainly located between the nation-states of Iran, Iraq, Turkey and Syria, Tyrolese ones between Austria and Italy, and Basque ones between France and Spain, to mention but a few. Indeed, an in-depth comparison would be worthwhile, as indicated, for instance, by Hartung (2017a).

pragmatics mentioned above, which, at times, commended collaboration between tendencies that were otherwise ideologically opposite, while, at others, the ideological divide appeared rather rigid, resulting in the respective advocates on either side standing somewhat apart from each other. Indeed, it is argued here that the world-view of the various socio-political manifestations of the "*taliban* discourse", including prominently the ṬIT / IEA, was strongly informed by sometimes even antagonistic positions on Islamic doctrine and practice, some of which have themselves emerged only from their creative interplay.

In this regard, "Salafism" and what is labelled here "Frontier Deobandiyyat" are the two ideational currents that stand out prominently. Yet, either one of them is the result of complex processes of intellectual cross-fertilization and an eventual synthesis of other, earlier, such threads: while "Salafism" represents the synthesis of "Salafi Islam" and "Islamism",[32] "Frontier Deobandiyyat" refers, first of all, to a distinctly local variety of the Sunni endeavours towards religious "reformulation"[33] associated with the *Dār al-ʿUlūm* seminary in northwest-Indian Deoband, but has, moreover, been burgeoning into a plethora of alternative and also conflicting interpretations, including explicitly militant ones. In keeping with the imaginary of a "*taliban* world-view" as a braid plaited from these currents, each one of them also represents an evolutionary step and is, therefore, investigated individually. Lastly, these analyses are rounded off by looking carefully into the dynamics of discourse caused by the emergence of what we may call "International Muslim Militancy" in the Pashtun Borderland, spearheaded by organizations such as *al-Qāʿida* in its various manifestations and, eventually, also the IS (Section 4.5). In contrast to a lot of the *al-Qāʿida*-centric literature, the focus here is much more on the rather ambiguous interactions of these various non-Pashtun outfits with the space-bound contemporary socio-political manifestations of the "*taliban* discourse", most prominently, although certainly not exclusively, the ṬIT / IEA and TṬP. Ultimately, the discussions of the separate ideational currents are brought together in the conclusion (Chapter 5), presented as the braid that makes up substantial parts, if not the entirety, of the world-view of "The Taliban".

***

32 For robust working definitions of each one of these academically and popularly contested categories, especially those that carry an "Ism", see the respective sections in the second part of the book.

33 This term, adopted from the title of the ESRC-funded research project "Islamic Reformulations: Belief, Violence, Governance" at the Institute of Arab and Islamic Studies, University of Exeter (2013–16, Principal Investigator Robert Gleave), is employed here and throughout the book, instead of "reform" and its derivatives, such as "reformation" and "reformism", all of which come with a rather heavy baggage of historical semantics.

From a *longue durée* vantage point, the pivotal argument made here is that the "*taliban* discourse" is very much informed by the topographical and geopolitical setting of the "Pashtun Borderland". This entity, of course, initially needs to be conceptualized, at least tentatively, in order for one to attach to it auxiliary conceptual terms, such as the already-mentioned "Borderland pragmatics". Moreover, this argument also accounts for the fact that, despite the division of the world along the lines of nation-states, we still have large communities, usually at the fringes of nation-state territories, which subscribe to such alternative forms of social and political organization that were regarded as somewhat primordial and archaic in the imperial narratives, which were increasingly informed by Enlightenment and post-Enlightenment ideas of civilizational progress. In the following, therefore, it is shown that a tribally structured society is by no means an anachronism, but rather a quite generic feature in the age of the nation-state, more often than not coinciding with particular topographies and geopolitical placement.

2

Setting the Stage: Conceptualizing the "Pashtun Borderland"

Admittedly, the region in focus here is rather difficult to hedge. If framed through political and cultural history, the notion of "borderland" makes sense only for certain historical periods; if one does so topographically, then the diversity of physical landscape prevents speaking of a coherent region. Even ethnically, the qualifier "Pashtun" suggests a homogeneity which, in empirical reality, does not exist, and has hardly ever existed. So, is the "Pashtun Borderland" perhaps an essentialism?

In view of these empirical incoherencies, it is useful to delineate a first limitation on the historical period for which the concept of "Pashtun Borderland" is applicable. Thus, in this book we are not much concerned with the fact that, between the fourth century BCE and the fifth century CE, the historical Gandhāra region covering largely the territory of our "Pashtun Borderland" was situated in the middle of successive larger imperial polities. It also played a key cultural role as an important cultural centre for the followers of the Buddha,[1] evidenced not least by the famous giant statues of the Buddha in Bamyān and the adjacent cave monasteries.[2] The formative period of the "borderland", therefore, must be assigned a later date, associated with the emergence of territorially confined and de facto independent polities under the suzerainty of the Islamic caliphate, ruled predominantly by former Turkic slaves (*ghilmān*) to Iranian proxies for the Abbasid Caliphate in Transoxiana. Increasingly, successive slave dynasties established themselves in Iran and the Indian subcontinent, with the vast stretches of land around the Hindu Kush mountains and the plains around the Arghandāb River becoming their ever-shifting frontier, or truce lines.[3]

1 For reasons of consistency, readers will see even otherwise widely used "Isms" (e.g., "Sufism", "Shiʿism" or, as in this case, "Buddhism") carefully avoided in the present book as long as they do not refer to their respective politically ideologized varieties. In the case in point here, the word choice is determined by the Pali term *buddhᵃ-dharm*, which translates literally as "the path of the Buddha": see Bruckmayr and Hartung (2020), 152 n.58; also Sections 4.2 and 4.4.

2 See Neelis (2011), 94–181 and 229–56.

3 See Golden (1992), 189–94 and 216–23. The exception to the above is the Timurid period between the late fourteenth and late fifteenth centuries, during which the territory in

2.1 Imperial Landscaping: From Frontier to Borderline

The "frontier" in all the cases mentioned above constituted an ill-defined strip of land, usually guarded on its outer limits by an uneven sequence of fortifications from where control of the surrounding area decreased concentrically, oftentimes aided by extreme physical features of the environment.[4] As such, the "frontier" is quite distinct from the "border" of later times, the one on which most research in the academic field of Borderland Studies is focused.[5] Only with the advent of the modern nation-state and its bureaucratic apparatus did territorial confines become meticulously defined, mapped and, wherever possible, demarcated by a "borderline", which is generally patrolled. Because of this substantial difference between pre-modern and modern conceptions of "border" and "borderland", it is suggested here that it is necessary to distinguish terminologically between "frontiers" and "borderlines": "border", in turn, appears too polysemic to be unequivocally applicable. The term "borderland", finally, covers the lands of the pre-modern frontier and the spaces around a borderline. Further qualification to make such a generic definition of "borderland" operational for specific empirical cases is required, and, in each case, must be derived from the respective factual specifics that, by definition, differ from each other in each instance.

In our case, the physicality of the Hindu Kush region and the adjacent deserts to the south has historically constituted a convenient natural barrier to hostile attacks on imperial power, aptly cast by the first Mughal ruler Bābur in his memoirs: 'The country of Kabul is a fastness hard for a foreign foe to make his way into,'[6] and may, therefore, serve us as a first *definiens* for the Pashtun Borderland. Control of the population living in such lands-in-between was difficult and likely to be regarded as not worth the effort: the people living there seemed too diverse, too different, too impetuous and resilient to external attempts of domesticating them as true subjects of any claimant of *imperium*.

question was again situated in the centre, although the seat of power was based in Samarkand, later Herat. Also, see Maps 2.1 and 2.2.

4 High-altitude mountain ranges have frequently served to determine frontiers, such as in the case of the Pyrenees (see Sahlins [1989], 238–66; Leizaola [2000], 36f.), the Tyrolese Alps (see Schober [1982], 59–124, 418–38 and 564–9), the Pamirs (see Kraudzun [2012]) or the various parts of the Himalayas (see the various contributions in Yü and Micheaud [2018]). Rivers also seem to have played a similar role, as the case of the end of the eastward and north-eastward expansion of the Macedonian Empire under Alexander the Great vividly illustrates, see Plutarch (1852–4), III: 346–8; for the river Rubicon as northern limits (*finis*) of Republican Rome, see Cicero (1830), VI: 2 813f. (*Phillipica VI*); and for the Taklamakan and Gobi deserts and the Greater Xīng'ān Range, respectively, which marked the western and northern limits of the Chinese empires of the Qín, Hàn, Míng and their successors, see Edmonds (1985), 36–40.

5 For prominent examples, see Diener and Hagen (2010; 2012); Dell'Agnese and Szary (2015); Brambilla (2015a; 2015b).

6 Bābur (1905), 130a (translation largely follows W. Thackston).

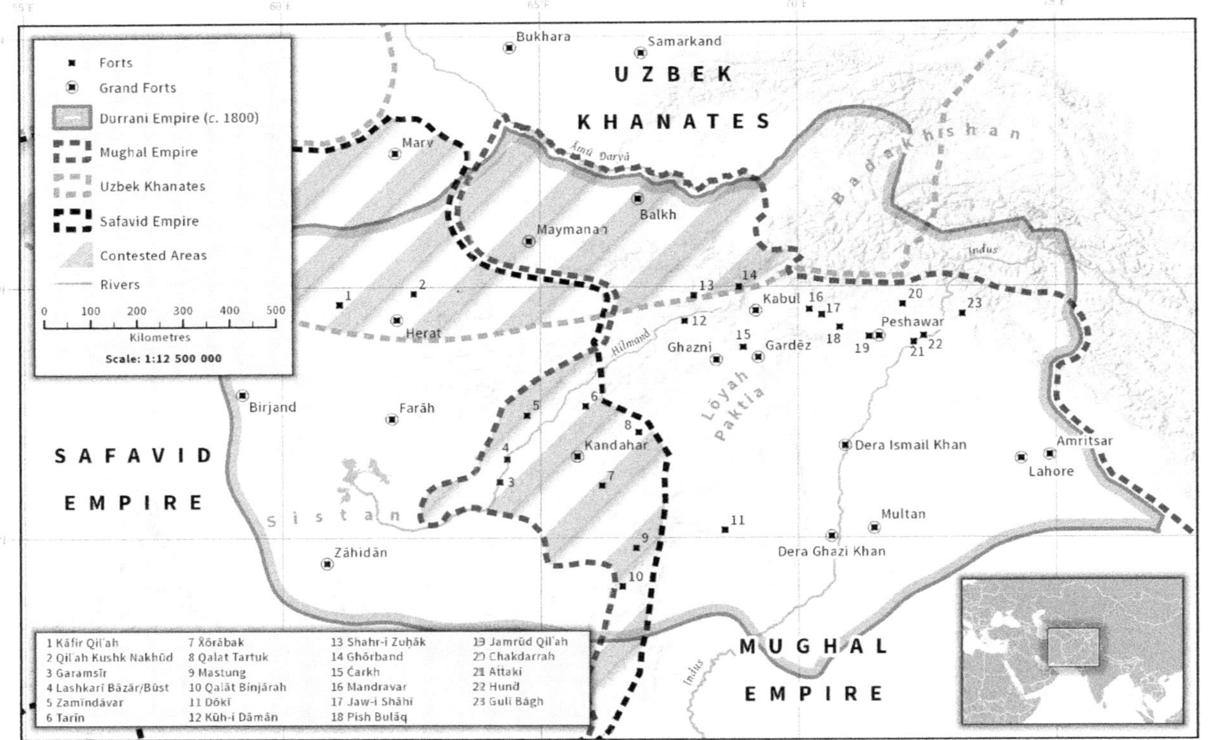

Map 2.1 Early-modern imperial boundaries in motion (c. seventeenth century).

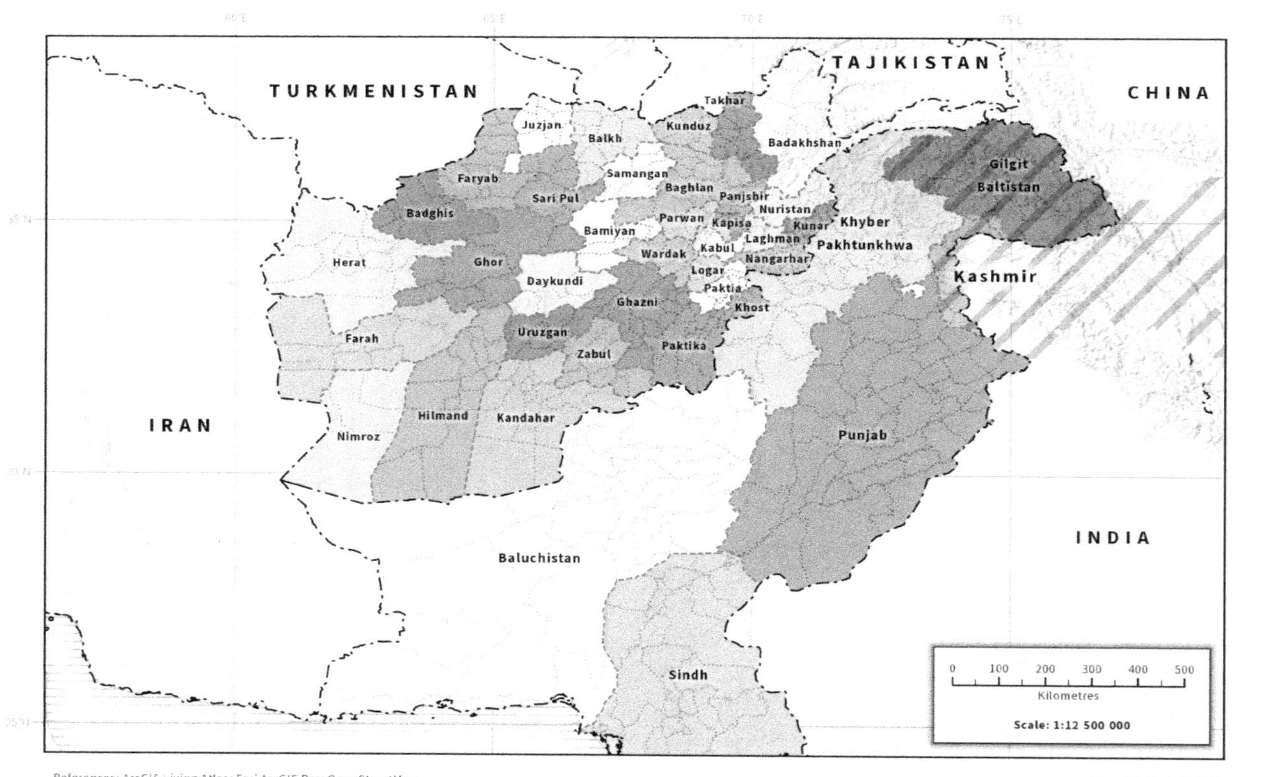

Map 2.2 The current administrative division of the Pashtun Borderland (2023).

Again, Bābur is a crown witness here when he stated that 'the Afghans between Kabul and Laghmān, even in times of peace [*amānlïqta*], are bandits and abettors of bandits [*duzd va duzd'afshār*]'.[7]

Consequently, in the lands of this particular frontier, the practice of denomadizing nomadic tribes, which played a crucial role in transforming the polities along sedentary lines since the days of "Aqsaq" Temür, the dreaded Tamerlane (r. 1330–1405), played a subordinate role at best. Where it still happened, tribal communities, especially from the plains, tried to elude the imperial grip by withdrawing to the upland of the ill-demarcated frontier region, driving out the local communities there themselves in the process. Still, the self-perceived cosmopolitan elites of the imperial courts had little interest in either welcoming such communities wholesomely into the folds of Persianate civility (*vaẓʿdārī*)[8] that, in their view, radiated from the royal courts, or even integrating them into the imperial structure, which, in the pre-modern period, is largely defined through the raising of revenue. Instead, local communities are employed as guardians of the frontier due to their intimate knowledge of the difficult environment, making mercenarism a major branch of the local economy in the course of time;[9] otherwise, they were predominantly left to themselves as long as they did not pose a security risk to the imperial domains.[10] As a result, social organization remained predominantly tribal, with the modes of life being principally between sedentariness and semi-sedentariness, in our case in point, with substantial nomadic and semi-nomadic communities. On the basis of this tribal element, expedient regulations of common interests, such as usage rights of pastures and forests or water rights, are established within each community.[11]

7 Ibid., 213b (translation largely follows W. Thackston).

8 For this term in the early-modern South Asian context, which is relevant for us here, see Naim (2011).

9 This has been the case in most frontier constellations: the County of Tyrol, for instance, was granted exclusive administrative rights by the Habsburg emperors in exchange for the Tyrolese defence of the southern border of the empire: see Schennach (2011); Forcher (2012), 56–61. Similarly, Kurdish communities were employed by the Ottomans to guard the eastern frontier of their empire: see van Bruinessen (1992), 152–61 and 185–9; Ateş (2015), 1–28; and Cossacks were granted a vast degree of autonomy by Czar Peter I (r. 1682–1725) in exchange for their services as defenders of the southern limits of the Russian Empire: see Boeck (2009).

10 A case in point here is that of the tribal confederation of the Yusufzay (*Yūsufzay*) Pashtuns, who had been forced to migrate from the southern plains to the mountainous regions of the Swat Valley and adjacent areas. From here, they resisted the adoption of the Mughal imperial framework to such an extent that Mughal *pādishāh* Akbar (r. 1556–1605) found himself compelled to repeatedly send out punitive expeditions, although with rather limited success: see, for example, ʿAllāmī (1877–86), III: 474–9, 481–6, 525f., 559 and 625f.

11 See Dupree (1973), 132–247; Nichols (2001), 15–21; compare van Bruinessen (1992), 50–132, for the Kurdish case; Forcher (2012), 32f., for the Tyrolese one.

By the mid 1500s, to a large extent, the bureaucratic estate of the vastly expanded Mughal Empire saw itself confronted with the security requirement of bringing some order into the thicket of the ethnic and cultural diversity within its dominion – ideologically framed and oftentimes romantically transfigured as "perpetual peace" (*ṣulḥ-i kull*)[12] – and began, subsequently, with ethnic profiling that also included the people(s) residing in the borderland.[13] About two centuries later, the Safavids, the main rivals of the Mughals to the west, pursued a less subtle and illusive course and tried to attain by the use of force a religious homogenization of their realm, including the southern plains of what began to evolve as the "Pashtun Borderland".[14]

Such imperial practices of policy enforcement triggered processes of ethnic, including religious, self-affirmation, gradually leading from the identification of tribal units, with their distinct agnatic pedigree and a certain territory claimed by them, to the formation of a streamlined ethnicity based on linguistic criteria and an overarching narrative of common descent, at the end of which stood a somewhat distinct Pashtun ethnic identity. However, below this ideological varnish, be it imperially ordained or devised by tribal elites, local descent- and territory-based identities strongly prevailed, and local idioms remained vastly different.

***

Let us pause here for a brief moment of reflection. What we have so far is the emergence of a certain territory wedged in between multiple and perpetually changing imperial claims, and a population that began to increasingly position itself vis-à-vis conflicting imperial ideologies. Indeed, this complex tension is regarded here as the first general feature of a borderland when framed in terms of geopolitics. The flexibility resulting from being accustomed to communal self-regulation in a difficult-to-navigate physical environment, symptomatically

[12] Ali (1980), 329–31, considers "ṣulḥ-i kull" the central ideological principle of domestic politics applied by Akbar and his immediate successor Jahāngīr (r. 1605–27), which found an organizational expression in the *silsilat-i irādah*, an exclusive religious circle of courtiers of various religious backgrounds, with the *pādishāh* as its spiritual pivot (see ʿAllāmī [1872–7], I: 160). Akbar's much trusted court physician Abū 'l-Fatḥ Gīlānī (d. 1018/1609), however, suggests more strategic considerations behind *ṣulḥ-i kull*, when he defines it as 'accommodating oneself to people, good or bad, and regarding oneself, with all of one's defects, as a necessary part of this world' (Gīlānī [1968], 150). Meanwhile, Jahāngīr (1359sh/1980), 36, stressed that his father highly recommended that he uphold 'this principle' (*īn maʿná*), whereas his own successor Shāh'jahān (r. 1628–58) no longer abided by this policy.

[13] See Section 3.1.1.

[14] One, if not *the*, major promoter of these attempts by the later Safavids to convert the Sunni Muslims within their realm to Imāmī Shiʿi Islam was the celebrated then-head of the Safavid clerical estate (*mullā bāshī*) Muḥammad Bāqir al-Majlisī (d. 1111/1699): see Arjomand (1981), 33; Foran (1992), 293f.

expressed in the "formally informal" ways of conflict resolution on a case-to-case basis in a perpetually changing assembly of usually male community representatives agreeable to all the conflicting parties,[15] stands in opposition to the imperial aspiration for stability of a much larger political entity with a, therefore, much less homogeneous population. "Stability", in turn, is a highly charged ideological term, going hand in hand with the equally ideological concept of "order" as the basis for political organization. "Order", finally, demands the power of "coercion", to be used as a last resort against those who threaten it, which, in turn, requires some kind of conceptualization of "disturbance", "threat" and the like.[16] To this end, imperial powers employ administrative measures, including the codification of rules and regulations as "law", which – and here we come full circle – promotes the myth of continuous stability of the "order".

The imperial notions of "stability" and "durability" are defied by the inhabitants at the frontiers of imperial territories, who have their own alternative and quite flexible mechanisms of managing communal affairs, and consequently perceive such notions as constituting a merely ideologically grounded imaginary. This, in turn, is already a sufficient reason to cast these communities as the unruly "Other" within the imperial ideological framework, subsequently presenting them as some kind of bogeyman to the other subjects under rule as well as providing a convenient pretext for exercising coercion against them whenever doing so would be seen as beneficial for the heads of the imperial estate.

Imperialist statecraft, however, was not exclusively based on either a *laissez-faire* attitude or the coercive subjugation of all subjects within a dominion to "the law". The Mughals, for one, strategically prudent under the ideological pretext of "perpetual peace" (*ṣulḥ-i kull*), attempted to lure the leading representatives of the various local status groups into what turned out to have really been only an illusion of participation, under the pretext of full toleration of differences in norms and values that are more often than not carried by religious beliefs and practices, all for the sake of achieving as much internal stability as possible.[17] Temporary rewards for loyalty, however, were never confined solely to existing

[15] This is expressed in Pashtun tribal communities in the institution of *jirgah*, an ad hoc council of almost exclusively male community elders agreeable to all conflicting parties that aims at arbitration for the sake of maintaining community cohesion: see, for example, ʿAṭāyī (1357sh), 73–6; Wardak (2002).

[16] See Thomä (2016), 32 and 56f.

[17] That the imperial policy of *ṣulḥ-i kull* was devised primarily as a strategic tool for the maintenance of internal stability and security, and not, as is often romantically transfigured, an indication of the tolerance of the Mughals for religious differences in their dominion is graphically illustrated by the execution of Gurū Arjun Dēv, the sixth *gurū* of the Sikhs, by order of Jahāngīr in the first year of his reign (1605 CE). Although Arjun Dēv was executed on the pretext of treason for allegedly submitting himself to Jahāngīr's rebellious son Khusraw Mīrzā (d. 1031/1622), the passage in his memoirs in which the

local elites; in fact, the creation of new ones by such means was most helpful in breaking up prevalent local power structures and establishing a greater degree of imperial control through loyal beneficiaries. Indeed, this resembles less the *divide et impera* approach of the ancient Romans and rather more one that we may call *restructure et impera*. In order to succeed, the imperial apparatus required information on the social, economic and political structures in the communities under its dominion: imperial historiographies that claim authoritative force are, therefore, an inevitable part of the political project to bring these communities under imperial control as much as is required for the safety and stability of the polity by exploiting and manipulating their socio-political particularities, be they real or imagined.

Thus, the Mughal rulers gained information on the existing tribes and their various relationships, intelligence that could be well employed for their own ends. A prominent case in point, especially because of his ambivalence, is certainly the celebrated tribal elder and renowned Pashto poet Khūshḥāl Khān Khaṫṫak (d. 1100/1689): taking advantage of the rather recent intertribal rivalries between Khattak (*Khaṫṫak*) and Yusufzay,[18] the Mughals co-opted Khūshḥāl's father, Malik Akōṛ Khān, and later Khūshḥāl himself, through their sophisticated reward system and had, thus, won a mighty ally to further their imperial aspirations in the Pashtun Borderland.[19] According to Ẓafar Kākā Khēl, the Khattak had until then been a rather insignificant tribe;[20] the

monarch gave an assessment of Arjun Dēv is indicative of *ṣulḥ-i kull* having been little more than a politically convenient smokescreen (Jahāngīr [1359sh/1980], 42):

> In Gobindwal [. . .] there was a Hindu named Arjun, in the attire of a Sufi [*dar libās-i pīrī va shaykhī*], so much so that, by his ways, he had not only captured many of the simple-hearted of the Hindus, but even of the ignorant and foolish followers of Islam [*nādān* (sic) *va safīhān-i islām*], and they had loudly sounded the drum of his sainthood [*pīrī va valāyat*]. They called him "Gurū", and from all sides stupid people [*kūlān*] crowded and manifested complete faith in him. For three or four generations [of spiritual successors] they had kept this shop warm. Many times it occurred to me to close down this shop, to either finish this fabrication [*sākht*] or to bring him into the assembly of the people of Islam.

18 See the imperial stocktaking in ʿAllāmī (1872–7), I: 585f., 591 and 593, and indications of the imperial politics towards the Yusufzay in ʿAllāmī (1877–86), I: 92 and III: 474–626. For the instigation of the intertribal rivalries between Khattak and Yusufzay, see Yūsufī (1960), 267–9; Kākā Khēl (1986), 235–8.

Editorial note: For the sake of convenience, it has been decided not to discriminate between the grammatical singular and plural in the spelling of the names of Pashtun tribal configurations that indicate descent from an eponymous ancestor by adding the Pashto word "zay" (descendant). The respective designations will invariably be given in their singular form throughout this work.

19 Khān Khaṫṫak (2001), 11: 'My own truth, I say, is that / I have been faithful and loyal to the Mughals' (*kih lah khpalah ḥaqīqatah dar tah vāyim / zah źāyay yam də mughal namak ḥalāl*). See also Kākā Khēl (1965), 759f.

20 Kākā Khēl (1965), 697–9.

Mughal interference did, thus, alter the socio-political dynamics in the region in their geostrategic favour. Indeed, tribal and clan rivalries, a most common feature of such organized societies, indicate a second line of conflict and tension, this time, however, not between an imperial centre and the borderland areas of its dominion, but within the wider Pashtun Borderland itself.

2.2 Lines of Conflict Criss-Crossing the Borderland

While the main drivers are certainly what, in the Indo-Afghan region, is popularly cast as the three "z": *zan* (woman), *zar* (gold) and *zamīn* (land), in other words, economical gains and the enhancement of one's own social status, tribal groups keep discriminating themselves from each other on the basis of each other's foundational genealogy, which is usually reflected in personal names, assigning superiority and inferiority according to skin complexion, and so on. After the establishment of the Pashto language as a common denominator in most communities in the Pashtun Borderland, the various dialects became a marker of distinction between superiority and inferiority of respective tribal communities. Last, but certainly not least, regionality has played an important part, one, in fact, that will concern us repeatedly in the chapters below in the topographical binary of "highland" and "lowland". It is, of course, largely impossible to draw an exact line here, thus, every reference to this conceptual pair is necessarily only an approximation, which, however, can be ruthlessly employed by Borderland residents with polemical intent. The "highland" covers roughly the eastern ranges of the Hindu Kush as far to the west as the Kabul Valley and, to the east, as far as the upper Kashmir Valley and the Indus river. The "lowland", in turn, covers the large arid southern areas from the Hilmand Valley and the Sistan Basin in the west, and to the east again as far as the Indus river. The division along the latitude is more difficult: while the city of Dera Ismail Khan (*Ḋērah Ismāʿīl Khān*) usually serves as a marker for the lowland–highland divide in the eastern parts, in the west, it would be the southern limits of the culturally quite homogeneous Greater Paktia region, and further west still, the northern extent of the Rīgistān desert and the Dasht-i Mārgū / Dasht-i Khāsh, respectively.[21] Urban centres representative of the highland are Kabul and Peshawar, both situated on the Kābul River, and of the lowland, Dera Ismail Khan on the western banks of the Indus, Kandahar on the Arghandāb and Lashkar'gāh on the Hilmand River.

The physical conditions in the two regions are indeed quite distinct, especially if one ignores the vast transitional area in between, and they have subsequently led to rather distinct economies, socio-political configurations and cultural frameworks. The very moment, however, that Aḥmad Khān ibn Muḥammad Zamān Khān Sadōzay, or Pōpalzay (d. 1182/1773), leader of the

[21] See Map 2.1.

southern Abdālī tribe, had himself crowned "Aḥmad Shāh Durrānī" in 1747 and, from his capital Kandahar, established an empire that comprised, among others, almost the entire Pashtun Borderland, and paternalistically claimed suzerainty over all "Afghans", the so-far physical divide between highland and lowland became a line that separated conflicting hegemonic claims. While, at a glance, all this seems to be of rather little relevance for the matter at the core of this book, we will discover that the conflict between competing claims for cultural and, subsequently, political superiority flared up perpetually all the way into the present and, thus, also shaped what is called here the "*taliban* discourse".

Religiosity, as we will see, served repeatedly as a benchmark criterion for sustaining hegemonic claims, as well as counterclaims, a fact that results in the growth of religious polemics, alongside normative treatises regarding the nature of proper religiosity and how it is to be made manifest. Moreover, a religiosity measured against a normative benchmark appears to have always been a powerful motivator for all sorts of socio-political resistance, including its armed variety. With the passing of time, and the aggravation of the conflict between imperial and communally confined aspirations for power in the era of the nation-state, religiosity developed into an ever stronger argument to activate resistance to imperial claims.

The conflict between the imperial aspirations of the Mughal ruler, Akbar, and those of the Rawshaniyyah, a subaltern socio-religious movement in the Pashtun Borderland around the "Pīr Rōx̌ān" Bāyazīd ibn ʿAbdallāh Anṣārī (d. c. 993/1573), who had staged a general and Islamically sustained rebellion from the Barakī, or Ōrmuṛ, territories of South Waziristan in and around the town of Kānīgūram, will serve as an illustration of the importance of religiosity in negotiating conflicting power claims for the pre-modern context – we will have to turn to the modern one in a dedicated section. Initially, the Mughals employed their freshly elevated local proxies to crush the Rawshaniyyah, but, in addition, Akbar had also commissioned his court chroniclers to construct and disseminate an image of the Rawshanis – the followers of the Pīr Rōx̌ān – as religiously highly questionable.[22] This imperial image of a heretical group that, because of its misguided religious persuasion, rebelled against the

[22] The most prominent and influential pejorative appraisal of the Rawshaniyyah was that of Badāʾunī (2001), II: 241–3, from whose writing distinct phrases were adopted verbatim by Haravī (1911–35), II: 398, for example. Badāʾunī's polemics, however, including the mock epithet "Pīr of Darkness" (*pīr-i tārīk*) for the Pīr Rōx̌ān, were preceded just a little by Darvīzah (n.d.), 31f.; (1885), 155f., although there is the so far still uncorroborated claim that the label was actually coined a little earlier by Ḥājjī Muḥammad "Zangī Pāpīnī", one of the spiritual guides of the Ākhūnd Darvīzah ibn Gadā Nangarhārī (d. 1048/1638), see Qāsimī (1967), 63. On Zangī Pāpīnī, hardly any further information could be located; the only contemporaneous reference appears to be the passing remark by Darvīzah (n.d.), 123f.

imperial order in a marginal space of the empire served as a justification to take active countermeasures;[23] the same image was revived even in later times – now as a polemical label – to sustain the persecution of adherents to certain beliefs and practices.[24]

On the other hand, Akbar and his own religiosity were looked upon quite contemptuously on account of its distance from the language and precepts of the Islamic *shari'a*. A highly important bearer of this was the eminent Naqshbandi Sufi *shaykh* Aḥmad Fārūqī Sirhindī (d. 1034/1624), who had already been honoured during his lifetime with the epithet "Renewer [of the Religious Standard] of the Second [Islamic] Millennium" (*mujaddid-i alf-i s̱ānī*).[25] Therefore, the Naqshbandiyyah-Mujaddidiyyah, the branch of the Naqshbandiyyah leading off from Sirhindī, would, not by accident, emerge in the Pashtun Borderland and beyond as a major reservoir for criticism of religious beliefs and practices in general, and of ruling elites in particular, even leaning towards armed enforcement of a rather conservative interpretation of the Islamic *shari'a*.[26] Conversely, however, we need to acknowledge

[23] Although this negative image eventually emerged, ʿAlī Muḥammad Mukhliṣ (d. unknown), nephew of an important *khalīfah* of the Pīr Rōx̌ān, suggests in his admittedly partial hagiography that Akbar had initially been positively inclined towards the Pīr Rōx̌ān and even wished to become his disciple: see Shinvārī (1388sh/2009), 344. If this narrative does indeed correspond to the historical events (which are not corroborated in any of the standard Mughal chronicles), then Akbar may still have seen in the Pīr Rōx̌ān a counterweight to the rebellious Yusufzay in the Pashtun Borderland. Be that as it may, these sympathies soon faded away when overzealous tribal followers of the millenarian teachings of the Pīr Rōx̌ān tried to hasten the advent of the Last Days by attacking an imperial caravan on its way to Kabul, and prompted severe punitive measures: see Shinvārī (1388sh/2009), 346–53. From there it was only a small step to the embrace of the heresiographical image created by the Ākhūnd Darvīzah and others in the orbit of his spiritual guide, the "Pīr Bābā" Sayyid ʿAlī Tirmiẕī (d. 991/1583), moreover, since the arguments presented by them provided a convenient rationale for the Mughals to subjugate the Rawshaniyyah. For illustration, see, for example, the narration of the persecution of Aḥdād ibn ʿUmar (killed 1035/1626), a grand-nephew of Bāyazīd Anṣārī and fourth leader of the movement, by Jahāngīr (1359sh/1980), 113f., 149f. and 174f. Perhaps the most comprehensive official Mughal account of the Rawshaniyyah is the eighteenth-century *Maʾās̱ir al-Umarā* of Navvāb Mīr ʿAbd al-Razzāq "Ṣamṣām al-Dawlah Shāh Navāz Khān" Awrangābādī (killed 1171/1758), which proves the solidification of the imaginary prominently created by the Ākhūnd Darvīzah, see Navāz Khān (1888–96), II: 241–8.

[24] Navāz Khān (1888–96), II: 248–50 (on Allāh'dād ibn Jalāl al-Dīn Anṣārī [d. 1038/1648], the later "Rashīd Khān" in the service of *pādishāh* Shāh'jahān, who 'in most habits and manners [*dar aks̱ar-i ʿādāt va awẓāʿ*] resembled the people of Persia', i.e., he had been well assimilated by the Persianate culture at the Mughal court).

[25] See Sirhindī (1397/1977), III: 467–9 (no. 88); ʿAlī (1894), 110; Friedmann (1971), 26–9. According to the quite compelling discussion by ter Haar (1992), 145–60, however, the matter of who was the first to use the epithet and when might actually be much more complex than so far acknowledged.

[26] See Chapter 3.

that, as long as these elites were in line with this and expressed their piety in public, leading representatives of the Naqshbandiyyah-Mujaddidiyyah would also accept courtly patronage and extend spiritual support to them in return.[27]

The imperial strategy of striving to tie local elites to a far-away seat of political and administrative power by bestowing privileges has also had an irreversible impact on the entire social fabric of the Borderland communities. In a society 'where status, be it social, tribal, political or other, is always present, even in patterns of discourse',[28] the creation of new status elites results inevitably in shifts in loyalty by those of lesser significance, in the hope of gleaning some of the eminence of the new elite, that is, of enhancing their own status by association. In fact, the creation of imperial proxies in local communities indicates a third line of potential conflict, in addition to those already mentioned that run between empire and tribes and between rivalling tribes. This third line, while strongly shaped by geopolitical constellations, plays out solely in the local community, impacting its socio-economic, political and, eventually, also religious and wider cultural constitution. What is referred to here is the deepening gap between socio-economic and political elites (*məshərān*) and those who have neither sufficient material nor social capital (*kəshərān*).[29] Among the latter in the Pashtun tribal society are females in general, who are regarded more as property that can also be traded or destroyed,[30] economically disadvantaged men, usually those who do not own land and are, therefore, forced to work the land of those who possess it, and also – if only to a limited extent – male unmarried youths. True, some of them would eventually inherit their fathers' estates and sometimes also socio-political positions, but, for as long as they remain unmarried and have not yet set up a household of their own, they continue to be fully dependent on the grace of their fathers and elder male relatives and are not given any independent choice.

It seems that distinct, though ideal-typical, notions of ethics apply to either group of Pashtun Borderland actors, discursively filtered through two – again ideal-typically – distinct forms of religious disposition, which are, nonetheless, both rooted in the specific regional and ethnic context of the Pashtun Borderland and can, thus, both serve as motivators for resistance to imperial claims of power. The *məshərān* follow what has been called "*khān*-ethics", a rather worldly morality that pivots on the individual maximizing of power

[27] See Edwards (1993); Ziad (2017), 227–85.

[28] Grima (2005), 15. "Discourse" seems to be understood here less in the strict Foucauldian sense than as a general synonym for "speech" on a certain subject matter.

[29] The Pashto binary *məshər–kəshər* seems to correspond, by and large, to the Indo-Persian and Urdu *ashrāf* (nobles)–*ajlāf* (ignoble), which, scholars claim, has been derived from the ancient Indian system of social stratification, commonly called the "caste system" (Sanskrit: *varṇāśramadharma*). For the former, see Ahmed (1980), 141–9; for the latter, see Ahmad (1966); Dumont (1966), 260–9.

[30] See Tapper (1991); Khan (2012).

and status. This, in turn, requires a great deal of flexibility in negotiating everyday affairs, which is referred to here as "Borderland pragmatics". Khūshḥāl Khān Khaṫṫak can serve here again as a paradigmatic example: at one time 'faithful and loyal to the Mughals',[31] at another, the ardent champion of Pashtun self-determination against the Mughals, his poetry is that of a nobleman at ease with the conventions of intricate Persianate eloquence, reflecting on falconry, the courting of women and other qualities associated with a noble warrior.[32] The *məshərān*'s habituation to the taste of political and economic power and related social status also translated into a kind of religiosity that highlighted rather mundane qualities, such as honour, manliness, and boldness to the extent of aggression, which were traditionally accepted within the wider community as a means to enhance and preserve individual socio-political status.

Such qualities are highlighted in their religious interpretation, as is reflected, for instance, in poetic imaginaries of the Prophet Muḥammad by representatives of the tribal elite: Muḥammad the warrior, Muḥammad the statesman or Muḥammad the community leader.[33] Max Weber devised the concept of "governance-orientated religiosity" for such a religious disposition, juxtaposing it with a "guidance-orientated religiosity",[34] and both, again ideal-typical, concepts will play a prominent role in the chapters to come, because they have proven useful in relating religious perspectives to socio-economic and political realities in what is framed here as the Pashtun Borderland.

Indeed, a guidance-orientated religiosity, pivoting greatly on eschatological themes, is a prominent expression of a "subaltern ethics" of justice and equity (*ʿadl aw inṣāf*). In fact, it is alleged here that "subaltern ethics" reflects the mundane side of the coin, one that expresses 'the composite culture of resistance to and acceptance of domination and hierarchy',[35] while guidance-orientated religious disposition emphasizes otherworldly transcendence.

However, while the two sets of ethics and associated religious dispositions are far apart analytically, in application, they actually show a tendency to

[31] See above, n.19.

[32] See, for example, his *Bāz'nāmah*, in Khān Khaṫṫak (2001), 974–1 016; or his numerous *qaṣā'id* on themes of warfare, political constellations and the qualities expected in a nobleman, in ibid., 4–105; even more so in Khān Khaṫṫak (1345sh), 92–129.

[33] See Hartung (2022a).

[34] See Weber (1972), 267f. and 355–9. For the meaningful practical application of this analytical binary, see Mukarram (1992); Hartung (2004), 123–5; Bruckmayr and Hartung (2020), 165–9.

[35] Chakrabarty (1985), 376. It is emphatically argued here against the provocative contribution of Spivak (1988), according to which subalternity is denied voice or agency, a criticism much in line with the current state of discussion of this term: see, for example, Ludden (2002), esp. 19f.; Green (2011); Hartung (2022a), esp. 421f. n.9. Here, "subaltern" is understood as relational to "elite" and entirely context-bound: the "subaltern" in one hierarchical constellation may well be part of the "elite" in another.

converge. This is especially the case with representatives of guidance-orientated religiosity, who, once empowered within their respective communities, shift over to a much more governance-orientated one, in this way buying into the same coercive framework as the formerly despised elites and, thus, testifying that the subalterns too are in no way immune to elitist tendencies. In fact, the ṬIT / IEA and the TṬP are prominent cases in point here.

Let us once more pause for a moment and take stock of what we have presented so far. We have identified three lines of perpetual conflict that determine the Pashtun Borderland: one between imperial and local forms of governance within a tribal setting, both interlaced with distinct religiosities; a second that is intertribal and also responds to a territorial division of "highland" and "lowland" communities; and a third that runs between tribal elites and subalterns within these local communities. All three together constitute what in Borderland Studies has been conceptualized as a "borderscape", a space in which practices of "bordering", "de-bordering" and "re-bordering" – in other words construction, deconstruction and reconstruction of spatially connoted boundaries that heavily impact the formation of distinct identities – take place, one that is not static but fluid; established and at the same time continuously traversed by a number of bodies, discourses, practices and relationships that highlight endless definitions and shifts in definition between inside and outside, citizens and foreigners, hosts and guests across state, regional, racial and other symbolic boundaries.[36] The term "threshold" which defines the significance of a demarcation at a given moment or time-span, depending on its width, which determines duration, and height, signifying the degree of solidity of such a boundary, appears crucial in this regard.

The arguments of political philosopher Dieter Thomä in favour of the term "threshold" rather than "border", while so far not playing much of a role in the conceptual discussion of the "borderscape", may be well worth considering here in order to be better able to account for the actor-centric perspective against an observer-centricity:

> First of all, a threshold is usually *low*. You can step over it, stumble over it, or come to a stop right on top of it. The permeability of the threshold is far more variable and negotiable than that of the border. Second, a threshold can be used to divide two spaces and define one as being inside and one outside. This kind of distinction is also possible with borders, but in the case of a border the definition of inside and outside depends entirely on the position of the observer. One person's outland is another person's inland, and vice versa. By contrast, the most prominent version of a threshold is an *entrance*, which definitely marks the boundary between inside and outside. It is not possible for someone standing outside a door

[36] Brambilla (2015a), 19; see also Brambilla (2015b). For a survey of the career of the "borderscape" concept, see Dell'Agnese and Szary (2015).

> to convince themselves that they are actually inside. The border, with its variable classifications, is less well suited to the political problem of order and disturbance than the threshold. The threshold relates to an interior space delineated by edges where members of the political order are confronted with outsiders. This is precisely what makes the permeability of the threshold a key issue.[37]

The term "threshold" seems useful to appreciate the micro-perspective, vis-à-vis the imperially determined geopolitical one, because the story of religiously sustained discontent in the Pashtun Borderland is deliberately told in the present book not from the aerial view of the various empires involved in the narrative, but more from that of the discontents themselves. Still, "borders", both as pre-modern frontiers and as modern borderlines, have an immediate impact on all the various thresholds in existence in the Pashtun Borderland, and, therefore, we cannot, as was perfectly possible in Thomä's purely philosophical deliberations, merely substitute "border" with "threshold". In fact, the very materiality of the border necessitates operating rather with both terms and, in this way, integrating the "threshold" into the concept of the "borderscape".

A related problem is that the "borderscape" concept has been applied so far almost exclusively for contemporary situations, hence, dealing with the implications that the nation-state has for those existing on its margins. The matter becomes more complicated still when applied to pre-modern settings, where the idea of a precise demarcation of spaces as national territories has not yet played much of a role. Indeed, the shift from the only loosely defined frontiers between pre-modern polities to the eventual meticulously defined borderlines of the modern period intensifies the three lines of conflict, cascading down from the imperially-versus-tribally informed local aspirations for governance to the intertribal and intratribal ones, making the need to determine who belongs where in which particular socio-political space ever more urgent.

2.3 Imperial Ideology: From Octopus to Jellyfish

We need to understand the shifts in conceptions of politics that directly impacted the region under review with the establishment of direct European colonial rule in succession to the earlier Muslim empires of the Mughals in the east and the Uzbeks in the north and northwest to be better able to appreciate these dynamics of interrelated "bordering" processes, triggered by an aggravated line of conflict between imperial and tribally local aspirations for power and control.

The pre-modern polity did not need an open affirmation by each and every subject under rule. Governance received its legitimacy through the person of

[37] Thomä (2016), 16f. (translation J. Spengler; italics in the original).

the sovereign (Max Weber called this type of domination "patrimonial"[38]), a fact that explains the many attempts at palace revolution and the regular succession disputes after the death of a monarch. This was very much the case in all the Muslim empires that touched upon the Pashtun Borderland, be it the Mughals, the Safavids or the Uzbeks to the north.[39] It was usually perfectly sufficient to pay one's due to the imperial treasury and maintain a submissive attitude. Only if one of these two obligations, or both, were violated would the imperial centre have reacted with a forceful intervention. As such, the pre-modern polity appears to resemble a "cephalopod" (or, more colloquially, an "octopus"):[40] a living organism possessing a central nervous facility in which various major ganglia have been coalesced into a complex structure that is considered to represent something like a brain. Its numerous limbs contain large axons which, while being connected to the central brain, can bring about autonomous nerve activity, at least to a significant extent: certain directed reflexes in the limbs, prominently during foraging, happen independently of the brain; they are visible in the temporary swelling or contracting of the limbs.[41]

Applied to the pre-modern polity, the image of the octopus highlights the fact that there is a central institution – the seat of power – that itself is the result of an intense interaction of various elements, to such an extent that they form an inseparable unit. The central institution attempts to reach out in a quest for total control – the enforcement of "order" – far beyond the confines of its own physical location, but does so successfully only to a limited extent. Rather, its locally distinct deputies assigned to this task may actually choose to act upon their own ideas regarding what constitutes "order" and how it is to be enforced. Still, the central institution is not fully at the mercy of the autonomous actions of its deputies. It is still, to a certain degree, in a position to control them by sending out strong signals that aim at making a deputy refrain from a certain action, because the central power has a generally stronger and more sophisticated anatomy, one that is able to at least attempt to oversee all of the affairs of any part of the administrative body. For our purposes, the most important factor highlighted by the metaphor of the cephalopod is that of reach, because

[38] See Weber (1972), 133f. and 583–653. Weber's ruler-centric image of a polity under patrimonial rule, however, appears unsatisfying in the light of historical documentation and has, therefore, given rise to the emergence of hybrid types, such as "patrimonial-bureaucratic": see, for example, Blake (1979). Weber (1972), 153f., himself conceded what he called 'the combination of different types of authority', indicating 'that "ruling organizations" which belong only to one or another of these pure types are very exceptional' (translation T. Parsons).

[39] See here the excellent contributions assembled in Trausch (2019).

[40] It has to be admitted that this metaphor has been hijacked here from Anton Escher (Mainz), who stimulatingly proposed it in July 2011 for conceptualizing "diaspora".

[41] See Sumbre, Gutfreund, Fiorito, Flash and Hochner (2001).

control over the extension of power is not exclusively situated in the central institution of the polity, the imperial court.

Yet, there is even more to the octopus that can be productively employed in a metaphor for the pre-modern empire: its way of movement, the ability to change its colour and its surface character according to situation and environment,[42] and its haematological particularities that are the cause of the short intervals between activity and inactivity. The octopus keeps on the move almost at random, although within a distinct hunting territory, its movement, therefore, resembling the mobile princely courts of the pre-modern era. However, what appears random at first sight is actually dependent on the octopus's very own agenda: its hunting strategies, for instance, are quite diverse and, consequently, require appropriate agility.[43] In turn, however, such nimbleness is limited by the fact that the blood of the octopus employs haemocyanin, which has a lesser capacity to bind oxygen than haemoglobin, and this causes the octopus – despite its three hearts – to tire rather quickly.

Applying this to the concept of the pre-modern empire, we see that periods of intense activity were rather short, followed by – equally short – intervals of recuperation: this, in turn, also means that the outreach of the arms of the imperial centre was confined predominantly to the periods of heightened activity of the empire as a whole. The octopus's ability to change its colour and even the character of its surface is a mechanism employed predominantly both for individual protection and as camouflage for hunting. This makes the octopus appear as if it could live in virtually any environment, to which it would formally adapt.

The inability to fully control its empire the further one gets away from its centre of power is, in fact, a matter of serious concern regarding the stable maintenance of "order" across the entire polity. Alongside the acknowledgement that effective border control would exhaust resources needed elsewhere, the Borderland, already in pre-modern times with all its constituents, was systematically vilified as epitomic spaces of "disorder".[44] This vilification, in turn, provided a convenient pretext to use any coercive means at liberty, triggering potentially violent responses. As long as the government is still an octopus, enough spaces are provided which are – at least temporarily – not under its control, so that mobile dissenters can always evade the imperial grip. This rather convenient situation changed irreversibly with the advent of the modern, or bureaucratic, state, that Weber, in his typology of dominion outlined above, had considered as the substitution of traditional and charismatic authority for bureaucratic rule, which he lauded as "rational".[45]

[42] See Kühn (1950), 583–9; Hanlon and Messenger (1998), 31–46.

[43] See ibid., 47–56; Yekutiel et al. (2002).

[44] See, for example, Nichols (2013), 2–7 *et passim*.

[45] See Weber (1972), 126–30 and 815–68.

It is quite suggestive to take a closer look at modern bureaucracy, mainly because bureaucratic practices have emerged as the modern state's principal techniques of control, resulting in the appearance of the state being entirely depersonalized. The state, even in its contemporary modern garb, still consists of actual people and the structures devised and enforced by them. Yet, the bureaucratic state which had emerged from paradigmatic shifts in human thinking in seventeenth- and eighteenth-century Europe and North America has quickly become so complex that it seems almost impossible to pinpoint the ultimate seat of power from which "order" emerges. In fact, because bureaucracy emerged as an effective tool for depersonalization, it is able to generate an illusion of "objectivity" beyond individual interest: the bureaucratic state does not require the endorsement of charismatic individuals, which had been the reason for Max Weber's rather optimistic assessment hinted at above.[46] After all, in practice, the "Copernican turn" in human thinking would not result in a greater appreciation of individuality, but rather in its great levelling. Moreover, what Enlightenment philosophers had envisioned as a social contract of equals turned out in its application to be just as oppressive as preceding forms of political domination, because the equality proposed was never given.[47] Nowhere was this becoming more apparent than in the rapidly changing economic field, and the entire Marxian theory was devoted to unveiling these inequalities and their causes.

Marx found them in the depersonalization of any economic activity, something to which he adapted the earlier Hegelian concept of "alienation": not only had the nexus of a labour force and consumable product become somewhat severed, but also the capitalist mode of production caused the emergence of a host of administrative measures. These measures were ostensibly introduced, first and foremost, to assist the better organization of labour. In reality, however, they provided mighty tools to more efficiently establish paramount control over economically disadvantaged people, not least because economic deprivation has a strong potential for social and political unrest – or, in other words, for jeopardizing the maintenance of "order".[48] Here, the nexus between a capitalist economy and political rule becomes plain: the foremost task of the "state" was to preserve the achievements of the "dual revolution",[49] which was first and foremost a new socio-economic "order", but an "order" nonetheless.

[46] See Graeber (2016).

[47] Isenberg (2017), 17–132, impressively unveils how socio-economic and resulting political inequalities were foundational to the colonial settlement of North America and how even the fathers of the Declaration of Independence of thirteen colonies from the British crown in 1776, usually lauded for their egalitarian persuasion, argued for the maintenance of socio-economic class differences in the former colonies.

[48] See Graeber (2016), 3–44.

[49] This term, designating the 'French revolution of 1789 and the contemporaneous (British) Industrial Revolution', is borrowed from Hobsbawm (1992), 11.

The bureaucratic practices that were devised served, in fact, as the prime representations of the "state"; the evergrowing army of bureaucrats and administrators, so-called "officials" or "incumbents", who have been tasked with 'a continuous rule-bound conduct of official business'.[50] Even more: 'The combination of written documents and a continuous operation by officials constitute [. . .] the central focus of all types of modern organized action.'[51] The "officials" comprise a distinct professional group that follows 'rules which regulate the conduct of an office', be they 'technical rules or norms', for which, 'if their application is to be fully rational, specialized training is necessary'.[52] That implies that one does not become an "official" by personal virtue, but by the mastering of technicalities. Consequently, individuality – at least in theory – does not have a place in bureaucratic governance; in fact, it would be deleterious for the effective administration of equally de-individualized subjects. Gathering as much information as possible on each subject within a given polity became a necessity for "structural planning"; "planning", in turn, also requires the highest degree of predictability possible, which is best achieved through control which is as absolute as possible. This control, finally, requires massive "human resources",[53] which helps to explain the numerical strength of the clerical estate.

As a consequence, the rather impulsive administrative measures of the pre-modern state gave way to the emotionless gathering of masses of all sorts of data, from the measuring of the material world and its various inhabitants to the comprehensive measuring of the individual subject to rule. The single octopus that was the pre-modern imperial power now, instead, began to increasingly resemble swarms of "scyphozoæ", or, more colloquially, "jellyfish".[54]

The use of this image reflects the paradoxical combination of individuality grounded in the philosophical anthropology of the Enlightenment period and socio-economic de-individualization that is also represented in the emergence of total bureaucracy. As such, the jellyfish represents a much lower level on the evolutionary ladder than the octopus, but its advantage over the latter is exactly the brainless and spineless uniformity of individuals bound together by some kind of swarm conscience. Jellyfish are highly invasive carnivores, and being

50 Weber (1972), 125 (translation T. Parsons).

51 Ibid., 126.

52 Ibid.

53 One may want to take a moment to reflect on the underlying anthropology of this nowadays rather common administrative term: it signifies that, structurally, a human being is no different from raw materials and manufacturing tools required to produce the intended outcome. This dehumanization has far-reaching social and political consequences for each actual individual living under such a framework.

54 This metaphor appears to have in fact first been considered by Jairus Grove (Manoa, HI), and was kindly brought to my attention by Syed Sami Raza (Peshawar).

resistant to all sorts of environments substantially aids them in this behavioural pattern. Moreover, jellyfish do not explore as octopuses do; their one and only pursuit is the intake of food, and this is an all-day activity. Because jellyfish often appear in very large swarms and have up to 150 viciously cnidocyte-equipped tentacles that can extend up to 60 metres, very little escapes their attention.[55] The eight arms of the octopus, which usually extend to four times the length of their pallium, are no match for them at all.

Now, what can the metaphor of the jellyfish contribute to the matter at hand? Here, it is contended that the evergrowing swarm with its invasive tendency shares the core characteristics of a modern bureaucracy: firstly, it is numerically massive, though largely devoid of individuality. Secondly, similarly to jellyfish, the bureaucracy thrives in any environment, no matter how hostile, and, consequently, spreads over regions so far only marginally impacted by its administrative measures. Finally, the number and density of the tentacles within a swarm of jellyfish are such that hardly anything remains untouched: the ever growing number of administrative procedures ensure that hardly any aspects of individual life remain unaccounted for. We may think here, for instance, of the periodically conducted censuses by the various ruling authorities in the Pashtun Borderland since 1865, of birth and death certificates, personal identification documents, or, over and above, tax codes.[56]

The jellyfish image of the modern "state" has serious consequences for borderlands in general, and the Pashtun Borderland in particular. Although, in the past, alternatively governed spaces were situated where the outreach of the octopus's law-enforcing limbs had only been sporadic and temporary, now, the extent of the borderland has shrunk dramatically under the bureaucratic "state" of the modern era. "Frontiers" disappeared, giving way to gapless demarcation lines between states based on mutual recognition expressed in administrative documents. The establishment of the Durand Line between the then-Emirate of Afghanistan and British India in 1896 is just one case in point.[57]

55 For a comprehensive account of the physiological and behavioural characteristics of jellyfish, see Arai (1997).

56 For the case of Kabul as the epitome of the modern, that is, centrally governed, nation-state of Afghanistan since the late nineteenth century, see, for example, Hanifi (2011), 41–50, 105–20 *et passim*; Askar (2019), esp. 126–9 and 135–51.

57 See Hayat Khan (2000), esp. 246–309 (Appendices II–XX). For the eventual demarcation of the border between Russia and Afghanistan, see Fuoli (2017). Other similar examples are the demarcation of the border between France and Spain in the period 1659–1868, cutting right through the ancestral territory of the Basque Country (*Euskal Herria*), that between republican Turkey, Iran, Iraq and Russia, which divided the ancestral homeland of the Kurds (*Kurdistân*), or the demarcation between Austria and Italy that divided the County of Tyrol in two: see Schober (1982), 416f. and 532–8; Sahlins (1989), 20; Ateş (2015), 284–315.

Bringing areas that have previously been alternatively governed under the control of the "state" had a number of decisive and lasting consequences for their inhabitants. One, which will concern us for much of the remainder of this book, is that the expansion of state control and the subsequent eradication of alternatively governed spaces did not go uncontested: the more the modern bureaucratic state expanded its authority, the more frequently we see serious resistance mounting in the borderlands.[58]

2.4 The Troublemaker and the Borderland

The resistance of Borderland actors was, however, not only a reaction to the imposition of "order" and the tools for its administration, but also an extreme response to representation. After all, the narrative regarding the territories formerly perceived as frontiers changed significantly with the new understanding of the "state" as a territorial entity with clearly defined political borders. The spaces that constituted borderlands, incorporated into the paradigmatic historicist narrative of linear development, were reappraised as rural areas, governed by tribal codes of conduct in which a human life was considered less valuable than the honour of a person or an agnatic group. Yet, what could have served merely as a functional differentiation was, in fact, highly charged with ideology, and "urbanity" was subsequently lauded as the most expedient spatial form of social, economic and political organization.[59]

Rurality, in turn, had to fulfil the role of the *alter ego*, either explicitly or implicitly woven into the powerful Enlightenment discourse on "civility" as an ultimate benchmark of timely development or backwardness.[60] The village was seen as an anachronism, yet conceptualized in a rather romantic way by critics of the capitalist economy as defined by the collective property of farmable land and "non-instrumental" egalitarianism.[61] From the perspective of the state within the capitalist world system,[62] rurality is a phased-out model to be overtaken by the nexus of industrialization and urbanization, wholesomely sold as "progress". Rurality in recalcitrant borderlands, however, was ultimately worse. Notwithstanding, such an appraisal did not result in concerted efforts to "develop" such regions along the lines of liberalist ideology pivoting

58 In this context, we must consider the various confrontations of the British colonial state, the Islamic Republic of Pakistan as its heir, and the Kingdom and later Republic of Afghanistan, and especially religiously motivated militant actors in the Pashtun Borderland: see Sections 3.2.3, 3.3.2 and 3.3.3.

59 See, for example, Rahim, Aurang Zeb and Shaukat (2007).

60 See Pernau, Jordheim, Bashkin et al. (2015), 30–3, 66, 126–8 and 254f. On the example of rural France, see Weber (1976), 3–22. On rural Appalachia around the time of the American Civil War, see Waller (1988), 1–8; Dunaway (1996), 1–5.

61 For a discussion of this term, see Hartung (2019a), 310–12.

62 For this quite convincing notion, see Dunaway (1996), esp. 8–21.

on industrialization, urbanization and parliamentarism as the corresponding form of governance. Looking into the Pashtun Borderland, the city of Peshawar remained a military outpost for most of the time with very little industrial development. Kabul met a slightly better fate, simply because it was the seat of the royal court, and, thus, the administrative and financial centre of what Hanifi fittingly calls the "Anglo-Durrani State", and would, therefore, especially in the modernist garb of the *Dār al-Amān* planned city of the 1920s, evolve as a representative national capital.[63]

The vast bulk of the Pashtun Borderland, however, remained deliberately "undeveloped". Consequently, its inhabitants had to subscribe to alternative economies, including, in addition to smaller cottage industries and gemstone mining, the manufacturing of arms of every conceivable variety, the cultivation of cannabis and poppies for the processing of hashish (*chars*) and raw opium (*khām apīn*), and, not least, providing logistics for discontent outsiders to the region who ended up in the Pashtun Borderland in their quest for a convenient operational basis as safe as possible from the reach of the state's security apparatus.[64] The central governments of Pakistan and Afghanistan both made sure to intervene in these local economies, especially the production and trade of drugs, as soon as they sensed that these would undermine the state's monopoly on production and trade within the capitalist world system.[65]

However, much more critical than the production and trade of narcotics for the modern imperial image of the "borderlander" is his provision of logistics to discontents from elsewhere, because abetting those classified as criminals or, worse, terrorists made the residents of the Borderland accessories to acts aimed at destabilizing "order" and, thus, to equally dangerous discontents. Once this stereotype had been created, it was immediately woven into the narrative of unchangeable "backwardness" indicated above, with a distinct religiosity

[63] See Nichols (2001), xv, 186 and 207f.; Hanifi (2011), 97–170; Askar (2019), 118–29.

[64] See Sections 3.2.1, 3.3.2, 4.4.2 and 4.5. A very prominent case in point is the aiding and abetting of the *al-Qāʿida* operative core in the western parts of the Pashtun Borderland under the first central government of the IEA, and in the eastern parts after this government had been overthrown in December 2001. This is even more vividly illustrated by the fact that, despite serious political pressure from the government of the USA for his immediate and unconditional extradition, Usāma ibn Lādin was able to reside undisturbed in his *Vazīristān Ḥavīlī* compound in Abbottabad between 2005 and his eventual killing on 2 May 2011.

[65] On 24 November 1957 (2 Qaws 1336sh), for example, Afghan King Muḥammad Ẓāhir Shāh (r. 1933–73) submitted to the emphatic request of the UN Office on Drugs and Crime and issued an edict prohibiting the cultivation of cannabis and poppy crops: see UNODC (1958). A few months before he was overthrown by his cousin Muḥammad Dāvūd Khān (assassinated 1978), Ẓāhir Shāh was said to have renewed the legislation on the cultivation of cannabis and poppies; however, no corresponding evidence could be found in the official bulletin of the Afghan government – the *Rasmī Jarīdah-yi Dawlat-i Pādishāhī-yi Afghānistān* – for the months in question here.

identified as a prime manifestation of this explosive mix: inhabitants of such inferior and marginal spaces are religiously either highly heterodox or, worse, fanatical. Consequently, the paradox that results from the deliberate neglect of the structural development of these regions and a perceived threat to the internal security of the state, on the one hand, and its monopoly of economic regulation, on the other, led to a deep and almost pathological suspicion in the Borderland community as a whole. From the administrative core, this premonition radiated into the wider population, where it established firm roots and led to the emergence of a certain public "*Stimmung*",[66] and provided the central government authorities with some kind of imaginary consensus of popular approval for its coercive measures directed at the Borderland communities.

The imperial conceptualization of borderlands as spaces of perpetual discontent and of extreme forms of religiosity and the resulting security threat to the integrity of the nation-state is the final feature to be highlighted here as constitutive for the "borderland" in general, and the Pashtun Borderland in particular. The roots of this trope reach way back into the history of imperial ideology, as we have already seen above in the case of how the Mughal establishment positioned itself in relation to the religiously charged subaltern militancy of the Rawshaniyyah movement in the sixteenth and seventeenth centuries. However, the trope of the "discontent" or "troublemaker" gains systematic necessity in early modern and modern political theory only in the modern conception of governance that is based on the idea of secular nationhood.[67] If Thomä is to be believed, it all started with the systematic conception of the troublemaker – as *puer robustus* – by Thomas Hobbes,[68] and it is this very systematic negative alterity that has continued to dominate political discourse since then.

Without going into the rather chauvinistic conception of the *puer robustus* as mentally challenged or worse, and, therefore, not able to act according to its inscribed natural law,[69] what needs to be highlighted is the disturbingly

[66] The German term "*Stimmung*" – recently made the focus of sociological inquiry by Bude (2016; 2017) and since then discussed by Borneman and Ghassem-Fachandi (2017), Cabot (2017) and Hann (2017) – is difficult to render into other European languages: it encompasses, for instance, the three English terms "atmosphere", "mood" and "tuning". The earliest theorist of "Stimmung", however, and, thus, the anchor point for Bude's deliberations, appears to have been the French criminologist and social psychologist Gabriel Tarde (d. 1903), a contemporary as well as adversary of Émile Durkheim.

[67] A pivot of political theory since Thomas Hobbes is the idea of a universal "natural law" that subsequently serves as the logical foundation for the concept of the "commonwealth". It is important to recognize that this idea is, in fact, just as metaphysical in essence as the earlier justifications of "patrimonial" imperial rule were divinely ordained.

[68] See Thomä (2016), 56–68; compare Hobbes (1835–45), III: 147f. (*Leviathan*).

[69] See, for example, Hobbes (1839–45), II: 148 (*Præfatio ad lectores*): 'ut vir malus idem fere sit quod puer robustus, vel vir animo puerili, et malitia idem quod defectus rationis ea ætate'.

consistent way in which such arguments have been used for the justification of coercive measures by imperial actors. Examples include pushing the perceived discontents collectively to the margins of society, both in terms of socio-economics and in physical space, and the self-confident justification of their discontent with the imperial framework by the *pueri robusti*, for which more often than not, religious and ethno-culturalist arguments are put forward.[70] Here, finally, Thomä's analytical typology of the *puer robustus* as an egocentric, eccentric, nomocentric or massive troublemaker constitutes a useful attempt at a systematization, even though it is always useful to recall that in reality, of course, these types overlap most of the time.

Along the three lines of conflict outlined above, all four types can be discerned in the Pashtun Borderland and can be framed through the prism of "borderland religiosities". Along the line of conflict between imperial claims of power and local ones, ethnocentric discontent, as in the case of the *Khudāy Khidmatgār* movement of the early twentieth century[71] or the so-called *Pashtun Tahaffuz Movement* (*Paẋtūn Žghōrənē Ghūrźang*; PTM) in Pakistan since 2014, has also been strongly supported by Pashtuns in Afghanistan. This form of discontent usually plays out in a non-violent manner, having adopted forms of protest such as civil disobedience, made famous by "Mahātma" Gandhi (Mohandās Karamcand Gāṅdhī; assassinated 1948) during the Indian Independence Movement: remonstration, which, thus, takes the shape of political mass rallies, usually in the Pashtun majority areas themselves; sit-in protests (*dharnē*); and protest marches, usually to the seat of the imperial government. While there is a constant allusion to religious precepts, the rhetoric is, first and foremost, ethno-nationalist, a fact that gives rise to serious concerns in the central governments about possible secessionism and, thus, in its ultimate consequence, the threat of territorial loss.

It appears that the egocentric troublemaker and the eccentric troublemaker in the Pashtun Borderland fall into one category, perhaps best epitomized by members of the socio-economic and political elites of a given tribal community, the *məshərān*. These social actors aim at maintaining and ideally increasing their regional dominance by displaying a high degree of flexibility in forging and dissolving temporary alliances with just about everyone useful to their own ends, something that in the present book is termed "Borderland pragmatics".

The eccentric Pashtun troublemaker is little bothered by the imperial setting; he operates firmly within the confines of the Borderland setting. It is

[70] In the latter case, one may think of the justification of armed resistance by the *Euskadi ta Askatasuna* ("Basque Country and Freedom"; ETA) in the Basque Country, the *Partiya Karkerên Kurdistanê* ("Kurdistan Workers Party"; PKK) in the Turkish parts of the "Kurdish Borderland" or the *Befreiungsausschuss Südtirol* ("South Tyrolean Liberation Committee"; BAS) in South Tyrol: see Hartung (2017a), 48f.

[71] See Section 3.3.3.

usually those troublemakers whose regional influence the imperial centre regularly aims at "normalizing"[72] by co-opting them into the imperial framework: a graphic example is the incorporation of influential warlords into the Afghan central governments since 2002 or their appointment as provincial governors.[73] However, egocentric troublemakers also appear along the line of conflict between elites and subalterns, although their thrust remains essentially elitist. Here belong established religious dignitaries, such as the principals of various significant places of Islamic learning, who use an egalitarian rhetoric for the mobilization of subalterns, but aim at furthering their own cause, which consists of gaining and fortifying a monopoly of definition in all matters religious. More often than not, they are also part of the local elites co-opted by the central government; they mostly have clear affiliations to a political party and, coupled with the traditional socio-political position of religious dignitaries in the Pashtun Borderland (as well as in other predominantly rural areas), can, therefore, influence the voting behaviour in their constituencies and, by implication, the distribution of seats in provincial and central governments and, subsequently, the course of politics.[74]

The further we move away from the imperial and local elitist framework, the more violently the troublemaker of the Pashtun Borderland expresses himself. He is the subaltern machine-breaker of the era of industrialization (Luddite), the young participant in race riots, antiglobalization protests and right- and left-wing extremism, he is the ṬIT / IEA, the TṬP and the IS: the massive troublemaker, who, in the course of action, also tends towards nomocentricity. The nomocentric massive troublemaker posits an entirely different political order vis-à-vis the existing one, grounded in a subaltern ethics that emphasizes such societal values as social justice, equity, even freedom – something that one hardly associates with entities such as the ṬIT / IEA, the TṬP or the IS. Yet, when investigating what sparked them off initially, we must acknowledge their metaphysically sustained ideological basis in subaltern ethics, while needing to remain equally aware of the fact discussed above, namely that their ethical framework tends to shift further towards an elitist governance-orientated religiosity the closer they come to the realization of their alternative political vision. Once in charge, they express the same imperial aspirations for power as the representatives of the political order that they aim at overthrowing with all available means.

This, finally, is the "Pashtun Borderland", at least for the present book: a distinct physical and geopolitical space, projected to the outside as quite homogeneous while on the ground it is highly fractioned and conflictual. It is

[72] This is the Foucauldian term aptly chosen by Thomä (2016), 165, 286f. and 493f. See also Foucault (1994), III: 124–30.

[73] See, for example, Mukhopadhyay (2014).

[74] See, for example, Shah (2019), 211–35.

determined by several distinct conflict lines, some of which run inside the space and others vis-à-vis larger political entities. This larger and overarching line of conflict between state-based and tribal local frameworks gives rise to imperial and ethnic self-ascriptions, both of which are highly normative and yet discursively entangled. The former, in turn, is part of the wider imperial ideology which, over time, pivots ever more strongly on the notions of "order", "stability" and "security", and conceptualizes the space at the margins, where control is difficult to maintain, as its *alter ego*. Consequently, these are spaces imagined as being of little or no civility and refinement, inhabited by people whose way of life seems incompatible with imperial order and can, therefore, not be governed in the conventional way. As a consequence, they can only be "normalized", not "civilized", that is, coerced by various means into neutrality and non-interference with the "order" of the state. By definition, such a fundamentally different space cannot be orderly but, at best, may be transitional; more likely, however, is that it is a locus of perpetual unrest and a threat to the stability of the imperial order. Once a space at the margins of empire is essentialized in this way, all its inhabitants are potential or actual troublemakers, *pueri robusti*, who are more in cahoots with their peers elsewhere than with the representatives of imperial law and order.

3

Chief Trajectories of Militant Religious Activism in the Pashtun Borderland: The Antecedents

3.1 Prelude: The Early Modern Period

After having already probed here and there into the earlier political history of the region, our archaeological endeavour proper sets in at the pivotal moment that inhabitants of the Pashtun Borderland developed manifest imperial aspirations themselves.

At that time, the region had been dominated more by views on community and society, alongside mechanisms to put these into practice, which were somewhat at odds with the various forms of imperialism to which they had been subjected. Yet, without the latter, a distinct Pashtun ethnic identity would perhaps not have emerged to such an extent that it could serve as a major element in the ideological justification of their own imperial ambitions. After all, while larger empires around the Pashtun Borderland had emerged and disappeared, the Borderland itself, alongside a distinct ethnic identity which was considered worth defending against external forces, remained rather fluid in shape until the early eighteenth century. In fact, Gommans makes a convincing case for the need to consider the nexus of wider Central and South Asia as the space in which the ethnogenesis of Pashtuns and others took place, as ethnically confined habitats emerged here rather late.[1] In fact, those who communicated in a language later identified as Pashto had mostly been highly mobile communities who combined a pastoral nomadic lifestyle with trading activities that spanned from the Caspian Sea to the Deccan.[2] The main trading commodities that made their way from Central Asia to the Indian subcontinent were (war-)horses, camels and military slaves; the traders themselves sometimes offered their services as mercenaries.[3]

Over time, some of these mobile trading communities, which – as is predominantly the case in pastoral nomadic societies – were tribally organized (*ūlūsī/vūlusī*), succeeded in establishing a monopoly in the trade with certain

[1] See Gommans (1995), 10–12.

[2] See ibid., 13–33.

[3] See Digby (1971); Gommans (1995), 77–83 and 113–43; (2002), 44–6, 68–73 and 116f.; Green (2008), 174f.

imperial trading partners and particular commodities, not least because they established local representations at strategic market places, thus forming a largely reliable chain in the exchange of distinct goods. Two communities more successful than others were the originally rivalling Abdālī and the Ghilzay of Kandahar, with representations eventually in Herat and Multan, thus connecting the trade between late Safavid and Afsharid Persia, Uzbek-controlled Transoxiana, Mughal India and numerous smaller local polities.[4] Yet, ethnic identity appears to have rested fully with the tribe; whatever ethnogenesis of the Pashtuns existed by then was restricted to imperial ascriptions, especially by the Mughals, meant to help to keep track of all the subjects claimed by imperial rule.[5]

3.1.1 Pashtun Ethnogenesis: From Ascription to Identity

Very early categorizations of these mobile trading-cum-service communities (see Figure 3.1 and Map 3.1) as ethnically distinct took place in the memoirs of the first Mughal *pādishāh* Bābur,[6] and were repeated in ʿAbbās Khān Sarvānī's (d. after 988/1580) account of the reign of Shīr Shāh Sūrī, commissioned by the Mughal *pādishāh* Akbar.[7] The label "Afghan" was employed for them in both works. A few decades later, imperial chronicler Niʿmatallāh Haravī (d. c. 1040/1630) was commissioned by a courtier of Jahāngīr, Akbar's eventual successor to the throne, to compose a genealogy of 'this folk' (*īn ṭāʾifah*).[8] When Haravī identified them as descendants of an "Afghanah", son of the Semitic prophet Dāwūd,[9] "this folk" had now been given a mythical genealogy and could, therefore, rightfully be labelled as "Afghans".

However, the success of a label depends on whether or not it can be established as a norm: for this, recognition by those labelled is paramount.

4 See Gommans (1995), 34–6.

5 Green (2008), among others, rightly points out that so-far dominant and rather flexible clan identities of the various trading networks across the region between the eastern Iranian Plateau, Transoxiana and the Indian subcontinent were forced by the Mughals under a broader collective identity. This, however, happened not only to those now lumped together as "Afghans", but to other ethnic and religious groups as well – the "Rajputs" would be a case in point here. In fact, we need to remind ourselves that labelling and categorizing are core bureaucratic practices, aiming at better control by those in power, and are therefore certainly not confined to the Mughal–Afghan context.

6 See Bābur (1905), 131a f.: 'There are different peoples [*aqvām*] living in the province of Kabul: in the plains [*čälgäsidä*] there are Turks, Aymāq and Arabs, in the towns and some villages [*baʿẓï kentläridä*] are Sarts, in some other villages and throughout the province live Pashāyī, Parājī, Tajiks, Barakī and *Afghans*. [. . .] To the south [of Kabul Province] lies the land of the *Afghans* [*janūbī Afġānistān dur*]' (emphases added, translation roughly follows W. Thackston).

7 See Sarvānī (1964), I: 2f.

8 al-Haravī (1379/1960), I: 6.

9 See ibid., I: 29–75.

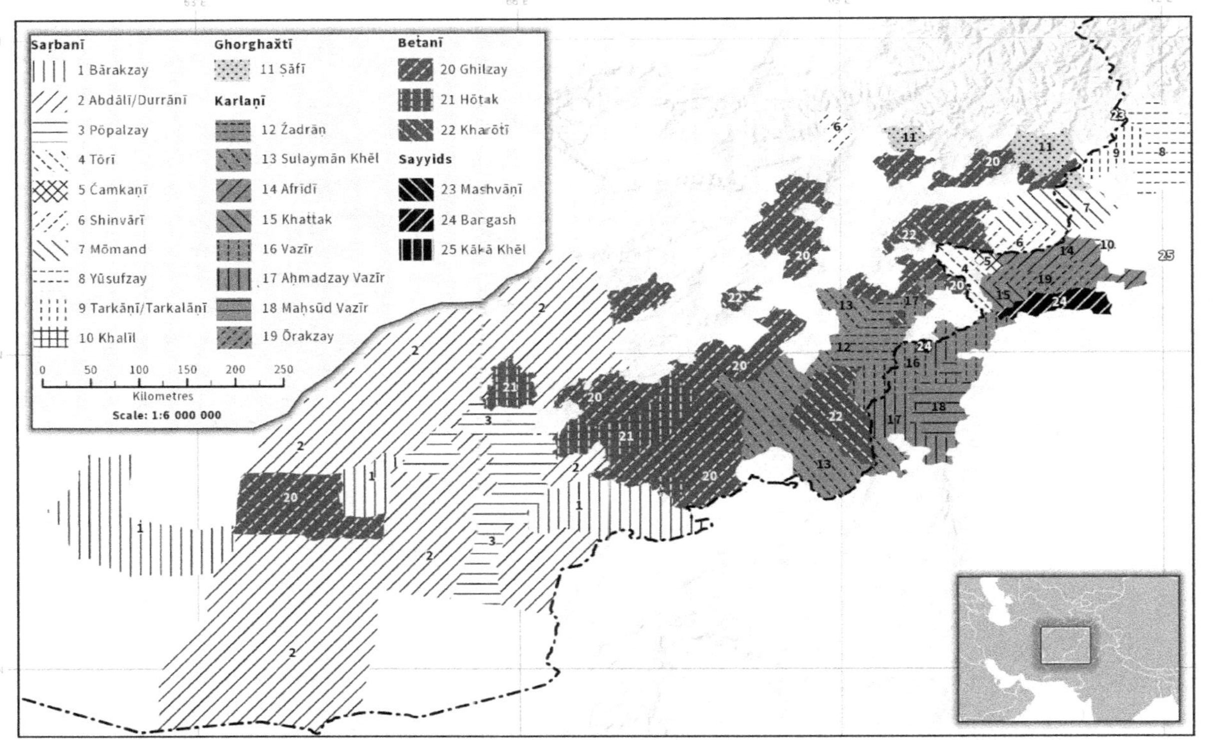

Map 3.1 Distribution of tribal communities across the Pashtun Borderland (simplified).

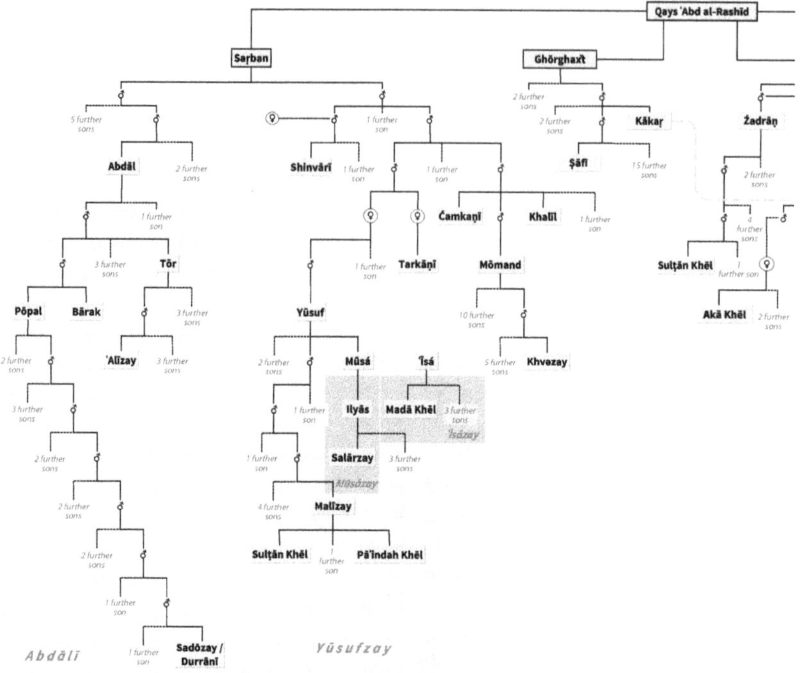

References: Darvīzah (n.d.); Haravī (1379/1960); Ḥayāt Khān (1867); "Shāh'jī" (1930); "Syāl" Mōmand (1365/1986).

Figure 3.1 Pashtun tribal genealogies.

In the case at hand here, Haravī's earlier genealogy was indeed absorbed by members of these communities themselves, as, for example, the Persian *Tazkirat al-Abrār va 'l-Ashrār* of the Ākhūnd Darvīzah Nangarhārī mentioned above testifies.[10] Now that the label had entered the realm of literary expression, it was on the way to potentially become "common wisdom". This process, however, was convoluted by the fact that, roughly around the same time, Ḥāfiẓ Muḥammad Ṣiddīq (d. unknown), a vassal of the Yusufzay-Rōhillah chief of North-Indian Baraylī,[11] brought in an alternative term: a number of tribes that had originated from the area around Kandahar and moved north, towards

[10] See Darvīzah (n.d.), 58–62. Interestingly, while he identified himself clearly as a native of Nangarhar (see ibid., 10), in the various and usually much later materials available his place of origin remains ambivalent. According to Quddūsī (1966), 229, for instance, Ākhūnd Darvīzah was born in the Mughal subdivision (*parganah*) of Laghmān, but flourished for most of his life somewhere unspecified in Nangarhar, from where his ancestors hailed. Undisputed, however, is that he died in Peshawar and is buried there.

[11] On the Rōhillah, "the people from Rōh", originally settled in the Peshawar Valley, and the eventual formation of their own polity in seventeenth-century northern India, see Gommans (1995), 104–8 and 144–9.

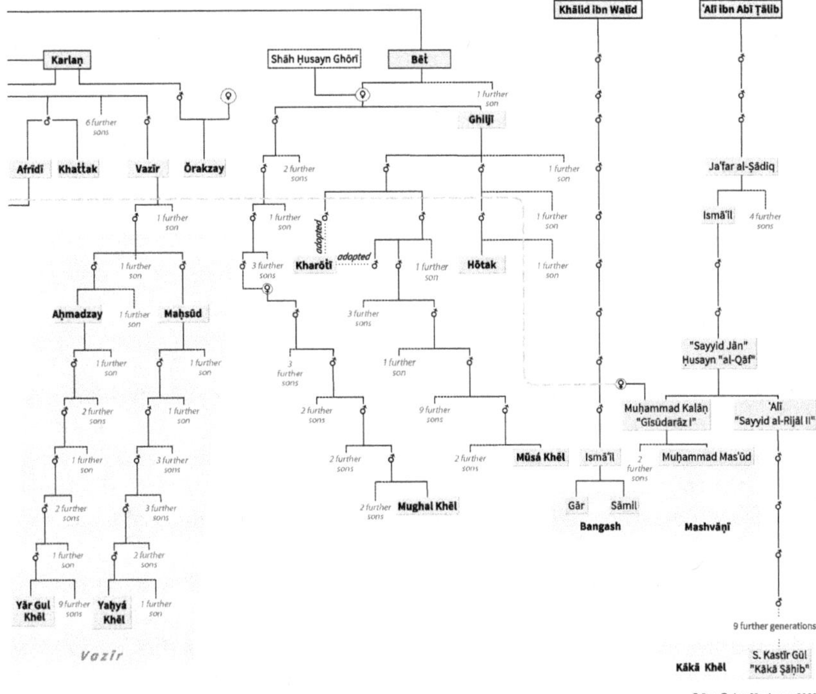

Figure 3.1 (cont.)

Kabul, and then east into the Peshawar Valley, are labelled as "Pashtun" in his *Tavārīkh-i Ḥāfiẓ Raḥmat'khānī*.[12] Yet, while these two terms were often used synonymously, they are semantically distinct: "Afghan" refers to the acknowledgement of the mythical genealogy as constitutive, and "Pashtun" became the epitome of its qualitative signification.

Discourse-determining authors, such as Khūshḥāl Khān Khaṭṭak, a wilful member of the lower Mughal elite for quite some time,[13] stressed in their poetry certain qualities as essentially "Afghan" or "Pashtun" (Khūshḥāl used the two terms synonymously),[14] qualities which – as late as in the twentieth

12 See Muʿaẓẓam Shāh (1976), *passim*.

13 See Hartung (2019a), 313f. None of the standard chronicles for the reign of Shāh'jahān, the *Bādishāh'nāmah* of ʿAbd al-Ḥāmid Lāhawrī (d. 1064/1654) and Muḥammad Amīn Qazvīnī (d. after 1042/1632), respectively, and the *ʿAmal-i Ṣāliḥ* of Muḥammad Ṣāliḥ Kanbūh (d. c. 1085/1675), mentions Khūshḥāl among the listed military ranks of the nobility. A lot of the narrative on Khūshḥāl's earlier amicable relationship with the Mughals seems to originate rather from Ḥayāt Khān (1867), 321–4, and [A.] Khān Khaṭṭak (1893), 230–40.

14 See [Kh.] Khān Khaṭṭak (2001), for example 24–6: 'də Awrangzīb nah shikāyat aw də khpalē maṛānē stāʾīnah'.

century – would ultimately feed into the widespread and, therefore, discursively powerful romantic notion of a distinct Pashtun code of conduct, *paẍtūnvalī*.[15] Khūshḥāl himself, however, turns out to be an interesting case. It seems that his ostensible attitude towards the Mughals was not that of a submissive subject to a superior power, but rather the vivid expression of the maintenance of the instrumentally rational flexibility of collaboration that was so characteristic of the pre-Mughal trading communities in various parts of India. Now, however, this flexibility became recast as a distinct Pashtun "sense of independence" that was consistent with concepts of "pride" and "honour" – concepts not exclusive to the Pashtuns – and a readiness to go to the extreme in defending the latter.

The sense of independence, in turn, coupled with the willingness (and ability) to take up arms in its defence, gave rise to the notion of the sturdy mountain warrior who uses the roughness of his habitat to stubbornly elude "order", or to subvert it: Mughal *pādishāh* Bābur had already complained about the intransigence of, for example, the inhabitants of the Kunar (*Kunaṛ*) Valley, who eluded payment of their dues to the imperial treasury,[16] and asserted that dacoity was indeed their prime activity.[17]

The process of ethnogenesis had finally arrived on the field of literature with Khūshḥāl's self-confident Pashto poetry and began to constitute what Caron calls 'counter-empires of Pashto verse'.[18] While there are earlier documents that position Pashto as a language of equal import to the imperial Persian and Arabic,[19] it took a representative of the tribal elite, such as Khūshḥāl, to establish the language as a literary idiom. Indeed, Caron suggests reading his poetry as an expression of a cultural, or aesthetic, as well as political

15 This rather loose concept, which has been around for a while as an expression of communally acceptable conduct that may vary according to the respective context, has eventually been embraced by Afghan nationalist intellectuals. A case in point is Qiyām al-Dīn Khādim (d. 1979), a leading member of the Leftist *Vīẍ Zalmiyān* movement of the late 1940s, to whom we owe the monograph *Paẍtūnvalī* (Kabul: Də paẍtō ṫōlānah 1331sh), a very early attempt to enshrine the constituents of *paẍtūnvalī* independent of the respective context in which they are applied. On Khādim, the *Vīẍ Zalmiyān* and its role in the creation of Afghan ethnic nationalism, see Bezhan (2017).

16 See Bābur (1905), 133b: 'Although it [i.e., the district of Kunar and Nūr Gul] is about as large as the Laghmān districts [*Lamğānāt* (sic)], the revenue coming from there is little [*bu jihattïn mālï kesim dur*], because the area is remote and the people do not pay' (translation largely follows W. Thackston).

17 See ibid., 213b; also Section 2.4.

18 All the following owes a considerable amount to the ideas of James Caron (London), which he – generous as always – has shared even before they were published. This sign of trust is much appreciated, moreover, as it seems to have become an increasingly rare commodity in academic circles.

19 A core reference for this is the *Khayr al-Bayān*, a Sufi spiritual text by the "Pīr Rōẍān" Bayāzīd Anṣārī: it contains parallel translations in Arabic, Persian, Hindko and Pashto, without privileging one idiom over the others. See also Hartung (2019a), 314f.

negotiation with empire, oscillating between approval of imperial order as a representation of "civility"[20] and fierce rejection, while establishing a Pashto "counter-civility". Khūshḥāl's *qaṣīdah* "Poetry is the Discharge of Men" (*shiʿr ḥayẓ al-rijāl day*) comprises, according to Caron, all the core themes in this discourse: the relationship between mundane and divine beauty, imperial economy and politics vis-à-vis communal ones, and youthful virility that, nonetheless, requires disciplining and channelling into concerted action within a patriarchal framework.[21] It is significant that, in this context, Khūshḥāl relied less on religious rhetorical figures to sustain his views,[22] but much more on social values distinctly held by the communities to which he spoke.

The one author finally able to combine the socio-political pragmatism that shines through Khūshḥāl's verses with the subaltern spirituality of the vilified Bāyazīd ibn ʿAbdallāh Anṣārī, the "Pīr Rōx̌ān", and those who, in his wake, have been regarded with suspicion as a Rawshaniyyah movement,[23] appears to be ʿAbd al-Raḥmān Mōmand, commonly referred to as "Raḥmān Bābā" (d. 1123/1711), of a village very close to Peshawar. Raḥmān Bābā, in fact, presents a kind of egalitarian message that is strongly informed by his leanings to a less ritualistic and more introspective form of Sufi Islam, and which we shall repeatedly encounter in our discussion of the centuries to come. This internal egalitarianism appears to have, indeed, been born out of a perceived discrepancy between the egalitarian ethos of a tribally organized society and its socio-economic realities, which are hierarchical between Pashtuns and larger imperial power structures, but also within the Pashtun communities themselves. Most revealing in this regard is an often-cited *ghazal* of his in which he reflected on the erosion of communal socio-economic practices, here prominently the institution of *vēsh* – the periodic redistribution of land and water

[20] On this concept and its political dimensions, though dominantly for the context of nineteenth-century European Imperialism, see fundamentally Pernau (2014); Pernau, Jordheim, Bashkin et al. (2015).

[21] See Khān Khaṫṫak (2001), 6–12. It is interesting to note that Amīr Krōṛ Sūrī (fl. second/eighth c.), the celebrated poet-warrior of the nascent Ghorid dynasty in the ninth and tenth centuries CE, has already been credited with verses that serve stereotypes of Pashtun masculinity which we later find prominently in Khūshḥāl's compositions, culminating perhaps in the foot of a poem called "Pride" (*viyāṛənah*): 'There is no one braver than me!' (*lah mā atal nəstah*): Hōtak (1339sh), 34. Still, what little we have that is claimed to be Amīr Krōṛ's is clearly devoid of the refinement of habits and customs that distinguished the Persianate court culture of the Mughals and has clearly shaped the poetic imaginary of their one-time vassal Khūshḥāl Khān Khaṫṫak.

[22] Khūshḥāl's poetry is certainly not devoid of religious references, as are prominently present in his *Faẓl'nāmah*, but also shorter *qaṣāʾid* on divine and Prophetic attributes prove (see Khān Khaṫṫak [2001], 2–5 and 801–972). Yet, such references were little used to sustain the socio-political arguments in his poetry.

[23] For a brief introduction, see Yaqubi (2010).

rights among members of settled agrarian upland communities under the supervision of a morally upright religious functionary[24] – by the incorporation of the Peshawar Valley into the hierarchical Mughal system of land tenure (*zamīndārī*).[25] When referring to a *məshər* who, 'in parcelling out water [rights] he is not just, even if his hand grips pages of The Book',[26] Raḥmān Bābā combined socio-economic critique with religious ethics and, thus, sustained a trope that, so Ibrāhīm ʿAṭāyī claims, had already been a major driver for the Rawshaniyyah movement in the sixteenth century CE,[27] consequently resulting in a barrage of polemical remarks on their subaltern religiosity by privileged members of the Mughal establishment.[28]

This *ghazal* contains further significant pointers which, as we shall see throughout the present study, are maintained and frequently referred to by subaltern Pashtun actors well into the present, ultimately including those who identify as *taliban* of whatever shade. After all, Raḥmān Bābā established an almost causal relationship between social, economic and political equity, resistance to perceived injustices in all these departments, and "Pashtun-ness":

> Tenant he is, sharecropper he was, he will rise to be Pashtun / even if a cobbler or butcher by origin.
> Speaking mildly has no effect on him [i.e., the landlord] / since in his heart is neither shame nor *ḥijāb*.[29]

By writing this, Raḥmān Bābā established a powerful trope: a "Pashtun" is whoever resists injustice and maintains a strong social conscience, and, even more, a "Pashtun" is essentially subaltern.[30] It is, in fact, these two conflicting conceptions of "Pashtun-ness", represented by Khūshḥāl Khān Khaṫṫak and Raḥmān Bābā, respectively, which, it shall be argued, have played a significant role until today in legitimizing either fraternization with the strong and powerful, or their militant rejection.[31] In fact, we may even go so far as to suggest that a lot of the perpetual violence inside the Pashtun Borderland is

[24] See ʿAṭāyī (1357sh), 292–5. For a historical account on the practice in the sixteenth century CE, see Muʿaẓẓam Shāh (1971), 36–43. Also, see Section 3.2.1.

[25] See ʿAbd al-Raḥmān (1963), 109–12; also, see the less literal, but more poetic, translation by J. Enevoldsen in Nichols (2001), 53–5.

[26] ʿAbd al-Raḥmān (1963), 164, ll. 13f.: 'də ōbō pah vēsh chih varshī inṣāf nah kā / kih lās yē varaqūnah də kitāb vī'.

[27] See ʿAṭāyī (1357sh), 295. This view has been adopted by Nichols (2001), 21.

[28] See Section 2.2.

[29] ʿAbd al-Raḥmān (1963), 165, ll. 17–20: 'hamsāyah yē chalēkār vu paẋtānah shī / aw pah aṣl bah mōchī yā bah qaṣṣāb vī // mulāyīm vəyəl aṣar var bāndī nah kā [*sic*] / chih pah zṛəh kẋī yē tah sharm nah ḥijāb vī'.

[30] We have to acknowledge, though, that Raḥmān Bābā's notion of equity (*inṣāf*) was curtailed by the male-dominated socio-cultural orbit he inhabited. Consequently, the notion was never meant to apply to women, too. For intimate insights into gender inequalities among Pashtuns, see Tapper (1991); Grima (2004; 2005); Khan (2012).

[31] See Hartung (2024), 27–32.

related to contestation over the notion of "Pashtun-ness", alternating between the stress on "manliness" (*nar'tōb*) that radiates from Khūshḥāl's poetry and Islamically inspired and socially conscious "softness" (*narmī*), as presented by Raḥmān Bābā.

3.1.2 An Early Taste of Nationhood: Durrani Imperialism, 1747–1826

The most incisive case of enacting what shall here be called the "*khān* ethics" of Khūshḥāl was certainly the emergence of Pashtun dynasticism, emerging from the first attempt at empire under the Durrani-turned Abdālī tribe, then of Kandahar. Their aspiration grew out of their rise to wider eminence as brokers in the long-distance trade that connected the west of the Iranian Plateau, southern Transoxiana and the north of the Indian subcontinent during a period in which the larger polities of the Safavids and Mughals struggled to maintain their imperial claims. As a result, the Durrani, led by Aḥmad Shāh ibn Zamān Khān Sadōzay, later "Abdālī", and finally "Durrānī", embraced to some extent Khūshḥāl's take on external imperial powers[32] and gave up the practice of seeking their endorsement of any eventual political action.[33] Gommans's argument that, apart 'from expanding their economic base, the Durrani rulers also attempted to furnish their empire with an idea of legitimacy which had more widespread appeal than the indigenous Islamic folk tradition of their Afghan homeland',[34] however, appears too elite-centric to have sufficient currency.

Instead, their attempt at empire building, also consisting of shifting the centre of gravity to their ancestral Kandahar, would be seriously challenged, especially by those from the uplands of the Pashtun Borderland. This, however, does not necessarily contradict the fact that the economic successes of the Durrani enabled them to offer financial incentives to rivalling Pashtun tribal groups to submit jointly to their imperial patronage. Beyond the Borderland, the "*khān* ethics", pivoting greatly on military virtues such as "courage" (*maṛānah*), even "boldness" (*zṛəva'tōb*), and "determination" (*ʿazm*) to the extent of self-sacrifice,[35] served for the Durrani to style themselves the legitimate heirs of the Safavid, Afsharid and Mughal empires.[36] Aḥmad Shāh, the

[32] This view, however, developed only after Khūshḥāl had broken off his once-subservient relationship to the Mughal court at Delhi: see Khān Khaṫtak (2001), 16–29; also Hartung (2019a), 313.

[33] See Gommans (1995), 45–7.

[34] Ibid., 45.

[35] Revealing in this regard is, once again, Khān Khaṫtak (2001), for example 30–7 (*Məshərān aw Źān Stā'īl aw Khēl'khānē Nah Faryād*).

[36] See Gommans (1995), 47–66; Noelle-Karimi (2017); Tarzi (2017). Indeed, Maḥmūd al-Ḥusaynī, author of the *Tārīkh-i Aḥmad'shāhī*, had been commissioned by Aḥmad Shāh around 1754 to emulate the style of the *Tārīkh-i Jahān'gushā-yi Nādirī* of

progenitor of the Durrani dynasty, was certainly not in any urgent need to have his claims religiously legitimized outside the frame of Borderland pragmatics and, thus, from actors outside the confines of the Pashtun Borderland. This strong attachment to Borderland pragmatics, in turn, was most probably misapprehended by the celebrated Delhiite scholar Shāh Valiyallāh ibn Shāh ʿAbd al-Raḥīm (d. 1176/1762) when he purportedly invited Aḥmad Shāh to come to Delhi and take over the reins from the Mughals.[37]

For Shāh Valiyallāh, the disintegration of the Mughal Empire was to be blamed on a serious decline of sound Islamic religiosity; yet, his deep investment in religious matters seems to have made him unable to think of legitimate political power outside an Islamic legal framework.[38] The matter was made even more complicated by the fact that Aḥmad Shāh had indeed initially styled himself a champion of Muslims under threat, a mission that he and his contemporaneous chroniclers claimed had imposed itself on him by divine intervention during Aḥmad Shāh's early life, during which he claimed to have spent some time in the day in a hermitage in 'contemplation over the external beauty of the unseen world' (*mutaraṣṣid-i ẓuhūr-i laṭīfah az ʿālam-i ghayb*).[39] Moreover, his coronation was reportedly conducted by his own *murshid*, the *Chishtī shaykh* Muḥammad Ṣābir Shāh Darvīsh, or "Majẕūb", of Kabul (killed 1160/1747), who is also credited with predicting the downfall of the Afsharids and the rise of his *murīd* Aḥmad Shāh Abdālī in their stead.[40] However, such religious self-dramatization may have been the result of mere Borderland pragmatics. After all, when Aḥmad Shāh finally ransacked Delhi in 1757, but left the Mughal *padishāhī* formally intact,[41] he delivered some conclusive proof

Muḥammad Mahdī ibn Muḥammad Naṣīr Astarābādī (d. c. 1174/1760), one of the two imperial chronicles of the reign of Nādir Shāh Afshār, Aḥmad Shāh's imperial predecessor and, apparently, role model: see Jāmī (1384sh), 49–57, esp. 56f.

37 See Dihlavī (1388/1969), 6–17. This infamous letter, however, is directly addressed to neither Aḥmad Shāh nor any of his leading courtiers, but appears to have rather been a circular to 'some sultans' (*bah baʿẓī salāṭīn*), of whom Aḥmad Shāh might have been only one.

38 Interestingly, the Mughals themselves most of the time did not legitimize their claims to rule within an explicitly Islamic framework, an omission which resulted in the persistent existence of a religious opposition in court and wider society, see, for example, Hartung (2017b), 91–102.

39 Durrānī (1346sh), 9. Also, see pp. 8–10 of this 240-folio-long letter of Aḥmad Shāh to the Ottoman Sultan Muṣṭafá III (r. 1757–73), written sometime after 1761. In addition, Gommans (1995), 50, refers to the *Mujmal al-Tārīkh-i Baʿd-i Nādiriyyah* of Abū 'l-Ḥasan Muḥammad Amīn-i Gulistānah, completed around 1781. Remarkably, similar strategies to gain legitimacy in view of a weak royal pedigree were adopted only a little later by Shāh Murād of the Mangïts of Bukhara (r. 1785–1800), as indicated by von Kügelgen (2002), 337–47.

40 See Jāmī (1384sh), 68; Kashmīrī (1970), 186; Ziad (2017), 231f.

41 See Amīn-i Gulistānah (1896), 97–114.

that his political claims did not necessarily depend on being religiously sanctioned, much to the indignation of Shāh Valiyallāh.

Still, the symbolic force that Aḥmad Shāh's spiritual proclivities carry for posterity, as well as his investiture by a subaltern dervish rather than by confident self-anointment à la Napoléon Bonaparte, can hardly be underestimated. This is vividly proven by the iconic image of IEA cadres posing for a photograph at an elaborate writing desk inside Kabul's Arg, the Presidential Palace, upon the second capture of the Afghan capital in August 2021. Instead of posing at the president's personal desk, another one had been chosen for the occasion, one that shows the popular painting of renowned Afghan artist ʿAbd al-Ghaffūr Brēx̌nā (d. 1392/1974) depicting Aḥmad Shāh's purported coronation by Ṣābir Shāh Darvīsh on the wall behind them. Coupled with the devoutly downcast eyes and, alternately, index fingers pointing upwards, the message radiating from this is that power results ultimately from humility and unconditional trust in God, not from the self-aggrandizement of contenders for political leadership that characterizes election campaigns in the Global North and, by implication, those of the two cabinets in charge of Afghanistan by the grace of the USA and its allies between 2002 and 2021.

Aḥmad Shāh's invasion of Mughal North India and the sack of its imperial centre, however, indicates that there might be alternative and probably less favourable perspectives of him, ones that make him appear not so much a humble servant of God and His "friends" (*awliyāʾ allāh*) but rather more aligned with those contemporary Afghan politicians that cadres and supporters of the IEA despised. Given the utter disappointment of the celebrated Shāh Valiyallāh of Delhi in the Pashtun ruler, the IEA reference to Aḥmad Shāh is actually quite surprising. After all, it was the politically rather gormless Shāh Valiyallāh and his descendants who were eventually appropriated by Pashtun Borderland actors from outside the circles of the *məshərān*, while Aḥmad Shāh's legacy remains at best a reference perhaps for those ruling Afghanistan from Kabul. In fact, those associating themselves with the ṬIT / IEA are significant contemporary proponents of subaltern attempts to establish a counter-narrative sustained by religious precepts to the "*khān* ethics" as the epitome of "Pashtun-ness". In reality, however, these two conceptual frameworks are almost impossible to keep strictly apart, as the allusion of IEA personnel to Aḥmad Shāh's coronation in the photograph mentioned above indicates.

Historically, this appears to have, at least to an extent, something to do with the fact that, with the Durrani, the so far scattered, often antagonistic and only loosely integrated Pashtun tribal communities across the Borderland have been given a patriarchal political structure that helped a Pashtun proto-nationalism to emerge. It may, therefore, be reasonable to conclude that under Durrani rule, lasting at least from the coronation of Aḥmad Shāh in 1747 to the incorporation of much of the eastern territories into the dominion of the Sikhs (*sikh̄ khālsā rāj*) under Mahārāja Raṇjīt Sing̣h̄ (r. 1792–1801) and his immediate successor, the Borderland had been dissolved. However, a closer look reveals that this was certainly not the case, as the matter was, indeed, considerably more complex.

Aḥmad Shāh rose to prominence in an environment heavily shaped by imperial Iranian court culture, because after the Abdālī had been given Kandahar by Nādir Shāh Afshār (r. 1736–47) as a reward for their military services,[42] they greatly facilitated the trade between there and Safavid Iran. Pragmatics demanded a rather tolerant stand on the particular religious orientation of their trading partners to the west, an attitude that was taken over into Durrani imperial policy.[43] Similarly to the Abdālī control of the trade between Kandahar and the west, the Khattak, Khūshḥāl's tribe which had been elevated to prominence for their services to the earlier Mughals,[44] had established their command over the northern trading routes between Kabul and Delhi. The almost equal economic standing of lowland Abdālī and upland Khattak put them, at least potentially, in competition over political and cultural prevalence in the Pashtun Borderland. In his attempt to control the potential for intertribal conflict across the dominion of the Durrani, whose political influence radiated from its homebase in Kandahar, which would therefore indeed be situated almost right in its centre,[45] Aḥmad Shāh pursued a dual strategy, designed to overcome the disparity between "*khān* ethics" and its egalitarian counterpart sustained by religious precepts. Firstly, he appealed to a common "Afghan" political identity, intended to overcome intertribal conflict, which is perhaps one of the reasons why the Durrani dominion is commonly seen as the nucleus of the nation-state of "Afghanistan":

> All are one, whether a Ghilzay or an Abdālī; / He, whose heart is of clear glass is good. [. . .]
>
> May all Pashtuns join hands as one, / since today we have a war for faith upon us on all fronts.
>
> When has tranquillity ever been found without labour? / This is why Aḥmad fights a war for faith on all sides.[46]

The poem, ascribed to Aḥmad Shāh himself,[47] emphasizes, similarly to those of Khūshḥāl earlier on, the virtue of submitting to patriarchal authority. This

[42] See Jāmī (1384sh), 66f.

[43] See Gommans (1995), 51–3.

[44] See Kākā Khēl (1965), 697–9.

[45] See Map 2.1; compare also the one provided in Gommans (1995), 44.

[46] Durrānī (1388sh), 89: 'ṫōlah yaw dī kih Ghiljī kih Awdalī [*sic*] dī / ẍah haghah chī yē də zṛəh ẍīẍah ṣafā dah // [. . .] Paẍtānah dī ṫōlah lās sarah yaw kāndī / chē mū nən ghazā har lōrī shāw'khvā dah // bē zaḥmatah rāḥat chīrī [*sic*] mūndah nah sī / də "Aḥmad" źakah par har lōrī ghazā dah.'

[47] The authorship of the poems collected as Aḥmad Shāh's *Dīvān* is just as unproven as its circulation at the time. Yet, it is regarded as an established fact that they all belong in the

time, however, the authority was not justified by manly virtues alone, but embedded in a wider religious argument, also aimed at bringing the advocates of egalitarianism sustained by religious precepts on board.

Secondly, to reinforce this strategy, Aḥmad Shāh, and even more so his successors to the throne, offered courtly patronage to a varying extent to a wide range of Sufis, many of them of the Naqshbandiyyah-Mujaddidiyyah, as has only recently been unearthed by Waleed Ziad.[48] Many of these possessed a host of adepts in various regions of the Durrani dominion, especially including the uplands to the northeast. Offering courtly privileges to those who were increasingly disfavoured by the Mughals[49] translated into mutual loyalties of the numerous *murīdūn* of these Sufi *shaykhs* across tribes and clans. The importance of the establishment of this net of loyalties can hardly be underestimated: in fact, it potentially created a strong layer of transregional and intertribal identity that complemented the rootedness in locally distinct tribal identities.

Because religious dignitaries – especially those Olesen calls 'maraboutic' – hold an exceptional degree of authority in the predominantly tribally organized communities and, therefore, enjoy unconditional submissiveness,[50] they also exercise a considerable influence over the political fortunes of the entire region. Religious competition is, therefore, always also political competition; for most of the time, however, this remained the prerogative of self-proclaimed elites, while most of the population remained – cynically spoken – mere "human resources" for the various ambitions underlying what appear at first glance to be purely religious controversies.

With the rise of the Durrani-run polity in the eighteenth century, however, the controversies over Islamic orthodoxy and orthopraxy in the Pashtun Borderland now also had to reflect on the adherence of the Durrani ruling elites to the precepts of the *shari'a*. This, in fact, appears critical in

context of the early Durrani courts at Kandahar, and provide, therefore, a good reflection of its imperial ideology.

48 See Ziad (2017), for example 209 and 227–70, here esp. 238 n.20, the information of which, however, is based on the rather recent *Kābul-i Qadīm* of Nēk Muḥammad Pōpalzay (first published in 1375sh/1996). It is also worth noting that, other than the Mughal imperial chronicles, none of those for the Durrani era contained a section on famous scholars, Sufis and poets.

49 These disfavours did not necessarily result from dissent in doctrinal matters, but were rather due to the fact that the Mughal treasury was in an increasingly precarious state, due to costly military campaigns and an increasing sense of factual independence by the governors of Mughal imperial provinces, which resulted in a substantial decrease in the revenue that reached the treasury. Incidentally, a similar strategy was also employed by the Durrani's new neighbours to the north, the Khanate of the Turco-Mongolian Mangïts of Bukhara: see von Kügelgen (2002), 97–101.

50 See Olesen (1995), 51–3; also, although much less differentiated, Wieland-Karimi (1998), 45–83. Somewhat more to the point are Haroon (2007), 69–75 (here all religious dignitaries in the region figure under the common yet rather pejorative term "mullah") and Green (2008). The most reasonable discussion so far appears to be Caron (2016a).

determining, firstly, to what extent, if at all, the new rulers of Pashtun ethnic origin deserved obedience from everyone residing in the territories claimed as their dominion and, secondly, who would succeed in establishing supreme authority in religious matters within the Durrani dominion.

Aḥmad Shāh himself appears to have been clearly aware of these dynamics, otherwise he would perhaps not have staged his coronation as an act of submission to his own *murshid* Ṣābir Shāh Darvīsh, vividly depicted in Brēx̌nā's popular painting mentioned above. This, of course, is not to deny the ruler any such personal inclination,[51] but to ignore the political utility of spiritual backup would surely be short-sighted. The *məshərān* were far too well aware of the immensely high esteem at least some of the Sufi *shaykh* enjoyed among the *kəshərān* for their pious and simple lifestyle that rewarded them, in turn, with charisms (*karāmāt*)[52] and the ability to work miracles (*khawārīq*), ceaselessly stressed in the hagiographical literature, to be able to simply ignore them. Still, *məshərān* have tried to use the blessings (*barakāt*) of renowned Sufis to their own rather worldly ends, as the story of the Hōtak-Ghilzay rebellion against the Safavid occupation of Kandahar in 1709 testifies: for the justification of the uprising, Mīr Vays Khān Hōtak (d. 1127/1715), progenitor of the dynasty that was to rule over the region for the next three decades, read – ostensibly at random – two lines of a *ghazal* from the *Dīvān* of Raḥmān Bābā and interpreted it generously as affirmation of the legitimacy of rising against the Safavid governor. A month later, Raḥmān Bābā's *Dīvān* had once more to serve legitimization purposes: another passage from a *ghazal* was read:

> It has been narrated that the sky was cloudy that day, but by the might of God the clouds disappeared and the sun broke when the late Ḥājjī Mīr [Vayz Khān] read this couplet. Also the people regarded this as a [sign of] divine support [*yaw ilāhī maddad*]. Then the Khān – the "Heavenly Abode" – spoke to the people: 'The love and favour of God the Ever-Highest is with us! Now is the time to draw the sword and free ourselves from the enemy's regime [*dux̌manah* (sic)]!' Thus, on the 29th of Muḥarram of the year 1119 [AH] the people gathered and, with the support of the "Heavenly Abode", the Mīr, they entered Kandahar and killed off the enemy.[53]

In view of such powerful prospects for the utilization of Sufis for Aḥmad Shāh's imperial project, it appears quite consistent to tie as many of these gifted

[51] Aḥmad Shāh's own collected poetry clearly proves a deep familiarity with the mystical lexicon, see Durrānī (1388sh), for example 23 (*ghazal* no. 2), 27f. (nos. 10 and 14), 37 (no. 39) and 189–93 (*murabbaʿ*). Nonetheless, it is contended here that acquaintance with a certain vocabulary does not necessarily testify to a corresponding inner disposition.

[52] The rather particular translation of this, as well as other technical Sufi terms, has been adopted from the late Annemarie Schimmel. Her versions are to be considered the most appropriate among the various alternatives extant.

[53] Hōtak (1339sh), 98. The passages from Raḥmān Bābā's *Dīvān*, cited there, are ʿAbd al-Raḥmān (1963), 68 ll. 6–10 and 69 ll. 9f.

community representatives as possible to the courts of the Durrani ruler and his governors. Regrettably, we do not have sufficient and reliable data to assess which of the various reputed Sufi masters had actually followed the invitation to settle in and around the imperial courts of the Durrani. There are, however, a few pointers and considerations that allow us to at least stage a hypothesis. The first is the great emphasis on piety (*birr*), ascetic discipline (*riyāẕat*) and contemplation (*murāqabat*), which are divinely rewarded with visions (*futūḥāt*), revelations (*mukāshafāt*) and especially charisms (*karāmāt*) in the few contemporaneous hagiographies available[54] that already points in the direction of the very popular Chishtī *ṭarīqa*.[55] Another and perhaps most significant hint is provided by the little story above. Indeed, we need to ask what purpose the royal patronage of Sufi *shaykh*s from all over the Durrani lands was to serve, aside from the possibility of some of Aḥmad Shāh's personal mystical leanings. Patronage of the arts and sciences is clearly a commonly stipulated marker of exemplary royal conduct in the mirrors for princes, and

54 See, for example, Mākū (1379sh/2000), 23f. and 26; al-Haravī (1379/1960), II: 711–830; Hōtak (1339sh), 8, 18, 23f., 62, 64f., 74, 100 and 132–4.

It is remarkable that, for all the emphasis on the exceptional socio-cultural importance of the Sufi *shaykh* in the Pashtun Borderland (and beyond), there are still precious few published studies that shed light on this phenomenon before the late eighteenth / early nineteenth century, especially outside the urban centres. The reason for this may well be that we still have only a very few contemporaneous texts available that would allow us to acquire some more reliable insight. As it stands, the authenticity of some of the core materials, for instance, the anthology of Pashto poets by Muḥammad ibn Dāvūd Khān Hōtak (d. after 1141/1729), edited as *Pəṭah Khizānah* by ʿAbd al-Ḥayy Ḥabībī (d. 1984), is seriously disputed for a number of specifically linguistic reasons. Another is the early seventeenth-century Persian *Makhzān-i Afghānī* of Niʿmatallāh Haravī, which contains a hagiographical section on sixty-six renowned Sufis descending from one of the three major tribal confederacies he himself laid out in the very same work, composed in 1018/1609 with a purpose within the context of the Mughal court and based on a number of rather standardized Persian and Arabic chronicles (see al-Haravī [1379/1960], I: 4–6). Later hagiographies, such as *Də Kandahār Mashāhīr* of Muḥammad Valī Źalmay (d. 1395sh/2018), rely heavily on these two works, in addition to the extant fragment of the *Tazkirat al-Awliyā* of Sulaymān Mākū Sābzay (fl. around 1220 CE in the Arghastān region of today's south-eastern Afghanistan), purportedly the earliest extant prose text in Pashto (see Mākū [1379sh/2000], 23): see Źalmay (1349sh).

The major exceptions to this rather sobering assessment appear to be those Sufis who have left behind writings that, in the times to follow, were repeatedly copied and disseminated across the entire Pashtun Borderland, such as the Pīr Rōx̌ān, the Ākhūnd Darvīzah and Raḥmān Bābā.

55 Indeed, the core theological doctrine and spiritual practice of the Chishtiyyah fit the above list of Sufi technical terms quite well, and it corresponds to the forms and contents of relevant poetry from the southern Hilmand–Arghandāb basin in the *Pəṭah Khizānah*: see Hōtak (1339sh), 24–30, 84–8, 100–2, 116–8 *et passim*; Ernst and Lawrence (2002), esp. 14–8 and 34–46. The prominence of the Chishtiyyah in the Pashtun Borderland, especially before the advent of the Naqshbandiyyah-Mujaddidiyyah, had already been remarked upon by Badakhshī (1140h), 75a–76b.

necessary for unfolding an elaborate court culture, even more so as Aḥmad Shāh needed to show himself as sufficiently emancipated from his former Safavid overlords.[56] Moreover, the drafting in of renowned clients from across the dominion suggests that the ruler, having sought their wise counsel, would issue decrees that were indeed reflective of the particular situation of his subjects in all the various localities and, therefore, truly equitable (*inṣāfī*).

However, the co-option of Sufi *shaykh*s to the Durrani court at Kandahar turned out to be rather a double-edged sword. Firstly, not every one of them could enjoy the amenities of courtly life, which may have left one or other of them somewhat disgruntled. Secondly, and perhaps more importantly, not every one of them would have wanted these amenities, as they potentially conflicted with the Sufi virtues of modesty, chastity and detachment from mundane desires, although most of those who could be persuaded to relocate to the Durrani courts of Kandahar and Kabul appear to have mainly been of that rather world-rejecting kind that is epitomized by followers of the Chishtiyyah approach.

Still, a critical mass of Sufi *shaykh*s generally suspicious of worldly power of whatever provenance remained in existence in the various parts of the Pashtun Borderland, and – as the Pīr Rōx̌ān's earlier confrontation with Mughal imperial claims indicates – could also activate their networks of followers to challenge the rule of the Durrani. The Naqshbandiyyah-Mujaddidiyyah, with its strong track record of theological and socio-political critique,[57] was almost predisposed to be the carrier of such articulations. In this light, it had perhaps been rather short-sighted of Aḥmad Shāh to affront Shāh Valiyallāh Dihlavī, who, after all, was widely regarded as a major representative of the Naqshbandiyyah-Mujaddidiyyah in eighteenth-century northern India, and would, in the centuries to come, eventually evolve into a core reference point for socio-political discontent sustained by religious precepts, not least in the Pashtun Borderland. In this regard, the distinction between what Brown and Rassler call "lowland" and "highland Pashtuns"[58] turned out to play a significant role.

3.1.3 The Other Side of the Coin: Negotiating "Islam" in the Pashtun Borderland

What would gradually develop into a cultural conflict between "lowland" and "highland Pashtuns" is already somewhat foreshadowed by the historiographical dispute over who it was that actually bestowed the title "Pearl of Pearls"

[56] See Hartung (2011), 302–7; (2017b), 92–8.

[57] The prime example here is the progenitor of the Naqshbandiyyah-Mujaddidiyyah, Aḥmad Fārūqī Sirhindī, the "Renewer of the Second Millennium" (*mujaddid-i alf-i s̱ānī*) mentioned above; see also Section 2.2. In fact, as we shall see below (e.g., in Section 3.3.4), Sirhindī himself would become a reference point, albeit a comparatively marginal one, for later political discontents in the Pashtun Borderland.

[58] See Brown and Rassler (2013), 22–7.

upon Aḥmad Shāh and was, thus, giving the subsequent dynasty its name. While chronicler Maḥmūd al-Ḥusaynī at the court of lowland Aḥmad Shāh ascribed this to Ṣābir Shāh Darvīsh, who was mentioned above,[59] others – mostly from the highlands and all of them rather distanced from the courtly circles – claim this, for instance, for the Naqshbandi ʿUmar ibn Ibrāhīm Ćamkanī.[60] The latter, after all, came with a mighty pedigree: his own *murshid* was a discipline of Aḥmad Sirhindī's important *khalīfah* Sayyid Ādam ibn Ismāʿīl Banūrī (d. 1053/1643); in addition ʿUmar Ćamkanī himself claimed to have been initiated to the spiritual path by a vision of the Prophetic light.[61] The *shaykh* himself reflected upon his relationship with Aḥmad Shāh,[62] who, in later *taẕkirāt*, is listed as one of ʿUmar Ćamkanī's disciples.[63] Still, it seems as if the *shaykh*, who carried the epithet "Helper of the Age" (*ghawṡ-i zamān*), had not attended the court at Kandahar, but remained firmly in the Peshawar Valley. More importantly, Banūrī himself played an important role in challenging the balance of power in the delicate ethnic set-up of the Mughal polity: combining his well-respected descent from the family of the Prophet Muḥammad with his socio-political rootedness in the Pashtun context as a purported member of the Mashvāṇī tribal community, he is said to have initiated so many Pashtun disciples that he earned himself the epithet

59 See Jāmī (1384sh), 68f; also Kashmīrī (1970), 188; Kātib-i Hazārah (1331sh), I: 10. The fact, however, that the couplet ascribed to Ṣābir Shāh in the *Tārīkh-i Aḥmad'shāhī* contains the Arabic term *luʾluʾ-i lālā* (shining pearl) instead of the Persian epithet "Pearl of Pearls" (*durr-i durrān*) for Aḥmad Shāh, from which the name of the dynasty was purportedly derived, suggests that someone else might indeed have been responsible for bestowing the latter title upon the monarch.

60 See, for example, Khān (1894), 172; Quddūsī (1966), 453f. The claim by the latter is based on Shīr Muḥammad Khān's *Ansāb-i Ruʾasah-yi Ḍērah Ismāʿīl Khān*, the manuscript of which it has unfortunately not been possible to trace to date.

61 See Gīlānī (1972), I: 96, who quotes from the preface of ʿUmar Ćamkanī's own *Tawẓīḥ al-Maʿānī Sharḥ Khulāṣah-yi Kaydānī*; compare also Ḥanīf (1979), 427–30. The text, a commentary on a short Hanafi *fiqh* work by Luṭfallāh al-Nasafī al-Fāḍil al-Kaydānī (d. 750/1349) on the correct execution of the ritual prayer, seems to have been lost, as both Gīlānī (1972), I: 97f., and Ḥanīf (1979), 427, have quoted from secondary texts. The latter two, however, as well as "Aṡr" Afghānī (1965), II: 736f., mention at least two manuscripts in private collections in KP, as well as a printed version from Delhi's Maṭbaʿ Fayẓ-i ʿĀmm in 1298h (1881). Finally, there is a reasonable possibility that MS no. 414 (*Rasāʾil-i Taṣawvuf*) in the Muḥammad Iqbāl Mujaddidī Collection of the Punjab University Library, Lahore, contains that very text.

62 Unfortunately, the consulted manuscript Ćamkanī (1138/1725) does not contain these particulars. The copy held by the Library of the National Museum of Pakistan in Karachi, which had been checked and approved by ʿUmar Ćamkanī himself, has not been available to me. For an account on his still rather nebulous relationship with Aḥmad Shāh Durrānī by one of Ćamkanī's disciples, see Mōmand (1164h), 18a–19b and 30a f.

63 See, for example, Ḥanīf (1979), 523–32. This perspective, based by and large on the narrative perpetuated by the Durrani imperial historiographer, has also been adopted by Khan (2022).

"Shaykh of the Afghans" (*shaykh-i afghānān*).[64] Such a degree of spiritual power could easily translate into political influence, which eventually caused the Mughal *padishāh* Shāh'jahān to have Banūrī and a large contingent of his following exiled to Mecca, where they would confront other eminent Naqshbandis in residence with Sirhindī's teachings towards Islamic reformulation.[65]

Moreover, on top of the historical account, the portrayal of the banishment of Ādam Banūrī and his large entourage from the Mughal lands in the *Manāqib-i Ādamiyyah* of the shaykh's contemporary and spiritual *khalīfa* Muḥammad Amīn Badakhshī (d. 1102/1691)[66] contains another point of great significance for our quest to unearth the various discursive strands that provide for the polysemy of the term "talib", and its plural form "taliban", within the Pashtun Borderland: instead of "murīdūn", namely, which would certainly have been expected here, Badakhshī denoted the followers and *khulafā*ʾ of Banūrī's throughout the entire text as "taliban". Because this word choice is not substantiated by the author in the least, it appears as if the application of the term "talib" to the follower of a Sufi *shaykh* was a familiar occurrence in the Pashtun Borderland of the seventeenth century CE, and, therefore, Badakhshī's audience needed no further explanation. For the moment, however, we shall file away this observation of ours and continue with investigating the sequence of historical events that resulted in the firm and durable rooting of the Naqshbandiyyah-Mujaddidiyyah as perhaps *the* major pivot of intra-Islamic reformulation attempts in the Pashtun Borderland prior to the late nineteenth and early twentieth centuries.

64 See Badakhshī (1140h), 6b. This author, himself a leading disciple of Banūrī, estimated the number of Pashtun adepts at 100 000, which, however, may not be factually correct but, instead, only a way to indicate a massive following. For a list of disciples who left with Banūrī for the Hijaz, see ibid., 49a f.

65 See ibid., 42b–44a. The most renowned debate was that with Aḥmad ibn Muḥammad al-Qushāshī (d. 1070/1680), teacher of the later crucially important Ibrāhīm ibn Ḥasan al-Kurānī (d. 1101/1690) and himself a Naqshbandi *shaykh*. On both, see İnce (2014), 15–7, 120–9, 192, 245f. and 270f. The controversy pivoted on the question of the pre-eminence of the Prophet Muḥammad vis-à-vis the Kaʿba, as an expression of the fundamental doctrinal dispute over the "unity of existence" (*waḥdat al-wujūd*), advocated by al-Qushāshī and his circles, versus the "unity of testimony" (*waḥdat al-shuhūd*) that was argued for by the followers of Sirhindī: see Badakhshī (1140h), 80a–94a and 142b–3b. In fact, ʿUmar Ćamkanī's own *Ẓavāhir* contains an explanation of the very same issue, which indicates his firm doctrinal adherence to the tradition of Sirhindī: see Ćamkanī (1138/1725), 81–8.

66 Muḥammad Amīn Badakhshī, who had fled his native Badakhshan from the invading Uzbeks to the greater safety of the Punjab, was a disciple of Aḥmad Sirhindī's son Muḥammad Maʿṣūm (d. 1097/1686) and, moreover, one of those who actually accompanied Ādam Banūrī to Mecca, where he stayed on with him until the *shaykh*'s demise in 1102/1691: see Badakhshī (1140h), 49b.

Banūrī's banishment by a political sovereign for fear of losing power to the intimidating following of a spiritual figure appears, in fact, somewhat symptomatic. Firstly, it points to the exceptional degree of authority of the Sufi *shaykhs* of the Borderland as a whole, which had frequently been used to raise ad hoc militias (*laẋkarūnah*) from their substantial followings and confronted political authorities whenever their particular interests were at stake. Here, in fact, we seem to already have an early instance of the convergence of *taliban* and religiously inspired militant activism, which, again, we shall keep in mind for later. Secondly, authorities usually aimed at channelling these powers into acquiescence, if not support, of the respective ruling regime; they would turn to coercive measures only if their attempts to do so were unsuccessful. This approach towards the *shaykhs* of the Borderland would remain almost unchanged from the time of the Mughals onwards: the Durrani, the Barakzay (*Bārakzay*) of Afghanistan as its successor, the British colonial authorities and, later, even the national governments of Afghanistan and Pakistan would employ similar strategies to handle this delicate matter of power in their respective interest. The co-option of influential socio-religious dignitaries emerged as a major tool in negotiating the lines of conflict between "lowland" and "highland" communities and creating the imaginary of the entire Pashtun Borderland as a single and, thus, manageable, unit, while imperial hierarchies remained intact.

The investigation of these strategic patterns, however, confronts us with a source problem: while complacent religious dignitaries are often identifiable through the biographical sections on religious dignitaries in imperial historiography, those who did not submit themselves to the temptations of courtly privileges remain difficult to identify. As a result, the known case of ʿUmar Ćamkanī needs to serve us as a stand-in for the real figure of other such Sufis of eminence, especially from the highlands. Most of those who are included in the translocal *taẕkirāt* do not figure as discontents to imperial power claims. In view of the potential competition between Durrani and Khattak over prevalence indicated above, however, one is prompted to assume that the most likely opposition radiated from the spiritual descendants of the patron saint of the Khattak tribe, Sayyid Kasṭīr Gul "Raḥm'kār" "Kākā Ṣāḥib" (d. 1063/1653), whose most eminent disciples are – probably erroneously – said to have included Khūshḥāl Khān,[67] the then-chief of the Khattak.[68] Yet, these spiritual successors would perhaps also perpetuate imperial claims, not just those of the Durrani. It appears, therefore, inevitable to engage with local *taẕkirāt* as what

[67] See, for example, Quddūsī (1966), 312–65; Gīlānī (1972), I: 45. While repeatedly quoted with reverent verses and statements about the Kākā Ṣāḥib, Khūshḥāl is not listed among the *shaykh*'s fifty-one *khulafāʾ* in Kākā Khēl (1986), 186–95; for the passages quoted from Khūshḥāl, see ibid., 196f. and 245.

[68] See Dās (1878), 377.

Caron calls 'borderland historiographies';[69] yet, those appear, more often than not, rather difficult to locate and, if one has successfully done so, to access.

It is easier to establish the image of competition between "lowland" and "highland" imperial claims based on contrasting imperial chronicles. The Durrani universe, first laid out in Maḥmūd al-Ḥusaynī's *Tārīkh-i Aḥmad'shāhī*, was further elaborated by Imām al-Dīn Chishtī in his *Tārīkh-i Ḥusayn'shāhī* (completed 1798) and, subsequently, by Shāh'zādah ʿAlī Muḥammad Khān Sadōzay of Multan (d. 1255/1939) in the *Tazkirat al-Mulūk-i ʿAlī'sha'n* (completed 1835) and Sulṭān Muḥammad ibn Mūsá Durrānī in the *Tārīkh-i Sulṭānī* (completed 1864).[70] At the other end, the descendants of Khūshḥāl Khān, such as his grandson Afẕal Khān ibn Ashraf Khān (d. 1160/1747), fortified similar claims for the supremacy of the Khattak in their own historiographies – here the *Tārīkh-i Muraṣṣaʿ*.[71] These pretensions were not necessarily based on military superiority, but rather on a cultural one that pivoted on a refined morality, as expressed in the Pashto verse of the highlands, prominently represented by poets as diverse as Khūshḥāl Khān and Raḥmān Bābā.

It appears that the latter set the tone for the justification of claims for moral superiority by "highland Pashtuns", while the former served to vindicate corresponding political ones. Most probably relying on expositions in the *Tārīkh-i Muraṣṣaʿ*, Rāʾī Bahādur Munshī Gōpāl Dās (b. 1843) of Lahore, Extra Assistant Commissioner to the British colonial administration for the District (*band va bast*) of Peshawar between 1869 and 1874, kept justifying the authoritative claims of the Khattak as historically derived from their earlier servitude to the Mughals.[72] By doing so, he was putting them implicitly at odds with the Sadōzay-Abdālī-Durrani as former vassals of the Persian Safavids and Afsharids, who had been major rivals of the Mughals.

More importantly, still, Dās stressed in his preface that his views on administrative and cultural matters were, first and foremost, based on his own observations and communications with community representatives.[73] What emerges here is an image of the wider Peshawar Valley, rather than the Durrani heartland around Kandahar, as the cultural and, subsequently, political centre of the Borderland, partially defined by a generous understanding of the ancestral territory (*tappah*) of the Khattak tribe.[74] Alongside this political

[69] See Caron (2016b), 333–8.

[70] See Chishtī (1826), 3a–4b; Durrānī (1298sh), 52–69 and 93–134; Noelle-Karimi (2017), 66–74.

[71] See Khān Khaṭṭak (1893), for example 233–40.

[72] See Dās (1878), 306f. and esp. 376–82, where he wrote of 'the rule of the Akōṛah branch of the Khattak-family' (*riyāsat-i khāndān-i Khaṭṭak-i shākh-i Akōṛah*), meaning that around Khūshḥāl Khān.

[73] See ibid., 1.

[74] See ibid., 303–58, esp. 323–6.

geography, Gōpāl Dās also presented a religious one, which revolved very much around spiritual centres in the Peshawar Valley, first and foremost, that of the Kākā Ṣāḥib, patron saint of the Khattak, to the southeast of Nowshera (*Nawshahr* / *Nawx̌ār*).[75] A century before Shaykh ʿUmar Ćamkanī, the Kākā Ṣāḥib was also affiliated – among others – to the Naqshbandiyyah, although not its Mujaddidiyyah branch that started in the Pashtun Borderland with Sirhindī's legatee Ādam Banūrī.[76]

All these affiliations, however, were somewhat overridden by his claim of a later Uwaysi initiation,[77] that is, obtaining spiritual affiliation without the need to interact physically.[78] This is a remarkable fact, because initiation into a *ṭarīqa* usually served for the subordination of the Uwaysi identity to that of the *ṭarīqa*.[79] As a consequence of his dominant Uwaysi self, the Kākā Ṣāḥib remained unaffiliated to any of the established Sufi *salāsil*, a fact that exempted him from submitting to their disciplining chain of authority, and this, subsequently, allowed him to remain outside the intricate web of delicate spiritual, socio-economic and political hierarchies in the Pashtun Borderland. His vast and diverse following across the region, including some spiritual descendants

[75] See ibid., 333–42.

[76] See Kākā Khēl (1986), 123–5.

[77] The picture that emerges from the hagiographical material available at the time of writing is that the Kākā Ṣāḥib received spiritual guidance from the Prophet Muḥammad, renowned Sufi personalities of the formative period, Bāyazīd Bisṭāmī (d. 261/874) and Sayyid ʿAlī Hujvīrī (d. *c.* 464/1072) prominently among them, as well as many of the eponymous founders of a *silsila*, such as Muʿīn al-Dīn Chishtī (d. 627/1236) and Bahāʾ al-Dīn Naqshband (d. 791/1389), see "Asr" Afghānī (1965), II: 577–81; Kākā Khēl (1986), 121–3. Both scholars have based much of their exposition on the *Maqāmāt-i Quṭbiyyah va Maqālāt-i Qudṣiyyah*, a collection of the teachings of the Kākā Ṣāḥib by the dignitary's fourth-eldest son ʿAbd al-Ḥalīm "Ḥalīm Gul" (d. 1092/1681). Unfortunately, despite best efforts, no print copy of this work could be located. However, large parts are available for download as audio lectures in Urdu, delivered at the *khānaqāh* of the Kākā Ṣāḥib in Nowshera, at: www.tazkia.org//ur/bayanat/audio/makamat-e-qutbiyah (accessed 28 August 2020).

[78] The Uwaysi current of Sufi Islam, tracing its origins back to the enigmatic Uways al-Qaranī (allegedly killed 37/657) as the first to have claimed spiritual communication with the Prophet by telepathy, is still little explored in comparison with other more institutionalized traditions, such as the Naqshbandiyyah. Yet, the eponymous founder of the Naqshbandiyyah, Bahāʾ al-Dīn Naqshband of Bukhara, had received his initiation from ʿAbd al-Khāliq Ghiždūvānī (d. 617/1220), who himself is said to have been a Uwaysi; Aḥmad Sirhindī had also received, besides his earlier initiation into the Naqshbandiyyah by his father Khᵛājah Muḥammad Baqī bi'llāh of Kabul (d. 1012/1603), direct spiritual instruction by the Prophet and had, therefore, been a Uwaysi. Foundationally, see Baldick (1993); DeWeese (1993); on Uways al-Qaranī himself, see Zakharia (1999).

[79] DeWeese (1993), 21 and 25f., refers to the example of Bahāʾ al-Dīn Naqshband, whose Uwaysi identity was soon assimilated into the *Khᵛājah'gān* tradition which eventually morphed into the Naqshbandiyyah and 'marked the rise of the *silsila* (literally, "chain") as a principle of legitimizing Sufi activities and teaching' (Paul [2017], 72).

of the "Pīr Bābā" Sayyid ʿAlī Tirmiẕī, who remains until today the pivotal spiritual figure especially for the Yusufzay of Bunēr and Swat,[80] as well as his general aloofness from worldly affairs, predisposed the Kākā Ṣāḥib to mediate in intertribal conflict. Perhaps the most important such conflict occurred between the Khattak, in whose territory the Kākā Ṣāḥib flourished, and the northern Yusufzay, instigated by Mughal ruler Akbar and continued during the reign of his successors Jahāngīr and Shāh'jahān.[81] Despite the Kākā Ṣāḥib's efforts, the conflict remained latent even after Khūshḥāl Khān's break with the Mughal court, albeit then slightly toned down in view of the more immediate conflict of the highland tribes as a whole with the imperialist southern Durrani.

The latter, in turn, had established their formal sovereignty over the Peshawar Valley in 1749, and had been assured a declaration of loyalty from numerous *məshərān* of the dominant tribes there.[82] This, however, should not lead us to assume that the Durrani rulers – even Tīmūr Shāh ibn Aḥmad Shāh (r. 1773–93), who had made Peshawar his winter residence[83] – had been fulsomely accepted as rulers over the Peshawar Valley and the adjacent mountainous territories to the east and north.[84] First, the shift of the rulers' residence (*dār al-salṭanat*) from Kandahar to Kabul,[85] aimed at avoiding an escalation of conflict with the formerly dominant and similarly southern tribe of the Ghilzay,[86] established a more direct presence of Durrani rule in the former Mughal imperial province of Kabul and the Frontier, thus suggesting a firmer grip on their own territories to the communities of "highland" Pashtuns. Secondly, and this we owe once more to Gōpāl Dās, the religious policies of the Durrani in these lands appear to have exhausted themselves in the

80 See "Aṣr" Afghānī (1965), II: 579; Yūsufī (1960), 250–2.

81 See Yūsufī (1960), 256–69; Kākā Khēl (1986), 240–4.

82 See Jāmī (1384sh), 115; Khān (1894), 172; Kākā Khēl (1965), 681.

83 See Chishtī (1826), 61b.

84 Obviously, authors such as Qadir and Asghar (2016), 58f., have taken a slightly different stand when going as far as styling Peshawar the second capital of the Durrani empire.

85 Given the fact that wider Kandahar served almost instantly as a base for the Ghilzay tribal resistance to Sadōzay-Durrani rule, Kabul, to which neither tribal group had any hereditary claims, was certainly considered quite early on as a feasible option for an administrative centre of the territorially growing Durrani polity. Still, the fact that Aḥmad Shāh had a new city created in the vicinity of the Shrine of Shīr Surkh to the south of the older cities of Kandahar (see Trousdale [2021], 22–4) clearly suggests that the city in which the dynasty was founded was indeed initially intended to serve as its administrative centre. In fact, Aḥmad Shāh's efforts to lure dignitaries from all parts of the new polity to settle in Kandahar sustain this perspective even further: by assembling a diverse array of representatives of the entire Durrani polity in Kandahar, he was able to shift the perception of the city from its being the ancestral territory of distinct tribal groups to that of a more cosmopolitan place.

86 See Chishtī (1826), 58a–59a; Kātib-i Hazārah (1331sh), I: 38 (though much less detailed); Khān (1894), 132–70 and 173f. We shall see below that the Ghilzay claims of political dominance resurged in the late twentieth century with the rise of the ṬIT / IEA.

appointment of a nomenclature of religious functionaries: *qāẕī*, *muftī*, *muḥtasib* and a *shaykh al-islām* as the highest religious authority served as officials for the Durrani court.[87] While we lack comprehensive and trustworthy registers of these appointees, circumstantial evidence suggests that the Durrani made their appointments, at least in part, on the basis of tribal affiliation, as indicated, for instance, in the case of the ancestors of mufti ʿAbd al-Raḥīm ibn ʿAbd al-Ḥakīm of the Durrani subtribe of Pōpalzay (d. 1363/1944), who will play a prominent role in our narrative at a later point.[88]

Such an imposition of a religious service elite by the "lowland" Durrani certainly did not go uncontested. In 1779, the "Ṣāḥib'zādah of Ćamkanī", son of Shaykh ʿUmar mentioned above,[89] was blamed for instigating Fayẕallāh Khān, an elder (*arbāb*) of the Khalīl tribe of the village of Tākāl in today's western part of Peshawar city, to assassinate Tīmūr Shāh and have him replaced by his younger and presumably more suggestible brother Sikandar Shāh.[90] While the plot ultimately failed, this episode, nonetheless, indicates a serious opposition to the Durrani regime among "highland" Pashtuns, carried out mainly by local spiritual authorities and directed against the perceived infringement of the political and cultural autonomy of the various "highland" communities. Again, the legitimacy of such autonomy was rooted in the proclamation of moral superiority that had been derived from distinct religious interpretations as put forth by such regionally important personalities as ʿUmar Ćamkanī, who in this way continued the tradition of religious criticism especially of popular Sufi beliefs and practices often associated with the Chishtiyyah, which runs along the same line of thinking as that of the Naqshbandiyyah-Mujaddidiyyah.[91]

Consequently, the tenacious orientation towards the example of the Prophet Muḥammad and his Companions, as well as a strong understanding of God's fundamental Oneness (*tawḥīd*),[92] both cornerstones of the religious universe of the Naqshbandiyyah-Mujaddidiyyah, also radiated from the teachings of the

87 See Dās (1878), 382f.

88 See Gīlānī (1972), I: 258f.; Pōpalzaʾī (1992), 12. For more on ʿAbd al-Raḥīm Pōpalzay, see Section 3.3.2.

89 This appears to have been Miyāṇ Muḥammadī Ćamkanī (d. 1220/1805), to whom we owe the *Burhān al-Uṣūl fī Bayān al-Uṣūl*, an Arabic work on legal hermeneutics (MS Islamia College Peshawar 581, dated 1210/1795), the *Rayāḥīn al-Salawāt fī Basātīn al-Barakāt* on the salutations upon the Prophet (*durūd*) (MS purportedly at the Kutub'khānah Bahānah Māṛī Peshawar) and, finally, his seminal *Maqāṣid al-Fiqh* (MS Pashto Academy Peshawar University 16, dated 1787), see Kātib-i Hazārah (1331sh), I: 38; Ḥanīf (1979), 469–79.

90 See Chishtī (1826), 61b–64b; Kātib-i Hazārah (1331sh), I: 37f.; Kākā Khēl (1965), 703f.

91 For comprehensive discussions of Aḥmad Sirhindī's open criticism of Sufi beliefs and practices that have played a prominent role even in the Mughal court, see Friedmann (1971), 41–68 and 77–85.

92 See Faruqi (1940), 117–39; Friedmann (1971), 13–21 and 33–40; ter Haar (1992), 117–22 and 137–60.

Kākā Ṣāḥib. Yet, there is a substantial difference between the Kākā Ṣāḥib and ʿUmar Ćamkanī regarding political authority and servitude, as well as taking part in worldly affairs in general, which makes them somewhat paradigmatic representatives of two distinct positions of spiritual authorities in the Peshawar Valley of the seventeenth and eighteenth centuries vis-à-vis the respective imperial establishment.

The Uwaysi Kākā Ṣāḥib served, as we saw above, as someone able to mediate between diverse religious and socio-political perspectives and claims, without forcing anyone under the umbrella of his own personal views and convictions. Salvation for him was apparently a very personal affair, and he would, therefore, not go out and preach uniformity of belief and / or practice. Instead, he represented the individualistic and detached ethos of the early Sufis, that is, before the advent of the socio-religious organization of Islamic spirituality in the Sufi *ṭuruq*;[93] obedience to the *shari'a*, as he interpreted it, was an individual matter of the heart, not an outward expression of conformity.[94] A little over a century after that, ʿUmar Ćamkanī, and others in his wake, took a rather different stand on this and related matters. For them, heart and hand needed to correspond to allow the recognition of true obedience to the *shari'a*. Full compliance with the *shari'a*, in turn, was suitable for claiming religious and, subsequently, political authority across the Pashtun Borderland, something that had already been found in the late sixteenth century in the arguments the Ākhūnd Darvīzah Nangarhārī presented in his condemnation of the "Pīr Rōx̌ān" Bāyazīd Anṣārī, enshrined first and foremost in his bilingual *Makhzān al-Islām*.[95] In fact, the way in which he presented his reckoning with a competitor for socio-religious and political influence in the Pashtun Borderland bequeathed ʿUmar Ćamkanī and later writers with a blueprint; it is, therefore, deemed reasonable to briefly take a closer look.

Surprisingly, the *Makhzān al-Islām* has been recognized in the academic and semi-academic literature so far almost exclusively for its explicit critique of the Pīr Rōx̌ān and popularizing the infamous epithet "Pīr of Darkness" – *pīr-i tārīk* – for the author's adversary.[96] Yet, the *Makhzān* is, in fact, much less straightforward heresiographically, although the events around the Pīr Rōx̌ān and his massive following constituted explicitly the inducement for the composition of this work.[97] Its bulk, instead, consists of translations of four classical Arabic texts on the core tenets of faith and basic ritual practices into Pashto. This, the Ākhūnd Darvīzah emphasized, was necessitated by his own observation that the inhabitants of the Pashtun Borderland are not even

[93] Comprehensively on these developments, see Melchert (2020).

[94] See Kākā Khēl (1986), 71–121.

[95] See Darvīzah (n.d.).

[96] See Section 2.2, n.22.

[97] See, for example, Darvīzah (1885), 14 and 72.

familiar with what he would regard as the "bare minimum", and, as a result, they had become gullible victims of manipulation at the hands of local religious dignitaries of questionable authority:

> An additional explanation is that because the community has split into seventy-two groups, one after another they have all forsaken [their] faith of the Sunni creed [*i'tiqādī az maẕhab-i sunnat va jamā'at*], and, one by one, they went to the fringes and, by following the winds and [inadmissible] innovation, submitted to heresy and error, so that nowadays most beliefs of the *ahl-i bid'at* are now widespread among the Afghans. Because the sheer number of seditious shaykhs and pirs – human in appearance, but diabolic in nature – is the reason for the overabundance of worldly scholars who inquire into religious matters on earth and therefore imagine themselves as having the exclusive right to it – In God I seek refuge from error! The Afghans love the friend [of God; *mawlá*] fervently and are eager to know the *dīn*, but because of their gullibility and ignorance [*nā-dānī va jāhilī*] they are deprived of the religious sciences. They do not know the truth from a lie and [therefore] accept from them what to believe [*mu'taqāt*]. They affirm and exaggerate a lot in emulation [*taqlīd*], so that, [even] if the respected elders and all of today's pious people are saying something to the contrary, they will not accept or acknowledge. Therefore, because of exaggeration in corrupt imitation the unbeliever and innovator is killed [*pas binā'bar ghuluv dar taqlīd-i fāsid kāfir va mubtadi' kashtah va mīkardand*] – In God I seek refuge from the blind followers of unbelief![98]

Publicizing concise introductory works on creed and jurisprudence among a Pashto-speaking audience deemed a reasonable way forward to rectify this situation,[99] targeting especially the religious functionaries in the communities to whom the ability to read was, and, in fact, in some areas of the Pashtun Borderland still remains, very much confined.

From this observation, coupled with the recognition of the exceptionally important role of religious functionaries in the Pashtun Borderland for all kinds of community affairs, it appears reasonable to contend that the Ākhūnd Darvīzah was establishing an elite discourse about a sustainable "bare minimum" of Islamic belief and practice, which had an almost immediate impact on various kinds of socio-political activism. At the same time, the various passages in Persian suggest that he also wrote implicitly with the Mughals as

98 Ibid., 71f.

99 The very short works rendered here into Pashto were the *'Aqā'id* of the Maturidi *mutakallim* Najm al-Dīn Abū Ḥafṣ 'Umar al-Nasafī (d. 537/1142), four select articles of the *'Aqīda* of 'Uthmān ibn Muḥammad al-Shāmī al-Ḥanafī (d. 607/1210), the panegyrical *Kawākib al-Durriyya fī Madḥ Khayr al-Bariyya*, better known as *Qaṣīdat al-Burda*, of the North African Berber poet Abū 'Abdallāh Muḥammad al-Būṣīrī (d. 691/1294) and, last but not least, the aforementioned (see n.61 in this chapter) *Khulāṣa* of Luṭfallāh al-Kaydānī on the correct execution of the ritual prayer.

the representatives of the imperial superstructure at that time in mind, somewhat insinuating that he and his circles were the exponents of an authoritatively grounded Islamic orthodoxy in the Pashtun Borderland and, therefore, politically serene and rather loyal, at least as long as Islamic core principles were not violated.

Although, to date, there is no solid textual evidence to prove that either the Ākhūnd Darvīzah or any of his disciples[100] provided authoritative religious support to the punitive measures of the Mughals against the Rawshaniyyah movement, the legally substantiated condemnation of the Pīr Rōx̌ān and his followers as heretics, innovators and apostates would certainly have contributed to a general acceptance of the persecution of the Rawshaniyyah across the communities of the upper Pashtun Borderland. By doing so, the Ākhūnd Darvīzah, indeed, evolved as a reference point for later and equally nomocentric elite actors in the region, eventually culminating in those who are, in fact, responsible for narrowing down the semantic range of the term "*taliban*" to its currently dominating meaning, prominently represented by ṬIT / IEA and TṬP.[101] Moreover, in this train of thought, they also devised a standard pattern of engagement with religious opponents in the Pashtun Borderland: a handful of short and, therefore, barely explanatory classical texts are singled out to serve as an authoritative backdrop to justifying the claim of the respective author to be a, if not *the*, rightful custodian of Islamic normativity. The other side of the coin is that everyone who rejected those claims was branded as a deviant, the scale of which ranged from a mere sinner (*fāsiq*) and hypocrite (*munāfiq*) to a heretic (*mulḥid*) and apostate (*kāfir murtadd*).

Moreover, by invoking the Qur'anic injunction to 'enjoin the commendable and prevent the reprehensible' (*al-amr bi'l-maʿrūf wa-nahy ʿan al-munkar*; henceforth truncated) emphatically as obligatory,[102] like the Ākhūnd did

[100] Two important cases in point here were Ākhūnd Miyāṇdād ibn ʿAlī al-Dīn (d. 1079/1668) and Ākhūnd Muḥammad Ćāllāk (d. 1068/1658), purportedly two chief upholders of Ākhūnd Darvīzah's programme for Islamic reformulation: see, for example, Ḥakīmzay and Muḥammad (2018); Ḥakīmzay and Akbar (2018); Yūsufzay (2012).

[101] For a rather random example, see Ḥāfiẓ ʿAbd al-Ghaffūr Qārī, 'Ḥazrat Akhūnd [*sic*] Darvīzah kē ḥalāt awr taṣānīf', *al-Ḥaqq* 21/1 (1406/1985), 45–9. Tellingly, of the at least seven known writings of the Ākhūnd, four of which were printed during the British Raj and would have been, therefore, more easily available, only the *Makhzān* is covered in this article. Incidentally, a section of the same passage quoted above is cited and additionally translated into Urdu on p. 48.

[102] This precept is rooted especially in Q3.104 and 110: 'And let there be a people among you, inviting to the good, enjoining the commendable and preventing the reprehensible. [...] You are the best people brought forth among humankind. You enjoin the commendable and prevent the reprehensible, and you believe in God' (*wa-'ltakūn minkum ummatun yadʿūna ilá 'l-khayri wa-yamurūna bi'l-maʿrūfi wa-yanhawna ʿani 'l-munkari* [...] *kuntum khayra ʾummatin ʾukhrijat li'l-nāsi taʾmurūna 'l-maʿrūfi wa-tanhawna ʿani 'l-munkar*).

explicitly in his rather expansive *Irshād al-Ṭālibiyīn*,[103] the doors are pushed wide open for the emergence of self-righteous intracommunal vigilantism, quite often adopted by younger males whom the Ākhūnd Darvīzah envisioned as the core audience for this tract. When explaining the actual practical implementation of *amr bi'l-maʿrūf* [...], the Ākhūnd drew on an accepted *ḥadīth* in which the Prophet Muḥammad was asked about details on how to discipline an apostate from Islam: after all, the Prophet had already decreed elsewhere that 'Whoever changes his religion, kill!' (*man baddala dīnahu fa'qtūluh*), a rather blunt statement which the Ākhūnd also quoted in this discussion.[104] Yet, this declaration became somewhat moderated by the *ḥadīth* mentioned that the Ākhūnd Darvīzah chose as a starting point for elaborating on his own position, one which seems to have been derived more from his understanding of the respective discussions among the early Islamic jurists than the *ḥadīth* itself.[105] After all, prominently among the things of which the Ākhūnd accused the Pīr Rōx̌ān and his followers figure gross exaggeration and extremism in religious interpretation and practice, and it is, thus, quite comprehensible that the Ākhūnd himself took great care not to fall into a similar trap by being excessively harsh. True, he went as far as accusing the Pīr Rōx̌ān and his followers of apostasy (*ridda*, or *irtidād*) – something that he discussed with little differentiation alongside "sin", "heresy", "hypocrisy" and "inadmissible innovation in matters of religion". However, he stressed that the imposition and execution of the death penalty was to remain the very last resort in dealing with those Muslims perceived as religiously deviant, the more so as judgement and the corresponding penalty were contingent upon certain general socio-political conditions.[106] What adds an interesting twist to the whole discussion is that the Pīr Rōx̌ān, however, and to some extent also his successors as leaders of the Rawshaniyyah movement, maintained an equal claim to represent Islamic orthodoxy and based their beliefs and practices on their own interpretation of the Islamic *shariʿa*.

For the moment, let us retain that religious dignitaries in the diverse Muslim communities across the Pashtun Borderland had already cultivated at this early stage in our present narrative a binary image of "us" as a small righteous elite,

[103] See Darvīzah (1310/1893), 70f.

[104] See ibid., 71. The "*man baddala* [...]" *ḥadīth* is attested in *Ṣaḥīḥ al-Bukhārī*, k. istitābat al-murtaddīn wa'l-muʿānidīn wa-qitāluhum, b. ḥukm al-murtadd wa'l-murtadda, no. 1 (ḥadīth 7 009); *Sunan Ibn Māja*, k. al-ḥudūd, b. al-murtadd ʿan dīnih, no. 1 (ḥadīth 2 632); *Sunan Abī Dāwūd*, k. al-ḥudūd, b. al-ḥukm fīman irtadda, no. 1 (ḥadīth 4353); and *Sunan al-Nasāʾī*, k. taḥrīm al-damm, b. al-ḥukm fi'l-murtadd, no. 3 (ḥadīth 4 076).

[105] See Darvīzah (1310/1893), 71f. The *ḥadīth* in question, on the singular authority of Abū Saʿīd al-Khudrī, is found in *Ṣaḥīḥ Muslim*, k. al-īmān, b. bayān kawn al-nahy ʿan al-munkar min al-īmān wa-ʾanna 'l-īmān yazīdu wa-yanquṣu wa-ʾanna 'l-amr bi'l-maʿrūf wa'l-nahy ʿan al-munkar wājibān, no. 1 (ḥadīth 186).

[106] For the various positions regarding the grave offence of apostasy in early Islamic *fiqh*, see Friedmann (2003), 121–59 *et passim*.

and "them", which is the majority of the residents there, who are sweepingly characterized by a severely defective understanding of even basic Islamic principles and who are steeped in popular superstition and practices that are difficult to sustain from a normative Islamic perspective. Such a nomocentric perspective of Muslim religiosity in general also had immediate implications regarding whether or not political rule could be endorsed as legitimate, because, according to classical Islamic political theory, the fidelity of the subjects to rule is entirely dependent on that of the ruler as their shepherd. In the eyes of the religious dignitaries, especially in the upper Pashtun Borderland, this would be expressed as the extent to which rulers would be willing to listen to their advice on good governance and facilitate structural developments within the dominion to increase the prosperity of the community. In other words, what was called for was a different kind of religious guidance of the mighty and powerful from the rather world-rejecting spirituality of those who assembled around Aḥmad Shāh's court at Kandahar.

Urbanite *shaykh*s, such as the prominent ʿUmar Ćamkanī already repeatedly mentioned, expressed these sentiments quite well and, consequently, would rather have rulers come to them, thus indicating a new level of self-confidence as a mark that set them apart from their peers of past and present.[107] Their preoccupation with matters of *ʿaqīda*[108] and *fiqh* appears conspicuous; this is evident, not least, in the fact that they presented their arguments with a strong emphasis on *shari'a*, which stands in stark contrast to those that highlight more the higher stages of individual Sufi spirituality, that is "inner truth" (*ḥaqīqa*) and "gnosis" (*maʿrifa*), as seemed much more common in non-urban contexts.[109] It looks as if the urban element, seemingly stronger in Peshawar and Kabul than in Kandahar, played a substantial role in this readjustment of focus, a role that demands our due appreciation.

[107] This, of course, does not necessarily make them even *proto*-bourgeois, even though the comparison with developments in Europe after the Thirty Years' War certainly appears quite tempting, as has most sustainably been undertaken by Pernau (2008), 63–71, 216–40 *et passim*, and already by Malik (1993; 2018), although significantly for imperial Delhi under British colonial rule and with due attention to the cultural impact of the respective contemporaneous European conceptual universe on urbanite Indo-Muslim ideas of socio-political order.

[108] ʿUmar Ćamkanī had contributed a comprehensive Persian commentary on the versified *Badʾ al-Amālī* of Sirāj al-Dīn ʿAlī ibn ʿUthmān al-Ūshī al-Farghānī (d. 575/1173), entitled *al-Maʿālī Sharḥ Qaṣidah-yi Amālī*, to this field. A photocopy of the manuscript is held in the Muḥammad Iqbāl Mujaddidī Collection of the Punjab University Library, Lahore, R[otograph]. no. 231.

[109] The emerging – admittedly much simplified – binary categorization of Sufi dignitaries across the Pashtun Borderland is already clearly discernible for the earlier instance of the Pīr Rōxān versus Ākhūnd Darvīzah: while the focus of the latter on all matters *shari'a* had been comprehensively fleshed out above, the writings of the Pīr Rōxān leave little doubt that he regarded the *shari'a* as subordinate to the more esoteric stages *ḥaqīqa* and *maʿrifa*, mediated by *ṭarīqa*: see Rōxān (1396sh/2017), 140–87.

Traditionally regarded as spatial nodes of larger polities, urban settlements have often been established at strategically convenient spots along transregional trading or pilgrim routes and were subsequently serving as either market places or, especially at the fords of rivers or mountain passes, concentration points for tax collection and military defence posts. Because of these utilities, they are marked by a high degree of periodic fluctuation in their respective population, especially among traders, commissioned administrators and military service personnel, while possessing only a small stable core of permanent residents. Intrinsically dependent on the yield of agricultural production in the rural surroundings and its "human resources", urban residents have, in turn, emerged as increasingly specialized artisans, stretching as far as the art of administration, and prided themselves on the comparatively high degree of cultural production in these places.[110]

Peshawar, the domain, not least, of ʿUmar Ćamkanī, fulfilled all these criteria: situated at a ford of the Kabul river and in close proximity to the Khyber Pass, it had served both functions as a transregional marketplace on the overland route to Jalalabad, Kabul and on towards Persia and Transoxiana, and as a garrison town, a function that,[111] according to popular etymologies, was even responsible for its name: *pīsh'āvar*, Persian for "head of what lies ahead".[112] Moreover, as Puruṣapura, it had served the Buddha-following Kuṣāṇa rulers between the first century BCE and the fifth century CE and served as a major hub of Gandhāra cultural production and a node on the routes to pilgrim sites for Buddha-followers[113] to the west, such as Haḋḋah near Jalalabad, which will figure more prominently in our investigation further below.[114] Peshawar's main purpose under Muslim rule, however, seems to have been that of a frontier post garrison.

What is of significance at this particular point are the differences in social interaction between rural and urban spaces. Certain elements in this regard have been highlighted by thinkers as diverse as Ibn Khaldūn in fourteenth-century (CE) Tunis and the so-called "Chicago School" of sociology in the 1920s and 1930s, prominently among them the disintegration of "traditional" forms of solidarity and social organization, based on the heterogeneity of and the high fluctuation in the urban population:[115] 'The close living together and working together of individuals who have no sentimental or emotional ties

[110] See Kleniewski and Thomas (2006), 138, 152–4, 159f., 213, 255, 272–4 and 279f. This perspective is said to have been advocated most vigorously by Australian archaeologist V. Gordon Childe (d. 1957). It occurs, however, that he had been much more considerate than later authors would credit him with having been: see Childe (1950).

[111] See Dās (1878), for example 31–5 and 69–75.

[112] See Davies (2007), 427.

[113] See Chapter 2, n.1.

[114] See Dās (1878), 75–82; Neelis (2011), 244–53.

[115] See Ibn Khaldūn (1425/2004), II: 48–50 and 55f.; Wirth (1938), 14–18.

foster a spirit of competition, aggrandizement and mutual exploitation.'[116] This is why urbanite scholar Ibn Khaldūn, and, by inference, also *shaykh* ʿUmar in suburban Ćamkanī, saw the necessity of enforcing Islamic precepts as compensators for the lack of alternative means to establish community cohesion in the urban context: for either, it is the Islamic *shari'a* that provides the reliable framework of a society not based on traditional modes of organization and community control.[117] Community cohesion is envisioned to be achieved by a common ideational framework and expressed in the public performance of the ritual obligations, first and foremost, the congregational prayer (*ṣalāt*).

Therefore, it is hardly surprising that ʿUmar Ćamkanī was quite concerned about the correct performance of the *ṣalāt* in all its details, and a text that had already been introduced to a Pashto-speaking audience by the Ākhūnd Darvīzah, namely the short exposition of eighth / fourteenth-century Transoxianian Hanafi-Maturidi scholar Luṭfallāh al-Nasafī al-Fāḍil al-Kaydānī in the *fiqh al-ʿibādāt*, commonly known as *Khulāṣat al-Kaydānī*, held a special significance for him in this regard.[118] ʿUmar Ćamkanī did not merely appropriate this text as a template, but – inspired not least by his own *murshid*, the Kākā Ṣāḥib[119] – commented on it.[120] Moreover, in this way, ʿUmar Ćamkanī initiated an exegetical tradition that was kept very much alive by his successors and, thus, sustained his own authority in this matter.

The ostensibly very minor issue on which this commentary tradition pivots is the question of the correct performance of the affirmation of faith during the ritual prayer (*tashahhud*). As we shall see, this matter of seemingly marginal importance would from now on be re-evoked time and again by following generations of Pashtun religious actors in their respective attempts to justify their own aspirations to communal leadership against those of any competitor. Therefore, when also ʿUmar Ćamkanī's spiritual heir Miyāṇ Muḥammadī "Ḥaẕrat Ṣāḥib'zādah" treated the matter at some length in the section on prayer of his *Maqāṣid al-Fiqh*,[121] he reinforced the claim of supreme religious authority of the *khānaqāh* in Ćamkanī.

The way in which Pashtun religious dignitaries in the mountainous regions of the north got on their high horse in matters of orthopraxy fitted well with an increasing sense of the necessity to enforce what they regarded as the right conduct and belief. This was even more so the case as the Durrani rulers and their Barakzay successors were regarded as not paying sufficient heed to what

116 Wirth (1938), 15.
117 See Ibn Khaldūn (1425/2004), I: 364–8 and 400f.
118 See Darvīzah (1885), 82–92.
119 This claim has been made by "Aṣr" Afghānī (1965), II: 579.
120 See n.61 in this chapter.
121 See Ḥanīf (1979), 450 and 478.

leading Sufi *shaykhs* and *ʿulamāʾ* considered an indispensable duty of the sovereign in any Muslim polity. In fact, this tendency can also be traced back to Aḥmad Sirhindī, progenitor of the Naqshbandiyyah-Mujaddidiyyah, to which ʿUmar Ćamkanī and his circles adhered, and a staunch critic of the Mughal monarchs for their purported negligence in matters of the Islamic *shariʿa*. The responsibility for safeguarding the Prophetic Sunna in Sirhindī's concept of the "common Muslims" (*ʿavāmm-i ahl-i islām*)[122] falls ultimately upon every righteous believer, not least because the supremacy of the *ʿālim* and Sufi *shaykh*, including Sirhindī – as "Renewer of the Second Millennium" – himself, is herein dissolved.[123] The benchmark is the Sunna of the Islamic Prophet Abraham (*millat Ibrāhīm*), and it is exclusively the community on this path which can be considered righteous.

This, in fact, is an important reference, as we shall see in due course that the concept of the Abrahamic creed – the *millat Ibrāhīm* – would gain an ideologically pointed emphasis in the late twentieth century among Arab theorists with closer links to ṬIT/IEA and TṬP.[124] Even more, however, Sirhindī also commented on the *tashahhud* issue in a manner that foreshadowed the momentum it would gain two links further down the spiritual chain. Dwelling on the relevant *aḥādīth* on this matter and various Hanafi legal works, Sirhindī concluded that, firstly, the different *aḥādīth* conflicted with each other, subsequently leading to great varieties of interpretation even within a single canonical tradition of Islamic jurisprudence. As a result, secondly, he strongly recommended suspending *taqlīd* in this question and abstaining from the practice of moving the index finger during the *tashahhud* at all, be it only in pointing.[125]

Coupled with his earlier considerations of the individual responsibility to ensure orthodoxy and orthopraxy alike, it was only a small step for those in Sirhindī's wake to embrace a more exoteric agenda: grounded, once again, in the Qur'anic directive of *amr biʾl-maʿrūf* [. . .], which would evolve in the times to come as an ever more powerful rhetorical – and eventually also practical – instrument,[126] the authors of various later *tazkirāt* attested strong inclinations to act upon this precept to ʿUmar Ćamkanī.[127] Indeed, the combination of dogmatically following one distinct opinion among at least three regarding an

122 See Sirhindī (1397/1977), II: 145f. (no. 54).

123 See ibid., for example, I: 410–18 (nos. 251f.). In this context (I: 411), Sirhindī quoted from Q16.123: 'Then We revealed to you: Follow the faith of Abraham (a man of pure faith, who was no idolater).' (*thumma ʾawḥaynā ʾilayka ʾani ʾttabiʿ millata ʾIbrāhīma* [*ḥanīfan wa-mā kāna mina ʾl-mushrikīn*]). Also, see the discussion in Friedmann (1971), 18–21; ter Haar (1992), 80–5.

124 See Section 4.5.

125 See Sirhindī (1397/1977), I: 658–62 (no. 312).

126 See above in this chapter, also Sections 3.2.2, 3.2.3, 4.2.1 and 4.4.

127 See Gīlānī (1972), I: 96f. On the normative basis of this moral imperative, and its interpretations in early *fiqh* and *kalām*, see Cook (2006), although developments in the Islamic East go widely unrecognized there.

ostensibly minor issue of the ritual prayer (*ṣalāt*)[128] with a firm inclination towards *amr bi'l-ma'rūf* [. . .] appears to have served as an indicator of orthodoxy in the Pashtun Borderland and beyond. While Cook suggests that the concept 'is at home' in Islamic jurisprudence and politics, and contends that both 'are not constituents of Ṣūfism as such',[129] our case here suggests otherwise. Indeed, functional differentiation of authority – religious as well as worldly – might have been much more advanced in the Islamic West of the Middle Period – the region and period of Cook's immediate expertise, and especially in its urban centres as hubs of scholastic text production.

However, these diverse forms of authority in the Pashtun Borderland were concentrated on the person of the Sufi *shaykh*, who would then frequently enter into confrontation with the various other claimants of the trusteeship of orthodoxy and orthopraxy, as well as those who claimed socio-political authority. In the former case, the constantly simmering conflict was eventually played out in fierce learned disputations (*munāẓarāt*)[130] and heresiographical writings, and would, on occasion, even take a somewhat violent form.[131]

What apparently manifested itself here once more is a certain kind of ethics sustained by religious precepts, which we had already encountered with Raḥmān Bābā in the late seventeenth century. Now, however, we may reframe the binary "*khān* ethics" and "subaltern ethics" introduced above into more socio-religious terms, here as "governance-oriented" and "guidance-oriented".[132] Both Sirhindī

128 Kaydānī's decree on the matter of the *tashahhud*, according to which it is compulsory (*wājib*) to proclaim the Islamic creed during the sittings (*qu'dāt*) between prostration, and commendable (*mustaḥabb*) to place the hands on the thighs and raise the index finger (see al-Kaydānī [n.d.], 8f. and 13) is controversially discussed by other Hanafi authorities. Earlier scholars, such as Abū Ja'far Aḥmad al-Ṭaḥāwī (d. 321/933), Abū 'l-Ḥasan Aḥmad al-Qudūrī (d. 427/1037), 'Alī ibn Abī Bakr al-Marghinānī (d. 593/1197) and Muḥammad al-Bazzāzī (d. 827/1424), were of the view that the person praying should not raise the finger at all (see al-Ṭaḥāwī [1370h], 27; al-Qudūrī [1418/1997], 27; al-Marghinānī [1417h], II: 51; al-Bazzāzī [2009], I: 60f.). Later scholars, such as Muḥammad ibn 'Alī al-Ḥaṣkafī (d. 1004/1596), opined instead that the correct way was to point with the index finger while not clenching the others (see al-Ḥaṣkafī [1423/2002], 84), whereas the even later legal systematizer Muḥammad Amīn ibn 'Umar ibn 'Ābidīn (d. 1252/1836) held that the fingers should be clenched with the index finger raised for negation and lowered for affirmation (see Ibn 'Ābidīn [1423/2003], II: 249).

129 Cook (2006), 460.

130 See Section 3.2.

131 See Zaman (2012), 300f., who refers to a much later incident reported by Muḥammad Rashīd Riḍā (d. 1354/1935): in a not further specified mosque in Lahore, some Pashtun *madrasah* students broke the index finger of a man who had raised his index finger during the testimony of faith (*tashahhud*) after the second prostration in prayer not in accordance with al-Kaydanī's legal position. Riḍā (1344/1925), 282, himself quoted one of the students who affirmed that, 'Yes, it was a punishment ['*iqāb*] for opposing the Prophet (ṣ) and abandoning his Sunna, that is, for enmity towards the law [*shar'*] of God, the Most Exalted, and for deeming permissible what He had forbidden [*wa-istiḥlāl mā ḥarramah*].'

132 For this binary, strongly inspired by Weber (1972), 267f. and 355–9, see Chapter 2, n.34.

and Banūrī had been representatives of the latter, expressed by their emphasis on conformity with the *shari'a* and uneasy relationship with political power-holders, especially those who, in their eyes, failed on the former. ʿUmar Ćamkanī also appears to fall into this category, despite his spiritual relationship with Aḥmad Shāh Durrānī. The dissociation of his son and successor, Miyāṇ Muḥammadī, from the administration of the Peshawar Valley by the Durrani, with their home base in far-away Kandahar, once again emphasizes the prominence of the "guidance orientation" over "governance orientation" in this particular thread of religious authority in the Pashtun Borderland. It seems that the systemic antagonism between the representatives of these two paradigmatic types of moral action kept playing out in competition between the various claimants to socio-religious authority, which, as shall be hypostatized at this point, crystallizes in, among other things, the controversies over the performance of the *tashahhud* during the ritual prayer. In the following, therefore, we shall constantly be on the lookout for traces of this controversy in the Pashtun Borderland across the entire span of time that is covered in this book.

3.2 The Nineteenth Century

The fate of the Pashtun Borderland in the early nineteenth century was shaped very much by the rise and westward expansion of the dominion of the Sikhs under Mahārāja Raṇjīt Siṅgh, in direct contestation with the territorial claims of the Durrani in the region. Having been transformed into a militant brotherhood by their tenth and last *gurū*, Gobind Siṅgh, in the late seventeenth century, the Sikhs began to successfully erode Mughal imperial rule in the Punjab in the early eighteenth century.[133] Various of the – mainly Mughal – fortifications, representing claims of political and administrative authority, changed hands back and forth in the turbulent times of the Durrani excursions into the eastern Gangetic Plain. In the end, however, the representatives of the Durrani ultimately had to concede them to the Sikhs, while withdrawing to their strongholds in the Peshawar Valley, including the city itself. The Durrani rulers had installed a governor of the equally southern Barakzay there, a fact that led to increasing tensions with the Yusufzay as the dominant tribal confederacy in the uplands of the Pashtun Borderland.[134] Moreover, this points emblematically to the continuation of the political and cultural conflict between southern "lowland" and northern "highland" Pashtuns that had

[133] See Alam (1986), 138–205; Syan (2013), 48–104 and 239–50.

[134] See Qadir (2015a), 61f.; Qadir and Asghar (2016), 59f. The points made there are based on an undated later edition of Gōpāl Dās's *Tārīkh-i Pishāvar* (Lahore: Glob[e] pablisharz), but appear to have been interpolated from Ḥayāt Khān (1867), 69–74. As the *Ḥayāt-i Afghānī* had been published only a few years before the work of Gōpāl Dās, it may indeed have served the latter as a historiographical core reference.

crystallized during the rule of the Durrani, a line of conflict that, as outlined above, is regarded here as a constitutive feature of the Pashtun Borderland.[135]

Finally, when Peshawar was taken by Sikh forces in 1811 and the attempts of the former Durrani governor of Peshawar, Yār Muḥammad Khān of the Barakzay (killed 1245/1829), to recapture the city had been checked, the latter did not have many options left but to declare his allegiance to Raṇjīt Siṅgh. In fact, the Barakzay governorship over the Peshawar Valley, firstly, on behalf of the Durrani court of Kandahar and later on behalf of the Sikhs in Lahore, another of the three ideal-typical lines of conflict that shape the Pashtun Borderland,[136] would become increasingly manifest. This new rift now occurred between local power-holders, with their willingness to align themselves pragmatically with larger imperial powers outside the Borderland in attempts to retain their regional, political and economic power, and more subaltern regional actors who subscribed, and still do subscribe, to strong sentiments of political autonomy, cultural integrity and socio-economic egalitarianism. Therefore, when a large band of Muslim activists from the Gangetic plains arrived at Peshawar in November 1826, via eastern Sindh, Baluchistan and the lowlands of the Pashtun Borderland, these multifarious tensions crystallized further.

3.2.1 *The Ṭarīqah-yi Muḥammadiyyah: Sowing the Seeds of Proto-Salafi Islam*

Those who arrived at Peshawar in November 1826 were following the lead of two personalities from the de facto independent Mughal imperial province of Awadh and the imperial capital Delhi, respectively: Sayyid Aḥmad ibn ʿIrfān of Raʾī Baraylī and his *murshid* Shāh Ismāʿīl ibn Shāh ʿAbd al-Ghanī Dihlavī. The latter was a grandson of Shāh Valiyallāh of Delhi, and both were students of Shāh Ismāʿīl's paternal uncle Shāh ʿAbd al-Qādir ibn Shāh Valiyallāh Dihlavī (d. 1230/1815). The expressed aim of their campaign was to redress the fact that, with the formal establishment of Sikh rule, Muslims in the Greater Punjab were forced to submit to non-Muslim domination for the first time in centuries. Consequently, Sayyid Aḥmad and Shāh Ismāʿīl saw the ability of Muslims to conform to the requirements of the Islamic *shari'a* seriously jeopardized, which would ultimately impair their chances of salvation in the Hereafter. Both were fully prepared to use any means sustainable by *shari'a* injunctions, prominently including a militant option in the guise of a defensive *jihād*, to counter this great peril for the Muslim community as a whole.

Now, much has already been written on various religious and political aspects of the movement which the two learned activists initiated and which became alternately known as *Ṭarīqah-yi Muḥammadiyyah*, *Jamāʿat-i Mujāhidīn* and,

135 See Chapter 2.
136 See Section 2.2.

eventually, in the powerful British colonial discourse, as the "Wahábi [sic]" movement.[137] For that reason, the focus here is narrowed down to their distinct religio-political legacy in the Pashtun Borderland and beyond, zooming in on the socio-political implications of a particular Islamic legal hermeneutic that has elsewhere been argued for as a pointer to a persuasion that would eventually solidify as "Salafi".[138] In this light, we shall reflect, first and foremost, on the category of "imāma", as stressed by the masterminds of the *Ṭarīqah-yi Muḥammadiyyah*, especially Shāh Ismāʿīl. After all, the Imamate, to be led initially by *imām-i ʿaṣr* Sayyid Aḥmad,[139] combines the spiritual and political aspects in the early Islamic conception of communal leadership.[140] It would consistently fall upon Sayyid Aḥmad to lead the response of the – potentially entire – Muslim community to non-Muslim rule, such as that of the Sikhs and their Barakzay collaborators. Accordingly, it was his sole privilege to proscribe it an individual duty to either migrate to a Muslim dominion (*hijra*) or actively resist non-Muslim rule (*jihād*). Moreover, it would be his prerogative to ensure the prevalence of *shari'a* law in the community under his leadership, which would technically require him to also act as the foremost of the *fuqahāʾ*.[141]

The emphasis on *jihād* in the *Ṭarīqah-yi Muḥammadiyyah*, however, added momentum to the discussion about what to do in view of the steadily encroaching non-Muslim rule to which Muslims were increasingly subjected, experienced across almost the entire former Mughal dominion: Sayyid Aḥmad's teacher and Sufi *pīr* Shāh ʿAbd al-ʿAzīz of Delhi (d. 1239/1823), the eldest son of Shāh Valiyallāh, had stressed the call for *hijra* as obligatory for the "Imam of all Muslims", but remained by and large silent on the matter of armed *jihād*.[142] It

137 See, for example, Nadvī (1406/1986); Ahmad (1994); Gaborieau (1996; 1999; 2010); Mihr (2008); Qadir (2015a); Hartung (2004; 2019a).

138 See Hartung (2020), 176–83.

139 The crucial text here is Shāh Ismāʿīl's Persian *Manṣib-i Imāmat*, completed around the formal declaration of Sayyid Aḥmad as *imām-i ʿaṣr* on 12 Jumādá II 1242 / 10 January 1827. For an analysis, see Gaborieau (2010), 200–2. Moreover, Shāh Ismāʿīl also penned an introduction (*tamhīd*) to Shāh Valiyallāh's *Hamaʿāt*, entitled *ʿAbqāt*, in which the social practice of spiritual discipleship is defended: see Dihlavī (1963), 7. Last but not least, Shāh Ismāʿīl rigorously defended the legitimacy of Sayyid Aḥmad's Imamate against anyone objecting to it, as exemplarily shown in the two letters edited and presented by Maiello (1996), 257–64.

140 See Crone (2004), 21f. The concept of "imāma" was central not least to al-Māwardī (1422/2002), 5.

141 See Dihlavī (1877), 22–8. These named duties and prerogatives of the political and spiritual head of the Muslim community had already been set out in classical standard works on Islamic governance, such as al-Māwardī (1422/2002), 15f. and 35–64. Yet, Shāh Ismāʿīl added momentum by making the militant enforcement of belief, as stipulated in *Taqviyyat al-Īmān*, a crucial right, if not duty, of the *imām*: see Dihlavī (1877), 25.

142 See Dihlavī (1321h), I: 30f. For an analysis, see Rizvi (1982), 225–37. Later Indo-Muslim historiography as well as academic scholarship has credited Shāh ʿAbd al-ʿAzīz's *fatwa* "On the Issue of When the Abode of Islam Becomes an Abode of War" (*Masʾalah-yi dār*

may, thus, be argued that the legal pragmatics of Shāh ʿAbd al-ʿAzīz were subsequently trumped by a more normative interpretation that would not allow for any concessions to prevailing social, economic and political circumstances. This turn towards a stronger and more inflexible normativity in the *Ṭarīqah-yi Muḥammadiyyah* was also indicated by the fact that the mental map of the two leaders of the movement went beyond the confines of the subcontinent: they had already alluded to a classical notion of "Khurāsān" as an administrative unit of an Islamic caliphate in their letters to rulers in Transoxiana;[143] this was a concept that would gain exceptional importance about two centuries later in the territorial conceptions of the IS.[144]

Yet, we may well assume that Shāh ʿAbd al-ʿAzīz was very familiar with the use of the "imām" in the Islamic literary canon[145] and used this term, therefore, with deliberation. After all, the caliphate – then held by a succession of seven Ottoman sultans – played a subordinate role at best for North Indian Muslims in the eighteenth and early nineteenth centuries. We may infer from this that Shāh Ismāʿīl did not imply "caliphate" either when discussing the concept of "imāma", allegedly in reference to Sayyid Aḥmad.[146] Instead, he wished to legitimize the latter as the definite religious authority in the areas under his control, even though we may have to concede the possibility that the semantic ambivalence of the term played into the hands of Shāh Ismāʿīl.

al-ḥarb shudan dār al-islām) with exceptional importance for all the discussions on that matter in Muslim India ever since. Chaudri (2019), 108–14, however, proves that the purported significance of this *fatwa* is widely unwarranted before the first decades of the twentieth century. The personal dependence of Sayyid Aḥmad on Shāh ʿAbd al-ʿAzīz, however, suggests at least a strong relevance of the latter's views on the leaders of the *Ṭarīqah-yi Muḥammadiyyah*.

143 See Sayyid Aḥmad (1395/1975), 46f., 62, 66, 114 and 120–5. Additionally, see the analysis of the letter of Sayyid Aḥmad to Amīr Naṣrallāh ibn Ḥaydar Tūrah of the Mangït dynasty of Bukhara (r. 1827–60) in Gaborieau (1996), 272–7. It is noteworthy that the declaration of Sayyid Aḥmad as *imām-i ʿaṣr* in January 1827 and the drawing up of the *Manṣib-i Imāmat* by Shāh Ismāʿīl immediately after, in conjunction with the frequent allusion to "Khurasan" in Sayyid Aḥmad's correspondence, abetted his later millenarian elevation. Sunni conceptions of the "coming Imam" (*al-imām al-mahdī*) revolve a lot around Prophetic *aḥādīth* such as: 'Black banners will come from Khurasan, nothing shall turn them back until they are planted in Jerusalem [*bi-Iliyāʾ*]' (*Jāmiʿ al-Tirmidhī*, k. al-fitan, b. {yaʾtī zamānun man ʿamila minhum bi-ʿushr mā ʾamira bihi najā}, no. 2 [ḥadīth 2438]).

144 See Section 4.5.5.

145 The most succinct classical definition, cited by Calder (1984), 262, appears to be that of Muḥammad ibn Idrīs al-Shāfiʿī (d. 203/820), eponymous founder of one of the four canonical traditions in Sunni Muslim jurisprudence.

146 See Dihlavī (1877). Still, in the text itself there is no explicit indication that Shāh Ismāʿīl, as suggested, for example, by Gaborieau (2010), 201f. and Qadir (2015a), 175, wanted his purely legal considerations to be applied in justification of Sayyid Aḥmad's *imāma*. Consequently, all such interpretations must necessarily be based on circumstantial evidence, such as the coincidence of its composition with the declaration of Sayyid Aḥmad's *imāma*.

Indeed, the institution of the Imamate in the distinct political vision of the *Ṭarīqah-yi Muḥammadiyyah* for the time after the anticipated defeat of the Sikhs served as an expression of the Salafi social ideal, which Gaborieau describes as aiming at a 'resurrection of the primitive Muslim community [. . . in which] Sayyid Aḥmad modelled himself on the Prophet and his close associates like his Companions'.[147] However, while this normative staging of Sayyid Aḥmad as a supreme spiritual and political authority does indeed appear to be a magic formula to ensure that the *Ṭarīqah-yi Muḥammadiyyah* was accepted and could establish hegemonic control over numerous communities in the upper Pashtun Borderland, the case in point appears to have been slightly more complex.

On the one hand, the beacons of the *Ṭarīqah-yi Muḥammadiyyah* were still very much entrenched in Persianate cultural elitism,[148] indicated not least by the fact that all the literature they produced still preferred the regionally established literary idiom over Arabic, as one usually more associated with the normative Islamic framework. On the other hand, however, the elaborate scholarship in the *ʿulūm al-ḥadīth*, the *ʿilm al-rijāl* prominently among them, that would characterize most of the later works considered to be "Salafi" is still largely absent in the works of Shāh Ismāʿīl and Sayyid Aḥmad; the general historical reference points serve the Prophet Muḥammad and the so-called "Rightly Guided" Caliphs alone. However, regarding its epistemology, theology and *fiqh*, the scholar-activists show remarkable closeness to "Salafi" traditionism, at least in its very early forms, which allows us to speak here of "proto-Salafi" inclinations.

While most North Indian Muslim scholars at that time, including Shāh ʿAbd al-ʿAzīz and most of his learned family members, maintained their Hanafi-cum-Maturidi persuasion, the works of Shāh Ismāʿīl and Sayyid Aḥmad indicated a clear departure from this so far dominant framework in the north of the subcontinent towards what has elsewhere been called "Salafi reduction":[149] the Qur'an and the Prophetic Sunna were declared the sole yardstick for any matter with religious connotation. While both scholars would still acknowledge 'the responses of the wise [*buzurgōṇ kī javābāt*], deliberations of the scholars and the customs one may observe within his community [*barādarī kī jō rusum unkē mavāfiq hō*]',[150] this would

[147] Gaborieau (2010), 206f. (translation mine).

[148] For the underlying understanding of "Persianate [cultural] elitism", see Hartung (2017b), esp. 87–102.

[149] See Hartung (2020), 178–83.

[150] Dihlavī (1998), 10. Compare the Arabic version of the text in al-Dihlawī (2003), 47, where the statement appears with a bit of momentum: 'One may resort to the stories of saints [*quṣaṣ al-mashāʾikh waʾl-ṣāliḥīn*] and the words of the scholars, preachers and celebrities [*kalām al-ʿulamāʾ waʾl-wuʿāẓ waʾl-madhkūrīn*] as long as they correspond to the foundations and texts [*al-uṣūl waʾl-nuṣūṣ*]; whenever they stray from the word [of

apply only as long as there was no contradiction with the injunctions of the Qur'an and Prophetic *ḥadīth*.[151]

Where exactly these "proto-Salafi" persuasions in Shāh Ismāʿīl and Sayyid Aḥmad came from is still not entirely clear. Two distinct influences that may have informed these proclivities will be proposed here. The first of them is the spiritual tradition of the Naqshbandiyyah-Mujaddidiyyah, in which both dignitaries had been initiated. As we have already seen, the great importance assigned to redressing what was considered a set of transgressing beliefs and customs, especially in Sufi circles and subaltern local practices, had its progenitor Aḥmad Sirhindī as early as in the late sixteenth century CE, and was, consequently, reflected in many works on matters of creed (*ʿaqīda*) and ritual practice (*fiqh al-ʿibādāt*) that were produced in those circles, not least, in the Pashtun Borderland.[152] Moreover, it appears that the "Shaykh of the Afghans" Ādam Banūrī was already inclined to denounce contrary views as unbelief (*kufr*),[153] a practice that would gain increasing significance in the Pashtun Borderland from the activities of the *Ṭarīqah-yi Muḥammadiyyah* and its eventual heirs.

Most important among the practices criticized were, of course, the pious visitation of graves (*ziyārāt*) and the related custom of asking the deceased for intercession with God on behalf of the practitioner (*tawassul*). The correct performance of the ritual prayer, a subject matter that we have already encountered with ʿUmar Ćamkanī and his circle, pivoting on interpretations of al-Kaydānī's short epitomé on the matter discussed above also figured prominently. We owe one short exposition from the perspective of the *Ṭarīqah-yi Muḥammadiyyah* to Vilāyat ʿAlī of ʿAẓīmābād / Patna (d. 1269/1853), who succeeded Sayyid Aḥmad Barēlvī as its *amīr* in 1831. In this text, the discussion became emphatically tied to the practice of the Prophet's Companions as the ultimate benchmark for compliance with the *shari'a* and points, thus, once more, to the proto-Salafi proclivities of the *Ṭarīqah-yi Muḥammadiyyah*.[154] However, its leading representatives were still strongly attached to the Indian Hanafi-Maturidi tradition; their "Salafi reduction" was, at least in places, softened by later Hanafi legal views, as explicit references to, for instance, Shāh ʿAbd al-ʿAzīz Dihlavī indicate.[155] By and large, their elite approach appears to sweep under the

God] and the *aḥādīth*, as well as from customs and conventions [*al-ʿādāt wa'l-taqālīd*], one is to refrain from it.'

151 See, for example, Dihlavī (1998), 60f.

152 See Section 3.1.3.

153 See, for example, Badakhshī (1140h), 89b.

154 See ʿAẓīmābādī (1284/1868), 3.

155 See ibid., 4. Other standard Hanafi references, indicated in the margins of the treatise, are the *Sharḥ al-Wiqāya* of the "Ṣadr al-Sharīʿa al-Thānī" ʿUbaydallāh ibn Maʿsūd al-Bukharī (d. 747/1346), the *Fatḥ al-Bārī* of Ibn Ḥajjar al-ʿAsqalānī (d. 852/1449), the *Fatāwá Ḥindiyya*, the *Fatḥ al-Qadīr* of Kamāl ibn al-Humām (d. 861/1457), the *Baḥr*

carpet more subtle points in their various discussions of the *ʿibādāt* as a whole, perhaps because they perceived their co-religionists, especially in the Pashtun Borderland, as failing even in the very basics. In this light, therefore, a discussion of issues such as the manner in which to perform the *tashahhud* during prayer might have been regarded by Vilāyat ʿAlī either as premature or as potentially jeopardizing the cohesion of his already fairly fragmented following and was subsequently left out. Instead, he spent a lot of ink on the non-negotiable compulsory character of the ritual prayer, even if work or travel seems to prevent this. Surely, the cultural elitism of the leaders of the *Ṭarīqah-yi Muḥammadiyyah* prevented them from even remotely recognizing the regional contributions of ʿUmar Ćamkanī and other early Borderland commentators on al-Kaydānī's work, especially as they were produced in an idiom foreign to them. Consequently, their attitude to Borderland religiosities remained an utterly patronizing one for a long time, a feature that would be shared by all the later manifestations of Salafi Islam in the region well into the present day.

It is certainly legitimate to entertain the theory that the "proto-Salafi" inclinations of Sayyid Aḥmad and Shāh Ismāʿīl were boosted, if not sparked off in the first place, by their purported contact with the celebrated traditionist and legal scholar Muḥammad ibn ʿAlī al-Shawkānī (d. 1250/1837) from Sana'a in Yemen, who served many later Salafis across the Muslim world as a major source of inspiration. In the two dominant hagiographical accounts on which all the later ones are based,[156] their mutual acquaintance was owed to an exchange of correspondence during a stopover of Sayyid Aḥmad and Shāh Ismāʿīl at Moka in southern Yemen during their pilgrimage to the Hijaz between 1822 and 1824.[157]

The extent of that correspondence is not really known, but it seems that Shawkānī responded mainly out of respect for a direct descendant of Shāh Valiyallāh of Delhi.[158] Be that as it may, with Shawkānī, the two Indian scholars-cum-activists were at least able to claim back home an endorsement of their religious views by a crucial figure in the genesis of contemporary Salafi

al-Rāʾiq of Ibn Nujaym al-Miṣrī (d. 970/1562) and, finally, the *Radd al-Muḥtār* of Ibn ʿĀbidīn.

156 The later accounts of Nadvī (1406/1986) and Mihr (2008) are both based predominantly on Vazīr Khān (1428/2007) and Bastavī (1434/2012). The latter is originally a Persian work, entitled *Manẓūrat al-Suʿadāʾ fī Aḥvāl al-Ghazāt al-Shuhadāʾ* and composed by Sayyid Aḥmad's *mīr-munshī* and *khalīfah* Sayyid Jaʿfar ʿAlī Naqvī of the Bastī district in Awadh (d. 1247/1832). It needs to be acknowledged here, however, that only a partial Urdu translation by an ʿUbaydallāh al-Asʿadī is currently available.

157 See Vazīr Khān (1428/2007), 1049f.; Bastavī (1434/2012), 94f. Gaborieau (2010), 170, refers to this incident as well, although based on secondary readings that do not reveal their respective sources. The actual letters to and from Shawkānī have not been included in the collection of Sayyid Aḥmad's correspondence (see Sayyid Aḥmad [1395/1975]), and the facticity of this exchange, therefore, still remains open to doubts.

158 See Bastavī (1434/2012), 95.

Islam. What is more, two of Shawkānī's students would even eventually settle in the Indian princely state of Bhopal and become highly instrumental in the creation of the *Ahl-i Ḥadīs̱*.[159] The traditionist *Ahl-i Ḥadīs̱* movement, in turn, which received much inspiration from Shawkānī's firm arguments in favour of normativity-grounded *ijtihād* for the derivation of Islamic legal judgements, would later emerge as a major reference point for central actors in our present narrative, both in terms of orientation and in terms of affiliation.[160] Finally, it is the *Ṭarīqah-yi Muḥammadiyyah* that has been considered by the *Ahl-i Ḥadīs̱* themselves as their true precursor.[161]

For the moment, however, we need to linger a little longer in the early nineteenth century, not least because we still need to establish the second ideal-typical line of conflict mentioned which was constitutive for the Pashtun Borderland: the one that runs between local power elites and their subaltern counterparts. The markedly elitist approach of the leaders of the *Ṭarīqah-yi Muḥammadiyyah* on matters of religious belief and practice was apparently badly suited to succeed easily among the *kəshərān* within the complex social, political and cultural environment that they encountered in the Pashtun-dominated Frontier. A litmus test for the actual efficacy of rigid arguments such as those made in *Taqviyyat al-Īmān* would certainly be the extent to which its advocates are able and willing to communicate them to the various communities in ways that do not alienate them. The fact, however, that this programmatic text had been translated into Urdu during the lifetime of its author(s), presumably even by himself or themselves, must certainly not trick us – as has occasionally happened – into interpreting this as a step for reaching out to the subalterns in the rural communities of the Pashtun Borderland. Urdu, after all, had emerged towards the end of the eighteenth century as the up-and-coming idiom of the literary elites in urban centres such as Hyderabad in the Deccan, Lucknow and Delhi, and it seems, therefore, reasonable to expect its target audience rather there, even more so as Urdu was not a dominant idiom in the Frontier region.[162] It can, therefore, be stated with some confidence that the leaders and advocates of the *Ṭarīqah-yi Muḥammadiyyah* perpetuated the deeply rooted patronizing attitude of the North Indian urban Muslim elites towards the rural and, moreover, tribal communities on the Frontier, something that was going to become a continuous feature of later Salafi and Salafist enterprises in the Pashtun Borderland.

[159] See Hartung (2004), 224–8 *et passim*; Preckel (2005), 110–13, 164–8, 336–8 *et passim*. On Shawkānī's legal theory that emphasized revelation as the only firm point of departure for legal reasoning, see Peters (1980); Haykel (2003).

[160] See Sections 3.3.1, 4.1.2 and 4.4.2.

[161] See Preckel (2005), 94–106.

[162] On the role of Urdu in nineteenth century Delhi, see Lelyveld (1994); Pernau (2008), 113f. and 264.

Unsurprisingly, the initial appeal of Sayyid Aḥmad and Shāh Ismāʿīl's agitation for an armed defensive *jihād* against the Sikh Empire on the Frontier soon gave way to disillusion among the local Pashtun communities: almost instantly, Sayyid Aḥmad and Shāh Ismāʿīl started to criticize their newly won allies for certain belief and practices that they found in contradiction with their rigid programme for socio-religious change. The strong impact of tribal customs in regulating community affairs was central to their criticism.[163] Local forms of conflict resolution in those areas under the control of the *Ṭarīqah-yi Muḥammadiyyah*, led by the now *imām* Sayyid Aḥmad, were officially abolished and replaced by *shariʿa* jurisdiction, and the *imām* demanded full obedience of his religious decrees.

The legitimacy of these claims was enhanced by the fact that all partisans had to pledge an oath of allegiance, and this is where the ambiguity of *bayʿa* to Sayyid Aḥmad seems to have been strategically exploited: with Shāh Ismāʿīl's justification of Sayyid Aḥmad's *imāma*, the latter became a Sufi *shaykh* and a religio-political authority in one, and a *bayʿa* given to him in one capacity could, therefore, equally well be considered a binding pledge in the other.[164] This ambiguity would eventually be increased by the appellation of Sayyid Aḥmad with the caliphal honorifics: 'Commander of the Faithful, Leader of the Muslims, Caliph of God on Earth, Shadow of God over the Worlds in the Times of Wickedness, Vessel of Virtue, Pathway through The Book, the One Admitted to the Halls of the Almighty'.[165] Elevated in such a way, it is no surprise that Sayyid Aḥmad would expect total obedience, and the defection of tribal leader X̌ādī Khān of Hunḍ in the Peshawar Valley – equivalent to breaking his oath of allegiance – had, therefore, consistently to result in his killing on 14 August 1829 by associates of Sayyid Aḥmad and Shāh Ismāʿīl; this, at least, is the tenor of the retrospective legal justification by the latter.[166]

[163] See Gaborieau (2010), 193; Qadir (2015a), 108–10. The latter account is based almost entirely on Mihr (2008), II: 93–105. Ghulām-i Rasūl "Mihr" (d. 1391/1971), in turn, refers to the reproduction of a letter of Sayyid Aḥmad in Jaʿfar ʿAlī Naqvī's *Manẓūrat al-Suʿadāʾ* in which he registered his strong objections to various customs of the people on the Frontier. This particular letter, however, does not appear in the partial Urdu translation, although the collected correspondence of Sayyid Aḥmad and Shāh Ismāʿīl contains a few similar items, dated between August 1827 and April 1829: see Sayyid Aḥmad (1395/1975), 138–45 (69b–73a), 193–6 (97a–98b) and 146–53 (123b–127a).

[164] This alone already indicates that any attempt to frame the *Ṭarīqah-yi Muḥammadiyyah* as a Sufi brotherhood, which appears to be a common reduction that is effective until today (see, e.g., Hopkins and Marsden [2011], 87f.), misses the organizational and semantic complexities.

[165] Sayyid Aḥmad (1395/1975), 138 (69b): 'amīr al-muʾminīn, imām al-Muslimīn, khalīfat allāh fi'l-arḍīn [the plural here is probably used owing to the rhyme], ẓill allāh ʿalá 'l-ʿālamīn bi-tārīkh-i mughulān, faẕīlat'maʾāb, manāqib al-kitāb, maqbūl-i bārgāh-i rabb-i qadīr'.

[166] See the letter from Shāh Ismāʿīl to Sayyid Aḥmad, dated 11 Jumādá I 1246/7 November 1829, in Sayyid Aḥmad (1395/1975), 146–53 (123b–127a). See also Qadir (2015a), 113–19 and 151–6.

What, probably because of their elitism, they could not anticipate was that tribal customs would instantly kick in: the resulting *tabūrvalī* – rivalry between paternal cousins – has been interpreted as the ultimate reason for the disintegration of the *Ṭarīqah-yi Muḥammadiyyah* and the eventual defeat in the Battle of Balakot (*Balākōṫ*) on 6 May 1831.[167]

The genie, however, was out of the bottle: neither the religio-political ideas of the *Ṭarīqah-yi Muḥammadiyyah*, nor its supporter base, now including countless Borderland residents, would vanish entirely from the Frontier, as we shall see in a later chapter.[168] In the course of the aftermath of Balakot, however, when new volunteers arrived in the Pashtun Borderland, mainly from Bihar and Bengal, the *Ṭarīqah-yi Muḥammadiyyah* transformed gradually into something new, eventually known – at least historiographically – as *Jamāʿat-i Mujāhidīn*.[169]

It is in this context that the matter of the correct performance of the *tashahhud* during the ritual prayer, of eminent importance within the Pashtun Borderland since, at least, ʿUmar Ćamkanī's commentary of al-Kaydānī's *Khulāṣa*, also made its entrance in *Ṭarīqah-yi Muḥammadiyyah* circles. Although the issue was still disregarded by its *amīr* Vilāyat ʿAlī of Bihar after the Battle of Balakot, it was some of its local associates who brought the matter back into the limelight, now as a fine measuring needle in their considerably less technical and increasingly polemical contestations over local religious authority. The crux of these contentions, as we shall encounter in the following, was the claim to be the true heir to the *Ṭarīqah-yi Muḥammadiyyah / Jamāʿat-i Mujāhidīn* in the Borderland, a trope that would come to the fore every now and again as the ultimate benchmark for *shari'a*-conforming religiosity and, subsequently, religious and socio-political authority.

3.2.2 Local State Formation: The Princely States of Swat and Dir

The chaotic aftermath of the Battle of Balakot offered numerous local actors the opportunity of having the balance of power tipped in their favour. One of the local figures of eminence who almost immediately took advantage of the

167 See Qadir (2015a), 151–6

168 See Section 3.3.

169 However, the terminology in the relevant historiographies is unclear, especially since most of them are of a significantly later date. The use of the label "Jamāʿat-i Mujāhidīn" for the group around Sayyid Aḥmad and Shāh Ismāʿīl by Mihr (2008), 111, for instance, already indicates the strong possibility that different labels were employed to highlight various aspects of this enterprise: whereas "Ṭarīqah-yi Muḥammadiyyah" emphasizes the spiritual one, "Jamāʿat-i Mujāhidīn" puts the spotlight on its militant activities. It appears that none of its leaders after Balakot could fill the spiritual void left by the death of Sayyid Aḥmad, and even more so Shāh Ismāʿīl, a fact that suggests one way in which a reduction to militancy sustained by religious precepts became a grossly permanent feature in the region.

situation was ʿAbd al-Ghaffūr, a Safi from Maṫṫah Shāmzay in the upper Swat River valley, commonly known as "Sayyidō Bābā" or "Ākhūnd of Swat" (d. 1295/1878). He was eventually able to project a local Yusufzay principality in the Swat Valley, with its pivot in Bālīgrām, better known by its honorific "Sayyidō Sharīf", where he resided by playing the game of Borderland pragmatics in a most accomplished manner.

The Yusufzay had, after a long history of involuntary migration, forcefully introduced themselves to Swat in the sixteenth century CE and established their political and economic dominance over the old-established Tajik communities there (see Map 3.2).[170] Once settled there for good, they began to establish a quite momentous reputation for themselves, one that would soon contribute to increasingly encrusted stereotypes of "Pashtuns" and "Pashtunness", conveniently invoked by representatives of Yusufzay communities themselves to gain an advantage in the intertribal contestations over who represents the ethnicity in its purest form that we have already encountered above. The abundance of colourful accounts in the Mughal imperial historiography regarding the difficulties *pādishāh* Akbar and his successors experienced in trying to coerce them into obedience was certainly conducive in this process:[171] later imperial administrations and auxiliary scholarship have taken Yusufzay intractability as an indicator that they have continued to preserve their communal institutions in a much less adulterated form than others have managed.[172] Accordingly, in subsequent academic studies, a conservative religiosity is stressed as a crucial qualification for the appointment of communal leadership,[173] and it seems that the Sayyidō Bābā was most successful in establishing himself as possessing the utmost credibility in this regard. Among other affiliations, he traced his spiritual pedigree back to the "Pīr Bābā", already mentioned above as a spiritual predecessor of the Kākā Ṣāḥib.[174]

The Pīr Bābā, who had settled in adjacent Bunēr, emerged next to his disciple Ākhūnd Darvīzah as one of the foremost voices in opposition to the subaltern religiosity of the Pīr Rōx̌ān and his followers,[175] and was, thus,

170 See, for example, ʿAllāmī (1877–86), III: 475; Ḥayāt Khān (1867), 176–88; Yūsufī (1960), 45f. and 217–28. On the Tajiks of the earlier Kingdom of Gibar in Swat, see Akhtar (2002); Akhundzada (2017).

171 See prominently ʿAllāmī (1877–86), III: 481–6; Badāʾunī (2001), II: 243–50 and 254; Haravī (1911–35), III: 410–24; al-Haravī (1379/1960), II: 405–8.

172 Consequently, the Yusufzay received a lot of attention from later ethnographers, first and foremost the Norwegian Fredrik Barth (d. 2016), whose works have lastingly shaped the prevalent views on this particular tribal confederation as an ultimate reference point regarding the social mechanisms in Pashtun communities in general: most prominently, see Barth (1959).

173 See ibid., 58–60.

174 See Section 3.1.3.

175 See, for example, Darvīzah (n.d.), 11f. and 31f. See also Gīlānī (1972), I: 11f.

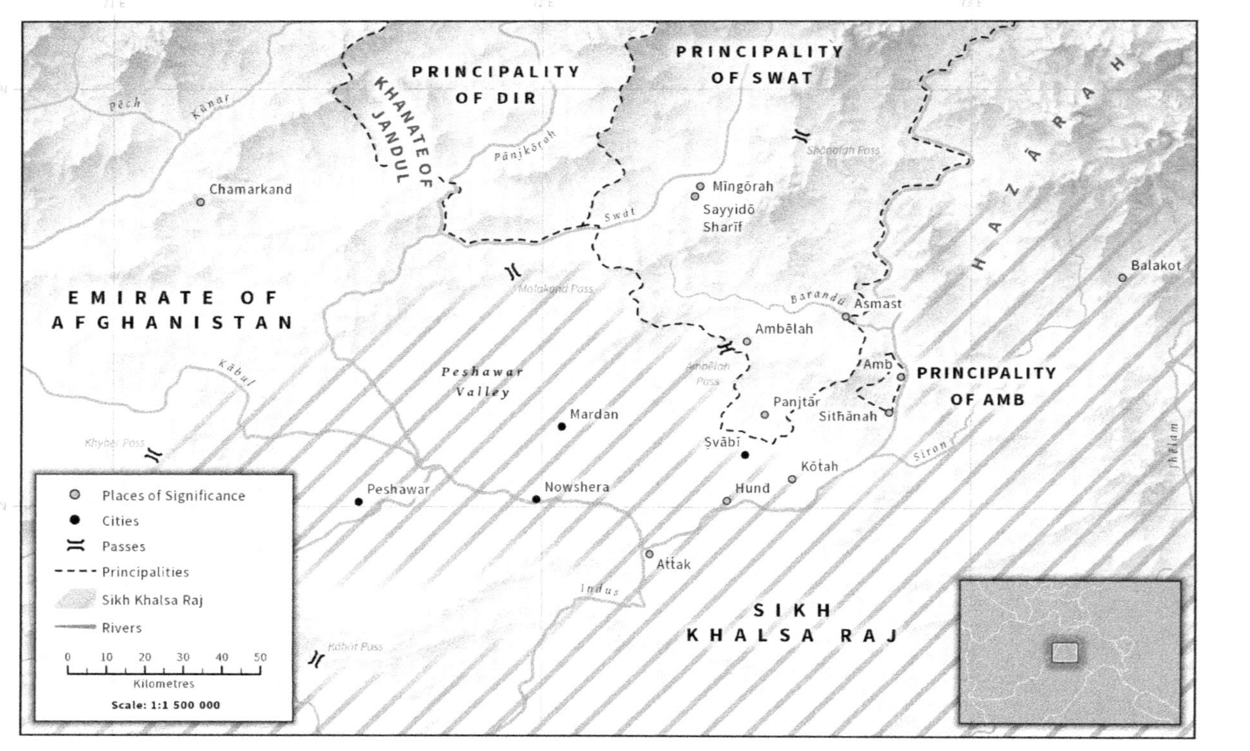

Map 3.2 Local state formation: the principalities of Dir and Swat (mid nineteenth century).

widely perceived as an embodiment of conservative Islamic beliefs and practices. Additionally, the Sayyidō Bābā embraced other *salāsīl*, chiefly that of the Naqshbandiyyah-Mujaddidiyyah,[176] which tied him to earlier religious dignitaries in the northern part of the Pashtun Borderland, such as the Kākā Ṣāḥib and ʿUmar Ćamkanī, and enabled him to concentrate a variety of spiritual lineages in his person. Subsequently, his large following would eventually also transcend the confines of agnatic groups.[177] However, because the wider societal influence of a "saint" (*zbərgah*) depended on popular recognition, their leadership claims, as we have already seen in the previous chapter, never went entirely uncontested.

It was quite often some core event in the Borderland that triggered a surge in the negotiation of religious normativity and, almost inseparably tied to it, sociopolitical claims. Such events were, as we have already seen, the imperial expansion of the Durrani polity in the second half of the eighteenth century or the spread of the Sikh Empire in the early nineteenth. The Battle of Balakot also turned out to be one of those events, because the death of the two charismatic leaders of the *Ṭarīqah-yi Muḥammadiyyah / Jamāʿat-i Mujāhidīn* left an immediate vacuum of communal leadership sustained by religious precepts to be filled, especially in those territories of the Pashtun Borderland within which there was a substantial following of the *Ṭarīqah-yi Muḥammadiyyah*. However, competition over leadership took place not only within these hermetically closed confines, but also very much with other and differently justified forms of political authority in the Pashtun Borderland, as we shall encounter later on in the case of Dir (*Dīr*).

Consequently, we encounter a fresh wave of hot contestations over religious and associated political claims in the aftermath of Balakot, mostly carried by fierce learned arguments and heresiographical writings. Quite similarly to the leaders of the *Ṭarīqah-yi Muḥammadiyyah*, whose political claims were based very much on their dismissive assessment of the fidelity of the top-level community leaders in the Pashtun Borderland because of their acquiescence in the rule of the Sikhs, those in their wake kept challenging local religious and political authority on matching grounds. Yet, these processes seem to have

[176] Sayyidō Bābā's *murshid* in this context was Ghulām-i Muḥammad "Ḥaẕrat Jī" Pishāvarī (d. 1175/1761), allegedly a direct descendant of Aḥmad Sirhindī, see Ḥayāt Khān (1867), 209–11; Gīlānī (1972), I: 101–3 and 150. Moreover, the latter stresses that Ḥaẕrat Jī, who had been born in Sirhind, was instrumental in establishing the Naqshbandiyyah-Mujaddidiyyah in the courtly circles of Kabul, leading Haroon (2007), 39, to speak of him as of the "Kabul-Mujaddidiyyah line". Conversely, Ziad (2017), 241–54, argues, firstly, that the more appropriate term, as appears in the contemporaneous texts, would be "Ḥaẕarāt-i Maʿṣūmiyyah", named after Shāh Ghulām Muḥammad "Maʿṣūm-i S̲ānī" (d. 1161/1748); and secondly, that it was the "Qayyūm-i Jahān" Khᵛājah Ṣafiyallāh (d. 1213/1798), rather than his elder brother "Ḥaẕrat Jī" Pishāvarī, who succeeded in establishing a lasting presence of the Mujaddidiyyah in Kabul.

[177] See Barth (1959), 100–2.

now gained some additional momentum, as the religious and subsequent political contention increasingly took place within associations in the region that were active in the pursuit of Islamic reformulation.[178]

A good illustration of these developments is provided by the onslaught on the spiritual and political authority of the Sayyidō Bābā over the Yusufzay of the Swat Valley by Sayyid Amīr (d. 1281/1865), the "Ṣāḥib", or – pejoratively – "Mullā", of Kōṫah, a locality situated roughly twenty miles southwest of Sayyidō Bābā's abode in what, for that very reason, became "Sayyidō Sharīf".[179] Both of these competitors were affiliated to the Naqshbandiyyah-Mujaddidiyyah and, moreover, had been in contact with the leadership of the *Ṭarīqah-yi Muḥammadiyyah*, although to a varying degree.[180] Subsequently, both had served as a proxy in the attempts of Sayyid Aḥmad Barēlvī and Shāh Ismāʿīl Dihlavī to obtain the support of the various tribal communities, as well as a potential provider of sanctuary for the forces commanded by them.[181] Consequently, the debate, pivoting on various matters of religious belief and practice, was strongly informed by the ripples which the impulses of the proto-Salafi persuasion of the *Ṭarīqah-yi Muḥammadiyyah* created especially in the lower Swat Valley, accompanied by distinct political manoeuvrings of the two rivals.

Unfortunately, no written evidence has come down to us directly from either the Sayyidō Bābā or the Kōṫah Ṣāḥib, so, we are left with little choice for the reconstruction of their respective positions in the argument but to rely on records from their disciples, who, after all, kept the controversy alive and going. The side of the Kōṫah Ṣāḥib was chiefly represented by his foremost disciple, Mullā Ṣafiyallāh (d. 1273/1856), commonly known as "Mullā-yi Bāndah".[182] His Persian *Naẓm al-Durar fī Silk al-Siyar*, a half-hagiography and half-heresiography, completed in May 1876,[183] must be considered the

178 It has already been suggested by Yūsufī (1960), 522, that this controversy was actually about establishing and expanding local power bases of the respective adversaries.

179 This controversy is mentioned to a varying extent in most of the later hagiographical dictionaries, for example, Quddūsī (1966), 565–73; Gīlānī (1972), I: 152. Since Ahmad (1994), 263–8, it has also received increasing recognition in the academic literature, see Haroon (2007), 44f.; Qadir (2015a), 176. Yet, the numerous primary texts reflecting the dispute have not yet been studied in depth; this task is currently being undertaken by Altaf Qadir.

180 For the *silsila* of the Kōṫah Ṣāḥib, see Ṣafiyallāh (1305h), 9f.; for that of the Sayyidō Bābā, see Farīd (1979), 11–101.

181 See, for example, the Shāh Ismāʿīl's letter to the Sayyidō Bābā, dated 2 Dhī 'l-qaʿdah 1245 / 24 April 1830, in Sayyid Aḥmad (1395/1975), 243 (122a). Haroon (2007), 42f., has portrayed the relationship between Sayyid Aḥmad and the Sayyidō Bābā as much closer and more amicable than is sustainable from the available contemporaneous documents. Mihr (2008), IV: 360f., 410, 420f. and 434–6, for example, suggests quite strongly that the Sayyidō Bābā's stance was actually more one of etiquette and blatant political pragmatics.

182 See Ṣafiyallāh (1305h), 2.

183 See ibid., 4.

primary reference to the positions of the Kōtah Ṣāḥib, at least, until we have a more comprehensive study of the religious developments in the Pashtun Borderland post-Balakot.

The *Naẓm al-Durar* opens by exposing a rather general aspiration of the author in correcting the religious practices of people who were led astray by religious and worldly office-holders – both functions were joined in the person of the Sayyidō Bābā. Once again pivoting on the Qur'anic commandment of *amr bi'l-maʿrūf* [. . .], which the Sayyidō Bābā emphatically stressed himself,[184] the Kōtah Ṣāḥib and his disciples also pledged to work towards the eradication of all 'obscurity [*ẓilmat*], innovation [*bidʿat*] and darkness [*tārīkī*] that contradicts the intoxicating and elevated Sunnah'.[185] What he saw in the 'parts of the province of the Afghans' (*ufq-i vilāyat-i Afghānān*), and, more explicitly still, 'in the homeland of the Yusufzay' (*dar vaṭan-i Yūsufzay*),[186] however, were exactly these obscurities and innovations which, given the eminence of the Sayyidō Bābā there, must inevitably result from his religious influence. Therefore, somewhat implicitly projected as a continuation of the unfinished work of Sayyid Aḥmad Barēlvī and Shāh Ismāʿīl, the Kōtah Ṣāḥib and his disciples styled themselves true warriors for the pure faith and, thus, legitimate community leaders.

Such heresiography, while remaining widely polemical, appears to have still been regarded as threatening the position of the Sayyidō Bābā to such an extent that, at one point, the latter proclaimed his adversaries formally to be infidels.[187] The castigation of the Kōtah Ṣāḥib himself for an extreme self-elevation to a prophet-like status[188] meant that the controversy was conducted equally polemically from this side. Yet, Mawlavī Aḥmad ʿAlī Yūsufzay's *Burhān al-Muʾminīn ʿalá ʿAqāʾid al-Muḍillīn* especially indicates other dimensions of the dispute that would gradually become more manifest in the area in the centuries to come: other than Mullā Ṣafiyallāh's, this refutation was composed in Arabic and is spiked with numerous references from classical works on *fiqh* and *ʿaqīda*, and it concludes with a legal declaration of the Kōtah Ṣāḥib and those who hold similar views as unbelievers, affirmed by the seals of 100 of the Sayyidō Bābā's retainers.[189] To have the text composed in Arabic rather than Persian was certainly suitable for radiating a sense of profound scholarly erudition. The many references seem to have catered towards the same end; however, the frequent misspellings of the names of authors and works, alongside the fact

[184] See Gīlānī (1972), I: 151 and 154.
[185] Ṣafiyallāh (1305h), 5.
[186] Ibid.
[187] See ʿAlī (1291h), esp. 112–16. This is also alleged in Ṣafiyallāh (1305h), 242–56, esp. 249 and 255.
[188] See ʿAlī (1291h), 23–40; compare Ṣafiyallāh (1305h), for example 20–37, 74–81 and 85–96.
[189] See ʿAlī (1291h), 113–20.

that, whenever Aḥmad ʿAlī was quoting from them, he did so in Persian rather than in the original Arabic of these works, suggests that the author was actually less firmly acquainted with them than he wanted to let on.[190] As we shall see in subsequent chapters,[191] full command over the classical legal reference works would become a marker of the intellectual capacity and trustworthiness of religious Borderland actors from the middle of the nineteenth century onwards, with enough well-trained competition around to dismantle sloppy scholarship.

Besides the learned appearance of this tract, which stood in stark contrast to the expositions of the Kōtah Ṣāḥib's retainers, the rhetoric of Aḥmad ʿAlī's exposition carried a distinct sectarian note, epitomized in the use of the term "rejectors [of the legitimacy of the caliphates of Abū Bakr al-Ṣiddīq and ʿUmar al-Khaṭṭāb]" (*ravāfiẓ*), usually applied in the polemical depreciation of the Shiʿi Muslims.[192] It all culminates in the question of the attached *fatwa*, in which the Kōtah Ṣāḥib and his disciples were declared unbelievers: 'What do you call him who keeps advocating such Shiʿi positions?' (*mā qawlakum dāma faḍlikum fī qāʾil hādhā al-aqwāl al-shīʿa*).

At this point, it is commendable to take a moment again and appreciate the still subliminal implication that such a ruling had on the religious and socio-political dynamics in the Pashtun Borderland in general, that is, beyond the immediate circles of the two parties in this particular controversy: by singling out Shiʿi Muslims in the Pashtun Borderland communities as potential adversaries to social cohesion, both sides pushed forward a trend that, while clearly

[190] Among these works figure the voluminous *al-Muḥīṭ al-Burhānī fi'l-Fiqh al-Nuʿmānī* of Burhān al-Dīn ibn Māza (d. 616/1219) (see ʿAlī (1291h), 22, 30, 49, 61, 66, 78 and 82), the *Sharḥ Adab al-Qāḍī* by ʿAbd al-ʿAzīz al-Halwānī (d. 448/1056) (see ibid., 47), Muḥammad ibn Aḥmad al-Sarakhsī's (d. 490/1090) commentary of the *K. al-Siyar al-Kabīr* of Muḥammad ibn al-Ḥasan al-Shaybānī (d. 189/750) (see ibid., 70f.), the *Nasīm al-Riyāḍ fī Sharḥ Shifāʾ al-Qāḍī ʿIyāḍ* of Shihāb al-Dīn al-Khafājī (d. 1069/1659) (see ibid., 74), the *Tuḥfat al-Mukhtāj bi-Sharḥ al-Minhāj* of Aḥmad ibn Ḥajar al-Haytamī (d. 973/1567) (see ibid., 39), the *K. al-Musāmara*, a super-commentary by Kamāl al-Dīn ibn Abī Sharīf al-Shāfiʿī (d. 906/1500) on the *Sharḥ al-Musāyara* of Ibn Humām (see ibid., 51), the *Fatāwá Hindiyya* (see ibid., 28, 65, 77 and 80), the *Durr al-Mukhtār Sharḥ Tanwīr al-Abṣār* of Muḥammad ibn ʿAlī al-Ḥaṣkafī (d. 1088/1677) (see ibid., 26, 88 and 95), the *Ghurar al-Fawāʾid Durar al-Qalāʾid* of the Sharīf al-Murtaḍá (d. 436/1044) (see ibid., 38, 44 and 86, misspelled each time), al-Shahrastānī's heresiographical *al-Milal wa'l-Niḥal* (see ibid., 52f.), as well as a couple of works by ʿAbd al-Ghanī al-Nabulusī (d. 1143/1731), which, to this day, are available only as manuscripts (a prominent case in point here is *al-Maṭālib al-Wafiyya*: see ibid., 54 and 74). Qur'anic commentaries referred to here are the *Tafsīr al-Jalālayn* of Jalāl al-Dīn al-Suyūṭī (d. 911/1505), the *Madarik al-Tanzīl wa-Haqāʾiq al-Taʾwīl* of Abū Barakāt Maḥmūd al-Nasafī (d. 710/1310) and the Persian *Tafsīr-i Ḥusaynī* of Kamāl al-Dīn Ḥusayn "Vāʿiẓ" Kāshifī (d. 910/1504) (see ibid., 55–7).

[191] See Chapter 4.

[192] See ʿAlī (1291h), 31, 44 and 110.

visible already in earlier centuries,[193] would see its major escalation only in the late twentieth century.[194] After all, the disciples of the Kōtah Ṣāḥib also used the anti-Shiʿi label "ravāfiẓ" blithely to denounce their opponents,[195] which suggests that an attitude hostile towards religious minorities was already very much a feature of the ideological legacy of the *Ṭarīqah-yi Muḥammadiyyah* in the Pashtun Borderland, alongside an increasingly fierce contestation in Pashtun Naqshbandiyyah-Mujaddidiyyah circles over what *amr bi'l-maʿrūf* [...] was supposed to consist of. By the later nineteenth century, it seems, its understanding had radicalized from Ādam Banūrī's already quite pronounced opposition to *shirk*, via its even more emphatic rejection by Sayyid Aḥmad Barēlvī and Shāh Ismāʿīl Dihlavī,[196] to a rather casual employment of the practice of accusing a Muslim of infidelity, or apostasy (*takfīr*), as espoused in the controversy between the respective circles of the Sayyidō Bābā and the Kōtah Ṣāḥib. Moreover, it is also in this context that, finally, the issue of the correct way of performing the *tashahhud* during the ritual prayer resurfaced again with verve and now carried even more severe implications for those accused of misperforming it.[197] Yet, besides such liturgical matters in the evaluation of belief, its propriety would – true to the legacy of the *Ṭarīqah-yi Muḥammadiyyah* – be determined not least by the readiness to actively confront non-Muslim rule over Muslim communities.

In fact, it seems that the Kōtah Ṣāḥib and the Sayyidō Bābā represented the two distinct aspects in the legacy of Sayyid Aḥmad Barēlvī and Shāh Ismāʿīl Dihlavī which are expressed in the respective nomenclature *Ṭarīqah-yi Muḥammadiyyah* and *Jamāʿat-i Mujāhidīn*. While the Kōtah Ṣāḥib represented especially the millenarian religious views that are encapsulated in the first label much more than did the Sayyidō Bābā, it was, in fact, the latter dignitary who employed his adherents first in major confrontations with the successors to the Sikh rule over the Punjab, the British East India Company (EIC), represented in the label "Jamāʿat-i Mujāhidīn".

The aggravation of the conflict between the Kōtah Ṣāḥib and Sayyidō Bābā, however, was much less doctrinal than it seemed on the surface. The controversy over which of the two was the true heir to Sayyid Aḥmad and Shāh Ismāʿīl also turned out to be little more than just a convenient strategic tool in

193 No less an authority than Khān Khaṭṭak (1358sh), 37 and 40 (verses 217 and 231), had infamously employed the *ravāfiẓ* label in order to polemically brand his Yusufzay adversaries in Swat.

194 See Section 4.5.

195 See, for example, ʿAlī (1291h), 31f., 44 and 110.

196 See, for example, Dihlavī (1998), which is entirely devoted to the refutation of certain beliefs and practices as one of four forms of *shirk*: in religious knowledge (*fi'l-ʿilm*), in the right of disposal (*fi'l-taṣarruf*), in religious worship (*fi'l-ʿibādāt*) and in local custom (*fi'l-ʿādāt*).

197 See Ṣafiyallāh (1305h), 254–6.

settling the rather profane matter of rule over the Swat Valley, which was still meant to determine their respective prerogative of religious interpretation and authority. For the Sayyidō Bābā, this consisted, first and foremost, of his desire to ensure the continuous independence of the Swat Valley from colonial rule, which, after all, was the *conditio sine qua non* for the reaffirmation of his own religious and, subsequently, socio-political status in that area, as well as that of his closest associates.[198] After all, the threat of losing the independence of the Swat Valley communities to the British had become quite real when the British had occupied Peshawar, following their annexation of the Punjab after the victory in the so-called Second Anglo-Sikh War on 21 February 1849, which effectively ended fifty years of Sikh rule over the Greater Punjab and adjoining territories.

A grand *jirgah* at Sayyidō Sharīf eventually agreed on proclaiming Sayyid Akbar Shāh (d. 1273/1857) of Sithānah, a descendant of the Pīr Bābā, as *amīr-i sharʿiyyat* of Swat, thus, making him the effective ruler over the entire region, while simultaneously establishing a distinct political entity: the State of Swat (*riyāsat-i Svāt*).[199] Sayyid Akbar Shāh, in turn, had been a faithful retainer of Sayyid Aḥmad Barēlvī, expressed, not least, in the fact that it was he who, already before the defeat at Balakot, offered lasting sanctuary to the adherents to the *Ṭarīqah-yi Muḥammadiyyah* / *Jamāʿat-i Mujāhidīn* at Sithānah,[200] where they would establish a colony that was seen as the hotbed of the "Wahhabis" in later British intelligence reports.[201] As Sayyid Aḥmad's spiritual deputy in the Hazārah region around 1824 – a period locally known as "Muslim rule" (*landəy musalmānī*) – he had already gained some experience in community administration according to *shari'a* regulations, which, as in the case of Sayyid Aḥmad himself, revolved a lot around the issues of Islamic taxation (*zakāt* and *ʿushr*) and communal conflict resolution.

It has been suggested that the Sayyidō Bābā was a driving force behind Sayyid Akbar Shāh's elevation to King of Swat,[202] particularly because his descent from the House of the Prophet Muḥammad put him outside the tribal arrangement in the region, which came in handy for settling long-standing communal feuds.[203] Yet, Sayyid Akbar's firm affiliation to the *Ṭarīqah-yi*

198 See Ahmad (1994), 114f., 155, 187 and 190.

199 See Mihr (2008), II: 200–2; Sultan-i-Rome (2008), 25 and 38f.

200 See Vazīr Khān (1428/2007), I 186f.; Mihr (2008), II: 202–4, IV: 153–5; Ṣābir (1990), 99.

201 For the British colonial perspective on the colony at Sithānah after the Battle of Balakot, see Hopkins and Marsden (2011), 78–94; compare and contrast the indigenous portrayal in Ḥāẕiq (1900). Remarkably, the polemical label "Wahhabi", frequently blamed on the British colonial establishment thanks to such influential writings as Hunter (1871), and the lengthy apologetics by "Sir" Sayyid Aḥmad Khān (d. 1315/1898) one year later, had indeed first been used in intra-Muslim polemics, such as the "Kōtah Ṣāḥib vs Sayyidō Bābā" controversy: see ʿAlī (1291h), 22.

202 See Khān (2004), 63f.

203 See Jahanzeb (1985), 14f.

Muḥammadiyyah entailed further important implications, proof of the Sayyidō Bābā's ability for canny political manoeuvring. After all, by proposing a candidate with such an ideological pedigree, the Sayyidō Bābā would have been able to deflect the attention of the British colonial security apparatus away from his own ambitious activities in Swat and Bunēr, which he carried out as the *shaykh al-islām*, the *éminence grise* behind Sayyid Akbar.[204] While it is difficult to date the exact beginning of the Sayyidō Bābā's controversy with the Kōtah Ṣāḥib, we may consider situating it at the time of Sayyid Akbar Shāh's rule in Swat. As a staunch supporter of Sayyid Aḥmad Barēlvī, the Kōtah Ṣāḥib may have considered himself, rather than the Sayyidō Bābā, as the most appropriate religious authority in Swat and Bunēr, which, in turn, would have centred politics and spiritual authority consistently on the legacy of the *Ṭarīqah-yi Muḥammadiyyah*. When, in November 1857, only half a year after Sayyid Akbar Shāh had passed away and had been succeeded by his much less capable son Mīr Mubārak ʿAlī Shāh (d. unknown), the Kōtah Ṣāḥib travelled to Mīngōrah to meet with the Sayyidō Bābā,[205] affairs seemingly climaxed: by then, it had already become a more or less open battle for religious and political authority in Swat between these two eminent figures. Eventually, both aimed at showing their capability of securing the independence of Swat by leading military campaigns against the British colonial state between 1860 and 1863, using large contingents of Sayyid Aḥmad Barēlvī's former retainers in their respective *laẍkar*.[206]

In the same year in which the Sayyidō Bābā confronted the British colonial troops on their "Ambēlah Campaign" against what the latter called the "Indian Wahhabis" in Bunēr,[207] Sayyid Mubārak Shāh, the son of Sayyid Akbar Shāh and his successor as ruler of Swat, faced a rebellion and in the end had to abdicate his throne, thus clearing the way for the family of the Sayyidō Bābā – known as the Miyāṇgul – to eventually establish their own dynastic rule over Swat. However, their ascent to power, which finally – though posthumously – sealed the religious and political triumph of the Sayyidō Bābā, was far from straightforward, and it was especially prominent Borderland actors, such as the Kōtah Ṣāḥib Sayyid Amīr, who saw to that. Among those contesting for the

204 See ibid.

205 See Ṣafiyallāh (1305h), 228f.

206 For the Kōtah Ṣāḥib's attacks on the English garrison at Mardan in 1860–1, see ibid., 265f. For the Sayyidō Bābā's leading participation in resisting the so-called "Ambēlah Campaign" of 1863, see Ḥāẕiq (1900), 66–70 and 139–54; Khān (2004), 66–74; Mihr (2008), IV: 434–6. On the remainders of the *Ṭarīqah-yi Muḥammadiyyah* in the Pashtun Borderland, see Section 3.2.

207 Hunter (1871), 61 *et passim*, was perhaps the one most responsible for establishing this label in the British colonial discourse, with repercussions continuing to the present. On the "Ambēlah Campaign" and its context, see ibid., 27–39; Mihr (2008), IV: 422–42; Ahmad (1994), 181–92; Hopkins and Marsden (2011), 86f.

throne was also Raḥmatallāh Khān of the neighbouring principality of Dir (d. 1343/1925),[208] established in the early seventeenth century by Ākhūnd Ilyās Khān Malīzay, better known as "Ākhūnd Bābā" (d. 1087/1676). Swat, for Raḥmatallāh Khān, also became an interesting proposition for the territorial expansion of his polity based on religious precepts, which existed already.

***

As in Swat, political authority in Dir evolved on a firm basis of spiritual and social capital, pivoting on the Ākhūnd Bābā and his descendants who, subsequently, came to be known as "Ilyāszay" instead of "Malīzay"; their retainers, in turn, became known as "Ākhūn[d] Khēl". The Ākhūnd Bābā, born in the village of Kōhān in eastern Upper Dir, had been yet another disciple of Aḥmad Sirhindī's *khalīfa* Ādam Banūrī, whom he even accompanied to his final abode in Mecca, before returning to Dir.[209] There, he elected to establish his own pendant to Sayyidō Sharīf, although not in his native Kōhān, but instead in Lājbōk Darrah: situated around ten miles north of Tīmargarah, today's district capital of Lower Dir, and some forty-five miles from the settlement of Dir in today's district of Upper Dir, the town that would serve as the eventual capital of the principality until its dissolution.[210] Still, because the Ākhūnd Bābā died and was buried in Lājbōk Darrah, this location can be considered the spiritual core of the Khanate, which again mirrors the spatial division between Sayyidō Sharīf and Mīngōrah as the spiritual vis-à-vis administrative pivot of the principality of Swat.

The Ākhūnd Bābā's son Ismāʿīl (d. 1165/1752) succeeded his father as spiritual and legal authority in Dir,[211] still profiting from his father's charisma, as well as that of Shaykh Malī ibn Khᵛājō Bābā (d. unknown), their great ancestor,[212] who, in the fifteenth century, devised, against the so far prevalent aggressive Yusufzay elite hegemony, the system of land rotation known as *vēsh*, under which no one can accumulate the more fertile plots of land forever.[213] Interestingly enough, despite the political rivalry between the tribes of Khattak

[208] See Sultan-i-Rome (2008), 40–2. It is quite understandable that these contestations of the Miyāṇgul claims are not mentioned in the personal accounts of family members, such as Khān (2004).

[209] See Badakhshī (1140h), 49b. The fact that, apart from this one mention in the list of Ādam Banūrī's *khulafāʾ*, the Ākhūnd Bābā, named "Mullā Ilyās Bājawṛī", is not discussed in the subsequent account on them (see ibid., 49a–116a) suggests that, at least in the eyes of the early eighteenth-century author, he had been not as significant as many of the other spiritual successors.

[210] See "Aṣr" Afghānī (1965), II: 612–16.

[211] See Shāhid (2005), II: 14.

[212] See ibid., II: 13.

[213] See Khān Khaṭṭak (1358sh), 31f.; Muʿaẓẓam Shāh (1971), 143–9; Ḥayāt Khān (1867), 195–7; Yūsufī (1960), 83–9; Nichols (2001), 18–20. On the term "*vēsh*", see ʿAṭāyī (1357sh), 292–5.

and Yusufzay, Khūshḥāl Khān, leader of the former, had expressly recognized the role of Shaykh Malī's *Institutions (daftar)*,[214] which, after all, turned out to become a crucial element in later Pashtun self-perceptions as an essentially egalitarian, or, in the words of Raḥmān Bābā, subaltern people.[215] Yet, the idea behind Shaykh Malī's provision of an egalitarian administrative measure was not rooted in tribal custom and lacks, therefore, a distinct ethnic reference, but lies in his understanding of the universal Islamic *shari'a*, or so the secondary materials suggest in the absence of any contemporaneous written copy of the *Daftar*.[216] For Shaykh Malī, tribal custom was identified as a cause for injustice in the Yusufzay lands, benefited by what Khūshḥāl Khān – with his usual bias – had dismissed as an only superficial religiosity.[217] If some of Khūshḥāl's deliberations in this regard are still to be considered apt, then Islamic religiosity had indeed declined over the generations, and it required dignitaries such as the Sayyidō Bābā and the Ākhūnd Bābā to revive societal practices based on Islamic precepts, practices which appeared socio-economically more inclusive than the prevalent "*khān* ethics". In this way, they were able to build a strong supporter base among the subalterns in the region, one that could not easily be ignored by the mighty and powerful. In order to become effective, however, the *shari'a*-based practices necessitated enforcement, something we have already encountered as the Qur'anically sustained imperative of *amr bi'l-ma'rūf* [...] against any kind of competing normativity to that of the *shari'a*, as was emphatically stressed especially by Ādam Banūrī, the spiritual guide of the Ākhūnd Bābā, who posited the latter as yet another representative of the guidance-orientated paradigm of religiosity in the Pashtun Borderland.

American social anthropologist Charles Lindholm has applied an earlier typology of communal leaders to the cases of Dir and Swat, indicating the situational confluence of roles assumed by the two seminal figures, the Ākhūnd Bābā and the Sayyidō Bābā, respectively. Accordingly, they sometimes served as religious dignitaries, at others as warriors, communal arbitrators, or what Lindholm calls an "inspirational leader",[218] and they filled each of their roles against the backdrop of local expansion efforts of the communal territories, in the case of Swat into the Kohistan region to the northeast, in that of Dir into

214 See Khān Khaṭṭak (n.d.), 349: 'Two works are reputed in Swat, in secret as in the open [*dvah kārah day pah Svāt kx̌ī kih khafī day kih jalī*]: Darvīzah's *Makhzān* and Shaykh Malī's *Daftar*'. Thankfully, Sultan-i-Rome (Swat) has provided a copy of the relevant pages, the more so as this line could not be located in other published collections of Khushḥāl's *rubā'iyāt*.

215 On the romantic imagination of Pashtun society as fundamentally egalitarian, see Hartung (2019a).

216 See n.86 in this chapter.

217 See Khān Khaṭṭak (1358sh), 33–42.

218 See Lindholm (1986), 5–8.

the principality of Chitral.[219] Moreover, Lindholm makes the convincing point that the dissimilarities in the increasingly centralized polities which emerged in both Swat and Dir are rooted in the confrontation with the distinctly different manners in which community affairs in these two regions were administered.

The principality of Chitral, predominantly Khuvār-speaking, had been under central dynastic rule since 1320 CE, first by the Raʾīs and, from 1595 onwards, by the Katūr, originally from around Herat. During both dynastic periods, revenue was collected into the treasury of the ruler (*mahtār*), who parcelled out land in exchange for military services, and a central court existed in the capital town of Chitral with a definite nomenclature and protocol. All civil, military and judiciary matters pivoted on the *mahtār*, and the dominion was administratively divided and managed by a hierarchy of royal governors.[220] Kohistan, in turn, was also populated by distinct ethnic communities with their own respective languages, but its inhospitable terrain had not provided for much centralization. Instead, it 'form[ed] an autarchic political society [and], hav[ing] resisted political domination, they also form moral autarchy, acting upon unwritten rules and social norms validated and sanctioned by themselves'.[221]

Lindholm argues, for the case of Dir, that the successful attempts of its Yusufzay communities to expand into Chitral led to the adoption of the effective administrative patterns of its northern neighbour, increasingly developing its own centralized statehood, a process which he calls the 'evolution of secondary state systems'.[222] The Yusufzay of Swat, in turn, aligned instead with the Eastern Kohistani patterns of administering community affairs, resulting – at least initially – in a lack of centralization of political and economic power and the building of the respective institutions. This, of course, is not yet the end of the story: by the beginning of the twentieth century both Dir and Swat had become recognized by the British colonial establishment as "Princely States" (*riyāsāt*), and their leaders had been bestowed with the titles "duke" (*navvāb*) and "king" (*bādⁱshāh*), respectively. At this point in time, both principalities had evidently come a long way from their origins.[223]

219 Remarkably, Shāhid (2005), II: 14, writes of campaigns of the Sulṭān Khēl and Pāʾindah Khēl under Ẓafar Khān (r. 1804–14) against 'the unbelievers of Kohistan'. However, because he does not mention Chitral in this regard, we may assume that what is meant here is neither the contemporary District of Kohistan, nor Swat-Kohistan, but its westernmost spur around the Pānjkōṛah Valley, which borders on Chitral. Incursions into Chitral, however, did take place in 1895, during the interim rule of the usurper Khān ʿUmarā Khān (d. 1321/1903) of the Tarkaṇī, or Tarkalāṇī, tribe of Jandul in today's district of Lower Dir, on the instigation of the British colonial authorities, see ibid., II: 16; Jahanzeb (1985), 18f.

220 See Baig (2004), 3–55.

221 Knudsen (2009), 29. For a breakdown of the "community management strategies" in Indus Kohistan, see ibid., *passim*.

222 See Lindholm (1986), 5f.

223 See Jahanzeb (1985), 21 and 32; Shāhid (2005), II: 17–9; Sultan-i-Rome (2008), 48–56.

This was even more apparent in Dir, where Khān Ẓafar Khān relocated his base from the home of his two more spiritually oriented predecessors in Bībyavaṛ to the town of Dir, situated only about ten miles further north, and where, in this way, once again some spatial division of the spiritual and political seats of authority was created.[224] The descendants of the Ākhūnd Bābā now began to mould the various rather charismatic roles the latter had assumed as a spiritual leader into a bureaucratic set-up; something similar happened eventually in Swat under Miyāṇgul ʿAbd al-Vadūd (r. 1918–49).[225]

Before this, however, both the Khān of Dir and the Walī of Swat had even joined hands in an armed anti-colonial activity: side-by-side with the Sayyidō Bābā, Khān Ghazan Khān (d. 1285/1868) of Dir led a substantial tribal militia into confrontation with the British during their "Ambēlah Campaign" of 1863.[226] After having sustained substantial casualties, the British nonetheless succeeded in the end in what turned out to be only one, though important, punitive expedition of finally almost forty of them in total, mostly directed against individual tribal communities, between 1849 and 1897.[227] The most significant outcome of this encounter for the continuation of our present narrative is that, after the British victory in December 1863, the Sayyidō Bābā pragmatically struck an agreement with the British in order to retain his position in Swat, while the Khāns of Dir became embroiled in local tribal conflict with the Khāns of Jandul (*Jandūl*) until the mid 1890s, when the British colonial forces helped to settle this conflict and reinstated Muḥammad Sharīf Khān (d. 1322/1904), although now as *navvāb* by grace of Queen Victoria.[228] Such an accord required, of course, some firm commitment to the British position on the "Wahhabis", something that the Sayyidō Bābā and his retainers were obviously willing to make.[229]

The surrender of the two local authorities to British suzerainty triggered responses from politically less established religious dignitaries in the region,

[224] See Dīravī (2003), 24f.

[225] See Lindholm (1986), 8–12. The institution-building is very much what Weber (1972), 661–81, had described as the 'transformation of charismatic authority' for the sake of its continuity, during which an individual "pure charisma" becomes routinized as "office charisma".

[226] See Ahmad (1994), 181–92; Shāhid (2005), II: 15.

[227] See Hayat Khan (2000), 244f. (Appendix I).

[228] See Jahanzeb (1985), 15; Shāhid (2005), II: 15–7; Sultan-i-Rome (2008), 27.

[229] In this context belongs what is perhaps – despite its brevity – the most systematic refutation of Shāh Ismāʿīl's depiction of certain beliefs and practices as *bidaʿ*, entitled *Iḥqāq al-Ḥaqq*, composed in Persian by Miyāṇ Naṣīr Aḥmad "Miyāṇ Ṣāḥib Qiṣṣah'khᵛānī" (d. 1308/1891), one of the foremost disciples of the Sayyidō Bābā, after the open dissociation of the latter from the *Ṭarīqah-yi Muḥammadiyyah*, see [Qiṣṣah'khᵛānī] (1297h). See also Gīlānī (1972), I: 153 and 168. This work also foreshadows a theological debate on the state of the Prophet in his grave, which would gain considerable momentum in the Pashtun Borderland in times to come, see Hartung (2020), 195–201. See also Section 4.1.2.

among them the Ṣāḥib of Kōṫah in the very south of the Swat Valley, who might, however, also have entered an alliance with the British had they supported his claim for political leadership against that of the Sayyidō Bābā and his disciples. After all, in the later 1830s, when the Sayyidō Bābā had aligned himself with the ruler of Kabul, Dūst Muḥammad Khān Bārakzay (r. 1826–40 and 1843–63),[230] the Kōṫah Ṣāḥib is said to have received at least some moral encouragement from Shāh Shujāʿ Khān (r. 1803–9 and 1839–42), the last Durrani ruler of Afghanistan and a chief opponent of Dūst Muḥammad.[231] After the demise of the Kōṫah Ṣāḥib in 1865 and the Sayyidō Bābā thirteen years later, however, new religious actors, formally affiliated to either dignitary, came to the fore, who departed from the willingness of their spiritual masters to make concessions to larger political powers for the sake of their own regional authority.[232]

3.2.3 Anti-imperialist Religious Borderland Activism: The Beginning

The disciples of the Sayyidō Bābā and the Kōṫah Ṣāḥib from various parts of the Pashtun Borderland found themselves in a geopolitical setting towards the end of the nineteenth century quite different from that of their respective spiritual masters. The communities of which they were part now found themselves at the centre of the geostrategic manoeuvring of the British and Russian Empires, as well as the Barakzay polities of Kabul/Afghanistan, successors to the Durrani, with rather similar imperial aspirations.

Kabul's new ruler, the "Iron Emir" ʿAbd al-Raḥmān (r. 1879–1901), began to consolidate the authority of his family by forcing large territories under his rule to negotiate border treaties with neighbouring imperial powers and to centralize his administration, cutting out the religious dignitaries in the course of this process.[233] Thus, while British colonial forces campaigned against insubordinate Pashtun tribes, these communities could not expect much support from the ruler of Kabul either. This must have become even more painfully plain to them after, in November 1893, Emir ʿAbd al-Raḥmān signed a border agreement with the then-Foreign Secretary of India, Sir Henry Mortimer Durand (d. 1924), ratifying the still effective national borderline between British India

230 Dūst Muḥammad had also been one of the political dignitaries frequently approached by Sayyid Aḥmad and Shāh Ismāʿīl for support and recognition, either directly or through family members and leading courtiers, although, at best, with marginal success, see Sayyid Aḥmad (1395/1975), 46f. (23b f.), 63–6 (32b–34a) and 114–18 (57b–59b).

231 See Ḥayāt Khān (1867), 135–7 and 303; Yūsufī (1960), 542–47; Noelle (1997), 15 and 168; Haroon (2007), 39f.

232 The view elaborated in Haroon (2007), 43–64, that the following generation of religious borderland actors derived its 'revivalist agenda' (57) from a spiritual line that goes back to the Sayyidō Bābā is somewhat challenging. Instead, it shall be argued here that the spiritual affiliation to him was not much of a legitimizing force in the socio-political activities of those religious dignitaries in the Pashtun Borderland.

233 See Kakar (1979); Olesen (1995), 61–93, esp. 71–5; Noelle (1997), 278.

(and its successor state Pakistan) and Afghanistan by disregarding local property and usage rights of the tribal communities of the area through which the so-called "Durand Line" was to run.[234]

The Ṣāḥib of Hadḋah, or The Primordial Talib

One pivotal case of those who epitomized the deep distrust of religious community representatives towards all the political actors who were reaching out from their far-away metropolises of London and Delhi, St Petersburg and Tashkent, as well as Kabul, and who opposed any colonization of the Pashtun Borderland with increasing vigour was Najm al-Dīn Ākhūnd'zādah of Hadḋah near Jalalabad, the "Hadḋah Ṣāḥib" (d. 1320/1901).[235] As one of the foremost disciples of the Sayyidō Bābā, he consequently succeeded him as the spiritual head of the principality in Swat after the passing away of his celebrated *shaykh*. As he was a tribal outsider – he originated from one of the Mūsá Khēl majority areas around Ghazni[236] – this is surprising, and then again, it is not.[237] Sayyid Akbar Shāh, as ruler of Swat during the Sayyidō Bābā's spiritual tenure, is just a case in point to indicate that bringing in outsiders was actually a common means of arbitration in intracommunal conflict, which, in the case of the Hadḋah Ṣāḥib's nomination, suggests the great likelihood of succession disputes between the Sayyidō Bābā's own progeny and other disciples from among the Yusufzay. The Hadḋah Ṣāḥib's chief adversary from among the disciples of the Sayyidō Bābā, however, turned out to be Sayyid ʿAbd al-Vahhāb, then the "Pīr Ṣāḥib [of] Mānkī-yi Sharīf" (d. 1322/1904) in today's Nowshera District, who, like he himself, stood outside the tribal setting, courtesy of his descent from the family of the Prophet Muḥammad.[238] Interestingly, the conflict between these two luminaries, most likely to determine who owned the legacy of the Sayyidō Bābā, crystallized once again, and now with renewed intensity, on the correct execution of the *tashahhud* during the ritual prayer, culminating in a week-long disputation on the subject in April 1896 in Gandāb, situated in the then Mōmand Tribal Agency of the British NWFP, in front of a massive gathering of local religious dignitaries.[239] Purportedly, the Hadḋah Ṣāḥib defended the

234 See Hayat Khan (2000), 53–174 and Appendices II–VI; Kakar (1979), 49 and 64–6.

235 See Gīlānī (1972), I: 207f.; Kakar (1979), 156f.; Jāvīd (1982), 43f.; Ṣābir (1990), 25–36; Olesen (1995), 84–7; Haroon (2007), 45–53 *et passim*; Qadir (2015b), 21f.

236 See Quddūsī (1966), 575; Edwards (1996), 133f. See also Map 3.2.

237 Reliable biographical material on the Hadḋah Ṣāḥib is extremely scarce, the information in later hagiographies rather thin; so, most information on him is, in fact, derived from British colonial records. Edwards (1996), 126–71, went laudably farther and used a host of oral information, unfortunately still with little more solid outcome insofar as historical data are concerned.

238 On his pedigree, see Kākā Khēl (1990), 13.

239 See Edwards (1996), 157. This information is based on a British colonial intelligence report, indicating the apparent need of the imperial authorities to monitor the activities of the Hadḋah Ṣāḥib.

practice of raising the index finger during the *tashahhud* as a sound Prophetic practice, supported by commonly acknowledged *aḥādīth*;[240] the Pīr Ṣāḥib of Mānkī-yi Sharīf, in turn, 'marshaling his scriptural evidence',[241] argued that raising the finger constitutes, in fact, an inadmissible religious innovation (*bid'a*).[242]

This portrayal of the argument, as presented by Edwards on the basis of a colonial intelligence report, however, does somewhat conflict with the history of the dispute over the *tashahhud* matter in the Pashtun Borderland, and, in the absence of additional textual evidence, it does indeed seem as if the positions held by the Haḋḋah Ṣāḥib and the Pīr Ṣāḥib of Mānkī-yi Sharīf, respectively, were in fact rather the reverse. Accordingly, it would have been the Haḋḋah Ṣāḥib rather than the latter who, in the tradition of Aḥmad Sirhindī, Ādam Banūrī, 'Umar Ćamkanī and also the Kōṫah Ṣāḥib, would be the one representing the guidance-orientated paradigm of religiosity, emphasizing, firstly, conformity with the stipulations of the *shari'a* in the footsteps of the Prophet.[243]

Secondly, this particular hermeneutical approach went hand in hand with a deep suspicion of any kind of imperial aspiration. The Pīr Ṣāḥib of Mānkī-yi Sharīf, for one, showed easy willingness to collaborate with the British colonial authorities in exchange for adequate privileges, in order to gain an upper hand in the fierce competition for the monopoly of religious authority in the Pashtun Borderland.[244] For the Haḋḋah Ṣāḥib, in turn, concessions to political office-holders, even more so to those with imperial aspirations, were preferably not to be made, especially as long as their rule ran counter to the precepts of the

[240] See, for example, *Sunan Abī Dāwūd*, k. al-ṣalāt, b. al-ishāra fi'l-tashahhud, no. 3 (ḥadīth 991): 'Ibn Zubayr remembered that the Messenger – God's blessing be upon him and peace! – used to point with his finger when he offered [the *tashahhud*], and he did not stir it. Ibn Jurayj said: "And 'Amr bin Dinār added: 'He [i.e., Ziyād, a Companion in the chain of transmitters] said: "'Āmir [ibn 'Abdallāh] informed me from his father that he saw the Messenger – God's blessing be upon him and peace! – supplicating like that [*yad'ū kadhalika*] and bore his left hand on his left thigh.'

[241] Edwards (1996), 157.

[242] It remains unclear of what the Pīr Ṣāḥib of Mānkī's 'scriptural evidence' actually consisted. For now, we may well entertain the possibility that it was various Hanafi texts, especially the *Khulāṣat al-Kaydānī*, which had been somewhat trailblazing for Shaykh 'Umar Ćamkanī a century earlier (see Section 3.1.3): 'The unlawful [acts in prayer; *muḥarramāt*] are fourteen: [. . .] Pointing with the index finger as the People of *ḥadīth* do [*wa'l-ishāra bi'l-sabbāba ka-'ahl al-ḥadīth*]' (al-Kaydānī [n.d.], 15f.). Besides, it is a fact that the reliability of the *ḥadīth* above had been, and still remains, disputed.

[243] This fact is reflected well in the Haḋḋah Ṣāḥib's alleged reliance on *ḥadīth* in this matter, rather than on legal works of one particular tradition of Islamic jurisprudence, which were presumably what the Pīr Ṣāḥib of Mānkī-yi Sharīf had "marshalled".

[244] This friendly attitude of Sayyid 'Abd al-Vahhāb towards an imperial establishment would be continued by at least some of his successors: see Kākā Khēl (1990). See also Section 3.3.

shari'a and the "common good" (*maṣlaḥa*). In fact, this attitude of the Haḋḋah Ṣāḥib marked his entire position vis-à-vis Emir ʿAbd al-Raḥmān, and his vast network of disciples disseminated that stance particularly among the subalterns across the Pashtun Borderland, to such an extent that both imperial powers, the British in India and the Barakzay ruler of Kabul, perceived these activities increasingly as a serious threat to their own respective political aspirations. As a matter of fact, the conflict between the Emir and the Haḋḋah Ṣāḥib initially became manifest shortly after the demise of the Sayyidō Bābā, on whose instruction Najm al-Dīn had set up base at Haḋḋah on today's southern outskirts of Jalalabad, an important node in the network of pilgrimage sites and a place of religious learning for the followers of the Buddha in Kushan Gandhāra around the first century CE,[245] but then a place with very little infrastructure.[246]

Yet, it was close to the North-West Frontier of the British infidels, thus making Haḋḋah into a fortress of faith and its inhabitants guardians of the frontier, somewhat emulating the institutions of *ribāṭ* and *futuwwa* associations during the formative period of Islam.[247]

Apparently, the Emir had become firmly convinced by 1880 that the community which established itself around Najm al-Dīn at Haḋḋah posed more than only a potential threat to his own political aspirations, for which, after all, he claimed a divine mandate.[248] Indeed, what manifested itself in this particular constellation was, once more, the antagonism between "*khān* ethics" and its subaltern pendant mentioned above, an epitome of which the religious poetry of Raḥmān Bābā had introduced:[249] what Edwards calls 'the single-mindedness of his piety and his disregard for the normal demands of the body',[250] radiating from many of the popular stories about him in circulation, stood in

245 Apparently, the name of the place had been derived from the Sanskrit word for "bone" (*haḍḍa*), suggesting that relics of the historical Buddha Siddhārta Gautama had been kept there, see Neelis (2011), 246–8. The Sanskrit term was eventually appropriated into Pashto as *haḋūkay* ("small bone").

246 See Edwards (1996), 133 and 138–41.

247 See ibid., 138. On the two early Islamic institutions, see Taeschner (1979), 13–9; Chabbi (1995). See also Chapter 5. Meanwhile, the abode and shrine (*āstānah ʿāliyyah*) of the Pīrān-i Mānkī-yi Sharīf remained a major spiritual centre in the Peshawar Valley, with its respective heads deeply involved in regional and national politics.

248 See Khan (1900), I: 217–19, 224, 250–3 and 263–66; Kakar (1979), 156 (once again based on a British colonial document); Olesen (1995), 85. On the religious underpinnings of the Emir's claim to rule, see ʿAbd al-Raḥmān (1306sh), 62–71. Moreover, Kātib-i Hazārah (1331sh), III: 567, puts the following words into the mouth of the Emir in a missive to the Haḋḋah Ṣāḥib in August 1887: 'Now that I am here, and thanks to the Most-Exalted One Who Decrees Fate [*va az faẕl-i qādir-i subḥān*], the thread of the Emirate has become strong [*mustaḥkam*] and the business of governance steady [*va kār-i salṭanat muntaẓim ast*] [...]'

249 See Section 3.1.1.

250 Edwards (1996), 143.

stark contrast to the "*khān* ethics" displayed by Emir ʿAbd al-Raḥmān and offered the people of the land a viable societal alternative.[251] The Haḋḋah Ṣāḥib initially appears to have kept very much aloof from politics, seemingly accepting the necessity of a Muslim ruler for the "management of the flock", even if he was a tyrant.[252] This, however, was to change dramatically in around 1887, when the Haḋḋah Ṣāḥib was informed about an allegedly immanent assassination attempt on him during his presence in the courtly circles of Kabul, and subsequently fled to the ancestral territory of the Shinvari (*Shinvārī*) around the Khyber Pass.[253] This particular tribal community was already in a rebellious mood, following the royal decree that the entire revenue from the traffic across the Khyber was to go into the imperial treasury, and no longer, as was established custom, proportionally to the Shinvari community.[254]

The various materials available present us with a host of different and, at times, even conflicting narratives for all the developments from this crucial moment on. For one, the account of "Kātib-i Hazārah" Fayẕ-i Muḥammad (d. 1349/1931), chronicler and secretary at the royal court of the Barakzay Emir Ḥabīballāh at Kabul (r. 1901–19), suggests that the Haḋḋah Ṣāḥib maintained his stance towards obedience to the ruler and, consequently, tried to discourage the elders of the Shinvari from an armed response to what was regarded as an open and deliberate assault on the collective honour of this community.[255] When they went on to embark on what the Kātib-i Hazārah called a "tribulation" (*fitnah*), the Haḋḋah Ṣāḥib left them for Lālpūrah in the Mōmand territories of today's Nangarhar Province; from there, he petitioned Emir ʿAbd al-Raḥmān for permission to return to his abode, stating that 'those people [with an agenda; *ahl-i gharaẕ*] have falsely accused me of having a desire to claim kingship [*havā-yi shāhī*] and taking the path of rebellion against the ruler whom one must obey [*va rāh-i baghāvat bā-bādishāh vājib al-iṭāʿat*

[251] This does indeed correspond exactly to the point Edwards makes in ibid., 144–55.

[252] This impression emerges especially from Kātib-i Hazārah (1331sh), III: 562. Yet, we must, of course, remain aware of the fact that the author himself was an imperial chronicler, something that would have shaped his own attitude towards the monarchic rule of the Barakzay. Islamically, the imperative of obeying whoever rules over the Muslim community is rooted in Q4.59; for the stress on obedience even if the ruler was a tyrant (*imām jāʾir*), sustained by references to *aḥādīth*: see Ibn Taymiyya (1426/2005b), 138.

[253] See Kātib-i Hazārah (1331sh), III: 562.

[254] See Olesen (1995), 87. This somehow calls into question the unconditional loyalty of the Pashtun tribes to the Afghan ruler, expressed in the *kalimah bādⁱshāhī*, as Khan (2014), 67f., suggests from his scrutiny of British colonial documents. Quite likely, what had informed the perspective of the British colonial administration was Emir ʿAbd al-Raḥmān's own *Kalimah-yi Amīr al-Bilād fī Targhīb ilá 'l-Jihād* (see ʿAbd al-Raḥmān [1304sh]).

[255] See Kātib-i Hazārah (1331sh), III: 562.

khᵛāhad sipārd]'.[256] The stern response of the latter, however, ignited the fire of open discontent in the Haḍḍah Ṣāḥib:

> Whatever "people with an agenda" might say, they do not attribute to you any lordship, pre-eminence or superiority [*sarvarī va buzurgī va bartarī*]. [. . .] Your flight is clear proof that something is bothering you. You fail to heed the words:
>
> > When Abū Musaylimah claimed prophethood / the only
> > outcome [for him] was that people called him a liar //
> > Let us imaging a firefly glowing. / How do you equate that to the
> > moonlight? [. . .]
>
> You stopped acting in accordance with the word of God – Honoured and glorified He shall be! – who said: 'Why do you not practice what you preach?' [. . .] You claim to be a mystically endowed one, pious and of the divine folk [*ʿārifī va pārsāʾī va ahl-i ilāhī*], [yet] you were the one who ran away and turned your back on the royal audience. Well done! Following your "intuition" and "certainty" [*maʿrifat va īqān*], and boasting of "guidance" and "righteousness" [*hidāyat va irshād*], you went to the rebellious Shinvari tribe and did what you did. [. . .] We do not think that your general welfare [*ḥāl-i khayr-i shumā*] lies in your being inside Afghanistan. It is better that you go away. Know that it is no longer permitted for you to stay another night within [its] borders.[257]

The unmistakably derogatory tone of this response appears to have changed the Haḍḍah Ṣāḥib's understanding of politics and the imperative of obeying the ruler whatever the circumstances. Political rule for him now had to conform with the religiously grounded precepts of "equity" (*inṣāf*) and "justice" (*ʿadl*), to be measured by the extent to which a community leader cares for the "common good" (*maṣlaḥa*), which would almost necessarily emanate from the appropriate implementation and monitoring of the Islamic *shariʿa*. It was the Haḍḍah Ṣāḥib, rather than Emir ʿAbd al-Raḥmān, who could deliver on this basis for the common people in the Pashtun Borderland, a fact that is underlined by the emphasis on his ability to work miracles (*karāmāt*, or *khawārīq*) by the grace of God, and expressed by the immense popularity of his *langar'khānah* prior to his withdrawal into the mountainous Borderland proper.[258]

The Haḍḍah Ṣāḥib now demanded "good governance" (*siyāsa sharʿiyya*) in return for obedience, or else he would provide a religious justification for open

[256] Ibid., III: 567.

[257] Ibid., III: 567f. The passage quoted in this letter is Q61.2: [*yā ʾayyuhā alladhīna ʾāmanū*] *lima taqūlūna mā lā tafʿalūna*; the couplet had been taken from the *Dīvān* of the eighteenth-century Iranian poet Ḥabīballāh Shīrāzī "Qāʾānī" (d. 1270/1857).

[258] See Edwards (1996), 126–8.

opposition with whatever means deemed necessary. Emir ʿAbd al-Raḥmān's own repeated stress on the fact that some of the "mullahs" he so despised had openly declared him an unbeliever[259] resonates well with that, and the popular stories about the Haḋḋah Ṣāḥib collected by Edwards and British colonial intelligence reports provide some corroboration that he had, indeed, been one of those exercising *takfīr al-ḥākim*,[260] a theologically sustained legal practice that would gain enormous momentum in the centuries to follow.[261] Furthermore, if one of the justifications for this particular *takfīr* was actually, as suggested by Olesen, a religious deviation of the monarch caused by his rather amicable contacts with the unbelieving Europeans,[262] then we have some indication of the odd proto-Salafi leaning of the Haḋḋah Ṣāḥib: the doctrine of "association and disengagement" – *al-walāʾ wa'l-barāʾ* – was an early cornerstone of Salafi thought and would, by the end of the twentieth century, emerge as one of the strongest arguments in the legitimization of *takfīr* in general.[263]

All these various threads in the personality of the Haḋḋah Ṣāḥib could be meshed into the single image of the archetypal "talib" as suggested by Edwards, in view of his formative years in the area around Ghazni.[264] The indicators that sustain this categorization for the anthropologist are the Haḋḋah Ṣāḥib's upbringing as a son of a religious functionary at the village level (*ākhūnd*), his belonging to the more inferior strata within the tribal hierarchy and his subsequent pursuit of a religious education rather than engaging in more materialistic activities. Still, it is suggested here that one should cast the view a bit wider, very much in line with our understanding of the term "talib" above as a rather colourful and highly discursive trope in the Pashtun Borderland, by bringing Edwards's observations into conversation with the diligent attempt of James Caron to correlate the literary phenotype of the "talib", based especially on the image that emerges from the popular folk story of Ṭālib Jān,[265] with the more empirical one of the ṬIT/IEA and TṬP in the late twentieth and twenty-first centuries. In fact, Caron's point is that it was precisely the existence of the phenotypical image in the collective perception throughout the Pashtun Borderland that 'political activists (that is, "The Taliban") are able to inhabit and control – [if] only to some extent'.[266] We encounter in the person of the Haḋḋah Ṣāḥib for the first time in the present narrative a person who

[259] See Khan (1900), 1: 212f. and 225.
[260] See Edwards (1996), 160.
[261] See below, esp. Sections 4.2.2, 4.4.2, 4.5.2 and 4.5.5.
[262] See Olesen (1995), 85.
[263] On the history and present interpretations of this doctrine, which is derived from Q60.1, see Wagemakers (2012), 148–53; Nedza (2020), 110–18. On its role in the Pashtun Borderland, see below, esp. Sections 4.4.2 and 4.5.3.
[264] See Edwards (1996), 134.
[265] See Nūrī (1387sh/2008).
[266] Caron (2012a), 61. See also Hartung (2024), 40f.

appears as a true embodiment of the collective and poetically shaped imaginary of a "talib"; therefore, it seems only logical to sketch out the phenotype at this point, even more so as the image will accompany us in the subsequent chapters.

Indeed, Caron conceptualizes the literary phenotype of the "talib" as 'a specific romantic countercultural social type',[267] a highly mobile, yet morally respectable, youth whose preoccupation with spiritual matters stands in contrast to a fixation on material wealth and highly pragmatic political power.[268]

It is not really hard to relate all this to the personality of the Haḋḋah Ṣāḥib. He came from a subaltern background within the Pashtun tribal context and adopted an itinerant lifestyle, one that brought him eventually to the feet of the Sayyidō Bābā in distant Swat. His *langar'khānah* in Haḋḋah epitomized the conceptual contrast to the *ḥujrah*, the public guesthouse usually attached to the homes of the village *məshərān*, which, according to Edwards, 'is one of the prime elements in the tribal khan's social persona'.[269] The Haḋḋah Ṣāḥib was initially not in conflict with the structures of mundane powers, and focused on spiritual refinement through an ascetic disposition and service to the lower socio-economic strata of the tribal community. Moreover, we need to consider him entirely unfamiliar with the novel ways of contemporaneous politics, because his conflict with Emir ʿAbd al-Raḥmān originated more in a misapprehension which the latter then chose to exploit to make a firm statement against the role of religious community leaders in the Pashtun Borderland. In the Haḋḋah Ṣāḥib's hagiographical glorification, of course, this had been recast as his unwillingness to make any concessions to political power-holders, a consequent result of his religious steadfastness. To this end, the Haḋḋah Ṣāḥib resorted to a return to the itinerant life, now, however, swapping the earlier focus on ascetic exercises for an active resistance to any imperial attempt to impair the traditional societal structures in the Pashtun Borderland, structures which, after all, secured – at least to some extent – the continued socio-political eminence of religious dignitaries such as himself.

The Sartōr Faqīr, or The Warrior Intoxicated

Another such character, though quite distinct from the Haḋḋah Ṣāḥib, rose to prominence in the Pashtun Borderland at around the same time, eventually

267 Caron (2012a), 63.

268 Once again, the popular story of Ṭālib Jān (see Nūrī [1387sh/2008]) and his romance with Gul Bashrah, daughter of the *bāchā* of a village, presents this image well: inhabiting different concrete characters in the many variations in circulation, the common denominator in all the various subaltern imaginaries of Ṭālib Jān is his breaking with the social norms defined and controlled by the more worldly minded heads of the social hierarchy, the *məshərān*, arguably because they conflict with the sublime religious precepts that define Ṭālib Jān's own moral universe.

269 Edwards (1996), 151. See also ibid., 67f.

joining hands with the latter in what later Pashtun nationalist historiographers exaggerate as the first concerted anti-colonial resistance in that region:[270] Saʿdallāh Khān, son of Malik Ḥamīdallāh of Bunēr, better known as "Sartōr Faqīr" – the "Bare-Headed Mendicant", or "Mullā Mastān" – the "Mad Mullah", as he is pejoratively referred to in the British colonial archives. Yet, those appear to be the primary textual evidence for the reconstruction of his biography – even later authors writing in Urdu and / or Pashto were forced to rely heavily on such specimens as young Winston Churchill's *The Story of the Malakand Field Force* (1898).[271]

Saʿdallāh's early life, thus, remains shrouded in mystery. He is said to have actively participated in the resistance to the British "Ambēlah Campaign" in 1863. Soon after, however, he had to flee the repercussions from his own community after an argument with his brother had got out of hand,[272] and he spent the subsequent years at the shrine of Muʿīn al-Dīn Chishtī (d. 627/ 1236) in Ajmēr. There is word that from there he travelled on even as far as Baghdad, from where he proceeded to Mazār-i Sharīf in northern Afghanistan and spent about a decade at its Blue Mosque, believed to be the burial site of the Prophet Muḥammad's nephew and son-in-law ʿAlī ibn Abī Ṭālib.[273] If any of this information is reliable, then Saʿdallāh passed prolonged periods in centres of highly emotional religious worship,[274] which may have shaped his own ecstatic-cum-ascetic Sufi practices that he added to his exceptional taste for *jihād* of the militant variety against all forms of unbelief.

A British colonial document also indicates that Saʿdallāh even went as far as presenting himself to Emir ʿAbd al-Raḥmān at the court in Kabul and offering his services as warrior for the faith. After all, the Barakzay ruler had begun in the late 1880s to emphasize an offensive *jihād* against "unbelievers" in general as a pillar of his imperial ideology,[275] so Saʿdallāh's offer actually followed a

[270] See, for example, Ahmad (2017).

[271] The most prominent of such later works are Allāhbakhsh Yūsufī's *Yūsufzāʾī* (1960) and Khān Rōshan Khān's *Yūsufzaʾī Qawm kī Sar'guzasht* (1986). Renowned local historian Sultan-i-Rome (1994) necessarily relied heavily on them, yet he adds valuable oral information from living members of the Sartōr Faqīr's family.

[272] This is apparently a common strategy after bloodshed in Pashtun tribal communities: see Grima (2005), 3–13.

[273] The various secondary accounts, however, are fairly inconsistent and, moreover, lack sustainable references: see Ṣābir (1986), 714; (1990), 138; Sultan-i-Rome (1994), 93; Ahmad (2017), 87 n.93.

[274] On the shrine in Ajmēr, see Currie (1989), 117–40; on that of ʿAbd al-Qādir al-Jīlānī in Baghdad, see Al-Gailani (2015), esp. 77–83. On the shrine of ʿAlī ibn Abī Ṭālib in Mazār-i Sharīf, although exclusively on its economy and administration across the centuries, see McChesney (1991). For a brief anthropological account, see Canfield (1993).

[275] See Kakar (1979), 176–9; Olesen (1995), 68–71. His imperial doctrine of *jihād* was enshrined in ʿAbd al-Raḥmān (1304sh), and even more elaborate in ʿAbd al-Raḥmān (1306sh).

certain logic. Still, since we already know of ʿAbd al-Raḥmān's aversion to these kinds of religious figures, it might not be surprising that the Emir regarded him as insane and chose to relinquish his services. After this, Saʿdallāh, now known as "Bābā Mastān", returned to Bunēr via the Mōmand territories, where allegedly he spent time in the company of the Haḋdah Ṣāḥib. Back home in Bunēr, he is said to have been appointed the custodian (*mutavallī*) of the shrine of the Pīr Bābā;[276] yet, this rather sedentary duty does not appear very compatible with his otherwise rather mendicant lifestyle, which is why this claim may well be questioned for the time being.

Finally, he set up his base in Landākay on the southern bank of the River Swat in 1897 and began to rally volunteers for a *jihād* against the infidel British, declaring that he was acting entirely under the orders of Muʿīn al-Dīn Chishtī, who had appeared to him in a vision while in Ajmēr.[277] Interestingly, similarly to the Haḋdah Ṣāḥib, the person of the Sartōr Faqīr is also surrounded by numerous popular stories and poems about his supernatural abilities: he was claimed to be able to rally heavenly troops to ensure victory, feed thousands from only one handful of rice or make himself invisible.[278]

British colonial intelligence reports relate that the Sartōr Faqīr was rhetorically quite accomplished, a quality he seems to have shared with other mendicants in borderland communities.[279] Remarkably still, his agitation in favour of *jihād* was presumably based on Emir ʿAbd al-Raḥmān's imperial doctrine on the matter, the text of which, as established by a British colonial intelligence report from August 1897, had been in wide circulation particularly in Swat.[280] If those reports are to be trusted, then this is a remarkable difference from the approach to *jihād* taken by the Haḋdah Ṣāḥib: after all, the acknowledgement of ʿAbd al-Raḥmān's proclamations on the matter meant, by and large, an acknowledgement of the Emir himself, in this manner following the classical legal understanding of the conditions for a legitimate *jihād*, according to which *jihād* can be declared only by the supreme leader of (all) Muslims from out of the "Lands of Islam".[281] Indeed, ʿAbd al-Raḥmān's relevant communiqués on the matter emphasize – with reference to the Qur'an and the Sunna of the

[276] See Ahmad (2017), 87 n.93.

[277] See Sultan-i-Rome (1994), 94; Ahmad (2017), 73.

[278] See, for example, Hamdānī (1981), 237f.; Khaṫtak (1385sh/2007), 73.

[279] See Sultan-i-Rome (1994), 94. The comparison with mendicant agitators in borderland communities elsewhere had, in fact, already been made by contemporaneous British war correspondent H. Woosnam Mills (d. 1925), in Mills (1897), 34f. For myself, it actually resonates quite well with the Capuchin preacher Joachim Haspinger (d. 1858), one of the central figures in the Uprising in Tyrol in 1809 against the Bavarian–French occupation: see Hartung (2017a), 43f.

[280] See Ahmad (2017), 74.

[281] See, prominently, al-Māwardī (1422/2002), 15, 35–7. See also Crone (2004), 297–300.

Prophet – generally fighting unbelief,[282] as well as safeguarding the Lands of Islam and especially its frontiers (*ribāṭ*).[283]

Such a privileging of the Borderland and its inhabitants by the Afghan ruler, in stark contrast to the image painted by the British colonial administration (as well as its Orientalist and journalist auxiliaries both in the region and back home), certainly did not fail in its appeal to the Borderland communities. Therefore, we may assume that especially ʿAbd al-Raḥmān's rather concise exposition on *jihād*, emphasizing its compulsory nature and religious virtue, was indeed in circulation in the eastern parts of the Borderland and facilitated a favourable attitude towards it. It provided a particularly fertile ground for the Sartōr Faqīr's agitation to rise in defence of the Land of Islam against the British intruders. He was supported in this by Mullā Sayyid Akbar of Spīnkāy Tīģah (b. c. 1265/1849), spiritual pivot of the Ākā Khēl branch (*ćāngah*) of the Afridi (*Afrīdī*) tribe in the Tīrah Valley region, who, as a competitor of the Haḋḋah Ṣāḥib, presented himself as a loyal outpost of the Afghan Emirate to the court at Kabul, just like the Sartōr Faqīr.[284]

For the Haḋḋah Ṣāḥib, however, it was also necessary to direct this Frontier *jihād* against the Barakzay establishment. After all, had they not disqualified themselves as proper Islamic rulers by their disrespectful attitude towards the religious dignitaries, something the Haḋḋah Ṣāḥib could personally relate to, and had they not, moreover, amicably associated with non-Muslim powers? It is apparent that the early anti-imperialist activities sustained by religious precepts in the Pashtun Borderland did not pull in one direction only. It is useful to savour this insight here, because this multidirectionality of force

282 See, for example, ʿAbd al-Raḥmān (1306sh), 8, where he quoted Q8.39: 'And fight them [i.e., unbelievers, although in this context rather apostates], until there is no *fitna*, and the *dīn*, all of it, is for God [alone].'

283 See ibid., 67–74. The references here are to such prophetic *aḥādīth* that stress the extraordinary religious benefits in this world and the Hereafter for those who guard the frontiers of the Muslim territories: *Ṣaḥīḥ al-Bukhārī*, k. al-jihād wa'l-sayr, b. faḍl ribāṭ yawmin fī sabīli 'llāh wa-qawli 'llāh taʿālá, no. 1 (ḥadīth 2930); k. al-raqāq, b. mithli 'l-dunyā fi'l-ākhira wa-qawli 'llāh taʿālá, no. 1 (ḥadīth 6491); *Ṣaḥīḥ Muslim*, k. al-imāra, b. faḍl al-ribāṭ fī sabīli 'llāh – ʿazza wa-jalla, no. 1 (ḥadīth 5047). ʿAbd al-Raḥmān's perhaps most interesting reference in this context (p. 72) is to al-Bayhaqī (1423/2003), VI: 145 (ḥadīth 3987, version no. 3), who is quoted here from Ibn ʿĀbidīn (1423/2003), VI: 197f. The *ḥadīth* from Muslim had also already been cited in ʿAbd al-Raḥmān (1304sh), 25; alongside a variety from the first one of the two above from al-Bukhārī, as found in *Jāmiʿ al-Tirmidhī*, k. faḍāʾil al-jihād, b. mā jāʾ fī faḍl al-murābiṭ, no. 4 (ḥadīth 1768).

284 See Ahmad (2017), 71f. *et passim*. Surprisingly, Haroon (2007), 59, has Sayyid Akbar down as a disciple of the Haḋḋah Ṣāḥib; this is supported neither by Quddūsī (1966), 574–84, nor by contemporaneous colonial documents (prominently, see Anon., 'Leading Mullahs on the Punjab Frontier', Khyber Pakhtunkhwa Provincial Archives Peshawar, Foreign Ex. D.D. 1897, serial no. 2080, bundle no. 19, 46–8. See also Warburton (1900), 291–7. Thanks are due to Altaf Qadir (Peshawar) for kindly sharing the materials from the KP Provincial Archive).

would constitute a standing feature of religio-political Borderland activisms in the region until the very present, and has, therefore, a significant bearing on all those contemporary varieties associated with ṬIT / IEA and TṬP.

The situation became even more intricate because the political and economic elites in the Pashtun communities took a rather pro-British position, mindful of the fact that their loyalty had been bought with material incentives as well as socio-political privileges.[285] They even received religious justification of sorts prominently from Sayyid ʿAbd al-Vahhāb, then the Pīr Ṣāḥib of Mānkī-yi Sharīf, who instructed his substantial following to refrain under all circumstances from engaging in hostilities against the British colonial establishment.[286] This all contours the situation at the eve of the outbreak of the first major upheaval against – predominantly British – imperialism, the so-called "Frontier Uprising of 1897".

The Frontier Uprising of 1897

The insurrection received its initial spark from attempts of the British colonial establishment for over a year to enforce a collective fine on the Madā Khēl, a clan of the ʿĪsāzay branch of the Yusufzay tribal confederation,[287] for the unsolved murder of a local Hindu scribe at Mayzār, situated in the Tōchī Valley of North Waziristan, close to the border with Khost. When the British political officer arrived at the locus on 10 June 1897, shots were fired at him and his escort by unidentified villagers, resulting in his urgent call for reinforcements and the swift administration of a severe penalty, in other words, a punitive expedition.[288] Given that militant agitation in various tribal communities by religious figures such as the Haḍḍah Ṣāḥib, the Sartōr Faqīr, Mullā Sayyid Akbar and others had already been going on for some time, the British punitive expedition against the Madā Khēl was little less than the final straw that broke the camel's back.

There were, in fact, a lot of local grievances, starting with the British endeavour to bring about a systematic land policy after their decisive victory over the Sikhs in 1849 and the subsequent incorporation of the Greater Punjab into the British dominion.[289] The measures applied by the British ranged from taking certain community representatives into their service as intermediaries between the British authorities and their respective tribe, the reversion of communal land to hereditary landed property, attempts to codify local customs into an overarching legal framework, which, in 1872, fed into the amended *Punjab Frontier Crimes Regulation* (FCR), all the way to the precise

285 See Section 2.2.
286 See Khan (2014), 34f., 63–7 and 153–7; Ahmad (2017), 271f. and 273f.
287 See Ḥayāt Khān (1867), 171.
288 See Mills (1897), 10–5; Ahmad (2017), 90–127.
289 See Appendices I–VIII in Ahmad (2017), 307–15, consisting of a sample of petitions by local tribal representatives to the British colonial administration.

demarcation of the imperial territories by the Durand Line: in short, all attempts to incorporate the eastern parts of the Pashtun Borderland into the capitalist "world system".[290] The administrative measures benefited a new socio-political service elite – the *khāns* – more than others,[291] while seriously impairing local custom, traditions and mechanisms of communal self-administration. Therefore, Robert Nichols argues rightly that the Frontier Uprising of 1897 represented primarily various simultaneous local attempts to retain the traditional institutions and their supremacy against the encroaching colonial state at the interface of "settled", that is, state-controlled, and "tribal" territories.[292] The "Frontier Uprising of 1897" strongly represents an attempt by traditionally established socio-political and spiritual authorities to maintain their respective positions in the face of the newly created imperial service elites in the Pashtun Borderland, and this is reflected well in the backgrounds of the three religious dignitaries mentioned above who were at the centre of the various insurrections.

Consequently, a success of the various risings led by local spiritual dignitaries against what was perceived as a British and Barakzay intrusion into sovereign communal territories would help to ascertain the continuity of their position within the Borderland communities. Accordingly, just one month after the so-called "Mayzār Incident", the Sartōr Faqīr instigated an attack on the British garrison in Malakand (*Malākanḋ*), thereby, setting off a chain reaction of similar uprisings in numerous tribal communities across the north-eastern Pashtun Borderland. The Mōmand, following the battle cry of the Haḋḋah Ṣāḥib, were the next to rise. The fact that this tribe inhabits a territory on either side of the Durand Line, with the Haḋḋah Ṣāḥib's base near Jaṛōbī Darrah in the Mōmand Agency somewhat as its pivot, made the attack staged from there one that – in spirit at least – went against the domination both by the British and by the Barakzay. The Mōmand rising was followed by that of the Afridi in Tīrah, encouraged and led by Mullā Sayyid Akbar.[293] Each

290 See Nichols (2001), 133–91; (2013). The reading of these transformations as ways of incorporating a certain territory into the "capitalist world system" is inspired by Waller (1988), 77–101 and 139–57, and, even more so, by Dunaway (1996), both of whom looked at similar developments in Southern Appalachia in the first half of the nineteenth century. Dunaway explicitly utilizes Immanuel Wallerstein's "world-systems theory" for her analysis.

291 See Khan (2014), 34f. and 60 n.32.

292 See Nichols (2001), 221–52. See also Khan (2014), 63–75 and 83–5. In fact, this view is strongly supported by contemporaneous local Pashto poetry which reflects on the Uprising: see Hamdānī (1981), 232–41; Khaṫṫak (1385sh/2007), 66–81. The emphatic stress on conscious – and distinctly Pashtun! – anti-colonial sentiments in the Uprising of 1897 in later Pashto and Urdu historiography, in turn, is not really warranted by the contemporaneous materials available.

293 See Ahmad (2017), 128–247. Interestingly, the uprising in Tīrah was strongly supported by the local Ćamkanī tribe, who, other than the followers of the Sartōr Faqīr, were also

local eruption was met with a severe punitive expedition by British colonial forces, well documented in the colonial archive that especially comprised the eyewitness accounts of the young Winston Churchill and H. Woosnam Mills mentioned above.[294] By the middle of October 1879, however, all the various revolts had been crushed and their leaders forced to go into hiding. A little later, the FCR was tightened, and the way was thus paved for the separation of the Pashtun Borderland from the Punjab and the establishment of the NWFP of British India in 1901 in order to impose more direct control of the area.[295]

Reasons for the disintegration of the various militant upheavals commonly known as the Frontier Uprising in what the British colonial administrators in 1895 had roped together into the Malakand Agency – comprising the principalities of Dir, Chitral and Swat, plus Bunēr – were manifold. Yet, the most important cause was perhaps the disparity between an opportunistic landholding local elite, many members of which had been enticed to show loyalty towards the British by the various privileges bestowed upon them, and the uncompromising and idealistic representatives of one kind of traditional socio-political community leadership, that is, charismatic religious dignitaries. Apparently torn between the two poles, many of the recruits of the Sartōr Faqīr, the Haḋḋah Ṣāḥib, Mullā Sayyid Akbar and others had eventually forsaken the rebels in view of the military superiority of the British colonial forces engaged in the punitive campaigns, something that Mills was quick to highlight.[296]

Still, the mere fact of defection and flight does not tell us whether the traditionalist sentiments were also discarded in the process. Other than, for example, Muḥammad Sharīf Khān of Dir, mentioned above, who rewarded the British for their assistance in heaving him back into position against the usurper ʿUmarā Khān of Jandul with unconditional loyalty,[297] the matter was certainly more complicated with the bulk of the predominantly subaltern insurgents. In some respects, similar patterns of initial support of all kinds and its eventual withdrawal, occasioned by severe military responses that no longer discriminated between actual combatants and civilians, are also clearly discernible in the era of ṬIT / IEA and TṬP and should, therefore, actually not be surprising. Taking a stand against a religiously inspired militant movement of such a kind does not necessarily clarify much about sympathies and

inclined to oppose Barakzay domination (see Anon. [1910]). This is somewhat reminiscent of the ambivalent position of Shaykh ʿUmar Ćamkanī and, even more so, his son and successor, towards Durrani rule in the late eighteenth / early nineteenth century. On the latter, see Section 3.1.3.

294 On both works and the colonial discourse on the Frontier Uprising of 1897 in general, see Edwards (1996), 172–219.

295 See Nichols (2001), 258f.; (2013), 178–92.

296 See Mills (1897), 44, 47, 51, 96f., 162f. and 186.

297 See ibid., 34, 73f. and 182.

antipathies, but, cynically, says more about the effectiveness of punitive military campaigns against the entire population of the immediate Borderland. In fact, it is to be assumed that, just like after the Battle of Balakot in 1831, general sympathies for Islamically justified militancy remained very much alive in the region, be they only simmering for much of the time.

It can, therefore, be argued that the agendas of the *Ṭarīqah-yi Muḥammadiyyah* and of the various circles of local religious dignitaries at the helm of the Frontier Uprising of 1897 showed certain overlaps, despite their distinct origins. As we shall see in the following, these overlaps would become larger in the course of the anti-colonial activism in the Pashtun Borderland during the early twentieth century, and they would in some sense replay the earlier fierce competition between the respective circles of the Kōṭah Ṣāḥib and the Sayyidō Bābā over who owns the legacy of the *Ṭarīqah-yi Muḥammadiyyah*, but now, however, with even greater intensity.

3.3 The Early Twentieth Century

The developments which we have seen emerging towards the end of the nineteenth century, leading to increasing contestation between the advocates of different political instances of activism sustained by religious precepts gained further momentum at the beginning of the twentieth century. Its predominant reason was the growing entanglement of these vigorous Borderland actions with similar ones across the Indian subcontinent, thus embedding them into a much wider socio-political and religious context. While the political context would soon be dominated by a large-scale anti-imperialist and anti-colonial discourse, responding to the increasingly oppressive colonial policies of the British imperial administration, the religious one was rooted in developments that even predated the establishment of direct British colonial rule, in the aftermath of the "Sepoy" Uprising of 1857.

Numerous and diverse religious interpretations emerged and steadily found their respective institutional base, largely in response to the socio-political situation in the urban centres of late Mughal India, but decisively impacted by the deposition of the last Muslim Mughal ruler and the beginning of non-Muslim political rule.[298] While, on the surface, debating with each other the "correct" interpretation of the Islamic precepts, such as the *conditio sine qua non* for a sustained claim to authoritative religious guidance of all Sunni Muslim communities in the now British crown colony, the leadership of these

[298] A wealth of academic studies on Muslim intellectual responses to what had been perceived as decline of Mughal political rule and British colonization has emerged since the late 1970s, prominently including Lelyveld (1978), 3–68; Metcalf (1982), 16–86; Rizvi (1982); Sanyal (1996), 15–48; Malik (1997), 129–200; Zaman (2002), 38–74; Riexinger (2004), 23–108; Preckel (2005); Pernau (2008), 25–94.

various new currents – cast in the literature as "pathways" (*masālik*) – soon also claimed a political voice. Positioning themselves vis-à-vis the non-Muslim British colonial establishment, they would not leave any region in the subcontinent untouched, thus necessitating that the local actors – such as in the Pashtun Borderland – commit themselves in this shifting and increasingly politicized religious landscape that also had an irreversible impact on the socio-political state of the Borderland.

Predominantly two of the *masālik* made headway into the Pashtun Borderland from quite early on, both strategically using the legacy of the *Ṭarīqah-yi Muḥammadiyyah* there as a common thematic anchor, despite their otherwise hotly debated differences:[299] the *Ahl-i Ḥadīs̱* and what has elsewhere been called the "Deoband Project" – or "Deobandiyyat".[300]

3.3.1 *The* Ahl-i Ḥadīs̱

Although the advent of the *Ahl-i Ḥadīs̱* somewhat predates direct British colonial rule, it was still tied to British pursuits in India. In fact, some authors attribute their origin to a split of the remnants of the *Ṭarīqah-yi Muḥammadiyyah* after the defeat at Balakot in the Eastern Gangetic plains. According to this narrative,[301] the rift occurred over the adherence to the Hanafi *madhhab*, which was advocated by Karāmat ʿAlī Jawnpūrī (d. 1290/1873), the man who was responsible for the movement's missionary campaigns in Assam and the Ganges delta.[302] Meanwhile, the brothers Vilāyat and ʿInāyat ʿAlī (d. 1275/1858) from ʿAẓīmābād in Bihar turned away from it and began to promote the practice of independent legal reasoning (*ijtihād*) instead. Apart from this rather methodological issue, the view on inadmissible religious innovations (*bidaʿ*) and piety derived from the Prophetic example remained largely uniform.[303] The turn to a legal methodology outside the confines of the Hanafi tradition, however, had at least one important consequence: zealous practitioners who would not shy away from armed confrontation with everyone they deemed an unbeliever were now not primarily required; the need was rather for scholars solidly trained in the religious fields of knowledge. It is at

[299] Indeed, both claimed a close ideational relationship with the *Ṭarīqah-yi Muḥammadiyyah* and its leaders, differing only in the accentuation of particular aspects in its heritage: see, for example, Siyālkōṭī (1995), 419–22. Compare Madanī (n.d.) 418–47.

[300] See Hartung (2016b), 359–61.

[301] See prominently Riexinger (2004), 121.

[302] See Nadvī (1430/2009), 31–54. For his explicit advocacy of the Hanafi *fiqh* as the legal framework for the evaluation of religious innovations, see Jawnpūrī (1281h), esp. 5f.

[303] See Jawnpūrī (1311/1894), 17–39 *et passim*. In this text, Karāmat ʿAlī also relied heavily on the Hanafi legal tradition to justify a strict view on the matters of God's *tawḥīd*, His attributes and knowledge (pp. 39–91). Compare ʿAlī (1341h), 30–45 (*Risālah-yi ʿAmal bi'l-Ḥadīs̱*).

this point that the *Ṭarīqah-yi Muḥammadiyyah* and a rising scholarly movement, which became known as *Ahl-i Ḥadīs̱*, parted ways, at least for the time being.

Its emergence owes a lot to the impact of the methodological considerations of the Yemenite ʿAlī al-Shawkānī, with whom, as we saw above, Sayyid Aḥmad and Shāh Ismāʿīl had also been in contact upon their return from their *ḥajj* in 1823.[304] At least two of their retainers, ʿAbd al-Ḥayy Baṛhānavī (killed 1243/1828) and ʿAbd al-Ḥaqq Banārasī (d. 1276/1860), stayed behind with Shawkānī and obtained from him the formal authorization to teach his works (*ijāza*), which, in fact, they did upon their return to India.[305] After the defeat at Balakot, Vilāyat ʿAlī is also said to have travelled to the Yemen in pursuit of an *ijāza* from al-Shawkānī.[306] ʿAbd al-Ḥaqq Banārasī, author of the programmatic *al-Durr al-Farīd fī Manʿ ʿan al-Taqlīd*, evolved as a key figure in the emergence of the scholarly movement: the two scholars mainly associated with the foundation of the *Ahl-i Ḥadīs̱* proper, Naẕīr Ḥusayn Bihārī, later Dihlavī (d. 1320/1902), and Ṣiddīq Ḥasan Khān Qannawjī (d. 1307/1890), had either been his direct students or at least studied with scholars in his environment.[307] Ṣiddīq Ḥasan, in turn, was personally responsible for luring two of al-Shawkānī's Yemenite students to the princely court of Bhopal,[308] where he had established himself as a major player by virtue of marriages, firstly to princess Ẕakiyyah Bēgam (d. 1301/1884) and then to the reigning Shāh'jahān Bēgam (r. 1868–1901).[309] In fact, Ṣiddīq Ḥasan must be considered an organizational pivot of the nascent *Ahl-i Ḥadīs̱* movement,[310] whereas its learned hallmark was derived much more from Naẕīr Ḥusayn and his students.

Bhopal, however, is important here in yet another way. The principality was established in 1723 when Dūst Muḥammad Khān (r. 1723–8), an Ōrakzay Pashtun from Tīrah who had briefly served the Mughal emperor Shāh ʿĀlam I (r. 1707–12) as a mercenary, declared himself sovereign.[311] He favoured his own tribesfolk, whom he recruited into a mighty *laxkar* of around 100 000

[304] See above, Section 3.2.1.

[305] For Baṛhānavī, see al-Ḥasanī (1412–13/1991–3), vii: 277f.; for Banārasī, see ibid., vii: 266–72.

[306] See ibid., vii: 576f.; Ahmad (1994), 86.

[307] For the educational background of Naẕīr Ḥusayn, see al-Ḥasanī (1412–13/1991–3), viii: 523f.; for Ṣiddīq Ḥasan Khān, see ibid., viii: 203. See also Riexinger (2004), 122f. and 129; Preckel (2005), 138–43.

[308] The two scholars in question were the brothers Zayn al-ʿĀbidīn (d. 1297/1879) and, more importantly, Ḥusayn ibn Muḥsin (d. 1327/1909) of Ḥudayda, whose descendants would continue to play important roles in Indian scholarly circles: see Qannawjī (1289/1872), 88. On the careers of the two brothers and their heirs, see Hartung (2004), 224–8; Preckel (2005), 164–73.

[309] See Preckel (2005), 153f. and 160–3. See also Shāh'jahān Bēgam (1290h), iii: 25–36.

[310] See Preckel (2005), 157–259.

[311] See Shāh'jahān Bēgam (1290h), i: 4–9.

men, to consolidate his political power. In the following roughly 100 years, these Pashtuns formed a critical mass for the socio-political destiny of the polity: non-Pashtun contenders to the throne had to forge alternative political and military alliances to sustain their respective claims, and it is this constellation that is largely responsible for the close relations between the Bhopal State and the British EIC, and the British Raj as its later manifestation.[312] Under Qudsiyyah Bēgam (r. 1819–37), the first of four successive female rulers, a programme of Islamization was initiated,[313] at the end of which stood Ṣiddīq Ḥasan Khān and the development of the Bhopal State into an early centre of the *Ahl-i Ḥadīs̱*.

Ṣiddīq Ḥasan, however, was content neither with the forms nor with the degree of the Islamization efforts, especially under Qudsiyyah Bēgam: he harshly criticized the influence of Imāmī Shiʿi Muslims and Sufis throughout the principality, which, according to him, absolutely had to be curbed.[314] His pre-eminent position as the husband of ruler Shāh'jahān Bēgam enabled him to restructure the composition of scholarship in the state, and also to attract like-minded scholars in the Arabian Peninsula to the court at Bhopal.[315] This, in turn, is of significance for our narrative in a twofold way. Firstly, these transregional links would become more sustained over the years, thus perpetuating an agenda of Islamic reformulation in a Persianate environment that was heavily Arabicized, a process which solidified the imaginary of a universal notion of Islam that pivots on its formative period in the Arabian Peninsula and the Fertile Crescent.[316] Secondly, it is important to acknowledge that Pashtuns, who, although having settled in Bhopal, still maintained close relations with tribal affiliates in the Borderland, now came into immediate contact with protagonists of religious views that appeared quite alien to the socio-religious fabric in the Borderland.

The more solidly provable emergence of the *Ahl-i Ḥadīs̱* movement in the Pashtun Borderland, however, pivots around Naẕīr Ḥusayn Dihlavī, the "Shaykh al-Kull", and was mediated by the movement's representatives in the Punjab. Naẕīr Ḥusayn, born in Bihari Mōngīr, grew up in an environment in which the religious and political ideas of the *Ṭarīqah-yi Muḥammadiyyah* were omnipresent. His own grandfather reportedly rallied a troop of about 1 000 volunteers and led them into the Pashtun Borderland; his father, too,

312 See ibid., I: 14f. and 36–9.

313 See Preckel (2005), 45–53 and 64–71.

314 See Qannawjī (1315/1898), 14.

315 See al-Bassām (1398h), I: 156–8, 205f. and II: 84–95; Preckel (2005), 231–52.

316 Although Ṣiddīq Ḥasan Khān would distance himself especially from militant elements in dominant legal interpretations within the Wahhabiyya, he still continued to share crucial doctrinal views, especially regarding certain popular religious practices: see al-Qannawjī (1288h), 413–16; (1978), III: 194–211; (1428/2007), 301–3. See also Preckel (2005), 547–53.

maintained close contacts with Pashtun allies. As a young man, he actually heard Shāh Ismāʿīl himself preaching in Patna, an event that his hagiographers highlight as the trigger for his relocation to Delhi, where he could be nearer to him.[317] Naẕīr Ḥusayn's marriage to the daughter of the *mutawallī* of Delhi's Awrangābād Mosque, finally, tied him into the wider family of Shāh Valiyallāh and provided him, at the same time, with a domain for disseminating his increasingly *ḥadīth*-centred ideas.[318] Among his students were Muḥammad Aʿẓām "ʿAbdallāh" Ghaznavī (d. 1297/1881), who had studied previously with Ḥabīballāh ibn Fayẓallāh Qandahārī (d. 1265/1849), author of the seminal *Mughtanim al-Ḥuṣūl fī ʿIlm al-Uṣūl* and an earlier acquaintance of Shāh Ismāʿīl Dihlavī and Sayyid Aḥmad Barēlvī,[319] as well as ʿAbd al-ʿAzīz Raḥīmābādī (d. 1330/1912), who would later be one of those responsible for linking up the remnants of the *Ṭarīqah-yi Muḥammadiyyah* and the *Ahl-i Ḥadīs̱* in the Pashtun Borderland.[320]

Naẕīr Ḥusayn, in turn, enjoyed the continuous patronage of the increasingly self-confident Punjabi Muslim traders in Delhi, and they most probably served as a transmission belt for disseminating the ideas of the *Ahl-i Ḥadīs̱* into the Punjab.[321] This process was facilitated further by the fact that adherents to the movement in Afghanistan, such as ʿAbdallāh Ghaznavī, mentioned earlier, were subjected to persecution under the Barakzay ruler Muḥammad Afẕal, the son of Dūst Muḥammad (r. 1866–7), and probably also under his successors.[322] After all, ʿAbdallāh Ghaznavī appears to have received his firm introduction to an *Ahl-i Ḥadīs̱* world-view – a deep inclination towards *ḥadīth* as the supreme source for theology and jurisprudence, and for his rejection of *taqlīd* as a *modus operandi* within Hanafi *fiqh* – already prior to his arrival in Delhi to subject himself to the tutelage of Naẕīr Ḥusayn. If his hagiographers are to be believed, then *Taqviyyat al-Īmān* – the programmatic work by Shāh Ismāʿīl and Sayyid Aḥmad – was emphatically read in Kandahar and, thus, presumably also in the

317 See Siyālkōṭī (1995), 425.

318 See ibid., 427; Pernau (2008), 123.

319 See Nadvī (1406/1986), II: 540; Ṣāḥib-i Islām (1421/2001), 56f.; ʿIrāqī (2003), 32; Riexinger (2004), 179.

320 See Ahmad (1994), 133. For his biography, see al-Ḥasanī (1412–13/1991–3), VIII: 274.

321 See Riexinger (2004), 123; Pernau (2008), 201–7 and 225–9.

322 See Ghaznavī (n.d.), 15–19; ʿIrāqī (2003), 34–9. The same persecution was also observed by Muḥammad Rashīd Riḍā during his travels to India in 1912: see Riḍā (1297/1919), 232. The alienation of the *Ahl-i Ḥadīs̱* was based, first and foremost, on particulars during worship, especially the raising of the hands during prayer (*rafʿal-yadayn*) and the loud affirmation to God (*āmīn bi'l-jahr*), both of which are justified by references to canonical *aḥādīth*; see prominently *Ṣaḥīḥ al-Bukhārī*, k. al-adhān, b. rafʿ al-yadayn idhā kabbara wa-ʾidhā rakaʿa wa-ʾidhā rafaʿa, no. 1 (ḥadīth 743), and b. jahri ʾl-maʾmūmi bi'l-taʾmīn, no. 1 (ḥadīth 790). The loud affirmation to God at the end of prayer particularly made *Ahl-i Ḥadīs̱* stand out discernibly from their Hanafi co-religionists during congregational prayer, which, in turn, required them to establish designated places of worship.

circles of Ḥabīballāh Qandahārī; besides, Naẕīr Ḥusayn himself quoted from Ḥabīballāh's *Mughtanim*, which contains a firm refutation of the *Musallam al-Thubūt* of Muḥibballāh Bihārī (d. 1118/1707) that had meanwhile evolved as a core text in Hanafi *uṣūl al-fiqh*.[323]

When various places in the Punjab became sanctuaries for early Pashtun followers of the *Ahl-i Ḥadīs̱*, such as ʿAbdallāh Ghaznavī, they would eventually even adopt a *nisba* which refers to a place there rather than in the Pashtun Borderland: his first-born son ʿAbd al-Jabbār (d. 1331/1913), who changed his *nisba* after his final migration to the Punjab from "Ghaznavī" to "Amritsarī",[324] is a vivid example of this. Members of the Ghaznavī family would occupy key positions in the religious infrastructure of the *Ahl-i Ḥadīs̱* in Punjab in the time following and, thus, provide a hub for the dissemination of the ideational universe of that *maslak* between Northern India and the Pashtun Borderland. The *Dār al-ʿUlūm Taqviyyat al-Islām* in Amritsar, established in 1902 by ʿAbd al-Jabbār and relocated to Lahore in 1947,[325] and the Chīniyāṇvalī Mosque in Lahore, where ʿAbd al-Jabbār's younger brother ʿAbd al-Vāḥid (d. 1349/1930) served as *imām*, were of crucial importance here.

It was important for this role as interface, as Riexinger reasonably infers, that the family members maintained their ability to converse in Pashto,[326] as was the fact that, judging from their literary output, they acted as popularizers of classics rather than developers of genuine ideas of their own.[327] Alongside the scholarly thread, the family also produced a number of entrepreneurs and traders,[328] which seems to support the widespread view that the emerging *Ahl-i Ḥadīs̱* were indeed firmly rooted in the nascent urban Muslim middle class.[329] The reality,

323 See Dihlavī (2007), 112f. Remarkably, the passage could not be traced in the editions of Qandahārī's text, based on three extant manuscripts, respectively held at Peshawar, Lahore and Quetta, by Ṣāḥib-i Islām (1421/2001), 98–531. It is, therefore, to be assumed that Naẕīr Ḥusayn had only paraphrased the salient points. On the role and prominence of the *Musallam al-Thubūt* at the time in focus here, see Hartung (2021b), 1 200, 1 224 and 1 228.

324 See al-Ḥasanī (1412–13/1991–3), VIII: 234; Fīrūzpūrī (1996), 338.

325 See Ghaznavī (1994), 445–62.

326 See Riexinger (2004), 181 (based on a contemporaneous report from the 1914 meeting of the *All-India Ahl-i Ḥadīs̱ Conference* [AIAḤC] in Peshawar, where ʿAbd al-Tavvāb [d. unknown], a grandson of ʿAbdallāh Ghaznavī, is said to have delivered his address in Pashto).

327 ʿAbdallāh Ghaznavī is credited with translations of works by Taqī al-Dīn Aḥmad ibn Taymiyya (d. 728/1328), Ibn Qayyim al-Jawziyya (d. 751/1350) and Ṣāliḥ al-Fulānī (d. 1218/1803) into Persian and Urdu: see Ghaznavī (n.d.), 23; Fīrūzpūrī (1996), 339; Riexinger (2004), 181. These translations, however, have unfortunately not been traced so far.

328 See Riexinger (2004), 181 and 524f.; ʿIrāqī (2003), 88 and 91.

329 This view, frequently connected to the hypothesis of the emergence of an indigenous Indo-Muslim middle class, is advocated, for example, by Preckel (2005) and, even more pronouncedly by Pernau (2008), 224–32 *et passim*.

however, may have been slightly more complex. After all, the *Ahl-i Ḥadīs̱* rose in the Punjab as the result of particular family networks – the Ghaznavis having been one of them – which extended well into rural space.[330] The efforts of the Ghaznavis in popularizing rather complex and mainly Arabic works through the publication of vernacular translations and synopses were of crucial importance to reach out to the communities there.

In addition, there is another piquant element that makes the Ghaznavis and their oftentimes Pashtun followers stand out from many other *Ahl-i Ḥadīs̱*, and may, in fact, have had a decisive bearing on the Borderland manifestation of this very *maslak* in the Pashtun Borderland: the positive appraisal of *jihād* against perceived unbelievers and among nominal Muslims, something that became increasingly enshrined in the ethos of the "talib". This particularity seems to be rooted, on the one hand, in the close proximity of the *Ṭarīqah-yi Muḥammadiyyah* and, on the other, in the attraction that Central Arabian Wahhabi thought exerted on them: in an encounter of ʿAbd al-Vāḥid and ʿAbd al-Raḥīm Ghaznavī with ʿAbd al-ʿAzīz ibn Saʿūd (d. 1373/1953) in 1894, during the latter's exile to Kuwait, they were presented with a stack of shorter works representing the gist of Wahhabi thought, all of which they subsequently had reprinted as a single edition entitled *Majmūʿat al-Tawḥīd* at one of Delhi's foremost *Ahl-i Ḥadīs̱* publishing houses.[331]

The choice of texts, most probably conceived by its two editors as constituting an *Ahl-i Ḥadīs̱* textbook, is quite revealing: it is comprised of mainly shorter works of Ibn Taymiyya, Muḥammad ibn ʿAbd al-Wahhāb (d. 1206/1792), some descendants of the latter, the early Wahhabi scholar Ḥamd ibn ʿAlī ibn ʿAṭīq (d. 1301/1884) and the medieval *muḥaddith* Abū Saʿīd Muḥammad ibn al-Fayḍ al-Anṣārī (d. 616/1219). Classics such as Ibn ʿAbd al-Wahhāb's *K. al-Tawḥīd* and Ibn Taymiyya's *al-Wāsiṭa bayn al-Khalq wa'l-Ḥaqq* are not so much of special interest here,[332] but three works that deal with the dangerous matter of interacting with unbelievers, polytheists and apostates,[333] a matter that would eventually assume a central position in contemporary Salafi and Salafist *manāhij*, are important.[334]

330 Riexinger (2004), 135–8 and 189–95, argues for a more diverse socio-economic background even of the early *Ahl-i Ḥadīs̱* in the Punjab, where entire villages converted to this *maslak*. See also Fīrūzpūrī (1996), 499f. and 508f.

331 See al-Ghaznawī and ʿAbd al-Raḥīm (1894); also referred to in Riexinger (2004), 524f. and 644. On Ibn ʿAṭīq, see al-Bassām (1398h), I: 228–32.

332 See al-Ghaznawī and ʿAbd al-Raḥīm (1894), 60–75 (here titled *al-Qāʿida al-Wāsiṭa*) and 105–49 (*K. al-Tawḥīd*).

333 The texts in question here are the [*al-Dalāʾil fī*] *Ḥukm Muwālāt Ahl al-Ishrāk* of Sulaymān ibn ʿAbdallāh ibn Muḥammad ibn ʿAbd al-Wahhāb (d. 1233/1818), Ibn ʿAṭīq's *K. Bayān al-Najāt wa'l-Fakāk min Muwālāt al-Murtaddīn wa-Ahl al-Shirk* and Ibn Taymiyya's renowned *al-Furqān bayn Awliyāʾ al-Raḥmān wa-Awliyāʾ al-Shayṭān*: see ibid., 149–61, 161–98 and 288–363.

334 See, for example, Wagemakers (2012), 147–89; Nedza (2020), 110–18.

From this selection, we may infer the evidence that the Ghaznavis, more than other prominent early authors of the *Ahl-i Ḥadīs̱*, expressed a rather confrontational attitude towards non-Muslims and all those who adhered to any alternative interpretation of the Islamic creed and practice. This, in turn, resonates very well with the earlier attempts of Sayyid Aḥmad Barēlvī and Shāh Ismāʿīl Dihlavī in the Pashtun Borderland to actively purge what they perceived as violations of the fundamental doctrine of *tawḥīd*, as well as social practices in contravention of the *shari'a* as they interpreted it. Moreover, these principles have been upheld by their successors, who remained in various colonies on Pashtun tribal territory, and provided them with the justification to continue their hostile activities against the British colonial establishment.[335] The common world-view, pivoting on the concept of armed *jihād*, contributed to the emergence of the *Dār al-ʿUlūm Taqviyyat al-Islām* in Amritsar as one of the major recruitment centres in the Punjab of prospective *mujāhidīn* for deployment to the Pashtun Borderland, while those scholars and students who did not join the train of active fighters supported them financially.[336] Of equal, if not even greater, importance for strengthening the relationship between the former *Ṭarīqah-yi Muḥammadiyyah* in the Pashtun Borderland, which had finally solidified as the *Jamāʿat-i Mujāhidīn*, and the *Ahl-i Ḥadīs̱* of the Ghaznavī persuasion was the Chīniyāṇvalī Mosque in Lahore, especially under its then-*imām* ʿAbd al-Raḥīm ibn Raḥīm Bakhsh (d. 1353/1934), who, after joining the *Jamāʿat-i Mujāhidīn* in around 1914, had changed his name to "Muḥammad Bashīr" (assassinated 1353/1934).[337]

During this time, the *Jamāʿat-i Mujāhidīn* became increasingly entangled with the *Ahl-i Ḥadīs̱*, owing extensively to the activities of Naẕīr Ḥusayn Dihlavī's student ʿAbd al-ʿAzīz Raḥīmābādī mentioned above, and also reflected in the decreasing significance of some of their earlier operational bases and the rise of others instead. After all, the large band of followers of Sayyid Aḥmad and Shāh Ismāʿīl, most of them from abroad, were always in need of a local *məshər* as bailsman, to sustain their stay on tribal land.[338] So, when, for whatever reason, those relationships deteriorated, as we have seen above in the case of X̌ādī Khān of Hund in 1829, they were forced to move on in search of a new base. When they established themselves at Sithānah, Panjtār

335 See, for example, Hopkins and Marsden (2011), 88–97.

336 See Rauf (2005), 425f.

337 See ibid., 416; Riexinger (2004), 444. On Muḥammad Bashīr, see Mihr (2008), IV: 678f. and 697–701; Khalil (2000), 153–62 and 350–4.

338 In fact, this is the standard mechanism underlying the rights of hospitality in the Pashtun Borderland (*mēlmastiyā*, or *mēlmah pālənah*), enshrined in the rather abstract concepts of "convoy" (*badragah*) and "sanctuary" (*nənavātay*). In the case in point here, the responsibility of the local host for the adherents to the *Ṭarīqah-yi Muḥammadiyyah* was sealed with an oath of allegiance (*bayʿa*) to Sayyid Aḥmad: see, for example, Mihr (2008), I: 477 and 485.

and Amb, they set up more durable colonies there,[339] and could conveniently fall back on them after losing the battle at Balakot. Still, this major defeat, the culmination point of a sequence of earlier ones, caused many *məshərān* in the region to call off their support,[340] one of the most prominent having been the Sayyidō Bābā in Swat. Consequently, the remaining retainers of Sayyid Aḥmad Barēlvī and Shāh Ismāʿīl were forced to search for new local allies to grant them sanctuary and allow the establishment of new colonies, which soon became places from which the *Ahl-i Ḥadīs̱* interpretation of Islam radiated into the wider Pashtun Borderland.

Two of the later colonies stand out: one at Asmast in Bunēr, established in 1902, and the other at Chamarkanḍ in Bajawr (*Bājawṛ*), created in 1915 on a former base of the Haḍḍah Ṣāḥib,[341] which was colonized as tributary to the former.[342] The colony at Asmast was inseparably tied to the leadership of ʿAbd al-Karīm (d. 1333/1915), son of former *amīr* Vilāyat ʿAlī of Ṣādiqpūr / Patna, over all the *mujāhidīn* in the Pashtun Borderland and their various auxiliaries across Northern India. Moreover, it became, as we shall see below in greater detail,[343] a centre of gravity of all anti-British activities in the Pashtun Borderland during World War I. When ʿAbd al-Karīm was succeeded as *amīr al-mujāhidīn* by his grandnephew Niʿmatallāh (killed 1339/1921), however, successful British attempts to negotiate a truce with the *mujāhidīn* resulted not only in the assassination of the *amīr* by a young retainer, but also, and more importantly, in the evolution of the colony at Chamarkanḍ – as an increasingly independent centre of continued anti-British militant activities.[344] It was there that the *Ahl-i Ḥadīs̱* finally established their lasting presence in the Pashtun Borderland, a process that had already begun when ʿAbd al-Karīm Qannawjī, later Chamarkanḍī (d. 1339/1921), was in command of the colony. However, exceptional momentum was gained under his successor Faẕl-i Ilāhī Vazīrābādī

339 On the various colonies, see Khattak (2016), 47–68. For the location of Sithānah as the major colony, see Map 3.2. See also the map in Nadvī (1406/1986), II: 35f. For the colony's layout, see the image in Hopkins and Marsden (2011), 79.

340 However, other members of the local elites who had earlier submitted to the leaders of the *Ṭarīqah-yi Muḥammadiyyah*, such as prominently Sardār Fatḥ Khān of Panjtār (d. 1257/1841), would continue to employ remaining bands of *mujāhidīn* in the region to re-establish their own eminence, because they had lost substantial amounts of political and, more importantly still, economic influence in the aftermath of the Battle of Balakot, see Mihr (2008), II: 93–102; almost verbatim Nadvī (1406/1986), II: 84–9. See also Khattak (2016), 48f.

341 See Khalil (2000), 121.

342 See Mihr (2008), IV: 597–600 and 608f.; Khalil (2000), 70–121 (here the name of the first colony is given as "Asmas"); Riexinger (2004), 442–7 (here the name of the first colony is given as "Samasta"). Rauf (2005), 419, gives 1898 as the year in which the colony at Asmast was founded, but does not corroborate this. It has, therefore, been decided to stick, for the time being, to the dating by Mihr and Khalil.

343 See Section 3.3.3.

344 See Mihr (2008), IV: 604–12; Khalil (2000), 121–62; Rauf (2005), 419f.

(d. 1370/1950), who eventually succeeded in luring the *imām* of Lahore's Chīniyāṇvalī Mosque, ʿAbd al-Raḥīm "Muḥammad Bashīr", into the Borderland, only to see the latter rise as one of his own major competitors over the *imārat al-mujāhidīn* in Chamarkand. Another important early *Ahl-i Ḥadīs̱* to be named in this context was Muḥammad ʿAlī Qaṣūrī (d. 1375/1956), a Cambridge-educated layman who arrived at Chamarkand from Kabul.[345] Still, Borderland pragmatics required a rather flexible attitude to doctrinally opposing orientations, and, therefore, it does not really come as any surprise that, regarding educational infrastructure and content, the colonists at Chamarkand also turned to Deoband and even the otherwise much despised Aligarh-affiliated *Anjuman-i Ḥimāyyat-i Islām*, established in Lahore in 1884, for inspiration.[346]

Leadership disputes aside, the closing of the ranks between the *mujāhidīn* colonists and the *Ahl-i Ḥadīs̱* in the Pashtun Borderland around this time is not deniable, thus raising the contestations of locally prevalent beliefs and practices to a new level: the emphatic dissociation of the *Ahl-i Ḥadīs̱* from any of the *madhāhib fiqhiyya*, derived from their systematic re-evaluation of the sources and methods of jurisprudence (*uṣūl al-fiqh*), provided them with mighty legal arguments to sustainably attack those who were holding opposing views. Their prime target turned out to be the one orientation currently devoted to Islamic reformulation that claimed similar origins and an interpretation of Islamic beliefs and practices related to the *Ahl-i Ḥadīs̱* themselves, although holding uncompromisingly fast to the Hanafi legal orientation: "Deobandiyyat".[347] The immensely growing popularity of that *maslak* all over the subcontinent made this orientation arguably one of the main competitors of the *Ahl-i Ḥadīs̱* in the quest for influence in and dominance over all religious matters under colonial and post-colonial conditions, and the Pashtun Borderland was certainly not spared from this competition.

345 See Qaṣūrī (1986). Muḥammad ʿAlī belonged to an important family of *Ahl-i Ḥadīs̱* laymen in Punjabi Qaṣūr. His grandfather Ghulām-i Aḥmad (d. 1361/1942) had studied with Ghulām-i Rasūl "Qilʿavī" (d. 1291/1874), beside his close acquaintance ʿAbdallāh Ghaznavī the second important propagator of the *Ahl-i Ḥadīs̱* in the Punjab: see Bhaṭṭī (1433/2012), 308f.; Fīrūzpūrī (1996), 360–5; Riexinger (2004), 490–2.

346 See Khalil (2000), 151. On the *Anjuman-i Ḥimāyyat-i Islām*, see Lelyveld (1978), 303; [M.-M.] Fuchs (2019).

347 Generally, on the points of conflict between *Ahl-i Ḥadīs̱* and Deobandis, see Riexinger (2004), 232–8; Preckel (2005), 353–74; Hartung (2016b), 361. It appears that it was the claim of common heritage that caused *Ahl-i Ḥadīs̱* and Deobandis to clash most severely over sometimes rather tiny details of interpretation. In those arguments, neither side used velvet gloves, which made for a highly polemical encounter.

3.3.2 Deobandiyyat in the Early Twentieth Century: Reaching Out to the Subalterns[348]

On 30 May 1866, in the small rural town Deoband, roughly 100 miles northeast of Delhi, the foundation stone was ceremoniously laid for a *madrasah* that would eventually evolve into one of the most influential Muslim educational institutions worldwide.[349] Yet, when it was established by a number of Sunni Muslim scholars linked through multiple channels to the circle of the Shāh Valiyallāh family in Delhi, its aspiration, in the absence of state patronage after the failed Uprising of 1857 against the meanwhile massive British colonial encroachment in the subcontinent, was merely to provide a place for the training of the Muslim communal leaders of tomorrow. As such, this indeed constituted just one more pathway (*maslak*) among numerous others that ranged from the *Ahl-i Ḥadīs̱* to Sir Sayyid Aḥmad Khān's much more acculturational "Aligarh movement".

The *Ahl-i Ḥadīs̱* slightly aside, underlying most of these communal responses to the aggravated colonial situation was the necessity for renegotiating religious authority on the basis of socio-economic status: Sir Sayyid, for instance, himself a product of the established urban elites of the late Mughal court (*ashrāf*), would plead for a continuation of dominance, albeit modified, by these former Mughal elites, which also suggested a large degree of flexibility when interacting with the new political powers that many would see as opportunism and almost unconditional servitude as long as former privileges could be maintained. The college at Deoband, the *Dār al-ʿUlūm*, emerged as a vanguard of more subaltern (*ajlāfī*) claims to communal leadership. Its chief competitor materialized only some 160 miles to the southeast in the town of Baraylī, where the Hanafi jurist and Sufi *shaykh* Aḥmad Riẕá Khān (d. 1340/1921) laid out yet another pathway, colloquially known by the loconym "Barelviyyat", in which authority is derived from ancestral and spiritual connections to the Prophet Muḥammad and his immediate family.[350] Disentangling the competing claims of Deobandis and Barelvi was made more complicated by the fact that the founding fathers of the *Dār al-ʿUlūm* in Deoband also had strong Sufi affiliations and, in fact, made this cognitive approach into a cornerstone of its educational model. We shall have to return to this point.

A pivotal figure of the *maslak* that would eventually grow out of the *Dār al-ʿUlūm* in Deoband was Muḥammad Qāsim Nānawtavī (d. 1297/1880), who would eventually even be considered the true embodiment of the Deobandi

348 Substantial portions in this and the following section follow closely Hartung (2016b), esp. 352–5.

349 See Riẕvī (1413–4/1992–3), I: 57–66.

350 The followers of this *maslak* call themselves "Ahl al-Sunnat va 'l-Jamāʿat", announcing in this way their claim to be the only true representatives of Sunni Islam, vis-à-vis competitors such as the Deobandis and the *Ahl-i Ḥadīs̱*. Sanyal (1996) still remains the standard reference for the origins of Barelviyyat.

world-view.[351] Whether or not the claim that he was descended from the Prophet's father-in-law and first Medinese Caliph Abū Bakr is sustainable, the fact that his *nisba* "Ṣiddīqī", especially in the then-United Provinces, may also refer to descent from the indigenous Kāyasth[352] served him well in gaining the support of the *ajlāf* Muslims who would eventually constitute the core clientele of Nānawtavī's later "Deoband Project".

Trained, first and foremost, by Mamlūk al-ʿAlī Nānawtavī (d. 1267/1851) in Delhi in the 1840s, he became well acquainted with the hybrid approach to education of the *Delhi College*.[353] Additionally, he was also noticed by Sir Sayyid Aḥmad Khān, with whom he developed a critical, yet mutually very respectful relationship.[354] However, his close personal and spiritual relationship with Ẓafar Aḥmad Imdādallāh Fārūqī Tħānavī (d. 1317/1899) was even more important for the formation of Nānawtavī's religious thought, which would subsequently give shape to the devotional dimension of "Deobandiyyat".

Similar to Nānawtavī, Imdādallāh also originated from Nānawtah and had established a *khānaqāh* at Tħānah Bħavan some seventy-five miles northwest of Delhi, which reportedly soon served as a hub of Muslim spirituality in the region, but could only avoid persecution for his active involvement in the Uprising of 1857 by escaping to Mecca, and, therefore, he was subsequently known as "Muhājir Makkī". Surprisingly, other than that, only a little reliable biographical information on him is available.[355] Apparently, it was once again

351 See Ṭayyib (1407/1988), 100.

352 See Ahmad (1966), 274f. The Kāyasth are originally a North Indian Hindu caste (*jātī*). Converts from this community to Islam have, nonetheless, retained their caste identity, most probably by external ascription. Many of them belonged to the clerical estate, serving there as scribes, accountants and registrars: see Bellenoit (2014).

353 The *Delhi College*, situated in the *Madrasah-yi Ghāzī al-Dīn Khān* at the northern city walls of Delhi, constituted, in fact, one of the very early attempts of British EIC officials to introduce European teaching contents in formerly traditional Islamic places of learning through the medium of Urdu, thus, preparing a new local service elite for the time after the establishment of direct colonial rule: see, for example, Pernau (2008), 109–17.

354 In his obituary for Nānawtavī, published in the bilingual *Aligarh Institute Gazette* 14 (24 April 1880), 467f., Sir Sayyid hailed him as follows: 'People thought that after Mawlavī [Muḥammad] Isḥāq [Dihlavī, a grandson of Shāh Valiyallāh] there would be no one like him, bearing all of his qualities [*tamām ṣifāt*]. However, the late Mawlavī Muḥammad Qāsim, through his perfect piety, faith, austerity and simplicity [*kamāl nīkī awr dīnvārī awr taqvá awr varʿ awr maskīnī sē*], has proved that God Almighty did procure another person with these qualities, perhaps even superior than him as far as these issues are concerned. [...] At this time and age, everybody would agree that he had no match – he might perhaps not have been as knowledgeable [*maʿlūmātī ʿilm mēṇ*] as Shāh ʿAbd al-ʿAzīz [ibn Shāh Valiyallāh], but in other aspects, he was greater than him. If he was not superior to Mawlavī Isḥāq in matters of humility, piety and virtuousness [*sādah mizājī*], then he was certainly not inferior either.'

355 Even information on his educational background differs greatly. Compare, for example, al-Ḥasanī (1412–13/1991–3), VIII: 79f., and Muḥammad Riẓá ʿUs̱mānī in Muhājir Makkī (1397/1976), 2.

the Mamlūk al-ʿAlī mentioned already who was very responsible for bringing Imdādallāh to Delhi, where the latter developed a keen interest in the esoteric fields of knowledge; this spiritual orientation, in turn, prompted him to become the disciple of Naṣīr al-Dīn Thānēsarī, later Dihlavī (d. 1256/1840), a former student of Shāh Rafīʿ al-Dīn (d. 1233/1818) and Shāh Muḥammad Isḥāq (d. 1262/1845) of the Valiyallāh family. Naṣīr al-Dīn, finally, constitutes an important link in the institutional narrative of "Deobandiyyat" to the *Ṭarīqah-yi Muḥammadiyyah*, because he had apparently joined the military campaign of his teacher's uncle Shāh Ismāʿīl and Sayyid Aḥmad Barēlvī in the Pashtun Borderland[356] and, after the defeat at Balakot, emerged as one of the new leaders of the movement that secured its continuous presence there.[357]

It might have been the activist inclination of Imdādallāh's spiritual guide, who would increasingly shift the thrust of his activities from the Sikhs to the British, that he carried on to Thānah Bhavan and cultivated further among his own ever growing following, including most of the founders of the "Deoband Project". With the outbreak of the Uprising of 1857, Imdādallāh began to utilize the Sufi network he had created for the organization of armed resistance to the British EIC. In May of that year, following a successful attack on a military convoy at Thānah Bhavan's main thoroughfare, he led a contingent of volunteers into open battle with British forces at Shāmlī, a larger town some twelve miles to the south of Thānah Bhavan, but was defeated this time and subsequently had to go into hiding.[358] Remarkably, an exceptional role in these ventures has been ascribed to Nānawtavī in the later Deobandi historiography, while, at the same time, the significance of Imdādallāh in this regard was substantially downplayed. In retrospect, this might be understandable because, when Imdādallāh vanished somewhat from the Indian scene due to his emigration to the Hijaz, Nānawtavī and his close associate Rashīd Aḥmad Gangōhī (d. 1323/1905) – the second founder figure – were left behind and had to deal with the severe repercussions the failed Uprising of 1857 had on the Muslim communities in the subcontinent.

Nonetheless, Imdādallāh's exemplary life and his writings provided the early scholars and students at Deoband with a pattern for a distinct style of pious conduct (*adab*)[359] that was practised by them right from the onset.[360] Accordingly, material wealth or noble descent was considered by and large irrelevant, which again helped these scholars to connect with their predominantly subaltern clientele. In fact, much of the early "Deobandiyyat" seems to have revolved around the notion of "social justice" (*ʿadālah-yi ijtimāʿī*) and

356 See Khān (2000), 559; al-Ḥasanī (1412–13/1991–3), VII: 551f.

357 See Mihr (2008), IV: 175–264; Ahmad (1994), 78–83.

358 See Merathī (n.d.), I: 73–9; Gīlānī (1373h), II: 134–63; al-Ḥasanī (1412–13/1991–3), VIII: 80.

359 See Muhājir Makkī (1397/1976), 92–7 (*Irshād-i Murshid*).

360 See Metcalf (1982), 167f.

"equity" (*inṣāf*) that was soon sustained by references to the Qur'anic revelation: human "equity" is ultimately measured supratemporally, and worldly "riches and progeny" (*māl va awlād*) in such a perspective pale significantly against the permanence of the Hereafter.[361] Consequently, it is one's personal attitude to "riches and progeny" that becomes the yardstick for one's fidelity; their mere existence in this world is to be considered only a divinely decreed test of faith. The semantically complex Qur'anic term "*fitna*" had been consistently rendered by the early Deobandi Qur'anic commentators as "review" (*jāṇch*) and "examination" (*imtiḥān*):[362] both terms clearly suggest that the – divinely caused – existence of "riches and progeny" in this world poses a viable test of one's fidelity, as God's final reckoning will be based on how each individual human being positions themself towards it. This, again, resonates very well with the interrelated Sufi concepts of "self-reckoning", or "soul searching" (*muḥāsaba*), and "spiritual surveillance" (*murāqaba*) that constitute a dominant feature especially in Naqshbandi circles.[363]

In view of the empirical realities, the eschatological promise of salvation is arguably shared by many subaltern world-views.[364] Because of such structural commonalities, cross-fertilizations have been quite common, as we shall see further below. What increases the potential for such mutual enhancement, however, is that this new kind of subaltern "salvation anxiety"[365] does not result in world-renunciation but instead is translated into socio-political agendas. For this purpose, "noblesse" (*sharāfa*) became, again in recourse to the Qur'an, reinterpreted as exclusively spiritual capital,[366] which, by inference, makes the economically and socially disadvantaged Muslims, the *ajlāf*, a vanguard in redressing any kind of deprivation (*ẓulm*). In other words, it is these *ajlāf* who are the true *shurafā'* and, as such, they have an exceptional societal responsibility. Consequently, any *madrasah* that had emerged out of a positive response to the message that radiated from the *Dār al-ʿUlūm* at Deoband was regarded as a "deputy" (*nā'ib*) of the Prophet, which, once again, emphasized the centrality of the Prophet as a reference point for the justification of social and political activism.[367]

However, no clear and singular strategic instructions can be derived from the Prophetic example, which is why the early representatives of

[361] See ʿUs̱mānī (1428/2007), for example II: 449 (on Q18.48) and 647 (on Q23.56).

[362] See ibid., III: 708f.

[363] Generally, on *muḥāsaba* and *murāqaba* in the Naqshbandiyyah, see Netton (2000), 40–7. For the context in focus here, see, for example, Muhājir Makkī (1397/1976), 29–34, 42–4 and 51–4 (*Ẓiyā' al-Qulūb*).

[364] These include prominently the political ideologies of Communism and Fascism, see Hartung (2013a), 44–59.

[365] For this quite diligent term, see Lange (2016), 5–11.

[366] See ʿUs̱mānī (1428/2007), III: 748 (on Q68.14f.).

[367] See Hartung (2022a).

"Deobandiyyat" already had to negotiate conflicting positions within the *maslak* itself. Yet, the relationship of some of its founding figures and their spiritual forerunners to various militant endeavours sustained by religious precepts appears to have reinforced a pattern of militantly inclined socio-political activism that was soon to be adopted by various individuals from within the early Deobandi context. Such inclinations were certainly facilitated by a discourse on *jihad*, in which, once again, Muslim jurisprudence and Sufi spirituality coincided. While sections on this and related matters are conspicuously absent especially in the early Deobandi collections of *fatāwá*[368] – certainly out of political prudence post-1857 – later ones reconnected well with the earlier tradition in which *jihād* against one's own lesser soul and physical *jihād* against an external opponent have coalesced.[369] Nānawtavī's student and allegedly first graduate of the *Dār al-ʿUlūm*, Maḥmūd al-Ḥasan of Baraylī, better known by his later epithet "Shaykh al-Hind" (d. 1339/1920), was the one who stood more than any other of the early Deobandis for this return to socio-political activism, prominently including the militant option.

From Deoband to Delhi, and on, into the Borderlands

Among the many possible expressions of Muslim piety (*taqwá*, or *birr*) that constituted what was perhaps the smallest common denominator of "Deobandiyyat", socio-political activism was a controversial matter among Deoband's early scholars and students, most certainly informed by the elders' memories of the tragic events of 1857. The Shaykh al-Hind, however, was only six years old at the time of the Uprising,[370] which might explain why his views on this question were quite different: this would be even more so for the next generations, who did not have any first-hand experience of the Uprising itself.

The conflict over the permissibility of socio-political activism at that point in time was, in fact, part of the negotiation process of what constitutes "Deobandiyyat", in contrast to the other competing *masālik*. If we follow later protagonists of this enterprise who tried to establish a synonymy of "Deobandiyyat" with Muḥammad Qāsim Nānawtavī,[371] then true authenticity

[368] See, for example, Gangōhī (1987).

[369] See, for example, Ẓafīr al-Dīn (2002), xii: 162–266; Akōṛavī (1422/2002), v: 285–355; Ludhiyānavī (1425h), vi: 11–366. For a historical link, see Imdādallāh's versified treatise on the "Greater *jihād*", in Muhājir Makkī (1397/1976), 106–27 (*Jihād-i Akbar*).

[370] See Riẓvī (1413–4/1992–3), ii: 34; ʿUs̱mānī (1428/2007), i: 8. Still, the Uprising affected the family of the Shaykh al-Hind directly, as his father Ẕū 'l-Fiqār ʿAlī ibn Fatḥ ʿAlī (d. 1322/1904), renowned as a literary scholar and poet, had studied in imperial Delhi also with Grand Mufti (*muftī-yi aʿẓam*) Ṣadr al-Dīn "Āzurdah" Dihlavī (d. 1285/1868), who had been severely persecuted by the British for his active endorsement of militant resistance against them in 1857: see Hartung (2013b), 140f., (2021b), 1 213–15.

[371] See prominently Ṭayyib (1407/1988), 100.

can be assured only by the closest possible proximity to and subsequent emulation of him. In this regard, the dispute between the Shaykh al-Hind, the adept,[372] and his main opponent "Shams al-ʿUlamāʾ" Ḥāfiẓ Muḥammad Aḥmad (d. 1348/1928), the son of Muḥammad Qāsim, was a fierce struggle not only over the advisability of anti-colonial activism, but also very much over the ownership of the embodiment of "Deobandiyyat". The emergence of distinct factions was, thus, an almost inevitable result, each pivoting around a distinct office-holder in the Deobandi nomenclature: Ḥāfiẓ Muḥammad Aḥmad served as head administrator (*muhtamim*) of the *Dār al-ʿUlūm* during the Shaykh al-Hind's terms as principal (*ṣadr al-mudarrisīn*) and superintendent (*sar'parast*).

The passionately presented arguments of the Shaykh al-Hind and his inner circle of mainly former students in favour of potentially anti-British socio-political activism led initially to their alienation from the proclaimed mainstream of the other and, in the beginning, more powerful faction. This increasing alienation was facilitated by the fact that the most active of the Shaykh al-Hind's students in this regard was ʿUbaydallāh Sindhī (d. 1363/1944), a rather recent convert to Islam, whose polarizing views even led to accusations of unbelief (*takfīr*) against him.[373] ʿUbaydallāh was instrumental in establishing in October 1909 the *Jamʿiyyat al-Anṣār*, a Deobandi alumni organization, designed especially to further a pragmatic rapprochement between them and the graduates of Sir Sayyid Aḥmad Khān's *Muhammadan Anglo-Oriental College* at Aligarh.[374] By 1913, the pressure placed on ʿUbaydallāh by the faction around Ḥāfiẓ Muḥammad Aḥmad in the controversy over what constitutes "Deobandiyyat" had become so heavy that, on the advice of the Shaykh al-Hind, he retreated from Deoband to Delhi and set up the increasingly successful *Naẓārat-i Maʿārif-i Qurʾāniyyah* college in the old city's Fatḥpūrī Mosque.[375]

The spatial arrangement of this institution is remarkable: first of all, while being situated in the very capital of the British Raj, its location in the old Mughal residence of Shāhjahānābād proper clearly indicated a frame of reference that could well do without any collaboration of whatever kind or extent with the colonial establishment. This strategic choice of location was perhaps

[372] The exceptional closeness of the Shaykh al-Hind to Nānawtavī was – probably for strategic reasons – stressed, first and foremost, by Sindhī (1942), 188: 'From among the three who attained knowledge from him [i.e., Muḥammad Qāsim Nānawtavī], it was our own teacher [*shaykhnā*], the Shaykh al-Hind, who loved his teacher the most. He was the chief inheritor of his knowledge [*maʿrifa*], and was one of the most ardent followers of his [*ittibāʿan lah*].'

[373] See Minault (1982), 29. So far, however, confirmation by primary materials is still pending.

[374] See Madanī (n.d.), 143 and 570; Riẓvī (1413–4/1992–3), I: 221f. and II: 65.

[375] See Madanī (n.d.), 563–6 and 570f.; Lighārī (1998), 21; Minault (1982), 28–30.

also targeted at the emergence of administratively supported hierarchical power structures in Deoband itself,[376] epitomized in some of Ḥāfiẓ Muḥammad Aḥmad's otherwise rather difficult-to-explain schemes. As such, the *Naẓārat-i Maʿārif-i Qurʾāniyyah* run by ʿUbaydallāh Sindhī emulated to a great degree the more egalitarian classical tradition of teaching Islamic contents in some corners of a religious, functional building, be it a mosque, a Sufi shrine or a convent. As a result, this seminary turned out to be a most important meeting ground for various religiously grounded socio-political ideas, blurring otherwise important doctrinal lines.[377] The activist and increasingly anti-colonial sentiments that were stirred up in the *Naẓārat-i Maʿārif-i Qurʾāniyyah* did not, of course, go unnoticed by the colonial administration: it was explicitly mentioned in the report of the Sedition Committee as late as 1918, which then fed directly into Act No. XI/1919 of the Imperial Legislative Council, the *Anarchical and Revolutionary Crimes Act*, more commonly known by the name of the head of the committee as the "Rowlatt Act".[378] Sir Sidney Rowlatt's (d. 1945) assessment was, of course, retrospective, most certainly influenced by the fact that the Shaykh al-Hind and his close circle of companions had by then already been ascribed the stigma of political rebelliousness. Their activities during the early years of World War I were again responsible for this, and resulted in their conviction and imprisonment between 1916 and 1920 in the Citadel of Gozo on Malta on the count of treason against the British Crown.[379]

[376] Metcalf (1982), 92, makes a valuable point by stressing that the seminary at Deoband was indeed 'emulating the British bureaucratic style for educational institutions, [. . .] conceived of as a distinct institution, not relegated to a wing of a mosque or home and dependent on the parent institution'.

[377] Among those who took classes in this institution was, for example, Sayyid Abū 'l-Aʿlá Mawdūdī (d. 1399/1979), the systematic mastermind of Islamism and *spiritus rector* of the *Jamāʿat-i Islāmī* (JiI) that was founded in late August 1941 in Lahore and will play a quite pronounced role in our narrative further on: see Nasr (1996), 18f.; Hartung (2013a), 19.

[378] See Sedition Committee (1918), 177. See also Madanī (n.d.), 143 and 565f. The *Rowlatt Act*, emerging out of the *Defence of India Act* of 1915 (Act IV/1915) and remaining valid until its abolition in March 1922, allowed the apprehension and indefinite preventive incarceration of those suspected of seditious activities without any trial or judicial review.

[379] The actual occasion of the detention of the Shaykh al-Hind and his compatriots was their attempt to rally Ottoman support for their anti-colonial activities during their *ḥajj* in 1915. In return, they offered the unconditional loyalty to and support of the Indian Muslims for the Ottoman sultan as holder of the Islamic caliphate. Under this proposition, it is not really surprising that the Shaykh al-Hind in an audience with Sharīf Ḥusayn ibn ʿAlī al-Hāshimī of Mecca (r. 1908–24) denied the latter the legitimacy of his claims to power against those of the Ottoman sultan Meḥmed V (r. 1909–18). Still, the Shaykh al-Hind and his compatriots seem to have overlooked the fact that, in their war alliances, the British had sided with the Arab opposition to the Ottomans that was led by the same Sharīf Ḥusayn. He, in turn, reacted to what he had to perceive as an insult by the

Indeed, the outbreak of World War I, which would force Indian Muslim soldiers to fight as members of the British army against their Muslim brethren of nations at war – particularly the Ottoman Turks – with the Kingdom, served the Shaykh al-Hind and his companions as the trigger for intensified activities. The gravity of the situation called for the mass mobilization of Muslims in the Raj for an eventual armed uprising against their current Christian overlords. The Shaykh al-Hind directed the mobilization efforts towards the rural regions and areas difficult to control in the west, where he could rely on the support of those local Sufi dignitaries who were somewhat linked to him by numerous of his students, among whom, once again, ʿUbaydallāh Sindhī stood out. After having rallied for support in rural Sindh,[380] Sindhī's activities were finally relocated to the adjacent Pashtun Borderland in 1915.[381]

The recruitment of support in both regions, Sindh and the Pashtun Borderland, followed a compelling logic. While the colonial establishment had been well aware of the fact that, other than in ethnically and religiously more heterogeneous areas in the subcontinent, the *pīr*s formed the chief representatives of the local communities and had consistently attempted to co-opt leading Sufi personalities through a system of awarding official honours to them,[382] it seems to have missed the point that their real power base remained in their local communities. Those, in turn, were regularly regarded as unruly and lawless,[383] and, therefore, required on occasion what Ansari calls

Indian dignitary by reporting him to the British representatives, who had the Shaykh al-Hind and his companions apprehended, and subsequently deported them to Malta: prominently, see Madanī (1920), 17–25 and 27–64.

380 ʿUbaydallāh had close contacts with leading Sufi figures in Sindh, notably Rashīdallāh Shāh Rāshidī (d. 1340/1922) and his son Rashīd al-Dīn of Gōtħ Pīr Jħandō, north of Hyderabad, and their circles. He had already established a *madrasah* in the very same place in 1901, thus linking his own institutional affiliation to Deoband with that of the regional Sufi *pīr*. For the role of these Sufi dignitaries in anti-colonial activities, see Ansari (1992), 79f.

381 Abdūl Ḥāmid Kħān Bħaṣānī from Sirājganj in Bengal (d. 1396/1976), another important member who had briefly been part of the circle of the Shaykh al-Hind in Deoband, carried the spirit of anti-colonial and anti-hegemonic subaltern activism to the massive river deltas in his native Bengal, which we may regard in many ways as the eastern pendant to the Pashtun Borderland. The most in-depth analysis of Bħāṣānī's socio-political activities currently available is Uddin (2016).

382 See Ansari (1992), 36–56.

383 Indicative in this regard is the so-called *Criminal Tribes Act of 1871* (Act XXVII/1871), tabled by the lawyer Sir James Fitzjames Stephen (d. 1894) and passed and enforced by the then-Viceroy Sir Richard S. Bourke (d. 1872). In this important piece of legislation, various rural and pastoral–nomadic groups, especially in the NWFP, Sindh and Baluchistan, were branded "criminal" and, together with others, subjected to a restriction of movement up to internment in specially designed settlements (a procedure infamously put into practice in the final phase of the Second Boer War in South Africa at the turn to the twentieth century), along with hard manual labour.

'intimidatory action',[384] which would subsequently result in more concerted subversive action with the support of the *pīr*s as leaders of communities that, more often than not, consisted mainly of their own *murīdūn*.[385]

However, it is precisely this stigma of "unruliness" and "lawlessness" in colonial legislation[386] that made the rural population in both areas strongly susceptible to the highly egalitarian rhetoric employed by the Shaykh al-Hind and his associates. After all, the scholar himself would emerge as a role model in this regard: his was a service to God and to His community, not one to satisfy his own vanities, exemplarily expressed in his 'most sincere' (*baṛī maʿṣūmiyyat sē*) refusal to accept the title "Shaykh al-Islām" – traditionally reserved for the highest legal authority for the Muslims in India, regardless of their respective adherence to particular legal traditions – when it was offered to him only a few months before his death by leading members of the *Central Khilafat Committee*.[387] In addition, the Shaykh al-Hind seems to have been well aware of the danger of losing this local support by assuming the patronizing attitude of an outsider to the region, as had happened to the *Ṭarīqah-yi Muḥammadiyyah* less than a century earlier. This is a major reason why, for his agitation, he particularly employed a number of his own students who had originated in the Pashtun Borderland communities as local proxies,[388] causing the emergence of a distinct regional form of "Deobandiyyat" on the way, which, for its ability to relate to the life-world experiences and subsequent aspirations of the local population, became much more successful in establishing a lasting dominance in the Pashtun Borderland than many of the other *masālik*.

"Frontier Deobandiyyat"

In the aftermath of the socio-political activism sustained by religious precepts of the Shaykh al-Hind and his personal network in the Pashtun Borderland, the "Deoband Project" – now increasingly solidified as a distinct *maslak* of

384 Ansari (1992), 59.

385 A case in point here would be the rebellions of the "Ḥurr" in Sindh of the 1890s (see ibid., 58–76). The Ḥurr were the adepts of the Pīr Pagāṛō of Pīr Jō Gōṫh, the leading Sufi institution in the then-British-Indian Princely State of Khayrpūr since the early nineteenth century, whose name resulted from them being declared free of any responsibilities towards the British by Ṣibghatallāh Shāh I, the first Pīr Pagāṛō (d. 1276/1831), when he joined the *Ṭarīqah-yi Muḥammadiyyah* in early July 1826: see Nadvī (1406/1986), I: 473–7 and II: 370.

386 The most effective instrument to discriminate the population of the Borderland, based on the understanding that their societal specifics would necessitate a special legal framework, had certainly become the FCR of 1901 and its subsequent legislative derivatives, see Nichols (2013), ix–xvi.

387 See Malīḥābādī (1960), 34–6, esp. 35, where the Shaykh al-Hind's declination of the offer is quoted; for a rather liberal translation of this passage, see Minault (1982), 104.

388 See Hartung (2016b), 355–9.

reformulated Islamic learning – manifested itself in the shape of a network of religious seminaries across the Borderland and well into Afghanistan (see Map 3.3). One person of vital importance in this regard was Faẕl-i Vaḥīd of the village of Turangzay, situated just a few miles northwest of Chārsaddah. He was perhaps the most prominent disciple of the Haḋdah Ṣāḥib,[389] and is better known as the "Ḥājjī Ṣāḥib of Turangzay" (d. 1356/1937).

Indeed, the Ḥājjī Ṣāḥib stood out not so much because of his elaborate writings, but rather by virtue of his religiously inspired socio-political activism, which was very much in the tradition of the Shaykh al-Hind. The latter, in fact, prompted the Ḥājjī Ṣāḥib, alongside many other acquaintances of his, to privately open places for religious instruction and thus subvert the attempts of the British colonial establishment to control the educational sector.[390] The Ḥājjī Ṣāḥib enthusiastically complied, much to the annoyance of the British authorities. Subsequently, much of what we know about the Ḥājjī Ṣāḥib is filtered through the lens of colonial intelligence officers, while indigenous information is almost entirely hagiographical in nature.[391]

Despite the resulting vagueness of what can indeed be factually stated, the Ḥājjī Ṣāḥib's relationship with the Shaykh al-Hind and his circle appears to have begun when he spent some time at the *Dār al-ʿUlūm* in Deoband, ostensibly as early as in the mid 1870s.[392] At that time, the founding fathers of the seminary in Deoband, Muḥammad Qāsim Nānawtavī and Rashīd Aḥmad Gangōhī, were still very much flourishing, while the Shaykh al-Hind had completed his formal studies only five years earlier. One can, therefore, assume that, despite Shaykh al-Hind having been seventeen years senior to the Ḥājjī Ṣāḥib, the chief reasons purportedly for the latter joining the official Deobandi delegation for *ḥajj* in 1877 were perhaps rather the two grandees Nānawtavī and Gangōhī.[393] This is further supported by the fact that, while in Mecca, the Ḥājjī Ṣāḥib took discipleship (*bayʿa*) at the hand of Imdādallāh

389 See Section 3.2.3.

390 See Mihr (2008), IV: 665.

391 See the literature review in Qadir (2015b), xiii–xv.

392 See Jāvīd (1982), 44f. There are, however, various points that render it advisable to regard the year 1878 given here for the Ḥājjī Ṣāḥib's sojourn in Deoband with some suspicion. Firstly, the *ḥajj* of Deobandi dignitaries he is said to have joined took place one year earlier, see Riẕvī (1413–4/1992–3), I: 187. Secondly, all the others with whom the Ḥājjī Ṣāḥib had reportedly struck up a lasting association while at the *Dār al-ʿUlūm* in Deoband had not enrolled there before the 1910s: see, for example, Shalmān (2016), 50–5.

393 See Jāvīd (1982), 45–7. While still awaiting corroboration by primary materials, the assessments in the more recent secondary literature allow for either interpretation: whereas, according to Haroon (2007), 55, the Ḥājjī Ṣāḥib predominantly wanted to accompany the Shaykh al-Hind; Qadir (2015b), 21f., whose view is being followed here, suggests that he wanted to join the travelling party because of Gangōhī and Nānawtavī.

Map. 3.3 Centres of anti-imperialist borderland activisms (early twentieth century).

"Muhājir Makkī", who, as we have already seen, had been the *murshid* of both of the founding figures of Deoband.

The Ḥājjī Ṣāḥib evolved into one of the most important of the Shaykh al-Hind's assets in the Pashtun Borderland, alongside a rather diverse array of its residents, such as ʿUzayr Gul from Ziyārat Kākā Ṣāḥib near Nowshera (d. 1410/1989), Faẕl-i Maḥmūd "Makhfī" (d. 1365/1946) and the "Muhtamim Ṣāḥib" Mīr Aḥmad Khān (d. 1398/1978) from around Peshawar, Sayf al-Raḥmān Qandahārī (d. 1369/1950), Faẕl-i Rabbī of Hazārah, Muḥammad Akbar, mufti ʿAbd al-Raḥīm Pōpalzay and especially Khān ʿAbd al-Ghaffār "Bāchā" Khān from near Chārsaddah (d. 1408/1988).[394]

In fact, it would be personalities like these who formed the nucleus of what, from an ideological perspective, is termed here "Frontier Deobandiyyat". From an empirical perspective, however, the notion of a single uniform ideological foundation is not really sustainable and suggests, therefore, that it should be more appropriately regarded, in the plural, as "Frontier Deobandiyyāt". Still, the use of the singular form is also appropriate for systematic reasons. After all, it would be almost impossible to take into account adequately the complexities on the ground, a dilemma for the solution of which sociologist Max Weber proposed the idea of the "ideal-type": 'a scientifically formulated pure type [. . .] of a common phenomenon'.[395] Indeed, our category of "Deobandiyyat" constitutes exactly such a type. Any concept derived from adding further attributes, such as a spatial denominator, remains essentially heuristic and cannot, therefore, be regarded as what Weber called a "real type", that is, the true representation of an empirical fact. Consequently, the term "Frontier Deobandiyyat" also requires, as an ideal-type, at least a working definition: for the moment, the term shall be used to signify any distinct combination of a normativity-instilled Deobandi agenda for religious reformulation as enshrined in the institutional narrative of the *Dār al-ʿUlūm* of Deoband and socio-political specifics of the Pashtun Borderland, associated with members of various distinct Pashtun Borderland communities.

It was perhaps the Ḥājjī Ṣāḥib of Turangzay who personified this in the most unadulterated way, and his activities are, therefore, to be regarded as the epitome of "Frontier Deobandiyyat". While his educational efforts remained, by and large, within the scope outlined by the Shaykh al-Hind,[396] it was the

[394] See Madanī (n.d.), 600–19. By far the most space in this breakdown of the Shaykh al-Hind's compatriots from the Frontier was devoted to the Ḥājjī Ṣāḥib (pp. 600–8). See also Jāvīd (1982), 90, 227–33 *et passim*. For short biographies of Sayf al-Raḥmān, Faẕl-i Rabbī and ʿUzayr Gul, see Riẕvī (1413–4/1992–3), II: 69–71, 102f. and 117f. On ʿUzayr Gul, see also Shah (1983); on "Makhfī", see Shalmān (2016), esp. 25–53; on the "Muhtamim Ṣāḥib", see "Rix̌tīn" (1367sh/1988), esp. 11–15.

[395] Weber (1972), 4 (translation by T. Parsons).

[396] See the Shaykh al-Hind in Kāndhalavī (1392h), I: 119: 'In India previously knowledge was so scarce [. . .] that one could hardly find anyone to perform the funeral prayers

religiously grounded socio-political changes the Ḥājjī Ṣāḥib demanded on top of that which were met with resistance, especially by the *məshərān* of old and new in the Borderland localities. This opposition should come as no real surprise, given that most of the Ḥājjī Ṣāḥi's clamour was directed at them: thus, for example, he targeted the frequent breach of truce (*tīǵah*) by tribal leaders, their co-option by the British for personal socio-economic gains and the distortion of the institution of *jirgah* by internal and external forces.[397]

Nevertheless, the Ḥājjī Ṣāḥib would perhaps not have succeeded had his religious authority been based exclusively on his links to the North Indian scholars from Deoband. In fact, while "Deobandiyyat" was the source of his normative arguments for or against certain beliefs and practices, it was his embeddedness in the local authority structures that made people susceptive to his calls. Years before he embarked on his travel to Deoband, the Ḥājjī Ṣāḥib had already gone to Haḋḋah near Jalalabad, where he pledged his spiritual allegiance to the Haḋḋah Ṣāḥib, introduced above as the "primordial *talib*".[398]

Indeed, it was the eminence of the Haḋḋah Ṣāḥib and his disciples in the Pashtun communities on either side of the Durand Line, which had been established in the meantime, that endowed the Ḥājjī Ṣāḥib with the spiritual and social capital needed for successfully campaigning in the Pashtun Borderland. However, in his struggle for self-determination and local autonomy, the Haḋḋah Ṣāḥib appears to have still been drawn to the regional circles of power and would, therefore, let them remain largely uncontested.

In contrast, the Ḥājjī Ṣāḥib's buying into the egalitarian rhetoric of the Shaykh al-Hind and his associates opened a gate for subaltern socio-political activism that went simultaneously against the British imperial attitudes and local power structures.[399] On the other hand, having been very much a son of the Borderland, the Ḥājjī Ṣāḥib did not shy away from the use of armed force when verbal admonitions did not yield the desired result.[400]

By confronting the British colonial establishment through subverting their various administrative measures in the Frontier as well as alienating their socio-economically privileged allies in the region, the Ḥājjī Ṣāḥib had indeed developed into a major nuisance for them. The outbreak of World War I and the subsequent activities of the circle around the Shaykh al-Hind, predominantly at the various frontiers of the British Raj,[401] tipped the scale of the Ḥājjī

[*janāzah kī namāz*]. Today, however, knowledge is so widespread that every town, in fact, every *qaṣbah*, and indeed perhaps every village has now its own *mawlavī* present.'

397 See Qadir (2015b), 28–31 and 39–52.

398 See Gīlānī (1972), I: 207f.; Jāvīd (1982), 43f.; Ṣābir (1990), 125–36; Qadir (2015b), 21f. Haroon (2007), 43–64, makes a viable point in this regard when she focuses on the regional Naqshbandi networks in which the Ḥājjī Ṣāḥib was integrated.

399 See Qadir (2015b), *passim*; Caron (2016b), 329–31 and 335–7.

400 See Qadir (2015b), 29–31 and 43–56.

401 See Hartung (2016b), 355–9.

Ṣāḥib's activities ultimately in favour of the subversion of the colonial establishment, especially because of the detrimental impact its co-option of local elites had had on the socio-economic and political fabric of the Pashtun Borderland. It was others from within the folds of "Frontier Deobandiyyat" who carried the torch of intracommunal Islamic reformulation and, thus, also indicated alternative responses to the Ḥājjī Ṣāḥib's militant activism to improve the current socio-political conditions in the Pashtun Borderland. ʿAbd al-Raḥīm Pōpalzay and Bāchā Khān, mentioned above, and their respective circles represent two further directions of Deobandi political activism, and both were seemingly rooted in their respective local environment.

ʿAbd al-Raḥīm Pōpalzay was descended from a long line of religious functionaries to the rulers of Peshawar, who had lost their prestigious offices when the city became part of the Sikh polity of Raṇjīt Singh in 1818. The family, nonetheless, remained eminent, with ʿAbd al-Raḥīm's father, ʿAbd al-Ḥakīm (d. 1348/1929), again serving as Grand Mufti (*muftī-yi aʿẓam*) of Peshawar and, if the hagiographical accounts are to be believed, of the entire Pashtun Borderland.[402] ʿAbd al-Ḥakīm had already spent time at the *Dār al-ʿUlūm* in Deoband, and it was, therefore, not surprising that he also sent his son there, where the latter became part of the Shaykh al-Hind's circle.[403] Yet, other than those members of the early Frontier Deobandis who came from a rural background, ʿAbd al-Raḥīm had also been sent to Rampur, where he studied the rational religious sciences in the tradition of the scholars of Khayrābād, developing a strong liking for logic and philosophy in its course.[404] This is an important difference, because it made ʿAbd al-Raḥīm less reluctant to be open to other – and not necessarily Islamic – interpretations of reality, about which we still have to talk.

Upon his return to Peshawar from Deoband and like the Ḥājjī Ṣāḥib of Turangzay, with whom he shared spiritual allegiance to the Haḍḍah Ṣāḥib,[405] ʿAbd al-Raḥīm set up a religious educational institution in his native place at the behest of the Shaykh al-Hind, benefiting herein from the reputation that his family enjoyed. The egalitarian proclivities of the Shaykh al-Hind, along with his personal attitude, left such a lasting impression on ʿAbd al-Raḥīm that he soon turned to emulate the ascetic *adab* of his teacher.[406] Moreover, his reconsideration of socio-economic status in the light of the Shaykh al-Hind's egalitarian teachings made him susceptible to the concerns of the rural

402 See Gīlānī (1972), I: 234–38 and 258f.; Pōpalzaʾī (1992), 15–22.

403 See Pōpalzaʾī (1992), 31–4; Gīlānī (1972), 234 and 259.

404 See Gīlānī (1972); Pōpalzaʾī (1992), 31–7. See also Khān (1970), 14f., where ʿAbd al-Raḥīm is said to have named Faẕl-i Ḥaqq Khayrābādī (d. 1278/1861) as one of the three formative and lasting intellectual and spiritual influences on him. On the so-called "School of Khayrābād", see Hartung (2021b), 1 206–43.

405 See Pōpalzaʾī (1992), 35.

406 See ibid., 31f.

population, which he began to increasingly frame in a class terminology that caused later authors to style him as alternately a communist, Marxist or Leninist.[407] This appears very much in line with the fact that especially the latter variety of socialism was most popular among mainly urban South Asian revolutionary activists at that time.[408] While solid evidence is lacking, we may still assume that ʿAbd al-Raḥīm's had a certain acquaintance with Leninism: after all, he was working mainly in and out of an urban context, where the impact of the inclusion into a capitalist world economy against which Marx and his revolutionary epigones developed their ideological alternative was felt most severely. As a result, ʿAbd al-Raḥīm took into account, perhaps more than did the other representatives of "Frontier Deobandiyyat" during that period, the profound socio-economic changes that had been brought to the region by British colonial imperialism and which irreversibly changed the fabric of the Pashtun Borderland: labour migration to cities and town, wage labour and centrally administered structural measures that aimed at increasingly predicting the flow of capital.[409]

Thus, while the militant activism of the Ḥājjī Ṣāḥib of Turangzay and his local allies was still rooted in a conservative understanding of Pashtun Borderland culture and politics, ʿAbd al-Raḥīm Pōpalzay's activism, while frequently overlapping with that of the Ḥājjī Ṣāḥib and others, was very informed by the drastic socio-economic changes of capitalism that aligned the concerns of those suffering under these conditions beyond geographical and cultural boundaries. This focus on the general human condition in the environment of a capitalist market economy enabled ʿAbd al-Raḥīm to eventually transcend the boundaries of his own religious universe. In this, he joined hands with luminaries such as Ḥusayn Aḥmad Madanī and Abū 'l-Kalām Āzād (d. 1377/1958), both of whom argued Islamically for the viability of a composite Indian nationalism, as counter-draft to the colonial reality, as well as with communalist models that were most prominently advocated by the *All-India Muslim League* (AIML), the *Akhil-Bhāratīya Hindū Mahāsabhā* or the

407 See, for example, Khān (1970); Marwat (2005). Tellingly, all of the works on him by his grandson ʿAbd al-Jalīl bear cover illustrations with suggestive images, for example cuffed hands raised in a prayer gesture (see Pōpalzaʾī [1992]) or chains with broken links (see Pōpalzaʾī [1991]), reminiscent of the famous Marxian line that '[t]he proletarians have nothing to lose but their chains' (Marx and Engels [1956–90], IV: 493 (translation by Samuel Moore), or a mass gathering of people with a fist rising from it (see Pōpalzaʾī [n.d.]).

408 For early twentieth-century Calcutta, see Ray (1985); more generally, see Hartung (2013a), 46–9.

409 While published research on the socio-economic impact of introducing a capitalist market economy in the Pashtun Borderland is still scarce, perhaps apart from Nichols (2001), 192–220, and Hanifi (2011), there are plenty of studies on the same phenomena elsewhere which may provide us with a *tertium comparationis*. For Southern Appalachia around the time of the American Civil War, see, for example, Waller (1988), 135–205; Dunaway (1996).

Śiromaṇī Akālī Dal of the Sikhs, all established at around the same time.[410] It is, therefore, not surprising that ʿAbd al-Raḥīm was committed to the composite bodies of the anti-colonial independence movement, the *Indian National Congress* (INC) and its Deobandi ally, the *Jamʿiyyat al-ʿUlamāʾ-i Hind* (JUH).[411]

However, his commitment especially to the INC did not last for long when he realized that the organization was led mainly by urban elites who did not greatly object to the capitalist mode of production as such.

It was then that ʿAbd al-Raḥīm withdrew himself somewhat and, in 1928, associated himself with the *Naw-Javān Bhārat Sabhā* (NJBS) around Bhagat Siṅgh (executed 1931),[412] which, due to their disappointment over Mahatma Gandhi's abolition of the Non-Cooperation Movement in early 1922, maintained an increasingly militant strategy for improving the socio-economic conditions of the weakest of society. Accordingly, Lenin's *What Is to Be Done?* (*Čto delat'?*; 1902) emerged as a mighty provider of slogans, which were adopted alongside other radical Communist concepts, here particularly Trotsky's "Permanent Revolution", which Bhagat Siṅgh appropriated in the slogan "Long Live Revolution!" (*inqilāb zindabād*).[413] ʿAbd al-Raḥīm Pōpalzay also lined up behind this slogan as the provincial president of the NJBS, but – and this seems significant – embedded it in an anti-colonial agenda:

> I do not doubt that, finally, the view has become dominant among the majority of this people that a socialist revolution needs to be preceded by a nationalist revolution. For this nationalist revolution [, in turn,] all the Indian groups who represent various interests need to unite to one common front to defeat British imperialism.[414]

In the following, ʿAbd al-Raḥīm referred explicitly to similar constellations worldwide, from which all sorts of anti-imperialist independence movements arose:[415] by doing so, he raised the situation of the Pashtuns under British rule from its exclusivity and tied it into a universalist model of explanation which he upheld quite consistently. Imperialism, as a political practice, emerges from capitalism as the corresponding economic one. However, as ʿAbd al-Raḥīm elaborated in 1937 in a letter to the managing director of the newspaper

410 See Madanī (1395/1975), 27–92; Āzād (2010), I; (2012), 48–51 (Presidential Address to the *All-India Khilafat Conference* on 25 August 1921 at Agra). See also Hartung (2022b). On the various communalist organizations, see Hartung (2004), 143–55.

411 See Tariq (2018), 5.

412 See Gīlānī (1972), I: 260, who, however, attributes the establishment of the NJBS to Pōpalzay. Recent research on Bhagat Siṅgh and the NJBS, however, suggests otherwise: see Moffat (2016), 75f.

413 See ibid., 73 and 76f.

414 Pōpalzaʾī (n.d.), 115.

415 See ibid., 116.

Mazdūr Kisān, capitalism is a force that comprehensively affects all walks of human life. Thus, the political enslavement of India is only the consequence of its economic enslavement, which can be overcome only if the condition of the workers and peasants is rectified, and this may be by force.[416] His interpretation of the 1857 Uprising as an – albeit unsuccessful – subaltern attempt to counteract the increasingly aggressive attitude of the British EIC was, in fact, also based on this line of argument.[417]

This subordination of all societal praxes under the economic one is, in fact, clearly reminiscent of Marx's political theory and suggests that ʿAbd al-Raḥīm was, at least to a degree, familiar with and certainly sympathetic to its ideational underpinnings. The extent and depth of his concrete affinity with communist thought, however, remains to be unearthed by future research. For the time being, he shall, therefore, remain here as a religious Borderland actor who sympathized with certain ideas to an extent, but would, very much in line with the pragmatics that characterize the navigating of Borderland politics, remain rather flexible in his ultimate commitment.

The British colonial establishment was well aware of the potential pull of an eminent and publicly very active scholar such as ʿAbd al-Raḥīm for the subalterns, especially in the Pashtun Borderland. It may well be that his appointment as Grand Mufti of the NWFP in the footsteps of his father was an attempt to co-opt him for the colonial establishment, as they had succeeded in doing with many of the power-holders in the local communities.[418] Given the eminence of the family,[419] ʿAbd al-Raḥīm might have considered himself entitled to this position, without seeing any necessity to reciprocate the favour, and he is, therefore, to be regarded as a prime example of the fact that the imperial strategy of making and breaking Borderland elites did not always yield the results desired.

As mufti, ʿAbd al-Raḥīm seems to have interpreted his constituency as being not only the population of the British NWFP but, in fact, the entire Pashtun Borderland. On behalf of especially the subalterns on either side of the Durand Line, he petitioned the colonial administrators in the province and the political establishment in Kabul alike, in his attempt to negotiate a favourable treatment for those who had become a pawn in the hands of the mighty pursuing their

416 See ibid., 97f.

417 See ibid., 82–92 (Preface to the Urdu translation of *The Other Side of the Medal* [1925] by Edward J. Thompson [d. 1946], a work that was deeply unsettling for the British colonial authorities because of its pro-Indian stand). Remarkably, this interpretation of the Uprising of 1857 as a "War of Independence" even though, in fact, there was still nominal Mughal rule in large parts of the subcontinent, was adopted by Marxist social and economic historians, such as prominently Bipan Chandra (d. 2014) of the Jawaharlal Nehru University of New Delhi.

418 See Khan (2014b), 41f. and 62.

419 See Pōpalzaʾī (1992), 12–26.

own ulterior agendas.[420] It is, therefore, not surprising that his persistent refusal to be hitched before the cart of the British colonial administration and his choice, instead, to act on the behalf of those who, in the eyes of these administrators, he was rather meant to keep in check, resulted in punitive measures: from May 1940 until January 1943, that is less than a year before his death, ʿAbd al-Raḥīm served a sentence in various prisons of the NWFP as a C-Class prisoner for instigating social and political unrest in the Pashtun Borderland and beyond.

In contrast to Bāchā Khān, to whom we shall turn in a moment, ʿAbd al-Raḥīm was not at all adverse to the use of violent means as a last resort, and it is in this regard that his views coalesced with those of Bh̄agat Sing̈h̄ and the other activists of the NJBS. Yet, as the quote above from ʿAbd al-Raḥīm's presidential address to the provincial NJBS in Peshawar on 26 March 1939 also suggests, the reason for this may have been less to do with an affinity with communist ideology in its Leninist and Trotskyist garb than with the fact that he, just like the Ḥājjī Ṣāḥib of Turangzay, had been a disciple of the politically active Haḋḋah Ṣāḥib.[421] Furthermore, ʿAbd al-Raḥīm was also one of the liminal Borderland actors who would enter into pragmatic alliances with dogmatically opposed groups in the region.[422] His increasingly radical position regarding the use of force in the struggle to improve the socio-economic conditions of marginalized communities in the Pashtun Borderland and beyond had gained momentum during his involvement in the agrarian revolt at the village of Ghallah Ḋh̄ēr near Mardan (*Mardān*) in the summer of 1938;[423] the acceleration in radicality can be traced in his few preserved public addresses to gatherings of those communities in the years to follow, as well as in the short introductory writings of his from that period.[424]

420 A showcase in this regard is ʿAbd al-Raḥīm's leadership of a delegation of Borderland *ʿulamāʾ* to Kabul in 1928–9, which tried to negotiate on behalf of various rebellious tribes in the east of the Durand Line that had been encouraged by Afghan Emir Amānallāh Khān, as these tribes had been subjected to severe punitive measures by the British colonial forces: see Pōpalzaʾī (n.d.), 35–76; Jāvīd (1982), 344–8.

421 See Gīlānī (1972), I: 266; Khān (1970), 14f.; Pōpalzaʾī (1992), 35.

422 His pragmatic relationship with the *Jamāʿat-i Mujāhidīn* at Chamarkanḋ, which he shared with the Ḥājjī Ṣāḥib of Turangzay, is significant in this regard, see Pōpalzaʾī (1992), 166–8; (n.d.), 77f. (here, the reproduction of an article in the journal *al-Mujāhid*, which was published from the colony at Chamarkanḋ between autumn 1923 and the 1940s and is not to be confused with the later publication of the same name; on the journal itself, see Rauf [2005], 427–9).

423 See Pōpalzay's introduction to Nagīnah (1994), 17–19. For comprehensive accounts of this and related agrarian revolts in the region, see Shah (2015), 68–75.

424 See here his presidential address to the *Peasants Conference* in Punjabi Talagang on 5 February 1938 in Pōpalzaʾī (n.d.), 100–5; his presidential address to the *First Hazārah District Kisān Conference* on 25 February 1939 in Mansehrah (*Mānsihrah*), in ibid., 106–13; Pōpalzaʾī (1994), 95–104; the one in Sarāʾī Ṣāliḥ on 20 December 1939 in Pōpalzaʾī (n. d.), 123–8; and his address to the people of Bannū on 12 April 1940, which led once more

ʿAbd al-Raḥīm Pōpalzay's deep sympathies for the socio-economically deprived and his commitment to better their situation were shared by Bāchā Khān, although the latter would not endorse at all Pōpalzay's approval of violence as a viable strategy against a British establishment that would not, as numerous examples prove, shy away from using its monopoly of structural violence against civilian protesters, especially in the colonies.[425] Yet, while figures such as Bhagat Singh and ʿAbd al-Raḥīm Pōpalzay would respond to this with rallying especially young subalterns for local revolts and the employment of other common means of violence in grossly asymmetrical conflicts, others – prominently Gandhi – would rather call off confrontational strategies in order to avoid further bloodshed. Bāchā Khān would evolve into the most prominent local actor with Deobandi affiliations in the Pashtun Borderland on that end of the spectrum.

In contrast to Pōpalzay and the Ḥājjī Ṣāḥib, however, Bāchā Khān had not actually studied at the *Dār al-ʿUlūm* at Deoband itself. Instead, he stated in his memoires that he travelled there a couple of times with his compatriots Faẕl-i Maḥmūd "Makhfī" and Faẕl-i Rabbī, and that it was during these visits that he developed a friendly relationship with the Shaykh al-Hind and ʿUbaydallāh Sindhī.[426] Born in the village of Utmānzay, a little west of Chārsaddah, he had received his education from the padres at the *Edward Memorial Mission High School* in Peshawar, thus having been confronted with the Christian values of compassion, benevolence and also of learning in general.[427] Thus, similarly to ʿAbd al-Raḥīm, Bāchā Khān was able to combine the Islamic egalitarianism of the Shaykh al-Hind with ideas from elsewhere from which he had derived inspiration. While being in cahoots with the Ḥājjī Ṣāḥib of Turangzay insofar as the establishment of schools outside the colonial power of disposition was concerned,[428] his attitude to socio-political change, as has already been indicated, was decidedly different.

In fact, its theological basis was derived from a distinctly mundane understanding of "service to God": 'Because God has no need of service, service to God is service to the creation of God.'[429] Tellingly, the term "khidmat" was used, which, in Bāchā Khān's understanding, merges the service to God (*ʿibādāt*) with the service to the community (*muʿāmalāt*). The foundation of

to his arrest under Section 124 A (Seditionist Activities) of the *Indian Penal Code* from 1860, in Pōpalzaʾī (1991), 39–44.

425 One may think here of the massacre at Jaliyāṅwālā Bāgh in Amritsar on 13 April 1919, which strikingly resembles the events of the "Bloody Sunday" in Dublin's Croke Park on 21 November 1920 and suggests that this was actually a systematically employed response of the British authorities to local protest in their colonies.

426 See Khān (1983), 70–4 and 94f.

427 See ibid., 65–8.

428 See ibid., 69f. and 526f.

429 Ibid., 356.

service to humanity as God's creation, again, was love (*mīnah*), and, in this conceptual universe, love of humanity became equal to love of the Divine. On the concept of mutual love, finally, rests the doctrine of non-violence (*ʿadam tashaddud*) that became fundamental for Bāchā Khān's *Khudāy Khidmatgārān*, a socio-political protest movement, and matched well the doctrine of *ahiṃsā*,[430] as advocated by Gandhi and many of his compatriots from the INC, which too was sustained by religious precepts.[431] Consequently, the *Khudāy Khidmatgārān* and affiliated organizations agreed in April 1930 to join the *Civil Disobedience Movement* spearheaded by the INC, a decision that instantly resulted in the arrest of leading *Khudāy Khidmatgārān* and, only a few days later, in the massacre of about 200 unarmed protesters in Peshawar's *Bāzār Qiṣṣah Khᵛānī* by British military forces.[432] Other than in armed confrontation with militant expressions of protest, here the extreme asymmetry of the conflict was most vividly exposed and the colonial claims of authority were subsequently eroded.

Besides the non-violent form of protest adopted by Bāchā Khān and the *Khudāy Khidmatgārān*, the British colonial establishment was also uneasy concerning two other matters, one of which had quite some significance also for the heir to the British Raj, the state of Pakistan. The first uneasiness arose from the red shirts worn by the *Khudāy Khidmatgārān*: Viceroy Lord Halifax (r. 1925–31) informed Secretary of State William Wedgewood Benn on 16 August 1930 that, despite the acknowledgement that the movement was not, as initially suspected, inspired by Leninism, the ambiguity was, nonetheless, intentional, so this imaginary association could well be used as a pretext to persecute members of the movement.[433] The second concern of the British colonial establishment was even more severe, and had, in fact, already led to Bāchā Khān's imprisonment years before the establishment of the *Khudāy Khidmatgār* movement:[434] his ethnocentric orientation, which aligned the movement only temporarily with various others, all of which had their own distinct agendas.

Bāchā Khān's strong affinity to his Pashtun ethnicity, which he saw explicitly targeted by the introduction of the FCR in 1901,[435] was largely responsible for

[430] See Schmidt (1968).

[431] One may wish to compare the related passages of Gandhi's autobiography *The Story of My Experiments with the Truth* (Gujarati: *Satyanā prayōgō athavā ātmakatthā*; 1927) with Bāchā Khān's deliberations on the matter.

[432] See Khān (1983), 354–6, 372–4 and 376.

[433] See Shah (2015), 30f. n.39. Members of the movement have denied outright any association with Bolshevism, as indicated, for example, in ibid.

[434] See Khān (1983), 143–65 and 189–300. These arrests were based on Bāchā Khān's active participation in the *Khilafat Movement* and its auxiliaries, such as the *Hijrat Movement* of 1919: on the latter, see Reetz (1995).

[435] For a comprehensive edition of all the relevant documents that fed into the eventual FCR, and an analysis, see Nichols (2013).

his unfettered political loyalty to Amānallāh Khān (r. 1919–29), the Barakzay Emir of Afghanistan. For him, Pashtun tradition was the cultural reference point and the Borderland communities the socio-political reference point, and not India, as for the INC, not Pakistan, as for the AIML, and not even the Muslim *umma*, as for the Shaykh al-Hind. He saw in Amānallāh an enlightened ethnic Pashtun monarch whom he considered able to overcome all the social and economic obstacles that kept the Pashtuns an assemblage of fractioned communities rather than a nation.[436] Thus, Bāchā Khān perceived his own activities to be fully in line with Amānallāh's modernistic endeavours in Kabul, which, in turn, made him an ally to a hostile neighbouring state in the eyes of the British colonial officers and, eventually, their Pakistani heirs. Consequently, Bāchā Khān was repeatedly jailed for subversive and secessionist activities under both imperial powers.

It is the reminder of the irrelevance of the national borderline between British India / Pakistan and Afghanistan for the definition of the Borderland by its inhabitants that forms the lasting legacy of Bāchā Khān for the present study. Moreover, Bāchā Khān and the *Khudāy Khidmatgārān* remain a core reference point for those Borderland residents who subscribe to the political doctrine of non-violence as a precondition to any conflict resolution and societal progress. However, against such culturalistic arguments, which perpetuate personalized forms of Muslim piety, stand those that project "Islam" as a universal normative framework which, because of its universality, needs necessarily to override any cultural and linguistic specifics. The Ḥājjī Ṣāḥib of Turangzay and his partisans represented the latter, and this thread would be spun further by some of the following generation of Pashtun graduates from Deoband, who returned to the Borderland and eventually established their own educational institutions in that particular scholarly tradition. This development was boosted by the gradual success of the various Indian independence movements and the resulting loss of hope for the British colonial establishment of being able to retain its crown colony for much longer.

An important aspect of these developments in the Pashtun Borderland, which reflects very well what has been conceptualized in this study as "Borderland pragmatics", was the purpose-bound alliances between elite actors in the region, such as Deobandis of different persuasions and *Ahl-i Ḥadīs̱*, as well as more subaltern religious figures, especially in the communities of the region that has been administratively framed as "Tribal Areas" and in which the FCR was applied with full force.

[436] See Khān (1983), 339–47 *et passim*.

3.3.3 *Borderland Alliances, in View of an Overpowering Enemy*

Indeed, doctrinal differences needed to be set aside for the time being in the face of political circumstances with a profound and extensive impact on all the communities in the Borderland, and hands joined against common adversaries. While this does not at all suggest that the doctrinal differences, especially in the field of jurisprudence and its methodology, became insignificant, it nonetheless indicates a certain flexibility in matters of religious dogma that generally allows for – temporary – pragmatic collaboration of otherwise fiercely opposed religious camps. Once the common goal was achieved, however, the old trenches were dug up again and the disputes resumed with undiminished vigour.

Perhaps no other condition was equally suited to the putting aside of doctrinal differences than British colonial rule and the subsequent resistance that, in the early twentieth century, took the shape of a mass movement for the eventual independence of India from British domination. The almost epic might of this conflict called for all sorts of pragmatic concessions that would, at times, also transcend even denominational divides and put leading representatives of all the religious communities in the Crown Colony on the same side. The confrontation between the colonial establishment and its Indian subjects reached a first culmination point during World War I, not least because the various alliances of the warring parties put Britain and various Muslim powers in opposite camps. One of those was, in addition to the Ottoman Empire, the Kingdom of Afghanistan, a fact that left Pashtuns on the eastern side of the Durand Line in an emotionally highly charged moral conflict. After all, the overwhelming majority of the *ʿulamāʾ* in those parts had already affirmed the rulers of Afghanistan as supreme political authorities over the Pashtuns also on the eastern side of the Durand Line in the late nineteenth century; the important socio-political role of these scholars, especially in the rural communities, in turn ensured that the spirit of loyalty towards the Afghan monarchs instead of the British crown permeated the subaltern population of the Borderland.[437] Allegiance to the latter, in turn, was pledged only by those who benefited directly from it: the old and newly created landed elites and political power-holders.[438]

As a result, resistance to colonial rule was chiefly carried out by religious community leaders with a sympathetic attitude towards subaltern concerns. It is, therefore, not surprising that a lot of the active opposition to colonial rule during World War I pivoted once more on the circle around Maḥmūd al-Ḥasan, the "Shaykh al-Hind". This network of local supporters which he managed to establish across the Pashtun Borderland also drew in numerous activists from the *Ahl-i Ḥadīs̱–Jamāʿat-i Mujāhidīn* nexus, who, for the time being, seem to have ignored the Shaykh al-Hind's earlier public defence of the

[437] See Khan (2014b), 67f. The term used for these affirmations was "the avowal of the king" (*də kalimah bādʾshāhī*).

[438] See ibid., 32–5.

cornerstones of Hanafi *fiqh* against the sustained criticisms by those labelled "*ghayr-muqallidūn*" – those who reject following any of the canonical jurisprudential traditions, the *madhāhib fiqhiyya*.[439]

In fact, the Shaykh al-Hind actively sought an alliance with the *mujāhidīn*, especially of the colony at Chamarkand, which, from a strategic point of view, was conveniently situated between two nations at war. While the Deobandi scholar appreciated the manpower, the fierce anti-British sentiments and the resulting fighting spirit of the *mujāhidīn*, they, in turn, benefited financially and logistically from the Deobandi network, at least indirectly.[440] The proxy in mediating between the dogmatically opposed parties was, once again, the Ḥājjī Ṣāḥib of Turangzay,[441] but also Grand Mufti ʿAbd al-Raḥīm Pōpalzay[442] as well as, at a later stage, even their own *murshid*, the Ṣāḥib of Haḍḍah: all three actors qualified for this task because of their deep entrenchment in the socio-religious fabric of the Pashtun Borderland. The normative Islamic argument for reaching out into the tribal areas on the Durand Line was, as had already been the case with the *Ṭarīqah-yi Muḥammadiyyah* of the nineteenth century, the idea that these territories, nicknamed "Yāghistān" – "Land of the Rebels", were not subject to any state regulation and constituted, therefore, a *dār al-islām*, to where Muslims from the *diyār al-ḥarb* could migrate, and from which a *jihād* in defence of the Muslim lands could be legitimately conducted.

Much of this, however, evolved while the Shaykh al-Hind and some of his companions remained in war captivity in Malta; when, upon his release, he arrived back in India in June 1920, he had only five more months to live. Others, many of whom were not Deobandis, took over the baton: on 30 July 1920, Abū 'l-Kalām Āzād released his *fatwa* in support of Muslim mass migration to Afghanistan, which was published in the weekly *Ahl-i Ḥadīs̱*.[443] A second *fatwa* in this regard was issued only nineteen days later by ʿAbd al-Bārī

439 See Dēobandī (1990), 21f. This work is a response to an earlier criticism of Hanafi *fiqh* by the renowned *Ahl-i Ḥadīs̱* writer and publisher Muḥammad Ḥusayn Baṭālavī (d. 1338/1920). On the latter, see Riexinger (2004), 212–22.

440 See Madanī (n.d.), 630–2: 'The *mujāhidīn* of Yāghistān ([i.e.,] the Land of the Free Tribes) informed His Excellency Maḥmūd al-Ḥasan that, due to their shortage of ammunition and aliments, they were not able [anymore] to carry out their *jihād* activities against the British government. [... Therefore] They requested some Muslim government to be persuaded to support the *mujāhidīn*. [... For this reason,] The Shaykh al-Hind sent Mawlānā ʿUbaydallāh Sindhī to Kabul and concluded for himself the need to reach Istanbul.'

441 See ibid., 579 and 629f.

442 See Pōpalzaʾī (1992), 166–8.

443 See Minault (1982), 103–6; Riexinger (2004), 224f., 454 and 512–17. The journal had been published since 1903 from Amritsar by S̱anāʾallāh Amritsarī (d. 1367/1948), the initiator of the AIAḤC and its first Secretary General between 1912 and 1947. With the AIAḤC, in turn, the *Ahl-i Ḥadīs̱* evolved from an association with a focus purely on theological and legal matters into an organization of political significance: see Riexinger (2004), 451f.

Farangī Maḥallī of Lucknow (d. 1344/1926).[444] Yet, neither Āzād nor ʿAbd al-Bārī cared much about proper logistic arrangements for what they were calling for, or was sufficiently well connected to Afghanistan to make sure that the roughly 30 000 mainly North Indian Muslim peasants who sold all their worldly possessions and set out for the Khyber Pass could indeed find sanctuary there: consequently, the whole affair turned out to be, by and large, a disaster.[445] Minault argues convincingly in this regard that this debacle demonstrated in a painful way, especially to the newly emerging urban Muslim elites, the importance of a tight support network of the religious dignitaries in the rural areas. Indeed, this could have been learned by paying more attention to the activities of the Shaykh al-Hind and his companions, because, other than elitist actors such as Āzād or ʿAbd al-Bārī Farangī Maḥallī, they had actually begun to establish such networks, as well as sustainable relationships to the relevant circles of power in and around Kabul, including the royal court, already by 1915. The pivot of these arrangements was, once more, ʿUbaydallāh Sindhī, who, alongside three companions, arrived at Kabul in October 1915.[446]

In January of the same year, a group of fifteen students from Lahore had already disembarked to Kabul on the instigation of *Ahl-i Ḥadīs̱* supporter ʿAbd al-Raḥīm "Muḥammad Bashīr",[447] who at that point in time was still the *imām* of Lahore's Chīniyāṇvalī Mosque, with the objective of proceeding to Istanbul and joining the Ottoman forces there in their war with the Entente. En route, they received logistical support from the *Ahl-i Ḥadīs̱–Jamāʿat-i Mujāhidīn* network and used the various colonies of the *mujāhidīn* in the Borderland as convenient stopovers.[448] When these students were arrested in Kabul by order of Afghan Emir Ḥabīballāh (r. 1901–19), who attempted to maintain amicable relationships with the British despite serious opposition in court,[449] it was supposedly Sindhī whose contacts and influence secured their release.[450] As a result, one of them, Ẓafar Ḥasan Āybak (d. 1409/1989), became a close associate of Sindhī, regardless of the almost insurmountable doctrinal differences between Deobandis and *Ahl-i Ḥadīs̱*.[451]

In the following years, other notable figures from this realm, such as Muḥammad Bashīr, Muḥammad ʿAlī Qaṣūrī and ʿAbd al-Karīm Chamarkandī, acted as intermediaries between ʿUbaydallāh Sindhī's semi-permanent circle in

444 See Minault (1982), 240 n.147 (quoted from the *Abdul Bari Papers*, Farangī Maḥall, Lucknow).

445 For a comprehensive account on the course of the Muslim mass migration from Northern British India to Afghanistan, see Reetz (1995).

446 See Lighārī (1998), 43f.; Madanī (n.d.), 562f.

447 See Āybak (1990), 14; Pākrāy (1368sh), 99f.

448 See Āybak (1990), 42–52.

449 On Ḥabīballāh's reign, see Olesen (1995), 95–106.

450 See Āybak (1990), 97f.; Lighārī (1998), 60; Mihr (2008), IV: 670.

451 See Āybak (1990), 100–5 *et passim*.

Kabul, the various centres of the *mujāhidīn* in what had once again become a frontier in a war and various centres of the *Ahl-i Ḥadīs̱* in the Punjab by going back and forth.[452] The chief intermediaries, it appears, were once again the Ḥājjī Ṣāḥib of Turangzay and ʿAbd al-Raḥīm Pōpalzay.[453] Meanwhile, Sindhī and his compatriots set up their base in Kabul's Shōr Bāzār, the abode of the highly influential descendants of the "Ḥaẕarāt-i Maʿṣūmiyyah", the Mujaddidī Sufi family which will play a more pronounced role in our narrative a little later.[454] It is quite likely that the common spiritual affinity of the Deobandi scholars and the Mujaddidis, who, in turn, were exceptionally close to the royal family, provided a solid enough basis for Sindhī to strike up a quite useful relationship with "Nūr al-Mashāʾikh" Faẕl-i ʿUmar ibn Qayyūm Jān Mujaddidī (d. 1376/1957), the then-head of the Mujaddidī family and a gatekeeper to the royal palace.[455] The fact that Emir Ḥabīballāh's successor to the throne, Amānallāh Khān, affirmed as ruler of Afghanistan by the Nūr al-Mashāʾikh, met with Sindhī almost instantly and informed him of his unfettered support of the anti-colonial resistance in the Pashtun Borderland might corroborate this assumption.[456]

On the eve of the Third Anglo-Afghan War (May 1919), therefore, all of the strategic constellations finally fell into place. From a normative perspective, Shāh ʿAbd al-ʿAzīz Dihlavī's *fatwa* on whether or not colonial India can still be regarded a place where Muslims can legitimately live, already radicalized by the proclamations of Shāh Ismāʿīl and Sayyid Aḥmad Barēlvī, was now boosted by a proclamation of the legitimacy of resistance of Indian Muslims against their British colonial masters by the Ottoman governor of the Hijaz, Ghālib Pāṣā, which was solicited by the Shaykh al-Hind during his sojourn in Mecca in late 1915.[457] This manifesto, popularly known as *Ghālib'nāmah*, represented for the Indians the official endorsement of their activities by an authorized representative of the Ottoman sultan-cum-caliph. The internal power politics in the Arabian Peninsula which caused Ghālib Pāṣā to surrender to the British-supported Arab tribes under the Sharif of Mecca, Ḥusayn ibn ʿAlī, only one year later, however, did not seem to have

452 See Madanī (n.d.), 578f.; Chamarkandī (1981), 17–22; Qaṣūrī (1986), 35–40.

453 See Jāvīd (1982), 179–82, 236–40 *et passim*.

454 See Āybak (1990), 98. For the significance of the Ḥaẕarāt-i Maʿṣūmiyyah of Kabul's Shōr Bāzār in the eighteenth and nineteenth centuries, see Ziad (2017), 246–85; for the twentieth century, see Section 4.3.

455 On the Mujaddidis during that period, see Olesen (1995), 133, 135 and 146f.; Wieland-Karimi (1998), 125f. In both cases, however, the identity of the respective family members, especially when only their epithets are used, appears confused.

456 See Lighārī (1998), 189–93; Āybak (1990), 163–70; Olesen (1995), 113f. and 146.

457 Madanī (1920), 14–16; (n.d.), 634–6; Lighārī (1998), 162f.; Āybak (1990), 111f.; Mihr (2008), IV: 672–4; Jāvīd (1982), 214–17 (here a transcript of the text of Ghālib Pāṣā's missive, together with the related petition [*ʿarẕ'dasht*] of the *Jamʿiyyat-i Ḥizballāh*, signed by the Ḥājjī Ṣāḥib of Turangzay, the "Bābaṛah Ṣāḥib" Sayyid Amīr Jān (d. 1343/1925), Faẕl-i Rabbī and a Mawlavī ʿAbd al-ʿAzīz).

been fully comprehended by the Shaykh al-Hind and his compatriots. Meanwhile, Emir Amānallāh of Afghanistan, upon his accession to the throne, proclaimed *jihād* to religious dignitaries from either side of the Durand Line, supposedly assembled at a strategically well-chosen place: the mosque of Haḋdah Sharīf.[458] Reinvigorating the traditional affirmation of the Afghan ruler by the *ʿulamāʾ* in the Borderland as stipulated by Emir ʿAbd al-Raḥmān's *Kalimah* of 1886,[459] he could now place himself at the helm of a legitimate *jihād* against an infidel power that threatened the integrity of a Muslim population.

The proclamation elicited fervent support from two directions that confirm the underlying pragmatism adopted by the many diverse parties involved. On the one hand, there were the various religious figures in the rural areas, especially those with roots in the areas classified by the British colonial administration as "tribal", claiming authority to represent their respective local communities. Trans-communal representation, however, was claimed by Deobandis and *Ahl-i Ḥadīs̱* who were active in the region, first and foremost, the Ḥājjī Ṣāḥib of Turangzay and Muḥammad Bashīr of Chamarkanḋ.[460] On the other hand, Emir Amānallāh's proclamation was also wholeheartedly supported by the self-appointed Provisional Indian Government in exile, led by "Minister of the Interior" ʿUbaydallāh Sindḧī and his inner circle.[461]

Borderland pragmatics, however, caused the multilayered alliances between various political and religious elites, and elites and subalterns in general, to break down the very moment that the objectives were no longer aligned. The potential temporality of these alliances was stressed emphatically in the petitions of Borderland community representatives: full recognition of their general autonomy from any imperial rule was a non-negotiable condition for their active support of the Emir during his armed conflict with the British.[462] After

458 See Źalmay (1346sh), 40–5; Olesen (1995), 113f.; Haroon (2007), 107. Regrettably, the statements in this regard in the second and third sources cited are based solely on secondary readings, pointing to the predicament that, so far, no primary reference has been found that could confirm the location of this proclamation.

459 See ʿAbd al-Raḥmān (1304sh), 33–9.

460 See, for example, Jāvīd (1982), 122–6 and 234f. Also see the petition (*ʿarīẓah*) to Amānallāh Khān by representatives of the various Pashtun Borderland communities from 24 Dhī ʾl-ḥijjah 1337 / 7 September 1919, as reproduced and transcribed in Źalmay (1346sh), 78–83 (including a facsimile of the document between pp. 82 and 83).

461 See Źalmay (1346sh), 83–5; Lighārī (1998), 189–93; Chamarkanḋī (1981), 137–42; Jāvīd (1982), 236–40; Āybak (1990), 125–7 and 163–6; Olesen (1995), 113–15; Haroon (2007), 106–12. On the Provisional Government of India in Exile, see, once again, Āybak (1990), 101–5; Pākrāy (1368sh), 98–105 *et passim*.

462 See n.162 in this chapter. See also Źalmay (1346sh), 83–5 (undated Persian letter of the Khᵛəzay Mōmand to ʿUbaydallāh Sindḧī, in which the latter was authorized to represent them before Amānallāh).

Amānallāh had secured the sovereignty of Afghanistan in the Treaty of Rawalpindi on 8 August 1919 and, in return, confirmed the Durand Line as the legitimate border between Afghanistan and British India, the various tribal communities of the Pashtun Borderland began to gradually withdraw their support.[463] The members of the Provisional Indian Government were also utterly disappointed when Amānallāh's true objectives became clear:

> Afghanistan, in line with her old and legendary custom, once again left her war ally, the Indian Muslims, to their fate. Subsequently, the British applied their cruelties on the Indians for which they are renowned all over the world. Meanwhile, Emir Amānallāh Khān was confirmed as king [of Afghanistan] and put the laurels of success on his own head.[464]

As a result, the strategic alliances began to break apart: in October 1922, ʿUbaydallāh Sindhī and most of his close associates left Kabul for good, and when, in February 1923, Amānallāh publicly presented his Constitution (*niẓām'nāmah-yi asāsī*) for Afghanistan to the grand *jirgah* of Jalalabad,[465] ever louder voices among his former supporters arose which questioned the Islamicity of the new Constitution and the related modernization projects of the king.[466] Nevertheless, various prominent local religious leaders, such as the Ḥājjī Ṣāḥib of Turangzay, maintained their support of the king,[467] perhaps on the basis of the traditional endorsement of the Afghan ruler as sovereign over the Pashtun Borderland communities also to the east of the Durand Line, at least as long as until 1929. Others, in contrast, rallied tribal militias and contested both the British and the Afghan imperial claims.[468] Mufti ʿAbd al-Raḥīm Pōpalzay, finally, issued a *fatwa* as late as April 1920, in which he stipulated the religious obligation of unfettered support of the Ottoman sultan-cum-caliph,[469] thus, continuing to challenge the British on loyalty by all Britain's colonial subjects. In addition to all that mounting chaos, the *Jamāʿat-i Mujāhidīn* became riddled by internal conflicts more than ever before. When, on 15 Ramaḍān 1353/9 December 1934, Muḥammad Bashīr, *amīr* of the Chamarkand colony, met a violent death, the *Jamāʿat-i Mujāhidīn*

463 For the text of the Treaty, see Hayat Khan (2000), 265f.

464 Āybak (1990), 170.

465 See Anon. (1302sh).

466 ʿUbaydallāh Sindhī went first to the Soviet Union and then to what by then had become republican Turkey, before he finally reached Mecca, where he remained until he was finally granted permission by the colonial authorities to return to British India in 1939: see Lighārī (1998), 221–53; Āybak (1990), 223–326. For Amānallāh's reformist policies, see Olesen (1995), 116–33; Navid (1999), 73–81 *et passim*; for his continuous manoeuvring with the Borderland tribes, see Navid (1999), 85–104; Haroon (2007), 113–20.

467 See Jāvīd (1982), 218–26.

468 See Navid (1999), 161–70; Qadir (2015b), 68–72.

469 See Pōpalzaʾī (n.d.), 79–81.

began to finally discharge into other religio-political organizations in the Eastern Pashtun Borderland.[470]

With World War I over, the various religious actors from the British-held parts of the Pashtun Borderland inclined to Islamic reformulation shifted their focus more firmly to their own colonial situatedness and, consequently, sought new alliances with various bodies inside the Indian independence movement. In this more transregional orientation, they emulated, in part, the cosmopolitan attitude of the more urban Muslim community leaders, many of whom were associated either with the centres of the Deoband or the *Ahl-i Ḥadīs̱* movements. This tension between local, national and cosmopolitan aspirations would contribute significantly to shaping the religious landscape in the Pashtun Borderland in the aftermath of World War I.

When the Indian mass movement for the preservation of the Ottoman-held caliphate finally collapsed in 1924, various Deobandis and *Ahl-i Ḥadīs̱* members of the many *Khilafat Committees* that had emerged throughout the entire subcontinent associated themselves more closely with the JUH.[471] In British India's NWFP, however, this political organization of Muslim scholars established in 1927 its own regional branch as *Jamʿiyyat al-ʿUlamāʾ-i Sarḥadd* (JUS) that was soon to be led by mufti ʿAbd al-Raḥīm Pōpalzay,[472] a fact that indicates once more the self-perceived distinctiveness of the Borderland and its inhabitants from the rest of the Indian subcontinent. In fact, the further fate of the region's religio-political set-up was largely shaped by these anti-colonial forms of communal organization.

The president of the JUH from 1923 onward was Ḥusayn Aḥmad Madanī, one of the Shaykh al-Hind's closest companions. In fact, "Shaykh al-Islām" Madanī would be styled by his supporters and by himself as the deceased scholar's true heir,[473] a claim that was certainly disputed by the partisans of "Imām-i Inqilāb" ʿUbaydallāh Sindhī. In reality, both represented particular aspects of the legacy of the Shaykh al-Hind, aspects that over time would

[470] See Chamarkandī (1981), 132–4: only the very early stages of the disputes within the colony are covered here, because the narrative ends in around 1929. For the developments after 1929, see Rauf (2005), 421 and 439.

[471] See Minault (1982), 79–84; Qureshi (1999), 131f. and 249. The initiative for the establishment of the JUH is claimed by Deobandis and *Ahl-i Ḥadīs̱* alike. The former traces their origins back to a *fatwa* of Rashīd Aḥmad Gangōhī from as early as 1888 that permitted political association with the INC as in conformity with the *shariʿa*: see Rauf (2005), 415. (This *fatwa*, however, could not be located in the standard edition of the *Fatāvá-yi Rashīdiyyah*.) At the same time, S̱anāʾallāh Amritsarī, president of the AIAḤC, regarded himself as sole initiator of the JUH: see Riexinger (2004), 453, esp. n.148.

[472] See Pōpalzaʾī (1992), 79; Haroon (2007), 155–8. The most comprehensive history of the JUS so far is Tariq (2018).

[473] See Metcalf (2009), 79f. and 88f. See also the carefully crafted self-portrayal in Madanī (n.d.), 636–8 and 676–92.

become exacerbated to the extent that, eventually, they became very distinct from one another.

Sindhī, detached from the daily events in British India due to his involuntary exile in the Hijaz, devoted his thirteen years in Mecca to more systematic contemplation, at the end of which he arrived at quite significant conclusions, especially regarding Islamic textual and legal hermeneutics. These may well have been influenced by the fact that the Hijaz was ultimately conquered by the Najdi troops of then-Emir ʿAbd al-ʿAzīz ibn Saʿūd (d. 1373/1953) only shortly after Sindhī's arrival and subsequently tied into what, in 1932, was finally proclaimed as the Kingdom of Saudi Arabia. The religious legitimization of that new polity was provided by Wahhabi scholars; because of their long-standing relationship with the nascent *Ahl-i Ḥadīs̱*, the latter now possessed a politically quite powerful ally.[474] When, in the summer of 1926, the King of the Hijaz, Ibn Saʿūd, convened the first *Islamic World Congress* (*Muʾtamar al-ʿĀlam al-Islāmī*) in Mecca, Sindhī was briefly reunited with former compatriots and acquaintances of the *Ahl-i Ḥadīs̱*, with whom he now began also to discuss religious matters.[475] They all belonged among the Ghaznavis, who had come to Mecca as a counter-delegation to the one led by S̱anāʾallāh Amritsarī, with whom they had entered into a fierce factional dispute over doctrinal matters:[476] consequently, Sindhī's own understanding of the *Ahl-i Ḥadīs̱* positions was rather limited to those advocated by the conservative Ghaznavis.

The personal closeness of the Deobandi ʿUbaydallāh Sindhī to leading representatives of the *Ahl-i Ḥadīs̱*, as well as his exposure to the religious and political changes in the Hijaz under new Saudi rule, may indeed have had a decisive impact on the systematic elaboration of his religious thinking that began to pivot ever more strongly on the legacy of Shāh Valiyallāh Dihlavī. Sindhī's reading of aspects of Shāh Valiyallāh's *taṣawwuf*, for instance, is said to have made a lasting impression on mufti ʿAbd al-Raḥīm Pōpalzay after lengthy discussions with Sindhī on this matter during the *ḥajj* season of the Hijri year 1353h (1935–6).[477]

[474] Perhaps still the best in the ever growing body of literature on the Wahhabiyya and its political significance for the creation of the Kingdom of Saudi Arabia is Steinberg (2002). On the socio-religious consequences of the Saudi conquest of the Hijaz, see ibid., 511–68.

[475] According to the list of attendees in Schulze (1990), 82f., which is based on the information in the newspaper *Umm al-Qurá* 2/75 (30 Dhī 'l-qaʿda 1344/11 June 1926), the delegates from the *Ahl-i Ḥadīs̱* comprised the AIAḤC President S̱anāʾallāh Amritsarī, ʿAbd al-Vāḥid Ghaznavī and Sayyid Ismāʿīl Ghaznavī (d. 1379/1960). See also Riexinger (2004), 359f.; ʿIrāqī (2003), 88 and 95.

[476] See Riexinger (2004), 339–61, esp. 360f. Lighārī (1998), 248f., meanwhile, highlights the historically close links between the Ghaznavis and the Saudi religious establishment, thus corroborating the impression above that ʿUbaydallāh Sindhī was more drawn to the radically inclined *Ahl-i Ḥadīs̱*.

[477] See Pōpalzaʾī (1992), 80–2 and 85f. As a result of these discussions, especially on Shāh Valiyallāh's reconciliation of the controversial philosophical concept of "unity of existence" (*waḥdat al-wujūd*) with Aḥmad Sirhindī's counter-draft "unity of testimony"

However, Sindħī's styling of Shāh Valiyallāh as the leader of a political movement had an even deeper impact.[478] Yet, a so far perhaps less acknowledged contribution of Sindħī in this regard was Shāh Valiyallāh's methodology of Qur'anic exegesis, laid down by the latter in the rather short Persian *Fawz al-Kabīr fī Uṣūl al-Tafsīr*. In fact, Sindħī's own exegetical efforts were closely modelled on the principles laid out there,[479] and it was these efforts that would eventually have a lasting impact on the further religious developments in the Pashtun Borderland, although in a radicalized form. The bearer of the popularization and radicalization of ʿUbaydallāh Sindħī's understanding of Qur'anic exegesis was Muḥammad Ṭāhir ibn Āṣif of Panjpir (*Panjpīr*) in the Swabi (*Ṣvābəy*) region of the Peshawar Valley (d. 1407/1987), who will play a prominent role further on in our narrative.[480] Muḥammad Ṭāhir studied *tafsīr* with Sindħī in Mecca only one year before the latter was finally allowed to return to India, and also one year before the establishment of the *Dār al-Qurʾān* at Panjpir. The confluence of some representations of "Frontier Deobandiyyat" and the Islam of the *Ahl-i Ḥadīs̱* – now home to the bulk of the *Jamāʿat-i Mujāhidīn* – would be taken to its ultimate limits in this institution [481]

On the other end of the eventual disentanglement of the temporary alliance of Deobandis and *Ahl-i Ḥadīs̱* was the emergence of a more institutionalized framework of "Frontier Deobandiyyat" in which the political agenda of the JUH / JUS coalesced with the firm maintenance of the theological and jurisprudential characteristics of the Deobandi *maslak*. A young Pashtun student and *murīd* of Ḥusayn Aḥmad Madanī from Akōṛah Khaṫṫak near Nowshera, by the name of ʿAbd al-Ḥaqq (d. 1409/1988), was chiefly responsible for this. While, interestingly, his hagiographers tried to gloss over his political involvement with the JUH, the regional JUS and the later JUI, they put some stress on his father Gul Ṣāḥib's association with the Ḥājjī Ṣāḥib of Turangzay.[482] This, however, may well be only a strategic measure to tie Madanī,[483] who spent

(*waḥdat al-shuhūd*), ʿAbd al-Raḥīm Pōpalzay is said to have developed his idea of the "unity of religions" (*vaḥdat-i adyān*). While this concept is reminiscent of Abū 'l-Kalām Āzād's "unity of religion" (*vaḥdat-i dīn*) (see Āzād [2010], I: 210–334; Hartung [2022b]), ʿAbd al-Raḥīm's use of the plural is significant, as it points more to the ability to coexist rather than to "dīn" as a metaphysical principle.

478 On this, see Sindħī's ultimate work *Shāh Valiyallāh awr unkī Siyāsī Taḥrīk*, first published in Lahore in 1942. This work was succeeded only two years later by *Shāh Valiyallāh awr unkā Falsafah, yaʿnī Imām Valiyallāh kē Ḥikmat kā Ajmālī Taʿāruf.*

479 See Zaman (2012), 16–18; Chaudri (2019), 220f.

480 See Sections 4.1.2 and 4.4.1.

481 See Ilyās (2012), 98–103. For an in-depth discussion of the enterprise at Panjpir and its later ramifications in the Pashtun Borderland, see Sections 4.1 and 4.4.

482 See Mukhtārallāh Ḥaqqānī, 'Pish lafẓ' in Akōṛavī (1422/2002), I: 87. See also Ḥaqqānī (1422/2001), 25.

483 As he is not identifiable from the lists of followers of the Ḥājjī Ṣāḥib in the British Intelligence Files, reproduced with comments in Qadir (2015b), 102–19, it remains open

only a little time in the NWFP of British India and had only laudable things to say about the Ḥājjī Ṣāḥib,[484] closer into the circles of the various representations of "Frontier Deobandiyyat". Other than the Ḥājjī Ṣāḥib, ʿAbd al-Ḥaqq had actually completed the full course of studies at the *Dār al-ʿUlūm* of Deoband itself[485] and, therefore, returned to his native lands as a true and accomplished representative of the scholarly aspects of "Deobandiyyat". The college which he established on the eve of Partition at his native Akōṛah Khaṫṫak would, therefore, perhaps more than all the earlier and smaller ones in the Pashtun Borderland, evolve as the epitome of "Frontier Deobandiyyat" in Pakistan. It was subsequently lauded by Deoband's own then-principal Qārī Muḥammad Ṭayyib (d. 1403/1983), to be considered as the driving force behind canonizing "Deobandiyyat", a "second Deoband".[486]

3.3.4 "Frontier Deobandiyyat" 2.0: Ḥaqqāniyyat – Singular

Indeed, it seems as if the *Dār al-ʿUlūm-i Ḥaqqāniyyah* at Akōṛah Khaṫṫak lived up to the expectations that come with glorifications, such as the one by Qārī Muḥammad Ṭayyib. In theology and jurisprudence, they remained entirely within the Hanafi-Maturidi tradition that had constituted a core feature of the Deobandi *maslak* right from its inception. Yet, especially for a region where the literacy rate is rather low, such a comparatively complex and normative approach required some kind of cultural translation that made "Deobandiyyat", as a scholarly thread and beyond the activist networks in our focus so far, digestible for a predominantly subaltern audience in the Pashtun Borderland, beyond the earlier grassroots efforts of the Ḥājjī Ṣāḥib of Turangzay or Bāchā Khān.

The translatability of "Deobandiyyat" into the Pashtun Borderland context required a thorough appreciation of the hermeneutical universe of the latter,

to debate whether or not Gul Ṣāḥib, 'the *imām* of a mosque', had indeed 'spent all of his life with *ʿulamāʾ* and *mujāhidīn*, because whenever something in his vicinity was not in conformity with the rules of the *shari'a*, unlawful innovations and rituals [*bidʿāt va rusūmāt*], he would always report this to ʿAllāmah ʿAbd al-Nūr Kharavī and the Ḥājjī Ṣāḥib of Turangzay' (Ḥaqqānī [1422/2001], 25).

484 See Madanī (n.d.), 600–8.

485 See Ḥaqqānī (1422/2001), 36–47.

486 See Samīʿ al-Ḥaqq (n.d.), 52f. Qārī Muḥammad Ṭayyib is the author of many works that bear the term "Deobandiyyat" in their title and in which a catalogue of constituents of this particular religious persuasion is given that pivots especially on the establishment of a pantheon of "elders" (*akābirīn* [sic]) whose works had defined the limits of what can rightly be considered "Deobandiyyat". Metcalf, to whom we owe the first major academic monograph on this *maslak*, follows, by and large, Ṭayyib's notion of it, which may be down to the fact that Metcalf spent a prolonged time in his household, see Metcalf (1982), xxix; even more, Metcalf (2004), 9f. Recently, on the basis of a rigorous investigation of the writings of the so-called *akābirīn*, this institutional narrative has been profoundly challenged by Chaudri (2019).

which, in turn, was benefited by ʿAbd al-Ḥaqq's regional rootedness. Owing to this, he was able to shift the weight of certain constituents of "Deobandiyyat" without giving up on any of them, in order to meet the complex and multilayered concerns of the subaltern Borderland communities that remained the prime target audience of the Deobandis in this region. In this regard, the *Ḥaqqāniyyah* differed, for example, from the *Jāmiʿat al-ʿUlūm al-Islāmiyyah* in Karachi that was founded in 1954 by fellow Pashtun Muḥammad Yūsuf Binōrī (d. 1397/1977) and emerged as a major centre for the in-depth study of Hanafi *fiqh* in Pakistan and beyond. In Akōṛah Khaṫṫak, in turn, the legal pursuit was conspicuously ingrained in the exceptionally strong popular Prophetic piety prevalent across the Pashtun Borderland, prominently reflected in the thought and devotional practices of local Sufi Islam.[487]

However, this very common persuasion among mainly rural Pashtuns caused a dilemma for ʿAbd al-Ḥaqq, which, in fact, proved difficult to dissolve. On the one hand, ʿAbd al-Ḥaqq and his associates aligned their own deep veneration of the Prophet Muḥammad with culturally deep-rooted modes of expression, reflected, for instance, in *naʿt* poetry, that is, devotional poetry in praise of the Prophet, that they were composing themselves.[488] On the other hand, and despite its strong and desirable social implications in the Borderland, not all expressions of Sufi Islam could be sanctioned with a clear conscience from within the normative Hanafi-Maturidi framework of the Deobandis, within which, after all, ʿAbd al-Ḥaqq and his associates also operated.[489] The phenomenon of dervishes and intoxicated mendicants that was widespread in the Borderland was problematic, as an undated *fatwa* of ʿAbd al-Ḥaqq on that matter suggests.[490]

True to the claimed origins of "Deobandiyyat" that, as we have already seen, began to emerge vigorously with ʿUbaydallāh Sindħī's considerations of this

487 Vivid illustration provide the various fatwas issued by the various muftis of Akōṛah Khaṫṫak on matters related to Sufi-Islam in Akōṛavī (1422/2002), II: 243–86.

488 See, for example, Ḥaqqānī (1422/2001), 173–94. Generally, on *naʿt* poetry in the Pashtun context, see Schimmel (1985), 176–8; Gohar (1422/2001). Furthermore, ʿAbd al-Ḥaqq's own take on Prophetic piety is also well expressed in the account of his own pilgrimage to the Ḥaramayn in 1964: see Samīʿ al-Ḥaqq (2011a), 244–65, esp. 248–54.

489 The respective references are consistent with those in other areas of inquiry and include Hanafi standards such as Ibn ʿĀbidīn (1423/2003), I: 139, II: 291 and VI: 408f.; al-Ḥaṣkafī (1423/2002), 665; al-Miṣrī (n.d.), III: 155 and VIII: 352; and the *fatwa* collections of Qāḍī Khān (2009), I: 355f. (the exact quote in Akōṛavī [1422/2002], II: 274 n.2, however, could not be traced); al-Anṣārī (1407/1987), I: 633; al-Bazzāzī (2009), I: 28; [R. A.] Gangōhī (1987), 225f.; [M. Ḥ.] Gangōhī (1430/2009), IV: 457. The Maturidi core reference is al-Taftāzānī (1408/1988), 92.

490 See Akōṛavī (1422/2002), II: 282. The reference here is to the expansive treatise *Sharīʿat va Ṭarīqat* by Ashraf ʿAlī Thānavī (d. 1362/1943), he himself being a core reference author for ʿAbd al-Ḥaqq throughout this section. Remarkably, this work does not receive any special appreciation either in Zaman (2007) or in Mian (2015), the latter being otherwise the most comprehensive study of Tħānavī to date.

theme, the paradigm of what was and was not acceptable in Sufi beliefs and practices was ultimately established by Shāh Valiyallāh Dihlavī and, although to a somewhat lesser extent, by Aḥmad Sirhindī, the progenitor of the Naqshbandiyyah-Mujaddidiyyah.[491] ʿAbd al-Ḥaqq's decision in favour of urban elite Sufi Islam by emphasizing the tradition of the Naqshbandiyyah-Mujaddidiyyah over all other prevalent ones, especially in what by then had become the Federally Administered Tribal Areas (FATA) of Pakistan, meant, in fact, a closing of ranks with the very orientation from which the *Ṭarīqah-yi Muḥammadiyyah* had sprung in the early nineteenth century, and which had also been patronized in Afghanistan under the suzerainty of the Emir ever since the Emirate of Dūst Muḥammad Khān Bārakzay at around the same time.[492] Still, ʿAbd al-Ḥaqq, a true son of the Borderland environment that he thrived in, maintained amicable relationships with numerous Sufi dignitaries of different affiliation in the local communities of the Borderland.[493]

The second thread that tied the constituents of "Deobandiyyat" into the popular Prophetic piety that has been so deeply enrooted in Pashtun Borderland culture was the focus of ʿAbd al-Ḥaqq and his associates on the *ʿulūm al-ḥadīth*.[494] In combination with the endorsement of the Sufi Islam of the Naqshbandiyyah-Mujaddidiyyah, this was well suited to ultimately justify one of the most significant emphases of Hanafi-Deobandi legal practice, that is, wholesomely and unquestionably following the legal opinion of one's own teacher – *taqlīd shakhṣī*,[495] and can perhaps best be exemplified by the instructions ʿAbd al-Ḥaqq received in the *Jāmiʿ al-Tirmidhī* from his teacher and *murshid* Ḥusayn Aḥmad Madanī, who himself had studied this very collection with the Shaykh al-Hind. The latter, in turn, had acquired the *ijāzat* to teach

[491] Five works from within reformulation-inclined Naqshbandiyyah circles account for the bulk of the references in Akōṛavī (1422/2002), ii: 243–86: al-Dihlawī (1355/1936), i: 85; Dihlavī (1963), 61; (1970), 13, 18–34, 49, 68–74 and 93–102; Sirhindī (1397/1977), i: 111 (no. 43), 135 (no. 57), 143f. (no. 61), 213–17 (no. 107), 329–35 (no. 209), 421–4 [no. 256], ii: 150–8 [no. 55] and 175–7 [no. 63]; and al-Ḥanafī (1316h), 13, 526, 542–4, 549, 555, 558, 564, 567, 593, 605f., 643 and 656. The latter work was composed by Faqīrallāh ibn ʿAbd al-Raḥmān Shikārpūrī (d. 1195/1781) from Jalalabad, who reportedly had been one of the most prominent *shuyūkh* of the Naqshbandiyyah-Mujaddidiyyah in Aḥmad Shāh Durrānī's eighteenth-century confederal polity.

[492] See Noelle (1997), 279f.; Buehler (1998), 172–4.

[493] See his correspondence in Samīʿ al-Ḥaqq (2011a), 130f. (with Amīn al-Ḥasanāt, the then-Pīr Ṣāḥib of Mānkī-yi Sharīf), 150f. (with the Pīr Ṣāḥib of Karbūghah Sharīf in Kohat [*Kōhāṭ*]), 265–75 (with Siyāḥ al-Dīn Kākā Khēl of Ziyārat Kākā Ṣāḥib) and 471f. (with Pīr ʿAbd al-Laṭīf of Zakōṛī Sharīf in D.I. Khan). Besides these local dignitaries, ʿAbd al-Ḥaqq also corresponded quite intimately with the heads of a number of Punjabi *khānaqāhs*.

[494] See, for example, Ḥaqqānī (1422/2001), 228–51.

[495] On the centrality of *taqlīd shakhṣī* in Deobandi legal practice since the inception of this *maslak*, see prominently Gangōhī (1987), 233–8; Dēobandī (1990), 73–88; Akōṛavī (1422/2002), ii: 25–38. See also Metcalf (1982), 143; Chaudri (2019), 61f., esp. n.193; Hartung (2021a), 130–7.

what is said to have been his favourite collection from the deeply spiritual Rashīd Aḥmad Gangōhī, one of the two founder figures of the *Dār al-ʿUlūm* at Deoband, who, in turn, had obtained his *ijāzat* from Shāh Valiyallāh's great-grandson Shāh Muḥammad Isḥāq Dihlavī.[496]

Indeed, the *Jāmiʿ al-Tirmidhī* is widely considered to be the one of the six canonical collections of *ḥadīth* that, because of its exceptional systematics and explicitness, presented itself as an obvious choice for teaching, especially to students with limited prior knowledge of this particular field.[497] Yet, Imām al-Tirmidhī appears even more significant because of his al-Tirmidhī, Muḥammad ibn ʿĪsá *K. al-Shamāʾil,* or *Shamāʾil Muḥammadiyya*, on the qualities and attributes of the Prophet: the fact that ʿAbd al-Ḥaqq's son and successor as principal of the *Ḥaqqāniyyah* Samīʿ al-Ḥaqq (assassinated 1440/ 2018), as well as other products of the college, have focused prominently on this particular work in their teaching and research[498] confirms the initial suspicion that the extraordinary Prophetic piety across the Pashtun Borderland is the one element that entwined its popular manifestation, as expressed so fervently in Pashto *naʿt* poetry, into a single plait with Naqshbandi Sufi Islam and Deobandi *fiqh*. Spiritual authority descended from the Prophet equally onto Sufis and *fuqahāʾ*; both represent only the two sides of one and the same coin and both require, therefore, unquestioning obedience from the apprentice.

The practice of *taqlīd shakhṣī*, however, was impairing with respect to the pragmatic flexibility that the Borderland context demanded to a not insignificant extent. After all, ʿAbd al-Ḥaqq and his early jurist colleagues at the *Ḥaqqāniyyah* followed a similar agenda in their *fiqh* to that of, for instance, the Ḥājjī Ṣāḥib of Turangzay when he challenged numerous social practices in the Pashtun communities that he saw as not being in line with the injunctions of the *shariʿa* and, thus, as fundamental obstacles to social justice. Consequently, the *Fatāvá-yi Ḥaqqāniyyah* contains plenty of (unfortunately mostly undated) *fatāwá* in sections on marriage, land and finance, or reprehensible religious innovations (*bidaʿ*) in which the questioner (*mustaftī*) explicitly refers to social practices in the community and even in his own family.[499] Yet, other than the Ḥājjī Ṣāḥib,

496 See Merathī (n.d.), I: 29 and 88–96; Madanī (n.d.), 56; Ḥaqqānī (1422/2001), 37.

497 I am indebted to Zeeshan Chaudri (London) for this information.

498 Indicative of this is Samīʿ al-Ḥaqq's two-volume *Zayn al-Maḥāfil Sharḥ al-Shamāʾil li'l-Imām al-Tirmiẕī* (2007) and the three-volume *Sharḥ-i Shamāʾil-i Tirmiẕī* (2002) by ʿAbd al-Qayyūm Ḥaqqānī (b. 1376/1956). Also, Ḥāfiẓ Muḥammad Ibrāhīm Fānī (d. 1435/2014), the previous *shaykh al-hadīs̱* at the *Ḥaqqāniyyah*, had specialized in the teaching of al-Tirmidhī's works: see Muftī Muḥammad Asʿad S̱ānī, 'Ḥaẕrat Fānī kā ḥadīs̱-i nabavvī sē ʿāshiqānah awr vālihānah taʿalluq', *al-Ḥaqq* 49/6–8 (1435/2014): 256–9.

499 See Akōṛavī (1422/2002), IV: 393–440 (*K. al-Nikāḥ*). Questions of general nature and on the issue of dowry (*mahr*), which refer explicitly to local customs ('In some areas I saw [. . .]'; 'Among common people of this area the following matter is renowned: [. . .]'; 'My own marriage took place [. . .]'; 'Among us Pashtuns there is the custom [*rivāj*] [. . .]';

the scholars and students of the *Ḥaqqāniyyah* were bound by the confines of their legal trade in the Deobandi tradition, which, by force of *taqlīd shakhṣī*, was even more restrictive. Consequently, all these matters were responded to exclusively through this normative framework, which included prominently also the official collection of *fatāwá* of the *Dār al-ʿUlūm* of Deoband, issued by mufti ʿAzīz al-Raḥmān ʿUs̱mānī (d. 1347/1928), who was yet another former student of the Shaykh al-Hind.[500]

Remaining firmly within the confines of Deobandi scholarship, the *ʿulamāʾ* of the *Ḥaqqāniyyah* were not agents as flexible as the Ḥājjī Ṣāḥib of Turangzay; they would also employ physical force as a religiously legitimate way to redress socio-political wrongs in the Pashtun communities. Their prime tool remained legal opinions – *fatwa*s, at least until the late 1970s, and it is in this very context that the issue of the correct execution of the *tashahhud* during the ritual prayer came once more to the fore, explicitly recognized by Mufti ʿAzīz al-Raḥmān ʿUs̱mānī at the *Dār al-ʿUlūm* in Deoband as a particular issue in Borderland debates.[501] ʿAbd al-Ḥaqq affirmed the Deobandi position[502] in his own *fatwa* on the issue, but, being a true specimen of the Pashtun Borderland, presented his response in a much more elaborate manner than his learned colleague at North Indian Deoband. Using Mullā ʿAlī al-Qārī's seventeenth-century commentary on the *Mishkāt al-Maṣābīḥ* of Khaṭīb al-Tabrīzī (d. 741/1340), perhaps the most popular *ḥadīth* collection in the Deobandi curriculum for those still less advanced in this field, ʿAbd al-Ḥaqq concedes that, from the sound *aḥādīth*, three different Prophetic practices are discernible, which are, therefore, all to be regarded in accordance with the Sunna (*masnūn*).[503] Even

etc.), are mentioned on pp. 293f., 298f., 303f., 309f., 312, 314, 318–20, 322–6, 330, 338, 341–5, 357–9, 364, 366, 368 and 373f. For the virulence of these customs in Pashtun communities, many of them revolving around the place and status of females, see, for example, Grima (2005).

500 The responses to all the community-specific cases and those listed above have been taken from al-Ḥaṣkafī (1423/2002), 177f., 183, 188f., 192, 194 and 667; Ibn ʿĀbidīn (1423/2003), IV: 61f., 72, 215, 274 and 315, V: 323, VI: 399f. and X: 607f.; al-Kasānī (1424/2002), III: 433 and 608; al-Miṣrī (n.d.), III: 144, 147, 177, 187, 251 and 383; al-Anṣārī (1407/1987), III: 178 and V: 365; Qāḍī Khān (2009), I: 379 and III: 402; [al-Burhānfūrī] et al. (1421/2000), I: 332, 347 and 358; al-Marghinānī (1417h), III: 3f. and 5f., and IV: 340f.; al-Shawkānī (1428/2007), 163; ʿUs̱mānī and Gamthalavī (1400h), III: 237; Ẓafir al-Dīn (2002), VIII: 245; al-Tabrīzī (1399/1979), 939 (nos. 3 138f.).

501 See Ẓafir al-Dīn (2002), II: 142: 'Question 345: Scholars from the Frontier have forbidden to raise the index finger during *tashahhud*, [saying] that this act is not to be done during prayer. We, however, say that doing this during prayer is established by the Sunna, and, therefore, established in the best possible manner.' The mufti justifies this practice by quoting from al-Ḥaṣkafī (1423/2002), 70, though stressing that there are conflicting views, this being the accepted one within the Hanafi legal tradition.

502 See n.203 in this chapter.

503 See Akōṛavī (1422/2002), III: 110f. (*K. al-Ṣalāt*); compare al-Tabrīzī (1399/1979), I: 285 and 287; al-Qārī (1422/2001), II: 574f.

so, he himself determined that the conclusive argument is derived – unsurprisingly – from a *ḥadīth* in al-Tirmidhī's collection, and additionally Rashīd Aḥmad Gangōhī's endorsement of that *ḥadīth*.[504]

By observing *taqlīd shakhṣī* in this way, ʿAbd al-Ḥaqq identified himself unmistakably as Deobandi, both regarding the legal views of earlier authorities and in relation to the *ḥadīth* collection at the core of his own education in this area. As such, he positioned himself vis-à-vis those who put such views into question, foremost among them the *Ahl-i Ḥadīs̱*, with whom the Deobandis were engaged in a serious confrontation over technical matters of worship right from the very beginning.[505] Still, the 'scholars from the Frontier [who] have forbidden to raise the index finger during *tashahhud* '[506] appear – in line with the above argument on this matter[507] – to have rather been Borderland actors with a very strong affiliation to the Naqshbandiyyah-Mujaddidiyyah, and who, moreover, were rather suspicious, if not entirely adverse, to any kind of imperial incorporation. By assigning the observance of *taqlīd shakhṣī* a higher priority than the local Naqshbandiyyah-Mujaddidiyyah heritage of rejecting the predominant Hanafi views on the correct performance of the *tashahhud* during ritual prayer, ʿAbd al-Ḥaqq exhibited his leanings towards the "governance-orientated" paradigm of religiosity. By doing so, he appears to have dissociated himself and his associates from any discontent with political domination from outside the Borderland, at least insofar as such formal matters of Islamic jurisprudence are concerned: eventually evolving as a party politician in post-Partition Pakistan,[508] he seems to have accepted the top-down approach to societal change within the given constitutional framework, which is indeed a defining feature of "governance orientation".

This development proper, however, was still a couple of decades away from the formative period of the *Ḥaqqāniyyah* project which is our focus at this point. For the moment, therefore, this enterprise shall be loosely defined as an institutional provision for a nexus of Sunni traditionism, rigid Hanafi *fiqh* and Sufi-inspired Prophetic piety of Pashtun Borderland provenance. This concatenation was further strengthened by the impact of an additional manifestation of "Deobandiyyat", that is, the *Tablīghī Jamāʿat* (TJ), officially established in

[504] See Akōṛavī (1422/2002), III: 111; compare Gangōhī (1987), 312f. The crucial *ḥadīth* here, on the authority of ʿAbdallāh, son of the second caliph ʿUmar, is *Jāmiʿ al-Tirmidhī*, k. al-ṣalāt, b. mā jāʾ fi'l-ishārati fi'l-tashahhud, no. 1 (ḥadīth 295).

[505] Core matters of contestation between Deobandis and *Ahl-i Ḥadīs̱* remained – in fact, up to this very day – *rafʿ al-yadayn* and *āmīn bi'l-jahr*, see, for example, Gangōhī (1987), 310f., who is here fencing off the earlier arguments from al-Dihlawī (1256h); see also n.25 in Section 3.3.1. In contrast, however, the legal and theological problems around the execution of the *tashahhud* during ritual prayer were, at best, of subordinate importance to this debate.

[506] Ẓafīr al-Dīn (2002), II: 142.

[507] See Sections 3.1.3 and 3.2.3.

[508] See Section 4.3.1.

1926. Originating in a socio-economic environment quite similar to that of the Pashtun Borderland, the efforts of its founder figure, Muḥammad Ilyās Kāndhalavī (d. 1363/1944), and those who succeeded him in the leadership of the TJ towards Islamic reformulation aimed first and foremost at instilling a form of deep Islamic piety, yet again modelled on the *sunna* of the Prophet Muḥammad and his Companions, in a subaltern rural and tribally organized population traditionally drawn to what Deobandis would consider unmistakably heterodox forms of religiosity.[509]

The initial target of the missionary activities of Muḥammad Ilyās and his compatriots was the Meo communities of Mēvat, today a region some forty miles to the south of New Delhi's city limits. Just like the Pashtuns, the Meo have repeatedly attempted to elude becoming political subjects of the larger imperial polities, and have, thus, gained a historical reputation of being notoriously rebellious.[510] Politically marginalized and discriminated against, and adhering to forms of religiosity which Mayaram tagged as "liminal" in her seminal study on the TJ, these rural communities became a natural target for communalist activists among Hindus and Muslims alike, aiming at pulling them to either side.[511] In order to succeed in this quite merciless competition, Muḥammad Ilyās resolved that the ground needed first to be prepared in these communities even for *madrasah* education. Subsequently, he stripped "Deobandiyyat" of its strong tradition in Hanafi jurisprudence and shifted the focus more onto a confined and simplified set of regular practices.[512] This comprised a strict adherence to the ritualistic duties to affirm the Islamic creed (*shahādah*) and perform the obligatory prayer (*namāz*), complemented by the combined practice of the constant recollection of God (*ẕikr*) with the acquisition of knowledge (*ʿilm*), all of which should feed into the personal disposition of deference to fellow Muslims (*ikrām-i muslim*) and sincerity of intention (*ikhlāṣ-i niyyat*).

Finally, once one has realized all of those basic requirements for oneself, one is obliged to actively propagate them to others (*tablīgh*). Eventually, all these components were tied together in the famous "Six Matters" (*Chh̠ah Bātēṇ*) of the TJ, publicly proclaimed by Muḥammad Ilyās to a congregation of leading Mevatī community representatives on 2 August 1934.[513] The benchmark for what, in fact, constitutes an interesting blend of exoteric and Sufi practices was, once more, the precedent established by the Prophet and his Companions: respective collections of *ḥadīth* and stories about the life and conduct of the

509 For an authoritative account, see Mayaram (1997), esp. 44–9.
510 See Mayaram (2003), 74–176.
511 See Mayaram (1997), 64–71.
512 See Muḥammad Ilyās in Nadvī (1991), 136–44 (six letters to TJ activists in Mēvat, all dated around 1938).
513 See Bulandshahrī (1992).

Prophet and his *ṣaḥāba*, which, however, were deliberately not subjected to rigorous *isnād* criticism,[514] formed the overwhelming majority of the literary canon of the TJ.[515] Distinct appearance and dress in public, modelled once more on the Prophetic example, played an important role as a communal identifier and was to distinguish "proper" Muslims, that is, the adherents of the TJ, from those whose religious practice they considered wrongfully entrenched in local customs of often dubious origin.[516] Similarly, especially the tribal communities in the Pashtun and Baluch Borderlands were seen as religiously not firm enough by TJ standards, which is why, in February 1945, the then-*amīr* of the TJ, Muḥammad Yūsuf Kāndhalavī, decreed an expansion of the missionary work of the movement from Punjab into that region, starting with a large public congregation in Peshawar in early March 1945.[517] However, the TJ did not succeed in growing firm roots in the area until after the tragic events around Partition and the establishment of Pakistan.

It was agreed at the 1953 general *ijtimāʿ* of the Pakistani TJ in Sakkhar, Sindh, to set up seven permanent TJ centres in various Pakistani cities, one of them being Peshawar. All of these new foundations, however, were answerable to the new Pakistani headquarters at Raʾēvinḍ, some thirty miles south of Lahore.[518] The efforts of the TJ in the Pashtun Borderland intensified in 1957: the centre at Kohat was inaugurated in that year, and the first delegation travelled to Afghanistan to extend the missionary work of TJ to the neighbouring country.[519] The fact that none of the ten members of that delegation was of Pashtun ethnicity, or indeed any of the other ethnicities prevalent in Afghanistan, was remarkable: sermons were, therefore, delivered exclusively in Arabic. While this somewhat conveys the elitist aspirations of an ostensibly rather subaltern movement-cum-organization, which could easily alienate them from their Afghan audiences, their stay was, in fact, facilitated by the Faẕl-i Rabbī mentioned above as well as former students of Madanī from those lands. Moreover, Madanī, having meanwhile risen to the

514 See, for example, Ṭālib al-Raḥmān (1995), 6 and 19–53. See also the allusion to criticism by other scholars of *ḥadīth*, presumably of *Ahl-i Ḥadīs̱* provenance, in, for example, Metcalf (1993), 600 n.15; Masud (2000), 103.

515 In this canon belong prominently the *Faẓāʾil-i Aʿmāl* (1966–7), compiled by Muḥammad Zakariyyā Kāndhalavī (d. 1402/1982) and following the sequence of the "Six Matters", as well as the multivolume *Ḥayāt al-Ṣaḥābah* (1959) by Muḥammad Ilyās' son and successor as *amīr* of the TJ, Muḥammad Yūsuf Kāndhalavī (d. 1384/1965).

516 See Mayaram (1997), 154f.

517 See Ḥasanī (1420/1999), 246–9. Apparently, already in early 1944, that is still during Muḥammad Ilyās' lifetime, a small group of TJ activists existed in Peshawar, see Haq (1972), 136f. and 162. The first contact with Afghanistan was also established during this time, through the acquaintance of a TJ activist with a Mujaddidī pedigree from Sindh with the "Nūr al-Mashāʾikh" Faẕl-i ʿUmar Mujaddidī: see Haq (1972), 135.

518 See Ḥasanī (1420/1999), 374–7.

519 See ibid., 390 and 488–90. Places visited in Afghanistan were Kabul, Ghazni and Kandahar.

position of the principal of the *Dār al-ʿUlūm* in Deoband, supported the sojourn of the TJ delegation by bestowing it with a favourable letter of introduction.[520] While not an active part of the TJ himself, the rector was, nonetheless, highly sympathetic to it,[521] which, in turn, reflects once again the grassroots approach to religious reformulation already strongly advocated by the Shaykh al-Hind. It was this inclination which the latter also passed on to his own students and adepts, among whom we find ʿAbd al-Ḥaqq of Akōṛah Khaṫṫak. Moreover, Madanī, as the principal of the motherhouse at Deoband since 1933, needed to ensure the maintenance of a common direction in all Deobandi establishments, a matter that was becoming especially virulent after Partition. Subsequently, ʿAbd al-Ḥaqq seemingly received regular missives from Deoband, in one of which a meeting between ʿAbd al-Ḥaqq and Muḥammad Ilyās was explicitly referred to, presumably at Akōṛah Khaṫṫak, where ʿAbd al-Ḥaqq was running his first seminary, called *Anjuman-i Taʿlīm al-Qurʾān*.[522]

In the years to follow, ʿAbd al-Ḥaqq maintained friendly relationships with all three leaders of the TJ in Pakistan: Muḥammad Shafīʿ Qurayshī (d. 1391/1971), Ḥājjī Muḥammad Bashīr (d. 1413/1992) and Muḥammad ʿAbd al-Vahhāb (b. 1340/1922), besides leading TJ activists from the Pashtun Borderland, such as ʿAbd al-Ḥafīẓ Dīravī, a teacher at the *Maẓāhir al-ʿUlūm* in Sahāranpūr and one of the closest disciples of its founder, Muḥammad Zakariyyā Kāndhalavī.[523] ʿAbd al-Ḥaqq seems to have developed a very close personal relationship with the latter, starting in the early 1960s.[524]

Yet, with the dramatic geopolitical developments that thrust Afghanistan and, at least by implication, the wider Pashtun Borderland into the limelight from late 1979 onwards, the relationship between the TJ and the scholars and students of the *Ḥaqqāniyyah* seems to have seriously deteriorated. After all, in none of Muḥammad Zakariyyā's letters to ʿAbd al-Ḥaqq from that time did he refer to the difficult situation at Akōṛah Khaṫṫak due to the Soviet invasion of Afghanistan and the resulting mass migration of Afghans into the Pakistani side of the Pashtun Borderland, which strongly suggests that the leading TJ

520 The letter is reproduced in ibid., 489f. In it, Madanī emphasized the non-political objectives of the TJ, and stated that 'some of our close friends [*hamārē chand aḥbāb*] [...] perform only religious services and fulfil the preaching obligations [*khidmāt-i dīniyyah awr farāʾiẓ-i tablīghiyyah*], with the goal of refreshing the memory of the Muslims of Afghanistan of what common Muslims may have forgotten'.

521 This closeness is underlined by the fact that it was Muḥammad Zakariyyā Kāndhalavī, of the TJ cadre training ground *Maẓāhir al-ʿUlūm* in Sahāranpūr, who led the funeral prayer at Madanī's burial on 22 November 1957 in Deoband: see Riẕvī (1413–4/1992–3), II: 84.

522 See Samīʿ al-Ḥaqq (2011a), 179 (letter no. 9, dated 26 March [1939]). On ʿAbd al-Ḥaqq's educational efforts prior to the establishment of the *Ḥaqqāniyyah*, see Akōṛavī (1422/2002), I: 86. See also Section 4.3.4.

523 See Samīʿ al-Ḥaqq (2011a), 144, 208, 284, 357f. and 493–9.

524 See ibid., 207–15.

scholar was not really concerned with matters of such a mundane nature. Subsequently, the correspondence dried up in August 1981 and was never again resumed before Muḥammad Zakariyyā's demise some nine months later.[525] Meanwhile, the official business of the *Ḥaqqāniyyah* was increasingly overseen by ʿAbd al-Ḥaqq's ambitious son, Samīʿ al-Ḥaqq, who took over the rectorate of the institution after the death of his father in 1988.

Under him, the significance of the TJ in and for the *Ḥaqqāniyyah* appears to have largely evaporated.[526] Instead, a different force came to the surface, against the dangerous impact of which Ḥusayn Aḥmad Madanī had already warned his former student and *murīd* ʿAbd al-Ḥaqq in 1957: "Islamism".[527] Yet, what Madanī had obviously been less concerned with, or aware of, is that there happened to be developments within "Frontier Deobandiyyat" already during his lifetime which facilitated a distinct entrance point for Islamist ideas and concepts into the still strongly Deobandi-dominated religious landscape of the Pashtun Borderland. In addition, this particular socio-cultural and geopolitical setting also provided a conducive environment for other perhaps rather unusual hybridities, with which we will be increasingly confronted in the following chapters.[528]

***

Now we have completed our survey of the socio-political context which developed over a period of roughly three centuries, up to the pivotal moment when Soviet troops crossed the Āmū Daryā river on Christmas Eve 1979 and, thus, caused the Pashtun Borderland to come dramatically into the focus of global awareness. In fact, this event, much more even than the inseparably related coup d'état of the *People's Democratic Party of Afghanistan* (PDPA) of 27 April 1978 – euphemistically called the "S̲awr Revolution" – altered the political, and subsequently also religious, dynamics in the Borderland

525 See ibid., 213–15 (letters nos. 14–19).

526 This is inferred from the fact that none of the letters published in the six volumes of Samīʿ al-Ḥaqq (2011b) are to or from any distinct member of the TJ.

527 See Samīʿ al-Ḥaqq (2011a), 177f. (letter no. 7, dated 3 Dhī 'l-ḥijjah 1376 / 28 June 1957). In this letter, Madanī informed ʿAbd al-Ḥaqq of the proclivities of former *Ḥaqqāniyyah* graduate Muḥammad Yūsuf, then a teacher at the girls' *Madrasah-yi Amīniyyah* in Delhi, towards the thinking of Sayyid Abū 'l-Aʿlá Mawdūdī, of which Madanī emphatically disapproved.

528 This shall serve us as yet another reminder of the fact that clear-cut identities along ideational lines, as well as coherent biographies, are, in reality, highly illusory and can, therefore, serve solely heuristic purposes. Mere affiliation with the TJ, for example, by no means rules out other and seemingly contradictory religious and political affinities, also including much more militant ones, as we shall see, for example, in the case of Abū Yazīd ʿAbd al-Qāhir al-Khurāsānī, a native of Kunar, who, despite his expressed sympathies for the TJ, serves currently as one of the religious authorities of the IS in the Pashtun Borderland: see, for example, al-Khurāsānī (1433h; 1435h). See also Section 4.5.5.

irreversibly. Indeed, the bloody takeover of power by communist cadres served as a combustive agent for the ultimate triumph of Islamism, beyond the confines of the urban contexts in which it was conceived as a distinctly Islamic response to the various other political ideologies of the day. Eventually, it would also add a distinct conceptual edge to all other socio-religious currents prevalent in the region which could claim older and more firmly established legacies there, and this is what we shall now be looking at in greater depth.

4

Chief Trajectories of Militant Religious Activism in the Pashtun Borderland: Acceleration in the Twentieth and Twenty-First Centuries

Religious discourse in a specific environment, such as the Pashtun Borderland, was decidedly shaped by highly localized, traditional Islamic articulations, while ideational cross-pollination with more universalist ones appears to have historically been rather limited, especially among the subaltern strata of society. The most dominant expressions belong, first and foremost, to a spectrum of Sufi Islam that ranged from the ecstatic kind of the mendicant dervish to the sober variety epitomized in the Naqshbandiyyah-Mujaddidiyyah. During the first decades of the twentieth century, as we have seen, the latter especially was widely absorbed into diverse local manifestations of "Frontier Deobandiyyat", which turned this particular Islamic response to the challenges of an aggressively expanding global modernity into the one that, despite its origins outside the region, had been establishing itself across the Pashtun Borderland much more successfully than any of its various competitors.

A major opponent, despite the temporary pragmatic alliances that have been discussed above, was certainly the *Ahl-i Ḥadīs̱*, particularly because each *maslak* claimed for itself the true heritage of the *Ṭarīqah-yi Muḥammadiyyah*, although with quite different emphases. The essence of its enlarged forebear for many of the leading adherents to "Deobandiyyat" in the Pashtun Borderland was apparently its socio-political grassroots activism that was born out of a deep and unreserved submission to God and Prophetic piety that originates therein. It was these spiritual roots of the activisms both of the *Ṭarīqah-yi Muḥammadiyyah* and of the Deobandi circles around the Shaykh al-Hind and his regional epigones that coalesced in the Naqshbandiyyah-Mujaddidiyyah; the decidedly anti-elitist approach of the proponents of "Frontier Deobandiyyat" was, moreover, highly conducive to developing a more patient and charitable attitude towards local norms, beliefs and practices, even if they were seen as generally objectionable from a purely Islamic legal perspective.

However, the physical proximity of Deobandis and *Ahl-i Ḥadīs̱* in the region and the many intersections whenever Borderland pragmatics required them provided a fertile ground for eventually less confrontational encounters on core doctrinal matters that, in fact, serve as clear-cut demarcations of the one *maslak* from the other. It was thus only a question of time before a faction of adherents to "Frontier Deobandiyyat" would boost its sense of heritage from the *Ṭarīqah-yi Muḥammadiyyah* by receiving hermeneutical inspiration from the *Ahl-i Ḥadīs̱* and, subsequently, loosen its ties with the theological and legal underpinnings of this *maslak* and, thus giving rise to a further distinct religious current in the Borderland, namely "Salafi Islam".

4.1 Pashtun Salafi Islam

It was the *Ahl-i Ḥadīs̱* who took the hermeneutical programme of the "Salafi reduction"[1] of the *Ṭarīqah-yi Muḥammadiyyah* to a new and, in their view, purified level across the entire Indian subcontinent. Their emphasis on the Qur'an and the Prophetic Sunna as the sole reference points for all matters of belief (*ʿaqīda*) and religious practice (*manhaj*) went hand in hand with a theologically sustained deep suspicion of the exegetical traditions, prominently including all four canonical *madhāhib fiqhiyya*, that had developed over almost one and a half millennia.[2] As a consequence, a new surge in the critical evaluation of Prophetic *aḥādīth* emerged, alongside a corresponding jurisprudence that firmly rejected any kind of emulation of historically generated scholarly authority (*taqlīd*).

The ultimate goal of the "Salafi reduction" is the purification of religious belief and practice from later "fabrications" (*bidaʿ*), in other words, their readjustment to those of the formative period of Islam, represented in their most authentic form by the Prophet Muḥammad himself and handed down to posterity by the so-called "pious elders" (*al-salaf al-ṣāliḥ*). Who exactly they comprised, however, has been subject to serious debate within Salafi circles from the very early days on, and is again very dependent on a careful re-evaluation of the quality of the Prophet's Companions and usually the first two generations following them, rooted in the widely accepted Prophetic saying: 'The best people are those of my age [*qarnī*], then those who come after them, and then those who come after them. Then, after them, there will be folk whose

[1] See Hartung (2020), 178–83.

[2] The theological rationale consists of the fact that, being part of God's creation, all human beings are inherently fallible, which makes any contemporary exegetical effort as valid as those of the past. Moreover, the importance of what would eventually be known especially, although certainly not exclusively, in Salafi circles as *fiqh al-wāqiʿ*, translatable only awkwardly as "the legally constitutive appreciation of (ever-changing) actuality", renders many earlier exegeses insignificant, especially if they do not provide any opportunity to relate the historical circumstances to the prevalent ones by analogy (*qiyās*). For more on this hermeneutical principle and its role in the Pashtun Borderland from the early 1990s onwards, see Section 4.5.3.

testimony [*shahādatuhum*] precedes their belief [*īmānahum*], and whose faith precedes their testimony.'[3]

The closing of ranks between those inspired by the "Salafi reduction" of the *Ṭarīqah-yi Muḥammadiyyah* and the *Ahl-i Ḥadīs̱* in the Pashtun Borderland, already alluded to above, was initiated from within the nexus of early "Frontier Deobandiyyat" and Naqshbandiyyah-Mujaddidiyyah at around the same time that ʿAbd al-Ḥaqq Akōṛavī established the *Dār al-ʿUlūm* at his native Akōṛah Khaṫṫak, and thus evolved in a very particular religious environment that appears quite at odds with those parts of the Middle East and North Africa (MENA) region in which what will be called here "Salafi Islam" originated.[4]

4.1.1 *The Nucleus of Indigenous Salafi Islam: The Legacy of the* Ṭarīqah-yi Muḥammadiyyah

As indicated above, the hermeneutical programme of the *Ṭarīqah-yi Muḥammadiyyah* movement was, after 1831, kept somewhat alive across the upland regions of the Pashtun Borderland at the various colonies at Sitħānah, Amb and Panjtār on the western banks of the Indus river,[5] as well as initially in neighbouring Swat, to which the remnants of the movement – the nucleus of the later *Jamāʿat-i Mujāhidīn* – relocated in the aftermath of their ultimate defeat at the Battle of Balakot. Even a century later, however, these early colonies, as well as the later ones at Asmast and Chamarkand, which were serving as strategically convenient bases for the pragmatic anti-colonial alliances of Deobandis, *Ahl-i Ḥadīs̱* and the *Jamāʿat-i Mujāhidīn*,[6] remained quite aloof from regional specifics, despite the fact that they were clearly situated on tribal land and thus required the approval of, or at least toleration by, the *məshərān* of the respective communities. That many of them did extend such acquiescence was most certainly not out of sympathies for the religious views and the way in which they were enacted within the colonies, but, once again, was informed more by typical Borderland pragmatics. Leaders of various tribes and clans utilized the military power of the *mujāhidīn* colonists for their respective ends, be it to decide intratribal disputes in their own favour, or to

[3] See *Ṣaḥīḥ al-Bukhārī*, k. al-riqāq, b. mā yuḥdharu min zahrati 'l-dunyā wa'l-tanāfusi fīhā, no. 5 (ḥadīth 6505). For the contemporary Salafi controversy over who in fact constitutes the *salaf ṣāliḥ*, see Nedza (2014), 96–100.

[4] In accord with recent conceptual (re)considerations, "Salafi Islam" and "Salafism" are kept heuristically distinct in the present work, while, at the same time, their underlying commonalities should be kept in mind. For an elaborate justification of this analytical terminology, including a breakdown of the academic debate so far, see Bruckmayr and Hartung (2020), 145–59.

[5] See Vazīr Khān (1428/2007), I 196; Mihr (2008), IV: 153–9 (this passage is based on a section of the *Vaqāʾiʿ-i Aḥmadī* that was not available at the time of writing), 342f., 380–3 385f. and 402.

[6] See Section 3.3.1.

employ them as *laxkar* for raids on trading caravans or into Sikh- and later British-held territories.[7] As a result of these raids, certain tribal communities became targets of British punitive expeditions themselves, thus the temporary pragmatic alliances with the *mujāhidīn* as a significant military factor in the region became further reinforced.[8] The religious persuasion of these militiamen, however, would still not have any notable bearing on these alliances and, thus, the gradually evolving Salafi orientation of the *Jamāʿat-i Mujāhidīn* remained exclusive.

An important reason for this indifference to the actual conditions on the ground was certainly that, for the first years after Balakot, the ideational centre of the *Ṭarīqah-yi Muḥammadiyyah* became distant Patna, the native place of Sayyid Aḥmad's two successors, Vilāyat and ʿInāyat ʿAlī ʿAẓīmābādī. While both were trying to revive the *Ṭarīqah-yi Muḥammadiyyah* as a unified movement with a transregional agenda,[9] their analysis of the causes of the movement's failure at Balakot did not include any self-critical assessment of their rather harsh elitist attitude towards the local population in the Pashtun Borderland. Ultimately, they still aspired to the establishment of a distinct polity based exclusively on their own rigid interpretation of Islam, for which the regional cultural set-up remained of subordinate importance at best.

Because of this sustained indifference to regional cultural specifics, the fortified colonies in the Pashtun Borderland under their supreme command remained strategically most convenient hideouts, which, in the following years, attracted new contingents of mainly subaltern Muslims from the plains of northern India, who were largely indifferent to the cultural environment in which they were now located. Apparently, the numbers of the new arrivals were quite substantial: the colony at Sitȟānah, for instance, was inhabited by a steady number of around 600 people by the late nineteenth century, most of them male and from outside the Pashtun Borderland.[10]

The colonists continued to follow their own religiously inspired agenda inside their outposts at Sitȟānah, Panjtār and Amb, supplemented by serious military training, although generally within the limits of what was acceptable for the local tribes whose hospitality they enjoyed. The first signs of an opening-up occurred only when their colony at Chamarkand evolved as a

[7] The most comprehensive discussion to date is Khattak (2016), esp. 219–36. Also see Khalil (2000), 39–42. Soon, however, the colonists of the *Jamāʿat-i Mujāhidīn* also embarked occasionally on self-motivated raids on Sikh political representatives and Hindu merchants, something that has prompted some contemporaneous observers and later authors to see a distinct "class dimension" in the whole enterprise. This is based on a colonial document from September 1863: see Hopkins and Marsden (2011), 78.

[8] See, for example, Paget (1907), I: 82–320; Mihr (2008), IV: 350–7 and 573–84.

[9] See Ahmad (1994), 47f., 118–20 and 131–61.

[10] See Hopkins and Marsden (2011), 78, 89f. and 92.

joint operational base for the anti-colonial activities discussed above from around the time of World War I and the temporary closing of ranks between the proponents of "Frontier Deobandiyyat" and the *Ahl-i Ḥadīs̱*.

Regarding the successive confluence of the religious ideas of the *Ṭarīqah-yi Muḥammadiyyah* with that of the *Ahl-i Ḥadīs̱* in the Borderland, greatly propelled by scholars such as ʿAbd al-ʿAzīz Raḥīmābādī, who has already been mentioned, the still quite millenarian activism of the former would increasingly be sustained through the sound hermeneutical programme of the *Ahl-i Ḥadīs̱*. This tied the "proto-Salafi reduction" of Sayyid Aḥmad and Shāh Ismāʿīl, as well as the ʿAẓīmābādī brothers, to various fields of higher Islamic learning propelled by the *Ahl-i Ḥadīs̱*, foremost among which were the critical study of *ḥadīth* and an Islamic jurisprudence liberated from the restrictions posed by the canonical Islamic legal traditions. In this regard, the *Ahl-i Ḥadīs̱* also introduced their new acolytes in the Borderland to the fundamental controversy with the learned representatives of "Deobandiyyat", pivoting on matters of legal hermeneutics (*uṣūl al-fiqh*) and the resulting differences in ritual practice.[11] While it has been suggested that the *Ahl-i Ḥadīs̱* position on the latter had already been propagated among Pashtuns by the leaders of the *Ṭarīqah-yi Muḥammadiyyah*,[12] we may assume that – provided this had indeed been the case – they had not engaged much in explaining to their Pashtun hosts the complex legal baggage that is behind the issue. In fact, this would change only gradually with the influx of the *Ahl-i Ḥadīs̱* into the Pashtun Borderland.

After the pragmatic temporary alliance of the various *Jamāʿāt-i Mujāhidīn* and the Deobandis in the Pashtun Borderland for concerted anti-imperialist activities had ended, one of the main objectives of the *Ahl-i Ḥadīs̱* was to ensure that these relationships were fully severed, in order to prevent any further advance of the Hanafi "Deobandiyyat" in the region and strengthen the Salafi approach and, subsequently, its own position there instead. Still, given the repeatedly mentioned absolute dominance of "Frontier Deobandiyyat", it might not come as too much of a surprise that the next stage in the evolution of a Pashtun Salafi Islam emerged from within the folds of "Deobandiyyat".

[11] As a reminder: the core issues of contestation were the firm rejection of any form of emulation of earlier authorities (*taqlīd*) in exegetical pursuit, which results in the radical repudiation of all the canonical *madhāhib fiqhiyya*, and, resulting from their distinct textual hermeneutics, the performance of the ritual prayer, epitomized in the diametrical position regarding *rafʿ al-yadayn* and *āmīn bi'l-jahr*: see Riexinger (2004), 232–8; Preckel (2005), 340–74.

[12] See Preckel (2005), 354. Shāh Ismāʿīl's treatise on the *rafʿ al-yadayn* (al-Dihlawī [1256h]) is circumstantial evidence, as well as the fact that the Hanafi position on the matter had already been rejected in favour of the Shafiʿi one by his grandfather Shāh Valiyallāh: see al-Dihlawī (1426/2005), II: 12f. and 16f.

4.1.2 *Deoband Meets* Ahl-i Ḥadīs̱*: The Dār al-Qur'ān in Panjpir, Swabi*

The remnants of the *Ṭarīqah-yi Muḥammadiyyah* had managed to establish themselves quite firmly in the region by the turn to the twentieth century, using to this end a combination of keeping a low profile and political manoeuvring, and by eventually making at least some concessions to the locally established norms, values and customs that the leaders of the movement in the first decades of the nineteenth century had been unwilling to make. Meanwhile, however, the impact of the *Ahl-i Ḥadīs̱* as a distinctly scholarly movement in the Pashtun Borderland had still been rather marginal, so that the expansion of "Deobandiyyat" here was not met by any serious resistance from its religious opposition.

Around the time that ʿAbd al-Ḥaqq Akōṛavī established the *Dār al-ʿUlūm* at his native Akōṛah Khaṫṫak, however, another Deoband-affiliated institution had been established in the small town of Panjpir in the Swabi Division of the Mardan District of what was then the NWFP,[13] spearheaded by local *ʿālim* Muḥammad Ṭāhir. The locality of Panjpir had, just like Akōṛah Khaṫṫak, already been penetrated by the *Ṭarīqah-yi Muḥammadiyyah* in the early nineteenth century,[14] thus providing a fertile ground for certain religious persuasions to prevail. Muḥammad Ṭāhir was only a few years younger than ʿAbd al-Ḥaqq Akōṛavī, and appears to have belonged to a new generation of Deobandis that no longer obtained their entire academic pedigree from the *Dār al-ʿUlūm* in Deoband, but benefited from the ever-evolving network of affiliated institutions closer to home. Thus, the various hagiographical materials indicate – with different emphases, depending on their concrete provenance – that Muḥammad Ṭāhir was initially introduced to "Deobandiyyat" by the Ḥājjī Ṣāḥib of Turangzay himself, before joining several *madāris* in the far west of the Punjab, where he began to study under a number of transregionally prominent Deobandi *ʿulamā'*. Finally, however, he still enrolled at the motherhouse in Deoband itself.[15]

While celebrities such as Ḥusayn Aḥmad Madanī figured among his teachers in the *ʿulūm al-ḥadīth*, what was perhaps the most formative influence came from Ḥusayn ʿAlī Alvānī (d. 1363/1944), who, like the Shaykh al-Hind, had been an early student of Rashīd Aḥmad Gangōhī and, moreover, of Muḥammad Maẓhar Nānawtavī (d. 1302/1885), founder of the TJ cadre factory *Maẓāhir al-ʿUlūm* in North Indian Sahāranpūr. Remarkably, neither Alvānī nor Nānawtavī have been granted an entry into the various official Deobandi hagiographies, somewhat suggesting that their respective contributions did not fit the canonical understanding of "Deobandiyyat" as a distinct

13 For a survey of this locality, see Dās (1878), 250f.

14 See Sayyid Aḥmad (1395/1975), 107 (21a); Nadvī (1406/1986), II: 233f.

15 See Panjpīrī (n.d.), 18–44; Bukhārī (1419/1999), 467; Ilyās (2012), 7f. and 77–94.

and well-defined learned tradition (*maslak*), something that was vigorously undertaken by the leadership of the *Dār al-ʿUlūm* of Deoband from the second half of the twentieth century onwards.[16] While the same certainly holds true for the Ḥājjī Ṣāḥib of Turangzay, the cases of Nānawtavī and Alvānī differ in one crucial respect: both scholars made themselves a name in the field of Qur'anic hermeneutics.

Muḥammad Maẓhar Nānawtavī obtained his knowledge in that field from Muḥammad Qāsim Nānawtavī,[17] and it was in this field that he again taught Ḥusayn ʿAlī Alvānī, who, in turn, was responsible for training Muḥammad Ṭāhir of Panjpir therein. Yet Alvānī, who later hagiographers attest to have 'raised the voice for the unalloyed oneness of God [*tawḥīd-i khāliṣ*] like no other at that time',[18] appears to have somewhat departed from the exegetical principles upheld by Nānawtavī, thus causing the latter to ultimately distance himself from his former student. The bone of contention appears to have been Alvānī's seminal *Bulghat al-Ḥayrān fī Rabṭ Āyāt al-Qurʾān*,[19] an attempt at a hermetic commentary of the Qur'an which, in fact, is regarded as a defining feature of the Salafi approach to Qur'anic exegesis.[20] Eventually, Muḥammad Ṭāhir would produce his own work on the matter, almost emulating the programmatic part of the title of Alvānī's earlier work when he chose to name it *Simṭ al-Durar fī Rabṭ al-Āyāt wa'l-Suwar*. Acknowledging that leading *Ahl-i Ḥadīs̱*, here prominently S̱anāʾallāh Amritsarī, followed similar hermetic principles in their *tafāsīr*,[21] we can already sense a departure from the folds of "Deobandiyyat" and a turn towards the hermeneutics of the *Ahl-i Ḥadīs̱* and other Salafis. Yet, when Muḥammad Ṭāhir, his disciples and successors were explicitly expelled from the Deobandi *maslak* by a *fatwa* of Mufti ʿAṭāʾ al-Raḥmān of the *Jāmiʿah Binōriyyah* in Karachi (d. 1433/2012) as late as in 2012,[22] it seems to have come as somewhat of a surprise to everyone who had gathered at the *Dār al-Qurʾān* in Panjpir since its establishment in 1940.

After all, had Muḥammad Ṭāhir not also studied with ʿUbaydallāh Sindhī when they met in 1938 during the *ḥajj* of the former, while Sindhī himself spent this period of his life in exile in the Ḥaramayn?[23] Did he not follow the

16 See Chaudri (2019), 5f. and 200–30. Bukhārī (1419/1999), 467, mentions only Ḥusayn ʿAlī as a teacher of Muḥammad Ṭāhir (although here strangely as a teacher in the study of *ḥadīth*), who, in contrast, was granted a dedicated entry in the list of canonical "elders" (*akābirīn* [sic]) of the Deobandi *maslak*.

17 See al-Ḥasanī (1412–13/1991–3), VIII: 480.

18 Nadvī (1416/1995), 388. See also Ghumman (2014), 85f.

19 See Kāndhalavī (1428/2007), 105f.

20 See Rohman (2012), 201–6. The principles of hermetic *tafsīr* had already been laid out by Ibn Taymiyya (1392/1972), 93–102, who, after all, constitutes a cornerstone of the Salafi pantheon of reference authors.

21 See Riexinger (2004), 337f.

22 See ʿAṭāʾ al-Raḥmān (1434/2012; 1435/2013). See also Hartung (2020), 190–4.

23 See Panjpīrī (n.d.), 46–65; Bukhārī (1419/1999), 467.

exegetical principles of Shāh Valiyallāh Dihlavī,[24] whom ʿUbaydallāh substantially helped to firmly enshrine the image of the "Deoband project" as the true continuator of the endeavours to Islamic reformulation of Shāh Valiyallāh Dihlavī and his successors – an image that has since then been perpetuated in Deobandi historiography?[25] Last but not least, had not, twenty-five years earlier, the Deobandi historiographer Ḥāfiẓ Muḥammad Akbar Shāh Bukhārī from Rawalpindi honoured Muḥammad Ṭāhir in his obituary in the monthly *Taʿlīm al-Qurʾān* as a Deobandi scholar of fame?[26]

Perhaps an even closer look at Muḥammad Ṭāhir's Qur'anic hermeneutics and its implications regarding authority is conducive for dissolving this apparent puzzlement, which, however, requires an investigation of the exegetical principles of ʿUbaydallāh Sindhī beforehand.

Unsurprisingly, the guiding star for the latter remained Shāh Valiyallāh throughout, expressed in the fact that ʿUbaydallāh followed the exegetical principles laid down by the eighteenth-century celebrity unconditionally in his rather concise Persian *Fawz al-Kabīr*, supplemented with insights from his seminal *Ḥujjat Allāh al-Bāligha.*[27] The *Fawz al-Kabīr*, in turn, has apparently become the ultimate yardstick for most exegetical efforts on the Qur'an by Indo-Muslim scholars striving for Islamic reformulation since then; in fact, the doyen of the early *Ahl-i Ḥadīs̱*, Ṣiddīq Ḥasan Khān, modelled his own *Iksīr fī Uṣūl al-Tafsīr* closely on Shāh Valiyallāh's earlier work.[28]

The compatibility of Shāh Valiyallāh's deliberations on the matter with that of the *Ahl-i Ḥadīs̱* in its formative phase is clearly indicated by his stress on the absolute preference of exegesis in correlation with the sayings of the Prophet and his Companions (*tafsīr bi'l-maʾthūr*, or *tafsīr bi'l-riwāya*) against any such endeavours based on human rational consideration (*tafsīr bi'l-raʾy*, or *tafsīr bi'l-dirāya*), complete with some leaning even towards a hermetic interpretation as had already been advocated by Ibn Taymiyya and his epigones.[29] Shāh Valiyallāh stipulated

[24] ʿUbaydallāh's own exegetical efforts were assembled in around 1933 as *Maqām al-Maḥmūd* by his disciple ʿAbdallāh Lighārī (d. 1378/1958): see Sindhī (2009), 15f.

[25] See prominently Riẓvī (1413–4/1992–3), I: 11–23 and 86–109. See also Chaudri (2019), 217–28. ʿUbaydallāh's two works on particular aspects of Shāh Valiyallāh's thought mentioned above (see Section 3.3.3, n.181), alongside his Urdu commentary on Shāh Valiyallāh's seminal *Ḥujjat Allāh al-Bāligha*, were also instrumental in this regard.

[26] See Bukhārī (1419/1999), 467f.

[27] See Sindhī (1977), for example, 24–6, 123, 170–2, 213, 238 and 457. Honesty demand to acknowledge that here an Urdu translation of the original Arabic text had been used. Still, this translation was authorized by the influential Tatar scholar Mūsá Jārullāh Bigiev (d. 1368/1949), who hosted ʿUbaydallāh for some time during the latter's sojourn in Moscow and assisted in developing the first draft of Sindhī's *Ilhām al-Raḥmān* (see ibid., 22).

[28] See Preckel (2005), 265.

[29] For a long time, and perhaps thanks to Calder (1993), the *Tafsīr al-Qurʾān al-ʿAẓīm* of Ibn Taymiyya's retainer ʿImād al-Dīn ibn Kathīr (d. 774/1373) was considered the prime representative of a *tafsīr bi'l-maʾthūr*. This hypothesis has been critically discussed, for

five core subject matters of the Qur'an, and emphasized that 'these fields of knowledge appear in the style of the early Arabs, not in the style of the moderns [*va bayān-i īn ʿulūm ba-ravish-i taqrīr-i ʿarab-i avval vāqiʿ shud na ba-ravish-i taqrīr-i mutaʾakhkhirān*]'.[30] This perspective has a firm impact on crucial matters pertinent to Qur'anic exegesis: the abrogation of earlier verses by later ones (*naskh*), the understanding of the "obscure verses" (*āyāt mutashābihāt*), even the contextual reasons for the revelation of Qur'anic content (*asbāb al-nuzūl*) and the congruity of the Qur'anic revelation with those that preceded it, alongside the trope of corruption of these earlier revelations by the communities to whom they were revealed.[31] Consequently, individual opinion would be justifiable only if either the Prophet or any of his Companions had not stipulated some interpretation of their own:[32] this is where the study of *ḥadīth* comes in as the inevitable tool for establishing both authenticity and authority of meaning. Without delving into the discussion himself, Shāh Valiyallāh seems to have followed the arguments of Ibn Taymiyya on the issue of disagreement (*ikhtilāf*) between those regarded as *salaf ṣāliḥ* in their interpretation, arguing that their disagreements were, in fact, still in correspondence (*tanawwuʿ*) with, not in opposition to, one another (*taḍāḍ*), which is why the later exegetes had to seriously engage in the assessment of the virtues of the *salaf*, in order to sustain their decision for the variation proposed by one *salaf* against their possible alternatives.[33]

ʿUbaydallāh, while adhering to the hermeneutical principles outlined by Shāh Valiyallāh, gave his own exegetical efforts a distinct interpretative twist: the five Qur'anic core themes identified by the latter were now supplemented with a strong leaning towards societal affairs and directives instructing how to realign societal affairs with the Qur'anic benchmark, sustained with quotes from Shāh Valiyallāh's relevant works.[34] The Qur'an, it seems, had been revealed to humankind to serve as the ultimate criterion for communal belonging, thus, as a distinguishing mark between "us" and "them", "us" being those 'aware of the Divine Domain [*ḥaẓīrat al-quds*]' vis-à-vis those 'who are negligent' of it.[35]

example, by Saleh (2010), 124 and 153; Pink (2011), 26f. and 39f. While the arguments of both are entirely convincing, the prominence of Ibn Kathīr's *tafsīr* in contemporary Salafi and Salafist circles suggests, nonetheless, that regarding it as paradigmatic for a *tafsīr bi'l-maʾthūr* is certainly widespread and, therefore, requires some further thought: see, for example, Lauzière (2016), 27, 101 and 141; Saleh (2020), 53f.

30 Dihlavī (1249h), I: 5.

31 See ibid., I: 38f., 46–54 and 69–86.

32 See ibid., I: 38–40 and 46f.

33 See Ibn Taymiyya (1392/1972), 38–93; compare Dihlavī (1396/1976), I: 50 (on the authority of the Prophet's cousin Ibn ʿAbbās, one of the first exegetes of the Qur'an, known especially for his elucidation of incomprehensible terms by drawing heavily on pre-Islamic Arab poetry).

34 See Sindhī (2009), 22–6; compare al-Dihlawī (1426/2005), I: 101; (1355/1936), I: 82f. Also see Panjpīrī (n.d.), 66–83.

35 Sindhī (2009), 52.

This, in fact, is a good example to illustrate the overlapping of the various ideational currents which are discussed here as if they existed independently from one another. ʿUbaydallāh's language here appears somewhat Islamist, strongly reminiscent of that of Sayyid Abū 'l-Aʿlá Mawdūdī, a mastermind of the Islamist ideology in general, which is not necessarily surprising. After all, Mawdūdī had for some time been a frequent visitor to the *Naẓārat-i Maʿārif-i Qurʾāniyyah*, which the Shaykh al-Hind had requested ʿUbaydallāh Sindhī to establish at Delhi's Fatḥpūrī mosque for the religious instruction of the educated urban laypeople, after ʿUbaydallāh had been forced out of Deoband by his opponents there.[36]

It seems as if ʿUbaydallāh's impact on Muḥammad Ṭāhir, besides emphasizing the hermeneutical principles of Shāh Valiyallāh, was prominent in translating the Qur'anic message into a socio-political programme, with which Muḥammad Ṭāhir, his associates and followers around the *Dār al-Qurʾān* at Panjpir eventually performed a turn to "Salafism". We shall, therefore, have to take up this thread again in the following section,[37] while, for the moment, remaining focused solely on Muḥammad Ṭāhir's Salafi Qur'anic hermeneutics and its implications for related fields of Islamic learning, especially the *ʿulūm al-ḥadīth* and its auxiliaries.

Indeed, Muḥammad Ṭāhir's hermeneutics appear to be informed, in addition to ʿUbaydallāh's, very much by the approach of Ḥusayn ʿAlī Alvānī, reinforced by the fact that it was the latter who initiated Muḥammad Ṭāhir into the Naqshbandiyyah-Mujaddidiyyah in November 1936 and, subsequently, made him study Aḥmad Sirhindī's *Maktūbāt* as well as his own Persian *Fuyūẓāt-i Ḥusaynī*.[38] The *silsila* which Muḥammad Ṭāhir would continue through his initiation by Alvanī did not include either of the two founding figures of the *Dār al-ʿUlūm* at Deoband, as one would have expected from a student of theirs.

Rather, and much to Ḥusayn Aḥmad Madanī's regret, Alvānī decided against taking the *bayʿa* from his Deobandi teacher Muḥammad Maẓhar Nānawtavī and chose instead his initiation into a Borderlands branch of the Naqshbandiyyah-Mujaddidiyyah, running through Khᵛājah Muḥammad ʿUs̱mān of Mūsázay near D.I. Khan (d. 1314/1897), who belonged to the Naqshbandi network around Ḥājjī Dōst Muḥammad Qandahārī (d. 1284/1868).[39] It was, in turn, under the tutelage of elders within these circles that Alvānī had developed his hermetic understanding of the Qur'an, eventually

36 See Minault (1982), 30; Nasr (1996), 18; Hartung (2013a), 19; (2016b), 355.

37 See Section 4.4.2.

38 See Panjpīrī (n.d.), 44; Ilyās (2012), 95. The rather concise *Fuyūẓāt-i Ḥusaynī* appears to be, first and foremost, a primer of Naqshbandiyyah-Mujaddidiyyah core tenets, emphatically on the relationship of master and adepts, including the breakdown of the eight different *salāsil* of which Ḥusayn ʿAlī himself was part, as well as a couple of *manāqibāt*: see al-Ḥanafī (1387h), 104–204.

39 See ʿAbd al-Ḥamīd Svātī in al-Ḥanafī (1387h), 14–20. On Muḥammad ʿUs̱mān and Dōst Muḥammad Qandahārī, see Buehler (1998), 152, 154f., 164–6, 174 and 254–7.

fleshed out in his *Bulghat al-Ḥayrān*,[40] while Muḥammad Ṭāhir appears to have laid down most of his own hermeneutical considerations in the 1950s.[41]

Muḥammad Ṭāhir's fixation on the Qur'an resulted from an unease with the strong reliance of the Islamic jurists on the chain of authority of their respective legal tradition that appears quite similar to that of the *Ahl-i Ḥadīṣ*: in his view, it is this blind dependence on any of the *madhāhib fiqhiyya* that has sustained the somewhat naïve popular acceptance of religious authority. This, in turn, has resulted in the attribution of exceptional and superhuman qualities to religious dignitaries in a manner that is not in any way sustainable from the word of God as revealed in the Qur'an. For Muḥammad Ṭāhir, this results ultimately in a variety of manifestations of the "association of any other entity with God" (*shirk*), which he understood, as most would, as an antonym to "Islam".[42]

Now, while we have encountered this theme already in the writings of the leaders of the *Ṭarīqah-yi Muḥammadiyyah*, Sayyid Aḥmad Barēlvī and Shāh Ismāʿīl Dihlavī, Muḥammad Ṭāhir took this discussion to a new level, one on which he joined hands firmly with other Salafi and Salafist Muslims elsewhere. For him, *shirk* would not solely be manifest in customs rooted in local tradition rather than Islamic normativity, or in religious rituals that have grown out of some Sufi traditions, such as the pious visitation of graves and the practice of praying there for intercession (*tawassul*), as had been the chief concern of Sayyid Aḥmad and Shāh Ismāʿīl. Instead, *shirk* for him was rooted in the general acceptance of any authority but, or besides, God, be it a spiritual or a political one.[43] Thus, in addition to the rejection of various ritual Sufi practices, Muḥammad Ṭāhir had also been highly critical of the millenarian element that had emerged strongly within the remnants of the *Ṭarīqah-yi Muḥammadiyyah* after the Battle of Balakot,[44] because, to him, this meant an unwarranted exaltation of Sayyid Aḥmad.[45]

40 See ʿAbd al-Ḥamīd Svātī in al-Ḥanafī (1387h), 20.

41 See Ilyās (2012), 192–208. Most of the twenty-seven works authored by Muḥammad Ṭāhir appear to be undated; the reprints do not bear the year of the first edition either, nor can it be ascertained that, upon completion, they were immediately published. Some crucial works, however, have been dated by Panjpīrī (n.d.) and Ilyās (2012) to the second half of the 1950s and early 1960s, in this way sustaining the hypothesis that all the hermeneutically relevant works were completed in and around those one and a half decades.

42 See Panjpīrī (1980b), 18–63.

43 See ibid., 21–34; compare Dihlavī (1998), 21–79.

44 Sayyid Aḥmad's status had been posthumously enhanced by declaring him to be not dead, but only physically absent, to reappear as "mahdī" at the end of time. See Gaborieau (2010), 217–70, whose assessment is based on later and increasingly popular literature produced by adherents to the movement, most prominently among them ʿAlī (1341h), 46–63 (*Arbaʿīn fī Mahdiyīn*; c. 1840).

45 See Panjpīrī (1980b), 60f.

Such a radical take on authority, which somewhat resembles the Islamist onslaught on it, as we shall see further below, had a fatal consequence: it would not only question the legitimacy of contemporary learned, spiritual or political authority, but was also suspicious of the widespread superexaltation of the *salaf ṣāliḥ* as well as, in its ultimate consequence, the Prophet Muḥammad. It was of vital importance for Muḥammad Ṭāhir to emphasize the humanity of the Prophet, rather than making him a focus of devotion, as is exceptionally widespread in the Pashtun Borderland and the mainly rural areas beyond.[46] The Qur'an offers plenty of authoritative references to emphasize the humanity of the Prophet and, thus, allow for his own fallibility, as well as for the acknowledgement of his limited knowledge vis-à-vis God, and one may assume that Muḥammad Ṭāhir, and his epigones with him, would, therefore, be eager to highlight them. The strategy they adopted, however, was different.

Challenging Learned Authority: Qur'anic Hermeneutics, Panjpir-Style

At the beginning stood, as indicated, an extensive and in-depth treatment of *shirk*, which drew its inspiration seemingly not so much from the earlier and less elaborate discussion of Sayyid Aḥmad Barēlvī and Shāh Ismāʿīl Dihlavī as from the core-Salafi reference authors Ibn Taymiyya and Ibn Qayyim al-Jawziyya, or even only from the Qur'anic text itself.[47] Muḥammad Ṭāhir and his associates, most prominently among them his son and heir, Muḥammad Ṭayyib Ṭāhirī (b. 1376/1957), and his former associate ʿAbd al-Salām Rustamī (d. 1436/2014), elaborate meticulously in their respective writings which aspect of the first part of the Islamic creed – the affirmation of God's oneness (*tawḥīd*) – is violated by which form of *shirk*. They were following here the generally accepted tripartite understanding of *tawḥīd* as *tawḥīd al-rubūbiyya*, that is, the affirmation of God's supremacy, divinity and creative powers, *tawḥīd al-ulūhiyya* (or *tawḥīd al-ʿibāda*), that is, the affirmation of God's oneness through worship, and *tawḥīd al-asmāʾ wa'l-ṣifāt*, that is, the affirmation of God's qualities as expressed in his numerous epithets.[48]

46 See Schimmel (1985), 35, 74 and 195–215; "Gohar" (1422/2001); Hartung (2020), 174f.

47 See Panjpīrī (1980b), 21–62. Core references here are Ibn Taymiyya (1424/2003) and al-Jawziyya (1432h), whereas al-Rustamī (1428h[a]), 9–60, derived all his arguments exclusively from the text of the Qur'an instead, sustained in only two instances by a paraphrased Prophetic *ḥadīth*.

48 See Panjpīrī (1433h), 17–31; al-Rustamī (1428h[a]), 9–13, 35–42 and 52–60. Traces of this tripartition can already be found, for example, in Ibn Taymiyya (1396/1976a); (1426/2005a), XVII: 60–80; al-Jawziyya (1423/2003), I: 48–60, 125–8 and III: 411–17; and it figures prominently in Wahhabi theological writings, see, for example, Ibn ʿAbd al-Wahhāb (1406/1986), 106f.; al-Najdī (1417/1996), for example I: 64–6 and 508f., II: 249–52 and 362f., III: 267f., XI: 360–2 and XII: 547; Ibn Bāz (1420h), I: 34–42; Ibn ʿUthaymīn (1407h), I: 17–23.

Violating any of these three forms of *tawḥīd* is mostly considered a form of "great association" (*shirk akbar*) and, therefore, results in the very serious pronouncement of excommunication (*takfīr*),[49] although the scholars of Panjpir did not initially argue this immediate causality. Instead, their focus shifted to an unlawful "innovation" in belief and religious practice (*bidʿa*), because, for Muḥammad Ṭāhir, it is its three varieties – in belief, utterance and act – that result inevitably in *shirk*.[50] Proceeding retrogressively, the scholar then investigated the roots of *bidaʿ*, identifying as many as twenty of them, which, in the end, are all related to the matter of interpretative authority.[51] At this point, Muḥammad Ṭāhir had already abolished *taqlīd shakhṣī* and, thus, broke with a cornerstone of Deobandi legal hermeneutics when he emphasized the important semantic distinction between "acknowledgement of authority" (*taqlīd*) and "conformity" (*ittibāʿ*), one that is of utmost importance for Salafi hermeneutics everywhere: that is, *Ittibāʿ* requires necessarily the exact knowledge of the textual proof (*dalāʾil*) provided by someone to sustain a judgement, as well as the way in which these are established; conformity with such a person's arguments has, therefore, to be based on its firm comprehension and justification by someone who aligns himself to this person. *Ittibāʿ*, however, for Muḥammad Ṭāhir, precludes an inference by analogy (*qiyās*), as all proof must necessarily correspond to the authoritative texts, if it is to be regarded as valid.[52]

Consequently, Muḥammad Ṭāhir always began his arguments with Qur'anic references, if possible, drew his own conclusions from them and only then listed statements of earlier authors on the subject at hand. His selection of reference authors indicates a sensitivity for the arguments presented, rather than paying much heed to whether they belonged to certain theological or legal traditions.[53]

This, in fact, already constitutes more of an *Ahl-i Ḥadīs̱* approach that breaks clear of the Deobandi emphasis on *taqlīd shakhṣī*. Perhaps this is an implicit reason why Hanafi authors are less referred to than others, prominently among them those who have been labelled "Neo-Hanbali" by the classical French

49 See Nedza (2020), 100; compare Ibn Bāz (1420h), I: 43f.

50 See Panjpīrī (1980a), 10–12.

51 Unsurprisingly, a core reference for Muḥammad Ṭāhir in this regard is the *K. al-Iʿtiṣām fī Ahl al-Bidaʿ wa'l-Ḍalālāt* of the medieval Maliki jurist Abū Isḥāq al-Shāṭibī (d. 790/1388), because it is widely regarded one of the most detailed classical treatments of the matter, see, for example, ibid., 14f., 32, 42, 44, 51f., 62, 70f., 103, 112, 128, 133, 136, 140, 144f. and 158f.; Panjpīrī (1980b), 186 and 189; (1427/2006), 21, 68 *et passim*.

52 Panjpīrī (1427/2006), 66–73; (1980b), 62 and 81–91. On *ittibāʿ* in Salafi hermeneutics, see Nedza (2020), 211, 215, 219 and 267f.

53 With this approach, even the otherwise highly controversial gnostic philosopher Muḥyī 'l-Dīn ibn ʿArabī (d. 638/1240), whose monistic ideas are rejected outright by Mujaddidi-Naqshbandis, appears a possibility for *ittibāʿ*: see Panjpīrī (1980b), 128 (here, Ibn ʿArabī's *tafsīr*, the *Aḥkām al-Qurʾān*, is referred to).

Orientalist Henri Laoust (d. 1983) and by many academics since: first and foremost, Ibn Taymiyya and his closest disciple Ibn Qayyim al-Jawziyya.[54] Both scholars of the Middle Period serve as chief representatives of a reassessment of the classification of the sources of Islamic law (*uṣūl al-fiqh*) so far accepted within the Hanbali *madhhab*, especially regarding the role of the human intellect in the process of deriving positive law.

It is, therefore, especially Ibn Taymiyya's refutation of the validity of the Aristotelian logic herein with which Muḥammad Ṭāhir conformed, a fact that ties well into his argument that 'analogous reasoning is [a form of] corruption [*al-qiyās al-fasād*]',[55] initially derived from Q12.77, 16.74 and 36.78. In what followed, Muḥammad Ṭāhir confirmed his own conclusions with those of prominently Ibn Taymiyya in his *Radd ʿalá 'l-Manṭiqiyīn* and Ibn al-Qayyim in his *Miftāḥ Dār al-Saʿāda*.[56] The Hanafi scholar closest to the hermeneutics of these "neo-Hanbali" ones is Shāh Valiyallāh Dihlavī, which made his works feasible reference points for Muḥammad Ṭāhir: interesting in this regard is the allusion to the *Fawz al-Kabīr* in the same breath as Ibn Taymiyya's *Muqaddima fī Uṣūl al-Tafsīr* and *Radd ʿalá 'l-Manṭiqiyīn*, in this manner indicating their hermeneutical similarities.[57] However, Muḥammad Ṭāhir's discussion did not remain entirely theoretical: on occasion, he referred to the cultural environment in which he himself was living, and analysed the wrongs he perceived,[58] identifying, as we may expect by now, a superstitious trust of the common people in the miraculous powers of saints as the main reason for the emergence of certain customs. This goes as far as taking oaths in the name of such a person instead of, as would be appropriate, in the name of God.

Significantly, however, this rejection of many practices associated with Sufi Islam did not make Muḥammad Ṭāhir condemn this variety of Islam wholesale, something that appears at first sight at odds with the tenets of Salafi Islam, at least insofar as some of the prominent academic literature on the relationship between these two intellectual currents is concerned.[59] Instead, what is

54 See Laoust (1962), 29. See also Lav (2012), 9 and 41–9; Nedza (2020), 6 and 204–14.

55 Panjpīrī (1980b), 62; compare Ibn Taymiyya (1424/2003), *passim*. See also von Kügelgen (2005), 209–12.

56 See Panjpīrī (1980b), 27–9, 39, 104, 116–18, 152 and 182; compare Ibn Taymiyya (1424/2003), 47, 232f., 309 and 458; al-Jawziyya (1432h), 117, 138 and 500. Notably, in some instances (e.g., on pp. 127, 132, 174 and 186) Muḥammad Ṭāhir's references to the latter work are not unequivocal: whether the "*Miftāḥ al-Saʿāda*" he referred to in those places is supposed to be this work, in which case the title would be erroneous, or yet another work of the title provided (such as, for instance, that of Abū ʿAbbās ibn ʿArīf [d. 536/1141]) is not entirely clear.

57 See Panjpīrī (1980b), 189; compare Dihlavī (1249h), I: 98–100; and Ibn Taymiyya (1392/1972), 92f.; (1424/2003), 309.

58 See Panjpīrī (1980b), 37 and 92

59 See, for example, Sedgwick (2004), 130f.; (2015), 105f.; Knysh (2007), 507. The reason for this perspective may be the so far prevalent assumption that Salafi Islam, and its political

required is a reformulated approach to Sufi Islam and, for this, Muḥammad Ṭāhir agreed once more with arguments put forth by Ibn al-Qayyim, and, further on, Shāh Valiyallāh Dihlavī. The former, for example, is referred to for his quote to al-Junayd al-Baghdādī (d. 297/910), the epitome of what many scholars of Sufi Islam had called "sober Sufism": 'Junayd always said: "Our knowledge of such is restricted by the Book and the Sunna [. . .] If one does not memorize the Qur'an, writes down *ḥadīth* and does not comprehend does not follow his [i.e., the Prophet's] example."'[60] In the same context, Shāh Valiyallāh is also referred to for his definition of the erroneous practices known as *bidaʿ* and the resulting necessity to adhere to the principles laid out by God and His Messenger.[61] Sufi Islam remained permissible both for Ibn al-Qayyim and Shāh Valiyallāh, and for Muḥammad Ṭāhir in their wake, as long as its epistemology is firmly and exclusively rooted in the Qur'anic revelation and does not, therefore, give way to unwarranted beliefs and practices, in other words, *bidaʿ*.[62] The argument here comes somewhat full circle: no one is to be followed blindly for an alleged spirituality, but only after their alignment with the authoritative texts of Sunni Islam has carefully been confirmed.

This rather receptive attitude towards Sufi Islam within the nascent Salafi tradition in the Pashtun Borderland, however, gave way over time, probably due to the increasing exposure of Panjpiri scholars – that is, those who are formally affiliated to the *Dār al-Qurʾān* in Panjpir or have studied there and maintained some intellectual affiliation with it – to their counterparts in Saudi Arabia. Thus, the matter is almost entirely absent in the writings of ʿAbd al-Salām Rustamī mentioned earlier, for instance; where it is not absent, it is dealt with in a manner that now followed the respective Wahhabi position. Though no stay in Saudi Arabia is mentioned in the brief hagiography on him, a strong affinity to the Wahhabiyya can, nonetheless, be inferred from the fact that Rustamī used to wear a long tunic (*thawb*) as worn in the Arabian Peninsula, along with the traditional headdress (*ghutra*), but – Wahhabi style – without the usual cord (*ʿiqāl*).[63] Indeed, Rustamī's vita is more complex still:

twin Salafism, originated very much in the Arabian Peninsula, where it was shaped by the distinctly anti-Sufi attitude of the Wahhabiyya. While the latter definitely plays a major role in the formation of contemporary Salafi Islam and Salafism, the Arabo-centricity – or, more precisely, Saudi-centricity – of most researchers in this field somewhat obscures alternative developments elsewhere, as has already been critically remarked, *inter alia*, in Bruckmayr and Hartung (2020), 139–44.

60 al-Jawziyya (1423/2003), III: 136; cited in Panjpīrī (1980a), 172.

61 See al-Dihlawī (1355/1936), II: 64; cited in Panjpīrī (1427/2006), 28.

62 See, for example, Anjum (2010), 176f.

63 See ʿAlī (n.d.), title page. On the Wahhabi view concerning headdress, see al-Najdī (1417/1996), IV: 257–60. Al-Fahad (2004) explains comprehensively the socio-religious issues underlying the omission of the *ʿiqāl* by Wahhabi scholars: the doubly worn cord had served generally as a worldly status symbol in the Bedouin society of the Najd from where the Wahhabiyya originated.

the *Dār al-Qur'ān* at Panjpir was only one in a range of educational institutions to which he went for training; after completion, he would then teach in a variety of *dīnī madāris* in the Pashtun Borderland and in the Punjab, thus providing a special impetus to the development of Salafi thought in the region.

Ghulāmallāh Khān (d. 1400/1979), yet another student of Ḥusayn ʿAlī Alvānī at his *madrasah* at Gujranwala in north-eastern Punjab, was also significant for informing his religious views, all of which were, just like Muḥammad Ṭāhir's, shaped exclusively through the prism of the Qur'an. Ghulāmallāh also adopted Alvānī's hermetic approach for understanding the Qur'an, reflected in the fact that he was instrumental in posthumously editing Alvānī's own *tafsīr*, the *Javāhir al-Qur'ān* (1966). By this time, Ghulāmallāh, based in Miyaṇwālā in the farthest north-western corner of the Punjab, had already somewhat broken away from "Deobandiyyat" after having radicalized Ḥusayn ʿAlī Alvānī's views enshrined in a small pamphlet named *Maslak-i Shaykh al-Qur'ān*, and initiated an organization called *Jamʿiyyat-i Ishāʿat al-Tawḥīd va 'l-Sunnah* as a platform for their propagation.[64] The main bone of contention with the leading representatives of "Deobandiyyat" was Ghulāmallāh's position on the status of the Prophet Muḥammad in his grave, an issue which would soon be embraced also by the scholars and students at Panjpir and which would serve as the straw that finally broke the camel's back and led subsequently to their formal expulsion from the folds of "Deobandiyyat", mentioned above, as late as 2012.[65]

At the heart of the matter was the question of whether – as accepted by the majority of Sunni Muslims – the Prophet was alive in his grave, or – as advocated by those regarded here as Salafi scholars – dead, the same as every other human being.[66] The controversy which now evolved pivoted essentially on the respective status of the various authoritative texts: for the Qur'an-centric Salafis, there was no sustainable indication in the text of the divine revelation that would allow one to attribute extra-human qualities to the Prophet. Those with a stronger focus on *ḥadīth* as enshrined especially in the canonical collections would present ample textual evidence from there and point out that, already in the eyes of the primordial Muslim community, the Prophet was regarded as having been graced by God with superhuman properties for the sake of remaining a benevolent guide to the community until the end of time.

The issue seems scholastic at first sight, but has important implications for the religious practice that the grandees of the *Ṭarīqah-yi Muḥammadiyyah* had already been concerned with: after all, the aliveness of the Prophet in his grave provides a good justification for also worshipping the graves of the Prophet's

64 See ʿAbd al-Maʿbūd (1433/2012), 9 and 22f.

65 See Section 4.1.2.

66 For a first analysis of this issue, see Hartung (2020), 195–200.

descendent or the so-called *awliyā*ʾ, the "friends of God", as Sufi masters are commonly regarded. Once again, the dominant view in the Salafi circles with which we are concerned here is that an excessive focus on the Prophet bears the danger of grossly violating the Islamic core doctrine of God's oneness (*tawḥīd*) and, consequently, paving the way for all kinds of *shirk*.

Thus, Muḥammad Ṭāhir had already made abundantly clear that the Prophet ought to be venerated, first and foremost, as the recipient of the divine communication and its transferor to humanity; his prophethood is, indeed, confined to the period during which he revealed the Qur'an, whereas he was an ordinary human being outside of that.[67] ʿAbd al-Salām Rustamī, who had briefly replaced Ghulāmallāh Khān after his death as headteacher of *tafsīr* at the *Jāmiʿah Taʿlīm al-Qurʾān* in Rawalpindi,[68] followed suit: quoting Q33.40, he stressed the humanity of the Prophet Muḥammad, as one of a given community, the same as all the Messengers before him. Possessor of many refined qualities, none of them is of such kind as would justify worship (*ṣifāt al-ulūhiyya*). Thus, he possessed neither knowledge of the unseen by himself (Q72.26 f.), nor universal powers of disposal of heavenly or earthly treasures (Q63.7), and neither did he hold the powers to benefit or harm (Q7.188). Because the Prophet does not inherently manifest any of the divine qualities, he serves primarily as a role model for the believers, one 'that must be obeyed and confirmed in principle [*wa-tajibu ʾiṭāʿatahu wa-ʾittibāʿahu fi'l-uṣūl / aw vājib day də haghah iṭāʿat aw tābiʿdārī pah aṣl*]'.[69]

The same, of course, applies to members of the Prophet's family, the so-called *sādāt*, who are popularly venerated throughout South Asia and beyond, the Companions and those generations who are considered *salaf ṣāliḥ*, as well as Sufis of any shade. The approach of the *salaf ṣāliḥ* served Rustamī, much more than Muḥammad Ṭāhir, as the ultimate benchmark of Qur'anic hermeneutics: while the latter was still quite open to considering the exegetical efforts of the *mufassirīn* of the past, Rustamī tried to remain solely within the confines of the various reporters of Prophetic *aḥādīth*.[70] In fact, the acknowledgement of the exceptional role of the *salaf ṣāliḥ* for an appropriate understanding of the Qur'an required a high degree of proficiency in the various sciences of *ḥadīth*, something that was closer to the domain of the *Ahl-i Ḥadīs̱*.

Moreover, while Muḥammad Ṭāhir still adhered to Naqshbandi practices highlighted by his own *murshid* Ḥusayn ʿAlī Alvānī, such as the imagining of the face of the *murshid* by the adept for the control of the appetitive soul (*taṣawwur al-shaykh*);[71] Rustamī was not known for any inclination towards

[67] See, for example, Panjpīrī (1980b), 64–6.
[68] See ʿAlī (n.d.), 5.
[69] al-Rustamī (1428h[a]), 89. The thirty-eight undated sermons in this collection are provided both in Arabic and in Pashto.
[70] Compare Panjpīrī (1421/2000) and Rustamī (1436/2015a).
[71] See al-Ḥanafī (1387h), 152f.

Sufi Islam at all, something which again he had in common with the later *Ahl-i Ḥadīs̱*.[72] Therefore, it is not really surprising that ʿAbd al-Salām Rustamī, after having served a prison sentence for his involvement in a violent clash in 1989 in Rustam between his considerable following and opposing groups, finally took up the offer by a *madrasah* of the *Ahl-i Ḥadīs̱* in Peshawar to teach Qur'an and *ḥadīth* there, a position in which he remained until his death.[73] That, by then, he was likely to be considered an *Ahl-i Ḥadīs̱* proper is probably indicated by the fact that the weekly *Ahl-i Ḥadīs̱* from Lahore, the official mouthpiece of the organization, carried a comparatively long obituary for him.[74]

Meanwhile, however, Muḥammad Ṭāhir's heir in leading the *Dār al-Qurʾān* in Panjpir, Muḥammad Ṭayyib Ṭāhirī, had also closed ranks with the *Ahl-i Ḥadīs̱*, following the expulsion of the Panjpiris from the folds of "Deobandiyyat". However, even then, their full commitment to following the *madhhab al-salaf*, the path which is meant to define Salafi Islam, was put in question by Shams al-Dīn ibn Muḥammad Ashraf al-Afghānī (d. 1420/1999), a Borderlands scholar who was actually raised within the confines of "Panjpiriyyat".

4.1.3 *The Cage Rattled: The Systematic Critique of Shams al-Dīn "al-Salafī" al-Afghānī*

Salafi Islam in the Pashtun Borderland would receive a major boost with Shams al-Dīn, who was born in an unspecified place in Afghanistan[75] and would later choose to call himself "Shams al-Afghānī", although, by way of seriously confronting its so far present manifestations in the region, first and foremost, "Panjpiriyyat".

This thrust, in fact, is hardly surprising in view of the fact that Shams al-Dīn was initially trained by Muḥammad Ṭāhir, *inter alia*, which suggests that he had spent at least a while at the *Dār al-Qurʾān* at Panjpir.[76] What exactly he had

72 See Riexinger (2004), 246–8. The author rightly points out that many of the early *Ahl-i Ḥadīs̱* had still been openly affiliated to the Naqshbandiyyah, while this nexus was increasingly lost after around 1900.

73 See ʿAlī (n.d.), 7–10. It was there and then that Rustamī wrote his seminal *al-Tibyān fī Tafsīr Umm al-Qurʾān*, an attempt at Qur'anic exegesis through a critical evaluation of the various relevant *ḥadīth* reports.

74 See Ḥāfiẓ Riyāẕ Aḥmad "ʿĀqib", 'Yād raftagān: Āh! Shaykh al-Qurʾān ʿAbd al-Salām Rustamī – raḥmat allāh [ʿalayh]', *Ahl-i Ḥadīs̱* 46/2 (24–30 Rabīʿ I 1436/16–22 January 2015), 24.

75 See al-Afghānī (1419/1998), I: 172f. The circumstances of Shams al-Dīn's demise at the rather young age of forty-eight remain, at least for the time being, just as obscure as the name of his actual native place in Afghanistan. It is noteworthy that the search for an obituary that reveals some more concrete information on these blind spots in his biography has so far not been successful.

76 See ibid., I: 173; Anon. (1426h). Among the other early teachers mentioned were ʿAbd al-Raḥīm Chitrālī, Naqīb Aḥmad al-Rabāṭī and, electively, ʿAbd al-Ẓāhir Afghānī or

studied remains unclear for now, but we may infer that he was exposed, more or less, to the usual Deobandi course of study, alongside Muḥammad Ṭāhir's peculiar take on Qur'anic exegesis and the issue of *taqlīd* which is so dominant in the Deobandi Hanafi universe. There is, however, a plausible reason for why we know so little about Shams al-Dīn's formative religious education: his biography is overshadowed by the second phase of his educational journey, the one that took place in the Kingdom of Saudi Arabia and reshaped his religious thought to such a profound extent that his earlier life faded – certainly helped by his biographers – almost into oblivion.[77]

While it is also not clear when exactly Shams al-Dīn moved to Saudi Arabia, the fact that he joined the *Islamic University of Medina* (IUM) is highly significant, because this institution, established in 1961 under the aegis of Saudi King Saʿūd ibn ʿAbd al-ʿAzīz (r. 1953–64), was created alongside the *World Muslim League* – the *Rābiṭat al-ʿĀlam al-Islāmī* (RAI) – to propagate the distinct Saudi interpretation of Islam throughout the entire (Sunni) Muslim world against any competing one.[78] Enrolled in the Faculty of Mission Studies (*kulliyyat al-daʿwa*), Department for Creed (*qism al-ʿaqīda*), the list of nineteen teachers with whom Shams al-Dīn claimed to have studied at the IUM reads like a "Who's Who" of Salafi core reference authors, prominently among them ʿAbd al-ʿAzīz ibn Bāz (d. 1419/1999), at one time principal of the university and later Grand-Mufti of the Kingdom, *shaykh al-ḥadīth* Nāṣir al-Dīn al-Albānī (d. 1419/1999) and Muḥammad ibn Ṣāliḥ al-ʿUthaymīn (d. 1421/2001).[79] In fact, many other eventual spearheads of Salafi Islam or Salafism outside Saudi Arabia would, at one time or other, have belonged to the circle around these Saudi scholars.[80]

Badīʿ al-Dīn Sindhī Rāshidī, on whom no further biographical information could be gleaned. Naqīb Aḥmad al-Rabāṭī had apparently authored two works to which Shams al-Dīn kept referring, although neither is available to me: *ʿIqd al-Laʾāliʾ waʾl-Durar fī Taḥqīq al-Masāʾil al-Arbaʿa ʿAshar* and *al-Kawākib al-Durriyya fī Taḥqīq al-Wasīla al-Sharʿiyya*, both reportedly published in Lahore, see al-Afghānī (1416/1996), III: 1757.

[77] See prominently his short biography in al-Afghānī (1419/1998), I: 172–8, where his secondary studies 'in Afghanistan and Pakistan until the completion of the "dars niẓāmī"' are mentioned only in general terms.

[78] See Schulze (1990), 156–9; Hartung (2004), 350f.; Farquhar (2017), 67–85; al-ʿAbbūd (1424h), esp. I: 306–10 and 336. Over the next few decades, the IUM established satellite institutions in other parts of the Muslim world, for example, in Pakistani Islamabad (IIUI; established 1980, restructured 1985), the Malaysian capital Kuala Lumpur (1983) and in Chittagong, Bangladesh (1993). The IIUI is of special importance for the present study, even more so as it benefited substantially from an exceptionally large contingent of Afghan refugee students, see Dürr (2016), 92 nn.3f., and 97f.

[79] See al-Afghānī (1419/1998), I: 173f.

[80] A case in point here is the Yemenite Muqbil al-Wādiʿī (d. 1422/2001), who later on emerged as a pivot of both Salafi Islam and Salafism in Yemen, see Bonnefoy (2011), 56. See also Section 4.4.2.

In April 1989, Shams al-Dīn submitted his Master's thesis, written under the supervision of Ṣāliḥ ibn ʿAbdallāh (Āl) al-ʿAbbūd (b. 1385/1939), one of Ibn Bāz's successors as the principal of the IUM, entitled *The Enmity of the Māturīdiyya against the Creed of the Salafiyya – ʿAdāʾ al-Māturīdiyya li'l-ʿAqīda al-Salafiyya*. This work would quickly override all of the few other Salafi refutations of the Maturidi theology of causation (*kalām*) and, subsequently, establish something like the heresiographical standard in this particular regard.[81] Bruckmayr makes the convincing point that 'al-Afghānī, particularly due to his origins in a region of the Muslim world dominated by Hanafi-Maturidi tradition, was instrumental in raising the spectre of a "modern Māturīdiyya" as a serious doctrinal challenger and impediment to Salafi expansion in South Asia and elsewhere.'[82] Because of the historical nexus between Maturidi *kalām* and Hanafi *fiqh*, which was especially strong in Muslim South Asia, it is not really surprising that Shams al-Dīn decided to continue his research into this matter in his doctoral studies, still at the IUM and still under the supervision of al-ʿAbbūd, a quest which resulted in his second major work, entitled *The Efforts of the Hanafi Scholars in the Refutation of the Tenets of the Grave-Worshippers – Juhūd ʿUlamāʾ al-Ḥanafiyya fī Ibṭāl ʿAqāʾid al-Qubūriyya* – which was successfully defended in May 1994.[83] Unsurprisingly, the thrust of this work is similar to that of Shams al-Dīn's earlier Master's dissertation. Although, at first sight, the argument is directed mainly against those Hanafi scholars in South Asia who maintain a strongly affirmative position on the theological underpinnings of Hanafi jurisprudence, here especially the Barelvis and many mainstream Deobandis,[84] the true target appears to have been much closer to home. Without being too obvious about it, those in the focus are the ones to whom Shams al-Dīn owed his own initiation into Salafi thought, that is, the scholars of Panjpir and affiliates.

81 See Bruckmayr (2020), 298–302. The most elaborate refutation until then was perhaps the *Ẓāhirat al-Irjāʾ fi'l-Fikr al-Islāmī* (1986) of Ṣafar al-Ḥawālī (b. 1375/1955). For an analysis, see Lav (2012), 86–119. Ibn ʿUthaymīn's *Qawāʿid al-Muthlá* from 1984, thus, from the time when Shams al-Dīn was studying at the IUM, contains at least two polemical references to the Maturidiyya: see Gharaibeh (2012), 382f.

82 Bruckmayr (2020), 297.

83 See al-Afghānī (1416/1996), i: i (facsimile of the title page of the doctoral dissertation).

84 Indeed, the pantheon of Deobandi adversaries of Shams al-Dīn includes the founding fathers Muḥammad Qāsim Nānawtavī and Rashīd Aḥmad Gangōhī, as well as their *spiritus rector* Imdādallāh Thānavī "Muhājir Makkī". Among luminaries of the second and third generations, which constitute the core of the so-called *akābirīn*, he engaged dismissively with "Shaykh al-Hind" Maḥmūd al-Ḥasan, Ashraf ʿAlī Thānavī, Ḥusayn Aḥmad Madanī, Anvar Shāh Kashmīrī (d. 1352/1933), Shabbīr Aḥmad ʿUs̲mānī (d. 1369/1949) and Khalīl Aḥmad Sahāranpūrī (d. 1346/1927). Among the later Deobandis figure Qārī Muḥammad Ṭayyib, Muḥammad Shafīʿ (d. 1396/1976) and his son Muḥammad Taqī ʿUs̲mānī (b. 1362/1943), see al-Afghānī (1416/1996), i: 29, 107, 133, 517–22 and 548, ii: 632f., 712–14 and 771–807, iii: 705, 771 and 805; (1419/1998), i: 199, 286–93, 365–80 and 484–6, ii: 20–2, 587–600 and 609–22, iii: 112–287, 309f. and 329–43.

Therefore, while his academic achievements must have appeared as a true fulfilment of the mission of the IUM stated above, they might have also had some cathartic meaning for Shams al-Dīn, and were, at the same time, a mighty instrument to establish himself as the chief authority in all matters "Salafi" in the Pashtun Borderland. As the systematic features of Shams al-Dīn's polemics have already been comprehensively analysed by Bruckmayr,[85] we shall here zoom in very much on his arguments against the scholars of Panjpir, most prominently among them his own teacher Muḥammad Ṭāhir and renowned affiliates, such as ʿAbd al-Salām Rustamī. Consequently, Shams al-Dīn keeps adding the *nisba* "al-Ḥanafī al-Māturīdī" to the names of both, moreover expanding that for Muḥammad Ṭāhir by the addition of "al-Naqshbandī al-Dēobandī".

However, before looking a little closer into Shams al-Dīn's points of critique on his former associates from Panjpir and its surrounds, it appears quite important to acknowledge that he had no qualms about the Hanafi *madhhab* as such: in fact, its eponymous founder remains highly regarded as one of the *salaf ṣāliḥ*, whose consideration had only later been distorted by its infestation with first Muʿtazili and later Maturidi theological thought.[86] It is, thus, the matter of the theological underpinnings of legal considerations, including the textual hermeneutics that inform the *uṣūl al-fiqh*, which needed to be bared and, subsequently, weeded out, in order to realign the *ʿaqīda* and *manhaj* of contemporary Sunni Islam to that of the *salaf ṣāliḥ*. For Shams al-Dīn, the authentic and undistorted Hanafi creed was ultimately laid down by Abū Jaʿfar al-Ṭaḥāwī and affirmed by its subsequent commentators of "neo-Hanbali" and, later, Wahhabi background.[87] While this initially appears of only marginal importance, Shams al-Dīn attributed the origins of the tripartite concept of *tawḥīd* to this very text, which then helped him to sustain his claim that its disappearance from the Hanafi tradition is only to be blamed on the later Maturidi prism, a fact that led even the scholars of Panjpir and those around them to inevitably violate the fundamental Islamic creedal tenet of God's oneness.[88]

From the Maturidi – and, by implication, also the Panjpiri – point of view, ignorance of the oneness of His names and attributes (*tawḥīd al-asmāʾ wa'l-ṣifāt*), which constitutes the third facet of *tawḥīd* besides the oneness of lordship (*tawḥīd al-rubūbiyya*) and the oneness of Him who entails exclusive worship (*tawḥīd al-ulūhiyya*), results in a categorical error, which, in its

85 See Bruckmayr (2020), 306–13.

86 See al-Afghānī (1419/1998), I: 11 and 193–200.

87 See ibid., *passim*; also Shiliwala (2018); Bruckmayr (2020), 313–15. The most prominent commentator in this context was Ibn Abī ʿIzz al-Ḥanafī (d. 792/1390); the most renowned contemporary commentary on the *ʿAqīda Ṭaḥāwiyya*, in turn, is surely the one by Nāṣir al-Dīn al-Albānī.

88 See al-Ḥanafī (1426/2005), 77–87; compare al-Afghānī (1416/1996), I: 105.

utmost consequence and whether intended or not, leads to worshipping other entities alongside God, in other words, to *shirk*.[89]

Does this argument really compute with the theological and legal positions cultivated in and around the *Dār al-Qur'ān* of Panjpir? For Shams al-Dīn, this was beyond question, and he aims at demonstrating this at length, consistently starting with Ḥusayn ʿAlī Alvānī and Ghulāmallāh Khān, via Muḥammad Ṭāhir, to Rustamī, though the latter was examined on the basis of only two of his works.[90] All four are noted for their explicit acknowledgement of the *tawḥīd al-rubūbiyya* and *tawḥīd al-ulūhiyya*,[91] but marked down for their failure in comprehending the true meaning of *tawḥīd al-asmā' wa'l-ṣifāt*. In the eyes of Shams al-Dīn, however, this is something that must remain uncompromisingly aloof from any allegorical approach at explanation if one is to avoid the possibility of stepping into the pothole of *shirk*.[92] According to the Wahhabi view on the matter, which, after all, is what Shams al-Dīn had been trained in at the IUM, the only matter permissible regarding *tawḥīd al-asmā' wa'l-ṣifāt* is the distinction of the attributes between *in esse* (*dhātiyya*) and *in actu* (*fiʿliyya*).[93] For Shams al-Dīn, either theological persuasion results in dramatic consequences in legal theory and practice, and, as such, they will have a grave material impact on the communities in which such ideas flourish: the popular veneration of deceased human beings in their graves – *al-qubūriyya* – is an important case in point.[94]

There is no doubt that the Deobandis were utterly critical of such practices, which, in fact, became a major point of their perpetual conflict with the equally Hanafi Barelvis.[95] However, and this appears to be the crux of Shams al-Dīn's argument, as long as the Deobandis maintained their theological underpinnings and strong affiliation with the Naqshbandiyyah-Mujaddidiyyah, the Deobandi critique of those practices would remain merely superficial: in Salafi parlance, it would aim to redress only the *manhaj*, the external manifestation of the *ʿaqīda*, without touching the latter in the least. This discrepancy can apparently be

[89] See al-Afghānī (1416/1996), I: 175–351; (1419/1998), III: 177–346.

[90] The bibliographical entry on Rustamī in al-Afghānī (1416/1996), III: 1 764f., appears somewhat exaggerated: in fact, the two works exclusively referred to are *al-Tibyān fī Tafsīr Umm al-Qur'ān* and *Tanshīṭ al-Adhhān fī Uṣūl Tafsīr al-Qur'ān*.

[91] See, for example, ibid., I: 203f.; compare al-Ḥanafī (1385/1966), I: 47f.; Panjpīrī (1980b), 26–8; al-Rustamī (1436/2015a), 53f. In fact, these two facets of *tawḥīd* were also acknowledged in his explanation of the two Qur'anic concepts "lord" (*rabb*) and "deity" (*ilāh*) by the Islamist mastermind Sayyid Abū 'l-Aʿlá Mawdūdī, who is, therefore, referred to by al-Afghānī (1416/1996), I: 91f.; compare Mawdūdī (1996), 11–80 (note: al-Afghānī cites the Arabic translation of this work by Muḥammad ʿĀṣim al-Ḥadād as *Mabādi' al-Islām* [Damascus: Maktabat al-shabāb al-musallam 1373/1954]).

[92] See al-Afghānī (1419/1998), I: 501–82 and II: 235–401.

[93] See ibid., II: 467–78; compare Ibn ʿAbd al-Wahhāb (1406/1986), 6, 34–6, 128–30, 134, 139 and 148. On the position of Ibn ʿUthaymīn, see Gharaibeh (2012), 107–20.

[94] See al-Afghānī (1416/1996), I: 455.

[95] See Metcalf (1982), 296–314; Sanyal (1996), 231–55; Hartung (2004), 108–17.

traced back to Aḥmad Sirhindī, the progenitor of this particular branch of the Naqshbandiyyah,[96] and it runs all the way through this *silsila*, which explains why Shams al-Dīn is equally critical of the leaders of the *Ṭarīqah-yi Muḥammadiyyah*, here especially Shāh Ismāʿīl Dihlavī.[97] As an initiate into the Naqshbandiyyah-Mujaddidiyyah, Shams al-Dīn's own teacher, Muḥammad Ṭāhir, and Ḥusayn ʿAlī Alvānī, *murshid* of the latter, necessarily had to fall into the same trap. Even Rustamī, who appears to have remained outside the confines of discipleship in a Sufi community, is relentlessly regarded by Shams al-Dīn as still caught within the selfsame vicious circle.[98]

Shams al-Dīn's accusations against his earlier teachers at Panjpir and their circles seem somewhat scholastic and petty, a fact which reinforces the impression that with his two major works he was specifically aiming at freeing himself with a vengeance from their legacy.[99] Still, petty as this might appear, it certainly did not fail to make a decisive impact on the wider – not to say "global" – Salafi Muslim community,[100] and on the Deobandis, who, after all, can be regarded as the most prominent of the various learned Sunni *masālik* in South Asia and beyond, especially in the Pashtun Borderland. To put it bluntly: his extensive investigation was well suited to pull the rug out from under the feet of even the conservative religious authorities in this region, especially the representatives of the Naqshbandiyyah-Mujaddidiyyah and "Deobandiyyat" among them. Whatever the efforts of the scholars of Panjpir, their intellectual progenitors in the Punjab and even renegades from "Panjpiriyyat" proper, such as ʿAbd al-Salām Rustamī, they were still 'evidence of [their] Deobandiyyat', hence of their attachment to the Hanafi-Maturidi hermeneutic universe, for Shams al-Dīn.[101]

96 See ter Haar (1992), 60–8; Bruckmayr (2009), 77–81; (2014), 125f.; (2020), 295. The role of Sirhindī in promoting Maturidi perspectives is acknowledged in al-Afghānī (1416/1996), I: 154 and 164, II: 753 n.1 and 987, and III: 1 490–2; (1419/1998), II: 638; compare Sirhindī (1397/1977), I: 111–14 (no. 43) and 421–4 (no. 256); II: 114–18 (no. 43) and III: 297–314 (no. 17).

97 See al-Afghānī (1416/1996), esp. I: 335–42 and II: 1 166–8; compare Dihlavī (1998), 46–56; al-Dihlawī (1256h), 27; (2003), 131–45.

98 See al-Afghānī (1416/1996), for example I: 318f., 332, 394–6 and 431, II: 882f., 1 109f. and 1 195f., and III: 1 468; but most uncompromisingly I: 136 n.1.

99 Remarkably, Shams al-Dīn's own supervisor at the IUM, Ṣāliḥ ibn ʿAbdallāh (Āl) al-ʿAbbūd, distanced himself publicly from the exceedingly sectarian tone of the published versions of both dissertations, stressing that their revision and subsequent publication had at no point been authorized by any scholar in the higher echelons of the IUM, see al-ʿAbbūd (1416h). In hindsight, however, al-ʿAbbūd's public dissociation appears somewhat hypocritical, because around one decade later the examination board of the same academic unit of the IUM that had once approved of Shams al-Dīn's works passed at least two more works of the same kind, see al-Ṣāfī (1441/2019); Ibn Jamīl al-Raḥmān (1434h). See also Section 4.2.2.

100 See Bruckmayr (2020), 309.

101 al-Afghānī (1416/1996), III: 1 275 n.3. His reference at this point is Panjpīrī (1427/2006), 93, on the issue of allegorically rendering the opaque Qur'anic term *awtād* – "peg" (see Q38.12 and 89.10).

There is, however, one point in which Shams al-Dīn clearly shared the views of his teacher Muḥammad Ṭāhir of Panjpir, namely the issue of the Prophet being, or not being, alive in his grave, which, as we may recall, had served the upper echelons of Deobandi scholarship to cast the Panjpiris out of their fold.[102] In this point, too, Shams al-Dīn blamed the impact of Maturidi *kalām* on Hanafi thought, which he attempted to sustain by correlating early Maturidi statements on this matter with later Hanafi ones.[103] This anachronism is an important observation, because it indicates the difficulties of categorizing the Panjpiris vis-à-vis Deobandis and Salafis, respectively, and in this way suggests considering "Panjpiriyyat", at least before the proper closing of ranks with the *Ahl-i Ḥadīṣ*, rather as a hybrid form of "Salaficized Deobandiyyat". Because of this perceived hermeneutical incoherence, Shams al-Dīn could not but castigate their adherents.

Having dissociated himself so profoundly from the tradition in which he was brought up, Shams al-Dīn consequently had to seek an operational base for himself after his return from Medina in 1994, which he found in Ćamkanī on the eastern outskirts of Peshawar, where he established the *Jāmiʿah Aṣariyyah.*[104] It was from there that a network eventually evolved to send out the new and purified Salafi message into the wider Pashtun Borderland, a message that would finally be embraced by some who, in the 1990s, would identify themselves as "*taliban*" within the ṬIT / IEA.

4.1.4 A Distinct Environment: Afghan Salafi Networks in the Borderland and Beyond

The pillars set up by Shams al-Dīn's undermining of the religious authority of the Deobandis were ultimately further cemented and modified by local Salafi scholars in his wake. While Shams al-Dīn had confined himself mainly to a theological critique, Abū Muḥammad Amīnallāh Pishāvarī (b. sometime between 1961 and 1973) set out to attack the second source of Deobandi spiritual authority, that is, the above-discussed Hanafi legal practice of *taqlīd shakhṣī.*[105]

[102] See Section 4.1.2, n.34.

[103] See al-Afghānī (1419/1998), I: 484–6 and III: 317–23; (1416/1996), II: 831–9; compare al-Māturīdī (1426/2005), I: 595f.; even more pronounced is al-Nasafī (1419/1998), I: 143f. ('We do not know this, as the life of a martyr is not known beyond a feeling.'); al-Miṣrī (n.d.), II: 299–301 and V: 119–37; Ibn ʿĀbidīn (1423/2003), III: 150–57; Gangōhī (1987), 273–8; al-Kashmīrī (1426/2005), II: 496f.; Ludhiyānavī (1425h), I: 36. However, the Ottoman Hanafi scholar Shihāb al-Dīn Maḥmūd al-Ālūsī from Baghdad (d. 1270/1854), in his renowned Qur'anic commentary *Rūḥ al-Maʿānī fī Tafsīr al-Qurʾān al-ʿAẓīm wa'l-Sabʿ al-Mathānī*, appears here as Shams al-Dīn's crucial reference for the Hanafi position in this point: on this work, see Pink (2011), 42f.

[104] See al-Afghānī (1419/1998), I: 178.

[105] See al-Bishāvarī (1422h), 264–83. On *taqlīd shakhṣī* in Deobandi legal practice, see Section 3.3.2.

Amīnallāh originally hailed from Kunar Province, where he might have encountered a particular manifestation of the Panjpiri world-view active there for a short period after the Soviet withdrawal from Afghanistan,[106] and set up his base in Peshawar when he established himself as *shaykh al-ḥadīth* of the *Jāmiʿat Taʿlīm al-Qurʾān va ʾl-Ḥadīs̱* in the Munavvar Shāh Colony in Ganj, situated, like Shams al-Dīn's later *Jāmiʿah As̱ariyyah*, on the eastern outskirts of the city. In this capacity, Amīnallāh soon emerged as the dominant voice of the *madrasah* that had been established to cater for Afghan refugees in the early 1980s. While many of them were educated at ʿAbd al-Ḥaqq Akōṛavī's *Dār al-ʿUlūm-i Ḥaqqāniyyah* at Akōṛah Khaṫṫak,[107] Amīnallāh's mission appears to have consisted of the provision of a counterweight to the Deobandi scholarship there and elsewhere. In order to succeed, Amīnallāh devoted much of his effort to the firm refutation of *taqlīd shakhṣī* as a cornerstone of Deobandi legal practice and, subsequently, guarantor of Deobandi religious authority in the Pashtun Borderland and beyond. Yet, he himself had emerged from that very persuasion, having studied with ʿAbd al-Salām Rustamī, who, after all, was regarded by Shams al-Dīn as a prime representative of the ongoing attachment of the Panjpiris to the core elements of the Deobandi theological and legal universe.[108] Then, again, it may be possible to still perceive Rustamī's positions as an expression of his Borderland pragmatism: as an acknowledgement, namely, of the need for a more accommodating attitude if one wished to succeed in spreading one's message in this distinct environment.[109]

Amīnallāh Pishāvarī, however, would be leaning more towards Shams al-Dīn's ruthless reckoning with the theological and subsequent legal positions widely held by the followers of the Deobandi *maslak* and not making any concessions to the ever-changing context. Consequently, he, too, distanced himself from his former teacher, and, by doing so, deliberately violated the practice of *taqlīd shakhṣī*. In fact, he took this matter to heart, as is attested by his many encounters with Deobandi scholars whom he aimed to refute.[110]

This onslaught on the Deobandi pattern of authority formation and sustenance could initially be regarded as a rejection of a monopoly of definition arising from a radical egalitarian persuasion that has repeatedly been

[106] See Section 4.4.2.

[107] See Malik (1996), 202–8, 235f. and 241.

[108] See Ḥāfiẓ Riyāẓ Aḥmad "ʿĀqib", 'Yād' (see above, n.73), 24.

[109] See, for example, al-Rustamī (2009), 105–57 and 199–210.

[110] See al-Bishāvarī (1422h), 264–83; Anon., 'Taqlīd shakhṣī: fāḍilat al-shaykh Amīnallāh Pishāvarī mā bayna muftī Mujīb al-Raḥmān Dēobandī' (Pashto in four parts). URL: munazarah.org/index.php/ur/pashto-debate/audios-pushto/sheikh-ameen-ullah-peshawari (accessed 20 January 2017).

attributed to the inhabitants of the Pashtun Borderland.[111] Such a view is certainly supported by the evident fact that most Salafi scholars, prominently among them Amīnallāh, would set up their own small centres of learning and scholarly enquiry, thus indicating that no authority should be accepted before a position is satisfactorily affirmed in the course of one's own enquiries. Such an interpretation may indeed carry some weight, yet still seems to fall short of the mark: after all, we may assume that undermining the hitherto established Deobandi learned authority would only serve attempts to establish one's own interpretation as authoritative instead.

In contrast to Shams al-Dīn, however, Amīnallāh, who had not been trained in Saudi Arabia, was not as adverse to certain beliefs and practices commonly associated with Sufi Islam as the former; on this point he appeared to be more in line with the views of ʿAbd al-Salām Rustamī, and, by inference, also with those of Ibn Taymiyya and Ibn al-Qayyim.[112] Thus, while severely challenging Deobandi legal authority, and not sparing his own teacher in the course of this, that Amīnallāh was able to flourish in the same cultural environment as that from which he originated in the first place appears to have induced in him a sense of the practicability of Sufi Islam in the Pashtun Borderland. Accordingly, he did not alienate his target audience from its cultural roots and was, therefore, rather successful at spreading a variety of Salafi Islam that appeared somewhat soft in comparison with the dry and scholastic one of Shams al-Dīn. In fact, Amīnallāh's Sufi Islam greatly resembles that of Deobandis and Nadvis by virtue of emphasizing a departure from worldly attachment and a return to true piety (*taqwá*) and asceticism (*zuhd*) that takes its model from the religious conduct (*adab*) of the *salaf ṣāliḥ*,[113] while sticking firmly to Salafi theological precepts.[114]

Let us halt here for the moment and turn next to the one ideational current that irreversibly added the element of "governance orientation" to all the others, be it Salafi Islam or "Frontier Deobandiyyat", and, in this way, conferred on them an ultimately political thrust: "Islamism". The significance of this particular current for reshaping earlier ones can hardly be underestimated: as we shall see below, it was indeed "Islamism" that begat "Salafism" out of "Salafi Islam", as well as contemporary more militant varieties of "Frontier Deobandiyyat".

[111] See Caron (2016a), 136, 145 and 147f.; Caron and Dasgupta (2016), 108f.; Hartung (2016b), 348–50, 353, 356–8 and 361; (2019a).

[112] See, for example, the quite nuanced discussion of the matter of "intercession" (*tawassul*) in al-Rustamī (1436/2015), 133–48, esp. 144–8; compare al-Jawziyya (1423/2003). On the position of Ibn Taymiyya, see Makdisi (1973); Meier (1981); on that of Ibn al-Qayyim, see Anjum (2010). The proximity of Amīnallāh Pishāvarī and Rustamī is perhaps well reflected in the two eulogies which the latter contributed to the former's *Də Taqlīd Ḥaqīqat aw də Muqallidīnō Aqsām* (2001): see al-Bishāvarī (1422h), 1 and 255.

[113] On the complex intra-Salafi debate over who is and is not considered a *salaf*, see Nedza (2014), 96–100.

[114] See al-Bishāvarī (1430/2009), I: 6–32 and II: 547–53.

4.2 Islamism

"Islamism" denotes the attempts to systematically recast "Islam" as a comprehensive governance-orientated ideology. Its classical theorists, such as the Indian Sayyid Abū 'l-Aʿlá Mawdūdī and the Egyptians Ḥasan al-Bannā (assassinated 1368/1949) and Sayyid Quṭb (executed 1386/1966), all argued for the Qur'an as the sole primary reference point, thus relegating the *ḥadīth* that is held so dearly by Salafis to a backseat. The text of the Qur'anic revelation, argued Mawdūdī, for example, contained, in addition to historically and geographically rooted elements, messages which are invariant in time and space and can be boiled down to a limited number of axiomatic concepts that, in their entirety, point to

> its main task, which is not only to present the intellectual and moral foundations of the Islamic System [*niẓām-i islāmī kī fikrī awr akhlāqī bunyādōṇ*] in full clarity. Rather, it is a rational proof as well as a passionate appeal, from both of which results reinforcement [*mustaḥkam*]. [...] The task of the Prophet – Peace be upon him and prayer! – was to give a practical form to the Islamic life, by offering the world a model of an individual character as well as the pattern of a society and state [*muʿāsharat awr riyāsat kā numūnah*], as a practical interpretation [*ʿamalī taʿbīr va tafsīr*] of the principles of the Qur'an.[115]

What distinguishes "Islamism" from Salafi Islam and "Deobandiyyat" of whatever kind is exactly this immanent emphasis on state and society, not on an individual piety that is very closely linked to what had aptly been called 'salvation anxiety':[116] humans require a distinct socio-political framework as the *conditio sine qua non* for their ability to lead their lives in accordance with the injunctions of the *shari'a*, however defined. The ultimate aim of Islamists is, therefore, to define "Islamic governance" (*ḥukūmat-i islāmī*) in line with Qur'anic injunctions and actively strive for its realization.

In view of this wider agenda, particulars, such as the correct performance of the ritual obligations (*ʿibādāt*), receded into the background: other than Deobandis and *Ahl-i Ḥadīs̱*, to whom such matters were of such crucial importance that they would even go as far as questioning each other's fidelity, none of the early theorists of Islamism had bothered much with ostensibly nitpicking details such as raising one's hands during prayer, the formulaic acclamation on its conclusion, or – with an eye on the Pashtun Borderland in particular – the raising and moving of one's index finger during the *tashahhud*.[117] Fidelity, for them, was entirely contingent on the commitment

[115] Mawdūdī (1949–72), I: 37f.
[116] See Lange (2016), 5–11.
[117] The only mention of the issue of *tashahhud*, for example, in classical Islamist texts that could so far be located is by Mawdūdī (1972), 155, and differs quite significantly from those *ḥadīth*-centric legal arguments we have encountered elsewhere: 'At the point in

to object to all present forms of governance while actively striving for the establishment of their Islamic alternative. Consequently, all the *ʿibādāt* are subjected to this very end: prayer, for example, had been reconsidered both by Mawdūdī and by Quṭb rather philosophically as a means to the personal realization of God's Absolute Sovereignty (*ḥākimiyyat allāh*). For Quṭb, this makes it a most important exercise of individual cultivation (*tarbiyyat al-shakhṣiyya*), in the course of which each individual practitioner becomes liberated from the fear of other created beings;[118] for Mawdūdī, moreover, the congregational prayer especially also has an essentially communitarian function, something that is denoted by the uniformity of movement. Consequently, this is invoked for a "governance-orientated" thinker such as Mawdūdī as the main reason why the congregational prayer was declared compulsory: 'During the time of the Revelation and the time of the Companions, no one was considered a Muslim unless he joined the prayer in congregation.'[119] Moreover, for a congregational prayer to be valid, it necessarily requires a leader, and, as such, each prayer congregation also serves as a true analogy to the global political community of Muslims, led by an inspired figurehead.

The subordination of even a religious obligation as fundamental as the ritual prayer to a distinct socio-political agenda is, in fact, a clear reflection of the paradigm shift in Islamic thought brought about by Islamism. Historically rooted in the prevalence of numerous political ideologies in Muslim societies predominantly under European colonial rule, its early theorists were eager to devise an Islamic equivalent as a sustainable alternative to the Liberalism which was prevalent then, as well as its two mighty counter-projects: communism and fascism.[120]

While Liberalism appears to have been the ideology of choice for all those colonial subjects who aimed at raising their individual status by integrating themselves into the "capitalist world-system", communism in its various shapes had a most powerful pull for the socially and economically marginalized groups under colonial rule.[121] Communism and Islamism overlap almost congruently in their fundamental criticism of the prevalent socio-economic and subsequent political conditions and the advocacy of a radically alternative

time the testimony [of faith] is given, you raise the index finger, because this is the affirmation of your creed during prayer [*namāz mēṇ tumhārē ʿaqīdē kā iʿlān hē*], and while performing it verbally, it is a requirement to give exceptional attention and emphasis.'

118 See Quṭb (1430/2009), I: 40 (on Q2.3).

119 Mawdūdī (1972), 143 (see also 159–66).

120 See Hartung (2013a), 43–59, 113–22, 132–48 and 163–73.

121 In this regard, one may recall the case of mufti ʿAbd al-Raḥīm Pōpalzay discussed above (Section 3.3.2) as an ardent advocate of a communist solution to the economic and socio-political imbalance in the Pashtun Borderland of the first half of the twentieth century.

draft. Moreover, both ideological orientations maintain a distinction between the masses that are deprived of a voice of their own and a benevolent and well-organized intellectual vanguard that leads them in the struggle. The advocates of communism certainly enjoyed an advantage in that regard, being the recipients of the open and covert ideological and material support of the leadership of the Soviet Union and other members of the various *Communist Internationals*.[122]

Given these significant parallels, it is not really surprising that, of all the alternative political ideologies with which increasingly regimented Islamists competed, their rivalry with the adherents to communism stood out most in terms of intensity and intransigency. There is a further crucial element which accounts for the exceptional ferocity of this altercation: the fact that communism was the only political ideology expressly not in need of any divine entity as the ultimate source of its metaphysical foundations, while God and His revelation to humankind are the solitary anchor and permanent and immediate reference of the Islamist ideology.

The same as elsewhere, the urban and urbanite youth, somewhat epitomized by the university student, are more attracted than others to those ideologies that fundamentally challenge the political status quo within the capitalist world-system. As a result, university campuses evolved as a major field in which ideological contestations are acted out.[123] These developments also found their way into urban Afghanistan with the various modernization policies since the reign of Emir-cum-King Amānallāh Khan, while the colonial system of higher education in neighbouring Pakistan was, by and large, continued, complete with the deliberate structural disadvantaging of its western borderlands.[124] When, on New Year's Day 1965, the PDPA was founded on the debris of the earlier nationalist "Constitutionals" (*mashrūṭiyyah*) –

[122] In this light, we may well consider the nine-month sojourn of the "Imām-i Inqilāb" ʿUbaydallāh Sindhī and a band of close associates in the Soviet Union in 1923, after they were no longer made welcome in Afghanistan by King Amānallāh Khan: see Āybak (1990), 210–63.

[123] Ideologically charged student activism goes back as far as the early nineteenth century in what had then been the German Confederation. Since the early twentieth century, this form of political engagement has also splashed over into the actual and former colonies of states of the Global North, including British India, although its most decisive boost was finally received in the late 1960s.

[124] In addition to the *Islamia College* in Peshawar, established in 1913 in the spirit of the *Muhammadan Anglo-Oriental College* in Aligarh on the initiative of NWFP politician and educationist Ṣāḥib'zādah ʿAbd al-Qayyūm Khān (d. 1356/1937) and the then-Chief Commissioner of the NWFP, Sir George O. Roos-Keppel (d. 1921), the adjacent University of Peshawar (established 1950) remained the only institution for higher education in the province for the following two years. Most of the currently active ones were not established before the early twenty-first century.

popularly known as "Young Afghans" (*afghānān-i javān*) – of the 1920s and the *Vīx̌ Zalmiyān* of the 1940s,[125] the conflict between the proponents of the two antagonistic ideologies finally made its entrance onto the Afghan stage with full force.

4.2.1 The Islamist Circles of Afghanistan's University Campuses

Just like other university campuses throughout the Muslim world of the 1960s and 1970s, that of Kabul University, established by royal decree in November 1932, developed into a hotbed of political activism of all sorts. Soon, however, any wider variety of articulation got absorbed into the two major factions already indicated: those inspired by a Marxist world-view, often in its Stalinist, Maoist and Trotskyist garb, stood in opposition to more conservative and predominantly religiously inspired groups.

In Afghanistan, these tendencies received additional boosts from study trips to various destinations, which can be regarded as sources of inspiration for either faction. While many of those with secular and Leftist inclinations would go to study in France, which at that time was rocked by increasingly violent political protests by left-wing students, those who were more religiously oriented went to Cairo to join al-Azhar. A prominent representative of the former was Sayyid Bahā' al-Dīn Majrūḥ, born in 1928 in Kunar, while a leading exponent of the latter was Ghulām Muḥammad "Niyāzī", a native of Ghazni. Both had already left Afghanistan for their studies in the late 1950s.

Majrūḥ appears to have also become personally acquainted with some of the chief representatives of contemporary philosophy in France, such as Michel Foucault and Jean-Paul Sartre, during his higher studies at the Sorbonne and the University of Montpellier. He is, therefore, credited with subsequently bringing existentialist thinking in the wake of Sartre to Afghanistan,[126] where, upon his return from France, he joined the Faculty of Literature at Kabul University. Niyāzī, who became a professor at the Shariʿa Faculty of the same institution after his return from Cairo, in contrast, was impacted by the new religious–political thought in and, even more, outside the student cohort at al-Azhar, carried, first and foremost, by the *Society of the Muslim Brethren* (*Jamāʿat al-Ikhwān al-Muslimīn*; MB).

[125] See Arnold (1983), 9–26.

[126] Florence Shahabi is currently working at SOAS, University of London, on her doctoral dissertation "Sayyid Bahodine Majrouh: An Intellectual Biography", which will certainly enhance our still rather superficial knowledge on Majrūḥ. For some indication of Sartre's impact on him, see Majruh (1976/1355sh), 47; Majrūḥ (1356sh), 154.

To Modernity through Tradition: The "Madrasah-yi Tawḥīd"

Yet, perhaps even more important for the constitution of an Islamist movement in Afghanistan than the studies abroad of a select few were – at least initially – Sufi circles inclined to Islamic reformulation, predominantly those of Muḥammad ʿAṭāʾallāh Fayẓānī (presumably executed 1400/1979) of Herat and Ṣibghatallāh Mujaddidī (d. 1437/2016) of Kabul. The former, especially who represented a more individualist spiritual approach outside the established *ṭuruq*, is said to have been a pivot in the emerging Islamist circles in Kabul. His *Madrasah-yi Tawḥīd*, established after he had moved there in 1969, became a port of call for numerous religiously conservative young urbanite men eager for societal change; the fact that he had repeatedly been jailed for his fierce public criticism of prevalent social and political practices gained him additional credibility. In this, he differed substantially from the traditional spiritual authority of the Mujaddidī family of Kabul's Shōr Bāzār, which has been quite close to the royal palace since the rule of the Durrani in the eighteenth century.[127] Fayẓānī was much less willing to join the circles of political power, which he regarded as one of the roots of evil in Afghanistan at the eve of the downfall of the Barakzay monarchy.

An important proposition was Fayẓānī's attempt to link an Islamic worldview, deeply rooted in the belief in the authoritative texts, to other epistemic systems as promulgated by the natural sciences.[128] While this development took place in India about a century earlier and is associated with thinkers such as Sir Sayyid Aḥmad Khān,[129] the fact that Afghanistan had not been subject to direct colonial domination may have delayed the necessity for this kind of intellectual engagement. The new generation of urbanite youths, especially in the larger cities, exposed to an increasingly global urban culture, which was hardly compatible with religiously shaped and regionally specific norms and values,[130] required new approaches that could negotiate the conflicting epistemic systems without having to necessarily sacrifice the Islamic one. Fayẓānī's *Madrasah-yi Tawḥīd* seems to have been a prime address for this kind of endeavour, and it is thus not surprising that his study circle was frequented by students and teachers from Kabul's two chief educational institutions at that time: Kabul University and Kabul Polytechnic University. Subject matters in these circles were established by Fayẓānī in the form of a catalogue of "general questions": they ranged from the status of the human in

[127] See Wieland-Karimi (1998), 125–7; Ziad (2017), 263–73.

[128] See, for example, Fayẓānī (2012b).

[129] See prominently Troll (1978), 144–70 and 303–7.

[130] In this context, one should remember the role that the imagination of Afghanistan, as a major destination on the so-called "Hippie Trail", played for European and North American youth culture from the 1950s to the late 1970s, see Gemie and Ireland (2017), 18f. and 209–14. See also Zaeef (2010), xiii.

the order of beings and its emotional and social discomforts (*nā ārāmī'hā*), to the question of its physical death, and, finally, the dilemma of explaining empirical reality through the prism of the Qur'anic revelation, in full awareness of the existence of powerful alternative scientific models of explanation.[131]

Political and other societal matters appear only subordinately to the general epistemological problem. Yet, they can be logically deduced from there, and Fayẕānī is, therefore, to be considered at least a groundbreaker for the eventual Islamist ideas in Kabul. However, while the majority of the theorists of Islamism would arrive at similar conclusions by rational speculation and a rather liberal and selective approach to Qur'anic hermeneutics,[132] Fayẕānī's approach was decidedly that of mystic contemplation and intuition as the primary modes of cognition; he shared this, to an extent, more with Ḥasan al-Bannā or even more so the Āyatallāh Rūḥallāh Khumaynī (d. 1409/1989).[133] Fayẕānī developed a severe critique of a society based on different world-views from the unfettered affirmation of the absolute truth of the Qur'anic message derived in this way and all of its components, which he tied to a political message that is worth quoting in its entirety:

> Yet, careless heretics [*ighfāl'girān-i mulḥid*] who, to further expanding their own colonialist plans, call the creation of the world a coincidence [*khūd ba-khūd paydah shudah*], indulge in nothing more than mere speculation, clear falsehood, and pure ignorance [*jahl-i maḥẕ*].
>
> Sure enough, the propagation of such an ideology [*mafkūrah*] follows two basic objectives:
>
> Firstly, the new colonizers have experienced the inhumane and repressive behaviour of the greatest colonizers of the world in history (England and others) vis-à-vis oppressed people during hundreds of years of colonization. Colonizers witnessed that, as soon as the oppressed tribe or nation [*qawm yā millat*] rose to power, they drove them off their land in a most humiliating way. Consequently, these [new] colonizers have established a novel narrative for the [current] state of confusion, namely that the foundations of creed, faith, culture, traditions, as well as the preservation of honour and soil [*khāk*], are [all] born out of religion [*dīn*]. Consequently, before they could stretch out their colonizing arm, reel in their dominion and establish hegemony over oppressed peoples and nations, they had to destroy all religious principles and put everything under the banner of heresy and atheism [*livā'-i ilḥād va 'adam-i vujūd-i khudā*], as well as the denial of the unparalleled and exalted Artificer [*ṣāni'*]. They first give the youth, which is already wary of dry-hearted

131 See Fayẕānī (1354sh), 4–10.

132 Among such theorists, Sayyid Abū 'l-A'lá Mawdūdī and Sayyid Quṭb hold the dominant position. On their respective approach to the Qur'an, see Hartung (2013a), 83–99; al-Khālidī (1421/2000).

133 For their respective affinity to Sufi Islam, see al-Bannā (1422/2001), 20–3, 42, 52 and 62–4; Knysh (1992).

> religions, a taste of indulgence and obscenity. By such deceit, they attract them to become used in accomplishing the second objective: to defeat undeveloped countries by means of their own people is the best of strategies.
>
> It is well known that corruption [*taṭmīʿ*] works best among the unaware among the youths [*javānān-i nāʾkhūd*]. With the poison of indulgence and obscenity they lure them and, thus, deprive the oppressed nations of their own fruits. Secretly and undetected by careless ruling powers, they stage revolutions across the world, as happened in Bukhara, Eastern Germany, Georgia, Poland, Czechoslovakia, and elsewhere. From these various colonial deceptions over hundreds of years nothing has been, and will ever be, extracted from the thoughts [*fikr va maghz*] of intellectuals [*ahl-i dānish*] of earlier and contemporary times but head-ache, disaster, murder, expansion, and, in short, domination over [other] people. Now that we have entered the particular nuclear age, the most powerful [*buzurgʾtarīn*] states engage in a crazy armed race, instead of racing towards tranquillity for humanity, and this cannot be called by any other name but madness!
>
> Indeed! We should be leading and guiding those insane ones, who pretend to be oh so perfect, through direction and gnosis, the sound guidance of the Qur'an, an Islam of extended hands, through the efforts of the teachers of the Qur'anic schools, and with the help of God Almighty and with modesty, to a flood of universal mercy, [thus] just the opposite to the wrathful times of Noah – Peace be upon him.[134]

In contrast to the most renowned early theorists of Islamism, Fayẕānī's argument did not pivot on God's commandment to establish the rule of the revealed law, the *shariʿa*. Instead, his truth resulted from a deep personal mystic experience, and his objective was to convince others of that truth for the moral betterment of humanity. In doing so, he was perhaps still more a representative of guidance-orientated religiosity, convinced that the truth as he experienced it would prevail in the long run against any opposition, no matter how strong it is. However, those who, like Ghulām Muḥammad Niyāzī, attended his circle would move away from mystic introspection and develop more proscriptive arguments that they were also willing to see through by the use of force. In this, they certainly merely reciprocated the growing willingness to apply violent means among their secular and leftist opponents on and off the university campuses.

Campus Politics: The Left versus the Religious Right

The politicization of the university campuses in the cities of Afghanistan, especially Kabul University, can be attributed directly to the emergence of a new social stratum among its clientele that originated in the rural setting, but was somewhat alienated from it by its education and the related exposure to an increasingly Westernizing urban culture. On the basis of earlier works of

134 Fayẕānī (2012a), 18f.

Michael A. Barry and Detlev Khalid, Olesen convincingly argues that the gap between these two distinct social spaces was much more severe than, for instance, in neighbouring Iran or the Central Asian Soviet republics: in fact, communication between those inhabiting one space and those in the other was almost non-existent.[135] Yet, those villagers who ventured to Kabul or Herat for work or education were clearly confronted with two conflicting sets of societal norms and values which they were inescapably required to negotiate. That this task had been thrust especially upon the youth had, as we have seen, already been markedly acknowledged by Fayẕānī.

Indeed, a substantial number of young people were drawn to alternative socio-political ideas which were derived from their intensive engagement with various ideological offers that ranged from Liberalism to Marxism and even Maoism.[136] Each of these new propositions had, in the eyes of its respective advocates, relevance for solving perceived social, economic and political problems in Afghanistan: in the end, all these ideologies aimed at nation-building proper, which in Afghanistan required primarily overcoming the confines of ethnic and religious identities. The problem, however, remained that the affinity to "development narratives"[137] of this kind was confined very much to the urban educated strata of Afghan society and, therefore, ultimately elitist.

Vis-à-vis the monarchs' inclination to Liberalism since the early twentieth century, which for them consisted primarily of technological advancement and cultural "Westernization",[138] Leftist ideologies, perhaps because of their revolutionary rhetoric, appear to have exerted an exceptional pull on the new urbanite educated youth. Interestingly, the Soviet Union – standard-bearer of these political persuasions – had been unsuccessful in expanding the influence of its ideological underpinnings beyond the shores of the Āmū Daryā for many decades.[139] Yet, the so-called "Young Afghans", or "Constitutionals" (*Mashrūṭah Khᵛā*), concentrated strongly around the only recently established *Amānī High School* in Kabul,[140] paved the way for anti-religious sentiments that would eventually become solely associated with Communism when they demanded the violent 'subversion of the existing government and of its basis,

[135] See Olesen (1995), 227f.

[136] See ibid., 203–19; Barry (2002), 215–18.

[137] For the discourse on "development" in colonial India, which, mediated especially by the *Khudāy Khidmatgārān*, appears to have had some impact on its Afghan neighbours, see Zachariah (2005).

[138] For a comprehensive account, see Olesen (1995), 111–212.

[139] See Arnold (1983), 5–7; Hyman (1984), 41–5.

[140] The *Amānī High School* (*Līsah-yi 'Ālī-yi Amānī*), later *Madrasah-yi Najāt*, which ran under the auspices of the Embassy of the Federal Republic of Germany in Kabul until 1964, was established by order of King Amānallāh Khān in 1924 and soon developed into a training centre for the future elites of Afghanistan: see Anon. (1353sh), esp. 23–6.

the Islamic code'.[141] Finally, the attempt to organize the diverse Marxist cells, which had existed especially in Kabul since the late 1950s, resulted in the foundation of the PDPA mentioned above, which almost at once developed two distinct rival factions, the more moderate and Socialist *Parcham* ("Banner") and the Leninist *Khalq* ("People").[142]

Initially, however, the PDPA stood next to the Maoist *New Democratic Flow* (*Jarayān-i Dimūkrātīk-i Navīn*; JDN, established 1964) and the moderately leftist *Party of the Democratic Progress of Afghanistan* (*Ḥizb-i Mutaraqqī-yi Dimūkrāt-i Afghānistān*, established 1966).[143] The *Organization of the Progressive Youth* (*Sāzmān-i Javānān-i Taraqqī*; SJT), a clandestine reservoir of the JDN youth, in particular emerged as a militant agent of Leftist ideology on the university campuses. Violent clashes between various political factions among the students of Kabul University subsequently became more frequent in the early 1970s, particularly between activists of the SJT and those students with more Islamist leanings. In June 1972, finally, Gulbuddīn [Qulb al-Dīn] Ḥikmatyār (b. 1366/1947), a student of engineering from the Imām Ṣāḥib district of Kunduz, who was not well-known, made himself a name when he killed Saydāl Sukhandān of the SJT cadre during one of those clashes.[144]

The most important catalyst for the almost meteoric rise of Islamism in Afghanistan, however, was the beginning of socialist government in the country, starting on 17 July 1973, when Muḥammad Dāvūd Khān overthrew the rule of his cousin Muḥammad Ẓāhir Shāh and abolished the monarchy,

[141] This line is, in fact, taken from Arnold (1983), 8, complete with the parentheses. Despite sustained effort, the original text from which it had been quoted could not be located; regrettably, Arnold does not provide a solid reference for it. Moreover, the account of Ghubār (1397sh), 38–41, 60 and 113–38, who had actually participated in the Young Afghans' resistance to the regime of Muḥammad Nādir Shāh (r. 1929–33), clearly indicates that the *Amānī High School* was neither the only centre of gravity of what he and other Afghan contemporaneous historiographers labelled "those of a bright mind" (*rawshan'fikrān*), that is, modernist intellectuals, nor did it particularly stand out from all the others. It seems, therefore, reasonable to assume that the quote in question here represents the agenda of the Young Afghans at this time in general, possibly to be found in some issue of their underground newspaper *Ḥaqīqat-i Ḥaqīqat* (see ibid., 136f.), which was unfortunately not available at the time of writing.

[142] Arnold (1983), 34–51.

[143] See Ruttig (2006), 6–8. Edwards (1993), 185, mentions the fact that the communist leader cult in Afghanistan took distinctly religious forms: in 1970, for instance, the PDPA newspaper *Parcham* published a poem in which the Persian term "durūd" (benediction, praise [of the Prophet Muḥammad]) had deliberately been selected in reference to Lenin.

[144] See Ḥikmatyār (n.d.), 105f.; Sands and Qazizai (2019), 68f. The latter based their portrayal of the event also on interviews with three ḤiI-Ḥ cadres of the first generation. Because the narrative remains, thus, firmly within the confines of this Ḥikmatyār-led organization, material from outside these circles is vital to establish a more sustainable account of these events.

utilizing to this end the *Parcham* wing of the PDPA.[145] As a result, the PDPA began to operate with ever growing confidence; this, alongside Dāvūd's autocratic presidential rule, resulted in further heightened tensions between Leftist students and their political opponents, especially those with religious inclinations. They had, meanwhile, also organized themselves: in early 1969, the *Organization of the Muslim Youth* (*Sāzmān-i Javānān-i Musalmān*; SJM) was founded in Kabul under the aegis of Ghulām Muḥammad Niyāzī, then Dean of the Shariʿah Faculty of Kabul University.

The *Sāzmān-i Javānān-i Musalmān*

David B. Edwards conducted a series of interviews with former SJM member Qāẓī Muḥammad Amīn Vaqād (b. 1366/1947) in 1984 and 1986, in which the story of how the SJM was established appears a bit different from the standard account that has Ghulām Muḥammad Niyāzī as the driving force behind its formation.[146] Vaqād named instead the younger ʿAbd al-Raḥīm Niyāzī (d. 1390/1970) as the initiator of the organization, and Mawlavī Ḥabīb al-Raḥmān Nangarhārī (executed 1397/1977) of the Madrasah-yi Imām Abū Ḥanīfah, one of only a handful of important *dīnī madāris* in Afghanistan before 1979 and situated less than twenty miles to the west of the city of Kabul in Paghmān,[147] as the learned religious authority behind its formation.[148] Strictly speaking, these two competing narratives are symptomatic of the factional dispute that broke out among the members of the SJM almost immediately and would finally manifest itself in the emergence of various rival Islamist organizations.

There are, however, some arguments that support the narrative that establishes Ghulām Muḥammad Niyāzī as the pivot of the emerging Islamist scene among young Sunni Muslim students in Kabul. One was his comparatively older age and his subsequent professional status within the university.

145 The socialist leanings of the government of Dāvūd Khān are well reflected in the 1976 Constitution: in there, various elements of socialist rhetoric were widely invoked, for example, 'people's sovereignty' (*ḥākimiyyat-i millī*), the 'eradication of exploitation in all its forms and manifestations' (*burdan-i istis̱mār ba-har nawʿ va shaklī*), 'cooperatives, and cooperative companies for production and consumption with the participation of the people therein' (*kūprātīfʹhā va shirkatʹhā-yi taʿāvūnī-yi tavlīd va maṣraf bā ishtirāk-i mardum*), or the state's legal regulation of private property on the basis of the principle of non-exploitation: *Rasmī Jarīdah-yi Afghānistān* 360 (1356sh), 1–3.

146 The standard account was propelled predominantly by the JIA: see, for example, the serial 'Yadī az pōhānid ustād Ghulām Muḥammad Niyāzī – *muʾassis-i Nahẓat al-Islāmī* dar Afghānistān', *Mīs̱āq-i Khūn* 1/1 (1359sh/1401h) to 1/6–7 (1360sh/1401h) (italics added).

147 Khan (1993), 8, lists only six *madāris*, while Olesen (1995), 187, lists eleven of them.

148 See Edwards (2002), 199f. The narrative that assigns a more crucial role in the establishment of the SJM to personalities other than Niyāzī appears to be the official one maintained by the ḤiI-Ḥ. See, for example, the obituary for Engineer Ḥabīb al-Raḥmān: Anon., 'Yād-i ʿazīzān az dast-i raftah', *Shafaq* 2nd Series 3/2–3 (1364sh), 85f.

Secondly, in contrast to Mawlavī Ḥabīb al-Raḥmān, Niyāzī knew the traditional educational system of the *Madrasah-yi Imām Abū Ḥanīfah* in Kabul, from which he himself had graduated prior to his studies at al-Azhar in Cairo, as well as the modern university, and hence would have been more predisposed than the others to serve as a mediator between these two distinct academic worlds. Last but not least, it was during his stay in Cairo that he gained a first-hand experience of the Egyptian chapter of the MB, also in its more radical manifestations,[149] which would constitute the paragon for the SJM and other, as well as subsequent, Afghan Islamist organizations.

Another factor that, besides the exposure of Niyāzī and later some of his Afghan students to the MB during their respective sojourns to Cairo, contributed to a more governance-orientated approach in these circles was the increasing availability of classic Islamist readings that had been translated into Dari and Pashto since at least the late 1950s.[150] Nonetheless, we shall see that the careful establishment of an intellectual connection with various Islamisms from outside the Afghan cultural framework was concentrated in only one particular faction of the emerging Islamist movement in Afghanistan, while others developed a genuine approach of their own, one that centred most strongly on ethnicity.

A driving force in the endeavour of bringing foreign Islamist classics to a wider attention in Afghanistan was the by then middle-aged Deobandi scholar Muḥammad Yūnus Khāliṣ (d. 1427/2006), born in a village near Gandamak in Nangarhar Province, north of the Shpīn Ghar / Kūh-i Safīd mountain range that constitutes the border to the former Khurram Tribal Agency of Pakistan.[151] Given that he was based in Kabul since early 1950,[152] it is quite fathomable that Khāliṣ attended sessions at Fayẓānī's *Madrasah-yi Tawḥīd*; at least, he was personally acquainted with numerous of its participants. Khāliṣ probably knew Ghulām Muḥammad Niyāzī: after all, the latter had returned from Cairo only a short time before Khāliṣ himself. Khāliṣ was put in charge of a religious programme on Kabul Radio upon his return to Afghanistan, and concurrently oversaw a Dari

149 The nucleus of this internal development within the Egyptian MB was the so-called "Secret Apparatus" (*al-jahāz al-sirrī*, or *al-niẓām al-khāṣṣ*), a clandestine militant task force established as early as 1940, which became increasingly prominent after the beginning of the persecution of the MB in 1954, see Mitchell (1969), *passim*; Zalaf (2022).

150 Also highly instrumental in publicizing the ideational universe of the MB among Farsi-speakers were Iranian Islamists of renown, such as Sayyid Hādī Khusraw'shāhī (d. 1441/2020) and Sayyid ʿAlī Ḥusaynī Khāminaʾī (b. 1358/1939), the current *rahbar-i inqilāb* of the Islamic Republic of Iran: see Bohdan (2020).

151 See ʿAzīzallāh (1386sh), 1.

152 See Aḥmadzay (1385sh/1427h), 9–11. Brown and Rassler (2013), 39f., conclude from the fact that Khāliṣ was trained as a traditional *ʿālim* rather than in a "Western-style" university that he represented a "Highland Islamism" that was distinct from the urban variety. Realities on the ground, however, appear to have been even more complex than those acknowledged by these two authors.

translation of Sayyid Quṭb's seminal *al-ʿAdāla al-Ijtimāʿiyya fi'l-Islām* by Shāh Muḥammad "Rashād" and ʿAbd al-Sattār "Sīrat".[153] In the following years, he would provide further translations from works of leading members of the MB, for example, *al-Dīn wa'l-Ḥaḍāra al-Insāniyya* by Muḥammad al-Bahī (d. 1402/1982) who had been Minister of *awqāf* in Egypt in the 1960s.[154] Yet, as we shall see further on,[155] the relationship between Khāliṣ and the Islamist circles in Kabul would remain only informal; he was, instead, becoming more formally involved in a similar circle in Jalalabad from about 1968.[156]

Other Islamist organizations in the wider Pashtun Borderland, here particularly the JiI in Pakistan, took a proactive approach and had their core literature translated into other languages in order to spread their message, although Pashto ranged rather low on their priority list, and Dari / Farsi did not figure at all.[157] Presumably, at least some familiarity with Urdu was assumed by the JiI leadership, so that Pashto-speakers were required to come to terms with the Urdu texts.[158] However, this aspiration to perpetuate the message of the JiI and its mastermind Mawdūdī did not immediately stretch much beyond the Durand Line: at the time of Partition, reportedly only a single and not further specified work had been available in Afghanistan.[159] While this is seemingly only a marginal detail, it is, in fact, a quite significant one, because it actually helps a great deal to explain the fact that the paragon for the Afghan Islamists remained clearly the MB, predominantly in its Egyptian manifestation, while the JiI has hardly ever served them as an intellectual inspiration, at least until the outbreak of the resistance against the PDPA–Soviet nexus in Afghanistan in the early 1980s.[160]

153 See Khāliṣ (1339sh), I: Title page.

154 See Khāliṣ, ed. (1351sh), alif–bā. Bahī, however, is not mentioned as a cadre of the MB, only as an Egyptian scholar who was concerned with a "renewal of (social) theories" (*tajdīd naẓarūnah*), that is, the rethinking of the basic foundations of human society: in line with the classical Islamist theory of al-Bannā and Mawdūdī, the exposition starts with a reaffirmation of Islam as the only natural basis for society, derived from positing the Qur'anic narrative of Creation as easily recognizable "truth".

155 See below in the present chapter, as well as Section 4.3.4.

156 See Aḥmadzay (1385sh/1427h), 25–7. See also Ṭalāyī (1390sh), 33–6.

157 See Olesen (1995), 228. The decision to translate selected JiI literature into (predominantly Indian) languages other than Urdu had already been made in April 1945, see Markazī Shuʿbah-yi Tanẓīm-i JiI (1997), III: 39–42. Pashto, however, figured rather low on the list of priorities: by 1946, only two shorter and rather basic works of Mawdūdī had been translated (see ibid., IV: 73). By the time of Partition, however, this had already expanded to six works, the most prominent among them being Mawdūdī's controversial *Risālah-yi Dīniyāt* from 1937 (see ibid., V: 73f.).

158 Indicative is the fact that the first Pashto translation of Mawdūdī's seminal exegesis of the Qur'an – *Tafhīm al-Qur'ān* (1942–72) – seems not to have been published until June 2000, when it was brought out by Shafīq al-Raḥmān in Takht-i Bāhī.

159 See Markazī Shuʿbah-yi Tanẓīm-i JiI (1997), 68.

160 The view of Brown and Rassler (2013), 37, which has not been further corroborated, that 'by 1970 the Kabul Islamists had developed close organizational ties to their nearest

The affinity to the MB was reinforced by the fact that those urbanite Sunni Muslims with a penchant for higher religious learning would usually go to al-Azhar in Cairo, highly regarded as a place able to provide an education that catered for the needs of the contemporary world much better than, for instance, the various Deobandi institutions across the wider region of South Asia. Ghulām Muḥammad Niyāzī and Yūnus Khāliṣ went there in the late 1950s, and so did the younger Burhān al-Dīn Rabbānī, a native of Fayẕābād in Badakhshan, who had started teaching at Niyāzī's Faculty around the same time.[161] Rabbānī, in fact, turned out to be the closest to the universalistic spirit of the Islamist message from among the other young compatriots of Niyāzī. His eventual nemesis, Gulbuddīn Ḥikmatyār, but also to an extent ʿAbd al-Rabb Rasūl Sayyāf (b. 1364/1945) from the district of Paghmān, both ethnic Pashtuns and over a decade younger than Rabbānī, would eventually be conspicuously more inclined to culturalist delineations. For the time being, however, they had all joined ʿAṭāʾallāh Fayẕānī's circle in Kabul and, in addition, indulged in the reading of whatever writing from Sayyid Quṭb was available.[162]

Finally, in 1965, Niyāzī published his magnum opus *Maʾākhiẕ-i Duvvum-i Fiqh-i Islāmī*, in which he shifted the discourse away from Fayẕānī's more intuitive insight into the revealed truth to a more legally proscriptive approach. This work shows Niyāzī clearly as a jurist, and he, therefore, developed a more conciliatory attitude to the Prophetic *ḥadīth* than that of earlier and jurisprudentially less versed Islamist theorists, such as Mawdūdī. In fact, the entire work is devoted to *ḥadīth* as the second-most-important source of Islamic law-making, even more so, as the primary source – the Qur'an – would provide only the general principles of the *shariʿa* (*qavāʿid-i kulliyyah-yi tashrīʿ*). However, the ability to infer from Prophetic *aḥādīth* – embodiment of the Prophetic Sunna as a clear representation of the Qur'an[163] – is indispensable[164] for the various sub-areas of the law (*furūʿāt*) and for considering the viability of new forms of human transaction (*muʿāmalāt-i jadīd*) from an Islamic viewpoint. Nevertheless, Niyāzī denied the traditional *ʿulamāʾ* this ability, because, in his eyes, they were too steeped in mere emulation (*taqlīd*). Yet, because the

ideological cousins in Pakistan, the JI', as well as their – equally uncorroborated – claim that the later *Jamʿiyyat-i Islāmī* (JIA) in Afghanistan had named itself deliberately in reminiscence of the JiI (see ibid., 38), appear hardly sustainable in the light of the textual evidence available at present.

[161] In 1966, Rabbānī went to al-Azhar, where he stayed for two years, returning to Kabul with an M.A. in Islamic Philosophy, see Anon., 'Mukhtaṣar zindigī'nāmah-i ustād Burhān al-Dīn Rabbānī – rahbar-i Jamʿiyyat-i Islāmī-yi Afghānistān', *Mīṣāq-i Khūn* 1/2 (1359sh/1401h), 21f., here 21.

[162] See Olesen (1995), 231.

[163] See Niyāzī (1344sh), 19–22.

[164] See ibid., 1f.

exegesis of *ḥadīth* had historically been quite flexible,[165] a new stratum of Islamic legal experts needed to be produced that was once again appreciative of the need for its pliant interpretation in the light of current affairs and requirements.[166] Driving this forward was exactly what Niyāzī aimed at contributing to with this work of his.

Indeed, it seems to have left quite an impression on his students, as only six years after the publication of *Maʾākhiẕ-i Duvvum*, Sayyāf went to al-Azhar as well, but, differently from Rabbānī and Niyāzī himself, returning from there with an M.A. in Ḥadīth Studies.[167]

The indebtedness to Niyāzī's world-view, which is widely attributed to the strong impact that the writings of MB cadres had on him, was not generally shared. In fact, the continued popularization of their ideas in the Afghan context was tied to factional disputes over who was the true heir of Niyāzī's legacy. In these disputes, Rabbānī's circle has pushed their claim most vigorously. Consequently, they constructed the SJM as the nucleus of the *Islamic Awakening Movement* (*Nahẕat-i Islāmī*), which, they claimed, was basically identical to the *Jamʿiyyat-i Islāmī* of Afghanistan (JIA) soon to be led by Rabbānī.[168]

This, of course, is only one partisan version of the story, yet a concerted quest for impartial information in this regard turned out to be disappointing, giving rise to the suspicion that such information might not even exist.[169] Therefore, all that can be factually stated on the basis of the current and rather unsatisfying sources is that the JIA was the organization that most visibly strove to integrate into what, in loose reference to Reinhard Schulze's terminology, may be called here the "Islamist International",[170] thus carrying the banner of Niyāzī's *Nahẕat-i Islāmī* on to the next level.

[165] See ibid., 30–149.

[166] See ibid., 3.

[167] See ʿAbd Rabbih (1407/1987), 24.

[168] See Anon., 'Yādī az ustad Ghulām Muḥammad Niyāzī muʾassis-i Nahẕat-i Islāmī dar Afghānistān', *Mīs̱āq-i Khūn* 1/2 (1359sh/1401h), 8f.; Anon., 'Yādī az ustād pōhānid "Niyāzī"', *Mīs̱āq-i Khūn* 1/5 (1360sh/1401h), 13 and 1/6–7 (1360sh/1401h), 12f. The reproduction of Niyāzī's own 'Tarbiyyah aw aghrāẕ bəy', *Mīs̱āq-i Khūn* 1/3 (1359sh/1401h), 12–15, contains a picture of him, captioned "Founder of the JIA" (*də "Jamʿiyyat-i Islāmī-yi Afghānistān" muʾassis*).

[169] As a consequence, all we have to work from is strongly biased accounts from those directly involved in the contestations over the true heritage of the SJM. While, unfortunately, this does not provide a clear and straightforward picture, it perhaps tells us something revealing about how such conflicts over spiritual and intellectual legacy in the Pashtun Borderland play out more often than not.

[170] Schulze (1990), 104–22 and 149–56, uses the concept of the "Internationale of the Muslim Brethren" for the period of organizational fragmentation of the MB along national lines and the related attempts to concentrate them all within a transnational body, roughly between 1940 and 1960. Here, it is deemed reasonable to expand Schulze's

Consequently, its monthly magazine *Mīs̱āq-i Khūn* contained, especially in the first couple of years of its existence, numerous articles on Islamist pioneers from the MENA region,[171] or written by them and translated into either Dari or Pashto. Immediately after Sayyid Quṭb's account of his travels to the USA between 1949 and 1951 had been posthumously published in 1985, for example, its serialized Dari translation appeared in the JIA periodical.[172] Similarly, a few years earlier, the journal carried a Pashto translation of a short chapter from Quṭb's *Dirāsāt Islāmiyya* (c. 1953).[173] A series on "The Islamic Movements at the Twist and Turn of History" by the early JIA ideologue Sayyid Muḥammad Mūsá Tavānā (d. 1427/2006),[174] which, despite the plural in the title, was entirely focused on the history of the MB in Egypt,[175] is even more indicative of the JIA's orientation towards the Egyptian MB than those translations from the texts of Sayyid Quṭb. Yet, the extent to which the JIA's own ideology was indeed modelled after that of the MB, and hence that the JIA can, therefore, rightly be considered the one among the Afghan Islamist organizations that was most seriously orientated towards the "Islamist International", will still have to be investigated in more depth further below.

Nevertheless, as has already been indicated above, the alternative narrative of former SJM member Qāẓ̤ī Muḥammad Amīn Vaqād on the emergence of

term beyond the confines of the MB and its historical auxiliaries in the MENA region, potentially encompassing any Islamist organization anywhere.

171 This illustrious list includes thinkers as diverse as the Āyatallāh Rūḥallāh Khumaynī (1/3 [1359sh/1401h], 5f.), ʿAlī Sharīʿatī (1/2 [1359sh/1401h], 80f. and 1/4 [1359sh/1401h], 81), Necmettin Erbakan (1/2 [1359sh/1401h], 19 and 1/6–7 [1360sh/1401h], 60–2), Abū ʾl-Aʿlá Mawdūdī (2nd Series 1/9 [1365sh/1407h], 34–7, 2nd Series 1/10 [1365sh/1407h], 72–7, and 2nd Series 1/11–2 [1365sh/1407h], 14–16) and Qāẓ̤ī Ḥusayn Aḥmad (2nd Series 2/10 [1366sh/1408h], 30–6).

172 See "Fāẓ̤il" (trans.), 'Amrīka az dīd'gāh-i Sayyid Quṭb', *Mīs̱āq-i Khūn* 2nd Series 1/10 (1365sh/1407h), 54–9; 2nd Series 1/11–2 (1365sh/1407h), 39–44 and 136, 2nd Series 2/3–4 (1366sh/1407h), 94–7, 2nd Series 2/8–9 (1366sh/1408h), 34–8, 2nd Series 2/10 (1366sh/1408h), 83–5, 2nd Series 2/11 (1366sh/1408h): 49–55, and 2nd Series 2/12 (1366sh/1408h), 41–8. On the publication history of this work of Sayyid Quṭb, edited from various materials written around his study trip to the USA, see al-Khālidī (1414/1994), 579f.

173 See ʿIṣmat Qāṭiʿ (trans.), 'Sayyid Quṭb: navəy žvand aw birtarah naṛəy', *Mīs̱āq-i Khūn* 1/12 (1360sh), 28–30 and 2/1 (1360sh), 49–51; compare Quṭb (1422/2002), 79–85.

174 Tavānā was yet another of Niyāzī's students who, in 1973, would embark on a study trip to al-Azhar in Cairo and complete a degree in Legal Hermeneutics (*uṣūl al-fiqh*) there. A close associate of Rabbānī from the early days, the two would eventually part ways, with Tavānā subsequently joining the competing JMIA of Uzbek militia leader ʿAbd al-Rashīd Dūstam.

175 See Dr Sayyid Muḥammad Mūsá Tavānā, 'Junbish'hā-yi islāmī dar pīch va khamm-i tārīkh', *Mīs̱āq-i Khūn* 1/4 (1359sh/1401h), 11f., 1/5 (1359sh/1401h), 9–12, 1/7 (1360sh), 10f., 1/9–10 (1360sh), 15–17, 1/11 (1360sh), 27–30, 1/12 (1360sh), 8–11, 2/1 (1360sh), 8f., 2/3 (1360sh), 17f. and 2/4 (1360sh), 19–22.

the *Islamic Awakening Movement* claimed to establish the *Ḥizb-i Islāmī* (ḤiI) as the true heir of the SJM, instead of the JIA, and, thus, also placed its eventual supreme leader, Gulbuddīn Ḥikmatyār, more in the limelight. Apparently, this narrative is even supported by a speech of Ḥikmatyār himself in the early 1980s, in which he portrayed the origins of the ḤiI 'as a student group at Kabul University in the late 1960s'.[176] However, Ḥikmatyār's own personal involvement in the early phase of the *Islamic Awakening Movement* was somewhat curtailed by the fact that, after the killing of SJT activist Saydāl Sukhandān in June 1972, Ḥikmatyār had initially been jailed for murder, but was released in the course of Dāvūd Khān's coup d'état almost exactly one year later and fled further prosecution in Afghanistan by settling in Peshawar instead.

Ethnicity arguably played a substantially larger role in the ḤiI than it did in the JIA. Although the latter was led by an ethnic Tajik from Badakhshan, it had many Pashtuns and members of other ethnic communities in its upper ranks, whereas the ḤiI turned out to be the prime reservoir for Pashtuns alone. As such, its Islamism would – at least implicitly – accommodate elements of Pashtun ethnic norms and values; in fact, there might have already been an ethno-religious element in Ḥikmatyār's killing of Sukhandān that is indicative of an Islamist reframing of "Doing Pashto" (*paẋto kavəl*). Firstly, the JDN, the Maoist mother organization of the SJT, was established by members of the Hazārah community that had perpetually been oppressed ever since the establishment of Pashtun-dominated Afghanistan.[177] Hence, both the JND and the SJT had already been targets for Pashtun Islamists for ethnic reasons; in addition, however, this enmity now became charged in religious terms: after all, the Hazārah are overwhelmingly Imāmī Shiʿi Muslims. As such, they have been widely regarded as heretics in radical Sunni circles, a fact that, in turn, caused them to orient themselves politically much more towards Tehran than anywhere else.[178]

[176] Edwards (2002), 177 (see also 320 n.1). Apparently, the claim of authenticity of this version is further cemented by media representatives of the Global North, who seem to keep providing Ḥikmatyār with additional opportunities to radiate his preferred version of the developments in question. See, for example, the award-winning four-part German documentary *Afghanistan: Das verwundete Land* by Mayte Carrasco and Marcel Mettensiefel from 2020, which gave Ḥikmatyār ample opportunity to present his perspective on camera, without having it even remotely challenged by any alternative narrative.

[177] The first wave of what in later Hazārah historiography is confidently regarded as ethnic cleansing took place during the reign of Emir ʿAbd al-Raḥmān between 1891 and 1893 and continued perpetually under each of the successive Barakzay rulers, see, for example, "Riyāẕī" (n.d.), 247–60. A vivid example of the portrayal of the Hazārah as an essentially persecuted ethno-religious community in Afghanistan by its own contemporary historiographers is Dawlatābādī (1385sh).

[178] In fact, Shiʿi Hazārah students formed their own ethnocentric organizations on Afghan university campuses during the 1960s and 1970s. The most important one that emerged out of these early manifestations was the *Shūrā-yi Inqilāb-i Ittifāq-i Islāmī-yi*

The confluence of Hazārah ethnicity, Imāmī Shiʿi religious creed and Maoist emphatic atheism in the JDN and its youth wing appeared fully coherent for radical Sunni Muslims such as Ḥikmatyār, and ethnic violence appeared to them, therefore, perfectly justifiable by Islamic standards. This justification, however, would also seamlessly stretch to non-Hazārah members and sympathizers of the JDN, and Sukhandān, a Pashtun from Logar, had forfeited his life simply by virtue of his association with them. To kill him for this reason alone foreshadowed somewhat the brutal consequences of an extreme interpretation of the Islamic legal doctrine of "association and disengagement" (*al-walāʾ wa'l-barāʾ*), which Ḥikmatyār was evidently considering significantly earlier than most of his Islamist peers across the Pashtun Borderland.[179] The point in time, however, does not appear entirely arbitrary, because, in fact, this was exactly when this doctrine shifted increasingly into the focus of militant MB ideologues in Egypt,[180] and young Afghan Islamists, even if they were not as devoted to the MB as the cadres of the JIA, were certainly inspired by this.

Apparently, therefore, the SJM was not conceived as a reservoir for all the religious opposition to the increasingly secular political culture in Afghanistan. When Ṣibghatallāh Mujaddidī, leading representative of the powerful "Ḥaẓarāt-i Maʿṣūmiyyah" of Kabul's Shōr Bāzār, wanted to join hands with the SJM he was turned down, purportedly because of the family's long-standing relationships with the Barakzay court in Kabul and – perhaps more significantly – their representation of traditional Muslim religiosity in Afghanistan.[181] This particular episode also indicates quite strikingly that the understanding of the juncture of Islam and politics within the SJM circles was,

Afghānistān, led by Āyatallāh Sayyid ʿAlī Bihishtī Varasī (d. 1417/1996), see Dāvūdī (1390sh), I: 259–62. During the Soviet occupation of Afghanistan, Bihishtī stipulated the formation of Shiʿi Hazārah militias, the most important of which were the *Sāzmān-i Naṣr-i Afghānistān* and the *Sipāh-i Pāsdārān-i Jihād-i Afghānistān*, both led by a group of commanders around Muḥammad Ḥusayn Ṣādiqī (killed 1409/1990), see ibid., II: 255–61. In 1987, finally, many especially of the ethnocentric organizations would be dissolved into the Tehran-backed *Ḥizb-i Vaḥdat-i Islāmī-yi Afghānistān* (ḤVIA), led by ʿAbd al-ʿAlī Mazārī (killed 1415/1995): see ibid., III: 235–40. On the political organizations in general, see Wieland-Karimi (1998), 180; Rubin (2002), 221–3; Ruttig (2006), 25f.

179 See Ḥikmatyār (1365sh). See also Sections 4.4 and 4.5. Eventually, however, also ʿAbd al-Rabb Rasūl Sayyāf took up the theme and coupled it with the idea of transnational Muslim solidarity, see Sayyāf (1370sh), 77–82 (*Dūstān va dushmanān mā bāyad badānand!*).

180 A prime example in this regard is the Egyptian *Jamāʿat al-Muslimīn* (*al-Takfīr wa'l-Hijra*), led by former MB member Shukrī Muṣṭafá (executed 1398/1978), for which this legal doctrine played a crucial role in its ideological justification, see, for example, Shukrī Muṣṭafá's *Wathīqat al-Khilāfa* (1977), in Aḥmad (1991), II: 115–55.

181 See Edwards (1993), 185f. The fact that Mujaddidī was trained at al-Azhar (see Mujaddidī [n.d.], 6f.), however, did not, as Edwards presumes, prevent him from joining,

indeed, markedly different from more traditional conceptions, as will be shown below by a closer look into the ideological set-up of the three most important organizations that have grown out of the SJM: the JIA, the Ḥil-Ḥ and the *Islamic Union for the Liberation of Afghanistan* (*Ittiḥād-i Islāmī Barā-yi Āzādī-yi Afghānistān*; IIAA).

The SJM served as a model for similar organizations in other cities in Afghanistan, organizations which, nevertheless, remained at the margins of the Islamist spectrum. The most significant of those was certainly a distinct *Ḥizb-i Islāmī* under the leadership of Yūnus Khāliṣ (Ḥil-Kh), who claimed in this way the heritage of the *Ḥizb al-Tavābīn* of Jalalabad, established in 1965 by the elusive Minhāj al-Dīn "Jāḥiẓ", which he had prominently joined. While being part of an emerging Islamist network that would soon span the whole of Afghanistan,[182] it appears reasonable to assume that the *Ḥizb al-Tavābīn* utilized personal networks predominantly throughout Nangarhar Province, networks that would eventually form the power basis for the Ḥil-Kh and also making plausible its ideological independence from Ḥikmatyār. In fact, it shall be argued here that Khāliṣ, while clearly comfortable with regard to navigating the metropolises and without doubt seriously flirting with Islamist thought, was still more embedded in the "Frontier Deobandiyyat" of the rural Pashtun Borderland, which is why he will resurface more prominently later in this chapter.[183] Still, the fact that Khāliṣ and Ḥikmatyār both chose to name their respective organization "Ḥizb-i Islāmī" certainly begs further explanation.[184] For this, however, we need to fast forward to arrive finally at what is, in retrospect, perhaps the most incisive historical event in contemporary Afghanistan: the coup d'état of the Muḥammad Tarakī-led Khalq-faction of the PDPA on 27 April 1978 – euphemistically called the "Ṣawr Revolution".

Institutionalized Militant Islamism: The Peshawar Seven

The violent takeover of the government by the PDPA (Khalq) forced all those Islamists who had not yet migrated abroad during the rule of Muḥammad Dāvūd Khān to flee the country and instigate an insurgency from outside the national borders of Afghanistan (Map 4.1). With the PDPA's seizure of power, Afghanistan had finally become a major battleground in the Cold War, and its respective Communist and Islamist assets appeared in the geopolitical

given the fact that SJM activists such as Rabbānī and Sayyāf had obtained degrees from there as well.

182 See Hayat Khan (1993), 226.

183 See Section 4.3.4.

184 Once again exclusively on the basis of two interviews, this time conducted in 1983 and 1984 with Khāliṣ himself, Edwards (2002), 247–52, did not indicate that the information he received had been checked against possible alternatives, to make sure that Khāliṣ did not just convey his own preferred version of the sequence of events.

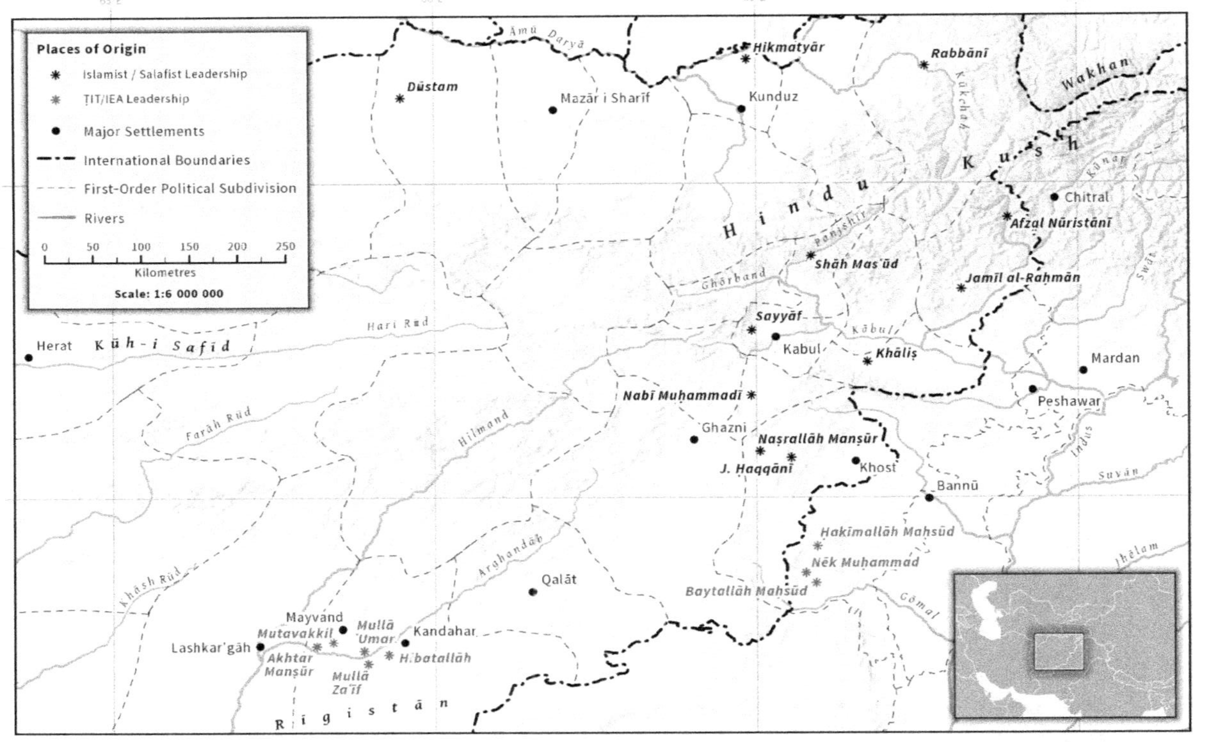

Map 4.1 The diverse leadership of militant Islamist resistance: places of origin (mid twentieth century).

calculations of the USSR and USA, alongside their various allies in the region, here predominantly India and Pakistan. As a result, the agendas of the Afghans involved did not play a role in these geostrategic calculations: the battle between the two ideological blocs was too fundamental to the justification of either side to seriously consider any aspiration outside that scenario.

The CIA had established an impressive track record of clandestine operations across the world over many years that aimed at destabilizing and removing any government with leftist inclinations. While its major area of operation in the 1970s was in Central and South America, close attention had also been paid to the developments in Afghanistan. The CIA was deeply concerned about the surge of left-wing activism in the major cities of Afghanistan, and, with the blessing of then-President James Carter (in office 1977–81), began to covertly support Islamist outfits there well before the Soviet invasion.[185] Finally, in June 1979, "Operation Cyclone" was initiated, with Carter's National Security Advisor Zbigniew Brzeziński (d. 2017), well known for his strong anti-Soviet sentiments, as its political driving force.[186] Almost instantly hastening to the support of the USA was the government of the Islamic Republic of Pakistan, which had been, since 5 July 1977, subjected to martial rule by General Zia-ul-Haq (Muḥammad Ẓiyāʾ al-Ḥaqq; killed in a plane crash 1409/1988),[187] and especially its military *Inter-Services Intelligence* agency (ISI).

A Special Operations Bureau had been established in 1973, in the aftermath of the unrest in the Pakistani province of Baluchistan that the power-holders in Islamabad perceived as a separatist action, and, from 1975 onwards, became the basis for all ISI operations in and around Afghanistan.[188] In 1979, this section was remodelled as the Afghanistan Bureau, which would become one of the largest and most important sections of the ISI.[189] Some years earlier, however, the ISI had been actively supporting religious adversaries of Dāvūd Khān financially and logistically. Among the beneficiaries, Ḥikmatyār turned out to be the one most agreeable to the agenda of the ISI, and initially – despite his open anti-Americanism – that of its mighty ally, the CIA.[190] The Soviet

[185] See Snider (2008), 283–5; Kiessling (2016), 48f.

[186] See Brzeziński's initially classified memo to Carter from 26 December 1979, in which he suggested that Afghanistan 'could become a Soviet Vietnam' (DNSA [1973–1990], AN unreadable).

[187] For the sake of better recognition, the common English rendering of the name of the sixth president of the Islamic Republic of Pakistan (as appears in official government publications from the years 1978–88) will henceforth be used throughout, despite it clearly appearing at odds with established academic conventions of Romanization of the Arabic script.

[188] See Kiessling (2016), 32–5.

[189] See ibid., 51–4. See also Sirrs (2017), 127–30.

[190] See Kiessling (2016), 34f.; Sirrs (2017), 113f. This information is based predominantly on an interview by investigative journalist Peter L. Bergen with Graham Fuller who, until the coup in 1978, was head of the Kabul Office of the CIA, see Bergen (2001), 69. Other

invasion, however, caused these relationships to deepen and intensify, while becoming more complicated at the same time.[191]

Moreover, the exile of Islamist leaders, such as Rabbānī and Ḥikmatyār, made Peshawar on the Pakistani side of the Durand Line into a convenient hub of all sorts of resistance activities against the PDPA and its Soviet ally. The crucial role of Peshawar as a hub of especially Islamist resistance turned out to have strong implications for the power dynamics in the Pashtun Borderland for many decades to come, underlined by the instantly mushrooming newspapers and periodicals that were published from there since around 1978 by the various factions of the Afghan resistance.[192]

It shall be contended here that these implications resulted from the ideologically distorted privileging of urban spaces over rural ones; ideologically distorted because it went hand in hand with the narrative of societal progress that finds its ultimate political expression in the "nation-state".[193] Because of the major attention devoted to the urban space, the actors within this frame mainly received the recognition by US-American and Pakistani authorities that translated into the much desired logistical and financial support. Subsequently, religio-political actors in the rural tribal areas who also longed for this kind of aid would have to use leading representatives of the predominantly Peshawar-based Islamist groups as proxies, or, alternatively, exploit their control over local commodities, here, predominantly narcotic plants and precious minerals, to finance their operations independently.[194] In fact, exploiting the wealth of green emeralds in the Panjshīr Valley enabled Aḥmad Shāh Masʿūd (assassinated 1422/2001) to retain a large degree of independence for his local *Shūrā-yi Naẓār*, and gave him a logistical advantage over other groups in the eventual war for power

former intelligence officers, such as Sayyid Raẓā ʿAlī, the first head of the ISI's Afghanistan Bureau, and his successor Muḥammad Yūsuf (b. 1937) between 1983 and 1987, corroborate these accounts to an extent: see Yousaf and Adkin (1992), 41.

[191] The US-American attitude especially towards Ḥikmatyār turned out to be a complicated one, in particular after the successful Islamic Revolution in Iran and the following wave of anti-Americanism across the Muslim world, epitomized in the hostage crisis in the Embassy of the USA in Tehran between November 1979 and January 1981: see Yousaf and Adkin (1992), 41, 103 and 208.

[192] See Faizi (1993), 275–9, who lists for the period between 1978 and 1981 twenty-seven newspapers and twenty-four journals issued from the various Afghan organizations in exile, in Dari, Pashto, Urdu Arabic and English.

[193] See, for example, Hobsbawm (1994), 24–33. See also Section 2.3.

[194] The number of research publications on what Schetter (2002) calls the Afghan "Bazar economy" is vast; their usefulness, however, depends a lot on the respective angle taken. Regarding the nexus of Islamically inspired militancy and the production and trade of narcotics, see Goodhand (2008); on the same constellation regarding precious minerals, see DuPée (2012), esp. 12f.

over Kabul that materialized almost instantly after the PDPA had given up its governing role.[195]

Both the CIA and the ISI, as well as the Saudi authorities, who saw an opportunity here to cement their own stake in the region as well as promoting the Kingdom's official brand of Islam, would, of course, not fund each and every supplicant who approached them for material support. Especially after this support no longer covered only the establishment of a religious and anti-Soviet propaganda machine, but, from January 1980 onwards, also catered increasingly for military support,[196] the funding bodies needed to streamline the beneficiaries, as virtually every group actively fighting the PDPA and the Soviets in Afghanistan demanded its share of the admittedly ample, yet ultimately limited, resources. This, after all, was the moment when the wheat had to be separated from the chaff even from among the meanwhile burgeoning Islamist organizations of various scales in Peshawar. Who was trustworthy enough to enjoy the material support of the US authorities – by proxy of their Pakistani counterpart – and deliver the results desired in Afghanistan, both in the short and in the long term? In answering this question, the contacts between the ISI, the CIA and the Afghan Islamists from before the Soviet invasion played a vital role, and led, finally, in late 1981, to the establishment of the IIMA, a coalition of seven distinct organizations. It was comprised of the JIA and the somewhat associated *Shūrā-yi Naẓār* of Shāh Masʿūd, the two distinct Ḥils led by Ḥikmatyār and Yūnus Khāliṣ, respectively, the IIAA headed by Sayyāf, as well as the two movements established by the heads of the two most influential Sufi families in the country, the *Maḥāẓ-i Millī-yi Islāmī-yi Afghānistān* (MMIA) of Sayyid Aḥmad Gīlānī (d. 1438/2017) and the *Jabhat-i Najāt-i Millī* (JNM) of Ṣibghatallāh Mujaddidī, and finally the *Ḥarakat-i Inqilāb-i Islāmī* (ḤII) led by Mawlavī Muḥammad Nabī Muḥammadī (d. 1423/2002).[197]

This coalition would appear to the outside as a by and large homogeneous bloc in the following years. Their collective leadership conducted political rallies on the Pakistani side of the Durand Line among the nearly two million Afghan refugees who had fled their country by the end of 1981,[198] and added

[195] See DuPée (2012). See also O'Donnell (1990). Generally on the *Shūrā-yi Naẓār*, see, for example, Qānūnī (n.d.).

[196] US-American military aid initially took place covertly, but, with the conservative Republican Ronald Reagan in the White House from January 1981 onwards, the budget was raised and the support became increasingly open, see Snider (2008), 284.

[197] See Hayat Khan (1993). On the two organizations led by Gīlānī and Mujaddidī, see Wieland-Karimi (1998), 199–204; on the Ḥil-Kh and the ḤII, see Section 4.3.4.

[198] For this figure, see Marchand, Siegel, Kuschminder et al. (2015), 30. For a report on one such rally in December 1986 in Peshawar, see Ustād Sayyāf, 'Afghān mujāhidīn kī sāt tanẓīmōṇ kē ittiḥād-i islāmī nē afghān ḥukūmat kī jang'bandī awr makhlūṭ ḥukūmat kī tajvīz kō mustaradd kar diyā', *al-Bunyān* 1/1 (1987), 15–8; Anon., 'Bayāniyyah-yi tārīkhī (18) jaddī-yi barādar Ḥikmatyār', *Shafaq* 2nd Series 2/7 (1365sh), 7–16; Anon., 'Bīsh az sih-hazār mujāhid va muhājir az qaṭaʿnāmah-yi haft tanẓīm-i jihādī-yi Afghānistān

two periodicals of their own to the ever more complex *jihādī* mediascape in and around Peshawar,[199] thus suggesting that they were all on the same page. This image would be fortified even further by the fact that the IIMA staged itself as the "Afghan government in exile", with an appropriately elaborate administrative structure. A closer look into those structures, however, and into the various periodicals of each organization under the umbrella of the IIMA, reveals a strong degree of subtle, and occasionally not so subtle, competition behind the public front of mutual affability.

However, it shall be argued here that this competition was not, as suggested elsewhere, entirely ideological,[200] but, in fact, more comprehensive. Ideological discord may, therefore, also turn out to be an extremely convenient cover for conflict that goes much deeper. In reality, the competition strongly signifies similar attempts to renegotiate the ethnic structure of governance in Afghanistan across all levels of society. After the ultimate collapse of the PDPA government in April 1992, this renegotiation turned into a bloody war for Kabul between the various armed Islamist organizations formerly under the umbrella of the IIMA, which continued until late September 1996 and left the hitherto hardly damaged capital reduced to rubble. That those militias who were responsible for this more than others, namely the Ḥil-Ḥ and Aḥmad Shāh Masʿūd's *Shūrā-yi Naẓār*, represented the two most prominent ethnic groups in Afghanistan – Pashtuns and Tajiks – underlines this point.[201] Democratic power-sharing, as was, perhaps naïvely, stipulated by the so-called "Peshawar Accord" of 24 April 1992 in which the 'structure and process for the provisional period of the Islamic State of Afghanistan'[202] was established, did not appeal wherever and whenever Afghan Islamism became compounded with ethnolinguistic chauvinisms. The various Islamist groups assembled under the IIMA represented distinct regional and ethnolinguistic constituencies;

mabnī bar radd-i ātish bas va maṣāliḥah-yi millī, Pishāvar namūdand', *Mīsāq-i Khūn* 2nd Series 2/10 (1365sh/1407h), 62–8; Anon., 'Afghānistan meṇ rūssī mudākhilat kē din kē mawqiʿah par *Ittiḥād-i Islāmī-yi Mujāhidīn-i Afghānistān* kā iʿlāmiyyah', *Maḥāẕ* [U] 1/4 (1987), 6–8.

199 These were the two monthly journals *Qiyām-i Ḥaqq* (in Dari) and *Də Shahīd Payghām* (in Pashto), both starting in autumn 1982.

200 See, for example, Wieland-Karimi (1998), 203f.

201 The prominence of these two groups in the conflict has a strong economic basis: while the Ḥil-Ḥ continued to receive the lion's share of material support from and through the ISI, the military advantage of the *Shūrā-yi Naẓār* was very much rooted in its extensive exploitation of the emerald deposits of the Panjshīr Valley that has continued well into the present.

202 UN General Assembly: Situation of Human Rights in Afghanistan. Note by the Secretary General, 17 November 1992 (A/47/656c), 34. The Islamic State of Afghanistan must not be confused with the current presence of the IS in the Pashtun Borderland, which will be discussed in Section 4.5.5. Here, however, it refers to the official designation of the government of Afghanistan between 1992 and 1996, as stipulated – although provisionally only – by the "Peshawar Accord".

therefore, their respective support bases expected them to enforce their particularistic interests if they wished to retain this support. In line with the borderland setting and the resulting socio-political specifics, this does not come as any surprise: we had already seen in the case of the nineteenth-century *Ṭarīqah-yi Muḥammadiyyah* how ethnically determined local interests frequently overrode universalist ideology in the Pashtun Borderland.

Still, ideological disparities – however illusory – remained a powerful driver for sustaining irreconcilable differences rooted elsewhere. In this respect, ideological particularities still require our attention, and this even more so as the subliminal competition between the various Islamist organizations under the umbrella of the IIMA was only one of the fatal miscalculations of the US-American authorities and their Pakistani allies. Another matter about which the CIA operatives remained almost entirely oblivious, and their Pakistani counterparts, at least on the surface, largely unconcerned, was the strong ideological drive behind the activities of those whom, in official documentation, they regarded as "dissidents", "insurgents" or "rebels".[203] Labels such as these frame them only functionally, as mere forces in opposition to the prevalent Afghan government, which the US administration had a vested interest in toppling. Yet, what they fall dramatically short of recognizing is the ideological direction of the Peshawar-based beneficiaries of American material and financial aid, a direction that would be as opposed to the market-driven neoliberal concept of governance that the USA was advocating, especially during the presidency of Ronald Reagan (in office 1981–9), as they were to communism of any variety. A similarly negative attitude was widely maintained among the Islamist organizations within the IIMA towards monarchism,[204] which put Saudi Arabia in the same boat as the representative democracies of the USA, Pakistan and other countries.

This misjudgement, the administrations of the USA, Saudi Arabia and Pakistan and their intelligence apparatuses would come to fully realize in the 2000s, cost them dearly.[205] By also offering material support to the media work

[203] See, for example, the confidential telegram from the US Embassy at Islamabad to the US State Department and other US Embassies and Consulates in Pakistan, Afghanistan, Iran and the Arabian Peninsula, dated 11 March 1985, regarding 'Afghan Dissident Activities' (DNSA [1973–1990], AN 790 113-1 325); or see the Briefing Paper of the US State Department on "Afghanistan and Pakistan" (ibid., AN 26 866, including substantial portions blackened out), dated 7 June 1983, where the Islamist resistance movement is cast as "rebels".

[204] It seems that not only the resistance organizations led by Gīlānī and Mujaddidī, but also the ḤII of Nabī Muḥammadī, were, presumably because of close relationships to the court that they had maintained during the Barakzay monarchy, not so averse to this model of governance: see, for example, Edwards (1993), 179–81; Wieland-Karimi (1998), 125–7, 179 and 202.

[205] Ironically, history seems to have been repeating itself during the two decades of direct military and political involvement of the USA and a host of allied nations of the Global

of the organizations under the umbrella of the IIMA – presumably because of the anti-communist propaganda it contained – the same foreign governments that would soon replace the Soviet Union as a deadly foe inadvertently contributed to the emphatic perpetuation of Islamist ideologies. In the end, core elements of these ideologies have manifestly become an integral component of the religio-political world-views associated with the ṬIT / IEA. This fact, in turn, provides all the justification we need to subject the respective ideology of three dominant Islamist organizations in the wake of the SJM – the JIA, the IIAA and, last but certainly not least, the ḤiI-Ḥ – to a detailed scrutiny. Predominantly on the basis of an investigation of especially the early volumes of the periodicals of each organization and writings of their leadership, the main objective will be to carve out their doctrinal differences, in order to subsequently be able to appreciate why and in what particular way some Islamisms have been of greater impact on the world-view of the ṬIT / IEA than others.

The Islamism of the *Jamʿiyyat-i Islāmī-yi Afghānistān*

In contrast to all of the other Islamist organizations under the umbrella of the IIMA, the JIA was the only one whose leadership at this point was actually ethnically diverse.[206] This is quite an important observation here, because the reasons for this are not to be found in the particular regional setting in which the JIA operated, but are probably to be inferred from its ideological set-up. Still, it is certainly commendable to bear in mind that, following the failure of the "Peshawar Accord" of 24 April 1992, the JIA and its closest ally, the Panjshīrī *Shūrā-yi Naẓār* of Shāh Masʿūd, emerged as the chief representatives of Tajik interests in the battle for Kabul. Whether or not this ethnocentric turn is owed to the political realities of the post-PDPA era in Afghanistan or also ideologically warranted will, therefore, also require investigation.

Accordingly, we shall begin by looking at its *Statutes* (*dastūr*), acknowledging that this is the core document that everyone who aspires to membership must affirm. According to this text, and very much in line with the general concept of Islamist organization, the JIA is headed by a consultative council (*shūrá*), presided over by a single leader (*rahbar*).[207] The choice of this term is quite significant, because it coincides semantically with the Arabic "murshid" that has been adopted into the nomenclature of the Egyptian MB,[208] thus highlighting

North in Afghanistan since late 2001, contributing significantly to its rather embarrassing outcome.

206 See Wieland-Karimi (1998), 178.

207 See Articles 5 and 16–18 of the JIA Constitution in JIA (n.d.).

208 The respective leader of the MB is known as *al-murshid al-ʿāmm*, or "general guide", a term consciously adopted from its usage in the Sufi context: see al-Bannā (1412/1992), 356–70 (*Risālat al-Taʿlīm*; 1937).

once more the strong impact of the MB both on the ideational universe and on the organizational design of the JIA. Equally revealing, though belonging to a denominationally distinct context, is the use of the address "rahbar" for the "Leader of the Revolution" in the Islamic Republic of Iran: both "murshid" and "rahbar" have a strong religious connotation that sheds light on the complex concept of leadership in the Islamic context. Communal leaders in the succession to the Prophet Muḥammad had hardly ever been exclusively political, but carried a strong salvific connotation of spiritual guidance.[209]

This spiritual dimension, in turn, was strongly emphasized by the JIA authors, especially regarding the first "General Guide" (*al-murshid al-ʿāmm*) of the MB in Egypt, Ḥasan al-Bannā,[210] and we may, therefore, safely assume that, despite the lack of explicit elaboration in its *Statutes*, the founding figures of the JIA were perfectly aware of these semantic particularities when they chose to adopt the term "rahbar" into its official nomenclature. In this light, the possession of actual charisma, in a Weberian sense, appears to be one, if not *the*, key criterion for anyone aspiring to the leadership of the JIA and, by implication, also the however vaguely envisioned polity-to-come. It is not surprising that this quality was instantly claimed by Rabbānī himself and resulted both in his uninterrupted leadership of the JIA until his assassination on 20 September 2011, his seventy-first birthday, by two suicide attackers allegedly from the wider orbit of the IEA, and in his sense of entitlement to the presidency of the Islamic State of Afghanistan, a claim which he and his retainers maintained throughout the first central government of the IEA. At that point, the baton of leadership in the JIA was passed on to Rabbānī's son, Ṣalāh al-Dīn (b. 1391/1971), who has since remained in this position, somewhat confirming Max Weber's systematic thoughts on the eventual transformation of "actual charisma" as a source of personal socio-political authority into "derivational" and finally "office charisma".[211]

If one accepts that Rabbānī's claim to leadership was sustained by the attribution of actual charisma by his followers, it seems reasonable to assume that his writings and public addresses will shed some authoritative light on the JIA's ideological set-up. However, apart from the voluminous *Irshād-i Jihād*, which, in

209 See Crone (2004), 17–32, who argues that the dominant term for the community leader in the foundational period of Islam had been that of "imām" not "khalīfa". This observation is consistent even with al-Māwardī (1422/2002), 5–22, which suggests that the salvific importance of communal leadership still remained undiminished during the late Abbasid period (c. fifth / eleventh century).

210 On al-Bannā's early compatriots in the MB, Aḥmad Afandī al-Sukkarī (d. 1411/1991), had, in one of his newspaper articles, stressed al-Bannā's predominant role as a "spiritual guide", while figures like himself would be more "political leaders": see al-Sukkarī, 'Kayf inzalaqa al-shaykh al-Bannā bi-daʿwat al-Ikhwān (3)', *Ṣawt al-Umma* 16 November (1947), 1.

211 See Weber (1972), for example 144.

fact, is a collection of speeches, sermons and interviews dating from between 1979 and 1989, that is, the period of active resistance against the Soviet occupation of Afghanistan, all of Rabbānī's separately published writings date only from the 1990s. The texts assembled in *Irshād-i Jihād* are instead motivational appeals aimed at aligning Rabbānī's various auditors to the coming and happening *jihād* against what is portrayed as unjust government, urging them to be prepared even for the ultimate sacrifice until – and this is noteworthy – the 'government of divine justice is established' (*dar jihat-i iqāmah-yi ḥukūmat-i ʿadl-i ilahī*).[212] The 'government of divine justice', in fact, emerged as a rather frequent expression in Rabbānī's speeches, which, towards the end of the Soviet occupation, became increasingly correlated with the notion of a "state of divine justice" (*dawlat-i ʿadl-i ilahī*)[213] that ultimately culminates in the "Islamic government of the Mujahidin".[214] However, what this post-occupation government of the *mujāhidīn* was actually supposed to look like remained, by and large, undeveloped in those public addresses, a fact that also marks Rabbānī's later writings. Instead, the emphasis in almost all of them remained on the dynamic element in the process of its establishment, captured in the concept of "revolution" (*inqilāb*).

"revolution" appears as a conceptual pivot both in Rabbānī's various published statements and in the JIA official periodical *Mīs̱āq-i Khūn*. While the titles of series of martyrologues and monthly accounts of the resistance activities in the various Afghan provinces suggest that it is mainly the armed opposition to the Soviet invasion and the PDPA regime that is regarded as "revolution",[215] one series in particular goes a lot deeper. Authored by a certain Sharīfallāh Faqīrī, the six instalments of "The Revolution within the Revolution" available, published between November 1981 and March 1982, present a systematic and differentiating perspective on the notion of "revolution", which is of special significance for any attempt to identify elements in the JIA ideology that distinguish it from other Islamisms, both inside and outside Afghanistan.

At first glance, Faqīrī's exposition seems pretty conventional: the opening paragraphs contain prominent terms from the lexicon of Islamism which, as the author later suggested, were prominently inspired by the works of Sayyid Quṭb and also Mawdūdī:[216] "divine sovereignty" (*ḥākimiyyat-i khudā*), Islam

[212] Rabbānī (1369sh), 134 (address to a large assembly of exiled *mujāhidīn* in Peshawar prior to their dispatch onto the battlefield, early April 1983).

[213] See, for example, Rabbānī (1367sh), 6.

[214] See ibid., 22.

[215] See the heading "The Martyrs of the Red Coffins of the Islamic Revolution" (*Də islāmī inqilāb sūr kafanī shahīdān*) for the regular martyrologues, and "What Is Happening in the Blood-Coloured Trenches of the Revolution?" (*Də inqilāb pah vīnō rang mōrchalō kx̌əy chah tīrīǵəy?*) for the monthly accounts from the provinces.

[216] See Sharīfallāh Faqīrī, 'Inqilāb dar inqilāb [part 3]', *Mīs̱āq-i Khūn* 2/3 (1360sh), 19–23, here 20.

as a "system of life" (*niẓām-i zindigī*) and "Islamic governance" (*ḥukūmat-i islāmī*) are prominent examples here.[217] Quṭb even got quoted, notably in a translation of his Qur'anic commentary by Rabbānī himself.[218]

Given its publication in the official periodical of the JIA, Faqīrī's line of argument may well be regarded as the organization's official ideological stand on the matter of "revolution". He set out by bisecting the concept into time-delayed parts: the first or immediate one would be the current armed struggle against the acute oppression by the PDPA and its Soviet allies. Once this is won – and won it undoubtedly will be by those who trust in and submit themselves to God! – comes the second and even more challenging part, consisting of the establishment of "Islamic governance". At this point, Faqīrī undertook an important differentiation between "war", "jihād" and "revolution". The latter two he regarded as synonymous as long as the revolution aims at establishing Islamic governance, or, in the words of Mawdūdī, who was cited here, the 'Islamic system of life'.[219] This meant that the participation of the JIA in the armed resistance against the PDPA–Soviet nexus was justified exclusively from the vantage point of its long-distance goal; at the same time, it discredited all of the many local resistance efforts across the Pashtun Borderland that were not necessarily driven by the desire to submit to the hegemony of any alternative political ideology, even if it came in an Islamic garb. In the eyes of the JIA cadres, those who did not participate in the resistance under an Islamist framework would have no right to perceive their activities as *jihād*, but would merely be waging war. As such, they were not of significance to the JIA and similar organizations other than as the future subjects of their rule, a view that strongly resembles the disdainful attitude towards rurality and subalternity which marked the rule of the Barakzay monarchs as much as that of Dāvūd Khān and also the PDPA.

217 See ibid. (part 1), *Mīṣāq-i Khūn* 2/1 (1360sh), 28f., here 28.

218 See ibid. (part 3), 20; compare Quṭb (1430/2009), I: 187 (on Q2.203). Rabbānī's translation of *Fī Ẓilāl al-Qur'ān* could not be located so far, and the quest for further details on it remains, therefore, open to future research.

219 See Faqīrī (part 4), *Mīṣāq-i Khūn* 2/4 (1360sh), 40–3, here 43f.; compare Mawdūdī (1994), 46. The Persian rendering of Mawdūdī's *Islāmī Ḥukūmat: Kis Ṭaraḥ Qā'im Hōtī Hē?* from 1941 was undertaken by Sayyid Ghulām-Riẓā Sa'īdī (d. 1409/1988) and published in 1964 in Tehran as *Bar'nāmah-yi Inqilāb-i Islāmī*. The Imāmī Shi'i cleric Sa'īdī, later compatriot of 'Alī Sharī'atī (assassinated 1397/1977) and Āyatallāh Rūḥallāh Khumaynī, was one of the foremost early translators of South Asian Islamist works into Persian.

To further sustain Mawdūdī's understanding here, Sayyid Quṭb was also quoted in this regard: see Faqīrī (part 4), 44; compare Quṭb (1402/1982), 171. The Persian translation of *al-Salām al-'Ālamī wa'l-Islām* (1951), as *Zīr'banā-yi Ṣulḥ-i Jahānī*, was prepared in 1977 by Sayyid Hādī Khusraw'shāhī and Zayn al-'Ābidīn Qurbānī Lāhījī (b. 1352/1934), two more of Khumaynī's early associates.

In the ideological set-up of the JIA, however, this attitude was sustained by the reference to Islamic precepts and would, therefore, yield potential consequences of a different degree of gravity: anyone's refusal to have local resistance efforts annexed by Islamist structures of predominantly urban provenance could well be used to deny such a person acknowledgement as a Muslim and decree their persecution for the offence of apostasy according to *shari'a* law.

The classical Islamist division of the world into the irreconcilable camps (*urdū'gāh'hā*) of Islam and of Unbelief, a cultural antagonism (*mubārizah-yi farhangī*) that is to be dissolved only through an uncompromising *jihād* in the Path of God or, in other words, the "Islamic revolution", serves as a theoretical basis for such an intensification. To support this argument, Faqīrī invoked not only Mawdūdī and Quṭb, but, this time, also the Shiʿi Muslim thinker ʿAlī Sharīʿatī, one of the masterminds of the Islamic Revolution of 1979 in Iran.[220]

For Faqīrī, a revolution can be regarded as genuine and legitimate only if it facilitates an instant "Islamic renaissance" (*nahẓat-i islāmī*): this – and here we come face to face with a central trope of the Islamist world-view – consists of a radical timely and socio-politically feasible reinterpretation of Qur'anic precepts, to be undertaken by those who would comprehend the requirements of the time.[221] Because of their educational and professional background, as well as having proved themselves in battle, the JIA cadres regarded themselves self-assuredly as predestined for this task, simultaneously denying traditionally educated *ʿulamāʾ* as well as other established community leaders the same privilege, including here even some with Islamist leanings, such as Mujaddidī and Gīlānī.[222]

Determining a purportedly "true" notion of "revolution" turns out to have been a rather diligent move by the JIA ideologues. After all, it was suitable to cater for the short-term goal, that is, the breaking of the monopoly of power held by the communist PDPA and militarily supported by the Soviet army, as well as for the long-term one, consisting of the complete transformation of the entire Afghan society exclusively on the basis of the JIA's interpretation of various Islamic precepts. Beyond this rather general declaration of intent, none

220 See Faqīrī, 'Inqilāb dar inqilāb [part 3]', 21f.; compare Sharīʿatī (1356sh), 133; Quṭb (1413/1993), 95. Especially in the latter case, the Persian translation of *al-Mustaqbal li-Hadhā al-Dīn* (1960), prepared in 1966 by Sayyid ʿAlī Khāminaʾī as *Āyindah dar Qalamrū-yi Islām*, introduces a consequential semantic nuance: rendering the Arabic terms "manhaj" (method) and "kifaḥ" (confrontation) synonymously as "jihād" has added a pointed meaning that could quite conveniently be utilized for their own ends by Afghan Islamist ideologues such as Faqīrī.

221 See Faqīrī, 'Inqilāb dar inqilāb [part 5]', *Mīs̱āq-i Khūn* 2/5 (1361sh), 22–5.

222 This point was emphatically made by the Egyptian jurist and early MB cadre ʿAbd al-Qādir ʿAwda (1405/1985), esp. 38–70, whose significance for the JIA ideologues will be highlighted later.

of the texts consulted revealed any practicable idea on the actual design of the polity envisioned, something that appears to be quite a common feature of Islamist ideologies in general.[223] Nonetheless, two further and rather early JIA texts allow us to, at least, infer some further conceptual details beyond the notion of "revolution". The first is a serialized Persian translation of the entire introductory part of ʿAbd al-Qādir ʿAwda's (executed 1374/1954) *al-Tashrīʿ al-Jināʾī al-Islāmī: Muqaranan biʾl-Qānūn al-Waḍīʿ* by the already repeatedly mentioned Sayyid Muḥammad Mūsá Tavānā;[224] the second is an anonymously authored series on "The Islamic Way of Governance", published in *Mīs̱āq-i Khūn* around the very same time.

ʿAwda himself turns out to have been an interesting choice. One of the few professional lawyers in the early generation of the MB, he represented the more systematic thinking within the organization that was then dominated by emotional revolutionary rhetoric. While this minority position put him over and over again in politically delicate situations, expressed by him oscillating between closeness to and distance from the top leadership of the MB,[225] his systematic thought represented, more than did the thinking of Ḥasan al-Bannā or Sayyid Quṭb, something approximating a theory of Islamic governance. The anonymous author of the series on "The Islamic Way of Governance", finally, seems to have fitted ʿAwda's ideas, as they appear from the passage translated by Tavānā, into the specific conceptual framework of JIA Islamism, in which armed *jihād* played a more pronounced role than for the very early theorists of Islamism, and a more systematic one than in the highly emotive expositions of Sayyid Quṭb.

The systematic integration of *jihād* takes off from ʿAwda's axiomatic stipulation that the "political system of Islam" (*niẓām-i siyāsī-yi islām*) grows out of the threefold root "equity" (*musāvāt*), "mutual consultation" (*shūrá*) and "justice" (*ʿadālat*).[226] From here, the anonymous author continued along the lines of Mawdūdī by ascribing the existing fundamental differences in the understanding of such basic anthropological provisions as "equity", and of resulting moral categories such as "justice", to distinct economic systems to which various societies adhere.[227] Human beings, however, have been

[223] This point has already been emphasized in Hartung (2013a), 225–59.

[224] See ʿAwda, Shahīd ʿAbd al-Qādir / trans. Dr Sayyid Muḥammad Mūsá Tavānā, 'Qānūn'jazāʾ dar islām', *Mīs̱āq-i Khūn* 1/3 (1359sh/1401h), 58f., 1/4 (1359sh/1401h), 56–9, 1/5 (1359sh/1401h), 45–9, 1/6–7 (1360sh), 70f. and 74, 1/9–10 (1360sh), 74–6, 1/11 (1360sh), 56–8, 1/12 (1360sh), 58–61, 2/1 (1360sh), 55–7, 2/2 (1360sh), 63–6, 2/3 (1360sh), 57–9 and 62, and 2/4 (1360sh), 56–8 and 82; compare ʿAwda (1400/1980), i: 12–63.

[225] On ʿAwda and his ambivalent manoeuvring between the various factions within the MB and their auxiliaries in the Egyptian military government of the early 1950s, see Mitchell (1969), *passim*.

[226] See Anon., 'Ṭarz-i ḥukūmat dar islām [part 1]', *Mīs̱āq-i Khūn* 1/2 (1359sh/1401h), 65–8, here 65; compare ʿAwda (1400/1980), i: 25–9 and 37–41.

[227] See Anon., 'Ṭarz [. . .] [part 2]', *Mīs̱āq-i Khūn* 1/3 (1359sh/1401h), 54f., and 'Ṭarz [. . .] [part 3]', *Mīs̱āq-i Khūn* 1/4 (1359sh/1401h), 72f.; compare Mawdūdī (1969), 21–67 and

benefited by God with reason and free will to individually choose the system under which they would live, provided that they are allowed to make their choice free from coercion. Yet, as the PDPA and its Soviet aides were all too willing to employ physical force in making all Afghans realize the – from their perspective, systematically consistent – inevitability of the Proletarian Revolution as part of a universal historical process, all those subscribing to any other ideological foundation were also prompted to respond with arms. Still, only the armed engagement of the adherents to Islamism can be rightfully regarded as *jihad*; every other armed confrontation between ideological adversaries would have to be merely a war (*jang*).

Devoting extensive space to the explanation of "jihād", especially regarding the limits of its legitimacy, appears reasonable for the time when these arguments were actually presented as a sound religious justification for the activities of all JIA-affiliated fighters.[228] It is, therefore, also plausible that most of Rabbānī's public and semi-public addresses at that time, published either in *Mīṣāq-i Khūn* or separately, pivot on the same theme. Yet, it certainly begs for some explanation that one such serialized treatise was reprinted without any modification or addition as a small booklet as late as 1994, that is, just two years before the IEA established its first central government. The situation for Rabbānī and those of his inner circle appeared as if the first phase of the "revolution", which, according to Sharīfallāh Faqīrī in 1981, consisted of the armed struggle against the PDPA–Soviet nexus, had never been completed. That, in fact, is quite consistent with the axiomatic leadership role that the JIA had bestowed upon itself and its *rahbar* Rabbānī: as long as there was any armed opposition to the presidency of Afghanistan that had been entrusted to Rabbānī and his allies by the ratification of the "Peshawar Accord", the establishment of civil Islamic rule in Afghanistan – phase two of the "revolution" – had once more to be postponed indefinitely.[229]

However, this is not to say that Rabbānī did not develop any idea at all of an Islamically grounded political reality in Afghanistan after the Soviet withdrawal and the subsequent collapse of PDPA rule. As in many instances where Islamists have been entrusted with actual government responsibilities, political pragmatics demanded certain concessions that were quite at odds with even fundamental positions of their ideology. Rabbānī's pragmatic

94–114; (1993), 66–71 and 114–25. On Mawdūdī's respective arguments, see also Hartung (2013a), 132–42.

[228] In this regard, see also ʿA.T. al-Ḥājj, 'Jihād az dīd'gāh-i Qurʾān al-Karīm', *Mīṣāq-i Khūn* 1/2 (1359sh/1401h), 31–4 and 59 (on Q2.190f.), 1/3 (1359sh/1401h), 26f. and 55 (on Q2.216), 1/4 (1359sh/1401h), 38f. and 74f. (on the first half of Q2.217), 1/5 (1360sh), 63–5, 1/6–7 (1360sh), 27–9 and 1/9–10 (1360sh), 38–42 (on Q3.121–7), and 2/4 (1360sh), 45f. and 64 (on the first half of Q29.6).

[229] This fact is, once again, indicated by the reissue of Rabbānī's *Āmūkhtānihāyī dar Masīr-i Inqilāb al-Islāmī* from 1981–2 as late as 1994: see Rabbānī (1372sh).

acknowledgement of the ethnic and religious diversity of Afghanistan was certainly conspicuous in this regard: it required the development of tolerance towards all other societal groups, particularly because it meant a clear departure from the earlier hegemonic attitude towards rural subalterns in the Pashtun Borderland who chose to resist the oppression by the PDPA and Soviet Army rather independently from Islamist organizations. Thus, less than a decade later, Rabbānī stressed, even repeatedly, the need to transgress the denominational divide between Sunni and Shiʿi Muslims,[230] which, however, may well have been born out of the realization that the Sunni Tajiks, to whom Rabbānī himself belonged, and the Imāmī Shiʿi Hazārah belong to the same linguistic group and thus form the largest opposition to the ethnocentricity of the Pashtun Islamist organizations, here, first and foremost, the fiercest rival of the JIA, the Ḥil-Ḥ.

Yet, Rabbānī's pragmatics in this regard could still be construed as an expression of his unfettered adherence to Islamist principles: the adherence to the "bare minimum"[231] of Islamicity transcends all existing ethnic and denominational boundaries and was, therefore, to be reasonably employed in post-PDPA Afghanistan. In fact, this approach was – at least on the surface – materialized in the *United National Islamic Front for the Salvation of Afghanistan* (*Jabhah-yi Muttaḥid-i Islāmī-yi Millī Barā-yi Najāt-i Afghānistān*), better known as the "Northern Alliance", which was pragmatically formed in early 1996 as a military reaction to the advance of the ṬIT by Sunni Tajik, Uzbek and Pashtun and Shiʿi Hazārah militias,[232] while the more ethnocentric Ḥil-Ḥ remained apart.

The Islamism of the *Ittiḥād-i Islāmī-yi Afghānistān*

The other major Islamist organization under the umbrella of the IIMA that did not join the "Northern Alliance" in 1996 was ʿAbd al-Rabb Rasūl Sayyāf's IIAA, a Pashtun-dominated organization which Wieland-Karimi has characterized as 'following a Wahhābite (Saudi Arabian) course'.[233] While it is certainly true that Sayyāf maintained a closer connection to the Kingdom than did the leaders of the other organizations, and was lauded for his proficiency and eloquence in Arabic,[234] this characterization still requires some

230 See Rabbānī (1369sh), 78–92, here 89f. (address to the publication wing of the *Shūrā-yi Naẓār* on 22 July 1988). On Rabbānī's friendly attitude towards Shiʿi Muslims, see also Fuchs (2017), 197f., who, however, also extends this assessment to the IIAA and Ḥil-Ḥ.

231 This term seems attractive enough to be borrowed from Tayob (2017), 30 and 41, despite him dropping it in rather casually and without any further conceptual substantiation.

232 See Ruttig (2006), 15.

233 Wieland-Karimi (1998), 179 (translation mine; spelling follows the German original); even Fuchs (2017), 189 and 200.

234 See Nadvī (1404/1984), IV: 296f., referring here to Sayyāf's address to the RAI in Mecca on 9 September 1990.

careful reassessment. After all, Sayyāf had been a core member of Niyāzī's circle that had eventually dissolved into the SJM, a fact that prompted observers to perceive the latter, the JIA and the IIAA as ideologically more or less identical.[235] This perspective also calls for closer inspection.

Sifting through the few available issues of the IIAA's Pashto and Dari journal *Ḥaqq Pāćūn*, which was started only as late as November 1985, a particularly strong relationship with Saudi Arabia is much less apparent than, once again, a strong connection with the Egyptian MB instead. In March 1988, for example, the journal printed the Dari translation of a message of greetings to the IIAA readership by the then *murshid ʿāmm* of the MB, Muḥammad Ḥāmid ʿAbd al-Naṣr (d. 1416/1996).[236] A serial by Engineer ʿAbd al-Vadūd "Khālid", which was published in *Ḥaqq Pāćūn* later the same year, was devoted to an extensive discussion of the activities of the MB in its formative period, including the respective ideological underpinnings of the two organizations.[237] In contrast, religious influences from Saudi Arabia are, at most, implicitly discernible. On the other hand, however, the IIAA was the only one of the prominent Islamist organizations under the umbrella of the IIMA that also ran a monthly journal in Arabic, *al-Bunyān al-Marṣūṣ*, alongside an Urdu one of the same title, a fact that prompts questions regarding their respective target audiences.

At this point, the issue of ethnolinguistic affinities comes into play for the IIAA, especially in the light of the JIA's capitalizing increasingly on its strong dominance by Dari-speaking Tajiks, and subsequently deriving the bulk of its support from other Persian-speaking communities, first and foremost among them the Islamic Republic of Iran. The Kharōṭī-Ghilzay Pashtun Sayyāf might possibly have sought support from his ethnic peers and their allies on the eastern side of the Durand Line had this support line not already been comprehensively exploited by the other Pashtun-dominated organization, the ḤiI. The IIAA, encouraged especially by Sayyāf's proficiency in Arabic mentioned previously and his academic background in the increasingly reviving *ʿulūm al-ḥadīth*, had, therefore, turned to the Arabic-speaking world for material and ideational support.[238] Consequently, Sayyāf emerged as the

235 Earlier in his memoirs, Indian scholar Sayyid Abū 'l-Ḥasan ʿAlī Nadvī (d. 1420/1999) stressed the common association with al-Azhar – and presumably also the leadership of the Egyptian MB, with which Nadvī himself enjoyed complex relationships – as the critical moment that united the initial efforts of Niyāzī, Sayyāf, Rabbānī and early JIA cadre Mūsá Tavānā mentioned above to advance their knowledge of 'faith-illuminating literature and Islamic movements' (ibid., II: 151 n.1).

236 See Anon. (trans.), 'Muṣāḥabah-yi kih bā murshid-i ʿāmm-i Jamʿiyyat-i Ikhvān al-Muslimīn pīrāmūn-i jihād-i Afghānistān ṣūrat giriftah ast', *Ḥaqq Pāćūn* 2/2 (1367sh/1408h), 6–8.

237 See Ingīnar ʿAbd al-Vadūd "Khālid", 'Ikhvān *al-Muslimīn* dar masīr-i daʿvat', *Ḥaqq Pāćūn* 2/14–5 (1367sh), 51–4 (fourth instalment; other issues are currently not available).

238 See, for example, Sayyāf (1366h).

public face of the Afghan Islamist resistance in that part of the world. He established closer contacts to the Mecca-based RAI from the mid 1980s onwards and subsequently figured in the organization's periodicals as a leading representative of the actually utterly diverse Afghan resistance to the PDPA–Soviet nexus.[239] Nonetheless, even his elevation in 1989 to membership in one of the RAI's bodies, the *Supreme World Council for Mosques* (*al-Majlis al-Aʿlá al-ʿĀlamī li'l-Masājid*), does not belie the fact that Sayyāf and his IIAA remained firmly within the Islamist rather than the Salafi-cum-Wahhabi ideological universe.[240] The creed (*shiʿār*) of the IIAA, printed at the head of the title page of the early issues of *Ḥaqq Pāćūn*, represents its world-view in a nutshell:

> Our goal is the pleasure of God – exalted He is! –; His Eminence Muḥammad – God's prayer upon him and peace! – is our leader [*rahbar*], the Noble Qur'an our law [*qānūn*], *jihād* in the Path of God our way, martyrdom in the Path of God our greatest hope, independence our honour, and the veil of the *shariʿa* our cloak [*sharʿī ḥijāb mū pət day*].[241]

Probably because of these rather obvious Islamist proclivities, Sayyāf would play much less of a role in the RAI than many other non-Saudi personalities, such as the above-mentioned admirer of Sayyāf's command of the Arabic language, Sayyid Abū 'l-Ḥasan ʿAlī Nadvī, president of the *Nadvat al-ʿUlamāʾ* in north-Indian Lucknow and a direct descendant of Sayyid Aḥmad Barēlvī.[242]

Nevertheless, while perhaps less significant for their ideological impact at that point in time, Sayyāf's networks in the Arabic-speaking world nonetheless had a decisive impact on the religio-political dynamics in the Pashtun Borderland and beyond. He and his IIAA emerged as an important facilitator for Arab Islamist volunteers who, from the second half of the 1980s onwards, started to join the Afghan resistance to the PDPA regime and its Soviet ally. His association with the Palestinian radical Islamist ʿAbdallāh ʿAzzām (killed 1419/1989), whom Sayyāf might have already met during his studies abroad at al-Azhar in Cairo, and who had moved to Pakistan in late 1980 at the instigation

239 See, for example, Anon., 'Tashkīl al-majlis al-aʿlá li-ʾittiḥād al-mujāhidīn al-afghānī', *Akhbar al-ʿĀlam al-Islāmī* 910 (1405/1985), 6 (picture of Sayyāf as representative of the IIMA); Anon., 'Sayyāf: al-jihād mustamirr ḥattá yawm al-naṣr', *Akhbar al-ʿĀlam al-Islāmī* 1 026 (1407/1987), 1 and 14.

240 See Anon., 'Aʿḍāʾ al-Majlis al-aʿlá al-ʿālamī li'l-masājid', *Akhbar al-ʿĀlam al-Islāmī* 1 108 (1409/1989), 14. A few years later, however, the scale had tipped in favour of the second Afghan member on that body, Muḥammad Hāshim Mujaddidī, from Ṭanḍō Sāʾīndād near Hyderabad, Sindh, see Anon., 'Intikhāb aʿḍāʾ jadduda fi'l-majlis al-aʿlá al-ʿālamī li'l-masājid', *Akhbar al-ʿĀlam al-Islāmī* 1 575 (1419/1998), 4. On the role and function of the *Mosque Council* within the RAI, see Schulze (1990), 284–91.

241 For example, *Ḥaqq Pāćūn* 1/1 (1364sh/1406h), title page.

242 On Nadvī's shifting role and significance in the RAI, see Hartung (2004), 421–36.

of Kamāl al-Dīn al-Sanānīrī (d. 1402/1981), a member of the Egyptian MB and brother-in-law of Sayyid Quṭb, was certainly of exceptional consequence in this regard.[243] Four years later, upon the release of his infamous appeal *The Defence of Muslim Lands Is the Highest of the Individual Obligations* (*al-Difāʿ ʿan ʿArāḍī al-Muslimīn Ahm Furūḍ al-Aʿyān*; 1984),[244] ʿAzzām finally set up shop in Peshawar's strategically convenient University Town and opened his *Maktab al-Khidamāt al-Mujāhidīn al-ʿArab* (MKh) there, designed to facilitate the processing of Arab volunteers, who, following his passionate appeal, began to arrive there in increasing numbers. ʿAzzām highlighted the reasons why he decided to issue what he self-assuredly called a *fatwa* in the prologue to this text, and claimed that these had already been explained to Sayyāf at length prior to its composition: 'I made clear to Sayyāf, the leader of the *mujāhidīn*, that, after three years of my life for the Afghan *jihād*, [I have arrived at the conviction that] this *jihād* needs [more] men.'[245] Leaving the theological and legal arguments provided by ʿAzzām aside for the moment,[246] it is important to note that Sayyāf, in a statement from 22 June 1985 which was purposefully included in ʿAzzām's text, appears to have assented to ʿAzzām's *fatwa* by putting the matter openly before a wider audience of *ʿulamāʾ* and Islamic preachers for their endorsement.[247] Still, he manifestly wished to restrict his own tacit approval of active Arab involvement in the Afghan resistance efforts to religious instruction and guidance of the *mujāhidīn* only, in order to advance and deepen their knowledge of all religious matters pertinent to their ultimate goal, the 'establishment of the state [on the principles] of the Qur'an' (*iqāma dawlat al-qurʾān*).[248] We may, therefore, safely conclude that Sayyāf was a driving force in bringing ʿAzzām to Peshawar and providing the necessary logistical support to the volunteers arriving from outside Afghanistan and the Pashtun Borderland.

Nevertheless, his recommendation (*naṣāʾiḥ*) to the Arab volunteers – the likely target audience of *al-Bunyān al-Marṣūṣ* – that they should refrain from harshly judging the religious beliefs and practices of their Afghan fellow fighters, issued just a few months later, puts things into perspective: they must not jeopardize the success of the *jihād* against the unbelieving PDPA

243 Although having, by and large, been rather unsuccessful, Sanānīrī is still highlighted in militant Salafist historiography as a pioneer in calling for a religiously inspired participation in the Afghan resistance and, thus, preparing the ground for the eventual surge of Arab volunteers arriving in the Pashtun Borderland, see, for example, al-Ẓawāhirī (1431/2010), 60–2.

244 See ʿAzzām (1417/1997), I: 119–46.

245 Ibid., I: 119.

246 For these, see Section 4.5.1.

247 See ʿAzzām (1417/1997), I: 128. Sayyāf's statement has been reprinted from *al-Jihād* 1/9 (1405/1985), frontispiece.

248 See *al-Jihād* 1/9 (1405/1985), frontispiece.

and its Soviet ally by wandering around and admonishing the Afghan *mujāhidīn* to give up various of their beliefs and practices which the Arab volunteers may consider a violation of the fundamental doctrine of *tawḥīd*:

> It is difficult for them [i.e., the Afghan fighters] to be assaulted with the blade of being charged with unbelief [*kufr*]. How can you declare them to be unbelievers? They have completely sacrificed life and property on the path of spreading the doctrine of God's Oneness [*fī sabīl nashr ʿaqīdat al-tawḥīd*] while you sit in your comfortable house with your family. If you see something objectionable, then there are gentle ways and a prudent manner to set the situation right.[249]

Apparently, there had been a significant rift between the Afghan and Arab fighters within the Afghan resistance, resulting ultimately in them establishing separate bases and only coming together for joint operations. Conflicting conceptions of *tawḥīd* and their respective practical implications, a constellation that we shall from now on encounter repeatedly, were obviously bones of contention. Underlying this conflict, however, was a methodical difference that was difficult to reconcile: while Borderland pragmatics commended suspension of dogmatic differences between the various factions of the *mujāhidīn* until the common enemy had been defeated, for the more theoretically informed Arab volunteers, the establishment of conformity with their own distinct interpretation of the *shari'a* among those fighters "in the Path of God" was declared *conditio sine qua non* for their eventual triumph over the infidels they were all fighting in Afghanistan at that point in time. The practice of *takfīr* was an indispensable part of that view, following consistently from the Qur'anic commandment to 'enjoin the commendable and prevent the reprehensible' (*amr bi'l-maʿrūf* [. . .]), which we have so far encountered most prominently in Naqshbandiyyah-Mujaddidiyyah circles, especially in the upper Pashtun Borderland, as well as the legal doctrine of "association and disengagement" (*al-walāʾ wa'l-barāʾ*), an increasingly prominent element in Salafi-cum-Salafist thought. As a cornerstone of the intellectual universe of the latter, it was most probably through the Arab volunteers facilitated by ʿAzzām's MKh in Peshawar that the practice of *takfīr* now also began to trickle into the Afghan Islamist circles.[250]

Nonetheless, it appears from the body of texts scrutinized here that the need to elaborate on their own conception of *tawḥīd* and put the agitated Arab volunteers at ease in that way had never really occurred to Sayyāf and his

249 Sayyāf, 'Akhī al-muslim', *Bunyān al-Marṣūṣ* 4 (1406/1985), 4–7, here 5. The translation follows largely Fuchs (2017), 200, who must be credited as the first scholar to bring this to the attention of a wider English-reading audience.

250 For ʿAzzām's own legal arguments for the necessity of *al-amr bi'l-maʿrūf* [. . .], which suggest that he was not as averse to the conduct of the Arab volunteers as his Afghan associates: see ʿAzzām (1417/1997), ɪ: 610–20 (*K. Ḥukm al-ʿAmal fī Jamāʿa*; n.d.), esp. 211–14.

compatriots of the IIAA. This lack of concern, however, is quite consistent with the Islamist attitude towards many of the established Islamic sciences as such: hardly any Islamist theorists have elaborated much on theological concepts; they have focused instead more on the elucidation of categories of Muslim societal practice, such as "state", "governance", "consultation" or "jihād". This, however, was clearly changing now: the new generation of Arab Islamists who arrived in Peshawar even disregarded classical Islamist authors such as Sayyid Quṭb as a solid reference on account of their not having engaged deeply enough in matters of faith (*iʿtiqādāt*).[251] Sayyāf and his compatriots in the IIAA, however, went further still and did not even bother to make any reference to readily available elaborations on *iʿtiqād*, which somewhat contradicts ʿAzzām's own judgement that Sayyāf was indeed a 'stern Wahhābite fundamentalist activist' (*wahhābī uṣūlī ḥarakī mutashaddid*).[252]

While being unwilling to accept the practice of *takfīr* against the IIAA cadres, Sayyāf operated with the concept of "unbelief" (*kufr*) himself to religiously justify the course of action of the IIAA. In an interview with the Saudi newspaper *al-Jazīra* in October 1981, for example, Sayyāf depicted the Soviets as naturally disposed to unbelief; their presence in Afghanistan, therefore, should be regarded as an assault on the – again not further elaborated – doctrine of *tawḥīd*. Because Sayyāf presented his perception of the situation in Afghanistan through an Islamic conceptual prism, all resistance to the PDPA–Soviet nexus in whatever form – with the tongue, the pen and the sword – counted for him as fulfilment of the individual obligation for defensive *jihād*. Evidently, the position of the IIAA leadership on this point, which actually echoes the exposition of Sayyid Quṭb on the matter almost verbatim,[253] differed quite strongly from that of the JIA at the same time.

One further difference in the respective ideological set-up of these two Islamist organizations is clearly discernible: while the frame of reference remained exclusively Afghanistan for Rabbānī and his JIA, for Sayyāf, as had been the case for Quṭb, too, the enemy was not to be regarded within national confines. Because the tyrants (*ṭawāghīt*) were many and potentially everywhere, matters could be remedied only by the establishment of 'God's rule on earth [*iqāma ḥukm allāh fi'l-arḍ*], the promotion of the word of God and service to the *dīn* of God',[254] as Sayyāf explained in May 1982 in another

[251] See, for example, Ibn ʿAbd al-ʿAzīz (n.d.), 693. Sayyid Imām ʿAbd al-ʿAzīz al-Sharīf (b. 1369/1950), author of this later text (1994) and one of the foremost ideologues of *al-Qāʿida*, fled from persecution in Egypt to Peshawar in around 1983, where he hooked up with ʿAzzām and other Arab volunteers who would soon rise to prominence, see Nedza (2020), 23–8.

[252] See ʿAzzām (1417/1997), III: 542 (*wa-Akhīran Shukkilti al-Ḥukūma*; c. 1988).

[253] See ʿAbd Rabbih (1407/1987), 49f.; compare Quṭb (1405/1985), 68–74. In his explication, however, Sayyāf did not refer to Quṭb at all.

[254] Cited in ʿAbd Rabbih (1407/1987), 31.

interview, this time with the Jordanian newspaper *al-Rāya*. Of course, as was to be expected, what the established divine rule on earth would eventually look like remained again, by and large, undefined. If all these observations are still not sufficient to ascertain that Sayyāf's political vision remained solidly based on an Islamist frame of reference and not on that of the Saudi Arabian Wahhabiyya, his explicit reference to Mawdūdī's and Quṭb's writings in an interview with the same newspaper almost exactly three years later, as well as both to the MB and to the JiI as organizational role models,[255] should serve as yet another testament to that.

However, Sayyāf made two important modifications to the conceptual framework of classical Islamism, as established especially in the writings of Mawdūdī, al-Bannā and Sayyid Quṭb, which might get easily overlooked, but play, in fact, an important role in the aggravation of socio-religious discourse in the Pashtun Borderland. The first one is discernible in Sayyāf's elaboration on the two non-militant forms of *jihād*:

> From among the categories of *jihād*, the *jihād* of the word and the pen consists in speaking out the Word of Truth [*kalimat al-ḥāqq*] and in its affirmation, in the rejection of falsehood and fending off the attacks of the unbelievers on the battlefield of ideas, in opposing the perversions of the enemy and his conspiracy, as well as his distortion of realities [*ḥaqāʾiq*] in the minds of the people. This all constitutes the framework of *jihād*: as long as man continues to investigate the realities and rejects the idle talk [*al-abāṭīl*] and courageously speaks out the truth wherever necessary then that all counts as an expression of *jihād*.[256]

What is conspicuous in this passage is the apparent departure from the concept of "ignorance" (*jahl*), which dominated the Islamist lexicon up to this point,[257] and its replacement with the concept of "unbelief" (*kufr*), a fact that points to a more traditionalist leaning in his thinking that might indeed have been the result of his exposure to the Wahhabi interpretation of Islam as officially recognized in Saudi Arabia. The implications of this terminological shift cannot be underestimated: while *jahl* and its various derivatives serve in the Islamist systematics as an epistemological category for all the accesses to reality outside the Qur'anic paradigm and this term implies, thus, no immediate consequence for anyone classified as *jāhil*, the term *kufr* has, at least potentially, immediate and severe legal repercussions. Therefore, by choosing the latter term over the former, Sayyāf provided, in fact, a justification for the

[255] See ibid., 33.

[256] Ibid., 37.

[257] The radical reinterpretation of the Qur'anic term "ignorance" (*jāhiliyya*) that evolved into a standard concept in Islamist thought was undertaken by Mawdūdī; it did not become a household term, however, until after its radicalization by Sayyid Quṭb: see Hartung (2013a), 62–72 and 200–5.

necessity of the proactive enforcement of a rigid interpretation of Islamicity on a potentially global scale, including very much Muslim majority communities, such as in the Pashtun Borderland, under pain of *takfīr*.

The second conceptual modification undertaken by Sayyāf concerns the term "revolution", which, for Mawdūdī and those like the JIA in his wake, constituted a central concept of the Islamic system.[258] Less concerned with the rather elaborate reinterpretation of that term by classical theorists of Islamism, and perhaps because of his own experience with a form of "revolution" that brought the PDPA into power and their Soviet allies into Afghanistan, Sayyāf pleads strongly for its disentanglement from the concept of "jihād":

> There is a major difference between *jihād* and revolution [*thawra*]: first of all, "*jihād*" is the word chosen by God – praised be He and exalted! – for the kind of action through which a Muslim is sincere in the eye of God, while "revolution" is an alien term that is not rooted in our Islamic culture.[259]

In extricating the Islamic nomenclature as provided by the Qur'anic revelation from a terminology of different provenance, Sayyāf broke away somewhat from the framework of classical Islamism and drew nearer to a more literal interpretation of the authoritative textual foundations of Islam that we have already encountered with the adherents of Salafi Islam. Once again, this also makes him to some degree linkable to Wahhabi interpretations. However, his reference to "our Islamic culture" suggests that this, in fact, is not a matter of legal interpretation, but one of culture, which ties him back into the Afghan hermeneutical universe. As such, Sayyāf and, by implication, the IIAA can rightly be framed as transitional borderland actors who are able to communicate across various ideational trends and communities in the Pashtun Borderland.

The Islamism of Ḥikmatyār's *Ḥizb-i Islāmī*

Perhaps the most graphic example of the divergence of consistent Islamist ideology and Borderland pragmatics, coupled, nonetheless, with a constant effort to fit the latter into the former, is provided by Gulbuddīn Ḥikmatyār and his ḤiI. Assessments of their ideological positions so far prevalent, rather epitomized in Wieland-Karimi's conclusion that 'the former Parchamī Hekmatyār adheres ideologically to Maudūdī',[260] seem, therefore, to still warrant some careful investigation.

It is true that Ḥikmatyār devoted comparatively more thought and ink to a systematic underpinning of the ideology of his ḤiI than his competitors of the

[258] See ibid., 157–73 and 212f.
[259] ʿAbd Rabbih (1407/1987), 37.
[260] Wieland-Karimi (1998), 179 (translation mine; spelling follows the German original).

JIA and IIAA discussed so far. On closer inspection, however, it turns out that Ḥikmatyār's direct references to Mawdūdī have been scarce at best, which indicates that the assumed ideological adherence to this classical Islamist thinker is certainly not straightforward and can, therefore, be established mainly by inference alone. This is certainly noteworthy, all the more so in contrast to the ample references to Islamist authorities beyond Afghanistan made by the ideologues of the JIA and IIAA.[261]

Moreover, during the time of armed resistance to the PDPA regime and its Soviet allies, Ḥikmatyār and his retainers contributed much less to the discussion of core concepts of Islamist ideology than Rabbānī and Sayyāf. Although he was certainly familiar with the general repertoire of Islamist thought commonly associated with its classical theorists in the MENA region and South Asia, Ḥikmatyār apparently began to elaborate on them at a much later point in time. In the 1980s, meanwhile, his own writings revolved predominantly around justification of violent engagement with the PDPA and those in its orbit as Islamically commendable.[262]

However, the more it transpired that the days of Soviet military occupation were numbered, the more Ḥikmatyār had to engage with the various possibilities of a post-war order. While generally agreeing with the vision of all other forces under the umbrella of the IIMA, namely the need to establish a system of Islamic governance in Afghanistan, his ability to make pragmatic compromises was clearly limited. When more conciliatory forces within the IIMA considered the option of what he called "coalition government" (*ḥukūmat-i iʾtilāfī*) with the PDPA, he began to chastise them for compromising on the idea of an "Islamic government" (*ḥukūmat-i islāmī*), especially as such a government would be based not on Islamic precepts, but rather on the PDPA's programme for "National Reconciliation" (*qawmī muṣālaḥat*).[263] This objectionability extended consistently from the government as such to its central organs, prominently among them the "Grand Assembly" – the *Lōyah Jirgah* – as a decision-making body under the Constitution. The institution as such was not a problem for Ḥikmatyār from an Islamic perspective,

[261] The non-consecutive issues of the ḤiI-Ḥ periodical *Shafaq* available contain references of uneven depth only to Muḥammad Quṭb (Muḥammad Quṭb, 'Miʿyār-i akhlāq va rawsh-i tarbiyyat pas ān rā nikār!', *Shafaq* 2nd Series 3/1 [1364sh], 52–60 and 91), Jamāl al-Dīn al-Afghānī (Mawlavī Shīr Āqā, 'Sarguẕasht-i ḥayrat-angīz: Sayyid Jamāl al-Dīn-i Afghānī dar Miṣr', *Shafaq* 2nd Series 3/2–3 [1364sh], 72–4), Necmettin Erbakan (Muḥammad Zamān Muzammil, 'Də Turkiyəy safar'nāmah: də Istanbūl tēr majd pātəy pēghōr', *Shafaq* 2nd Series 3/10 [1365sh/1986], 40–3) and Ḥasan al-Tūrābī (ʿAwẓ al-Dīn "Ṣiddīqī" [trans.], 'Pah Sūdān kē pawźəy kūditā', *Shafaq* 2nd Series 4/12 [1368sh], 17–19). References to standard classical authors, such as Mawdūdī and Sayyid Quṭb, are, meanwhile, entirely absent.

[262] See, for example, Ḥikmatyār (1365sh; 1366sh; 1367sh).

[263] See Ḥikmatyār, 'Rāh'hā-yi ḥall-i buḥrān-i Afghānistān', *Shafaq* 2nd Series 3/3–4 (1368sh), 9–22, here 10f.; Ḥikmatyār (1379sh), 8–13.

but the fact that it would be chaired by the king or president of Afghanistan and subject to the constitutional framework was.[264] His main concern, however, was not so much the fidelity of the chairman of the *Lōyah Jirgah*, but the fact that this institution was rooted in tribal customs that stood counter to the Islamic principle of social justice and equity.

In his critique, Ḥikmatyār appears to have taken the respective stipulations made in the various Constitutions seriously and has come to the consistent conclusion that the appointment of the tribal socio-economic and political elites to the supreme representation of the Afghan people would necessarily perpetuate tribal hierarchies which have no basis in the Islamic framework. Interestingly, he, who is well known for his ever-shifting alliances for the sake of maintaining and enhancing his own position,[265] also extends the allegation of un-Islamic governance to his competitors within wider Islamist circles:

> Ẓāhir Shāh, Sardār Dāvūd, Babrak Kārmal, Najīb, Rabbānī and Mullā Muḥammad ʿUmar, each one of them took successively advantage of the tribal and legally adorned power politics of the *jirgahs*: [...] Mullā Muḥammad ʿUmar Ākhūnd'zādah maintained a circle in Kandahar which elected him there as Commander of the Faithful. Burhān al-Dīn Rabbānī kept a circle in Kabul and Herat, and the governors extended extra-judicial support to him. Najīb and Kārmal entertained a circle in Kabul and rode on Russian tanks and by the force of arms of the Soviet gunmen, yet presenting themselves as elected presidents. And was not Dāvūd, having himself unanimously elected president after deposing of Ẓāhir Shāh in a bloodless coup d'état, dealing out favours to them [i.e., those in his circle]?[266]

Such a strong aversion to tribal institutions, as espoused here by Ḥikmatyar, was one of the reasons for the growing distance between him and Yūnus Khāliṣ, who had pragmatically joined right after Dāvūd Khān's coup d'état in 1973, alongside many other Islamist opposition leaders who had, at that time, congregated around Rabbānī.[267] Another reason for the eventual split between

264 See Ḥikmatyār (1379sh), 14–20; Ḥikmatyār, 'Rāh'hā-yi ḥall', 13f. This subordinate role of the *Lōyah Jirgah* was already implied in amendments to the first Afghan Constitution of 1923, and further cemented by the subsequent Constitutions of 1963, 1976, 1987 and 1990, as well as by the current one, promulgated in 2004: see Anon. (1302sh), 15f.; 'Ḥavādis̱-i dākhiliyyah: lūyah jirgah-yi ʿumūmī va khuṣūṣī dar Jalālābād', *Amān-i Afghān* 3/19 (1301sh/1341h/1923), 11–14; Anon. (1343sh), 57f.; Anon. (1355sh), 30 and 32. See also Noelle-Karimi (2002).

265 A vivid example of Ḥikmatyār's own temporary tribal alliances, as emerged from the conversation with a person associated with the Baraval Ṣāḥib of Upper Dir, held on 10 August 2017 in Bāṛah Galī (KP), is that with Malik Muḥammad Zarīn (killed 1432/2011), a *məshər* of the Mashvāṇī tribe from Binshāhī in Lower Dir. Additionally, see below in the present section.

266 Ḥikmatyār (1379sh), 16.

267 See ʿAzīzallāh (1386sh), 33f. See also Section 4.3.4.

the two, which is as clear a reflection of their different frames of reference as the first, was Ḥikmatyār's complete rejection of the common belief, especially among rural subalterns in the Pashtun Borderland, that socio-religious authority results from personal charisma, as was frequently expressed in narratives of extraordinary spiritual capabilities.[268] Ḥikmatyār, after all, trained in engineering science, had little tolerance for forms of Muslim piety that prove to be rather elusive to the rationalistic mind, a fact that he has in common with most other Islamists. Nonetheless, considering his upbringing in the cultural environment of the Kharōṫī-Ghilzay in the village of Vartāpūr in the Imām Ṣāḥib district of Kunduz, such a fervently displayed repudiation of tribal values and customs is certainly surprising. As it transpires, however, Ḥikmatyār was clearly not averse to socio-political practices of Pashtun tribal provenance as such: the fact that hardly any of the other commanders of Islamist militias has shifted alliances as often and for however short a period as he did clearly marks him out as a most accomplished Borderland pragmatic.

His almost unmoving strategic making and unmaking of alliances with a surprisingly wide array of local community leaders and militia commanders, as well as his utter disregard for civilian lives during the battle for Kabul, which the ḤiI-Ḥ fought especially against Aḥmad Shāh Masʿūd's *Shūrā-yi Naẓār* in contravention of the Peshawar Peace Accord of April 1992, however, consistently follow a clear principle: everything is to be subordinated to the ultimate objective, the absolute rule of Ḥikmatyār over an Islamic state of his vision into which Afghanistan was to be turned. The legitimacy of this aim is especially implicitly rooted in Ḥikmatyār's more systematic considerations of the ideological foundations of his ḤiI that he began to undertake from the early 1990s onwards.

Many elements in this eventual ideological set-up resemble core ideas of Mawdūdī, with whom, after all, Ḥikmatyār is said to have had some direct dealings during the early days of the resistance.[269] Its core foundation, as

[268] An interesting case in point here is the nineteenth-century figure of the Haḋḋah Ṣāḥib (see Section 3.2.3), who was much revered by Ḥikmatyār for his later anti-colonial activism; his deep spirituality, manifest in the miracles he worked, however, caused an Islamist such as Ḥikmatyār some serious unease. Edwards (2002), 129 and 147, for instance, informs us that, when the Soviet army moved into Afghanistan, the entire library at the *khānaqāh* in Haḋḋah Sharīf, including the sole manuscript of the Haḋḋah Ṣāḥib's disciple ʿAbd al-Bāqī on the miraculous works of his master, had been evacuated by ḤiI-Ḥ cadres to some unknown destination in Pakistan. The fact that the current whereabouts of these holdings is unknown suggests that the evacuation of the library was, in fact, a convenient opportunity for Ḥikmatyār and his lieutenants to take control of the extant narratives on the Haḋḋah Ṣāḥib, thus purging them of the various spiritual aspects in favour of his anti-colonial activities, which were much more compatible with an Islamist world-view.

[269] See ibid., 245. It is not entirely clear whether this statement is also based on Edwards's interview with Muḥammad Nabī Muḥammadī, the leader of the ḤII, in Peshawar in 1983. On Nabī Muḥammadī and the ḤII, see Section 4.3.4.

emerges from one of Ḥikmatyār's earlier theological texts from 1990, is the total and unconditional submission (*iṭāʿat*) to God as the supreme Lord, and the acceptance of His all-encompassing and all-pervasive divine system according to nature. This submission also extends to the Prophet Muḥammad, predominantly because God's revelation to him was an act of divine grace.[270]

Ḥikmatyār distilled several social principles from this metaphysical superstructure, some of which are quite remarkable because they appear somewhat in stark contradiction to his own conduct. For one thing, he calls for the extension of one's "fervent love" (*klakah mīnah*) of God to all other human beings, which would eradicate all "oppression" and "cruelty" (*ẓulm*); for another, he stipulates that one should never act in the self-interest of divine reward.[271] These are also necessary qualifications for "leadership" (*rahbarī*), which, in turn, is a crucial component in the Islamist imaginary of the Islamic polity, in stark contrast to the cruel and unjust ruler, whom Ḥikmatyār identified with the Qur'anic pharaoh.[272] Similar to Mawdūdī's concept of the *amīr* as the first among equals, the Qur'anically devised way to establish the leader is "consultation" (*mashvarah*) among qualified contenders for the role.[273] Still, and also herein, Ḥikmatyār overlapped with Mawdūdī and other Islamist theorists, each of those who qualify must, according to *sharʿ*, be identifiable as a member of an organized vanguard, which for Ḥikmatyār is the "party" (*ḥizb*).[274] This word choice is, of course, obviously based on a strategic decision: as Mawdūdī's concept of the *jamāʿat* as vanguard resonates well with the JiI, Ḥikmatyār's does with the ḤiI, and, more precisely, with him as the leader.

His self-assertive claim to be best qualified for this position, in line with the ten properties Ḥikmatyār derived from his reading of the Qur'an, rested exponentially on his "erudition" (*ʿilm*) and "eloquence" (*fuṣāḥat*).[275] Similarly to Mawdūdī, whose scholarship was equally questioned by a vast array of *ʿulamāʾ*,[276] Ḥikmatyār aimed at proving his qualification by producing a host of partly quite expansive writings on theological and legal matters, and his countless speeches and sermons. Epistemologically, too, Ḥikmatyār appears in

270 See Ḥikmatyār (1387sh), esp. 36–58 and 177–83.

271 See ibid., 109–16 and 140–7.

272 See Ḥikmatyār (1378sh), 1–37.

273 See ibid., 38–46.

274 See ibid., 85–96.

275 See ibid., 1–26, esp. 5f. and 23–6. The other eight properties are "trustworthiness" (*amānat*), "merit" (*kifāyat*), "being a role model" (*asvah būdan*), the "absence of lust for reward" (*ʿadam-i ṭamaʿ-i pādāsh*), "trust in God" (*tavakkul bar khudā*), "courage" (*shujāʿat*), being a "walker on the path of God" (*az̤īb-i rāh-i khudā*) and possessing a "compassionate heart" (*ẓamīr-i ḥisās*).

276 See Nasr (1996), 115–22; Hartung (2004), 133–42. Meanwhile, most of the polemics of *ʿulamāʾ* against Mawdūdī had been collectively published in two volumes as *Mawlānā Mawdūdī par Iʿtirāẓāt kā ʿIlmī Jāʾizah* (2010), edited by Muftī Muḥammad Yūsuf of the *Dār al-ʿUlūm-i Ḥaqqāniyyah* at Akōṛah Khaṭṭak.

league with Mawdūdī: the firm basis for his elaborations is the text of the Qur'anic revelation, supplemented by *aḥādīth* only whenever the Qur'an is silent or leaves substantial room for conflicting interpretations.[277]

Consequently, disregarding, in the same way as Mawdūdī, the exegetical tradition and most established principles of *tafsīr*, Ḥikmatyār would also not grace the pioneering Indian Islamist thinker with a reference. Instead, he would do as Mawdūdī and other pioneers of Islamism, such as Sayyid Quṭb, did and compile his own *tafsīr*, which was released in eight volumes under the title *Rays of the Qur'an* (*Də Qur'ān Palvashē*). In this, Ḥikmatyār differed greatly from Rabbānī, Sayyāf and other Afghan Islamist leaders, with the possible exception of Yūnus Khāliṣ, who is said to have begun to engage in translating and interpreting the Qur'an already in the 1950s, during his time at Kabul Radio, although no substantial publication resulted from this.[278]

Also like Mawdūdī, Ḥikmatyār regarded substantial portions of the Qur'an as historically fastened to the time and place in which the revelation took place. Consequently, he opted for a rather free translation of the Arabic text into Pashto, in order to also connect those sections to the here and now.

After all, it appears that the common assessment according to which Ḥikmatyār would adhere ideologically to Mawdūdī is indeed mainly correct. There are, however, some issues on which Ḥikmatyār departs from the latter, and some in which he goes way beyond Mawdūdī and, somewhat like Sayyāf, thus provides connection points for the adherents to other ideational currents prevalent in the Pashtun Borderland, here primarily Salafi Islam and "Frontier Deobandiyyat". Even such a fashioned compatibility of the ḤiI-Ḥ ideological universe with that of others, however, underlies a single aim: to assert the eventual hegemony of the ḤiI-Ḥ ideology across all of Afghanistan and possibly beyond, with Ḥikmatyār as its unquestioned authority. To this end, the conceptual focus in Ḥikmatyār's deliberations needed to be shifted: after all, none of the other Islamist leaders under the umbrella of the IIMA, nor a large proportion of the Afghan people after more than a decade of oppressive PDPA rule and Soviet military occupation, needed much convincing that the post-war order in Afghanistan needed to be a profoundly Islamic one. It is, therefore, not really surprising that an explicit statement about "governance" as a core theme of the Qur'an, which is found both in Mawdūdī's *Tafhīm al-Qur'ān* and in Sayyid Quṭb's *Fī Ẓilāl al-Qur'ān*,[279] is largely absent in the preface to Ḥikmatyār's *tafsīr*.

Instead, the most pressing issue for Ḥikmatyār to solve appeared to be the fact that not everyone had already subscribed to the idea of the ḤiI-Ḥ as the supreme choice among the competing representatives of Islamist ideology in

[277] See, esp., Ḥikmatyār (1385sh).
[278] See ʿAzīzallāh (1386sh), 4f.
[279] See Ḥikmatyār (1385–90sh), I: 2–18; compare Mawdūdī (1949–72), I: 13–40, and Quṭb (1430/2009), I: 11–18.

Afghanistan, and Ḥikmatyār himself, subsequently, as the most suitable option for the highest governmental authority. The classical jurisprudential term "dissent" (*ikhtilāf*) and the Qur'anic "hypocrisy" (*nifāq*) proved to be highly convenient conceptual weapons for fitting the fact of their opposition to the axiomatic leadership role of the ḤiI-Ḥ into an Islamically sustainable model of explanation. It is, therefore, only a little surprising that Ḥikmatyār aimed at eradicating both with his comprehensive *tafsīr*, thereby paving the way for the desired dissolution of all disagreement among the Islamist forces in Afghanistan into the ideological and organizational set-up of the ḤiI-Ḥ. His first step towards achieving this was to extinguish any dissent over Qur'anic interpretation by a recourse to sound *aḥādīth*, which, in fact, constitutes a significant departure from the principles of Islamist Qur'anic hermeneutics laid down by Mawdūdī: the only correct *tafsīr* is the one that at no point conflicts with any of the interpretations of the Prophet Muḥammad as enshrined in the canonical collections of sound *aḥādīth*, the *Ṣaḥīḥayn*.

The same, in fact, applied to the severe challenges Ḥikmatyār found himself eventually confronted with, especially by Arab militants and their theorists who had been roaming the Borderland since the mid 1980s with growing self-confidence and were, as we have seen above in Sayyāf's stern words directed at the first wave of volunteer fighters, never shy of accusing those with a different opinion of apostasy – *takfīr*.[280] In a quite bulky work from 2010, Ḥikmatyār consequently expanded his attempts to overcome dissent to the field of *fiqh*, prominently including in the discussion one pathway of legal interpretation he labelled "Salafi". *Ikhtilāf* in matters of religious obligations against God (*ʿibādāt*), such as the matter of the correct performance of the *tashahhud* during the ritual prayer that had been so virulent in the Pashtun Borderland, concern, according to Ḥikmatyār, exclusively individual legal matters (*furūʿ al-fiqh*). In the fundamentals (*uṣūl*), however, which according to him are the Qur'an and the Sunna of the Prophet Muḥammad, there was always utter agreement.[281] Even the doctrinal matters that ultimately divide Shiʿis and Sunnis were for him only matters of the *furūʿ*, but not fundamental ones.[282] In the preface to this very work, Ḥikmatyār is actually quite upfront

[280] See Ḥikmatyār (1389sh), 1.

[281] See ibid., 3. Here, Ḥikmatyār's lack of solid legal training is fully evident, as he did not refer to the other *uṣūl al-fiqh*, such as consensus (*ijmāʿ*) and analogical reasoning (*qiyās*), which have been firmly established since the systematic methodological efforts of al-Shāfiʿī (1358/1939), 471–86, 559–600 *et passim*. In addition, the matter of independent reasoning (*ijtihād*), which for Mawdūdī carried quite some currency, remained unmentioned.

[282] See Ḥikmatyār (1389sh), 250–75. This assessment of the roots of the major disagreements between Shiʿis and Sunnis does, of course, conveniently ignore the fact that the former have additional sources of absolute authority, which materialized in alternative collections of *aḥādīth* and *akhbār*.

about why he is devoting so much space and ink to his attempts to level even incommensurate disagreements:

> This is the way chosen by the Ḥil: to make all Muslims form one front against all the families [of notables] and foreign enemies. Because of this approach, it not only organizes most of the pious and wise [*ṣāliḥ aw hōx̌iyār*] *mujāhidīn* of the Afghan nation, it moreover unites also the sincerest [*dēṛ mukhliṣ*] among the adherents of the *maẕāhib* and Salafis with the Ḥil. Even volunteers from countries other than Afghanistan would be regarded as *mujāhidīn*, as long as they came into the fortresses of the Ḥil and fought the *jihād* alongside them. 'Oh God, make us see the Truth as true and inspire us to follow it, show us falsehood as false and inspire us to avoid it!'[283]

To facilitate this closing of ranks, Ḥikmatyār turns to the second core term that he substituted for that of "Islamic governance": *nifāq*. To this end, he had already, two years earlier, presented a very simplified *ʿaqīda* which would constitute the bare minimum of "Muslimness": the unconditional belief in God, all of His Messengers, all of His revelations, the angels and the Hereafter would be the only non-negotiable factors[284] On this basis, most of the instances of *takfīr* at the hands of Salafists with which he was concerned in his work from 2010 would not be legitimate, because those accused of apostasy are, in most cases, mere hypocrites (*munāfiqūn*) whose lapses in faith could be redressed without having to necessarily expel them from the Muslim community. This, of course, is a quite particular understanding of *nifāq*: we shall see further below that the line between *nifāq* and *kufr*, especially in militant Salafist circles of Saudi Arabian provenance active in the Pashtun Borderland, is considered quite blurred, and *nifāq*, therefore, equally results in *takfīr*.[285]

Ḥikmatyār, however, had already engaged with this matter before the actual coup d'état which brought the PDPA to power when he published his *tafsīr* of the sixty-third chapter of the Qur'an, Sūrat al-Munāfiqūn, in Dari.[286] From there it emerges that the hypocrites, that is, those whose faith is "swinging" (*taẕabẕab*), constitute the critical mass to tip the scale either in favour of the believers or possibly also the unbelievers.[287] Undecided in their loyalty, they bear the potential to stab the community of believers in the back by often

[283] Ibid., 5. The internal quote is a common supplication affirmed by tradition (*duʿāʾ maʾthūr*), which, in this exact wording, is prominently attested in Ibn Shāhīn (1415/1995), 36, and Ibn Kathīr (1421/2000), II: 281 (on Q2.123).

[284] See Ḥikmatyār (1387sh), 1.

[285] See Nedza (2020), 119–23.

[286] See Ḥikmatyār (1377sh), 1. The text was originally serialized in the Ḥil-Ḥ weekly *Mīs̲āq-i Īs̲ār* in 1977; a Pashto translation was later incorporated into Ḥikmatyār's *tafsīr*: see Ḥikmatyār (1385–90sh), VII: 657–748, esp. 657–60.

[287] See Ḥikmatyār (1377sh), 126–30.

inadvertently aiding the forces of unbelief, which is why it is vital to find them out and reel them firmly back into the community of believers.

This Qur'anic chapter, however, also includes a reference to the focus on "wealth and offspring" (*amwāl wa-awlād*) as a sign of hypocrisy; a Qur'anic trope that, as we have seen earlier on, had strongly informed the religiously charged rhetoric of egalitarianism prominently espoused by the early Frontier Deobandis around Shaykh al-Hind Maḥmūd al-Ḥasan in the early twentieth century.[288] The emphasis for Ḥikmatyār, however, was clearly not on the socio-political elitism that derives from such a worldly focus, but rather on the fact that those in question were 'diverted from [. . .] remembrance of God' (*tulhi*[*hum*] *ʿan dhikr allāh*).[289] By invoking Q3.104 and 110, Ḥikmatyār brings the practice of "moral coercion" (*ḥisba*) into play to redress this wrong. This injunction would have to be realized for him and, therefore, the ḤiI-Ḥ in the larger "revolutionary" (*inqilābī*) project of Islamic awakening and amelioration (*nahẓat va iṣlāḥ*), aiming, as so often in Islamist rhetoric, at the eradication of oppression and the firm establishment of social justice, and spearheaded by the ḤiI-Ḥ as the vanguard of this revolution.[290] However, one's belonging to the vanguard needs to be actively earned, which, in fact, is the very thrust of Ḥikmatyār's brief exposition on Q3.110:

> There are several reasons for which you are the chosen [people]: enjoining the commendable, prevent the reprehensible, and believe in God. You have forsaken these distinctions [*źāngəṛtiyāvī aw khuṣūṣiyāt*], do not fall from your elevated position, because then you will become like the People of the Book. How were the People of the Book? Few of them had faith, most of them were sinners [*akṯar yē fāsiq vū*]. The believers did not prevent the sinners, so they were stripped of that position and this obligation [*dā dandah*] was entrusted to you. If you are divided into two groups like them, the majority of you being sinners, and a limited number of you being believers and righteous ones [*muʾmin aw ṣāliḥ*], and you do not prevent the sinners, then you shall end up like them.[291]

288 See Section 3.3.2. See also Hartung (2016b; 2019a).

289 See Ḥikmatyār (1377sh), 183–93, esp. 185f. The passage in question here is Q63.9: 'yā ʾayyuhā alladhīna ʾamanū lā tulhikum amwālukum wa-lā awlādukum ʿan dhikri ʾllāh [. . .]'.

290 This tendency is well expressed in Ḥikmatyār's exegesis of Q3.104 in Ḥikmatyār (1385–90sh), I: 264: 'So, for this work all of you need to come together as one group [*yawah ḋalah*] whose work is to call for the good, to be engaged in the commendable, to direct good works, and refrain from hateful and reprehensible works. For such a group and people there will be prosperity and triumph [*falāḥ aw baryā bah də daghasī ḋalī aw ummat pah barkhah kēǵī*]. [. . .] In practice, this means to prevent injustice and enforce the truth, which is quite different from abstract criticism and objection. You will defeat the oppressor and the corrupt, you will prevent oppression and corruption, and you will extend support and friendship to those devoted to the Truth [*də ḥaqq'pālvankō marastah aw malgərtiyā bah kawəy*].'

291 Ibid., I: 266.

Of course, those whose world-views and actions can no longer be regarded as merely hypocritical but outspokenly anti-Islamic still remain. Here belong, in Ḥikmatyār's view, prominently the cadres of the SJT and JDN, ḤDMA and, ultimately, the PDPA; their transgressions are regarded as being so severe that they fall well outside the frame of intra-Islamic ways in which to deal with deviation. They must be dealt with as outright unbelievers-cum-apostates and, therefore, subjected to uncompromising armed *jihād* – the core issue of many of the publications to which Ḥikmatyār and other leading ḤiI-Ḥ cadres gave birth. It is in this context that Ḥikmatyār reflected, perhaps for the first time, on the issue of distinguishing *kufr* from *nifāq*, a matter that would eventually inform another of his conceptual contributions to the Islamic discourse, which turned out to be a docking point for more governance-orientated Salafis in the Pashtun Borderland, that is, the legal concept of "association and disengagement" (*al-walāʾ wa'l-barāʾ*).

To this end, however, the understanding of *nifāq* needed to be further modified: what additional conditions need to be met to tip the scale of hypocrisy towards unbelief? After all, the standard bearers of competing ideologies were quite dexterous in luring the unsuspecting into their orbit and, thus, stealthily affecting their thinking. The people Ḥikmatyār had in mind here were, therefore, those who did not – at least, not instantly – wholeheartedly embrace the atheism which increasingly characterized the government of Afghanistan, especially since the deposition of King Ẓāhir Shāh, but who, nonetheless, collaborated with them out of whatever motivation, some of them surely because they regarded their religiosity as a personal and private matter. For Islamists generally, however, there is no such thing as private religiosity, and any kind of association (*muvālāt*) of anyone calling herself or himself a Muslim with proclaimed unbelievers needed, therefore, to be emphatically discouraged.

Ḥikmatyār's engagement with this question, which dates back to the year 1986, drew closer to the ideational universe of initially predominantly Arab Salafi-cum-Salafist circles: the issue of "association and disengagement" (*al-walāʾ wa'l-barāʾ*). We have so far encountered this only in the case of the Naqshbandi-Mujaddidi Ṣāḥib of Haḋḋah in the nineteenth century, and it was increasingly becoming one of the core elements of Salafi internal debate over the correct execution of their creed (*manhaj*). In fact, two of the most relevant treatises in this regard: *Millat Ibrāhīm* (1984) and *al-Kawāshif al-Jaliyya fī Kufr al-Dawla al-Saʿūdiyya* (1989) by the Palestinian-Jordanian Abū Muḥammad ʿĀṣim al-Maqdisī (b. 1379/1959),[292] at which we shall have to take a closer look further below,[293] were published in Peshawar in the years around Ḥikmatyār's own respective work. As for al-Maqdisī and his various

[292] See Wagemakers (2012), 38–41 and 153–64.
[293] See Section 4.5.3.

earlier references,[294] an anchor point of Ḥikmatyār's argument is Q60, in conjunction with an array of other verses, all of which provide a rather differentiated discussion of the issue. The backdrop of his deliberations was clearly the actual situation in PDPA-ruled Afghanistan, which, for him, is clearly reflected in Q60.9: 'God only forbids you as to those who have fought you in religion's cause, and expelled you from your lands, and have supported in your expulsion, that you should associate yourself with them.'[295]

In an escalation of this divinely decreed prohibition, Ḥikmatyār also invoked the popular verse Q5.51, in which God warns against fraternizing with Jews and Christians, because whoever does so inevitably becomes one of them.[296] The interpretation of that verse he conferred to Sayyid Quṭb, who made a point of differentiating between the situation in pre-Islamic Medina and the situation after the arrival of the *muhājirūn*.[297] Moreover, Quṭb was emphatic about the fact that "becoming one of them" does not mean taking over their religious views (*walāya fi'l-dīn*), but referred exclusively to forms of active support (*tanāṣir*) and co-operation (*ta'āwūn*), especially in their military pursuits. The same applies to nominal Muslims seeking the help of non-Muslims, *al-isti'āna bi'l-kuffār*, the rediscovery of which had been credited to Abū Muḥammad al-Maqdisī,[298] but which Ḥikmatyār had also been considering at around the same time and without any evidence at all that he did so inspired by al-Maqdisī. The fact that Ḥikmatyār's deliberations seriously lack the jurisprudential depth of al-Maqdisī's still not very systematic treatment of the issue seems to support the assumption that the two of them developed their respective thoughts on *al-walā' wa'l-barā'* rather independently from one another. Moreover, these two authors responded to quite different local contexts with, subsequently, different objectives, which resulted in the fact that al-Maqdisī arrived at a justification of the practice of *takfīr* even against nominal Muslim rulers of Muslim majority states as legally mandatory individual duty. In the case of Ḥikmatyār, the arguments appear to have fed into his overall task of sustaining the justification of armed *jihād* against those infidel forces which, at that time, held Afghanistan quite firmly in their grip, as well as their abetters, who, by mere association, have also become legitimate targets of armed retribution.

294 See Wagemakers (2009), 88–92.

295 Q60.9: 'innamā yanhākumu 'llāhu 'ani alladhīna qātalūkum fi'l-dīni wa-akhrajūkum min diyārikum wa-ẓāharū 'ālá ikhrājikum 'an tawallawhum' (translation above largely follows Arberry).

296 See Ḥikmatyār (1365sh), 33–6.

297 See ibid.; compare Quṭb (1430/2009), II: 909. The first two volumes of *Fī Ẓilāl al-Qur'ān* had been translated into Farsi as early as 1954 by Aḥmad Ārām (d. 1998), see Ünal (2016), 42f.; Bohdan (2020), 249. The latest translation of the entire text, published by Iḥsān in Tehran in 2007, was undertaken by Muṣṭafá Khurram'dil.

298 See Wagemakers (2012), 153–6; compare Ḥikmatyār (1365sh), 44–51.

It is remarkable that Ḥikmatyār did not consider association to be confined to direct interactions between Muslims and non-Muslims, but also extended it to a more intellectual engagement, in which – very much in line with Sayyid Quṭb's arguments in this regard – he saw the seed sown for subsequent direct interactions:

> Those [Muslims who associate themselves with non-Muslims] forget what the Noble Qur'an asserts of the People of the Book, of their being allied one with another in fighting the Muslim community [*fī ḥarb al-jamāʿa al-muslima*]. This is their constant attitude [*shaʾn thābit*]. They are hostile to the Muslim because of his Islam. They will not be satisfied with the Muslim unless he abandons his religion [*dīnah*] and follows theirs.[299]

The "People of the Book", of course, are to be understood allegorically here: in the case of Afghanistan, communists were as much subsumed under the term as liberals, especially as both were successful in securing for themselves the loyalty of the heads of state, thus causing the latter to feed these dangerous thoughts into their policies and, subsequently, leading the entire Muslim people of Afghanistan into the abyss. Ḥikmatyār referred to Q2.120 to support this perspective; Q2.120 clearly states that 'neither will the Jews ever be satisfied with you, nor the Christians, not until you follow [the creeds of] their community'.[300] An example of the ultimate proof of the veracity of this perspective is that the PDPA's seizure of power in 1978 turned them fully into the true representatives of the non-Islamic creed of their Soviet masters in Afghanistan, and everyone performing even the meanest of services for the new regime would consequently become one of them, too. Should any further evidence for this still be required, the collaboration of the PDPA government of Babrak Kārmal with the invading Soviet troops and the subsequent concerted efforts to supress any especially Islamically inspired opposition to their rule was certainly designed to serve this purpose. In this, we find another coincidence between Ḥikmatyār and al-Maqdisī: in the case of the latter, it was the call of the Saudi Arabian government for foreign military support to end the occupation of the Great Mosque in Mecca in November 1979 by young Saudi militants around Juhaymān al-ʿUtaybī (executed 1400/1980) that served as the straw that broke the camel's back and triggered his harsh reaction, culminating in accusing the entire Saudi state of apostasy.[301]

299 Quṭb (1430/2009), II: 910.

300 Q2.120: 'wa-lan tarḍá ʿanka 'l-yahūdu wa-lā 'l-naṣārá ḥattá tattabiʿa millatahum', see Ḥikmatyār (1365sh), 38f.

301 On the Occupation of the Great Mosque of Mecca, see Hegghammer and Lacroix (2007). Apparently, Juhaymān al-ʿUtaybī and his surviving compatriots had been an influence on shaping al-Maqdisī's views during the latter's stay in Saudi Arabia in the early 1980s: see Wagemakers (2012), 35–7 and 154.

Interestingly, just like Arab Salafists, especially with those ties to the Pashtun Borderland, would soon extend their *takfīr* of alleged deviant Muslim governments and their various executive bodies to fellow Salafists who were accused of having made concessions to such political authorities,[302] Ḥikmatyār also expanded the group of those he considered to be fraternizing with the non-Muslims to his own *mujāhidīn* compatriots. The actual occasion was their acceptance of an invitation by the then-President of the USA Ronald Reagan in July 1986 – the very year that Ḥikmatyār wrote his treatise on *muvālāt* – and the subsequent sojourn in Washington as an official delegation, headed by Ḥikmatyār's competitor Burhān al-Dīn Rabbānī, and including Ṣibghatallāh Mujaddidī, Muḥammad Nabī Muḥammadī and Sayyid Aḥmad Gīlānī.[303] In contrast, Ḥikmatyār prided himself on having declined a meeting with Reagan only one year earlier, when he was elected the spokesperson of the IIMA and led a delegation to the Headquarters of the UN in New York to convey an appeal of the IIMA for international sanctions against the USSR.[304] He could now self-righteously portray himself as about the only leader of a *mujāhidīn* party within the IIMA not to fraternize with either superpower of the Cold War era and ask them for military and logistic assistance, and, thus, the Ḥil-Ḥ as the only Afghan Islamist organization that remained uncompromisingly true to the Islamically sustained principle of not associating with any unbeliever.

This, of course, is a case of hypocrisy in itself, because, after all, most of the funding the Ḥil-Ḥ received through the Pakistani ISI was US-American money.[305] These pragmatics, in turn, defy the ostensibly sole reliance of the Ḥil-Ḥ on its ideological framework. Consequently, the officially published agenda (*marām'nāmah*), as well as the constitution (*asās'nāmah*) and also all other Ḥil-Ḥ publications, remain vague when filling ideological catchwords with concrete meaning. This very fact, however, poses a rather serious problem for anyone wishing to unearth the ideological differences between the Ḥil-Ḥ and the two other Afghan Islamist organizations under review here, because it is actually the semantics of individual core concepts, not the conceptual universe as such, that are the points of contestation. After all, all three organizations shared a framework that resonates exceptionally well with

302 See esp. Sections 4.5.2 and 4.5.5.

303 See Ḥikmatyār (1365sh), 51–64. For the meeting itself, see Reagan Library (2017a). One year later, in November 1987, Yūnus Khāliṣ also led a delegation of the IIMA to Washington, D.C., to meet with Reagan: see Reagan Library (2017b).

304 See HIA (1986), Title page; Sands and Qaziaminzai (2019), 211f. The latter based their own portrayal of the incident on interviews with Muḥammad Dāvūd ʿĀbidī, former Ḥil-Ḥ representative to the USA, and Ḥikmatyār confidant Muḥammad Zamān Muzammil, as well as the respective statement in the memoirs of Zalmay Khalilzad, a US-American politician of Afghan origin.

305 See Kiessling (2016), 62, 68 and 283f. n.9.

Mawdūdī's early systematic elaborations on this matter, and, consequently, in the relevant writings from the Ḥil-Ḥ orbit we find the common idea of Islam as a "complete system of life" (*kāmil niẓām-i zindigī*), to be comprehensively governed by the Islamic *shari'a*, which, in turn, has to be derived exclusively from the Qur'an and the Prophetic *aḥādīth*. This "system of life" splits up into numerous subsystems: societal (*ijtimāʿī*), economical (*iqtiṣādī*), moral (*akhlāqī*), all of which need to be regulated according to the same sources,[306] and executed by a leadership to be similarly elected from within the Ḥil-Ḥ on each territorial level.[307]

As has already been established, the Ḥil constitutes, just as does Mawdūdī's Jil, the vanguard in the ambitious project for religious awakening – or, as stated elsewhere, for the 'vivification and renewal of the religion' (*də dīn iḥyā aw tajdīd*).[308] It, therefore, exclusively provides the elite in the "Islamic polity" (*ḥukūmat-i islāmī*), with its *amīr* as the supreme commander who requires complete loyalty and obedience (*iṭāʿat*),[309] while simultaneously acknowledging the supreme sovereignty of God (*ḥākimiyyat-i ilāhī*).[310]

Yet, again, beyond the ideological catchphrases, in its pursuit of power the Ḥil-Ḥ was, more than the JIA and IIAA, rooted in the highly flexible and pragmatic socio-political tradition of the Pashtun Borderland. As such, and despite the occasional acknowledgement of Islamist activities elsewhere,[311] the Ḥil-Ḥ was less orientated towards the Islamic ecumene, but more towards regional power structures. Indeed, references to the Islamic revolution and awakening beyond Afghanistan are incredibly rare, and the Ḥil-Ḥ would

306 See Ḥil-Ḥ (n.d.); (1369sh), 5f.

307 See Ḥil-Ḥ (1369sh), 2 and 7–32. In the first instance, the text contains the translation of part of a *ḥadīth* attributed to ʿUmar ibn al-Khaṭṭāb: 'There is no Islam without a community [*illā bi-jamāʿatin*], no community without leadership [*illā bi-ʾimāratin*], and no leadership without obedience.' See *Sunan al-Dārimī*, b. fī dhahab al-ʿilm, no. 12 (ḥadīth 257). Also see Qāẓī Muḥammad Ḥakīm, 'Pah islām kī ḥukūmatī niẓām', *Shafaq* 2nd Series 5/9 (1369sh), 51–4.

308 See the serialized translation of Mawdūdī's *Tajdīd va Iḥyā-yi Dīn* (1940) by Muḥammad Naṣīm "Tāʾib", 'Də dīn iḥyā aw tajdīd', *Shafaq* 2nd Series 3/12 (1367sh), 35–7; *Shafaq* 2nd Series 4/3–4 (1367sh), 43–5 and 66; *Shafaq* 2nd Series 4/12 (1368sh), 29f.; *Shafaq* 2nd Series 5/3 (1368sh), 41–4. It needs to be acknowledged that the collection of the journal currently at my disposal contains major gaps, while issues of *Mīṣāq-i Īṣār* from the 1970s to the 1990s have unfortunately not been available to me at all.

309 See Ḥil-Ḥ (1369sh), 7–13 and 48f.

310 See Tūrən ʿAbd al-Salām, 'Zmūǵ yavāzinəy armān pah Afghānistān kī də ilāhī niẓām ḥākimiyyat dī', *Shafaq* 3rd Series 1/1 (1370sh), 14–16 and 26.

311 See, for example, "Aʿẓāmī", 'Dāʿiyyah-yi Filasṭīn dar būtah-yi farāmūsh', *Shafaq* 3/4–5 (1364sh), 72–5; Muḥammad Shīr "Mahjūr" (trans.), 'Afzāyish-i tablīghāt-i ilḥād dar Turkmanistān', *Shafaq* 2nd Series 3/12 (1367sh), 8–10; Anon., 'Pah khatīźah Ifrīqā kē də musalmānānō də ḥālat pah haklah də shaykh ʿAbd al-Karīm sarah də al-mujtamāʿ majalləy marakah', *Shafaq* 2nd Series 5/3 (1368sh), 25–31; as well as those items listed in n.147 of this chapter.

eventually share this feature with the ṬIT/IEA. In view of the potential implications for the inner stability of the Pakistani state, its intelligence agencies, above all the ISI's Afghanistan Bureau, tried to control these configurations by strategically financing the activities of the ḤiI-Ḥ and its immediate allies.[312] However, while much of the funding for the ḤiI-Ḥ continued to come through these channels even after the dissolution of the IIMA in the course of the Afghan Civil War, the actual control of the Pakistani agencies over the activities of the ḤiI-Ḥ remained partial at best.

After all, as true borderland actors, Ḥikmatyār and his compatriots engaged in ever-shifting strategic alliances with friends and foes of their Pakistani sponsors alike. Yet, while other Islamist organizations, such as the JIA and the IIAA, built and dissolved similar strategic networks, the ḤiI-Ḥ sought its allies almost exclusively within the confined local context of the Pashtun Borderland. A complex concoction of local tribal militias and the JiI in its Pashtun-dominated constituencies was of exceptional importance in this regard.

4.2.2 Islamisms in Pakistan's Pakhtunkhva

Indeed, the JiI, who had been active in the Peshawar Valley since before Partition,[313] had significantly transformed during the armed resistance to the Soviet occupation of Afghanistan, undergoing a transformation which was exponentially facilitated by the programme of proactive "Islamization" initiated by the military dictator Zia-ul-Haq in 1977,[314] and had begun to expand into the more rural areas of the then-NWFP of Pakistan. Yet, the JiI had been successful in establishing a major presence in two of its PATA regions already decades before that, and it was especially here where the JiI converged with the ḤiI-Ḥ and other formally independent smaller tribal militias more vigorously

312 See Kiessling (2016), 68, 149 and 270 n.2. The last passage is especially enlightening: there the author makes clear that the majority of the support for Ḥikmatyār was owed to the personal sympathies of the then-Director-General of the ISI, Ḥamīd Gul (d. 1436/2015) for the JiI, which, in turn, prompted him to offer disproportional financial support to the ḤiI-Ḥ.

313 In fact, this is still an assumption based on an official report of the JiI General Assembly in 1946, where it had been decreed that some of the JiI literature was to be translated into Pashto by its active members (*arkān*) in the NWFP in order to advance its mission in the Pashtun borderland: see Qayyim-i JiI Pākistān (1989–96), IV: 72f. Hard data could not be obtained, even in a personal meeting with the provincial *amīr* KP, Senator Mushtāq Aḥmad Khān, at the JiI provincial headquarters, the *Markaz-i Islāmī*, in Sardār Gaṛhī, Peshawar, on 18 April 2019.

314 The literature on and debate over Zia-ul-Haq's measures to establish state control over the religious infrastructure (prominently *zakāt*, religious education, and the judiciary) is vast. Despite the host of later ones, Malik (1996) still remains one of the most comprehensive studies on the matter.

than elsewhere in the Pashtun Borderland. We shall have to investigate the reasons for this and its implications, but will do so, however, only after a more general account of the JiI in the region has been presented.

The *Jamāʿat-i Islāmī* in the North-West Frontier Province

It still remains rather nebulous when exactly the JiI first established its presence in the Pashtun Borderland. Sayyid Asʿad Gīlānī (d. 1412/1992), a prominent historiographer of the JiI, lists ten members for April 1946; however, the membership had already reached twenty-three in March 1947. One of them must have been Khān Sardār ʿAlī Khān, the provincial representative in the Central Consultative Council (*markazī majlis-i shūrá*) of the JiI in 1946.[315] Yet, the Borderland seems to have played only a marginal role for the organization in the early years, partly perhaps because of the language barrier, and partly because of the strained political relationship between Pakistan and Afghanistan.[316]

It seems that the JiI grew firmer roots in the region by using as a proxy its student wing, the *Islāmī Jamʿiyyat-i Ṭalabah* (IJṬ), which became increasingly active on the university campuses of the Peshawar Valley, and, more precisely still, in Peshawar itself. After all, most universities in the Borderland were established only in the 2000s, whereas Peshawar was home to the Islamia College, which had been founded in 1913, and the University of Peshawar, inaugurated in 1950. It is, therefore, eminently conceivable that Pashtun students of the Islamia College in Lahore, where the IJṬ was founded around 1945, brought its ideas and its activist fervour back to Peshawar. When the organization launched its first journals – in Urdu and *Student's Voice* in English, which would soon be supplemented by others – its ideology spread even faster in the literate youth circles.[317] Just like its Afghan counterparts, especially the SJM, the IJṬ saw itself as a spearhead against left-wing student bodies and, consequently, unleashed waves of increasingly violent action against the supporters of the *Democratic Student Federation* and the *National Student Federation*, a Stalinist–Maoist outgrowth of the former.[318] However, another federation established itself in the competition over the student body in Peshawar and beyond in 1967: the *Pakhtun Student Federation* (*Paẋtūn Pōhānō Ghūnḋ*; PSF), the student wing of the secular-leftist-cum-Pashtun nationalist *Awami National Party* (ANP), which had grown out of the *Khudāy Khidmatgār* movement of the 1930s and 1940s.[319] That the IJṬ was violently opposed to ethno-nationalism had been vividly

315 See Gīlānī (1992), 210, 212 and 226.

316 See, for example, Qayyim-i JiI Pākistān (1989–96), VII: 238f.

317 See Nasr (1994), 64f.

318 See Gilani (1978), 78. See also Nasr (1994), 65.

319 See Nasr (1994), 73. On the student associations and campus politics in Pakistan in general, see Nelson (2011).

proven during the Bangladesh War of Independence in 1971, when many of the paramilitary forces on the side of the Pakistani army – the *al-Badr* and *al-Shams* brigades being the most notorious of them – formed from the IJṬ demographic.[320] Over the years, the IJṬ and PSF have perpetually clashed violently on campuses across Pakistan, demonstrating the staunch unwillingness of the IJṬ cadres to give in to expressions of ethno-nationalism, which often cherished cultural practices that were seen as violations of Islamic ones.[321]

Another organization affiliated to JiI, with intricate relationships to the IJṬ, especially in the Pashtun Borderland, finally turned out to become a catalyst for the eventual collaboration of the JiI and militant Afghan Islamist organizations, first and foremost, the ḤiI-Ḥ: the paramilitary *Ḥizb al-Mujāhidīn* (ḤM), that owed its existence to the continuous conflict in and over Kashmir.[322] In fact, the ḤM emerged contemporaneously with the breakdown of the strategic IIMA in 1989, and its own alliances with other militant organizations were as pragmatic as those of the ḤiI-Ḥ. There are, however, certain elements that also align the ḤM and the ḤiI-Ḥ ideologically, the most striking one perhaps being the emphasis on the "enemy within" the wider society and increasingly also the Islamic and Islamist circles, legally enshrined in the concept of *walāʾ bi-kuffār*. The assassination of *mīr vāʿiẓ* Muḥammad Fārūq, for instance, holder of the hereditary highest religious office in the Kashmir Valley, on 21 May 1990 by activists of the ḤM appears to have, at least implicitly, been grounded in this legal precept which Ḥikmatyār, Abū Muḥammad al-Maqdisī and others had already theorized some years earlier.[323]

Still, the JiI nexus with its various affiliates, as well as their Afghan counterparts, benefited exceptionally from the structural advantage which was created by Zia-ul-Haq's proactive "Islamization" programme. It was through the patronage received from the hands of the military dictator-turned-president that the JiI was able to grow firm roots in hitherto untouched territories in the Pashtun Borderland and beyond. Apparently, the axiomatically governance-orientated approach of the JiI made them a more productive asset to the top-down institutionalization of important parts of the religious infrastructure in Pakistan, aiming at the establishment of the government's monopoly of definition over "Islam" in the Islamic Republic of Pakistan, which Zia-ul-Haq claimed was based entirely on the "Muhammadan system" (*niẓām-i muṣṭafá*).[324] Consequently, JiI cadres were

320 See Hartung (2013a), 238f.

321 Some of the more recent major clashes on the campuses of Islamia College (2017) and the University of Peshawar (2014), as well as that of the University of Punjab in Lahore (2017), were triggered by PSF-organized Valentine's Day (*yawm-i ḥayāʾ*) celebrations.

322 On the emergence of the ḤM and its connection to the JiI, especially in Jammu & Kashmir, see Hartung (2013a), 246–8.

323 See Behera (2000), 180f.; (2006), 52.

324 See Malik (1996).

heavily involved in these efforts: Khurshīd Aḥmad (b. 1350/1932), for example, a leading IJṬ activist earlier in his life, directed the preparation of the albeit short-lived "Zakat and Ushr Ordinance" of 1979.[325] In exchange, the JiI benefited directly from the creation of this new source of government revenue by receiving generous funds for establishing its own network of religious seminaries (*dīnī madāris*).[326] The outbreak of the Afghan resistance to the regime of the PDPA and its Soviet ally, which came as a timely asset to Zia-ul-Haq's general political agenda, ensured that almost half of the JiI *dīnī madāris* were set up along the entire national borderline with Afghanistan, where they catered for young refugees from Afghanistan as well as Pashtuns on the Pakistani side of the Durand Line.[327]

Although the close alliance between Zia-ul-Haq and the JiI began to dissolve around 1984, to a significant extent because the IJṬ began to question the sincerity of the president's commitment to see through his "Islamization" programme without any concessions to his political opponents, the structural benefits that the JiI had received over the previous seven years remained very much in place. Moreover, with the election of Qāẕī Ḥusayn Aḥmad (d. 1434/2013) in 1987 to supreme *amīr* of the JiI, a Pashtun native of Nowshera took over the reins of the organization, as a result of which the Borderland received even more attention by the JiI than it had before.[328] A leader who was pro-Zia-ul-Haq, Qāẕī Ḥusayn evolved into an epitome for the closing of ranks between the JiI, the IJṬ, the ḤM and various Afghan Islamist organizations, first and foremost the ḤiI-Ḥ, as well as – if only to a limited extent – the JUI.[329] However, he was still a representative of the Peshawar Valley, the so-called "settled districts"; his successor as *amīr-i aʿlá*, Sirāj al-Ḥaqq Khān (b. 1382/1962), hailed from Upper Dir in what used to be the Malakand Division of the former FATA.[330]

325 See ibid., 90; Nasr (1994), 67 and 188–93.

326 In order to receive government funding, all *dīnī madāris* had to submit to one of the contemporary five Boards of Religious Seminaries. The JiI established its own, the *Rābiṭat al-Madāris al-Islāmiyyah*, as late as 1983, and subsequently received generous funds from the Zia-ul-Haq administration: see Malik (1996), 130–53.

327 See ibid., 208f.

328 See Nasr (1994), 195. The various contributions by fellow JiI cadres can be found in ʿU̱smān (2014), 67–178.

329 See Ḥikmatyār, 'Afghān qawm kā ēk sar'parast,' in ʿU̱smān (2014), 56–9; Sayyid Ṣalāḥ al-Dīn (qāʾid-i Ḥizb-i Mujāhidīn), 'Kashmīriyōṇ sē vālihānah muḥabbat', in ibid., 191–3; Anon., 'Imtiyāz Aḥmad bhī ḥayāt jāvidān pā gaʾē', *Jihād-i Kashmīr* 7/4 (1998), 12; Samīʿ al-Ḥaqq (2015), III: 180–93.

330 In fact, the former princely states of Dir, Chitral and Swat, as well as the districts of Bunēr, Malakand and Shānglah in the FATA, had been administratively tied up into the Malakand Agency since 1895. This unit was succeeded in 1969 by the Malakand Division, which existed as an administrative unit until 2000, when it was finally dissolved under military ruler Parvēz Musharraf's (in office 1999–2002) Devolution of Power Plan.

Beyond the logistical facilitation of a more pronounced impact of the JiI on the Borderland affairs through Zia-ul-Haq's domestic and foreign policies, as well as internal shifts in the JiI leadership, the "Afghanistan problem" was also reflected upon in ideological terms. Prolific JiI historiographer Sayyid As'ad Gīlānī embedded the matter into the wider JiI narrative of the inexorable battle between the "*dīn* of ignorance" and the "*dīn* of Islam", which transcends all national confines. Like Mawdūdī, Gīlānī was strongly associated with the competing ideologies of Communism and Liberalism, which required a firm and conceptually pure counter-draft to maintain Muslim integrity. Gīlānī stressed the fact that the former colonies of European imperial powers still formed a critical mass in the systemic battle between Communism and Liberalism, manifest in the so-called "Cold War", and that the Soviet invasion of Afghanistan, therefore, had to be viewed from such a wider perspective.

The (Sunni) Muslim majority regions of the Soviet Union, where Islamicity had become degraded to mere folklore and Islamic ideas of political order had been substituted by secular narratives of "progress" and "development", were prime examples of forcing larger Muslim communities into either camp.[331] As a consequence, the very foundations of Islam under such conditions would reflect intellectual slavery, expressed in such common labels as "Islamic Socialism" or, even worse, "Arab Socialism", which Gīlānī unmasked as a mere form of what he somewhat inexpertly called "National Socialism".[332] The only way out of that dilemma was active resistance (*'amalī muzāḥamat*), manifest either in active propaganda or in armed opposition, both of which, Gīlānī claimed, took their core inspiration from the works of Mawdūdī.[333]

What followed was a justification of armed *jihād* as the only Islamically acceptable option: here migration (*hijrat*) only serves the purpose of setting up a convenient base from which armed resistance can be launched. Consequently, the migrations of the Islamic Prophets were not framed as a quest for sanctuary of a community under threat, but as a strategic move to obtain an advantageous position for the inevitable armed attack on its enemies: 'Migration is the gateway for the Islamic conquest [*hijrat islām kī fatḥ kā darvāzah hē*],'[334] Gīlānī concluded. From such a perspective, the Afghan refugee camps in the Pashtun Borderland could serve no other possible purpose than the recruitment, physical and ideological training, and management of *mujāhidīn*, and it was in this context that the involvement of foreign personnel also found its justification.[335]

331 See Gīlānī (1989), 41–50.

332 See ibid., 42.

333 Ibid., 50: 'In Afghanistan a movement rose from within that is bound in gratitude to the revolutionary Islamic literature of Sayyid Mawdūdī from Pakistan.'

334 Ibid., 64.

335 This is also reflected by the reproduction of fifteen personal accounts of the migration (*hijrat'nāmah*) by select individuals, all of whom support the concept of the refugee camp as projected by Gīlānī: see ibid., 108–54.

On the other hand, and this indicates once more the tug of war among the various *mujāhidīn* factions, some camps were preferable to others, and in this context, especially those run by the Ḥil-Kh, Ḥil-Ḥ and the IIAA were highlighted.[336] However, and probably for systematic reasons, Gīlānī needed to maintain the illusion of unity among the various and more often than not bitterly opposed factions among the *mujāhidīn*, referring to the successful opposition to British colonial rule (or – in the case of Afghanistan – colonial aspiration) as a historical case in point and making, therefore, a firm plea for the maintenance of the IIMA.[337] Yet, and this seems most significant, Gīlānī did not discuss any scenario for the time after the inevitable victory of the *mujāhidīn*. Qāẕī Ḥusayn Aḥmad, the supreme *amīr* of the JiI at the time of Gīlānī's writing and a contributor of forewords to these works, instead expressed hopes for the realization of the *ḥukūmat-i islāmī* after Mawdūdī's design in Afghanistan, which would have positive repercussions for the Islamic development of Pakistan.[338] Hopes of this kind, however, were instantly shattered when the IIMA disintegrated and, following the withdrawal of the Soviet Army in February 1989, the race for Kabul resulted in a disastrous civil war that would be ended only by the successful campaign of a new force from the southern lowlands of the Pashtun Borderland: only six and a half years after the Red Army had pulled out of Afghanistan, the ṬIT around Mullā Muḥammad ʿUmar would establish its supreme rule over the entire country.

Tribalizing the *Jamāʿat-i Islāmī* in the Borderland: The Role of the Former Princely States

In addition to their constituencies in urban centres and university campuses in Pakistan, a further bastion of the JiI and its affiliates, predominantly the IJṬ, in the Pashtun Borderland are the former principalities of Dir and Swat, as well as, though to a slightly lesser extent, the district of Malakand, which connects Swat to the Peshawar Valley. In fact, the JiI voter bank in Dir is considered so strong and reliable that the former *amīr* of the central JiI, Qāẕī Ḥusayn Aḥmad, decided in 2002 to stand for election to the national parliament there rather than in his JUI-dominated home district Nowshera in order to secure his seat.[339]

It is certainly highly beneficial to inquire into why these districts have such a strong affiliation to Islamist thought and politics, whereas a different religio-political landscape had emerged in other districts further to the south. One is almost immediately drawn to the idea that a, if not the, dominant reason is the political legacy of the formally independent principalities of Dir and Swat

[336] See ibid., 84–91.
[337] See ibid., 309–18.
[338] See Qāẕī Ḥusayn Aḥmad, 'Dībāchah', in ibid., 19–22. Gīlānī's own outlook on the matter can be found in ibid., 331–5.
[339] See Shah (2019), 74f.

between the nineteenth century and their annexation by Pakistan in 1969, in both cases rooted in the *shari'a*-mindedness of their respective founders, the Ākhūnd ʿAbd al-Ghaffūr in Swat and Ākhūnd Ilyās Khān Malīzay in Dir. However, at the time of Partition, both polities had widely departed from these aspirations and had opted either for a more modernizing course of governance under the Miyāṇgul dynasty between 1915 and 1969, as in the case of Swat,[340] or for a conservative autocracy, as in the case of the Ākhūn Khēl dynasty in Dir between 1897 and 1969.[341] While both principalities had received their seal of approval from the British colonial authorities, thus rewarding their respective regent for his loyalty to the British crown, the rulers of Dir were not really inclined to make concessions to any kind of modernization wished for by the colonial establishment as part of its "civilizing mission" in the colonies: even the revision of its *Official Manual of Governance* (*dastūr al-ʿamal*) in March 1963 clearly reflects the ultra-conservative attitude of the last *navvāb*, Muḥammad Shāh Khusraw Khān (r. 1961–9), which, moreover, was deeply entrenched in local custom.[342] Because of the latter fact, the *navvāb* was not inclined to tolerate any agenda that aimed at establishing a transregional narrative for social and political change, be it secular or religious. Driven mainly by his desire to maintain his power, he thus opposed by force the spread of education[343] and potentially rivalling religio-political groups.[344] The JiI, fully introduced to Dir in the early 1960s by Jahānzēb Khān, the district's first Deputy Commissioner and brother of the IJṬ *amīr* of Swabi, turned out to be one of the latter.

Its arrival, however, was preceded by what local JiI historians call the "Takht-i Bāhī Movement" around Sayyid Masʿūd al-Ḥasan Bukhārī (assassinated 1371/1951) from the village of Narhand in Upper Dir. The fact that, as a Sayyid, he was not bound to conforming with the normative expectations of any particular tribal community allowed him to put himself forward to *navvāb* Shāh Jahān Khān (r. 1924–60) as a viable asset. Subsequently, in exchange for representing the regent's interests against possible conflicting ones in that locality, the *navvāb* appointed Masʿūd al-Ḥasan *qāẓī* of Baraval Bāndī and caretaker of its mosque, in addition to allotting him some land.[345] Yet, he who would eventually be known as the "Baraval Ṣāḥib" instead used his position to raise strong public objections to *navvābī* rule, rooted in his understanding of "good governance", or *siyāsa sharʿiyya*, probably developed

340 See Sultan-i-Rome (2008), 212–53. See also Jahanzeb (1985), esp. 18–32 and 106–27.

341 See Shāhid (2005), 91–111. See also Riyāsat-i Dīr (1963).

342 See, for example, the regulations for the treatment of women in Riyāsat-i Dīr (1963), 33–5, for which one would not easily find support in Islamic precepts. The same goes for all of the many regulations relating to tribal feuds.

343 See Shah (2013), 134.

344 See, for example, Shāhid (2005), 120f.

345 See Yaʿqūb Khān (2009), 11–13.

during his studies in pre-Partition India that might quite possibly also have taken him to one of the many institutions affiliated to the then highly politicized *Dār al-ʿUlūm* of Deoband. The relationship between the *navvāb* and the Baraval Ṣāḥib unsurprisingly deteriorated rather fast, culminating in the latter's eventual expulsion from the principality.[346] Masʿūd al-Ḥasan moved south to Takht-i Bāhī, a town about nine miles north-west of Mardan, which is home to the well-preserved ruins of a monastery of followers of the Buddha from around the turn of the common era. It was there that he gathered his followers around him and 'made [the place] into a centre of *jihād*'[347] against the ruler of Dir. Moreover, it was also there that the Baraval Ṣāḥib hooked up with cadres of the JiI, among them ʿAbd al-Ḥamīd Kākā Khēl (d. 1415/1994), a leading representative of the JiI in the NPFP Provincial Assembly in the late 1980s,[348] and moved successively closer to the organization, which had by then morphed into a political party.[349] The *navvāb* tried from a remote distance to enforce sanctions against ʿAbd al-Ḥamīd for spreading Islamist propaganda and, according to the JiI narrative, eventually even instigated the assassination of the Baraval Ṣāḥib in his exile. However, after *navvābī* rule was finally abolished by the decree of the military dictator Muḥammad Yaḥyá Khān (r. 1969–71) in July 1969 and Dir was incorporated into the NWFP of Pakistan, the descendants of the Baraval Ṣāḥib returned to Baraval and subsequently established themselves as one of the two major hubs of the JiI in Dir.

The other one formed around Ṣūfī ʿInāyat al-Raḥmān of the "Ṣāḥib'zādah" family of Rayḥānkōṫ (d. 1403/1983), whose paternal grandfather Khalīl al-Raḥmān had been a disciple of the Sayyidō Bābā,[350] and he was connected in this way to important figures such as the Haḋḋah Ṣāḥib. Ṣūfī ʿInāyat al-Raḥmān himself had been educated at the *Dār al-ʿUlūm* of Deoband; another of his teachers, his paternal uncle Fa̤zl al-Raḥmān, the "Bābā Jī" of Kōṫkay in neighbouring Kunar, is said to have been a retainer of the Ḥājjī Ṣāḥib of Turangzay and was certainly sympathetic to the thoughts of Mawdūdī, with whose writings he was acquainted.[351] Earlier, Ṣūfī ʿInāyat al-Raḥmān was

[346] See ibid., 14–17. It is interesting to note that author Muḥammad Yaʿqūb Khān (d. 1423/2002), an early activist of the JiI in Dir and its most prominent historiographer, uses terminology to characterize the rule of *navvāb* Shāh Jahān Khān which resonates very well with Islamist symbolical language: the comparison with the Pharaoh in the Qur'anic story of Prophet Mūsá (Moses) and, even more pointedly, addressing the *navvāb* with the Qur'anic term for "idol" (*ṭāghūt*), a term that was reinterpreted by theorists such as Sayyid Quṭb as "tyrant" or "oppressor", one who would not submit to the absolute sovereignty of God (*ḥākimiyyat allāh*), are cases in point here. Compare Quṭb (1430/2009), I: 292 (on Q2.256); Faraj (1981), 2 and 15.

[347] Yaʿqūb Khān (2009), 16.

[348] On him, see ibid., 112–25.

[349] See ibid., 17f.

[350] See ibid., 32; compare Farīd (1979), 113–18, esp. 114.

[351] See Farīd (1979), 31–4.

affiliated to the circle around the Baraval Ṣāḥib at Takht-i Bāhī, became a formal member of the JiI in 1963 and, after the abolition of *navvābī* rule in Dir six years later, was instantly elected its *amīr* for the Malakand Agency.[352]

The activities of the JiI in Dir, from which the organization also eventually splashed over to neighbouring Swat, pivoted on two somewhat related issues. One was informed by its history of opposition to the autocratic *navvābī* regime and consisted of raising an increasing awareness of democratic political participation in the formerly completely disempowered local population. The other resulted from insight into the cultural specifics of the highland Pashtun Borderland and, on the personal suggestion of Mawdūdī, was comprised of instilling a sense of collective discipline. The ultimate tool for awakening the respective sentiments was religious education, for which the JiI set up a network of *dīnī madāris* across the entire district, in conjunction with a civic education that strongly emphasized the modes of democratic participation available, such as voting. This strategy appears to have yielded the results desired: in the first General Elections after the dissolution of the princely state in 1970, the JiI candidate in the constituency of Dir (then NW-18) secured the only seat for the entire NWFP in the National Assembly of Pakistan (PNA).[353] Over the next couple of General Elections, the JiI fared rather well; its top candidates until more recently were predominantly from among the Ṣāḥib'zādah family.[354] The repeated success of "Ṣāḥib'zādah" Fatḥallāh in the 1988 and 1993 General Elections and, although only as runner-up, in 1990, each time as the representative of an alliance of religiously conservative political parties,[355] is once again an indication of the high degree of Borderland pragmatics which, as we have already frequently encountered, would trump ideological rigidity more often than not. There is perhaps no better illustration of this fact than that the current main political representative of the Ṣāḥib'zādah family, Ṣibghatallāh, son of former JiI-MNA Ṣafiyallāh, is now representing the *Pākistān Taḥrīk-i Inṣāf* (PTI) instead of the JiI. Such a shift in affiliation is surprising only at first glance, even more so as current research on electoral behaviour in Lower Dir indicates that the stress of the JiI on social justice (*ʿadālat*) is very compatible with the notion of "equity" (*inṣāf*) that forms the backbone of the PTI agenda, consequently providing floating voters with more options that would ostensibly address their concerns.[356]

While it appears that the JiI in Dir initially deferred its ideological proclivities in favour of local hands-on politics, the Soviet invasion of Afghanistan

352 See Yaʿqūb Khān (2009), 40f.

353 See, for example, Nasr (1994), 166 (Table 9).

354 See the election results by constituency at http://electionpakistan.com/constituencies-list (accessed 10 February 2024); Shah (2019), 28–52.

355 For the first alliance, the *Islāmī Jumhūrī Ittiḥād* (IJI), see Nasr (1994), 206–18; for the second, the *Muttaḥidah Majlis-i ʿAmal* (MMA), see Shah (2019), 72–4.

356 See ibid., 186–210.

brought its transregional agenda to the fore and, moreover, reeled the eventually bipartite district of Dir – Lower (*kūz*, or, in Urdu, *zīrēṇ*) and Upper (*bar*, or, in Urdu, *balā*) – into the wider Pashtun Borderland. In addition, it was in these circumstances that the family of the Baraval Ṣāḥib gained revived recognition. A critical element in this was the ḤM, which deployed a contingent from the Kashmir Frontier to set up a base of operations in Dir and the wider Malakand region. Receiving generous funds from the strategic nexus of ISI and JiI during the early years of the war, they subsequently engaged in guerrilla warfare against the Soviet occupation force and its PDPA allies across the border along the entire Malakand borderline, yet without any formal submission to any of the Afghan Islamist forces under the umbrella of the IIMA.

While the latter operated mainly out of the more cosmopolitan urban space of Peshawar, the ḤM was based in a distinctly rural environment, which meant that paying heed to the local ethnic sentiments was absolutely critical for the success of any campaign staged from there. The utterly nomocentric ḤM, however, appeared, at least in the beginning, just as incapable of putting its rigid ideological framework aside as were the leaders of the *Ṭarīqah-yi Muḥammadiyyah* in the early nineteenth century. Because the activists of the ḤM who arrived at the Durand Line from the Kashmir frontier were clearly orientated towards the Pakistani nation-state, they failed to recognize the importance of tribal affiliations in the Pashtun Borderland. To overcome the initial alienation from the local population for the sake of concerted action against a common enemy, the JiI, as the political umbrella under which the ḤM operated, needed to employ a number of pragmatic approaches towards other activist religious currents in the eastern part of the Pashtun Borderland, regardless of the profound ideological differences.

Exemplarily, while the JiI used a large proportion of the funds made available to it by Zia-ul-Haq and the ISI to substantially expand the network of its own *dīnī madāris* in Dir and Bajawr, an increasing number of young JiI cadres from there also enrolled in the *Dār al-ʿUlūm-i Ḥaqqāniyyah* at Akōṛah Khaṫṫak. Using this opportunity to perpetuate JiI views in this Deobandi environment, they themselves became, in turn, influenced by the various debates circulating in the *Ḥaqqāniyyah* at this time.[357] Alongside this growing confluence of "Frontier Deobandiyyat", JiI-Islamism and ḤM militancy, tribal leaders with vested personal stakes in matters of governance from both sides of the Durand Line helped to negotiate the various interests at play, regardless of whether these were ideologically, politically or economically motivated. A very prominent case in point was Malik Muḥammad Zarīn of the Mashvāṇī tribe mentioned previously,[358] who owned land on either side of the Durand Line

[357] See Malik (1996), 208f.

[358] See Section 4.2.1, n.151. Generally on the Mashvāṇī, see Ḥayāt Khān (1867), 443f.; "Shāh'jī" (1930). See also Christensen (1980), 81.

and eventually even acted for some time in the early 2000s as the quasi-governor of Kunar Province.[359] We find in Malik Zarīn once again a vivid example of a governance-orientated, yet utterly pragmatic, Pashtun Borderland actor, who would easily make or break political and ideological alliances, depending solely on their utility for furthering his own ends.

Malik Zarīn's core contacts in the JiI on the eastern side of the Durand Line included the brothers ʿInāyatallāh Khān (b. 1392/1972) and Ḥājjī Muḥammad Anvar Khān of the Baraval Ṣāḥib family, as well as his fellow tribesman Sirāj al-Ḥaqq Khān, the eventual *amīr-i aʿlá* of the national JiI.[360] All of them had, at times, been active in the ḤM, entering the folds of party politics only later in their lives. The proximity of Malik Zarīn to prominent JiI cadres may have been the reason why his own son Malik Ayyūb has also been pursuing a political career in Lower Dir since 2001 on a JiI ticket. On the other side of the Durand Line, however, Malik Zarīn entered the circles of leading Afghan *mujāhidīn* commanders, prominently among them Gulbuddīn Ḥikmatyār and Ṣibghatallāh Mujaddidī, and started to successfully operate his own *lax̌kar* in Kunar against the Soviet occupying forces, although formally under the umbrella of Mujaddidī's JNM.[361]

After the withdrawal of the Soviet army from Afghanistan, the ḤM redirected the main focus of its attention back to Kashmir, while their former fighters from the JiI circles of Dir and beyond would lay down their arms and involve themselves more in provincial and national politics, eventually standing successfully for election to the Provincial and National Assemblies.[362] Still, the relationship between the JiI and the ḤM in Khyber Pakhtunkhwa, while being publicly downplayed, still appears very much alive.[363] Meanwhile, on the other side of the borderline, the erupting civil war in Afghanistan, followed by the first central government of the IEA, demanded even more flexibility than before from regional operators with vested interests on either side of the national divide, such as Malik Zarīn. Therefore, it is not really

359 His portrayal in Akbar and Burton (2005), 269, 290f. and 332, appears to be a rather biased one, probably because Malik Zarīn was a competitor to the author's own father Sayyid Faẕl Akbar, the first governor of Kunar Province appointed by Ḥāmid Karzay in 2001, but, moreover, also perhaps because the author, thanks to his political socialization in the USA, was not entirely aware of the subtler points of Borderland pragmatics.

360 Conversation with an affiliate to the family of the Baraval Ṣāḥib of Upper Dir, Bāṛah Galī (KP), 10 August 2017.

361 See UNHCR (1989), 11 and 26.

362 ʿInāyatallāh Khān, mentioned above, for example, has served as MPA for the JiI since 2002, and has, so far, headed two departments within the provincial government of Khyber Pakhtunkhwa.

363 On a visit to the provincial headquarters of the JiI in Sardār Gaṛhī, Peshawar, on 18 April 2019, the armed guards of the compound were observed to carry the ḤM badge on their uniform. Furthermore, imagery shared on various social media platforms proves that the relationship between the JiI and the ḤM is also quite openly displayed in Dir.

surprising to see this tribal leader entering into temporary alliances with the Ḥil-Ḥ and the government of Karzay, supporting a particular position on one day and going against it on the next. The efficacy of such a pragmatic flexibility is evident from the great material wealth and political power that Malik Zarīn was able to accumulate, as well as the fact that he survived well into his eighties, before, on 13 April 2011, he finally fell victim to a successful assassination attempt by an anti-government suicide bomber.

Meanwhile, a more radical organization grew out of the JiI in Dir in the early 1990s, which is as difficult to clearly assign to the Islamist ideational current as was the case earlier with Yūnus Khāliṣ, described above. Although, on the one hand, this clearly indicates the limitation of ideal-typical framing of distinct ideational threats, on the other hand, it nonetheless points to the fact that Borderland pragmatics demand an ability to overcome doctrinal divides in the face of possible discord within individual organizations for the sake of retaining, and possibly increasing, one's own reputation and influence.

Aggravation: The *Taḥrīk-i Nifāẕ-i Sharīʿat-i Muḥammadī* (Part I)

Ṣūfī Muḥammad ibn al-Ḥaẕrat Ḥasan (d. 1440/2019), a JiI activist from Maydān in Lower Dir, was put in charge of a JiI *madrasah* in his hometown. A lot of his educational background is shrouded in mystery, a fact that is responsible for the parallel existence of diverse narratives, depending on the particular interests of the respective relator. Thus, while those with a strong affinity to the JiI claim that Ṣūfī Muḥammad was trained solely within this party's educational framework, others suggest that he was yet another graduate from the *Dār al-Qurʾān* in Panjpir.[364] Amīr Ḥamzah (b. 1378/1959), a native of Punjabi Shaykhūpūrah who evolved into a major figure in the *Ahl-i Ḥadīs̱*-affiliated militant organization *Lashkar-i Ṭayyibah* (LiṬ), indicates that Ṣūfī Muḥammad studied – among others – with a certain Muḥammad Ḥusayn Ṣāfī from Kunar, *nom de guerre* "Jamīl al-Raḥmān" (killed 1412/1991), who will figure quite prominently further below.[365]

Ṣūfī Muḥammad had been a faithful cadre of the JiI for three decades, and was even twice elected as its representative in the District Council of Lower Dir. Yet, in contrast to the majority of JiI cadres there, Ṣūfī Muḥammad acquired a reputation of being overtly emotional, a fact that dissociated him somewhat from the more sober and rationalistic rhetoric of the JiI leadership. On the other hand, his emotive way of teaching, which, since 1979, revolved much around the need for support of the Afghan *jihād*, turned out to be quite

[364] Conversation with an affiliate to the family of the Baraval Ṣāḥib of Upper Dir, Bāṛah Galī (KP), 10 August 2017. Conversely, Khan (2010), 140f., claims that Ṣūfī Muḥammad had studied with Muḥammad Ṭāhir at Panjpir, but does not support this claim with evidence.

[365] See Ḥamzah (1423/2002), 272. On Jamīl al-Raḥmān, see Section 4.4.2.

effective with the local attendees of the *madrasah* in his charge, even more so with the influx of Afghan refugees into the region.

This tension within the JiI in one of its prime constituencies did not go unnoticed. The military dictator Zia-ul-Haq's relationships with the initially very supportive JiI had cooled down significantly around the Islamization Programme Referendum in 1984, during which the then-*amīr-i aʿlá* of the JiI, Miyāṇ Ṭufayl Muḥammad (d. 1430/2009), had critically distanced himself from the dictator's aspiration to use "Islam" for the solidification of his own military regime.[366] In anticipation of the elections to the National and Provincial Assemblies in February 1985, Zia-ul-Haq started to exploit internal dissent within the JiI for his own benefit: the overall bad performance of the JiI in these elections[367] suggests that Zia-ul-Haq's strategy paid off. One of the dissenters that the dictator successfully pulled over to his side appears to have been Ṣūfī Muḥammad.

As said previously, there are alternative narratives, and one of them Amīr Ḥamzah claimed had been presented to him by Ṣūfī Muḥammad himself when they met in Maydān in July 1991. According to this, the rift between the JiI leadership in Dir and Ṣūfī Muḥammad did not begin to crystallize until Bēnaẓīr Bhuṭṭō's first term in office (1988–90). The break occurred when the then-Commissioner of Kohat and the Malakand Division, Shakīl Durrānī (b. 1366/1947), informed the leadership of all political parties in his constituency of the government's plans to replace the hitherto-valid "jirgah system" with Pakistani common law in the FATA and PATA. According to Ṣūfī Muḥammad, there was agreement across all political parties involved that, while the "jirgah system" should indeed be abolished, it could under no circumstances be replaced by an un-Islamic legal framework inherited from the former colonial master Great Britain, but must instead be supplanted exclusively and indispensably by *shari'a* law. The parties in Dir jointly organized a massive sit-in outside the District Commissioner's office in Tīmargarah in early July 1989 to place emphasis on this demand, voicing their firm opposition to the current legal system and demanding what they called the "preservation of the *shari'a*" (*nifāẕ-i sharīʿat*) in Dir. At the same time, the representatives of the JiI in the National and Provincial Assemblies tabled this demand in their respective bodies, and, towards the end of that month, a boycott of the Pakistani state judiciary was announced and a *shari'a* judiciary in Dir established instead.[368]

The government authorities, alarmed by the sheer scale of the so-far regionally confined protests, backed down and offered the people in Dir, and possibly also in adjacent areas, a choice between maintaining the FCR, under which the

366 See Richter (1985), 148; Nasr (1994), 195f.
367 See Nasr (1994), 196–9.
368 See Ḥamzah (1423/2002), 272–4.

"jirgah system" had been enshrined, and embracing the Pakistani common law, or would even relent and grant the full implementation of *shari'a* law.[369] The general decision in favour of the last option, however, bore in itself the seed for dissent within the JiI and for aggravated violence: the bone of contention was the 1990 general elections, following the dismissal of Bēnaẓīr Bhuṭṭō by President Ghulām Isḥāq Khān (in office 1988–93) on charges of corruption and the general deterioration of law and order, in which the developments in Dir had certainly played a considerable role. When the elections were announced, a fundamental debate broke out inside the JiI in Dir and adjacent areas that resembled those in the early days of Pakistan over the direction of its eventual Constitution and the role of the JiI herein: did the implementation of *shari'a* law not cause political parties and their perpetual contestation in elections to become redundant? After all, one could still compromise with the metamorphosis of the JiI from an elitist model community into a political party as a strategic move to pave the way for the establishment of a *shari'a*-based societal framework. However, once this objective had been achieved, the JiI should return to its original form as the pioneering nucleus of the Islamic community that would successively expand and absorb all other citizens into a uniform Islamic polity, Mawdūdī's *ḥukūmat-i islāmī*.[370]

Consequently, Ṣūfī Muḥammad and his retainers argued for a boycott of the 1990 General Elections, while especially those JiI cadres who, as members of the Provincial and National Assemblies or the Senate of Pakistan, were already immersed in the political structures of the Islamic Republic and would be forced to give up their responsibilities, reputations and privileges, argued strongly against it. As neither side would relent from its respective position, a crack emerged that, over time, would widen into a trench and further into an insurmountable canyon, culminating in Ṣūfī Muḥammad's eventual expulsion from the JiI. The dissenter, namely, used his influence in and around Maydān to enforce a full boycott of the elections, resulting in a severe loss of parliamentary seats for the JiI. As a consequence, so Ṣūfī Muḥammad said as quoted by Amīr Ḥamzah, the JiI withdrew its support from the *Movement for the Preservation of the Muḥammadan Shari'a*, the *Taḥrīk-i Nifāẕ-i Sharī'at-i Muḥammadī* (TNSM), led by Ṣūfī Muḥammad and, thus betrayed its original objective, the relentless work for the "establishment of the (Islamic) *dīn*".[371]

[369] See ibid., 274. On the role and scope of "jirgah" under the FCR, see Nichols (2013), 151–7 (Chapter III of the Punjab FCR of 1887 as amended in July 1900). Nichols himself makes clear in his introduction to this edition of FCR-related documents that 'the FCR jirga was an artificial institution [. . .] appointed by colonial officers and composed of three or more approved leading men' (p. xv).

[370] On the strategic shift from community vanguard to political party in 1951, see Nasr (1994), 28–43. On Mawdūdī's original conception of the Islamic state, see Hartung (2013a), 99–192.

[371] See Ḥamzah (1423/2002), 275. On Mawdūdī's concept of *iqāmat-i dīn*, see Nasr (1996), 80–3; Hartung (2013a), 75f. and 230–2.

Ṣūfī Muḥammad now saw himself as the only righteous one left to carry this torch further, and, certainly encouraged by the effect of the election boycott he had instigated, he now began to extend the demand for the full introduction of *shari'a* law to the national government, assembled those loyal to him and started to march on Islamabad. The convoy was intercepted at Aṭṭak by various provincial ministers who assured the marchers that they had been heard by the government, but that conduct bordering on insurgency in Dir was not tolerable under any circumstances.[372]

What followed was the growth of conspiracy theories about the JiI and certain government authorities – first among them, the ISI – being in cahoots with each other, and about the JiI central leadership under Qāẓī Ḥusayn Aḥmad claiming ownership of the TNSM.[373] Ṣūfī Muḥammad furiously severed his long-standing ties with the JiI.

After his split from the JiI, a religious disputation (*munāẓarah*) is said to have been held in Maydān between Ṣūfī Muḥammad and notable JiI cadre Zāhid Shāh from Dir (b. 1389/1970) to determine the future deanship of the *madrasah* that Ṣūfī Muḥammad had so far held. The defeat in this publicly held disputation led to Ṣūfī Muḥammad being stripped of his position and subsequently establishing a *madrasah* of his own design in Maydān,[374] where he began to arouse *jihādī* sentiments further, soon, however, directed no longer against the defeated Soviets, but instead against the national governments on either side of the Durand Line. In 1992, Ṣūfī Muḥammad finally affirmed his supreme leadership over the now distinct TNSM, which drifted ideologically ever further away from the Islamism represented by the various Afghan organizations that grew out of the SJM and the JiI / IJṬ on the Pakistani side. In contrast to them, the TNSM advocated a general aloofness from party politics and the parliamentary framework; it also stood for firm rejection of the possibility of any man-made legislation based on *ijtihād*. Consequently, the TNSM resembled, in fact, various radical splinter groups of the MB, especially in the Egypt of the 1970s and 1980s, foremost among them the so-called *Tanẓīm al-Jihād al-Islāmī* around Sayyid Imām al-Sharīf, *nom de guerre* "Dr Faḍl" (b. 1369/1950), and Ayman al-Ẓawāhirī (killed 1444/2022), who, in 1991, even went as far as to accuse the founder of the MB, Ḥasan al-Bannā, and his successors of apostasy (*irtidād*) for their advocacy of parliamentary participation and non-violence.[375]

These parallels between the positions of Ṣūfī Muḥammad and people such as al-Ẓawāhirī and Abū Muḥammad al-Maqdisī mentioned above regarding

372 See Ḥamzah (1423/2002), 275f.

373 See ibid., 276f.

374 Conversation with an affiliate to the family of the Baraval Ṣāḥib of Upper Dir, Bāṛah Galī (KP), 10 August 2017.

375 See al-Ẓawāhirī (1426/2005). See also Nedza (2020), 31 n.53 and 42 n.103.

democracy as a political system indicate that Ṣūfī Muḥammad had moved well out of the ideological thread of Islamism and into another, albeit related, one by the early 1990s: Salafism. We will, therefore, have to pick up our narrative on the TNSM again; however, this time treating it as a representative of "Pashtun Salafism". Before embarking on that journey, however, we will first have to investigate what impact, if any, the prominence of Islamism in the Pashtun Borderland during the armed resistance against the PDPA regime in Kabul and its Soviet allies had on the distinct regional manifestations of "Deobandiyyat", the most widespread and, therefore, important contemporary current in the Pashtun Borderland.

4.3 Militant Frontier Deobandiyyat

Although, as we have seen, the Sunni Islamic cultures of the Pashtun Borderland have been penetrated by Islamist ideas with increasing force since the 1950s, the PDPA coup d'état and the subsequent Soviet invasion of Afghanistan in late 1979 raised this ideational pollination to an unprecedented level of significance. However, this process of acceleration had already been triggered a few years earlier when Muḥammad Dāvūd Khān deposed his uncle Ẓāhir Shāh, and the powerful inspiration of Islamism for politically savvy young Afghan Muslims, especially in the urban centres of the north and west of the country, was translated into political action. It was then that the influence of Islamism also became notable in rural areas of the Borderland, where it entered a highly consequential alliance with those forms of Muslim religiosity pivoting on Islamic reformulation that dominated in the rural spaces east and west of the Durand Line.

The sort of piety-focused "Frontier Deobandiyyat" that, after 1947, had emerged most prominently in the shape of the *Dār al-ʿUlūm-i Ḥaqqāniyyah* at Akōṛah Khaṫṫak was at the forefront of this. However, the focus on personal and Prophet-inspired piety, which was then playing itself out in the TJ-associated activities of the *Ḥaqqāniyyah* teachers and students, did not preclude any political investment. In fact, the strong personal ties of the seminary's founder, ʿAbd al-Ḥaqq Akōṛavī, with Ḥusayn Aḥmad Madanī, the then-president of the JUH and principal of the *Dār al-ʿUlūm* of Indian Deoband indicated some interest in participating in political processes, which was later construed by former students of ʿAbd al-Ḥaqq as fulfilment of his civic duty.[376] ʿAbd al-Ḥaqq successfully competed for the JUI for a seat in the PNA in the controversial General Elections of 1970, which triggered the eventual secession of East Pakistan and the subsequent establishment of the independent People's Republic of Bangladesh,[377] a victory which he repeated seven years later.

376 Sayyid ʿAbdallāh, 'Shaykh al-ḥadīs̱ Ḥaẓrat Mawlānā ʿAbd al-Ḥaqq – rḥ – marḥūm kī yād mēṇ', *Nuṣrat al-Jihād* 1/11–12 (1370sh/1412/1991), 28.

377 See Pirzada (2000), 34.

Such an involvement in actual political affairs was certainly encouraged by Madanī himself and, following his death in 1957, also by his son and successor As'ad Madanī (d. 1428/2006).[378] The close contacts of 'Abd al-Ḥaqq with leading JUI members had existed since the 1950s,[379] suggesting that the scholar himself had been actively involved in that enterprise right from the moment that the JUS dissolved into the JUI.

4.3.1 Ḥaqqāniyyāt *(Plural), Post-1979 (Part I)*

During 'Abd al-Ḥaqq's election campaign of 1969–70, one of the recent graduates of the *Ḥaqqāniyyah* went out enthusiastically canvassing for him.[380] This man, Jalāl al-Dīn ibn Khᵛājah Muḥammad Khān of the Sulṭān Khēl Źadrāṇ, better known by his *nom de guerre* "Jalāl al-Dīn Ḥaqqānī", had been born thirty years earlier to a rather wealthy landowner in the village of Kārezgay of the Źadrāṇ District of the Afghan province of Paktia, which borders the province of Khost. In the years to come, he would play a central role in the upsurge in militancy sustained by religious precepts in the Pashtun Borderland. His death in 2014 was just as assiduously covered up by his associates as that of Mullā 'Umar, the first supreme commander of the ṬIT / IEA.

Jalāl al-Dīn turned out to be yet another of the liminal Borderland actors; his pedigree drew on a long-standing involvement in tribal warfare legitimized by

378 This is somewhat reminiscent of the conditions Madanī stipulated before accepting the rectorate of the *Dār al-'Ulūm* of Deoband, which emphatically included an acknowledgement of his political work as part of his official routines: see Metcalf (2009), 92f. The relationship with As'ad Madanī, in turn, is more difficult to grasp, as by the time he assumed the presidency of the JUH, the two states, India and Pakistan, had already significantly grown apart. Letters to 'Abd al-Ḥaqq's son Samī' al-Ḥaqq, however, kept invoking the role of the Pashtun Borderland activists in the early anti-colonial activities of the Shaykh al-Hind and, by inference, their significance for the institutional narrative of the JUH: see Samī' al-Ḥaqq (2011b), I: 247f. (letters dated 17 July 1969 and 7 August 1974). Also, see the four speeches As'ad Madanī delivered at the *Dār al-'Ulūm-i Ḥaqqāniyyah* in March 1970, December 1980, December 1984 and April 2001 in Samī' al-Ḥaqq (2015), I: 328–53.

379 See the published correspondence with Iḥtishām al-Ḥaqq Thānavī of Ṫandō Allāhyār in Sindh (d. 1400/1980), Zāhid al-Rāshidī, then-head of the publication department of the JUI, and especially with Muftī Maḥmūd (see below in this section), president of the JUI since 1970. The correspondence with 'Abd al-Ḥanān Hazāravī, descendent of some members of the *Ṭarīqah-yi Muḥammadiyyah* in the early nineteenth century and, until the withdrawal of the JUI from activities in nascent Pakistan, its head administrator appears of equal importance: see Samī' al-Ḥaqq (2011a), 48–51, 206f., 376–90, 477–80 and 596–604.

380 See Anon., 'al-Ḥājj Mawlavī Jalāl al-Dīn Ḥaqqānī lah (al-Naṣīḥah) sarah paḥ marakah kē: ćangah chih malgarī millatūnah də kufrī ṭāqatūnō tar tāṣīr lānday dī gaḋūn hīć bīrūnī qawt tah də hēvād pah dākhilī chārūkay', *Manba' al-Jihād* [P] 2/5 (1369sh/1411h), 36–42 and 52, here 41.

religious precepts. Some of his family members had allegedly been active in the tribal resistance to Amānallāh Khān's modernization efforts in 1924 and 1928.[381] In June 1929, members of the Źadrāṇ tribe answered the call of "Nūr al-Mashā'ikh" Faẕl-i 'Umar Mujaddidī – the then-Ḥaẕrat of Shōr Bāzār – to help to redress the fact that the ethnically Tajik Amīr Ḥabīballāh ibn Hidāyatallāh Kalakānī, mock-epithet "Bachah-yi Saqqāw" – "son of a water-carrier" (executed 1348/1929), had taken advantage of the very same tribal revolt and installed himself on the throne of Kabul. Again, the tribes rose to help remove an ethnically different usurper of the regality, which they themselves are said to have considered the exclusive prerogative of a Pashtun dignitary.[382] Surely, Jalāl al-Dīn must have grown up with these events as part of the local tribal folklore, and which, moreover, appeared to have been re-enacted immediately before Jalāl al-Dīn's birth on the other side of the Durand Line by the anti-British insurgency of Ḥājjī Mīrzālī Khān Vazīr, the "Faqīr of Īpī" (d. 1379/1960), and his followers and disciples.[383] Brown and Rassler have, therefore, rightly concluded that the 'world into which Jalaluddin Haqqani was born was thus a maelstrom of similar types of borderland violence that he would find himself at the centre of later in adulthood'.[384]

This maelstrom to which the two authors refer has an even greater systematic significance, because it points back to what might be called "the essence of the borderland constellation": a substantial proportion of the endemic violence in these regions is a conservative and community-conscious reaction to multifarious pulls from imperial centres, in the modern era mainly under the banner of "civilizational progress". A paradigmatic frame of reference for these agendas has been urban development; rural space, in turn, is conceived as a reservoir of socio-cultural traditions belonging to an earlier stage in the civilization process that will die out sooner or later. Jalāl al-Dīn, similarly to

381 See Olesen (1995), 134–8 and 145–9.

382 See ibid., 149. For a meticulous contemporaneous day-to-day account of the controversial nine-month interregnum of Ḥabīballāh Kalakānī, the complete text of which has only recently been made available to a wider audience, see Kātib-i Hazārah (2013). In addition, Robert McChesney has published two English translations of it, the first (McChesney [1999]) still solely based on the 1988 Russian translation by A. I. Škirando), the second (McChesney and Khorrami [2019]) based on the above edition of the Persian text, as well as a contemporaneous manuscript held by the National Archives of Afghanistan in Kabul.

383 See Warren (2000), 85–105, 129–70 and 232–73. This work is based exclusively on British colonial records and, thus, tells the story with an understandable bias. The opposite perspective, based primarily on extensive interviews with former adepts and compatriots of the Īpī Faqīr, is provided by Maḥsūd (2000). In his insurgency against British colonial domination, the Īpī Faqīr also enjoyed the support of 'Abd al-Raḥīm Pōpalzay: see Pōpalza'ī (1992), 70–5. The Grand Mufti of the NWFP, however, passed away before the Īpī Faqīr's turn to religious zeal, of which the former would probably not have approved.

384 Brown and Rassler (2013), 31.

the overwhelming majority of the *Ḥaqqāniyyah* clientele, represented exactly these rural spaces with all their various and allegedly anachronistic norms and values. Indeed, most of the students at Akōṛah Khaṫṫak hailed from the meanwhile integrated Federally and Provincially Administered Tribal Areas (FATA) and PATA of the Islamic Republic of Pakistan and its former NWFP, respectively, and increasingly the Pashtun-dominated provinces of Afghanistan, Jalāl al-Dīn's native region Paktia being prominent among them.[385]

The urban paradigm represented a serious challenge to these people's distinct understanding of socio-economic and political organization: the urban market economy that depended so much on wage labour triggered migration from rural spaces into the cities, at the expense of a highly restrictive yet solid social solidarity network that the labour migrants had in their respective home communities. This estrangement, in turn, results in the loss of significant socio-cultural norms and values, making the cities appear as dens of iniquity to the representatives of rural communities. The emerging vicious circle runs as follows: turning a peasant into a worker is accompanied by the loss of values which are highly important to maintain the overall cohesion within the rural communities.[386] This existential threat to the socio-cultural fabric of the rural communities leaves only two options: one, to bow to the might of the rather recent urban paradigm; or, two, to actively defend these values by declaring rurality the paradigm. Because the latter option results basically in the collision of two incompatible paradigms, it is almost inevitably violent. For borderland actors, such as Jalāl al-Dīn, this battle could be decided in his favour only if governance were brought under his control. Then, and only then, would it be possible to redress all the perceived wrongs, especially moral ones, that the nexus of urbanity and capitalism had produced.

Bearing all of this in mind, it is not surprising that Jalāl al-Dīn emerged at the helm of agitation for a militant response to Muḥammad Dāvūd's coup d'état in the Lōyah Paktia region. While, once again, conclusive evidence is lacking,[387] Jalāl al-Dīn is credited by his associates with having issued a

385 See Malik (1996), 208f. Malik's data cover the period between 1977 and 1984 (which, of course, encompasses the time of the Soviet invasion of Afghanistan and the subsequent mass exodus of Afghans into Pakistan that had had a decisive impact on student numbers). According to these data, students from FR Bannū and the North Waziristan Agency constitute the majority of those from the FATA region of Pakistan (about 16.7 per cent). The substantially smaller contingent from Dir (4.9 per cent) is also of significance for the religio-political orientation of the *Ḥaqqāniyyah*, as we shall see.

386 Consequently, the PDPA government was defamed in the later anti-communist rhetoric of Jalāl al-Dīn and his associates as the "workers' regime": see, for example, Sayyid Muḥyī 'l-Dīn "Hāshimī", 'Də *mazdūr rižīm* pah zindānūnō kē də bandbānō līdlay ōrēdlay ḥālāt', *Manbaʿ al-Jihād* [P] 2/5 (1369sh/1411h), 28f. (italics added).

387 Brown and Rassler (2013), 46, rightly remark that the factuality of this episode remains still to be proven beyond the mere myth-making of Jalāl al-Dīn and his associates.

declaration (*iʿlān*) of *jihād* against the "godless" republican government of Kabul in July 1973, utilizing the network of *dīnī madāris* in Lōyah Paktia that he had established a few years earlier to rally a *laẋkar* from among their students.[388] In this endeavour, Jalāl al-Dīn happened to have allied for the first time with Gulbuddīn Ḥikmatyār, who had fled Kabul for Peshawar when Dāvūd Khān seized power.[389] This is quite an important observation, as it indicates a link between some representations of "Frontier Deobandiyyat" and Islamism that predates the surge of Islamist activities in the Pashtun Borderland with the S̱awr Revolution and the subsequent Soviet military invasion of Afghanistan. In fact, Islamism, especially of the JiI variety, was already well established in the *Ḥaqqāniyyah* in the early 1970s; yet, it gained even wider currency during the martial rule of General Zia-ul-Haq in Pakistan between July 1977 and August 1988.

ʿAbd al-Ḥaqq Akōṛavī had been a JUI representative in the PNA before and during Zia-ul-Haq's rule,[390] with his son, Samīʿ al-Ḥaqq, serving in the Senate of Pakistan between 1985 and 1991.[391] Three years prior to that, the latter was a member of Zia-ul-Haq's *Majlis-i Shūrá*, which substituted for the PNA under martial law and turned the parliamentary system of Pakistan into a kind of technocracy. In fact, the occurrence of Samīʿ al-Ḥaqq increasingly taking over his father's responsibilities in the administration of the *Ḥaqqāniyyah*, as well as within the JUI, strongly indicates that the closing of ranks between students and staff of the *Ḥaqqāniyyah*, as chief representatives of "Frontier Deobandiyyat", and Islamists was predominantly to his credit. This is also supported by the fact that, in 1986, Samīʿ al-Ḥaqq was joined in the Senate of Pakistan by Qāẓī Ḥusayn Aḥmad, the then-Secretary General, and later *amīr-i aʿlá*, of the JiI, who, like him, was a native of Nowshera and, therefore, yet another borderland actor who would put doctrinal differences pragmatically aside whenever the situation necessitated it.[392] In fact, both were instrumental in bringing the Shariat Bill onto the national political agenda,[393] for which the *Muttaḥidah Sharīʿat Maḥāẕ*, established by ʿAbd al-Ḥaqq Akōṛavī in 1973, had been fiercely campaigning.

388 See ʿAbd al-ʿAzīz Khān, 'Pah Afghānistān kē də jihād də lumṛanī ʿamaliyāt aw də kamūnistānō pah muqābil kē də ʿulamāʾō paćūn', *Manbaʿ al-Jihād* [P] 1/4 (1368sh/1410h), 17–22, here 19.

389 See ibid.

390 See the respective rosters of members of the fifth (1972–10 January 1977), sixth (28 March–5 July 1977) and seventh (1985–8) PNA on the official website of the PNA, URL: www.na.gov.pk/en/content.php?id=121 (accessed 23 May 2018).

391 See Senate of Pakistan (1991), 8, 49 and 122.

392 See ibid., 8, 42 and 122.

393 The "Shariat Bill", proposed to the PNA on 28 August 1998 by the government of Miyāṇ Muḥammad Navāz Sharīf (r. 1990–3, 1997–9 and 2013–17), refers to the attempt at amending the Constitution of Pakistan, aimed at replacing all state law with the *shariʿa*. The proposal was eventually blocked by the Senate of Pakistan.

Subsequently, they would act in cahoots in a variety of constellations over the years to come.[394]

On the surface, the efforts of the JUI and JiI in the national politics of Pakistan were driven by a motivation similar to those of the various Islamist organizations in Kabul, as well as those of Jalāl al-Dīn Ḥaqqānī and his associates and comparable groups in the rural areas of the Pashtun Borderland. All of them were deeply concerned about the possible impact of alternative socio-political ideologies on the Islamicity of their respective nation-state frameworks. Yet, the most virulent question that consistently followed from this for most involved in national politics was who would acquire the power to define "Islamicity". Thus, they had clearly elitist aspirations and, because this battle was fought within the various governmental bodies, they would also not challenge the existence of the state and its basic structures. That was not necessarily so for Jalāl al-Dīn and similar borderland actors.

The Faqīr of Īpī, for example, remained highly suspicious of the new national elites and, therefore, continued his confrontational course with the government of Pakistan which, allegedly, he saw explicitly as a British creation, with Jinnāḥ as their agent.[395] Immediately after the establishment of the new Republic, the Īpī Faqīr began to needle the new imperial authority by attacking the main post of its locally sourced military representatives (*khāṣṣah'dārān*) in North Waziristan's Dattā Khēl, aiming just one year later at capturing that strategic post for himself.[396] From his stronghold, an elaborate cave system in Gūrvēk only a few miles from the Durand Line, he had already proclaimed his emirate over the *mujāhidīn* in 1938.[397] Now, he began to disseminate propaganda that combined the idea of an independent "Pashtunistan", as prominently advocated by Bāchā Khān and the *Khudāy Khidmatgārān*, with his rather narrow religious vision of *shari'a*-based rule, which he did not see being advocated by the Pakistani state.[398] The Pashto paper *Ghāzī* that the Īpī

394 See Senate of Pakistan (1988), 59f., 86, 146f. and 272–6. See also Nasr (1994), 204f.; Samī' al-Ḥaqq, 'Bachpan mēṇ bhī barōṇ kī ṭaraḥ sōchtē thē', in 'Usmān (2014), 189f.

395 Uncorroborated by documentary evidence, it is widely held that, on 12 May 1948, that is, almost exactly four months before Jinnāḥ's death, the Īpī Faqīr had a poster issued from his headquarters at Gūrvēk in which he defamed the "Father of the Nation" as an agent of the British. Jinnāḥ, in turn, did not shy away from accusing the Īpī Faqīr of being in cahoots with the Afghan government and the Nehru-led INC, see Jinnah (1993–2012), III: 164f. (no. 68, Col. Shah Pasand Khan to M. A. Jinnah, dated 8 July 1947), 471 (no. 183, Letter from Maulvi Abu Sulaiman to Zafar Ahmed Ansari, dated 17 July 1947).

396 See Warren (2000), 260–3. Notably, while nationalistic historiographers seem less interested in historical accurancy (see, e.g., Źalmay [1368sh], 266–70), the account of Maḥsūd (2000) stops short in 1945.

397 See ibid., 210–23.

398 The short interview that American journalist Christopher Rand (d. 1968) conducted with the Faqīr of Īpī at the latter's base at Gūrvēk, in which the latter stressed that his

Faqīr and some of his learned adepts and associates published irregularly from Gūrvēk, alongside corresponding pamphlets, was highly instrumental in this regard. Their message, in all its confusing inconsistency, is well summed up in the following statement:

> From 19 August 1947, when the British appointed Mr Jinnāḥ as the Governor General of Pakistan, the Pīr Ṣāḥib [Amīn al-Hasanāt] of Mānkī-yi Sharīf, the Pīr [ʿAbd al-Laṭīf] of Zakōṛī Sharīf, Doctor Khān [ʿAbd al-Jabbār Khān] Ṣāḥib, ʿAbd al-Ghaffār Khān and other prominent figures from among the Pashtuns raised their voice for the introduction of *shari'a* law and freedom for "Pashtunistan". Yet, against these demands, and with the intention of bringing the Pashtuns into slavery with the help of gold and bayonets, the so-called "Islamic government" began to promote the religion of Mīrzā Ghulām Aḥmad Qādiyānī and continued the enforcement of British supremacy. [...] The Pashtuns are one body, and cannot be divided into two. Generosity [*sakhāvat*] and a sense of honour [*nang*] is the heritage of the Pashtuns. They also possess the sharpest sword. Despite fourteen years of bombardment by the British, the people of Waziristan did not submit to slavery. [Therefore,] Be courageous like the Īpī Faqīr, who did not [once] desert the battlefield in these past fourteen years! [...]
>
> These are the two main defects [of the current Pakistani state]: first, the introduction of man-made laws, and, second, the encroachment on the legal rights of the Pashtuns. [...]
>
> According to the Noble Qur'an, killing [in the Path of God] is permissible. The one who dies in that effort will be a martyr. [...] We shall either achieve freedom, or will bring destruction to the entire country.[399]

It is important at this point, despite such state-focused rhetoric, that the Faqīr of Īpī never ventured beyond the confines of the Tribal Areas, which, under the Pakistani Constitution, would eventually be termed FATA.[400] It seems, therefore, as if his aspiration was not the expansionist "Islamization" envisioned by the Islamists, but instead just a quest for the self-determination of the Pashtun Borderland communities. Self-determination provided, the Faqīr of Īpī and his associates would – unmolested by external imperial foes – still have entered the intracommunal contest regarding who exerts command over the binding norms and values. It is this very attitude that unites him with Jalāl al-Dīn Ḥaqqānī much more than with elitist politicians of the Pashtun Borderland, such as Samīʿ al-Ḥaqq.

main objective, unchanged since colonial times, was independence from any imperial force is also illuminating in this regard, see Rand (1955).

399 *Ghāzī* (9 December 1949), cited in Hussain (2000), 133. The original text could not be located. For the relationship of the Faqīr of Īpī with the Pīr Ṣāḥib of Mānkī-yi Sharīf Amīn al-Ḥasanāt mentioned, see Kākā Khēl (1990), 45–9.

400 See Maḥsūd (2000).

It is true that, especially from the second half of the resistance to the Soviet occupation of Afghanistan, Jalāl al-Dīn and Samīʿ al-Ḥaqq intensified their communication, at least as far as can be deduced from their published correspondence.[401]

A closer look, however, reveals that the bulk of the correspondence actually consists of mere field reports from Jalāl al-Dīn to the *Ḥaqqāniyyah*, which is probably the reason why they have also featured in the in-house magazine *al-Ḥaqq*.[402] More indicative still is the rather deferential tone of Jalāl al-Dīn's communication with his own teacher's son, who was of almost similar age,[403] as well as the protocols of a number of gatherings with Samīʿ al-Ḥaqq and delegations of Jalāl al-Dīn's *mujāhidīn* commanders at Akōṛah Khaṫṫak in January 1983. Here, the former is clearly staged as the religious authority over the latter, something that serves Samīʿ al-Ḥaqq's public image as "(god) father of the Taliban" rather well.[404] In contrast, the quite extensive correspondence of the *Ḥaqqāniyyah* principal with his senator colleague Qāẓī Ḥusayn Aḥmad of the JiI is markedly more at eye level,[405] which, in turn, suggests that the elite actors preferred to interact among themselves.

It seems, thus, that Jalāl al-Dīn represented a darker side of the particular "Frontier Deobandiyyat" that emanated from the *Ḥaqqāniyyah*: he would not contribute much to shaping the discourse of Deobandi learning,[406] but was doubtlessly appreciated as one who would enact whatever messages he had received during his training at Akōṛah Khaṫṫak and which he merged with a personal religiosity shaped by his distinct rural background in the Pashtun Borderland.

The learned discourse, in turn, which would eventually incite large numbers of *Ḥaqqāniyyah* students to swap their pen for the sword and set out to take an active part in combat on the other side of the Durand Line, was shaped instead

401 See Samīʿ al-Ḥaqq (2011b), VI: 60–140.

402 See ibid., VI (vii), 66–9, 78–80 and 81f.; compare *al-Ḥaqq* 16/9 (1401/1981), 12–15; 16/11 (1401/1981), 17–19; 23/1 (1408/1987), 45–9. Other communications published by Samīʿ al-Ḥaqq are, in fact, reports by compatriots of Jalāl al-Dīn which had also been published before in *al-Ḥaqq*, a report on a JUI delegation to Jalāl al-Dīn's basecamp in March 1988 or even interviews with Jalāl al-Dīn that had previously been published in other journals or newspapers.

403 See, for example, Samīʿ al-Ḥaqq (2011b), VI (vii), 63 (letter no. 9, dated 23 April 1986).

404 See ibid., VI (vii), 100–30 and 306–31.

405 See ibid., II (iii), 672–85 (comprising twenty-five letters from Qāẓī Ḥusayn Aḥmad to Samīʿ al-Ḥaqq, dated between November 1978 and December 2006).

406 This is indicated, for example, by the fact that Jalāl al-Dīn authored only three short pieces for the *Ḥaqqāniyyah* in-house journal *al-Ḥaqq*, all of which reflect rather the religiosity of the rural tribal context in which he was operating and, because the two later ones were edited by ʿAbd al-Qayyūm Ḥaqqānī, may actually date back to his student days in Akōṛah Khaṫṫak: see Anon., 'Mawlānā Mawlā Bakhsh Jhāvariyāṇ', *al-Ḥaqq* 17/1 (1402/1981), 49; Anon., 'Kalimah-yi ṭayyibah va kalimah-yi shahādat', *al-Ḥaqq* 18/8 (1403/1983), 62; Anon., 'Faẓīlat va ahmiyyat-i duʿā', *al-Ḥaqq* 20/2 (1405/1984), 63.

by a number of *ʿulamāʾ* inside the seminary, as well as, interestingly, some Deobandi scholars with their roots more in the Punjab than in what used to be the NWFP of the Islamic Republic of Pakistan. Sayyid Shīr ʿAlī Shāh Madanī (d. 1437/2015), a scholar of *ḥadīth* and *tafsīr* at the *Ḥaqqāniyyah* who is better known by his epithet "Ustād-i Mujāhidīn", and the two Karachi-based muftis Rashīd Aḥmad Ludhiyānavī (assassinated 1422/2002) and Niẓām al-Dīn Shāmzay (assassinated 1425/2004) were outstanding in this regard.

4.3.2 *The Karachi Connection*

The ethnically highly diverse megacity and port of Karachi, Pakistan's capital between 1947 and 1959, provided a conducive space for religious actors of different ethnic backgrounds to combine. Ludhiyānavī and Shāmzay are just two cases in point: while the latter was ethnically a Yusufzay Pashtun, originating from Maṫṫah Shāmzay in Swat,[407] the older Ludhiyānavī hailed from pre-Partition Eastern Punjab. Consequently, the two of them received their formative religious education in geographically distinct locations, owing not least to the fact that this took place before and around 1947 for Ludhiyānavī: a classmate of ʿAbd al-Ḥaqq Akōṛavī in Deoband, he studied, like the latter, under the tutelage of Ḥusayn Aḥmad Madanī.[408] Shāmzay, however, born after Partition, received his initial education at the *Jāmiʿah ʿArabiyyah-yi Maẓāhir al-ʿUlūm* in Mīngōrah, only about twelve miles south-east of his native village, and when he arrived in Karachi to continue his studies at the Saudi-sponsored *Jāmiʿah Fārūqiyyah*,[409] Ludhiyānavī had already been settled there for almost a decade.[410]

Yet, despite the age difference and the respective educational institutions where they had been trained, these two scholars shared their scholarly orientation – "Deobandiyyat" – as well as, related to it, their spiritual affiliation: Ludhiyānavī himself, as well as his hagiographers, never tired of emphasizing that the Deobandi affinity in his family had been so strong that he was actually named after Rashīd Aḥmad Gangōhī, one of the two founder figures of the *Dār al-ʿUlūm* at Deoband.[411] Moreover, Ludhiyānavī took the *bayʿa* from Ashraf ʿAlī Thānavī, a *khalīfah* of the one among Gangōhī's disciples who was widely regarded as the most authentic embodiment of his master.[412] Shāmzay was also linked to him, although not as directly as Ludhiyānavī, but by way of his spiritual bond with one of Thānavī's *khulafāʾ*.[413]

[407] See Shāmzay (1424h), 46.
[408] See Ludhiyānavī (1424h), I: 69–72.
[409] See Shāmzay (1424h), 46f. On the *Fārūqiyyah*, see Zaman (2002), 175f.
[410] See Shāmzay (1424h), 46; Ludhiyānavī (1424h), I: 205. With a different chronology, see Ludhiyānavī (1425h), I: 15.
[411] See Ludhiyānavī (1425h), I: 7; (1424h), I: 49f.
[412] See Bukhārī (1418/1997), 85–7; Mian (2015), 311 n.2.
[413] See Shāmzay (1424h), 51.

In fact, the spiritual proximity both of Ludhiyānavī and of Shāmzay to Tħānavī is highly significant, as he represented an antipode to Madanī's political vision of "composite nationality":[414] insofar as the involvement in politics and the rational re-examination of religious precepts and earlier traditionist interpretations were concerned, the ascetic Ashraf ʿAlī Tħānavī took a far more conservative stand.[415] While still belonging to an elite, as indicated by his Arabic-heavy literary output, Tħānavī's stress on unconditional piety and "worldly asceticism"[416] derived from the Prophetic role model also made his views quite digestible for more subaltern laypeople. Among the fifty-eight people whom he – directly or indirectly – authorized to counsel such commoners (*majāzīn-i suḥbat*) figured especially Rashīd Aḥmad Ludhiyānavī.[417]

During his fifteen years of active involvement with Karachi's *Jāmiʿah Fārūqiyyah*, where he established himself as an authority in the exegesis of the *Mishkāt al-Maṣābīḥ*,[418] Shāmzay also pledged his allegiance to two other significant Sufi scholars: the first was the leading TJ scholar Muḥammad Zakariyyā Kāndhalavī, who had permanently relocated to Medina in the spring of 1973 and is, therefore, referred to by Shāmzay himself as "Muhājir-i Madanī", while the second was Muḥammad Yūsuf Ludhiyānavī (assassinated 1421/2000), then head of the strongly sectarian *Majlis al-Aḥrār-i Islām* and the equally sectarian *ʿĀlamī Majlis-i Taḥaffuẓ-i Khatam al-Nubūvat.*[419] It is quite conceivable that Shāmzay's sectarian proclivities gained exceptional strength through the influence of the latter. Yet, just as Rashīd Aḥmad Ludhiyānavī's eventual role in providing militancy in the Pashtun Borderland and beyond with a sustained religious justification can be understood through the prism of his spiritual relationship with ʿAbd al-Ghanī Pħūlpūrī (d. 1383/1963), there might also be similar reasons for Shāmzay's views which we would have to look for in the more distant past.

Ludhiyānavī's *murshid* had begun his own studies at Jawnpur in what were then the United Provinces of British India under Muḥammad Abū 'l-Khayr

414 This opposing stand on the place of political activism has led, for example, Nasr (2000), 170–9, to constitute two groups of Deobandi scholars in Pakistan, one in the wake of Madanī, the other following on from Tħānavī. This attempt at a systematic categorization has been criticized as being too schematic and detached from the empirical realities by Zaman (2002), 133f.

415 See Mian (2015), 76–114 and 266–91.

416 This useful term is borrowed from Weber (1950), 95 *et passim*, as translated in 1930 by Talcott Parsons.

417 See Bukhārī (1418/1997), 235f. Shāmzay's *murshid* Faqīr Muḥammad Pishāvarī (d. 1412/ 1991), however, is not listed here among those retainers of Tħānavī authorized to counsel laypeople: see ibid., 99–101.

418 This is already indicated by the prominence of this text among Shāmzay's references: see, for example, Shāmzay (1433/2012), 33, 39, 45, 61, 89, 98–100, 117, 125, 143, 150, 154, 156, 214, 233, 240, 243f., 306–8, 335 and 341.

419 See Shāmzay (1424h), 51.

Makkī ibn Sakhāvat ʿAlī Jawnpūrī (d. 1341/1923). Abū ʾl-Khayr's father, in turn, had been an active participant in the militant activities of the *Ṭarīqah-yi Muḥammadiyyah* in the early nineteenth century and was also one of the countless *khulafāʾ* of Sayyid Aḥmad Barēlvī,[420] which strongly suggests that he was quite familiar with the tenets of proto-Salafi hermeneutics. Consequently, we may well assume that Abū ʾl-Khayr was deeply influenced by his father's Salafi proclivities, testified by the *Risālah-yi Naṣāʾiḥ* from which Nadvī quotes,[421] and it was this inclination that he would finally have handed down to P̄hūlpūrī. The latter, according to Ḥakīm Muḥammad Akhtar (d. 1434/2013), his own hagiographer and *murīd*, developed subsequently some liking for the violent enforcement of his understanding of religiously grounded morals, which, given the high communalist tension especially in Northern India at that time, was enthusiastically approved of by Ashraf ʿAlī T̄hānavī.[422] The morality P̄hūlpūrī strove to see things from the perspective of was based on his understanding of the three core concepts: *tawḥīd* – God's oneness, *risālat* – the divine message and *qiyāmat* – resurrection, as laid out in numerous of his short epistles.

P̄hūlpūrī's proof of God's oneness was, just like the divine message, predominantly informed not by the Qur'an itself, but rather by "Mawlānā" Jalāl al-Dīn Rūmī's (d. 672/1273) famous *Ma̱snavī-yi Maʿnavī*,[423] or the related deliberations by other spiritual poets, such as Muḥammad Iqbāl. More important than his derivation of these concepts themselves, however, is what P̄hūlpūrī inferred from their – in his eyes – proven truthfulness. From a rather mechanistic understanding of God's *tawḥīd* and the resulting Creation, he deduced the necessity for positive law (*qānūn*), almost as if the law were the instruction manual for the proper use of any artifice by which P̄hūlpūrī comprehended Creation. As such, and here he was in concordance with contemporaneous Islamist concepts, only the Creator can reasonably issue the law, as only He could know the exact mode of operation of anything He had brought forth.[424] Yet, he differed greatly from Islamist thought in that for him the mere existence of the law does not necessarily imply that especially humankind, as the only part of creation endowed with reason, would act obediently. Relentlessly,

420 See, for example, Nadvī (1406/1986), II: 540. On Muḥammad Abū ʾl-Khayr and his father, respectively, see al-Ḥasanī (1412–13/1991–3), VII: 214f. and VIII: 481f.

421 See Nadvī (1406/1986), I: 53 and II: 535.

422 See Akhtar (1418/2014), 14–21, esp. 17, where T̄hānavī is quoted as saying: 'If the Hindus had been fighting us and *jihād* had to be conducted, then our army [*fawj*] will come from Aʿẓamgaṛh under the command of the venerable ʿAbd al-Ghanī P̄hūlpūrī – God's blessing be upon him.' T̄hānavī would even condone P̄hūlpūrī's quick temper as fully appropriate under the prevalent conditions.

423 See P̄hūlpūrī (n.d.), 11–15 and 50f.

424 See ibid., 22–9 and 41. Here, interestingly, almost all of his references are, which is similar again to Islamist ways of argument, Qur'anic. Compare, for example, Mawdūdī's expositions on the matter, in Mawdūdī (1997), 20–8. See also Hartung (2013a), 101–5.

Pħūlpūrī kept pointing out improper traits of the human character as he saw them at large in the world that surrounded him: "greed" (*bukhl*), "hypocrisy (*riyā'*), "vanity" (*ṭama'*) and "self-aggrandizement" (*takabbur*).[425]

Actual obedience to the Divine Law, however, can reasonably be demanded only if it has become known to humankind, and revelation and prophethood were necessary for this reason alone. Prophets have been sent to establish the acknowledgement of God's lordship (*rubūbiyyah*) in humanity, and to provide examples of norm conduct under this *conditio sine qua non*.[426] After all, individual salvation is at stake here, as Pħūlpūrī never tired of reminding his audiences.[427] The safest way to attain salvation in the Hereafter, which must be a believer's prime concern, is to follow God's Law as guidance onto "the Straight Path" (*al-ṣirāṭ al-mustaqīm*). For Pħūlpūrī, and, once again, sustained predominantly by references to Rūmī's *Masnavī*, this path is supremely embodied in the way of the Sufi, because it is he more than anyone else to whom "piety" (*taqvá*), "righteousness" (*ṣidq*) and "certitude" (*yaqīn*) have become a natural disposition (*fiṭrī awr ṭab'ī mizāj*). Whoever is of such a state of mind will not be in need of philosophical speculation or scientific explanation, but follows God's commandment uncompromisingly and exclusively instead: 'Oh ye who believe, fear God and be with the righteous ones!'[428]

Of Shāmzay's three spiritual guides, the most eloquent seems to have been Muḥammad Yūsuf Ludħiyānavī. From his writings and sermons assembled in his multivolume anthology *Iṣlāḥī Mavā'iẓ* radiates a world-view quite similar to that of Pħūlpūrī: the aim of life is not worldly gain, but preparation for the Hereafter; that is why otherworldliness – not asceticism, but rather an inner disposition of non-attachment – is undisputably to be preferred.[429] The testing ground (*imtiḥān'gāh*) regarding which material world (*dunyā*) has been designed can be meaningfully navigated only with well-developed Sufi-cum-TJ virtues, prominently among them patience: 'Patience', Yūsuf Ludħiyānavī wrote, 'is the cure for all problems and afflictions.'[430] This patience, coupled with the fear of God – or, in other words, "salvation anxiety" – and love for the Prophet and his companions, however, does not preclude the firm rejection of practices and beliefs associated with wrongful innovation (*bid'a*) or worse. Patience aside, in such instances one is called upon to hold fast to the Truth

425 See Pħūlpūrī (n.d.), 29–41.

426 See ibid., 48–113 (*Jalālat-i Sha'n-i Risālat*).

427 See ibid., 115–42 (*K. al-Qiyāmat*).

428 See ibid., 144–95 (*Ṣirāṭ-i Mustaqīm, ya'nī Sīdħā Rāstah*), esp. 148–64. The quote on p. 162 is Q9.119: 'yā 'ayyuhā alladhīna 'amanū uttaqū 'llāha wa-kūnū ma'a 'l-ṣādiqīn'.

429 See Ludħiyānavī (1999), I: 26–47 (*Maqṣad-i Ḥayāt Dunyā Nahīṇ – Ākhirat*), II: 357–70 (*Qabr kī Tayyārī*), and VII: 203–70 (*Māl, Ahl va 'Iyāl awr A'māl: Ziyādah Mufīd Kawn?* and *Ākhirat kī Tayyārī*).

430 Ibid., VI: 229–44 (*"Ṣabr" Tamām Masā'il kā 'Ilāj Hē*). See also ibid., I: 356–72 (*Ṣabr kē Darjāt*), and II: 246–70 (*Ṣabr va Shukr*).

and actively defend it, however adverse the circumstances may be: the conduct of the Prophet and his companions prior to their migration to Yathrib serves as an ultimate yardstick.[431]

So this, finally, is the spiritual environment in which both Rashīd Aḥmad Ludhiyānavī and Niẓām al-Dīn Shāmzay evolved into major religious inspirations for many of those who would later be involved in the ṬIT and the subsequent IEA, earning the latter's sermons the epithet "summons of the *mujāhid*" (*mujāhid kī aẕān*).[432] Ludhiyānavī, in turn, considered his formal education and especially his spiritual affiliation outspokenly as the 'ferment for his passion for *jihād*' (*khamīr-i jōsh-i jihād*).[433] He recalls, in fact, that military training during his student days was regularly conducted in Deoband under the supervision of two younger faculty members, thus suggesting that his later spiritual bond with ʿAbd al-Ghanī Phūlpūrī only served to reinforce the taste for armed confrontation which Ludhiyānavī had already acquired at Deoband.[434] Indeed, in this regard he would later invoke the precedent of the Prophet and his companions, aimed at bringing back the ascetic Sufi warrior as had for a long time been imagined to have existed in the early phases of the Muslim territorial expansion.[435] Just as for them, for Ludhiyānavī, too, the enemy was roaming all around the community of the righteous: in his view this included adherents to any religious creed other than the Sunni Islamic one, therefore including here the Ahmadi and Shiʿi Muslims of every shade, as well as those who held what he considered 'wrongfully innovative ideas' (*bidʿatī manāẓir*), foremost among them any of the political ideologies prevalent at that time, and also the natural sciences.[436]

The overwhelming threat scenario created, alongside a fixation on *shari'a* conformity and a similarly obsessive "salvation anxiety", called inevitably for an actively defensive response. Nomocentricity and strong eschatological proclivities are already central in all the extant works of ʿAbd al-Ghanī Phūlpūrī and, to an extent, also those of Ashraf ʿAlī Thānavī. The latter, however, subsumed within an all-encompassing concept of *jihād* that also included necessarily the militant variety, shifted into the limelight in the life and works of Rashīd Aḥmad Ludhiyānavī, and in this, finally, he was wholeheartedly joined by Niẓām al-Dīn Shāmzay.

431 See Ludhiyānavī (1999), for example v: 261–79 (*Shahādat kī Faẓīlat va Aqsām*), and vi: 82–96 (*Muhājirīn – rẓ – va Anṣār – rẓ – kī Faẓīlat*).

432 See Shāmzay (1424h), 36.

433 Ludhiyānavī (1424h), i: 77.

434 See ibid., i: 77–81.

435 See ibid., i: 85–114. For the warrior Sufis of the formative period of Islam, see Taeschner (1979). For a recent and more critical perspective, see Melchert (2020), esp. 131–9.

436 Ludhiyānavī (1424h), i: 127 (see also 127–40, 153–74 and 179–237). Ludhiyānavī's anti-Shiʿi polemics are most vividly expressed in his *Ḥaqīqat-i Shīʿah* from 1981.

Both scholars combined the ethos of the TJ,[437] represented, for instance, in Ludħiyānavī's meticulous legal advice on matters of compulsory *ʿibādāt*[438] or Shāmzay's marital counsel and elaborations on the sighting of the moon,[439] with a deep-rooted suspicion against any interpretation other than a conservative religious one by earlier Deobandis, prominently among them Tħānavī and Pħūlpūrī. Added to this was the conviction that the community of believers itself is fully responsible for maintaining its proper Islamicity, be it by coercive measures or not. The *ʿulamāʾ* bear the highest degree of responsibility from among the community members: in the absence of a Muslim ruler and because of their familiarity with all matters *shari'a*, it remained their prerogative – and simultaneously their burden – to ensure the community's conformity with the law and, thus, guide the common believers onto the Straight Path. Shāmzay put some pithy stress on this by referring to the popular sound *ḥadīth* "The Scholars are the Heir of the Prophets" (*al-ʿulamāʾ warathat al-anbiyāʾ*).[440] Moreover, for him, the authority of the *ʿulamāʾ* descended also upon their students, or *taliban*, as expressed in the equally catchy slogan "The Religious Seminaries are the Bastions of the Islamic *dīn*."[441]

Ludħiyānavī's "Deobandiyyat" contained a much stronger and more visible Sufi element other than that of the Pashtun scholar who had spent most of his own education in Saudi-sponsored institutions,. After all, in his view, the heavy responsibility placed on the *ʿulamāʾ* for the legal and spiritual guidance of the community required them to maintain a high degree of self-reflexivity and humility regarding their own directives,[442] for which the Sufi *khānaqāh* appeared to be just as conducive a space as the *madrasah*.[443] In this way, he appears to make a strong case for the inevitability of combining the daily pursuit of the *ʿālim* with a deep spiritual inclination that is generally so characteristic of "Deobandiyyat". The responsibility for guiding the community in the absence of a Muslim ruler rests, therefore, both with the scholar and with the Sufi, and Ludħiyānavī consequently blamed any possible deviation of

437 See, for example, Ludħiyānavī (1425h), IX: 167–85 (*Tablīghī Jamāʿat awr Unchās Krōṛ kā Ṣavāb*; 1422/2001).

438 See, for example, his extensive elaborations on prayer times in ibid., II: 243–563 (*Irshād al-ʿĀbid ilá Taḥrīj al-Awqāt wa-Tawjīh al-Masājid*; 1389/1970). Remarkably, so far, no evidence that Ludħiyānavī also ruled on the matter of *tashahhud* during the ritual prayer could be located.

439 See Shāmzay (2000; 1433/2012).

440 See Shāmzay in Aẓhār (1414h), I: 18; compare *Jāmiʿ al-Tirmidhī*, k. al-ʿilm, b. mā jāʾ fī faḍl al-fiqh ʿalá ʾl-ʿibāda, no. 2 (ḥadīth 2898).

441 See Shāmzay (1424h), 134–8 (*Dīnī Madāris, Dīn-i Islām kē Qilʿē*; 2002).

442 See, for example, Ludħiyānavī (1420–5h), I: 13–6 (*ʿUlamāʾ kē liʾē Ẓarūrī Dustūr-i ʿAmal*).

443 See ibid., III: 12f. (*Khānaqāh mēṇ Ḥāẓirī kī Ẓarūrat*); V: 30 (*Madāris awr Khānaqāhēṇ Dīn kē Kārʾkhānē*).

the common believer on the "wrongfully innovative scholar" (*bidʿatī mawlavī*) and "ignorant (*jāhil*) Sufi".[444]

The epitome of a Sufi-cum-scholar to be turned to for proper guidance was for him once again Ashraf ʿAlī Thānavī. Accordingly, Thānavī embodied the perfect blend of detachment from worldly affairs, a focus on the Hereafter as a supreme reality and the – unfortunately necessary – acknowledgement that one must actively work in the community to ensure that the former two proclivities remained possible.[445]

***

Here is perhaps a good point to pause once more for a moment of systematic reflection, this time on the two forms of "Frontier Deobandiyyat" that we have so far encountered in this chapter, both of which fed eventually into its militant variety as represented by scholars-cum-warriors such as Jalāl al-Dīn Ḥaqqānī: one that is epitomized by the *nomenklatura* of the *Dār al-ʿUlūm-i Ḥaqqāniyyah* at Akōṛah Khaṫṫak, and the other personified by the two Karachi-based Deobandi muftis Rashīd Aḥmad Ludhiyānavī and Niẓām al-Dīn Shāmzay.

Ultimately, it seems that Vali Nasr's occasionally criticized distinction between two Deobandi traits in Pakistan, one following Ḥusayn Aḥmad Madanī and the other following Thānavī, still has some currency.[446] While, on the one hand, the two scholars from Karachi and, on the other, Samīʿ al-Ḥaqq all served ultimately as inspirations and facilitators of the initial ṬIT, they represent quite different takes on the role and significance of politics: Samīʿ al-Ḥaqq – son of a *khalīfah* of Madanī – evolved into a professional politician who would enjoy all the amenities of a parliamentarian,[447] whereas Ludhiyānavī and Shāmzay remained political theorists of necessity, following therein their direct or indirect spiritual mentor Ashraf ʿAlī Thānavī. Subsequently, relationships between those two and Samīʿ al-Ḥaqq appear to have been cordial, but ultimately distant, and neither regarded the other as a credible reference point.[448]

[444] See ibid., I: 14f. and IV: 38f. (*Jāhil Ṣūfī Marīẕ-i Vahm*).

[445] See prominently Muḥammad Taqī ʿUṣmānī, 'Ḥakīm al-Ummat – raḥmat allāh taʿālá – kē siyāsī afkār', in Ludhiyānavī (1425h), VI: 85–140 (originally published in *al-Balāgh* 24/9 [1410/1990], 23–49). See also Ludhiyānavī (1420–5h), XI: 38f. (*Ḥaẕrat Ḥakīm al-Ummat – raḥmat allāh taʿālá – kā Ṭarīq-i Iṣlāḥ*).

[446] See n.414 in this chapter. Yet, it has to be conceded to Nasr's critics that especially his view of Madanī is a bit too reductive, and that various of the conclusions he draws from his schematic do indeed appear a little too simplistic.

[447] This includes even the morally rather questionable habit of visiting luxury brothels in Islamabad, as leaked to the national media in late 1991, which, according to interviews with the madam of his favourite establishment about the sexual services he preferred, earned him the derogatory nickname "Sandwich Sammy".

[448] The published collected correspondence of Samīʿ al-Ḥaqq includes only two letters from Ludhiyānavī, one undated, the other from October 1973. The first one comments on the

The major problem for scholars such as Rashīd Aḥmad Ludhiyānavī and Niẓām al-Dīn Shāmzay was that participation in the parliamentary culture of Pakistan inevitably had to be based on an acknowledgement of the Pakistani political set-up as legitimate, if also in dire need of reform. In comparison with Samīʿ al-Ḥaqq, both of the Karachi-based scholars were much less inclined to concede any legitimacy at all to the existing state of Pakistan. For them – and this moved them much closer to the Salafi approach which Shāmzay may have become exposed to courtesy of the Saudi funds that financed the seminaries in which he studied – no human-made law was to prevail as long as it was not entirely derived from the Qurʾanic revelation, regardless of whether or not it could be rationalized.[449] It can be quite firmly established, particularly for Ludhiyānavī, that this perspective was wholesomely taken over from his own *murshid*, ʿAbd al-Ghanī Phūlpūrī, who, in turn, claimed to be following in this regard the Shaykh al-Hind.[450]

Yet, his fierce polemics against Mawdūdī and the mindset of the JiI demonstrate impressively that Phūlpūrī wanted to have this view of his clearly dissociated from the Islamist epistemic reduction.[451] He regarded these views rather as a logical continuation of the "Deobandiyyat" of the Shaykh al-Hind and his associates, prominently including the young Ḥusayn Aḥmad Madanī, which had been dominant in the Pashtun Borderland of the early twentieth century. Consequently, Ludhiyānavī's views also appealed greatly to those who, like him, rejected the idea of loyalty towards the nation-state, even though perhaps for alternative reasons.

After all, "patriotism" indicated to Ludhiyānavī an excessive attachment to this world (*dunyā*) rather than the coming one (*ākhirah*),[452] even though a lot of especially subaltern residents of the Pashtun Borderland were not necessarily so otherworldly inclined. Instead, their deep-rooted suspicion of externally defined larger collective identities such as "nationhood" was more a reaction to the vivid collective memory of marginalization, abuse and deceit by representatives of larger political entities, all of which maintained their centres of

schism in the JUI caused by the activities of Ghulām Ghaws̱ Hazāravī (d. 1401/1981) that, in around 1970, turned the JUI into a proper political party with some socialist leanings, thereby becoming unfaithful to Thānavī's views on politics that had so far determined the form and agenda of the JUI: see Samīʿ al-Ḥaqq (2011b), II: 824.

449 It needs to be emphasized, though, that Ludhiyānavī remained firmly within the Hanafi legal tradition, which, among other markers, is constitutive for "Deobandiyyat", and firmly rejected the approach of the *Ahl-i Ḥadīs̱*, which does not recognize the authority of any *madhhab fiqhiyya*: see Ludhiyānavī (1420–5h): III: 49f. (*Ghayr-Muqallidīn kō Javāb*).

450 See Phūlpūrī (n.d.), 42–4 (*Ḥaẓrat Shaykh al-Hind – raḥmat allāh ʿalayhi – kā Irshād*).

451 See Ludhiyānavī (1425h), I: 297–330 (*Mawdūdī Ṣāḥib awr Takhrīb-i Islām*; 1386/1966); (1420–5h), IX: 78 (*Mawdūdī Jihādī Tanẓīm sē Taʿalluq*).

452 See Ludhiyānavī (1420–5h), I: 77 (*Shawq-i Vaṭan-i Ākhirat*), VI: 96 (*Vaṭan kī Maḥabbat*), VII: 36 (*Shawq-i Vaṭan*).

gravity outside the Pashtun Borderland. Still, there was sufficient overlap to provide fertile ground for Ludhiyānavī's ideas in these Borderland communities, where they took root with much greater ease than in others. Apart from Samīʿ al-Ḥaqq, whose rather pragmatic *jihād* rhetoric really took off only after the Soviet invasion of Afghanistan,[453] *jihād* of any variety served as a pivot for Ludhiyānavī's much more systematic considerations that were visibly less dependent on actual political developments. In this, he followed closely the positions of his spiritual predecessors Phūlpūrī and Thānavī, all the way back to the Shaykh al-Hind and his spiritual predecessor Imdādallāh "Muhājir Makkī".

In fact, all of Ludhiyānavī's ideas on socio-political order are inseparably tied to the concept of *jihād* as the ultimate form of Muslim worship that evolves solely from a truly pious disposition: 'From piety [*taqvá*] comes comfort and tranquillity, from trust in God Almighty [*tavakkul va iʿtimād*] results humility [*istighnāʾ*].'[454] *Jihād*, in turn, is the supreme way to atone for one's imperfection (*nuqṣān*) and keep one's mind clean:[455] 'By the blessing of *jihād*, God Almighty provides for the entire world [the means] to be delivered from Hell and to enter Paradise, and this will continue until the present world is ended.'[456]

This is a significant point, as it allows for the complete atonement of one's own sins, however great, if one is only prepared to make a return to God and His *dīn* through *jihād*. Ludhiyānavī elaborated in one of his *fatāvá* from April 2002 that *jihād* does *not*, first and foremost, refer to the practice of preaching (*tablīgh*), as was the standard notion in the TJ, but was unequivocally recognized in all four canonical legal currents as "killing an enemy (in the Path of God)" (*qitāl maʿa ʿadūw* [*fī sabīl allāh*]): 'a special act that begins in the proclamation of God's greatness [*takbīr*] and ends in peace [*salām*]'.[457] All "righteous acts" (*aʿmāl-i ṣāliḥ*), in Ludhiyānavī's opinion, are ultimately hierarchically tiered, while the less significant ones are fully absorbed into those of a higher order. Therefore, just as, for example, the concept of "supplication" (*duʿāʾ*) is already contained in the Qur'anic concept of "prayer" (*ṣalāt*), the specific act of *takbīr* is fully absorbed into the more general act of *jihād*.[458] Ludhiyānavī tellingly stipulated only conformity with the *shariʿa* as conditions for *jihād*,[459] while not bothering

453 See, for example, Samīʿ al-Ḥaqq (n.d.), 343–82.
454 Ludhiyānavī (1420–5h), II: 63 (*Taqvá kī Barakat*).
455 See ibid., III: 36 (*Jihād mēṇ Nuqṣān par Istighfār*).
456 Ibid., IX: 39 (*Jihād Raḥmat Hē!*)
457 Ludhiyānavī (1425h), VI: 28 (*fatwa* dated 15 Ṣafar 1423 [15 April 2002]). Ludhiyānavī's reference here is al-Kasānī (1424/2002), IX: 379.
458 See Ludhiyānavī (1425h), VI: 29.
459 See ibid., VI: 17 (*fatwa* dated 9 Jumādá I 1398 [4 April 1978]). His references here are al-Maghribī (1418/1998), II: 478 (no. 6 144), and Q6.129, 30.41 and 42.30. The *ḥadīth* from al-Maghribī has been taken from *Jāmiʿ al-Tirmidhī*, k. al-diyāt, b. mā jāʾ fīmā qutila dūna mālihi fa-huwa shahīdun, no. 1 (ḥadīth 1 481).

to substantiate what he wished to be understood as "shari'a" beyond the observance of Qur'anic penalties for grave offences (*ḥudūd*), talion law (*qiṣāṣ*) and other punitive regulations. This rather common eschewal of a clear-cut definition of "shari'a", however, left some *fatāvá*, such as this one on the conditions for *jihād*, open to a wide array of interpretations.

Shāmzay's positions on these matters were quite similar. His starting point was the Qur'anically derived ethical concept of the "objective of life" (*maqṣad-i zindigī*) that consists in the all-comprehensive subservience to God (*ʿibādat*).[460] The paradigm for what this service entailed was set forth once more by the Prophet Muḥammad, which necessitates, therefore, the close investigation of his *sīra*, in conjunction with a perpetual self-reflexive reckoning of one's own thoughts and actions against this benchmark.[461] Whosoever follows that path, which Shāmzay called "investigation into the objective" (*maqṣad'shināsī*), would, in fact, be a "seeker of knowledge", a *ṭālib-i ʿilm*.[462] These *taliban*, Shāmzay argued, constitute the vanguard on the "path of Truth" (*rāh-i ḥaqq*), and their way of achieving this goal, finally, is *jihād* in all of its varieties, predominantly, however, in its militant one.[463]

The later stages in Shāmzay's line of argument, which pivot on notions such as "vanguard" (*qiyādat*), "Islamic revolution" (*inqilāb-i islāmī*) and "system" (*niẓām*), reek quite strongly and distinctly of Islamism, a facet that is generally absent in Ludhiyānavī's published views. Shāmzay's Islamist leanings can be explained, firstly, by the fact that the JiI was historically quite present in his native Swat and has, thus, strongly impacted the religious atmosphere in the principality.[464] Secondly, however, they may result from the influence of Muḥammad Masʿūd Aẓhār (b. 1388/1968), one of his students at the *Jāmiʿat al-ʿUlūm* in Karachi's Binori Town.[465]

Aẓhār is the son of a close friend of a Mufti Abū Bakr Saʿīd al-Raḥmān from southern Punjabi Bahāvalpūr, and it was this scholar who was responsible for bringing this young man into the institution where Shāmzay had served as *shaykh al-ḥadīth* since 1988.[466] Masʿūd Aẓhār would eventually gain notoriety

460 See Shāmzay (1424h), 71–82 (*Maqṣad-i Zindigī*; Ṣafar 1422h).

461 See ibid., 54–69 (*Ḥuẓūr – sallá 'llāh 'layhi wa-salam – kī Sīrat-i Mubārakah*; July 1999) and 347–59 (*Apnē Aʿmāl sē Ḥuẓūr – sallá 'llāh ʿalayhi wa-salam – kō Taklīf nah Pahunchāʾēṇ*; April 2002).

462 See ibid., 76.

463 See ibid., 286–99 (*Ṭulabāʾ awr Siyāsat*; August 2001), 302–18 (*Islāmī Inqilāb Lānē kā Ṭarīqah*; 1998).

464 See Section 4.2.2.

465 Conversely, for Rahman (2018), 220, it was the elder Shāmzay who had been a crucial influence on Aẓhār, which would appear instantly plausible if we had convincing alternative explanations for Shāmzay's Islamist proclivities. As solid textual evidence is lacking for either perspective, both must remain viable possibilities for the time being.

466 See Aẓhār in Swami (2001), 19. Shāmzay owed his employment there to the invitation of Muftī Aḥmad al-Raḥmān (d. 1411/1991), epithet "Mujāhid-i Millat" and, at that time,

as the founder and leader of the *Jaysh-i Muḥammad*, a militant outfit which had grown out of the *Ḥarakat al-Mujāhidīn* and *Ḥarakat al-Jihād al-Islāmī*. These two organizations, in turn, had been established in the mid 1980s to actively support the Afghan *mujāhidīn* against the nexus of the PDPA and Soviet Union, and had, in 1993 – with the decisive involvement of former Arab volunteers – merged finally into the *Ḥarakat al-Anṣār*.

It is not entirely clear how this young man, who graduated from the *Jāmiʿat al-ʿUlūm al-Islāmiyyah* in 1989 at the age of twenty-one, could gain such great influence over seasoned scholars such as Niẓām al-Dīn Shāmzay, and possibly also Rashīd Aḥmad Ludhiyānavī. It is a fact, however, that Masʿūd Aẓhār, who was soon involved in a transnational network of young Muslim militants at the *Dār al-ʿUlūm*, emerged as a major advocate of the obligatory character of armed *jihād* in Afghanistan and Kashmir, and soon also beyond.[467] Perhaps it was his rhetorical skills, which he refined while editing the two *Ḥarakat al-Mujāhidīn* journals *Ṣadā-yi Mujāhid* and *Ṣawt al-Kashmīr*, and which he later employed in an extensive literary output exclusively on the matter of *jihād*.[468] Be that as it may, the ideological affinity of the two established scholars and Masʿūd Aẓhār is evident, for example, from Shāmzay's foreword to Aẓhār's collected sermons, published in 1993 and dedicated to all the jailed Kashmiri militants.[469] Shāmzay praised Aẓhār, 'our compatriot and determined young scholar and *mujāhid*',[470] as well as his scholarship in these few pages. Moreover, with reference to the popular *ḥadīth* "The Scholars are the Heir of the Prophets" cited above,[471] Shāmzay pleaded that Aẓhār's deliberations are recognized as 'sound interpretation and analysis' (*ṣaḥīḥ taʿbīr va tashrīḥ*) of the Islamic normativity revealed – an assessment that aligns Aẓhār with the *ṭulabāʾ-i ʿilm* in Shāmzay's broader world-view outlined above.

Jihād is just one of those indisputable compulsory principles which Shāmzay aimed at proving by his reference to Q8.65, which is not further contextualized: 'Oh Prophet, urge the believers to battle!'[472] Moreover, and this perhaps is one

the highest legal authority at the *Jāmiʿat al-ʿUlūm* in Karachi's Binori Town, see Shāmzay (1424h), 48f.

467 See Aẓhār in Swami (2001), 19. The militant's own admission that, 'partly because of my poor physique [. . .] I did not complete the mandatory forty days of training' in a ḤuM training camp at Yāvar, in Tarkhān Province in northeast Afghanistan, is interesting. Glossing over this admission by Aẓhār himself is editor Sulṭān Maḥmūd Ẓiyāʾ in Aẓhār (1414h), I: 12.

468 Masʿūd Aẓhār's *opus magnum* appears to be the four-volume *Fatḥ al-Javād fī Maʿārif Āyāt al-Jihād* (2009), which has almost instantly, though only partly, been translated into English and Pashto. This rather late work was preceded by other core writings, such as *Fażāʾil-i Jihād-i Kāmil* (1998). On both works, see Rahman (2018), 221–7.

469 For the dedication, see Aẓhār (1414h), I: 6.

470 Shāmzay in ibid., I: 18.

471 See n.440 in this chapter.

472 Shāmzay in Aẓhār (1414h), I: 18: 'yā ʾayyuhā ʾl-nabīyu ḥarriḍi ʾl-muʾminīna ʿalá ʾl-qitāl'.

further pointer to the Islamist undercurrent in Shāmzay's ideational universe, he dissolved the classical Islamic legal concept of territoriality – the distinction between a sphere governed by *shari'a* law (*dār al-islām*) and one governed by opposing principles (*dār al-ḥarb*) – and declared, like many Islamist theorists have done before him, the *dār al-islām* wherever there is a righteous Muslim. Defensive *jihād*, in turn, is, therefore, legitimately conducted wherever such a righteous Muslim confronts those not as righteous as them, which, in turn, allows one to legally sustain militancy within a Muslim environment as *jihād*.[473]

Such militant proclivities may well be the result of the influence of Masʿūd Aẓhār over Shāmzay and perhaps, to some extent, also over Rashīd Aḥmad Ludhiyānavī. Laurent Gayer affirms that the *Jāmiʿat al-ʿUlūm* in Karachi's Binori Town had 'from the 1980s onwards [...] been at the forefront of Pakistan's sectarian wars',[474] and this has undoubtedly been the result of various external circumstances in both Pakistan and Afghanistan coming together at this point in time. The first was the coup d'état of Pakistan's then-Chief of Army Staff General Zia-ul-Haq on 5 July 1977, the subsequent imposition of martial law and the change of the political structure of Pakistan into a military–bureaucratic technocracy under presidential rule. Under this revised constellation, the president was empowered to initiate his programme of bringing core areas of the religious infrastructure of the country under the exclusive control of the central government, something that has become known in the literature as "Islamization", but is perhaps much better captured by Malik's "dissolution of traditional institutions in Pakistan".[475] While local religious functionaries viewed these policies with ambivalence, religious educational institutions, especially in more remote areas of the country, benefited from the centralized structures that made them financially less dependent on their respective local communities.[476]

The "Ṣawr Revolution" and the subsequent Soviet invasion of Afghanistan added a wider political stimulus to the distribution of centrally collected *zakāt* among religious educational institutions in Pakistan: those seminaries particularly now benefited to an exceptional degree from it and accepted – and often simply had no choice but to accept – a fast and ever growing number of Afghan refugees among their students. Karachi had almost instantly become a – if not *the* – magnet for Afghan refugees beyond the NWFP and Baluchistan, and the institutions with which Rashīd Aḥmad Ludhiyānavī and Niẓām al-Dīn

473 See Shāmzay (1424h), 118–33 (*Jihād kē bi-Dawlat Dīn-i Ghālib Hūʾā*; 2000). See also Rahman (2018), 230. Compare the views of Abū 'l-Aʿlá Mawdūdī on the same matter in Hartung (2013a), 18.

474 Gayer (2014), 174.

475 See the subtitle of Malik (1996).

476 See ibid., 133–6 and 143–53.

Shāmzay were involved witnessed a surge of new enrolments from among the refugees, especially because of the free provision of boarding.[477]

In addition, Zia-ul-Haq's policies regarding the central administration of religious affairs also resulted in an upsurge in communal tension, fuelled by various pieces of legislation,[478] and Karachi consequently emerged as a centre of sectarian unrest. The founder of Shāmzay's *Jāmiʿah Fārūqiyyah*, Muḥammad Salīmallāh Khān (d. 1439/2017), who had studied immediately before Partition at Deoband with Ḥusayn Aḥmad Madanī and could, thus, well have been a fellow student of ʿAbd al-Ḥaqq Akōṛavī and Rashīd Aḥmad Ludhiyānavī, established the *Savād-i Aʿẓam-i Ahl-i Sunnat va Jamāʿat* movement in 1980, an explicitly anti-Shiʿi closing of ranks of Deobandis, Barelvis and, although to a much lesser degree, *Ahl-i Ḥadīs̱*. According to Gayer, 'the core of this group [. . .] was composed of Pashtun Deobandi *ulama*',[479] which raises the possibility that Shāmzay had been one of them. Similar and later Sunni sectarian pressure groups, movements and militant outfits aimed at pressurizing the political decision-makers into extending another piece of Zia-ul-Haq's legislation onto the Shiʿi Muslims of whichever denomination: the infamous Ordinance XX of 1984, which declared members of the Aḥmadiyyah community – the so-called "Qadiyanis" – infidels.[480]

Last but not least, the surge of Afghan refugees into Karachi resulted in a massive increase in the number of *dīnī madāris* in the city. As stated by Gayer, only four of the twenty *madāris* in Karachi were affiliated to the Deobandi *maslak* in 1971, and that number had risen to an impressive 1 500 by 2007. The mushrooming of new religious educational institutions, which catered more for the education of refugees than public schools, was also facilitated by a new wave in the more often than not chaotic expansion of the city. Binori Town evolved during this period around the *Jāmiʿat al-ʿUlūm al-Islāmiyyah*, one of the four early Deobandi *madāris* in Karachi, to cater for the ever growing number of especially Afghan students, and, around the same time, the city authorities also began to develop the "Mujāhid Colony" in Karachi's affluent middle-class Nāẓimābād area to provide housing for displaced Afghans. Only a few years earlier, Rashīd Aḥmad Ludhiyānavī had already complied with the dying wish of his late *murshid* ʿAbd al-Ghanī Phūlpūrī to establish a *Dār al-Iftāʾ wa'l-Irshād* in the place of Phūlpūrī's *Khānaqāh-yi Ashrafiyyah*, situated exactly where the "Mujāhid Colony" would emerge only a few years later.[481]

[477] See AREU (2005), 4f. and 19; Alimia (2013), 30 and 52–6.

[478] The infamous amendments B and C of Article 293 of the Pakistan Penal Code, from March 1982 and October 1985, respectively, on the matter of "blasphemy" are a special case in point.

[479] Gayer (2014), 171.

[480] See Abou-Zahab (2009b), 161.

[481] See Ludhiyānavī (1424h), I: 208–10.

While it is difficult to establish cause and effect in this relationship, the synergies between the location of Ludhiyānavī's seminary and a predominantly Pashtun population in that area, which, moreover, would identify with the idea of armed *jihād*, are rather difficult to ignore. Ludhiyānavī's few dated writings, prominently including sermons and other forms of oral presentation, also indicate that his views became more explicitly radical from the 1980s onwards and finally culminated in his open support for the ṬIT, which went well beyond mere spiritual nourishment: in February 1996, Ludhiyānavī set up the *al-Rashīd Trust* (ART), a charity to actively finance *jihād* activities not only in Afghanistan but also in the Caucasus, the Balkans and Kashmir. The generous logistical aid bestowed on the Kandahar-based ṬIT / IEA leadership around Mullā Muḥammad ʿUmar through this channel secured Ludhiyānavī and his close associates, here especially his former students Mufti Abū Lubābah Shāh Manṣūr and Mawlavī Ṣibghatallāh, the privilege of unhindered access to the innermost circle.

Niẓām al-Dīn Shāmzay, in turn, would be even more directly involved with the ṬIT leadership: after all, it was he who had declared that the "seekers of knowledge", the vanguard of the Islamic revolution, had framed their scope of action and, thus, provided public legitimacy to the military pursuits of the ṬIT since 1994 and, moreover, to their regime of the IEA. Shāmzay hailed the ṬIT in a sermon delivered at the *Muftī Maḥmūd Academy* of Karachi as late as 1999 as the one and only force that had been able to check the various other Islamist militias which competed for power and influence across Afghanistan, thus, in fact, reunifying and pacifying the country. It was the adherents of the ṬIT who, in contrast to the JIA, the ḤiI-Ḥ, Shāh Masʿūd's *Shūrā-yi Naẓār* or the ḤVIA, walked in the footsteps of the Prophet, embraced his *sīra* and were, again in contrast to the Islamist militias, able to successfully establish the true "Islamic system". In return for their sincerity (*ikhlāṣ*), the Islamic *dīn* was safeguarded, especially as their example would encourage other Muslims across the world to accomplish the same.[482] Consequently, Shāmzay advanced to become a leading jurisconsult for the ṬIT.

Ludhiyānavī also provided ideological backup for them, on top of his logistical support via the ART. The capstone of his religio-political universe was his concept of leadership, ultimately laid down in his treatise *Iṭāʿat-i Amīr*, which Michael Semple dates to around the year 2000, that is, after the scholar had extensively toured areas in Afghanistan under the control of the IEA.[483]

482 See Shāmzay (1424h), 239–55 (*Imārat-i Islāmī-yi Afghānistān awr Hamārī Ẓimmidāriyāṇ*; 1999).

483 See Semple (2014), 10. The year 2000 as the date of composition is, however, not entirely certain. While this title does not appear on the earliest list of Ludhiyānavī's writings in the first volume of his collected *fatwas* published in 1398/1978, a corresponding list in his *Anvār al-Rashīd*, first published in 1416/1995, has the title already included: see Ludhiyānavī (1424h), III: 120; (1425h), I: 18f. Yet, even if the text itself appears to

Semple further states that this work had quickly become a primer for its conception of governance, with the movement's commander-in-chief, the elusive Mullā Muḥammad ʿUmar, personally distributing copies of its Pashto and Dari translations to all visitors to his office.[484] Yet, the recurrence to this classical theme of Islamic political thought in itself was not as spectacular as it seems at first glance. A similar text, originally written in Dari by ʿAbd al-Rabb Khān (d. 1337/1919), the then-*mullā-yi darbār*, had already been published in Kabul in 1855, with its Pashto translation by Ṣāliḥ Muḥammad of the *Madrasah-yi Ḥabībiyyah* first issued in 1916. This commissioned work aimed at justifying the rule of Emir Ḥabīballāh Khān as being in accordance with the *shari'a*,[485] and was, just like Ludhiyānavī's later text, distributed from the palace of the Emir free of charge.[486] Mullā ʿUmar, holding Ludhiyānavī's work in esteem and disseminating it generously from his office, appears, therefore, to have been following a long-established precedent of strategically legitimizing new political rulers in Afghanistan.

Both ʿAbd al-Rabb Khān and Ludhiyānavī derived their respective visions on governance, consisting of a clear chain of authority sustained by religious precepts that culminates in the supreme office of the *amīr*, from Q4.59.[487] Yet, there are certain elements in Ludhiyānavī's text that are still noteworthy. The ultimate aim of the *imāra* of the *mujāhidīn*-cum-*muʾminīn* for him is to prevent dissension (*fitna*) within the community from happening, which is why unconditional obedience to the *amīr* is paramount for the maintenance of community cohesion. Indeed, this cohesion, created by way of a strict implementation and observance of *shari'a* law, provided Ludhiyānavī with adequate proof that God was, in fact, pleased, a point that could also be inferred from the arguments of Niẓām al-Dīn Shāmzay.

have been composed some years before the date suggested by Semple, Ludhiyānavī might indeed have updated it substantially around 2000.

484 See Semple (2014), 10. In 2015, Semple, together with Yameema Mithra, had an annotated English translation of this meanwhile hard-to-get-hold-of text published as *Mufti Rasheed Ludhianvi: Obedience to the Amir. An Early Text of the Afghan Taliban Movement* (Berlin: First Draft Publishing). Unfortunately, however, this annotated translation contains too many flaws and, moreover, does not fully appreciate Ludhiyānavī's critical apparatus, so it cannot be taken to be a trustworthy and useful tool for the present book.

485 See ʿAbd al-Rabb Khān (1234sh), 27–30; (1334sh), 73–83.

486 See ibid., frontispiece.

487 See ʿAbd al-Rabb Khān (1234sh), 7f.; Ludhiyānavī (1421h), 14. The most important passage of this Qur'anic verse reads: 'Oh ye who believe! Obey God, obey the Messenger and those among you who are in authority [*wa-ūlī 'l-amri minkum*].' In addition to this Qur'anic verse ʿAbd al-Rabb Khān and Ludhiyānavī both cited and succinctly commented on a – rather motley – plethora of *aḥādīth*, in order to sustain God's commandment and establish the unquestionable authority of the *amīr*, in Ludhiyānavī's words, 'as long as he does not pass a decree counter to the *shari'a*' (Ludhiyānavī (1421h), 16).

How could the community ascertain that the *amīr* was indeed acting exclusively within the frame of the *shari'a* and not out of a personal disposition for power and control, which Ludħiyānavī – similarly to Shāmzay – saw as having been the case with numerous Afghan Islamist outfits under the umbrella of the IIMA in Peshawar,[488] and implicitly also applied to savvy politicians such as Samīʿ al-Ḥaqq? Here, Ludħiyānavī, once again similarly to Shāmzay, made a case for the nexus of rural subalternity and sincerity, which revolves a lot around the fairly well-established literary trope of the *talib* in the Pashtun context.[489] This persona, unlike the urbane Islamist and the equally worldly member of the rural elites, combines the simplicity and truthfulness of the young male rural subaltern with an otherworldly focus that also prominently embraces a passionate longing for the Hereafter, expressed in romanticized martyrdom: 'May God be praised! What a brotherhood we had among the *mujahedeen* [sic]! We weren't concerned with the world or with our lives; our intentions were pure and every one of us was ready to die as a martyr,'[490] remembers Mullā ʿAbd al-Salām Ẓaʿīf (b. 1388/1968), a Ghilzay Pashtun from Zangāvāt in the Panjvāyī District of Kandahar Province and later ambassador of the first IEA central government to Pakistan.

In fact, this is precisely the *mujāhid* that Ludħiyānavī had in mind, and, in this, he was following his *murshid* ʿAbd al-Ghanī Pħūlpūrī closely. For them, to be a *mujāhid* was not just an episode, but a way of life that transforms one's entire being: 'A *mujāhid* who sets out to resolve upon *jihād* becomes a friend of God [*valī allāh*] even before leaving his house; as the decision to offer one's soul to the Beloved cannot be possible without friendship [*valāyat*].'[491] This, to Ludħiyānavī, is an act of divine grace (*niʿmat*), which is also reflected in how the body of the *mujāhid* is supremely transformed, starting with the build-up of the desire to set out "in the Path of God".[492] This all-consuming desire, finally, evolves from a personal disposition to renunciation and sacrifice (*qurbānī*),[493] which, tellingly, appears very compatible with various forms of socially

488 Ludħiyānavī explicitly referred in his foreword to *Iṭāʿat-i Amīr* to Ḥikmatyār, Shāh Masʿūd, Sayyāf and Rabbānī as having caused substantial 'damage to Islam and Muslims. They brought *jihād* into discredit all over the world. [...] Hardly can be expressed what they have done to perturb peace and security, to offend against the divine decrees and to trample around everything that is considered blessed' (Ludħiyānavī (1421h), 20). Once more, this resonates well with Shāmzay (1424h), 239–55 (*Imārat-i Islāmī* [...]), here esp. 242–6.

489 See Caron (2012a); Hartung (2024). See also the discussion of that trope in the case of the Haḋḋah Ṣāḥib in Section 3.2.3.

490 Zaeef (2010), 43. See also Gharvāl (1360sh), 104f., who briefly discusses forms of poetic expression, and Malgarē (1352sh), 8f., where a distinct style of the traditional Pashtun tribal dance (*ataṇ*) is highlighted.

491 Ludħiyānavī (1420–5h), II: 28 (*Mujāhid awr Maqām-i Valāyat*).

492 See ibid., IV: 83f. (*Mujāhid kē Jism mēṇ Dhātōṇ kā Tanāsub*); X: 17 (*Mujāhid kī Ziyārat Shawq-i Jihād kā Ẓarīʿah*).

493 See Ludħiyānavī (1429h), VII: 331–80 (*Qurbānī kī Ḥaqīqat*; 1419/1999).

commendable conduct in the Sunni Muslim Pashtun Borderland communities. It is, therefore, quite conceivable that Ludhiyānavī's prominence, especially among Pashtuns, is owed to the synergies between traditional ethical values of Pashtun Borderland communities and a distinct religious interpretation of moral conduct by Ludhiyānavī himself. Applied to the theory of legitimate governance above, the significant difference in the conception of *imāra* between Emir Ḥabīballāh Khān's *mullā-yi darbār* ʿAbd al-Rabb Khān in the middle of the nineteenth century and Ludhiyānavī one century and a half later lies in the stipulation of a distinct moral environment which, both for Ludhiyānavī and for Shāmzay, was conducive to the legitimacy of *imāra*.

By and large, these two Karachi-based scholars shared the same world-view: Ludhiyānavī emphasized more the ascetic and world-disdaining aspect of "Deobandiyyat" which provides justification for a distinct moral attitude being publicly instilled,[494] while Shāmzay's introduction of certain Islamist ideas highlighted the necessity of actively implementing a comprehensive *shariʿa*-based political and social practice throughout.[495] Still, the views of either scholar remained entirely within a normative framework, which may have impaired their ability to appreciate that the world-view of the ṬIT / IEA was never really static. Instead, it has been subject to Borderland pragmatics, especially in the decade prior to the release of the so-called "Taliban Code of Conduct" (*Də Mujāhidīnō Lapārah Lāʾiḥah*), first published in 2006 predominantly for the members of the Leadership Council which, by then, had been forced to relocate across the border to Quetta.[496]

Indeed, it seems that the early ṬIT high command regarded these views by respected Deobandi scholarly authorities as being conducive to their objectives, and had, therefore, no qualms about facilitating their kind of *daʿwa*. Still, Mullā ʿUmar and his inner circle appear to have hardly felt bound by these scholarly views, as later developments would testify. After all, however much those in charge of the early ṬIT liked the religious visions of Ludhiyānavī and Shāmzay, they were also in dire need of extensive logistical support and a steady supply of "human resources", which is why they also allied with less idealistic supporters, prominent among them various non-Afghan actors[497]

494 See, for example, Ludhiyānavī (1420–5h), IX: 25 (*Imārat-i Islāmiyyah mēṇ Futbāl Mēch*). See also Shāh Manṣūr (1430–2/2009–11), for example I: 16 and 44–52, who tied his apocalyptic world-view and salvation anxiety to "Deobandiyyat" as well as the agenda of the ART in Afghanistan.

495 In addition, Rahman (2018), 229f., stresses the strong apocalyptic sentiments of Shāmzay, which tie in well with all kinds of conspiracy theories that are equally to be found in many writings of Ludhiyānavī's student and the person in charge of the ART, Muftī Abū Lubābah Shāh Manṣūr: see Shāh Manṣūr (1430–2/2009–11). See also Hartung (2021a), 137–42.

496 See Də Afghānistān Islāmī Imārat (1431/2010).

497 The most prominent support from that direction was probably the Arab *al-Qāʿida* network in the Pashtun Borderland, then led by Usāma ibn Lādin, and its auxiliaries,

and others who were equally well disposed towards them, for all sorts of reasons. The one institution that turned out to be a major supporter – both in material and non-material ways – was, once more, the *Dār al-ʿUlūm-i Ḥaqqāniyyah* at Akōṛah Khaṫṫak.

4.3.3 *Ḥaqqāniyyāt (Plural), Post-1979 (Part II)*

Thanks to the political circumstances, the *Ḥaqqāniyyah* turned out to be a main beneficiary of Zia-ul-Haq's efforts to bring the entire religious infrastructure in Pakistan under state control. In conjuncture with the alarming political developments in Afghanistan since the passing of the Republican Constitution under Dāvūd Khān in 1977 and the massive influx of Afghan refugees after the "Ṣawr Revolution" in April 1978, the focus of Zia-ul-Haq and the Pakistani security apparatus now shifted fully to the "Second Deoband"[498] in Akōṛah Khaṫṫak as a major asset to the foreign politics of Pakistan. Thus, the funding of the seminary, as distributed from the centrally accumulated *zakāt*, increased substantially in the first half of the 1980s, to 18.8 per cent of the total receipts in 1984.[499] The political role of ʿAbd al-Ḥaqq Akōṛavī as a member of the PNA and his son's later membership in the Senate of Pakistan were certainly helpful when negotiating the share for the *Ḥaqqāniyyah* with the officials in the Ministry of Religious Affairs. Indeed, their deep involvement in Pakistani policy-making might well have helped these two subsequent principals of the *Ḥaqqāniyyah* in successfully convincing the president of Pakistan of the position of the seminary as a major spearhead of the Afghan *jihād*, thus justifying its claim to the lion's share of funds and other government support. In the same breath, the leadership of the *Ḥaqqāniyyah* began to actively perpetuate a corresponding self-image in public: according to Samīʿ al-Ḥaqq, all the leading heads of the Afghan *jihād* had studied with his father and continued to consult him until his natural death in September 1988, while ʿAbd al-Ḥaqq himself had laid the foundation stone for the *jihād*.[500]

Moreover, the notion of the "Second Deoband", with which the former principal of the Indian mother house, Qārī Muḥammad Ṭayyib, had chosen to honour the *Ḥaqqāniyyah*, has provided a convenient pretext to publicly evoke a genealogy that ties the nineteenth-century *Ṭarīqah-yi Muḥammadiyyah* of Shāh Ismāʿīl Dihlavī and Sayyid Aḥmad Barēlvī to the anti-imperialist activities of the Shaykh al-Hind and his circles, and from there to Deoband under Ḥusayn Aḥmad Madanī and, finally, the Afghan *jihād*.[501] This, however, we

such as the Arab charity *al-Wafāʾ al-Ighātha al-Islāmiyya* that is rumoured to have co-ordinated its activities in Afghanistan quite closely with the ART: see Burr and Collins (2006), 98.

498 Qārī Muḥammad Ṭayyib cited in Samīʿ al-Ḥaqq (n.d.), 52f.

499 See Malik (1996), 206, Table 37.

500 See ibid., 207.

501 See Samīʿ al-Ḥaqq (n.d.), 323–8.

may interpret rather as an attempt of an accomplished Pashtun Borderland actor to seize the opportunity created by favourable external conditions and establish a monopoly of definition over what can rightly be regarded as "Deobandiyyat" even beyond the Pashtun Borderland. In addition, Samīʿ al-Ḥaqq attempted in this way to assert himself politically as the supreme representative of the JUI in all of Pakistan.

The widespread view of Samīʿ al-Ḥaqq as "(god)father of 'The Taliban'", and the *Ḥaqqāniyyah* as the "University of *jihād*", which has been gullibly embraced especially by mainstream media and security analysts all over the world, is a clear demonstration of how successful and efficacious its own publication strategy has been.[502] In reality, however, this image is lopsided at best. Firstly, there is neither any indication that the ṬIT leaders who had congregated in Kandahar have indeed received substantial spiritual nourishment from Samīʿ al-Ḥaqq, nor evidence that the *Ḥaqqāniyyah* served as the exclusive recruitment ground for the ṬIT. Yet, as the largest religious seminary in Pakistan's NWFP by far, it would appear only natural for it to produce comparatively higher numbers of volunteers, and these numbers increased dramatically with the growing influx of Afghan refugees among its students since early 1978.

Politically, too, Samīʿ al-Ḥaqq's aspirations to supremely represent the JUI did not withstand any reality check. Samīʿ al-Ḥaqq and his father, as staunch supporters of Zia-ul-Haq's policies of bringing the religious infrastructure under state control in their respective political fora, headed for conflict when the then-JUI President and former Chief Minister of the NWFP Muftī Maḥmūd (d. 1400/1980), a member of the Pashtun Yaḥyá Khēl clan of southern D.I. Khan, firmly rejected them as being not in conformity with the injunction of the *shariʿa*.[503] When Muftī Maḥmūd passed away and the staff of leadership was passed to his son Faẓl al-Raḥmān (b. 1372/1953), Samīʿ al-Ḥaqq refused to acknowledge as new *amīr* someone who had followed his father's firm instructions not to take any sessions with Samīʿ al-Ḥaqq while studying at the *Ḥaqqāniyyah*,[504] and, subsequently, created his own JUI, known today as JUI-S, while the remnants of the original organization are now recognized as JUI-F.[505]

502 See, for example, Ali (2007); Craig (2016).

503 For a sample of various legal responses regarding the relation between state and religious authorities in Pakistan, see Maḥmūd (2001–8), III: 269f., 297–9 and 310 (on taxation); VIII: 43 and 222f. (on matters of finance); IX: 205 (on military service). See also Malik (1996), 138 and 211f.

504 See Mahsūd (n.d.), 6.

505 In fact, the JUI-S continued its existence even after the assassination of Samīʿ al-Ḥaqq in November 2018. It is now led by his eldest son Ḥāmid al-Ḥaqq Ḥaqqānī (b. 1388/1968) who, like his grandfather ʿAbd al-Ḥaqq before him, served as a member of the PNA between 2002 and 2007.

Remembering the constructed and hard-to-corroborate nature of the now dominant image of the *Ḥaqqāniyyah* and its current principal, however, is not to question the fact that the issue of *jihād* shifted irrevocably into the centre of discourse at the *Ḥaqqāniyyah*, even though this began to blossom properly only with the establishment of the PDPA regime in Afghanistan. The various subjects now began to be taught with a clear focus on that theme in order to prime students for their eventual engagement in combat. In the study of *ḥadīth*, for instance, which, after all, is regarded as the most prominent field of religious learning in this institution, the emphasis was now ultimately placed on the sections in the various *ḥadīth* collections that concern the Prophet's military campaigns (*maghāzī*) and on warfare sustained by religious precepts (*jihād wa-sayr*). These were supplemented by relevant classical literature on the same subject, here especially the works of al-Wāqidī (d. 207/823) on the conquests of Syria, Mesopotamia and Persia. Samīʿ al-Ḥaqq again claimed that the teaching faculty selected these texts with a practical reason in mind: the students should

> not only be familiar with the particulars of the means of communication of current and previous eras, such as the postal system, telegram, telephone, television, video, mobile phone, internet and newspapers, but also with the miraculous way [*muʿajizātī ṭawr*] in which the hands of the third generation of companions [*ṣaḥābah-yi tābiʿīn*] have laid down and preserved all these war reports. In this way the Battle of Qādisa, the conquests of Egypt, Syria, Andalusia and Khurasan, Muḥammad ibn Qāsim, Ṣalāḥ al-Dīn Ayyūbī, the conquests of the Ghaznavids and the Abdālī, Ṫīpū Sulṭān's Battle at Śrīraṁgapaṫṭaṇa, the caravan of mission and resolve of Shāh Ismāʿīl and Sayyid Aḥmad Shahīd, the Freedom Movement of 1857, the Battles of Pānīpaṫ and Shāmlī, the Silk-Letter Movement, the Pakistan Movement and other smaller and larger movements and *jihād* activities have adorned the pages of history.[506]

While this passage reflects once again Samīʿ al-Ḥaqq's politically motivated desire to publicly stage the *Ḥaqqāniyyah* as heir to the early Muslim conquests conducted under the Medinese Caliphs, as well as to the anti-imperialist activism sustained by religious precepts of early "Deobandiyyat", we must

506 Samīʿ al-Ḥaqq, 'Pish lafẓ', in Samīʿ al-Ḥaqq (2011b), VI: 43. The reference to the Battle of Shāmlī, which was fought in May 1857 near Ṫhānah Bḣavan, is actually implicitly to Imdādallāh "Muhājir Makkī": see, for example, Meraṫhī (n.d.), I: 73–9; Hartung (2016b), 352f. The reference to the "Silk-Letter Movement" (*taḥrīk-i rashmī rumāl*), in turn, has, despite not really referring to something that would fit any extant definition of a "social movement" as such, become a standard label in Indo-Pakistani historiography for the activities of the Shaykh al-Hind and his associates around World War I. It derived its name from the fact that some of the missives sent by the Shaykh al-Hind from the Hijaz to ʿUbaydallāh Sindḣī and his associates in Kabul were written on small pieces of silk and sewn into the garments of the couriers, see Metcalf (2009), 24f.

bear in mind that it is not he alone who represents the *Ḥaqqāniyyah*. Indeed, some of its leading faculty[507] were of a less mundane persuasion than their current principal, deriving their notion of piety rather from ʿAbd al-Ḥaqq Akōṛavī and a distinct TJ environment which matched much more Rashīd Aḥmad Ludhiyānavī's disposition to ascetic and otherworldly oriented religious activism and were, thus, of greater appeal to those who would later be associated with the ṬIT / IEA. One of the foremost scholars here, idealized as "Imām al-Mujāhidīn" by one of his hagiographers,[508] was Shīr ʿAlī Shāh Madanī, *shaykh al-tafsīr wa'l-ḥadīth* at the *Ḥaqqāniyyah*, mentioned above.

Shīr ʿAlī Shāh, a native of Akōṛah Khaṫṫak, represents the first generation of Ḥaqqānī scholars, alongside later luminaries such as Yūnus Khāliṣ and Jalāl al-Dīn Ḥaqqānī. He was spiritually tied to the family of ʿAbd al-Ḥaqq Akōṛavī, began to study under the latter at the *Anjuman-i Taʿlīm al-Qurʾān*, the pre-Partition forerunner of the *Ḥaqqāniyyah*, and, after 1947, was the first local to enrol as a student in the *Ḥaqqāniyyah* itself.[509] Five years later, ʿAbd al-Ḥaqq sent him, alongside his son Samīʿ al-Ḥaqq, to the *Jāmiʿah Ashrafiyyah* in Lahore, to study *ḥadīth* for some months with some former students of Ashraf ʿAlī Thānavī. Another study trip to Lahore in 1958, now with Aḥmad ʿAlī Lāhōrī (d. 1381/1962), one of ʿUbaydallāh Sindhī's foremost students and disciples, however, turned out to be even more formative.[510] Shīr ʿAlī Shāh found in Lāhōrī a scholar quite similar to Rashīd Aḥmad Ludhiyānavī, insofar as the combination of an ascetic pious lifestyle, which also received a lot of inspiration from the revivalist programme of the TJ, and religiously grounded political activism against dominant and oppressive government structures are concerned. Shīr ʿAlī Shāh seems to have somewhat parted way here with the

507 The eminence of deceased scholars of the *Ḥaqqāniyyah* is measured here by whether or not a special commemorative issue of the in-house journal *al-Ḥaqq* has been dedicated to someone. In addition to ʿAbd al-Ḥaqq Akōṛavī and Samīʿ al-Ḥaqq, this privilege has so far been granted only to Shīr ʿAlī Shāh Madanī and Muḥammad Ibrāhīm Fānī. Another one who, upon his eventual demise, will most certainly enjoy a special commemorative issue is ʿAbd al-Qayyūm Ḥaqqānī, currently principal of the *Ḥaqqāniyyah*-affiliated *Jāmiʿah Abū Hurayrah* in Khāliqābād near Nowshera.

508 See Shawkat ʿAlī Ḥaqqānī, 'Dēoband-i s̱ānī (Ḥaqqāniyyah) kā rūḥ-i ravāṇ', in Madanī (1437/2016), 217–25, here 221.

509 See Shīr ʿAlī Shāh al-Madanī, 'al-Sīra al-dhātiyya li'l-shaykh al-Duktūr Shīr ʿAlī Shāh al-Madanī', in ibid., 17–19, here 17.

510 On him, see Hartung (2004), 247–50 and 252–7. On the basis of the laudatory references for Aḥmad ʿAlī Lāhōrī's interpretations of Qur'anic passages on the matter of armed *jihād*, Rahman (2018), 220f., also introduces him as a major influence on Masʿūd Aẓhār. While it is true that Lāhōrī's glosses are repeatedly recommended in the later *Fatḥ al-Javād* (see Aẓhār [1428–30/2007–09], e.g., I: 9, 363, 456 and 512), in the earlier *Faẓāʾil-i Jihād*, it is ʿAbdallāh ʿAzzām whom Masʿūd Aẓhār regarded as the ultimate learned authority in this regard (see Aẓhār [1419h], 66). For this reason, the influence of Aḥmad ʿAlī Lāhōrī was perhaps not as exceptional as it seems at a cursory glance. Rashīd Aḥmad Ludhiyānavī also figures quite prominently among other authorities referred to.

younger Samīʿ al-Ḥaqq, whose aspirations for political eminence he did not share. Instead, he focused on teaching introductory classes at the *Ḥaqqāniyyah* for the next decade and a half, while ʿAbd al-Ḥaqq took over the responsibility for instructing the more advanced levels.[511] Finally, in 1973, Shīr ʿAlī Shāh evaded the controversial government of Ẕū ʾl-Fiqār ʿAlī Bhuṫṫō (executed 1979) and his *Pakistan People's Party* (PPP) by moving to Medina, where he enrolled in the Shariʿa Faculty of the only recently established IUM, then headed by Ibn Bāz. Specializing in the *ʿulūm al-tafsīr*, he graduated five years later with an M.A. as well as a Ph.D. in hand.

Both of his dissertations, supervised by ʿAbd al-ʿAzīz ibn Muḥammad ibn ʿUthmān (d. 1430/2009), can serve as an excellent illustration of his particular religious world-view: his M.A. dissertation was an exegesis of the eighteenth chapter of the Qur'an, while, for his doctorate, Shīr ʿAlī Shāh investigated the scattered contributions of the great early ascetic Ḥasan al-Baṣrī to the interpretation of the Qur'an.[512] The exegetical principles which he claimed he had been following consistently since his studies with Aḥmad ʿAlī Lāhōrī were those laid down by the latter, which Sayyid Abū ʾl-Ḥasan ʿAlī Nadvī, another student of Lāhōrī already repeatedly mentioned, characterized as Sufic *tafsīr* of "contemplation and allegorical interpretation" (*iʿtibār va taʾvīl*) in the tradition of Ibn ʿArabī, the Indian *mufassir* Makhdūm ʿAlī al-Mahāʾimī (d. 836/1432) or the Ottoman mystical exegete Ismāʿīl Ḥakḳī Bursevi (d. 1137/1725).[513] The foundational text at the first stage of instruction, aimed at training the ability to translate all that one has rationally comprehended into a persistent emotive religious disposition (*taqvá awr rūḥāniyyat, awr ikhlāṣ va īshār*), was Shāh Ismāʿīl Dihlavī's seminal *Taqviyyat al-Īmān*.[514]

How to remain a steadfast believer in a contingent world full of temptation and miscreed – already a core theme for Ashraf ʿAlī Thānavī, ʿAbd al-Ghanī Pḣūlpūrī, Rashīd Aḥmad Ludḣiyānavī and Niẓām al-Dīn Shāmzay – was clearly also a chief concern to Shīr ʿAlī Shāh Madanī. It is, therefore, not surprising that the choice of his first exegetical effort fell on the one chapter of the Qur'an which, in the famous story of the Men of the Cave (*aṣḥāb al-kahf*), contains crucial authoritative references to the theme of how to preserve one's piety in a world of affliction. It is the story of a few pious youths who fled their idolatrous community and took refuge in a cave, where God graced them by making them sleep for an indefinitely long period. When they

511 See ʿAbd al-Qayyūm Ḥaqqānī, 'Shaykh al-ḥadīs̱ Mawlānā Ḋākṫar Sayyid Shīr ʿAlī Shāh – rḥ – ēk jāmʿ al-kamālāt shakhṣiyyat', in Madanī (1437/2016), 47–51, here 50f.

512 See al-Madanī (1429/2008); al-Madanī, 'al-Sīra [. . .]', in Madanī (1437/2016), 18f.; ʿIrfān al-Ḥaqq Ḥaqqānī, 'Hayāt va khidmāt', in Madanī (1437/2016), 25–38, here 31–7.

513 See Nadvī (1414–19/1994–8), I: 137f. The exemplary *tafāsīr* mentioned here by Nadvī are Ibn ʿArabī's *Aḥkām al-Qurʾān*, al-Mahāʾimī's *Tabṣīr al-Raḥmān wa-Taysīr al-Mannān* and Ismāʿīl Ḥakḳī's *Rūḥ al-Bayān*.

514 See ibid., I: 139; Khān (1964), 114–16.

eventually reappeared from the cave, they were able to convince the community outside of the truth of all of God's promises, not least thanks to an inscription (*al-raqīm*) which God Himself left in the cave.[515]

Indeed, it is this Qur'anic story that contains all the salient points that shaped the world-view of scholars such as Shīr ʿAlī Shāh Madanī: the threat to fidelity by an increasingly areligious world is one of them; another one is the ontic supremacy of the Qur'anic narrative over the contingent external world and the many conflicting narratives; a third is the need to preserve one's belief even in the most adverse circumstances, in which case, the believer can be sure of God's sublime support; and, finally, the firm conviction that the Final Days, and thus the ultimate reckoning, are imminent. Repeatedly invoked in the Qur'anic story of the *aṣḥāb al-kahf*, the core belief to be sustained under any circumstances however adverse is in God's Oneness (*tawḥīd*). This, at least, is the reading strongly affirmed by prominent classical Sufi exegetes such as Ibn ʿArabī,[516] which was more than enough for Shīr ʿAlī Shāh to regard the spiritual universe of the Sufi as a credible and *shari'a*-compliant frame of reference and integrated, thus, into a set of like-minded scholars of past and present, prominently including Shāh Ismāʿīl Dihlavī and Sayyid Aḥmad Barēlvī in the early nineteenth and Tȟānavī, Pȟūlpūrī, Ludȟiyānavī and Shāmzay in the twentieth century. What all these personalities, including Shīr ʿAlī Shāh, had in common was the strong conviction that the only appropriate action for a believer to prove her or his faith under such adverse circumstances was to wholesomely engage in *jihād* of whatever kind, crossing at ease between the individual inner struggle with one's appetitive soul, so typical for the path of the Sufi, and the armed variety.

Let us, however, return to the chronology. After graduating from the IUM, Shīr ʿAlī Shāh decided to stay on in Medina, where he established a traditional teaching circle in the Prophet's Mosque. Contrary to what one might expect from a graduate of the IUM, even more so in the light of the case of Shams al-Dīn al-Afghānī discussed above,[517] Shīr ʿAlī Shāh remained a firm Hanafi, who would always give preference to the opinion of that particular canonical tradition in legal hermeneutics. In fact, the frequent interaction with Saudi Wahhabi scholars[518] and South Asian *Ahl-i Ḥadīs̱* seems to have rather

[515] The exegetical tradition of this chapter is strong, with different emphases laid by various *mufassirūn*. As a true follower of Aḥmad ʿAlī Lāhōrī's approach, Shīr ʿAlī Shāh would engage much less in philological or *ḥadīth*-based exegesis, but instead built on earlier more esoteric interpretations, such as Ibn ʿArabī's *Aḥkām al-Qurʾān*.

[516] See Ibn ʿArabī (1424/2003), III: 220–45 (on Q18.7, 19f., 23–6, 39, 46, 60–3, 66f., 69, 73, 76f., 79, 82, 94 and 103f.).

[517] See Section 4.1.3.

[518] A case in point here is Ibn Bāz, the president and chancellor of the IUM at that time, with whose thinking Shīr ʿAlī Shāh had already engaged in late 1969 when he published his Urdu translation of the Saudi scholar's comments on the occasion of the Moon landing

consolidated his traditional orientation,[519] instead of leading him to embrace a more Salafi orientation that radiates strongly from the officially decreed Wahhabi interpretation of Islam in the Saudi Kingdom.[520] This suggests a general understanding of and mutual respect for conservative scholars beyond the confines of the *madhāhib fiqhiyya*, which ultimately allowed the crossing over of various dogmatically sustained denominations, as we have already seen in the case of the Panjpiris.[521] Be that as it may, Shīr ʿAlī Shāh seems to have been respected well enough, even by a Wahhabi grandee such as Ibn Bāz, that he was officially commissioned to lead a delegation of ṬIT representatives to Saudi Arabia in 1996, and actually succeeded in soliciting the spiritual and material support of the Saudi religious and political establishment for the IEA.[522]

However, before this eventually happened, there were other developments that demand our attention. After having spent three years teaching at the Prophet's Mosque in Medina, Shīr ʿAlī Shāh returned to Pakistan, though not, as one might expect, to his *alma mater* at Akōṛah Khaṫṫak, but rather, for reasons not yet entirely clear, to Karachi. Thus, the two threads of "Militant Frontier Deobandiyyat" distinguished in this chapter, associated with Akōṛah Khaṫṫak and Karachi, respectively, coincided in the person of Shīr ʿAlī Shāh.

In Karachi, he first began to teach at the city's *Dār al-ʿUlūm*, established in 1951 by the Deoband's former mufti Muḥammad Shāfiʿī (d. 1396/1976), before heading on to the *Jāmiʿat Aḥsan al-ʿUlūm*, founded by Muḥammad Zarvalī Khān (b. 1374/1955) as late as in 1978. This scholar from Khān Khēl in Swat is yet another case of a Pashtun Borderland actor who, similarly to Shīr ʿAlī Shāh, combined personal and ideational threads that we have already encountered in previous chapters: not only was Zarvalī Khān educated at the *Ḥaqqaniyyah* as well as the *Dār al-ʿUlūm* in Deoband itself, but also one of his principal

of Apollo 11 in the same year: see Shīr ʿAlī Shāh (trans.), 'Taskhīr-i mahtāb (chānd tak insānī rasāʾī) kē khilāf kōʾī dalīl nahīṉ', *al-Ḥaqq* 5/3 (1969), 20–3. This text, in fact, relates to the widespread sarcastic allegation by literati of the nascent *Progressive Party* (*Ḥizb al-Tajammuʿ al-Waṭanī al-Taqaddumī al-Waḥdawī*) of Egypt that Ibn Bāz was denying the scientifically established view that the earth is a revolving globe (*al-arḍ kuriyya wa-tadawwur*), but would rather maintain the perspective of the Qur'an (e.g., Q88.20) and Prophetic *aḥādīth*. For one of his numerous refutations of that allegation: see Ibn Bāz (1420h), IX: 226–9 (*Radd ʿalá ʾl-Muftirīn ʿalá ʾl-ʿUlamāʾ* [1397/1977]).

519 See Aḥmad Saʿīd Jān Ḥaqqānī, 'Madīnah Yūnīvarsiṫī mēṉ "Abū Ḥanīfah-yi s̱ānī" laqab pānēvālā', in Madanī (1437/2016), 371–5, here 374f.

520 In fact, matters of state and religion in Saudi Arabia are ultimately much more complex than, unfortunately, is acknowledged in many academic and journalistic works, in which a rather reductive narrative is perpetuated. New research, ideally with an empirical component, is, therefore, highly desirable.

521 See Section 4.1.2.

522 See ʿAbd al-Bāqī Ḥaqqānī, 'ʿIlm awr jihād kā sangam', in Madanī (1437/2016), 258–63, here 261f.

teachers was a brother-in-law of Qāẓī Ḥusayn Aḥmad, the *amīr-i aʿlá* of the JiI between 1997 and 2009 . Moreover, having studied *tafsīr* in the tradition of Anvar Shāh Kashmīrī, one of the celebrated so-called *akābirīn* of "Deobandiyyat", he finally emerged as one of the most outspoken critics of the Qur'anic hermeneutics of Muḥammad Ṭāhir Panjpīrī, whom he repeatedly confronted in learned disputations.[523]

Enticed by Muḥammad Yūsuf Binōrī (d. 1397/1977), a native of Mardan and also a student of Anvar Shāh Kashmīrī himself, Zarvalī Khān moved to Karachi to join Binōrī's enterprise, the *Jāmiʿat al-ʿUlūm al-Islāmiyyah* in the neighbourhood that would later become "Binori Town" and where Niẓām al-Dīn Shāmzay had also been flourishing since the late 1980s. After the death of Yūsuf Binōrī, finally, Zarvalī Khān, who had also developed strong leanings towards the TJ, established his own institution and, presumably, utilized his personal network extending into the Pashtun Borderland to recruit the faculty. One of those whose services he succeeded in securing for the year 1993 was Shīr ʿAlī Shāh Madanī.

Thus, Shīr ʿAlī Shāh entered a major hub of manifold Deobandi activities in Karachi, with strong personal and ideational ties extending into the Pashtun Borderland. The interconnectedness of the various major Deobandi scholars there and the relative proximity of Zarvalī Khān's *Aḥsan al-ʿUlūm* in Gulshan-i Iqbāl Town to Rashīd Aḥmad Ludhiyānavī's *Dār al-Iftāʾ wa'l-Irshād* in Nāẓimābād makes it quite likely that the two scholars were very familiar with one another and mutually shaped their respective views. They may even have taught, or at least spoken to, the same people, and have, thus, kept the fires of *jihād* in whichever form alive, as the only viable way to prove oneself worthy of salvation in view of the presence of what both scholars regarded as clear portents of the Hour.

Yūsuf Binōrī also apparently encouraged such sentiments among his students. In June 1985 , while Shīr ʿAlī Shāh was still in the Hijaz, the young scholar Arshad Aḥmad "Shahīd" started a militant organization called *Ḥarakat al-Jihād al-Islāmī al-ʿĀlamī* at the *Jāmiʿat al-ʿUlūm al-Islāmiyyah* and began to undertake raids into Afghanistan.[524] All this markedly underscores once more the great significance of Karachi regarding the origins of the ṬIT around Mullā Muḥammad ʿUmar. What is more, at the same time, it also contradicts somewhat the institutional narrative in which the *Ḥaqqāniyyah* leadership claims to have been the major, if not sole, cradle of that movement. Nonetheless, Shīr ʿAlī Shāh's major reference points among the *mujāhidīn* after the Soviet withdrawal from Afghanistan were not, as one might well have expected, graduates from any of the Karachi institutions, but rather graduates

523 See Mughal (1425/2004), 19–28.

524 See Ḥāfiẓ Muḥammad Ṣiddīq Arkānī, 'Musnad-i tadrīs sē maydān-i kārzār tak', in Madanī (1437/2016), 268f.

of his own *alma mater*, the *Ḥaqqāniyyah*: the people in question are none other than Jalāl al-Dīn Ḥaqqānī and his circle.[525]

Jalāl al-Dīn had, by then, already evolved into a major player in the tricky borderland game of asserting oneself, while, simultaneously, conceding the need for temporary alliances even with fierce opponents, while faced with a mighty common enemy.[526] While he was still alive, ʿAbd al-Ḥaqq Akōṛavī remained his former student Jalāl al-Dīn's prime interface to the *Ḥaqqāniyyah*;[527] after that, it seems, Shīr ʿAlī Shāh shouldered this responsibility. Indeed, a few matters are important in this context.

Firstly, and if only to reiterate what has already been said above, not all of the faculty of the *Ḥaqqāniyyah* were actively inclined to continued armed *jihād* to the same degree after the Soviet withdrawal from Afghanistan and the subsequent civil war that was triggered by the *mujāhidīn* commanders' greed for power.[528] While the interrelated practices of *jihād* and sacrifice both needed constant reaffirmation and have, therefore, been pivotal in the learned discourse at the *Ḥaqqāniyyah*, especially during the early years of the resistance to the PDPA–Soviet nexus, when casualties among the *mujāhidīn* were enormously high,[529] this was significantly less so in the following period. While the majority of the faculty certainly still supported *jihādī* thinking, Shīr ʿAlī Shāh

525 See, for example, ʿAbd al-Bāqī Ḥaqqānī in ibid., here 260.

526 The limited number of issues from the Jalāl al-Dīn-edited periodicals *Manbaʿ al-Jihād* (two distinct versions appeared in Pashto and Arabic, respectively) and *Nuṣrat al-Jihād* (Urdu) available still contain enough telling images that show Jalāl al-Dīn with almost all the major *mujāhidīn* commanders of the IIMA, including even the otherwise much despised Aḥmad Shāh Masʿūd: see, for example, *Manbaʿ al-Jihād* [A] 2/7–8 (1411/1991), 46 (with Rabbānī); *Manbaʿ al-Jihād* [P] 1/8–9 (1368sh/1410h), 47 (with Qāẓī Ḥusayn Aḥmad); 2/3–4 (1369sh/1411h), title page, 33 and 35; *Nuṣrat al-Jihād* 1/1 (1411/1990), 48 (with Shāh Masʿūd); 1/11–12 (1412/1991), 17 (with Faẓl al-Raḥmān, the son of Muftī Maḥmūd). See also Nangiyāl (1370sh), 46 and 109 (with Rabbānī).

Postscript: Unfortunately, the third major periodical published in the early 1990s at the behest of Jalāl al-Dīn Ḥaqqānī, the Pashto weekly *Də Jihād Hindārah*, has come to attention only too late in the writing process of this book, and has, therefore, informed neither the present account nor my analysis.

527 See Ḥaqqānī (1419/1998), 201–3 (on a meeting at ʿAbd al-Ḥaqq's house in December 1986) and 358–93 (on a meeting in January 1983).

528 For the time around the ṬIT's proclamation of the *Islamic Emirate of Afghanistan*, Muḥammad Ṣiddīq Arkānī, *shaykh al-ḥadīth* at Karachi's *Jāmiʿah Iḥtishāmiyyah*, declares that, in fact, only three Pakistani *ʿulamāʾ* had actually been actively involved in providing religious instruction to *mujāhidīn* in Afghanistan: in addition to Muḥammad Ḥasan Jān (killed 1428/2007) there were Niẓām al-Dīn Shāmzay and Shīr ʿAlī Shāh Madanī: see Arkānī in Madanī (1437/2016), 269. On Muḥammad Ḥasan Jān, see his interview with *Manbaʿ al-Jihād* [A] 2/11 (1412/1991), 20f.

529 This changed only when the *mujāhidīn* obtained man-portable surface-to-air missiles, the legendary FIM-92 Stingers, from their US-American supporters, in 1986. Only then could the *mujāhidīn* respond reasonably effectively to the massive and thus far successful attempts of the Soviet armed forces to establish control over the difficult territory from

stood well out from the crowd by virtue of the extent of his commitment to the cause, also fuelled perhaps by the need he felt to compensate for having spent the entire war of resistance to the PDPA–Soviet nexus abroad. Now that various Islamist militias were tearing each other apart over the ownership of Kabul, all in the name of an "Islamic system" they claimed they would realize upon their respective victory, Shīr ʿAlī Shāh set out to make a significant contribution to "Islamic character formation", with which most of the Afghan Islamist organizations were, at least initially, not overtly concerned.

In early 1992, after having distinguished himself as a top military commander, Jalāl al-Dīn made a trip to Karachi, where he was honourably received at various Deobandi educational institutions, among them the *Jāmiʿat al-ʿUlūm al-Islāmiyyah* in Binori Town and the *Jāmiʿat Aḥsan al-ʿUlūm.*[530] Shīr ʿAlī Shāh figures most prominently in the extensive report on this tour, suggesting that Jalāl al-Dīn Ḥaqqānī and he took an instant liking to each other.[531] While certainly not discounting the possibility that the two were simply just sympathetic to each other, a closer relationship between them also clearly carried the prospect of gaining some logistical advantage for Jalāl al-Dīn himself. After all, in his address in honour of the esteemed guest from Lōyah Paktia, Shīr ʿAlī Shāh highlighted the readiness of students and staff of the *Dār al-ʿUlūm* of Karachi to participate in the *jihād*, saying: 'This seminary has 5 000 students and 200 faculty and, while teaching follows a schedule and the students go to their homes during vacation, if needed they would all join their *mujāhidīn* brethren [in combat].'[532]

It is hardly surprising for someone so dedicated to the cause of the *mujāhidīn* that Shīr ʿAlī Shāh volunteered as *shaykh al-ḥadīth* at Jalāl al-Dīn's flagship *madrasah*, the *Manbaʿ al-ʿUlūm* in Mīrāmshā, North Waziristan, in 1994–5,[533] after having already been a frequently visiting member of the faculty there while still regularly employed at the *Dār al-ʿUlūm* in Karachi.[534]

Jalāl al-Dīn appears to have made the idea of the fountainhead, the *manbaʿ*, a symbolic pivot of all his and his associates' activities: Muslim activists prepared to use armed violence would receive from that well all the nourishment they could possibly need to fulfil their tasks. The *Manbaʿ al-ʿUlūm*, established in

the air, while also systematically releasing landmines and cluster bombs across the entire country to disrupt the logistics of the resistance efforts.

530 See Shuhrat Nangiyāl, 'al-Ḥājj Mawlavī Jalāl al-Dīn Ḥaqqānī də Karāchī lah dīnī jāmʿiyō aw madrasō ćakhah līdanah vakṛah', *Manbaʿ al-Jihād* [P] 3/9–10 (1371sh/1412h), 13–25.

531 Jalāl al-Dīn Ḥaqqānī also authored a preface to the published version of Shīr ʿAlī Shāh's Ph.D.: see al-Madanī (1429/2008), I–II: ḥa–ya.

532 Shīr ʿAlī Shāh in ibid., I: 16.

533 See Asrār ibn Madanī, 'Ḥayāt va khidmāt qadam bah qadam', in Madanī (1437/2016), 42.

534 See Anon., 'Də dawrah-yi ḥadīṣ-i sharīf ṭālibānō tah yawah lōyah khūsh'khabarī', *Manbaʿ al-Jihād* [P] 1/11 (1369sh/1410h), 29.

1980 and further developed over the following years, represented herein the aspect of religious instruction and spiritual guidance in Jalāl al-Dīn's constantly growing militia. The *madrasah* was complemented by the *Manbaʿ al-Jihād* in Žavarah, Khost, a complex of military training camps, which would also be frequented by Arab volunteers from early on, that served as the practical preparation for Islamically inspired combat.[535] The locations of these two operations under a single command demonstrate impressively how insignificant the Durand Line was in reality for local Pashtun Borderland actors and that movement in either direction remained indeed rather unchecked.

The *Manbaʿ al-ʿUlūm* also represents a significant shift away from the tradition of "Frontier Deobandiyyat" proper. Rather than what had previously been assumed,[536] the *Manbaʿ al-ʿUlūm* did *not* follow the Deobandi curriculum of the *Ḥaqqāniyyah*. Instead, it taught a specifically developed hybrid curriculum which emphasized the need for independent legal reasoning (*ijtihād*) outside the confines of any of the *madhāhib fiqhiyya*, something that was rather difficult to accept for those of a stern Hanafi orientation and possibly a reason why Shīr ʿAlī Shāh remained only a visiting member of the faculty at the *Manbaʿ al-ʿUlūm.*[537] Besides the traditional Islamic disciplines, with the typical stress on the *ʿulūm al-ḥadīth*, the early curriculum also included practically applicable subjects, such as mathematics, English language, physics and medical studies, all of which had an immediate relevance for those in combat during the resistance to the PDPA regime and its Soviet allies. At the same time, the religious education had been somewhat customized for the sake of providing spiritual comfort amidst horrid warfare of extreme asymmetry. After the Soviet withdrawal, however, the dynamics changed and religious knowledge in general became increasingly important, especially for an institution that, in early 1990, made the same boastful claim as the *Ḥaqqāniyyah*, namely that it was the prime educational institution for the Afghan *jihād.*[538]

The appropriation of this pretence by Jalāl al-Dīn Ḥaqqānī is a clear pointer to the fact that the universe of the *Ḥaqqāniyyah* had only a limited impact on the *Manbaʿ al-ʿUlūm* beyond its formative phase in the early 1980s. That

535 The network of the militia under Jalāl al-Dīn's command and the Arab volunteers who would eventually form the nucleus of *al-Qāʿida* is the major concern of Brown and Rassler (2013). In the present work, these relationships are discussed only in Section 4.5, although from an angle quite distinct from that of Brown and Rassler.

536 See ibid., 55.

537 See Anon., 'Manbaʿ al-ʿulūm – manbaʿ al-jihād: qilʿa ʿilmiyya li-taḥrīj al-ʿulamāʾ al-mujāhidīn', *Manbaʿ al-Jihād* [A] 1/1 (1410/1990), 6–10, here esp. 9. Emphatically on the firm Hanafi stand of the *Ḥaqqāniyyah*, after all the "Second Deoband", see Ḥaqqānī (1419/1998), 203–5 (*Dār al-ʿUlūm Dēoband Ḥanafiyyat kī Ḥifāẓat awr Difāʿ kā Maẓbūṭ Qilʿah Hē*).

538 See Anon., 'Manbaʿ al-ʿulūm – manbaʿ al-jihād' [see above, n.537]: 8.

instruction there was predominantly provided by former *Ḥaqqāniyyah* graduates[539] appears, therefore, to have been primarily owing to logistical convenience. Beyond that, the overlap between the two institutions seems to have been rather slim: careful perusal of a substantial number of published obituaries of combatants from the militia commanded by Jalāl al-Dīn from the final years of armed resistance against the PDPA regime in Kabul reveals that only a very few of them actually had a *Ḥaqqāniyyah* background profound enough to be worth mentioning.[540] Yet, almost all of the recruits on whom we have some biographical information came from conservative rural backgrounds throughout the Pashtun Borderland of Afghanistan, but overwhelmingly from Jalāl al-Dīn's native Paktia Province, thus making his militia, at least initially, a strongly local one, although with manifold ties to actors in the wider Pashtun Borderland.[541] Unsurprisingly, therefore, the *Manbaʿ al-ʿUlūm* seemed predestined to serve as a major cadre training facility for those who eventually merged into the ṬIT.

The complex, yet rather ambivalent, relationships of former *Ḥaqqāniyyah* graduate Jalāl al-Dīn Ḥaqqānī with his *alma mater*, and, by extension, also between *Ḥaqqāniyyah* and Jalāl al-Dīn's various "*Manābiʿ*" projects are, in fact, important observations, as they strongly invite a reassessment of the adequacy of the widely used label the "Ḥaqqānī Network", defined by Brown and Rassler as

> an intertwined group of Haqqaniyya graduates who deployed distinctive practices of Islamist mobilization in the highland tribal regions of Afghanistan and Pakistan during the 1970s and 1980s and from which some of the Taliban leadership emerged in the 1990s.[542]

539 See Anon., 'Də Manbaʿ al-ʿUlūm madrasah də yaw lōṛ taʿlīmī markaz pah ḥayṣ̱', *Manbaʿ al-Jihād* [P] 1/1 (1368sh/1409h), 12–15, here 14f. See also Brown and Rassler (2013), 55.

540 The following is based on a survey of 324 obituaries in the twenty-six copies of *Manbaʿ al-Jihād* [P] that were available at the time of writing from the period August 1989 to November 1993. Among them, only five are explicitly described as *Ḥaqqāniyyah* graduates, see *Manbaʿ al-Jihād* [P] 1/2 (1368sh/1410h), 60–2 and 66; 1/12 (1369sh/1410h), 61. Eight others received their religious training instead in *dīnī madāris* which are not further named and presumably local (see *Manbaʿ al-Jihād* [P] 2/3–4 [1369sh/1411h], 69 and 81; 2/6 [1369sh/1411h], 60 and 71; 2/12 [1370sh/1411h], 62; 3/1 [1370sh/1411h], 64; 3/9–10 [1371sh/1413h], 59; 4/1 [1371sh/1413h], 64).

541 Among the deceased was, for example, one originally from Gardēz in Paktia and educated at the *Jāmiʿah Nuʿmāniyyah* in Lahore (see *Manbaʿ al-Jihād* [P] 3/1 [1370sh/1411h], 64); another one was from Jānī Khēl in Paktia and taught at the *Dār al-ʿUlūm* in Kohat (see *Manbaʿ al-Jihād* [P] 1/6–7 [1368sh/1410h], 70); a third hailed originally from Nangarhar Province and had studied at the *Madrasah Imām Abū Ḥanīfah* in Peshawar (see *Manbaʿ al-Jihād* [P] 3/9–10 [1371sh/1412h], 60); and one from Nīkah District in Paktika Province was a student at Jalāl al-Dīn Ḥaqqānī's own *Manbaʿ al-ʿUlūm* in Mīrāmshā (see *Manbaʿ al-Jihād* [P] 1/6–7 [1368sh/1410h], 71f.).

542 Brown and Rassler (2013), 40.

In the light of the above, it seems rather difficult to maintain the position that the personnel basis of Jalāl al-Dīn's enterprise consisted by and large of *Ḥaqqāniyyah* graduates, although the pointer to Islamist practices of mobilization is significant, if only to an extent. Here, it is argued instead that it was not *Ḥaqqāniyyah* graduates who embraced these strategic tools of the various existing Islamist organizations. Rather, what has been labelled the "Ḥaqqānī Network" is structurally, in fact, not very different from various other regionally operative militias that kept entering, and again dissolving, purpose-driven coalitions much as they submitted to, and withdrew from, larger and more transregionally active entities, such as the ṬIT / IEA. Whenever the circumstances suggest it expedient for these militias to subordinate themselves to any larger armed formation for a certain period of time, the territories under their control become distinct regional sections of the front (*maḥāẕūnah*), with the militia leaders as commanders responsible for them and answerable, like in any military hierarchy, to those on the next higher level in the overall command structure. As such, they resemble very much the self-conception of the various Islamist groups under the umbrella of the IIMA during the resistance to the PDPA regime and the Soviet military presence in Afghanistan in the 1980s.[543]

Thus, what Brown and Rassler call the "Ḥaqqānī Network" and Giustozzi labels the 'Miran Shah Shura', a 'largely autonomous branch [...] of the Taliban which existed at that time',[544] namely in the early 2010s, actually called itself the *Manbaʿ al-ʿUlūm Jihādī Maḥāẕ* (MʿUJM): a regional front in Lōyah Paktia, consisting of local militias of different persuasions under the supreme command of Jalāl al-Dīn Ḥaqqānī, with his brothers Muḥammad Ismāʿīl (killed 1410/1990), Ibrāhīm (b. c. 1378/1958) and Khalīl al-Raḥmān (b. 1385/1966) as his deputies. From early 2005 onwards, the supervision of all day-to-day activities was overseen by Jalāl al-Dīn's eldest son Sirāj al-Dīn (b. c. 1399/1979),[545] the current commander-in-chief of the MʿUJM and, since September 2021, Interior Minister of the IEA.

543 In addition, there are also a few systematic reasons why the label "Ḥaqqānī Network" appears rather misleading. The first is the singular framing of the *maḥāẕ* led by Jalāl al-Dīn and later Sirāj al-Dīn as a "network", somewhat suggesting that a network is an empirical entity rather than a sociological model in which social configurations are viewed from a transactional perspective. As a consequence, if employed, it needs to be done consistently for all social configurations under investigation; that is, it would need to be equally applied, for example, to the ḤiI-Ḥ or the ṬIT / IEA. Secondly, assigning different labels for structurally rather similar groups of local actors, such as "network", "group", "force", "party" or even "shūrá", amounts to ignoring clear sociological distinctions among these terms. Using these loaded categories as if they were synonymous is neither empirically sustainable nor, at least for the moment, heuristically useful.

544 Giustozzi (2018), 22, whose term seems actually much more to the point, see Section 4.5.4.

545 See Ruttig (2009), 63. We need to be aware, however, that these data are based solely on an interview with Sirāj al-Dīn by late Pakistani journalist Rahimullah Yusufzai. This

True to their firm roots in the rural Pashtun Borderland, the leadership of the Mʿ UJM, secured by agnatic ties, entered temporary strategic alliances with whoever would provide an advantage in the negotiation of the various power claims in the region. Once the objective had been achieved and no further benefit could be expected from a particular ally, these associations were dissolved just as easily. During the armed resistance to the PDPA government and the Soviet occupation forces in Afghanistan, the strategic coalition partners of choice for local militias, such as the Mʿ UJM, were usually the various larger and ideologically more cohesive Islamist organizations under the umbrella of the IIMA.[546] Those who could relate better than others to the specifics of the rural and strongly tribal cultural environment dominant in those parts of the Pashtun Borderland in which actors like Jalāl al-Dīn Ḥaqqānī and his associates flourished were, however, preferable. Moreover, these strategic alliances were additionally fortified by the fact that, at some point in time, their leaders have had a spiritual relationship with ʿAbd al-Ḥaqq Akōṛavī and, as a result, they appear to have been much more durable. In this regard, it is important to recall that these are, first and foremost, personal relationships with the founder of the *Ḥaqqāniyyah*, not so much with the institution itself.[547]

What remains, therefore, is not so much a network of *Ḥaqqāniyyah* graduates, but one of religiously conservative actors strongly ingrained in the tribally structured rural world of the Pashtun Borderland, yet, with exposure to the Islamist thought that began its rise in Afghanistan's cities of the 1960s and 1970s. Jalāl al-Dīn, however, who, apart from his pilgrimage to Mecca in 1970, had mainly remained in his native environments and, like so many residents of the rural parts of the Pashtun Borderland, shunned the city and its dwellers. His Islamist influences must, therefore, have come from somewhere other than Kabul: indeed, they seem to have come rather directly from the MENA region, be it by reading the original Islamist classics or via personal acquaintances made during his sojourn in Mecca. Jalāl al-Dīn must have been so deeply impressed that, earlier than anyone else, he and his lieutenants actively encouraged the migration of Arab volunteers, many of

causes some suspicion regarding the veracity of the information: after all, we have already repeatedly encountered how prominent interviewees try to use the official media to their own advantage, often to create a public image of their own eminence that might not always correspond to the reality.

546 A good illustrative example is, once again, Malik Muḥammad Zarīn of the Mashvāṇī tribe mentioned above, who entered into temporary alliances with just about everyone seen as suitable for achieving short-term goals, including otherwise mutually exclusive forces, such as the ḤiI-Ḥ and the Karzay administration. See Section 4.2.2.

547 Although often listed as such (see, e.g., Rashid [2010], 84 and 90), neither Muḥammad Yūnus Khāliṣ, originally from Nangarhar, and Muḥammad Nabī Muḥammadī from Logar, the two most prominent alliance partners for local militias such as the Mʿ UJM, have actually been graduates of the *Ḥaqqāniyyah*: for the case of Khāliṣ, see Aḥmadzay (1385sh/1427h), 5f.; for Muḥammadī, see Bārakzay (2015). Also, see below, ch. 4.3.4.

whom had a background in the more radical groups within and around the MB in Egypt.[548] The call was responded to well, and the first Arab volunteers began to trickle into the Pashtun Borderland as early as June 1979, that is, four months before the invasion of Afghanistan by the Red Army.[549] It seems that this is what Brown and Rassler had correctly in focus when speaking of the "Ḥaqqānī nexus": the active recruitment of Arab radical Islamists to the battlefields of Afghanistan and their facilitation once they had arrived, which went as far as eventually securing their stay in the *Islamic Emirate of Afghanistan*, a fact that had the most serious consequences for the IEA after the summer of 2001.[550]

However, focusing solely on organization, the almost inevitable result of a prime interest in geopolitical strategy and national security matters that informs studies such as that of Brown and Rassler, blanks out the ideological consequences of the encounter between the diverse militias involved in the Afghan resistance to the Soviet-backed PDPA regime and the equally variant Arab *francs-tireurs* who assembled at the Hindu Kush. It seems as if a proactive promoter of a joint military effort, such as Jalāl al-Dīn Ḥaqqānī and his M'UJM, had also grossly underrated the might of the ideological stimuli brought along by these new arrivals, impulses that would change the landscape of religiously motivated militancy in the Pashtun Borderland irreversibly. As we shall see in greater detail below, the migration of Arab radical Islamists to the Pashtun Borderland offered – all rhetoric aside – an especially convenient way for them to evade severe persecution in their respective home countries. Consequently, their baggage contained their own actually quite local debates, which, under the illusion of a colourful sample of the entire Muslim *umma* in the training camps in Afghanistan, were rhetorically raised to a universal level as soon as the hated PDPA regime had been ended and commanders of various Islamist *mujāhidīn* forces, starting with Ḥikmatyār, rushed for Kabul, each aiming to seize power for himself alone, thereby breaking the "Peshawar Accord" of April 1992. We have already seen that there was tension between Pashtun combatants and Arab volunteers right from the start, when the latter began to criticize the beliefs and conduct of their Pashtun hosts, even going as far

548 These links began to be more formally established as early as 1978: Ḥanīf Shāh ibn Ḥājjī Ẓāhir al-Dīn, also a native of Paktia and a classmate of Jalāl al-Dīn when the latter finally joined the *Ḥaqqāniyyah*, was dispatched by the latter to Saudi Arabia, while ʿAzīz Khān, the later principal of the *Manbaʿ al-ʿUlūm* at Mīrāmshā, had been sent with others to the UAE: see Mawlavī ʿAzīz Khān, 'Pah Afghānistān kē də jihād lumṛanē ʿamaliyāt aw də kamūnistānō pah muqābil kē də ʿulamāʾō paćūn', *Manbaʿ al-Jihād* [P] 1/4–5 (1368sh/1410h): 17–22, here 22; also n.n.: 'Də jihād də sangar lah yaw zṛavār qōmāndān sarah yawah pah zṛəh pōrē marakah', Ibid., 23–7, here 24.

549 See Muṣṭafá Ḥāmid, 'Jalāl al-Dīn al-Ḥaqqānī: asṭūra fī taʾrīkh jihād Afghānistān (1)', *al-Ṣumūd* 4/45 (1431/2010), 34–41, here 34. See also Muḥammad (1991), 89.

550 See Brown and Rassler (2013), 70f.

as declaring them unbelievers.[551] Apparently, those who joined the activities at the *Manbaʿ al-Jihād* in Žavarah, among them leading figures of what would later gain global notoriety as *al-Qāʿida*, did in no way any better, and had to overcome their disgust with beliefs and practices of which they did not approve.[552]

Had both camps kept ideologically to themselves and concentrated on joint military action, greater ideational warpages could perhaps have been avoided. Yet, and this is almost inevitable in any socio-political action sustained by religious precepts, practical preparation for combat went hand in hand with religious education that was to provide the necessary ideological underpinning for the military activities. This was the case with the various Islamist organizations under the umbrella of the IIMA and their command centres in Peshawar, and it was certainly no less so for Jalāl al-Dīn Ḥaqqānī and the MʿUJM in Paktia. Just like the various *dīnī madāris* established by the JIA, IIAA and others in and around Peshawar, the *Manbaʿ al-ʿUlūm* in Mīrāmshā too constituted a vital part of the whole approach to active resistance against the non-Islamic government in Kabul, and eventually elsewhere. However, due to the comparatively much larger contingent of ideologically primed Arab fighters in the orbit of the MʿUJM, it was probably here more than elsewhere that some representatives of a "Frontier Deobandiyyat", already somewhat impregnated by an Islamist ideological framework, now also entered into a fateful alliance with Salafi thought in its most politicized form: "Salafism". This, in fact, was a development of most dramatic consequences that we shall, therefore, be looking at much more closely in a later section.[553]

Meanwhile, when the commanders of the various Islamist organizations formerly under the IIMA began to vie for power over Kabul in the late 1980s, the various regional militias of a more strongly rural and predominantly Deobandi background that had aligned themselves on and off with the Islamist militias during the resistance to PDPA rule and Soviet occupation were now forming the critical mass that could make or break the new "king of Kabul". Jalāl al-Dīn Ḥaqqānī also found himself in this dilemma. Which of the Islamist parties, if any, should enjoy the support of the MʿUJM, and why? It was at this moment that the Islamicity of the various rivalling parties shifted more into the focus, and it was the Arab volunteers, fairly well established in the Pashtun Borderland, who could potentially provide an argument sustainable by religious precepts on the basis of experiences and debates in their home countries.

Sayyāf's old associate ʿAbdallāh ʿAzzām turned out once more to be the spider in this highly complex and sensitive web of agents, and we will,

551 See Section 4.2.1.

552 See al-Shaybānī (2003). It is also noteworthy in this context that the *naʿt* poetry, which was a regular feature in the Pashto and Urdu periodicals of Jalāl al-Dīn in the early 1990s, was largely absent in the Arabic one.

553 See Section 4.5.

therefore, have to turn to him in more detail below.[554] In addition to his close relationships with the leaders of the various Peshawar-based Islamist organizations and the operation of his own training camps to facilitate new arrivals from the various Arab countries,[555] ʿAzzām also developed equally if not even more intimate links with traditionalist *mujāhidīn* commanders in the rural areas of the Pashtun Borderland, Jalāl al-Dīn Ḥaqqānī and Yūnus Khāliṣ most prominently among them.[556]

Yet, there is at least one crucial difference in dealing with urbanite Islamists such as Sayyāf and those whose frame of reference was essentially rural and who had received their ideational priming by "Frontier Deobandiyyat" of some kind. Consequently, the matter of involving foreign volunteers in their military operations was predominantly pragmatic for the likes of Jalāl al-Dīn Ḥaqqānī and Yūnus Khāliṣ. Other than for those Islamists whose ideological awakening was strongly linked to the few urban spaces within the Pashtun Borderland, loyalty to lofty ideas of a potentially global Islamic polity was subordinate to concrete matters on the ground to be dealt with in an as pragmatic a manner as possible: therefore, while the Arab *francs-tireurs* remained fully dependent on the express permission to stay on – and operate out of – tribally governed territory, Jalāl al-Dīn and Khāliṣ both had no qualms about actively involving them in major operations to further their own respective ends.[557] The commanders of the larger Islamist organizations, in contrast, appeared much more disturbed by the sometimes serious disagreements over core matters of doctrine that frequently translated into the excessive zeal of the Arab volunteers and tried to check their ardour by trying to freeze them out of most military operations.[558] Jalāl al-Dīn, again, could not refrain from praising his Arab combatants for their devotion to fight against the common enemy which, until April 1992, remained the PDPA government and the Afghan National Army.[559]

554 See, for example, *Bunyān al-Marṣūṣ* 4 (1406/1985), 12f.; 5 (1406/1996), 13f.; 28 (1409/1989), 42; 30 (1410/1990), whole issue; 31 (1401/1990), 38f.; *Mīṣāq-i Khūn* 2nd Series 4/9–10 (1368sh), 3–26 and 98. Tellingly, none of the fourteen available copies of the ḤiI-Ḥ journal *Shafaq* from between 1980 and 1990 contains any reference to ʿAzzām.

555 See, for example, al-Lūjarī (n.d. [c. 2003]), 41–75; Faraj (1422/2002), 24–6.

556 For references to ʿAzzām on the side of Jalāl al-Dīn, see *Manbaʿ al-Jihād* [P] 1/7–8 (1368sh/1410h), 48–50; 2/7 (1369sh/1411h), 15–17; *Manbaʿ al-Jihād* [A] 1/1 (1410/1990), 17 and 46; 2/7–8 (1411/1991), 48–52; *Nuṣrat al-Jihād* 1/2 (1411/1991), 21–5. For references to Jalāl al-Dīn Ḥaqqānī by ʿAzzām's MKh, see *al-Jihād* 1/5 (1405/1985), 7; 1/10 (1405/1985), 25–7; 2/2 (1406/1985), 18–22; 2/8 (1406/1986), 6–9; 2/11 (1406/1986), 28f.; 3/4 (1407/1986), 23; 3/5 (1407/1987), 16; 5/11 (1409/1989), 14; 7/4 (1411/1991), 16f.; 8/1 (1412/1992), 6 and 12–15.

557 See Ḥāmid (1997).

558 See ibid., 81 (quoting the Yemeni volunteer Abū Salmān al-Ṭāʾifa).

559 See, for example, his laudatory remarks on ʿAbd al-Raḥmān al-Miṣrī (killed 1408/1988) in Dirāz (1409/1989), 36f.

This attitude follows an interesting logic in which Islamic arguments became linked with socio-cultural norms common in the Pashtun tribal communities, especially those of rural provenance, and provides us with a vivid demonstration that the two frames of reference are actually not, as is often claimed especially regarding the ideological underpinnings of the ṬIT/IEA, completely discrete. The Islamic argument, as presented by Jalāl al-Dīn in 1980,[560] pivots on the conception that *jihād* against the atheist regime in Kabul was indeed the individual duty of every Muslim all over the world, an argument to which he might have been introduced by some early arrival in the Hindu Kush with affiliation to the Egyptian *Jamāʿa Islāmiyya* (JIM), an organization in which this idea was first cultivated and that will play quite a significant role in our narrative later on.[561] If *jihād* against an unbelieving regime was indeed an individual religious obligation for Muslims, regardless of their place of residence, then any Muslim arriving in the Pashtun Borderland to perform this duty had to be warmly welcomed there and supplied with shelter and the necessary logistics, including ample opportunities for military training.[562] Even more, they were to be provided with sanctuary should they be in need of it, a matter that strongly informed the IEA's position regarding Usāma ibn Lādin after the authorities of the USA demanded his extradition. While all these social norms are, at least conceptually, embedded in the tribal customs of Pashtun communities, they can equally be sustained by corresponding Islamic concepts (e.g., the Islamic pendant to the Pashto *mēlmastiyā* – hospitality – would be *ḍiyāfa*).

It seems, nonetheless, that Jalāl al-Dīn was following here the local socio-cultural conventions rather than the universalistic Islamic ones because alliances of great distinction are also customarily buttressed by intermarriage in the Pashtun context. Thus, Egyptian volunteer ʿAbd al-Raḥmān al-Miṣrī, for instance, married a tribal refugee woman soon after his arrival at Mīrāmshā, while Jalāl al-Dīn himself took a woman from the UAE as his second wife in turn.[563] By doing so, the normative expectations that derive from family relationships in the Pashtun

[560] See Brown and Rassler (2013), 61–3. Jalāl al-Dīn's statement, which preceded the more renowned declaration of ʿAbdallāh ʿAzzām by about four years, was made during an interview with the Abu Dhabi-based newspaper *al-Ittiḥād* on 11 June 1980. The original text could unfortunately not be located; the passage in ibid., 62, is cited from a translation provided by the Foreign Broadcast Information Service (FBIS) of the CIA. A Pashto translation by Jamīl al-Raḥmān "Sāʾil" was published in *Manbaʿ al-Jihād* [P] 3/2–3 (1370sh/1411h), 29–40.

[561] See Section 4.5.3.

[562] This also applied to Usāma ibn Lādin, who had already been provided with a base near Žavarah in early 1985, which the infamous Saudi had developed further into his *Maʾsadat al-Anṣār*, see, for example, al-Lūjarī (n.d. [c. 2003]), 87–98; Faraj (1422/2002), 25f.

[563] See Anon., 'Thulla min al-ākhirīn: ʿAbd al-Raḥmān al-Miṣrī (al-rukn alladhī thawá)', *al-Jihād* (1408/1988), 35f., here 36. On Jalāl al-Dīn's marriage no further details could be

Borderland were added to strengthen those transcultural military, and soon also ideological, alliances of exceptional importance.

Yet, however intimate the relationships with the Arab *francs-tireurs* became, they were still regarded as guests in Afghanistan, and were as such expected to fully respect the cultural particularities of their hosts, even if they clashed with norms and values utterly dear to the volunteers. To make sure that this remained the case even after the Arab contingent in the Pashtun Borderland had grown substantially in number and begun to act increasingly self-confidently and independently, Jalāl al-Dīn and his lieutenants banked heavily on a continuously strong Deobandi environment at their cadre-training facility at Mīrāmshā. This is most probably the constellation in which Shīr ʿAlī Shāh arrived at the *Manbaʿ al-ʿUlūm* for a teaching stint of two years, and it was during that time that he wrote for the first time explicitly about the ṬIT as a distinct Islamic movement,[564] something that we will have to investigate in some more detail towards the end of our journey.[565]

Properly situating the MʿUJM religiously, however, is perhaps best done by looking more closely at the content of the issues of its periodicals available from 1989, 1990 and 1992, respectively. The fact that the employment of these propaganda tools began comparatively late sets the MʿUJM somewhat apart from the various Islamist organizations under the umbrella of the IIMA that started publishing their periodicals almost instantly upon the beginning of the armed resistance to the Soviet occupation. Even when *Manbaʿ al-Jihād* finally began to be published, its content throughout the early 1990s hardly matched the more conceptual discussions in the periodicals of the JIA, IIAA and ḤiI-Ḥ.[566]

This is not to say that pieces on conceptual matters were entirely absent. We have frequently encountered translations from Islamist classics of Sayyid Quṭb and others in the periodicals of the aforesaid Islamist organizations; however, the respective articles in *Manbaʿ al-Jihād* were almost exclusively written by members of the faculty of the *Manbaʿ al-ʿUlūm*.[567] Most of them are concerned with the legal justification of the ongoing *jihād* after the Soviet withdrawal,[568]

found, other than that this second wife gave birth to three of his nine sons, including the later IEA commander Naṣīr al-Dīn (killed 1435/2013).

564 See Shīr ʿAlī Shāh al-Madanī, 'Taḥrīk-i islāmī-yi "Ṭālibān"-i Afghānistān kā ajmālī taʿāruf', *al-Ḥaqq* 31/14 (1417/1996), 17–21 and 28.

565 See Section 4.5.

566 Compare the respective discussions in Section 4.2.1.

567 The major exception is the serialized Pashto translation of *Qādāt al-Gharb Yaqulūn: Dammirū al-Islām Ubīdū ʾAhlah* (1974, expanded 1978) by the Syrian writer ʿAbd al-Wadūd Yūsuf al-Dimashqī (d. 1403/1983), pen name "Jalāl al-ʿĀlam", by Sulṭān Maḥmūd "Ṣalāḥ" as 'Də islām pah aṛah də ṣalībiyānō aw yahūdiyānō naẓariyyatī' between issues 2/12 (1370/1411) and 3/7 (1370/1412). This text is further discussed in Section 4.5.5.

568 See, for example, Mawlavī Bashīr, 'Də Ḥaẓrat payghambar jihādī risālat', *Manbaʿ al-Jihād* [P] 1/3 (1368sh/1410h), 11–16; Mawlavī Ghulām Ḥaqqānī, 'Də Jihād də faẓāyīl',

and similarly the need to maintain unity within the Muslim *umma* in the light of what Niẓām al-Dīn Ḥaqqānī, a fellow tribesman of Jalāl al-Dīn and his deputy commanders of the Žavarah base,[569] called the "forces of unbelief" (*kufrī ṭāqatūnah*).[570] The sources of inspiration for the authors are important: while the normative example of the Prophet Muḥammad dominates, homage is paid to the founding fathers of the Hanafi orientation in *fiqh*[571] and, last but not least, to Shāh Ismāʿīl Dihlavī.[572] This, finally, points to the most important feature of the Pashto journal regarding situating Jalāl al-Dīn Ḥaqqānī and his local compatriots religiously: the editors of *Manbaʿ al-Jihād* employed strongly traditional forms of conveying cultural norms and values for the religious and, moreover, moral education of its readership across Pashtun communities, here, first and foremost, didactic and devotional poems (*shiʿrūnah*), short stories (*landē kīssē*) and folk literature (*vuləsī adabiyāt*). These literary forms appear markedly less in the Urdu journal *Nuṣrat al-Jihād*,[573] but are entirely absent in the Arabic *Manbaʿ al-Jihād*. Yet, instead, the Urdu journal carries pieces that, because of the vocabulary employed, may appeal strongly to readers with Islamist inclinations,[574] in addition to regular ones on the Kashmir conflict and other international

Manbaʿ al-Jihād [P] 1/3 (1368sh/1410h), 53–6; Mawlavī Muḥammad Shāhān, 'Qitāl fī sabīl allāh', *Manbaʿ al-Jihād* [P] 1/6–7 (1368sh/1410h), 32f.; Naẓar Aḥmad, 'Də Jihād də ādāb aw faẓāyil', *Manbaʿ al-Jihād* [P] 1/8–9 (1368sh/1410h), 13–15; Mawlavī ʿAzīz Khān, 'Jihād tah ẓarūrat aw də qurʾān, aḥādīṣō aw ʿulamāʾō də naẓariyātō pah ṛnā kē də haghah ahmiyyat', *Manbaʿ al-Jihād* [P] 1/8–9 (1368sh/1410h), 56–8.

569 At the time of writing, no further biographical information on Niẓām al-Dīn Ḥaqqānī was available but that he is, or was, the brother of Ḥabīb al-Raḥmān ibn Mawlavī ʿAbd al-Raḥīm, a.k.a. Fatḥallāh Ḥaqqānī (killed 1405/1985), of the Źadrāṇ tribe and had, alongside his brother, enrolled at the *Dār al-ʿUlūm-i Ḥaqqāniyyah* at Akōṛah Khaṫṫak in 1959/60, see Anon., 'Də shahīd Mawlavī Fatḥallāh "Ḥaqqānī" landạh pīžandənah', *Manbaʿ al-Jihād* [P] 1/2–3 (1368sh/1410h), 60f., here 60. A claimed affiliation to the ḤiI-Kh (see Haroon [2007], 206), however, appears rather unsustainable.

570 See Mawlavī Niẓām al-Dīn Ḥaqqānī, 'Mujāhidīn bāyad də kufrī ṭāqatūnō pah vṛandē mutaḥid aw piyāvəṛē də rīź ghvərah kaṛī', *Manbaʿ al-Jihād* [P] 2/8 (1368sh/1411), 35–40.

571 See Mawlavī ʿAbd al-Majīd, 'Də Imām Abū Ḥanīfah (rḥ) žvand tah yaw katənah', *Manbaʿ al-Jihād* [P] 3/8 (1370/1412), 10–12; Muḥammad Surūr Ṣiddīq Mal, 'Də Ḥaẓrat Imām Abū Yūsuf də fiqāhat darjah', *Manbaʿ al-Jihād* [P] 3/8 (1370/1412), 13–15.

572 See [Shuhrat] Nangiyāl, 'Ismāʿīl Shahīd shō: khō, də vīnō ḋevay bah yay də jihād sangarūnah taw dah aw də muqāvimat lār rōx̌ānah sātay', *Manbaʿ al-Jihād* [P] 2/2 (1369/1411), 72–5.

573 A third of the available issues of *Nuṣrat al-Jihād* contain short stories (*afsānē*), half of them translated from the original Pashto.

574 See, for example, Mawlavī Zāhidī Aḥmadzay, 'Islāmī tahẕīb awr islāmī taṣawvur-i zindigī kī khuṣūmiyāt', *Nuṣrat al-Jihād* 1/5 (1411/1991), 53–5; Sayyid ʿAbdallāh, 'Mukammal islāmī ḥukūmat kē qiyām awr jihādī quvvatōṇ kō iqtidār kī muntaqilī tak hamārī jadd va juhd jārī rahēgī', *Nuṣrat al-Jihād* 2/3–4 (1412/1992), 45–7; Miyān Gul, 'ʿĀlam-i islām kī baqāʾ kē liʾē jihād ēk ahm ẓarūrat hē', *Nuṣrat al-Jihād* 2/3–4 (1412/1992), 56–8.

incidents of perceived oppression of Muslim communities.[575] The ability to address different audiences in ways sensitive to their respective expectations and preferred semantics in order to ensure the widest possible support for one's own ends is, in fact, a common feature of borderland pragmatism. Liminal actor that Jalāl al-Dīn was, he had been fully aware of the fact that the M'UJM had also been joined by substantial numbers of ḤM cadres; these were, of course, more strongly invested in the Kashmir issue than a predominantly locally operating militia in Afghanistan would be.[576]

In view of the whole complex constellation, we must ask how much Islamism generally and especially Islamism of its militant variety, and, inseparably with it, a global frame of reference, was actually present in the thinking of Jalāl al-Dīn, and how much his focus also remained firmly and ideologically within the long-established and commonly recognized traditions of religious interpretation, primary among them the colourful range of "Frontier Deobandiyyat". It is true that, to his negotiation partners in the UAE, the agenda of the M'UJM was expressly advertised as 'our war is not a national or tribal war, but a *jihād* in the path of God Most Exalted'.[577] Yet, at a time when "jihād" was widely understood as a generally global affair in Arab Muslim circles, and, although Jalāl al-Dīn's interlocutors from that part of the world may, therefore, have seen a potential for the expansion of that effort beyond the limits of Afghanistan, the vision of the warrior-scholar and those in his wake remained very much confined to the Pashtun Borderland and its tribally informed culture, even aesthetically expressed in the architecture of the *Manba' al-'Ulūm* in Mīrāmshā[578] and the flag of the first fourteen issues of the Pashto journal *Manba' al-Jihād*.

It is, thus, very likely that the stimulus for Jalāl al-Dīn's increasingly positive attitude towards Islamist actors and their respective agendas came from a different direction, namely, from Yūnus Khāliṣ and Muḥammad Nabī Muḥammadī, the leaders of two of the Peshawar-based armed resistance organizations under the eventual umbrella of the IIMA, who, both regarding their biographies and in terms of their ideology, were, nonetheless, liminal

575 See, for example, Matī'allāh "'Ābid", 'Kashmīr bulātā hē', *Nuṣrat al-Jihād* 1/2 (1411/1990), 26–8; Sayyid 'Abdallāh, 'Bābarī Masjid kī āṛ mēṇ kā musalmanōṇ kā qatl-i 'āmm karnēvālē hindū!', *Nuṣrat al-Jihād* 1/3 (1411/1990), 37f. and 40; Sajjād Gul, 'Khalīj mēṇ hawlnāk jang: tāzah'tarīn ḥalāt', *Nuṣrat al-Jihād* 1/4 (1411/1991), 17f. and 35; Anon., 'Arākān (Birmā) kī islāmī taḥrīk', *Nuṣrat al-Jihād* 1/5 (1411/1991), 33; Abū Rayḥān Ṣiddīqī, 'Bhārat kī bhalā'ī kashmīriyōṇ kō ḥaqq khūd-irādiyyat dēnē mēṇ hē', *Nuṣrat al-Jihād* 1/8 (1411/1991), 30f.

576 See Jamal (2009), 169; Hartung (2013a), 245–8.

577 Jamīl al-Raḥmān "Sā'il" (trans.), 'Zmūǵ jang qawmī aw qabīlī jang nah day, balkih də khudāy (j[alla jalālah]) pah lār kē jihād day', *Manba' al-Jihād* [P] 3/2–3 (1370sh/1411h), 29–40, here 29.

578 See the image on the title-page of *Manba' al-Jihād* [P] 1/1 (1368sh/1409h), and the images in *Manba' al-Jihād* [A] 1/1 (1410/1990), 6–10, one of which has also been reproduced in Brown and Rassler (2013), Figure 8.

actors just like Jalāl al-Dīn Ḥaqqānī himself. Even though they were fringe players in relation to the universe of "Militant Frontier Deobandiyyat" to various degrees, it is argued here that, despite their differences, both of these personalities still represented quite the same ethos as those subsumed under that label, which is why this seems the most appropriate place to look at them more closely.

4.3.4 The Ḥizb-i Islāmī *of Yūnus Khāliṣ and the* Ḥarakat-i Inqilāb-i Islāmī *of Nabī Muḥammadī*

Khāliṣ, a proper liminal actor of the Pashtun Borderland, actually defies categorization as "Deobandi" in the same way as that in which he eluded clear classification as "Islamist", a characteristic he shared with someone like Niẓām al-Dīn Shāmzay. Yet, it will be argued here that his attachment to the traditional norms and values of rural Pashtun society, as is reflected more by "Frontier Deobandiyyat" than by Islamism, was the more dominant persuasion in him. The same, in fact, applies to Muḥammad Nabī Muḥammadī. In comparison with their Islamist allies-cum-competitors Rabbānī, Sayyāf and Ḥikmatyār, as well as with Jalāl al-Dīn Ḥaqqānī and those in his circle, however, both Khāliṣ and Nabī Muḥammadī appear much more elusive, a feature which, in fact, they shared somewhat with Mullā Muḥammad ʿUmar and others within the later ṬIT / IEA high command of the first generation.

Nabī Muḥammadī especially, who is said to have been closest to the religiously driven political activism of the ṬIT, continues to evade successfully the grasp of anyone wishing for a better understanding of his personality and the ḤII, the militant organization he was responsible for. In contrast even to the versatile Yūnus Khāliṣ, Nabī Muḥammadī moved neither in the early Islamist circles of Kabul and Jalalabad, nor in the large and prominent institutions of "Frontier Deobandiyyat" to the east of the Durand Line. Neither did he work in various media, as Khāliṣ has done, nor had he produced any writing of lasting prominence. Instead, he moved almost exclusively in the local religious networks of the Pashtun-dominated provinces around Kabul, that is, his native Logar, Wardak and Laghmān.[579] Born in 1921 into a family of local religious dignitaries in the village of ʿAbbās Kalā of the Barakī Barak district of Logar Province, Nabī Muḥammadī left his tutelage at home only at the age of fourteen and spent the next decade in ten different *dīnī madāris* in the three provinces named. He eventually graduated in October 1946, and the ceremonial turban (*dastar*) was bestowed on him by the regionally eminent *shaykh al-ḥadīs̱* Mawlavī Dād Muḥammad of the Mughal Khēl (d. 1370/1950).[580] This

[579] See Ḥikmat (2015).

[580] See ibid. (based on Nabī Muḥammadī's own notes as received from his family by ʿAbd al-Raʾūf Ḥikmat). On Mawlavī Dād Muḥammad, see Rashīdī (1387sh/2003), 93–8. The

coincided with the death of his father, and Nabī Muḥammadī spent the following few years teaching at his father's *madrasah* in ʿAbbās Kalā. In 1950, however, for unknown reasons, he left home again and travelled the north of Afghanistan preaching and teaching, returning to ʿAbbās Kalā, via Mecca, four years later. From the late 1950s, news of increasing communist activities in Afghanistan also began to arrive there, accompanied by the rumours of atheist and anti-Islamic propaganda spread through them. This marks the beginning of Nabī Muḥammadī's political involvement: having moved his household to the northern Sar-i Pul Province, he now emerged as an ever more vocal admonisher of the anti-religious communist "infestation", a fact that was duly registered in the long memory of the local communists.

However, he made a lasting impression among the religious representatives across Logar Province, to which Nabī Muḥammadī had returned in 1968, as a fierce anti-communist agitator, and was subsequently persuaded to stand for elections to the thirteenth national *Vuləsī Jirgah*, the lower house of the PNA. He was elected as the representative for Logar in September 1969 and, over the following four years, crossed swords with the likes of later president-at-the-behest-of-Moscow Babrak Kārmal.[581] Consequently, he evolved into a target high on the PDPA's list of wanted men right after the "S̱awr Revolution" and slipped, like other later leaders of the Islamic resistance to PDPA rule, away to Pakistan, where he joined their ranks and soon served as a convenient compromise for the leadership of the conflicting Islamist organizations.

This, in fact, also marks the beginning of the ḤII: not as Nabī Muḥammadī's own distinct organization, but initially as a reflection of a settlement between all the groups involved.[582] This agreement, however, became void almost instantly, and the well-intended enterprise dissolved into the seven dominant factions that, from late 1981 onwards, made up the IIMA. The ḤII was now

relevant academic literature is full of myths regarding the educational background of Nabī Muḥammadī: while, for example, Wieland-Karimi (1998), 179, speaks of one *madrasah* only, the uncorroborated statement of Brown and Rassler (2013), 41 and 51, that Nabī Muḥammadī had – similarly to Khāliṣ – been a *Ḥaqqāniyyah* graduate (something that, as we have seen above, does not even fully apply to Khāliṣ), is probably based on the uncorroborated claim of Rashid (2010), 84 and 90.

581 See Edwards (2002), 244f.; Rashīdī (1387sh/2003), 265–9; Ḥikmat (2015). Whether the fact of Nabī Muḥammadī's term in the national *Vuləsī Jirgah* warrants the claim that he had 'close contacts to the central elite prior to 1973' (Wieland-Karimi [1998], 179 [translation mine]), remains still to be supported by solid primary evidence. Even Ruttig (2009), 80, erroneously states that Nabī Muḥammadī represented the Mārjah sub-district of Hilmand Province in the *Vuləsī Jirgah*, while he had actually moved to Hilmand only after Muḥammad Dāvūd Khān's coup d'état in 1973, that is, after the dissolution of the National Assembly, to become the *imām* of the Sulaymān Khēl Mosque in Zarghūn Kalay, Nād ʿAlī District, Hilmand Province: see Rashīdī (1387sh/2003), 270; Ḥikmat (2015).

582 See Ḥikmat (2015).

only one of them, and appeared to be internally closest to the MMIA of Aḥmad Gīlānī and to Ṣibghatallāh Mujaddidī's JNM.

Each of these three personalities represented, quite distinctly from the leaders of the Islamist organizations and even more than Yūnus Khāliṣ, a traditional conservative Afghan Islam which derived its authority from erudition in the religious disciplines and spiritual genealogies that have already surfaced time and again in our present narrative. While Gīlānī and Mujaddidī represented the genealogical aspect, Nabī Muḥammadī epitomized the aspect of profound scholarship. It was, in fact, his teaching sojourns in the northern provinces of Faryāb, Balkh, Sar-i Pul and Juzjān that led to his transregional eminence, bolstered by the acknowledgement of his anti-communist activities during his term at the *Vuləsī Jirgah*. The political activism sustained by religious precepts of all three appears, therefore, almost like a recourse to the legacy of Muḥammad ʿAṭāʾallāh Fayẕānī and his *Madrasah-yi Tawḥīd*.[583]

It was no surprise, therefore, that the bilingual ḤII journal *Khuddām al-Furqān*, published in Peshawar, and a monthly paper of the same title coming out of Tehran carried the name of a religio-political party of the mid 1960s and early 1970s, whose origins are alternatively attributed to Fayẕānī and "Ẕiyāʾ al-Mashāʾikh" Muḥammad Ibrāhīm Mujaddidī (executed 1399/1979), the then-Ḥaẕrat of the Shōr Bāzār of Kabul and Ṣibghatallāh's uncle.[584] The paper from Tehran especially appears to have carried frequent and reverential information on the "Ḥaẕarāt-i Shōr Bāzār", which somewhat fortifies the impression of a certain affinity between the ḤII and the JNM.[585] The creed of the journal, and presumably everything affiliated to it, consists of the first half of Q25.1: 'Blessed is He who sent down the mark of distinction [*al-furqāna*] upon his servant' and a modification of the sound Prophetic *ḥadīth* 'I fear what I fear for my *umma*: a hypocrite with knowledge on the tongue [*munāfiqin ʿalīmi ʾl-lisān*].'[586] Moreover, a single available copy of an English version of the journal from Peshawar carries an interesting alternative mission statement, which combines Sufi-inspired piety with a strong emphasis on the precedent established by

583 On Fayẕānī, see Section 4.2.1.

584 See Olesen (1995), 230.

585 See, for example, Anon., 'Sih va chahārumīn sālgar dar riḥlat-i ḥujjat allāh al-shāmikh Ḥaẕrat Faẕl-i ʿUmar Nūr al-Mashāʾikh – rḥ – az bunyād'guẕārān-i nahẕat-i jahānī-yi islām', *Khuddām al-Furqān* 1/6–7 (1369sh/1411h), 2 and 5, and 1/8 (1370sh/1411h), 8; Anon., 'Khuddām al-Furqān aw də Mujaddidī kōranī', *Khuddām al-Furqān* 2/3 (1370sh), 51–6 and 2/4 (1370sh), 43–5; ʿAbd al-Bārī "Ghayrat", 'Də Afghānistān nāmtū ʿulamāʾ: janāb Nūr al-Mashāʾikh Faẕl-i ʿUmar Mujaddidī', *Khuddām al-Furqān* 2/8 (1370sh), 29–34. The rather careful wording here has been chosen deliberately because the very limited selection of copies of *Khuddām al-Furqān* currently at one's disposal does not allow one to make more definitive statements.

586 Both creeds are printed on the flag of the *Khuddām al-Furqān* publication from Tehran. The *ḥadīth*, narrated on the authority of ʿUmar ibn al-Khaṭṭāb, is preserved in Ibn Ḥanbal (1416/1995), I: 296 (no. 310).

the Prophet and his Companions, spiced with militant rhetoric about *jihād* as its sole path and the longing for martyrdom therein.[587]

It needs to be acknowledged, however, that *Khuddām al-Furqān* began its run only towards the end of the resistance against the PDPA–Soviet nexus, and represented not Nabī Muḥammadī, but rather a split-off faction led by Naṣrallāh Manṣūr ibn al-Ḥājj Ghulām Muḥammad Khān (killed 1413/1993). Naṣrallāh, a native of Zurmat in Paktia Province, was, in contrast to Nabī Muḥammadī, firmly attached to the Mujaddidī family. He had received his education at the *Nūr al-Madāris* in the Andaṛ district of Ghazni Province, the large *madrasah* established in the later 1920s by the later Ḥaẓrat of Kabul's Shōr Bāzār, "Ẕiyā' al-Mashā'ikh" Muḥammad Ibrāhīm, of whom Naṣrallāh Manṣūr is also very likely to have become a personal disciple (*murīd*).[588] Little else is known about his earlier life, prior to his migration to Peshawar via Jalāl al-Dīn Ḥaqqānī's base at Mīrāmshā in North Waziristan, and his joining the resistance. In 1982, apparently the ḤII split up into several factions, the most successful and durable one led by Naṣrallāh Manṣūr (ḤII[N]), and this despite being cut off from the cash flow to the Islamist organizations under the umbrella of the IIMA controlled by the Pakistani ISI.[589]

Ruttig, to whom we owe the currently most detailed exposition on the ḤII [N], characterizes it as 'the one *tanzim* [i.e., organization] [...] closest to the radical, anti-Shiite Deobandi doctrine of Sunni Islam'.[590] He even remarks on a strong opposition to Mujaddidī's JNA and Gīlānī's MMIA.[591] Apparently, neither statement seems to be entirely correct: the fact that one version of *Khuddām al-Furqān* was published from Tehran, as well as the frequent reverential references to the Mujaddidī family in it, indicate that the reality might have been somewhat more complex. It is entirely plausible, however, despite the imaginary of at least national import radiated from its publications, that the scope of the ḤII[N] was indeed regionally confined to Lōyah Paktia, if not even more so to Zurmat and its immediate environs in the south of Paktia

587 See Anon., 'Our Slogan', *Khuddam-ul-Furqan* 1/2 (1989), endpaper.

588 See "Rayān", 'Pah Ghaznī kī də jihād pah haklah (ćalōrəmah barkhah)', *Khuddām al-Furqān* 2/8 (1370sh), 16–18, esp. 16. Brown and Rassler (2013), 112f., make the uncorroborated claim that Naṣrallāh Manṣūr had been a graduate of the *Dār al-'Ulūm-i Ḥaqqāniyyah*. Moreover, none of the materials consulted for the present study contains any information in its support.

589 A detailed account of the strategic power games played by the leaders of the various resistance parties in Peshawar, including particulars about Sayyāf and Ḥikmatyār instigating the breakaway of Naṣrallāh Manṣūr from Nabī Muḥammadī's ḤII, is provided by Edwards (2002), 225–78, esp. 268. Although unquestionably valuable, these details are entirely based on interviews with the various high-end players in these power games themselves, without sufficient reflection about the possible strategic value that these statements may carry for each of the interviewees themselves.

590 Ruttig (2009), 80.

591 See ibid.

Province, where Naṣrallāh Manṣūr could effectively bank on strong tribal bonds as the basis of loyalty in his organization. The *Khuddām al-Furqān* badge, which Naṣrallāh, in contrast to Nabī Muḥammadī, employed widely and deliberately, served as another integrative element, sometimes at odds with the pragmatics of day-to-day power games in a perpetual war zone. One of those whom Ruttig states had associated themselves with this badge was a certain Vakīl Aḥmad ibn ʿAbd al-Ghaffār "Mutavakkil" from Mōrchah in the Mayvand District of Kandahar Province (b. c. 1391/1971), who eventually became the Minister of Foreign Affairs of the first central government of the IEA, a member of the Central *shūrá* and a personal advisor to Mullā Muḥammad ʿUmar.[592]

The obvious affinity to the Mujaddidī family, however, was certainly no bar to embracing classical Islamist thought, too,[593] and, by doing so, the leadership of the ḤII[N] also espoused the more transnational perspective on the "global Islamic *umma*"[594] – something that seems largely absent from whatever few statements of Nabī Muḥammadī we possess. Instead, his own influence over those who would eventually group together as ṬIT is less driven by distinct ideological proclivities, but stems more from his five years in charge of the Sulṭān Khēl Mosque in Zarghūn Kalay, Hilmand Province, while having been allotted some land in nearby Mārjah in the course of the application of state policies to ultimately settle the region defined as "Hilmand Province" as recently as 1963.[595] The implications of Nabī Muḥammadī's move need to be fully savoured: the region had been the centre stage for one of the most severe and long-standing tribal conflicts in the lowlands of the Pashtun Borderland – somewhat mirroring

592 See Ruttig (2009), 81. In his brief autobiographical account, however, Mutavakkil himself does not refer to the *Khuddām al-Furqān* at all, although he indicates that the ḤII was indeed one of the main umbrellas under which the later ṬIT assembled, see "Mutavakkil" (1384sh), 14.

593 Prominently, see Abū ʾl-Aʿlá Mawdūdī (trans. Anon.), 'Taʿlīm-i iqtiṣādī va siyāsī-yi Qurʾān', *Khuddām al-Furqān* 2/3 (1370sh), 14–17, 2/4 (1370sh), 8–11 and 2/5 (1370sh), 23–8; Abū ʾl-Aʿlá Mawdūdī (trans. ʿAbd al-Qayyūm), 'Dīmūkrāsī, sūsiyāliszm aw islāmī niẓām', *Khuddām al-Furqān* 2/8 (1370sh), 54f.

594 Programmatically, see Naṣrallāh Manṣūr, 'Də Khuddām al-Furqān də taʾsīs də pinźah vīshtamī kalīzī pah munāsibat də Ḥarakat Inqilāb Islāmī də amīr mukhtaram Mawlavī Naṣrallāh (Manṣūr) də payghām ćakhah yaw ćō muhimm ṫəkī: Khuddām al-Furqān s̱ābitah kṛah chī islāmī ummat yaw ummat dəy aw hīć ḋōl tabʿīẕ pah kay nishtah', *Khuddām al-Furqān* 2/5 (1370h), 4. See also Raḥmatallāh Raḥmat, 'ʿIrāq aw də Baʿs̱ gūnd', *Khuddām al-Furqān* 2/6 (1370h), 63–6; Muḥammad Fārūq "Jalālzay", 'al-Jazāʾir aw də islāmī žghōrənī ghūrzang', *Khuddām al-Furqān* 2/7 (1370h), 14f.; Muḥammad Fārūq "Jalālzay", 'Kashmīr yā də ʿālam islām nah jabīrah kīdūnkī zakhm', *Khuddām al-Furqān* 2/8 (1370h), 22f.

595 See Ḥikmat (2015). On the administrative measures enforced in the territories to the east and west of the Hilmand River, starting in late 1945, but receiving a major push under Dāvūd Khān: see Dupree (1973), 482–5 and 499–507; Scott (1980).

the rivalry between Yusufzay and Khattak in the uplands – dating back at least to early Barakzay rule.

The Barakzay tribal community (*qawm*) had been granted the central part of the later Hilmand Province, then known as Pusht-i Rūd, by Nādir Shāh Afshār as a reward for their participation in Nādir's overall rather disastrous Daghestan campaigns (1735–43), while the even more fertile northern part, Zamīndavār, was given to the ʿAlīzay.[596] Once Aḥmad Shāh had taken the throne in Kandahar, Ḥājjī Jamāl Khān, the then-leader of the Barakzay, allegedly persuaded the new ruler to always have a Barakzay as his prime minister,[597] thus gaining an advantage over the competing ʿAlīzay that would eventually help to facilitate the eventual takeover of power by Dūst Muḥammad Khān Bārakzay in 1823.

All three tribal communities – the Abdālī-Pōpalzay, ʿAlīzay and Barakzay – trace their origins back to a common ancestor, which probably explains the strong rivalries between them in their shared ancestral homeland.[598] As soon as Dūst Muḥammad Khān Bārakzay established the rule of his tribal community on the debris of the Durrani empire, the ʿAlīzay of Zamīndavār were heavily taxed and their payment enforced by severe punitive measures, leading the latter to stage a series of desperate uprisings between 1840 and 1938, accompanied by a massive rural exodus.[599] As a result of the violent subjugation of the local communities by the various Kabul-based Barakzay rulers,[600] the central government and its politics lost entirely whatever little credibility they had possessed to begin with, while alternative forms of community administration and economic pursuit emerged and prevailed instead.[601]

596 See Ḥayāt Khān (1867), 127f. See also Noelle (1997), 232f. For Nādir's final campaign in Daghestan in 1741–3, before he finally gave up on it, see Astarābādī (1875), 265–94.

597 This, without the provision of a solid historical text reference, was claimed by British colonial administrator Caroe (1958), 255.

598 The common progenitor of all three communities was ʿĪsá, the son of Zakhtar, son of Abdāl, son of Tarīn, son of Sharkhabūn, son of Saṛban, son of the Prophet's companion Qays "ʿAbd al-Rashīd" (d. c. 41/663) who, according to the dominant southern narrative, had been the progenitor of the ethnic Pashtuns: see Ḥayāt Khān (1867), 111–18 and 121–33.

599 See Kātib-i Hazārah (1331sh), II: 328 and III: 472f.; Tapper (1973); Scott (1980), 19; Noelle (1997), 238–40 and 295–7.

600 The policies of British-subsidized Amīr ʿAbd al-Raḥmān towards the concentration of the state administration in Kabul, the chosen capital of the Durrani rulers since 1776, which resulted in severe consequences for the role of Kandahar and the wider Hilmand–Arghandāb basin as a long-established major hub of transregional commercial activities are extremely important in this regard: see Hanifi (2011), 6–13, 18f., 23–9 and 147–52.

601 The large-scale cultivation of poppies for the production of raw opium is perhaps the most significant of these alternative economies, trade in which allowed the communities in the region to retain a substantial degree of autonomy from the various central governments, including the current one: see Pain (2006); Mansfield (2017), esp. 26–32. Ironically, however, and counter to its public self-portrayal (see, e.g., Amīr al-Muminīn Mullā

These processes of deterioration were slowed down only by a succession of government development programmes, including the "domestication" of nomadic communities and the resettlement on and recultivation of abandoned land, from which ultimately Nabī Muḥammadī also benefited.[602] Still, the top-down administrative measures continued to cater for inequalities – often along tribal lines – regarding access to all sorts of commodities. As it turned out, the government programmes advantaged almost exclusively the central areas of Hilmand, those within immediate reach of the Hilmand River, but grossly neglected the communities elsewhere in the province. The ʿAlīzay, who lost their landed property by virtue of their exodus from Zamīndavār in the nineteenth century, turned out to be among the biggest losers, alienating them even further from the other tribal groups in that region.

To what extent Nabī Muḥammadī was able to consolidate grievances of such dimensions while based in Hilmand is difficult to establish. Yet, his voluntary entrenchment into this rather particular setting indicates that, in contrast to most leaders of the Islamist organizations under the umbrella of the IIMA, Nabī Muḥammadī was – at least in general terms – somewhat sensitive to subaltern concerns within a rural and tribal setting, and to the ways in which tribal mechanisms function outside the grasp of central governments. The failed attempt of some communists from his former home of Barakī Barak in Logar to bring about his prosecution[603] served especially the subaltern public as proof and, consequently, enhanced his status among a growing number of students and retainers from Hilmand and the adjacent Kandahar Province.

Moreover, his credibility was underlined by the fact that he seemed unwilling to give in to the political manoeuvring of the leaders of the Islamist organizations and their attempts to pull him to their respective side, as well as his firm rejection of any position in Rabbānī's government in 1992.[604] Nabī Muḥammadī's ḤII could well be turned into an important asset, especially in the light of the very negative reputation the various Islamist militias and their

Muḥammad ʿUmar [Mujāhid], 'Farmān-i maqām-i Imārat-i islāmī-yi Afghānistān dar bārah-yi maḥw-yi chars va kār'khānah'hā-yi chars [6 Jumādá I 1422h]', *Də Afghānistān Islāmī Imārat Rasmī Jarīdah* 799/2 [1422h]), the cultivation and trade of narcotics continued well under the first central government of the IEA: see Kursawe (2011). The discrepancy between religious–political rhetoric and actual reality has led sensation-seeking journalists and policy advisors in their wake to perpetually point this out, to the extent even of claiming that the production and trade of narcotics had evolved into a major pillar of the IEA's national economy: prominently, see Peters (2009); Rashid (2010), 117–24. For a fervent defence of the IEA's policies on narcotics, see Ḥāmid (2007), 103–20.

602 See Scott (1980), 8f.

603 See Ḥikmat (2015).

604 See ibid.; Edwards (2002), 246f. Also, see his own warning of the temptation to abuse power once the *mujāhidīn* were in charge in Kabul, delivered already on 24 April 1989, that is, three days before the so-called "Peshawar Peace Accord": Muḥammadī (1368sh), 12.

commanders had gained, particularly among the subaltern strata of Afghan society during the Civil War, which had started at almost the same moment as the *mujāhidīn* took over the government in Kabul. It might, thus, well be that he saw in the growth of the ṬIT a remedy to the egocentricity especially of the leaders of JIA, ḤiI, the IIAA or even Dūstam's JMIA, which provided for what Mukhopadhyay calls "strongman governance" and was widely regarded as being responsible for the cynical disregard of the ordinary population in Afghanistan.[605] Nabī Muḥammadī was a traditionally educated *ʿālim*, and would have also seriously objected to the rather contemptuous attitude of especially the ḤiI leadership and, subsequently, their cadres towards the Islamic religiosity of common Afghans,[606] which, after all, is a common trope of Islamist rhetoric everywhere. Lastly, Nabī Muḥammadī had ample opportunity during his time among subaltern communities in southern Afghanistan to confirm the initial suspicion that the leaders of the Islamist militias regarded these lands as not worth fighting over. The ṬIT, which sprang from exactly this environment, must, therefore, have seemed to him a remedy to counteract the destructive prevalence of Islamism in Afghanistan. Still, his view may have been somewhat clouded, allowing him to miss how deeply entrenched the entire religio-political landscape of Afghanistan had become in various types of Islamism during the armed resistance to the PDPA regime and its Soviet ally, how much his own ḤII had actually already been entrenched in Islamist thinking, and how much Islamism was, therefore, in the ṬIT right from the onset.

Be that as it may, in 1994, Nabī Muḥammadī finally declared his ḤII, which had been in control of the northern part of Hilmand, to have dissolved into the ṬIT,[607] a fact that caused its leadership to regard him as one – if not *the* – major inspiration for the religious and political world-view of the movement.[608] The same, apparently, happened with the ḤII[N], run, after the assassination Naṣrallāh Manṣūr on 8 February 1993, by his son Sayf al-Raḥmān (killed 1423/2002) and his brothers, who would eventually become major local IEA field commanders themselves.[609] Throughout the remainder of his life, Nabī Muḥammadī, who had been seriously marginalized in the public eye, kept vocally defending the ṬIT and later the IEA against all odds, especially after the UN-sanctioned military intervention in the late autumn of 2001, which went hand in hand with bringing back into positions of power exactly those Islamist

605 See Mukhopadhyay (2014), esp. 1–75.

606 See Edwards (2002), 249f.

607 See Mustaʿīd (1375sh), 103f.; Rashīdī (1387sh/2003), 297–9.

608 See Anon., 'Pah Qandahār kē də ʿulamāʾō kirāmō tārīkhī ghūndah', *Khilāfat* 1/2–3 (1417/ 1996), 37–50, here 48.

609 See Qārī Ḥabīb (trans. Ḥabībī Samangānī), 'Yād raftagān: nigāhī bah zindigī-yi qahramān-i Shāhīkūt Shahīd Mullā Sayf al-Raḥmān Manṣūr – rḥ', *Ḥaqīqat* 4/6 (1438/ 2017), 38–43; Ruttig (2009), 81.

militia leaders who had been chiefly responsible for the atrocities committed during the first phase of the Afghan Civil War between 1992 and 1996.[610] The fact, however, that the IEA's resistance against the euphemistically named "Operation Enduring Freedom" of the USA-led military coalition and, later on, against the Afghan National Army's presence in the province proved exceptionally stubborn and, moreover, quite effective in Hilmand Province, suggests a continuous legacy in this region of Nabī Muḥammadī's deep suspicion of central administration and the power games played both behind closed doors and, rather frequently, in plain sight.

***

Khāliṣ, on the other hand, had been much more at ease with Islamist ideology proper, and, as such, he represented – similarly to Jalāl al-Dīn Ḥaqqānī – the interface of certain manifestations of "Frontier Deobandiyyat" and Islamism. Yet, differently from the latter, Khāliṣ appears to have also been quite comfortable in the urban context that constituted the backdrop against which the Islamist ideology in its various varieties crystallized. Proof of this substantially different attitude is the expansive literary *œuvre* which Khāliṣ left behind, a collection in Pashto and Arabic which included works of entirely theological and Islamic legal nature, as well as Islamist writings (either by himself or, as we have already seen above, by the classical theorists of this ideological current), political pamphlets, articles and speeches, and his own poetry. Regrettably, only a small selection was available at the time of writing, so that, as in the case of Nabī Muḥammadī, most of that which can be said about him here remains rather tentative.

Among the key religious works which he purportedly authored, mainly before the Soviet invasion, are *Dīnī Malghalərē* (1957), *Islām aw Insānī Tamddun*, *Rūḥ al-Ijtimāʿ*, *ʿAql, Taqlīd aw Dunyavī Gaṭē-Vaṭē* and *Islāmī Rūḥ* (1979).[611] The driver was, similarly to that for Nabī Muḥammadī, a deep disgust for communism and all that it represented in and for Afghanistan. Yet, teaching and preaching in the traditional way was clearly not Khāliṣ's chosen approach: he probably attended ʿAṭāʾallāh Fayẓānī's *Madrasah-yi Tawḥīd* from early on, and seemingly embraced the classic form of Islamist propaganda when starting to seriously engage in media and publishing activities. Initially, the Afghan government under Muḥammad Ẓāhir Shāh still provided quite attractive framework conditions, indicated by Khāliṣ's early employment at Kabul Radio, but even more so when the Afghan Ministry of Information and Culture is said to have commissioned him with the editorship of *Payām-i Ḥaqq*, a state-sponsored bi-monthly journal on Islamic culture

610 See Mustaʿīd (1375sh), 73–6 and 83–9. See also Rashīdī (1387sh/2003), 298–300; Ḥikmat (2015).

611 See Mubāriz (2014).

from an Afghan perspective, founded in 1955.[612] Whether or not he actually held this position,[613] Khāliṣ would continue such journalistic activities with his involvement in *Jāḥiẓ*, perhaps the first proper Islamist magazine published from Jalalabad,[614] and later on with his own journal *al-Nūr*, alongside engaging in translating the works of leading MB cadres in Egypt, prominently Sayyid Quṭb, Muḥammad al-Bahī and ʿAbd al-Qādir ʿAwda, as well as – interestingly – facilitating Shāh Muḥammad Rashād's Persian translation of Ibn Taymiyya's *K. al-Siyāsa al-Sharʿiyya* (1969).

After having joined the armed resistance to the PDPA regime quite early as a partisan of the Ḥil that was officially led by Qāẕī Muḥammad Amīn Vaqād but already dominated by Ḥikmatyār, the direction of Khāliṣ's writings shifted significantly to short-term political issues, all pivoting generally on the theme of *jihād*. Interestingly, however, most of these writings are, unlike those of Rabbānī, Ḥikmatyār or Sayyāf, hard to trace: we mostly have to be content with lists of works provided in secondary literature. The titles suggest that most of them were rather short pieces, probably based on public addresses: *The Islamic Jihad and Its Benefits* (*Islāmī Jihād aw Gaṭah Yē*), *Who Is the True Mujahid, and What Should He Do?* (*Ḥaqīqī Mujāhid Ćōk Day aw Bāyad Ćah Vakəṛī?*) and *The Path of Jihad and Guidelines* (*Jihādī Lār aw Lārx̌ōvunē*) are just three examples.

The rather limited visibility of Khāliṣ among the quite self-confident Islamist leaders of the resistance to the Soviet-backed PDPA regime who had assembled under the umbrella of the IIMA suggests that he carved out a rather distinct position for himself, one, in fact, that aligned him much more with Nabī Muḥammadī than with any of the others. This positioning owed a great deal to his firm adherence to traditional conceptions of religious authority, all of which revolved around seniority and religious knowledge, and which, however, began to undergo an almost paradigmatic shift towards increasingly activity-centred juniority during the resistance against the PDPA–Soviet nexus in Afghanistan.[615] Pursuant of the accepted Prophetic saying "The scholars are

612 See Aḥmadzay (1385sh/1427h), 11–13.

613 While most Pashto literature on Khāliṣ is hagiographical in nature, the exact years of his purported editorship of the journal are difficult to establish. While in the journal itself, of which only a few and moreover non-consecutive issues were available at the time of writing, as late as January 1966, a certain Muḥammad Yūnus "Ḥayrān" is introduced as its new editor-in-chief (see Anon., 'Mukhtaṣar-i savāniḥ-i Muḥammad Yūnus "Ḥayrān" kih akhīran baḥīs̱-i mudīr-i ʿumūmī-yi irshād-i vizārat-i maṭbūʿāt muqarrar shudah and', *Payām-i Ḥaqq* 13/11 [1344sh/1385h/1966], 41), none of the biographical data provided there matches any of Khāliṣ's, and we may, therefore, safely assume that these two men are not identical.

614 See Section 4.2.1. Unfortunately, not a single extant copy of *Jāḥiẓ* could be located.

615 See Hartung (2019a), 321–7. There, the focus is more on later developments in the aftermath of the first IEA central government, but it seems that the erosion of traditional conceptions of religious authority in the Pashtun Borderland had set in much earlier, perhaps indeed already in the late 1970s.

the heirs of the Prophets",[616] leadership, even more so in times as perilous as these, needed to rest solely in the hands of seasoned and well-trained scholars such as Khāliṣ himself, not young and hot-headed laypeople such as Ḥikmatyār with his degree in engineering. Khāliṣ's followers would sustain this claim to leadership even further by additionally quoting from Q8.65: 'Oh Prophet, urge the believers to battle!' (*yā ayyuhā al-nabī ḥarriḍi 'l-mu'minīna 'alá 'l-qitāl*), in conjunction with the *ḥadīth* that Khāliṣ himself had cited.[617]

Finally, however, when the power games at Peshawar pointed towards a different outcome, Khāliṣ split away from the ḤiI and formed his own organization under the very same name, thus suggesting, as in the case of the ḤII and ḤII[N], that his was the only genuine ḤiI, with Ḥikmatyār's Vaqād-fronted one little more than a deviant offshoot.[618] This, in fact, makes the ḤiI-Kh once more as unique as Nabī Muḥammadī's ḤII in the spectrum of the Peshawar-based Afghan Islamic resistance organizations: both parties were led by fully trained scholars, with concerns not only for day-to-day political affairs but also very much for Islamic learning as an important ideational underpinning of the Afghan society to come, once the PDPA government had finally been overthrown.[619]

Nabī Muḥammadī's approach followed to a great extent the traditional course of action of rural religious scholars as community leaders in the Pashtun Borderland: it was almost entirely hands-on and much less concerned with envisioning an Islamic societal utopia, however formulated. Khāliṣ, in turn, appears to have also been keen on establishing a lasting legacy for himself as a transregional community leader, reflected in the fact that he would seek a lasting permanence of his views – vis-à-vis especially those of his competitors from among the various Afghan Islamist leaders – through crafting, publishing and disseminating programmatic writing.

Two pieces of writing appear to stand out regarding his claim to religious authority. The first one is Khāliṣ's Arabic commentary on the *'Aqīda*

616 See *Sunan Abī Dāwūd*, k. al-'ilm, b. al-ḥathth 'alá ṭalabi 'l-'ilm, ḥadīth 1 (no. 3643); *Sunan Ibn Māja*, al-muqaddima, b. faḍl al-'ulamā' wa'l-ḥathth 'alá ṭalabi 'l-'ilm, ḥadīth 4 (no. 228); *al-Jāmi' al-Tirmidhī*, k. al-'ilm, b. mā jā' fī faḍl al-fiqh 'alá 'l-'ibāda, ḥadīth 2 (no. 2898).

617 See Mubāriz (2014). See also Khāliṣ (1393sh), 186f (*Məshər'tōb*), esp. ll. 6 and 11f. (also reproduced in 'Azīzallāh (1386sh), 182). In addition, Edwards (2002), 249, states that, in his two conversations with Khāliṣ on this matter in 1983 and April 1984, the latter would use terms such as "immature" (*khām*) and "schoolboys" (*maktabiyān*) to characterize the leaders of the various other Islamist organizations, above all his closest rival, Gulbuddīn Ḥikmatyār.

618 Judging from the titles, this may be reflected in Khāliṣ's two texts *Ḥikmatyār Ṣēb Ćah Vāyī?* and *Də Islāmī Ḥizb Nəvē Asās'nāmah*. Both texts were, unfortunately, not available at the time of writing.

619 See Edwards (2002), 247–9.

Ṭaḥāwiyya, alongside its Pashto translation, written as a provision for religious instruction in the Afghan refugee camps, especially in the Peshawar Valley, and, therefore, subsequently circulated by a rather obscure organization called *al-Hijrah wa'l-Jihād*.[620] The choice of this text is remarkable, as it appears to hold no special position in the Hanafi-Maturidi orb that informs the theological and legal perspectives of "Deobandiyyat". In fact, the creed by Abū Ḥafṣ ʿUmar al-Nasafī that had been somewhat popularized in the Pashtun Borderland by the annotated Pashto translation of the Ākhūnd Darvīzah in the sixteenth century CE,[621] and its commentary by Saʿd al-Dīn al-Taftāzānī (d. 791/1390), were historically much more common than the one by al-Ṭaḥāwī.[622] The latter's prominence is tied greatly to the commentary of Ibn Abī ʿIzz, who attained his intellectual maturity as a student of Ibn Taymiyya's prominent disciple Ibn Kathīr in Hanbali-dominated Damascus. Therefore, the *ʿAqīda Ṭaḥāwiyya* has assumed a much more prominent position in later Hanbali and, even later still, Salafi circles than among Hanafis.[623]

That someone like Khāliṣ, who had been trained firmly within the Deobandi framework, embarked on providing a commentary on al-Ṭaḥāwī's text of his own is certainly remarkable and requires some explanation. At a time when financial aid from Saudi Arabia for relief and guerrilla warfare was accompanied by subtle and not so subtle attempts to propagate the kingdom's official interpretation of Islam, Khāliṣ may well have attempted to put up a substantial Hanafi counterweight to the encroachment of the alien Hanbali traditionism of Wahhabi provenance. This explanation has even more currency in view of the tightening relationships between Sayyāf and various bodies in Saudi Arabia, alongside the increasingly offensive lashing out at the Hanafi legal tradition constitutive for all forms of "Deobandiyyat" by organizations that grew out of the Salafi universe of Panjpir.[624] Khāliṣ's preoccupation with the *ʿAqīda Ṭaḥāwiyya* outside the interpretative tradition based on Ibn Abī ʿIzz may, therefore, have served as his mission statement, and his ḤiI-Kh was directed against anyone who dared to challenge the traditional dominance of the Hanafi-Maturidi interpretation of Islam in the Pashtun Borderland.

The second text in question, the rather voluminous *Islāmī Rūḥ*, written at the crucial moment when religious propaganda against communism and its implications in general, as carried by Fayẕānī's *Madrasah-yi Tawḥīd* and the SJM, gave way to the religious legitimization of the armed resistance to the PDPA regime and its Soviet ally, however, appears to be of special significance for the internal ideological orientation of the ḤiI-Kh. Moreover, this appears

620 See Mubāriz (2014).

621 See Section 3.1.3.

622 See, for example, Bruckmayr (2009), 72f.

623 See Shiliwala (2018), 472–94. See also Bruckmayr (2020), 313–15.

624 See Section 4.3.4.

to be the only one of Khāliṣ's writings of which portions were still being republished in the Ḥil-Kh journal *Tōrah Bōṛah* almost a decade after his death and always in conjunction with an actual matter at hand.[625]

What, at first glance, seems to be little more than an exposition on the Islamic ritual obligations (*ʿibādāt*) and their underlying spiritual meaning, however, quickly emerges as an attempt to justify *jihād* as a supreme duty to God. According to Khāliṣ, *jihād* takes five different forms, all of which he derived from Q9.122: 'It is not for the believers to go forth [to battle] all together: so why does not a section of each tribe [*firqatin minhum ṭāʾifatun*] go forth and obtain an understanding in the *dīn* and warn their people when they return to them, so that they may beware?', and two trusted sayings of the Prophet Muḥammad: 'Strive against the polytheists with your wealth, your selves [*anfusikum*] and your tongues' and 'The best *jihād* is speaking a word of justice against an unjust power-holder [*ʿinda sulṭānin jāʾirin*].'[626] For Khāliṣ, these three authoritative statements translate into a distinction of verbal *jihād*, financial *jihād*, *jihād* of body and mind, political *jihād* and, last but not least, educational *jihād*.[627] While this pattern certainly goes beyond the classical binary of *jihād akbar* and *jihād aṣghar*, there is some reason in devising such a more refined taxonomy.

The five forms may – at least partly – represent Khāliṣ's own path and could, thus, support his claim of greater eminence and experience over the leaders of the various Islamist bodies. Did he not start out as early as the 1950s, that is, earlier than most of the others, to fight the verbal (*lisānī*) *jihād*, firstly at Kabul Radio, later as an editor and contributor to religious magazines, and an author and translator of religious treatises, with ever more vigour the more the communist sentiments spread across Afghanistan? Did he not contribute all his worldly possessions to the cause, as he would continue to do? Did his publications and – albeit rather informal and infrequent – teaching activities not clearly prove his commitment to spreading the true teachings of Islam against any other ideology? Was not all this embedded in his taking up arms against those forces of unbelief that had usurped power in Afghanistan and gone against the righteous ones with a heavy hand?[628]

625 See, for example, the instalments in *Tōrah Bōṛah* 9/1 (1391sh), 89–92, 11/1 (1393sh), 33–5, 11/2 (1393sh), 48–51, and 12/1 (1394sh), 65–9; compare Khāliṣ (1366sh), 11–8, 20–34 and 69–78. Regrettably, only a very limited number of copies of the *Tōrah Bōṛah* magazine from between 2012 and 2015 were available at the time of writing, which did not allow one to properly trace the sequence and frequency of the instalments.

626 All cited in Khāliṣ (1366sh), 107f. The two Prophetic sayings are from *Sunan Abī Dāwūd*, k. al-jihād, b. karāhiyya tarki 'l-ghazw, no. 3 (ḥadīth 2 506), and k. al-malāḥim, b. al-amr wa'l-nahy, no. 8 (ḥadīth 4 347).

627 See Khāliṣ (1366h), 107.

628 See ibid., 110–38 and 156–212.

The most significant among the five varieties of *jihād*, however, appears to be what Khāliṣ called the "*jihād* of body and mind" (*pah lās aw sar jihād*), because, in elucidation of what he meant by that, Khāliṣ presented an argument that would later align him with renowned Arab militant Salafists, most infamously Usāma ibn Lādin and other leading cadres of *al-Qāʿida*:

> Whoever hears the call of *jihād* thinks instantly of fighting the unbelievers, and that we attack them for the exaltation of the word of God. Or we defend ourselves against an attack, or in case our land is occupied: 'Get out of our land by force of the sword!' Doubtlessly, such a *jihād* can be called a "*jihād* of the body and mind", but the point is that such a *jihād* is not only directed against foreigners, but also necessary to carry out against the internal apostates inside a country, as well as the rebels and sinners [*də yaw mamlakat də dākhilī murtaddānō, bāghiyānō aw fāsiqānō*]. That is why we are dividing it into two types: the first one is internal *jihād*, the second is external *jihād*, directed at non-Muslims.[629]

To reiterate, what Khāliṣ called here "internal *jihād*" (*dākhilī jihād*) is not the fight against one's own appetitive soul, one's drives and desires, which is usually called *jihād akbar*, but, in fact, also directed at others. This, of course, requires not only a firm understanding of the legal dichotomy of *dār al-islām* and *dār al-ḥarb*, but also a certain inner disposition of righteousness, nourished by an "unconditional trust in God" (*tavakkul*), "humility" (*tavāẓuʿ*) and "true piety" (*ḥaqīqī taqvá*).[630] In Khāliṣ's opinion, the paradigmatic embodiment of these qualities, which are cultivated by a strict observance of the *ʿibādāt* and the realization of their inherent spirit, appears to have been the late seventeenth-century Pashtun poet Raḥmān Bābā,[631] which seemingly aligns Khāliṣ with the guidance-orientated paradigm of religiosity that is focused more on life in the Hereafter than on the temporary affairs of this finite world. This impression, in fact, is also to some extent maintained in some of Khāliṣ's own poetry.[632] Yet, Khāliṣ was a pragmatic enough Pashtun Borderland actor to also have some serious aspiration for worldly power, and herein his argument reconciled with standard Islamist tropes.

629 Ibid., 138f.

630 See ibid., 217–21.

631 See ibid., 26. Here, Khāliṣ quoted the following couplet commonly attributed to Raḥmān Bābā, although not found in his *Dīvān*: 'If the blindfold is not in the middle / you know your foot is stepping wrongly' (*chī də stragō pəṭavəl pah manź kx̌ī nah vī / maʿlūmīǵī* [sic] *khpalah px̌ah praday paṇah*). On Raḥmān Bābā as a key representative of the "guidance-orientated" paradigm, which, in the Pashtun Borderland, is somewhat associated with subaltern ethics, see Section 3.1.1.

632 See Khāliṣ (1393sh), for example 104–7 (*Ḥurriyyat aw Musāvāt*), 154f. (*Mīnah aw Insāniyyat*), 205f. (*Də Bashar də Khayr Lapārah*) and 218–20 (*Musāvāt*). This argument has already been developed in Hartung (2022a), 433–5, but it needs to be acknowledged that so far only one of Khāliṣ's purportedly six collections of poems has been investigated.

Authority (*ḥukmarānī*) and the exercise of power is, according to Khāliṣ, an ontic condition of all living beings, based entirely on physical and mental strength. Human intellect, however, is there to realize the highest possible power, that is, that of the Creator. The most natural way is, therefore, to acknowledge the supreme power of God and submit to His commands, which He had laid down in the succession of revelations to humanity, culminating in the Qur'an. Naturally, however, each human being also aspires to be in authority over any living beings that are less mighty, a fact that ultimately results in statecraft. Governance according to nature, however, and here we are back to arguments systematically presented by Mawdūdī as early as in the 1930s, requires the recognition of God's supreme power and, therefore, governance in this world that is based exclusively on the precepts ordered by God by way of the Qur'anic revelation. Governance based on any other framework is consistently against nature, therefore, entirely inadmissible and subsequently in need of active redressal: the reference here, unsurprisingly, is once more Q3.110, and the only way to go about it is *jihād*.[633]

By arguing in this manner, Khāliṣ opened a gateway to ideological collaboration with Muslims elsewhere. In contrast to his later Arab associates, and also the IEA-affiliated *Tōrah Bōṛah Jihādī Maḥāẓ* (TBJM) – the remnants of the Ḥil-Kh under the leadership of Khāliṣ's eldest son, Anvār al-Ḥaqq "Mujāhid" (b. 1387/1967) – Yūnus Khāliṣ did not embrace the clear-cut distinction between the "near enemy" and the "far enemy", which would inform much of the activity of *al-Qāʿida* and various of its affiliates.[634] Despite the respective ideological docking points, Khāliṣ clearly did not operate on any transnational agenda, perhaps not even on a national one, but remained very much confined to the Pashtun Borderland that defies national borderlines. This is perhaps best expressed in his view on gender-related matters, which, although shrouded in an Islamic garb, reflects greatly the traditional positions on these as prevalent in the conservative environment of the rural Pashtun Borderland.[635]

***

[633] See Khāliṣ (1366sh), 11–8 and 78. For the parallels to Mawdūdī and later "classical" Islamist theorists, see Hartung (2013a), 99–122 and 205–13. For Khāliṣ's position towards Mawdūdī, see ʿAzīzallāh (1386sh), 151f.

[634] On Anvār al-Ḥaqq's positions, see Anon., 'Də Afghānistān də Islāmī Ḥizb də amīr aw star jihādī shakhṣiyyat muḥtaram Khāliṣ Bābā – raḥmat allāh [ʿalayh] – źōy aw źāy'nāstī aw də Tōrah Bōṛah Jihādī Maḥāẓ masʾūl Mawlavī Ṣāḥib Anvār al-Ḥaqq Mujāhid sarah marakah', *Tōrah Bōṛah* 12/2 (1394sh), 24–9.

[635] These views are most certainly laid out in his tellingly titled *Woman and Men, or the Two Wings of Human Society* (*X̌aźah aw Nārīnah yā də Insānī Ṫōlənē Dvah Vazarūnah*), which, despite best efforts, has also proven impossible to locate for now. Interestingly, eight years after Khāliṣ's death, the *Tōrah Bōṛah* magazine published the Pashto translation of an article by the late Saudi Arabian Grand-Muftī Ibn Bāz on the dangers of mixed-sex working spaces that carried a quite similar message, see Ibn Bāz (trans. ʿAndalīb), 'Də Nārīnah aw x̌aźē də gadʾkār khaṭar', *Tōrah Bōṛah* 11/1 (1393sh), 61–4.

Why the militant kind of "Frontier Deobandiyyat", as represented by Yūnus Khāliṣ and the Ḥil-Kh, Nabī Muḥammadī and Naṣrallāh Manṣūr with their respective ḤII, as well as the M'UJM of Jalāl al-Dīn Ḥaqqānī and his successor Sirāj al-Dīn, was of much greater significance for the eventually emerging ṬIT than, for example, the large Islamist organizations formerly under the IIMA, or Samīʿ al-Ḥaqq and most of the *nomenklatura* of the *Dār al-ʿUlūm-i Ḥaqqāniyyah* certainly requires some further explanation. The autobiographical account of former IEA ambassador Mullā ʿAbd al-Salām Ẕaʿīf, made accessible to a wider audience by Strick van Linschoten's and Kuehn's meritorious translation, to which ample oral material has been added, is helpful in this regard.

The "talib" to which Ẕaʿīf introduces us reduces the traditional polysemy of the concept somewhat to its material manifestation in the lowlands of the Pashtun Borderland at the crucial moment in time when the ṬIT emerged around the elusive Mullā Muḥammad ʿUmar.[636] Students of *dīnī madāris* in southern Afghan villages clearly actively opposed the ruthless enforcement of anti-religious and anti-traditional policies of the PDPA government under Tarakī, which included the abduction of local dignitaries and violent assaults on the representatives of the religious infrastructure in these tribally organized rural communities, including *madrasah* students. It is similarly plausible that *madrasah* students who continued their religious education in and around refugee camps in Pakistan along the southern borderline with Afghanistan after the Soviet military invasion in December 1979 were eager to return to Afghanistan as *mujāhidīn* and fight both the occupation and the anti-religious PDPA regime. Yet, and this is revealing, many partisans of the various Islamist organizations involved in the armed resistance were active in these camps, spreading fiery *jihād* propaganda while also recruiting for the cause. Those who, like Ẕaʿīf, returned to Afghanistan as *mujāhidīn* submitted to the command either of independent local militia leaders or of those affiliated to one of the large Islamist organizations.[637]

However, the cynical attitude of Islamist militia personnel towards the general civilian population during the Civil War of the early 1990s, coupled with the gross disregard of their supreme commanders in Kabul for the lowlands of the Pashtun Borderland, brought these organizations, with all they represented, into deep discredit in the communities affected. What little

[636] See Rashid (2010), 25–9; "Mutavakkil" (1384sh), 12–14; Zaeef (2010), 62–5; Ẕaʿīf (1396sh/2018), 32–6.

[637] See Zaeef (2010), 13–46; Ẕaʿīf (1396sh/2018), 6–10. One needs to be aware that Ẕaʿīf's presentation of "the Taliban" as a somewhat closed and homogeneous entity before autumn 1994 (see Ẕaʿīf [1396sh/2018], 32–42; it is even stronger in Zaeef [2010], 65–80) is entirely aimed at creating a consistent narrative of the origins of the ṬIT, in order thereby to legitimize them as a mere contemporary manifestation of something with deep roots in the cultural universe of the Pashtun Borderland.

political vision existed among activist *madrasah* students in the south beyond the defeat of the PDPA–Soviet nexus appears to have been rooted in Islamist catchphrases – "Islamic government" (*islāmī ḥukūmat*) and "Islamic system" (*islāmī niẓām*) being two of the most popular of them – consisted less in the adoption of an Islamist frame of reference than in a conservative Islamic ethic which, more often than not, overlapped with the traditional socio-cultural universe of the rural Pashtun Borderland. Representatives of "Militant Frontier Deobandiyyat", such as Khāliṣ, Nabī Muḥammadī, Naṣrallāh Manṣūr, and Jalāl al-Dīn Ḥaqqānī and his son Sirāj al-Dīn, appear to have represented a similar perspective and, despite them still retaining enough independence to follow various other trajectories, this made them almost natural allies for the nascent ṬIT.[638] A distinct political agenda of this new formation seems to have been evolving only on the go, necessitated by the surprising speed at which the ṬIT succeeded in bringing an ever growing territory under its control. On its advance, Borderland pragmatics demanded from regional power-holders of a "Militant Frontier Deobandiyyat" persuasion, especially in the uplands of the Pashtun Borderland, such as Khāliṣ and Jalāl al-Dīn Ḥaqqānī, that they align themselves with the militarily successful ṬIT and, by doing so, they successfully made lasting impressions on its – at this point still rather crude – ideological set-up.

Such rather intangible personalities and organizational networks as the *Khuddām al-Furqān*-ḤII nexus, which was especially important on a more practical local level in the southern and south-western regions of the Pashtun Borderland, were equally important. Still, these ideational threads and interpersonal networks provided only one impetus, if certainly a mighty one, to the currently dominant manifestation of the "*taliban* discourse": in fact, its formation clearly goes beyond the single figuration that established itself in 1996 as the IEA and enjoyed its first spell of central rule over Afghanistan until 2001.[639]

Further ideological developments, however, which shaped not only the religious and political thought of later adherents to and affiliates of the ṬIT, but also that of later organizational manifestations of the wider "*taliban* discourse", such as the TṬP, were triggered more from outside the colourful universe of "Frontier Deobandiyyat", and even from outside the Indo-Afghan cultural space. After all, ideologues of Islamic militancy from abroad, predominantly from, but not limited to, the Arab world, who made their first appearance in the Pashtun Borderland in the mid 1980s, succeeded in making an increasing impact on ideological adjustments within the IEA universe after the dramatic conclusion of its first central government in December 2001. The

[638] Prominently, see ʿAzīzallāh (1386sh), 80–132.

[639] The current second central government of the IEA since August 2021 is still deemed too recent to allow for any serious assessment of its current ideological set-up. Some possible influences, however, are provisionally indicated in Section 4.5.5.

eventual pervasion of the ideological framework of "Militant Frontier Deobandiyyat" with religious ideas hotly debated in Sunni Muslim activist circles across the MENA region at that time but rather alien to Frontier Deobandis, however, required some mediation.

The facilitators for the absorption of new or refined concepts into the ṬIT/IEA ideological universe that had so far been shaped more by "Militant Frontier Deobandiyyat" as represented by MʿUJM, ḤII and ḤiI-Kh, it shall be argued here, were Pashtun Salafists who grew out of the Salafi circles of Panjpir and Peshawar. Therefore, prior to finally being able to delve deeper into the formative role that especially Arab volunteers have played in further shaping the "*taliban* discourse" since the armed resistance to the PDPA–Soviet nexus in Afghanistan, we shall have to turn to the historical developments and particular ideological cornerstones of Salafism in the Pashtun Borderland.

4.4 Salafism, or Pashtun Islamism Salaficized

Before being able to turn to the investigation of Salafism in the Pashtun Borderland proper, some terminological clarification is necessary, even more so as the term "Salafism" is, by and large, employed conceptually vaguely in the vast body of literature on the matter. On the basis of an emphasis on either "guidance" or "governance", however, scholars in the field have quite recently suggested a clear distinction between "Salafi Islam" and "Salafism".[640] In this regard, the suffix "-ism" in "Salafism" is considered as an analytically meaningful marker for the governance-orientated form of the otherwise rather guidance-orientated "Salafi Islam", which, for the Pashtun Borderland, has already been discussed above. "Salafism", in a nutshell, emerges from the confluence of Salafi Islam and Islamism.

The distinction between "Salafi Islam" and "Salafism" is, of course, predominantly analytical as, in reality, the two forms are frequently intertwined, making it rather difficult to identify the respective fault lines other than analytically. This holds true for these phenomena in the Arab world, and is clearly also the case in the Pashtun Borderland. After all, in the initial *Ṭarīqah-yi Muḥammadiyyah*, a combination of a puritan movement for the reformulation of Islamic beliefs and practices – hence "guidance-orientation" – is as easily discernible as the political aspiration to enforce – as *Jamāʿat-i Mujāhidīn* – a distinct legal system in the areas under its control, also, if necessary, by violent means. Similar combinations of Salafi hermeneutic persuasion and socio-political aspiration can subsequently also be found in "Panjpiriyyat" – the form of Salafi Islam outlined above developed by Muḥammad Ṭāhir and associates in and around the *Dār al-Qurʾān* in Panjpir – as well as among the students and associates of their

[640] See, for example, Nedza (2014), 86–90; (2020), 5–16; Hartung (2019b); Bruckmayr and Hartung (2020), 145–57.

internal critic Shams al-Dīn al-Afghānī, such as Amīnallāh Pishāvarī.[641] After all, Pishāvarī's immediate entourage included numerous leading activists inclined to use violent means to see through their own vision of an Islamic society in the region, a fact that has led top US Law Enforcement Agencies to want him for questioning regarding his alleged material support of various militant organizations active in the Pashtun Borderland, including *al-Qāʿida*, the IEA and LiṬ.[642]

The origins of the developments that led up to this point, however, date back as far as the early 1960s, to the moment in time when Muḥammad Ṭāhir of Panjpir initiated a socio-political movement to finally enact in the wider community what he and his associates had gleaned from the authoritative Islamic texts through the distinct hermeneutical approach described above as "Panjpiriyyat".[643]

4.4.1 *"Panjpiriyyat" Organized: The* Jamāʿat-i Ishāʿat al-Tawḥīd va 'l-Sunnah

Let us recall that, at the core of the religious world-view of the Panjpiris and those associated with them, such as ʿAbd al-Salām Rustamī, lies an unconditional belief in the oneness of God, conceived in the tripartite form that is generally traced back to Ibn Taymiyya. The medieval Damascene scholar, alongside contemporary acolytes, such as Ibn al-Qayyim, and later epigones, for example, Muḥammad ibn ʿAbd al-Wahhāb in eighteenth-century Central Arabia, however, believed that God's *tawḥīd* would be fully realized only once the insight translated into distinct conduct in public as well as in private, and, in this regard, Muḥammad Ṭāhir followed suit. Indeed, and perhaps the common tribal background of both was conducive here, the Pashtun scholar emerged in regard to this question as exceptionally close to the Central Arabian scholars of the early Wahhabiyya, who considered *shariʿa*-compliant conduct the exclusive criterion of proper beliefs.[644] This conduct, moreover, was not an individual affair; rather, its establishment and maintenance were the responsibility of the entire community of righteous believers.

It is at this point that Muḥammad Ṭāhir connected with the local activism of the Ḥājjī Ṣāḥib of Turangzay, whose, at times, militant resistance movement against the British colonial state he claimed to have joined earlier, as well as with the Haddah Ṣāḥib's spiritually inherited taste for *amr bi'l-maʿrūf* [...], and, finally, even with that of Muḥammad ibn ʿAbd al-Wahhāb.[645] Much in

641 See Section 4.1.

642 See URL: http://ucr.fbi.gov/wanted/terrorinfo/shaykh-aminullah/@@poster.pdf (accessed 10 February 2023).

643 See Section 4.1.2.

644 See al-Najdī (1417/1996), XI: 111–14 and 134–6.

645 See Gīlānī (1972), 211. For Muḥammad Ṭāhir's own – although meagre – recollection of his brief participation in what he himself associated with the Ḥājjī Ṣāḥib's religio-political

line with Muḥammad Ṭāhir's less accommodating stance on conduct that he perceived as a violation of the unconditional belief in God's oneness, he would actively promote what amounts to little other than a culture of religious vigilantism. Accordingly, he initiated the *Jamāʿat-i Ishāʿat al-Tawḥīd va ʾl-Sunnah* (JITS[a]) on 1 August 1963, with its headquarters at the almost simultaneously founded *Dār al-Qurʾān* in Panjpir:[646] these two enterprises, in fact, are mutually dependent, constituting merely two indispensable aspects of one ideological whole.

A few years before the coming into existence of these two entities, however, a similar development had already taken place in the northern Punjabi city of Gujarat, spearheaded by ʿInāyatallāh Shāh Bukhārī (d. 1421/2000), Muḥammad Ṭāhir's fellow student and adept of Ḥusayn ʿAlī Alvānī.[647] Inspired by the teachings of his *pīr*, which in themselves had been strongly informed by the alarmingly successful growth of the Ahmadiyyah Muslim community in rural Punjab at that time, ʿInāyatallāh initiated among his fellow students and adepts the establishment of the *Jamāʿat-i Ishāʿat al-Tawḥīd va ʾl-Sunnah* (JITS[b]) in November 1957.[648] Even though the two organizations, JITS[a] and JITS[b], would eventually remain distinct and establish independent regional zones of influence, the fact that they converge in Alvānī as the *spiritus rector* and, consequently, share similar doctrinal views and resulting agendas would lead their opponents to regard them as one and the same[649] and affirm in this way that the Salafism of "Panjpiriyyat" was actually not exclusive to the Pashtun Borderland.

The objectives of the JITS[a][650] are clearly stipulated in its statutes (*manshūr*): its main mission has been 'the propagation of God's oneness and the Sunna [of the Prophet]', which is directed against 'the rituals, inadmissible

activities between roughly April and November 1930, at the age of around fourteen, see Panjpīrī (n.d.), 17f.

646 See Panjpīrī (1433/2011), 14.

647 See al-Ḥanafī (1387h), 43–5.

648 See Ghumman (2014), 83–8.

649 See ibid., 88f. The one amongst their various theological positions which stood out clearly and would ultimately be responsible for their being cast out from the fold of "Deobandiyyat" was the rejection of the belief that the Prophet Muḥammad was alive in his grave. In fact, some early Muslim traditionists would sustain a similar conclusion *qua* analogy (see, e.g., al-Bayhaqī [1414/1993], 84f. and 111; directly referring to the former is al-ʿAsqalānī [1379h], VI: 487f. [see also III: 235, VII: 29–33, 210, and XI: 167]), and the leaders of the *Ṭarīqah-yi Muḥammadiyyah* in the early nineteenth century by drawing from al-Shawkānī (1408/1988), 42; (1426/2005), IV: 334. Both Muḥammad Ṭāhir and ʿInāyatallāh Shāh, however, rejected this on methodological grounds, arguing instead that it was inadmissible to expand crucial Qurʾanic statements in this regard beyond the martyrs in the Path of God explicitly mentioned there. On the entire debate in more detail, see Hartung (2020).

650 Unfortunately, no similar text could be located for the JITS[b], which is why the following exposition will be confined to the JITS[a] only.

religious innovations and forms of association [of God] with created entities [*aw makhlūq də rusūmātō aw də bidʿātō (aw) shirkiyātō*]'.[651] The propagation of *tawḥīd* has to follow the Prophetic precedent, which, in turn, is not based on rational speculation or reasoning by analogy: spreading this particular course of action is also an inevitable part of the agenda of the JITS[a].[652] Consequently, the socio-political agenda of the organization, with the emphasis still more on the social rather than the political, is extremely consonant with the Qur'anic injunction of *amr bi'l-maʿrūf* [. . .], understood here explicitly as *daʿwa*, and justified with Q2.159: 'Verily, those who conceal the clear signs and the guidance [*al-bayināti wa'l-hudá*] that We have sent down after We made it clear for humankind, those will be cursed by God and those who curse [*al-lāʿinūna*].'[653]

While fully sharing the firm conviction of the classical Salafi reference authors that the verbal proclamation of the Islamic creed alone was not sufficient to make someone a Muslim, but that the active discouragement of everyone from any leanings towards *shirk* was equally required, both JITS organizations did, at least initially, not go as far in their vigilant outreach as prominently suggested by Muḥammad ibn ʿAbd al-Wahhāb:

> He [i.e., the Prophet] – God's blessing and peace be upon him! – stated on this matter: 'The one who professed that there is no deity but God and denies everything which the people worship beside God [*wa-kafara bi-mā yuʿbadu min dūni 'llāh*], [only] his property and blood became inviolable, and his account [*ḥisābuh*] rests with God.' It is one of the greatest manifestations of the meaning of 'There is no deity but God,' because he did not do make this pronouncement as an asset for [the preservation of his] wealth and blood. Yet, there is neither a deeper comprehension [*maʿrifa*] of its meaning by mere utterance, nor affirmation [*iqrār*], even for him who calls on none other than God, Who is Alone and without partners. Therefore, his wealth and blood do not become inviolable [*lā yaḥrumu*], unless he adds to this disbelief [*al-kufr*] the one in what is worshipped besides God. If he has doubt or hesitates in this, neither his wealth nor his blood is safe. What greater and more splendid an example could be given, what to elucidate the point in more clear manner? What more proof [*ḥujja*] is there to cut off any dispute?[654]

Why, one may want to ask, is one's wealth and life at stake if one confines herself or himself to what most traditions of Islamic jurisprudence regard as a perfectly sufficient indicator for faith? Because, so Ibn ʿAbd al-Wahhāb and

651 Panjpīrī (1433/2011), 14.
652 See ibid., 21–3.
653 Quoted in ibid., 24.
654 Ibn ʿAbd al-Wahhāb (1406/1986), 26. The internal quote is *Ṣaḥīḥ Muslim*, k. al-īmān, b. al-amr bi-qitāl al-nās ḥattá yaqūlū «lā ʾilāha ʾillā 'llāh Muḥammadun rasūlu 'llāh», no. 7 (ḥadīth 139).

those in his wake would argue, if one does not actively renounce any other authority but God, one ceases to be a Muslim and becomes an apostate (*murtadd*) or unbeliever (*kāfir*), for whom there are clear punitive procedures stipulated in all of the four canonical traditions of Sunni Islamic *fiqh*.

The JITS[a], however, would not subscribe to the practice of *takfīr* in its full legal range, at least not at this point in time. Instead, its members would go around the neighbourhoods of Swabi district and beyond, preach their interpretation of Islam, severely admonish those whose practices they considered an infringement of the core doctrine of *tawḥīd*, and go from door to door emphatically urging believers to join the congregational prayers, close their shops during prayer times and maintain chaste conduct in public. They would even go so far as deprecating those who did not share their interpretation of Islam as unbelievers – *kuffār*, but the label itself remained predominantly polemical. Still, the statutes stipulate at least one action for the members of the JITS[a] vis-à-vis perceived unbelief: in explicit recourse to Q60.4, they are required to practice *al-walāʾ wa'l-barāʾ* (association and disengagement), a legal precept which had already been enacted by the Ḥājjī Ṣāḥib of Turangzay in his anti-colonial militant activity and which Muḥammad Ṭāhir may indeed have become acquainted with during the short time he purportedly spent as the Ḥājjī Ṣāḥib's retainer.[655]

While the vigilant activities of the JITS[a] cadres caused, first and foremost, a nuisance and the disruption of public life, the imperative of *al-walāʾ wa'l-barāʾ* is certainly not devoid of socio-political implications, just as Muḥammad ibn ʿAbd al-Wahhāb's stipulated course of action – euphemistically presented as a "mission" (*daʿwa*) – had: to dissociate oneself from perceived unbelievers – that is, those who do not share the particular interpretations of Muḥammad Ṭāhir and associates – one needs to, firstly, openly identify and admonish them before finally withdrawing physically. The first serious effect of such an approach for the accused is their public stigmatization and possible resulting social isolation, the significance of which can hardly be underestimated in communities as tightly knit as those in the rural Pashtun Borderland.[656] Beyond that, however, the identification of someone as an unbeliever also constitutes the first step in the legal process of *takfīr*,[657] which some of those following in the wake of the JITS[a] would eventually see through in its entirety.[658] Last but not least, special attention in this regard is given to political office-holders, as they are seen as having failed to meet their responsibility to safeguard the *shari'a* as an exclusive

[655] See Panjpīrī (1427/2006), 6–17; (1433/2011), 26. For Muḥammad Ṭāhir's relationship with the Ḥājjī Ṣāḥib, see Section 4.1.2.

[656] During a brief visit to Swabi in autumn 2017, it was very observable that the frequent pro-JITS graffiti across the district do not fail to have a certain intimidating effect on the local residents.

[657] See Nedza (2020), 96–123 and 136–61.

[658] See Section 4.5.5.

legal framework in the territories under their administration and, thus, provided fertile ground for the spread of all forms of unbelief among the common people.

To counter this, the JITS[a] finally opened its gates wide to the "governance-orientated" framework of Islamism in whatever variety and thus completed the turn from a Salafi to a Salafist organization. In this process, they complemented what would eventually rise to prominence in Salafist circles everywhere as *takfīr al-ḥākim*[659] with the provision of an alternative structure of authority, one that is indicative of the growing impact of Islamist organizations, here, first and foremost, the JiI that, as we have seen above, was actively present in the area around Mardan and Swabi since around the same time that the JITS[a] was established.[660] This affinity to Islamist thought would also be reflected in the take of its leadership and, subsequently, its basis on "prayer": it was important for the activists of the JITS[a] that prayer was observed in congregation; nitpicking details on its correct execution, such as the issue of moving or not moving the index finger during the *tashahhud*, had been reduced to insignificance, details to be left to the scholars of *fiqh*.[661] However, this is a central feature of the ritual prayer for Salafi scholars and must, therefore, under no circumstances be ignored.

Still, the major push towards politicization for the JITS[a] came only in the late 1970s when the PDPA established its regime in Afghanistan with the logistical, ideological and military support of the USSR. Now that parts of the Pashtun Borderland had come under the control of an explicitly anti-religious force, cadres of the JITS[a] were prompted to engage increasingly in the religious justification of, as well as active participation in, defensive armed *jihād*.[662]

However, organized militant activities do not appear to have been at the top of the JITS[a]'s agenda, if they were on it at all, in the decade and a half before. It still differed from the agenda of the JiI in this regard, because the alternative structures of authority advocated by the JITS[a] did not necessarily mean the establishment of government structures as the only framework to ensure everybody's adherence to the precepts of the *sharīʿa*; the taking of this step remained very much the prerogative of some former students of the *Dār al-Qurʾān* at Panjpir from the northeast of Afghanistan, in the light of the

[659] The most comprehensive study on this matter to date remains Nedza (2020).

[660] See Panjpīrī (1433/2011), 27–32. For the activities of the nascent JiI in this region, see Section 4.4.2.

[661] See Section 4.2. Indicative in this regard is Rustāmī (1438/2017), 51, who merely alludes to the general significance of the issue of moving the index finger during the *tashahhud* by providing a list of six relevant *aḥādīth* here from al-Khaṭīb al-Tabrīzī's *Mishkāt al-Maṣābīḥ* (compare al-Tabrīzī [1399/1979], 285–9 [aḥādīth 906f., 911–13 and 917]).

[662] One such justification, although rather implicit, based on the particular textual hermeneutics of the scholars from and associated with Panjpir, was provided by Rustamī (1428h[b]).

aggravated political situation in their home country since the late 1970s. The religious universe of "Panjpiriyyat" and the activism of the JITS[a] encountered rather specific local conditions, especially in the mountainous environment of north-eastern Afghanistan, which eventually fed into the rise of "Pashtun Salafism" proper. At the forefront of these developments was Jamīl al-Raḥmān from Kunar, already mentioned above, who will consequently figure more prominently in our narrative in just a moment. Before that, however, we have little choice but to appreciate some important particularities of the space in which Jamīl al-Raḥmān and like-minded activists operated. To do so, we need to go back in time once again, in fact, all the way back to the 1890s when the imperial project of Emir ʿAbd al-Raḥmān of the Barakzay made a formative impact on the mountainous north-east of contemporary Afghanistan.

4.4.2 *The Role of Salafist Polities in the Pashtun Borderland*

Preliminaries: North-Eastern Afghanistan, 1895–1970s

It is perhaps not surprising that those who would take the symbiosis of Salafi Islam and Islamism further operated in and from the particular region that today covers the Afghan provinces of Kunar and Nuristan, as well as the even more remote Badakhshan (Map 4.2). Firstly, the area is difficult to access; even Kunar, whose capital Asadabad (*Asʿadābād*) is no more than sixty miles from low-lying Jalalabad, appears physically remote and difficult to access.[663] Nuristan, adjacent to the north-east, is even less accessible, which explains the persistence of distinct polytheistic religious beliefs and practices well into at least the early 1980s.[664] Indeed, until late in 1895, when Emir ʿAbd al-Raḥman of the Barakzay ordered his troops to invade the territory which Muslims called "Kāfiristān",[665] the region remained rather cut off from affairs in the plains, helped by the fact that its inhabitants spoke a range of distinct mother-tongues, which linguists have situated between early Indic and Iranian languages.[666] Their main commodity to trade, it seems, was slaves, something they had in common with other regions in the north, such as Badakhshan and Chitral.[667] The conquest of Kafiristan under ʿAbd al-Raḥmān was meant to serve as the crowning finish of his Islamization programme as a means to bind the various

663 Akbar and Burton (2005), 134–6, provide a vivid account of the difficulty in travelling from Jalalabad to Asadabad by road as late as summer 2003.

664 Prominently, see Jettmar (1965); (1975), 29–185; Frembgen (1983); Klimburg (1999).

665 See Khan (1900), 287–92; Kātib-i Hazārah (1331sh), III: 1 117f.

666 See Degener (2002), 107–16.

667 See Kakar (1979), 174–6. For contemporaneous references for slaves as a long-established commodity among inhabitants of the Lāndai S'inValley, see Robertson (1896), 99–103. For Badakhshan, see Kūshkakī (1367sh), 217f.

territories under his rule into the one centralized entity that would eventually be the nation-state of Afghanistan.

Once again, we are facing a frontier situation here, which subsequently shaped both Kunar and what, after the conquest and the forced conversion of its non-Muslim inhabitants, was officially named "Nūristān" – the "Land of Light". British colonial officer George Scott Robertson (d. 1916), who had ventured into Kafiristan, via Chitral, from his posting at Gilgit in autumn 1889 (thus, more than five years before ʿAbd al-Raḥmān's incursion) observed that inhabitants of the Bašg'al – or Lāndăi S'in Valley – had frequent interactions with their Muslim neighbours in Chitral, resulting in voluntary conversions and the dilution of their religious tradition by Islamic elements.[668] With the conquest, however, forced conversion took place on a large scale, local elders were resettled to break down any possible resistance from the communities[669] and, finally, a formal Islamic infrastructure was introduced, particularly reflecting suspicion regarding the sincerity of the conversion of the Nuristani tribes. Intelligence reports from the British agencies in Kabul, Khaybar and Malakand indicate that the religious functionaries dispatched to the region were numerous, and they were armed, partly to protect themselves against rather frequent outbreaks of hostility from locals, especially from those areas that did not share a border with Chitral,[670] but predominantly also to enforce their obedient execution of the Islamic norms.[671]

In addition, the frontier constellation suggests that many champions of Islam gathered on the southern limits of Nuristan, as well as among the inhabitants of the Lāndăi S'in Valley, who had – however superficially – converted to Islam before the annexation of the region. In fact, these historical events play an important role in the collective memory of many restive communities in upper and central Nuristan, the Kāt'a and Kaḷaśa, as they do among the K'om of lower Lāndăi S'in, although, as we shall see further below, in a somewhat reverse manner. Kunar, with its eastern borders with Chitral, Lower Dir, Mōmand and Bajawr, appears to have been a chief deployment zone during

668 See Robertson (1896), 72–4 and 378f. Also, compare the rare historical account on the region prior to its incorporation into the Barakzay Emirate of Afghanistan in Khān (1894), 317–19.

669 See the four poetic oral reflections on these matters in the Väigali language, collected in 1969 in the village of Nišaigrām in the Väigal Valley, bordering in the south entirely on Kunar, by Buddruss (1983), 75–81. See also the analysis by Degener (1998), 52–4. Thanks to Alberto M. Cacopardo (Florence), we now have access to the contemporaneous written account of Shaykh Muḥammad ʿAbdallāh Khān "Azar" – both as a facsimile and in an English translation prepared by the Norwegian linguist Knut Kristiansen (d. 1999), presented in 1929 to Kristiansen's teacher Georg Morgenstierne (d. 1978) by the author in his exile in Chitral, to which his family fled in early 1896: see Cacopardo and Smith (2006).

670 See Cacopardo and Smith (2006), 53; Kakar (1979), 151.

671 See ibid.

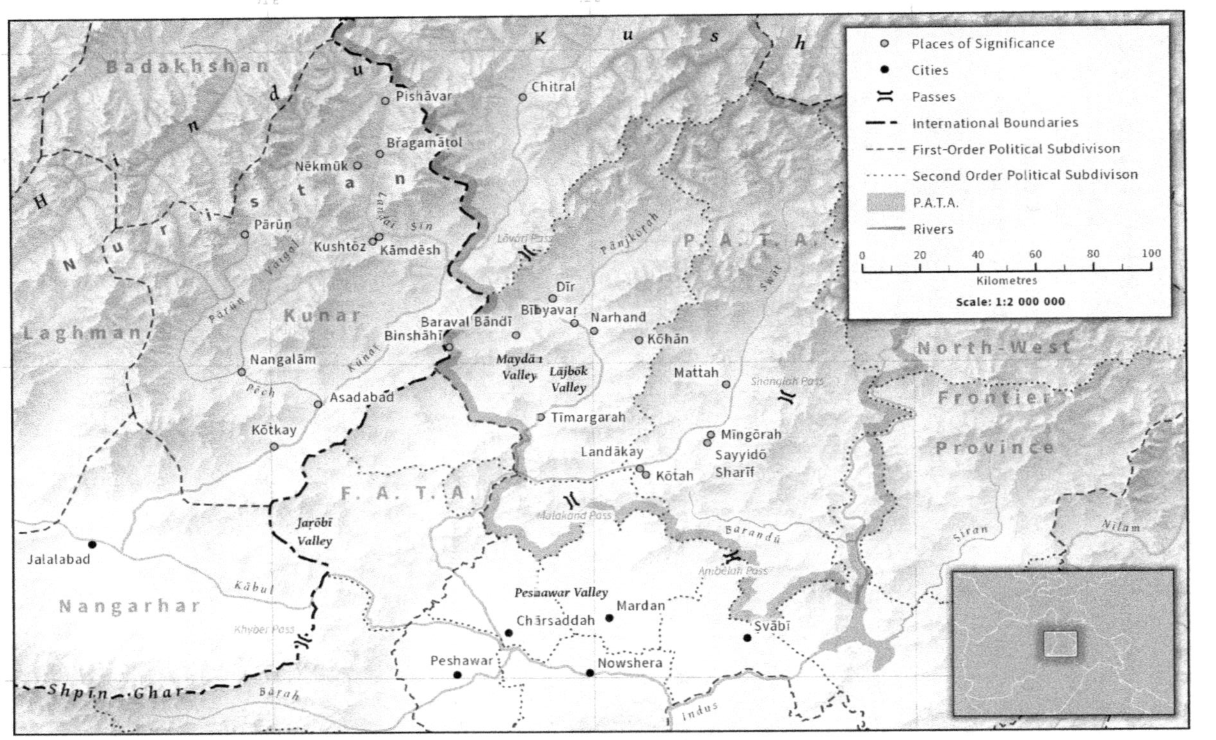

Map 4.2 The territorial setting of the early Salafist polities in the Pashtun Borderland (late twentieth century).

this period. Moreover, while some religious practices from the period before the annexation of Nuristan may have survived in one form or other,[672] the "frontier of faith" image – to borrow Sana Haroon's phrase – had further solidified: here, we may recall the selfsame interpretation of these very localities by the Ṣāḥib of Haḋḋah in the context of the Frontier Uprising of 1897.[673]

The fact that the Durand Line, established by a series of treaties[674] as a firm borderline between the British Empire and the Afghanistan of the Barakzay, cut straight through traditionally established territorial taxonomies is also important: consequently, members of one and the same tribal unit have ended up on either side of this line, and those on the eastern side may, therefore, have somewhat legitimate claims to landed property on the western side, and vice versa. The topography, however, made effective border control next to impossible, resulting in more or less unhindered movement across the Durand Line, which continued well into the present.[675] Such movement was not restricted to communal land on both sides, but went farther still, as is indicated by the various anti-colonial activities along this divide in the first half of the twentieth century as well as the fact that young males from Kunar and Nuristan were prominent among the students of the *Dār al-ʿUlūm-i Ḥaqqāniyyah* at Akōṛah Khaṫṫak right from its inception – one prominent case being Muḥammad Afẕal ibn Sayyid Muḥammad (d. 1433/2012), who would soon move entirely towards a Salafi persuasion.[676] Meanwhile, Shams al-Dīn al-Afghānī from Nangarhar and Jamīl al-Raḥmān from Kunar became prominent students at the *Dār al-Qurʾān* at Panjpir,[677] and it might have been there and then that they struck up a relationship of such closeness that it eventually outlasted even them.

Today, the male children of both of them are still in close contact and are still carrying on the strict Salafi hermeneutical legacy of their fathers. All of those who could be identified have studied for some time at the IUM and, while

672 See Frembgen (1983), 143f.

673 See Section 3.2.3.

674 For transcripts of these various treaties, arranged in chronological order, see Hayat Khan (1993), 246–67.

675 Akbar and Burton (2005), 221–5, provide a graphic description of how easy it still was to cross from Kunar into Bajawr and vice versa as late as 2003. In fact, only two years later, in September 2005, the then-Pakistani President Parvēz Musharraf decreed the plan to fence and mine the national border with Afghanistan, which the governments of the latter keep refusing to recognize. In 2011, the first short section of the border fortification had been completed, and in late 2018 Pakistani military spokesman Maj. Gen. Āṣif Ghaffūr declared in an official tweet that the work along the entire border should be completed by the end of 2019: see DG ISPR <@OfficialDGISPR> (15 December 2018).

676 See Ẓakī al-Raḥmān Lakhvī, 'Dawlat-i Inqilābī-yi Afghānistān: pas manẓar awr taʿārif [*sic*]', *Muḥaddiṡ* 14/9 (1404/1984), 33–48, here 40.

677 See Malik (1996), 208; al-Afghānī (1419/1998), I: 173; Anon., 'Tarjama mawjiza ʿan al-shaykh Jamīl al-Raḥmān (raḥmahu allāh)', *al-Mujāhid* 3/10 (1412/1991), 10f., here 10.

most of them have returned to Pakistan and are now engaged in religious instruction, Jamīl al-Raḥmān's son Ẓiyā' al-Raḥmān remained in Medina after completing his Ph.D. at the Faculty of Propagation and the Principles of Religion (*da'wa wa-uṣūl al-dīn*) of the IUM under the guidance of 'Abd al-Qādir Muḥammad 'Aṭā' Ṣūfī.[678] Both this work and his M.A. thesis, supervised by Ghālib bin 'Alī 'Awājī (d. 1438/2017), already show the programmatic continuation of the heresiographical efforts of Shams al-Dīn al-Afghānī in their titles, a fact that is underlined by the selection of well-reputed staunch Salafi heresiographers for advisors. The M.A. thesis, published in two volumes, is titled *The Efforts of the Hanafi Scholars in the Warning against Illicit Innovation in the Ritual Duties – Juhūd 'Ulamā' al-Ḥanafiyya fi'l-Taḥdhīr al-Bida' fi'l-'Ibādāt* (1426/2005), and the still unpublished Ph.D. dissertation is titled *The Efforts of the Hanafi Scholars in the Refutation of the "Dissenters" – Juhūd 'Ulamā' al-Ḥanafiyya fi Radd 'alá 'l-Khawārij* (1434/2013).[679] With such an emulation of the title of Shams al-Dīn's earlier work, in conjunction with the fact that Muḥammad Ṭāhir Panjpīrī remained a prime target of this polemic,[680] it is certainly remarkable, if not calling for an explanation, that across the almost 750 pages Ẓiyā' al-Raḥmān did not mention either the name or the work of the former even once. Instead, however, Amīnallāh Pishāvarī's voluminous collection of *fatwas*, entitled *Fatawá al-Dīn al-Khāliṣ* (1995–2013), serves here repeatedly as a credible Salafi reference vis-à-vis those of the Hanafis, who prominently include Rashīd Aḥmad Ludhiyānavī and Muḥammad Yūsuf Ludhiyānavī.[681] Furthermore, it is certainly noteworthy that, despite almost 550 pages of the M. A. thesis in its published form pivoting on the issue of the ritual prayer, the matter of whether or not to move one's forefinger during the *tashahhud* has also not received any treatment here at all.[682] Apparently, what in the eighteenth century emerged as a most virulent matter in the *fiqh al-'ibādāt* in the Pashtun

678 See the publicly accessible Twitter accounts of Jamīl al-Raḥmān's sons Hādī al-Raḥmān <@hadijamil800>, Ḥamīd al-Raḥmān <@HameedU54903733> and Ẓiyā' al-Raḥmān <@zieasafi>, as well as of Shams al-Dīn's son 'Ubayd[allāh] <@obaidshams1983> (all accessed 20 November 2021).

679 See al-Ṣāfī (1441/2019), I: 28f.; Ibn Jamīl al-Raḥmān (1434h), frontispiece.

680 Ẓiyā' al-Raḥmān's criticism of Muḥammad Ṭāhir's positions as demonstrably Hanafi-Maturidi is based on merely two works of the latter: the *Ḍiyā' al-Nūr min Iḥyā' al-Sunna* from 1961 and the *Uṣūl al-Sunna li-Radd al-Bid'a* (1986), see al-Ṣāfī (1441/2019), I: 70f., 181f., 200, 245, 308, 312, 318f., 320, 322–5, 328–33, 357, 375 and 424, II: 10f., 18, 23, 25f., 42f., 49, 52f., 68, 71f., 75, 83, 88, 90, 111, 128f., 159f., 170, 195, 198, 203, 217–19, 226, 230f., 241, 255f. and 349.

681 See ibid., I: 98f., 81, 276, 318f. and 419f., II. 35f., 39 and 46. Perhaps it is not just by accident that the title of Amīnallāh's collected legal opinions resembles that of early *Ahl-i Ḥadīs̱* heavyweight Ṣiddīq Ḥasan Khān Qannawjī's earlier extensive work on *tawḥīd* versus *shirk* and *bid'a*.

682 In fact, across the entire work only a single mention of the term "tashahhud" could be established, and this was in a passage in which it did not play any substantial role at all, see ibid., II: 238.

Borderland had little to no significance elsewhere. And, besides lashing out at the Deobandi *akābirīn* and Muḥammad Ṭāhir in the same fashion Shams al-Dīn had done some decades earlier, there is precious little indication that the specific cultural setting of the Pashtun Borderland was in any way relevant to the adherents of Salafi Islam for shaping their particular religious views.

As we have seen, such a more universalistic orientation has also been a distinct feature of Islamism, but, as in this case in point here, only on its conceptual side. In practice, however, the socio-cultural specifics of the Pashtun Borderland as a whole, and of various of its localities in particular, tend to play a substantial role in the concrete formulation of Islamic socio-political identities in that region, as "Frontier Deobandiyyat" and "Panjpiriyyat" testify. Therefore, in contrast to what occurred in the urban centres of Kabul and Peshawar, the combination of relative remoteness and impassability of regions such as Kunar, Nuristan and the adjacent regions-cum-provinces of Panjshīr and Badakhshan, as well as the porousness of the border with the former PATA territories of the NWFP, facilitated a formative impact of the JiI of Dir and Malakand on the area's religious landscape from the mid 1960s onwards.

While there is virtually no research available to shed a more concrete light on these ideological pollinations across the national borderline, it seems fair to assume that it was indeed the JiI chapters in the PATA of Pakistan's NWFP who were chiefly responsible for the Islamist transformation of the religious thinking in these north-eastern Afghan provinces which had hitherto been dominated by varieties of "Frontier Deobandiyyat" or the Salafi Islam of Panjpir. Coupled with the strong sense of effective autonomy in communal affairs in Kunar and Nuristan, originating from the limited accessibility of these provinces for administrators and law enforcement agencies from the various central governments in Kabul, it is not surprising that it was here that the PDPA faced the first armed resistance against its regime and that the Soviet military forces were pushed to the utmost limits of their ability to subdue and control the population.[683] However, besides actively participating in and facilitating the armed resistance against the military display of the PDPA–Soviet nexus across the borderline during the 1980s, the profound impact of the JiI on the region finally became manifest in the rise of Salafism among former graduates and people in the wider orbit of the *Dār al-Qurʾān* in Panjpir, and the subsequent establishment of two locally confined Salafist polities in Kunar and Nuristan, respectively.

[683] See Saharī (1368sh/1989), 1f. See also Vakīl Muḥammad Kabīr, *The Anti-Communist Revolt in Kombřom*, rec. in 1979, ed. and trans. Richard F. Strand, 2019, URL: http://nuristan.info/Nuristani/Kamkata/Kom/KomTexts/KhalqiWar.html (containing a link to Strand's recording in Kâmv'iri, the Nuristani language spoken by the K'om of Lāndăi S'in); Muḥammad Anvar Amīn, *Imo sta ǰāhot sta ṣṭalviri purǰik / The True Story of Our Jihad*, rec. in 1992, ed. and trans. Richard F. Strand, 2002 (1997), URL: http://nuristan.info/Nuristani/Kamkata/Kom/KomTexts/AnvarJihad.html (both websites accessed 1 April 2020).

The "State of the Islamic Revolution of Afghanistan" in Nuristan, 1980–1997

In September 1978, that is, less than half a year after the PDPA had seized power in Kabul, the *ʿulamāʾ* of Lāndāi S'in in eastern Nuristan, according to a rather hagiographical account, congregated and swore an oath of allegiance (*bayʿa*) to Muḥammad Afẕal ibn Sayyid Muḥammad, mentioned above, and committed themselves to actively strive for the ubiquity of the Qur'an and the Prophetic Sunna in each and every affair throughout Afghanistan.[684] This, in fact, resonates well with the accounts of other community representatives on hurt sentiments in view of the insolent attitude towards religious beliefs and customs by the PDPA officials, resulting in the general attitude that

> (i)n Afghanistan, whoever has faith, whoever believes in Islam, should hit this cuckold Tarakī; [like] this [. . .] this [. . .] this [. . .] [and] this, across there, this Soviet Union's [. . .] this Russians' bootlicker. 'From here, we should drive him out of our Islamic soil', we said, and right away we said, 'In the name of God'.[685]

The popular uprising against the PDPA regime that had started in Kunar in May 1978[686] soon took hold of much of north-eastern Afghanistan, followed by brutal attempts at suppression by the PDPA forces and the subsequent beginning of a fierce resistance from the first contingents of *mujāhidīn* in this conflict.[687] As a result of this, various areas came under the control of such early local *mujāhidīn* contingents, something that changed the whole balance of power and allowed particular ideological positions to establish a firm presence. In 1980, therefore, Muḥammad Afẕal and his followers suggested the establishment of the *State of the Islamic Revolution of Afghanistan* (*Dawlat-i Inqilāb-i Islāmī-yi Afghānistān*; DIIA) in the Lāndāi S'in Valley, vowing to bring security and stability by submitting all personal and private affairs exclusively to the dictates of the Qur'an and the Prophetic Sunna. A grand council of *ʿulamāʾ* from across all the prevalent learned orientations endorsed this plan and elected Muḥammad Afẕal *amīr al-muʾminīn*.[688]

Little reliable biographical information on the latter is available, something that, in fact, applies to many of the socio-political and religious developments in Nuristan in general. Written materials from the DIIA are difficult to obtain, and most social anthropologists who worked on Nuristan at this time were still more interested in more conventional ethnographic matters, such as kinship, material culture or the remains of the unique pre-Islamic religiosities in the

684 See Lakȟvī, 'Dawlat-i Inqilābī' [see above, n.676], 43.

685 Kabīr, *The Anti-Communist Revolt in Kombřom* (see above, n.683), at 4′47″–5′03″ .

686 See Saharī (1368sh/1989), 1f.

687 For a breakdown of the results of the PDPA's and, from December 1979 on, the Red Army's retaliation strikes in this region, see al-Rustamī (1428h[b]), 27–9.

688 See Lakȟvī, 'Dawlat-i Inqilābī' (see above, n.676), 46.

region.[689] Therefore, as yet, little reliable can actually be said on Muḥammad Afẕal, the DIIA and especially its ideological underpinnings, apart from what can be found in the meagre and partly biased secondary material.

According to those, Muḥammad Afẕal was born in Badamūk in today's Břagamāṭol (Barg-i Matāl) District of Nuristan, only about an hour by foot from Kāmdēsh, the largest settlement and district headquarters in the Lāndải S'in Valley.[690] Muḥammad Afẕal himself is said to have claimed descent from the K'om and, moreover, that it was one of his own ancestors who was instrumental in the successful submission of the hitherto not Islamized region to Emir ʿAbd al-Raḥmān.[691] The fact that there is no conclusive evidence to support this claim suggests that, at some point, Muḥammad Afẕal was designing a historical continuum which could enhance the legitimacy of his political endeavours sustained by religious precepts. That this strategy eventually worked out is reflected in the fact that little concrete information about his education is available either: the rather hagiographical article by LiṬ's Ẕakī al-Raḥmān Lakȟvī (b. 1380/1960) in the Lahore-based *Ahl-i Ḥadīs̱* journal *Muḥaddis̱* is conveniently vague about any biographical data: a three-year study stay in Mīngōrah, Swat, is mentioned, followed by others in Kabul and places in Logar, Peshawar and Mardan, until, as already mentioned, he enrolled in the study of *ḥadīth* at the *Ḥaqqāniyyah* in Akōṛah Khaṫṫak. At some point along the way, presumably in Peshawar, Muḥammad Afẕal met Muḥammad Ibrāhīm ibn Khān Muḥammad (b. 1352/1933), a Nuristani like himself, who introduced him to the hermeneutical programme of Salafi Islam that he himself had been initiated into by his own teacher of *tafsīr* and *ḥadīth*, a certain ʿAbdallāh Jān.

It seems that Muḥammad Ibrāhīm was actually the real driving force in rooting Salafi Islam in Nuristan.[692] He began teaching *ḥadīth* and *fiqh* in his

689 Symptomatically, see Cacopardo and Cacopardo (2001). Incidentally, in 1984, Swiss social anthropologists Iren von Moos, who tragically died four years later under suspicious circumstances in her hotel room in Peshawar, and Edwin Huwyler took photographs in Badamūk (today's Nēkmūk) of clearly discernible DIIA offices and activists, seemingly without being able to contextualize them, see von Moos (1996), 170–2.

690 See Lakȟvī, 'Dawlat-i Inqilābī' (see above, n.676), 39.

691 See van der Schriek (2005), 2. Indeed, Strand (2011) presents the local myth that this person was a certain Akram Jān of the K'om, who had only recently converted to Islam and whose subservient assistance in the forced conversion of his own tribespeople resulted finally in him being killed by them. This account, however, conflicts with Kātib-i Hazārah (1331sh), III: 1 116: 'At this moment, one of the *Āskant Kāfir* [i.e., the Āṣkuňu of the upper-middle Pēch Valley to the west] leaders came to Awliyāʾ Qūl Khān [the governor of Laghmān between April 1895 and March 1896] to offer allegiance. He bestowed on him a robe of honour [*khilʿat*] and ordered him to convince his people to embrace Islam. He [i.e., the leader] accepted this charge and returned home' (italics added).

692 Lakȟvī, 'Dawlat-i Inqilābī' (see above, n.676), 40f., is equally vague about Muḥammad Ibrāhīm's course of education. Klimburg (2001), 54, meanwhile, speaks of 'groups of mullahs, educated in a *madrasah* in the village of Panjpir close to Mardan [. . . who, in the

paternal village of Pishāvar in the Břagamāṭol District, an activity that soon brought him into conflict with the prayer leader of the local mosque, a government appointee originally from northern Afghanistan. After he had eventually succeeding in causing his competitor to leave the battleground for good, locals reported Muḥammad Ibrāhīm to the political authorities for inciting dissent within the community. Spells in jail were followed by a flight to Pārūṇ, where again he quickly built a reputation for causing civil unrest, similar to the public activities of the JITS[a] in and around Swabi. Muḥammad Ibrāhīm would initially abide by the constitutional requirement that every government official had to follow the Hanafi tradition in jurisprudence as a binding interpretation in Afghanistan.[693] However, when those officials began to claim authority in matters of *fiqh* and had dissenting local *ʿulamāʾ* exiled from their communities, Muḥammad Ibrāhīm's position towards the government authorities became increasingly less accommodating. His firm opposition to all forms of *shirk* and *bidʿa* fell on fertile ground, even among local Hanafi scholars: after all, their position too was threatened by the increasing monopolization of important religious and communal functions by government authorities, including matters of religious jurisdiction.[694]

In fact, the allusion to *shirk* and *bidʿa* seems to have been a common one among *ʿulamāʾ* in Nuristan, especially among the descendants of those *ʿulamāʾ* who had been officially dispatched from elsewhere and settled there after the Barakzay appropriation of this region in 1896, as well as local *ʿulamāʾ* who received most of their education outside Nuristan. Indeed, the ethnographically established fact that earlier non-Islamic practices continued in a loose Islamic garb, especially among those Muslim religious functionaries whose descendants had converted only after the Barakzay annexation,[695] makes the high sensitivity to the persistence of non-Islamic beliefs and practices among Nuristani Muslims somewhat relatable. Moreover, numerous practices rooted in local custom were portrayed as rather disruptive to social justice, equity and, thus, community harmony, such as the payment of exorbitant amounts as dowry, violent retribution for defilement, adultery and the mixing of the sexes during congregational prayer, alongside the secret persistence of religious practices dating from before the Barakzay annexation of Nuristan and the forced conversion of its population to Sunni Islam. In a way, the situation is somewhat reminiscent of that of Central Arabia in the eighteenth century, which prompted the fierce

1960s,] started to preach throughout Nuristan the "true Islam" according to orthodox tenets'. If this is correct, then one of those "mullahs" may well have been Muḥammad Ibrāhīm.

693 See Anon. (1343sh), 3 (art. 2), 7 (art. 8), 49 (art. 69) and 72 (art. 102). The pagination of the Pashto and Dari versions of the 1964 Constitution is identical.

694 See Lakhvī, 'Dawlat-i Inqilābī' (see above, n.676), 42f.

695 See Jones (1974), 234–7. See also Frembgen (1983), 143.

criticism of Muḥammad ibn ʿAbd al-Wahhāb and the subsequent rise of the Wahhabiyya.

The theological assumptions that one's belief is comprehensively expressed in one's actions and that the enforcement of a *shari'a*-conforming conduct would, therefore, lead straight to the necessary correction of beliefs were both, once again, foundational. However, a political structure that wielded the judicial and executive powers was deemed utterly conducive to the pursual of such a programme, and this is exactly the purpose that the DIIA was meant to serve.

It is, therefore, not at all surprising that one of the first actions of the *amīr al-muʾminīn* Muḥammad Afẕal was the establishment of an institutional framework for the introduction and execution of the *shari'a*-based *ḥudūd* penalties through far-reaching supervision (*ḥisba*), in accord with the Qur'anic commandment to enjoin the religiously permissible and prevent the reprehensible – *al-amr bi'l-maʿrūf* [. . .]. After the public display of a number of rather drastic penalties for alleged grave offences in early 1984,[696] transgressions seen as contradictory to the precepts of the *shari'a* had indeed quickly dropped in number, leading supporters of such a regime to rejoice over the provision of security for life and material possession, as well as honour.[697] Those subjected to such encroaching and punitive measures instituted by the DIIA and its executive bodies, however, would certainly have a different story to tell.

This rather laudatory narrative of the emergence of the DIIA is, nevertheless, complemented by an alternative one unearthed by Alain de Bures, representative of a French NGO in Nuristan between 1984 and 1985.[698] According to this, the DIIA owed its emergence more to a locally confined and heavily ethnicized competition for religious and, implicitly, political leadership in eastern Nuristan between Muḥammad Afẕal and other contenders. This conflict was confined to the Lānḍāi S'in Valley, crystallizing between northern Břagamāṭol, inhabited predominantly by Kāt'a, and southern Kāmdēsh, dominated by K'om. The traditional feud between the residents of the two parts of the Lānḍāi S'in Valley revolved a lot around natural resources: the large southern village of Kāmdēsh required more of them, transported downhill

[696] To illustrate this point, the official Facebook page of the DIIA contains a graphic image of a public hanging of twelve offenders, see URL: www.facebook.com/1436287689997878/photos/a.1449868221973158/1589588078001171/?type=3&theater (accessed 10 February 2024).

[697] See Lakħvī, 'Dawlat-i Inqilābī' (see above, n.676), 47f.

[698] Unfortunately, despite multiple efforts, no copy of de Bures's unpublished report to his organization MADERA, entitled *Historique de la succession de conflits qui opposent les communautés de Koustoz et de Kamdesh au Nouristan-est et qui a abouti à la destruction des quatre villages de Koustoz*, could be secured. Therefore, we are forced to rely for now solely on the brief exposition by Klimburg (2002), who had used the report by de Bures, but regrettably had no copy available which he could have shared.

via a canal from the tributary Kushtōz River. In around 1984, the villagers of Kushtōz, who had earlier submitted to protection by the DIIA, closed the canal and, thus, provoked serious armed clashes with the residents of Kāmdēsh, which would keep flaring up repeatedly over the following two decades.[699] At least after losing this initial combat, if not earlier, people in the lower Lāndāi S'in Valley submitted to the Peshawar-based Islamist parties under the umbrella of the IIMA, especially to the ḤiI-Ḥ, which subsequently served as their armed proxy in the violent confrontations with the DIIA on behalf of the people of Kushtōz.[700] Thus, the ethnically coloured local conflict over natural resources played itself out eventually as a contestation between Ḥikmatyār's "Pashtun Islamism" and the "Salafism" of the DIIA.

This constellation does not appear to have changed much after the Soviet withdrawal and the eventual downfall of the PDPA regime or after the end of the Rabbānī-led Islamic State of Afghanistan in 1996. Even the ṬIT had little desire to strain its limited resources in order to fully integrate remote Nuristan into its Islamic Emirate and was instead content with administering the inhospitable region by means of a local proxy, prominently Muḥammad Afẕal. As a result, his power base Břagamāṭol was officially elevated to the administrative centre of the region during the first central government of the IEA. However, and this points once again to the fact of the DIIA firmly belonging to the local setting of the Lāndāi S'in Valley, the conflicts with Kāmdēsh continued on an escalating spiral, drawing IEA forces into it as much as the Shāh Masʿūd- and Dūstam-led "Northern Alliance". With the ground they won from the IEA, however, Muḥammad Afẕal's own gave way: in 1997, he was heavily wounded in one of their attacks, losing an eye; soon after he abandoned his base and moved to Jalalabad, later to Peshawar, where he retired by and large from his political activities.

It is perhaps an irony of fate that the DIIA regime in Nuristan's Lāndāi S'in Valley, on which we have so little information, lasted substantially longer than the second of the Salafist polities in north-eastern Afghanistan: Jamīl al-Raḥmān's Islamic Emirate of Kunar, for which we have disproportionately more material at our disposal. It may well be that the ethnic component played a significant role in the neat local confinement of the DIIA: after all, its upper echelons were comprised exclusively of non-Pashtun Nuristanis, with their own cultural identity and vested interests in regionally confined issues. It is, thus, not really surprising that the only diplomatic representation of the DIIA was in neighbouring Chitral.[701] The same was certainly not the case with Jamīl al-Raḥmān: his Safi (*Ṣāfī*, or *Ṣāpī*) tribespeople lived on both sides of the Durand Line, resulting in a much higher rate of traffic between Kunar and

[699] See Lakhvī, 'Dawlat-i Inqilābī' (see above, n.676), 56–60.
[700] See ibid., 56.
[701] See Klimburg (2001), 57.

adjacent areas to the east, and, subsequently, in a much greater exposure to the range of *jihād*-minded views formed and articulated in and around Peshawar.

The Islamic Emirate of Kunar

The negotiations of power after the end of the PDPA–Soviet nexus did not take such a dramatic turn everywhere as they did in the race of Islamist organizations formerly under the umbrella of the IIMA for Kabul that effectively resulted in civil war between 1992 and the proclamation of the IEA in 1996. Local leaders in north-eastern Kunar, for instance, including representatives of all the prominent *mujāhidīn* factions in the region, congregated in October 1989 to discuss the options for post-occupation governance. Among the many rivalling aspirants for rule, the *Jamāʿat al'Daʿwa ilá 'l-Qurʾān wa'l-Sunna* (JDQS), a local Salafist organization with a strong presence across the entire province, finally prevailed and subsequently declared its *Islamic Emirate of the Kunar Region of Afghanistan* (*Də Afghānistān də Kunaṛūno Islāmī Imārat*), with its own leader Jamīl al-Raḥmān at the helm of this new polity.[702] Modelled on the precedence of the *salaf ṣāliḥ*, the other military commanders were called upon to formally pledge their allegiance to him (*bayʿa*),[703] thus following a procedure that would later become a distinct practice of political empowerment in Salafist and Salafist-influenced circles.[704] As a result, Jamīl al-Raḥmān's authority appeared widely accepted and remained, therefore, little challenged at first.

This man, born in 1941 as Muḥammad Ḥusayn to an ʿAbd al-Manān of the Safi tribe in the village of Nangalām in the Pēch Darrah district of Kunar, actually started out as a further product of the more acculturative Salafi Islam of "Panjpiriyyat". During his more than two decades of education, he studied *tafsīr* and *ḥadīth* with Muḥammad Ṭāhir and ʿAbd al-Manān Salafī at Panjpir, and his high esteem for the founder of the JITS[a] is well expressed in referring to him as 'a famous scholar in the field of *tawḥīd ulūhiyya*',[705] even though later Pashtun Salafi scholars, such as Shams al-Dīn al-Afghānī, would most certainly have objected to this assessment.

Yet, Jamīl al-Raḥmān's anonymous hagiographer suggests that he had already been primed for the Salafi *ʿaqīda* before enrolling at Panjpir, picking

702 See Samīʿallāh, 'Kunaṛ kī kahānī dastāvīzāt kī zabānī', *Daʿvat* [U] 5/3 (1412/1991), 6–15, here 6–8. See also Ḥamzah (1423/2002), 243–50.

703 See Bell (2016), 10. Unfortunately, it needs to be pointed out here that most of Bell's references seem rather flawed, and the trustworthiness of his account is thereby seriously impaired.

704 On the role and recent exceptional importance of the oath of allegiance in Salafist circles, see, for example, Hartung (2016a), 139–41; Wagemakers (2015).

705 Anon., 'Tarjama mawjiza ʿan al-shaykh Jamīl al-Raḥmān (raḥmahu allāh)', *al-Mujāhid* 3/10 (1412/1991), 10f., here 10. The Panjpiri affiliation is also mentioned in Dorronsoro (2000), 255, and Edwards (2002), 153, although neither provides any primary reference to support this claim.

up this trait immediately after his move across the Durand Line to Bajawr and Kohat. Although we do not have any further details on what he had studied there prior to his enrolment in Panjpir, it was probably no accident that Jamīl al-Raḥmān received his initiation into Salafi Islam in the northern parts of the former FATA of Pakistan. After all, we should recall that proto-Salafi thought and the more legalistic thought of the *Ahl-i Ḥadīs̱* had prevailed through the *mujāhidīn* colony at Chamarkand, established in the aftermath of the defeat of the *Ṭarīqah-yi Muḥammadiyyah* at Balakot in 1831, especially in Bajawr, home to a substantial number of fellow Safi tribespeople.[706] Whether or not Jamīl al-Raḥmān developed his Salafi proclivities there or in Panjpir, around 1965 he returned to Kunar and began to actively preach his newly acquired interpretation of Islam. In this activity, he would soon be joined by students and local *ʿulamāʾ*, who carried the Salafi mission all over north-eastern Afghanistan, as well as the adjacent territories to the east of the Durand Line.

The increasingly vocal criticism of the constitutional monarchy of Ẓāhir Shāh and its course of modernization by the circle that had formed around Jamīl al-Raḥmān eventually alerted the political authorities in Kunar, and he was subsequently forced to relocate momentarily to Kandahar, where he, nonetheless, kept spreading his message. One of those who allegedly quite regularly attended his study circle in the southern metropolis was Gulbuddīn Ḥikmatyār, with whom Jamīl al-Raḥmān had been developing a rather ambiguous relationship over the years: while he is said to have joined the Kabul-based SJM in the early 1970s, he soon seems to have been drawn more towards Ḥikmatyār's circle, culminating in him joining what would eventually emerge as the ḤiI-Ḥ.[707]

This appears to have been the very moment at which Jamīl al-Raḥmān turned from being a Salafi into a Salafist, a fact, however, which may have alienated him from Ḥikmatyār's Islamism: Jamīl al-Raḥmān rose quickly through the ranks of the ḤiI-Ḥ and was subsequently appointed its leading representative in his native Kunar Province immediately before the PDPA coup d'état.[708] By the early 1980s, however, his relationship with Ḥikmatyār had cooled down considerably – be it over leadership claims or their respective interpretations of Islam – and, consequently, Jamīl al-Raḥmān left the ḤiI-Ḥ for good,[709] only to finally establish his own JDQS at some time in 1985, that is, at the height of the armed resistance against the PDPA–Soviet nexus.

[706] See Sections 3.2.1 and 4.1.1; also Figure 3.1 and Maps 3.1–3.3.

[707] See Anon., 'Tarjama' (see above, n.705), 11. On the SJM and the ḤiI, see Section 4.2.1.

[708] Interestingly, though, Saharī (1368sh/1989) does not mention Jamīl al-Raḥmān in his account of the early armed resistance to the PDPA regime in Kunar.

[709] Edwards (2002), 271, suggests that Jamīl al-Raḥmān had already severed his ties with the ḤiI-Ḥ in 1980; this information seems to have been gathered from an oral source which is not further specified. As for possible reasons for the rift, however, Edwards also remains silent.

The deliberately Arabic designation of this organization clearly encapsulated its sole reference points in all matters of belief and practice, much in contrast to those of the various Islamist organizations under the umbrella of the IIMA. Interestingly, one of Jamīl al-Raḥmān's early retainers, ʿAbd al-Raḥīm Muslim Dōst (b. 1379/1960), who will play a prominent role in our narrative later,[710] considered the Salafi hermeneutical underpinnings of the JDQS one way, if not the only way, to overcome the increasing infighting among the IIMA organizations.[711]

The readily available body of primary textual material from the JDQS allows us to investigate the ideological underpinnings of Pashtun Salafism much better than in the case of the JITS[a] and even more so the DIIA. Courtesy of the later King of Saudi Arabia, Salmān ibn ʿAbd al-ʿAzīz,[712] the JDQS ran the Arabic-language monthly *al-Mujāhid* between autumn 1988 and early summer 1994, alongside the Urdu- and Pashto-journal *Daʿvat* between November 1987 and September 1992, as well as a monthly of the same name in Pashto between autumn 1989 and November 1995. Interestingly, differently from most of their Islamist counterparts, the JDQS does not seem to have published an equivalent in Dari, pointing to the fact that the reach of the organization was territorially confined to an almost exclusively Pashtun-inhabited area. Nevertheless, the relative ethnic homogeneity of Kunar did not prevent an explicit ethnic bias in the JDQS and its later political enterprise.[713]

There remains, however, a considerable margin of incertitude regarding the few years between the establishment of the JDQS and the launch of its periodicals, which is all the more serious because crucial relationships with major intellectual sources of inspiration, especially in the Arabic-speaking world, were forged during exactly this period. Unless fresh primary material is unearthed, we will remain largely in the dark about the actual circumstances

710 See Section 4.5.5.

711 See Muslim Dōst and Badr (1385sh/1427h), 4, 9f. and esp. 13.

712 See ibid., 14. Prince Salmān's only condition for financing *al-Mujāhid* was that the word "*ṭāghūt*" – "idol" or "tyrant" – was never employed. The background to this stipulation was the increasing application of that term by militant Salafists to Muslim rulers, especially in the MENA region, who were regarded as having deliberately lapsed in their faith and which, since the armed occupation of the Grand Mosque in Mecca by the *Jamāʿa al-Salafiyya al-Muḥtaṣiba* – the millenarian movement around Juhaymān al-ʿUtaybī (executed 1400/1980) – in late November 1979, also became increasingly employed in reference to the Saudi royal family. Prominently, see al-Maqdisī (1421h). For the use of this term by later militant Saudi Salafist scholars, see Nedza (2020), 79f., 93 and 187.

713 So far, the only serious investigation of the various periodicals of Islamist organizations in Afghanistan during the war against the Soviet occupation remains Fuchs (2017). Yet, while single issues of the JDQS's *al-Mujāhid* have also been used there (see ibid., 304 nn.48f.), a systematic appraisal of the journal as a whole was certainly beyond the scope of that paper.

under which these transnational relationships came about. For the moment, we may, therefore, assume that the militia run by Jamīl al-Raḥmān under the banner of the JDQS as part of the wider Afghan Islamist resistance to the PDPA–Soviet nexus was recognized by religious and political dignitaries in the Arabic-speaking world, especially in Saudi Arabia and the other Gulf states, just as were all the larger organizations under the umbrella of the IIMA. However, the dominant Salafi world-view of the JDQS allowed especially the religious *nomenklatura* of the Kingdom to relate to them much more and in a different way than to the others, who were, nonetheless, financially and logistically subsidized by the House of Saʿūd.

As a consequence of their shared tenets, leading representatives of Salafi Islam within the Wahhabi framework, such as Ibn Bāz, Ibn ʿUthaymīn, Naṣīr al-Dīn al-Albānī, Ṣāliḥ ibn Fawzān (b. 1354/1935) and Rābiʿ ibn Hādī al-Madkhalī (b. 1352/1931), appeared regularly in *al-Mujāhid* either as interviewees or as the authors of letters to the editor and of dedicated articles, or had various of their published *fatāwá* reprinted there.[714] The most important of these illustrious Saudi scholars was certainly Ibn Bāz, who indeed seems to have taken a personal interest in the fortunes of the JDQS and its *amīr* Jamīl al-Raḥmān. From the journal's first issue on, he advised the organization and its sympathizers on Salafi core issues, such as the doctrine of *tawḥīd*, Salafi piety, or, closer to the actual establishment of the Islamic Emirate of Kunar, the ethico-legal principle of enjoining the commendable and preventing the reprehensible.[715] However, JDQS cadres themselves also reflected on Salafi themes: Ibn Yaqīn, for instance, deliberated on creed (*ʿaqīda*) – constricted very much to the matter of *tawḥīd* – exclusively through the prism of a small number of Qurʾanic verses that were interpreted only within the very narrow confines of a literalist (*ẓāhirī*) approach.[716] Ibn Yaqīn's exposition reflected the Panjpiri hermeneutical position well, something that was later elucidated by Muḥammad ibn Jamīl Zīnū (d. 1431/2010), the exceptionally conservative

[714] For examples of *fatwa*s of Ibn ʿUthaymīn, see *al-Mujāhid* 3/7 (1411/1991), 46f., or 4/6 (1412/1992), 48f. For a *fatwa* of Ibn Bāz on matters related to fasting during Ramaḍān, see *al-Mujāhid* 4/3 (1412/1992), 48f. For three short *fatwa*s of Ibn Fawzān on prayer-related matters, see *al-Mujāhid* 3/7 (1411/1991), 47. For a *fatwa* of al-Albānī on Khumaynī's position towards the first three caliphs of Islam, see *al-Mujāhid* 4/6 (1412/1992), 34.

[715] See ʿAbd al-ʿAzīz ibn ʿAbdallāh ibn Bāz, 'Bayān maʿnī "lā ilāha ʾillā ʾllāh"', *al-Mujāhid* 1/2 (1409/1989), 11f. (I); 1/3 (1409/1989), 6f. (II) and 1/4 (1409/1989), 26–8 (III). This article was in fact republished in Urdu translation in an abridged form under the same title in *Daʿvat* [U] 4/1–5 (1411/1990), 21–3 and 46. Also, see ʿAbd al-ʿAzīz ibn ʿAbdallāh ibn Bāz, 'Wujūb al-taʿāwun ʿalá ʾl-birr waʾl-taqwá', *al-Mujāhid* 2/4 (1410/1990), 16–21; ʿAbd al-ʿAzīz ibn ʿAbdallāh ibn Bāz, 'Wujūb al-amr biʾl-maʿrūf waʾl-nahy ʿan al-munkar', *al-Mujāhid* 2/6 (1410/1990), 20–6.

[716] See Ibn Yaqīn, 'Taʾammulāt fiʾl-ʿaqīda', *al-Mujāhid* 1/1 (1409/1989), 25 (I) and 1/2 (1409/1989), 18 (II).

Syrian-born Salafi scholar, in the same journal, remarkably under the heading "In the Shades of the Qur'an" (*fī ẓilāl al-qurʾān*), which somewhat suggests a certain appreciation for the Qur'anic interpretation of the selfsame title by Sayyid Quṭb.[717] However, subject matters of heresiography were the most dominant issue throughout: initially focused on unbelief (*kufr*) and inadmissible religious innovations (*bidaʿ*) in more general terms, they became increasingly concrete when discussing the status of the few remaining non-Muslim Kaĺaśa in Chitral (adjacent to Nuristan), until they eventually zoomed in on the various Shiʿi denominations within the Pashtun Borderland and beyond.[718] The emphasis on these matters is also indicative of the strong influence on the JDQS of the world-view that radiated from Panjpir; moreover, it also served very much as a crossover point from Salafi Islam to more concrete Salafist socio-political agendas, in a manner quite similar to the earlier case of the JITS[a].

The proclamation of the Islamic Emirate of Kunar in May 1990 finally caused the orientation of the JDQS periodicals to shift visibly towards practical matters of Islamic legal administration and statecraft. The most pressing issue at the beginning appears to have been an arbitration with the ḤiI-Ḥ in Kunar, necessitated especially by the fact that it had played a major role in the liberation of the province from the grip of the PDPA and, therefore, had a substantial presence both in Kunar and southern Nuristan on the Afghanistan side, and, in cahoots with the local JiI, across the Malakand Division to the east of the Durand Line. This settlement, in fact, was achieved after lengthy negotiations and the signing of a number of documents that detailed the territorial arrangements.[719] What apparently united the leadership of JDQS and ḤiI-Ḥ was their firm rejection of UN Special Envoy Benon V. Sevan's (b. 1937) plan to have Ẓāhir Shāh reinstalled as king, once the PDPA regime had ended all over Afghanistan.[720] Regarding how an Islamic polity was to be run, the Salafist JDQS and the Islamist ḤiI-Ḥ remained clearly distinct: while the

[717] See Muḥammad [ibn] Jamīl Zīnū, 'Kayfa nafham al-qurʾān?', *al-Mujāhid* 2/4 (1410/1990), 34–8; Muḥammad [ibn] Jamīl Zīnū, 'Mawqif al-rāsikhīn fi'l-ʿilm wa'l-zāʾighīn min al-mutashābih', *al-Mujāhid* 2/6 (1410/1990), 32f.; Muḥammad [ibn] Jamīl Zīnū, 'Mafhūm al-ṣaḥīḥ li-āyat al-hidāya', *al-Mujāhid* 2/7 (1410/1990), 26f.; Muḥammad [ibn] Jamīl Zīnū, 'Yā ʾayyuhā alladhīna ʾamanū […] tuḥsharūna (al-Anfal: 24)', *al-Mujāhid* 2/10 (1411/1991), 40f. These all seem to have served as preliminary studies for Zīnū's own later books, suggested especially by the fact that his *Kayfa Nafham al-Qurʾān?: Anwāʿ al-Tafsīr wa-Sharḥ baʿḍ Āy al-Qurʾān* was published in Jeddah around the same time.

[718] Emblematically, see the sixteen lessons by ʿAbdallāh al-Muhājir, 'al-Shīʿa fī Afghānistān', *al-Mujāhid* 1/12 (1410/1989) to 3/3 (1411/1990).

[719] Facsimiles of the forty-two relevant documents, alongside transcripts, were published in the extensive appendix of Samīʿallāh, 'Kunaṛ kī kahānī' [see above, n.702], 16–91, as well as in 'Dastāvīzāt', *Daʿvat* [P] 2/11–12 (1412h), 31–126.

[720] See 'Iḥrāj-i ʿasākir-i rūssī az Afghānistān: tashkīl-i ḥukūmat-i ʿubūrī-yi mujāhidīn', *Afghān Jihād* 2/2–4 and 3/1 (1367–8sh), 8–11, esp. 9. See also Olesen (1995), 287f.

latter remained very much indebted to the religious universe of the MB and the JiI, the JDQS took its respective guidance almost exclusively from particular Wahhabi scholars in Saudi Arabia and other Salafi scholars active there or in other Gulf states. In fact, there is a strong rationale for this, which even has a historiographical component: while neither the MB nor the JiI had any practical experience in running a polity at that particular point in time, Saudi Arabia constituted, especially for sympathetic observers from the outside, a shining example of an actual state run on *shari'a* principles that were derived from a particularly austere interpretation which the scholars of the Wahhabiyya at least claim to safeguard. Moreover, JDQS cadres drew a strong parallel between their own contemporary socio-political and religious situation and the Najd during the times of Muḥammad ibn ʿAbd al-Wahhāb. A remedy to the problems in wider Kunar – including adjacent areas such as Bajawr – similar to that in the Arab Peninsula two and a half centuries earlier appeared, thus, as simply a logical consequence.

Cultivating Punishment: Pashtun Salafism in Application

Much of the conception of *shari'a*-based statecraft by Ibn ʿAbd al-Wahhāb and increasingly more so of the following generations of Wahhabi scholars pivots on the Qur'anically grounded precept, already repeatedly mentioned, of enjoining the commendable and preventing the reprehensible – *al-amr bi'l-maʿrūf* [. . .], now decreed a binding collective obligation (*farḍ ʿalá 'l-kifāya*). According to the standard Wahhabi historiographies, Ibn ʿAbd al-Wahhāb led by example in fulfilling it through practical enforcement, later being politically aided by Imam ʿAbd al-ʿAzīz ibn Saʿud (d. 1218/1803),[721] although Michael Cook convincingly argues that communal supervision based on this precept did not begin to shift more into the centre of Wahhabi legal thought until 1802, when the dominion of the Āl Saʿūd expanded beyond the confines of the central Najd.[722] It made its ultimate breakthrough with the successful reconquest of the Hijaz by the troops of ʿAbd al-ʿAzīz ibn Saʿūd, who eventually became the first king of the newly founded Saudi Arabia, because now it could become, in fact, a feasible task for the new state's executive force, since 1926 lastingly institutionalized in the "Committees for Enjoining the Commendable and Preventing the Reprehensible", the *Hay'āt al-Amr bi'l-Maʿrūf wa'l-Nahy ʿan al-Munkar*.[723]

Needless to say, a lot of inspiration for the Wahhabi interpretation of the precept was derived from Ibn Taymiyya's treatise on the matter, usually considered in conjunction with his one on supervision (*ḥisba*) and the late exposition on good governance, the *K. al-Siyāsa al-Sharʿiyya*. In fact, the

721 See, for example, Ibn Bishr (1402/1982), I: 34f. and 38f.; al-Najdī (1417/1996), I: 147–58.
722 See Cook (2006), 175–9.
723 See ibid., 180–91; Steinberg (2002), 397–421.

medieval Damascene traditionist had already undertaken a somewhat similar constriction to that of Ibn ʿAbd al-Wahhāb some 500 years later when making the rather bold claim that God had revealed Himself repeatedly to humankind for the sole reason of getting this concept across. Consequently, *al-amr biʾl-maʿrūf* [...] constitutes the very essence of the *dīn* and consistently, therefore, a collective duty,[724] to be supremely administered, as stipulated in Q4.59, by 'those among you in command' and subsequently obeyed, regardless of whether or not they rule justly.[725]

As both Ibn Taymiyya and Ibn ʿAbd al-Wahhāb are indispensable cornerstones of the entire Salafi hermeneutical universe, everyone claiming to follow what is called in these circles the *madhhab al-salaf* is required to engage with the concept of *amr biʾl-maʿrūf* [...] and its practicalities. Consequently, enterprises in the Pashtun Borderland, such as the JITS[a], and even more so the DIIA and JDQS, also paid great heed to it. Proper implementation of the precept, however, necessitates a firm understanding of what constitutes the "commendable" and what the "reprehensible", and, even more importantly, how the two relate to one another. The JDQS, it seems, had relied for this, first and foremost, on the authority of Ibn Bāz, with additional input from the Algerian Salafi scholar Abū Bakr Jābir al-Jazāʾirī (d. 1439/2018), one of the first members of the faculty of the IUM, and, later, also the younger Wahhabi grandee ʿAbd al-ʿAzīz ibn Muḥammad Āl ʿAbd al-Laṭīf (b. 1380/1961). The last two, especially as scholars active in Saudi Arabia, had first-hand experience of *al-amr biʾl-maʿrūf* [...] in application, an experience which was deemed helpful for the establishment of an adequate legal framework in the Islamic Emirate of Kunar.

Just to anticipate: the yield turned out to be rather meagre. Ibn Bāz, unsurprisingly, echoed Ibn Taymiyya's valuation of the status of the precept as the 'root of the *dīn* and basis of Islam', which it was necessary to carefully 'analyse for the common good [*maṣlaḥa*] of the *umma* and its salvation, which, if neglected, bears great danger and greatest turmoil, and makes the virtues disappear and gives way to the vices'.[726] Of course, the threat scenario sketched out here is highly suggestive and probably helps to explain why the emphasis was tacitly shifting to the prevention of the reprehensible alone. Ibn Bāz, however, confined his exposition of what is commendable to the practice of the various messengers of God as enshrined in numerous Qur'anic verses, namely, the emphatic invitation of the people to the oneness of God. This invitation (*daʿwa*), in turn, seems to consist, by and large, of the implementation of the *ʿibādāt*, which is meant to prevent the reprehensible from happening: the ritual prayer, for instance, is a way to instil the fear of divine

724 See Ibn Taymiyya (1396/1976b), 9–14; (n.d.), 11–3. See also Cook (2006), 151–5.

725 See Ibn Taymiyya (1396/1976b), 15; (1426/2005b), 137f. See also Cook (2006), 156f.

726 Ibn Bāz, 'Wujūb al-amr biʾl-maʿrūf [...]' [see above, n.715], 20; compare Ibn Taymiyya (1396/1976b), 9f.

punishment (*khawf al-ʿadhāb*) into a practitioner and, subsequently, cause submission and obedience; and the payment of the alms tax is a way to secure equity (*inṣāf*) and, thus, cohesion in the community.[727]

Yet, every Muslim who knows better than his or her peers is called upon to instantly correct practices, which is justified with a reference to the accepted *ḥadīth* on the authority of Abū Saʿīd al-Khudrī to which the Ākhūnd Darvīzah in the Pashtun Borderland of the sixteenth century had already referred, in order to call for prudent moderation in dealing with all sorts of deviation in religious matters, but ultimately with apostasy from Islam:[728]

> He who amongst you sees something reprehensible should modify it [*faʾl-yughayyirhu*] with his hand; and if he has not strength enough to do it, then he should do it with his tongue, and if he has not strength enough to do it, then he should [abhor it] from his heart, and that is the least of the belief [*aḍʿaf al-īmān*].[729]

As soon as there is someone invested with political powers, it remains – in line with Ibn Taymiyya's emphasis on the necessity of a Muslim ruler regardless of his actual moral integrity – the prerogative of this person to take care of the supervision over what is commendable and what reprehensible; the pre-eminence of redressing a perceived violation of divine decrees in a physical manner – with the hand – in the quoted *ḥadīth* explains the implementation of the *ḥudūd* jurisdiction.[730]

Consequently, it is this very measure that Jamīl al-Raḥmān and his government of the Islamic Emirate of Kunar, just like Muḥammad Afẓal Nūristānī in the DIIA, established as the first visible sign of their regime, severely punishing preferably the interaction of the sexes outside of wedlock and the traditional consumption of drugs, such as snuff and hashish, but even tobacco in the region, all backed up with a recourse to the weak *ḥadīth* 'A *ḥadd* punishment that is carried out in the land is better for the people of that land than if it were to rain for forty days.'[731] The breaking up of the customary practice of blood

[727] See Ibn Bāz, 'Wujūb al-amr biʾl-maʿrūf [. . .]', 22f.; Abū Bakr al-Jazāʾirī, 'al-Amr biʾl-maʿrūf waʾl-nahy ʿan al-munkar', *al-Mujāhid* 1/4 (1409/1989), 62; compare Ibn Taymiyya (1396/1976b), 15f. Interestingly, ʿAbd al-ʿAzīz ibn Muḥammad stresses the responsibility of those who practice *al-amr biʾl-maʿrūf* [. . .] to lead by example, invoking Q2.44: 'Do you enjoin the piety [*al-birr*] in the people while you forget yourself in reciting the Book? Will you not use your reason?': see ʿAbd al-ʿAzīz ibn Muḥammad Āl ʿAbd al-Laṭīf, 'Taṣḥīḥ mafāhim shubha wa-jawābuhā fiʾl-amr biʾl-maʿrūf waʾl-nahy ʿan al-munkar', *al-Mujāhid* 3/4–5 (1411/1991), 44f.

[728] See Section 3.1.3, n.105.

[729] Cited in Ibn Bāz, 'Wujūb al-amr biʾl-maʿrūf [. . .]' [see above, n.715], 22 and 26; al-Jazāʾirī, 'al-Amr biʾl-maʿrūf [. . .]' [see above, n.727].

[730] See Ibn Bāz, 'Wujūb al-amr biʾl-maʿrūf [. . .]' [see above, n.715], 24; compare Ibn Taymiyya (n.d.), 45–7.

[731] See Anon., 'Imārat "Kunar" wa-iqāmat al-ḥudūd al-sharʿiyya', *al-Mujāhid* 3/3 (1411/1991), 4f., here 5. The *ḥadīth*, reported by the not entirely undisputed Abū Hurayra, and considered "sound" (*ṣaḥīḥ*) by the JDQS author, is *Sunan Ibn Māja*, k. al-ḥudūd, b.

revenge (*qiṣāṣ*) was of special importance, not least because this would bring disparate forms of communal conflict management under a centralized jurisdiction, something which the JDQS government regarded as a way to dispense equal justice.[732]

Dealing out *ḥadd* punishments, however, requires, firstly, the firm establishment of guilt: consequently, the institution of supervision (*ḥisba*) had necessarily to come into play, in this case, carried out by the seriously armed JDQS cadres themselves. In their logic, this was only the consistent continuation of their *jihād* against the unbelief of the PDPA and its Soviet allies, which they vowed to continue until the end of all *fitna* – yet another prominent term in the Salafist lexicon which points towards how twisted this world has already become.[733] Consequently, the *jihād* against the unbelievers (*kuffār*), that is, those outside the Muslim community, and the hypocrites (*munāfiqūn*) as their counterpart on the inside, takes the priority of rank, vis-à-vis all efforts directed at the appetitive soul of an individual believer for strengthening her or his piety.[734] What constitutes *fitna*, finally, is somewhat apparent from the various familiar bogeymen the JDQS established in their publications and which are apparently also shared by adherents to other interpretations of Islam in the Pashtun Borderland, as exemplified by "Frontier Deobandis" of the more militant variety, such as Niẓām al-Dīn Shāmzay, Rashīd Aḥmad Ludhiyānavī and especially Abū Lubābah Shāh Manṣūr:[735] communism, Zionism, Freemasonry, as well as – and here matters take a much more tangible shape – the various manifestations of Shiʿi and Sufi Islam in the region.[736]

iqāmat al-ḥudūd, no. 2 (ḥadīth 2 635); there are two variations in *Sunan al-Nasāʾī*, k. qaṭʿi al-sāriq, b. al-targhīb fī ʾiqāmat al-ḥadd, nos. 1f. (aḥādīth 4 921f.). For its classification as "weak" (*ḍaʿīf*), see Ibn Bāz (1420h), XXVI: 300.

732 See Anon., 'ʿAdl aw inṣāf pah Islāmī Imārat kḳ̌ī', *Daʿvat* [P] 2/1 (1411h), 11–14. Immediately following this article is Anon., 'Islāmī Imārat aw sharʿī ḥudūdō taṭbīq', *Daʿvat* [P] 2/1 (1411h), 15f. and 29.

733 See Abū Ayyūb, '"wa-qātilūhum ḥattá lā takūna fitnatun wa-yakūna al-dīn kulluhu li'llāh"', *al-Mujāhid* 2/9 (1411/1990), 42f. The quote in the title is once again Q8.39: see Section 3.2.3, n.150.

734 See Samīʿallāh al-Afghānī, 'Marātib al-jihād fi'l-islām', *al-Mujāhid* 2/11 (1411/1990), 33–5, esp. 35.

735 See Section 4.3.2.

736 Prominently, see Abū Jalāl, 'al-Māsūniyya', *al-Mujāhid* 1/1 (1409/1988), 32f.; Naẓr Muḥammad al-Fāryābī, 'al-ʿAlmāniyya', *al-Mujāhid* 1/5–6 (1409/1989), 62–4; Naẓr Muḥammad al-Fāryābī, 'al-Yahūdiyya', *al-Mujāhid* 1/7 (1409/1989), 31–3; Muḥammad [ibn] Jamīl Zīnū, 'al-Ṣūfiyya fī mīzān al-Kitāb wa'l-sunna', *al-Mujāhid* 2/8 (1410/1990), 26–9; Safar al-Ḥawālī, 'al-Shuyūʿiyya bayn al-suqūṭ wa-iʿādat al-bināʾ', *al-Mujāhid* 2/11 (1411/1990), 10–15; Ḥusām al-Dīn, 'Qabāʾil "Kalāsh" al-kāfira: hal lahā man yadaʿūhā ʾilá ʾl-islām?', *al-Mujāhid* 3/8 (1411/1991), 44–7; Muḥammad Raḥīm Khaṫṫak, 'Dar ḥaqīqat avliyāʾ allāh kawn hayṇ?', *Daʿvat* [U] 5/11 (1412/1992), 43f.; Anon., 'al-Shīʿa fī Kābul: mādhā yurīd "Ḥizb-i Waḥdat" al-rawāfiḍī?', *al-Mujāhid* 4/7 (1413/1992), 52f.; Ḥāfiẓ

In a way, this perspective bore a striking resemblance to the arguments put forth by Ibn ʿAbd al-Wahhāb and those in his wake, until the dust began to settle with the proclamation of the Kingdom of Saudi Arabia in September 1932: 'Mind that Islam remains deficiently performed unless hostilities [*muʿādāt*] are directed against idolaters. Whoever fails to act in a hostile manner against them is one of them',[737] Ibn ʿAbd al-Wahhāb stressed in one of his epistles to the people of the oasis of ʿUnayya on whom he is said to have executed the *amr bi'l-maʿrūf* [. . .] himself for the first time. These historical parallels were well acknowledged by Jamīl al-Raḥmān and his compatriots, and they undertook efforts subsequently to explain to the people within their reach that the negative image that the term "Wahhabi" had assumed in the nineteenth century was entirely unwarranted.[738] Yet, in an undated letter to Jamīl al-Raḥmān, the then-Grand Mufti of Saudi Arabia Ibn Bāz recommended a much more moderate approach than the one adopted by the JDQS to achieving what he also regarded as the desired result of the Salafi quest for purity of beliefs and practices:

> It is incumbent upon you to [carry the banner of the Salafi *ʿaqīda* and to spread the correct knowledge from the Book of God and the Sunna of His messenger – God's blessing upon him and peace! – and [judgements grounded in] the *ijtihād* of the leaders of the *salaf* based thereupon] with patience and kindness [*bi'l-ṣabr wa'l-rifq*], for the adherent to illicit innovations and disobedience [*ṣāḥib al-bidaʿ wa'l-maʿṣiyya*] is like the patient who is won by kindness and wisdom. [. . .] God provides with kindness what He does not give upon violence and the like. Know [therefore] that [only] with patience comes victory, repose with anguish, and ease with hardship.[739]

Despite the professed general veneration for this Saudi Arabian beacon of Salafi Islam, the activists of the JDQS seem to have been sufficiently self-confident borderlanders to rather disregard this gentle intervention and remained faithful to their more confrontational course. On top of that, the more the Islamic Emirate asserted itself, the more this approach began to also include two further socio-legal practices that scholars in the field have recently started to regard as defining constituents of "Salafism", vis-à-vis "Salafi Islam": the accusation of unbelief, or apostasy (*takfīr*), and the doctrine of "association

Ḥāmid, 'al-Firqa al-Ismāʿīliyya: nashāṭ al-Aghā'khāniyya (taḥarrukāt al-ṭāʾifa al-Ismāʿīliyya al-Aghā'khāniyya fī Afghānistān)', *al-Mujāhid* 4/8 (1413/1992), 36–9.

737 Ibn Ghannām (1415/1994), 372.

738 See, in proper sequence, Anon., 'Shaykh al-islām Muḥammad bin ʿAbd al-Wahhāb, 1115–1206h', *al-Mujāhid* 1/8 (1409/1989), 28–31; Anon., 'Də Vahhābiyyat iṣṭilāḥ chārā manź tah kṛah?!', *Daʿvat* [P] 2/10 (1412h), 26–8; Anon., 'Ḥaqīqat daʿvat shaykh Muḥammad bin ʿAbd al-Vahhāb', *Daʿvat* [P] 2/11–12 (1412h), 19f. and 22; ʿAbd al-ʿAzīz ibn Muḥammad Āl ʿAbd al-Laṭīf, 'Jawānib tajdīdiyya fī daʿwat al-shaykh Muḥammad ibn ʿAbd al-Wahhāb', *al-Mujāhid* 3/10 (1412/1991), 44–7; its Urdu translation by Anon., 'Shaykh Muḥammad bin ʿAbd al-Vahhāb kī daʿvat kē tajdīdī pahlū', *Daʿvat* [U] 5/8 (1412/1992), 11–13.

739 Ibn Bāz (1420h), IV: 35f., here 36.

and disengagement" (*al-walāʾ wa'l-barāʾ*).[740] While the first clearly targets the perceived enemy within, the second helped to demarcate the range of action for the Islamic Emirate. In these two matter, however, the JDQS bowed first to the superior knowledge of their learned counterparts in Saudi Arabia: for one thing, they evidently owed the thematic introduction to *al-walāʾ wa'l-barāʾ* to Ṣāliḥ ibn Fawzān.[741] Yet, other, more radical Salafists from various parts of the Arab world, by then already present in fair numbers in the Pashtun Borderland, would refine its meaning further and argued for disengagement (*barāʾ*) as an inseparable component of the religious duty of *jihād*, firmly directed against the association (*walāʾ*) of the unbelievers.[742]

At this point, one is tempted to ask whether the scrupulous observance of the correct form of the ritual prayer, especially regarding the moving of the index finger during supplication (*tashahhud*), which had, after all, been a hotly contested issue in the Pashtun Borderland since at least the eighteenth century and was usually argued about in reference to the normative practice of the Prophet and the *salaf ṣāliḥ*, played any pronounced role for the practicing of *takfīr* and *al-walāʾ wa'l-barāʾ* in the Emirate. Remarkably, however, not even the periodicals targeted at a Pashto and Urdu readership carry any discussion of that matter, be it from a JDQS scholar or one of their learned Saudi Arabian authorities. True, in November 1990, the *al-Mujāhid* journal carried a piece by Ibn Bāz on the legal necessity to remain aloof from anyone not adhering to the proper Salafi ʿ*aqīda*; praying together with them would indeed lead inevitably to the further spread of serious unbelief.[743] Still, the Saudi Arabian scholar did not discuss how such corrupting influences could be identified in the way that prayers are actually performed, not to mention the particular issue of pointing the finger during the *tashahhud*. The three short *fatāwá* on prayer-related issues by Ṣāliḥ ibn Fawzān in the same journal are also silent on this matter.[744] Nevertheless, the deference of the JDQS leadership to these Salafi luminaries of Saudi Arabia, rather than, for instance, the more militant circle around Ḥamūd ibn ʿUqlāʾ al-Shuʿaybī (d. 1422/2002),[745] suggests that they have tacitly taken

740 See Nedza (2020), 12–15; to an extent also Wagemakers (2012), 7–20.

741 See Ṣāliḥ ibn Fawzān al-Fawzān, 'al-Walāʾ wa'l-barāʾ fi'l-islām', *al-Mujāhid* 3/2 (1411/1990), 20–5, which, apart from two small instances, consists of Ibn Fawzān's entire text: compare al-Fawzān (1411h). See also ʿAbd al-ʿAzīz ibn Muḥammad Āl ʿAbd al-Laṭīf, 'Ḍawābiṭ fi'l-waʿd wa'l-waʿīd … maqāl yuʿālij qaḍiyyat al-wasaṭiyya bayn al-irjāʾ wa'l-takfīr', *al-Mujāhid* 4/1–2 (1412/1992), 26–9.

742 For a more detailed discussion, see Sections 4.5.2 and 4.5.4.

743 See ʿAbd al-ʿAzīz ibn ʿAbdallāh ibn Bāz, 'Ḥukm min dars al-qawānīn al-waḍʿiyya aw tawallī tadrīsihā', *al-Mujāhid* 3/2 (1411/1990), 68–70.

744 See n.714 in this chapter.

745 Although al-Shuʿaybī had, like Ibn Bāz, also been trained by the then-Grand Mufti of Saudi Arabia, Muḥammad ibn Ibrāhīm Āl al-Shaykh (d. 1389/1969), he was apparently not offered by the Āl Saʿūd monarchy priviliges similar to those accorded to his two peers Ibn Bāz and Ibn ʿUthaymīn. While, as was expected from them in return, they would

up their views on the matter as authoritative. A look in their writings is, therefore, deemed conducive to elucidation.

Given the unmistakable "governance-orientation" of Jamīl al-Raḥmān and the other JDQS cadres, it is indeed rather surprising that al-Shuʿaybī and those of his inner circle do not serve much more prominently as reference authors than they actually do. This, however, is easily explained by the fact that neither al-Shuʿaybī's own writings, nor those of his alleged former student Ṣāliḥ ibn Fawzān[746] pertaining to this matter, include a discussion of the fine points of distinction between those a righteous Muslim should associate with and those to dissociate from. The one Saudi Arabia-based Salafi authority to turn to for an insight in this matter is, therefore, Nāṣir al-Dīn al-Albānī, which might appear surprising at first glance, because hardly any of his peers has been as outspoken as he was against Islamist interpretations of the *shari'a* and how to ensure its prevalence:

> We firmly believe that any congregation [*jamāʿa*] not grounded in those fundamentals of the Book [of God], the Sunna [of the Prophet] and the practice of the virtuous forefathers [*manhaj al-salaf al-ṣāliḥ*], as most comprehensive treatment [*dirāsa wāsiʿa jiddan muḥīṭa*] of all the commandments of Islam, its major and minor, its hermeneutical principles and its casuistry [*uṣūluhā wa-furūʿuhā*], such a congregation is not part of the saved community [*al-firqa al-nājiyya*] and does not proceed on the

largely refrain from challenging even government policies that appeared religiously problematic, al-Shuʿaybī had obviously chosen a rather different path by actively supporting the learned opposition that began to grow among a younger generation of Wahhabi scholars and would eventually be known as *Ḥarakat al Ṣaḥwa al-Islāmiyya*, or the *Islamic Awakening Movement*. With its main proponents, first and foremost among them Salmān al-ʿAwda (b. 1376/1956) and Ṣafar al-Ḥawālī, changing their attitude towards the monarchy upon their release from custody for contempt, al-Shuʿaybī dissociated himself from them and developed instead an increasingly militant attitude towards governance that did not in correspond to his interpretation of the *shari'a*. Verifiably inspired by the writings of Sayyid Quṭb, he eventually emerged as a spiritual anchor point for militant Salafists associated with *al-Qāʿida*, among them Yūsuf al-ʿUyayrī (killed 1424/2003), allegedly also Usāma ibn Lādin,as well as the triumvirate of the former *ṣaḥwiyūn* ʿAlī ibn Khuḍayr al-Khuḍayr (b. 1374/1954), Nāṣir ibn Ḥamad al-Fahd (b. 1388/1968) and the native Kuwaiti Aḥmad ibn Ḥamūd al-Khālidī (b. 1389/1969), see Hegghammer (2010), 95–8 and 147–55, to whom we might owe the exclusively etic label "Shuʿaybī school": see also Lacroix (2011), 168–72 and 250–2; Nedza (2020), 51–63.

746 See Lacroix (2011), 169. See also his sole reference al-Jafān (1423h), 13. Ibn Fawzān himself, however, does not refer to al-Shuʿaybī as one of his teachers, although they would most probably have had contact while at the *Maʿhad al-ʿIlmī* in Riyadh, see, for example, part 1 of the quinquepartite ʻal-Sīra al-dhātiyya al-shaykh al-duktūr Ṣāliḥ Fawzān al-Fawzān', presented to the *Noble Quran Broadcasting* platform (*Idhāʿat al-Qurʾān al-Karīm min al-Mamlaka al-ʿArabiyya al-Saʿūdiyya*) in its programme "Fī Mawkab al-Daʿwa" from 7 September 2017, URL: http://dralfawzann.com/file/6410 (accessed 25 November 2021).

> Straight Path implied by the Prophet – God's blessing upon him and peace! – in the sound [*ṣaḥīḥ*] *ḥadīth*. [. . .] We disbelieve that such parties [*aḥzāb*] are on the Straight Path, in fact we are certain that they are on pathways at the end of which stands the devil, beckoning the people towards him.[747]

In contrast to those of an Islamist persuasion, al-Albānī had developed a very strict *ḥadīth*-centred procedure by his programme of "purification and rearing" (*al-taṣfiyya wa'l-tarbiyya*) to derive what he regarded as the authentic and untainted Islamic creed as well as the resulting practical norms in utmost detail. Naturally, therefore, al-Albānī also subjected all those *aḥādīth* that had so far served as authoritative references in the controversies over the correct performance of the ritual prayer to a rigid re-evaluation,[748] including the issue of the *tashahhud*. Dismissing numerous canonically accepted *aḥādīth* as weak in the process, al-Albānī ultimately took the side of al-Ṭaḥāwī, whose *ʿAqīda* is held in high esteem by the adherents to Salafi Islam, when he explained that the Prophet himself had moved his finger during the *tashahhud*: '"When he raised the finger, he would move it, supplicating with it", and he would say: "It is surely more powerful against Satan than iron, meaning the index finger".'[749] Elsewhere, al-Albānī specified this by pointing to the different views on the matter held by the four established Sunni legal traditions, before he concluded:

> These definitions and directions [*hādhihi 'l-taḥdīdāt wa'l-kayfiyyāt*] are without basis in the Sunna. Closest to the correct view comes the path [*madhhab*] of the Hanbaliyya, would they not confine the moving of the finger to the remembrance of The Sublime. The apparent meaning of the *ḥadīth* of Wāʾil [ibn Ḥujr] is that he [i.e., the Prophet] continued the movement until the end of the *tashahhud*, without any restriction of qualification. Ṭaḥāwī has been pointing this out in [his] *Sharḥ al-Maʿānī*.[750]

747 al-Albānī (1414/1994), 114. The main targets of al-Albānī's various criticisms of the Islamist *manhaj* were Ḥasan al-Bannā and even more Sayyid Quṭb, whom he regarded solely as a *litterateur* (*adīb*), lacking sufficient qualification to prowl the highly complex field of Islamic jurisprudence. Because Sayyid Quṭb did this regardless, al-Albānī characterized his writings as faulty (*khāṭiʾ*) and his thoughts as ignorant and deviant (*jāhilī wa-munḥarif*): see al-Albānī (1426/2005), 29–36 and 41.

748 These controversies include not only that on the correct performance of the *tashahhud* that appears to have been particular to the Pashtun Borderland, but also those between the *Ahl-i Ḥadīs̱* and their Hanafi opponents regarding the practices of the *rafʿ al-yadayn* and *āmīn bi'l-jahr* since the nineteenth century, see Section 3.3.1, n.327.

749 See al-Albānī (1429/2008), 158f. The reference to al-Taḥāwī here is given in note 6. In line with what has been said above about the preoccupation of Islamists and those fraternizing with them with it, al-Shuʿaybī's own commentary on the *ʿAqīda Ṭaḥāwiyya* is demonstrably more concerned with general matters of belief, such as the concept of *tawḥīd* and its taxonomy, than with the subtler details of ritual practice: compare, therefore, al-Shuʿaybī (n.d.).

750 al-Albānī (1408h), 223. The *ḥadīth* referred to here is in *Sunan Ibn Māja*, k. iqāmat al-ṣalāt wa'l-sunna fīhā, b. al-ishāra fi'l-tashahhud, no. 2 (ḥadīth 966).

As a consequence, Salafis and Salafists both began to adopt the custom of wiggling their index finger during the *tashahhud*, a practice that, as succinctly put by Richard Gauvain, 'has become a symbolic marker of difference'[751] between Salafis of any shade and the adherents to other interpretations, just as the practices of the *rafʿ al-yadayn* and *āmīn bi'l-jahr* at the end of the ritual prayer have become a mark of distinction for the *Ahl-i Ḥadīs̱*.[752] Regrettably, however, we do not yet possess any information about whether or not this particularity in a core ritual obligation was actually enforced in the Islamic Emirate along the lines of al-Albānī's conclusion, or if its leadership was, in fact, more inclined to simply follow the *Ahl-i Ḥadīs̱*' way of conducting the prayer.

Whatever the details of the situation, the Emirate itself was rather short 'lived anyway. After an attack on the market of Asadabad by two Soviet Scud missiles on 20 April 1991, which killed many of the JDQS cadres, the ḤiI-Ḥ seized the opportunity and moved in with their full force, thus effectively ending the JDQS administration.[753] With the subsequent assassination of Jamīl al-Raḥmān at his headquarters in Bajawr about four months later,[754] the JDQS seemed ultimately finished; this, at least, is the view held almost unanimously by the few analysts who have so far commented on this political experiment in Kunar.[755] The issue, however, appears a bit more complex. After all, if the Emirate indeed no longer existed, why would the JDQS bother to elect Samīʿallāh ibn Najīballāh "Najībī" (b. c. 1354/1936), a native of Rudāt in the centre of Nangarhar Province,[756] as a successor to Jamīl al-Raḥmān as *amīr* over the polity? While its publications after Jamīl al-Raḥmān's assassination indicated clearly how severe an incision the loss of his leadership was for the JDQS,[757] there are also indicators that this did not mean necessarily the end of the Emirate, not to speak of the movement.[758] In fact, it shall be argued here that the clinging of the JDQS to the idea of a persistent polity that was only

751 Gauvain (2013), 127.

752 Prominently, see Nūrpūrī (1973), 39–44, esp. 41.

753 On the missile attack, see Bermudez Jr. (1992). See also Sulṭān Ṣiddīqī, 'Rūssī skuḍ mīzāʾil kā ḥamlah', *Daʿvat* [U] 4/10–11 (1411/1991), 6–9.

754 See Samīʿallāh, 'Bayān min Jamāʿat al-Daʿwa ilá 'l-Qurʾān wa'l-Sunna ḥawla ḥādith ightiyāl al-shaykh Jamīl al-Raḥmān (raḥmat allāh)', *al-Mujāhid* 3/10 (1416/1991), 8f.

755 See, for example, Ruttig (2010); Bell (2016), 12.

756 For a brief biography, see Anon., 'Shaykh Samīʿallāh fī suṭūr', *al-Mujāhid* 3/10 (1412/1991), 13.

757 See, for example, 'al-Shaykh Jamīl al-Raḥmān kī shahādat kē baʿd Jamāʿat al-Daʿvat [ilá Qurʾān va 'l-Sunnah] kē naʾī amīr al-shaykh Samīʿallāh kī prēss kānfrans', *Daʿvat* [U] 5/4–5 (1412/1991), 5f.

758 Articles especially in the more regionally oriented *Daʿvat*, both in Pashto and in Urdu, in the early months of 1992 suggest that the Islamic Emirate of Kunar was still considered an existing entity. For an example, see its monthly press review 'Imārat-i Islāmī z̤arāʾiʿ-i iblāgh mēṇ', *Daʿvat* [U] 5/6–7 (1412/1992), 44f.

temporarily not under its control provided a blueprint for later movements, especially for the various groups who all claimed the label "*taliban*" for themselves.

Aggravation: The *Taḥrīk-i Nifāẕ-i Sharīʿat-i Muḥammadī* (Part II)

The TNSM, led by Ṣūfī Muḥammad in neighbouring Dir and the wider Malakand region, was one of the groups who explicitly drew their inspiration from Jamīl al-Raḥmān as a charismatic leader, the JDQS as the organizational manifestation of his Salafist perspective and the Islamic Emirate of Kunar as the attempt to realize this world-view in practice. After all, Ṣūfī Muḥammad may have developed an amicable relationship with Jamīl al-Raḥmān already during his time at the *Dār al-Qurʾān* of Panjpir and, in the same way as the latter had broken off his former ties with the plainly Islamist ḤiI-Ḥ, Ṣūfī Muḥammad had done so with the JiI. The close ideological ties between the leaders of the JDQS and the TNSM was further underlined by the fact that Ṣūfī Muḥammad is said to have been given the honour of leading the prayers at Jamīl al-Raḥmān's funeral (*ṣalāt al-janāza*), and this even gave rise to the contention that Ṣūfī Muḥammad was indeed the true heir to Jamīl al-Raḥmān, and that the TNSM was the tool to fulfil his mission.[759]

There are indeed various points which speak in favour of this claim. The first is the wholesale adoption by Ṣūfī Muḥammad of the theological and legal universe of Salafi Islam, which views everything through the prism of the fundamental binary of *tawḥīd* in its tripartite conception versus *shirk*. For Salafists in general, and other than for Salafis, *shirk* is utterly manifest in all non-*shari'a*-based forms of government and legal administration, because they would ultimately elevate man-made legislation above the divinely decreed *shari'a*, and, subsequently, demand obedience to created beings instead of to God alone. For this reason, Salafists appear rather uncompromising and tend to accuse all those who submit to any form of government other than one based solely on the *shari'a* of apostasy. Above, we have already mentioned Ayman al-Ẓawāhirī accusing the leading figures of the Egyptian MB of that most serious offence;[760] Salafists in the Pashtun Borderland and beyond would follow suit and eventually administer the appropriate penalty as established by the Prophet Muḥammad himself. The uncompromising stance which Ṣūfī Muḥammad developed in the early 1990s towards the Pakistani constitutional framework and everyone who participated in it points very much in this direction.

Indeed, it became the practice of *takfīr* that empowered hardened Salafists around Ṣūfī Muḥammad to continue the earlier course of the JDQS of ruthlessly persecuting members of religious minorities, first and foremost Sikhs

[759] See Ḥamzah (1423/2002), 278 and 281.
[760] See Section 4.2.2.

and Shiʿi Muslims of whatever denomination, but – on the basis of their affirmation of the Prophet being alive in his grave[761] – increasingly also Deobandis and Deobandi affiliates. That branding Deobandis as apostates appears legally rather complicated did not apparently bother the TNSM activists too much, as they were hardly inclined to provide good legal counsel to their victims.[762]

More crucially, however, the TNSM appears to have brought into the militant rhetoric the distinction between the "near" and "far enemy" that – thanks to the influence of Arab Salafist volunteers – had become *en vogue* in *mujāhidīn* circles during the later stages of the resistance to the Soviet occupation and the following civil war in Afghanistan.[763] Yet, the Pashtun Salafists of the TNSM would modify it to the extent that the "far enemy" did not reach farther than the Pakistani state, while the immediate communities in the former Malakand Division constituted the "near enemy". This observation is remarkable in two ways at least. Firstly, it confirms one of the core hypotheses of this present work, namely, that residents in borderlands generally, and of the Pashtun Borderland in particular, do not necessarily identify themselves as fully belonging to any of the national entities that resulted from the various border treaties signed in the late nineteenth and early twentieth century. Secondly, by confining themselves to their native environment, the Pashtun Salafists of the TNSM still differed greatly from the global aspirations of Arab-dominated militant outfits that had started to permeate throughout the Pashtun Borderland since the late 1980s. The TNSM, however, was certainly not hermetically closed to any external stimulus. As we shall see below, the presence of militant Salafists from the MENA region resulted increasingly in the integration of Pashtun Salafists into their own ever more elaborate theological and legal debates which they had brought with them to the Borderland and kept refining there.

Initially, though, the TNSM would not even target the Pakistani state authorities outside the Malakand Division, even though they regarded them and the underlying political system that they used for their own legitimization as infidel.[764]

761 See Hartung (2020), 183–7 and 195–201.

762 Saʿīd (1406/1986) states that the programme of the "Establishment of the Revealed Law" (*nifāẕ-i sharīʿat*) originated from the *Ahl-i Ḥadīs̱*: in their estimate, Ḥanafis – eponymous to Deobandis – would be considered identical with Jaʿfaris, because both affirm the exceptionality of the Prophet and his House, in the case of the latter in affirming that, in contrast to ordinary human beings, the Prophet is alive in his grave. This very fact, however, constitutes a clear form of *shirk*, which, for the *Ahl-i Ḥadīs̱*, is a grave offence (*kabīra*) and consequently to be punished with expulsion from the Muslim community and the subsequent execution of the offenders.

763 This binary, first used in the infamous *al-Farīḍa al-Ghāʾiba* of the Egyptian militant Islamist ʿAbd al-Salām Faraj (executed 1402/1982), will be discussed in greater detail below, esp. Section 4.5.1.

764 See Ḥamzah (1423/2002), 273, who refers to the slogans used by the participants of the initial protest against the government's plans to substitute the FCR with Pakistani

Indeed, there is a certain element of community service here, which made locals as susceptible to the agenda of the TNSM as they were to that of the DIIA and JDQS: the substitution of prevalent state law with sound *shari'a* legislation[765] served, on the communal level, to bypass the utterly convoluted, highly formalized and cost-intensive legal procedures under the federal and provincial frameworks.

Things, however, would change drastically when, on 3 November 1994, TNSM volunteers took up arms and began, under the slogan "Divine Law or Martyrdom" (*sharīʿat yā shahādat*), to confront the Pakistani state with violence.[766] They certainly benefited from the increasingly unstable situation in the immediate vicinity of the national borderline that cuts through the Pashtun Borderland, owing to a great extent to the speedy advance of the ṬIT in Afghanistan in the mid 1990s; it is, therefore, hardly surprising that the two movements joined hands almost instantly and helped to sustain one another ideologically and logistically. When the ṬIT forces advanced on the north-eastern provinces of Afghanistan, Ṣūfī Muḥammad raised a *laǩkar* and went over to Kunar to assist them.

At around the same time, the JDQS, whose ability to enforce its own version of Islam there became at least temporarily limited when the ḤiI-Ḥ established its control in Kunar and reduced the Islamic Emirate to a Salafist aspiration only, also began to openly express its sympathies for the ṬIT as the new and mighty contender for power in the whole of Afghanistan.[767] In fact, this appears quite reasonable, because Ḥikmatyār, the leader of their direct competitor for political power in Kunar, had stood against the advancing ṬIT forces in early 1995 and, subsequently, lost many of his major bases, including his headquarters at Chahār Āsyāb on the southern outskirts of Kabul.[768] With Ḥikmatyār thereafter in Iranian exile and the ṬIT, despite sustaining heavy losses, gaining ever more ground, the JDQS leadership obviously saw an opportunity to be reinstated, even if at the expense of remaining a vassal to the ṬIT/IEA. It may well be that they had also counted on support from the TNSM in this regard, yet unfortunately the materials currently at hand do not extend to covering the eventual capture of Kunar by ṬIT militias in September 1996.

common law: 'The present law is unbelief, is unbelief indeed!' and 'We do not recognize the present system, we do not recognize!'

765 See Anon., 'Taḥrīk-i Nifāẕ-i Sharīʿat-i Muḥammadī: ēk jāʾizah', *Muḥaddis̱* 31/2 (1419/1999), Title page.

766 See ibid.; Sultan-i-Rome (2012), 118.

767 See [Samīʿallāh], 'Də Ṭālibānō taḥrīk aw də Afghānistān kashālah', *Daʿvat* [P] 7/3 (1415h), 2–5, here 5; [Samīʿallāh], 'Ṭālibān də žavərō taḥavvulātō', *Daʿvat* [P] 7/4 (1415h), 2–5. In fact, these two articles appeared alongside others which were highly critical of the Rabbānī-led government in Kabul and the various on–off alliances during the civil war, see, for example, Samīʿallāh "Najībī", 'Də Ustād Rabbānī də iqtidār pah intiqāl sarah nūr də jagṛī nah pātah kīğī', *Daʿvat* [P] 8/2 (1416h), 5.

768 See Rashid (2010), 33f.

However, that the last issue of the Pashto *Daʿvat* appeared in January 1996 suggests that the JDQS had actually already disintegrated some months prior to the ṬIT assuming control over Kunar, probably over severe disagreements regarding how to position themselves in relation to the ṬIT / IEA. For a Salafist organization, this was surely not a trifle: should they pragmatically close ranks with an – admittedly mighty – militia that did not submit to the Salafi interpretation of Islam, but was deeply entrenched in the Hanafi-cum-Maturidi universe, just so that the JDQS could expand its activities with renewed political authority? Would those affiliated to the ṬIT be inclined to listen to their *daʿwa* and eventually embrace what the JDQS regarded as the most authentic and sustainable interpretation of Islam? Otherwise, the small but significant differences between Hanafis, *Ahl-i Ḥadīs̱* and Salafis of every shade in the performance of ritual prayer – epitomized in such practices as *rafʿ al-yadayn* and *tashahhud bi'l-ishāra* – already make it rather difficult to imagine an amicable coexistence without either side having to seriously compromise. Once the ṬIT / IEA were in charge of large parts of Kunar, it is rather hard to imagine them making such concessions to the JDQS, while, on dogmatic grounds, the same applies the other way around.

All the same, such considerations appear to have been of subordinate importance at best for Ṣūfī Muḥammad and his TNSM. As one of his *Ahl-i Ḥadīs̱* sympathizers expressed years later in an opinion piece in the Lahore-based journal *Muḥaddis̱*, Ṣūfī Muḥammad would actually support everyone who advocated a form of governance based exclusively on Islamic precepts, which, by implication, means one that is fully opposed to the concept of "democracy", at least as enacted across the globe.[769] From this perspective and, at least, for the time being, doctrinal differences took second place, and, in this way, the closing of ranks between the ṬIT / IEA, with its strong roots in the south of the Pashtun Borderland and the Hanafi universe of "Frontier Deobandiyyat", and Pashtun Salafists from the uplands was not a serious obstacle to collaboration, especially if the result was an Islamic Emirate.

We do not have reliable information on where and how exactly Ṣūfī Muḥammad and his *laẋkar* spent the years in IEA-ruled Afghanistan. He resurfaced only in November 2001, after the Emirate was effectively destroyed by the USA-led combat mission in response to the ṬIT / IEA leadership's refusal to extradite Usāma ibn Lādin from Afghanistan. In fact, the successful *al-Qāʿida* attacks of 11 September 2001 had dramatically impacted the entire geopolitical situation, all the more so in the Pashtun Borderland, because the then-president of Pakistan, General Parvēz Musharraf, had joined the so-called "War on Terror" and began to support the military operations in Afghanistan with similar action from the Pakistani side. One of the first steps in this regard

769 See Dr Muḥammad Amīn, 'Svāt mēṇ nifāẕ-i sharīʿat awr talibanāʾizēshan', *Muḥaddis̱* 31/5 (1430/2009), 2–20.

was to officially outlaw various militant Islamic organizations, among them the *Jaysh-i Muḥammad*, the *Anjuman-i Sipāh-i Ṣaḥābah* (ASṢ) and its Shiʿi counterpart, the *Taḥrīk-i Jaʿfariyyah-yi Pākistān* (TJP), for their sectarian violence, and, finally, the TNSM. Accordingly, when Ṣūfī Muḥammad returned with his combatants to Pakistan, he was instantly apprehended and jailed for anti-Pakistani terrorist activities, where he remained until April 2008.[770]

However, after the official banning of the TNSM and Ṣūfī Muḥammad's subsequent imprisonment, the latter's former favourite student (*lāləy*) at Maydān and son-in-law, Faẕl-i Ḥayāt "Mullā Faẕlallāh Khurāsānī" (killed 1439/2018), commonly known as "Mullā Radio" for his regular sermons and lectures on his own radio station in Swat,[771] assumed the leadership of the now officially banned TNSM. Finally, in summer 2007, he, whose retainers bestowed upon him the title "Imām-i Inqilāb"[772] that had so far been reserved exclusively for ʿUbaydallāh Sindhī, entered into a strategic alliance with a force that, although endorsed by the IEA supreme commander Mullā Muḥammad ʿUmar, claimed the label "*taliban*" for itself:[773] having emerged after the end of the first central government of the IEA on the eastern side of the Durand Line, they went by the name of *Taḥrīk-i Ṭālibān-i Pākistān*, initially led by Baytallāh Maḥsūd (killed 1430/2009), about whom we shall read more further below.[774] The straw that had broken the camel's back and served retrospectively as a basis of legitimacy for this merger was an event in the Pakistani capital, which provided religiously inspired militants with the rationale to take up their arms against the Pakistani state authorities: the siege and storming of the *Lāl Masjid* in the heart of Islamabad by Pakistan Army special operations forces between 3 and 11 July 2007.[775]

For Salafist sympathizers in Pakistan, this violent course of action by state actors against those perceived as pious guardians of the religious tenets which, in their eyes, were to actually constitute the sole basis of the Islamic Republic since its inception in 1947, including the female students of the adjacent *Jāmiʿah Ḥafṣah*, was regarded as conclusive proof of the anti-religiosity, indeed infidelity, of the Pakistani government. By administering the legal procedure of *takfīr al-ḥākim*, the government and especially its security apparatus was turned into an unbelieving aggressor, which requires every righteous Muslim

770 See Ali (2009), 6.

771 See Yousafzai and Lamb (2013), 92–97; Rafi (2016), 26; Hartung (2019a), 324.

772 See the various articles in the special commemorative issue of the *Majallah-yi Taḥrīk-i Ṭālibān-i Pākistān* (Rabīʿ II 1440 / November 2018).

773 See Maḥsūd (2017), 631.

774 See Section 4.5.5.

775 See Ḥāfiẓ Ḥasan Madanī, 'Sāniḥah-yi Lāl Masjid: ēk lamḥah-yi fikriyyah', *Muḥaddiṯ* 39/8 (1428/2007), 2–11. For TṬP perspectives, see Maḥsūd (2017), 160–2, 169, 210, 440 and 631f.; Anon., 'Savāniḥ-i ṭālib-i ḥaqq Mawlānā Faẕlallāh Khurāsānī', *Majallah-yi Taḥrīk-i Ṭālibān-i Pākistān – khuṣūṣī ishāʿat* (Rabīʿ II 1440 / November 2018), 5–14, here 9f.

to embark on a defensive *jihād* (*jihād difāʿī*).[776] Concurrent action did not take long: while the *Lāl Masjid* siege was still under way, an assassination attempt was made on President Musharraf, government employees and security forces were targeted by suicide bombers across Pakistan, and this all culminated in the assassination by a suicide squad of the new Prime Minister Bēnaẓīr Bhuṭṭō on 27 December 2007 after a political rally in Rawalpindi.[777]

However, while neither Ṣūfī Muḥammad, who remained the *éminence grise* of the TNSM during his years of internment, nor Mullā Fazlallāh appears to have left us any writing, their learned sympathizers from the *Ahl-i Ḥadīṣ* did not really go into detail about the formal specifics of *takfīr* in general, and *takfīr al-ḥākim* in particular. On the other hand, these matters of legal technicality were at the core of intense and controversial debates in Arab militant Salafist circles which had been present in the Pashtun Borderland since the mid 1980s, and after the autumn of 2001 kept on fermenting in the FATA of Pakistan and the PATA of its NWFP. It appears, thus, safe to conclude that the views on these matters held by Salafists in Pakistan, and particularly in the Pashtun Borderland, were predominantly informed by these debates in which they do not appear to have been actively involved. We, therefore, in a penultimate step, need to shift the focus of our attention to these influences and the resulting dynamics. Important early facilitators in this were the DIIA and, even more so, the JDQS, because their respective Salafist polities provided a practical testing ground for the comprehensive implementation of the *shariʿa*. Mullā Fazlallāh's Emirate in Swat between October 2007 and – on and off – September 2009 seems, thus, to have been only an emulation of these earlier Salafist polities, as well as the result of inspiration drawn from the IEA.[778]

***

The JDQS, meanwhile, appears still to have been less willing to strategically compromise, especially insofar as the IEA was concerned. In fact, when the

[776] See Amīn, 'Svāt mēṇ [. . .]' [see above, n.769], 13; Ḥāfiẓ Muḥammad Zubair, 'Taḥrīk-i Nifāẕ-i *Sharīʿat-i Muḥammadī* – ṣ – awr ʿulamāʾ kī ẕimmi'dāriyāṇ', *Muḥaddiṣ* 31/5 (1430/2009), 28–39, here 32.

[777] For years, the instigators of the assassination remained unidentified; although *al-Qāʿida* had almost immediately claimed responsibility, the TṬP leadership was soon indicted, too. Ten years later, however, the fourth supreme *amīr* of the TṬP, Muftī Nūr Valī Maḥsūd, *nom de guerre* "Abū Manṣūr ʿĀṣim" (b. 1398/1978), emphatically restated the TṬP's claim of responsibility for Bhuṭṭō's assassination: see Maḥsūd (2017), 397f.

[778] Remarkably, Ṣūfī Muḥammad was subsequently released from jail in late April 2008 as part of the negotiations between the Pakistani state authorities and the TNSM government in Swat. Having failed to broker a robust peace agreement, he was re-apprehended in Peshawar only fifteen months later and charged once more with sedition, anti-state conspiracy and involvement in terrorist activities in the Malakand region in thirteen cases. He was finally released, on bail for medical grounds, in January 2018, that is only roughly one and a half years before his passing away in Peshawar.

ṬIT assumed control over Kunar in September 1996, the JDQS had already fragmented into an opportunistic, or pragmatic, wing headed by Ḥājjī Rōzī Khān (b. c. 1377/1958), who was subsequently rewarded with the deputy governorship of Kunar, and another around Jamīl al-Raḥmān's nephew Ḥājjī Rūḥallāh Vakīl Palavyān (b. c. 1382/1962), regarded as the then-'Salafi provincial commander for Kunar',[779] which remained fully in resistance to the first IEA central government.[780] Regardless of Ḥājjī Rūḥallāh being alleged to have been spending most of his time in Peshawar, the JDQS resistance to the IEA moved up to the more remote parts of the Pēch Valley, including the notorious Kuṛangal Valley, where it continued to relentlessly implement the JDQS's stern vision of religious beliefs and socio-cultural practices. The JQDS was aided in this by numerous foreign volunteers, including LiṬ and later *al-Qāʿida* cadres, all of whom very much followed their own agendas.[781] It was this strategic alliance which eventually broke Ḥājjī Rūḥallāh's neck: in August 2002, he was detained by US military forces and deported to its Guantánamo Bay Detention Camp, from where he was moved in 2008 back to Afghanistan and soon released.

The case of Ḥājjī Rūḥallāh can actually serve very well as an illustration of the complex and yet quite flexible handling of socio-political affairs in the tribal setting of the uplands of the Pashtun Borderland, captured in the present work by the term "Borderland pragmatics". In fact, it all goes back to the assassination of Jamīl al-Raḥmān: his very early retainer ʿAbd al-Raḥīm Muslim Dōst, first editor-in-chief of the Urdu *Daʿvat*, accused Ḥājjī Rūḥallāh of having been the driving force behind the killing of his uncle.[782] Reading the relevant passage in Muslim Dōst's account of his detention in Guantánamo closely, however, it seems that his derogatory portrayal of Ḥājjī Rūḥallāh resulted more from a serious disgruntlement about having been left out of the list of contenders for the succession of Jamīl al-Raḥmān, especially as Muslim Dōst attested the eventual new *amīr*, Samīʿallāh Najībī, a 'very weak personality'.[783] Unsurprisingly, therefore, Muslim Dōst regarded the detention of Rūḥallāh Vakīl in Guantánamo as fully justified, while he himself protested his innocence in the same breath. The story of traditional tribal rivalry, double crossing, deceit and betrayal, greed increasingly also for economic power, and hurt vanity, however, becomes more complicated still. After his release from jail in 2008, the then-President Ḥāmid Karzay met with Rūḥallāh and apologized for the detention, stating that Muslim Dōst had been denounced by the already repeatedly mentioned Malik Zarīn of the Mashvāṇī tribe, because Ḥājjī

779 Ruttig (2010).
780 See ibid.
781 See, for example, Ibn Lādin (1436/2015), 688–97 (*al-Mursila ilá 'l-Shaykh ʿAṭiyyatallāh al-Lībī*; 8 October 2010), here 689.
782 See Muslim Dōst and Badr (1385sh/1427h), 18f. See also *Daʿvat* [U] 1/1 (1408/1987), 2.
783 Muslim Dōst and Badr (1385sh/1427h), 19.

Rūḥallāh and his JDQS forces had started a systematic attempt at eradicating the large-scale cultivation of poppy in Kunar, in which Malik Zarīn is said to have had a personal stake.[784]

While Ḥājjī Rūḥallāh was in jail, Samīʿallāh Najībī, his former competitor and *amīr* of the JDQS, took the opportunity offered by the new Political Parties Law of October 2003 and had the JDQS officially registered as a political party with the Ministry of Justice in Kabul. While the party is no longer listed on the Ministry's official website, the *Country of Origins Information Report: Afghanistan* by the British Home Office has it still on record in August 2008; Ruttig situates their main dependency in Badakhshan.[785]

Less than two years later, on 9 January 2010, the elusive spokesperson for Eastern and Central Afghanistan at that time, Ẕabīḥallāh "Mujāhid", finally officially announced the formal submission of the JDQS to the command of the meanwhile Quetta-based Supreme Leadership Council of the IEA.[786] Which splinter of what had once been the JDQS it was that had actually submitted to the supreme command of Mullā Muḥammad ʿUmar, however, continues to remain obscure. Moreover, given the very fluid making and unmaking of alliances, especially in north-eastern Afghanistan, it is equally unclear whether the deference to the IEA high command was primarily confined to military considerations, or also implied some kind of merger in terms of ideology.

For the IEA, as convincingly pointed out by Ruttig, the submission of the JDQS under its high command served above all as an asset to its claim of representing the entire armed resistance against the nexus of the Afghan government and USA-led international military presence, but not necessarily an ideological stimulus. Then again, even if there was no discernible ideological cross-pollination, the subsumption of Salafist organizations such as the JDQS under the umbrella of the IEA is a clear indicator that Pashtun Salafism does indeed constitute a distinct intellectual thread in the wider "*taliban* discourse". This hypothesis is further sustained by the fact that a student wing that went by the name of *Tanẓīm Ṭalabah-yi Salafiyyah*[787] had already been inaugurated in April 1985 under the umbrella of the JDQS, with representations not only in Kunar, but also in the FATA of Pakistan, first and foremost in adjacent

[784] See Youssef (2013). How easy it is for the little initiated to buy into one or other of the many conflicting narratives around, without necessarily seeing through their strategic underpinnings, is well illustrated by the way in which Ḥājjī Rūḥallāh is portrayed by Akbar and Burton (2005), 46–9.

[785] See Ruttig (2010); Home Office / UK Border Agency (2008), 215.

[786] See Ruttig (2010). See also Roggio (2010). Both quote from the official statement released on the website of the IEA as it was at that time, one referring to the Pashto version, the other to its English pendant. This URL is long since defunct; none of the five language versions of the currently active homepage of the IEA (URL: www.alemara.af [accessed 10 February 2024]) any longer carries any item that dates from before 2017.

[787] See Anon., 'Də Tanẓīm Ṭalabah-yi Salafiyyah taʿāruf', *al-Daʿvah* 4/51 (1368sh/1410h/1990), 4.

Bajawr.[788] Its self-portrayal, in fact, resembled very much that of the ṬIT: a group of rural Salafi *madrasah* students, devoted to putting into practice their distinct interpretation of Islam, and be it by force if necessary.

Their increasingly obvious incompatibility with the still predominantly Hanafi proclivities of the ṬIT / IEA, however, would eventually result in the departure of Salafist contingents within the various ṬIT / IEA and TṬP militias across especially the northern parts of the Pashtun Borderland in the autumn of 2014 and their subsequent forging of a new alliance of serious consequence, not only militarily, but also and above all ideologically: with the IS. ʿAbd al-Raḥīm Muslim Dōst would play a pronounced role in this process. However, such an ideological alliance, which in this case reached well beyond the spatial confines of the Pashtun Borderland, required more than only religious zeal, which characterized the TNSM and its own attempts at governance. Instead, as already indicated, some more serious theological and legal knowledge was required to participate in a now trans-territorial Salafist project heavily imprinted, at least in its formative phase, with imperatives brought by Arab activists. The fully intentional intellectual fertilization of Pashtun Salafists by their brethren in spirit from other parts of the Muslim world had been, so it shall be contended, initiated by Jamīl al-Raḥmān right at the inception of the Islamic Emirate of Kunar in 1990.

Fashioning the First Salafist International

Only two months after the proclamation of the Islamic Emirate of Kunar, Jamīl al-Raḥmān publicly advertised his project to 'the Arab brethren' (*li'l-ikhwa al-ʿarab*).[789] The obvious thrust of this "offensive" was to gain an advantage over the ḤiI-Ḥ, which, despite the agreement of a large cross-party *shūrá* of which it had been a vital part,[790] remained a competitor to the JDQS. It was, therefore, a matter of the heart first of all to justify Jamīl al-Raḥmān's leadership as fully in line with the precepts of the *shariʿa*[791] and, secondly, to

[788] See Anon., 'Də Bājawṛ Ījansəy də Tanẓīm Ṭalabah-yi Salafiyyah ripōt [sic]', *al-Daʿvah* 4/55 (1369sh/1410h/1990), 3.

[789] See Jamīl al-Raḥmān, 'Taṣḥīḥ mafāhīm ḥawla ʾImārat «Kunar» al-Islāmiyya: ḥadīth li'l-ikhwa al-ʿarab', *al-Mujāhid* 2/10 (1411/1990), 20–22, here 22.

[790] See Aḥmad Zaydān, 'Kayfa yudīr al-mujāhidūn wilāyat "Kunar"?', *al-Mujāhid* 2/8 (1410/1990), 10–13; Samīʿallāh, 'Kunaṛ kī kahānī' [see above, n.702], 6–14; Samīʿallāh, 'Kunaṛūnah də jihād lah payl nah tar ōsəh', *Daʿvat* [P] 2/11–12 (1412h), 25–30.

[791] See Anon., 'Imārat-i Islāmī kē sharʿī qiyām par fatvá-yi ʿulamāʾ-i Bājawṛ', *Daʿvat* [U] 5/3 (1412/1991), 86–91 (including a transcription of the facsimile of the *fatwa*). In his argument, mufti Muḥammad Abū Bakr Ṣiddīq Kūhistānī made ample use of standard Salafi references, such as *Minhāj al-Sunna* of Ibn Taymiyya, *Faṣl al-Milal wa'l-Niḥal* of Ibn Ḥazm al-Andalusī (d. 456/1064) and the *tafsīr* of Muḥammad Amīn ibn Muḥammad Mukhtār al-Shinqīṭī (d. 1393/1974): compare al-Ẓāhirī (1416/1996), v: 13–18; al-Shinqīṭī (1426h), i: 51. The passage referring to Ibn Taymiyya (1406/1986), i: 526–31, is actually only a synopsis of the latter and has been taken verbatim – though

extend a warm invitation to the Islamic Emirate to Salafist volunteers from abroad.[792] Since this was, at that time, the only effective polity based on Salafi underpinnings outside the Kingdom of Saudi Arabia – the DIIA had by then been very much confined to the southern part of the Břagamāṭol district in eastern Nuristan – there was certainly an attraction for especially militant Salafists from elsewhere to acquire first-hand experience in Salafist state-building.

As a result, Arab former volunteers in the war against the Soviet occupation who, after the withdrawal of the Soviet forces, had begun to use the rough terrain of eastern Afghanistan as a convenient base for their own operations were drawn to the enterprise in Kunar. Simultaneously, prominent ideologues of militant Salafism, such as the Yemenite Muqbil al-Wādiʿī, ʿAbd al-Munʿim Muṣṭafá Ḥalīma, *nom de guerre* "Abū Baṣīr al-Ṭarṭūsī" (b. 1379/1959), and eventually also Usāma ibn Lādin, extended strong ideological support.[793] This ideological impetus, in turn, brought the cadres of the JDQS into closer conversation with theological and legal debates that had seriously sparked off in Salafist circles, especially across the Arabic-speaking world. In fact, that distinguishes the JDQS significantly from more or less all of the other Afghan Islamist organizations involved in the armed resistance against the PDPA regime and the Soviet military occupation of Afghanistan: while they had apparently been happy to utilize foreign volunteers in combat, they chose to remain otherwise rather aloof, as we shall see shortly in more detail. The same seems to have actually been the case with the ṬIT/IEA during its formative period and first central government, and was to change only when the USA-led military intervention pushed them into making fresh alliances with *francs-tireurs* of various origins, prominently among them Arabs of various nationalities and increasingly also Uzbek militants of the *Özbekiston Islomiy Harakati* (IMU), founded as late as 1998 by Jumaboi Khodžaev, *nom de guerre* "Juma Namangani" (killed 1422/2001), and Tohir Yol'doshev (killed 1430/2009).[794]

without acknowledgement – from al-Shinqīṭī (1426h), I: 73. Interestingly, however, Kūhistānī also used Hanafi and Maturidi works which Borderland Salafis such as Shams al-Dīn al-Afghānī would have abhorred: compare al-Kasānī (1424/2002), IX: 137f.; al-Taftāzānī (1408/1988), 96f.; al-Dihlawī (1426/2005), II: 233.

792 See Jamīl al-Raḥmān, 'Taṣḥīḥ mafāhim ḥiwal: Imārat "Kunar" al-Islāmiyya', *al-Mujāhid* 2/10 (1411/1990), 20–2.

793 See Ḥamzah (1423/2002), 137f. Also see the statements of al-Wādiʿī (1421/2000), 31–59; al-Ṭarṭūsī (1430/2009), 3; Ibn Lādin (1436/2015), 82–93 (*al-Jihād wa-Tajāwiz al-ʿUqubāt*; undated), esp. 82–9. Also see the documents published under the heading 'ʿArab mujāhidīn kī faryād: dard'mand musalmānōṇ kē nām', *Daʿvat* [U] 5/3–4 (1412/1991), 147–52. Generally, see Lav (2012), 143; Bell (2016), 12.

794 See, for example, Anon., 'Muṣāḥabah-yi istūdiyavī "Jund Allāh" bāh Qārī Valiyallāh Mazārī, ʿaẕuw-i kumīsiyūn-i Imārat-i Islāmī-yi Afghānistān', *Lashkar-i Khurāsān* 1/5 (1434h): 10–18.

The Islamic Emirate of Kunar, in contrast, and, albeit to a much lesser degree, the DIIA provided foreign Salafist volunteers not only with a platform to gain some first-hand practical experience in establishing a Salafist polity, but also with a conducive environment for further refining their ideological tenets in direct conversation with their peers from elsewhere. Thus, radical *Ahl-i Ḥadīs̱* from other parts of Pakistan, such as Amīr Ḥamzah mentioned above,[795] who were initially only interested in assisting their Afghan brethren in combat, would also increasingly open up to Salafi theological and especially legal arguments prominently presented by Arab Salafist volunteers on site and eventually embraced them as ideological foundations of their own organizations, the most important of which, the LiṬ, was indeed actually formed on Afghan soil during that period.[796]

Initially, a small contingent of radical *Ahl-i Ḥadīs̱* students at the *Jāmiʿah-yi Muḥammadiyyah* in Punjabi Gujranwala, led by Ẕakī al-Raḥmān Lakhvī, who has been mentioned above, had already ventured into Nuristan in 1983 to extend practical support to Muḥammad Afẕal and the DIIA; upon Lakhvī's return five months later, he became a chief recruiter for the further deployment of radical *Ahl-i Ḥadīs̱* to Nuristan.[797] That they ended up in Nuristan in the first place, however, was not necessarily owing to a prior acknowledgement of the ideological underpinnings of the DIIA. Lakhvī was trained courtesy of the ISI in the Lōyah Paktia region for general deployment in the Afghan armed resistance against the PDPA–Soviet nexus,[798] and owed the fact that he found himself eventually in Nuristan rather to the *Ahl-i Ḥadīs̱* networks that his teachers in the Punjab were tied into. Only after his first return from there did the reality of a Salafist polity emerge as a major selling point for further recruitment. One of those attracted by the ideological underpinnings of the DIIA project was Amīr Ḥamzah, who, in the summer of 1986, accompanied Lakhvī and nine others on the latter's second sojourn in Nuristan. Ḥamzah's extensive account of this "mission", while – perhaps unsurprisingly – resembling in parts Lakhvī's earlier favourable portrayal in the *Muḥaddis̱* magazine,[799] still remains a reasonably valuable resource, especially since other materials on Nuristan during the days of

795 See Section 4.2.2.

796 See Ḥamzah (1423/2002), 127–34, 141f. *et passim*. On the LiṬ and its political arm, the *Jamāʿat al-Daʿvah*, see Iqtidar (2011), 104–11; Tankel (2013); Yasmeen (2017), 37–80, esp. 50–2.

797 See Ḥamzah (1423/2002), 40–2.

798 See ibid., 25–40.

799 See ibid., 45–89. Amīr Ḥamzah also mentions the published memoirs of Ḥāfiẓ ʿAbd al-Manān Nūrpūrī (d. 1433/2012) on his participation in these early cross-border activities, entitled *Āʾinah-yi Nūristān* (see ibid., 40). Regrettably, no copy of this work could be found, perhaps because it may have been officially banned by the Pakistani state authorities because of its inciting content. Another two untraceable works mentioned in this regard by Amīr Ḥamzah are *ʿArabistān sē Nūristān tak* and *Sarguzasht-i Nūristān*, both by Mawlānā ʿAbd al-Raḥmān Kaylānī (d. 1416/1995), see ibid., 98.

the DIIA are so utterly scarce. Yet, the eleven *Ahl-i Ḥadīs̱* students-cum-*mujāhidīn* from Gujranwala stayed only some three weeks in Nuristan before returning to their studies, which makes the whole episode appear rather like a kind of adventure excursion of young men in their late adolescence.

Be that as it may, they were well received by Muḥammad Afẕal upon their arrival at Nēkmūk, although communication needed to be facilitated by Muḥammad Afẕal's nephew as interpreter. Here, they also met a certain Abū ʿAlī al-Saʿūdī and Abū Baṣīr al-Filasṭīnī, two Arab volunteers, indicative of the growing number of fighters from abroad in the Afghan resistance since around 1984.[800] The later nucleus of the LiṬ command then moved, with the blessings of the DIIA government, towards the frontline on the border with Kunar, but does not seem to have been involved in any combat, before they returned to Nēkmūk and, bidding farewell to Muḥammad Afẕal and companions, went back to Gujranwala.[801]

There, however, they began, together with some of the more radical members of the faculty at the *Jāmiʿah-yi Muḥammadiyyah*, to radiate the news of an existing Salafist polity across upper Punjab and the NWFP. Logistically supported by none other than ʿAbd Rabb al-Rasūl Sayyāf, these young *Ahl-i Ḥadīs̱* activists then extended their Salafist *daʿwa* to the various training camps established for the different militias in the immediate vicinity of the Durand Line,[802] an activity vital for the further sophistication of militant Salafism, as will be unravelled in greater detail in the next section. Their acquaintance with a like-minded commander of a local militia in Bajawr, Jamīl al-Raḥmān, who already counted some Arab Salafist volunteers among his retainers, was of crucial importance at this point. He introduced the young *Ahl-i Ḥadīs̱* militants to his educational and missionary activities across the Pashtun Borderland and successfully roped them in to his cause, which culminated in the establishment of the Islamic Emirate of Kunar. Suitably trained, the *Ahl-i Ḥadīs̱* around Amīr Ḥamzah were employed in preaching the tenets of Salafi Islam to the people in Kunar as soon as they arrived in Asadabad. Jamīl al-Raḥmān had a distinct military camp set up for his foreign retainers, which would also serve as a convenient first contact point for all new arrivals.[803]

Two of them who should be mentioned here were the Indonesians Ja'far Umar Thalib (b. 1381/1961) and Abu Nida (b. 1374/1954). In fact, both brought the legacy of Jamīl al-Raḥmān and the JDQS back to Indonesia, underlined not least by the fact that, in 1995, Abu Nida founded the *Ma'had Jamilurrahman As Salafy*, a religious seminary (*pesantren*) in the village of

800 See ibid., 63f. On the emergence of the so-called "Arab Afghans", see Section 4.5.1. It is rather unlikely, however, that "Abū Baṣīr al-Filasṭīnī" is, in fact, identical with the above-mentioned Abū Baṣīr al-Ṭarṭūsī.

801 See ibid., 66–85.

802 See ibid., 98–127.

803 See ibid., 200–66.

Wirakertèn, situated in the Bantul District of the Special Region of Yogyakarta and established for the dissemination of a militant and governance-orientated interpretation of Salafi Islam.[804] In 2000, finally, both Ja'far Umar Thalib and Abu Nida emerged as spearheads of *Laskar Jihad*: this paramilitary wing of the *Forum Komunikasi Ahlus Sunnah Wal Jama'ah* provided further evidence for the inspirational impact of Jamīl al-Raḥmān and the JDQS, as became manifest in the *Laskar*'s violent activities against Christians during the ethno-political conflict in the Moluccas between 1999 and 2002.[805] *Laskar Jihad* was dissolved only two years after its inception, giving way to serious factional disputes among its former leading members, among them Thalib and Abu Nida, who found themselves on different ends of the dispute that pivoted greatly on the issue of how Salafists are to position themselves towards the Indonesian government and the constitutional framework of the republic. Interestingly, those of the former leadership of the *Laskar Jihad* who began to advocate a state-supportive attitude, were former students of the *Dār al-Ḥadīth* in Yemeni Dammāj, established and run by Muqbil al-Wādiʿī, who, in turn, was also actively involved with the Islamic Emirate of Kunar.[806] Yet, after the dissolution of the *Laskar Jihad*, his former students turned away from his rather uncompromising positions and embraced those of Rābiʿ al-Madkhalī instead.[807]

While al-Madkhalī's rather loyalist viewpoints seem to be growing into the dominant form of Salafism in Indonesia, this does not mean that its militant, or – euphemistically – "revolutionary" variety ceased to exist. Yet, the fragmentation of the Salafi scene in Indonesia in the aftermath of 2002 indicates that the element of armed *jihād*, which had served to bind potentially conflicting groups and individuals together in a common cause, had ceased to carry effective force. As we shall see in the following, dissenting views could not be supressed much

804 See Hasan (2006), 71–3. On the *Ma'had Jamilurrahman As Salafy* in Wirakertèn (homepage URL: http://pondokjamil.atturots.or.id [accessed 23 April 2020; currently defunct]), there exists an unfortunately still unpublished 2014 ethnographic study by Ahmad Bunyan Wahib (UIN Sunan Kalijaga Yogyakarta) and his two assistants Alfarabi and Haidarullah, *Pola Engagement dan Disengagement Aktivis Muslim Militan di Yogyakarta (Studi terhadap Komunitas Pesantren Jamilurrahman)* (Yogyakarta: Lemlit UIN Sunan Kalijaga). Sunarwoto (Yogyakarta) must be thanked for providing a copy of the report, as well as additional information on this *pesantren* and its later affiliates, the *Ma'had Tahfidzul Quran* (added in 1996) and the *Markaz Syaikh Bin Baz* (added in 2000). Further thanks are due to Martin van Bruinessen (Utrecht) for bringing this institution to my attention in the first place.

805 On the stay of these two in Kunar, see Hasan (2006), 52 and 71–3. On the *Laskar Jihad* in general, see ibid.

806 See Ṣafāʾ al-Ḍawī, '"al-Mujāhid" taltaqī bi-faḍilat al-shaykh Muqbil bin Hādī al-Wādiʿī', *al-Mujāhid* 4/10 (1414/1994), 12–16. On Muqbil al-Wādiʿī and his role within the wider Salafist discourse, see Bonnefoy (2011).

807 See Sunarwoto (2016; 2020).

longer even within the militant spectrum of Salafism and caused further fragmentation on ideological grounds, in addition to the rather pragmatic making and unmaking of strategic alliances during times of war.

4.5 Challenges by Outsiders: The Local Impact of *al-Qāʿida* and the IS

The role of Afghanistan during the 1980s and 1990s as a refuge and connecting point for radical Muslims from the MENA region, as well as for the genesis of the *al-Qāʿida* organization, is perhaps so far the best-researched issue of all the various intricate developments in the Pashtun Borderland within the focus of the present book. This is only mildly surprising: after all, it was the activities of *al-Qāʿida* that brought Islamically sustained militancy to the heartlands of the Global North in a dramatic fashion.[808] Similarly, the history and background of the IS has for some time been frenetically researched, first and foremost because of its very concrete bearings on these industrial nations.[809] Yet, the impact of these two genetically related organizations on the Pashtun Borderland itself appears to be of significantly lesser academic interest. In most studies, "Afghanistan" figures mainly as a deployment zone for predominantly Arab militant Muslim activists, and their Pashtun counterparts are treated only as their facilitators,[810] which is why many of them had to join *al-Qāʿida* activists in detention at the Guantánamo Bay Naval Base and elsewhere. All these studies are undoubtedly useful in putting together a map of those non-Afghan activists who organized themselves into *al-Qāʿida* and other Arab-dominated militias on Afghan (and, although largely neglected, Pakistani) soil. However, here the focus will emphatically be on the repercussions that the Afghan–Arab alliance during the resistance against the PDPA–Soviet nexus and in the immediate aftermath had for the religious landscape of the Pashtun Borderland.

Of course, the Islamic Emirate of the ṬIT between 1996 and 2001 served as an important facilitator and a link between the presence of *al-Qāʿida*, the IMU and others in the Pashtun Borderland: having been handy assets, especially in ṬIT/IEA combat action, they were readily granted the use of Islamic Emirate territory as their own operational base, at least as long as there were no negative consequences for the IEA central government itself.

808 See here, for example, Gunaratna (2002); Steinberg (2005); Wright (2006); Hegghammer (2010), 24–30 and 38–50. Even the brief study by Bell (2013) appears a little lopsided in this regard.

809 See, for example, McCants (2015); Lister (2015); Bunzel (2015), 13–16.

810 Also Brown and Rassler (2013) are predominantly concerned with the emergence of *al-Qāʿida* under the protection of Jalāl al-Dīn Ḥaqqānī and his compatriots, rather than with the Pashtun commander himself, not to speak of how and to what degree the "Ḥaqqānī nexus" actually impacted the religious landscape in the Pashtun Borderland.

In order to be able to appreciate the lasting impact of the prolonged presence of non-Afghan Muslim militants in the Pashtun Borderland better, however, we need to recapitulate – if only in a woodcut-like manner – the history of migration of non-Afghan combatants to the region and the socio-religious dynamics triggered by their lasting presence. This will take us, firstly, back to the mid 1980s, when, as had already occurred in connection with Mʿ UJM and JDQS, the first volunteers began to trickle into the Pashtun Borderland. Stretching across the time of the Afghan civil war between 1992 and 1996, the era of the IEA between 1996 and 2001, and the entire period of the USA-led military intervention since 2001, our narrative will finally reach very much into the present. This cursory review is, hereby, facilitated by the fact that many especially of the Arab volunteers have published written accounts of their time in the Pashtun Borderland, albeit ones that vary in length and attention to detail.

According to the convincing reconstruction of the emergence of a Pashtun–Arab nexus by Brown and Rassler, based in large part on the same body of textual material as the exposition here, the first Arab volunteer known to appear on the scene was the Egyptian journalist Muṣṭafá Ḥāmid (b. 1364/1945), *nom de guerre* "Abū Walīd al-Maṣrī".[811] This former adherent to the MB[812] and two Egyptian associates of his moved to the Pashtun Borderland of their own volition, following a meeting with a delegation dispatched by Jalāl al-Dīn Ḥaqqānī to the UAE to rally material support and any other form of assistance.[813] Yet, we need to bear in mind that, by that time, the Pashtun Borderland also already hosted a growing number of local graduates from the IUM, who, although they were not necessarily participating actively in the resistance against the PDPA–Soviet nexus, were, nonetheless, of vital importance for preparing the ground on which religious thought strongly associated with the Saudi Arabian Wahhabiyya could grow firmer roots in the Pashtun Borderland. After all, as has been repeatedly hinted at above, important doctrinal differences between the Afghan *mujāhidīn* of Islamist and Frontier Deobandi persuasion and their Arab supporters had already become apparent at the very instant this liaison of convenience was forged, and we must, therefore, ask why these disagreements did not result in a cancellation of the arrangement, as is inferable from Sayyāf's already highlighted admonition to the Arab volunteers in late 1985.[814]

It is actually quite likely that especially the returning IUM graduates, such as, prominently, Shams al-Dīn al-Afghānī, played a substantial role in sensitizing the wider local Pashtun population to an interpretation of Islam that was

811 See Brown and Rassler (2013), 64f.
812 See Ḥāmid (1994), 15f.
813 See ibid., 31–7.
814 See Sayyāf, 'Akhī al-muslim', *Bunyān al-Marṣūṣ* 4 (1406/1985), 4–7.

quite alien, especially to the tribally organized subalterns in the rural areas of the Pashtun Borderland, while clicking rather well with the religious universe of many of the Arab (and non-Arab) volunteers in the Afghan *jihād*, whose numbers increased significantly after 1984. Another important proxy in this regard, who has only very recently received appropriate acknowledgement by a dedicated academic monograph,[815] was ʿAbdallāh ʿAzzām and the various activities he undertook with his MKh: as a first point of call for foreign volunteers, constituting a centre for their distribution to the various Afghan Islamist militias and provider of logistics, as well as a publicistic node for processing the various ideological impulses from outside the Pashtun Borderland.

4.5.1 *ʿAbdallāh ʿAzzām: Raising the Pashtun Borderland to Global Islamic Awareness*

By the time he set up his MKh in Peshawar, ʿAzzām had already departed fully from the organizational structure and the ideology of the MB to which he had enthusiastically subscribed ever since his encounters with the then-*murāqib al-ʿāmm* of the Jordanian MB, Muḥammad ʿAbd al-Raḥmān Khalīfa (d. 1427/2006), in the mid 1950s.[816] However, differently from many of especially the Egyptian MB, his advanced degrees in Islamic *fiqh*, obtained from the University of Damascus and al-Azhar in Cairo,[817] made him – at least initially – less prone to the standard criticisms of Islamists by the formally trained *ʿulamāʾ*. Indeed, his ability to handle the normative literature in the manner of a classical *faqīh* made criticizing his hermeneutics quite challenging. His various teaching stints in Jordan, Saudi Arabia and, finally, one step away from settling down in Peshawar, at the IIUI,[818] added significantly to his reputation as a scholar to be taken rather seriously. Yet, ʿAzzām's religious conservatism and his temperament, attractive to his students but discomforting for his employers and the local state authorities, already pointed to his activist inclinations and, according to his hagiographers, earned him the telling epithet "Sayyid Quṭb of Jordan".[819] Apart from Sayyid Quṭb's brother Muḥammad (d. 1435/2014), who purportedly facilitated ʿAzzām's appointment to the Malik ʿAbd al-ʿAzīz ibn Saʿūd University in Jeddah, it was the encounter with Kamāl al-Dīn al-Sanānīrī, cadre of the Egyptian MB, member of the Quṭb family and possibly the very first Arab

815 See Hegghammer (2020).
816 See Abū Mujāhid (1398h), 39.
817 See ibid., 5, 7 and 42f.
818 See ibid., 17.
819 See ibid., 16 and 49–52.

activist to join the Afghan resistance, instead of Abū Walīd al-Maṣrī, that decisively set ʿAzzām's future agenda in that direction.[820]

Shortly after, a disagreement between ʿAzzām and ʿAbd al-Raḥmān Khalīfa over the appropriate course of action for the Jordanian MB regarding the "Afghanistan Question" resulted in such a severe cooling-off of the relationship between the organization and ʿAzzām that some commentators have even suggested that he had, in fact, been formally expelled from it.[821] This strain, in turn, had an important impact on the further development of ʿAzzām's religious and political thought, which now began to shift ever closer towards Salafist positions. Already in 1975, that is, some five years before ʿAzzām's move to Pakistan, he had published his *al-ʿAqīda wa-Atharihā fī Bināʾ al-Jīl*, carrying the subtitle "An Abridgement of the Creed of the (Pious) Elders, which is the Creed of the Author, as is the Creed of the Saved and Victorious Community at the Final Hour, that is, the Sunni Muslims".[822] This, in fact, is an important and so far surprisingly little recognized text for shedding light on ʿAzzām's hermeneutical foundations to his more prominent *jihād*-centred deliberations expressed a few years later in works such as *al-Difāʿ ʿan ʿArāḍī al-Muslimīn Ahm Furūḍ al-Aʿyān*, mentioned above, or *Ilḥaq al-Qāfila* (1987).[823]

In fact, this *ʿaqīda* is regarded here as an early document of the process described by Lav as a 'plank of the salafī jihādī project – the regrouping of Quṭbist concepts in neo-Ḥanbalism and Wahhābism'.[824] Although ʿAzzām remains strongly indebted to the thought of Sayyid Quṭb, especially regarding the assessment of the contemporary realities and the various temptations by the scientific world-view and forms of entertainment,[825] he did not refer

820 See ibid., 9.

821 See Hegghammer (2005), 193 and 192 n.32. For a decidedly more considered approach regarding ʿAzzām's alleged expulsion from the MB, see Hegghammer (2020), 200f.

822 *Khulāṣat ʿAqīdat al-Salaf, wa-hiya ʿAqīdat al-Muʾallif, wa-hiya ʿAqīdat al-Firqa al-Nājiyya al-Manṣūra ilá Qiyām al-Sāʿa (Ahl al-Sunna waʾl-Jamāʿa)*, see ʿAzzām (1417/1997), I: 2–44.

823 According to Hegghammer (2020), 130, '[t]he book places Azzam squarely in the Muslim Brotherhood intellectual tradition. The topic itself, religious education, was central to the Brotherhood's ideology. Moreover, it copiously cites Sayyid Qutb and other Muslim Brotherhood thinkers.' This assessment, however, is not shared here, for reasons stated further below.

824 Lav (2012), 133. "Neo-Hanbalism", in fact, is a category introduced by Laoust (1962), 29, which has become widely used in academic circles, as indicated by Lav (2012), 45–9. For a thorough and critical discussion of it, see Nedza (2020), 6 and 204–20. An additional critical point here is the use of the "-ism" suffix both in "Neo-Hanbalism" and in "Wahhabism", which so far remains to be properly substantiated: in this regard, see the valuable arguments by Marjanen (2018), as well as the arguments on "Islamism" and "Salafism" in Sections 4.2 and 4.4, respectively.

825 See ʿAzzām (1417/1997), I: 10–12, 16f., 28f. and 38; compare Quṭb (1962), 80f.; (1426/2005), 146 (this is actually a quote from Mawdūdī's *Pardah/al-Ḥijāb*; 1940); (1430/2009), II: 697 and 976, III: 1 217 and 1 478; IV: 2 131.

to him in any matter of doctrine or *fiqh*. There, his references remain firmly within the realm of classical exegesis, citing the disciplines of *ʿulūm al-ḥadīth* and *uṣūl al-fiqh*, with a strong leaning towards Hanbali authorities, such as Ibn Taymiyya, Ibn Qayyim al-Jawziyya and Abū ʾl-Faraj ibn al-Jawzī (d. 594/1201),[826] as well as the earlier Wahhabi scholars ʿAbd al-Raḥmān ibn Ḥasan Āl al-Shaykh (d. 1285/1869)[827] and Ḥamd ibn ʿAlī ibn ʿAṭīq. While not extensively used, these two Wahhabi scholars are represented by the *Fatḥ al-Majīd* and *Ibṭāl al-Tandīd*, respectively, both being commentaries on Ibn ʿAbd al-Wahhāb's *K. al-Tawḥīd.*[828]

The work lives up to its author's claim to represent the *ʿaqīda* of the *salaf ṣāliḥ* in terms of content, being 'midway between the repudiators (the Shiʿa) and those who had walked out' (*bayn al-rawāfiḍ (al-shīʿa) waʾl-khawārij*) – bearing in mind that, at least since Ibn Taymiyya, the term "Shiʿa" serves often as a mere stand-in for a quite broad range of classical theological orientations.[829] The heresiographical aspect that is alluded to here is, once again, a characteristic feature of especially Salafist agitation, an aspect that does not occur by default in Islamist writings, where opponents are usually rather vaguely cast as either "ignoramuses" (*juhhāl*) or "idol(ator)s" (*ṭāwāghīt*). Another indication of the strong Salafi element in ʿAzzām's *ʿaqīda* is the centrality of *tawḥīd* and his adoption of the Salafi tripartition of it.[830]

Still, ʿAzzām was perhaps not yet a full-fledged Salafist, especially when compared with even more radical authors who are said to have followed in his wake, prominently among them Sayyid Imām al-Sharīf, mentioned above, who eventually emerged as a major ideologue of what was to become *al-Qāʿida*. While ʿAzzām also crafted a commentary of the *ʿAqīda Ṭaḥāwiyya*,[831] which had been commented on by Nāṣir al-Dīn al-Albānī, for Sayyid Imām, both al-Ṭaḥawī and al-Albānī were theologically rather to be rejected as representatives of

826 See ʿAzzām (1417/1997), I: 13, 21f., 25, 30 and 38. The works ʿAzzām used have meanwhile all become standard references in Salafi writings: the *ʿAqīda Wāṣitiyya* of Ibn Taymiyya, *Talbīs Iblīs* of Ibn al-Jawzī, as well as Ibn al-Qayyim's *Iʿlām al-Muwaqqiʿīn*, *Ḥādī al-Arwāḥ ilá Bilād al-Afrāḥ* and *Ṭarīq al-Hijratayn wa-Bāb al-Saʿdatayn*.

827 On him, see al-Bassām (1398h), I: 56–62.

828 The full titles of these two rather voluminous works are *Fatḥ al-Majīd Sharḥ K. al-Tawḥīd* and *Ibṭāl al-Tandīd bi-Ikhtiṣār Sharḥ K. al-Tawḥīd*.

829 ʿAzzām (1417/1997), I: 3. For the Imāmī Shiʿa as representative of various classical forms of *kalām*, see Ibn Taymiyya (1406/1986).

830 See ʿAzzām (1417/1997), I: 7–16 and 21–3. For the historical antecedents, see prominently Ibn Taymiyya (1420/1999), 57–109; Ibn ʿAbd al-Wahhāb (1406/1986), 24–6, 106f., 116f. and 124. See also Lav (2012), 42f.; Nedza (2020), 105; and Section 4.1.2.

831 See ʿAzzām (1417/1997), I: 46–86 (*K. Tahdhīb Sharḥ al-ʿAqīda al-Ṭaḥāwiyya*). Unfortunately, the work itself has not been unequivocally dated.

"Murjiʾī jurists" (*murjiʾat al-fuqahāʾ*)[832] and, in the case of al-Albānī, even as one of the "extremists among the Murjiʾa" (*ghulāt al-murjiʾa*).[833] Indeed, a non-activist stand in view of anything religiously objectionable was clearly not acceptable in the Arab Salafist circles that congregated in Afghanistan from the mid 1980s onwards. Positions such as that of al-Albanī, who, after all, was (and still remains) a guiding star for Salafi Muslims worldwide, were interpreted by radical Salafists as a clear and deliberate denigration of the *tawḥīd rubūbiyya*, because of the implicit disjunction between an inner disposition and an externally discernible act.

The discussion over *takfīr* as an appropriate legal instrument to strip governments of their legitimacy and justify violent action as *jihād* for redressing that situation had been, in fact, a central bone of contention between Salafis and Salafists in the MENA region since the late 1970s. Even among the latter, however, this matter was not viewed in the same way by everyone, also leading to conflicting opinions over targets and strategy. Prompted for the first time explicitly by the Egyptian ʿAbd al-Salām Faraj, an early compatriot of the two trained physicians Sayyid Imām al-Sharīf and Ayman al-Ẓawāhirī in the *Tanẓīm al-Jihād al-Islāmī*,[834] the strategic discussions among the Arab Islamist and Salafist volunteers to Afghanistan pivoted initially on whether to concentrate their efforts on the "near" or the "distant enemy" (*adūw gharīb aw adūw baʿīd*):[835] should activists concentrate on their own infidel governments, or rather on those opposing forces identified as being behind these

832 This term was coined by Ibn Taymiyya and enthusiastically embraced by Sayyid Imām, see Ibn Taymiyya (1403/1983), 18–23; (1426/2005a), VII: 245f.; compare Ibn ʿAbd al-ʿAzīz (n.d.), 418–30, here 418: 'And this (the text of *al-ʿAqīda al-Ṭaḥāwiyya*), which speaks in the way of the Murjiʾa among the jurists [*ʿalá ṭarīqa murjiʾat al-fuqahāʾ*], is *not* the path of the Ahl al-Sunna.' (italics added).

833 This term, too, seems to originate in Ibn Taymiyya (1406/1986), V: 286, and was equally taken up by Sayyid Imām, see Ibn ʿAbd al-ʿAzīz (n.d.), 432f., 439, 444, 448, 464 and 470. For the application of this label to al-Albānī's commentary on the *ʿAqīda Ṭaḥāwiyya*, see Ibn ʿAbd al-ʿAzīz (n.d.), 503: '[. . .] and what he says is the speech of the extremist Murjiʾa, which limits unbelief to [active] denial and [its] proof, and considers this a separate condition for *takfīr* on the ground of infidel offences *in esse*'. See also Ibn ʿAbd al-ʿAzīz (n.d.), 502–5, 508f. and 710f.; (1420/1999), 284–90; Fuchs (2011), 104f.; Nedza (2020), 208 n.25.

834 The origins of the Egyptian *Tanẓīm al-Jihād al-Islāmī* still remain highly ambiguous. According to, for example, Gaffney (1994), 258f.; Möller (2001), 184, 187f. and 195 n.4; or Meijer (2009), 197f., this clandestine organization was founded in 1979 in Cairo by Faraj himself and almost instantly merged with the Cairene chapters of the JIM, which will play a distinct role in our narrative further on (see Section 4.5.3). An alternative version projects the *Tanẓīm al-Jihād* as a reservoir of militant renegades from the MB and activists of the JIM, leaving the actual role of Faraj herein open: see, for example, Ayubi (1991), 110 and 117. The standard reference for this narrative appears to be Kepel (1984), which, because the text is regrettably ill-referenced, seems of only limited use for gaining a closer understanding of the Cairene *Tanẓīm al-Jihād al-Islāmī*.

835 See Faraj (1981), 11.

infidelities? In other words, should Egyptians focus on Egypt, Saudis on Saudi Arabia and Afghans and Pakistanis on their own respective countries, or should Muslims rather unite as a global front against "forces of *kufr*" such as especially the USA, because their provision of ideological and logistical support to governments of Muslim majority states was regarded as largely responsible for sustaining the acts of unbelief by such rulers?

In fact, Faraj and ʿAzzām represent the two opposite sides of the same coin. For the former 'fighting the near enemy comes before fighting the distant enemy',[836] because the

> fundament [*asās*] for the prevalence of Imperialism in the lands of Islam are these [i.e., the Egyptian etc.] rulers [*al-ḥukām*]. To begin with, targeting the destruction of Imperialism is therefore not useful and, in fact, rather a waste of time. We need to rather concentrate on our own Islamic cause, which consists in the establishment of God's law [*iqāmat sharʿ allāh*] first of all in our own countries [. . .] There is no doubt that the scope of the *jihād* consists in the termination of these unbelieving leaderships and their replacement with the all-comprehensive Islamic system [*al-niẓām al-islāmī al-kāmil*].[837]

ʿAzzām, in contrast, envisaged the conceptual pair of near and far enemies differently. For him, all matters of unbelief were not nationally confined, but rather a concern to each member of the Muslim *umma*, regardless of their respective nationality. Accordingly, the oppression of Muslims under non-Muslim rule in Egypt would be of equal importance to, say, the persecution of the Muslim Rohingya by followers of the Buddha in Rakhine State in Myanmar:

> Whoever from among the Arabs is able to fight *jihād* in Palestine starts there; whoever is not capable should set out for Afghanistan. The rest of the Muslims, I propose, should start their *jihād* in Afghanistan. It is our view that we begin with Afghanistan before Palestine, not because Afghanistan is more important than Palestine: in fact, Palestine is the foremost matter of Islam. It is the heart of the Islamic world, and it is blessed soil, but there are [some good] reasons to make Afghanistan the starting point.[838]

One of those reasons stipulated by ʿAzzām was the convenient make-up of the Pashtun Borderland:

> There exist more than three thousand kilometres of open border [*al-ḥudūd al-maftūḥa*] in Afghanistan and, in addition, the tribal region [*minṭaqa al-qabāʾil*] which is not subject to [state] political rule and, therefore, provides an impenetrable shield [*dirʿan ḥasīnan*] for the *mujāhidīn*.[839]

[836] Ibid.
[837] Ibid.
[838] ʿAzzām (1417/1997), I: 127 (*al-Difāʿ* [. . .]).
[839] Ibid., I: 128.

ʿAzzām's appeal for *jihād* in Afghanistan did not, therefore, follow the logic of the distinction between a "near" and a "distant enemy", a binary that was of virtually no practical significance to him, but instead arose from a pragmatic reality check of the prevalent conditions[840] that he regarded as much more favourable in the Pashtun Borderland than, say, in Palestine.

Notably, however, Faraj and ʿAzzām both built their respective argument on divergent readings of Ibn Taymiyya. Using the same body of texts, they weighted certain statements of the medieval traditionalist differently:[841] For Faraj, the concrete advice Ibn Taymiyya gave to the people of Mardin, subjected to Mongol rule since the summer of 1299 CE,[842] allowed them to remain a steadfast believer in a land which was not governed by the rules of Islam (*aḥkām al-islām*), conditional on the ability to actively oppose the un-Islamic rule and work for its destruction and subsequent replacement by a proper Islamic framework. Only once this provision is no longer given does emigration (*hijra*) to a land under Islamic rules (*dār al-islām*) become a religious obligation.[843] For ʿAzzām, in turn, Ibn Taymiyya's legal concept of a hybrid (*murakkab*) between the definitions of *dār al-silm / īmān* and *dār al-ḥarb / kufr* informed his own view of the status of more or less the entire contemporaneous Muslim world,[844] which allows the righteous Muslim to stage the *jihād* for the liberation of Muslims from non-Muslim rule from everywhere, as all the targeted regions – for example, Afghanistan, Kashmir, Palestine, Bosnia and Chechnya[845] – were of equal value to him.

Such seemingly ideological reasoning, however, somewhat obscures the fact that ostensibly voluntary migration to the Pashtun Borderland presented itself as a convenient course of action for Muslim militants from across the MENA region at that particular point in time, when their own respective national governments were clamping down hard on those non-state actors who were

840 This pragmatic assessment of the ever-changing context for making an informed decision about the feasibility of armed *jihād* at a certain moment in time appears quite close to *fiqh al-wāqiʿ*, a concept which attracted exceptional attention in the course of the systematically justified abjuration of militancy by the leadership of the JIM in the early 2000s, see Section 4.1, n.2. There is, however, a valid reason to assume that ʿAzzām and his compatriots in and around the MKh were already familiar with this concept in 1990, although possibly only in a very superficial manner, see Section 4.5.1.

841 Michot (2006), 45–61, himself an academic authority on Ibn Taymiyya as well as, at the same time, religiously indebted to the medieval Damascene traditionist, criticizes later radical authors such as Faraj and ʿAzzām for decontextualizing statements that Ibn Taymiyya had made in response to concrete historical situations, an approach Michot calls 'l'islamisme mongolisant' (see Michot (1994), 27).

842 See Ibn Taymiyya (1426/2005a), XXVIII: 135. For an annotated translation, see Michot (2006), 63–5.

843 See Ibn Taymiyya (1426/2005a), XXVIII: 158–61. For an annotated translation, see Michot (2006), 66–85.

844 See ʿAzzām (1417/1997), I: 150–75, esp. 159f. (*Iʿlān al-Jihād*, c. 1988).

845 See ibid., I: 127 (*al-Difāʿ* [. . .]).

held responsible for the increasingly violent disturbances of public life. The option of migration sustained by religious precepts appears to have been especially attractive to the activists of various Egyptian organizations, the JIM and its later offshoot, the *Tanẓīm al-Jihād*, prominent among them.[846]

The ideologues especially of the latter who had, as stipulated by the title of one of ʿAzzām's treatises,[847] "joined the caravan" to the *jihād* in Afghanistan, began thereafter to blend the opposing views of Faraj and ʿAzzām. Two at the helm among them were, once again, the leading *Tanẓīm al-Jihād* cadres Sayyid Imām al-Sharīf and Ayman al-Ẓawāhirī. After the assassination of Egyptian President of State Anwar al-Sādāt on 6 October 1981 at the hands of one of the *Tanẓīm al-Jihād* activists, al-Ẓawāhirī was apprehended in the subsequent wave of arrests by Egyptian security forces and subsequently jailed, while Sayyid Imām managed to slip away, first to the UAE and, from there, to Peshawar. Once released, al-Ẓawāhirī followed him there, and both strove initially to reorganize their organization and plan their next assault on the – in their eyes – unbelieving and, therefore, illegitimate regime in Cairo.[848] Under these circumstances and strategic premises, in 1988, Sayyid Imām released his first major work, *al-ʿUmda fī Iʿdād al-ʿUdda li-Jihād fī Sabīl Allāh Taʿālá*, aiming at 'answering the following question: how can we fulfil the duty of *jihād* while we are in a state of weakness, fragmentation and a lack of opportunities?',[849] a question that relates very much to the controversial conceptual issue of the "far enemy" and "near enemy". For him, the answer to this question is provided in the Qur'an, as well as, once again, by Ibn Taymiyya: 'It is equally necessary to be ready for *jihād* by gathering strength and strap up the horse at a time when one has declined into inability [*fī waqt suqūṭihi li'l-ajz*]. Yet, this does not waive the compulsion for it, as it [i.e., *jihād*] is compulsory.'[850] Hence, Sayyid Imām concluded, the *mujāhidīn* were to train in the convenient environment of the Pashtun Borderland and prepare

846 While the leadership of the *Tanẓīm al-Jihād* exiled in Afghan soon emerged as a nucleus of *al-Qāʿida*, the presence of a substantial JIM quota in the Pashtun Borderland and its impact on the "ideoscape" there has so far received almost no scholarly recognition at all. Section 4.5.3 later in this chapter is, therefore, intended to serve as a first foray to redress this lopsided attention on *al-Qāʿida* and its immediate precursors. One who has actually acknowledged the active presence of the JIM in the Pashtun Borderland, even though still much focused on *al-Qāʿida*, is Stenersen (2017), for example 42, 47f., 120 and 154.

847 See ʿAzzām (1417/1997), I: 177–200 (*Ilḥaq bi'l-Qafīla*; 1987).

848 On these not fully vouchsafed biographical details, including a source-critical discussion, see Nedza (2020), 21–6.

849 Ibn ʿAbd al-ʿAzīz (1420/1999), 6.

850 Ibn Taymiyya (1426/2005a), XXVIII: 146; compare Ibn ʿAbd al-ʿAzīz (1420/1999), 6. His Qur'anic references in this regard are Q8.46 and Q60, pleading for unity and for the exertion of all possible effort to at least 'terrify the enemies of God and your own enemies' (*turhibūna bihi ʿaduwwa 'llāhi wa-ʿaduwwakum*).

themselves for the moment when an attack on the Egyptian regime became a viable option again.

While biding their time for that moment, the *mujāhidīn* were to be not only physically trained, but also ideologically primed, a process that was tremendously furthered by the fact that the Arab and other non-Afghan volunteers had established their own training facilities in the Pashtun Borderland by the mid 1980s (Map 4.3).[851]

Since these camps were prominently organized along the principle of common territorial association, the interaction between them and, even more so, with their Afghan hosts and compatriots became confined only to actual instances of combat. True, the language barrier may have added to this emergence of parallel Arab universes in the Pashtun Borderland: after all, most Arab volunteers did not bother to honour their hosts by acquiring even a bare minimum of the local idioms. That the proficiency in Arabic especially among the subaltern *mujāhidīn* from Afghanistan and Pakistan during the armed resistance against the PDPA–Soviet nexus was at best confined to the ability of reading classical Arabic religious texts and certainly not sufficient to participate in lively theological and legal debates among Arabic native speakers reinforced the separation even further.

As a result, very little of the debates and the literature that emerged from the Arab camps permeated the Afghan environment in which they were now cultivated, and especially the complex theological and legal matter of *takfīr*, on which an elaborate discussion emerged from those camps,[852] remained initially alien to their Pashtun hosts. Instead, their views on this matter were more informed either by the rather loose and polemical use of that practice in the Pashtun Borderland, as we have already encountered time and again in the earlier chapters of this book, or by the standard Hanafi arguments, as exemplified in the collected *Fatāvá* of the *Dār al-ʿUlūm-i Ḥaqqāniyyah* at Akōṛah Khaṫtak: with reference to al-Kasānī's *Badāʾiʿ al-Ṣanāʾiʿ*, the mufti highlighted, in his response to a query about the procedure of subjecting an apostate to the death penalty, the legal necessity to first invite the offender back to Islam, then give him three days respite to repent (*istitāba*),[853] something that the Arab militant Salafists in the Pashtun Borderland no longer considered.

In the diverging worlds of the Afghan and Arab *mujāhidīn* of the mid 1980s, it seems that ʿAbdallāh ʿAzzām was the one whose works enjoyed the widest

[851] See Steinberg (2005), 73–5.

[852] The works of such luminaries as Sayyid Imām, Ayman al-Ẓawāhirī, Abū Muḥammad al-Maqdisī, Abū Baṣīr al-Ṭarṭūsī and Muḥammad ʿAbd al-Majīd Ḥasan Qāʾid, *nom de guerre* "Abū Yaḥyá al-Lībī" (killed 1433/2012), belong to this discussion. In fact, most of them participated in a fierce internal debate from which non-Arabs had been largely excluded: see, for example, Lav (2012), 175–82; Wagemakers (2012), 137f. and 179–81; Nedza (2020), 11, 23–5 and 43–9.

[853] See Akōṛavī (1422/2002), I: 257f.; compare al-Kasānī (1424/2002), IX: 530f.

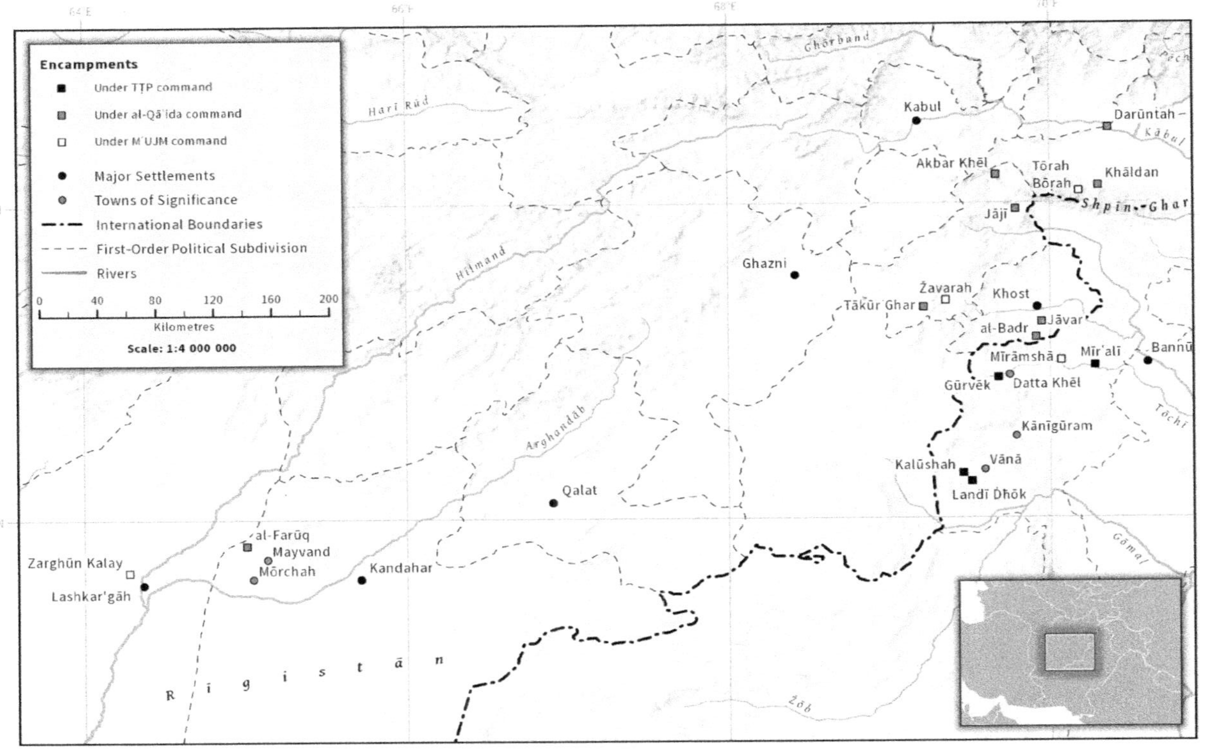

Map 4.3 Training facilities of the Islamist / Salafist International (late twentieth / early twenty-first century).

circulation beyond the Arab circles, all the more so as the occupants of the various training facilities became increasingly preoccupied anyway with fighting among themselves over the monopoly of definition in their circles.[854]

ʿAzzām, in contrast, was well placed in Peshawar, which had evolved into the primary hub for the organization of armed resistance against the PDPA–Soviet nexus and thus facilitated ample communication among the various armed Afghan Islamist organizations formerly under the umbrella of the IIMA and beyond. Yet, despite such favourable conditions, the internationally orientated agenda of ʿAzzām failed to impress his Afghan hosts. Even Islamists such as Sayyāf or Ḥikmatyār remained rather indebted to their own regional cause and had little apparent aspiration to extend their *jihād* beyond the Indo-Afghan region. Thus, collaboration was once more conceived rather as a pragmatic temporary alliance. ʿAzzām's ideological and, more importantly, logistical support was certainly as welcome as that of Usāma ibn Lādin later on; yet, it remained always conditional on the momentary interest of the diverse local commanders who granted the Arab *mujāhidīn* hospitality, as well as on honouring this privilege by abstaining from self-righteous criticism of the fidelity of the Afghan *mujāhidīn*.[855]

4.5.2 al-Qāʿida *and Pashtun Appropriations of Militant Salafist Concepts*

With the eventual rise of *al-Qāʿida* in the mid 1990s, however, and the again intensified collaboration with militant Muslim activists in the Pashtun Borderland, formerly rejected elements of the militant Salafist ideology, which had been developed during the 1980s in the exclusively Arab training camps, spilled over into like-minded circles among Pashtuns in the Borderland and began to tentatively grow roots there. The process, if not already latently at work, received a definite boost in 1996, when Usāma ibn Lādin, who in the meantime found himself in a rather precarious situation in Sudan, was offered sanctuary back in Afghanistan by three officially dispatched members of the Ḥil-Kh, the Ḥil-Ḥ and the IIAA. Their motivation, in turn, was once again informed by Pashtun Borderland pragmatics: as we have already encountered on various occasions, the infamous Saudi, who was not restrained by any

854 See the various laudatory statements by most of the leaders of the otherwise fiercely quarrelling Afghan and Pakistani Islamist organizations on the occasion of ʿAzzām's assassination, for example, in *Bunyān al-Marṣūṣ* 30 (1410/1990), 19–25; Anon., 'Payām-i Prūfisūr Burhān al-Dīn Rabbānī ... bah munāsibat-i shahādat-i buzurg'mard-i ʿālá'maqām Shaykh ʿAbdallāh ʿAzzām', *Mīṣāq-i Khūn* 2nd Series 4/9–10 (1367sh), 6f.; Ḥabīb Aḥmad, '... wa-raḥala al-duktūr ʿAbdallāh ʿAzzām: abʿād ightiyāl al-duktūr ʿAbdallāh ʿAzzām – raḥmahu allāh', *al-Mujāhid* 1/12 (1410h), 14f.; Anon., 'The great Mujahid Shaikh Aizzam [*sic*] martyred', *Khuddam-ul-Furqan* 1/2 (1989), 29f.

855 See, once again, Sayyāf, 'Akhī al-muslim' [see above, n.814], 4–7.

agnatic bonds with one of the tribal communities on the ground, was regarded as a suitable arbitrator between the Islamist government of Kabul and the ṬIT, which, by then, had emerged as a serious contender for power over Afghanistan.[856] Upon his arrival at Jalalabad Airport, Ibn Lādin was personally greeted by Sayyāf, then a representative of the Afghan government, and by Yūnus Khāliṣ, who had relocated from Peshawar back to his native province two years earlier and had turned down the offer to become a member of the Rabbānī administration. It was perhaps this independence from the power circles of Kabul that made Ibn Lādin decide to accept Khāliṣ's invitation to the *Najm-i Jihād* housing development in Jalalabad, a compound that would soon emerge as a major base of operations for what finally became known as *al-Qāʿida*.

For Islam and The Companions: Ideologizing an "Atmosphere" towards Religious Minorities

While it seems as if Khāliṣ had won the contest of courting Ibn Lādin, Sayyāf had meanwhile moved ideologically much closer to those who would soon emerge as the leadership of *al-Qāʿida*. The atrocities committed against Shiʿi Muslims during the so-called "Operation Afshār" in February 1993 by order of Sayyāf constituted a first indication of this closing of ranks between Arab Salafist militants and Afghan Islamists.[857] Yet, a closer look reveals that these actions were not only informed by strong anti-Shiʿi sentiments, but also very much part of the power game that was being played simultaneously in Kabul. Officially dispatched as a punitive expedition against an alliance of ḤiI-Ḥ forces with the Iran-supported ethnically Hazārah ḤVIA of ʿAbd al-ʿAlī Mazārī, which was challenging the Rabbānī administration by shelling Kabul from its positions in the city's Afshār area, neither Sayyāf's IIAA nor Shāh Masʿūd's *Shūrā-yi Naẓār* was in second place insofar as the bloodshed was concerned. Yet, Sayyāf's men going purposefully after the Hazārah Shiʿi Muslims implies a combination of ethnic and religious cleansing, invoking the painful memories of Emir ʿAbd al-Raḥmān's ethnically informed politics of subjugation in the late nineteenth century. Unfortunately, however, the archive of currently available IIAA periodicals does not extend to the period after April 1990, which makes it almost impossible to firmly trace a theologically grounded rejection of Shiʿis in the thinking of Sayyāf and his commanders. Circumstantially, however, there are various factors that point to an increasingly sectarian atmosphere in the region, factors which would certainly have

856 See Muždah (1382sh), 66; ʿAzīzallāh (1386sh), 202; Ḥāmid (2002), 58. Apparently, Ibn Lādin's later bodyguard Nāṣir al-Bahrī, *nom de guerre* "Abū Jandal" (d. 1437/2015), and the young Syrian militant Muṣṭafá ibn ʿAbd al-Qādir al-Rifāʿī, *nom de guerre* "Abū Muṣʿab al-Sūrī" (b. 1378/1958), have also remarked on Ibn Lādin's arrival in Jalalabad, although neither was an actual eyewitness.

857 See Dāvūdī (1390sh), III: 239.

had an impact on Sayyāf's position on the matter and which we, therefore, need to appreciate.

The take on Shiʿi Muslims of whatever provenance did, in fact, not emerge in isolation from a wider and rather deep-rooted discourse of increasing stigmatization and subsequent marginalization of religious minorities in the Pashtun Borderland and beyond, something that had contributed over time to a certain public "*Stimmung*" or "atmosphere" towards religious and ethnic minorities.[858] It will be contended here that the processes shaping this discourse have merely gained some further momentum since the beginning of the IIMA-dominated resistance against the PDPA–Soviet nexus; that it fell on fertile ground, however, required an already widespread predisposition to the ostracizing of local minorities from the communities residing in the Pashtun Borderland. In fact, an anti-Shiʿi rhetorical lexicon was quite happily invoked already in earlier centuries for denouncing one's ethnic and/or religious opponents in the Pashtun borderland.[859] In this, Borderland actors, such as Khūshḥāl Khān Khaṫṫak in the late seventeenth century or the Ṣāḥib of Kōṫah in the late nineteenth century, contributed actively to further cementing the long-standing history of communal violence between Sunni and Shiʿi Muslims in the Indo-Afghan lands, as well as a tradition of mutual polemics in which each side accuses the other of infidelity (*kufr*), or at least heresy (*zandaqa*). While this violence appears to have previously been largely unsystematic and predominantly tied to situations of economic, social and political disparity between these respective communities in localities across the subcontinent,[860] at least from the eighteenth century onwards there have been prominent attempts at providing it with a theological and legal justification. These efforts include prominently the explicitly anti-Shiʿi heresiographical *Izālat al-Khafāʾ ʿan Khilāfat al-Khulafāʾ* of Shāh Valiyallāh Dihlavī, the *Tuḥfat-i Iṡnā ʿAshariyyah fi'l-Kalām ʿalá Maẕhab al-Shīʿah* of his son Shāh ʿAbd al-ʿAzīz and *Taqviyyat al-Īmān* and *Ṣirāṭ al-Mustaqīm* of Shāh Ismāʿīl and Sayyid Aḥmad Barēlvī.[861] All these works would subsequently be employed as standard references for the justification of Sunni supremacism across the Indo-Afghan region that finally broke with full force in the second half of the twentieth century and in which the hostile take on Shiʿi Muslims, and,

[858] See Bude (2016), 47–63; (2017). See also Section 2.4.

[859] See, for example, the respective cases of Khūshḥāl Khān Khaṫṫak and the Ṣāḥib of Kōṫah, as discussed in Sections 3.1.1 and 3.2.2.

[860] See, for example, the case of post-Partition Punjab in Zaman (2002), 124–31.

[861] See, for example, Dihlavī (1998), 21, 30f., 51f. and 75–7. Interestingly, while Shiʿi Muslims were not explicitly targeted either in *Taqviyyat al-Īmān* or in *Ṣirāṭ al-Mustaqīm*, the next generation of *Ṭarīqah-yi Muḥammadiyyah* activists would eventually turn the branding of certain beliefs and rituals commonly adhered to by Shiʿis and Sufis alike as forms of *shirk* and *bidʿa* into full-fledged anti-Shiʿi heresiographies: see Gaborieau (2010), 145–7.

subsequently, all other religious minorities in Sunni-dominated environments, evolved into a *definiens* of normatively grounded Sunni Muslim identity.

Various external factors contributed to this dramatic development: while the victorious Islamic Revolution in Iran provided especially Imāmī Shiʿis all over the world with a mighty and theologically sustained political reference point, Zia-ul-Haq's seizure of power and subsequent regime of comprehensive Sunnitization in Pakistan at around the same time aggravated the already fairly deep denominational divide and added material implications to the ever more firmly grounded public atmosphere, not least in and around the Pashtun Borderland. This solidification of discourse was further boosted by the resistance against the PDPA–Soviet nexus in Afghanistan spearheaded by the various Afghan Islamist organizations and local militias of Frontier Deobandi background. The constant reiteration of the "*īmān – kufr*" binary in the literature which they produced, even though initially intended simply to legitimize the armed resistance to the Soviets and their PDPA stooges in Kabul, would make their respective audiences also increasingly susceptible to ideational influences from the outside, here, first and foremost, from Saudi Arabia, one of the chief stakeholders in the armed conflict. Benefiting greatly from the hostile public atmosphere already prevalent regarding religious minorities, the explicitly anti-Shiʿi attitude which emerged as a direct legal consequence of the Wahhabi doctrine of *tawḥīd*[862] could well serve as theological and legal justification for this atmosphere and for the devising of an appropriate course of action at the same time, as was wholeheartedly adopted, as we have seen, by local parties of Salafist persuasion in the conflict, such as the DIIA and the JDQS.

Others, however, such as prominently the representatives of militant "Frontier Deobandiyyat" which have so far been discussed, hardly required the support of key reference authors from the Wahhabi-cum-Salafi universe, such as Ibn Taymiyya, Ibn ʿAbd al-Wahhāb and other Hanbali grandees in their wake. Their own theological and legal deliberations on the role and status of Shiʿis in their own local communities could well remain within the hermeneutical universe of Hanafi *fiqh* and, even more specifically, within the confines of "Deobandiyyat". Starting with Rashīd Aḥmad Gangōhī, the heresiographical current of "Frontier Deobandiyyat" set out from the arguments presented in the works of Shāh Valiyallāh Dihlavī and his descendants mentioned above, but took them to their ultimate legal consequence by declaring Shiʿi Muslims outright unbelievers.[863] Despite the gravity of Gangōhī's conclusion, however, at this early point in time it had not yet resulted in serious material consequences for Shiʿis other than contributing to the further concretization of the hostile atmosphere towards them among the Sunni Muslim majority.

[862] See Steinberg (2009), 111–16; Matthiesen (2015), 1–10 *et passim*.
[863] See Gangōhī (1987), 54. Also, see Metcalf (1982), 152 and 211f.

The main reason for the Deobandi defamation of the Shiʿis was not, as for the Wahhabi-cum-Salafi approach, the violation of the dogma of the finality of prophethood by the Imāmī Shiʿi dogma of the sinlessness and infallibility (*iṣmāʿ*) of their *aʾimma*, but rather the deliberate disrespect towards certain companions of the Prophet Muḥammad who play a pivotal role in the self-conception of Sunni Islam, for example, the first Medinese Caliph Abū Bakr and his daughter and wife of the Prophet, ʿĀʾisha.[864] This point of dissent, in fact, seemed much better suited to fuel the already fairly widespread hostile atmosphere towards Shiʿi Muslims by appealing to the general sentiments of reverence towards these early figures of Islamic history, especially among subaltern Sunni Muslims in the Indo-Afghan region, sustained by the constant emphatic reiteration of their unreserved significance by the activists of popular pietistic Sunni mass movements, such as prominently the TJ.[865]

For many decades, the Deobandi had taken on the religious beliefs and practices of Shiʿi Muslims, firmly rooted in the Hanafi tradition of Islamic *fiqh*, appearing, thus, more befitting to the general public atmosphere regarding non-Sunni minorities than demanding the actual enforcement of the legal consequences. This was clearly no different in the Pashtun Borderland, as, in fact, is once again well illustrated by the published *fatwa*s of ʿAbd al-Ḥaqq Akōṛavī, founder of the *Dār al-ʿUlūm-i Ḥaqqāniyyah* at Akōṛah Khaṭṭak, on this matter. All five – unfortunately undated – legal opinions on the evaluation of the Shiʿi creed and resulting practices, also including the practical question about interdenominational marriage, have been answered exclusively with recourse to classical Hanafi authorities, in one instance, also including Shāh Valiyallāh Dihlavī.[866]

Yet, except perhaps for the latter, none of these references actually corroborates ʿAbd al-Ḥaqq's depiction of Shiʿi creed and rite as expressions of

864 The Shiʿi debasement of these pivotal figures for Sunni Islamic identity is rooted in the original schism in the early Muslim *umma* over the succession to the Prophet in the leadership of the community, as well as the subsequent armed confrontations, such as the so-called "Battle of the Camel" (*maʿrakat al-jamal*) in 36/656, in which those who would eventually emerge as the *Ahl al-Sunna wa'l-Jamāʿa* were goaded on site by the Prophet's widow ʿĀʾisha bint Abī Bakr al-Ṣiddīq. Over time, the antipathic sentiments gave rise to a number of communal practices in the polities ruled by Imāmī Shiʿis that were designed to cause a strong sentiment of indignation among Sunni Muslims under their rule, such as the public dissociation (*tabarrāʾ*) from the first three of the so-called "Rightly guided Caliphs" in the call to prayer and the ritual invocations at the beginning of the Friday sermon. In the majority of cases, however, Shiʿi rulers apparently decided to waive these practices for the sake of maintaining communal harmony within their realm: see, for example, Astarābādī (1875), 273–5.

865 Symptomatically, see Nuʿmānī (1405/1984), 191–223.

866 See Akōṛavī (1422/2002), I: 385–8 and 400. For the Hanafi-Maturidi references, see al-Ḥaṣkafī (1423/2002), 199 and 344; Ibn ʿĀbidīn (1423/2003), VI: 378; al-Miṣrī (n.d.), V: 206f.; al-Bazzāzī (2009), II: 439f.; [al-Burhānfūrī] et al. (1421/2000), II: 286; al-Taftāzānī (1408/1988), V: 227, al-Qārī (1416/1995), 114–16.

unbelief, but instead they contain rather general statements on the pronunciation of *takfīr* if certain offences have been committed. The actual *takfīr* would, therefore, ultimately be based on ʿAbd al-Ḥaqq's personal assessment of the creed and religious practices of the two major Shiʿi denominations, informed perhaps not so much by a careful study of the authoritative textual corpuses of the Imāmī and Ismāʿīlī Shiʿis as by either personal observation shaped by communal hearsay or – as would befit a proper Deobandi *faqīh* – *taqlīd shakhṣī*. The latter, however, is hardly ever explicit, even though ʿAbd al-Ḥaqq's conclusions clearly resemble those of Rashīd Aḥmad Gangōhī more than half a century earlier. Still, his ruling on the contours of Sunni Islam consists of a quote of the Deobandi grandee Ẓafar Aḥmad ʿUs̱mānī (d. 1394/1974),[867] which has not even been commented on further, while his position of the Shiʿis regarding the dogma of the finality of prophethood, which still remains rather general, consists almost verbatim of the legal view expressed in Shāh Valiyallāh's commentary on Malik ibn Anas's *Muwaṭṭaʾ*.[868]

As most of the criticisms resemble the arguments against exaggerating the beliefs and practices of Sufi Islam, ʿAbd al-Ḥaqq's line of argument still contains the legally less precise ideas that were propagated by the adherents to the *Ṭarīqah-yi Muḥammadiyyah*. In September 1987, however, the public atmosphere seems to have been aggravated to such an extent that it provided a sufficiently conducive environment for further escalation: Samīʿ al-Ḥaqq now declared the active defence of the integrity of the Prophet's companions to be an individual religious compulsion for every Muslim (*farẓ-i ʿayn*), implying that those who do not meet this requirement would be in danger of being expelled from the community of believers.[869]

The point in time here appears to be quite significant, because this declaration coincided with the imminent withdrawal of the Soviet Army from Afghanistan, the heavier influx of Arab and other non-Afghan volunteers in the Pashtun Borderland and a possibly somewhat related upsurge of militant anti-Shiʿi activities across Pakistan. Two antagonistic, yet deeply intertwined, developments facilitated the latter. On the one hand, there was the emergence of a public representation of Imāmī Shiʿi interests in the *Taḥrīk-i Nifāẕ-i Fiqh-i Jaʿfariyyah* (TNFJ) in 1979, spearheaded by Mufti Jaʿfar Ḥusayn (d. 1403/1983) from Punjabi Gujranwala.[870] On the other hand, Ḥaqq Navāz Jhangvī (killed 1410/1990), a graduate of Ashraf ʿAlī Thānavī's *Jāmiʿat Khayr al-Madāris* in Multan, responded to the growing impact of the TNFJ by establishing the ASṢ

[867] See Akōṛavī (1422/2002), I: 379; compare ʿUs̱mānī and Gamthalavī (1400h), I: 169.

[868] See Akōṛavī (1422/2002), I: 387; compare al-Dihlawī (1403/1983), II: 269.

[869] See Samīʿal-Ḥaqq, 'Fitnah-yi rafẓ, difāʿ-i ṣaḥābah awr hamārā farẓ', *al-Ḥaqq* 22/12 (1407/1987), 4f.; partly reprinted in Akōṛavī (1422/2002), I: 527f.

[870] See Fuchs (2019), 137–46.

in September 1985, the first of a plethora of Sunni supremacist militant organizations that has been mushrooming ever since.

By then, the increasingly violent confrontation between the TNFJ and its Sunni opponents had already found a prime battleground in the Pashtun Borderland, very much because the young Sayyid ʿĀrif Ḥusayn al-Ḥusaynī (assassinated 1409/1988), who had been entrusted with the leadership of the TNFJ after the demise of Mufti Jaʿfar Ḥusayn, was actually a Pashtun Shiʿi of the Tūrī tribe in Parachinar (*Pāṛah Chinār*). Educated first at the *ḥawza* of Najaf and later Qom during the highly politicized late 1960s and 1970s, al-Ḥusaynī brought the legacy of scholars such as Khumaynī, whom he had personally encountered during the years in Najaf, back to Pakistan, and, to be more specific still, to his native Khurram Agency, situated immediately at the Durand Line and separated from the ḤiI-Kh base at Tōrah Bōṛah only by the – though admittedly mighty – Shpīn Ghar / Kūh-i Safīd range.[871] What started out as a movement to merely safeguard the Imāmī communities in Pakistan in cultural terms was now turned, as the TJP, into a proper political organization that would also not shy away from employing violent means, reciprocated with equal fervour by the ASṢ.

Very much in line with Samīʿ al-Ḥaqq's declaration of the active defence of the unconditional respectability of the Prophet's companions as an individual religious duty for every Muslim in 1987, the ASṢ targeted especially those Shiʿi Muslims who had been accused of deliberate disrespect towards them.[872] After Jħangvī himself was killed by a Shiʿi activist in retaliation for his anti-Shiʿi militancy, some of his lieutenants broke away and finally formed the *Lashkar-i Jħangvī* (LJħ), a name that clearly indicates that their former leader remained the spirit behind all their actions. While both have since their inception been involved in countless attacks on Shiʿi Muslims throughout Pakistan, neither group appears to have produced any substantial ideological writing.[873] For ideological nourishment, groups like them, which have emanated from the wider universe of "Deobandiyyat", would, therefore, rely heavily either on works that have been appropriated into the Deobandi master narrative or texts produced in Deobandi / TJ circles.

The immensely popular polemic of Muḥammad Manẓūr Nuʿmānī (d. 1417/1997), a Deoband-educated scholar with substantial influence on the TJ with his base in Indian Lucknow, turned out to be of exceptional importance in this regard. Written in 1984 as a reckoning with Khumaynī and the Islamic

[871] See Zaman (2002), 114–18; Fuchs (2014); (2019), 135f.

[872] See Zaman (1998), 693–714; (2002), 118–24; Abou-Zahab (2004), 141–8.

[873] The voluminous *Tārīkhī Dastāvīz* (1994), compiled by the then-leader (*sar'parast*) of the ASṢ, Abū Rayḥān Ẓiyāʾ al-Raḥmān Fārūqī (executed 1418/1997), is, in fact, not a genuine text by ASṢ cadres, but rather a compilation of sections of heresiographical and classical legal works on the religious status of the Shiʿi Muslims. Other writings of Fārūqī comprise primarily short eulogies of prominent companions of the Prophet.

Revolution in Iran,[874] this polemic instantly became a fast selling item, especially in Deobandi / TJ circles, also in the Borderland, and added its share to the further deterioration of the already taut situation there. In the very same year that Nuʿmanī published his polemic, Zia-ul-Haq is said to have given his explicit blessing concerning violent attacks of activists of the Ḥ M on the TJP stronghold in Parachinar.[875] What for the military dictator may have been only a punitive expedition against the TJP also had, similarly to "Operation Afshār" nine years later, some much more down-to-earth Borderland reasons which dated back to as far as the eighteenth century. The Shiʿi Tūrī tribesfolk had then pushed their former lords, the Sunni Bangash, to the south of Khurram, creating constantly simmering disputes in the wake of this event between the two tribal communities over land and natural resources.[876] For local Bangash, therefore, the clash between ḤM and TJP cadres in Parachinar also appeared to be a convenient opportunity to settle old scores.

***

What applies to the Shiʿi communities in the Pashtun Borderland and beyond pertains even more to the even smaller non-Muslim minorities there, first and foremost among them Sikhs and Hindus. The emotionally charged public attitude in Pakistan especially towards them had never been exceptionally cordial thanks especially to the collective memory of atrocities committed by Hindus in India during the course of Partition in 1947, which are kept fresh by making them a vital part of political rhetoric towards Pakistan's neighbour in the east. In Afghanistan, however, this attitude had seemingly deteriorated at a much later moment, yet with a similar long-term effect.

As soon as the communist enemies had been ousted from power and country, the binary morphed increasingly into a legal argument suitable for the ideologically sustained privileging of Sunni Islam above all other religious expressions, and to grant its adherents the right to claim the status and possessions of community members of other religious beliefs. At first glimpse, the situation in the FATA Agencies inside Pakistan's then-NWFP appeared quite like that of Afghanistan. However, one must remember that the annexation of the Peshawar Valley by the Sikhs under Mahārāja Ranjīt Siṅgh in the aftermath of the militant activities of the *Ṭarīqah-yi Muḥammadiyyah* in the Pashtun Borderland has been well logged in the collective memory of Muslim Pashtuns, especially to the east of the eventual Durand Line. In addition, the persistent presence of the spiritual descendants of the *Ṭarīqah-yi Muḥammadiyyah* in their colonies across the eastern Borderland was a constant reminder of the imperial attitude of the

[874] On Nuʿmānī, see Hartung (2004), 326–9 *et passim*. Nuʿmānī's work in question here is *Īrānī Inqilāb, Imām Khumaynī awr Shīʿiyyat* (1984).

[875] See Abou-Zahab (2009a), 8.

[876] See ibid.; compare Ḥayāt Khān (1867), 339f.

Sikhs in the early nineteenth century, which, if properly essentialized, could well be used to cultivate at least some suspicion towards Sikhs, thereby pushing them into a potentially very vulnerable position.[877]

Yet, the spreading of the idea of religious uniformity under the umbrella of a stern and conservative Sunni Islam in the Pashtun Borderland was not exclusive to Islamists of whatever shade. In fact, the travelling activists of the TJ turned out to be the most instrumental in these processes. They did not merely contribute significantly to the hostile atmosphere towards Shiʿis by fervently propagating the unimpeachable virtues of the Prophet and his companions: approaching villages and reprimanding their Sunni inhabitants for their adherence to allegedly Hindu customs served the purpose of establishing a sense of Sunni supremacy in these localities well, and increased the social pressure to clearly dissociate oneself from all beliefs and rituals declared to be un-Islamic.[878] The activities of the TJ regarding the few remaining Kaĺaśa, a distinct ethnic community in Chitral and a few valleys in Afghan Nuristan that adheres to a polytheistic religion which pivots much on the annual life cycle and its gregarious cattle, have been most fatal for that community. Although they successfully withstood forced conversion, the massive theft of cattle from the few Kaĺaśa-populated valleys by TJ activists, who redistributed the animals among Sunni Muslims in adjacent Nuristan, resulted in the near extinction of the Kaĺaśa religion.[879]

Countless members of the non-Muslim religious communities in the Pashtun Borderland, who lacked similar political and military community representation to the Imāmī Shiʿis, responded to the increasing manifestation of hostile sentiments towards them in the wider public on either side of the Durand Line by increasingly giving up their homes and worldly possessions and emigrating to India,[880] or to countries in Europe or North America, while

877 Conversely, Hussain (2018), 113 and 126–59, in what seems to be the only study so far in English expressly dedicated to the Sikh communities in the Pashtun Borderland, conveys the rather optimistic impression that the Sikh communities in Peshawar are currently quite well integrated into the majority society and hardly subject to any discrimination on ethno-religious grounds by the Sunni Muslim majority of the population.

878 So far, no proper investigation of the role of the TJ in mainstreaming religiosity in the Pashtun Borderland and beyond could be identified, and such a study appears, therefore, to be a major research desideratum. Yet, glimpses of the activities of the TJ in the region can be gained from marginal remarks in ethnographic work, as well as more popular travel accounts: see, for example, Marsden (2005), 144f. and 181f.; Knudsen (2009), 31–3, 99 and 179.

879 Muhammad Kashif Ali (University of Gujrat, Pakistan), ‘Kalasha of Chitral: Victims of Extremism and Mal-Governance’ (paper delivered at the 26th Pakistan History Conference, University of Peshawar, 10 October 2017). Apart from Ali’s, there seems, so far, to have been hardly any academic work on the very manifest existential threat to Kaĺaśa cultural identity.

880 On Hindu and Sikh migration from Afghanistan to India, see, for example, Bose (2004), 4, 699f.

those of them who did not have the means to migrate increasingly sought safety by at least moving into the better secured compounds of their respective places of worship.[881] As discomforting as this is, this strategy of evading the looming material consequence for life and limb by leaving their ancestral homes for good appears quite sensible in view of the further aggravation of interreligious communal tension in the Pashtun Borderland from the late 1980s onwards. This time, however, it was pushed forward by the visibly growing impact of increasingly self-confident militant Sunni Muslim actors, especially from the MENA region, that was to have an irreversible impact on the way in which religious discord is negotiated in the Pashtun Borderland.

Only a few months after Samīʿ al-Ḥaqq had declared the defence of the sacrosanctity of the Prophet's companions an individual religious duty, no lesser a protagonist than Usāma ibn Lādin is said to have been actively involved in the violent suppression of unrest in Gilgit-Baltistan,[882] dominated by non-Pashtun Ismāʿīlī Shiʿis, which ignited over a religious issue that their Sunni counterparts perceived as socially disruptive.[883] However, political Borderland issues also played an adjunct role here: the separatist *Tanẓīm-i Millat*, formed in Gilgit in 1971, demanded not only proper civil rights for the Shiʿi minorities in Pakistan, and ideally an independent polity, but also the abolition of the still effective FCR, which, after all, provided the legal backup for the punitive measures dealt out by the Pakistani state authorities and their substate Sunni allies from the Pashtun Borderland. Employing foreign mercenaries in the suppression of these aspirations turned out to be a smart strategic move by the agents of the Pakistani state: after all, Arab Salafists were known for their uncompromising rejection of Shiʿis, on a good day, as heretics (*zanādiqa*), or, on a bad one, as unbelievers (*kuffār*). Moreover, the overwhelming majority of

881 Personal observation of and conversation with a Hindu family living inside the Kālībārī Mandir, Ṣadr, Peshawar, on 8 August 2017.

882 So far, there has been no documented evidence of Ibn Lādin's direct involvement in atrocities against Shiʿi Muslims in the course of this punitive expedition which, in the collective memory of the communities in Gilgit, is known as the "Jalalabad incident", referring to the neighbourhood of Gilgit Town in which most of the cruelties were committed. Iẓhār ʿAlī Hunzāʾī, the General Manager of the Aga Khan Rural Support Programme in Pakistan, recalled local rumours that Ibn Lādin had been surveying Gilgit-Baltistan for its strategic suitability to stage transnational *jihādī* activities in all the adjoining nation-states. Dóra Günsberger (Budapest) generously shared the recordings of her interview with Hunzāʾī, conducted on 9 March 2017 in Islamabad.

883 Purportedly, the conflict arose over the sighting of the moon to determine the end of the fasting month of Ramaḍān 1408 (May 1988). After the Ismāʿīlīs had broken the fast earlier than their Sunni neighbours, the latter took serious offence and attacked the Ismāʿīlīs. The intervention by Pakistani armed forces escalated the situation further and led to violent protests of Ismāʿīlī and Imāmī Shiʿi Muslims, spearheaded by the *Tanẓīm-i Millat*, that were subsequently been crushed with the assistance of ad hoc militias prominently including militant Arab volunteers.

them did not, as we have already seen in various places, care about the delicate socio-cultural particulars of the environment in which they acted. Neither did they show the slightest degree of sensitivity towards any implication of their doings for the social fabric of the Pashtun Borderland, nor were they in the least passionate about the FCR under which, after all, many of their Pashtun hosts also suffered and which they, therefore, tried persistently to circumvent by establishing firm local control that would not tolerate any eventual interference by the Pakistani state authorities.

Remarkably, however, none of the available magazines of the various Islamist organizations under the umbrella of the IIMA in whatever language carried a report on these incidents, nor, in fact, did ʿAzzām's journal *al-Jihād*. Apparently, while fighting the Soviet army in Afghanistan, the focus was pragmatically on this enemy, rather than on getting involved in sectarian debates at the expense of their combat strength. The confidence which Usāma ibn Lādin and affiliated Arab fighters had seemingly gained during their involvement in government-sanctioned punitive expeditions against pronounced unbelievers, however, resulted in them demanding a more prominent role in the armed operations in Afghanistan. Their relative inexperience in combat strategy, coupled with a religious zeal that made them reckless, and their growing unwillingness to subordinate themselves to overall military command contributed substantially to the dismal failure of the battle between IIMA and PDPA forces for Jalalabad in March 1989, that is, roughly one month after the last Soviet soldier had pulled out of Afghanistan.[884]

Two years later, Jalāl al-Dīn Ḥaqqānī successfully led the IIMA operation for the "liberation of Khost" from PDPA rule,[885] this time with the much humbler and more obedient assistance of a substantially downscaled contingent of non-Afghan volunteers, proving that familiarity with the terrain and the societal specifics was more useful in actual combat than religious zeal. Yet, one may well argue that the non-Afghan contingents in this operation, consisting, according to a Libyan participant, of 'Saudis, Kuwaitis, Jordanians, Palestinians, Algerians, Tunisians, Syrians, Libyans and other nationalities',[886] constituted a critical mass

[884] See Ḥāmid (2002), 26–31. See also Anon., 'Də Jihād lah yawah takṛah qōmāndān Ḥājjī Maʿāfī Khān sarah marakah', *Manbaʿ al-Jihād* [P] 1/1 (1368sh/1409h), 31–42, here 36; ʿIṣām ʿAbd al-Ḥakīm, 'al-hujūm ilá "Jalālābād"', *al-Jihād* 53 (1409/1989), 10–17.

[885] See Anon., 'Khūst . . . aʿẓam al-futūḥāt', *Manbaʿ al-Jihād* [A] 2/7–8 (1411/1991), 30–47; special issue of *Nuṣrat al-Jihād* 1/6–7 (1411/1991). Interestingly, the successful operation was much less prominently covered in the Pashto version of *Manbaʿ al-Jihād* than in the Arabic and Urdu periodicals, suggesting that a certain message was to be conveyed to the non-Pashto speakers. For reports by the IIMA organizations, see, for example, Muḥammad Yūsuf "Qadr'dān", 'Fatḥ-i Khūst: itmām-i ḥujjat bā qarīb khᵛūrdagān', *Mīs̱āq-i Khūn* 6/1 (1370sh), 26f. In fact, this major military victory gave Jalāl al-Dīn Ḥaqqānī – now carrying the epithets "Conqueror of Khost" (*də Khōst fātiḥ*) and "Imām Shāmil II" – a huge boost to his public standing.

[886] Abedin (2005). The statement was made by Nuʿmān ibn ʿUthmān (b. 1386/1967), a native of Tripoli better known as "Noman Benothman". As the then-head of the *Jamāʿa*

ensuring the eventual military success. As commander of a regional force, Jalāl al-Dīn's powers appeared rather limited in comparison with those of the various factions of the *mujāhidīn* under the IIMA, which soon began to tear each other apart in their respective bid for supreme control. He had, therefore, to depend to a substantial extent on the active support also of non-Afghan combatants in the territory under his control. The delicate balance of power within the IIMA was easily disturbed over the question: 'After Khost, ... Where to?', rhetorically posed by the MKh journal *al-Jihād*,[887] which pointed clearly to the outbreak of factional disputes among the commanders under the IIMA – now acting as the legitimate government of Afghanistan in exile – immediately after the victory at Khost over the question of how to proceed, where to and to what end.

Implicit in the discussions over the further course of action was that, with this first territory in Afghanistan fully under the control of the IIMA, the various factions needed to keep their promise to establish Islamic law and order. The ideas about what this consists of were, however, manifold and conflicting,[888] and the matter was not helped by the fact that actors from Pakistan, here prominently Samīʿ al-Ḥaqq, as the leading representative of the JUI-S, and Qāẓī Ḥusayn Aḥmad of the JiI, used the occasion to tweak discussions in their own interests.[889] The branch of the JUI led by Faẓl al-Raḥmān also courted the "Conqueror of Khost" in the hope of gaining an edge over its Samīʿ al-Ḥaqq-led competitor in this way.[890]

al-Islāmiyya al-Muqātila bi-Lībiyā, he provided cadres for *al-Qāʿida* as prominent as Abū Yaḥyá al-Lībī and ʿAlī ʿAmmār al-Ruqayʿī, *nom de guerre* "Abū Layth al-Lībī" (killed 1429/2008).

887 Jamāl Ismāʿīl, 'Baʿd Khūst, al-qaḍiyya al-afghāniyya ... ilá ayna?', *al-Jihād* 78 (1411/1991), 18–20. See also Muḥammad Yūsuf ʿAbbās, 'Muʿallim bāriz', *al-Jihād* 78 (1411/1991), 4f.

888 See, for example, Anon., 'Qāla qāda: fi'l-dhikrī al-thāniyya li-insiḥāb al-quwwāt al-sūfiyītiyya al-ghāziyya min arḍ Afghānistān', *Manbaʿ al-Jihād* [A] 2/7–8 (1411/1991), 16f.; Anon., 'Qādat al-jihād yahnaʾūna al-muslim bi-fatḥ Khūst', *Manbaʿ al-Jihād* [A] 2/7–8 (1411/1991), 46. For Qāẓī Ḥusayn, see Ismāʿīl, 'Baʿd Khūst' [see above, n.887], 19; Anas (2002), 103–6.

889 Jalāl al-Dīn Ḥaqqānī was officially invited by Samīʿ al-Ḥaqq as the guest of honour to a large official press gathering of the JUI-S on 27 April 1991 in Lahore, to felicitate him and, at the same time, secure the JUI-S some influence in determining the religious and political future of Afghanistan, see Shuhrat Nangiyāl, 'Mujāhidīnō plān guẕārī kṛah chī mīnah aw havas yay pah zṛūnō kay nishtah', *Manbaʿ al-Jihād* [P] 2/11 (1370sh/1991), 35–47; Shuhrat Nangiyāl, 'Imām Shāmil-i s̱ānī – Jalāl al-Dīn Ḥaqqānī – fātiḥ-i Khōst zindah'dilān-i Lāhōr kē rū'ba'rū', *Nuṣrat al-Jihād* 1/6–7 (1411/1991), 42–52 and 32.

890 In fact, the visit of Jalāl al-Dīn Ḥaqqānī to various Deobandi institutions in Karachi in early 1992 (see Section 4.3.2) appears to have been organized by the JUI-F. While in the published report on this visit it is stated that 'the religious seminaries and schools of Karachi had extended an invitation to the Conqueror of Khost', a photo of this stay included in the report shows Jalāl al-Dīn Ḥaqqānī sitting next to Faẓl al-Raḥmān, see Shuhrat Nangiyāl, 'al-Ḥājj Mawlavī Jalāl al-Dīn Ḥaqqānī də Karāchī lah dīnī jāmʿiyō aw

With so many different stakeholders involved in pushing through their respective interests, the ethnic and ideological differences between the diverse militant Islamist groups were almost bound to become increasingly manifest after their pragmatic alliance appeared to have served its purpose. The heavy infighting which inevitably followed and was carried out at the expense of the Afghan civilians and whatever little infrastructure had remained in the country after the Soviet withdrawal, however, is said to have appalled some of the leading Arab volunteers. For example, it has been said that it was for this reason that Usāma ibn Lādin decided to stop his much-coveted financial support and leave Afghanistan alongside a considerable number of stalwarts on his payroll for Sudan, only, however, to return in 1994.

Meanwhile, other Arab volunteers stayed on at least for a little longer during what, in a title story of the MKh journal *al-Jihād*, had been labelled a 'painful *fitna*': the bloody race of the Islamist organizations for Kabul after the PDPA regime had finally come to its end in March 1992.[891] Those aligned over the whole period with Sayyāf's IIAA and other Islamist militias continued as part of these troops for a few more years, often returning to their native lands afterwards.[892] Others, such as Ayman al-Ẓawāhirī, would mostly stay away from the battle for Kabul and instead relocated either into areas that were difficult to access, where they continued their military and ideological training for their own independent ends, or to the Peshawar Valley and the city itself, where they commanded a solid and tightly knit support network.[893]

As a result of the changed situation on the ground, the conceptual debates conducted among the remaining Arab Salafists in the Pashtun Borderland gained consequential momentum. The new conceptual contributions emerging from there during the post-PDPA/civil war period in Afghanistan (1992–6) would also ultimately alter the discourse on religious minorities in the region by adding a much stronger legal element of compulsion, which had hitherto only been marginal at most. While a legal opinion, with which we have been mainly concerned so far, is not binding even for the one who requests it from a mufti, the conclusions drawn in works such as *Millat Ibrāhīm* and *al-Kawāshif al-Jaliyya* of Abū Muḥammad al-Maqdisī, mentioned already,[894] or *al-Jāmiʿ fī Ṭalab al-ʿIlm al-Sharīf* (1988) of Sayyid Imām al-Sharīf,[895]

madrasō ćakhah līdanah vakṛah', *Manbaʿ al-Jihād* [P] 3/9–10 (1371sh/1412h), 13–25, here 13 (quote) and 14 (image).

891 See Falāḥ al-Sumharī, 'Fitnat al-ṣirāʿ fī Kābul wa-athruhā ʾilá ʾl-shaʿb al-afghānī', *al-Jihād* 91 (1413/1992), 12–15, here 14.

892 See, for example, Anas (2002), 61–72.

893 See Ḥāmid (2002), 41–5; Anas (2002), 59f.; al-Lūjarī (n.d. [c. 2003]), 208.

894 See Section 4.2.1.

895 Also Abū Muṣʿab al-Sūrī", about whom we shall hear more in Section 4.5.3, belongs in this pantheon of Salafist theorists of lasting consequence, who developed their respective arguments while in the Pashtun Borderland.

stipulated the binding obligation on each and every righteous (Sunni) Muslim to see through the legal consequences of establishing *kufr*. In other words, what made these ideational impulses so significant is that they conveyed arguments for the necessary congruence of judicatory and executive force in the common believer under the adverse prevalent circumstances. The reasoning behind these conclusions of severe consequence was certainly appreciated by militant Islamic actors of Pashtun Borderland provenance, because it offered compelling arguments for their self-empowerment vis-à-vis the official judiciaries of the politically hegemonic powers in the region. Moreover, these conclusions contained an emphatic endorsement of continued armed engagement with opponents who were not, like the PDPA cadres and the Soviet military, decidedly anti-religious, but, in fact, nominally Muslim and claimed to govern according to Islamic principles. Hence, we may infer that the eventual proximity of *al-Qāʿida* and the ṬIT / IEA was not exclusively pragmatic, as IEA spokesmen would stress ever more vehemently the more governments of the Global North put increasing pressure on the IEA to severe its links with the *al-Qāʿida* leadership and extradite Usāma ibn Lādin for prosecution by the USA. Against this widely acknowledged narrative, it shall be contended here that the relationship between *al-Qāʿida* and ṬIT / IEA also facilitated an increasing ideological convergence of "Militant Frontier Deobandiyyat", Pashtun Borderland Salafism and its pendants of Arab provenance, and would subsequently, therefore, irreversibly impact the socio-religious dynamics in the Pashtun Borderland.

From an Anti-Shiʿi Atmosphere to *takfīr* Proper

As has already been alluded to, with the emergence of the ṬIT as a serious contender for power over Afghanistan in 1994, the already politicized conflict between Sunni Muslims and the members of smaller denominations as well as non-Muslim religious minorities in and around the Pashtun Borderland began to transform dramatically. While it had so far been confined mainly to stimulating and sustaining a general public atmosphere of contempt for the minorities by the constant reiteration of the traditional Hanafi line of argument, coupled with a significant increase of intercommunal violence carried out by Sunni supremacist groups such as the ASṢ, LiJ and ḤM, these trajectories now became systematically and increasingly embedded in a theory of radical *takfīr* as devised by Salafist theorists of MENA provenance.

A most pertinent question for Sayyid Imām, as a leading representative of this current, was whether *not* to pronounce *takfīr* and to carry out its legal consequences would render a Muslim herself or himself an infidel.[896] In other words, the matter pivoted on the question of whether or not *takfīr* is actually a constitutive element of belief, and whether this *takfīr* includes the compulsion

[896] The most comprehensive and detailed study of Sayyid Imām's elaborate discussions of *takfīr* remains Nedza (2020).

to see through its legal implications for the accused. In fact, this matter was, and to an extent still is, perhaps the most hotly debated one in Salafist circles, leading to the emergence of quite distinct factions within this spectrum that have, for heuristic reasons, been variously labelled by academics as "*jihādī salafī* " or, perhaps more pronouncedly, as "militant Salafist".[897] Although Sayyid Imām, as a former member of an Egyptian Salafist organization exclusively devoted to confronting the state authorities, never really left the Egyptian frame of reference, his theory of *takfīr*, a necessary element for the legitimization of armed *jihād* in conformity with the *shari'a*, still carried a strongly encouraged potential for its universal applicability.[898]

Sayyid Imām's ideas on belief and unbelief are inseparable from a theory of governance which pivots on the question of the responsibility of a political leader for the fidelity of his, or her, subjects. Buying into the classical argument that leadership over a community is absolutely necessary, which, for Ibn Taymiyya, included even the preference of tyrannical rule over none,[899] Sayyid Imām, however, stressed the significant difference between tyranny (*jawr*) and unbelief (*kufr*), claiming that Ibn Taymiyya had nowhere endorsed the necessity of *unbelieving* rule: in fact, he would have come to the same conclusion as Sayyid Imām.[900] For the latter, the unconditional compliance of political officeholders with the *shari'a* served as the *conditio sine qua non* of any legitimate political rule. If the fidelity of the ruler cannot be affirmed, then it becomes an individual religious duty for each and every Muslim to remove him, or her, if at all possible. Only if the enemy appears too powerful can the obligation for armed action be waived in favour of emphatic disengagement (*barā'*), while military training must be continued simultaneously in order to gather the strength for eventually overcoming the unbelieving enemy by force.[901]

Sayyid Imām did not, as was most commonly done, refer to the various classical lists of grave sins (*kabā'ir*), compiled by authors such as Shams al-Dīn al-Dhahabī (d. 748/1348) or Ibn Ḥajar al-Haythamī (d. 974/1567), to determine which offence would inevitably turn the perpetrator into an unbeliever.[902] Instead, he emphasized – once again with reference to Ibn Taymiyya, as well as

[897] The first label, as well as categorizing Salafi currents in general, goes back to the influential article of Wiktorowicz (2006). More recently, however, his categories have been critically revisited: Nedza (2014), 88 and 90–100, for instance, suggests the label "militant Salafist" instead, which limits the notion of *jihād* to its militant variety, as well as acknowledging the strong ideological imprint of Islamism in the views of activists like Sayyid Imām. Also see Bruckmayr and Hartung (2020), 166–8.

[898] See Ibn ʿAbd al-ʿAzīz (n.d.), 977–1 006.

[899] See Ibn Taymiyya (1426/2005b), 138; (1426/2005a), XXVIII: 216. The core reference in both of the identical passages is *Musnad Aḥmad*, no. 6 647 (narrated by ʿAbdallāh ibn ʿAmrū al-ʿĀṣ).

[900] See Ibn ʿAbd al-ʿAzīz (n.d.), 799.

[901] See Ibn ʿAbd al-ʿAzīz (1420/1999), 33, 290 and 299.

[902] See, for example, Lange (2016), 7f.

an early Wahhabi authority – the division of *kufr* into "greater" (*akbar*) and "lesser" (*aṣghar*). Only the former, consisting of offences that occur in the authoritative texts as a determined noun,[903] would inescapably lead to the pronunciation of *takfīr* and, subsequently, to the religious obligation to actively strive for the punishment of the perpetrator with his, or her, death.[904] Non-compliance with this commandment, however, constitutes an act of *kufr akbar* in itself and must be punished by death.[905]

Last, but not least, Sayyid Imām contributed to the conceptual discussion over *takfīr* by presenting a legal argument for the accusation of unbelief against less clearly defined groups, that is, collective actors, on the basis of Ibn Taymiyya's differentiation between a "general" (*muṭlaq*) and a "concrete" (*muʿayyan*) *takfīr*. While a general *takfīr* is limited solely to the assessment of certain acts as "unbelief", and those who commit them consequently are labelled as "unbelievers", it is exclusively the *takfīr muʿayyan* that is directed against specific individuals and can, therefore, result in a clear legal judgement.[906] There are, however, cases where the monopoly of coercive force by an unbelieving ruler helps to extend his, or her, rejection of the *shariʿa* to the various organs of government, as well as – further down the flagpole – to all the citizens under that government who abide by its legal framework and would even endorse it through democratic participation. In such an instance, the collective of offenders is, once more with recourse to Ibn Taymiyya, conceptualized as "the (*shariʿa-*) resisting group" (*al-ṭāʾifa al-mumtaniʿa*), that can then be treated as an individual legal entity which again can rightly be the object of a *takfīr muʿayyan*.[907] In pursuing this line of argument, Sayyid Imām was able to cast, for instance, the entire Egyptian government and all its administrative structures as a single *ṭāʾifa mumtaniʿa* and, thus, as a collective unbeliever, against which concerted action becomes again a religious obligation. Yet, those who would refrain from a clearly discernible commitment to destroy the structures of the state that has been found guilty of the grave offence of apostasy would, in turn, become members of the *ṭāʾifa mumtaniʿa* themselves and are subsequently to be fought against by the righteous believers as well.

In this context, Sayyid Imām also subjected various Muslim religious groups to critical scrutiny and came to the sobering conclusion that not only the various Shiʿi denominations or the Ahmadiyyah Muslim community are necessarily to be persecuted for their *kufr*, but even Islamist groups such as the Egyptian MB or

903 See Ibn ʿAbd al-ʿAzīz (n.d.), 469f. and 846f.; compare Ibn Taymiyya (1419/1998), I: 237. The cited Wahhabi scholar is ʿAbd al-Laṭīf ibn ʿAbd al-Raḥmān ibn Ḥasan Āl al-Shaykh (d. 1293/1876). On him, see al-Bassām (1398h), I: 63–71.

904 See Section 4.2.1.

905 See Ibn ʿAbd al-ʿAzīz (1420/1999), 296f.

906 See Ibn ʿAbd al-ʿAzīz (n.d.), 494–501; compare Ibn Taymiyya (1426/2005a), XII: 260f.

907 See Ibn ʿAbd al-ʿAzīz (n.d.), 564–78; compare Ibn Taymiyya (1426/2005a), XVIII: 172–5. See also Nedza (2020), 166–76.

the JIM – both highly rated among the various Afghan Islamist organizations – are to be held guilty of ultimately recognizing the Egyptian state and, especially in the case of the latter, having even publicly renounced a violent course of action.[908] By doing so, Sayyid Imām argued, they have joined the *ṭāʾifa mumtaniʿa* and had, therefore, also to be fought inexorably.

It appears that elements of arguments such as Sayyid Imām's had – presumably indirectly – already crossed over into the ideological stock of militant Islamic actors in the Pashtun Borderland around 1990. Brown and Rassler, for instance, have rightly observed a turn to anti-Americanism in the ideological mindset of Jalāl al-Dīn Ḥaqqānī and his direct associates,[909] which might well be explained as a clear indication of the impact of the concept of the *ṭāʾifa mumtaniʿa* that was being debated by the Arab Salafist volunteers in the Pashtun Borderland at the very same time and which would finally manifest itself in the rhetoric of the IS in this region. After all, Sayyid Imām had been a crucial figure in the establishment of *al-Qāʿida* as an organization operating out of Peshawar and beyond,[910] and Usāma ibn Lādin had a direct interaction with Jalāl al-Dīn Ḥaqqānī when setting up his own training facility in the territory controlled by the latter.[911]

Still, we might want to be careful not to automatically interpret this as evidence of a clear shift of the agenda of the MʿUJM towards a more global one.[912] While it is correct that various public statements of the MʿUJM leadership called for active support of Muslim struggles elsewhere from the 1990s onwards, and especially after the temporary relocation of Ibn Lādin and his retainers to Sudan,[913] this might not fully qualify as 'aid to al-Qa'ida's

[908] See Ibn ʿAbd al-ʿAzīz (n.d.), 635 and 793–6. After massive waves of persecution, the leadership of the JIM began to renounce violence in 1992, firstly, by the proclamation of a ceasefire, later by releasing a series of four publications under the title "Correction of the Concepts" (*taṣḥīḥ al-mafāhīm*), in which they provided a thorough legal and theological justification for their abjuration of violence (*mubādarat waqf al-ʿunf*): see Ḥāfiẓ and Muḥammad (1425/2004a; 1425/2004b); Munīb (2010), 102–272.

[909] See Brown and Rassler (2013), 91.

[910] See Nedza (2020), 23f.

[911] See Section 4.3.3.

[912] See Brown and Rassler (2013), 87–101.

[913] The first call for support was actually by the *Ḥarakat al-Jihād al-Islāmī al-Iritriyī*, the Eritrean militant Islamic movement that aimed at ousting the secular and Marxist government of the *People's Front for Democracy and Justice* (PFDJ) in Eritrea and replace it with *shariʿa*-based rule: see Anon., 'Bayān hāmm min Ḥarakat al-Jihād al-Islāmī al-Iritriyī ḥawla taṭawwurāt al-akhīra ʿalá sāḥatayn al-Ithiyūbiyya wa'l-Iritīriyya [*sic*]', *Manbaʿ al-Jihād* [A] 2/11 (1412/1991), 33. Other calls, however, were directed more to the liberation of Muslims in the Central Asian CIS states and the Muslim communities in the Xinjiang Uyghur Autonomous Region of western China, where *al-Qāʿida* at least initially had much less of a stake: see, for example, the quote from a Ḥaqqānī publication from 1988 that was not available at the time of writing, in Brown and Rassler (2013), 90 and 262 n.43.

earliest efforts in Africa'.[914] Instead, we may take the placement of MʿUJM activities exclusively in the Pashtun Borderland much more seriously, appreciating alongside this the prevalent mechanisms to enlist support for one's own objectives, conceptualized here as distinct "Borderland pragmatics". Local militias, such as the MʿUJM in Lōyah Paktia, were clearly in greater need of multifarious support if they were to stand any chance of retaining their regionally confined position in view of the more universally orientated Islamist organizations who aimed for power over the whole of Afghanistan and, although only in theory, beyond. Thus, apart from the special case of Sayyāf's IIAA, militias, such as the MʿUJM or Ḥil-Kh, that did not participate in the destructive race for power in Kabul appear to have been more at ease with welcoming non-Afghan combatants into their ranks, because these contingents could prove critical once the positions of these rather local commanders came under pressure from those who aspired for control over all of Afghanistan. In exchange for loyal support whenever needed, they offered their non-Afghan compatriots space and logistical support to carry on with whatever they were doing for their own ends. In addition, exhibiting moral support for the activities of non-Afghan combatants outside the Pashtun Borderland was also deemed a feasible way to ensure that their active and material support of groups such as the MʿUJM or Ḥil-Kh was maintained whenever the need for it might arise.

Thus, Jalāl al-Dīn's proclamations of support for militancy sustained by religious precepts outside Afghanistan may be rated only as lip service, given that documentary evidence for wider participation in *jihād* activities elsewhere has so far been entirely lacking. This conjecture is further supported by the fact that the labels "kāfir" and "kuffār", as well as "murtadd(ūn)" were hardly ever employed in any of the extant MʿUJM publications of the early 1990s,[915] and, where they were, there is no indication whatsoever of a deeper legal and theological engagement with the practice of *takfīr* as found in the works of Sayyid Imām and others of the so-called "Arab Afghans". This also includes the legal figure of the "(*shari'a*-)resisting group" – *al-ṭāʾifa al-mumtaniʿa* – which would allow one to legitimately consider the whole of the USA, its government and its citizens infidels and, thus, sustain the obligation to act against them.

It needs, therefore, to be reiterated that, in the 1990s, this kind of deeper engagement with the conceptual cornerstones of the Salafist legal theory of *takfīr* remained, by and large, confined to the Arab circles, as is indicated by an incomplete series of lectures on *takfīr muʿayyan* published in the Arabic journal *al-Murābiṭūn*,[916] organ of a radical JIM splinter group of the same name that

914 Brown and Rassler (2013), 90.

915 See, for example, Anon., 'Waṣiyyat al-Shaykh ʿAbdallāh ʿAzzām', *Manbaʿ al-Jihād* [A] 2/11, 11–17, here esp. 14.

916 See Anon., 'Takfīr al-muʿayyan bayn al-ghuluw wa'l-taqṣīr', *al-Murābiṭūn* 2/16 (1412/1991), 24–9; 2/22–3 (1412/1992), 30–6. The publication of *al-Murābiṭūn* seems to have ceased with this final issue.

had set up its base in Peshawar and provided manpower for numerous military operations in Afghanistan, mainly under the umbrella of the Mʿ UJM, the Ḥil-Kh or the IIAA. ʿAbdallāh ʿAzzām's MKh, once again, served as the logistics switchboard. The overwhelming majority of Arab volunteers to the Afghan armed resistance passed through there, at least immediately after their arrival in the Pashtun Borderland, and the JIM quota was certainly no exception. Besides the logistics services rendered by the MKh, its head office in the University Town of Peshawar and the various guesthouses it ran in the same and adjacent neighbourhoods provided a hub for the exchange, discussion and – possibly – modification of militant Salafist concepts among these arrivals from the MENA region. It is, therefore, quite reasonable to assume that the volunteers of the JIM and the *Tanẓīm al-Jihād*, among the latter Sayyid Imām and al-Ẓawāhirī, engaged in hermetically closed ideological activities of this kind while passing the time until their eventual deployment to the actual battle lines.

Indeed, it is suggested here that whatever ideological content eventually filtered through to the ṬIT / IEA probably did not reach them directly from *al-Qāʿida* circles, who had confined their focus solely to the resistance against existing political structures, but lacked a sustainable idea of what the Salafist Islamic alternative would look like in detail. It rather seems as if this owed more to the so far only little recognized *al-Murābiṭūn* group of the JIM, with their operational base in the Pashtun Borderland, much closer to its lowlands and their origins in a culturally and politically quite comparable environment to the one from which the ṬIT had sprung.

4.5.3 *The Missing Link? – The* Jamāʿa Islāmiyya *in the Pashtun Borderland*

The JIM is perhaps the most enigmatic of the various Muslim organizations with militant inclinations that had emerged in the early 1970s on the newly established regional campuses of the University of Asyūṭ in Upper Egypt, itself founded as a structure-building measure in the region as late as 1957. However, the JIM differed somewhat from Islamist organizations proper which also maintain a strong base in the university context, and it is argued here that it is these very differences that made it easier for similar actors in the Pashtun Borderland to relate to the JIM much more than to Islamist organizations proper. It is, therefore, highly desirable to properly comprehend these differences, for which, however, first the socio-cultural setting of Upper Egypt in which the JIM emerged needs to be appreciated.

Egypt, in fact, is split in this regard between the utterly fertile Nile Delta, including metropolises such as Cairo and Alexandria, and the arid south – the historical *Saʿīd Miṣr* – where agricultural pursuits are limited to the proximity of the banks of the Nile, becoming more pastoral the further one gets away from the river. As a result, the two parts of Egypt have developed very unevenly, thereby directly contributing to a distinct cultural attitude of

Lower Egyptians towards Upper Egyptians, who are widely regarded as rural and, thus, backward, less refined and, consequently, less civilized.[917] Their lack of education, so the commonly held view in the north goes, is compensated for by strong religious sentiments, which, however, are also not instantly relatable to those of their neighbours in the north. Yet, the resulting sense of detachment from one another appears to be quite mutual and had already resulted in agrarian revolts in the south in the eighteenth century against what was seen as a usurpation of the region by decision-makers in distant Cairo, or further away still.[918] In 1919, the land cultivators (*fallāḥūn*) of the south even appropriated the movement for national liberation from British colonial rule, carried out mainly by urban service elites (*afandiyya*), for their very own ends: the re-establishment of absolute regional autonomy. Such an agenda, in turn, also inevitably had to entail the rejection of any kind of national hegemony that would eventually radiate from Cairo.[919] Consequently, the Egyptian republican governments, whose policies alternated between a nationalist-secular and a nationalist-Islamic agenda, yet were almost always reliant on their approval by the military, considered Upper Egypt predominantly under the aspect of national security, especially since the state depended on the revenue generated from tourism to pre-Islamic attractions, many of which are situated in the south.[920] As a consequence, the government's structure-building measures in Upper Egypt, including the establishment of mass universities, remained inconsistent and unassertive.

However shallow these measures may have been, they still provoked substantial change in the socio-economic fabric of the region, especially with new – Lower Egyptian – forms of public interaction being implanted into the cities and towns of Upper Egypt, while the countryside remained by and large devoid of significant structural developments. In the universities, students who came predominantly from a rural background in the interior were confronted with norms and values rather alien to them, and quite a few responded to this by withdrawing into what they regarded as religious certainties. Initially, loosely organized Islamic student associations (*jamāʿāt islāmiyya*) at their universities started out as religious discussion and study circles that also engaged in welfare activities that were sustainable by religious

917 See, for example, all of the five contributions on "Issues of Regional Identity" in Hopkins and Saad (2004), 25–118.

918 See Schulze (1981), 79–94.

919 See ibid., 150–92.

920 See, for example, Gaffney (1994), 7–10; Auda (1994), 398; Möller (2001), 185. Remarkably, the lack of ethnographical studies on this region, apart from the Nubian communities in the far south, suggests that academics have also been gulled into embracing the ideological image of much of Upper Egypt as unrewarding and, in addition, a dangerous field of inquiry. With this in mind, the study by Gaffney (1994) is, despite its age, still to be regarded as pioneering.

precepts.[921] It was, first and foremost, their unofficial character that resulted in their frequent portrayal as "secret organizations" even in scholarly works. However, once we recall the strictly authoritarian nature of statehood in Egypt, which regarded all forms of communal self-organization as a threat to the security of the state's monopoly of power, these associations become much less conspicuous.[922] After all, although these circles were not actually engaged in shady business, student societies of all kinds were officially banned, subsequently leaving the student unions as the only authorized and, thus, legitimate student bodies in Egypt.

This, however, is not at all to imply that these *jamāʿāt* had their sphere of activities confined only to backrooms: during the initial stage, they had already become almost instantly known for their vigilante attitude towards campus life, and increasingly also beyond. This attitude, it appears, grew out of the understanding that overseeing the Islamically correct conduct of Muslims (*ḥisba*) constitutes a core religious duty, which the activists of these congregations derived not least from the already much mentioned Q3.110. Ibn Taymiyya's work *al-Ḥisba fi'l-Islām*[923] was a visible influence for this very interpretation, and, because of its controversial author, may have resonated better than other texts with a readership already predisposed by a serious scepticism of the ability of the governmental authorities to properly fulfil their public responsibility as *muḥtasib*.

***

Given the striking similarities between Upper Egypt and especially the lowlands of the Pashtun Borderland in terms of demographics, socio-economic and cultural constitution, and historical development vis-à-vis their respective imperial centres,[924] commonalities between the nascent JIM and the TJ, probably the largest organized religious representation of especially subaltern Muslims in the Indo-Afghan region, are not really surprising. Indeed, both organizations focus on a close study of didactically primed texts on the virtues

921 See, for example, al-Zayyāt (2005), 47–50; Fandy (1994), 611; Meijer (2009), 191–5. Still, the early history of the JIM remains largely obscure. Gaffney, unfortunately, did not conduct his fieldwork in Minyā until 1977, thus, at a time when the JIM appeared more organized and had already built up a reputation for confronting the state authorities violently. The lawyer Muntaṣir al-Zayyāt (b. 1375/1956), in turn, is widely reputed to be some kind of a wheeler-dealer, always eager and happy to feed to journalists and researchers alike whatever he assumes they want to hear from him.

922 See Gaffney (1994), 90f.

923 See Meijer (2009), 193f. and 195 n.28. The continued importance of Ibn Taymiyya in this matter could be inferred also from the references in the respective volume of the aforementioned "Correction of the Concepts" series of the JIM leadership: see Ḥāfiẓ and Muḥammad (1425/2004b), 97 and 140.

924 For a discussion of these issues in the lowlands of the Pashtun Borderland, see Section 4.3.4.

of each individual act of worship (*ʿibāda*) and subsequent communal outreach, aimed at redressing popular beliefs and practices not sustainable through these selections from authoritative texts, especially in rural spaces. A critical element in the approach of the TJ, enshrined in the *Chhah Bātēṇ* which was publicly proclaimed in 1934 by the movement's founder Muḥammad Ilyās, is the inclusion of *jihād* in the various methods declared suitable for spreading the message in public and private (*tablīgh*).[925] It is contended here that this positive attitude towards *jihād* in all of its varieties actually carries the potential for also employing coercive measures, despite the laborious efforts of activists of both the TJ and the JIM to assure everyone of the apolitical and non-violent attitude of the movement,[926] and made both organizations prone to politicization wherever their own respective agendas overlap with those of their Islamist counterparts. Therefore, the occasionally evident synergies between the TJ and the various representatives of "militant Frontier Deobandiyyat" and even the JiI and ḤiI also appear extraordinary only at first sight, even more so on recalling that they are predominantly based on pragmatics rather than ideological commonalities in the Pashtun Borderland.

Regarding this particular point, the case of the JIM is significantly different, because its growing proximity to the MB was also rooted in shared ideological tenets. It was, therefore, actually quite consistent that the JIM, then still a rather loose network of independent Islamic student associations, received the ultimate impulse towards becoming a political organization from an Upper Egyptian affiliate to the MB: while in jail, JIM cadre ʿAbdallāh al-Samāwī (d. 1430/2009), a native of al-Fayyūm, became acquainted with Shukrī Muṣṭafá, then a student of engineering, from the village of Abū Khurṣ in the Governorate of Asyūṭ, who was to emerge only a short time later as the leader of the short-lived radical *Jamāʿat al-Muslimīn*, better known as *Jamāʿat al-Takfīr wa'l-Hijra*.[927] In 1977, when the various and ever growing local *jamāʿāt* were, as succinctly put by Meijer, 'able to translate their numbers into power by electing their leaders to student unions',[928] al-Samāwī emerged as the driving force behind the transformation of the JIM into a more political

925 See Bulandshahrī (1992), 25.

926 For the TJ, see Masud (2000), 97–9; for the JIM, see Möller (2001), 185. The latter, however, draws his information once again from statements by Muntaṣir al-Zayyāt, which, despite the lawyer's early personal involvement with the JIM, ought to be treated with some care.

927 See Auda (1994), 399f. The assertion, however, that al-Samāwī and Shukrī Muṣṭafá had jointly 'developed the doctrine of takfir' while being jailed together remains uncorroborated here. Moreover, Auda does not duly recognize the complexities and long history in the development of the legal concept of *takfīr*. See also, with due wariness, al-Zayyāt (2005), 51–4.

928 Meijer (2009), 195. As in universities across the world, the student unions are regarded as a political representation of the entire student body of a single institution, a nation or even transnationally. As such, they are also closely associated with the student protests across Europe and North America in the late 1960s and early 1970s, even taking on, as

organization with a decidedly centralized structure. This development was ideologically accompanied by a wider and more systematic appropriation of the writings of Sayyid Quṭb by the cadres of the JIM, alongside literature of Salafi provenance that would henceforth define the core of the JIM's reference frame. Lastly, the various regional *jamāʿāt* had covertly begun to establish their own paramilitary wings, which responded to the increasing crackdown on Islamically inspired Muslim activists by the Egyptian government authorities from the end of the 1970s, with a spree of violence across the entire country, beginning with the assassination of President Sādāt in October 1981 and continuing until the atrocious attack on foreign tourists in Luxor in November 1997.[929]

From these ideological and related organizational developments, the commonalities between the JIM and the various associations of Islamically inspired subaltern activists in the Pashtun Borderland that range from the TJ to the MʿUJM, Ḥil-Kh and ḤII appear, by and large, confined to a similar background in deliberately marginalized parts of a wider national territory, hence the predominant subalternity of their activists and overlaps in their respective approaches. Still, these commonalities are of exceptional significance as they allowed for a less condescending attitude towards their Pashtun counterparts than was prevalent among the representatives of various Arab Islamist and Salafist organizations active in that part of the world. As a result, communication would be less constrained by mutual reservations caused by differences in religious ideas and practices, which is why it appears quite plausible that the JIM cadres who found themselves eventually in the Pashtun Borderland have been instrumental in communicating certain ideological reformulations undertaken by leading Arab militant theorists at that time in this environment to their Pashtun counterparts.

Other than that, however, the JIM remained rather firmly within the realms of Islamism and Salafism of MENA provenance, an assessment that is underlined by its increasing synergies with other and even more militantly inclined groups from those parts of the world that found a conducive environment in the Pashtun Borderland of the early 1990s. The Cairo-based *Tanẓīm al-Jihād al-Islāmī*, that began to reveal its contours on the eve of Sādāt's assassination, was perhaps the most important one of those groups. Although the origins of this group remain still somewhat disputed,[930] there are, nonetheless, pointers towards a substantial role of *al-Murābiṭūn*, a Cairene splinter-group of the JIM, in its formation.[931] Moreover, it was the core, if not the entirety, of this

happened in the Federal Republic of Germany, the ambitious epithet "extra-parliamentary opposition" (*Außerparlamentarischer Opposition*; APO).

929 See ibid., 207–10.

930 See Section 4.5.1, n.842.

931 This proposition, in fact, is backed by numerous articles and interviews on, or with, Sādāt's actual assassin Khālid Islāmbūlī (executed 1402/1982), *nom de guerre* "Abū

very faction that had evaded the ongoing persecution by the Egyptian state authorities in the aftermath of the Sādāt assassination by eventually "joining the caravan" to the Pashtun Borderland.

The driving force behind *al-Murābiṭūn*, and presumably the entire JIM quota in the Pashtun Borderland, was, despite his relatively late arrival there, Ṭalʿat ibn Fuʾād ibn Qāsim, *nom de guerre* "Abū Ṭalāl al-Qāsimī" (killed 1416/1995), a native of the Qinā Governorate of Upper Egypt. A former student of engineering at the University of Minyā, Abū Ṭalāl rose quickly to local prominence, consequently becoming the local representative at the central consultative council (*al-majlis al-shūrá al-markazī*) of the JIM that was presided over by ʿUmar ʿAbd al-Raḥmān (d. 1438/2017).[932] This al-Azhar-trained scholar had, while still teaching at the University of Asyūṭ, emerged right from the beginning as the ultimate legal authority for the various early *jamāʿāt* in Upper Egypt, as well as for the JIM after its eventual centralization.[933]

Abū Ṭalāl, who served a seven-year sentence despite the lack of sufficient evidence for his involvement in the Sādāt assassination and, soon after his release in 1988, was re-apprehended for his active involvement in Islamic *daʿwa*, which had been officially banned under emergency law, is said to have managed to escape from jail and, via Sudan, eventually reached Peshawar, where he was reunited with earlier JIM exiles.[934]

According to Muṣṭafá Ḥāmid, or "Abū Walīd al-Maṣrī", who has been identified as the first Arab volunteer of MB background who had joined the armed resistance in Afghanistan as a retainer of Jalāl al-Dīn Ḥaqqānī,[935] the contingent of JIM cadres was actively involved in the pivotal Battle for Khost in March 1991,[936] a circumstance that suggests that the Salafist ideas and concepts of the JIM began to grow roots in the Pashtun Borderland at least from that time. Ḥāmid, in turn, is significant not only for his prolific writings on the activities of the "Arab Afghans" there, but even more because he stands out as

Yāsir", in the Arabic *al-Murābiṭūn* journal that was issued from Peshawar by eponymous JIM group and in which the assassin is explicitly styled as one of its initial core members, see Anon., 'al-Murābiṭāt fī liqāʾ maʿa umm al-shahīd Khālid al-Islāmbūlī', *al-Murābiṭūn* 1/2 (1410/1990), 45–8; Muḥammad Shawqī Islāmbūlī, 'Ḥiwār maʿa shaqīq Khālid al-Islāmbūlī', *al-Murābiṭūn* 1/6 (1411/1990), 20–5; Anon., 'Risāla min Khālid al-Islāmbūlī ilá shaqīqih', *al-Murābiṭūn* 1/6 (1411/1990), 26–8.

932 See Anon., 'Shahr ramaḍān tharwa … wa-thawra', *al-Murābiṭūn* 1/1 (1410/1990), 6f.; Anon., 'Liqāʾ maʿa faḍīlat al-Duktūr ʿUmar ʿAbd al-Raḥmān', *al-Murābiṭūn* 1/2 (1410/1990), 14–9; Anon., 'Nidāʾ min al-Duktūr ʿUmar ʿAbd al-Raḥmān', *al-Murābiṭūn* 2/18–19 (1412/1991), 8f.

933 On some ideological positions of the blind scholar, who passed away in a US federal penitentiary in Butner, NC, where he was serving a life sentence for his involvement in the 1993 World Trade Center bombings, see Hartung (2013a), 218f. and 224.

934 See Mubarak, Shadoud and Tamari (1996), 41f.

935 See Brown and Rassler (2013), 64f.

936 See Ḥāmid (2001a), 53f.

having been pivotal in connecting various militant Arab Islamist and Salafist groups in the Hindu Kush region with their Pashtun counterparts, especially in the MʿUJM- and Ḥil-Kh-controlled areas, since at least the early 1990s. The emergent network, however, remained, first and foremost, one defined by Borderland pragmatics and not necessarily by ideological consensus. Thus, while Ḥāmid was about to emerge as a leading figure for *al-Qāʿida* – 'the best of the groups I was active with in Afghanistan'[937] – in the MʿUJM-controlled areas, neither an explicit relationship nor a manifest adoption of *al-Qāʿida*'s ideological framework by the JIM contingent in the Pashtun Borderland can be conclusively derived at least from the issues of the *al-Murābiṭūn* journal available.

Yet, the members of the JIM remained highly sceptical of party-like Islamic organizations, such as the MB, for their increasingly opportunistic attitude towards existing political frameworks.[938] At the same time, however, the fact that they opened their own ranks to volunteers from other mainly North African Muslim countries, prominently among them Tunisia and Algeria, because their distinct Islamist activism was strongly directed at the course that the societies in these countries were taking, nonetheless suggests at least some degree of overlap with the thrust of the *al-Qāʿida* agenda.

If further indication is needed, this more inclusionist attitude went hand in hand with an increasingly transnational agenda that was fed by an attention to precarious situations of Muslims all over the world,[939] something that would be a prominent feature in many later *al-Qāʿida* publications. The ultimate sign of the growing ideological nexus between JIM groups, such as *al-Murābiṭūn* and *al-Qāʿida*, was finally their collaboration in the "World Islamic Front of *jihād* against Jews and Crusaders" (*al-Jabha al-Islāmiyya al-ʿĀlamiyya li-Jihād al-Yahūd wa'l-Ṣalībiyīn*): after all, Ibn Lādin's controversial declaration of global *jihād* "against Jews and Crusaders" on 23 February 1998 was signed by, among others, leading JIM representative Rifāʿī Aḥmad Ṭāhā, *nom de guerre* "Abū Yāsir al-Maṣrī" (killed 1437/2016), thus openly declaring that *al-Qāʿida* and some radical factions of the JIM had a common agenda.[940]

937 Ḥāmid (2001b), 9.

938 See, for example, Anon., 'al-Luʿba al-ḥizbiyya . . . tilka al-fitna al-mubīra!!', *al-Murābiṭūn* 1/2 (1410/1990), 20–38.

939 Prominently, see Anon., 'al-Ḥawla al-fawqī . . . wa'l-muḥākama al-malaʾ min ahl al-khalīj!!', *al-Murābiṭūn* 1/12 (1411/1991), 4f.; Anon., 'al-Jazāʾir . . . maqbarat al-ḥulūl al-dīmuqrāṭiyya!!', *al-Murābiṭūn* 2/1–2 (1412/1991), 3; Anon., 'al-Ahdāf al-khafiyya li'l-muḥādithāt al-ʿarabiyya al-isrāʾīliyya', *al-Murābiṭūn* 2/7 (1412/1992), 6–10; ʿAbd al-Rashīd al-Jazāʾirī, 'Waṣiyya shahīd', *al-Murābiṭūn* 2/7 (1412/1992), 53f.; Anon., 'Fi'l-Jazāʾir: al-muwājaha al-shaʿbiyya . . . wa-li-tasaquṭ al-dīmuqrāṭiyya', *al-Murābiṭūn* 2/8 (1412/1992), 28–32; Anon., 'Man huwa Ḥāfiẓ al-Asad', *al-Murābiṭūn* 2/9–10 (1412/1992), 40–5; Anon., 'Turkiyya . . . al-dīmuqrāṭiyya wa-laʿibat al-ʿaskar', *al-Murābiṭūn* 2/9–10 (1412/1992), 48f.

940 See 'Naṣṣ bayān al-Jabha al-Islāmiyya al-ʿĀlamiyya li-Jihād al-Yahūd wa'l-Ṣalībiyīn', *al-Quds al-ʿArabī* 9/2732 (1418/1998), 3; also in Ibn Lādin (1436/2015), 249–51.

Despite many scholars having so far concluded that the declaration with its five signatories probably amounted to little more than an attempt to create the illusion of a truly global front, while the text itself reflects actually only the ideological positions of Ibn Lādin and *al-Qāʿida*, the very fact of the signatures by official spokespersons of their respective organizations could still be rightfully interpreted as an authoritative endorsement of these positions by others, not least the JIM.

Although it later became increasingly difficult to tell the various organizations within the conglomeration of Arab volunteers in the Pashtun Borderland apart, their ever-shifting alliances and blurred boundaries could still not prevent dissent over conceptual and strategic matters. Abū Ṭalāl and other ideological standard-bearers of the JIM were deeply involved in these fierce debates on ideology, and the predisposition to communicate certain content of these debates highlighted above, especially to their subaltern Pashtun counterparts, makes it quite feasible to assume that it was ultimately their positions, rather than those of their opponents, that filtered down into the conceptual universe of these particular Islamically inspired Pashtun activists from which eventually the ṬIT emerged. One of the most prominent points is perhaps a concept that is an inseparable part of the legal theories of *takfīr* as debated among the "Arab Afghans" at that time and which serves exceptionally well to illustrate clear ideological divisions within this seemingly homogeneous bloc of like-minded actors: the concept of "association and disengagement" – *al-walāʾ waʾl-barāʾ*.

Abū Ṭalāl had already become the target of open criticism by Sayyid Imām, a core founding member of *al-Qāʿida*, prior to the former's arrival in the Pashtun Borderland, for his particular understanding of *takfīr* in general, expounded in his rather short *Risāla al-Līmāniyya fiʾl-Muwālāt*, completed in early 1987 while he was still detained in Egypt's most dreaded high-security penitentiary, the Ṭūrah High Security Prison.[941] The pivot of Sayyid Imām's polemical disagreement with this work on the rules of engagement with those who have committed acts not sanctioned by the Islamic *shariʿa* was indeed Abū Ṭalāl's take on this concept that differed somewhat from Sayyid Imām's own and resulted finally in the latter's pronunciation of *takfīr muʿayyan* on the JIM, employing herein once again the concept of the *ṭāʾifa mumtaniʿa*.

Yet, Abū Ṭalāl's understanding of *al-walāʾ waʾl-barāʾ*, declared by Sayyid Imām to be 'nominal and ideational milestones [*al-maʿālim al-sharʿiyya waʾl-fikriyya*] of the *Jamāʿa Islāmiyya* of Egypt',[942] was less exceptional than one might be led to think. The most elaborate discussion of this concept within the "Arab Afghan" circles at that time is actually owed to Abū Muḥammad al-Maqdisī, who made it the fulcrum of the conceptual universe which he began to develop during his

941 See Qāsim (1987), 4.
942 Ibn ʿAbd al-ʿAzīz (n.d.), 638.

sojourn in Peshawar between roughly 1984 and 1990. This concept, especially in al-Maqdisī's interpretation, assumed such a significance that it would eventually transgress the confines of the circles of the "Arab Afghans" and permeate the minds of Pashtun Salafists as well. Thus, it is deemed appropriate to investigate the particulars of al-Maqdisī's arguments a bit more closely and against the backdrop of his own biography up to this time.

The Jordanian scholar had initially set out to the Pashtun Borderland to join the active *jihād*, but, discovering that his talents lay elsewhere, confined himself more to writing and disseminating his Salafist ideas among the Arab volunteers there, who, nevertheless, found them rather controversial.[943] In an interview with the Jordanian journal *al-Marʾāt* and online magazine *al-ʿAṣr* in 2003, al-Maqdisī elevated his role by staging himself as an instructor in religious matters for the *al-Qāʿida* cadres in their various camps across Afghanistan, as well as in what he called "their legal institute" (*maʿhaduhā sharʿī*) in Peshawar.[944] However, none of the periodicals of that time available in the Pashtun Borderland mentions him, which is why it seems that al-Maqdisī was really overemphasizing his impact on the ideological mindset of *al-Qāʿida*.

The pivot of his understanding of the legal practice of *al-walāʾ waʾl-barāʾ*, which he presented in the two works that frame his time in Peshawar, was al-Maqdisī's interpretation of Q60.4:

> You have had a good example in Ibrāhīm and those with him, when they said to their people, 'We are quit of you and that you serve, apart from God. We disbelieve in you, and between us and you enmity has appeared, and hatred forever, until you believe in God alone.'[945]

From al-Maqdisī's reading of this verse results the unconditional requirement to disavow clearly and openly those who, for him, do not belong to the "People of Abraham" (*millat Ibrāhīm*), and to dissociate oneself equally markedly from them, both in terms of space and in choice of attire. From his scrutiny of the existing governments in Muslim countries of the MENA region, al-Maqdisī arrived finally at the conclusion that righteous Muslims need to disavow them all: the logical consequence of *barāʾ* – disengagement – is *takfīr*, derived once again from the Qur'anic verse above by interpreting the enmity that has appeared 'between us and you' as a clear imperative to practice *takfīr*.[946] Yet,

943 See Wagemakers (2012), 38f.

944 See al-Maqdisī (1423h), 9.

945 The important internal quote runs in Arabic: 'innā buraʾaʾū minkum wa-mimmā taʿbudūna min dūni 'llāhi kafarnā bikum wa-badā baynanā wa-baynakum al-ʿadāwatu wa'l-baghḍāʾu ʾabadan ḥattá tuʾminū bi'llāhi waḥdah'. For this verse as pivot of his argument, see al-Maqdisī (1431h), 1, 5f., 18 and 24; (1421h), 237.

946 See al-Maqdisī (1431h), 19. Maqdisī's reference here is early Wahhabi scholar Isḥāq ibn ʿAbd al-Raḥmān Āl al-Shaykh (d. 1319/1901), who, in fact, is one of the core references in the entire work: compare al-Najdī (1417/1996), VIII: 297–209, here 305. On Isḥāq ibn ʿAbd al-Raḥmān's biography, see al-Bassām (1398h), I: 205f.

other than prominently Sayyid Imām, al-Maqdisī remained adamant that the standard legal process to establish an act as an expression of *kufr*, which usually consists of various procedures to evaluate the intention of the perpetrator and the circumstances of the act, must indispensably be followed. As a result, not all that theorists such as Sayyid Imām regard as *kufr akbar* would hold up if subjected to the proper legal procedures.

For al-Maqdisī, *barāʾ* – at least the way he derived it from the Qurʾanic verse above – also encompasses the concept of *jihād*: 'I say that *jihād* and battle [*qitāl*] is the highest level of showing hostility and hatred [*aʿlá marātib iẓhār al-ʿadāwa waʾl-baghḍāʾ*] towards the enemies of God.'[947] Indeed, in his second work written during his time in Peshawar, in which he brands the Kingdom of Saudi Arabia an abode of unbelief, he stated:

> The true Oneness of God consists of the unbelief in the idols [*al-kufr biʾl-ṭawāghīt*], that is *all* the idols, and in disengaging with its people. I mean not only the idols made from stone or wood that the scholars of Saudi Arabia are murmuring about, but, on the contrary, all idols, including the idols of ruling according to something other than what God has sent down, the idols of the law [. . .] and not just locally, but [also] in the Gulf, the Arab world, and globally.[948]

These are exactly the offences that al-Maqdisī blamed on the Saudi kingdom and for which he pronounced *takfīr* on it as a whole as well as on its various administrative parts,[949] consequently leaving righteous believers only two options to retain their fidelity: emigrate (to the *dār al-islām*) or fight – *hijra* or *jihād*.[950] Significantly, however, his elaborations on *jihād* remained comparatively rudimentary here, probably because, in his conceptual universe, *jihād* constitutes only one of many methods for practicing "disengagement" (*al-barāʾ*), ultimately dependent on the respective concrete circumstances.

Apparently, this anti-Saudi work alienated al-Maqdisī within the community of Arab volunteers in Peshawar, including ʿAbdallāh ʿAzzām.[951] This is quite understandable in the light of the time in which it was written: true, the Soviet army had already withdrawn from Afghanistan, but the PDPA was still in power and most of the Arab volunteer fighters in Peshawar had firmly subscribed to ʿAzzām's arguments for "Afghanistan First!", and served subsequently in the various military operations of the *mujāhidīn* until the ultimate breakdown of the PDPA and its successor, the *Ḥizb-i Vaṭan-i Dimūkrātīk-i Afghānistān*, in March 1992. Why, they wondered, would they rise against

947 al-Maqdisī (1431h), 47.
948 al-Maqdisī (1421h), 67.
949 See ibid., 68–164.
950 See ibid., 165–74.
951 See Wagemakers (2012), 38f.

far-away Saudi Arabia if there was a much worse "seducer" – *ṭāghūt* – right in front of them? At that point in time, however, they seem to have missed some of al-Maqdisī's core points.

After all, his general concern was to provide a legally and theologically sound Salafi argument for concerted action against administrative structures in general. Saudi Arabia served herein only as a prime example, exactly because its authorities kept affirming that the entire polity was based exclusively on the dogma of God's Oneness (*tawḥīd*), a claim which, as al-Maqdisī attempted to extensively demonstrate, was not warranted at all and needed, therefore, to be fought. Even then, however, he did not call for universal *jihād* against all the *ṭawāghīt* out there, as is also evident from his later writings, but continued to argue rather firmly within the then-current classical conceptual binary of the "near" and "distant enemy", pleading for a focus on the former alone.

Consistently, as soon as the "near enemy" of that time, the communist regime of Kabul, had been ousted and the battle among the various Islamist organizations for the Afghan capital had begun, numerous Arab volunteers went looking for new fronts on which to continue to fight. Prominent among them was al-Maqdisī's one-time confidant Abū Muṣʿab al-Zarqāwī (killed 1427/2006), who, despite his very late arrival in the Pashtun Borderland, his hagiographers claim had participated in the Battle of Khost while also serving as a reporter for the Arabic IIAA journal *Bunyān al-Marṣūṣ*.[952] Zarqāwī eventually ended up in Iraq, where he finally gained global infamy for being the driving force behind the eventual emergence of the IS around 2003.[953]

Abū Ṭalāl was the leader of the *al-Murābiṭūn* faction of the JIM in the Pashtun Borderland: inadvertently or not, his own understanding of *al-walāʾ wa'l-barāʾ* appears to have followed rather that of al-Maqdisī, which implies that Sayyid Imām's lengthy critique was directed as much at Abū Ṭalāl as at the Jordanian. The bone of contention and ultimate legitimation for Sayyid Imām's *takfīr muʿayyan* on the entire JIM turned out to be Abū Ṭalāl's distinction between an internal and an external form of "association" (*muwālāt*), which he inferred from his reading of Ibn Taymiyya[954] and which had profound consequences for legal theories of *takfīr* such as Sayyid Imām's. Only the internal variety (*muwālāt bāṭina*), comprising an affectionate relationship with unbelievers, an approval of their respective creed and even the desire to see them triumph over the Muslims, would ultimately render a Muslim an apostate and lead inevitably to the prosecution of the offender. The paradigm for this kind of *muwāla* constituted for Abū Ṭalāl the so-called

952 See Abū Qudāma (1428/2007), 58; al-Baghdādī (n.d.[b]), 2f. The journal's name is not given in either text.

953 See, for example, ʿAṭwān (2015), 66–8 and 94–105.

954 See Qāsim (1987), 6 and 8; compare Ibn Taymiyya (1426/2005a), XII: 262; (1419/1998), I: 551.

"hypocrites" (*munāfiqūn*) among the companions of the Prophet Muḥammad in their interaction with the Jewish tribes of Yathrib, prompting God to reveal verse 5:51 in response.[955]

The external variety (*muwālāt ẓāhira*), in turn, may be necessary for reasons of personal safety, and follows, therefore, by and large, the practice of "dissimulating one's own beliefs out of fear or as precaution" (*taqiyya*), which was historically most widely practised among Shiʿi Muslims.[956] Because such an external pretence does not inescapably touch the inner conviction and belief in the absolute veracity of the Islamic *shari'a*, mitigating circumstances have to be considered for this form of *muwālāt*, and subsequently *takfīr* is not inevitably pronounced.

In a socio-political environment as complex as the Pashtun Borderland, such a more pragmatic approach even towards former arch-enemies must certainly have had a much greater appeal than Sayyid Imām's dogmatic rigidity.[957] In fact, there is at least one further indicator that whatever filtered down from the circles of the "Arab Afghans" into the conceptual universe of various factions among their Pashtun hosts, which eventually included also the ṬIT / IEA, came from the interpretations favoured by the JIM rather than from those of the *al-Qāʿida* ideologues. There is a further concept that figured very prominently in the legal hermeneutics of the JIM and ties well into the line of argument adopted by Abū Ṭalāl: the principle of *fiqh al-wāqiʿ*, which, although commonly rendered into English as 'jurisprudence of reality, or current affairs',[958] translates more accurately, if admittedly also more awkwardly, as 'legally constitutive appreciation of (ever-changing) actuality'.[959] And, while this principle was not new and neither was its name tag a JIM invention, it became inseparably linked to the JIM when that organization's leadership in Egypt attempted a solid legal justification of the public abjuration from violence in the early 2000s.[960]

955 See Qāsim (1987), 5. The Qur'anic verse reads: 'Oh ye who believe, do not take Jews and Christians for friends [*awliyāʾ*], as they are friends with one another [*baʿḍuhum awliyāʾu baʿḍin*]. And whoever of you befriends them is one of them. Verily, God does not rightly guide the unjust people [*al-qawm al-ẓālimīn*].'

956 See ibid., 4f.

957 Highly illustrative in this regard is the composition of various Afghan governments since 1992, where the respective heads of state promoted and dismissed former adversaries according to purely pragmatic considerations. Examples here are the appointment of Ḥikmatyār as Prime Minister by the then-interim-President Rabbānī in June 1993, or the vice-presidency of ʿAbd al-Rashīd Dūstam in the Ashraf Ghanī administration between September 2014 and February 2020.

958 See, for example, Fawzi and Lübben (2004), 20f.; Wiktorowicz (2006), 224; Meijer (2009), 213; Wagemakers (2016), 84 and 237; Nedza (2020), 169.

959 See Section 4.1, n.2.

960 See prominently Ḥāfiẓ and Muḥammad (1425/2004a).

Fiqh al-Wāqiʿ – Conceptual Pivot of Intra-Salafist Contention

Perhaps not coincidentally, in January 1991, that is, around the time when the *al-Murābiṭūn* faction of the JIM had more firmly established itself in the Pashtun Borderland, ʿAbdallāh ʿAzzām's journal *al-Jihād*, now under the editorship of ʿIṣām ʿAbd al-Ḥakīm,[961] carried within its series "Towards the Right Path of Islamic Practice" (*naḥw masīra rāshida li'l-ʿamal al-islāmī*) a short piece by Bassām ʿAṭiyya, entitled "Fiqh al-Wāqiʿ".[962] Predating Nāṣir al-Dīn al-Albānī's short treatise on the matter by two years,[963] this article is testimony that the concept was current under the same label before Salafi scholars in the MENA region began to treat this issue increasingly commonly in their writings and, thus, to incorporate it into their own conceptual universe. ʿAṭiyya himself did not claim to have coined this label for a principle of legal hermeneutics that he, similarly to those writing in the wake of al-Albānī and others, traced back to Salafi core reference author Ibn Qayyim al-Jawziyya. Indeed, in the "Instructions to Those Who Are Entitled to Sign Off about the Lord of the Two Worlds" – the *Iʿlām al-Muwaqqiʿīn ʿan Rabb al-ʿĀlamīn* – the medieval Hanbali polymath had succinctly stressed that a legal opinion (*fatwá*) 'is liable to change [*taghayyur*], and its variation is contingent on the change in time, place, circumstances, intentions and utilities [*ʿawāʾid*]'.[964] As a consequence, 'he who is entitled to sign' – the mufti – is firmly reminded to always evaluate the contingent wider context as constitutive for his generally time- and space-bound legal decrees. A stable benchmark for such an evaluation for Ibn al-Qayyim, and his teacher Ibn Taymiyya before him, was always those decisions of the Prophet which were not directly guided by divine revelation and which, therefore, Ibn al-Qayyim regarded explicitly as the Prophet's *fatwa*s.[965]

What Bassām ʿAṭiyya presented in his short article from early 1991, however, is quite distinct from a situational assessment of very concrete circumstances that are pertinent to a specific legal case, but amounts instead rather to a socio-political agenda. His rather broad and general perspective of what he perceived as a disastrous state of the Muslim *umma* as a whole, as well as his statements on the underlying reasons, is reminiscent, at least in part, more of conspiracy theories, and his eventual conclusions "towards the right path of Islamic practice" – just to invoke once more the title of the series to which

961 Hegghammer (2020), 231, has tagged ʿIṣām ʿAbd al-Ḥakīm as an Egyptian; his reference (see Nadwat al-Jihād, 'Iʿmār Afghānistān masʾūliyyat al-muslimīn', *al-Jihād* 4/10 [1408/1988], 14–20, here 15), however, does not contain this information, and solid corroboration is, therefore, still pending.

962 See ʿAṭiyya, 'Fiqh al-waqiʿ', *al-Jihād* 75 (1411/1990), 50f.

963 See al-Albānī (1412h).

964 al-Jawziyya (1423h), IV: 337; paraphrased in the head paragraph of ʿAṭiyya, 'Fiqh *al-waqiʿ*' [see above, n.962]. Compare al-Ḥalabī (1420h), 23.

965 See al-Jawziyya (1423h), VI: 209–603.

ʿAṭiyya contributed his deliberations – follow suit. He outlines in rather broad strokes the image of opposing binaries throughout history, which are so characteristic for ideologies generally and for Islamism of whatever variety. The resulting image remains so rough and shallow that, in fact, it reduces the true purpose of *fiqh al-wāqiʿ*, as regarded by the likes of Ibn al-Qayyim, *al-Albānī* and epigones, as well as eventually the leadership of the JIM in their renunciation of a militant course of action, to absurdity. Actually, *fiqh al-wāqiʿ* offered al-Albānī a legitimate way to "de-ideologize" religiously charged *socio-political* positions and accept the complexity of the world, the intricate course of historical developments and the resulting necessity to keep constantly checking and rechecking the validity of one's position against the actual context, in view of the "common good" (*maṣlaḥa*) as the ultimate benchmark.[966]

Indeed, what the common good consists of is always dependent on the very fluctuating context; for those such as ʿAṭiyya, who are more ideologically inclined, however, it remained rather rigid and monolithic: for him, *maṣlaḥa* consists almost exclusively of the constant and active fight against the not further specified "enemies" (*aʿdāʾ*) of the Muslim *umma*. According to him, these enemies have first robbed the *umma* of its supreme leadership, the historical caliphate, then carved it up along ethnic and national lines, and, finally, by spreading the bug of secularism, prevented the Muslim inhabitants of these countries from politically reuniting. As a consequence, the Muslim *umma* is trapped in severe factional disputes over communal leadership and the appropriate course of action. The resulting socio-political agenda stipulates, consequently, the reunification of all the lands of Islam, reconquest of all the territories lost to the "enemy", an active 'attempt at preventing the conspiracies [*muʾāmarāt*] of the enemies and hindering the achievement of their goal' by 'uniting the efforts of the activists and preachers for Islam' and working against 'religious laxity [*ḍaʿf al-wāziʿ al-dīnī*]'.[967]

What exactly these activities are supposed to look like, however, ʿAṭiyya left to the imagination of his audience. Still, the fact that his deliberations appeared in a journal named "*al-Jihād* " might suggest that the range of methods he had in mind had been tapered to an active and, if necessary, violent enforcement, which is actually rather unusual; much more commonly than for sustaining a call to arms, *fiqh al-wāqiʿ* is invoked whenever a justification is needed for why such a call is not affirmatively responded to at a given time. Thus, when, almost two decades after ʿAṭiyya's article, the concept had evidently made its entry into the conceptual universe of the IEA, its high command had *fiqh al-wāqiʿ* presented instead as a highly convenient tool to justify its current policy of refraining from an offensive militant approach (*manhaj al-idʿāʾ*) while the

966 See, for example, ibid., IV: 337f.; al-Albānī (1412h), 36f.

967 ʿAṭiyya, 'Fiqh al-waqiʿ' [see above, n.962], 51.

USA-led military forces were still at large in Afghanistan. Instead, it was recommended that one should lie low, but remain highly alert, waiting for circumstances that would provide better prospects of success for an offensive militant approach than the present ones (*manhaj al-iʿtināʾ*).[968]

An illustration of the vital importance of prudently assessing the actual circumstances before committing to any action, the series of ever more reckless provocations of the USA by *al-Qāʿida*, culminating in the 11 September 2001 attacks, served the IEA as a powerful deterrent example. Clearly, these offensive militant acts had been committed without seeing any need for assessing the concrete circumstances regarding possible negative repercussions on the wider Muslim *umma*. These turned out actually to be most severe: they provided the ultimate justification for the USA-led military invasion of Afghanistan less than a month later, the manhunt for the supreme leadership of *al-Qāʿida* that resulted eventually in the targeted killing of Usāma ibn Lādin about one decade later and of al-Ẓawāhirī in 2022, and the overthrow of the first central government of the IEA, as well as a convenient pretext for invading Iraq, which was then still dictatorially ruled by the *Baʿth* party under Ṣaddām Ḥusayn (executed 2006).[969] Against such heedless demeanour of *al-Qāʿida*, the author of this article, who, judging by his name, was not a native of the Pashtun Borderland, posits the IEA as a beacon of due consideration:

> The Taliban movement is a blessed one [*ḥaraka mubāraka*], because it is aware of the battle it is waging, it knows the enemy that has lined up on the battlegrounds, and it knows the framework conditions of this battle [*taʿlam mulābasāt hādhihi ʾl-maʿraka*] as well as the potentially negative implications [*akhṭār*] that it may have for the region. It reviews the pages of history on the experience of the previous *jihād* against the Soviets, in order to avoid similar mistakes in the course of its own blessed *jihād*. The Taliban are [therefore] representatives of the action paradigm of considerateness [*aṣḥāb manhaj al-iʿtināʾ*].[970]

Apparently, the IEA high command has learned a lesson or two from the fact that the course of governance during its first period of central rule over Afghanistan had very much resulted in the alienation of the international community as well as the general local population. While continuing to receive unfettered support in many rural communities across the Pashtun Borderland, its government was then, as it is now, appraised from the outside almost

[968] See Aḥmad Jaʿfar Muhājir, 'Fiqh al-wāqiʿ bayn al-manhajayn «manhaj al-idʿāʾ wa-manhaj al-iʿtināʾ»', *al-Ṣumūd* 4/3 (1430/2009), 48.

[969] See *107th Congress of the United States of America*, Public Law 107–243: 116 Stat. 1 498 (16 October 2002): 'Whereas members of al Qaida [*sic*], an organization bearing responsibility for attacks on the United States, its citizens, and interests, including the attacks that occurred on September 11, 2001, are known to be in Iraq.'

[970] Aḥmad Jaʿfar Muhājir, 'Fiqh al-wāqiʿ' [see above, n.968].

exclusively in terms of the way it appeared especially in the metropolis of Kabul – which was, after all, the ultimate reference point in assessing the degree of modernization of the whole of Afghanistan.[971] This constricted focus, in turn, has largely shaped the public perception of the IEA, especially across the Global North, as a government still stuck 'in the stone age', as 'medieval', 'barbarian', 'terrorist' and so on, an image that was instantly revived in the mass media and the parlance of senior politicians when the IEA took Kabul in August 2021 and claimed the central government for the second time.[972]

However, some incredulity is certainly still expedient, because – to stress it once again – practising *fiqh al-wāqiʿ* does not at any point require necessarily a change of ideology, or, once in charge, even of practices of public administration. As such, *fiqh al-wāqiʿ* appears as little more than just a conveniently pragmatic strategy, and, as such, computes very well with the pragmatics so common in the Pashtun Borderland.

It must, therefore, be carefully appraised whether or not the ideology and practices of governance and public administration of the IEA have also been impacted by a 'legally constitutive appreciation of (ever-changing) actuality' or whether, as in almost all cases of "revision" of earlier positions held, for example, by the JIM or *al-Qāʿida* ideologue Sayyid Imām al-Sharīf,[973] the world-view is not touched at all and remains, thus, unchanged. For this, we need to broaden our gaze a bit and assess how the IEA leadership positions itself in relation to other concepts constitutive especially of militant Salafism and which have been introduced to its peers in the Pashtun Borderland especially by Arab fighters who had found a convenient operational base

971 For the paradigm of urbanity as the privileged space of modernity, see Askar (2019). See also Section 2.3.

972 The use of such charged language, which was overwhelmingly dominant during the first central government of the IEA, appears to have evolved from the rather cynical nonchalance of US-American political and military actors (as indicated by the controversy over the alleged threat of then-Deputy Assistant Secretary of State Richard Armitage to 'bomb Pakistan back to the Stone Age' if its government would not join the efforts of the US-American administration against "Islamic Terrorism" in late 2001). In the meantime, this rhetoric has become firmly rooted in media parlance, and, moreover, is re-invoked also by upper- and upper-middle-class urbanite Afghans. In an interview with Indian satellite television channel *WIONews* in early September 2021, for example, popular female Afghan singer Āriyānā Saʿīd said that '[T]hey [i.e., the IEA] are the same bunch of terrorists who came to Afghanistan and took Afghanistan back to [the] dark ages twenty years ago', a statement that, possibly for further dramatization, was rendered into the caption 'Taliban will take Afghanistan back to Stone Age' by the television studio (URL: www.wionews.com/videos/afghan-pop-star-aryana-sayeed-speaks-with-wion-411800 [9 September 2021, 11:35am IST], 00′10″ and 00′20″–00′29″ [accessed 10 February 2024]). Even blunter was the comparison of "Taliban" and "Nazis" by Afghan-American writer Tamim Ansary (2001).

973 See, for example, Ḥāfiẓ and Muḥammad (1425/2004a); Hartung (2013c), 89f.; Nedza (2020), 248–64.

there, courtesy, after all, of the IEA. Perhaps no conceptual issue reveals the complexity of these negotiations better than that of whether the thrust of the concerted action by all relevant parties assembled in the Pashtun Borderland was better to be directed at the "near" or the "far enemy".

4.5.4 *Renegotiating the Thrust of Action: Between the "Near" and the "Far Enemy"*

To this end, however, we must once again step back in time to the late 1990s, that is, before the *al-Qāʿida* attacks on US-American soil on 11 September 2001 unleashed a torrent of events that would result in severe and, so far, apparently irreversible consequences for the entire Muslim world and beyond. Then, *al-Qāʿida* ideologues such as Sayyid Imām, although not necessarily any longer in the Pashtun Borderland, were still maintaining an uncompromising stand regarding the unconditional duty of armed *jihād* and *takfīr*, and not taking much heed of *fiqh al-wāqiʿ*.[974] And, despite severe and detailed criticism by radical Salafist theoreticians such as Abū Muḥammad al-Maqdisī,[975] thanks to Ayman al-Ẓawāhirī and others in his orbit, elements of this radical conceptual universe eventually crossed the ethnic divide into that of their Pashtun peers, from where, as we shall see, at least some of them appear to have also been embraced by the IEA.

So far, at least one semantic cluster can already be identified. Pivoting on the old theme of *jihād*, what had been developed at the intersection of militant Islamists from various parts of the world in the Pashtun Borderland of the 1990s, from where it spread out into the notional universe of (Sunni) Muslim communities

[974] This, in fact, would change only after Sayyid Imām had been extradited by the state authorities of Yemen, where he had taken residence since 1994, and detained in an Egyptian high-security jail. In 2007, he presented what his ideological opponents perceived as an attempt to revise his earlier radical positions with reference to *fiqh al-wāqiʿ*, allegedly to propitiate the Egyptian authorities and to at least ease his detention conditions, if not to secure an early release: see Ibn ʿAbd al-ʿAzīz (1428/2007), for example 146, 12f. and 149, 12f.; Nedza (2020), 261–3.

In his staunch refutation of the arguments presented by his former compatriot, al-Ẓawāhirī (n.d.), 9, conjectured that 'these revisions were not only written under conditions of oppression, imprisonment and fear, but under the supervision, direction and management, and by the financial and military might of the Jewish crusaders; and those only dispensed these funds and efforts in it because it served their interest, because if they had not achieved by it what they wanted, they would not have allowed their comrade [i.e., Sayyid Imām] to speak at all.'

[975] This quite detailed legal and theological critique of Sayyid Imām's distinct conception of *takfīr*, written in March 1998 while he was in jail and released under the title "Shimmering Punchlines in Remarks on *al-Jāmiʿ*" – *Nukat al-Lawāmiʿ fī Malḥūẓāt al-Jāmiʿ*, revolved primarily on his understanding of governance counter the *shariʿa*: see Wagemakers (2011); Nedza (2020), 180f. and 226. Since its release, al-Maqdisī's *Nukat* has occasionally also been appended to editions of Sayyid Imām's *al-Jāmiʿ*.

elsewhere, was indeed a novelty: the concept of armed *jihād*, reformulated by theorists such as Sayyid Imām, was now systematically tied in to the formerly only loosely related Islamic legal concepts including *al-walāʾ wa'l-barāʾ* and *takfīr*. The finishing touches, however, were added by Abū Muṣʿab al-Sūrī, the one militant ideologue who was able to also establish a conceptual interface of *al-Qāʿida* and the IEA, and who supposedly referred to Sayyid Imām as his personal mentor during his first sojourn in the Pashtun Borderland in the late 1980s.[976] Indeed, it appears that, from that moment on, the direction of *jihād* has been irreversibly redefined, and this has, therefore, taken a lot of the ardour out of the earlier debates in militant Salafist circles over whether the battle against the "far enemy" was to take priority over the "near" one, or vice versa.

Seriously annoyed by the intra-Salafist debates over theological and legal concepts and over the strategic orientation of their *jihād*, al-Sūrī placed a strong emphasis on strategy instead.[977] He successfully dissolved the established binary of "near enemy" versus "far enemy" on over 1 600 pages by introducing a third way, one which he called "the global Islamic resistance" (*al-muqāwama al-islāmiyya al-ʿālamiyya*). According to al-Sūrī, no country in which Muslims lived took precedence over any other, which is why all *jihādī* activities, wherever they took place, needed to be weighted equally. A somewhat atomistic imaginary of an Islamic resistance results from this demand that, while organizationally decentred, is to be regarded in its sum as one single and global effort. Indeed, this perspective corresponds fully to the notion of the Muslim *umma* as a universal one that defies all other collective identities,[978] especially those that result from the colonial demarcations of allegedly "national" territories. The contrast between the idea of a single Muslim community that is naturally universal and the fragmentation into Muslim communities along artificially created national divides, finally, served al-Sūrī as a pointer to the true enemy: "The West", as the epitome of a persistent colonial attitude, typified, in turn, by "America" and the warfare the USA conducted in Muslim majority countries in retribution for the *al-Qāʿida* attacks on US-American targets in Saudi Arabia, Kenya, Tanzania, Yemen and eventually the USA itself:

> Hence, the enemy had globalized our cause [*ʿawlama qaḍiyyatunā*] by his attack on us, and Praise be onto God. This helps those who are not

[976] See al-Sūrī (1438/2018), 1 087; Markaz Razīz Qandahār (n.d.), 4f. Since the latter text does not have an identifiable author and, moreover, does not correspond to al-Sūrī's own portrayal of a certainly highly respectful, yet not explicitly deferential, attitude to the Egyptian, material like this brief biographical outline is best treated with an appropriate degree of caution, and information obtained from it should be presented – at least until more reliable material is located for corroboration – in a manner that demonstrates sufficient sensitivity regarding the source. For al-Sūrī's arrival in the Pashtun Borderland as late as 1987, see Lia (2007), 71.

[977] See Lia (2009), 283–9.

[978] See al-Sūrī (1438/2018), 1 366f.

> supported by belief and understanding [*al-muʿtaqad wa'l-fahm*], to move towards this *umma*-centric thinking [*al-tafkīr al-umamī*], which is among the constituents of our *dīn*. [. . .]
>
> Any Muslim eager to participate in the *jihād* and the resistance can participate in this battle against America in his own country, or elsewhere, which, on occasion, is thousands of times more effective than what he would be able to do if he arrived at the field of open confrontation [*sāḥat al-muwājaha al-maftūḥa*].
>
> However, it is inevitable to have a sense of commitment to the *umma* and its world [*al-iḥsās bi'l-intimaʾ li'l-umma wa-ʿālamihā*] [. . .]
>
> It is weird, though, that whoever looks at the frontlines, straight, curved and strangely twisted as they came when they draw maps of our countries, sees the drawings of the pens and rulers of the infidels in the ministries of the colonial powers [*al-kuffār min wizārāt al-mustaʿmarāt*], and they have been etched into the minds and hearts of the majority of the sons of this *umma*. Oddly, this tragedy is not much older than only a few decades, when the political entity of the entire *umma* collapsed in 1924, with the downfall of the last of the symbolic caliphs of this *umma* [*bi-suqūṭ ākhir al-khulafāʾ al-ramziyīn li-hādhihi 'l-umma*].[979]

With this image of a watershed event in Islamic-cum-Muslim history, al-Sūrī evoked another powerful symbol of Islamic political activism: that of the caliphate as the only political order sustainable by references to the authoritative Islamic texts and, therefore, exclusively suitable for Muslims. While not explicitly stated, the ultimate consequence of al-Sūrī's *jihād* would be the (re-) establishment of a caliphate, one, however, that was decidedly different from earlier Islamist thought. Had theorists like Mawdūdī conceived *khilāfa* as God's appointment of all humans 'who believe and work righteous deeds',[980] Salafists such as al-Sūrī – as well as, in fact, ʿAbd al-Salām Faraj two decades earlier[981] – (re-)envisioned this institution in continuation of the historical succession to the Prophet in the political and spiritual leadership of the Muslim *umma*.

In the early 1990s, most of these highly theoretical debates carried out by quite self-confident activists from the MENA region, predominantly within the various military training camps in the Pashtun Borderland,[982] were arguably still of little use and appeal to the nascent ṬIT. After all, these foreigners had established their presence in the region long before the emergence of the ṬIT, and the interface between them continued, by and large, to be kept

979 Ibid., 1 981–3.

980 This phrase, which Mawdūdī himself employed in this context, is taken from Q24.55: 'God has promised those of you who believe and work righteous deeds [*amanū minkum wa-ʿamilū al-ṣāliḥat*] to make them *khulafāʾ*, just as He has made those who lived before them *khulafāʾ*.' For Mawdūdī's interpretation of the *khilāfa*, see Hartung (2013a), 103–10.

981 See Faraj (1981), 4.

982 See al-Sūrī (1438/2018), 69–73 and 82.

deliberately slim,[983] particularly because especially those of Salafist persuasion among the Arab volunteers appear to have found it excruciatingly difficult to tolerate religious views and practices prevalent in the ṬIT / IEA, which they themselves regarded as clear signs of deviation in religious matters. In fact, the most ferocious among them, apparently concentrated around the infamous Khāldan training camp,[984] even went as far as openly building a case against the ṬIT / IEA that resulted in an estimation bordering on *takfīr*, which is, at least, how other renowned *al-Qāʿida* affiliates, prominently among them Abū Muḥammad al-Maqdisī and ʿUmar Muḥammad ʿUthmān, better known as "Abū Qatāda al-Filisṭīnī" (b. 1380/1960), have understood its message.[985] Yet, while Abū Muṣʿab al-Sūrī also saw 'some manifest loopholes [*maʿa baʿḍ al-thugharāt al-mawjūda*]' in the IEA's 'actual ruling according to the Islamic *shariʿa* as they perceive it',[986] he took a much more lenient, even amicable position towards them. As a result, he emerged as the most important go-between in the otherwise highly ambivalent and complex relationship between

983 See, for example, Nasiri (2006), 192–4 and 217. While Lia (2007), 242, considers the elaborations by Nasiri an 'eyewitness account', the fact that the person who uses the pseudonym "Omar Nasiri" volunteered between 1994 and 2000 as an informer to various European national intelligence agencies by infiltrating some Arab-run military base camps in Afghanistan under the pretext of wishing to embark on armed *jihād* makes him perhaps not the most credible character to rely on.

984 On this camp, purportedly established by the MKh on a plot of land in Lōyah Paktia formerly owned by the Ḥil, see Ḥāmid (2001a), 53; Brown and Rassler (2013), 80; Stenersen (2017), 50f. and 97f. See also Hegghammer (2020), 202 and 337, although what, on p. 202, is presented as ʿAbdallāh ʿAzzām's own words are, in fact, the words of former associate Noman Benothman, interviewed by Hegghammer more than twenty years after ʿAzzām's death (see Hegghammer (2020), 574 n.179).

985 A core document in this regard is *Kashf Shubuhāt al-Muqātilīn taḥta Rāyat Man Akhil biʾl-Aṣl al-Dīn* (April 2000) by the Syrian Bahāʾ Muṣṭafá Jaghl, also known as "ʿAbd al-Ḥamīd al-Sūrī" (b. 1396/1976), and Muḥammad Najāḥ Ḥasan ʿAbd al-Maqṣūd, *nom de guerre* "Abū Muṣʿab Rūyitīr [Reuter(s)]", after the London-based international news agency, a founding member of *al-Qāʿida* responsible for its media work (see *United States v. Usama Bin Laden et al.*, 146 F. Supp. 190–21 [S.D.N.Y. 2001], esp. 211f.). This text, sustained with a lengthy reference to Shams al-Dīn al-Afghānī's refutation of "Deobandiyyat" (see Anon. [1421h], 81–96; compare al-Afghānī [1419/1998], III: 329–43), pivots on the unchecked continuation of practices regarded as *shirk* under IEA rule, and concludes with a list of fourteen offences of which the IEA is accused: see Anon. (1421h), 99f.

Only six months later, Abū Qatāda released an equally comprehensive and systematic refutation of what, to him, appeared to be a collective *takfīr* on the IEA and the adherents to "Deobandiyyat", complete with a preface by Abū Muḥammad al-Maqdisī, see al-Filasṭīnī (n.d. [1421h]); also, compare al-ʿUyayrī (1422h). On the public dissociation of Ṣāliḥ ibn Muḥammad al-ʿAbbūd from the harsh sectarian tendencies in the language used in the published versions of his supervisee Shams al-Dīn's two theses, which, he claimed, are substantially different from the texts submitted for examination, see Section 4.1.3.

986 al-Sūrī (1436/2015), 31.

the IEA and *al-Qāʿida*,[987] possibly contributing to the incorporation of at least the symbolic term "caliphate" into the ṬIT / IEA frame of reference.[988]

However, al-Sūrī maintained the global scope of the militant Salafist International when he confined the significance of the *Islamic Emirate of Afghanistan* to little more than a convenient operational base for militant Salafists from all over the world, a destiny to be shared with Yemen and Muslim North Africa: from these bases, al-Sūrī proposed, the armed *jihād* was to spread out in ever wider concentric circles, eventually encompassing the entire globe.[989] Already at this early point, the ṬIT / IEA and al-Sūrī seem to have parted ways, because at no point did the IEA leadership indicate any aspiration to take their activities beyond the confines of the Afghan national territory, a fact that holds very much currency even today. We must, therefore, ask to what extent Arab militant Salafist theorists were able to instil – and interested in instilling – their ideological framework in whole or part into the various Islamically inspired local groups of militant activists, ultimately also including the ṬIT.

One is tempted to assume that both Salafis and Salafists native to the Pashtun Borderland have long since shared such sentiments that would ultimately catapult them beyond the confines of a regional frame of reference, from which it would, therefore, be easy to infer a certain predisposition to accepting the eventual re-establishment of the institution of a universal "caliphate" by the IS in June 2014. Yet, textual evidence is lacking to sufficiently corroborate this assumption. While Abū Muḥammad Amīnallāh Pishāvarī,[990] introduced above, for example, published his work on the so-called Rightly Guided Caliphs in the very same year that al-Sūrī released the first version of his *Daʿwat al-Muqāwama al-Islāmiyya al-ʿĀlamiyya*, and one might, therefore, be tempted to draw certain parallels, the text itself does not warrant this. Instead, Amīnallāh remained fully within the local frame of reference and merely continued in this work with what dominates all of his writings, namely, refutation of the influential Hanafi positions on the matter by pointing out the errors of their chief representatives in the region, the Deobandis. On the issue of the Rightly Guided Caliphs, he demonstrated how, contrary to the position ascribed to Abū Ḥanīfa and his *Fiqh al-Akbar*,[991] and which,

987 The relationship with Ibn Lādin had proactively been addressed by the ṬIT in response to the public accusations of hosting and abetting internationally wanted terrorists, responsible for the bomb attacks on the embassies of the USA in Kenya and Tanzania on 7 August 1998: see Anon., 'Də Usāmah bin Lādin də masʾalī siyāsay aw ḥuqūqay aṛkhūnō tah yavah katənah', *Khilāfat* 1/7–8 (1419h/1377sh), 22–5.

988 The fact that the term was adopted for the title of one of the, so far, earliest known ṬIT / IEA periodicals, if not the very earliest, the Pashto journal *Khilāfat*, published from spring 1996 to April 2001 from Kandahar, is indicative.

989 See al-Sūrī (1420/1999), 20f.

990 See Section 4.1.3.

991 The authorship of the *Fiqh al-Akbar*, while ascribed to Abū Ḥanīfa himself, is not securely established: see van Ess (1986), 332. Yet, as the text evidently continues to

according to Amīnallāh, has been followed in his eponymous current in Islamic jurisprudence, one is indeed able to find relevant information in the accepted *aḥādīth* which the Deobandis and other Hanafis ignored.[992] Nevertheless, nowhere in this or any other of the available works of Amīnallāh, who is, after all, a chief representative of the Salafi current in the Pashtun Borderland, is *khilāfa* considered a veritable and authoritatively grounded religio-political institution that Muslims are compelled to revive.

On the other hand, however, this observation still does not suffice to conclude that none of the significant actors of Pashtun Borderland provenance transcended their local focus by shifting to a more universalistic one, even though it has to be admitted that this is a much more complicated matter than assuming that the local frame of reference was entirely replaced by a global one. One of the prominent exemplars here is, once again, Jalāl al-Dīn Ḥaqqānī and, by implication, also Sirāj al-Dīn, his successor as leader of the MʿUJM. The JIM contingent in the Pashtun Borderland, whose magazine *al-Murābiṭūn* carried on a regular basis articles and reports on cases of oppressed Muslim communities in need of active support by their brethren in faith during its entire publication period, appears to have again been instrumental for their gradual opening up to a less locally confined focus. Apparently, this relentless reiteration has eventually paid off with genuine Borderland actors such as Jalāl al-Dīn Ḥaqqānī, who, in fact, was the only Pashtun commander besides Sayyāf[993] to merit a rather lengthy introduction to the *al-Murābiṭūn* readership, comprised overwhelmingly of JIM activists.[994] When, in the context of the capture of Khost, Jalāl al-Dīn was interviewed on the envisioned Islamic administration of the area under his control and eventually asked for his advice to the Arab volunteers who longed to stage *jihād* in their homelands and establish an Islamic government, he expressed his hope that they would eventually succeed in this pursuit, which may start out in one country and then spread into the others as well:

> I would neither say that they [i.e., the Arab volunteers] have suspended the *jihād* in their respective homelands for the sake of Afghanistan, nor

play a pivotal role within the Hanafi frame of reference, the actual authorship of this work seems of subordinate importance for the actual legal and theological praxis.

992 See al-Bishāvarī (1426h), 3–5. Pishāvarī listed more than 200 cases in this work, derived from a wide array of collections of accepted *aḥādīth* and contrasted with statements from the Hanafi legal literature, to show that the latter positions are not in line with the authoritative Islamic texts.

993 See 'Kalimat al-ustadh al-mujāhid "ʿAbd Rabb al-Rasūl Sayyāf" fī ḥafl taḥrīj al-difʿa al-khāmisa li'l-ṭullāb al-jāmiʿa al-ḥarbiyya', *al-Murābiṭūn* 1/7 (1411/1990), 12f.

994 The original interview with Jalāl al-Dīn Ḥaqqānī in *al-Murābiṭūn* was not available. However, a Pashto translation, although lacking a full reference to the Arabic original, was published as 'Mujāhidīn pah pawźī liḥāẓ shar maydalī mātay sarah', *Manbaʿ al-Jihād* [P] 2/12 (1370sh/1411h), 30–6.

> that this *jihād* can be waged everywhere at the same time, but rather in the form of a step-by-step *jihād*, starting first, for example, in Yemen, Syria and Libya, then later in Iraq, Tunisia and other countries.[995]

This, however, is as far as Jalāl al-Dīn Ḥaqqānī could be regarded as having subscribed to the embryonic idea of a "global Islamic resistance". However justified he saw such activities as being in each of the countries of the MENA region from which the Arab volunteers kept arriving in the Pashtun Borderland, he would clearly not compel his fighters to participate in *jihād* activities elsewhere: the battlefield for him and his retainers remained firmly local and would expand, at the most, to the whole of the national territory of Afghanistan.

Yet, there is no denial that, following the withdrawal of the Soviet Army from Afghanistan and the capture of Khost and Gardēz, the Mʿ UJM-run Urdu journal *Nuṣrat al-Jihād* began to carry an increasing number of pieces that suggested a growing anti-Americanism, especially in conjunction with the USA-led invasion of Iraq at around the same time. An article in the March 1991 issue of that journal, entitled "The New World Order of the Twenty-First Century", especially conveys the impression that the new lords over Khost had now subscribed to the "distant enemy" rhetoric that made the USA the prime target for the "global Islamic resistance". Referring to Henry Kissinger's article "False Dreams of a New World Order" in the *Washington Post* less than one month earlier, and citing from then-President George H. W. Bush's public "Remarks on the Observance of National Afro-American (Black) History Month" on 25 February 1991, the USA does indeed appear to be the new systemic enemy, replacing the then collapsing Eastern Bloc spearheaded by the Soviet Union.[996] The fact, however, that the articles appeared exclusively in the MʿUJM's Urdu journal and contained lengthy quotes from Qāẕī Ḥusayn Aḥmad, then-*amīr* of the JiI in Pakistan, who stressed the systemic incompatibility of an Islamic system of governance built on social justice and the system of US liberalism, built on the idea of the market economy and mutual competition, provides for a slightly alternative interpretation: far from being proof of the MʿUJM's embrace of the "distant enemy" trope, the anti-American articles in *Nuṣrat al-Jihād* were directed less at the "distant" government of the USA and much more at its "near" Pakistani counterpart, which had after all, been a main beneficiary of varied US aid since at least the late 1970s.

[995] Ibid., 36.

[996] See Sulṭān Ṣiddīqī, 'Ikīsvīṇ ṣadī [kā] nayā ʿālamī niẓām', *Nuṣrat al-Jihād* 1/5 (1411/1991), 19–21. Kissinger's article, which was actually rather critical towards the notion of the "New World Order" as coined by then-President Bush in his speech on 16 January 1991, during which he publicly announced hostilities with Iraq, appeared in *The Washington Post* (26 February 1991), 21. For an earlier assessment, see Brown and Rassler (2013), 263 n.51.

It seems that, while the strategic coalition between Pakistan and the USA during the PDPA regime and the Soviet military presence in Afghanistan was considered to conform with *shari'a* regulations by *mujāhidīn* commanders such as Jalāl al-Dīn Ḥaqqānī, the moment the USA led a military coalition against another Muslim nation, the Pakistani government was expected to put its loyalty towards Muslims above any economically and geostrategically beneficial alliances with a non-Muslim power. In other words, the Pakistani government, in order to live up to its claim to be administering an Islamic Republic, had to strictly observe the conditions of *al-walā' wa'l-barā'* if it were not to run into the danger of being accused of apostasy.

At this particular point in time, however, such *shari'a*-related implications remained still widely implicit, thus suggesting that the ideological transfer between the diverse Pashtun actors and the equally diverse Arab volunteers-turned-guests, alongside an increasing number of persecuted Muslim organizations especially from Central Asia,[997] was only sporadic.

Consequently, and countrary to the currently still dominant view, Yūnus Khāliṣ's success in persuading Usāma ibn Lādin to decline Sayyāf's invitation to Kabul and to instead take up residence at his own *Najm al-Jihād* compound in Jalalabad, for example, does not suffice to sustain the hypothesis of an ideological alliance with the Arab Salafist.[998] Again, it needs to be emphatically stressed that, also in the present book, little more than a mere sequence of circumstantial evidence could be indicated, because, even from the wealth of diverse primary materials that have been consulted here, it is possible neither to affirm confidently that there existed clear links between sender and recipient of the alleged ideological transfer, nor to ascertain the nature of these links beyond any doubt. What can be stated with some confidence, however, is that relationships between bustling Borderland actors such as Khāliṣ and infamous Arab militant Salafists such as Ibn Lādin amounted, in fact, primarily only to temporary marriages of convenience informed by Borderland pragmatics. In the case at hand, they aimed chiefly at stating Khāliṣ's intentions towards the Rabbānī-led government in Kabul in order for him to maintain as much of his independence as possible.[999] In reality, Khāliṣ himself remained rather in the

[997] Of special importance here is, firstly, the Uyghur-dominated *Shărqiy Türkistan Islam Hărkăti*, which, after 2001, had morphed into the more inclusive *Türkistan Islam Partisi*, see Brown and Rassler (2013), 111–13. The second major Central Asian organization in this regard is the IMU.

[998] A similar point has already been made by Bell (2013), 39–41 and 63.

[999] The common line adopted by Khāliṣ's hagiographers is, of course, rather different: in their accounts, Ibn Lādin appears as a man in dire need of sanctuary, which is exactly what Khāliṣ provided and, in this way, he fulfilled a religious as well as social obligation. With his generous financial contributions to the case of *jihād* against the PDPA–Soviet nexus, Ibn Lādin appears to have earned this sort of privileged treatment by his former Afghan brothers-in-arms: see, for example, Ṭalāyī (1390sh), 95f.; 'Azīzallāh (1386sh), 202–4; also already Muždah (1382sh), 67.

background and left the liaison with Ibn Lādin to his associate Muhandis (Engineer) Maḥmūd (killed 1417/1996).[1000]

In fact, Khāliṣ, as well as the Mʿ UJM high command and that of many other militias active across the Pashtun Borderland, had other matters to deal with that were more pressing than engaging in profound ideological cross-pollination with Ibn Lādin and the other *al-Qāʿida* activists. After all, during the last two years a new major player had entered the stage, had taken Kandahar and Herat – then governed by the JIA's commander Ismāʿīl Khān – and was fast advancing towards Kabul: the ṬIT.[1001] While its supreme commander, Mullā Muḥammad ʿUmar, is said to have fought as a member of the Ḥil-Kh against the PDPA regime in Kandahar Province after the Soviet withdrawal,[1002] Borderland pragmatics did not allow Khāliṣ and others to assume any continuous loyalty and, consequently, privileged treatment. Khāliṣ's situation would be rendered even more precarious by the fact that he, similarly to Jalāl al-Dīn Ḥaqqānī, was enjoying control over a distinct territory and rather reluctant to surrender his autonomy to the approaching ṬIT forces. Actually, Jalāl al-Dīn and his compatriots even considered armed resistance to the ṬIT's incursion into Khost.[1003]

Khāliṣ's *Najm al-Jihād* housing scheme, in turn, was conceived predominantly as a service to the local community, even though it hosted Ibn Lādin and other *al-Qāʿida* cadres for some time after their arrival in Jalalabad,[1004] before they finally moved on to the former Ḥil-Kh base at Tōrah Bōṛah, situated in the Pachīr aw Agām District of southern Nangarhar, just on the northern side of the Shpīn Ghar / Kūh-i Safīd range which separated it from the Khurram Agency with its strong Shiʿi Muslim population. When the ṬIT moved into Jalalabad in late August 1996, Ibn Lādin had just released his infamous proclamation of *jihād* against the "Occupying Americans in the Land of the Ḥaramayn", subtitled "They Expelled the Unbelievers from the Penninsula of the Arabs!", in which he firmly expressed his stand on the fact that the Saudi government had allowed US military forces to set up their base in the kingdom

[1000] See Muždah (1382sh), 66; (1391sh). Muhandis Maḥmūd and Ḥājjī Sāz Nūr, Sayyāf's lieutenants to serve as liaison with Ibn Lādin, were both killed in the same encounter at a checkpoint at Ṭōrkham near the border crossing with Pakistan, presumably in a case of blood revenge.

[1001] On the ṬIT campaigns of 1994 and 1995, see Rashid (2010), 18–40.

[1002] See ibid., 19 and 24 (based on a string of interviews of the author with the then-governor of Kandahar, Mullā Muḥammad Ḥasan Ākhūnd (killed 1435/2014), conducted between 1995 and 1997). Yet, Adamec (2003), 284, has Mullā ʿUmar down as a possible former member of the ḤII.

[1003] See Ruttig (2009), 65; Brown and Rassler (2013), 105. Why the MʿUJM commander eventually relented remains unclear; Davis (1998), 70, for instance, suggests pressure on him by the Pakistani ISI, which, by then, had shifted its major logistical support from the Ḥil-Ḥ to the ṬIT / IEA.

[1004] See ʿAzīzallāh (1386sh), 202f. and 265–7.

while being at war with Iraq.[1005] Thus, the head of *al-Qāʿida* had made clear that, at this time, he and his retainers were not planning to interfere in what they saw as Afghan domestic affairs, making sure in this way that the hospitality accorded to them as persecuted co-religionists could continue under alternating patrons, of which the ṬIT / IEA turned out to be just one among many.

When they took Nangarhar Province, some high-ranking commanders assured Ibn Lādin of continued protection by the IEA, reinforcing on the basis of religious precepts what would turn out to be a fatal relationship for both sides by referring to it as the relationship between the Meccan companions of the Prophet and their facilitators in Yathrib: 'You are the *muhājirūn*, while we are the *anṣār*'.[1006] While alluding to the formative period of Islam might have resonated especially well with the non-Afghans, references for the sake of the Pashtun commanders whom the leadership of the IEA courted were of a different kind. They all, in fact, appealed to the militant activism sustained by religious precepts of distinct historical Pashtun Borderland actors, extending from the Haḋdah Ṣāḥib, alleged patron saint of Yūnus Khāliṣ's *Najm al-Jihād* housing scheme,[1007] via the Ḥājjī Ṣāḥib of Turangzay, to the armed resistance of the Źadrāṇ tribe to the modernization policies of King Amānallāh and the very brief interim of the Tajik Ḥabīballāh Kalakānī, the "Bachah-yi Saqqāw", from January until October 1929.[1008] These references are highly significant, as they clearly confirm that the conceptual universe of the ṬIT was not yet populated by the sophisticated theological and legal concepts that were being fiercely discussed among the Arab and other non-Afghan Salafists. Moreover, and here the adherents to the early ṬIT differed greatly from regional Borderland actors such as the MʿUJM high command, they had clearly subscribed to a nationalistic agenda, which implies their recognition of the national boundaries of Afghanistan as the spatial limits to their political

1005 See Ibn Lādin (1436/2015), 182–200 (*Iʿlān al-Jihād ʿalá ʾAmrikān al-Muḥtalliyīn li-Bilād al-Ḥaramayn*). The subtitle of this proclamation was deliberately modelled after the popular – though not canonically recognized – Prophetic saying 'They expelled the polytheists from the Peninsula of the Arabs' (*akhrijū al-mushrikīn min jazīrat al-ʿarab*). For a considered discussion of this and related traditions, see Friedmann (2003), 90–3.

1006 al-Sūrī (1419/1998), 34.

1007 See ʿAzīzallāh (1386sh), 267: 'This settlement [*x̌ārgōṭī*] was named "Najm al-Jihād" because it was the previous location of the great fighting and spiritual personality [*lōy jihādī aw rūḥānī shakhṣiyyat*] Najm al-Dīn Ākhūnd'zādah, who truly was a great pioneer in bringing different communities [*qawmūnah*] of Afghanistan closer together.'

1008 For a reference to the Ḥājjī Ṣāḥib of Turangzay, see Muḥammad Nāṣir, 'Ḥājjī Ṣāḥib-i Turangzaʾī', *Navā-yi Afghān Jihād* 5/4 (1433/2012), 55–7. For the reference to the Źadrāṇ Uprising in 1929 by the then-ṬIT commander in Khost, Mullā Iḥsānallāh "Iḥsān" (killed 1418/1997), see Anon., 'Taliban Prepare to Attack Kabul', *AFGHANews* 11/10 (1995), 8.

aspiration, without any apparent reflection on the colonial roots of these demarcations.

In contrast, Jalāl al-Dīn Ḥaqqānī saw himself very much as a traditional borderland actor who defies territorial demarcations by imperial powers, knowing only too well that the ability of national administrators to establish firm control in the more mountainous areas of the upper Pashtun Borderland was limited at best.[1009] Thus, while he eventually complied with the call of the ṬIT to join them in capturing Kabul and ending the reign of the Rabbānī-led government and was subsequently rewarded with the Ministry of Frontier Affairs under the first central government of the IEA, he maintained a large degree of autonomy in Lōyah Paktia throughout.[1010] Moreover, his relationship with the IEA Leadership Council (*də rahbarəy shūrā*) in Kandahar,[1011] which was presided over by Mullā Muḥammad ʿUmar and in which all important matters were decided, was strongly informed by tribal rivalry between upland and lowland Pashtuns,[1012] going back to the attempts at establishing cultural hegemony over all Pashtuns under the southern Durrani confederation in the eighteenth century.[1013]

Even Yūnus Khāliṣ, who was more firmly rooted in the Islamist conceptual universe than Ḥaqqānī and, therefore, perhaps more open to a nationalistic agenda, stayed too independently minded to have himself and the ḤiI-Kh fully absorbed into the IEA. As we have seen above, this would in fact happen only under his eldest son and successor, when the ḤiI-Kh transformed into the TBJM, but even then a margin of independence remained.

In fact, the interaction between local power-holders in the Pashtun Borderland, whether or not they had transregional aspirations, like the ṬIT/IEA, or were content with their regional influence, like Jalāl al-Dīn or Khāliṣ, followed the well-established patterns of borderland pragmatics. At that time, also the relationships with Arab and other non-Afghans who operated in the Pashtun Borderland were exclusively informed by it. In fact, they resembled the local arrangements with the remnants of the predominantly non-Pashtun *Ṭarīqah-yi Muḥammadiyyah* after the Battle of Balakot in 1831: the *Ṭarīqah-yi Muḥammadiyyah* were permitted to establish their colonies of *mujāhidīn* on

1009 See Ḥaqqānī cited in Brown and Rassler (2013), 129 (from an interview for the Pakistani national broadsheet *The News*, 20 October 2001).

1010 See Ruttig (2009), *passim*.

1011 See ibid., 61. Ruttig has rightly reminded one of the fact that this council is not identical with the so-called "Kandahar *shūrā*", which, in fact, was one of four regional decision-making bodies in Afghanistan under the umbrella of the then-Quetta-based Leadership Council, with the others located in Herat and Badakhshan, as well as in Mīrāmshā.

1012 See Rashid (2010), 60 (based on an interview of the author with Jalāl al-Dīn Ḥaqqānī in Kabul in July 1997; also cited in Brown and Rassler [2013], 105). See also Ruttig (2009), 65f.

1013 See Section 3.1.2.

tribally owned land and do there whatever they wanted, where now the non-Afghan volunteers were granted space to set up their camps in which they would be allowed to do anything they wanted. In exchange, they were asked just to actively contribute men and logistics to the *laẍkarūnah* of their hosts, especially in socio-culturally sensitive situations where someone with no affiliation to any of the local tribes could come in handy as a proxy. We may view the active involvement of *al-Qāʿida* in the assassination of Aḥmad Shāh Masʿūd on 9 September 2001 in this light: instigated by the leadership of the IEA, whose advances were being seriously challenged by Masʿūd's forces, the act itself was committed by *al-Qāʿida* assets, which helped to divert responsibility away from the IEA and, thus, avoid any escalation according to the local traditions of conflict management.

Yet, such informal arrangements work out only if both sides stick to the terms agreed. Ibn Lādin and his *al-Qāʿida* compatriots, however, considered their relationships with the IEA high command to be on eye-level, if not – informed by a sense of ethnic supremacy – regarding themselves as superior. Hence, Ibn Lādin apparently cared little about the agreed framework for the granting of sanctuary from various Borderland actors. He repeatedly chose to ignore the order of Mullā ʿUmar to keep his head down and not cause any open conflict between the Islamic Emirate and the USA. Instead, he repeatedly snubbed the IEA leadership with his arbitrary media statements,[1014] and eventually dragged them into open military conflict with the USA, which ended the Islamic Emirate within two months of the invasion by allied forces.

This may have been Ibn Lādin's objective all along: to lure the US military into Afghanistan and wear them down in a prolonged guerrilla war, just as had been the case with the Soviet army, or with the British colonial forces between 1839 and 1919. Be that as it may, the severe consequences of the 11 September 2001 *al-Qāʿida* attacks for the central government of the IEA served as the ultimate combustive agent for a more widespread systematic appropriation of concepts devised by and refined in the Arab Salafist circles in the Pashtun Borderland by local actors than ever before.

The first indication, perhaps, is a special issue of the *Ḥaqqāniyyah* in-house journal *al-Ḥaqq* in the autumn of 2001 on "The Challenges of the Twenty-First Century and the World of Islam", in which the invasion of Afghanistan by the USA-led "Coalition of the Willing", as then-President George W. H. Bush labelled it, was situated within a wider historical and even eschatological context. Accordingly, the invasion was no mere retaliation for *al-Qāʿida* attacks on American high-profile targets, but – certainly as announced by the name "Enduring Freedom" that was chosen for this operation, as well as President Bush's emphatic use of Christian symbolic language – a systemic battle between the Islamic and the Christian worlds. The liberal application of

1014 See, for example, Brown and Rassler (2013), 114–17.

the term "crusaders", which had previously been used predominantly in the Arab Salafist circles, to the military coalition appears in this light, as well as reflecting the fact that the second millennium of the Gregorian calendar had only just begun and the "world of Christianity" had once again geared up to establish its absolute supremacy on earth, as it had done less than a century after the first millennium.[1015] Subsequently, the time for differentiated perspectives was over, and, only a few pages on, the "world of Christianity" became the "world of unbelief" (*ʿālam-i kufr*).

The wildly assembled essays had previously been published elsewhere;[1016] however, two core pieces set the agenda of the special issue *al-Ḥaqq*: an address by Ibn Lādin and an extensive interview with Samīʿ al-Ḥaqq. The exclusively written contribution of the former was to swear the community of believers to the ultimate *jihād* against the forces of unbelief, which will end only once Islam has ultimately triumphed. Here, too, an eschatological dimension is projected, emphasized with references to a plethora of acknowledged *aḥādīth*, according to which the Prophet had 'ordered [believers] to fight people [*uqātil al-nās*] until they testify that there is no deity but God and Muḥammad is His messenger'.[1017] Mundane concerns are to be deferred in view of the precarious situation that Muslims worldwide would find themselves in, as 'the extinction of the world upsets God much less than the killing of a Muslim'.[1018] Samīʿ al-Ḥaqq now followed suit and affirmed the agenda of global *jihād*, which had only started in Afghanistan, but will, via Pakistan, eventually take in the entire world.[1019]

Only a few months before Samīʿ al-Ḥaqq openly performed his closing of ranks with the leader of *al-Qāʿida*, the JUI-F had convened a large conference on the occasion of the 150th anniversary of the *Dār al-ʿUlūm* at Deoband in Peshawar, to which Mullā Muḥammad ʿUmar contributed a special address.[1020]

1015 See Rāshid al-Ḥaqq Samīʿ Ḥaqqānī, 'ʿĀlam-i islām kē khilāf ṣalībī jang kā āghāz ikīsvīṇ ṣadī kī bhayānak ibtidāʾ', *al-Ḥaqq* 36/11–2 to 37/1–2 (2001), 3–9, here 3.

1016 The array of authors, dead and alive, ranged from Abū ʾl-Ḥasan ʿAlī Nadvī to Yūsuf al-Qaraḍāwī (d. 1444/2022) and the British historian Francis Robinson, and they have – probably without their express consent – been assembled to indicate that the position taken by the *Ḥaqqāniyyah* establishment was one shared far beyond the confines of this seminary.

1017 *Ṣaḥīḥ al-Bukhārī*, k. al-īmān, b. fa-ʾin tābū wa-ʾaqāmū ʾl-ṣalāt wa-ʾātū ʾl-zakāt fakhallū sabīlahum, no. 1 (ḥadīth 25); compare Shaykh Usāmah ibn Lādin, 'Khuṣūṣ payghām ummat-i muslimah kē nām: ikisvīṇ ṣadī islām kī sar'bulandī awr ʿaẓimat kī ṣadī hōgī', *al-Ḥaqq* 36/11–2 to 37/1–2 (2001), 11–15, here 12.

1018 *Jāmiʿ al-Tirmidhī*, k. al-diyāt, b. mā jāʾ fī tashdīd qatl al-muʾmin, no. 1 (ḥadīth 1455); compare Ibn Lādin, 'Khuṣūṣ payghām' [see above, n.1 017], 14 (here given in a different and non-canonical variation, although whether this should be blamed on the author, or rather on the translator and editor, remains unknown).

1019 See Ḥāmid al-Ḥaqq Ḥaqqānī, 'Afghānistān kī tāzah ṣūrat'ḥāl awr ʿālam-i islām kī majmūʿī ḥālat-i zār awr mustaqbal kē bārē mēṇ Mawlānā Samīʿ al-Ḥaqq Ṣāḥib kā tafṣīlī intarvyū', *al-Ḥaqq* 36/11–2 to 37/1–2 (2001), 49–72.

1020 See Amīr al-Muʾminīn-i Afghānistān Mullā Muḥammad ʿUmar Mujāhid, 'Islāmī niẓām par sawdē-bāzī nahīṇ karēṇgē!', in Durrānī (2006), 124–8.

The fact that an address of the supreme head of the IEA was read on this occasion is significant; even more striking are the terminological parallels between this text and those exclusively written for the special issue of *al-Ḥaqq*. The short address begins with the dichotomy of the "world of Islam" and the "world of unbelief", against which the ṬIT had established its Islamic Emirate across Afghanistan. In view of the might of the enemy, unity remained key, and this accord should be firmly expressed by setting up an Islamic counterweight to the United Nations. However, and here the regional specifics again came back into play, the benchmark for Islamicity should be the culturally distinct interpretation of Islam of the founding fathers of the *Dār al-ʿUlūm* at Deoband rather than a more cosmopolitan one as advocated by Salafis of whatever kind.

This is, in fact, the crux of the matter: while the JUI-S rubbed shoulders with the advocates of a universal Salafist interpretation of Islam, the JUI-F stressed instead the distinctiveness of its ideological undercurrent as the exclusively suitable one for the Afghan–Indian region. Moreover, Faẕl al-Raḥmān was styled as the true heir to the Deobandi legacy in the reports of the Peshawar conference, thanks especially to the eminence of his father Muftī Maḥmūd.[1021] However, Samīʿ al-Ḥaqq recast himself as a champion of universal Salafism. Yet, once again, the issue of solidarity with regional and transregional manifestations of Islamically sustained militancy would be used to enhance the actor's own position in the highly complex and sensitive set-up of power in the Pashtun Borderland and, beyond that, in the Islamic Republic of Pakistan.

4.5.5 *A Time of Tribulations and End-Time Battles*

The forced removal of the IEA central government and its replacement with a hand-picked pro-USA provisional one, which would be affirmed in the controversial 2004 Afghan presidential elections, not only had severe political and operational consequences in the region, but would ultimately also find its corresponding ideological manifestation. The pivot appears to have been the already quite widespread eschatological world-view that radiated from the relentless reiterations in this regard by prominent militant Frontier Deobandis such as Rashīd Aḥmad Ludhiyānavī, Niẓām al-Dīn Shāmzay[1022] and Abū Lubābah Shāh Manṣūr, among many others. Their apocalyptic rhetoric tied in well with similar sentiments across large parts of the Muslim world at that time, where the sequence of events was understood against the backdrop of Sunni Islamic eschatology: the "Great Deceiver", the *dajjāl*, was roaming at large, causing the Islamic *umma* to fall apart by trying hard to pull its members over to his side, while the ever smaller community of righteous believers would have to hasten to prove itself worthy of salvation by the

1021 See Muftī Muḥammad Jamīl Khān, 'Muqaddimah', in Durrānī (2006), 13–59.

1022 See, for example, Shāmzay (1428/2007), esp. 10f.

imminent Judgement Day that would coalesce with God's termination of the material world as known. The disintegration of the *umma*, in turn, also did not spare the spectrum of those who considered themselves righteous: their formerly much-besought unity was increasingly sacrificed to the competing aspirations to affirm one faction or the other as the sole community among the countless fragments of the *umma* which the Prophet himself had assured of their salvation: alternatively labelled the "saved" or "victorious group" (*al-firqa al-nājiyya* or *al-firqa al-manṣūra*).[1023]

Consequently, as the IEA retreated from the former seat of its central government in Kabul to the less accessible regions of the Pashtun Borderland and subscribed to the guerrilla tactics once so successfully employed by the various Islamist organizations involved in the armed resistance to the PDPA–Soviet nexus, the situation across this entire area that defies national borderlines became exacerbated to a hitherto unprecedented degree. In fact, the Pashtun Borderland emerged as one of the central arenas in which the predicted tribulations (*fitan*) for the Islamic *umma* at the end of time materialized most graphically and in which the subsequent final battles with the forces of unbelief were fought. Under such aggravated conditions, pragmatics, which, in the case of the Islamist organizations of the 1970s and 1980s, had resulted in their submission to an alliance that persisted until it had served its cause, had to come second to ideological demarcation lines. Moreover, these lines – roughly assessed in the binary of *īmān* and *kufr* – needed to be constantly revisited by all those who regarded themselves as of the one community promised the exclusive privilege of salvation in the Hereafter. Appreciating the gravity of the situation and the little remaining time to prove oneself as a righteous believer, no one could be exempted from having his or her fidelity thoroughly scrutinized, not even those who adhered to the IEA, *al-Qāʿida* or any of the other governance-orientated militant groups in the Pashtun Borderland. Whoever failed the test of faith needed to be dealt with according to the legal theories of *takfīr* as devised by radical ideologues of various Arab provenances: by disengagement (*barāʾ*) and, ultimately, *jihād* in all of its varieties. The End-Time battles were, therefore, fought not only

[1023] The core reference in this regard is the accepted, though apocryphal, popular Prophetic "*Ḥadīth* of the Seventy-Three Factions", in which Muḥammad stated that 'The people of the Book before you have split into seventy-two factions, and this people [*inna hādhihi millata*] will break up into seventy-three: seventy-two of which will go into the fire and [only] one of them into Paradise, and this is "The Community" [*wa-hiya al-jamāʿa*]' (e.g., *Sunan Abī Dāwūd*, k. al-sunna, b. sharh al-sunna, no. 2 [ḥadīth 4 599]; *Jāmiʿ al-Tirmidhī*, k. al-imān ʿan rasūl allāh – ṣallá 'llāh ʿalayhi wa-sallam, b. mā jā aftirāq hādhihi 'l-umma, nos. 1f. [aḥādīth 2 852f.]). For extensive commentary on this *ḥadīth*, its significance for the constitution of an Islamic heresiography and also the shift of emphasis in its interpretation from the dangers of schism for the socio-political unity to eschatology around the second / middle of the eighth century, see van Ess (2011), I: 7–64.

against the US-led military coalition and the governments formed at their behest in Afghanistan, as well as the Pakistani authorities for their willingness to co-operate with the US government in its proclaimed "War on Terror", but also between the various factions involved in fighting the state authorities on either side of the Durand Line.

Many of these factions carved out territories for themselves within the Pashtun Borderland that were proclaimed emirates, thus constituting small enclaves of *dār al-islām* within a wider territory interspersed with unbelief, from which armed defensive *jihād* could legitimately be staged. The more the initially besought accord of all those activists in the Borderland who were persecuted by the various state actors in Afghanistan and Pakistan was sacrificed to ideological purity, the more the IEA was reduced to being only one actor, albeit a mighty one, in this increasingly incomprehensible thicket of groups in which each considered itself the sole representative of the *firqa nājiyya*.

Many of the eventual contenders who would hold the Pashtun Borderland in a tight grip for over two decades were swiftly subsumed under the catchy term "New" or "Neo-Taliban", which was generously (and interchangeably) employed in the subsequent research literature.[1024] Bearing in mind, however, that the prefix "neo-" appears more often than not attached to all sorts of already extant labels as a quick and convenient strategy to catch the attention of an audience, therefore complying more with marketing concerns than with purely academic criteria,[1025] it is certainly appropriate to pause our narrative

1024 The coiner of the term "Neo-Taliban", which has been willingly embraced especially by political think-tank personnel and investigative journalists, appears to have been the London-based defence and security analyst Antonio Giustozzi (2007). In Giustozzi (2009), "Neo-Taliban" and "New Taliban" are employed interchangeably, thus adding to the confusion that, unfortunately, results from not solidly conceptualizing either term in the first place. The meagre gesture towards a definition Giustozzi provides exhausts itself at this: 'Although their [i.e., the Neo-Taliban's] tactical skills remained weak throughout 2002–6, they made "creative" use of the modest human resources available. Indeed, compared to the "old Taliban" of 1994–2001, the insurgent of 2001– [*sic*] deserve to be described as *Neo*-Taliban. [. . .] The Neo-Taliban developed a passion for the new technologies completely at odds with the ostracism showed in the old days. It is not clear whether the top ranks of the Movement, who played a key role in 1994–2001 too, also personally adopted the new technologies or whether they only allowed their subordinates to use them. [. . .] The internationalisation of the Taliban is a third feature marking the Movement as "*neo*". The influence of the Arab jihadists was evident in this case.' (Giustozzi [2007], 236 [italics in the original]).

1025 We have already encountered the notion of "Neo-Hanbaliyya" as introduced by Henri Laoust, which has in the meantime started to become substantially challenged (see Section 4.5.1); other labels of that kind are Fazlur Rahman's "Neo-Sufism", "Neo-Salafiyya" and "Neo-Wahhabiyya", to name just a few, see, for example, Levtsiyon (1986), 53f.; Schulze (1990), 19–25. Critically regarding the first label, see O'Fahey and Radtke (1993); on the second, see Bruckmayr and Hartung (2020), 141 n.13.

once more and, first of all, subject the nowadays widely used labels "New" or "Neo-Taliban to a careful and critical cross-examination in order to ascertain to what extent they are empirically warranted and can, therefore, serve as useful analytical categories".

"New Taliban" . . . and the "New" Old Ones

Immediately after the fall of the central government of the IEA in December 2001, its leadership *shūrá* relocated from Kandahar to Quetta and almost simultaneously established a local leadership council in the same city, alongside others in Peshawar, Mīrāmshā and 'a separate *shura* for the North and North-East'.[1026] So far, the impression could be maintained that those who, from a government-centric perspective, were called "insurgents" were still united under a single banner and the decentralization of leadership was little more than a mere strategic necessity under the prevalent circumstances. Despite the continuous and increasingly professional efforts of a freshly established media office for the central co-ordination of the IEA's new multiple media strategies[1027] to maintain this image, however, it was bound not to last for very long.

The first who took advantage of the now more vulnerable state of the IEA after its first central government had been ended by force were disgruntled former retainers from the northern highland part of the Pashtun Borderland, who seized the opportunity to reignite the more-than-two-centuries-old dispute with their southern lowland counterparts over cultural supremacy in the entire Pashtun region. A handy carrier of such often rather implicit competition was constituted by a range of new IEA periodicals in various languages which began to emerge in the mid 2000s,[1028] somewhat resembling the modus

[1026] Ruttig (2009), 61 (italics in the original). No reference has been provided, which suggests that this information might be based more on popular hearsay than on firm evidence.

[1027] See Anon., 'al-Nashāṭāt al-iʿlamiyya'. See also Nathan (2009), who, however, doubts the impact especially of the virtual media employed by the IEA 'in a largely offline country such as Afghanistan' (p. 29). While this may indeed have been the case in the early 2000s, it was certainly no longer so at the time Nathan wrote her paper. Therefore, the lack of acknowledgement of the rapid spread of internet usage and cellular communication in Afghanistan since 2002 (see URL: www.internetworldstats.com/asia/af.htm [accessed 10 February 2024]) comes as something of a surprise from someone who was based in Kabul between 2003 and 2009.

[1028] The oldest of this second wave of official periodicals of the IEA is the bi-monthly Pashto journal *Ćrak*, publication of which started in 2004. In July 2006, it was joined by the two Pashto monthlies *Mōrchal* and *Shahāmat*, as well as the Arabic *al-Ṣumūd*. The Urdu journal *Sharīʿat* was launched as late as April 2012, and it took until January 2014 to complement the range with the Dari journal *Ḥaqīqat*, which, of all the periodicals, is the one published most irregularly. Nathan (2009), 30f., mentions two further periodicals, *Ẓamīr* and *Ilhām*, both Pashto weeklies, established in 2004 and 2005, respectively. Of these, only relatively few copies dating from 2005 and 2006, which, furthermore,

operandi of the various Islamist organizations during the resistance to the PDPA regime and the Soviet army in response to the mighty propaganda machines of their highly resourceful opponents.[1029] These efforts were – inadvertently – aided by the various pieces of legislation both in Afghanistan and in Pakistan regarding new information technologies which facilitated the electronic circulation of periodicals rather than necessitating, as was the case for the Islamist organizations in the 1980s, the use of a physical printing press. Nevertheless, even this more concerted and structured approach to print media, audio and video, which we shall look at more closely below, does not in itself amount to a deliberate and fundamental change of strategy that justifies the use of this label, as suggested by those who have coined and maintain the notion of a "Neo-Taliban".[1030]

because of serious formatting issues (caused probably by file conversion errors), are partly illegible, generously provided by the *Taliban Sources Project* (see Chapter 1, n.18), from the "Taliban Source Repository" run by the Norwegian Defence Establishment in collaboration with the University of Oslo, were available for scrutiny. *Ẕamīr* is also mentioned in Anon., 'al-Nashāṭāt al-iʿlamiyya li-ḥarakat Ṭālibān al-islāmiyya', *al-Ṣumūd* 2/6 (1428/2007), 5f., here 5, as are a number of affiliated periodicals, comprising the Pashto journals *ʿAzm* (2002–3), its successor *Tavakkul*, *Pāćūn*, *Tōrah Bōṛah* and *Də Mujāhid Ghaǵ*, the trilingual *al-Istiqāmah* (Pashto, Dari, English) and the Arabic *Nafīr*. Yet, all these new periodicals, whose emergence coincided somewhat with the spread of internet provision in the region, had, of course, been preceded by conventional printed ones, all of which were published under the auspices of the Directorate of Information and Culture (*Də Iṭṭilāʿātō aw Kultūr Riyāsat*) of the IEA in Kandahar: firstly, the Pashto monthly *Khilāfat*, with its first issue published in May 1996, secondly, the Pashto daily *Hēvād* and, finally, the *Majallat al-Imāra al-Islāmiyya*, an Arabic monthly, the first issue of which was released in July 2000. All three of these publications appear to have been terminated with the end of the first period of central rule of the IEA in December 2001 and the subsequent relocation of its Leadership Council to neighbouring Quetta.

1029 With some delay, the Urdu monthly *Sharīʿat* published the text of a speech by journalist-cum-translator Saʿd Kaṫavāzay on the vital importance of using media technologies against the dissemination of anti-IEA propaganda by those media outlets in the service of the Kabul government and its North American and European allies in what he calls a 'journalistic war' (*ṣaḥāfatī jang*): see Saʿd Kaṫavāzay, 'Jihādī mediyā kī ahmiyyat awr ẕarūrat', *Sharīʿat* 5/2 (1437/2016), 14–16. Against the popular sentiment among many followers of the IEA that the use of mass media is not endorsed by the *shari'a*, the author referred to two canonized Prophetic precedents: the first one served as an illustration of the virtue of control over information and the ability to spread misinformation while at war, the second as an indication that the Prophet himself had not been adverse to even pre-Islamic forms of public communication – here poetry – as long as they served the cause of Islam and the *umma* of the believers. The two Prophetic sayings which Kaṫavāzay paraphrased are *Ṣaḥīḥ al-Bukhārī*, k. al-maghāzī, b. ghazwat Uḥud, no. 3 (ḥadīth 4 093); and *Ṣaḥīḥ Muslim*, k. faḍāʾil al-ṣaḥāba, b. faḍāʾil Ḥassān ibn Thābit, no. 12 (ḥadīth 6 550).

1030 Studies on these late media developments in the region are numerous indeed, see, for example, Habibi, Ulman, Baha and Stočes (2017); Hanif, Shao and Hanif (2018).

There are two instances in which it is deemed appropriate to consider assigning the labels "Neo-Taliban" and "New Taliban", though not as a representation of actual realities, as is the case with the many security analysts who freely use these terms despite their academically problematic implications.[1031] Conversely, the term "Neo-Taliban" shall be proposed here as a distinct analytical category applicable principally to the TṬP, which had not existed before 2002 and owes its existence less to the end of IEA central rule in Afghanistan than to the disproportionately harsh domestic policy of the Pakistani government of four-star General Parvēz Musharraf towards the Pashtun Borderland as a general reservoir of anti-government militancy. Consequently, the frame of reference for the TṬP's activities was primarily not the prolonged presence of non-Muslim foreign military forces in Afghanistan and the national government established at their behest, but rather the Pakistani state and its ambiguous position towards (Sunni) Islam as a benchmark of good governance in the nation-state for the Indian Muslims. Clearly, therefore, the ideological setting for the emergence of the TṬP was quite distinct from that in southern Afghanistan after the end of the PDPA regime that gave rise to the ṬIT.

Moreover, as we shall see shortly, the ideological impact of especially Arab volunteer fighters in the orbit of *al-Qāʿida* is also clearly evident in the TṬP, but not so much among those who maintained IEA governance in a decentralized form until their second and equally fast sweeping advance across Afghanistan and the re-establishment of its central government in August 2021.

The term "New Taliban", however, does indeed have some empirical correspondence in the eschatologically charged religio-political culture of the Pashtun Borderland highlighted above decisively in the two decades following the bringing to an end of the first IEA central government by the USA-led military invasion in late 2001 and this is inseparably linked to the establishment of an official presence of the IS on Afghan territory on 29 January 2015. Taking the ideological demarcation between believers and unbelievers to a hitherto unprecedented level, cadres of the IS in its province of Khurasan began to distinguish between the "old", or "original" (*aṣlī*), pre-2002 IEA, to which most of them had originally belonged, and the present one, which was accused of having severely deviated from the conformity with the Islamic

[1031] Indeed, the terms "Neo-Taliban" or "New Taliban" both imply that the USA-led military campaign against the IEA between 26 September and 22 December 2001 had successfully ended not only its first central government, but the ṬIT / IEA as such, while the new "insurgent" actors draw inspiration from the ṬIT, but are essentially something distinct. While – given their strong institutional links with governments of the Global North – it may be understandable that political and security analysts are in need of such blunt narratives of comprehensive success, politically independent researchers may wish to be very careful before embracing such value-laden labels as categories to describe empirical realities.

shari'a for which the IEA was once renowned. As we shall see in some more detail further below, it is this very distinction between the "original" and "New Taliban" that allowed the ideologues of the IS to accuse everyone associated with the IEA of apostasy (*irtidād*) and, accordingly, to legitimize its own armed actions against them.[1032] "New Taliban" constitutes, thus, an exclusively polemical term, employed by IEA renegades to justify their exit from that organization as necessitated by the injunctions of the *shari'a*.

***

Yet, before we can embark on evaluating the impact that the presence of an IS contingent had on the religious dynamics in the Pashtun Borderland, some critical appreciation of the new stock of information that the various IEA magazines have provided since 2004 seems in order, all the more so because these materials are embedded in the wider "mediascape"[1033] of militant Salafist expression in the Pashtun Borderland. By now taking an active part in this, one may indeed be tempted to rush to conclusions similar to the ones drawn by those who introduced the label "Neo-Taliban". After all, it seems as if, once their central government had been overthrown, the representatives of the IEA became a conscious part of an increasingly global militant Salafist "ideoscape",[1034] in which cultural specifics and distinct territorialities are transcended by universalistic Islamic rhetoric and which would then indeed signify a new ideological direction.

In this regard, ʿAbdallāh ʿAzzām's MKh is to be considered a pioneering enterprise, with the monthly *al-Jihād* as a speaking tube of global militant Islamism. In the late 1990s, this growing entanglement of "ideoscape" and "mediascape" began to be raised to the next level by the ever-better-organized media activities of *al-Qāʿida*, which increasingly embraced the newly available virtual media.[1035] It all began with websites, such as the English-language <azzam.com> and <qoqaz.net>, run between 1997 and 2001 by British

1032 Prominently, see "Sar'bāz-i Khalīfah" (1397sh/1439h).

1033 The usage in the present book of this term, instead of analytically much weaker alternatives, such as "media landscape", follows Appadurai (1990), 298–300. The term "mediascape", in the way its originator wanted it to be understood, seems especially applicable to the context under review, in which hard-to-get print media are increasingly replaced by electronic ones, the reach of which is much less restricted to an actual physical presence in the region.

1034 See ibid.

1035 Dating the emergence of the various *al-Qāʿida* media platforms turned out to be quite difficult, as relevant primary material is oftentimes no longer available, while the mostly ill-referenced secondary works at hand have emerged predominantly within security policy think-tanks (e.g., the much-quoted study from 2007 *Al-Qaeda's Online Media Strategies: From Abu Reuter to Irhabi 007* by Hanna Rogan, courtesy of the Norwegian Defence Research Establishment FFI) or journalistic circles (e.g., Kāmil [2017]). Moreover, the dates provided in these materials differ significantly from each other.

national Babar Ahmad (b. 1974), and the Arabic-language <alneda.com>, run by the later *amīr* of the Saudi Arabian *al-Qāʿida* chapter, Yūsuf ibn Ṣāliḥ al-ʿUyayrī, which was live between March 2001 and the violent death of its operator. At that point in time, however, the preferred way to communicate with the wider public was still statements printed in Arab national newspapers, and telephone calls and videos which were passed on to major media outlets in the MENA region, prominently the Qatari television channel *al-Jazeera*.[1036] Sometime in the summer of 2001, that is, before the attacks that triggered the military invasion of Afghanistan by USA-led military forces, *al-Qāʿida*'s own media department, the *Muʾassasat al-Saḥāb li'l-Intāj al-Iʿlāmī*, gained public attention with the release of a two-hour video directed by Usāma ibn Lādin on "The State of the Islamic Umma and the Destruction of the American Destroyer «Cole»" (*Ḥāl al-Umma al-Islāmiyya wa-Tadmīr al-Mudammira al-Amrīkī «Kūl»*).[1037] In 2004, finally, *al-Saḥāb* and its only just established virtual distribution hub, the *Markaz al-Fajr li'l-Iʿlām*,[1038] became aligned with the newly established "Global Islamic Media Front" (*al-Jabha al-Iʿlāmiyya al-Islāmiyya al-ʿĀlamiyya*), a platform fashioned in Germany that aimed at centralizing all of the media efforts of militant Salafists anywhere, and of *al-Qāʿida* in particular.[1039]

This, finally, is what constitutes the paradigm of militant Salafist media work in the early 2000s.[1040] Since both *al-Saḥāb* and *al-Fajr* were operated by *al-Qāʿida*

1036 The website of *Azzam Publications* has been archived at URL: http://web.archive.org/web/20010720103119/http://azzam.com (accessed 14 July 2021). On al-ʿUyayrī's *al-Nidāʾ*, see Hegghammer (2010), 171f.

1037 The first part of the video, complete with English subtitles, can still be found on the official *al-Saḥāb* website, currently under the URL: http://sahabmedia.co/?p=531; the second is under http://archive.org/details/stateoftheummah2 (both accessed 17 July 2021).

1038 The mission statement of the distribution hub *al-Fajr* must be considered identical to that of its e-journal *Majallat al-Mujāhidīn al-Tiqanī*, of which only two issues appear to have been released, in December 2006 and February 2007, respectively. According to its editor, Abū Muthanná al-Najdī (b. 1403/1984), 'we are in the twenty-first century and have neither fixed offices nor conventional mail'; the consequently highly mobile hub was set up to 'publish announcements [*bayānāt*] of a number of jihādī groups around the world, spearheaded by our brethren of the *al-Qāʿida* organization in Afghanistan and our brethren in the Islamic State of Iraq in Mesopotamia, and by other blessed jihādī groups' ('al-Kalima al-iftitāḥiyya', *Majallat al-Mujāhidīn al-Tiqanī* 1/1 [1427h], iii).

1039 See Torres-Soriano (2012).

1040 Whether or not the media work by the IS does indeed constitute another paradigm shift is subject to scholarly debate. I, for one, tend to regard it as just a proliferation of the pattern established by *al-Qāʿida* and associates in the early 2000s. By utilizing all the newly available communication tools, however, and among them especially the so-called social media, control over the content is increasingly passed on from a numerically strictly confined leadership to the mass of individuals who post, discuss and comment on the personal views within their own select in-group. In a way, this

cadres, mainly from their various retreat areas on the eastern side of the Durand Line, we may well assume that the leadership of the various old and new militias that have embraced the label "Taliban" was primed in media strategies of the digital age. These, however, have not been an end in themselves, but rather recourse to them was caused by the fact that, at that time, it was far from certain that any territorial sovereignty would eventually accrue to the IEA, as well, in fact, as the TṬP, and the radiation of their propaganda in cyberspace was, therefore, simply a strategic necessity. Whether or not the adaptation and cultivation of a media strategy devised by Arab militant Salafists then operating out of the less accessible parts of the Pashtun Borderland by the IEA leadership has also had a significant impact on their ideological framework requires a closer look at the content of the official e-journals of the IEA listed above.[1041] This is even more relevant because all of the various militant groups in the Pashtun Borderland, be they the IEA, the TṬP or *al-Qāʿida*, subscribed increasingly to the same tools of extremely asymmetrical warfare: individual suicide attacks, abductions of individuals at random and the extensive use of improvised explosive devices.[1042] As they became almost instantly indistinguishable in terms of their activities, their respective ideological backgrounds would have to serve as a defining core feature to distinguish among these groups.

The first point to revisit to this end is the significantly increased linguistic variety of the media work of the IEA post-2004, especially in the light of the persistent view that the fact of IEA e-periodicals in Arabic and their financial support from some Gulf countries is a clear indication of their having joined what, in 1998, Ibn Lādin had conceived as a "Global Islamic Front (against Jews and Crusaders)". Indeed, the various contributions to all of these periodicals may instead be considered as a kind of seismograph for the flexibility of

corresponds to the currently final phase in the development of the militant Islamist "mediascape" in the four-stage model of Zelin (2013), 3f.

1041 This content analysis should actually also include the internet presence of the IEA. Unfortunately, various security agencies in the Global North, as well as well-meaning internet activists, have succeeded in repeatedly blocking access to the official website of the IEA, which has made the collection of data from there far too tedious for it to remain a feasible option at this time.

1042 In fairness it ought to be pointed out that, in autumn 2008, the leadership of the IEA still rejected these kinds of militant action at the expense of the civilian population, at least rhetorically: see Haćānd, 'Āyā rīx̌tiyānī Ṭālibān kitābūnah aw x̌ōvənźay svaźavī? – Nah, hīćkalah nah!', *Ćrak* 51 (1429/2008), 55–7. However, two years earlier, if not even before that, the IEA had begun to employ suicide attacks on their military opponents, while simultaneously risking Afghan civilian casualties as a consequence. The first issue of *al-Ṣumūd* carried an article in which suicide attacks were justified as an appropriate strategic tool in modern-day warfare, see Aḥmad Mukhtār, 'al-ʿAmaliyyāt al-istishhādiyya fī Afghānistān wa-atharuhā fi'l-istrātījiyya al-ḥarbiyya al-muʿāṣira', *al-Ṣumūd* 1/1 (1427h), 11f.

strategic and ideological orientations of local actors in the Pashtun Borderland that result from the perpetual forging and dissolving of alliances with a vast array of like-minded actors in the region and, whenever beneficial, increasingly also beyond. In other words, whereas the media work of *al-Qāʿida* and its various offshoots does indeed follow a very strong ideological directive and must, therefore, consistently act within a global framework, the emanations of the IEA and, if only to an extent, of the "Neo-Taliban" TṬP remained more expressions of Borderland pragmatics.

This impression is almost instantly sustained by the fact that all the official periodicals of the then-decentralized IEA maintained their firm focus on Afghanistan alone. Especially the three different Pashto journals investigated here appear very much modelled on those published by the various Afghan Islamist organizations in the 1980s: they contain hardly any contributions to doctrinal issues and are predominantly focused on *jihād* and exhortations to hold out, meticulously lauding the various successful IEA attacks on government structures and even more those on foreign military troops and installations. The extensive martyrologues which appeared in almost every issue of the Pashto *Mōrchal*, the Urdu *Sharīʿat* and the Arabic *al-Ṣumūd* are equally similar to those in the journals of the 1980s and 1990s. A significant novelty in the latter was a regular screening of the international media for reports on the IEA and, later, on Afghanistan in general, which was facilitated by the ever better internet coverage in the region, and a growing pool of internet-savvy youngsters in the movement.

The religious authorities presented in the three different Pashto journals – at least in the more than 100 issues of them that have been perused here – are exclusively homegrown, and the IEA evidently differs in this from the MB- and JIM-affine Afghan Islamists and militant "Frontier Deobandis" that we looked at earlier.[1043] The Arabic *al-Ṣumūd*, however, appears to be an exception to this rule, and a cursory glance might indeed trick us into regarding this particular journal as proof that the IEA has been, or was aspiring to be, integrated into an ever-growing Global Islamic Front. This impression is sustained even further by various boastful public statements of *al-Qāʿida* core cadre Abū Yaḥyá al-Lībī, in which he claimed to have been tasked in the early days of the digital media efforts of militant Salafists with extending technical support to the leadership of the IEA for the virtual dissemination of their announcements.[1044]

[1043] See Sections 4.2.1, 4.3.3 and 4.3.4.

[1044] In an interview with the *Tōrah Bōṛah* quarterly, al-Lībī apparently claimed that his 'mission was to transmit the word of the *mujāhidīn* through the internet and the particular website <al-imāra al-islāmiyya>' (cited in Nathan [2009], 33). Unfortunately, and despite sustained effort, no copy of issue 2/3 (1426h/1384sh) of the magazine could be traced and we must, therefore, rely for now on the translation cited by Nathan, courtesy of the *Middle East Media Research Institute* (MEMRI) with its headquarters in Washington, D.C. All attempts to locate the Pashto original text in order to check the translation have

That the first few issues of *al-Ṣumūd* carried pieces from al-Lībī[1045] and other renowned and less renowned Arab Salafist ideologues-cum-activists seems to reinforce the impression of the increasing inosculation of the IEA and the trans-territorially orientated militant Salafists of *al-Qāʿida*, its associates across Muslim communities worldwide and its offshoots, the most renowned of which would turn out to be its eventual nemesis: the IS.

Indeed, it appears significant that those Arab militant Salafist thinkers who figured in the initial stage of the extended media activities of the IEA and their auxiliaries were among those who are 'no part of *al-Qāʿida*'s core ideological or strategic leadership but who are nevertheless instrumental in shaping the broader radical Islamic movement around the organization';[1046] that is, this seems to apply for at least most of them and at that particular point in time.[1047] One who fits this description much better perhaps than the rather boastful Abū Yaḥyá al-Lībī was Maḥmūd Mahdī Zaydān, *nom de guerre* "Manṣūr al-Shāmī" (killed 1431/2010), a Jordanian commander somewhere at the interface of the IEA and *al-Qāʿida*, and, therefore, another "natural" contributor to the early media ventures of the IEA. He, alongside his brother ʿUmar Mahdī Zaydān, also known as "Abū 'l-Mundhir" (killed 1438/2017), were well connected within the Jordanian Salafist scene, and, thus, personally acquainted with such influential ideologues as Abū Muḥammad al-Maqdisī, Abū Muṣʿab al-Zarqāwī and Abū Qatāda al-Filisṭīnī.

This is clearly indicated by Manṣūr al-Shāmī's serial "In the Shades of the [Prophetic] Path" (*fī ẓilāl al-sīra*),[1048] a title strongly reminiscent of Sayyid Quṭb's influential commentary on the Qur'an. In its second instalment, he discussed – and this is the earliest textual evidence available at the time of writing – the matter of *al-walāʾ wa'l-barāʾ* explicitly within the context of the IEA, against the backdrop of his analysis of the Battle of Badr between the early Muslims under the leadership of the Prophet Muḥammad and the pagan Meccans in the second year after the Hijra. Remarkably, though, he did not quote the popular sound *ḥadīth* in which the Prophet turned down the offer of assistance by an unbeliever, despite the severe numerical disadvantage of the

so far been unsuccessful. A former member of staff at MEMRI indicated the great likelihood that the original text had been translated in Afghanistan itself and even the institute itself may, therefore, not possess a copy of the Pashto original.

1045 See Abū Yaḥyá al-Lībī, 'Ḥaqīqa mā yajrī warāʾ al-qaḍbān (wa-mā shahidnā ʾillā bi-mā ʿalimnā)', *al-Ṣumūd* 1/1 (1427h), 18–21.

1046 Wagemakers (2012), 39.

1047 The rather apodictic style in which Wagemakers presented this assessment of his would appear less so when we duly recognize the role of Ibn Lādin's most faithful retainer Abū Yaḥyá al-Lībī in this reconceptualization of the IEA's media strategies after 2001.

1048 See al-Shaykh Manṣūr al-Shāmī, 'Fī Ẓilāl al-sīra al-ʿiṭra', *al-Ṣumūd* 1/4 (1427h), 28f.; al-Shaykh Manṣūr al-Shāmī, 'Fī Ẓilāl al-sīra: ghazwat Badr al-kubrá', *al-Ṣumūd* 1/6 (1427h), 18–21; al-Shaykh Manṣūr al-Shāmī, 'Fiqh al-sīra: durūs min ḥādithatī al-rajīʿ wa-biʾr maʿūna', *al-Ṣumūd* 1/7 (1427h), 11–15.

Muslim forces.[1049] Instead, his first reference is a fatally abbreviated version of another sound *ḥadīth*, because in this form it privileges the opinion of ʿUmar bin al-Khaṭṭāb, which the Prophet himself had actually disapproved of in the *ḥadīth*.[1050] According to this reading, it is commendable to slay members of one's own community without any mercy if they show loyalty to any non-religiously defined community, such as the "Afghan nation". In the following, al-Shāmī points to prominent Muslim figureheads in the MENA region, such as Ḥasan al-Bannā and Yūsuf al-Qaraḍāwī, as examples of those who have violated the commandment of *al-walāʾ wa'l-barāʾ*,[1051] concluding that

> such scandals have been repeated throughout around the globe, and the aim is [therefore] to return the Truth to its origins. The real signposts for the association and dissociation are there in the life of every Muslim, for there is no point for Islam unless [the issue of] *al-walāʾ wa'l-barāʾ* is investigated.[1052]

Apart from these elaborations of al-Shāmī, however, precious little further direct doctrinal influence from Arab ideologues on the IEA is evident from *al-Ṣumūd*.[1053] Moreover, even al-Shāmī did not figure in any of the later issues of the journal, and the fact that he was killed in 2010 in a drone strike in South

1049 The *ḥadīth* in question is in *Ṣaḥīḥ Muslim*, k. al-jihād wa'l-sayr, b. karāhat al-istiʿāna fi'l-ghazwa bi-kāfir, no. 1 (ḥadīth 4 803), and the important passage reads: 'Go back, for I will not seek help from a *mushrik* [*fa-arjiʿfa-lan astaʿīna bi-mushrikin*].'

1050 See al-Shāmī, 'Fī Ẓilāl (11)', 20; compare *Ṣaḥīḥ Muslim*, k. al-jihād wa'l-sayr, b. al-imdād bi'l-malāʾika fī ghazwat Badrin wa-ibāḥat al-ghanāʾim, no. 1 (ḥadīth 4 687).

1051 See al-Shāmī, 'Fī Ẓilāl (11)', 21. While quoting al-Bannā, al-Qaraḍāwī and other leading representatives of the Egyptian MB, Manṣūr al-Shāmī provides neither their names nor a reference for his quotes. These were, in fact, taken from al-Bannā's *Hadhā Bayān li'l-Nās* (1949) and from 'Fatwá min al-Qaraḍāwī wa'l-ʿAwwā wa'l-Bishrī wa-ākhirīn tajīz li'l-ʿaskariyīn al-amrikiyīn al-Muslimīn al-mushāraka fi'l-ghārāt ʿalá Afghānistān', *al-Sharq al-Awsaṭ* 8 356 (1422/2001), 2. It has proved impossible to obtain a copy of al-Bannā's text, allegedly published in Cairo morning papers on 11 January 1949. However, friends and colleagues in the MENA region suggest that al-Shāmī himself did not quote directly from the text but, probably, from Ayman al-Ẓawāhirī's *al-Ḥiṣād al-Murr* (*1988*, revised in 2005), where the passage in question is quoted, too, see al-Ẓawāhirī (1426/2005), 199. Qaraḍāwī's *fatwa* was widely discussed on Abū Muḥammad al-Maqdisī's website *Minbar al-Tawḥīd wa'l-Jihād*, not least by Abū Baṣīr al-Ṭarṭūsī, see URL: www.ilmway.com/site/maqdis/MS_23355.html (accessed 23 May 2021). It is very conceivable that al-Shāmī made ample use of the texts provided by al-Maqdisī, rather than hunting for the original texts and quoting from there.

1052 al-Shāmī, 'Fī Ẓilāl (11)', 21.

1053 The only two exceptions are very brief essays by the young Saudi scholar Ibrāhīm ibn ʿAbd al-Raḥmān al-Turkī, also known as "Abū Salmān" (b. 1400/1980), and the Egyptian former associate of the *al-Qāʿida* leadership Hānī al-Sibāʿī (b. 1380/1961), both of which do not discuss doctrinal matters, see al-Turkī, 'Man sayaqṭif thamrat al-jihād fī ʿIrāq?', *al-Ṣumūd* 1/9 (1428h), 23f.; al-Sibāʿī, 'Taḥālufāt al-ikhwa al-aʿdāʾ fī Afghānistān', *al-Ṣumūd* 3/9 (1430/2009), 9.

Waziristan suggests that he had attached himself rather to those "New Taliban" who had emerged as a distinct entity on the eastern side of the Durand Line, who, shortly afterwards, were seriously reprimanded by the then-leadership of *al-Qāʿida* for not submitting properly to their command.[1054] Moreover, there is also little indication that the issue of *al-walāʾ wa'l-barāʾ* played any more pronounced role in the conceptual universe of the ṬIT / IEA. After all, their engagement in military action against occupying military forces, their contractors and their Afghan active supporters could well be legitimized in alternative and more pragmatic ways that were not really in need of a formal Islamic legal rationale. It appears, therefore, consistent that the religious authorities portrayed or interviewed in the early back runs of *al-Ṣumūd* were almost exclusively of local provenance.[1055] Two lengthy pieces on Jalāl al-Dīn Ḥaqqānī shine out, one being an extensive interview in which the seasoned commander implicitly affirmed Ibn Lādin's vision of the USA-led troops in Afghanistan heading towards a similar fate as the meanwhile disintegrated Soviet Union, the other a reminiscence of his rise to leadership in Khost.[1056]

Perhaps the most significant later development in *al-Ṣumūd*, insofar as the IEA–Arab interface is concerned, was the reappearance of Muṣṭafá Ḥāmid, or Abū Walīd al-Maṣrī, as the journal's dominant author from among the "Arab Afghans" towards the end of 2009.[1057] This seems to tie in well with the coverage of Jalāl al-Dīn Ḥaqqānī, who, after all, had brought Muṣṭafá Ḥāmid to Afghanistan as the first Arab volunteer to the *jihād* against the PDPA–Soviet

1054 Among the documents secured by US special forces in Ibn Lādin's compound in Abbottabad after the targeted killing of the *al-Qāʿida* leader on 2 May 2011 is a letter from Abū Yaḥyá al-Lībī and Maḥmūd al-Ḥasan "ʿAṭiyyatallāh" al-Lībī (killed 1432/ 2011) to Ḥakīmallāh Maḥsūd, the then-supreme *amīr* of the TṬP. In this missive, dated 3 December 2010, the two addressors conveyed the serious discontent of the *al-Qāʿida* leadership with certain 'ideas, method and conduct [*bi-fikr wa-manhaj wa-sulūk*] of the Movement of the Taliban of Pakistan' which they considered harmful to the cause of concerted action in the global *jihād* spearheaded by *al-Qāʿida* and, therefore, called for severe punitive action: see al-Lībī and al-Lībī (1431/2010).

1055 See, for example, *al-Ṣumūd* 2/2 (1428h), 6–10 (on Muḥammad Yāsir of Wardak); 2/3 (1428h), 8–13 (Mullā Amīnallāh of Kandahar); 2/4 (1428h), 8–11 (Mullā Muḥammad Ḥasan Raḥmānī of Uruzgan); 4/2 (1430/2009), 6–11 (Mullā Muḥammad Rabbānī of Kandahar); 4/4 (1430/2009), 18–20 (Mawlavī Aḥsānallāh of Zabul); 4/6 (1431/2010), 8–11 (Mullā ʿAbd al-Qahhār of Zabul), 20–3 (ʿAbd al-ʿAlī Dēobandī of Kandahar).

1056 See al-Shaykh Jalāl al-Dīn Ḥaqqānī, 'Hazīmat Amrīkā fī Afghānistān satakūna asraʿ min hazīmat al-ittiḥād al-sufiyātī al-munhār', *al-Ṣumūd* 3/2 (1429/2008), 9–15; Anon., 'Jalāl al-Dīn Ḥaqqānī . . . usṭūra min jihād Afghānistān', *al-Ṣumūd* 4/5 (1430/2009), 33–9.

1057 The first appearance of this trained journalist in *al-Ṣumūd*, following his reported service as a media adviser to the MʿUJM's Arabic *Manbaʿ al-Jihād* as well as the JDQS-journal *al-Mujāhid*, was in issue 4/4 (1430/2009), 22–5. He would later be present as an author numerous times per issue, writing as "Muṣṭafá Ḥāmid", as well as under his *nom de guerre* "Abū Walīd [al-Maṣrī]".

nexus in around 1981.[1058] Even so, however, fairly little changed in terms of content which could point to a strategic or ideological shift, an impression further sustained by the so-called "Code of Conduct" of the IEA, the so-called *Lā'iḥah*, first issued by its leadership council in 2006 and expanded in 2009 and 2010.[1059]

This sixty-nine-page document has already been analysed twice, first in 2011 by Kate Clark, former BBC journalist and currently with the *Afghan Analyst Network*, and a few years later by Yoshinobu Nagamine, former aid worker and current senior manager at the Geneva-based World Economic Forum. Both analyses contain English translations of the full text; Clark's even comprises all three of its versions.[1060] Her analysis also carries the important observation that 'this is an intra-Afghan affair – foreigners, whether civilians or military – are barely mentioned'.[1061] This is first indicated by the fact that the term "kāfir" is applied solely to the foreign forces, but not to the Afghan government, which, under the doctrine of *al-walā' wa'l-barā'*, would fall into the same category. Instead, it is labelled the 'administration enslaved by them, that is, the unbelievers' (*də haghūyə* [i.e., *də kuffārō*] *ghulāmah idārah*),[1062] which suggests that they were coerced into service and are, therefore, subject to mitigating circumstances when one is evaluating their fidelity.[1063] This, in fact, is fully in line with the standard Hanafi legal position, which provides the Islamic legal framework for the jurisprudence of the IEA as an explicit reference to al-Marghinānī's *Hidāya*, Ibn al-Humām's commentary on it and the *Fatāwá 'Ālamkīriyya*, or *Hindiyya*, indicates.[1064]

The core theme of the entire document is, once again, obedience in line with the command structures of the IEA, designed for the proper guidance of the common *mujāhidīn* and as a means to ensure that excessive indiscriminate attacks on those outside the IEA are kept in check. Moreover, this was a way to tighten the rein on all of its local representations and try, thus, to ensure that its outside appearance as a single uniform bloc, which it was perhaps only in the early days of the ṬIT, remained intact. After all, in some cases, ideological discrepancies started to leak to the outside – regardless of whether or not this leakage was conscious and deliberate – and, thus, potentially jeopardized the uniform framework that all the various local forces under the umbrella of the IEA were expected to abide by unquestioningly. A case in point here is the

1058 See Zaydan (1999), 92; Brown and Rassler (2013), 196.

1059 See Də Afghānistān Islāmī Imārat (1431/2010), 7; Clark (2011), 2 n.3.

1060 See Clark (2011), Appendix 1; Nagamine (2015), 145–62 (trans. Muhammad Munir).

1061 Clark (2011), 2.

1062 See, for example, Də Afghānistān Islāmī Imārat (1431/2010), 9.

1063 On coercion (*ikrāh*) as a mitigating circumstance in the legal practice of *takfīr*, see, for the pre-modern era, Friedmann (2003), *passim*; for the contemporary period, see Nedza (2020), 156–61.

1064 See Də Afghānistān Islāmī Imārat (1431/2010), 11; compare al-Marghinānī (1417h), IV: 356; Ibn al-Humām (1424/2003), VI: 99; [al-Burhānfūrī] et al. (1421/2000), II: 302f.

TBJM, formerly core of the Ḥil-Kh, whose eponymously named journal, which at that moment was still being issued exclusively in print, carried a piece on *al-walāʾ wa'l-barāʾ* in which its author concluded that any support extended by Muslims to the unbelieving foreign military and increasingly also civilian forces would render the former instantly unbelievers.[1065] Without needing to spell it out, and countrary to the official position of the IEA leadership on the status of the Afghan governments under Ḥāmid Karzay and later Ashraf Ghanī, the author of this piece declared them, alongside all of its personnel, to have become unbelievers and subsequently to be punished for this grave offence according to the stipulations of the *shariʿa* in the TBJM's own narrow interpretation.

Against such excesses, the IEA high command considered it necessary to emphatically remind all of its subordinates of the core theme of Rashīd Aḥmad Ludhiyānavī's *Iṭāʿat-i Amīr*, allegedly held in such high regard by Mullā Muḥammad ʿUmar himself,[1066] by declaring absolute obedience of the movement's command structure an essential condition stipulated by the *shariʿa*.[1067] Tied to the theme of "obedience", finally, is what was perhaps one of the most significant stipulations made in the 2006 *Lāʾiḥah*:

> If any governor [*vuləsvāləy*] or other commanding senior [*məshər*] already has an active group or military squad [*ḍalgəy*] in another province, he should introduce the relevant squad and *mujāhidīn* to the person responsible for the relevant province. After this, they will be obedient to the governor of the relevant area and will follow his instructions when executing their duties. The person responsible in the province will provide them with logistical supplies as they do for the other *mujāhidīn* of the province. In the structures [*tashkīlātūnah*] of the Islamic Emirate, communal fronts [*ʿumūmī maḥāẓūnah*] are prohibited. Such fronts will not be part of the Emirate's structures.[1068]

This, finally, is the watershed that separates the IEA from the TṬP, at least as per statutes. Although, in reality, numerous TṬP commanders submitted to the supreme command of the "Commander of the Faithful" whenever convenient, they equally commonly cut themselves loose from these command structures and either subscribed to different ones or established their own instead. By following this line of action, they confirm the above observation that interpreting reality through the prism of Sunni eschatology means that pragmatically commendable unity needs to be sacrificed for the sake of ideological purity, utilizing hereby the reinterpretation of theological and legal concepts put forward by militant Salafist theorists of mainly Arab provenance.

1065 See Mawlavī R. K. Ḥaqqpāl, 'Lah Musalmānānō sarah dōstī aw lah kāfirānō sarah duẍmanī', *Tōrah Bōṛah* 1/3 (1425/2004), 11–13, here 13.

1066 See Section 4.3.2.

1067 See Də Afghānistān Islāmī Imārat (1431/2010), 39.

1068 Ibid., 47.

This process would be further accelerated with the eventual arrival of the IS in the Pashtun Borderland, thus pointing to some link between TṬP and IS that we will have to look at more closely in due course, not least because it helps to situate the TṬP vis-à-vis the IEA better.

After all, the original nucleus of the TṬP had grown out of the latter, when IEA fighters originally from the former FATA of Pakistan – predominantly from North and South Waziristan – had organized the withdrawal of foreign Salafists, prominently among them the entire leadership of *al-Qāʿida* and of the IMU, from Afghanistan to Waziristan after the start of the USA-led military invasion of Afghanistan in early October 2001. Two who distinguished themselves in this pursuit were Nēk Muḥammad (killed 1425/2005),[1069] an Aḥmadzay Vazīr of the Yār Gul Khēl from around Vānā in South Waziristan, and arguably also Baytallāh of the traditionally rivalling Maḥsūd, originally from Landī Ḋhōk in District Bannū, with its border on North Waziristan. Both Nēk Muḥammad and Baytallāh Maḥsūd are said to have filled commanding positions during the first central government of the IEA, though Baytallāh was a retainer of the never completely integrated MʿUJM in Lōyah Paktia.[1070] The third key player in the emergence of the TṬP was Mawlavī Naẕīr Aḥmad (killed 1434/2013), an Aḥmadzay Vazīr like Nēk Muḥammad, but from the rival clan of Kākā Khēl.

Unsurprisingly, conflict arose first along these distinct socio-political lines; the close relatedness of the two clans led to extreme competition over pre-eminence, following the traditional institution of agnatic rivalry (*tabūrvalī*) that more often than not takes an extremely violent turn.[1071] In this case, the ethnically defined contention manifested itself in the emergence of two factions among the returnees from Afghanistan to South Waziristan, one led by Mawlavī Naẕīr Aḥmad, the other by Nēk Muḥammad. The former was fiercely opposed to the active presence of often rather wealthy non-Pashtun militants in the area, though not for ideological reasons but because they were generous benefactors of Nēk Muḥammad, who had facilitated their relocation to South Waziristan. For this reason, Naẕīr Aḥmad would even join hands with Pakistani government authorities in their compliance with the request by the US administration to help capture especially *al-Qāʿida* affiliates on the run.[1072]

Nēk Muḥammad, meanwhile, closed ranks with these foreign militants, to an extent that the ṬIT/IEA never had. In the first major clash with the Pakistani army in January 2004 at Kalūshah, some nine miles east of Vānā, this alliance showed its first major effect, while Nēk Muḥammad distinguished

[1069] On him, see Franco (2009), 275–9; Hartung (2019a), 323–5.

[1070] See Ruttig (2009), 71; Brown and Rassler (2013), 139.

[1071] See the extensive ethnographic literature on Pashtun community and society. For a special focus on Waziristan, see Ahmed (1983), 24–39.

[1072] See Franco (2009), 278f.

himself at the same time as a commander capable of successfully confronting even the well-equipped Pakistani military. This eminence, however, was only short-lived, because already in the very next offensive by the army, five months later, which was for the first time assisted by combat drones operated by the US-American military, Nēk Muḥammad was killed in the very first drone strike on 18 June 2004.

Eventually, Baytallāh Maḥsūd took over the baton and, in December 2007, tried to overcome the internal rift created by *tabūrvalī* by proclaiming the TṬP under his own leadership as a means to ensure at least some degree of unity among the various Islamically inspired local militias operating from the mountainous territories of the uplands of the Pashtun Borderland. That the actual establishment of the TṬP remains still somewhat shrouded in mystery[1073] need not worry us too much at this point, because our focus here remains on its ideological set-up and the degree to which this had been impacted by the conceptual universe of non-Pashtun militants in the Borderland.

Conducive for its appropriation to a substantially larger and more determined extent than with the ṬIT / IEA turns out to have been, once again, the political framework of Pakistan, not least because, as heir to the British Raj, the Islamic Republic continued the disdainful treatment of Pashtun borderland tribes by the British colonial authorities, epitomized in the FCR, in an almost identical manner until, on 24 May 2018, the FATA were finally integrated into the Province of Khyber Pakhtunkhwa.[1074] This perceived structural discrimination in Pakistani political practice, in turn, was regarded as an utter contradiction of the ideological foundations of the project "Pakistan" and resulted, thus, in legal justifications of concerted counteraction, all of which pivoted on the interpretations of the legal concept of *takfīr* by ideologues from the *al-Qāʿida* orbit. What for the IEA had so far been little more than mere theoretical speculations was now seen through to their utmost practical consequences by Borderland actors who had, at least officially, never full severed

1073 See ibid., 279–84. It needs to be borne in mind here that, maybe just because Claudio Franco himself is a journalist, he had apparently few qualms about relying solely on media reports, which, moreover, appear to be all in English. On the other hand, though, we need to acknowledge that other materials in this regard are utterly scarce and that, therefore, an ill-referenced work might still be better than none at all.

1074 Between 24 and 27 May 2018, the PNA and the Senate of Pakistan, as well as the Provincial Assembly of Khyber-Pakhtunkhwa, passed the 25th amendment to the Pakistani Constitution, which sealed the merger of FATA with the province, thus, extending the state's jurisdiction now fully up to the Durand Line. While those concerned about the extent of militancy in the area welcomed the full incorporation of semi-autonomous regions into the administrative structure of Pakistan, the JUI-F and the leftist-ethnocentric *Pakhtūnkhvā Millī ʿAvāmī Pārtī* (PMAP) opposed the merger, castigating it as a culturally insensitive tool to further limit the rights for autonomous decisions by the communal bodies.

their ties to the IEA, at least as long as Mullā Muḥammad ʿUmar remained its supreme head.

Consequently, Nēk Muḥammad was reported as having declared Pakistani soldiers legitimate killing targets already during the so-called "Operation Kalūshah";[1075] a few years later, proactive attacks on military installations in Pakistan claimed by the TṬP became almost a normality, beginning with the strike against the Pakistan Ordnance Factories in north-west-Punjabi Vāh in August 2008, and culminating perhaps in the attack on the Army Public School in Peshawar in December 2014. While all these onslaughts were publicly legitimated as retaliation for concrete operations of the Pakistani armed forces in the FATA,[1076] thus, as acts of self-defence, a closer look at the targets of some other lethal TṬP attacks clearly proves that their ultimate justification was much more ideological than just that.

Perhaps the most significant attack in this regard was the IED attack on 27 December 2007 in Rawalpindi that killed then-Prime Minister of Pakistan Bēnaẓīr Bhuṫṫō,[1077] a second major one being the bomb attack on a *jirgah* in Bajawr on 7 November 2008, in which *məshərān* of the Salārzay and government officials were discussing concerted measures to counter the TṬP activities throughout the FATA, for which the TṬP assumed full responsibility.[1078] Bearing in mind the close physical and ideological proximity of leading TṬP cadres and their *al-Qāʿida* peers, the respective targets of especially these two attacks indicate the strong imprint of the theological and legal debates among

1075 See Franco (2009), 275 (without, however, any indication of the source on which this is based).

1076 See, for example, Muṣʿab Ibrāhīm, 'Lākhōṇ muhājirīn ... Ay ahl-i Pākistān! Allāh sē ḍariyē!', *Navā-yi Afghān Jihād* 7/6 (1435/2014), 50–2; Ustād ʿAbd al-Raḥīm, 'Shimālī Vazīristān mēṇ maḥāẕ kī aṣl ṣūrat-i ḥāl', *Navā-yi Afghān Jihād* 7/8 (1435/2014), 24f.; and especially the series 'Shimālī Vazīristān ... ḥaqīqī taṣvīr' by Kāshif Kāshif ʿAlī al-Khayr, who even mocks the official name of this military operation – *Ẓarb-i ʿAẓb* (strike of anger) – as "ẓarb-i kaẕb", or "strike of lie", in *Navā-yi Afghān Jihād* 7/11 (1436/ 2014), 25–7.

1077 While initially blamed on the TṬP, it soon transpired that the Egyptian *al-Qāʿida* operative and former JIM cadre Muṣṭafá Abū 'l-Yazīd, *nom de guerre* "Saʿīd al-Maṣrī" (killed 1431/2010), had assumed responsibility in a telephone call to Italian news agency Adnkronos immediately after the attack. The information, although happily repeated by media outlets worldwide, remains uncorroborated. On Saʿīd al-Maṣrī's role in Pakistan, see, for example, Ustad Aḥmad Fārūq, 'Jinhēṇ dēkhkar allāh yād āʾē ...! Shaykh Saʿīd (Muṣṭafá Abū Yazīd) raḥmat allāh ʿalayh', *Ḥiṭṭīn* 9 (1438h), 117–38, here 123f.

1078 See Anwarullah Khan, 'Operation continues in Bajaur; 20 militants dead', *Dawn* 62/312 (8 November 2008), 1. A comprehensive justification for this and other related attacks on tribal institutions which were understood as siding with the Pakistani government is provided by the anonymous editor of *Ḥiṭṭīn*, e-journal of the *al-Qāʿida* dependance in the Indian subcontinent (*Jamāʿat Qāʿidat al-Jihād fī Shibh al-Qārra al-Hindiyya*; JQSQH), see Anon., 'Iftitāḥiyyah: Ahl-i Pākistān; ēk fayṣalah'kun dawrā hē par', *Ḥiṭṭīn* 6 (1431h), 7–36.

"Arab Afghans" since the mid 1990s. Despite the lack of solid textual evidence in the TṬP publications, it appears quite reasonable to assume a direct impact especially of the fierce debate over *takfīr* against a political ruler (*takfīr al-ḥākim*) and against everyone who, actively or passively, sustains a political regime whose head has been declared an apostate (*kāfir murtadd*) as a "(*sharī'a-*)resisting group" (*al-ṭā'ifa al-mumtani'a*), as was prominently and effectively elaborated in 1988 in Sayyid Imām's *al-Jāmi'* and in al-Maqdisī's critical response a decade later. That their conceptual contributions continued to play a significant role in the Pashtun Borderland even after Sayyid Imām had subjected his conceptual framework to revision is indicated by its strong and polemical refutation by Ayman al-Ẓawāhirī, who remained among those still safeguarded by the "New Taliban" east of the Durand Line and kept the theoretical orientation of *al-Qā'ida* alive.[1079]

Already in November 2002, *al-Qā'ida*'s then-second-in-command had released a short epistle on the organization's media channel *al-Saḥāb* on the matter of *al-walā' wa'l-barā'*, in which he reaffirmed the principle as constitutive for the *al-Qā'ida* world-view.[1080] Consequently, he also maintained his stance against Sayyid Imām's later ideological revision, which, on the basis of a careful employment of *fiqh al-wāqi'*, argued for the suspension of numerous religious duties formerly regarded as unconditional in the current state of weakness of the community of the righteous. This includes crucially the duty for armed *jihād*, a fact that once again points to the exceptional situation that presents itself through the prism of Sunni apocalyptic thought and, therefore, demands exceptional measures of one in order to prove oneself worthy of salvation in the Hereafter. The activists of *al-Qā'ida* would, therefore, continue deliberately targeting civilians, grossly including all Jews and Shī'ī Muslims, with an excessive employment of suicide attacks against them as the means of choice.[1081]

Abū Yaḥyá al-Lībī, who had escaped from US captivity in July 2005, most probably fleeing to Waziristan, went even further: his genuine, though cynical, contribution to this debate during these years was the theoretical affirmation of the legitimacy of killing Muslim civilians who, so it is claimed, are abused by the unbelievers as a protective shield (*tatarrus*).[1082] While the same discussion is found in Sayyid Imām's *al-Jāmi'*,[1083] it was not until al-Lībī's deliberations that this concept also informed the practice of militant Salafists, including very much the TṬP.

1079 On the whole debate between Sayyid Imām and al-Ẓawāhirī, see extensively Nedza (2020), 27f. and 249–64.

1080 See al-Ẓawāhirī (1423/2002), 19f.

1081 See Ibn 'Abd al-'Azīz (1428/2007), 148: 13, 151: 13, 152: 12f., 154: 12f. and 155: 12f.

1082 His infamous treatise on the subject, released after his escape in December 2005, is titled *al-Tatarrus fi'l-Jihād al-Mu'āṣir*. For an analysis, see Brachman and Warius (2008).

1083 See Ibn 'Abd al-'Azīz (n.d.), 617f. and 626; Nedza (2020), 92, 174, 235 n.63, and 251.

In fact, while the matter of *tatarrus* has not figured anywhere prominently in the TṬP literature of that period, *al-walāʾ waʾl-barāʾ* ultimately did: in April 2009, the TṬP journal *Navā-yi Afghān Jihād* carried a lengthy article on this concept by Abū ʿAmr ʿAbd al-Ḥakīm Ḥasan, *nom de guerre* "Shaykh ʿĪsá al-Maṣrī" (b. 1378/1959) and a major facilitator aiding the *al-Qāʿida* ideology as a whole to shape that of the TṬP,[1084] who provided the Islamic justification for attacks on the Pakistani government and its various appendages, such as the Pakistani armed forces. The TṬP followed suit and, as shown above, translated these words into immediate actions.

Even with this, however, the formulation of a distinct TṬP ideology that separated them more and more from the IEA, from which the TṬP had once sprung, was not yet complete. In fact, the increasing reference in its periodicals from around 2009 onwards to "Khurasan" for the region in which they operate foreshadowed dramatic developments in the TṬP itself that would substantiate its alienation from the IEA even further. While the latter maintained their sole focus on the re-establishment of the IEA's central rule in Afghanistan and had no real aspirations beyond its national borderlines, parts of the TṬP would tie themselves increasingly to a more global agenda of Islamically sustained militancy, necessitated once again by an eschatological interpretation of reality. The proclamation of a regional chapter of the IS in late January 2015, as the "Supreme Council for the Province Khurasan" (*al-shūrá al-ʿālá li-wilāyat Khurāsān*) was an ultimate combusting agent in aggravating this process.

The Pull of the IS in Its Province of Khorasan, and the Push Away

The formation of this formal presence of the globally orientated IS in the Pashtun Borderland resulted not so much from the great appeal of its ideological underpinnings, but, once more, rather from socio-political particulars in the region itself. The trigger was the increasingly fierce infighting over the leadership of the TṬP after the death of its *amīr* Baytallāh Maḥsūd on 5 August 2009 in a targeted US drone strike, when his former deputy Ḥakīmallāh Maḥsūd was elected as the new leader of the TṬP instead of Ḥāfiẓ Saʿīd Khān (killed 1437/2016), then-*amīr* of the TṬP for his native Ōrakzay Tribal Agency. When, on 1 November 2013, Ḥakīmallāh too was killed, in another US drone attack, history seemed to repeat itself and the Leadership Council of the

1084 See Mawlānā ʿAbd al-Ḥakīm Ḥasan, "ʻʻAqīdah-yi al-walāʾ waʾl-barāʾʼ" (dūstī awr dushmānī) Qurʾān va Sunnat kī rawshanī mēṇ', *Navā-yi Afghān Jihād* 2/4 (1430/2009), 3–7. This article, in fact, appears to be only a supplement to ʿĪsá al-Maṣrī's seminal *al-Īḍāḥ waʾl-Tibyān fī anna al-Ḥukkām al-Ṭawāghīt wa-Juyūshahum Kuffār ʿalá ʾl-Taʿiyīn*, written some time before 2006. On the author, see Marquardt and Bakier (2008). On his impact on the TṬP, see Brown and Rassler (2013), 113. Shaykh ʿĪsá was lauded by al-Ẓawāhirī (1431/2010), 177, for bringing Arabs and Pashtuns ideologically closer to one another.

TṬP choose former TNSM leader Faẕlallāh from Swat as its new supreme *amīr*, Ḥāfiẓ Saʿīd left the movement enraged. Other regional TṬP commanders followed suit.[1085] Now, the TṬP finally disintegrated fully into locality- and clan-based rival groups,[1086] which, since 2013, were also crossing swords with the IEA on the Afghan side, even if, for the sake of convenience, these militias were not above using the territories to the west of the Durand Line as their own operational zones of retreat. Under these circumstances, Ḥāfiẓ Saʿīd sought to gain an advantage over his competitors – especially those who still enjoyed the backing of non-Pashtun militants in the region – beyond the confines of his native Ōrakzay Tribal Agency by pledging his allegiance to Abū Bakr al-Baghdādī "Ibrāhīm" (killed 1441/2019), whose universal Islamic Caliphate was proclaimed in al-Raqqa on 29 June 2014.[1087]

In recognition of this *bayʿa*, about half a year later the then-IS spokesperson Abū Muḥammad al-ʿAdnānī al-Shāmī (killed 1437/2016) announced the establishment of a formal presence of the IS in its new province (*wilāya*) "Khurasan", led by Ḥāfiẓ Saʿīd, and called upon all Muslims in that region to submit to his command:

> We call upon all the *muwaḥḥidīn* in Khurasan to join the caravan of the Caliphate and abandon disunity and factionalism [*nabdh al-tafrīq wa'l-tashardhum*]. So, come to your state [*dawlatikum*], oh *mujāhidīn*! Come to your Caliphate, for you are the forerunners [*aṣḥāb al-sabq*]. You have fought the English, the Russians and the Americans, and upon you today is a new fight; a fight to enjoin *tawḥīd* and drive out *shirk*.

1085 See Rassler (2015), 7f.; Maḥsūd (2017), 519, 524f, 573, 577 and 583; Giustozzi (2018), 29–31.

1086 One result of these factional disputes during the TṬP central leadership of Faẕlallāh was the creation of the *Jamāʿat al-Aḥrār* by "ʿUmar Khālid Khurāsānī" (executed 1443/2021), at that time *nom de guerre* of a former ḤM cadre from the village of Qandahārō in Ṣāfī District of the Mōmand Agency in the then-FATA of Pakistan: see Anon., 'Amīr-i muḥtaram kumāndar ʿUmar Khālid Khurāsānī – ḥafiẓuhu allāh – kē sāth *Iḥyā-yi Khilāfat* kā khuṣūṣī intarviyū', *Iḥyā-yi Khilāfat* 3/3 (1434/2013), 7–11, here 7. After Khurāsānī had been formally expelled from the TṬP by Faẕlallāh for his disobedience to *amīr al-muʾminīn* Mullā Muḥammad ʿUmar, the *Jamāʿat al-Aḥrār*, which assembled many of the former retainers of Baytallāh and Ḥakīmallāh Maḥsūd, claimed to represent the genuine TṬP, see Anon., 'Jamāʿat al-Aḥrār kē taʾsīs kē din Jamāʿat kē qāʾidīn kē bayānāt', *Iḥyā-yi Khilāfat* 5/1 (1426/2014), 22–5. See also Khālid Sayfallāh, 'Taḥrīk-i Ṭālibān sē Taḥrīk-i Ṭālibān-i Jamāʿat al-Aḥrār tak', *Iḥyā-yi Khilāfat* 5/1 (1426/2014), 29. Sometime after January 2015, the *Jamāʿat al-Aḥrār* dissolved into the newly established IS chapter in the "province Khurasan", with ʿUmar Khālid Khurāsānī serving as its fourth *walī al-amr* between July 2018 and January 2019, see Zahid (2015).

1087 For Ḥāfiẓ Saʿīd's disappointment over the election of Faẕlallāh, see al-Shaykh Ḥāfiẓ Saʿīd Khān – walī Khurāsān, 'Idhā tajalat ḥaqīqat al-khilāfa li-ahl Khurāsān fa-innahum sayanḍammūna ilayhā bi-shakl akbar', *al-Nabāʾ* 1/17 (1437h), 8f. For al-Baghdādī's proclamation as Caliph Ibrāhīm, see al-ʿAdnānī (1441h), 167–75 (*Hādhā Waʿd Allāh*; Ramaḍān 1435/June 2014), here 171–5.

> So, come forth, humbling yourselves before God, and God will honour you and elevate you. Come forth, for this is an opportunity for the Muslims and it has not yet passed you by, so do not lose it. We call upon all the soldiers of the *Dawla Islāmiyya* who are in Khurasan to listen to and obey the governor [*walī*], Ḥāfiẓ Saʿīd Khān, and his deputy – May God preserve them both! – and to prepare for the tribulations [*ahwāl*] they will face: the factions will assemble against you and the rifles and bayonets will multiply against you. But, with God's permission, you are up to it![1088]

Two interrelated things are quite remarkable here. The first is the appellation of the "true Muslims" as *muwaḥḥidūn*, a term that resonates with the self-designation of those Central Arabian scholars otherwise known as Wahhabiyya, as well as with Salafis in their wake. The second point refers to the deputy of Ḥāfiẓ Saʿīd, former high-ranking IEA commander Mullā ʿAbd al-Raʾūf Khādim "Alīzā", a native of Hilmand and last governor of the IEA in Kunar (killed 1436/2015) before the overthrow of its first central government in late 2001. Kunar again, as discussed extensively above,[1089] continued to be a major stronghold of the Salafists of the JDQS that had been growing out of the Panjpir-based JITS[a], where, in turn, Ḥāfiẓ Saʿīd had received his Salafist priming. It is, therefore, easily conceivable that Khādim had gained a good taste of Salafism during his tenure in Kunar, which, in turn, had alienated him somewhat from the strongly Deobandi orientation of the ṬIT / IEA in matters of theology and, more importantly, *fiqh*.[1090] Deported for extrajudicial detention to the Guantánamo Bay Detention Camp in 2002, he spent five years in captivity, before he rejoined his former brothers-in-arms against the Karzay government over Afghanistan. In 2015, however, Khādim, too, cut off his ties with the IEA in the leadership dispute that was ongoing since Mullā ʿUmar had miraculously disappeared in 2013. When, on 30 July 2015, the supreme commander of the IEA was finally declared dead,[1091] and the baton passed

1088 al-ʿAdnānī (1441h), 190 (*Qul: «Mūtū bi-ghayẓikum!»*; Rabīʿ II 1436h / January 2015); also cited in 'Wilāyat Khurāsān wa'l-bayʿāt min Qawqāz', *Dābiq* 7 (05/1436h), 33–7, here 37.

1089 See Section 4.4.2. For an obituary of Khādim, see Anon., '«Min al-muʾminīna rijālun . . .»: al-shaykh Abū Ṭalḥa ʿAbd al-Rāʾuf Khādim al-Khurāsānī', *Dābiq* 8 (06/1436h), 30f.

1090 See ibid. Here, the anonymous author highlights the constant necessity for the IEA leadership to reprimand Khādim for his active dissemination of the Salafi creed and criticism of the respective Hanafi positions by divesting him of his command over, at times, fourteen provinces.

1091 See Anon., 'Də ʿālīʾqadr amīr al-muʾminīn Mullā Muḥammad ʿUmar Mujāhid – raḥmahu allāh – də vafāt də iʿlān pah aṛah də Islāmī Imārat də rahbarī shūrá aw də marḥum də kūranəy iʿlāmiyyah', *Shahāmat* 9/2 (1436/2015), 6f. The public announcement was released also in Arabic translation in *al-Ṣumūd* 10/5 (1436/2015), 2f., in Dari in *Ḥaqīqat* 2/4 (1337sh/1436h), 2f., and in Urdu in *Sharīʿat* 4/6–7 (1436/2015), 4–7.

on to Mullā Akhtar Manṣūr (killed 1437/2016),[1092] Khādim, himself initially a contender for this position, had already forsaken the movement and begun to fraternize with the IS instead.[1093] The catalyst for this increasing dissociation from the IEA and steering towards the IS was Khādim's captivity as an "unlawful combatant" at the Guantánamo Bay Detention Camp, alongside others who would eventually play a pronounced role in the IS province of Khurasan: ʿAbd al-Raḥīm Muslim Dōst, the younger Badr al-Zamān "Badr" (b. 1388/1968), who had been the teacher of the former at Shams al-Dīn al-Afghānī's *Jāmiʿah Asariyyah* in Ćamkanī,[1094] and his fellow student Ḥayātallāh ibn Muḥammad Shāh Khān "ʿAbd al-Ḥasīb al-Lūjarī" (killed 1438/2017).[1095] It was in this setting that the so far staunch adherent to the Hanafi-Maturidi cornerstones of "Frontier Deobandiyyat" embraced the Salafi *ʿaqīda* and the Salafist *manhaj*, which, as is clear from Muslim Dōst's and Badr's recollections of their detention at Guantánamo Bay, was actively disseminated among the inmates.[1096] Upon his release from US captivity and rejoining the IEA, Khādim began to challenge the authority of its Leadership Council by actively preaching the tenets of Salafi Islam, something for which he was repeatedly stripped of his command as a disciplinary measure, until he eventually broke off his ties with the IEA and turned towards the IS.[1097]

Yet, ʿAbd al-Raʾūf Khādim was not the only prominent commander of the IEA to have forsaken it around the time when Mullā Muḥammad ʿUmar was

[1092] See Hartung (2016a), 150f. For a short biography of Akhtar Manṣūr, see Anon., 'al-Sīra al-dhātiyya li-ʾamīr Imārat Afghānistān al-Islāmiyya al-jadīd Mullā (Akhtar Muḥammad Manṣūr) – ḥafiẓahu allāh taʿālá wa-raʿāh', *al-Ṣumūd* 10/6 (1436/2015): 6–10, its Dari version in *Ḥaqīqat* 2/5 (1394sh/1437h), 6–11, and the Urdu one in *Sharīʿat* 4/6–7 (1436/2015), 32–7.

[1093] See Giustozzi (2018), 21–6. While this work merits appreciation as the first monograph on the IS in "Khurasan", it nonetheless needs to be complemented by solid academic works that take a different angle and employ alternative materials which can serve to either confirm or refute the observations and conclusions drawn by Giustozzi. Until then, it does not really seem appropriate to consider this work the authoritative one on this subject; however, it is currently regarded as such, especially by political and military decision-makers.

[1094] See Muslim Dōst and Badr (1385sh/1427h), 153.

[1095] As his later adopted *nisba* "al-Lūjarī" suggests, the family of ʿAbd al-Ḥasīb originally belonged to Muḥammad Akbar Khēl in the Azrah District of Logar Province in Afghanistan. However, after they had fled the Soviet military invasion in 1979, ʿAbd al-Ḥasīb was actually born and grew up in the Khurram Agency of the former FATA of Pakistan, a region with a significant Imāmī Shiʿi population and subsequently a place of serious sectarian conflict (see Section 4.5.2). He went to Afghanistan only after completing his studies at Shams al-Dīn al-Afghānī's *Jāmiʿah Asariyyah* in Ćamkanī, where he eventually served the IEA in Kunar as a religious instructor: see Anon., 'al-Shaykh al-muḥaddith ʿAbd al-Ḥasīb al-Lūjarī – taqabbalahu allāh – tafaqqa qabl an yasūd wa-malik qulūb ikhwānihi bi-ḥusn akhlāqih', *al-Nabāʾ* 4/43 (1440), 10f., here 10.

[1096] See Muslim Dōst and Badr (1385sh/1427h), 215–24.

[1097] See Anon., '«Min al-muʾminīna rijālun [. . .]»' [see above, n.1 089], 30f.

publicly declared dead and command over the IEA bestowed upon Akhtar Manṣūr. Another very significant actor in this respect was Manṣūr Dādallāh (killed 1437/2015), the half-brother of the dreaded IEA commander Mullā Dādallāh Ākhūnd (killed 1428/2007). Having inherited command over the large forces in a region of strategically great significance for the IEA, he seems to have expected at least to be considered a candidate for the succession to Mullā Muḥammad ʿUmar. When the Leadership Council, however, passed over him and chose Akhtar Manṣūr instead, Manṣūr Dādallāh broke off his ties with the IEA and formed *Afghanistan's Islamic Movement of the Front of the Selfless Ones* (*Də Afghānistān Islāmī Taḥrīk Fidāʾī Maḥāẕ*; IMFF). His defection could possibly have been written off as caused by wounded vanity, had the IMFF not, on 10 September 2015, released a statement on its official website in which it challenged the decision of the Leadership Council as not in line with the stipulations of the *shariʿa*.

The legitimacy of their critical intervention, in turn, was derived by recourse to Q4.59, the famous verse on the obedience of God, His Messenger and 'those among you in command', which concludes: 'Then, if you disagree in any matter, refer it to God and the Messenger if you believe in God and the Last Day. That is better and more suitable for settlement [*khayrun wa-aḥsanu taʾwīlan*].' Having established such an authoritatively sustained basis for the permissibility of objecting to the decision of the Leadership Council, the IMFF cadres argued their case by presenting an array of points which they subsequently put in conversation with the textual frame of reference that was introduced above as "Salafi reduction".[1098] In addition, the bulk of their interventions, which concern the indispensable personal qualifications for leadership sustained by religious precepts (*shurūṭ al-imāma*), shows a remarkable similarity to the respective criteria listed in al-Māwardī's *K. Aḥkām al-Sulṭāniyya*.[1099] The resemblance is certainly not accidental, because this classic determination of the principles of Islamic governance soon became widely regarded as the final word on the subject by Sunni Muslim scholars from a diverse array of legal and theological persuasions.[1100]

1098 See Section 3.2.1.

1099 See Anon., 'Də Afghānistān Islāmī Imārat aw də shahīd amīr al-muʾminīn Mullā Muḥammad ʿUmar Mujāhid – raḥmat allāh ʿalayhi – pah žvand kē ṫākəl shəvay rahbarī shūrá sharʿī taḥaffuẓāt pah Manṣūr Akhtar Muḥammad' (19 Sunbulah 1394sh). URL: www.allfida.org/د-افغانستان-اسلامی-امارت-او-د-شهید-امیر/ (accessed 10 February 2024); compare al-Māwardī (1422/2002), 6.

1100 A vivid example from the early ninth / fifteenth century is al-Qalqashandī (1331–40/1913–22), II: 5, who stated that 'the "Supreme Judge of Judges" [*aqḍá 'l-qudāt*] Abū 'l-Ḥasan ʿAlī ibn Ḥabīb al-Māwardī – God's Mercy be upon him! – has laid down [the conditions for each governorate and what is necessary for the office-holder and what his duties] in *al-Aḥkām al-Sulṭāniyya* convincingly [*maqnaʿ*]. In this [present] book we shall provide a summary of each chapter, so that the reader [*al-nāẓir*] will not have to consult any other.'

While the matter certainly merits some more in-depth investigation,[1101] for the moment, it appears plausible to regard the celebrated Muḥammad Rashīd Riḍā's appraisal of this work, from which 'the words of all the theologians ['*ulamā' al-'aqā'id*] and jurists from all pathways of the *ahl al-sunna* do not depart',[1102] as the anchor point for the authority that al-Māwardī's text subsequently also assumed for the IS.[1103] In this context, we will shortly encounter it again.

The way in which the cadres of the IS in the Pashtun Borderland embraced the concept of the "caliphate" thus differs significantly from the allusions to it by the IEA. For the former, it was part and parcel of subscribing to the global frame of reference of the IS, whereas the IEA was increasingly compelled to make their satisfaction with the locally confined framework explicit. As a result, they received the pejorative attribute "national" in the parlance of the IS.[1104]

What sounds merely like a mocking epithet, however, had, in fact, extremely serious implications. Even the TṬP fared little better.

In an interview with the IS weekly *al-Nabā'*, Ḥāfiẓ Sa'īd denied not only the IEA, but also the TṬP, which he had once represented in the Ōrakzay Tribal Agency, any legitimacy to persist at a time when the IS raised the efforts of militant Salafists towards overcoming the division of the Muslim *umma* into nationalities by submitting to a global Islamic polity to a hitherto unprecedented level.[1105] Those who refused to join, so follows the logical consequence, are allowing the forced fragmentation of the *umma* along the confines of nation-states to prevail and thus contributing actively to the further aggravation of the prevalent *fitan* while, at the same time, endorsing all those whom Ḥāfiẓ Sa'īd regarded as illegitimate tyrants (*ṭawaghīt*). According to the

1101 While numerous renowned scholars in the Study of Islam have pointed out the quasi-canonicity of al-Māwardī's treatise, the only one who actually provides some concrete textual evidence is Mikhail (1995), 59f.

1102 Riḍā (1341/1922), 730.

1103 In Muḥarram 1436h (i.e., October 2014), the *Maktabat al-Himma*, one of the publishing enterprises of the IS, issued an abridgement (*mukhtaṣar*) of al-Māwardī's work, which saw its second edition as early as in March 2016 and is still being disseminated via the various and perpetually changing online distribution platforms of the IS. Consistently with what is seemingly standard practice in the IS, the compiler of this abridgement does not reveal his, or her, personal identity and remains 'a soldier of the IS', as the preface is signed.

1104 While the designation "Ḥarakat al-Ṭālibān al-Waṭaniyya" is, in fact, consistently used by the activists of the IS in its province Khurasan, its central authorities did not use this appellation, as the IS e-periodicals *Dābiq* (fifteen issues between July 2014 and July 2016) and *al-Nabā'* (weekly issue since October 2015) clearly reveal: compare, for example, Anon., 'Ba'd 'ām min i'lān al-bay'a li-amīr al-mu'minīn al-makāsib al-istrātījiyya li-dawlat al-khilāfa fī wilāyat Khurāsān', *al-Nabā'* 1/14 (1437h), 14, and Ḥāfiẓ Sa'īd Khān, 'Idhā tajalat' [see above, n.1087].

1105 See ibid., 9.

perpetually radicalized understanding of *al-walāʾ wa'l-barāʾ*, this situates them at the brink of apostasy and, consequently, compels every righteous Muslim to fight them to their death. It did not take long for this line of argument to translate into practical consequences: on 2 February 2015, only a few weeks after the official proclamation of a formal IS presence in the Pashtun Borderland, IS fighters ambushed and killed a local commander of the IEA in the Charkh District of Logar.[1106]

The resulting deteriorating situation forced the Leadership Council of the IEA to respond to what they regarded as an imminent threat to their own aspirations. In an official letter to the IEA's counterpart in al-Raqqa, they therefore warned the IS leadership against any interference with the internal affairs in Afghanistan.[1107] However, by doing so, they inadvertently triggered an ever-escalating spiral of mutual public defamation.[1108]

What had thus far been only a rhetorical exchange was now raised to the next level when, in March 2015, the high command of the IS in its Khurasan province released an official mission statement in which it aimed at sustaining its refutation of the IEA by attempting to cast their position into a legal argument. Two eventual successors to Ḥāfiẓ Saʿīd as *walī al-amr* in the Khurasan province of the IS were responsible for this document of some 100 pages: ʿAbd al-Ḥasīb al-Lūjarī and Ẓiyāʾ al-Ḥaqq "Abū ʿUmar al-Khurāsānī",[1109] who had formerly called himself "ʿUmar Khālid Khurāsānī" when he was *amīr* of the TṬP in the Mōmand Agency of the then-FATA of Pakistan by appointment of Baytallāh Maḥsūd.[1110] The pivot of their supposed legal argument was the establishment of proof for the supremacy of Abū Bakr al-Baghdādī over Mullā ʿUmar and, therefore, the non-negotiable obligation on all righteous Muslims to pledge their allegiance to al-Baghdādī, unless they wished to seriously jeopardize the chances of their own salvation in the Hereafter.[1111] The propositions on which they built

1106 See ʿAzīzī (2015).

1107 See editor, 'Risālat al-shūrá al-qiyādī li'l-Imāra al-Islāmiyya ilá 'l-shaykh Abī Bakr al-Baghdādī wa-ikhwānihi al-mujāhidīn', *al-Ṣumūd* 10/3 (1436/2015), 2–4. For its Urdu translation, see 'Muḥtaram Abū Bakr al-Baghdādī kē nām Imārat-i islāmiyyah-yi Afghānistān kē rahbarī shūrá kā khaṭṭ', *Sharīʿat* 4/5 (1436/2015), 3–6.

1108 Regrettably, because of spatial limitations, only a small selection from the ever growing body of available texts pertaining to this "propaganda war" can be given due consideration here.

1109 On him, see n.1086 in this chapter.

1110 See Anon., 'Amīr-i muḥtaram' [see above, n.1086], 6. The *Jamāʿat al-Aḥrār* that he established in the course of his leadership dispute with newly elected supreme *amīr* Faẓlallāh and his subsequent expulsion from the TṬP in September 2014 were entirely resolved in the IS, which al-Khurāsānī led briefly as *walī al-amr* of the province Khurasan between August 2018 and July 2019. He was apprehended by the Afghan National Army and jailed in the infamous Pul-i Charkhī prison in Kabul, where he was finally executed by IEA forces on 16 August 2021 upon their second takeover of Kabul.

1111 See [al-Lūjarī] and al-Khurāsānī (1436/2015/1394sh), 104–10.

their argument, however, were not really legal ones: they consisted, in fact, of the various requirements for the office of the Commander of the Faithful as listed, though not legally sustained, in al-Māwardī's *Aḥkām*.[1112]

Nevertheless, all their reasoning at this point was presented without a legal condemnation of any of those who were claiming for themselves the label "*taliban*". Rather, these arguments seem to have been directed more at the wider base of supporters of and sympathizers with the IEA, aiming at persuading them to shift their favour towards the IS instead. During the short tenure of ʿAbd al-Ḥasīb al-Lūjarī, however, the position of the IS towards the IEA became substantially more hostile, and the IS now put what they called the "Taliban National Afghan Movement" at the centre of their increasingly heresiographical argumentation. Responses by scholars from circles identifying as "*taliban*" on either side of the Durand Line were most probably to a large extent responsible for this exacerbation of the conflict.

A very prominent case in this regard is a treatise by TṬP cadre Abū ʿUs̱mān Salārzay, published simultaneously in Arabic and Pashto on various websites of the IEA only two months after the release of the mission statement by al-Lūjarī and al-Khurāsānī, that is, in early May 2015, with an Urdu version added only a few months later. Other than the IS text, to which it presumably responds, Salārzay's comprised a proper and comprehensive legal refutation of al-Baghdādī's – and, by implication, all of his retainers' – claim of a universal caliphate, therefore also providing a legally sustainable argument for the continuous legitimacy of the leadership model underlying the IEA and the TṬP.[1113]

The core of Salārzay's argument was the legal definition of "khilāfa" vis-à-vis "imāra", determining that al-Baghdādī would qualify only for the latter and hence his right to rule was just as territorially confined as that of the supreme commanders of the IEA and TṬP. In fact, this was also to be understood as an implicit warning to the IS to stay out of affairs in the Pashtun Borderland under the threat of serious armed retribution, a line that was taken almost identically by the IEA's Leadership Council in its official missive to the leadership of the IS five weeks later, as mentioned above.

Surprisingly, one of Salārzay's contemporary references for sustaining his legal position against al-Baghdādī's claim was a work of ʿAbd al-Raḥīm Muslim Dōst from Nangarhar,[1114] because Muslim Dōst had already in July 2014 pledged his allegiance to "Caliph Ibrāhīm" Abū Bakr al-Baghdādī, the Commander of all of the Faithful,[1115] and was, therefore, one of the most prominent representatives of the IS in the Pashtun Borderland. True to the

1112 See ibid., 11; compare al-Māwardī (1422/2002), 6.

1113 See Salārzay (1436/2015). For an analysis, see Hartung (2016a), 141–9; (2019a), 328–30.

1114 See Salārzay (1436/2015), 39; compare Muslim Dōst (n.d.[b]), 201.

1115 See Anon. (1435h), 10′04″–19′41″. Also, see above in the present chapter.

complex negotiation of allegiances in this particular environment, Muslim Dōst's adherence to the IS was not as straightforward as one might initially assume. After all, he, who had started out with the JDQS, was at some point also affiliated to the ṬIT and, after 2001, the TṬP, while – if Giustozzi's "sources" are to be believed – affiliating himself at the same time to various groups in Afghanistan that advocated the establishment of a caliphate as the most appropriate form of government in Afghanistan,[1116] but had little aspiration to carry the torch on to anywhere outside the country. These groups, however, appear to eke out a shadow existence, because the only one with a clear agenda towards the establishment of a caliphate roughly within the confines of the national boundaries of Afghanistan that could be corroborated is the still existing *Movement for the Islamic Caliphate of Afghanistan* (*Də Afghānistān də Islāmī Khilāfat Taḥrīk*), established and led by Rūḥallāh "Khilāfat'yār" Ḥaqqānī of Paghmān District in the mid 1990s.[1117]

Muslim Dōst's career, it seems, is a fine example to showcase the extent to which the lines between the various groups and ideational confessions in the Pashtun Borderland have become fluid under the prevalent strained circumstances, informed by Borderland pragmatics as the prominent and trusted course of action to secure and enhance one's own socio-political position within the local communities there. At the same time, this example should also serve as a reminder of how difficult it is for any observer from the outside to clearly assign someone to one grouping or other, because a certain ideological position does not automatically translate into a fully corresponding socio-political affiliation. Ideologically, Muslim Dōst has remained entirely consistent throughout his over sixty written works to date: he adheres firmly to a Salafi *ʿaqīda* and a Salafist *manhaj* that is very dismissive of the various Muslim religiosities prevalent in the Borderland, as well as of any political system that is not emphatically grounded in the unconditional acknowledgement of God's supreme authority and, subsequently, content with the limited power divinely granted to any human government.[1118] Thus, the Salafism of

[1116] See Giustozzi (2018), esp. 27–31, also 171 and 193f. However, it has not so far been possible to establish corroborating evidence for any of the various associations listed there as forerunners to the presence of the IS in Afghanistan.

[1117] On Rūḥallāh Khilāfat'yār, a product of the "Frontier Deobandiyyat" of Akōṛah Khaṭṭak rather than of one of the Salafi centres of learning in the Pashtun Borderland, see Sayyid Ḥabīballāh Shāh Ḥaqqānī, 'Fuẓalā-yi Ḥaqqāniyyah kī taʿlīfī awr taṣnīfī khidamāt: Mawlānā Rūḥallāh Khilāfat'yār Ḥaqqānī', *al-Ḥaqq* 50/1 (1435–6/2014), 56f. For the manifesto of the movement, which does not contain any allusion to Muslim Dōst or any of those early retainers of the IS, see Khilāfat'yār (1373sh).

[1118] See Muslim Dōst (1367sh/1409h), esp. 43–96; for systematic elaborations of his theologically grounded legal hermeneutics, see Muslim Dōst (1432h; 1437h). In the first of these two works, he even pointed towards the Islamic caliphate as their logical socio-political consequence, to be established even by force if need be: see Muslim Dōst (1432h), 314–19.

Muslim Dōst appears fully compatible with the ideological cornerstones of the IS,[1119] and his affiliation with it would, therefore, almost seem to be a logical consequence.

On the other hand, Muslim Dōst certainly did not share the universal aspirations of the IS, nor did he approve of many of the actions of his peers in the Leadership Council of the IS in Khurasan province. In particular, his expositions on the issue of *khilāfa* are a powerful proof of the rather pragmatic confinement of his focus to the Pashtun Borderland. While, in one of the two relevant works in this regard, his arguments resemble very much those of al-Māwardī,[1120] and would subsequently support the position of the IS leadership on this matter, in *Malāk al-Amjād*, the very work that Abū ʿUs̲mān Salārzay referred to in his refutation of al-Baghdādī's claim of universal political and spiritual authority over the entire Muslim *umma*, Muslim Dōst used the respective definitions by Ibn Khaldūn and Ṣiddīq Ḥasan Khān instead, which opened up a pathway for inferring the interchangeability of *khilāfa* and *imāra*, and, thus, the equivalence of al-Baghdādī and Mullā ʿUmar:

> *Imāma* is the deputyship of God's Messenger [*al-niyāba ʿan rasūl allāh*] – God's blessing upon him and peace! – in the protection of the *dīn* and the management of the world by it. Says Ibn Khaldūn: 'The caliphate means to cause the general public [*kāffa*] to act as required by religious insight into their interest in the Hereafter as well as this world. As, according to the Lawgiver [*al-shāriʿ*; i.e., the Prophet], the conditions of this world all have an impact on the benefits of the Hereafter, the succession of the Lord of the Law [*ṣāḥib al-sharʿ*; i.e., the Prophet] truly consists in safeguarding the *dīn* and management of the world through it.' Further he says: 'Thus, deputyship of the Lord of the Law, the preservation of the *dīn* and management of the world through it is called "caliphate" or "Imamate", and the one in charge of it "caliph" or "Imam". He is being called either a "leader" [*imāman*], just like the leader of the prayers by his followers who follow his example, for which is said: "Grand Imamate" [*al-imāma al-kubrá*], or he is called "successor" [*khalīfa*] as he is succeeding the Prophet – God's blessing upon him and peace! – in his community [*fī ummatih*], which is why he is called "successor" in the general sense, and "successor to the Messenger of God".'
>
> Says the learned Ṣiddīq Ḥasan Khān: 'The caliphate consists in the general supervision [*al-riyāsa al-ʿāmma*] of all the work required for the establishment of the *dīn* through the vivification of the religious disciplines, the institution of the pillars of Islam and the conduct of *jihād*, by taking care of the arrangement of armies and troops of fighters and showing us affection, by the installation of judges and the implementation of penal legislation [*iqāmat al-ḥudūd*], as well as the redressing of injustice [*maẓālim*] and execution of [the commandment to] enjoin the

[1119] See, for example, Muslim Dōst (1367sh/1409h), 52–7, 314–24 and 391–7.
[1120] See Muslim Dōst (1430h), 19–26 and 32f.; compare al-Māwardī (1422/2002), 5–21.

> commendable and prevent the reprehensible in substitution of the Prophet – God's blessing upon him and peace!'[1121]

Admittedly, to get from here to the synonymy of *imāma* and *imāra* that Salārzay was aiming at still required some serious interpretative effort. Still, Muslim Dōst's line of argument can easily be understood as an acknowledgement that the actual appellation for the leader of all Muslims might alternate between a number of terms, all of which, however, refer to one and the same office and set of responsibilities. By putting stress on the synonymy, his readership could well regard the position held by Mullā ʿUmar within the IEA as being equal to the position later claimed by Abū Bakr al-Baghdādī. Moreover, because Muslim Dōst also embraced the classical Islamist argument that without Islamic rule there cannot be a proper Islamic way of life,[1122] he could easily be understood – as Abū ʿUs̱mān Salārzay appears to have done – as legitimizing the claims both of the "commander" Mullā ʿUmar and of the "successor" al-Baghdādī.

With this in mind, Muslim Dōst's pledge of allegiance to the IS, while still affirming the legitimacy of Mullā ʿUmar, appears less of a contradiction. His main reason for advocating an Islamic caliphate was not, as for the principal ideologues of the IS, rooted in an obsession with an earlier form of governance simply because it was inferred from Prophetic practice and the normative example of the Prophet's companions. Instead, the institution of the "caliphate" represented for Muslim Dōst the most suitable guarantor of justice and equity (*ʿadl aw inṣāf*), which, because he considers this a crucial Islamic commandment, he derived from the Qur'an itself.[1123] As long as the leader of a Muslim community directs all his efforts towards the provision of justice and equity, it seems that Muslim Dōst never dogmatically vindicated the superiority of a "successor" over a "commander", as most of his fellow IS partisans would. Rather, he judged to whom the privilege of leading the Muslim community should be accorded on the basis of the ability and determination of a claimant to ascertain the needs of those subjected to his rule and to take care of the fulfilment of such needs within the limits prescribed by God in the Qur'an and, insofar as the technicalities of administering justice are concerned, in line with the precedent established by the Prophet and his companions.[1124] Muslim Dōst consistently distanced himself from the high

1121 Muslim Dōst (n.d.[b]), 17f.; compare Ibn Khaldūn (1425/2004), I: 365; al-Qannawjī (1294h), 7.

1122 See Muslim Dōst (n.d.[b]), 18–22; (1430h), 21. For the classical Islamist view on the same matter, see Hartung (2013a).

1123 See Muslim Dōst (1430h), 23–6. His authoritative references here are Q4.58 and 135, 5.8, 6.152, 16.90, 33.70 and 57.25.

1124 See ibid., 27–30. In this section, entitled "The System of Justice" (*də ʿadālat niẓām*), Muslim Dōst refers exclusively to *ḥadīth* material: *Ṣaḥīḥ al-Bukhārī*, k. al-aḥkām, b. hal yaqḍī al-ḥākim aw yuftī wa-huwa ghaḍbān, no. 1 (ḥadīth 7246); *Ṣaḥīḥ Muslim*, k. al-imāra,

command of the IS in Khurasan province at the very moment it transpired that, contrary to what he initially assumed, the atrocities committed against the civilian population on the Afghanistan side of the Pashtun Borderland had indeed been ordered by Ḥāfiẓ Saʿīd and his deputies. Meanwhile, his loyalty to al-Baghdādī, whom he still regarded as morally upright for quite some time, remained unfettered.[1125]

Increasingly, however, the transnational character of the IS became noticeable also in the Pashtun Borderland, when others of its adherents who were not, as Muslim Dōst and ʿAbd al-Ḥasīb al-Lūjarī, his fellow inmate at the Guantánamo Bay Detention Camp were, aware of or in the least concerned with the intricate socio-political patterns in the Pashtun Borderland, unleash their publisheded assaults on the IEA. In June 2018, for instance, the media outlet of the IS in Khurasan, the *Maktabat al-Muwaḥḥidīn*, released the concise Persian-language treatise of an IS activist who wrote under the pseudonym "Soldier of the Caliph" (*sar'bāz-i khalīfah*). With this publication, at least, the time of mere mud-slinging was ultimately over, because it contained a legal rationale for the necessity of *takfīr* on the "Taliban National Afghan Movement" as a whole and, consequently, on each of its adherents and even sympathizers.

The pivot of "Sar'bāz-i Khalīfah"'s argument is the concept of the "(*shariʿa*-) resisting group" (*ṭāʾifa mumtaniʿa*), the very one Sayyid Imām al-Sharīf had in the late 1980s creatively adapted from Ibn Taymiyya to provide a legal instrument for *takfīr* on collectives. Apparently, now this concept had also been transferred from the rather exclusive circles of the "Arab Afghans" to the conceptual universe of local militant Salafists. Just as *al-walāʾ wa'l-barāʾ* was first embraced by the activists of the TṬP, among whom many of the early leadership of the IS in the province of Khurasan had once belonged, to sustain

b. faḍīlat al-imām al-ʿādil wa-ʿuqūbat al-jāʾir wa'l-ḥathth ʿalá 'l-rifq bi'l-raʿiyya wa'l-nahy ʿan idkhāl al-mashaqa ʿalayhim, nos. 1f. and 14 (aḥādīth 4825f. and 4838), k. al-libās wa'l-zīna, b. al-nisāʾ al-kāsiyyāt al-ʿāriyyāt al-māʾilāt al-mumīlāt, no. 1 (ḥadīth 5704), k. al-birr wa'l-ṣilla wa'l-ādāb, b. al-waʿīd al-shadīd li-man ʿadhdhab al-nās bi-ghayr ḥaqq, no. 2 (ḥadīth 6824), k. al-janna wa-ṣifat naʿīmahā wa-ʾahlihā, b. al-nār yadkhuluhā al-jabbārūna wa'l-janna yadkhulunā al-ḍuʿafāʾ, no. 25 (ḥadīth 7375).

1125 Initially, Muslim Dōst staunchly defended the leadership of the IS in Khurasan, stating that al-Baghdādī himself would never endorse deliberate attacks on the civilian Muslim population, as was the case with the first suicide bombing in the Jalalabad branch office of the Kabul Bank on 18 April 2015. Rather, he resorted to common conspiracy theory that these crimes were actually the work of either the Pakistani or the Afghan intelligence agencies, intended to discredit the IS across the Pashtun Borderland, see Bārakzay (2015). Soon, however, his perception of the leadership of Ḥāfiẓ Saʿīd changed dramatically, when he finally acknowledged the responsibility of the provincial supreme commander for excessive acts of violence against Afghan civilians, blaming again, however, the Pakistani intelligence agencies for being the driving force behind Ḥāfiẓ Saʿīd's activities, see Aḥmad (2015).

the practice of *takfīr*, now further components of militant Salafist theories of *takfīr* were brought into play and realized their full potential in the extremely *takfīr*-centred IS.

Once again, this constitutes a clear mark of distinction from the IEA, which at no point used any of these legal tools to vindicate its armed activities against fellow Sunni Muslims, not even regarding the soldiers of the Afghan National Army, where this approach would have been easily utilizable. Not even the renegades of the IMFF, looking for authoritative justification to engage in warfare with their former compatriots of the IEA, have elected to go down that road, at least not as explicitly as is vividly illustrated by a respective *fatwa* issued on 30 July 2015 by IMFF mufti Zāhid al-Raḥmān al-Qurayshī, in which the problem is already presented in a way rather distinct from that of the IS a mere three years later:

> While our dear country is facing the night of oppression in the shadow of the invasion of the crusaders and is still maintaining its hope for deliverance from the darkness of oppression, is it permissible within the blessed *dīn* of Islam for one *mujāhid* to take up arms against another Muslim *mujāhid*, to kill, execute, burn down houses and seize property, just so he maintains his power and influence in the region and safeguards his regional interests and authority [*ḥākimiyyat*]? If someone is involved in such acts, can he [rightly] be called a *mujāhid*? Moreover, if he is killed in this situation, can he be called a martyr? What does the Islamic *shari'a* say about this?[1126]

As can clearly be seen, other than "Sar'bāz-i Khalīfah", whose major concern was to provide a legally sustainable argument for practising *takfīr* on everyone associated with the IEA and arrive, therefore, at a legitimization for military action against those who no longer constitute fellow Muslims, the IMFF went down a distinctly different path to arrive at a similar result. Therefore, while, as was to be expected, the positions of Ibn Taymiyya and Muḥammad ibn ʿAbd al-Wahhāb served as major references for the IS author,[1127] those of Zāhid al-Raḥmān al-Qurayshī remained entirely within the hermeneutical universe of Hanafi jurisprudence. And, even though the *aḥādīth* he employed have been classed in the canonical compilations under those sections that deal primarily with the capital offence of apostasy,[1128] the ones selected espouse rather the firm disapproval of causing bloodshed and exerting other forms of violence by

1126 IMFF (1394sh).

1127 See "Sar'bāz-i Khalīfah" (1397sh/1439h), 5–7; compare Ibn Taymiyya (1426/2005a), v: 315; xxviii: 273f. and 282f.; al-Najdī (1417/1996), x: 175–9, here 175.

1128 See IMFF (1394sh); compare *Sunan al-Nasāʾī*, k. taḥrīm al-damm, b. ḥukm fi'l-murtadd, no. 1 (ḥadīth 4074); *Sunan al-Nasāʾī*, k. taḥrīm al-damm, b. man qātala dūna ʾahlih, no. 1 (ḥadīth 4111); also in *al-Jāmiʿ al-Tirmidhī*, k. al-diyāt ʿan rasūl allāh – ṣallá 'llāh ʿalayhi wa-sallam, b. mā jāʾ fi-man qutila dūna mālihi fa-huwa shahīd, no. 5 (ḥadīth 1485); *Sunan Abī Dāwūd*, k. al-sunna, b. fi qitāl al-luṣūṣ, no. 2 (ḥadīth 4774). Moreover, Zāhid al-Raḥmān al-Qurayshī refers to al-Marghinānī's *Bidāyat al-Mubtadiʾ*, the text that he

one Muslim against another, emphasized even more by al-Qurayshī's references to Q4.93 and Q49.9, as well as the denial of martyrdom to every Muslim who is killed while being involved in such morally repulsive acts. At no point were those still loyal to the IEA and its new supreme leaders, Mullā Muḥammad Akhtar Manṣūr and Hibatallāh ibn Muḥammad Khān Ākhūnd'zādah (b. 1387/1967),[1129] respectively, called "unbelievers" or "apostates": the issue at hand is rather to at least put on a public show of striving for a de-escalation of the conflict between the IMFF and IEA:

> In case two Muslim sides are at war, peace should be called for, in line with the [respective] Qur'anic commandment [*də qurʾān də ḥukm par asās*]. However, if either side refuses to make peace or disobeys the terms of the peace [*də ṣulḥē sharāyiṭūnah*], all Muslims must take to the path of confrontation [*də muqābalē lār*] until peace is made and the terms of the peace abided by. Moreover, considering it permissible [*ḥalāl*] leads a Muslim to unbelief [*yaw musalmān kufr tah rasīğī*]. It is [therefore] the duty of the community of scholars to stop each transgressor and aggressor from affronting, even if only by killing him. [...]
>
> Instead of killing his own *mujāhid* brother for the sake of worldly gains, he should humble himself a little and take a lesson from how the infidels, polytheists and hypocrites of the world, despite all [their] international and religious differences, target us and our Islam as one. We must and we shall not lose power tomorrow. Your personal advantages cannot be allowed to jeopardize this in whatever name, nor to kill your own Muslim *mujāhid* brother, to disarm him, burn his house, loot his property and everything like that, in a state when we are deprived of [even] a single safe haven from the invading crusaders, and where alone we can protect our head.[1130]

For "Sar'bāz-i Khalīfah", in contrast, there was no valid common cause which would prompt him to consider refraining from his presentation of the evidence necessary in any trial to eventually pass a legal judgement: 'We declare the Taliban to be unbelievers [*takfīr mīkunīm*], because they are a "(*shariʿa*-)resisting group" [*ṭāʾifah-yi mumtaniʿah*]; we consider them apostates [*murtadd mīdānīm*]. For evidence, carefully follow our exposition.'[1131]

***

commented upon in his later and more famous *K. al-Hidāya*, to prove the agreement of his own interpretation with the Hanafi textual tradition.

1129 For a concise biography of Hibatallāh Ākhūnd'zādah, see Anon., 'al-Sīra al-dhātiyya li-zaʿīm Imārat Afghānistān al-Islāmiyya amīr al-muʾminīn al-Shaykh «Hibatallāh Ākhund'zādah» (ḥafiẓahu allāh taʿālá wa-raʿāh', *al-Ṣumūd* 11/10 (1438/2016), 2–6. For a Pashto version, see *Shahāmat* 10/4 (1438/2016), 5–14. Its Urdu version appeared in *Sharīʿat* 5/10 (1438/2016), 3–10.

1130 IMFF (1394sh).

1131 "Sar'bāz-i Khalīfah" (1397sh/1439h), 3.

Here seems to be a good place to halt once again for a moment of systematic reflection. As we have seen, those affiliated with the IS in the Pashtun Borderland were clearly not inclined to pragmatic solutions, which might have required the willingness to make the odd compromise, if only temporarily. This so far almost unprecedentedly uncompromising attitude, in fact, reveals a core feature that distinguishes the IS in whatever region of the Muslim world it has been able to establish a formal presence from the many Islamist and Salafist groups with a clearly local agenda and, therefore, it clearly demands some attempt at systematic explanation.

The fulcrum of the present attempt shall be the inexorable nomocentricity of the adherents to the IS, which political philosopher Dieter Thomä has attributed to one of his three basic ideal-types of the "troublemaker", or "discontent".[1132] The type of the "nomocentric troublemaker", that is, one 'who fights the existing order in anticipation of a different set of rules that will one day take its place',[1133] fits rather the classical Islamist as a person of the world in the here and now: because she or he adheres to a fundamentally different concept of morality as the foundation of any political ideology, all alternative discourse must necessarily be interpreted as being in stark opposition.[1134] As such, nomocentric troublemakers see themselves as essentially revolutionary, and, as revolutionaries, their major reference point is *in* the world. Some of it is clearly discernible in the IS and in the IEA, but neither fits the definition to the extent that the various Islamist organizations-cum-parties discussed above – the JiI, Ḥil, JIA, IIAA, JNM, etc.[1135] – do. To overcome this dilemma, Thomä concludes his analysis by proposing a fourth type, that of the "massive troublemaker", which seems to be intrinsically tied to one of the three pure ones, in the case at hand, to that of the "nomocentric troublemaker". Surprisingly, however, Thomä refrains from taking his typology further by discussing a hybrid "massive nomocentric troublemaker": for him, the transformation to a "massive troublemaker" originates, first and foremost, in the "egocentric" one, 'who – figuratively speaking – stamps his foot on the threshold [that defines the liminal space between order and disarray], bristles against the state order, and acts on his self-will'.[1136]

For the context under review here, however, this does not entirely seem to be the case, perhaps pointing to the limits within which occidental philosophical thought is applicable to alternative cultural frameworks. Still, regarding the IS, Thomä seems to be spot on: the personal experience of ostracization and humiliation of many of its adherents by the diverse majority societies in

[1132] See Section 2.4.
[1133] Thomä (2016), 21 (translation by Jessica Spengler).
[1134] See Hartung (2013a), where this is discussed extensively.
[1135] See Section 4.2.1.
[1136] Thomä (2016), 21 (translation by Jessica Spengler).

which they have lived has resulted in dysfunctional social relationships and self-appraisal that are at the core of socio-psychological investigations into political authoritarianism. This double alienation – firstly, from those sections of society that determine the dominant discourse and which is encountered as violently discriminatory, and, secondly, from oneself due to the induration arising from a sense of inferiority and extraneousness – results in the "egocentric discontent" becoming a "massive troublemaker", who 'hastily leaves his marginal or threshold situation and replaces inner and outer alienation with total assimilation'.[1137] In other words, such a person's individuality, which is shaped by the highly variant conditions of the environment in which one spends the formative period of life, is fully discharged into the new collective in which all these contingencies are entirely levelled.

All this applies very well to the activists of the IS, wherever they are: the humiliation which they have personally experienced within the societies and communities of which they were initially a however ill-fitting part is compensated for by a cathartic event: a rebirth through total submission to a new total society, in this case the IS. Figures such as Ḥāfiẓ Saʿīd, Abū ʿUmar al-Khurāsānī and ʿAbd al-Raḥīm Muslim Dōst all fit the bill quite well; the stress placed by Muslim Dōst on the caliphate as the best possible socio-political framework for ensuring that justice is comprehensively administered points, in fact, to these personal experiences of repeated subjection by captivity in the activists' background. Because the new collective is not closed, but has emphatically declared itself open to anyone following its call to completely commit herself or himself to it,[1138] it cannot be based on contingencies: how would it otherwise be possible to assemble people of such a vast array of cultural imprints under one banner, as successfully accomplished by the IS? In his first sermon as Caliph Ibrāhīm, Abū Bakr al-Baghdādī put this in a nutshell when he proclaimed:

> Raise your heads high, for today – by the bounty of God – there is a *dawla* for you and *khilāfa*, which will return your dignity and honour, reinstate your rights and your leadership [*taʿīdu karāmatakum wa-ʿizzatakum wa-tistarjiʿu ḥuqūqakum wa-siyādatakum*]. It is a state where the non-Arab and the Arab, the white and the black, the Easterner and the Westerner are [all] brethren. It is a caliphate that has brought together the Caucasian, the Indian, the Chinese, the Syrian and the Iraqi, the Yemeni, the Egyptian and the Moroccan, the American, the French, the German and the Australian. God has joined their hearts, and, by His grace, they became brethren, in harmony with each other; they are standing in one trench, defending each other, guarding each other and sacrificing

1137 Ibid., 452 (translation by Jessica Spengler).

1138 See the feature article 'al-Hijra min *nifāq* ilá 'l-ikhlāṣ', *Dābiq* 3 (1435h), 25–34; al-ʿAdnānī (1441h), 202–10 («*Yā Qawmanā ʾAjībū Dāʿiya ʾllāh*» [Q46.31]; Ramaḍān 1436 / June 2015).

> themselves for one another. Their blood got blended under a single flag and one single goal, under one canopy, [living in] amenity and delight by this blessing, the blessing of the faithful brotherhood [*niʿmat al-ukhuwwa al-īmāniyya*], so that, if kings were to savour this taste, they would [instantly] forsake their kingdoms and fight [each other] over it. So, praise be to God, and thanks![1139]

The totalitarian character of the IS enterprise lauded here by al-Baghdādī manifests itself not least in the fact that many authors in the service of the IS do not call themselves by their given name, but, if they provide a name at all, rather impersonally sign their texts as "soldiers of the Caliph", "of the *Islamic State*", or suchlike. This, in fact, speaks for itself just as much as does the quite common anonymizing visual self-presentation with a balaclava.

The extinction of individuality achieved in this way, finally, makes it easier to blank out socio-economic, cultural and political specificities that differ from region to region, to subsequently not relate to the local population with even the slightest degree of empathy, and, therefore, to subject each and every one to the same inflated standard. Thus, in its province Khurasan, as, in fact, everywhere else where the IS is present, both the world-view and the practice of its cadres refuse the necessity to acknowledge the complexities of a space like the Pashtun Borderland and exercise at least some degree of pragmatism. Such a deliberately chosen dearth of a local identity, derived from real-life embeddedness in a concrete socio-political and cultural context, turns out to be quite conducive to a literal interpretation of religious precepts, especially in matters of communal practice, and even more so their immediate and uncompromising implementation.

In the case of the IS, the binary world-view so common to all ideologies, according to which its activists are, by definition, positioned on the winning side, is more than elsewhere exacerbated by their interpretation of reality in terms of Sunni apocalyptic thought. At this point, where all signs seem to point towards the imminent end of the world and the advent of the last judgement, there can be no room for subtleties, or, in fact, for liminal spaces, such as borderlands, and everyone is consequently classed exclusively in terms of a

[1139] al-Baghdādī (n.d.[a]), 51f. See also, for example, Anon., 'al-Dawla al-Islāmiyya bāqiyya', *Dābiq* 5 (1436h), 32f. The various sermons by Abū Bakr al-Baghdādī's predecessor as *amīr* of what was then called *Dawlat al-ʿIrāq al-Islāmiyya*, Ḥāmid Dāwūd Khalīl Muḥammad al-Zāwī – *nom de guerre* "Abū ʿUmar al-Baghdādī" (killed 1431/2010), before the actual proclamation of the caliphate, are interesting in this regard here, esp. 'Ḥiṣād al-sannayn bi-dawlat al-muwaḥḥidīn' (2 Rabīʿ I 1428 / 20 April 2007), 37′56″–41′ 21″; and '«wa-Yamkurūna wa-yamkur allāh»' (3 Ramaḍān 1428 / 15 September 2007), 26′03″–27′19″. The audio files of both sermons were available in a collection named *Jamīʿ Kalimāt al-Shaykh al-Mujāhid Abū ʿUmar al-Baghdādī (taqabbalahu allāh) Kāmila*, uploaded by "Abū ʿAbdallāh" on 10 August 2020, under the URL: http://archive.org/details/20200810_20200810_0458 (accessed 9 November 2022).

binary distinction between those who will eventually prevail and those who are doomed to perdition.

This particular disposition of the ones attracted to the IS can well serve to explain why violence against nominal fellow Muslims has reached a hitherto hardly known level even in the Pashtun Borderland: among all the diverse groups that, since the end of the first central government of the IEA in Afghanistan, have competed with each other ever more fiercely over the claim to represent the "saved group", the *firqa nājiyya*, only the IS has made this eschatological dimension an essential constituent of its ideology. Therefore, its activists, be it in the Pashtun Borderland or elsewhere, appear to make a more sustainable claim than anyone else to the exclusive monopoly of judging the fidelity of those who call themselves "Muslims", as well as the supreme right to see through their particular understanding of *shari'a*-compliant conduct, including the powers to carry out their legal sentences.

Still, what proved quite easy to implement against the predominantly subaltern civilian population in this region turned out to be much less so when confronting other armed groups, especially if they were as powerful as the IEA.[1140] Here, all attempts by the IS detachment in Khurasan to establish those claims against its competitors evolved quickly into proper warfare, into which the IS entered recklessly, despite its conspicuous inferiority in terms of numerical manpower and logistics. Yet, the logic of compensating for eventual material shortcomings by exceptionally strong and unconditional trust in God's omnipotence and omniscience (*tawakkul*),[1141] which we have already encountered every now and again (and not least also with the ṬIT / IEA),[1142] had become a true cornerstone of the IS apocalyptic world-view.

Taking the Battle of Badr between the early Medinese Muslim community under the Prophet Muḥammad and the Quraysh of Mecca in the year 2/624 as

[1140] Similar to the scenario in the Pashtun Borderland was that in Syria and Iraq, where the IS stood in open confrontation with the *Jabhat al-Nuṣra*, another outgrowth of *al-Qāʿida* in the Fertile Crescent, as it did, in fact, with any other regional affiliate of *al-Qāʿida*. Other equally powerful Islamist militias in armed conflict with the IS also include prominently the Imāmī Shiʿi *Sarāyā al-Salām*, established in June 2014 by decree of Sayyid Muqtadá al-Ṣadr (b. 1394/1974) as the successor organization to the meanwhile dissolved *Jaysh al-Mahdī*. Its military engagement received almost immediate sanction by a *fatwa* of the supreme religious authority (*al-marjaʿ al-aʿlá*), Āyatallāh Sayyid ʿAlī al-Sīstānī (b. 1349/1930), in which armed *jihād* against the threat of the IS was declared a collective duty (see Alnasiri Tube, 'al-Sayyid al-Sīstānī yuftī bi'l-jihād al-kifāʾī', 14 June 2014. URL: www.youtube.com/watch?v=R7by5almGhA [accessed 10 February 2024]). Last, but not least, a similar constellation also occurred with various Kurdish militias in the Borderland between Iraq, Syria and Turkey, be they, like the *Islamic Movement of Iraqi Kurdistan* (*Bizûtinewey Islâmî le Kurdistânî-ʿIrâq*), of Islamist persuasion or, as in the case of the *People's Protection Unit* (*Yekîneyên Pârâstinâ Gel*), rather secular-orientated.

[1141] On the Qur'anic concept of *tawakkul*, see Eggen (2011), 57–60.

[1142] See Sections 3.2.3, 3.3.3 and 4.3.

an authoritative precedent, temporary success is, in conjunction with the eighth chapter of the Qur'an, which was revealed on this occasion, interpreted in IS circles as an indication of sufficiently strong *tawakkul*, whereas defeat is perceived as a sign of hypocrisy, or doubt in the unlimited powers of God.[1143] Still, temporary defeat certainly does not rescind God's promise of salvation to those

> whose hearts are fearful [*wajilat qulūbuhum*] when God is remembered, and when His signs [*āyātuh*] are recited faith makes them swell, and upon their Lord they rely; who establish the [ritual] prayer and bestow from what We have provided: these truly are the believers [*ulāʾika humu ʾl-muʾminūna ḥaqqan*].[1144]

Firm belief in the ultimate triumph over the multifarious unbelievers is, once more, sustained by references to the authoritative texts of Sunni Islam.[1145] Moreover, this serves as a viable explanation of the fact that, despite losing its territorial base in the Fertile Crescent to the concerted military efforts of an international alliance once more under the aegis of the USA, the IS remains relentlessly and uncompromisingly active, well sustained by Q8:39, the by far most frequently quoted verse of that chapter in the official periodicals of the IS: 'And fight them [that is, the unbelievers] until there is no infestation [*fitna*]

1143 See Ibn Hishām (1375/1955), I: 667–77. The Battle of Uḥud between the same two parties the following year serves, correspondingly, as an authoritative precedent for the causality of hypocrisy and military defeat: see ibid., II: 106–21. For the appropriation of these two narratives into that of the IS, see, for example, 'Indithār al-minṭaqa al-ramādiyya', *Dābiq* 7 (1436h), 55; 'Min ṣafaḥāt al-taʾrīkh: al-sarāyā wa'l-ghazawāt wa'l-futūḥāt fī shahr Ramaḍān', *Dābiq* 10 (1436h), 28; 'Durūs min fitnat al-maghūl', *Dābiq* 14 (1437h), 45; Abu Hamza al-Muhajir, 'Paths to Victory – Part 2.' *Rumiyah* 3 (1438h), 20–3, here 20, and 'Jihad through Du'a', *Rumiyah* 3 (1438h), 32–5, here 33; 'Disavowal of the Mushrikin in the Lives of the Prophet and the Sahabah', *Rumiyah* 7 (1438h), 26–9, here 27; Abū Muṣʿab al-Zarqāwī, 'And Likewise the Messengers Are Afflicted, Then the Final Outcome Is Theirs. Part 2', *Rumiyah* 9 (1438h), 16 and 19 (this is, in fact, the English translation of a sermon entitled "wa-ka-dhalika al-rusul tubtalá thumma takūnu lahā al-ʿāqiba", delivered on 21 January 2005 / 11 Dhī 'l-ḥijja 1425, see al-Zarqāwī [1427/2006], 182–209, here 192 and 195); 'Mushāhad min ḥirṣ al-ṣaḥāba ilá nayl al-shahāda', *al-Nabāʾ* 2/13 (1438h), 9.

1144 Q8.2–4.

1145 See, for example, Anon., 'Muqābala maʿa amīr junūd al-khilāfa fi'l-Banghāl, al-Shaykh Abū Ibrāhīm al-Ḥanīf', *Dābiq* 14 (1437h), 66; compare *Ṣaḥīḥ Muslim*, k. al-imāra, b. qawlihi – ṣallá 'llāh ʿalayhi wa-sallam – "lā tazālu ṭāʾifatun min ummatī ẓāhirīna ʿalá 'l-ḥāqq lā yaḍurruhum man khālafahum", no. 8 (ḥadīth 5 066); *Jāmiʿ al-Tirmidhī*, k. al-fitan, b. mā jāʾ fi'l-aʾimma al-muḍillīn, no. 1 (ḥadīth 2 393). Somewhat predictably, the Qur'anic term "naṣr" is translated within IS circles as "victory" in the military sense, although its semantic scope is certainly wider, and it is frequently also rendered as "aid", "assistance" or "strengthening" vis-à-vis an opponent. Thus, the IS-specific translation of verses such as Q8.10: 'There is no victory but through God' (*wa-mā 'l-naṣr ilā min ʿindi 'llāh*) clearly adds a pointed emphasis towards military pursuits.

and the *dīn* is God's entirely.'[1146] The Qur'anic text even specifies how the unbelievers are to be fought: 'And prepare against them whatever of force and of tethered horses you are able to do, to thereby terrify [*turhibūna bih*] the enemy of God and your enemy, as well as others besides them, whom you do not know, but [whom] God knows.'[1147]

In this light, spreading terror (*irhāb*) appears fully consistent with the literalist understanding of the Qur'an that characterizes the very particular Salafist hermeneutics of the IS ideologues. A necessary part of such a strategic set-up is a certain detachment from the material world, including one's own life, something that, as we have seen above, is not particular to the IS, but in fact applies also to many of those Islamic world-views that are heavily steeped in egalitarian Sufi concepts of piety, as adhered to, for example, by certain sections within the TJ and subsequently also the ṬIT / IEA.[1148]

Yet, all thoughts and especially practices associated with Sufi Islam, notably among them the pious visitation of graves of charismatic spiritual figures (*ziyāra*) and asking the deceased to intercede with God on their behalf (*tawassul*), which are very common among the subaltern population of the Pashtun Borderland, are for the IS cadres, as well as many of their forerunners in the TṬP, one of the main indicators of a religiosity so deviant that severe measures to redress them are required. The practice of the Emirate of the Āl Saʿūd in Dirʿiyya (1744–1818), sustained by religious precepts by the first generation of Wahhabi scholars, served them as a reference point in this regard: in July 2015, the *al-Ḥayāt Media Centre* of the IS[1149] had a lead feature published in its

1146 Across the fifteen issues of *Dābiq*, this verse was quoted twelve times, five of which appear in issue 10 alone. In *Rumiyah*, which replaced this magazine in September 2016, the verse figured comparatively less frequently; yet, the fact that it was cited already in the first issue (p. 7) indicates that the general thrust of the IS enterprise has not changed a jot.

1147 Q8:60. This verse has also been repeatedly cited in the official IS periodicals, in most instances to emphasize the necessity for as much preparation for battle as possible. The last one, however, which coincides with the USA-led anti-IS military coalition forces closing in on the IS strongholds and the battle for the IS capital al-Raqqa being imminent, stressed once again unconditional trust in God's omnipotence and omniscience as supreme to everything humans could do to influence the course of events, see Anon., 'Rely on Allah, not on Your Equipment', *Rumiyah* 7 (1438h), 12f.

1148 See Section 4.3.2.

1149 The editor-in-chief of *Dābiq* at that time was the Syrian-American Aḥmad Abū Samra, then known as "Abū Sulaymān al-Shāmī" or "Abū Maysara al-Shāmī" (killed 1438/2016), see Anon., 'Abū Sulaymān al-Shāmī – taqabbalu allāh – bayna ʿishq al-shahāda . . . wa-ṭams al-rumūs', *al-Nabāʾ* 2/24 (1438h), 12f.; Anon., '"Among the Believers Are Men": Shaykh Abu Sulayman ash-Shami – taqabbalahu allāh', *Rumiyah* 8 (1438h), 40–6. His superior at the top of all IS media ventures was Dr Wāʾil al-Ṭāʾī, *nom de guerre* "Abū Muḥammad al-Furqān" (killed 1438/2016), one of the very early militant Salafists in Iraq, a close confidant of Abū Muṣʿab al-Zarqāwī and, subsequently, of Abū Bakr al-Baghdādī. His association with them appears surprising only at first glance: after all, he had initially been

magazine *Dābiq* which included, among other things, a lengthy quote from a quite stern epistle of Imam Saʿūd ibn ʿAbd al-ʿAzīz (r. 1803–14):

> [You claim that] you do not submit to anything else but God, and that you are not pleased with such [beliefs and conduct contrary to Islam], that you do not encourage the people to do so: Yet, your actions – both outwardly and inwardly – disprove your words. These false majesties [*al-ḥaḍarāt al-bāṭil*], the accursed places of visitation [*al-mashāhid al-malʿana*], the structures over the graves, as well as alienating for them what is the [sole] entitlement of God Almighty, such as supplication, sacrifice, vows, [the expression of] fear and hope, and requesting from them what must not be requested but from God, performing the ritual prayer there, touching them [in devotion], offering gifts to them, and similar disgusting and heinous matters: all of this exists openly among you. And the one who does not do these things is [still] pleased with them, and [subsequently] defends those of his people with his wealth, his tongue, and his hands. [. . .]
>
> And that we are killing the infidels is a matter neither to apologize for nor be ashamed of. And – God willing – we shall do more of this, and we will advise our children to do likewise after us, and they will advise their children likewise after them, as the Companion said, 'Never will we refrain from *jihād*.' [. . .] We will rub the noses of the unbelievers into the dirt, shed their blood and seize their wealth by the might and power of God. This we do in conformity, not innovation [*ittibāʿan lā ibtidāʿan*], out of obedience to God and His Messenger, and as a sacrifice [*qurba*] by which we draw closer to God Almighty, and by which we hope for abundance in reward [*jazīl al-thawāb*].[1150]

The listing of 'disgusting and heinous matters' in this passage clearly points towards popular Shiʿi beliefs and practices, an impression sustained by the fact that it was Saʿūd ibn ʿAbd al-ʿAzīz who, on 21 April 1802, led a presumably mainly Bedouin force from the Najd into Ottoman Iraq and ransacked one of the pivotal Shiʿi devotional places, the shrine of Imām Ḥusayn ibn ʿAlī in Karbala, after having killed citizens of the town at random.[1151] In the *Dābiq*

affiliated with the so-called *Jamāʿat Fāʾiz*, named after its leader, the fervently staunch anti-Shiʿi Fāʾiz al-Zaydī, whose religious ideas combined Salafi hermeneutics with the political agenda of the Islamist *Ḥizb al-Taḥrīr* and the proselytising strategy of the TJ: see al-Maḥmūd (2017), 156; Anon., 'al-Shaykh al-mujāhid Abū Muḥammad al-Furqān – taqabbalahu 'llāh taʿālá – qāʾid maʿrakat al-iʿlām wa-murābiṭ ʿalá thughūr al-ʿaqīda. al-juzʾ al-awwal', *al-Nabāʾ* 6/37 (1442h), 3f., here 3.

1150 Saʿūd ibn ʿAbd al-ʿAzīz, 'wa-ʿAlayha atawakkala wa-lā quwwa ʾillā bi'llāh', in al-Najdī (1417/1996), IX: 264–89, here 275f. and 280. Compare 'A sharīʿat allāh ʾam sharāʾiʿ al-bashar? (hall muḥārabat al-khilāfa riddatun?)', *Dābiq* 10 (1436h), 50–64, here 60f. The internal quote is from the Prophet's companion Anas ibn Malik (d. 93/712), see *Ṣaḥīḥ al-Bukhārī*, k. al-sayr wa'l-jihād, b. al-taḥrīḍ ʿalá 'l-qitāl, no. 1 (ḥadīth 2 871).

1151 See Ibn Bishr (1402/1982), I: 257f. The attack acquired even more pointed emphasis by virtue of the fact that the date chosen for it coincided that year with ʿĪd al-Ghadīr, one of

article in which this passage was quoted, however, the scope has been considerably widened and targeted now also very much the adherents to Sufi Islam; something that – and here, finally, our excursion into IS ideology comes full circle – prominently included "Deobandiyyat" in its various manifestations, including the TJ and ultimately also the ṬIT / IEA.[1152]

***

Similarly to the fierce stricture on "Deobandiyyat", even in its Panjpiri garb, by Shams al-Dīn al-Afghānī, those who associated themselves with individuals trained at his *Jāmiʿah Asariyyah* in Ćamkanī now applied a similar critique to the IEA and, thus, attempted to delegitimize all its various legal efforts:

> The judges of the [Islamic] Emirate [of Afghanistan] are Deobandi "Maturidi Hanafi". They subscribe to the postponement of the judgement [*irjāʾ fi'l-ḥukm*] over "Muslim" spies who desert [from Islam] by aiding the infidels against the Muslims. They also have less severe punishments for this vicious act, as well as for the offence of sodomy, in comparison with other schools of jurisprudence [*al-madāris al-fiqhiyya al-ukhrá*].[1153]

the major Shiʿi religious festivals. It is certainly noteworthy that this attack, which left a traumatic impression on the Imāmī Shiʿi communities all over the region, has so far barely received due scholarly attention, which is surprisingly missing even in recent academic studies on the Shiʿi communities in the region, such as Matthiesen (2015), and is, therefore, something in dire need of rectification by future research.

1152 See Abū Jarīr al-Shamālī, 'al-Qāʿida fi Wazīristān: shahāda min al-dākhil', *Dābiq* 6 (1436h), 40–55, here 40 and 46.

1153 Ibid., 49 n.7. On *irjāʾ*, the postponement of a legal judgement to Judgement Day and its retransfer back to God, as a pivot of militant Salafist arguments against those legal scholars who refrain from the pronouncement of *takfīr* and the enforcement of this judgement, see Lav (2012); Nedza (2020), 124–36. The negative assessment of the legal position towards spies adhered to within the IEA, however, is a gross extrapolation from a single concrete instance, in which IEA judges had purportedly acquitted some *al-Qāʿida* affiliates in Mīrāmshā who, because of having become susceptible to blackmail for their adherence to sodomy, became informers of the Pakistani intelligence services, to a general legal position. Chronology is of key importance here: at the time al-Shamālī's diatribe was published, the IEA had already taken a much sterner stand on the issue of espionage for the enemy: see Də Afghānistān Islāmī Imārat (1431/2010), 20–5; discussed in Hartung (2021a), 155–7. Only three years earlier, however, in the first edition of the IEA *Lāʾiḥah*, the instructions regarding this matter did indeed fit al-Shamālī's portrayal, at least insofar as the strong dependence on the Hanafi legal procedure is concerned: espionage was not regarded as an offence that requires capital punishment (*ḥudūd*), and, considering even mitigating circumstances, such as coercion (*ikrāh*) into spying or simply a lack of awareness (*jahl*), the IEA leadership stipulates seriously admonishing the offender, threatening them with severe punishment after reoffending, and only at second reoffence carrying out execution, see Də Afghānistān Islāmī Imārat (1428/2007), 13; compare, for example, al-Kūfī (1399/1979), 138f.; Ibn ʿĀbidīn (1423/2003), VI: 279.

Even Mullā Muḥammad ʿUmar, otherwise highly respected,[1154] was now accused of serious deficiencies in matters of *shariʿa*,[1155] deficiencies that weighed all the heavier because, by insisting on a formalized relationship that demanded obedience to him, he accrued the blame for having led astray even those of otherwise sound Salafist persuasion, such as Mullā Faẕlallāh, the former supreme *amīr* of the TṬP.[1156]

From publicized positions such as the one above by former *al-Qāʿida* commander, Zarqāwī-confidant and eventual IS partisan Abū Jarīr al-Shamālī, allegedly of Jordanian origin, it is evident that the IS cadres and sympathizers in the Pashtun Borderland have fully subscribed to the official ideological framework of the IS venture, something underlined by the fact that, right from its inception, the short-lived magazine *Rumiyah* was published not just in English, but also in Pashto and Urdu, in addition to six other languages. The IS dependency in "Khurasan" did not release as much written material as one would wish, for studying it, even though it is reported to have issued a Pashto magazine called *Nidāʾ al-Ḥaqq*.[1157] Instead, it subscribed rather to audio and video as the preferred means for radiating its message, which seems a reasonable decision in view of the high degree of illiteracy in the region in which the IS had set up its bases of operation in the Pashtun Borderland.[1158] Right from its inception, it ran the Pashto language radio station *Də Khilāfat Ghaǵ – The Voice of the Caliphate* – on 90.00 FM, which could be received in most parts of Nangarhar Province, and also soon started to broadcast some hours per day in Dari,[1159] as well as a video channel called *Tōr Bayraghūnah Khparandōyah Idārah* – the *Black Banners Publication Centre.* At the time of writing, both were still very much alive, although under perpetually changing URLs.

1154 See, for example, al-Zarqāwī (1427/2006), 25 (*Ilḥaq bi'l-Qāfila*; 12 Dhī 'l-qaʿda 1424/4 January 2004) and 129 (*Waṣāyā hāmma li'l-Mujāhidīn wa'l-Radd ʿalá 'l-Mukhadhdhilīn*; 19 Jumādá I 1425/6 July 2004).

1155 See Anon., 'Qāʿidat al-Ẓawāhirī wa'l-Harārī wa'l-Naẓārī wa'l-ḥikma al-yamaniyya al-mafqūda', *Dābiq* 6 (1436h), 16–25, here 25f.

1156 See al-Shamālī, 'al-Qāʿida fī Wazīristān' [see above, n.1 152], 49.

1157 Despite best efforts, not even an image of a single issue of that journal could be located, partly due to the shutdown of various internet sites that did not require registration (see n.1 163 below in this chapter), but also because the claim that there is a somewhat regular Pashto publication by the IS might have been little more than a propaganda stunt. Be that as it may, the last post on the *Nidāʾ al-Ḥaqq* Facebook site <@KhurasanKhabrona> is dated 1 March 2016 (accessed 5 November 2021).

1158 *Postscript*: Since May 2022, the new media department of the IS dependency in Khurasan, the *Muʾassasat al-ʿAẓāʾim al-Iʿlāmiyya*, has consistently been publishing the monthly Pashto e-journal *Khurāsān Ghaǵ*, complemented since January 2023 by the Arabic monthly *Sawt Khurāsān*. Both periodicals, with distinct content, have since evolved into major platforms for publicizing ever harsher anti-IEA heresiographies.

1159 See Anon., 'Afghānistān khᵛāhān-i tavaqquf-i nasharāt-i rādiyū «Ṣadā-yi Khilāfat» shud', *Afghānistān-i Mā* 10/2754 (28 Qaws 1394sh / 19 December 2015), 5f.

There is yet another significant detail that occurs from al-Shamālī's influential piece in the sixth issue of *Dābiq*.[1160] The activists of the IS observed the publications of its competitors very closely, including the postings of official statements on their respective websites, and presented the contents therein as evidence of how seriously all of these organizations have strayed from the Straight Path, in contrast to the IS.[1161] To this end, they deemed it appropriate even to present positions from much older materials that had in the meantime become obsolete, as is indicated, for instance, by the above case of the IEA's procedure regarding prosecuting someone accused of spying for the enemy,[1162] to subtly alter statements or to tear them apart and reassemble them in a slightly different order for additional emphasis on one or other perceived transgression.[1163] Yet, it has to be conceded that the gist of the various IEA positions was, by and large, not presented incorrectly by the IS authors and, moreover, it cannot be denied that their publication had been authorized by the IEA high command. As the necessary final piece of the jigsaw that will enable us to appreciate the current dominant semantics of the term "talib", and its plural "taliban", even better and as a component of a much broader, more complex and much more colourful

1160 Much of the academic and semi-academic work on the IS in general, and its dependence on the Pashtun Borderland in particular, has taken note of this article and treated it as if it were the official IS position towards *al-Qāʿida* and the IEA: see, for example, Giustozzi (2018), 175. Still, and surprisingly, background information on its author is more or less non-existent.

1161 What is perhaps the most comprehensive list of quotes to prove the deviance of the IEA and its first supreme *amīr* Mullā Muḥammad ʿUmar was compiled by the editor-in-chief of *Dābiq*, Aḥmad Abū Samra, here as "Abū Maysara al-Shāmī", under the title *Fāḍiḥat al Shām wa-Kasr al-Aṣnām*: see al-Shāmī (1438/2017), 471–98, here esp. 477–93. Compare, for example, the various addresses of Mullā Muḥammad ʿUmar on the occasion of the two major Islamic holidays between 2009 and 2014: 'Bayān amīr al-muʾminīn al-Mullā Muḥammad ʿUmar al-Mujāhid – ḥafiẓuhu allāh – bi-munāsibat ʿīd al-fiṭr/al-aḍḥá al-mubārak li-ʿām [. . .]', *al-Ṣumūd* 4/6 (1430/2009), 1–4, here 3; 5/3 (1431/2010), 2–6, here 4f.; 6/3 (1432/2011), 2–6, here 3; 7/4 (1433/2012), 2–5, here 4; 7/6 (1433/2012), 2–5, here 4; 8/4 (1434/2013), 2–5, here 4; 8/6 (1434/2013), 2–4, here 4; and 9/4 (1435/2014), 2–4, here 3.

1162 See n.1153 in this chapter.

1163 Unfortunately, due to the shutdown of Islamist internet platforms mentioned above (n.1157 in this chapter), including the official website of the IEA, not all citations in the IS publications could be checked against versions posted there as authorized statements. The assessment provided here is, therefore, almost exclusively based on the versions eventually published in *al-Ṣumūd* alone, while bearing in mind the possibility that the pronouncements released originally may have been edited by the IEA media department before their reissue in the magazine. Still, adding crucial phrases such as "liberation of the homeland" (*taḥrīr al-waṭan*), and replacing the word "Afghānistān" in the original with "al-Imāra al-Islāmiyya" appears to provide good grounds not to suspect them of having been deliberately altered in *Dābiq*: compare Anon., 'Qāʿidat al-Ẓawāhirī' [see above, n.1 155], 24, with 'Bayān [. . .] bi-munāsibat ʿīd al-fiṭr [. . .] li-ʿām 1433[h]', *al-Ṣumūd* 7/4 (1433/2012), 4; 'Risālat amīr al-muʾminīn – ḥafiẓuhu allāh – bi-munāsibat ifrāj al-qāda al-khamsa min muʿtaqal Ghwāntānāmū', *al-Ṣumūd* 9/2 (1435/2014), 2.

discourse, we need to properly appraise these stances that appear so disturbing to the activists of the IS.

No other position seems to have bothered the IS activists, especially those with no background and no interest in the cultural particularities of the Pashtun Borderland, as much as that of international relations. While the IEA of the 1990s was well known for its predominantly indifferent, at times, however, even hostile attitude towards the wider geopolitical picture, following the forced termination of the IEA central government in 2001, its leadership carefully reassessed various of its earlier views and practices, including the IEA's attitude towards the political world outside Afghanistan. While now emphatically 'reassuring the world that [the IEA] will not', as persistently feared in particular by the three different administrations of the USA since the *al-Qāʿida* attacks on 11 September 2001, 'allow anyone to use its soil against any others', it was seeking instead

> to establish mutual relations with the world, especially with the Islamic world and the neighbouring countries in an atmosphere of mutual respect and joint interests [*min al-iḥtirām al-mutabādila wa'l-maṣāliḥ al-mutabadala*], in the light of Islamic teachings and our national interests. [. . .] Likewise, it declares to everyone that it respects all international laws and treaties in the light of the teachings of the Islamic *dīn* and our national interest [*maṣāliḥinā al-waṭaniyya*].[1164]

This radically changed attitude towards the world outside Afghanistan, still doubted by many even today, is in fact quite consistent with various points highlighted in the preceding chapters of the present study.

On the other hand, it also helps to explain the ever more categorical rejection of the IEA by the activists of the IS and the eventual escalation of the initially only polemical confrontation between the two entities in a formal collective *takfīr* on the IEA and everyone associated with or even sympathetic to it, by a certain Mufti Abū Ilyās Ḥanīfī on 10 Shaʿbān 1336 / 29 May 2015.[1165] Although no further information on him could be gleaned, it seems quite plausible to regard him as one of the IS *ʿulamāʾ* critically mentioned by Muslim Dōst whose narrow interpretations of the *shariʿa* would be regularly employed by the IS leadership in Khurasan to legitimize all those atrocities committed against the subaltern civilian population in the parts of the Pashtun Borderland that continue to be under its control.[1166]

For the IEA, however, to open up to the political world outside, unforgivably for the IS including even the Islamic Republic of Iran,[1167] was obviously the

[1164] 'Bayān [. . .] bi-munāsibat ʿīd al-fiṭr [. . .] li-ʿām 1433[h]', *al-Ṣumūd* 7/4 (1433/2012), 4.

[1165] See Ḥanīfī (1436h). Only one month after this *fatwa* had been issued, another, shorter, one with a similar tenor was published in *Dābiq* 2/6 (1436h), 18–24.

[1166] See Aḥmad (2015).

[1167] On 18 May 2015, an official delegation of the IEA from their office in Doha, led by Sayyid Muḥammad Ṭayyib Āghā (b. 1396/1976), the then-head of its Political

result of their *fiqh al-wāqiʿ* in application, which has obviously been on their radar at least since 2009.[1168] It is useful to recall two important matters in this regard. First of all, an altered course of action in appreciation of actual circumstances does not imply any change of their ideological positions. Secondly, in all the known cases, it is this very concession to the present conditions in which one had to operate that has earned those who argue for temporary tactical adjustments the accusation of apostasy by their more uncompromising counterparts: we have encountered this in the case of the JIM and *al-Qāʿida*, of the early *al-Qāʿida* and its later manifestations in Saudi Arabia and the Fertile Crescent, of *al-Qāʿida* of whatever stage and the IS, which, after all, had grown out of the former, and finally now also of the IEA and the IS.[1169]

This ever more aggravated conflict between former compatriots, something we have already encountered in the Pashtun Borderland in the cases of the quarrelling former associates to the *Ṭarīqah-yi Muḥammadiyyah* during the late nineteenth and early twentieth centuries, that of Frontier Deobandis and their renegade offshoot, the JITS[a], and eventually between the JITS[a] and its renegade offshoot constituted by those around Shams al-Dīn al-Afghānī, turns out to be indeed a standard feature of controversies over religious authenticity, especially in many governance-orientated Muslim circles actively devoted to Islamic reformulation.

This feature, while perhaps really a core marker of intrareligious debates on orthodoxy and orthopraxy in general, becomes more pronounced the more the rivalling parties are inclined to use physical force to see their respective interpretation through as the only truly authentic one.[1170] Since, philosophically speaking, "truth" cannot be established by logical conclusion procedures if the claims are solely based on religious creed, such conflict is bound to escalate to the extreme either verbally in polemical denunciation and theologically grounded legal judgements regarding the fidelity of the respective opponent, or physically in attempts to terminate the opponent by way of warfare. Such

Commission and close aide to Mullā Muḥammad ʿUmar, travelled to Tehran for informal talks on regional matters of mutual concern, see Anon., 'Hayʾat-i siyāsī-yi Ṭālibān vārid-i Īrān shud', *Rūz'nāmah-yi Kayhān* 73/240 (30 Ardībihisht 1394sh / 01 Shaʿbān 1436h), 3. This visit, which appears to have been rather clandestine (see, e.g., 'Foreign Ministry Claims Ignorance over Taliban Visit', *Tehran Times* 11 273 [31 Ardībihisht 1394sh / 02 Shaʿbān 1436h / 21 May 2015], 2), was instantly used by the IS establishment, both in the Fertile Crescent and in the Pashtun Borderland, to sustain their heresiological take on the IEA, see, for example, Ḥanīfī (1436h), 10; Anon., 'Qāʿidat al-Ẓawāhirī' [see above, n.1 155], 24f.; Anon., 'al-Rāfiḍa: min Ibn Sabāʾ ilá 'l-dajjāl', *Dābiq* 13 (1437h), 32–45, here 39f.; al-Shāmī (1438/2017), 375.

1168 See Section 4.5.3.

1169 See Nedza (2020), 261–4.

1170 This following argument has been presented in much greater detail in Hartung (2013c), esp. 80–94.

conflict actually cannot be settled by any kind of conciliation between the rivalling parties, but must – from the perspective of those involved in arguments of this kind – necessarily result in the ultimate victory of one over the other, because it is only in this ultimate triumph that one can find the proof that one belongs to the *firqa nājiyya*, which, according to the Prophetic "*Ḥadīth* of the Seventy-Three Factions",[1171] will be the only community worthy of salvation in the Hereafter. No wonder, therefore, that, despite the many overtly optimistic reports that have declared the IS in the Pashtun Borderland ultimately finished,[1172] their violent encounters with the IEA erupted again immediately after the former had taken over the central government of Afghanistan for the second time in August 2021,[1173] and, tragically, may continue to do so until only one side is left standing.

[1171] See n.1 023 in this chapter.

[1172] Prominently among those who went public with this evidently flawed assessment were not only numerous governments and military establishments in nation-states of the Global North, but also very much the IEA itself: see, for example, Bariyālay Khatīzvāl, 'DĀʿISHī fitnē kī ākhirī hichkiyāṇ', *Sharīʿat* 8/7 (1441/2019), 18f.; Shāhid Ghaznīvāl, 'DĀʿISH kā fanā hōtā manṣūbah', *Sharīʿat* 8/9 (1441/2019); Anon., 'al-Iftitāḥiyya: maqtal al-Baghdādī wa-taṣrīḥāt Trāmb al-fārigha', *al-Ṣumūd* 14/9 (1441/2019), 1; ʿAbd al-Matīn al-Kābulī, 'al-DAWĀʿISH lā al-islām naṣirū wa-lā al-aʿdāʾ kasirū!', *al-Ṣumūd* 15/4 (1441/2020), 18f.; also Ruttig (2015).

[1173] On 26 August 2021, IS cadre ʿAbd al-Raḥmān al-Lūjarī carried out a disastrous suicide attack outside Kabul International Airport where hundreds of civilians were waiting for their opportunity to leave Afghanistan after the takeover of the central government by the IEA only eleven days earlier: see Anon., 'bi-ʿAmaliyya istishhādiyya wa-malāḥim buṭūliyya junūd al-khilāfa yawaqiʿūna ʿasharāt al-qatlá wa'l-jarḥá fī ṣufūf mīlīshiyā Ṭālibān', *al-Nabāʾ* 7/9 (1443h), 1 and 4f.

5

Epilogue: Who and What Were – and Are – (The) Taliban?

Now, at least for the time being, we have reached the end of our journey across the Pashtun Borderland through the last few centuries, in our attempt to trace the ideational roots of those who gained international renown as "The Taliban". What emerges is a rather complex and multilayered picture that seems to make it even more difficult to adequately frame "The Taliban". However, it would perhaps have to be considered a disproportionate effort if the only result were to affirm that the ideational and ideological underpinnings of those who, as the ṬIT and IEA, governed most of Afghanistan between 1996 and 2001, and have done again, since the summer of 2021, are not so straightforward, as investigative journalist Ahmed Rashid prominently claimed back in 2000 (and confirmed in each of the subsequent editions and revisions of his best-selling *Taliban: Militant Islam, Oil and Fundamentalism in Central Asia*).[1] While there remains a need to challenge this still dominant narrative, because it serves as a reference point for such exceptionally crude characterizations as on the German Wikipedia site, where "The Taliban" are called 'a Deobandian-Islamist terrorist group' (*deobandisch-islamistische Terrorgruppe*),[2] the approach chosen here is rather special.

Instead of following the path of most extant works and putting the focus on political and military events between the early 1980s and now, as well as on the leading figures involved therein, the present work constitutes an attempt to understand the ideational background of these events and persons as a *longue durée* history of Islamically motivated socio-political activism in a topographically, geopolitically, socio-economically, politically, culturally,

1 See Chapter 1. Rashid's book has been republished under a variety of different subtitles, depending on the respective publisher. Eminent British journalist Patrick Seale (d. 2015), formerly of *The Observer*, reviewed this work for *The Sunday Times*, pointing out that it had been the prime source of background information for then-British PM Anthony Blair (r. 1997–2007) and his close associates. Almost every online bookseller uses this very review to advertise the singular importance of Rashid's work.

2 URL: http://de.wikipedia.org/wiki/Taliban (accessed 9 November 2022). Since the references in this entry stretch to 2020 and, moreover, this particular passage had not provoked any critical intervention in the adjacent discussion forum, we are left with little choice but to conclude that this is indeed regarded as currently valid and rather unproblematic.

ethnically and religiously distinct and highly complex landscape: the Pashtun Borderland.

From such a vantage point, the activists of the ṬIT / IEA appear as only one of many and often simultaneously occurring manifestations of a wider and historically rather deep discursive contestation over the monopoly of definition of the semantics of the term "talib", and its plural "taliban", in this region, which does indeed appear to be currently dominated by the IEA and its younger stepchild in the east, the TṬP. Even so, leading representatives of the ṬIT / IEA, such as prominently ʿAbd al-Salām Ẕaʿīf, have demonstrated their awareness of the discursive variety of meaning, a fact that also allowed them to toy around with the polysemy of the term and highlight one meaning over the others at their convenience.

In his memoirs, as edited and translated by Strick van Linschoten and Kuehn, Ẕaʿīf presented a very functional definition of "*taliban*", stating that

> [t]here is a common misconception that "the *Taliban*" came into being in 1994. In fact, the word *Taliban* is the plural form of *Talib*, meaning "student". As such, as long as there have been *madrassas*, there have been religious students or *Taliban*.[3]

Leaving aside the fact that Ẕaʿīf's grammatical explanation indicates his deep rootedness in the Persianate context, the one-time ambassador to Pakistan segues without any difficulty into the present of his narrative and continues that 'the *Taliban* have mostly eschewed politics, but the government tried to draw them in by pressuring them to be involved in the land reform, or by threatening them in other ways'.[4]

Rest assured, this is certainly not intended to accuse Ẕaʿīf of shrewd strategic thinking when presenting the above. It rather shows how easy it is to relate a functional definition of the term "*taliban*" to the very concrete religio-political organization of the 1990s within the semantic space that a distinguished Pashtun Borderland actor such as Ẕaʿīf inhabits. Besides, a functional definition such as Ẕaʿīf's is enmeshed in this particular space in a much older ethical one, exemplarily promoted in popular literary expression, such as the folk story of Ṭālib Jān and Gul Bashrah that has been diligently analysed and subsequently related to the adherents and supporters of the ṬIT / IEA by Caron.[5] This distinct moral universe, which is expressed in Pashto folk prose and even more so in poetry, has been traced back here to the seventeenth-century Sufi poet Raḥmān Bābā as some kind of a paradigmatic

[3] Zaeef (2010), 10. The spelling and italicization follow the original, whereas the punctuation has been harmonized. Also, compare the image of the *madrasah* student in Ẕaʿīf (1390sh), 14–23.

[4] Zaeef (2010), 10.

[5] See Caron (2012a). Admittedly, this perspective is already somewhat immanent in Edwards (1996).

representative of a guidance-orientated religious stance. This perspective, in turn, appears to appeal predominantly to the subaltern elements in Pashtun society; it poses a counter-draft to a rather self-confident elitist governance-orientated paradigm exemplarily expressed in the much more mundane poetry of tribal community leader Khūshḥāl Khān Khaṫṫak, Raḥmān Bābā's near contemporary.

The two ideal-typical ethical paradigms also very much reflect the socio-economic and political structures in the tribally organized communities of the Pashtun Borderland, encapsulated in the dichotomy of "senior" (*məshər*) and "have-not" (*kəshər*), the latter very often also applying to the rural youth, and almost comprehensively to females. One way to compensate for socio-economic and political deprivation is the stress on subaltern guidance-orientated religiosity that pivots on an exceptionally strong notion of Islamic piety (*taqvá*). This particular inner disposition, in turn, manifests itself to the outside by compassion (*raḥəm*), as well as a strong sense of social and economic justice (*ʿadl*) and equity (*inṣāf*). Coupled with the male youthfulness (*źəvān*) that characterizes the student of religion in popular Pashto literary expression, finally, this disposition carries a strong potential for uncompromising activism against any perceived injustice and inequity, be it even at the expense of one's own life.

Such an inclination towards activism, alongside an audacious disregard for one's own material existence, appears quite consistent in the light of the discursive marginalization of the subaltern in every aspect of mundane life, tellingly epitomized in the famous line from Marx's *Manifesto of the Communist Party* (1848) that '[t]he proletarians have nothing to lose but their chains', but, instead, '[t]hey have a world to win'.[6] Moreover, those who have little to lose in the here and now are said to be more prone than others to eschatological promises, regardless of whether they are embedded in the apocalyptic narratives of religious traditions or, as in the case of Marx, those referring to a social utopia.

However strictly locally confined these eschatologically charged subaltern socio-political activisms were, a historical recourse to the formative period of Islam provides a powerful universalistic reference point and makes it thus appear as if they were paradigmatically grounded in the phenomenon of the *futuwwāt*, or, Persianized, *javān'mardiyān*: associations of young unmarried men, in which pre-Islamic Arab tribal ethical ideals of bounty, hospitality and courage coalesced with the early Islamic ideals of fighting in the Path of God (*ghazwa*, or *jihād fī sabīl allāh*). Subsequently, during the early expansion of the Islamic caliphate in the seventh and eighth centuries CE, these associations were prominently found at the outer limits of the Islamic realm where such men had been charged with the active safeguarding of the standard of Islamic

[6] Marx and Engels (1956–90), IV: 493 (translation by Samuel Moore).

ethics in these delicate spaces, be it by setting individual examples of deep Islamic piety, by active dissemination of the core Islamic teachings, or, more often than not, also by the use of arms.[7] From the ninth century CE onwards, however, the public perception of *futuwwāt* was no longer exclusively positive, which resulted greatly from the fact that the intransigency of their adherents would increasingly threaten the political status quo after the era of the so-called Rightly Guided Caliphs: thus, historiographers tied to the various courts of the later caliphs and regional Muslim rulers portrayed them frequently as excessive, fanatical and violent, and, therefore, a constant danger to the refined Islamicate culture of the metropolis. Consequently, these writers expressed their general contempt of the *fityān*, or *javān'mardān*, by using such pejorative appellations as "vagrants" (*ʿayyārūn*) or "villains" (*shuṭṭār*), at least implicitly also pointing dismissively to their confidently acknowledged subalternity.[8] Still, from the fifth / eleventh-century Persian *Qābūs'nāmah* it can be gleaned first of all that these *javān'mardān* were quite a prominent feature in remote mountain regions, and, second, that they overlapped prominently with 'those who possess exoteric insight and the mendicant Sufis [*khudāvand-i maʿrifat-i ẓāhir'and va fuqarāʾ-i taṣavvuf*]',[9] the very societal stratum to which the cultural type of the *talib* in the Pashtun Borderland relates as much as he does to his various historically concrete manifestations in this region. What is more, even the observation of the rather contemptuous attitude of urbanite elite actors towards them is of great significance for our matter at hand, because it corresponds to a surprising degree to that of the *məshərān* and their respective retinue in the Pashtun Borderland, in fact, right up to the present day.

The reason for this is not difficult to see: while utilizing the universalistic Islamic moral frame of reference, the young male subaltern activists were deeply enough ingrained in the socio-political and cultural landscape of the Pashtun Borderland to focus their attention on, and thrust of action towards, its inside. By doing so, they posed a challenge first and foremost to the position of power of the *məshərān*; their counter-agitation was, therefore, utilitarian, to secure the equilibrium of power in the diverse Borderland communities intact. Because their positions were ultimately rooted in the materiality of the life-worlds around them, their references were informed by an alternative governance-orientated religiosity that was quite different from those that also prominently inhabit the cultural stereotype of the *talib* as expressed in popular literary articulation, and who have to resort to

7 See Taeschner (1979), 41–52. See also Hartung (2019a), 321f., 330 and 332.

8 See, for example, al-Ṭabarī (1426/2005), V: 1 790–805; Ibn al-Athīr (1407/1987), IX: 306; Ibn Iskandar (1312sh), 179–92.

9 ibid., 181.

eschatological arguments for pitting their moral superiority against worldly status based predominantly on material wealth.

The *məshərān* subscribed, therefore, much more to imperial ideologies, be it those on which the larger polities around the Pashtun Borderland rested in pre-modern times, or the one that was introduced to the discourse by the various colonial projects of European powers in the nineteenth and early twentieth centuries, to which eventually also the subsequent nation-states in the region subscribed. We have encountered examples of this every now and then across the previous chapters, starting with Khūshḥāl Khān Khaṭṭak in the late seventeenth century, if not earlier, and gaining decisive momentum with the establishment of the Durrani Empire.

Nonetheless, Khūshḥāl Khān would still complement his ethnocentric deliberations on governance with references to the universalistic Islamic framework and also the Persianate imperial ideology of early Durrani rule maintained a strong emphasis on the Islamicity of the dynasty's founder, Aḥmad Shāh. The more, however, modern imperial ideologies, such as nationalism and its auxiliaries "modernization" and "centralization", were embraced by "governance-orientated" local elite actors, the more the Islamic frame of reference got pushed into the background, suggesting that those who would still ground their demands for societal change in it were at best stuck in the mud, or worse, are to be considered *pueri robusti*, rendered recalcitrant by their distorted nature and, therefore, in constant dire need of being checked, more often than not by coercive force.

This process has, in fact, been continuous since the establishment of Barakzay rule over the increasingly firmly hedged territory of Afghanistan between 1826 and 1973, capitalizing on the proto-national identity the Durrani rulers had tried to instil in the hitherto very much locally confined and ethnically quite diverse communities across the wider Pashtun Borderland, as well as on the spread of ethno-nationalistic sentiments across the wider region at around the same time, sentiments which would eventually cause the political elites of the Islamic Republic of Pakistan serious worries. In this light, the republican governments of Muḥammad Dāvūd Khān, the PDPA and, finally, the governments of Ḥāmid Karzay and Ashraf Ghanī between 2001 and 2021, appear as little more than logical consequences of the groundwork laid much earlier.[10]

On the other side stood the countless and predominantly subaltern rural communities in the Pashtun Borderland, who had neither interest in nor understanding of centralization and modernization attempts by the respective governments in Kabul. Used for centuries to handling their community affairs themselves, and hardly ever dependent on subsidies dealt out by a central

[10] See, for example, Dupree (1973), 417–658; Kakar (1979); Olesen (1995), 20–198; Askar (2019).

government with little to no knowledge of the conditions on the ground, various tribal communities repeatedly tried to actively resist what they regarded as a usurpation of their long-standing autonomy.[11] The less sincere the references of the governing elites to the Islamic framework were perceived to be, the more it became consciously employed by many of those who resisted any imperial encroachment. Consistently, therefore, those who endorsed the armed resistance of Pashtun Borderland tribal communities to all such top-down attempts towards centralization and modernization were religious functionaries from the very same communities, prominently including here the Ṣāḥib of Haḋḋah and the Sartōr Faqīr in the late nineteenth century and the Ḥājjī Ṣāḥib of Turangzay in the early twentieth century.

Support from urban religious power centres, conspicuously here the Ḥaẕarāt of Kabul's Shōr Bāzār, whose earlier privileged position became equally vulnerable due to the ruler's increasingly secularist modernization efforts, added further weight to the legitimization of active disobedience by religious dignitaries from the subaltern rural communities of the Pashtun Borderland. Their rhetoric against the despised government policies was quite naturally Islamically charged, thus amplifying the local perception of righteous resistance as *jihād* against unbelieving enemies of Islam.

Here, finally, lies the crux of what, at least analytically, distinguishes the cultural stereotype of the *talib* from historically concrete socio-political phenomena such as the ṬIT / IEA and, although only to an extent, the TṬP. In the course of continuous conflict with societal elites who subscribed increasingly to secular political ideologies, an Islamically grounded "governance orientation" began to gradually impact the hitherto prevalent "guidance orientation" of the subaltern activists, forcing them increasingly to address the dilemma of subscribing to a universalistic frame of reference while simultaneously confining their activities solely to their native environment. To make matters more complicated still, the growing impact of an Islamic "governance orientation" went hand in hand with growing aspirations to establish the prevalence of a universally applicable interpretation of Islamic beliefs and practices, against the culturally distinct ones in the Pashtun Borderland. In this light, the advent of the *Ṭarīqah-yi Muḥammadiyyah* around Sayyid Aḥmad Barēlvī and Shāh Ismāʿīl Dihlavī and its later local manifestations as *Jamāʿāt-i Mujāhidīn* ties in well with the efforts of early Deobandi activists around "Shaykh al-Hind" Maḥmūd al-Ḥasan and "Imām-i Inqilāb" ʿUbaydallāh Sindhī towards a translocal notion of Islam that could, therefore, not permit any culturally grounded distinction. It intensified further with the rise of the at least initially culturally still rather distinct Salafi Islam from the *Dār al-Qurʾān* at Panjpir and its eventual confluence with the much more universalistic one of the *Ahl-i Ḥadīs̱*, and culminated finally in the decisive impact of the Islamist ideology as

[11] See Olesen (1995), 81–8, 133–8 and 144–65.

represented to the east of the Durand Line by the JiI and by the various Afghan organizations that grew out of the SJM in the 1970s.

Of course, this is not to say that such endeavours towards conformity with the Islamic *shari'a* never happened previously; the respective undertakings of the Ākhūnd Darvīzah in the seventeenth century and of ʿUmar Ćamkanī in the eighteenth century are only two cases in point. Yet, especially the efforts of the latter and his descendants regarding the issue of affirmation, *tashahhud*, during the ritual prayer are evidence of the continued confinement of these discussions to the Pashtun Borderland and its inhabitants, little suited to constitute a common ground with Muslim practitioners elsewhere, who reacted in a rather startled way to the vehemence with which their Pashtun peers tried to enforce what they regarded as sound Islamic practice. Unsurprisingly, therefore, the more Muslim activists in the Pashtun Borderland began to open up to the transregionally applicable interpretations of the Islamic *shari'a* that arrived there from outside the region, the less the *tashahhud* issue appeared to play a role in the mainstreaming of Islamic beliefs and practices across the region. Still, all these efforts did not deter Muslim communities across the Pashtun Borderland from continuing to express their religiosity as deemed sustained by local tradition.

This, in fact, was the ideational environment in which the ṬIT emerged in the mid 1990s. Hardened by a decade of strenuous and painful guerrilla war against the PDPA regime in Kabul and its Soviet allies, as well as the Afghan Civil War that followed immediately, its affiliates appear to have already adopted numerous elements from various of the ideological currents alive around them into their own ideological universe. Still, this did not necessarily result in the rejection of all the local Islamic beliefs and customs that the proponents of Islamism and Salafism, as the most significant ideologies at play in the Pashtun Borderland at that moment in time, would have outright spurned and persecuted, but leaned more towards the socially less disruptive approach to redressing them that the early Deobandis in the region had chosen. After all, it was the very successful spread of "Deobandiyyat" in the Pashtun Borderland, with its first major institutional expression in the *Dār al-ʿUlūm-i Ḥaqqāniyyah* at Akōṛah Khaṫṫak, that contributed substantially to a shift in the demographics of governance-orientated and guidance-orientated religiosity towards the latter, a ratio that would start to change only from the late 1960s onwards. Until the exceptionally strained situation in the Pashtun Borderland following the coup d'état of the PDPA in Afghanistan in 1978 finally caused leading representatives of "Frontier Deobandiyyat" to subscribe to a more violent approach, hitherto unprecedented religious mass education of predominantly subaltern rural young men had remained the means of choice in the Pashtun Borderland since the times of the Shaykh al-Hind.

Nevertheless, one must not overlook the impact of the "Deobandiyyat"-linked TJ on preparing the ground for this consequential shift towards a stronger "governance orientation": by adding an actively missionary component to the educational efforts of Deobandis in the Pashtun Borderland, young Deobandi students – *taliban*, in the sense of Mullā ʿAbd al-Salām Ẓaʿīf's functional definition above – were emboldened to spread this interpretation of Islam in their respective home communities and to openly confront all beliefs and practices, including socio-economic and political ones, that ran counter to it.

Even though organizations such as the TJ acted on a global scale, in the Pashtun Borderland even the Islamic frame of reference remained strongly local. At least initially, the ṬIT was no exception in this regard, as indicated by the great reverence its leadership showed towards Nabī Muḥammadī and which, in fact, established him as a principal role model for the movement, if, however, more implicitly. He was not one of those widely travelled local *ʿulamāʾ* with an expansive network of contacts in various parts of the Muslim world, especially the MENA region, but perhaps the last of the solely inward-looking traditional religious dignitaries in the immediate Pashtun Borderland, who was, nonetheless, deeply involved in political affairs, first as a local representative in the *Vuləsī Jirgah* of Afghanistan in the late 1960s and later as commander-in-chief of his own militia in resistance to the PDPA government, the ḤII. Yet, he would not want to play any role in any Islamic government that was to form after the PDPA had been ousted from power, a fact that increased his reputation especially among the rural subalterns in the most disadvantaged parts of the Pashtun Borderland, in hindsight of the devastating activities unleashed by the various former Islamist militia leaders in their quest for supreme power over Afghanistan. Thus, Nabī Muḥammadī very much embodied the popular cultural stereotype of the *talib*, while, at the same time, his political activities at a rather high level already foreshadowed the slightly different course that the ṬIT would eventually take.

In this light it seems that, although the establishment of the Islamic Emirate by the ṬIT in 1996 was more a matter of necessity than volition, it was soon to change, increasingly manifesting itself in their ideological set-up. Of crucial importance in this regard turned out to be the numerous volunteers to the *jihād* against the PDPA–Soviet nexus from other parts of the Muslim world, first and foremost the MENA region, many of whom evaded prosecution in their home countries for radical Islamist/Salafist activities. For this reason, many stayed put even after the end of PDPA rule and continued to use the distinct features of especially the uplands of the Pashtun Borderland as a convenient sanctuary and base of operations. Tolerated on tribal land on the condition that they would not interfere at all in local affairs, it was there and then that especially Arab militant Salafists elaborated and discussed intensively key components of their own ideological frame of reference, and, by virtue of ʿAbdallāh ʿAzzām's logistic hub, the MKh, their various reformulations were also published and disseminated inside the Pashtun Borderland, where some elements of their much more legally sustained ideological outlines fell on fertile ground and were subsequently adopted by their local peers. Yet, we must not forget that this process was facilitated by the fact that, despite the nowadays frequent averment that these elements were actually alien to the indigenous culture of the Pashtun Borderland and had been introduced solely by those mainly Arab *francs-tireurs*, practices such as the defamation of religious opponents as unbelievers have actually been a long-standing feature of socio-political discourse framed in religious terms in the region: the controversy between the Ṣāḥib of Kōṫah and his followers, on the one hand, and those of the Sayyidō Bābā, on the other, in the middle of the nineteenth century is just one case in point. What changed now, however, was the insistence on putting *takfīr* on a proper legal basis and, subsequently, seeing the process through to its ultimate material consequences for the accused.

The ṬIT initially stayed out of this; the severe punitive measures they dealt out during their first central government and which subsequently came to define them in the eyes of observers from the Global North were based on interpretations of Islamic criminal law and, thus, understood as castigation (*taʿzīr*) rather than deriving from the practice of expelling perceived culprits from the community of believers and persecuting them as unbelievers. This attitude is, by and large, maintained to this day, causing, of course, a need for strong justification, something that appears so far to be equally absent.

Nevertheless, this certainly does not imply that the leadership and supporter base of the ṬIT, in the meantime renamed the IEA, remained completely immune to external ideological influences. What was required, however, was a combusting agent in this process, and the severe consequences they faced for their refusal to extradite Usāma ibn Ladin to the US-American authorities on account of his crucial role in the violent attacks on their sovereignty, culminating in the strikes on US territory on 11 September 2001, seem to have served exactly this purpose. With its central government ousted by the military invasion of Afghanistan by a coalition of forces from the Global North, the focus of the IEA now shifted towards fighting what the *al-Qāʿida* leadership had already earlier epitomized in the USA as the new infidel occupational force in Afghanistan. Even though for quite distinct reasons, the fact that the IEA and *al-Qāʿida* nominally shared the same enemy made the IEA much more susceptible to external ideological influences than ever before. After all, its first central government, however cruel, appeared to manifest itself more as an expression of the urban–rural divide in the region and had its most vivid expression, therefore, in the metropoles of Afghanistan, first and foremost, Kabul, while in the traditionally very conservative villages of the Pashtun Borderland very little apparently changed in terms of everyday life. What applied here instead was the highland–lowland divide, as a contemporary manifestation of deeply rooted tribal rivalries, something that is well exemplified by Jalāl al-Dīn Ḥaqqānī's seeming unease with regard to subordinating his own position of command in the Lōyah Paktia region to an IEA leadership predominantly of lowland provenance. The deteriorating situation after 2001, however, resulting not least in the relocation of the operational bases for the resistance to the foreign military presence and its approved governments of Afghanistan to these very villages, would now also drastically impact the hitherto little perturbed rural communities of the Pashtun Borderland, especially those situated in what, until its formal integration into national territory as late as May 2018, constituted the FATA of Pakistan.

Under these circumstances, ideological stimuli from Arab Salafist circles active in the Pashtun Borderland were more readily received by the cadres and sympathizers of the nascent TṬP than by their peers in the IEA, which maintained the confinement in scope of its activities solely to Afghan national territory, with the aim of regaining its former position of power. While the IEA never provided a solid Islamic legal justification for going against the USA-sanctioned Afghan governments under Karzay and Ghanī, the TṬP's focus on the Pakistani state and all its executive bodies instead constituted a convenient intersection for the transfer of legal arguments from Arab Salafists that could serve the legitimization of such explicitly anti-government activities. Prominent in this regard was the extension of the applicability of the legal practice of *takfīr* to collectives as well as the highest government representatives, employing here what is subsumed under the concept of *takfīr al-ḥākim* and the related reinterpretation of Ibn Taymiyya's concept of the "(*shari'a-*)resisting group", the *ṭā'ifa mumtaniʿa*, as undertaken, discussed and gradually refined by the likes of Sayyid Imām al-Sharīf, Ayman al-Ẓawāhirī or Abū Muḥammad al-Maqdisī.

However, beyond merely discussing and further elaborating them, as these "Arab Afghans" did, the leadership of the TṬP actually employed these concepts for religious legitimization of their various violent activities: while, for example, the assassination of then-Prime Minister of Pakistan Bēnaẓīr Bhuṭṭō in December 2007 followed clearly the logic of *takfīr al-ḥākim*, there was an attempt to justify the atrocious massacre at the Army Public School in Peshawar on 16 December 2014, ordered by then-TṬP supreme *amīr* Mullā Faẓlallāh and outright condemned by the central leaderships both of the IEA and of *al-Qāʿida*,[12] by recourse to Sayyid Imām's recasting of the concept of *ṭā'ifa mumtaniʿa*, explicitly referring to the arguments provided by Wahhabi

[12] As indicated above (Section 4.5.5, n.1 054), the severe discord between the IEA leadership and *al-Qāʿida*, on one side, and the TṬP, on the other, is predominantly over the issue of supreme leadership and wider strategic orientation. The harsh criticism that the TṬP leadership faced from its *al-Qāʿida* counterpart extended explicitly to 'repulsive attitudes and clear legal errors' (*salbiyātin wa-akhṭā'an sharʿiyya wāḍiḥa*), prominently among them 'excess [*al-tawassuʿ*] in killing, excess in using [humans as a] shield [*tatarrus*] that is not executed in accordance with the *shari'a*, the unconcerned killing of common Muslim folk during operations of self-sacrifice in markets, mosques, roads, meeting places of the

scholar Sulaymān ibn ʿAbdallāh Āl al-Shaykh in his *al-Dalāʾil fī Ḥukm Muwālāt Ahl al-Ishrāk*.[13] Taken together, all of these various instances bear clear testimony to the development of strongly Salafist hermeneutical proclivities by the TṬP,[14] a circumstance that proved decisive for the eventual connectivity of substantial TṬP contingents to the IS, very much in opposition to the IEA.

As a result, however, the ruthless pursuit of this course of action provoked equally ruthless responses by the Pakistani state authorities, very much at the expense of the subaltern rural population in the former FATA. Besides becoming victims to the merciless retribution by Pakistani armed forces,[15] the TṬP cadres enacted their own understanding of "*taliban*-ness", in which what Caron had established as a trope of a rather fluid anti-elite male Pashtun youth culture counter to the otherwise highly regulated social etiquettes in sedentary local setting[16] coincided with an aggressive religious self-righteousness exacerbated by the interpretation of the current realities through

people and their congregations [. . .], and excess in accusing Muslims of apostasy' (al-Lībī and al-Lībī [1431/2010], 1).

This reproach, moreover by one of the chief propagators of using Muslim civilians as human shields in asymmetrical warfare (see Section 4.5.5, n.1 082), is, of course, not at all consistent with the fact that *al-Qāʿida* itself, as well as, from around 2004 onwards, the IEA, have systematically used suicide attacks against civilian targets themselves. Furthermore, such attacks, prominently that on the American University of Afghanistan in Kabul on 24 August 2016, had been somewhat pre-emptively justified, for example, by "Mujāhid" (1389sh/2010), 270–310. The reasons for the condemnation of TṬP attacks on civilian targets, such as the Army Public School in Peshawar in 2014, by the IEA must, therefore, be sought elsewhere. It is contended here, at least for the moment, that they were, at least partly, similar to the reprimand of Ḥakīmallāh Maḥsūd in 2010: the TṬP was treated like a recalcitrant youngster who had to toe the line specified by the two older organizations, otherwise 'we will have to take decisive public legal steps [*khuṭuwāt sharʿiyya ʿalaniyya ḥāsma*] from our side' (al-Lībī and al-Lībī [1431/2010], 2). Additionally, the then-decentralized IEA might also have been concerned about the repercussions that retaliatory measures by the Pakistani armed forces could possibly have on them.

[13] See, for example, Ḥuẓayfah Khālid, 'Pishāvar vāqiʿah . . . jurnaylī manṣūbē "zayr-i takmīl" hē', *Navā-yi Afghān Jihād* 8/1 (1436/2015), 37f. and 46.

[14] See Anon., 'Kyā favāj kē afrād par lafẓ "murtadd" kā aṭlāq jāʾiz hē? Javān mēṇ sē bi-Rāh-i Rast nah laṛē us kā sharʿī ḥukm kiyā hē?', *Iḥyā-yi Khilāfat* 9 (1436/2014), 16.

[15] According to an official estimate by the Geneva-based Internal Displacement Monitoring Centre, the conflict between the TṬP and its compatriots (among them *al-Qāʿida*, the IMU, the LJħ and the TNSM), on the one hand, and the Pakistani armed forces, on the other, in various parts of the former FATA since 2004 has resulted in over five million internally displaced civilians to date, many of whom are still not able to return to their homes (see URL: www.internal-displacement.org/countries/pakistan#overview [accessed 9 November 2022]). The number of civilian casualties remains undisclosed.

[16] See Caron (2012a), 62–76. See also, for example, Khaṫṫak (2005), 103–5; Gharvāl (1360sh), 104f.; Malgarē (1352sh), 8f. As such, the *talib* was also becoming an object of romantic phantasies, especially for secluded young females, who are usually not given

the prism of Sunni Islamic eschatology, resulting in intimidation and extortion of the local population from which many of these cadres originated.[17] This increasing alienation of those in the Pashtun Borderland who identify themselves as *taliban* of whatever kind from their socio-economic and political embeddedness has, therefore, consequently resulted in the increasing marginalization of the formerly so greatly appreciated 'folk symbol [of the *talib*] in Pashto expressive arts',[18] which has given way to one that is instead firmly associated with a cynical disregard for all traditional norms and values that constitute the distinct cultural environment of the Pashtun Borderland, as well as for human life in general. This most recent semantic shift is of exceptional significance, because it appears to be less ephemeral than one might wish, and instead rather irreversible.

Still, and this will conclude our deliberations, the old romantic imaginary of the *talib* has not yet vanished entirely. Instead, it seems as if at least elements of it have been appropriated by those who are either associated with, or at least openly sympathetic to, those who have assembled under the umbrellas of the ṬIT / IEA and TṬP. Under the adverse conditions of perpetual warfare since 1979 and strongly influenced by the various ideational threads discussed in detail in the present book, the formerly 'exuberant carefree happiness' (*mast aw khūshḥāl*)[19] of the fighting *taliban* has been replaced by the trope of honourable masculinity and unconditionally self-sacrificing spirit that radiates from *jihād*-focused Pashto poetry, which was also regularly published in the various Pashto periodicals of the different larger organizations involved in the resistance.[20]

This tradition was also notably carried on in the Pashto periodicals of the IEA.[21] It is reasonable to conclude that at least the adherents to the IEA, if not

much of a choice in the selection of a future husband by the male heads of the household: prominently, see Tapper (1991). See also Khan (2012), 131–48 and 154–6.

17 From informal conversations with numerous, here not further identified, residents of the former FATA at the University of Peshawar in September and October 2017, the impression received was that hardly any extended family is devoid of young male members who have joined either the TṬP or the IEA.

18 Caron (2012a), 60.

19 Khaṭṭak (2005), 105 (translation in Caron [2012a], 67).

20 All the magazines from the various Afghan resistance organizations which have been reviewed for the present book (see the list at the end of the bibliography) regularly carried *jihādī* poetry, predominantly in Pashto, but also in Dari and Urdu. Some of them even established a dedicated section for this: the JIA journal *Mīs̱āq-i Khūn*, for instance, contained a section entitled "In the Treasury of Poetry and Literature" (*Dar kanz-i ʿayn-i shiʿr va adab*), and Jalāl al-Dīn Ḥaqqānī's *Manbaʿ al-Jihād* [P] included one called "Jihad from the Point of Poetry and Literature" (*Jihād də shiʿr aw adab pah palū shūkay*).

21 *Jihādī* poetry regularly features in a dedicated section in all IEA Pashto magazines published from Kabul: *Mōrchal* carries one titled "Fragrances of 'The East'" (*Də Mōrchal vaǵmē*); *Shahāmat* one called "Chapters of Glory" (*Gulvarīne pāṇē*); and *Ćrak* one named "Flowery Coasts" (*Gulkaćūnah*). *Tōrah Bōṛah* carries no dedicated section,

to some extent also those of the TṬP, had consciously embraced the Islamically revised earlier poetic notion of "talib", something that Caron had also detected in the autobiographical statements of Mullā ʿAbd al-Salām Ẓaʿīf when he reminisced that 'we [i.e., the nascent ṬIT] weren't concerned with the world or with our lives; our intentions were pure and every one of us was ready to die as a martyr. When I look back on the love and respect we had for each other, it sometimes seems like a dream.'[22] Under the new circumstances, the theme of love and longing, earlier also carrying an erotic dimension that is implicit in the folk story of Ṭālib Jān and Gul Bashrah, was turned into one of brotherhood and Platonic affection between men joined together by a common and almost transcendent cause.

This, of course, covers only the somewhat elitist perspective of the IEA leadership. For the majority of those youths joining the movement, the erotic dimension remained very much alive, although now within the confines of the associations of young men. This, at least, is suggested by the collection of random studio photographs of young adherents to the ṬIT / IEA in Kandahar collected by German photographer Thomas Dworzak in 2002.[23] Elaborate turbans, extensive use of black eye-liner and soft-focus lenses, wallpapers with flowery gardens and traditional Alpine houses form, especially in shots of two or more men, a clearly homoerotic imaginary, that is socially enshrined throughout Afghanistan and the Pashtun Borderland in the widespread practice of *bachah'bāzī*, or "playing with the boy". In societies where relationships between the sexes outside of wedlock are severely curtailed and sharply monitored by the entire community, such homoerotic practices are not necessarily seen as something that must not be tolerated. The IEA leadership appears to have been conscious of the strong prevalence of this practice in Pashtun rural society, as is evident from the fact that a passage relating to this was added to the 2010 *Lāʾiḥah*: 'It is prohibited that pure boys [*ləghaṛ zənī*] (those who have not grown a beard due to their young age) accompany the *mujāhidīn* in residential areas and military bases.'[24] About one year later, Qārī Muḥammad Yūsuf Aḥmadī, a spokesperson of the IEA, released an authorized statement on the official website of the IEA in which he emphasized the full

but had this kind of poetry scattered throughout each issue. Even *Navā-yi Afghān Jihād* (Urdu), the monthly journal of the JQSQH, contains some *jihādī* poetry in each of its issues. Only *Iḥyā-yi Khilāfat* (Urdu), the magazine of the TṬP offshoot *Jamāʿat al-Aḥrār*, remained by and large aloof from the reproduction of poetry, something that foreshadows the increasing turn to a Salafism-inspired austerity that radiates from later exclusively online publications, such as *Ḥittīn* and *Majallah-yi Taḥrīk-i Ṭālibān-i Pākistān*, and already points towards the future of this group with the IS.

22 Zaeef (2010), 43; also cited in Caron (2012a), 72f.

23 These photographs have been published in Dworzak and Rees (2004).

24 Də Afghānistān Islāmī Imārat (1431/2010), 61.

implementation of the *Lā'iḥah* by their fighters, consequently calling the accusation that they would still adhere to the custom of keeping young adolescent boys with them false propaganda.[25]

From instances like this, we can indeed infer a serious tension between strong traditional local custom, deeply rooted in the Pashtun tribal society, and an Islamic normative framework that transcends ethnicity and territoriality: in other words, between the local reality of the Pashtun Borderland and a quite eclectic Islamic ideology. Just like the earlier poetic folk image of the *talib* and the later Islamically altered one, these two points constitute, in fact, further strands in the formation of the "discourse". Both the rootedness in a distinct local setting and a universalistic Islamic ideology are expressed in the increasingly frequent references to historical figures that serve as role models, almost all of whom have, therefore, consequently figured in the present work.[26]

It seems as if the eclectic character of these references is once more indicative of the difficult-to-resolve tension between the increasingly universal Islamic aspirations of those who are being considered here, especially after the fall of the first IEA central government in late 2001, and their roots in the culturally distinct space of the Pashtun Borderland. However, and here we finally come full circle, the traditional folk imaginary of the *talib* that is tied to the cultural specifics of this particular space, as well as the various and, admittedly, not always logically consistent self-conceptualizations of "The Taliban" that refer to ideational antecedents both from the wider Indo-Afghan region and the Muslim

[25] See Nagamine (2015), 40 and 88.

[26] During the supreme leadership of Ḥakīmallāh Maḥsūd, for example, the TṬP presented itself explicitly as the logical continuation of the anti-colonial activities of the Shaykh al-Hind and his compatriots during World War I: see, for example, Shaykh al-Hind Mawlānā Maḥmūd al-Ḥasan (raḥmat allāh), 'Muvālāt-i kuffār kā kō'ī shar'ī javāz nahīṇ!!!', *Navā-yi Afghān Jihād* 4/3 (1432/2011), back cover; Sayfallāh Khurāsānī, 'Taḥrīk-i Ṭālibān taḥrīk-i Shaykh al-Hind kā tasalsal hē', *Iḥyā-yi Khilāfat* 4/1 (1435/2014), 14f. and 11. On the occasion of the anniversary of the targeted killing of Usāma ibn Lādin in May 2011, the TṬP leadership elaborated this ideational thread further and now included Ṭīpū Sulṭān of Southwest-Indian Mysore, who was killed in 1213/1799 when he boldly confronted the British EIC, Imām Shāmil of Daghestan and Chechnya (d. 1288/1871), who tried to resist the military expansion of the Russian Empire into the Northern Caucasus region, via Sayyid Aḥmad Barēlvī, Sayyid Quṭb and ʿAbdallāh ʿAzzām: see Anon., 'Idāriyyah: ʿarsh-i valā hamārā ilāh ēk hē, kuch aḥad kē sivā ham nahīṇ jāntē!!!', *Navā-yi Afghān Jihād* 6/5 (1434/2014), 2. See also the front cover of the same issue. Finally, also the Ḥājjī Ṣāḥib of Turangzay received his appreciation as a role model *mujāhid* for the TṬP cadres, while, in a poem, Yūnus Khāliṣ was lauded as being on a par with the eighth-century conqueror of India Muḥammad ibn Qāsim al-Thaqāfī (d. 96/715), the vanquisher of the medieval crusaders Ṣalāḥ al-Dīn al-Ayyūbī (d. 589/1193), Aḥmad Shāh Durrānī and the Jordanian *al-Qāʿida* cadre Abū Muṣʿab al-Zarqāwī, see, for example, Sayfallāh Khurāsānī, 'Taḥrīk-i Ṭālibān . . . kā tasalsal hē' (above in this note), 15; Qārī Shuʿayb, 'Yawm-i Āzādī-yi Pākistān', *Majallat-i Taḥrīk-i Tālibān-i Pākistān* 1/1 (1438/2016), 14–17, here 15; "Shimʿūn", 'Khāliṣ Bābā aw Zarqāvī', *Tōrah Bōṛah* 10/1 (1392sh), 27.

world at large, and finally their various references to the earlier poetic image, although now clad in an Islamic garb, are certainly not the only constituents of the contemporary manifestations of the "*taliban* discourse". Very much integral to it is also what German linguist Siegfried Jäger has called "counter discourse", in this case consisting of the politically informed dominant hegemonic image of "The Taliban" in the Global North as terrorists and threats to the integrity of existing nation-states, which is perpetuated by mass media close to the state, as well as the "academic special discourse" dominated by certain disciplines that willingly offer learned support for the value judgements perpetuated by the "counter discourse". Still, what appears schematically plain is, in fact, tightly interlaced and entangled, resulting in the difficulty of trying to make sense of what Michel Foucault, foundational thinker of "discourse" as a societal practice of power relationships, called the 'proliferation of discourses'.[27]

Those not yet overwhelmed and intimidated by the might and complexity of these processes of discourse formation may, nonetheless, attempt to untie the Gordian knot in which the continuously rampant discourses appear by zooming in on collective symbols: cultural stereotypes which are collectively handed down and used. "Talib" and its Persianate plural "taliban" is just one such collective symbol that can, and does, mean different things at different times to different people, and it would, therefore, actually be wonderful if everyone were to make clear in advance from which vantage point she, or he, is speaking before using these terms. However, because this does not seem to fit with the way in which especially colloquial verbal communication works and will, therefore, tend to remain wishful thinking, in cases like the one presented here, some extra sensorium is advisable that allows one to remain constantly aware of the discursiveness of the label "*taliban*" and at least engage in some serious effort to distinguish between the various complexly interlaced discursive strands.

This, in fact, has been attempted in the present book. Considering the socio-economic, political, cultural and religious constitution of a very distinct topographical, socio-cultural and geopolitical space – the Pashtun Borderland – in a historical *longue durée* investigation, a different perspective has been offered on who, or what, the "Taliban", in all its manifestations, might be. Following this trajectory clearly exposes any monocausal explanation for this phenomenon as a rather problematic reduction and simplification of a historically developed complex reality, one that is quite likely to cause serious material consequences for the residents of the Pashtun Borderland at a time when the nation-state is finally out to merge the few remaining white patches on the map into its system of central territorial administration.

[27] See Jäger (2004), 133–57; Foucault (1976), 50–67. See also [M.J.] Hanifi (2004; 2011); [S. M.] Hanifi (2016; 2018); Hartung (2024).

BIBLIOGRAPHY

A[uswärtiges] A[mt] (2021). 'Entwicklungen der letzten Tage sind bitter und werden langfristige Folgen haben': Statement von Außenminister Heiko Maaß zur Lage in Afghanistan, 16 August 2021. URL: www.auswaertiges-amt.de/de/newsroom/maas-afghanistan/2477174 (accessed 24 February 2024).

al-ʿAbbūd, Ṣāliḥ ibn ʿAbdallāh (1416h). D. ʿAbbūd yaʿlanu barāʾat al-Jāmiʿa al-Islāmiyya min tadlīs al-Shams al-Afghānī. *al-Jumʿa* 16 (12 Rabīʿal-awwal / 9 August), 7.

(1424h). *Juhūd al-Mamlaka al-ʿArabiyya al-Saʿūdiyya fiʾl-daʿwa ilá ʾllāh taʿālá fiʾl-khārij min khilāl al-Jāmiʿa al-Islāmiyya*, 2 vols., Medina: Maktabat al-Malik Fahd al-waṭaniyya.

ʿAbd al-Maʿbūd, Mawlānā Muḥammad, ed. (1433/2012). *ʿAqīdah-yi Shaykh al-Qurʾān: fiʾl-ḥayāt baʿd al-wafāt li-Sayyid al-uns waʾl-jān – ṣallá ʾllāh taʿālá ʿalayhi wa-ʿalá aṣḥābihi wa-sallam taslīman kathīran kathīran*, Rawalpindi: Idārat al-taḥqīq va ʾl-taṣnīf.

ʿAbd al-Rabb Khān, Mawlavī (1234sh). *Iṭāʿat-i ūlī ʾl-amr*, Kabul: Maṭbaʿah-yi ʿināyat.

(1334sh). *Risālah-yi paxtō-yi iṭāʿat-i ūlī ʾl-amr*, trans. Ṣāliḥ Muḥammad, Kabul: Maṭbaʿah-yi dār al-salṭānat.

ʿAbd Rabbih, Nabīh Zakariyā (1407/1987). *ʿAbd Rabb al-Rasūl Sayyāf: qāʾid al-jihād al-afghānī*, Amman: Dār al-ḍiyāʾ liʾl-nashr waʾl-tawzīʿ.

ʿAbd al-Raḥmān (1963). *Dīvān-i ʿAbd al-Raḥmān Bābā*, ed. Mawlānā ʿAbd al-Qādir, Peshawar: Paxtō akēḋīmī, də Pəxavar yūnīvarsiṫī.

ʿAbd al-Raḥmān, Amīr (1304sh). *Kalimah-yi amīr al-bilād fī targhīb ilá ʾl-jihād*, Kabul: Dār al-salṭanah.

(1306sh). *Taqvīm al-dīn*, Kabul: Dār al-salṭanah.

Abedin, Mahan (2005). From Mujahid to Activist: An Interview with a Libyan Veteran of the Afghan Jihad. *Spotlight on Terrorism* 3(2). URL: http://jamestown.org/interview/from-mujahid-to-activist-an-interview-with-a-libyan-veteran-of-the-afghan-jihad (accessed 24 February 2024).

Abou-Zahab, Mariam (2004). The Sunni–Shia Conflict in Jhang (Pakistan). In *Lived Islam in South Asia: Adaptation, Accommodation & Conflict*, ed. Imtiaz Ahmad and Helmut Reifeld, New Delhi: Social Science Press, pp. 135–48.

(2009a). Sectarianism in Pakistan's Khurram Tribal Agency. *Terrorism Monitor* 7(6), 8–10.

(2009b). The SSP, Herald of Militant Sunni Islam in Pakistan. In *Armed Militias of South Asia: Fundamentalists, Maoists and Separatists*, ed. Laurent Gayer and Christophe Jaffrelot, London: Hurst / New York: Columbia University Press, pp. 159–75.

Abū Mujāhid, al-Duktūr (1398h). *al-Shaykh ʿAbdallāh ʿAzzām bayn al-milād wa'l-istishhād*, Peshawar: Markaz al-Shahīd ʿAzzām al-iʿlāmī.

Abū Qudāma, Ṣāliḥ Ilhāmī (1428/2007). *al-Zarqāwī al-jīl al-thānī li'l-Qāʿida: dirāsa manhajiyya wa-naqdiyya*, n.p.: Mawqiʿ minbar al-muslim.

Adamec, Ludwig W. (1972–85). *Historical and Political Gazetteer of Afghanistan*, 6 vols., Graz: Akademische Druck- u. Verlagsanstalt.

(2003). *Historical Dictionary of Afghanistan*, 3rd ed., Lanham, MD and Oxford: The Scarecrow Press.

al-ʿAdnānī, Abū Muḥammad (1441h). *K. Jāmiʿ li-kalimāt wa-khuṭubāt wa-rasāʾil al-shaykh al-mujāhid Abī Muḥammad al-ʿAdnānī – taqabbalahu allāh*, n.p.: Muʾassasat ṣarḥ al-khilāfa.

al-Afghānī, al-Shams al-Salafī (1416/1996). *Juhūd ʿulamāʾ al-ḥanafiyya fī ʾibṭāl ʿaqāʾid al-qubūriyya*, 3 vols., Riyadh: Dār al-ṣamīʿī li'l-nashr wa'l-tawzīʿ.

(1419/1998). *Adāʾ al-māturīdiyya li'l-ʿaqīda al-salafiyya*, 2nd ed., 3 vols., al-Ṭāʾif: Maktabat al-ṣiddīq.

Də Afghānistān Islāmī Imārat (1428/2007). *Də Afghānistān də Islāmī Imārat də məshər'tābah maqām ləkhvā və mujāhidīnō tah jihādī lāyiḥah*, n.p.: no publisher.

(1431/2010). *Də Mujāhidīnō lapārah lāʾiḥah*, n.p.: no publisher.

"Aḥmad" Kākā (1991). *Khudāʾī khidmatgār taḥrīk: vṛumbay ṫūk*, ed. ʿAbd al-Valī Khān, Peshawar: Yūnivarsiṫī buk ējansī.

Ahmad, Imtiaz (1966). The Ashraf–Ajlaf Dichotomy in Muslim Social Structure in India. *The Indian Economic and Social History Review* 3(3), 268–78.

Ahmad, Ishtiaq (2017). *Pakhtun Resistance against British Rule: An Assessment of the Frontier Uprising of 1897*, unpublished PhD thesis, University of Peshawar.

Ahmad, Qeyamuddin (1994). *The Wahhabi Movement in India*, rev. ed., New Delhi: Manohar.

Aḥmad, Rifʿat Sayyid, ed. (1991). *al-Nabī al-musallaḥ*, 2 vols., London: Riad El-Rayyes Books.

Aḥmad, Sayyid (2015). Muslim Dōst pah Afghānistān kē də DĀʿISH ḋaləy lah jināyātō pardah pōrtah kṛah. *Nən Ṫəkəy Asiyā* (21 October). URL: www.nunn.asia/ 55554/د-داعش-یو-لوړپوړی-مشر-په-افغانستان-کې (accessed 24 February 2024).

Aḥmadzay, Zāhidī (1385sh/1427h). *Khāliṣ Bābā: də abadiyyat pah lōr*, Peshawar: Amīr Krōṛ kitābtūn.

Ahmed, Akbar S. (1980). *Pukhtun Economy and Society: Traditional Structure and Economic Development in a Tribal Society*, Abingdon and New York: Routledge.

(1983). *Religion and Politics in Muslim Society: Order and Conflict in Pakistan*, Cambridge: Cambridge University Press.

Akbar, Said Hyder, and Susan Burton (2005). *Come Back to Afghanistan: Trying to Rebuild a Country with My Father, My Brother, My One-Eyed Uncle, Bearded Tribesmen, and President Karzai*, New York: Bloomsbury.

Akhtar, Muḥammad (2002). *Tājik-i svātī va mamlakat-i Gibar tārīkh kē āʾīnē mēṇ*, Abbottabad: Sarḥadd urdū akēḋimī.

Akhtar, Shāh Ḥakīm-i Muḥammad (1418/2014). *Lazẕat-i ẕikr kī vajd āfrīnī*, Karachi: Khānah'qāh-yi imdādiyyah-ashrafiyyah.

Akhundzada, Arif H. (2017). The Kingdom of Swat and the Lost Tajiks of North Pakistan. *Pashto* 46(4–6), 23–46.

Akōṛavī, Mawlānā ʿAbd al-Ḥaqq (1422/2002). *Fatāvá-yi ḥaqqāniyyah*, ed. Mawlānā Muftī Mukhtārallāh Ḥaqqānī, 6 vols., Akōṛah Khaṭṭak: Muʾtamar al-muṣannifīn-i dār al-ʿulūm-i ḥaqqāniyyah.

Alam, Muzaffar (1986). *The Crisis of Empire in Mughal North India: Awadh and the Punjab, 1707–1748*, Oxford: Oxford University Press.

al-Albānī, Muḥammad Nāṣir al-Dīn (1408h). *Tamām al-minna fi'l-taʿlīq ʿalá fiqh al-sunna*, 2nd ed., Riyadh: Dār al-rāya.

(1412h). *Suʾāl wa-jawāb ḥawla fiqh al-wāqiʿ*, ed. ʿAlī ibn Ḥasan al-Ḥalabī al-Atharī, Amman: al-Maktaba al-islāmiyya.

(1414/1994). *Fatāwá al-shaykh al-Albānī wa-muqāranatuhā bi-fatāwá al-ʿulamāʾ*, ed. ʿAbd al-Manān al-Ṭayyibī, Cairo: Maktabat al-turāth al-islāmī.

(1426/2005). *Ḥaqq kalimat al-imām al-Albānī fī Sayyid Quṭb wa-naqd aḥwālihi wa-naqḍ aqwālih*, ed. ʿAlī ibn Hasan al-Ḥalabī al-Atharī, Cairo: Dār al-tawḥīd wa'l-sunna.

(1429/2008). *Ṣifat ṣalāt al-nabī – ṣallá 'llāh ʿalayhi wa-sallam – min al-takbīr ilá 'l-taslīm ka-annaka tarāhā*, 10th ed., Riyadh: Maktabat al-maʿārif li'l-nashr wa'l-tawzīʿ.

Al-Fahad, Abdulaziz H. (2004). The *ʿimama vs.* the *ʿiqal*: Hadari–Bedouin Conflict in the Formation of the Saudi State. In *Counter-Narratives: History, Contemporary Society and Politics in Saudi Arabia and Yemen*, ed. Madawi Al-Rasheed and Robert Vitalis, New York: Palgrave Macmillan, pp. 35–75.

Al-Gailani, Noorah (2015). The Shrines of Shaykh ʿAbd al-Qadir al-Jilani in Baghdad and His Son in ʿAqra: Current Challenges in Facing Salafism. In *Sufis and Salafis in the Contemporary Age*, ed. Lloyd Ridgeon, London: Bloomsbury, pp. 71–90.

ʿAlī, Gawhar (n.d.). *Taẕkirah-yi Shaykh al-Qurʾān ʿAllāmah ʿAbd al-Salām Rustamī – raḥmat allāh*, Peshawar: self-published.

Ali, Imtiaz (2007). The Father of the Taliban: An Interview with Maulana Sami ul-Haq. *Spotlight on Terror* 4(2). URL: jamestown.org/interview/the-father-of-the-taliban-an-interview-with-maulana-sami-ul-haq (accessed 24 February 2024).

(2009). Militant or Peace Broker? A Profile of the Swat Valley's Maulana Sufi Muhammad. *Terrorism Monitor* 7(7), 6–8.

Ali, M. Athar (1980). Sulhi Kul [*sic*] and the Religious Ideas of Akbar. *Proceedings of the Indian History Congress* 41, 326–39.

ʿAlī, Mawlawī Aḥmad (1291h). *Burhān al-muʾminīn*, Bombay: Maṭbaʿah-yi ḥaydarī.

ʿAlī, Mawlavī Raḥmān (1894). *Tazkirah-yi ʿulamāʾ-i Hind*, Lucknow: Maṭbaʿ Munshī Naval Kishōr.

ʿAlī, Vilāyat (1341h). *Rasāʾil-i tisʿah*, ed. Ilāhī Bakhsh, Delhi: Maṭbaʿ-i fārūqī.

Alimia, Sana (2013). *The Quest for Humanity in a Dehumanised State: Afghan Refugees and Devalued Citizens in Urban Pakistan, 1979–2012*, unpublished PhD thesis, SOAS, University of London.

ʿAllāmī, Shaykh Abū 'l-Faẕl (1872–7). *Āʾīn-i akbarī*, ed. H. Blochmann, 2 vols., Calcutta: Baptist mīshan prēss.

(1877–86). *Akbar'nāmah*, ed. Mawlavī ʿAbd al-Raḥīm, 3 vols., Calcutta: Baptist mīshan prēss.

Amīn-i Gulistānah, Abū 'l-Ḥasan Muḥammad (1896). *Das Mujmil et-Târîkh-i Baʿdnâdirîje des Ibn Muḥammed Emîm Abuʾl-Ḥasan aus Gulistâne* [sic], ed. Oskar Mann, Leiden: Brill.

Anas, ʿAbdallāh (2002). *Walādat "al-Afghān al-ʿArab": sīrat ʿAbdallāh Anas bayna Masʿūd wa-ʿAbdallāh ʿAzzām*, London: Sāqī.

Anjum, Ovamir (2010). Sufism without Mysticism? Ibn Qayyim al-Ǧawziyyah's Objectives in *Madāriǧ al-Sālikīn*. *Oriente Moderno* 40 (1), 153–80.

Anon. (1910). Chamkanni [*sic*]. In *Encyclopædia Britannica*, vol. v, 11th ed., New York: Encyclopædia Britannica Inc., p. 826.

Anon. (1302sh). *Niẓām'nāmah-yi asāsī-yi dawlat-i ʿilliyyah-yi Afghānistān*, Kabul: Dāʾirah-yi taḥrīrāt-i majlis-i ʿālī.

Anon. (1343sh). Qānūn-i asāsī-yi Afghānistān / Də Afghānistān asāsī qānūn. *Də Afghānistān də Pādishāhī Dawlat Rasmı Jarıdah* 1(12), 1–3.

Anon. (1353sh). *Də Amānī ʿĀlī Līsah, 1303–1353, Kābul – Afghānistān*, Kabul: Maṭbaʿah-yi humā.

Anon. (1355sh). *Də Afghānistān də jumhurī dawlat asāsī qānūn / Qānūn-i asāsī-yi Dawlat-i jumhurī-yi Afghānistān*, Kabul: no publisher.

Anon. (1421h). *Kashf shubuhāt al-muqātilīn taḥta rāyat man akhil bi'l-aṣl al-dīn*, n.p.: no publisher.

Anon. (1426h). *al-Shaykh Shams al-Dīn ibn Muḥammad Ashraf al-Bashtūnī*. URL: www.alsoufia.com/main/1008-1/-al-shaykh-shams-al-dīn-al-afghānī-.html (accessed 19 November 2016).

Anon. (1435h). Rakāʾib al-ḥaqq: bayʿat al-Shaykh ʿAbd al-Raḥīm Muslim Dūst al-Afghānī – ḥafiẓuhu allāh – li-khalīfat al-muslimīn (4 Ramaḍān). URL: http://ia902508.us.archive.org/19/items/doost/rkaib.al7aaq.mp4 (accessed 24 February 2024).

al-Anṣārī, ʿĀlam ibn ʿAlāʾ (1407/1987). *Fatāwá tātār'khāniyya*, ed. al-Qāḍī Sajjād Ḥusayn, 5 vols., Hyderabad: Maṭbaʿat al-majlis dāʾirat al-maʿārif al-ʿuthmāniyya.

Ansari, Sarah F. D. (1992). *Sufi Saints and State Power: The* pirs *of Sind* [sic], *1843–1947*, Cambridge: Cambridge University Press.

Ansary, Tamim (2001). Think Taliban, Think Nazis. *Communalism Combat* 8 (10), 6f.

Appadurai, Arjun (1990). Disjuncture and Difference in Global Cultural Economy. *Theory, Culture & Society* 7(2–3), 295–310.

Arai, Mary N. (1997). *A Functional Biology of Scyphozoa*, London: Chapman & Hall.

AREU (Afghanistan Research and Evaluation Unit) (2005). *Afghans in Karachi: Migration, Settlement and Social Networks*, Kabul: AREU.

Arjomand, Said Amir (1981). Religious Extremism (*Ghuluww*), Ṣūfism and Sunnism in Safavid Iran, 1501–1722. *Journal of Asian Studies* 15(1), 1–35.

Arnold, Anthony (1983). *Afghanistan's Two-Party Communism: Parcham and Khalq*, Stanford, CA: Hoover Institution Press.

Askar, Mohammad Ali [Ali Karimi] (2019). *The Will Not to Count: Technologies of Calculation and the Quest to Govern Afghanistan*, PhD thesis, McGill University Montreal. URL: http://escholarship.mcgill.ca/concern/theses/2514nq70c (accessed 24 February 2024).

al-ʿAsqalānī, Aḥmad ibn ʿAlī ibn Ḥajjar (1379h). *Fatḥ al-bārī sharḥ Ṣaḥīḥ al-Bukhārī*, ed. ʿAbd al-ʿAzīz ibn ʿAbdallāh ibn Bāz, 13 vols., Beirut: Dār al-maʿārifa.

"Aṣr" Afghānī, ʿAbd al-Ḥalīm (1965). *Rūḥānī rābiṭah aw rūḥānī taṛūn*, 2 vols., Hōnī Sayyidān: Maktabah Ḥaẓrat Sayyid Najāt Qalandar.

Astarābādī, Naẓīr Muḥammad Mahdī ibn Muḥammad Naṣīr (1875). *Tārīkh-i jahān'gushā-yi Nādirī*, Bombay: Maṭbaʿḥaydarī.

ʿAṭāʾ al-Raḥmān, Muftī (1434/2012). Ishāʿat al-Tawḥīd va 'l-Sunnah kē ʿaqāʾid va naẓariyyāt. *Dār al-iftāʾ wa'l-qaḍāʾ al-Jāmiʿat al-Binūriyyah*. URL: http://web.archive.org/web/20170518112829/http://www.onlinefatawa.com/fatawa/view_scn/17570 (accessed 24 February 2024).

(1435/2013). Mamātī firqah Ishāʿat-i Tawḥīd va Sunnat kē barē mēṇ kiyā ḥukm hē? *Dār al-iftāʾ wa'l-qaḍāʾ al-Jāmiʿat al-Binūriyyah*. URL: http://web.archive.org/web/20200603235832/http://www.onlinefatawa.com/fatawa/view_scn/19107 (accessed 24 February 2024).

ʿAṭāyī, M. Ibrāhīm (1357sh). *Də Paxtanay qabīlō də ḥuqūqī, jazāyī, taʿāmulī iṣṭilāḥātō qāmūs*, Kabul: Də Paxtō ćēṛanō naṛīvāl markaz.

Ateş, Sabri (2015). *The Ottoman–Iranian Borderlands: Making a Boundary, 1843–1914*, Cambridge: Cambridge University Press.

ʿAṭwān, ʿAbd al-Bārī (2015). *al-Dawla al-islāmiyya: al-judhūr, al-tawaḥḥush, al-mustaqbal*, 2nd ed., Beirut and London: Dār al-Sāqī.

Auda, Gehad (1994). The 'Normalization' of the Islamic Movement in Egypt from the 1970s to the Early 1990s. In *Accounting for Fundamentalisms: The Dynamic Character of Movements*, ed. Martin E. Marty and R. Scott Appleby, Chicago: The University of Chicago Press, pp. 374–412.

ʿAwda, ʿAbd al-Qādir (1400/1980). *al-Tashrīʿ al-jināʾī al-islāmī: muqaranan biʾl-qānūn al-waḍīʿ*, Beirut: Dār al-kutub al-ʿarabī.

(1405/1985). *al-Islām bayna jahl abnāʾihi wa-ʿajz ʿulamāʾih*, Kuwait: Ittiḥād al-islāmī al-ʿālamī.

Āybak, Ẓafar Aḥmad (1990). *Khāṭirāt (āp bītī)*, ed. Ghulām-i Ḥusayn Ẕū ʾl-Fiqār, Lahore: Sang-i mīl.

Ayubi, Nazih N. M. (1991). *Political Islam: Religion and Politics in the Arab World*, London and New York: Routledge.

Āzād, Abū ʾl-Kalām (2010). *Tarjumān al-qurʾān*, 7th ed., 4 vols., New Delhi: Sāhitya akādimī.

(2012). *Khuṭbāt-i Āzād*, ed. Mālik Rām, 6th ed., New Delhi: Sāhitya akādimī.

Aẓhār, Muḥammad Masʿūd (1414h). *Khuṭbāt-i jihād*, ed. Sulṭān Maḥmūd Ẓiyāʾ, 4 vols. in two, Lahore: Maktabat Ḥasan.

(1419h). *Faẓāʾil-i jihād-i kāmil*, Lahore: Maktabat Ḥasan.

(1428–30/2007–9). *Fatḥ al-javād fī maʿārif āyāt al-jihād*, Lahore: Maktabat Ibn Mubārak.

ʿAẓīmābādī, Mawlānā Vilāyat ʿAlī (1284/1868). *Taysīr al-ṣalāt*, Lucknow: Maṭbaʿ-i ʿalavī.

ʿAzīzallāh (Ḥājjī Dīn Muḥammad) (1386sh). *Də Mawlavī Khāliṣ žvand, fann aw and*, Peshawar: Pīr chāpʼkhūnah.

ʿAzīzī, ʿAbd al-Maqṣūd (2015). Afrād-i musallaḥ-i DĀʿISH yak qūmāndān-i ṭālib rā kashtand. *Āžāns-i khabarī-yi Pažvāk*, 2 February. URL: http://pajhwok.com/fa/2015/02/02/%20افراد-مسلح-داعش-یک-قوماندان-طالب-را-%20کشت% (accessed 28 August 2023).

ʿAzzām, al-Shahīd ʿAbdallāh (1417/1997). *Mawsūʿat al-dhakhāʾir al-ʿiẓām fīmā uthar ʿan al-imām al-humām al-shahīd ʿAbdallāh ʿAzzām*, ed. Markaz al-shahīd ʿAzzām al-islāmī, 4 vols., Peshawar: Markaz al-shahīd ʿAzzām al-islāmī.

Bābur, Ẓahīr al-Dīn (1905). *The Bábar-Náma, Being the Autobiography of the Emperor Bábar [...] written in Chaghatáy Turkish; Now Reproduced in Facsimile from a Manuscript Belonging to the Late Sir Sálár Jang of Haydarábád*, ed. Annette S. Beveridge, London: Quaritch.

Badakhshī, Ḥājjī Muḥammad Amīn (1140h). *Manāqib-i ādamiyyah-yi ḥaẓrat-i aḥmadiyyah*, MS BL London Ethé 652.

Badāʾunī, ʿAbd al-Qādir (2001). *Muntakhab al-tavārīkh*, ed. Mawlavī Aḥmad ʿAlī, 3 vols., Tehran: Anjumān-i āṡār wa mafākhir-i farhangī.

al-Baghdādī, Abū Bakr (n.d.[a]). *Majmūʿ kalimāt amīr al-muʾminīn Abī Bakr al-Baghdādī*, al-Raqqa: Maktabat al-raqīm.

al-Baghdādī, Abū ʾl-Yamān (n.d.[b]). *Ḥiwār maʿa al-shaykh Abū Muṣʿab al-Zarqāwī*, n.p.: Muʾassasat al-furqān.

Baig, Rehmat Karim (2004). *Chitral: A Study in Statecraft (1320–1969)*, Karachi: IUCN Pakistan.

Baldick, Julian (1993). *Imaginary Muslims: The Uwaysi Sufis of Central Asia*, London and New York: I.B. Tauris.

al-Bannā, al-Imām Ḥasan (1412/1992). *Majmūʿat rasāʾil al-Imām al-Shahīd Ḥasan al-Bannā*, Cairo: Dār al-tawzīʿ wa'l-nashr al-islāmiyya.

(1422/2001). *Mudhakkirāt al-daʿwa wa'l-dāʿiyya*, Alexandria: Dār al-daʿwa.

Bārakzay, Mīrvays (2015). Muslim Dōst: də Jalālābād pēx̌ū də "sīmē istikhbārātō" kār vu. *Nən Ṫəkəy Asiyā* (22 April). URL: www.nunn.asia/42961/مسلم-دوست-د-جلال-اباد-پېښه-د-سيمي-استخ/ (accessed 24 February 2024).

Barry, Michael (2002). *Le royaume de l'insolence: L'Afghanistan (1504–2001)*, 2nd rev. ed., Paris: Flammarion.

Barth, Fredrik (1959). *Political Leadership among Swat Pathans*, London: The Athlone Press.

al-Bassām, ʿAbdallāh ibn ʿAbd al-Raḥmān (1398h). *ʿUlamāʾ Najd khilāla sitta qurūn*, 3 vols., Mecca: Maktabat wa'l-maṭbaʿat al-nahḍa al-ḥadītha.

Bastavī, Sayyid Jaʿfar ʿAlī Naqvī (1434/2012). *Ḥaẓrat Aḥmad-i shahīd kā ḥajj awr uskē as̱arāt*, Raʾī Baraylī: Dār-i ʿirfān.

al-Bayhaqī, al-Ḥāfiẓ Abū Bakr Aḥmad ibn al-Ḥusayn (1414/1993). *Ḥayāt al-anbiyāʾ – ṣalawāt allāh ʿalayhim – baʿd wafātihim*, ed. Aḥmad ibn ʿAṭiyya al-Ghāmidī, Medina: Maktabat al-ʿulūm wa'l-ḥikam.

(1423/2003). *al-Jāmiʿ li-shuʿab al-īmān*, ed. Mukhtār Aḥmad al-Nadwī and ʿAbd al-ʿAlī ʿAbd al-Ḥamīd Ḥāmid, 14 vols., Riyadh: Maktabat al-rushd.

al-Bazzāzī, Muḥammad ibn Muḥammad (2009). *al-Fatāwá al-bazzāziyya aw al-Jāmiʿ al-wajīz fī madhhab al-imām al-aʿẓam Abī Ḥanīfa al-Nuʿmān*, ed. Sālim Muṣṭafá al-Badrī, 2 vols., Beirut: Dār al-kutūb al-ʿilmiyya.

Behera, Navnita Chadha (2000). *State, Identity and Violence: Jammu, Kashmir, and Ladakh*, New Delhi: Manohar.

(2006). *Demystifying Kashmir*, Washington, D.C.: Brookings Institution Press.

Bezhan, Faridullah (2017). Nationalism, not Islam: The "Awaken Youth" Party and Pashtun Nationalism. In *Afghanistan's Islam: From Conversion to the Taliban*, ed. Nile Green, Oakland, CA: University of California Press, pp. 163–85 and 293–9 (notes).

Bell, Kevin (2013). *Usama bin Ladin's "Father Sheikh": Yunus Khalis and the Return of al-Qaʿida's* [sic] *Leadership to Afghanistan*, West Point, NY: The Combatting Terrorism Center at West Point.

(2016). The First *Islamic State:* A Look Back at the Islamic Emirate of Kunar. *CTCSentinel* 9(2), 9–14.

Bellenoit, Hayden (2014). Between Qanungos and Clerks: The Cultural Service Worlds of Hindustan's Pensmen, c. 1750–1850. *Modern Asian Studies* 48(4), 872–910.

Bergen, Peter L. (2001). *Holy War, Inc.: Inside the Secret World of Osama bin Laden*, Toronto: The Free Press.

Bermudez, Joseph S. Jr. (1992). Ballistic Missiles in the Third World – Afghanistan 1979–1992. *Jane's Intelligence Review* 4(2), 51–8.

Bhattī, Muḥammad Isḥāq (1433/2012). *Taẕkirah-yi Mawlānā Ghulām Rasūl Qilʿavī*, Qilʿah Mayhāṇ Singh: Ghulām Rasūl vēlfīʾar sosāʾitī.

al-Bishāvarī, Abū Muḥammad Amīnallāh (1422h). *Də taqlīd ḥaqīqat aw də muqallidīnō aqsām*, Peshawar: Maktabah-yi muḥammadiyyah.

(1426h). *Khulafā' rāshidīn aw aḥnāf*, Peshawar: Maktabah-yi muḥammadiyyah.

(1430/2009). *al-Favā'id: tazkiyyat-i nafs, 'ilm al-qulūb awr maḥabbat-i ilāhī kē favā'id*, trans. Muḥammad 'Alī Ṣiddīqī, 2 vols., Peshawar: Maktabah-yi muḥammadiyyah.

Blake, Stephen P. (1979). The Patrimonial–Bureaucratic Empire of the Mughals. *Journal of Asian Studies* 39(1), 77–94.

Boatcă, Manuela (2015). *Global Inequalities beyond Occidentalism*, Farham and Burlington, VT: Routledge.

Boeck, Brian J. (2009). *Imperial Boundaries: Cossack Communities and Empire-Building in the Age of Peter the Great*, Cambridge: Cambridge University Press.

Bohdan, Siarhei (2020). 'They Were Going Together with the *Ikhwan*': The Influence of Muslim Brotherhood Thinkers on Shi'i Islamists during the Cold War. *The Middle East Journal* 74(2), 243–62.

Bonnefoy, Laurent (2011). *Salafism in Yemen: Transnational and Religious Identity*, London: Hurst / New York: Columbia University Press.

Borneman, John, and Parvis Ghassem-Fachandi (2017). The Concept of *Stimmung*: From Indifference to Xenophobia in Germany's Refugee Crisis. *HAU: Journal of Ethnographic Theory* 7(3), 105–35.

Bose, Ashish (2004). Afghan Refugees in India. *Economic and Political Weekly* 39 (43), 4698–701.

Brachman, Jarret, and Abdullah Warius (2008). Abu Yahya al-Libi's "Human Shield in Modern Jihad". *CTC Sentinel* 1(6), 1–4.

Brambilla, Chiara (2015a). Exploring the Critical Potential of the Borderscapes Concept. *Geopolitics* 20(1), 14–34.

(2015b). Il confine come borderscape. *Rivista di Storia delle Idee* 4(2), 5–9.

Braudel, Fernand (1958). Histoire et sciences sociales: La longue durée. *Annales* 13(4), 725–53.

Brown, Vahid, and Don Rassler (2013). *Fountainhead of Jihad: The Haqqani Nexus, 1973–2012*, London: Hurst / New York: Oxford University Press.

Bruckmayr, Philipp (2009). The Spread and Persistence of Māturīdi [*sic*] Kalām and Underlying Dynamics. *Iran and the Caucasus* 13(1), 29–52.

(2014). Past and Present Aspects of Māturīdism [*sic*] in South and Southeast Asia. In *Uluğ Bir Çinar İmâm Mâturîdî Uluslararası Sempozyum Tebliğler Kitabı*, ed. Ahmet Kartal, Istanbul: Ofis Yayın Matbaacılık, pp. 123–31.

(2020). Salafi Challenge and Māturīdī Response: Contemporary Disputes over the Legitimacy of Māturīdī *kalām*. *Die Welt des Islams* 60(2–3), 293–325.

Bruckmayr, Philipp, and Jan-Peter Hartung (2020). Introduction: Challenges from "The Periphery"? – Salafi Islam outside the Arab World: Spotlights on Wider Asia. *Die Welt des Islams* 60(2–3), 137–69.

Buddruss, Georg (1983). Spiegelungen der Islamisierung Kafiristans in der mündlichen Überlieferung. In *Ethnologie und Geschichte: Festschrift für Karl Jettmar*, ed. Peter Snoy, Wiesbaden: Steiner, pp. 73–88.

Bude, Heinz (2016). *Das Gefühl der Welt: Über die Macht von Stimmungen*, Munich: Hanser.

(2017). What Does *Stimmung* Mean? *HAU: Journal of Ethnographic Theory* 7(3), 137–9.

Buehler, Arthur F. (1998). *Sufi Heirs of the Prophet: The Indian Naqshbandiyya and the Rise of the Mediating Sufi Shaykh*, Columbia, SC: University of South Carolina Press.

Bukhārī, Ḥāfiẓ Muḥammad Akbar Shāh (1418/1997). *Kāravān-i Thānavī: Ḥakīm al-Ummat Ḥazrat Mawlānā Ashraf ʿAlī Thānavī – rḥ – kē 192 khulafāʾ, majāzīn-i khulafāʾ awr mumtāz mutavassilīn kē ḥālāt va kamālāt kā jāmiʿ taẕkirah*, Karachi: Idārat al-maʿārif.

(1419/1999). *Akābir-i ʿulamāʾ-i Dēoband*, Lahore: Idārah-yi islāmiyyāt.

Bulandshahrī, Muḥammad ʿĀshiq-i Ilāhī (1992). *Chhah bātēṇ*, ed. Anīs Aḥmad, New Delhi: Idārah-yi ishāʿat-i dīniyyāt.

Bunzel, Cole (2015). *From Paper State to Caliphate: The Ideology of the Islamic State*, Washington, D.C.: The Brookings Institution Press.

[al-Burhānfūrī], Mawlānā al-Shaykh Niẓām et al. (1421/2000). *al-Fatāwá al-hindiyya, al-maʿrūfa bi'l-Fatāwá al-ʿālamkīriyya fī madhhab al-imām al-aʿẓam Abī Ḥanīfa al-Nuʿmān*, ed. ʿAbd al-Laṭīf Ḥasan ʿAbd al-Raḥmān, 6 vols., Beirut: Dār al-kutub al-ʿilmiyya.

Burr, J. Millard, and Robert O. Collins (2006). *Alms for Jihad: Charity and Terrorism in the Islamic World*, Cambridge: Cambridge University Press.

Cabot, Heath (2017). *Philia* and *phagia*: Thinking with *Stimmungswechsel* through the Refugee Crisis in Greece. *HAU: Journal of Ethnographic Theory* 7(3), 141–6.

Cacopardo, Alberto M., and Augusto S. Cacopardo (2001). *Gates of Peristan: History, Religion and Society in the Hindu Kush*, Rome: Istituto Italiano per l'Africa e l'Oriente.

Cacopardo, Alberto M., Augusto S. Cacopardo, and Ruth Laila Smith, eds. (2006). *Shaykh Muhammad Abdullah Khan 'Azar': My Heartrendering Tragic Story – Merī dilōṇ kō hilānē'valī dard'nāk kahānī*, Oslo: Novus forlag.

Calder, Norman (1984). The Significance of the Term *imām* in Early Islamic Jurisprudence. *Zeitschrift für die Geschichte der Arabisch-Islamischen Wissenschaften* 1, 253–64.

(1993). Tafsīr from Ṭabarī to Ibn Kathīr: Problems in the Description of a Genre, Illustrated with References to the Story of Abraham. In *Approaches to the Qur'ān*, ed. Gerald Hawting and Abdul-Kader A. Shareef, London and New York: Routledge, pp. 101–40.

Ćamkanī, Muḥammad ʿUmar (1138/1725). *Ẓavāhir*, paginated MS Punjab University Library Lahore, Shirani Coll. 388, Acc. No. 3 392.

Canfield, Robert L. (1993). New Year's Day at Ali's Shrine. In *Everyday Life in the Muslim Middle East*, ed. Donna Lee Bowen and Evelyn A. Early, Bloomington, IN: Indiana University Press, pp. 234–8.

Caroe, Olaf (1958). *The Pathans, 550 B.C.–A.D. 1957*, London: Macmillan.

Caron, James (2012a). Taliban, Real and Imagined. In *Under the Drones: Modern Lives in the Afghanistan–Pakistan Borderlands*, ed. Shahzad Bashir and Robert D. Crews, Cambridge, MA and London: Harvard University Press, pp. 60–82.

(2012b). Review of "Poetry of the Taliban" by Alex Strick van Linschoten and Felix Kuehn. *jadaliyya.com*, 27 May. URL: www.jadaliyya.com/Details/26082/Poetry-of-the-Taliban (accessed 24 February 2024).

(2016a). Sufism and Liberation across the Indo-Afghan Border: 1880–1928. *South Asian History and Culture* 7(2), 135–54.

(2016b). Borderland Historiography in Pakistan. *South Asian History and Culture* 7(4), 327–45.

Caron, James, and Ananya Dasgupta (2016). Popular Culture, Radical Egalitarianism, and Formations of Muslim Selfhood in South Asia. *South Asian History and Culture* 7(2), 107–16.

Chabbi, J[acqueline]. (1995). Ribāṭ. In *Encyclopaedia of Islam: New Edition*, vol. VIII, Leiden: Brill, pp. 493–506.

Chakrabarty, Dipesh (1985). Invitation to a Dialogue. In *Subaltern Studies*, vol. IV: *Writings on South Asian History and Society*, ed. Ranajit Guha, New Delhi: Oxford University Press, 364–76.

Chamarkandī, ʿAbd al-Karīm (1981). *Sarguzasht-i mujāhid*, ed. Muḥammad Ḥamīd, Lahore: Idārah-yi maṭbūʿāt-i sulaymānī.

Chaudri, Zeeshan (2019). *Demarcating the Contours of the Deobandi Tradition via a Study of the 'Akābirīn'*, unpublished PhD thesis, SOAS, University of London.

Childe, V. Gordon (1950). The Urban Revolution. *The Town Planning Review* 21(1), 3–17.

Chishtī, Imām al-Dīn (1826). [*Tārīkh-i*] *Ḥusayn Shāhī*, MS BL London Or.1662.

Christensen, Asger (1980). The Pashtuns of Kunar: Tribe, Class, and Community Organization. *Afghanistan Journal* 7(3), 79–92.

Cicero, Marcus Tullius (1830). *Orationes*, 7 vols., ed. J. A. Ernst, London: A. J. Alpy.

Clarke, Kate (2011). *The Layha* [sic] – *Calling the Taleban to Account*. AAN Thematic Report 6, Kabul: Afghanistan Analyst Network.

Cook, Michael (2006). *Commanding Right and Forbidding Wrong in Islamic Thought*, 4th rev. ed., Cambridge: Cambridge University Press.

Craig, Tim (2016). Pakistan's "University of Jihad" Is Getting Millions of Dollars from the Government. *The Washington Post* (22 June). URL: www.washingtonpost.com/news/worldviews/wp/2016/06/22/pakistans-university-of-jihad-is-getting-millions-of-dollars-from-the-government (accessed 24 February 2024).

Crone, Patricia (2004). *Medieval Islamic Political Thought*, Edinburgh: Edinburgh University Press.

Currie, P. M. (1989). *The Shrine and Cult of Muʿīn al-dīn Chishtī of Ajmer*, New Delhi: Oxford University Press.

Darvīzah, Ākhūn[d] (n.d.). *Tażkirat al-abrār va 'l-ashrār*, Peshawar: Islāmī kutub'khānah.

(1885). *Makhzan al-islām*, Delhi: Matbaʿ Fayẕ-i ʿāmm.

(1310/1893). *Irshād al-ṭālibiyīn*, ed. Ḥājjī Muḥammad Amīr, Lahore: Maṭbaʿ Naval Kishōr.

Dās, Munshī Gōpāl (1878). *Tārīkh-i Pishāvar: mushʿir-i rivājāt-i aqvām, mālikān va arāẕiyāt muṣaddaqah-yi ḥukkām-i band va bast ahd-i maʿdalat-i mahd*, Lahore: Kūh-i nūr prēss.

Davies, C. C. (2007). Peshawar. In *Historic Cities of the Islamic World*, ed. Clifford E. Bosworth, Leiden and Boston, MA: Brill, pp. 426–8.

Davis, Anthony (1998). How the Taliban Became a Military Force. In *Fundamentalism Reborn? Afghanistan and the Taliban*, ed. William Malley, London: Hurst / New York: Columbia University Press, pp. 43–71.

Dāvūdī, ʿAbd al-Majīd Nāṣirī (1390sh). *Mashāhir-i tashayyuʿ-i Afghānistān*, 3 vols., Tehran: Markaz bayn al-milalī tarjamah va nashr al-Muṣṭafá - ṣallá ʼllāh ʿalayhi wa-salam.

Dawlatābādī, Baṣīr Aḥmad (1385sh). *Hazārahʼhā az qatl-i ʿām tā iḥyā-yi huviyyat*, Qom: Ibtikār-i dānish.

Degener, Almuth (1998). Waigali-Lieder zur Islamisierung Kafiristans. In *Strany i narody vostoka*, ed. M. N. Bogulyubov, St Petersburg: Peterburgskoje vostokovedenie, pp. 51–61.

(2002). The Nuristani Languages. In *Indo-Iranian Languages and Peoples*, ed. Nicholas Sims-Williams, Oxford: Oxford University Press, pp. 103–17.

Dell'Agnese, Elena, and Anne-Laure Amilhat Szary (2015). Introduction: Borderscapes. From Border Landscapes to Border Aesthetics. *Geopolitics* 20(4), 4–13.

Dēobandī, Maḥmūd al-Ḥasan (1990). *Adillah-yi kāmilah, yaʿnī ghayr-muqallidōṇ kē das suʾālāt awr unkē taḥqīqī javābāt*, Karachi: Qadīmī kitābʼkhānah.

DeWeese, Devin (1993). *An "Uvaysī" Sufi in Timurid Mawarannahr: Notes on Hagiography and the Taxonomy of Sanctity in the Religious History of Central Asia*, Bloomington, IN: Indiana University, Research Institute for Inner Asian Studies.

Diener, Alexander C., and Joshua Hagen, eds. (2010). *Borderlines and Borderlands: Political Oddities at the Edge of the Nation State*, Lanham, MD: Rowman and Littlefield.

eds. (2012). *Borders: A Very Short Introduction*, Oxford: Oxford University Press.

Digby, Simon E. (1971). *War-Horse and Elephant in the Dehli* [sic] *Sultanate: A Study of Military Supplies*, Oxford: Oxford University Press.

Dihlavī, Mawlānā Shāh Ismāʿīl-i shahīd (1877). *Manṣib-i imāmat*, Delhi: Maṭbaʿ-i rawfāqī.

(1998). *Taqviyyat al-īmān*, Delhi: Kutubʼkhānah-yi ḥamīdiyyah.

Dihlavī, Shāh Valiyallāh Muḥaddis̱ (1249h). *Fawz al-kabīr fī uṣūl al-tafsīr*, 2 vols., Delhi: Maṭbaʿ-i aḥmadī.

(1963). *Hamaʿāt*, ed. Nūr al-Ḥaqq ʿAlavī and Ghulām Muṣṭafá Qāsimī, Hyderabad, Sindh: Akādīmiyyat al-Shāh Waliyallāh al-Dihlawī.

(1388/1969). *Shāh Valiyallāh Dihlavī kē siyāsī maktūbāt*, ed. Khalīq Aḥmad Niẓāmī, Delhi: Dār al-muṣannifīn.

(1970). *Shifā' al-'alīl tarjamat al-qawl al-jamīl*, with parallel Urdu trans. by Khurram 'Alī, 2nd ed., Karachi: Ejūkeshnal prēss.

(1396/1976). *Izālat al-khafā' 'an khilāfat al-khulafā'*, 2 vols., Lahore: Suhayl akēḋīmī.

Dihlavī, Shāh 'Abd al-'Azīz (1321h). *Fatāvá-yi 'azīzī*, 2 vols., Deoband: Kutub'khānah-yi raḥīmiyyah.

al-Dihlawī, Imām al-shahīd Ismā'īl ibn 'Abd al-Ghanī (1256h). *Risāla tanwīr al-'aynayn fī ithbāt raf al-yadayn*, [Delhi]: Maṭba'at raḥmānī.

(2003). *Risālat al-tawḥīd musammá bi-taqwiyyat al-īmām*, ed. Sayyid Abū 'l-Ḥasan al-Nadwī, Damascus: Dār waḥy al-qalam.

Dihlavī, Shaykh al-kull muḥaddis̱ Naẕīr Ḥusayn (2007). *Mi'yār al-ḥaqq*, ed. Muḥammad Yaḥyá Gūndalavī, Lahore: Jāmi'ah-i ta'līm al-qur'ān va 'l-ḥadīs̱.

al-Dihlawī, Shāh Waliyallāh ibn 'Abd al-Raḥīm (1355/1936). *al-Tafhīmāt al-ilāhiyya*, 2 vols., Bijnor: Madīnat-i Barqī Press.

(1403/1983). *al-Musawwá sharḥ al-Muwaṭṭa'*, ed. Jamā'at min al-'ulamā' bi-ashrāf al-nāshir, 2 vols., Beirut: Dār al-kutub al-'ilmiyya.

(1426/2005). *Ḥujjat allāh al-bāligha*, ed. Sayyid Sābiq, 2 vols., Beirut: Dār al-jīl.

Dīravī, Ḥabīb al-Raḥmān (2003). *Riyāsat-i Dīr tārīkh kē ā'inē mēṇ*, Dīr: A-One.

Dirāz, 'Iṣām (1409/1989). *Malḥamat al-mujāhidīn al-'arab fī Afghānistān*, Cairo: Maktabat al-usra.

DNSA (Digital National Security Archive) (1973–1990). *Afghanistan: The Making of U.S. Policy, 1973–1990*. URL: http://proquest.libguides.com/dnsa/afghanistan (accessed 24 February 2024).

Dorronsoro, Gilles (2000). *La révolution afghane: Des communistes aux tâlebân*, Paris: Karthala.

Dumont, Louis (1966). *Homo hierarchicus: Le système des castes et ses implications*, Paris: Gallimard.

Dunaway, Wilma A. (1996). *The First American Frontier: Transition to Capitalism in Southern Appalachia, 1700–1860*, Chapel Hill, NC: The University of North Carolina Press.

DuPée, Matthew (2012). Afghanistan's Conflict Minerals: The Crime–State–Insurgent Nexus. *CTC Sentinel* 5(2), 11–14.

Dupree, Louis (1973). *Afghanistan*, Princeton, NJ: Princeton University Press.

Dürr, Andreas (2016). Enjoining Good and Forbidding Evil: Islamic Education and Local Traditions in Afghanistan. *Asien* 138(1), 89–108.

Durrānī, Aḥmad Shāh (1346sh). *Nāmah-yi a'lī'ḥaẕrat Aḥmad Shāh Bābā ba-nām-i a'lī'ḥaẕrat sulṭān Muṣṭafá S̱āliṯ-i 'Us̱mānī*, ed. Ghulām-i Jīlānī Jalālī, Kabul: Də Tārīkh ṫōlanah.

(1388sh). *Də lōy Aḥmad Shāh Bābā dēvān (mashhūr pah Dēvān hərā)*, ed. Muḥammad Ma'ṣūm Hōtak, Quetta: Ṣaḥāf nashrātī mu'assasah.

Durrānī, Sulṭān Muḥammad Khān ibn Mūsá (1298sh). *Tārīkh-i sulṭānī*, Quetta: Shaykh 'Abd al-Razzāq Tājir.

Durrānī, Muḥammad Riyāẓ, ed. (2006). *Kāravān-i Dēoband: rū'idād-i ḋhēṛ ṣad sālah-yi khidmāt-i Dār al-ʿUlūm Dēoband kānfrans Peshāvar*, Lahore: Ishtiyāq A. Mushtāq prēss.

Dworzak, Thomas, and Thomas Rees (2004). *Taliban*, London: Trolley Press.

Edmonds, Richard L. (1985). *Northern Frontiers of Qing China and Tokugawa Japan: A Comparative Study of Frontier Policy*, Chicago, IL: Department of Geography at The University of Chicago.

Edwards, David B. (1993). The Political Lives of Afghan Saints: The Case of the Kabul Hazrats. In *Manifestations of Sainthood in Islam*, ed. Grace Martin Smith and Carl W. Ernst, Istanbul: Isis / Piscataway, NJ: The Gorgias Press, pp. 171–92.

(1996). *Heroes of the Age: Moral Fault Lines on the Afghan Frontier*, Berkeley, CA: University of California Press.

(2002). *Before Taliban: Genealogies of the Afghan Jihad*, Berkeley, CA: University of California Press.

(2017). *Caravan of Martyrs: Sacrifice and Suicide Bombing in Afghanistan*, Oakland, CA: University of California Press.

Eggen, Nora S. (2011). Conceptions of Trust in the Qur'an. *Journal of Qur'anic Studies* 13(2), 56–85.

Ernst, Carl W., and Bruce B. Lawrence (2002). *Sufi Martyrs of Love: Chishti Sufism in South Asia and Beyond*, New York: Palgrave Macmillan.

Faizi, Inayatullah (1993). Afghan Political Literature in Peshawar (1978–82). In *Afghanistan and the Frontier*, ed. Fazal-ur-Rahim Marwat and Syed Wiqar Ali Shah Kakakhel, Peshawar: Emjay Books, pp. 274–95.

Faizy, Mansoor (2017). Durand Line Will Remain Line; Pakistan Has No Legal Authority to Dictate Term on Durand Line: Karzai. *Afghanistan Times* 11(215), 1f.

Fandy, Mamoun (1994). Egypt's Islamic Group: Regional Revenge? *Middle East Journal* 48(4), 607–25.

Faraj, ʿAbd al-Salām (1981). *al-Jihād: al-farīḍa al-ghāʾiba*, n.p.: Minbar al-tawḥīd wa'l-jihād.

Faraj, Ayman Ṣābirī (1422/2002). *Dhikriyyāt ʿarabī afghānī Abū Jaʿfar al-Miṣrī al-Qandahārī*, Beirut: Dār al-shurūq.

Farīd, Ḥāfiẓ Ghulām (1979). *Aḥvāl al-ʿārifīn: taẕkirah-yi Qādiriyyah-Mujaddidiyyah-Ghafūriyyah*, Lahore: Naẕīr pablisharz.

Farquhar, Michael (2017). *Circuits of Faith: Migration, Education, and the Wahhabi Mission*, Stanford, CA: Stanford University Press.

Faruqi, Burhan Ahmad (1940). *The Mujaddid's Conception of Tawhid*, Lahore: Sh. Muhammad Ashraf.

al-Fawzān, Ṣāliḥ ibn Fawzān (1411h). *al-Walāʾ wa'l-barāʾ fi'l-islām*, Riyadh: Dār al-waṭan li'l-nashr.

Fawzi, Issam, and Ivesa Lübben (2004). Die ägyptische *jama'a al-islamiya* [*sic*] und die Revision der Gewaltstrategie. *DOI-Fokus* 15, 1–43.

Fayẕānī, Mawlānā Muḥammad ʿAṭāʾallāh (1354sh). *Prūgrām-i ibtidāʾī-yi Madrasah-yi Qurʾān*, reissue, Kabul: Markaz-i bayn al-milalī-yi Fayẕānī.

(2012a). *Khūd'shināsī – khudā'shināsī*, Kabul: Markaz-i bayn al-milalī-yi Fayẕānī.

(2012b). *Jamāl va kamāl-i ṣāniʿdar maṣnūʿāt*, Kabul: Markaz-i bayn al-milalī-yi Fayẕānī.

al-Filasṭīnī, al-Shaykh al-ʿAllāma Abū Qatāda (n.d. [1421h]). *Juʾnat al-muṭayyibīn fī bayān akhṭāʾ risālat Kashf shubuhāt al-muqātilīn taḥta rāyat man akhil bi'l-aṣl al-dīn*, n.p.: no publisher.

Fīrūzpūrī, Qāẕī Muḥammad Aslam "Sayf" (1996). *Tārīkh-i Ahl-i Ḥadīs̱: tārīkh kē āʾinē mēṇ*, New Delhi: al-Kitāb intarnēshnal.

Foran, John (1992). The Long Fall of the Safavid Dynasty: Moving beyond the Standard Views. *International Journal of Middle Eastern Studies* 24(2), 281–304.

Forcher, Michael (2012). *Kleine Geschichte Tirols*, rev. ed., Innsbruck and Vienna: Haymon.

Foucault, Michel (1966). *Les mots et les choses: Une archéologie des sciences humaines*, Paris: Gallimard.

Foucault, Michel (1976). *Histoire de la sexualité I: La volonté de savoir*, Paris: Gallimard.

Foucault, Michel (1994). *Dits et écrits, 1954–1988*, ed. Daniel Defert, François Ewald and Jacques Lagrande, 4 vols., Paris: Gallimard.

Franco, Claudio (2009). The Tehrik-e Taliban Pakistan. In *Decoding the New Taliban: Insights from the Afghan Field*, ed. Antonio Giustozzi, London: Hurst / New York: Columbia University Press, pp. 269–91.

Frembgen, Jürgen (1983). *Religiöse Funktionsträger in Nuristan*, Sankt Augustin: VGH Wissenschaftsverlag.

Friedmann, Yohanan (1971). *Shaykh Aḥmad Sirhindī: An Outline of His Thought and a Study of His Image in the Eyes of Posterity*, Montreal: McGill–Queen's University Press.

(2003). *Tolerance and Coercion in Islam: Interfaith Relations in the Muslim Tradition*, Cambridge: Cambridge University Press.

Fuchs, Maria-Magdalena (2019). *Islamic Modernism in Colonial Punjab: The Anjuman-i Himayat-i Islam, 1884–1923*, unpublished PhD thesis, Princeton University.

Fuchs, Simon Wolfgang (2011). *Proper Signposts for the Camp: The Reception of Classical Authorities in the Ǧihādī Manual al-ʿUmda fī Iʿdād al-ʿUdda*, Würzburg: Ergon.

(2014). Third-Wave Shiʿism: Sayyid ʿArif Husain al-Husaini and the Islamic Revolution in Pakistan. *Journal of the Royal Asiatic Society* 24(3), 493–510.

(2017). Glossy Global Leadership: Unpacking the Multilingual Religious Thought of the *Jihad*. In *Afghanistan's Islam: From Conversion to the Taliban*, ed. Nile Green, Oakland, CA: University of California Press, pp. 189–206 and 299–307 (notes).

(2019). *In a Pure Muslim Land: Shiʿism between Pakistan and the Middle East*, Chapel Hill, NC: The University of North Carolina Press.

Fuoli, Francesca (2017). *Colonialism and State-Building in Afghanistan: Anglo-Afghan Co-Operation in the Institutionalisation of Ethnic Difference, 1869–1900*, unpublished PhD thesis, SOAS, University of London.

Gaborieau, Marc (1996). L'Asie Centrale dans l'horizon de l'Inde au début du XIXe siècle: À propos d'une lettre de Sayyid Ahmad Barelwî à l'Emir de Boukhara. *Cahiers de l'Asie centrale* 1–2: 265–82.

(1999). Criticizing the Sufis: The Debate in Early-Nineteenth-Century [*sic*] India. In *Islamic Mysticism Contested: Thirteen Centuries of Controversies & Polemics*, ed. Frederick de Jong and Bernd Radtke, Leiden: Brill, pp. 452–67.

(2010). *Le mahdi incompris: Sayyid Ahmad Barelwî (1786–1831) et le millénarisme en Inde*, Paris: CNRS Éditions.

Gaffney, Patrick D. (1994). *The Prophet's Pulpit: Islamic Preaching in Contemporary Egypt*, Berkeley, CA: University of California Press.

Gangōhī, Ḥaẕrat Mawlānā al-Ḥājj al-Ḥāfiẓ Rashīd Aḥmad (1987). *Fatāvá-yi rashīdiyyah: mubavvab bi-ṭarz-i jadīd*, Delhi: Darsī kutub'khānah.

Gangōhī, Muftī Maḥmūd Ḥasan (1430/2009). *Fatāvá-yi maḥmūdiyyah*, ed. Salīmallāh Khān, 25 vols., Karachi: Dār al-iftāʾ Jāmiʿat fārūqiyyah.

Gauvain, Richard (2013). *Salafi Ritual Purity: In the Presence of God*, London and New York: Routledge.

Gayer, Laurent (2014). *Karachi: Ordered Disorder and the Struggle for the City*, London: Hurst / New York: Oxford University Press.

Gemie, Sharif, and Brian Ireland (2017). *The Hippie Trail: A History*, Manchester: University of Manchester Press.

Gharaibeh, Mohammad (2012). *Zur Attributenlehre der Wahhābīya unter besonderer Berücksichtigung der Schriften Ibn Uṯaimīns (1929–2001)*, Berlin: EBV.

Gharvāl, Muḥammad ʿĀrif (1360sh). *Gharaṇē sandaray (də Paktiyā źinay ūlusay sandaray)*, Kabul: Dawlatī maṭbaʿah.

Ghaznavī, ʿAbd al-Jabbār (n.d.). *Savāniḥ-i ʿumrī-yi Mawlavī ʿAbdallāh al-Ghaznavī al-marḥūm, va Majmūʿah-yi maktūbāt*, Amritsar: Maṭbaʿ al-qurʾān va 'l-sunnah.

al-Ghaznawī, ʿAbd al-Wāhid, and ʿAbd al-Raḥīm, eds. (1894). *Majmūʿat al-tawḥīd*, Delhi: Maṭbaʿal-anṣārī.

Ghaznavī, Abū Bakr (1994). Sayyidī va abī. In *Dāvūd-i Ghaznavī*, ed. Abū Bakr Ghaznavī, Lahore: Fārān akēḍimī, pp. 211–463.

Ghubār, Mīr Ghulām Muḥammad (1397sh). *Afghānistān dar masīr-i tārīkh: jild-i duvvum*, Kabul: Intishārāt-i muḥsin.

Gḥumman, Mawlānā Muḥammad Ilyās (2014). *Firqah-yi mamātiyyat kā taḥqīqī jāʾizah*, Lahore: Maktabah-yi ahl al-sunnat va 'l-jamāʿat.

Gilani, Syed Asad (1978). *Mawdudi: Thought and Movement*, trans. Hasan Muizuddin Qazi, 5th ed., Karachi: East & West.

Gīlānī, Sayyid Asʿad (1989). *Afghānistān mēṇ taḥrīk-i muzāḥamat*, Lahore: Fīrūzsanz.

(1992). *Jamāʿat-i islāmī 1941ʾ tā 1948ʾ*, Lahore: Fīrūzsanz.

Gīlānī, Abū ʾl-Fatḥ (1968). *Ruqaʿāt-i Ḥakīm Abū ʾl-Fatḥ Gīlānī*, ed. Muḥammad Bashīr Ḥusayn, Lahore: Idārah-yi taḥqiqāt-i Pakistān, Danishʾgāh-yi Panjāb.

Gīlānī, Faqīr Muḥammad Amīr Shāh Qādirī (1972). *Taẕkirah-yi ʿulamāʾ va mashāʾikh-i sarḥadd*, 2nd ed., 2 vols., Peshawar: Maktabat al-ḥasan.

Gīlānī, Mawlānā Sayyid Manāẓir Aḥsan (1373h). *Savāniḥ-i qāsimī, yaʿnī sīrat-i shams al-islām sayyidnā imām al-kabīr Ḥaẓrat Muḥammad Qāsim Nānawtavī – quddus allāh sirrah*, 2 vols., Deoband: Dār al-ʿulūm.

Giustozzi, Antonio (2007). *Koran, Kalashnikov and Laptop: The Neo-Taliban Insurgency in Afghanistan*, London: Hurst / New York: Columbia University Press.

ed. (2009). *Decoding the New Taliban: Insights from the Afghan Field*, London: Hurst / New York: Columbia University Press.

(2018). *The Islamic State in Khorasan: Afghanistan, Pakistan and the New Central Asian Jihad*, London: Hurst / New York: Oxford University Press.

'Gōhar', Muḥammad Islām (1422/2001). *Paẍtō kẍī də naʿtiyyah shāʿirəy irtaqāʾ*, unpublished PhD thesis, University of Peshwar.

Golden, Peter B. (1992). *An Introduction to the History of the Turkic Peoples: Ethnogenesis and State-Formation in Medieval and Early Modern Eurasia and the Middle East*, Wiesbaden: Harrassowitz.

Gommans, Jos J. L. (1995). *The Rise of the Indo-Afghan Empire c. 1710–1780*, Leiden, New York and Cologne: Brill.

(2002). *Mughal Warfare: Indian Frontiers and High Roads to Empire, 1500–1700*, London and New York: Routledge.

Goodhand, Jonathan (2008). Corrupting or Consolidating the Peace? The Drugs Economy and Post-conflict Peacebuilding in Afghanistan. *International Peacekeeping* 15(3), 405–23.

Gopal, Anand, and Alex Strick van Linschoten (2017). Ideology in the Afghan Taleban. *Afghanistan Analyst Network*. URL: www.afghanistan-analysts.org/wp-content/uploads/2017/06/201705-AGopal-ASvLinschoten-TB-Ideology.pdf (accessed 24 February 2024).

Graeber, David (2016). *The Utopia of Rules: On Technology, Stupidity, and the Secret Joys of Bureaucracy*, New York: Melville House.

Gramsci, Antonio (1977). *Quaderni del carcere: Edizione critica*, ed. Valentino Gerratana, 2nd ed., 4 vols., Turin: Giulio Einaudi.

Green, Marcus E. (2011). Rethinking the Subaltern and the Question of Censorship in Gramsci's Prison Notebooks. *Postcolonial Studies* 14(4), 387–404.

Green, Nile (2008). Tribe, Diaspora, and Sainthood in Afghan History. *Journal of Asian Studies* 67(1), 171–211.

ed. (2017). *Afghanistan's Islam: From Conversion to the Taliban*, Oakland, CA: University of California Press.

Grima, Benedicte (2004). *The Performance of Emotion among Paxtun Women: 'The Misfortunes Which Have Befallen Me'*, reprint from 1992, Karachi: Oxford University Press.

(2005). *Secrets from the Field: An Ethnographer's Notes from Northwest Pakistan*, Karachi: Oxford University Press.

Gunaratna, Rohan (2002). *Inside Al Qaeda* [sic]*: Global Networks of Terror*, New York: Columbia University Press.

Habibi, M. A., M. Ulman, B. Baha, and M. Stočes (2017). Measurement and Statistical Analysis of End User Satisfaction with Mobile Network Coverage in Afghanistan. *Agris On-Line Papers in Economics and Informatics* 9(2), 47–58.

Ḥāfiẓ, Usāma Ibrāhīm, and ʿĀṣim ʿAbdallāh Muḥammad (1425/2004a). *Ruʾya wāqiʿiyya wa-naẓra sharʿiyya*, Cairo and Riyadh: Maktabat al-ʿabikān.

(1425/2004b). *al-Nuṣḥ waʾl-tabiyīn fī taṣḥīḥ mafāhīm al-muḥtasibīn*, Cairo and Riyadh: Maktabat al-ʿabikān.

Ḥakīmzay, Badr al-Ḥakīm, and Faqīr Muḥammad (2018). Də Akhūn[d] Miyā[ṇ] dād Nūr'nāmah: də Darvīzah adabī maktab də astāzī pah ḥēṣ. *Paxtō* 47(2), 121–8.

Shahāb Akbar (2018). Akhūn[d] Ćāllāk: də Darvīzah adabī maktab də yaw naṣr'nigār ghəṛay pah ḥēṣ. *Paxtō* 47(2), 221–30.

al-Ḥalabī, ʿAlī ibn Ḥasan (1420h). *Fiqh al-wāqiʿ bayn al-naẓariyya waʾl-taṭbīq*, 2nd ed., Ramallah: Shirkat al-nūr.

Hamdānī, Raẓā (1981). *Razmiyyah dastānēṇ*, Islamabad: Lōk Virṣah.

Ḥāmid, Muṣṭafá (1994). *15 Ṭalqa fī sabīl allāh*, n.p.: no publisher.

(1995). *Maʿārik al-bawāba al-ṣakhriyya: Tanẓīm al-Qāʿida yūlad fī maʿrakat Jājī wa-Ḥaqqānī yudmá anf al-sūfiyat fī Jāwar*, n.p.: no publisher.

(1997). *al-Ḥamāka al-kubrá aw ḥarb al-maʿīz: maʿrakat Jalālābād yūliyū 1989 ahm maʿārik al-Qāʿida wa-Usāma bin Lādin fī Afghānistān*, n.p.: no publisher.

(2001a). *Fatḥ Khūst: ḥafl tatwīj li-ḥarb al-ʿiṣābāt al-afghāniyya*, n.p.: no publisher.

(2001b). *Mashrūʿ Ṭājīkistān: al-mujāhidūn al-ʿarab yantaqulūna min nahr Shamlī ilá nahr Jīḥūn*, n.p.: no publisher.

(2002). *Ṣalīb fī samāʿQandahār: qiṣṣat al-mujāhidīn al-ʿarab fī Afghānistān min dukhūl al-awwal ilá ʾl-khurūj al-akhīr*, n.p.: no publisher.

(2007). *Naẓara ghayr-taqlīdiyya ʿalá ʾl-jaysh al-amrīkī fī Afghānistān: ḥarb al-afiyūn al-thālitha*, n.p.: no publisher.

Ḥamzah, Mawlānā Amīr (1423/2002). *Afghānistān kī chūṭiyōṇ par qāfilah-yi daʿvat va jihād*, Lahore: Dār al-Andalus.

al-Ḥanafī, al-ʿAllāma Ibn Abī ʿIzz (1426/2005). *Sharḥ al-ʿaqīda al-ṭaḥāwiyya*, ed. Jamāʿa min al-ʿulamāʾ, Cairo: Dār al-salām.

al-Ḥanafī, al-Ḥājj Faqīrallāh ibn ʿAbd al-Raḥmān (1316h). *Quṭb al-irshād*, Quetta: Amīr Ḥamzah kitāb'khānah.

al-Ḥanafī, Mawlānā Ḥusayn ʿAlī (1385/1966). *Tafsīr javāhir al-qurʾān*, ed. Ghulāmallāh Khān, 3 vols., Rawalpindi: Kutub'khānah-yi rashīdiyyah.

(1387h). *Fuyūẕāt-i ḥusaynī, al-maʿrūf bah Tuḥfat-i ibrāhīmī*, trans. ʿAbd al-Ḥamīd Svātī, Gūjrānvālah: Idārah-yi nashr va ishāʿat-i madrasah Nuṣrat al-ʿulūm.

Ḥanīf, Muḥammad (1979). *Ḥayāt va ās̱ār-i ḥaẕrat Miyāṇ Muḥammad ʿUmar Chamkanī – raḥmat allāh ʿalayh*, unpublished PhD thesis, University of Peshawar.

Hanif, Muhammad Shehzad, Shao Yunfei, and Muhammad Imran Hanif (2018). Growth Prospects, Market Challenges and Policy Measures: Evolution of Mobile Broadband in Pakistan. *Digital Policy, Regulation and Governance* 20(1), 42–61.

Hanifi, M. Jamil (2004). Review of 'Before Taliban: Genealogies of the Afghan Jihad' by David B. Edwards. *American Anthropologist* 106(1), 185–7.

(2011). Vending Distorted Afghanistan through Patriotic "Anthropology". *Critique of Anthropology* 31(3), 256–70.

Ḥanīfī, Muftī Abū Ilyās (1436h). *al-Istiftāʾ: də islāmī khilāfat par ẕidd jang kavūnkī ćah ḥukm laray?*, n.p.: Anṣār al-khilāfah khparandōyah idārah.

Hanifi, Shah Mahmoud (2011). *Connecting Histories in Afghanistan: Market Relations and State Formation on a Colonial Frontier*, Stanford, CA: Stanford University Press.

(2016). The Pashtun Counter-Narrative. *Middle East Critique* 25(4), 385–400.

(2018). A Genealogy of Orientalism in Afghanistan: The Colonial Image Legacy. In *Middle Eastern Studies after September 11: Neo-Orientalism, American Hegemony and Academia*, ed. Tugrul Teskin, Leiden and Boston, MA: Brill, pp. 50–80.

Hanlon, Roger T., and John B. Messenger (1998). *Cephalopod Behaviour*, Cambridge: Cambridge University Press.

Hann, Chris (2017). Whose Moods? Anthropologists in a Bubble. *HAU: Journal of Ethnographic Theory* 7(3), 147–51.

Haq, M. Anwarul (1972). *The Faith Movement of Mawlānā Muḥammad Ilyās*, London: Allen & Unwin.

Ḥaqqānī, Mawlānā ʿAbd al-Qayyūm (1419/1998). *Ṣuḥbatē bā ahl-i ḥaqq: ifādāt-i muḥaddis̱-i kabīr Shaykh al-ḥadīs̱ Mawlānā ʿAbd al-Ḥaqq – raḥmat allāh ʿalayh*, Khāliqābād: al-Qāsim akēḍimī.

(1422/2001). *Savāniḥ-i Shaykh al-ḥadīs̱ Ḥaẕrat Mawlānā ʿAbd al-Ḥaqq – raḥmat allāh ʿalayh*, Nowshera: al-Qāsim akēḍimī.

al-Haravī, Khᵛājah Niʿmatallāh ibn Khᵛājah Ḥabīballāh (1379/1960). *Tārīkh-i Khān-i jahānī va Makhzān-i afghānī*, ed. Sayyid Muḥammad Imām al-Dīn, 2 vols., Dacca: Zaykū prēss.

Haravī, Niẓām al-Dīn Aḥmad ibn Muḥammad Muqīm (1911–35). *Ṭabaqāt-i akbarī*, ed. Brajendranath De and M. H. Ḥusayn, 3 vols., Calcutta: Maṭbaʿ-i baptist mīshan.

Haroon, Sana (2007). *Frontiers of Faith: Islam in the Indo-Afghan Borderland*, London: Hurst / New York: Columbia University Press.

Hartung, Jan-Peter (2004). *Viele Wege und ein Ziel: Leben und Wirken von Sayyid Abū l-Ḥasan ʿAlī Ḥasanī Nadwī (1914–1999)*, Würzburg: Ergon.

(2011). Enacting the Rule of Islam: On Courtly Patronage of Religious Scholars in Pre- and Early Modern Times. In *Court Cultures in the Muslim World: Seventh to Nineteenth Centuries*, ed. Jan-Peter Hartung and Albrecht Fuess, London and New York: Routledge, pp. 295–325.

(2013a). *A System of Life: Mawdūdī and the Ideologisation of Islam*, London: Hurst / New York: Oxford University Press.

(2013b). Abused Rationality? On the Role of maʿqūlī Scholars in the Events of 1857/8. In *Mutiny at the Margins: New Perspectives on the Indian Uprising of 1857*, vol. v: *Muslim, Dalit and Subaltern Narratives*, ed. Crispin Bates, New Delhi: Sage, pp. 135–55.

(2013c). The Limits of the Dialogical: Thoughts on Muslim Patterns of In- and Exclusion. *Culture and Dialogue* 3(1), 73–94.

(2016a). Between a Rock and a Hard Place: The *Ṭālibān*, Afghan Self-Determination, and the Challenges of Transnational Jihadism. *Die Welt des Islams* 56(2), 125–52.

(2016b). The Praiseworthiness of Divine Beauty – The "Shaykh al-Hind" Maḥmūd al-Ḥasan, Social Justice, and Deobandiyyat. *South Asian History and Culture* 7(4), 346–69.

(2017a). Frontiers – Pieties – Resistance. In *Dynamics of Change in the Pakistan–Afghanistan Region: Politics on Borderland. Conference Proceedings 2016*, ed. Shahida Aman and Muhammad Zubair, Peshawar: University of Peshawar, 39–54.

(2017b). Appropriations and Contestations of the Islamic Nomenclature in Muslim North India: Elitism, Lexicography and the Meaning of *The Political. Contributions to the History of Concepts* 12(2), 76–110.

(2019a). Of Pious Missions and Challenging the Elders: A Genealogy of Radical Egalitarianism in the Pashtun Borderscape. *Geopolitics* 24(2), 308–43.

(2019b). Making Sense of "Political Quietism": An Analytical Intervention. In *Political Quietism in Islam: Sunni and Shiʿi Practice and Thought*, ed. Saud al-Sarhan, London and New York: I.B. Tauris, pp. 15–32.

(2020). "He's Just a Man!": Pashtun Salafists and the Representation of the Prophet. *Die Welt des Islams* 60(2–3), 170–204.

(2021a). A Taliban Legal Discourse on Violence. In *Violence in Islamic Thought: From European Imperialism to the Post-Colonial Era*, ed. Robert Gleave and Mustafa Baig, Edinburgh: Edinburgh University Press, pp. 123–59.

(2021b). §§ 25–27: Südasien. In *Philosophie in der Islamischen Welt*, vol. iv.2: *19. und 20. Jahrhundert: Türkei, Iran und Südasien*, ed. Anke von Kügelgen, Basel: Schwabe, pp. 1189–365.

(2022a). Taking Lessons from the Prophet in Times of War: Muḥammadan Images during the Afghan Resistance, c. 1978–1992. In *Heirs of the Prophet: Authority and Power in Early Modern and Contemporary Islam*, ed.

Rachida Chih, David Jordan and Stefan Reichmuth, Leiden and Boston, MA: Brill, pp. 419–47.

(2022b). The Word of God for the Indian Muslim of Today: Abul Kalam Azad's *Tarjuman al-Qur'an*. In *Dynamics of Islam in the Modern Word: Essays in Honour of Jamal Malik*, ed. Saeed Zarrabi-Zadeh, Armina Omerika, Thomas K. Gugler and Michael E. Asbury, Leiden and Boston, MA: Brill, pp. 121–40.

(2024). On "Taliban", in Light of Current Events. *Afghanistan* 7(Suppl.) 19–49.

Hasan, Noorhaidi (2006). *Laskar Jihad: Islam, Militancy, and the Quest for Identity in Post-New Order Indonesia*, Ithaca, NY: Cornell Southeast Asia Program.

al-Ḥasanī, ʿAbd al-Ḥayy (1412–13/1991–3). *al-Iʿlām bi-man fī tārīkh al-Hind min al-aʿlām, yaʿnī nuzhat al-khawāṭir wa-bahjat al-masāmiʿ waʾl-nawāẓir*, reprint from 1947, 8 vols., Rāʾī Baraylī: Dārat al-Shaykh ʿAlamallāh.

Ḥasanī, Sayyid Muḥammad Ṡānī (1420/1999). *Savāniḥ-i Ḥaẕrat Mawlānā Muḥammad Yūsuf Kāndhalavī*, Lucknow: Majlis-i ṣaḥāfat va nashriyāt.

al-Ḥaṣkafī, Muḥammad ibn ʿAlī (1423/2002). *al-Durr al-mukhtār sharḥ tanwīr al-abṣār wa-jāmiʿ al-baḥār*, ed. ʿAbd al-Munʿim Khalīl Ibrāhīm, Beirut: Dār al-kutub al-ʿilmiyya.

Hayat Khan, Azmat (1993). Factional Organisation of the Afghan Mujahideens [*sic*] in Peshawar. In *Afghanistan and the Frontier*, ed. Fazal-ur-Rahim Marwat and Syed Wiqar Ali Shah Kakakhel, Peshawar: Emjay Books, pp. 214–34.

(2000). *The Durand Line: Its Geo-Strategic Importance*, Peshawar: Area Studies Centre, University of Peshawar.

Ḥayāt Khān, Muḥammad (1867). *Ḥayāt-i afghānī*, Lahore: Kūh-i nūr.

Haykel, Bernard (2003). *Revival and Reform in Islam: The Legacy of Muhammad al-Shawkani*, Cambridge: Cambridge University Press.

Ḥāẕiq, ʿAbd al-Ḥaqq (1900). *Ḥālāt-i jang-i Malkah va Sithānah*, paginated MS BL London Or.6651a.

Hegghammer, Thomas (2005). Abdallah Azzam. In *Al-Qaida dans le texte: Écrits d'Oussama ben Laden, Abdallah Azzam, Ayman al-Zawahiri et Abu Moussab al-Zarqawi*, ed. Giles Kepel, trans. Jean-Pierre Milelli, Paris: Presses Universitaires de France, pp. 113–215.

(2010). *Jihad in Saudi Arabia: Violence and Pan-Islamism since 1979*, Cambridge: Cambridge University Press.

(2020). *The Caravan: Abdallah Azzam and the Rise of Global Jihad*, Cambridge: Cambridge University Press.

Hegghammer, Thomas, and Stéphane Lacroix (2007). Rejectionist Islamism in Saudi Arabia: The Story of Juhayman al-ʿUtaybi Revisited. *International Journal of Middle East Studies* 39(1), 103–22.

HIA [Hizb-i Islami Afghanistan] (1986). Hekmatyars Schreiben an die UNO. *Al-Sobh* 13, 12.

Ḥikmat, ʿAbd al-Raʾuf (2015). Də marḥūm Mawlavī Muḥammad Nabī Muḥammadī žvand aw mubārizē tah katənah. *Nən Ṫəkəy Asiyā* 22 April. URL: www.nunn.asia/42916/د-مرحوم-مولوي-محمد-نبي-محمدي-ژوند-او-مبا/ (accessed 24 February 2024).

Ḥikmatyār, [Gulbuddīn] (n.d.). *Islāmī nahẕat: də nādirī kōrunəy lah ravastō də rūsānō tar īstō*, Peshawar: Idārah-yi mīs̱āq-i īs̱ār.

(1365sh). *Muvālāt va dūstī bā dushman*, n.p.: Riyāsat-i irshād va farhang.

(1366sh). *Də qawm məshərānō tah də vrōr 'Ḥikmatyār' vītā*, n.p.: Də shahādat nashratī argān.

(1367sh). *Də fatḥay karvān*, n.p.: Riyāsat-i irshād va farhang.

(1377sh). *Ḥaqīqat-i nifāq az dīd'gāh-i qur'ān*, Peshawar: Idārah-yi mīs̱āq-i īs̱ār.

(1378sh). *Rahbarī va shivah'hā-yi intikhāb-i ān*, Peshawar: Idārah-yi mīs̱āq-i īs̱ār.

(1379sh). *Buḥrān-i mushkilāt va rāh'hā-yi ḥall*, Tehran: Intishārāt-i maṭbūʿ.

(1385sh). *Də qur'ān qismūnah aw də asāsī qaẕāyā vū is̱bāt*, n.p.: no publisher.

(1385–90sh). *Də qur'ān palvashē*, 8 vols., Kabul: self-published.

(1387sh). *Pah allāh taʿālá īmān*, n.p.: no publisher.

(1389sh). *Mutaẕādd rivāyāt maẕhabī ikhtilāfāt salafi shum kih maẕhabī pātah shum?*, n.p.: no publisher.

ḤiI-Ḥ (Ḥizb-i Islāmī Ḥikmatyār) (n.d.). *Marām-i Ḥizb-i Islāmī*, n.p.: no publisher.

(1369sh). *Də Ḥizb Islāmī Afghānistān asās'nāmah*, n.p.: Də Ḥizb Islāmī Afghānistān.

Hobbes, Thomas (1835–45). *The Collected English Works of Thomas Hobbes of Malmesbury*, ed. W. Molesworth, 11 vols., London: Johann Bohn.

(1839–45). *Opera philosophica*, ed. W. Molesworth, 5 vols., London: Johann Bohn.

Hobsbawm, Eric (1992). *The Age of Revolution: Europe 1789–1848*, reprint from 1962, London: Abacus.

(1994). *The Age of Empire, 1875–1914*, reprint from 1987, London: Abacus.

Home Office / UK Border Agency (2008). Country of Origins Information Report: Afghanistan (29 August). URL: www.statewatch.org/media/documents/news/2009/mar/afghanistan-ukba-c-of-origin-report.pdf (accessed 24 February 2024).

Hopkins, Benjamin D., and Magnus Marsden (2011). *Fragments of the Afghan Frontier*, London: Hurst / New York: Columbia University Press.

Hopkins, Nicolas, and Reem Saad, eds. (2004). *Upper Egypt: Identity and Change*, Cairo and New York: American University of Cairo Press.

Hōtak, Muḥammad (1339sh). *Pətah khizānah*, ed. ʿAbd al-Ḥayy Ḥabībī, 2nd ed., Kabul: Də Pōhanəy vizārat də dār al-ta'līf riyāsat.

Hunter, W[illiam] W[ilson] (1871). *The Indian Musalmans: Are They Bound in Conscience to Rebel against the Queen?*, London: Trübner & Co.

Hussain, S. Iftikhar (2000). *Some Major Pukhtoon Tribes along the Pak–Afghan Border*, ed. M. Y. Effendi, Peshawar: Area Studies Centre / Hanns Seidel Foundation.

Hussain, Naheed (2018). *A Journey into the Lifeworld of* [*the*] *Sikh Community of Peshawar*, Islamabad: Iqbal International Institute for Research and Dialogue.

Hyman, Anthony (1984). *Afghanistan under Soviet Domination – 1964–83*, London: Macmillan.

Ibn ʿAbd al-ʿAzīz, ʿAbd al-Qādir (n.d.). *al-Jāmiʿ fī ṭalab al-ʿilm al-sharīf*, n.p.: Minbar al-tawḥīd waʾl-jihād.

(1420/1999). *al-ʿUmda fī iʿdād al-ʿudda liʾl-jihād fī sabīl allāh taʿālá*, Amman: Dār al-bayāraq.

(1428/2007). Serial "Wathīqat tarshīd al-ʿamal al-jihād fī Miṣr waʾl-ʿālam". *al-Jarīda* 145, 12f. to 159, 12f.

Ibn ʿAbd al-Wahhāb, Muḥammad (1406/1986). *Kitāb al-tawḥīd: ḥaqq allāh ʿalá ʾl-ʿabīd*, Beirut: Dār al-kutub al-ʿilmiyya.

Ibn ʿĀbidīn, Muḥammad Amīn (1423/2003). *Radd al-muḥtār ʿalá ʾl-durr al-mukhtār sharḥ tanwīr al-abṣār*, ed. ʿĀdil Aḥmad ʿAbd al-Mawjūd and ʿAlī Muḥammad Muʿawwaḍ, 12 vols., Riyadh: Dār ʿālam al-kutub.

Ibn ʿArabī, Abū Bakr Muḥammad ibn ʿAbdallāh (1424/2003). *Aḥkām al-qurʾān*, ed. Muḥammad ʿAbd al-Qādir ʿAṭā, 4 vols., Beirut: Dār al-kutub al-ʿilmiyya.

Ibn al-Athīr, Abū ʾl-Ḥasan ʿAlī ibn Muḥammad (1407/1987). *al-Kāmil fīʾl-taʾrīkh*, ed. Abū ʾl-Fidāʾ ʿAbdallāh al-Qāḍī, 11 vols., Beirut: Dār al-kutub al-ʿilmiyya.

Ibn Bāz, ʿAbd al-ʿAzīz (1420h). *Majmūʿa fatāwá wa-maqālāt mutanawwiʿa*, ed. Muḥammad ibn Saʿd al-Shuwwayʿir, 30 vols., Riyadh: Dār al-qāsim liʾl-nashr.

(1428/2008). *Fatāwá nūr ʿalá ʾl-ḍarb*, ed. Muḥammad ibn Saʿd al-Shuwwayʿir, 31 vols., Riyadh: al-Ruʾāsa al-ʿāmma liʾl-buḥūth al-ʿilmiyya waʾl-iftāʾ.

Ibn Bishr, ʿUthmān ibn ʿAbdallāh (1402/1982). *ʿUnwān al-majd fī taʾrīkh Najd*, ed. ʿAbd al-Raḥmān ibn ʿAbd al-Laṭīf Āl al-Shaykh, 4th ed., 2 vols., Riyadh: Dārat al-malik ʿAbd al-ʿAzīz.

Ibn Ghannām, Ḥusayn ibn Abī Bakr (1415/1994). *Taʾrīkh Najd*, 4th ed., Beirut: Dār al-shurūq.

Ibn Ḥanbal, Aḥmad ibn Muḥammad (1416/1995). *al-Musnad liʾl-imām Aḥmad ibn Muḥammad ibn Ḥanbal*, ed. Aḥmad Muḥammad Shākir, 20 vols., Cairo: Dār al-ḥadīth.

Ibn Hishām, ʿAbd al-Malik (1375/1955). *al-Sīra al-nabawiyya*, ed. Muṣṭafá al-Saqqā, Ibrāhīm al-Abyārī and ʿAbd al-Ḥafīẓ Shallabī, 2nd ed., 4 vols. in two, Cairo: Muṣṭafá al-Bābī al-Ḥalabī.

Ibn al-Humām, al-Imām Kamāl al-Dīn (1424/2003). *Sharḥ fatḥ al-qadīr ʿalá ʾl-Hidāya sharḥ bidāyat al-mubtadī*, ed. ʿAbd al-Razzāq Ghālib al-Mahdī, 10 vols., Beirut: Dār al-kutub al-ʿilmiyya.

Ibn Iskandar, Amīr ʿUnṣur al-Maʿālī Kaykāwus (1312sh). *K. Naṣīḥatʾnāmah, marʿūf bah Qābūsʾnāmah*, ed. Saʿīd Nafīsī, Tehran: Maṭbaʿah-yi majlis.

Ibn Jamīl al-Raḥmān, Ḍiyāʾ al-Raḥmān (1434h). *Juhūd ʿulamāʾ al-ḥanafiyya fīʾl-radd ʿalá ʾl-khawarij*, 2 vols., unpublished PhD thesis, al-Jāmiʿa al-islāmiyya biʾl-Madīna al-munawwara.

Ibn Kathīr, al-Ḥāfiẓ ʿImād al-Dīn Abī Fidāʾ (1421/2000). *Tafsīr al-qurʾān al-ʿaẓīm*, ed. Muṣṭafá al-Sayyid Muḥammad, Muḥammad Sayyid Rashād, Muḥammad

Faḍl al-Ajmāwī, ʿAlī Aḥmad ʿAbd al-Bāqī and Ḥasan ʿAbbās Quṭb, 15 vols., Gizah: Muʾassasat qurṭuba.

Ibn Khaldūn, ʿAbd al-Raḥmān (1425/2004). *Muqaddimat Ibn Khaldūn*, ed. ʿAbdallāh Muḥammad Darwīsh, 2 vols., Damascus: Dār yuʿarrib.

Ibn Lādin, Usāma (1436/2015). *Majmūʿ rasāʾil wa-tawjīhāt al-shaykh al-mujāhidīn*, n.d.: Nakhbat al-iʿlām al-jihādī.

Ibn Shāhīn, Abū Ḥafṣ ʿUmar ibn Aḥmad ibn ʿUthmān (1415/1995). *Sharḥ madhhab ahl al-sunna wa-maʿrifat sharāʾiʿ al-dīn waʾl-tamassuk biʾl-sunan*, ed. ʿĀdil ibn Muḥammad, Gizah: Muʾassasat qurṭuba.

Ibn Taymiyya, Abū ʿAbbās Taqī al-Dīn Aḥmad (n.d.). *al-Ḥisba fiʾl-islām, aw waẓīfat al-ḥukūma al-islāmiyya*, Beirut: Dār al-kutub al-ʿilmiyya.

(1392/1972). *Muqaddima fī uṣūl al-tafsīr*, ed. ʿAdnān Zarzūr, 2nd ed., Kuwait: Dār al-qurʾān al-karīm.

(1396/1976a). *al-ʿUbūdiyya*, ed. Maḥmūd Aḥmad Ghaḍanfar al-Salafī, Lahore: Ibn Taymiyya akēdīmī.

(1396/1976b). *al-Amr biʾl-maʿrūf waʾl-nahy ʿan al-munkar*, ed. Ṣalāḥ al-Dīn al-Munjid, Beirut: Dār al-kutub al-jadīd.

(1403/1983). *al-Ṣārim al-maslūl ʿalá shātim al-rasūl*, ed. Muḥammad Muḥyī al-Dīn ʿAbd al-Ḥamīd, Cairo: Maktabat Tāj.

(1406/1986). *Minhāj al-sunna al-nabawiyya fī naqḍ kalām al-shīʿa al-qadariyya*, ed. Dr. Muḥammad Rashād Sālim, 9 vols., Riyadh: Jāmiʿat al-Imām Muḥammad ibn Saʿūd.

(1419/1998). *Iqtiḍāʾ al-ṣirāṭ al-mustaqīm li-mukhālafat aṣḥāb al-jaḥīm*, ed. Dr. Nāṣir ibn ʿAbd al-Karīm al-ʿAql, 2 vols., Riyadh: Dār Ishbīliyā.

(1420/1999). *al-ʿAqīda al-wāṣitiyya*, ed. Abū Muḥammad Ashraf bin ʿAbd al-Maqṣūd, Riyadh: Aḍwā al-salaf.

(1424/2003). *K. al-Radd ʿalá ʾl-manṭiqiyīn*, ed. Muḥammad Ḥasan Ismāʿīl, Beirut: Dār al-kutub al-ʿilmiyya.

(1426/2005a). *Majmūʿat al-fatāwá*, ed. ʿĀmir al-Jazzār and Anwar al-Bāz, 37 vols., al-Manṣūra: Dār al-wafāʾ.

(1426/2005b). *K. al-Siyāsa al-sharʿiyya fī iṣlāḥ al-rāʿī waʾl-raʿiyya*, Beirut: Dār al-kutub al-ʿilmiyya.

Ibn ʿUthaymīn, Muḥammad ibn Ṣāliḥ (1407h). *Majmūʿal-fatāwá wa-rasāʾil*, ed. Fahd ibn Nāṣir al-Sulaymān, 29 vols., Riyadh: Dār al-waṭan liʾl-nashr.

Ilyās, Miyāṇ Muḥammad (2012). *Shaykh al-qurʾān Mawlānā Muḥammad Ṭāhir Panjpīrī – raḥmat allāh ʿalayhi – ḥayāt va khidmāt awr unkī qurʾānī taḥrīk*, 2nd ed., Peshawar: Ishāʿat akēdimī.

IMFF (1394sh). Fatvá. 29 July 2015. URL: www.allfida.org/فتوی/ (accessed 24 February 2024).

İnce, İrfan (2014). *Medina im 12. / 18. Jahrhundert: Politische Strukturen, Beziehungen und Konflikte, mit Einblicken in den Gelehrtendiskurs*, PhD thesis, Ruhr University Bochum. URL: https://hss-opus.ub.ruhr-uni-bochum.de/opus4/frontdoor/deliver/index/docId/4086/file/diss.pdf (accessed 24 February 2024).

Iqtidar, Humeira (2011). *Secularizing Islamists? Jama'at-e-Islami and Jama'at-ud-Da'wa in Urban Pakistan*, Chicago, IL and London: The University of Chicago Press.

ʿIrāqī, ʿAbd al-Rashīd (2003). *Ghaznavī khāndān*, Karachi: Imām Shams al-Ḥaqq Ḍiyānavī pablisharz.

Isenberg, Nancy (2017). *White Trash: The 400-Year Untold History of Class in America*, London: Atlantic.

Iṣfahānī, Muḥammad Yūsuf Vālah Qazvīnī (1382sh). *Īrān dar zamān-i Shāh Ṣafī va Shāh ʿAbbās-i duvvum (1038–1071 hijrī qamarī): ḥadīqah-yi shasham va haftam az rawẓah-yi hashtam - Khuld-i barīn*, ed. Muḥammad Riẓā Naṣīrī, Tehran: Anjuman-i āṣār va mafākhir-i farhangī.

al-Jafān, ʿAbd al-Raḥmān ibn ʿAbd al-ʿAzīz (1423h). *Īnās al-nubalāʾ fī sirat shaykhnā al-ʿUqlāʾ*, Ṭāʾif: no publisher.

Jäger, Siegfried (2004). *Kritische Diskursanalyse: Eine Einführung*, 4th ed., Münster: Unrast Verlag.

Jahāngīr, Nūr al-Dīn Muḥammad (1359sh/1980). *Jahāngīr'nāmah, yaʿnī tūzuk-i jahāngīrī*, ed. Muḥammad Hāshim, Tehran: Intishārāt-i bunyād-i farhang-i Īrān.

Jahanzeb, Miyangul (1985). *The Last Wali of Swat: An Autobiography as Told to Fredrik Barth*, Oslo: Universitetsforlaget.

Jamal, Arif (2009). *Shadow War: The Untold Story of Jihad in Kashmir*, New York: Melville House.

Jāmī, Maḥmūd [al-]Ḥusaynī (1384sh). *Tārīkh-i Aḥmad'shāhī: tārīkh-i tashkīl avvalīn-i ḥukūmat-i Afghānistān*, ed. Ghulām'ḥusayn Zargarī'nižād, Tehran: Muʾassasah-yi chāp va intishārāt-i Dānish'gāh-i Tihrān.

Jāvīd, ʿAzīz (1982). *Ḥājjī Ṣāḥib-i Turangzāʾī: barr-i ṣaghīr kī taḥrīk-i āzādī kā ʿaẓīm mujahid*, 2nd ed., Peshawar: Idārah-yi taḥqīq va taṣnīf-i Pākistān.

Jawnpūrī, Karāmat ʿAlī (1281h). *K. Maqāmiʿ al-mubtadiʿīn mashhūr bah Radd al-bidʿah*, n.p.: Maṭbaʿ-i [illegible].

(1311/1894). *Zād al-taqwá*, Calcutta: Maṭbaʿ-i saʿīdī.

al-Jawziyya, Abū ʿAbdallāh ibn Qayyim (1423h). *Iʿlām al-muwaqqiʿīn ʿan rabb al-ʿālamīn*, ed. Abū ʿUbayda Mashhūr ibn Ḥasan Āl Sulaymān, 7 vols., Riyadh: Dār Ibn al-Jawzī.

(1423/2003). *Madārij al-sālikīn bayna manāzil "iyyāka nabūdu wa-iyyāka al-nastaʿīn"*, ed. Muḥammad Muʿtaṣim bi'llāh al-Baghdādī, 3 vols., Beirut: Dār al-kutub al-ʿarabī.

(1432h). *Miftāḥ dār al-saʿāda wa-manshūr al-wilāyat al-ʿilm wa'l-irāda*, ed. ʿAbd al-Raḥmān ibn Ḥasan ibn Qāʾid, Jeddah and Mecca: Dār ʿālam al-fawāʾid.

Jettmar, Karl (1965). *Fruchtbarkeitsrituale und Verdienstfeste im Umkreis der Kafiren*, Heidelberg: Südasien-Institut.

(1975). *Die Religionen des Hindukusch*, Stuttgart: Kohlhammer.

JIA (*Jamʿiyyat-i Islāmī-yi Afghānistān*), ed. (n.d.). *Asās'nāmah va marām'nāmah-yi Jamʿiyyat-i Islāmī-yi Afghānistān*. URL: اساسنامه-و-مرامنامه- (accessed 30 January 2018).

Jinnah, Quaid-i-Azam Mohammad Ali [*sic*] (1993–2012). *Papers*, eds.-in-chief Z. H. Zaidi and M. Akram Shaheedi, 17 vols. to date, Islamabad: National Archive of Pakistan.

Jones, Schuyler (1974). *Men of Influence in Nuristan: A Study of Social Control and Dispute Settlement in Waigal Valley, Afghanistan*, London and New York: Seminar Press.

Kākā Khēl, Sayyid Bahādur Shāh Ẓafar (1965). *Paxtānah də tārīkh pah ranṛā kxē: də 550 q-m nah də 1964 pūrē*, Peshawar: Yūnivarsitī buk ējansī.

(1986). *Mukhtaṣar-i savāniḥ-i quṭb al-aqṭab shaykh al-mashāʾikh Ḥaẓrat Sayyid Kastīr, al-mulaqab bah Raḥm'kār – rḥ –, al-maʿrūf bah Kākā Ṣāḥib*, Peshawar: Chāp'źāy-yi Kōhāṫ rōḋ.

Kākā Khēl, Sayyid Vaqār-ʿAlī Shāh (1990). *Pīr ṣāḥib-i Mānkī-yi sharīf Sayyid Amīn al-Ḥasanāt awr unkī siyāsī jadd va juhd*, Islamabad: Qawmī idārāh barā-yi taḥqīq-i tārīkh va s̱aqāfat.

Kakar, Hasan Kawun (1979). *Government and Society in Afghanistan: The Reign of Amir ʾAbd* [sic] *al-Rahman Khan*, Austin, TX: The University of Texas Press.

Kāmil, Muṣṭafá (2017). Iʿlām "al-Qāʿida" minaṣāt nashr al-irhāb. *al-Bawāba News* (7 November). URL: www.albawabhnews.com/2791474 (accessed 24 February 2024).

Kānḋhalavī, Muḥammad Zakariyā (1392h). *Tārīkh-i maẓāhir*, 2 vols., Sahāranpūr: Kutub'khānah-yi ishāʿat al-ʿulūm.

Kānḋhalavī, Nūr al-Ḥasan-i Rāshid (1428/2007). *Taẕkirah-yi Ḥaẓrat Mawlānā Muḥammad Maẓhar Nānawtavī*, Kānḋhalah: Ḥaẓrat Muftī Ilāhī Bakhsh akēḋimī.

al-Kasānī, ʿAlāʾ al-Dīn Abū Bakr ibn Masʿūd (1424/2002). *Badāʾiʿ al-ṣanāʾiʿ fī tartīb al-sharāʾiʿ*, ed. ʿAlī Muḥammad Muʿawwaḍ and ʿĀdil Aḥmad ʿAbd al-Mawjūd, 10 vols., Beirut: Dār al-kutub al-ʿilmiyya.

Kashmīrī, Khᵛājah ʿAbd al-Karīm (1970). *Bayān-i vāqiʿ: sarguẕasht-i aḥvāl-i Nādir Shāh va safar'hā-yi muṣannif Khvājah ʿAbd al-Karīm ibn Khᵛājah ʿĀqibat Maḥmūd Kashmīrī*, ed. K. B. Nasīm, Lahore: Idārah-yi taḥqīqāt-i Pākistān, Dānish'gāh-yi Panjāb.

al-Kashmīrī, Muḥammad Anwar (1426/2005). *Fayḍ al-bārī ʿalá Ṣaḥīḥ al-Bukhārī, maʿa ḥāshiyyat al-Badr al-sārī ilá fayḍ al-bārī*, ed. Muḥammad Badr al-ʿĀlam Mīraṫhī, 6 vols., Beirut: Dār al-kutub al-ʿilmiyya.

Kātib-i Hazārah, Mullā Fayẓ-i Muḥammad (1331sh). *Sirāj al-tavārīkh*, 3 vols., Kabul: Maṭbaʿah-yi ḥurūfī-yi dār al-salṭānah.

(2013). *Taẕakkur al-inqilāb*, ed. ʿAlī Amīrī, Cologne: Bun'gāh-i intishārāt-i Kāvih.

al-Kaydānī, al-ʿAllāma Luṭfallāh al-Nasafī al-Fāḍil (n.d.). *Khulāṣah-yi Kaydānī, maʿa tarjamah-yi fārsī zayr-i matn va ḥavāshī nāfiʿah*, Lahore: Maktabah-yi raḥmāniyyah.

Kepel, Gilles (1984). *Le Prophète et Pharaon*, Paris: Gallimard.

al-Khālidī, Ṣalāḥ ʿAbd al-Fattāḥ (1414/1994). *Sayyid Quṭb min al-mīlād ilá ʾl-istishhād*, 3rd ed., Damascus: Dār al-qalam / Beirut: Dār al-shāmiyya.

(1421/2000). *al-Manhaj al-ḥarakī fī Ẓilāl al-qurʾān*, Amman: Dār ʿAmmār.

Khalil, Jehanzeb (2000). *The Mujahideen Movement in Malakand and Mohmand Agencies (1900–1940)*, Peshawar: Area Studies Centre at the University of Peshawar.

Khāliṣ, Muḥammad Yūnus, ed. (1339sh). *Sayyid Quṭb: Islām va ʿadālat-i ijtimāʿī*, trans. Shāh Muḥammad "Rashād" and ʿAbd al-Sattār "Sīrat", 2 vols., Kabul: Anjuman-i tarbiyyat va afkār.

trans. (1351sh). *Muḥammad al-Bahī: Dīn aw insānī tamaddun*, Kabul: Dawlatī maṭbaʿah.

(1366sh). *Islāmī rūḥ*, 3rd ed., Peshawar: Də Islāmī Ḥizb də farhangī riyāsat.

(1393sh). *Damūnah aw dānē (shiʿrī ṫōlgah)*, 2nd ed., Peshawar: Də Dānish khparandōyah ṫōlanah.

Khān, ʿAbd al-Ḥamīd (1964). *Mard-i muʾmin: Imām al-awliyāʾ Ḥaẓrat Mawlānā Mawlavī Aḥmad ʿAlī Ṣāḥib – nūr allāh marqad – kī pāk zindagī kē pākizah ḥālat*, Karachi: Fīrūzsonz.

Khan, Amanullah (2014). *The Pashtoon Resistance against the British Raj, 1897–1947*, unpublished PhD thesis, Quaid-i-Azam University Islamabad.

Khan, Anoosh Wisal (2012). *Contesting Subjectivities, Negotiating Agency, and Re-defining Boundaries: The Ideological Subject Formation and Positioning of Pakhtun Women*, unpublished PhD thesis, American University, Washington, D.C.

Khān, Khān ʿAbd al-Ghaffār (1983). *Zamā žvand aw jadd va juhd*, Kabul: Dawlatī maṭbaʿah.

Khān, Muḥammad Āṣif (2004). *Tārīkh-i riyāsat-i Svāt va savāniḥ-i ḥayāt-i Miyāṇgul Gul Shāh'zādah, yaʿnī Shāh ʿAbd al-Vadud Khān miʿmār-i riyāsat-i Svāt*, ed. Faẓl-i Rabbī "Rāhī", 3rd ed., Mingorah: Shuʿayb sanz pablisharz.

Khan, Muhammad Anwar (1993). The Emergence of Religious Parties in Afghanistan. In *Afghanistan and the Frontier*, ed. Fazal-ur-Rahim Marwat and Syed Wiqar Ali Shah Kakakhel, Peshawar: Emjay Books, pp. 1–21.

Khan, Navid Iqbal (2010). Tehreek-i-Nifaz-i-Shariat-i-Muhammadi in [the] Malakand Division (Khyber Pakhtunkhwa). A Case Study of the Process of "State Intervention". *Pakistan Journal of History and Culture* 31(1), 131–58.

Khān, Sayyid Aḥmad (2000). *Āsār al-ṣanādīd*, Delhi: Urdū akadimī.

Khān, Shīr Muḥammad (1894). *Tavārīkh-i khūrshīd-i jahān*, Lahore: Maṭbaʿ-i islāmiyyah.

Khan, Sultan Mahomed, ed. (1900). *The Life of Abdur Rahman, Amir of Afghanistan G.C.B. G.C.S.I.*, 2 vols., London: Murray.

Khan, Timur (2022). A "Good Qaṣba": Chamkanī and the Confluence of Politics, Economy and Religion in Durrānī Peshawar, 1747–1834. *Journal of the Economic and Social History of the Orient* 65(4), 618–47.

Khān, ʿUmar Fārūq (1970). *Ishtirākī ʿālim-i rabbānī Mawlānā ʿAbd al-Raḥīm Pōpalzāʾī*, Lahore: Sindȟ sāgar akādimī.

Khān Khaṫṫak, Afẕal (1893). Tārīkh-i Muraṣṣaʿ. In *Kalīd-i afghānī, yaʿnī muntakhabāt də nas̲r aw də naẓm də paẋtō žəbī*, ed. [Thomas] Patrick Hughes, Lahore: Mufīd-i ʿāmm, pp. 205–40.

Khān Khaṫṫak, Khūshḥāl (n.d.). *Kulliyāt-i Khūshḥāl Khān Khaṫṫak: qaṣāʾid – rubāʿiyāt – qiṭʿāt aw mutafarriqāt*, ed. Fahīm "ʿAẓīm", Peshawar: ʿAẓīm pablishing hāʾūs.

(1345sh). *Dastār'nāmah*, ed. Paẋtō ṫōlanah, Kabul: Dawlatī maṭbaʿah.

(1358sh). *Svāt'nāmah*, ed. ʿAbd al-Ḥayy Ḥabībī, Kabul: Də Afghānistān də ʿulūmō də akāḋīmī də žəbō aw adabiyātō instiṫūt.

(2001). *Armaghān-i Khūshḥāl*, ed. Miyāṇ Sayyid Rasūl "Rasā", 2nd ed., Peshawar: Yūniwarsitī būk ējensī.

Khaṫṫak, Ajmal (2005). *Qīṣṣah zamā də adabī žvand*, Chārsaddah: Riyāz būk ījansī.

Khaṫṫak, Yār Muḥammad Maghmūm (1385sh/2007). *Də āzādəy taḥrīk aw paẋtō shāʿirī, 1900ʾ–1947ʾ*, Peshawar: Də paẋtō akēḋimī.

Khattak, Naseem (2016). *The Mujahidin Movement in the North-West Frontier and the Role of the Local Tribes (1831–1901)*, unpublished PhD thesis, University of Peshawar.

Khilāfatyār, Rūḥallāh (1373sh). *Də Afghānistān də Islāmī Khilāfat Taḥrīk taḡ lārah*, n.p.: Də Afghānistān də Islāmī Khilāfat Taḥrīk khparavənah.

al-Khurāsānī, Abū Yazīd ʿAbd al-Qāhir (1433h). *Murtaddīn ćōk dī?*, n.p.: Abṭāl al-islām.

(1435h). *Tuḥfat al-Muslimīn fī bayān ahm masāʾil al-dīn: ḥaqīqī islām aw kalimah vayūnkī murtaddīn*, n.p.: Abṭāl al-islām.

Kiessling, Hein (2016). *Faith, Unity, Discipline: The Inter-Service-Intelligence (ISI) of Pakistan*, London: Hurst / New York: Oxford University Press.

Kirgis, Frederic L. (2001). Addendum: Security Council Adopts Resolution on Combating International Terrorism. *ASIL Insight* 6(18), 1 October. URL: www.asil.org/insights/volume/6/issue/18/terrorist-attacks-world-trade-center-and-pentagon (accessed 24 February 2024).

Kleniewski, Nancy, and Alexander R. Thomas (2006). *Cities, Change and Conflict: A Political Economy of Urban Life*, 3rd ed., Belmont, CA: Wadsworth.

Klimburg, Max (1999). *The Kafirs of the Hindu Kush: Art and Society of the Waigal and Ashkun Kafirs*, 2 vols., Stuttgart: Steiner.

(2001). The Situation in Nuristan. *Central Asian Survey* 20(3), 383–90.

(2002). A Tense Autonomy: The Present Situation in Nuristan. In *Afghanistan: A Country without a State?*, ed. Christine Noelle-Karimi, Conrad Schetter and Reinhard Schlagintweit, Frankfurt am Main: IKO-Verlag, pp. 53–64.

Knudsen, Are (2009). *Violence and Belonging: Land, Love and Lethal Conflict in the North-West Frontier Province of Pakistan*, New Delhi: Orient BlackSwan.

Knysh, Alexander (1992). Irfan Revisited: Khomeini and the Legacy of Islamic Mystical Philosophy. *Middle East Journal* 46(4), 631–53.

(2007). Contextualizing the Salafi–Sufi Conflict (from the Northern Caucasus to Hadramawt). *Middle Eastern Studies* 43(4), 503–30.

Kraudzun, Tobias (2012). From the Pamir Frontier to International Borders: Exchange Relations of the Borderland Population. In *Subverting Borders: Doing Research on Smuggling and Small-Scale Trade*, ed. Bettina Bruns and Judith Miggelbrink, Wiesbaden: VS Research, pp. 171–91.

al-Kūfī, Abū Yūsuf Yaʿqūb (1399/1979). *K. al-Kharāj*, Beirut: Dār al-maʿārifa.

Kühn, Alfred (1950). Über Farbwechsel und Farbensinn von Cephalopoden. *Zeitschrift für Vergleichende Physiologie* 32(6), 572–98.

Kuhn, Thomas S. (1962). *The Structure of Scientific Revolutions*, Chicago, IL and London: The University of Chicago Press.

Kursawe, Janet (2011). "Seeds of War"? Die Taliban und die Drogenökonomie. In *Der Taliban-Komplex: Zwischen Aufstandsbewegung und Militäreinsatz*, ed. Conrad Schetter and Jörgen Klußmann, Frankfurt am Main and New York: Campus, pp. 161–77.

Kūshkakī, Burhān al-Dīn, ed. (1367sh). *Rāh'numā-yi Qaṭaghān va Badakhshān*, crit. ed. Manūchihr Stūdah, Tehran: Muʾassasah-yi farhangī-yi jahāngīrī.

Lacroix, Stéphane (2011). *Awakening Islam: The Politics of Religious Dissent in Contemporary Saudi Arabia*, Cambridge, MA and London: Harvard University Press.

Lange, Christian (2016). Introducing Hell in Islamic Studies. In *Locating Hell in Islamic Traditions*, ed. Christian Lange, Leiden and Boston, MA: Brill, pp. 1–28.

Laoust, Henri (1962). Le réformisme d'Ibn Taymiya. *Islamic Studies* 1(3), 27–47.

Lauzière, Henri (2016). *The Making of Salafism: Islamic Reform in the Twentieth Century*, New York: Columbia University Press.

Lav, Daniel (2012). *Radical Islam and the Revival of Medieval Theology*, Cambridge: Cambridge University Press.

Leake, Elizabeth (2017). *The Defiant Border: The Afghan–Pakistan Borderlands in the Era of Decolonialization, 1936–1965*, Cambridge: Cambridge University Press.

Leizaola, Aitzpea (2000). Mugarik ez! Subverting the Border in the Basque Country. *Ethnologia Europaea* 30(2), 35–46.

Lelyveld, David (1978). *Aligarh's First Generation: Muslim Solidarity in British India*, Princeton, NJ: Princeton University Press.

(1994). *Zuban-e-Urdu-e Muʿalla* [*sic*] and the Idol of Liguistic Origins. *The Annual of Urdu Studies* 11, 57–67.

Levtsiyon, Neḥemiyah (1986). Tanûʿāh hitḥadshût va-repôrmâh 'isla'm vm'h 'adōnāi 18. *ha-Mizraḥ he-Ḥadash* 31(121–4), 48–70.

Lia, Brynjar (2007). *Architect of Global Jihad: The Life of al-Qaida Strategist Abu Musʿab al-Suri*, London: Hurst / New York: Columbia University Press.

(2009). "Destructive Doctrinarians": Abu Musʿab al-Suri's Critique of the Salafis in the Jihadi Current. In *Global Salafism: Islam's New Religious*

Movement, ed. Roel Meijer, London: Hurst/New York: Columbia University Press, pp. 281–300.

al-Lībī, Maḥmūd al-Ḥasan ʿAṭiyyatallāh, and Abū Yaḥyá al-Lībī (1431/2010). Letter to Hakimullah Mahsud. Reference Number SOCOM-2012-0000007. *Combating Terrorism Center at West Point: Harmony Program*. URL: www.ctc.usma.edu/harmony-program/letter-to-hakimullah-mahsud-original-language-2 (accessed 24 February 2024).

Lighārī, Mawlānā ʿAbdallāh (1998). *Mawlānā ʿUbaydallāh Sindhī kī sarguẕasht-i Kābul*, ed. Ghulām Muṣṭafá Khān, Lahore: Dār al-kitāb.

Lindholm, Charles (1986). Leadership Categories and Social Processes in Islam: The Cases of Dir and Swat. *Journal of Anthropological Research* 42(1), 1–13.

Lister, Charles R. (2015). *The Syrian Jihad: Al-Qaeda* [sic], *the Islamic State and the Evolution of an Insurgency*, London: Hurst.

Ludden, David (2002). A Brief History of Subalternity. In *Reading Subaltern Studies: Critical History, Contested Meaning and the Globalization of South Asia*, ed. David Ludden, London: Anthem, pp. 1–39.

Ludḧiyānavī, Muftī Rashīd Aḥmad (1420–5h). *Javāhīr al-rashīd*, 11 vols., Karachi: Kitāb'gaṛḧ.

(1421h). *Ṭālibān: mujāhidīn-i lashkar-i nabavī-yi aḥkām-i ʿāliyyah: iṭāʿat-i amīr*, Karachi: al-Rashīd trast̊.

(1424h). *Anvār al-rashīd*, ed. Aḥmad Nūr al-Muqtadá, 3 vols., Karachi: Kitāb'gḧar.

(1425h). *Aḥsan al-fatāvá*, 11th ed., 10 vols., Karachi: H.M. Saʿīd kampanī.

(1429h). *Khuṭbāt al-rashīd*, 7 vols., Karachi: Kitāb'gḧar.

Ludḧiyānavī, Muḥammad Yūsuf (1999). *Iṣlāḥī mavāʿiẓ*, ed. Saʿīd Aḥmad Jalālpūrī, 8 vols., Karachi: Maktabah-yi Ludḧiyānavī.

[al-Lūjarī], ʿAbd al-Ḥasīb, and Abū ʿUmar al-Khurāsānī (1436/2015/1394sh). *Də Islāmī Davlat vilāyat Khurāsān payghām*, n.p.: no publisher.

al-Lūjarī, Muṣṭafá Bādī Abū Ibrāhīm (n.d. [c. 2003]). *Afghānistān iḥtilāl al-dhākira*, Ṣanʿāʾ: no publisher.

Madanī, Muḥammad Asrār, ed. (1437/2016). *Yād: Shaykh al-tafsīr va 'l-ḥadīs̱ Mawlānā Ḋākt̊ar Shīr ʿAlī Shāh Madanī – rḥ: ḥayāt va khidmāt*, Akōṛah Khaṫṫak: Muʾtamar al-muṣannifīn-i dār al-ʿulūm-i ḥaqqāniyyah.

Madanī, Ḥaẓrat Mawlānā Sayyid Ḥusayn Aḥmad (1920). *Safarnāmah-yi asīr-i Mālṫā*, Deoband: Dār al-ishāʿat.

(1395/1975). *Muttaḥidah qawmiyyat awr islām*, 2nd ed., Lahore: Istiqlāl prēss.

(n.d.). *Naqsh-i ḥayāt: khūd'nivisht-i savāniḥ. kāmil dō jild*, reprint, Karachi: Dār al-ishāʿat.

al-Madanī, Shaykh Shīr ʿAlī Shāh (1429/2008). *Tafsīr al-Ḥasan al-Baṣrī*, 5 vols. in four, Akōṛah Khaṫṫak: Maktabah-yi rashīdiyyah.

al-Maghribī, Muḥammad ibn Sulaymān (1418/1998). *Jamʿ al-fawāʾid min Jāmiʿ al-uṣūl wa-Majmaʿ al-zawāʾid*, ed. Abū ʿAlī Sulaymān ibn Darīʿ, 4 vols., Kuwait and Beirut: Dār Ibn Ḥazm.

al-Maḥmūd, ʿAbd al-ʿAzīz ibn Ṣāliḥ (2017). *Juhūd ʿulamāʾ al-ʿIrāq fi'l-radd ʿalá 'l-shīʿa*, n.p.: no publisher.

Maḥmūd, Muftī (2001–8). *Fatāvá-yi Muftī Maḥmūd*, ed. Muḥammad Bilāl Durrānī, 11 vols., Lahore: Ishtiyāq A. Mushtāq prēss.

Maḥsūd, Muftī Nūr Valī (2017). *Inqilāb-i Maḥsūd-i Sāʾūth Vazīristān: farangī rāj sē amrīkī sāmrāj tak*, Barmāl: al-Shahāb.

Maḥsūd, Muḥammad Navāz Khān (2000). *Farangī rāj awr ghayrat'mand musalmān*, Gūrvēk: Gūrvēk markaz-i shimālī Vazīristān.

Mahsūd (sic), Sayfallāh "Sayfī" (n.d.). *Savāniḥ-i Mawlānā Faẓl al-Raḥmān*. URL: www.juidik.com/fazul.html (accessed 19 June 2016).

Maiello, Amedeo (1996). Sayyid Ahmad's Imamate According to Shâh Ismâʿîl Shahîd. In *Ex libris Franco Coslovi*, ed. Daniela Bredi and Gianroberto Scarcia, Venice: Poligrafo, pp. 251–64.

Majruh, Sayd [*sic*] B. (1976/1355sh). The Message of a Sufi for the Modern World: Text of a Lecture on the Occasion of the Thousandth Anniversary of Khwaja Abdullah Ansari Herawi's Birth. *Afghanistan: Historical and Cultural Quarterly* 29(3), 38–55.

Majrūḥ, [Sayyid Bahāʾ al-Dīn] (1356sh). *Źānźānī x̌āmār*, Kabul: Də adabiyātō aw basharay ʿulūm pōhanźəy.

Makdisi, George (1973). Ibn Taymīya: A Sufi of the Qādirīya Order. *The American Journal of Arabic Studies* 1, 118–29.

Mākū, Sulaymān (1379sh/2000). *Tazkirat al-awliyāʾ*, ed. ʿAbd al-Ḥayy Ḥabībī, Kabul: Də ʿAllāmah Ḥabībī də ćeṛənō markaz.

Malgarē, Ghulām Muḥyī al-Dīn Ghiljī (1352sh). *Pax̌tanəy milləy ataṇūnah aw maḥalləy naćāvəy*, Kabul: Dawlatī maṭbaʿah.

Malīḥābādī, ʿAbd al-Razzāq (1960). *Ẕikr-i Āzād: Mawlānā Abū 'l-Kalām Āzād kī rafāqat mēṇ aṛtīs sāl*, Calcutta: Ujālā prēss.

Malik, Jamal (1993). Islamic Institutions and Infrastructure in Shâjahânâbâd. In *Shâjahânâbâd/Old Delhi: Tradition and Colonial Change*, ed. Eckhart Ehlers and Thomas Krafft, 2nd rev. ed., New Delhi: Manohar, pp. 71–92.

(1996). *Colonialization of Islam: Dissolution of Traditional Institutions in Pakistan*, New Delhi: Manohar / Lahore: Vanguard.

(1997). *Islamische Gelehrtenkultur in Nordindien: Entwicklungsgeschichte und Tendenzen am Beispiel von Lucknow*, Leiden: Brill.

(2018). Literarische Salons im Indien des 18. Jahrhunderts: Ein Beitrag zur Moderne im Islam? In *Islam in der Moderne, Moderne im Islam: Eine Festschrift für Reinhard Schulze zum 65. Geburtstag*, ed. Florian Zemmin, Johannes Stephan and Monica Corrado, Leiden and Boston, MA: Brill, pp. 301–27.

Mansfield, David (2017). *Understanding Control and Influence: What Opium Poppy and Tax Reveal about the Writ of the Afghan State*, Kabul: AREU.

al-Maqdisī, Abū Muḥammad ʿĀṣim (1421h). *al-Kawāshif al-jaliyya fī kufr al-Dawla al-Saʿūdiyya* 2nd ed., n.p.: Minbar al-tawḥīd wa'l-jihād.

(1423h). *Ḥiwār maʿa al-Shaykh Abī Muḥammad al-Maqdisī "sana 1423"*, n.p.: Minbar al-tawḥīd wa'l-jihād. URL: www.ilmway.com/site/maqdis/MS_36954.html (accessed 3 September 2018).

(1431h). *Millat Ibrāhīm wa-daʿwat al-anbiyāʾ wa'l-mursalīn* [*wa-asālīb al-ṭughāt fī tamyīʿihā wa-ṣarf al-duʿāt ʿanhā*], n.p.: Minbar al-tawḥīd wa'l-jihād.

Marchand, Katrin, Melissa Siegel, Katherine Kuschminder, Nassim Majidi, Michaella Vanore, and Carla Bull (2015). *Afghanistan Migration Profile*, Kabul: International Organization for Migration.

al-Marghinānī, al-Imām Burhān al-Dīn (1417h). *al-Hidāya sharḥ bidāyat al-mubtadī, maʿa sharḥ al-ʿAllāma ʿAbd al-Ḥayy al-Laknawī*, ed. Naʿīm Ashraf Nūr Aḥmad, 8 vols., Karachi: Idārat al-qurʾān wa'l-ʿulūm al-islāmiyya.

Marjanen, Jani (2018). Editorial: Ism Concepts in Science and Politics. *Contributions to the History of Concepts* 13(1), v–ix.

Markazī Shuʿbah-yi Tanẓīm-i JiI, ed. (1997). *Rūdād-i Jamāʿat-i Islāmī*, 7 vols., Lahore: Shuʿbah-yi nashr va ishāʿat-i JiI Pākistān.

Markaz Razīz Qandahār (n.d.). *Tarjamat al-shaykh al-mujāhid Abū Muṣʿab al-Sūrī*, n.p.: Markaz Razīz Qandahār.

Marquardt, Erich, and Abul Hameed Bakier (2008). An Ideological and Operational Threat: Abu `Amr / Shaykh `Isa [*sic*]. *CTC Sentinel* 1(8), 4–8.

Marsden, Magnus (2005). *Living Islam: Muslim Religious Experience in Pakistan's North-West Frontier*, Cambridge: Cambridge University Press.

Marwat, Fazal-ur-Rahim (2005). Maulana Abdul Rahim Pōpalzai: A Marxist Maulana. *Journal of Humanities & Social Sciences* (University of Peshawar) 13(1–2), 182–202.

Marx, Karl, and Friedrich Engels (1956–90). *Werke*, ed. Institut für Marxismus-Leninismus des ZK der SED, 43 vols., Berlin: Dietz.

Masud, Muhammad Khalid (2000). Ideology and Legitimacy. In *Travellers in Faith: Studies of the Tablīghī Jamāʿat as a Transnational Movement for Faith Renewal*, ed. Muhammad Khalid Masud, Leiden: Brill, pp. 79–118.

Matthiesen, Toby (2015). *The Other Saudis: Shiism, Dissent and Sectarianism*, Cambridge: Cambridge University Press.

al-Māturīdī, al-Imām Abū Manṣūr Muḥammad (1426/2005). *Taʾwīlāt ahl al-sunna*, ed. Majdī Bāsallūm, 10 vols., Beirut: Dār al-kutub al-ʿilmiyya.

al-Māwardī, Abū 'l-Ḥasan ʿAlī (1422/2002). *K. al-Aḥkām al-sulṭāniyya*, Beirut: Dār al-fikr.

Mawdūdī, Sayyid Abū 'l-Aʿlá (1949–72). *Tafhīm al-qurʾān*, 4 vols., Lahore: Idārah-yi tarjumān al-qurʾān.

(1969). *Islām awr jadīd maʿāshī naẓariyyāt*, Delhi: Markazī maktabah-yi islāmī.

(1972). *Khuṭbāt*, Delhi: Markazī maktabah-yi islāmī.

(1993). *Akhlāqiyyāt-i ijtimāʿiyyah awr uskā falsafah*, Delhi: Markazī maktabah-yi islāmī.

(1994). *Islāmī ḥukūmat: kis ṭaraḥ qā'im hōtī hē?*, 5th ed., Delhi: Markazī maktabah-yi islāmī.

(1996). *Qur'ān kī chār bunyādī iṣṭilāḥēṇ*, 7th ed., Delhi: Markazī maktaba-yi islāmī.

(1997). *Khilāfat va mulūkiyyat*, Delhi: Markazī maktabah-yi islāmī.

Mayaram, Shail (1997). *Resisting Regimes: Myth, Memory and the Shaping of a Muslim Identity*, New Delhi: Oxford University Press.

(2003). *Against History, against State: Counterperspectives from the Margins*, New York: Columbia University Press.

McCants, William (2015). *The ISIS Apocalypse: The History, Strategy and Doomsday Vision of the Islamic State*, New York: St Martin's Press.

McChesney, Robert D. (1991). *Waqf in Central Asia: Four Hundred Years in the History of a Muslim Shrine, 1480–1889*, Princeton, NJ: Princeton University Press.

trans. (1999). *Kabul under Siege: Fayz Muhammad's Account of the 1929 Uprising*, Princeton, NJ: Wiener.

McChesney, Robert D., and Mohammad Mehdi Khorrami, eds. and trans. (2019). *Fayż Muḥammad Kātib Hazārah's "Afghan Genealogy" and "Memoir of the Revolution": Supplements to "The History of Afghanistan"*, Leiden and Boston, MA: Brill.

Meier, Fritz (1981). Das sauberste über die vorbestimmung: Ein stück Ibn Taymiyya [*sic*]. *Sæculum* 32, 74–89.

Meijer, Roel (2009). Commanding Right and Forbidding Wrong as a Principle of Social Action. The Case of the Egyptian al-Jama'a al-Islamiyya. In *Global Salafism: Islam's New Religious Movement*, ed. Roel Meijer, London: Hurst / New York: Columbia University Press, pp. 189–220.

Melchert, Christopher (2020). *Before Sufism: Early Islamic Renunciant Piety*, Berlin and Boston, MA: de Gruyter.

Merathī, Mawlānā Muḥammad 'Āshiq-i Ilāhī (n.d.). *Tazkirat al-Rashīd*, 2 vols., Sahāranpūr: Maktabah-yi khalīliyyah.

Metcalf, Barbara Daly (1982). *Islamic Revival in British India: Deoband, 1860–1900*, Princeton, NJ: Princeton University Press.

(1993). Living Hadīth in the Tablīghī Jama'āt [*sic*]. *Journal of Asian Studies* 52(3), 584–608.

(2004). *Islamic Contestations: Essays on Muslims in India and Pakistan*, New Delhi: Oxford University Press.

(2009). *Husain Ahmad Madani: The Jihad for Islam and India's Freedom*, Oxford: Oneworld.

Mian, Ali Altaf (2015). *Surviving Modernity: Ashraf 'Alī Thānvī* [sic] *(1863–1943) and the Making of Muslim Orthodoxy in Colonial India*, unpublished PhD thesis, Duke University.

Michot, Yahya (1994). Textes spirituels d'Ibn Taymiyya. XI: Mongols and Mamlûks: L'état du monde musulman vers 709/1310. *Le Musulman* 24, 26–31.

(2006). *Muslims under Non-Muslim Rule: Ibn Taymiyya on Fleeing from Sin; Kinds of Emigration; the Status of Mardin: Domain of Peace/War, Domain Composite; the Conditions for Challenging Power*, Oxford and London: Interface.

Mihr, Ghulām Rasūl (2008). *Taḥrīk-i Sayyid Aḥmad-i shahīd, reprint*, 4 vols., Mumbai: Maktabat al-ḥaqq.

Mikhail, Hanna (1995). *Politics and Revelation: Māwardī and After*, Edinburgh: Edinburgh University Press.

Mills, H. Woosnam (1897). *The Pathan Revolts in North-West India*, Lahore: The Civil and Military Gazette Press.

Minault, Gail (1982). *The Khilafat Movement: Religious Symbolism and Political Mobilization in India*, New York: Columbia University Press.

al-Miṣrī, al-Shaykh Zayn al-Dīn ibn Nujaym (n.d.). *al-Baḥr al-rāʾiq sharḥ Kanz al-daqāʾiq*, 7 vols., Beirut: Shirkat ʿAlāʾ al-Dīn.

Mitchell, Richard P. (1969). *The Society of the Muslim Brothers*, Oxford and New York: Oxford University Press.

Moffat, Chris (2016). Experiments in Political Truth. In *Revolutionary Lives in South Asia: Acts and Afterlives of Anticolonial Political Action*, ed. Kama Maclean and J. David Elam, London and New York: Routledge, pp. 73–89.

Möller, Jochen (2001). “Islamisch und noch einmal islamisch”. Die *Jamāʿa al-Islāmiyya* als politische Kraft Oberägyptens. In *Sendungsbewußtsein oder Eigennutz: Zu Motivation und Selbstverständnis islamischer Mobilisierung*, ed. Dietrich Reetz, Berlin: Das Arabische Buch, pp. 183–98.

Mōmand, Muʿizzallāh (1164h). *Majmaʿ al-asrār*, MS Ganj Bakhsh Library Islamabad 465.

Muʿaẓẓam Shāh, Pīr (1971). *Tavārīkh-i Ḥāfiẓ Raḥmat'khānī*, Peshawar: Paxtō Akīḍīmī.

Mubarak, Hisham, Sohail Shadoud, and Steve Tamari (1996). What Does the Gama`a Islamiyya Want?: An Interview with Tal`at Fu'ad Qasim [*sic*]. *Middle East Report* 198, 40–6.

Mubāriz, ʿAbd al-Rāʾuf (2014). Də muḥtaram Khāliṣ Bābā (raḥmat allāh [ʿalayhi]) ʿilmī žvand. *Tōrah Bōṛah Vēbpāṇah* (29 March). URL: www.tooraboral.com/archives/2980 (accessed 5 August 2020).

Mughal, Muḥammad Humāyūn (1425/2004). *Aḥsan al-burhān fī aqvāl shaykhnā Mawlānā Muftī Muḥammad Zarvalī Khān*, Karachi: Aḥsanī kutub'khānah.

Muhājir Makkī, Ḥaẓrat Ḥājjī Imdādallāh (1397/1976). *Kulliyāt-i imdādiyyah, yaʿnī das kitābōṇ kā majmūʿah*, ed. Muḥammad Riẓá ʿUs̱mānī, Karachi: Dār al-ishāʿat.

Muḥammad, Bāsil (1991). *Ṣafaḥāt min sijill al-anṣar al-ʿarab fī Afghānistān*, Riyadh: Idārat al-dirāsāt wa'l-tawthīq bi-lajnat al-birr al-islāmī.

Muḥammadī, Mawlavī (1368sh). *Payām-i Mawlavī Muḥammadī, amīr-i ʿumūmī-yi Ḥarakat-i Inqilāb-i slāmī va vazīr-i difāʿ-i ḥukūmat-i ʿubūrī-yi mujāhidīn-i*

Afghānistān bi-munāsib-i ʿīd-i saʿīd-i fiṭr 14/2/1368, Peshawar: Anjuman-i farhangī va maṭbūʿātī-yi Ḥarakat-i Inqilāb-i Islāmī-yi Afghānistān.

Mujaddidī, Āghā Ṣiddīq (n.d.). *Savāniḥ-i mukhtaṣar-i prūfīsūr ḥaẓrat Ṣibghatallāh Mujaddidī – rāʾis-i Dawlat-i Islāmī-yi Afghānistān*, Kabul: Āriyānā prēss.

"Mujāhid", Mawlavī ʿAbd al-Hādī (1389sh/2010). *Fikrī pōhānah*, 2nd ed., Peshawar: Ayyūb maktabah aw islāmī kīsət markaz.

Mukarram, Ahmed (1992). *Some Aspects of Contemporary Islamic Thought: Guidance and Governance in the Work of Mawlana Abul Hasan Ali Nadwi and Mawlana Abul Aala Mawdudi* [sic], unpublished PhD thesis, University of Oxford.

Mukhopadhyay, Dipali (2014). *Warlords, Strongman Governors, and the State in Afghanistan*, Cambridge: Cambridge University Press.

Munīb, ʿAbd al-Munʿim (2010). *Murājaʿāt al-jihādiyīn: al-qiṣṣa al-khafiyya li-murājaʿāt al-jihād wa'l-Jamāʿa al-Islāmiyya dākhil wa-khārij al-sujūn*, Cairo: Maktabat Madbūlī.

Muslim Dōst, ʿAbd al-Raḥīm (n.d.[a]). *al-Quyūd al-muḥaṭṭima*, n.p.: Markaz al-fajr li'l-iʿlām.

(n.d.[b]). *Malāk al-amjād*, n.p.: no publisher.

(1367sh/1409h). *Ittibāʿ al-rasūl*, Riyadh: Idāra iḥyāʾ al-daʿwa al-islāmiyya.

(1430h). *Islām də x̌ēgaṛō dīn*, n.p.: no publisher.

(1432h). *Tawḥīd raṇā aw shirk tayārē dī*, n.p.: Khilāfat khparandōyah ṫōlānah.

(1437h). *Tawḍīh al-maʾmūl fī tanqīḥ al-uṣūl*, Jalalabad: Dār al-qalam.

Muslim Dōst, ʿAbd al-Raḥīm, and Badr al-Zamān "Badr" (1385sh/1427h). *Də Guvānṫanāmō mātē-zōlanē*, Peshawar: "Khilāfat" khparandōyah ṫōlānah.

Mustaʿīd, Mullā [Muḥammad Ḥusayn] (1375sh). *Mawlavī Muḥammad Nabī (Muḥammadī) dar javāb-i pursish'hā-yi Ṭālibān*, trans. Mawlavī Faqīr Muḥammad Khanjirī, Peshawar: Asadallāh [Ḥanīfī].

"Mutavakkil", Mawlavī Vakīl Aḥmad (1384sh). *Afghānistān aw Ṭālibān*, 2nd ed., Mayvand: Də Mayvand khparandōyah ṫōlanē maṭbaʿah.

Muždah, Vaḥīd (1382sh). *Afghānistān va panj sāl sulṭah-yi Ṭālibān*, Tehran: Nasharānī.

(1391sh). Usāmah bin Lādin chigūnah bah Afghānistān bāz'gasht? *Hasht-i Ṣubḥ* (24 Mīzān). URL: http://8am.af/j8am/index.php?option=com_content&view=article&id=28004:1391%E2%80%9007%E2%80%9024%E2%80%9015%E2%80%9022%E2%80%9022&catid=3:2008%E2%80%9010%E2%80%9031%E2%80%9009%E2%80%9037%E2%80%9007&Itemid=554 (accessed 28 August 2023).

Nadvī, Muḥibballāh (1430/2009). *Tazkirah-yi Mawlānā Karāmat-i ʿAlī Jawnpūrī*, 2nd ed., Takiyah Kalāṇ: Dār ʿirfān.

Nadvī, Sayyid Abū 'l-Ḥasan ʿAlī (1404/1984). *Kāravān-i zindagī*, 7 vols., Lucknow: Maktabah-yi islām.

(1406/1986). *Sīrat-i Sayyid Aḥmad-i shahīd*, 2 vols., Lucknow: Majlis-i taḥqīqāt va nashriyāt-i islām.

ed. (1991). *Makātīb-i Ḥazrat Mawlānā Muḥammad Ilyās – raḥmat allāh ʿalayh*, New Delhi: Idārah-yi ishāʿat-i dīniyyāt.

(1414–19/1994–8). *Purānē chirāgh*, 3rd ed., 3 vols., Lucknow: Maktabah-yi firdaws.

(1416/1995). *Tārīkh-i daʿvat va ʿazīmat*, vol. IV, 3rd ed., Lucknow: Majlis-i taḥqīqāt va nashriyāt-i islām.

Nagamine, Yoshinobu (2015). *The Legitimization Strategy of the Taliban's Code of Conduct: Through the One-Way Mirror*, New York: Palgrave Macmillan.

Nagīnah, Rām Saran (1994). *Taḥrīk-i Ghallah Ḍhēr*, Lahore: al-Maḥmūd akēḍimī.

Naim, C[houdhri] M[uhammad] (2011). Individualism within Conformity: A Brief History of *Waz'dārī* in Delhi and Lucknow. *The Indian Economic and Social History Review* 48(1), 35–53.

al-Najdī, ʿAbd al-Raḥmān ibn Muḥammad (1417/1996). *al-Durar al-saniyya fi'l-ajwiba al-najdiyya: majmūʿat rasāʾil wa-masāʾil ʿulamāʾ Najd al-aʿlām min ʿaṣr al-shaykh Muḥammad ibn ʿAbd al-Wahhāb ilá ʿaṣrnā hādhā*, 6th ed., 16 vols., Mecca: Maṭbaʿat umm al-qurá.

Nangiyāl, Shuhrat (1370sh). *Žavarah də tārīkh pah spīdahdāgh kī* [sic], n.p.: Də jabhātō farhangī ṫōlānah.

al-Nasafī, Abū Barakāt ʿAbdallāh ibn Aḥmad (1419/1998). *Tafsīr al-Nasafī (Madārik al-tanzīl wa-ḥaqāʾiq al-taʾwīl)*, ed. Yūsuf ʿAlī Budaywī and Muḥyī al-Dīn Dīb Mistū, 3 vols., Beirut: Dār al-kalam al-ṭayyib.

Nasiri, Omar (2006). *Inside the Jihad: My Life with Al Qaeda* [sic]. *A Spy's Story*, New York: Basic Books.

Nasr, Seyyed Vali Reza (1994). *The Vanguard of the Islamic Revolution: The Jamaʿat-i Islami of Pakistan*, Berkeley, CA and Los Angeles, CA: University of California Press.

(1996). *Mawdudi and the Making of Islamic Revivalism*, New York and Oxford: Oxford University Press.

(2000). The Rise of Sunni Militancy in Pakistan: The Changing Role of Islamism and the Ulama in Society and Politics. *Modern Asian Studies* 34(1), 139–80.

Nathan, Joanna (2009). Reading the Taliban. In *Decoding the New Taliban: Insights from the Afghan Field*, ed. Antonio Giustozzi, London: Hurst / New York: Columbia University Press, pp. 23–42.

Navāz Khān, Nawwāb Ṣamṣām al-Dawlah Shāh (1888–96). *Maʾās̱ir al-umarā*, ed. Mawlavī ʿAbd al-Raḥīm, 3 vols., Calcutta: Maṭbaʿ-i urdū gāʾīḋ.

Navid, Senzil K. (1999). *Religious Response to Social Change in Afghanistan 1919–29: King Aman-Allah and the Afghan Ulama*, Costa Mesa, CA: Mazda.

Nedza, Justyna (2014). "Salafismus" – Überlegungen zur Schärfung einer Analysekategorie. In *Salafismus: Auf der Suche nach dem wahren Islam*, ed. Behnam T. Said and Hazim Fouad, Freiburg im Breisgau: Herder, pp. 80–105.

(2020). Takfīr *im militanten Salafismus: Der Staat als Feind*, Leiden and Boston, MA: Brill.

Neelis, Jason (2011). *Early Buddhist Transmission and Trade Networks: Mobility and Exchange within and beyond the Northwestern Borderlands of South Asia*, Leiden and Boston, MA: Brill.

Nelson, Matthew J. (2011). Embracing the Ummah: Student Politics beyond State-Power in Pakistan. *Modern Asian Studies* 45(3), 565–96.

Netton, Ian Richard (2000). *Sufi Ritual: The Parallel Universe*, Richmond: Curzon.

Nichols, Robert (2001). *Settling the Frontier: Land, Law and Society in the Peshawar Valley, 1500–1900*, Karachi: Oxford University Press.

ed. (2013). *The Frontier Crimes Regulation: A History in Documents*, Karachi: Oxford University Press.

Niyāzī, Ghulām Muḥammad (1344sh). *Maʾākhiẕ-i duvvum-i fiqh-i islāmī*, Kabul: Shuʿbah-yi nasharāt-i qavānīn va kutub, mudīriyyat-i ʿumūmī-i nashriyāt-i vizārat-i ʿadliyyah.

Niẓām al-Dīn, Pīr-i Ṭarīqat Mawlānā (2018). *Savāniḥ-i Sayyidō Bābā – quddisa sirruh*, n.p.: al-Khiṭāṭ grāfiks.

Noelle, Christine (1997). *State and Tribe in Nineteenth-Century Afghanistan: The Reign of Amir Dōst Muhammad Khan (1826–1863)*, London and New York: Routledge.

Noelle-Karimi, Christine (2002). The *Loya Jirga* – An Effective Political Instrument? A Historical Overview. In *Afghanistan: A Country without a State?*, ed. Christine Noelle-Karimi, Conrad Schetter and Reinhard Schlagintweit, Frankfurt am Main and London: IKO-Verlag, pp. 37–50.

(2017). Afghan Polities and the Indo-Persian Literary Realm: The Durrani Rulers and Their Portrayal in Eighteenth-Century Historiography. In *Afghan History through Afghan Eyes*, ed. Nile Green, Karachi: Oxford University Press, pp. 53–77 and 277–81 (notes).

Nuʿmānī, Muḥammad Manẓūr (1405/1984). *Īrānī inqilāb, Imām Khumaynī awr shīʿiyyat*, Lahore: Maktabah-yi madaniyyah.

Nūrī, Muḥammad Gul (1387sh/2008). Də Ṭālib Jān nakəl yā Mullā ʿAbbās aw Gul Bashrah. In *Millī hīndārah*, ed. Maṭīʿallāh Rōhiyāl, Kandahar: ʿAllāmah Rashād khparandōyah ṫōlanah, pp. 155–91.

Nūrpūrī, Ḥāfiẓ ʿAbd al-Manān (1973). *Ghunchah-yi namāz*, Lahore: Urdū ḋāʾijisṫ prinṫarz.

O'Donnell, Patrick (1990). Afghan Rebels Dig Up Financial Help: Guerrillas: Mining the Gem-Laden Panjshir Valley Is Helping to Pay for Their War Effort. *Los Angeles Times* 11 November. URL: www.latimes.com/archives/la-xpm-1990-11-11-mn-5919-story.html (accessed 24 February 2024).

O'Fahey, R. S., and Bernd Radtke (1993). Neo-Sufism Reconsidered. *Der Islam* 70(1), 52–87.

Olesen, Asta (1995). *Islam and Politics in Afghanistan*, Abingdon: Routledge.

Paget, William Henry, ed. (1907). *Frontier and Overseas Expeditions from India*, 6 vols., Simla: Government Monotype Press.

Pain, Adam (2006). *Opium Trading Systems in Helmand and Ghor*, Kabul: AREU.

Pākrāy, Mīr Muḥammad Sharīf (1368sh). *Ḥukūmat-i muvaqqat-i Hind dar Kābul*, Kabul: Maṭba'ah-yi dawlatī.

Panjpīrī, Mawlānā Muḥammad Ṭāhir (n.d.). *Baqiyyat al-āthār min ḥayāt al-mustaʿār, yaʿnī k. al-ibtilāʾ wa'l-miḥna fī ishāʿat al-tawḥīd wa'l-sunna fī bilād al-afāghina*, ed. Muḥammad Ṭayyib Ṭāhirī, Panjpīr: Maktabat al-yamān.

(1433h). *Simṭ al-durar fī rabṭ al-āyāt wa'l-suwar*, Panjpīr: Maktabat al-yamān.

(1980a). *Uṣūl al-sunna li-radd al-bidʿa*, Lahore: Markaz Jamāʿat ishāʿat al-tawḥīd wa'l-sunna.

(1980b). *al-ʿIrfān fī uṣūl al-qurʾān*, ed. Sulṭān Ghanī Ḥanafī Panjpīrī, Lahore: Dār al-qurʾān.

(1421/2000). *Nayl al-sāʾirīn fī ṭabaqāt al-mufassarīn*, 2nd ed., Panjpīr: Maktabat al-yamān.

(1427/2006). *Ḍiyāʾ al-nūr min iḥyāʾ al-sunna li-dakhiḍ al-fujūr wa-imātat al-bidʿa aw minhāj al-ḥayawāt al-sharʿiyya li-radd al-rusūmāt al-bidʿiyya*, Panjpīr: Maktabat al-yamān.

(1433/2011). *Manshūr*, Peshawar: Maktabat al-ishāʿat.

Paul, Jürgen (2017). The Rise of the Khwajagan-Naqshbandiyya Sufi Order in Timurid Herat. In *Afghanistan's Islam: From Conversion to the Taliban*, ed. Nile Green, Oakland, CA: University of California Press, pp. 71–86.

Pernau, Margrit (2008). *Bürger mit Turban: Muslime in Delhi im 19. Jahrhundert*, Göttingen: Vandenhoeck & Ruprecht.

(2014). Civility and Barbarism: Emotions as Criteria of Difference. In *Emotional Lexicons: Continuity and Change in the Vocabulary of Feeling, 1700–2000*, Ute Frevert, Christian Bailey, Pascal Eitler et al., Oxford: Oxford University Press, pp. 230–59.

Pernau, Margrit, Helge Jordheim, Orit Bashkin et al. (2015). *Civilizing Emotions: Concepts in Nineteenth Century Asia and Europe*, Oxford: Oxford University Press.

Peters, Gretchen S. (2009). The Taliban and the Opium Trade. In *Decoding the New Taliban: Insights from the Afghan Field*, ed. Antonio Giustozzi, London: Hurst / New York: Columbia University Press, pp. 7–22.

Peters, Rudolph (1980). *Idjtihād* and *taqlīd* in 18th and 19th Century Islam. *Die Welt des Islams* 20(3–4), 131–45.

Pĥūlpūrī, Shāh ʿAbd al-Ghanī (n.d.). *Barāhīn-i qāṭiʿah dar barā-yi tawḥīd, risālat, qiyāmat*, ed. Shāh Ḥakīm-i Muḥammad Akhtar, Karachi: Kitāb'khānah-yi maẓharī.

Pink, Johanna (2011). *Sunnitischer Tafsīr in der modernen islamischen Welt: Akademische Traditionen, Popularisierung und nationalstaatliche Interessen*, Leiden and Boston, MA: Brill.

Pirzada, Sayyid A. S. (2000). *The Politics of the Jamiat Ulema-i-Islam* [sic] *Pakistan: 1971–1977*, Karachi: Oxford University Press.

Plutarch (1852–4). *Vitæ parallelæ*, ed. K. Sintenis, 5 vols., Leipzig: Teubner.

Pōpalzaʾī, ʿAbd al-Jalīl, ed. (n.d.). *ʿAvāmī jadd va juhd-i āzādī: Imām-i Ḥurriyyat ʿAbd al-Raḥīm Pōpalzaʾī kī nigārishāt kē āʾīnē mēṇ*, Peshawar: ʿAllāmah ʿAbd al-Raḥīm Pōpalzaʾī akēḍimī.

ed. (1991). *Ḥurriyyat'nāmah-yi Bannūṇ: Imām-i Ḥurriyyat ʿAbd al-Raḥīm Pōpalzaʾī kē muqaddimah-yi Baghāvat-i rūdād*, Lahore: Istiʿārah pablīkēshanz.

(1992). *Rūḥāniyyat awr ʿavāmī taḥrīk: Imām-i Ḥurriyyat Muftī ʿAbd al-Raḥīm Pōpalzaʾī kī rūḥānī zindigī kē ḥavālē sē*, Peshawar: ʿAllāmah ʿAbd al-Raḥīm Pōpalzaʾī akēḍimī.

(1994). *Hazārah kē maẓlūm ʿavām awr ʿAllāmah ʿAbd al-Raḥīm Pōpalzaʾī*, Lahore: al-Maḥmūd akēḍimī.

Preckel, Claudia (2005). *Islamische Bildungsnetzwerke und Gelehrtenkultur im Indien des 19. Jahrhunderts: Muḥammad Ṣiddīq Ḥasan Ḫān (st. 1890) und die Entstehung der Ahl-e ḥadīth-Bewegung in Bhopal*, PhD thesis, Ruhr University Bochum. URL: https://hss-opus.ub.ruhr-uni-bochum.de/opus4/frontdoor/deliver/index/docId/2036/file/diss.pdf (accessed 24 February 2024).

Qāḍī Khān, Fakhr al-Dīn (2009). *Fatāwá Qaḍī Khān fī madhhab al-imām al-aʿẓam Abī Hanīfa al-Nuʿmān*, ed. Sālim Muṣṭafá al-Badarī, 3 vols., Beirut: Dār al-kutub al-ʿilmiyya.

Qadir, Altaf (2015a). *Sayyid Ahmad Barailvi: His Movement and Legacy from the Pukhtun Perspective*, New Delhi: Sage.

(2015b). *Reforming the Pukhtuns and Resisting the British: An Appraisal of the Haji Sahib Turangzai's Movement*, Islamabad: National Institute of Historical and Cultural Research.

Qadir, Altaf, and Fatima Asghar (2016). [The] Peshawar Valley under [the] Durrānīs with [a] Focus on Its Administration, 1747–1818. *Journal of the Pakistan Historical Society* 64(1), 57–66.

al-Qalqashandī, Abū 'l-ʿAbbās Aḥmad (1331–40/1913–22). *K. Ṣubḥ al-aʿshá* [*fī ṣināʿat al-inshāʾ*], ed. not known, 14 vols., Cairo: al-Maṭbaʿa al-amīriyya.

al-Qannawjī, Ṣiddīq Ḥasan Khān (1288h). *Itḥāf al-nubalāʾ al-muttaqīn bi-ʾiḥyāʾ athār al-fuqahāʾ al-muḥaddithīn*, Kanpur: Maṭbaʿ-i niẓāmī.

(1289/1872). *Riḥlat al-Ṣiddīq ilá bayt allāh al-ʿatīq*, Lucknow: Maṭbaʿat al-ʿalawī.

(1294h). *Iklīl al-karāma fī tibyān maqāṣid al-imāma*, Bhopal: al-Ṣiddīqī.

(1315/1898). *Tarjumān al-wahhābiyya*, Benares: Maṭbaʿ-i saʿīd.

(1428/2007). *al-Tāj al-mukallal min jawāhir maʾāthir al-ṭirāz al-ākhir wa'l-awwal*, Doha: Wizārat al-awqāf wa-shuʾūn al-islāmiyya.

(1978). *Abjad al-ʿulūm: al-washī al-maqrūm fī bayān aḥwāl al-ʿulūm*, ed. ʿAbd al-Jabbār Zakār, 3 vols., Beirut: Dār al-kutub al-ʿilmiyya.

Qānūnī, M[uḥammad Yūnus] (n.d.). *Dast-i āvārd'hā-yi Shūrā-yi Naẓār*, n.p.: Kamisiyūn-i farhangī-yi Shūrā-yi Naẓār.

al-Qārī, al-ʿAllāma al-Shaykh ʿAlī ibn Sulṭān (1416/1995). *Sharḥ k. al-Fiqh al-akbar, al-shirraḥ li'l-imām al-Mullā ʿAlī al-Qārī al-Ḥanafī*, ed. ʿAlī Muḥammad Dandal, Beirut: Dār al-kutub al-ʿilmiyya.

(1422/2001). *Mirqāt al-mafātīḥ sharḥ Mishkāt al-maṣābīḥ*, ed. Jamāl ʿAytānī, 12 vols., Beirut: Dār al-kutub al-ʿilmiyya.

Qāsim, Ṭalʿat Fuʾād (1987). *al-Risāla al-Īmāniyya fiʾl-muwālāt*, n.p.: no publisher.

Qāsimī, Ḥāfiẓ Muḥammad ʿAbd al-Quddūs (1967). Dībāchah. In Bāyāzīd Anṣārī. *Khayr al-bayān*, ed. Ḥāfiẓ Muḥammad ʿAbd al-Quddūs Qāsimī. Chaman: Pashtō adabī ṫōlanah, pp. 37–129.

Qaṣūrī, Muḥammad ʿAlī (1986). *Mushāhadāt-i Kābul va Yāghistān*, 2nd ed., Lahore: Idārah-yi maʿārif-i islāmiyyah.

Qayyim-i JiI Pākistān, ed. (1989–96). *Rūdād-i Jamāʿat-i islāmī*, 7 vols., Lahore: Shuʿbah-yi nashr va ishāʿat-i Jamāʿat-i islāmī Pākistān.

[Qiṣṣah'khᵛānī, Miyāṇ Ṣāḥib] (1297h). Iḥqāq al-Ḥaqq. In Muḥammad [Shāh] Ismāʿīl. *Īẓāḥ al-ṣarīḥ fī aḥkām al-mayyit al-ẓarīḥ*, ed. Mīr Muḥammad Muʿaẓẓam, Delhi: Maṭbaʿ-i Fārūqī, pp. 138–63.

al-Qudūrī, al-ʿAllāma al-Shaykh Abū ʾl-Ḥasan Aḥmad (1418/1997). *Mukhtaṣar al-Qudūrī fiʾl-fiqh al-ḥanafī*, ed. Kāmil Muḥammad Muḥammad al-ʿUwayḍa, Beirut: Dār al-kutub al-ʿilmiyya.

Quddūsī, Iʿjāz al-Ḥaqq (1966). *Taẕkirah-yi ṣūfiyyā-yi sarḥadd*, Lahore: Markazī urdū bard̊.

Qureshi, M. Naeem (1999). *Pan-Islam in British Indian Politics: A Study of the Khilafat Movement, 1918–1924*, Leiden: Brill.

Quṭb, Sayyid (1962). *Khaṣāʾiṣ al-taṣawwur al-islāmī wa-muqawwimātuh*, Cairo: ʿĪsá al-Bābī al-Ḥalabī.

(1402/1982). *al-Salām al-ʿālamī wa'l-islām*, 7th ed., Cairo and Beirut: Dār al-shurūq.

(1405/1985). *Maʿālim fiʾl-ṭarīq*, 18th ed., Beirut: Dār al-shurūq.

(1413/1993). *al-Mustaqbal li-hadhā al-dīn*, 14th ed., Cairo and Beirut: Dār al-shurūq.

(1422/2002). *Dirāsāt islāmiyya*, 10th ed., Cairo: Dār al-shurūq.

(1426/2005). *al-Islām wa-mushkilāt al-ḥaḍāra*, 13th ed., Cairo: Dār al-shurūq.

(1430/2009). *Fī ẓilāl al-qurʾān*, 38th ed., 6 vols., Cairo and Beirut: Dār al-shurūq.

Rabbānī, Burhān al-Dīn (1367sh). *Payām bah farmāndahān-i jihād va ham'mīhanān-i ʿazīz*, 2nd ed., n.p.: no publisher.

(1369sh). *Irshād-i jihād*, Tehran: Chāp'khānah-yi khawshah.

(1372sh). *Āmūkhtānihāyī dar masīr-i inqilāb-i islāmī*, 2nd ed., Kabul: Anjumān-i navīsandigān va sakhnūrān-i Jamʿiyyat-i Islāmī-yi Afghānistān.

Rafi, Ghazala (2016). *The Taliban Crisis in Pakistan: Implications for the Social Fabric of the Pukhtuns of Swat*, unpublished MPhil thesis, University of Peshawar.

Rahim, Tariq, Aurang Zeb, and Shaheen Shaukat (2007). Urbanization in [the] North West [*sic*] Frontier Province. *Sarhad* [sic] *Journal of Agriculture* 23(1), 233–42.

Rahman, Tariq (2018). *Interpretations of Jihad in South Asia: An Intellectual History*, Boston, MA and Berlin: de Gruyter.

Rand, Christopher (1955). From the Sweets to the Bitter. *The New Yorker* 19 February, 100.

Rashid, Ahmed (2010). *Taliban: The Power of Militant Islam in Afghanistan and Beyond*, rev. ed., London and New York: I.B. Tauris.

Rashīdī, al-Ḥājj Mawlavī Shīr Āghā (1387sh/2003). *Də Lōgar nōmiyālay ʿālimān*, Peshawar: Maktabat rawẕat al-qurʾān.

Rassler, Don (2015). Situating the Emergence of the *Islamic State* of Khurasan. *CTC Sentinel* 8(3), 7–11.

Rauf, Abdul (2005). The British Empire and the Mujāhidīn Movement in the N.W. F.P. of India, 1914–1934. *Islamic Studies* 44(3), 409–39.

Ray, Rajat K. (1985). Revolutionaries, Pan-Islamists and Bolsheviks: Maulana Abul Kalam Azad and the Political Underworld in Calcutta, 1905–1925. In *Communal and Pan-Islamic Trends in Colonial India*, ed. Mushirul Hasan, New Delhi: Manohar, pp. 101–24.

Reagan Library (2017a). President Reagan's Photo Opportunities in the Oval Office on June 16, 1986. *Youtube* (20 June). URL: www.youtube.com/watch?v=VaK_CZk-0Rg (accessed 24 February 2024).

(2017b). President Reagan's Remarks and Chairman Yunis Khalis Remarks Following a Meeting with Afghan Resistance Leaders and Members of Congress in the Roosevelt Room on November 13, 1987. *Youtube* (21 December). URL: www.youtube.com/watch?v=c9RWtx8myQc (accessed 24 February 2024).

Reetz, Dietrich (1995). *Hijrat – The Flight of the Faithful: A British File on the Exodus of Muslim Peasants from North India to Afghanistan in 1920*, Berlin: Das Arabische Buch.

Richter, William L. (1985). Pakistan in 1984: Digging In. *Asian Survey* 25(2), 145–54.

Riḍā, Muḥammad Rashīd (1297/1919). Dhat bayn al-Ḥijāz wa-Najd aw al-Khurma wa'l-wahhābiyya wa'l-mutadayyina. *al-Manār* 21(5), 226–34.

(1341/1922). al-Aḥkām al-sharʿiyya al-mutaʿalliqa bi'l-khilāfa al-islāmiyya. *al-Manār* 23(10), 729–52.

(1344/1925). Kalima fī fawāʾid kitābī al-Mughnī wa'l-Sharḥ al-kabīr. *Al-Manār* 26(4), 276–87.

Riexinger, Martin (2004). *Sanāʾullāh Amritsarī (1868–1948) und die Ahl-i-Ḥadīs* [sic] *im Punjab unter britischer Herrschaft*, Würzburg: Ergon.

"Rix̌tīn", Ṣiddīqallāh (1367sh/1988). *Də muhtamim ž̌vand*, Peshawar: Yūnivarsitī buk ējensī.

Riyāsat-i Dīr (1963). *Dastūr-i ʿamal-i Riyāsat-i Dīr tarmīm shudah-yi sāl 1963ʾ*, Dīr: no publisher.

"Riyāẕī", Muḥammad Yūsuf (n.d.). ʿAyn al-vaqāʾiʿ. In *Kulliyāt-i Riyāẕī*, n.p.: no publisher, pp. 58–267.

Rizvi, Saiyid Athar Abbas (1982). *Shāh 'Abd al-'Azīz* [sic]: *Puritanism, Sectarian* [sic], *Polemics and Jihād*, Canberra: Ma'rifat Publishing House.

Riẕvī, Sayyid Maḥbūb (1413–4/1992–3). *Tārīkh-i Dār al-ʿUlūm-i Dēoband*, 2nd ed., 2 vols., Deoband: Idārah-yi ihtimām-i Dār al-ʿulūm.

Robertson, Sir George Scott (1896). *The Káfirs of the Hindu-Kush*, London: Lawrence & Bullen.

Roggio, Bill (2010). Statement from Kunar-Based Salafi Group on joining Taliban. *Threat Matrix – A Blog of FDD's Long War Journal*, 10 January. URL: www.longwarjournal.org/archives/2010/01/statement_from_kunarbased_sala.php (accessed 24 February 2024).

Rohman, Izza (2012). Salafi Tafsirs [*sic*]: Textualist and Authoritarian? *Journal of Qur'ān and Ḥadīth Studies* 1(2), 197–213.

Rōshan Khān, Khān (1986). *Yūsufzaʾī qawm kī sar'guzasht*, Karachi: Rōshan Khān & Co.

Rōx̌ān, Bāyazīd (1396sh/2017). *Ṣirāṭ al-tawḥīd*, ed. Muḥammad Maʿṣūm Hōtak, Kandahar: ʿAllāmah Rashād khparandōyah ṫōlanah.

Rubin, Barnett R. (2002). *The Fragmentation of Afghanistan: State Formation and Collapse in the International System*, 2nd ed., New Haven, CT: Yale University Press.

al-Rustamī, al-Shaykh Abū Zakariyā ʿAbd al-Salām (1423/2002). *Tafsīr al-qurʾān al-karīm bi'l-lugha al-bashtū*, Riyadh: Dār al-salām.

(2009). *Inkār-i ḥadīs̱ sē inkār-i qurʾān tak*, Lahore: Dār al-salām.

(1428h[a]). *al-Khuṭbāt al-qurʾāniyya fi'l-uṣūl al-īmāniyya*, Peshawar: al-Jāmiʿa al-ʿarabiyya.

(1428h[b]). *Sīrat al-azm ʿan dasīsat sūshalizm wa-kumyūnizm aghná al-fawḍawiyya, al-shuyūʿiyya wa'l-ishtirākiyya*, 3rd ed., Peshawar: al-Jāmiʿa al-ʿarabiyya.

(1436/2015a). *al-Tibyān fī tafsīr umm al-qurʾān*, Peshawar: al-Jāmiʿa al-ʿarabiyya.

(1438/2017). *Badrat al-ṣalāt fī mustakhrajāt aḥādīth al-Mishkāt*, Peshawar: al-Jāmiʿa al-ʿarabiyya.

Ruttig, Thomas (2006). *Islamists, Leftists – and a Void in the Center: Afghanistan's Political Parties and Where They Came from*, Kabul: Afghanistan Office of the Konrad-Adenauer-Foundation.

(2009). Loya Paktia's Insurgency (I). The Haqqani Network as an Autonomous Entity. In *Decoding the New Taliban: Insights from the Afghan Field*, ed. Antonio Giustozzi, London: Hurst / New York: Columbia University Press, pp. 57–88.

(2010). Political Landscape: On Kunar's Salafi Insurgents. *Afghanistan Analyst Network*. URL: www.afghanistan-analysts.org/en/reports/war-and-peace/on-kunars-salafi-insurgents (accessed 28 August 2023).

(2015). *Afghan Taliban Contain Islamic State's Regional Reach. Oxford Analytica Daily Brief*, 17 November. URL: www.afghanistan-analysts.org/wp-content/uploads/2016/02/oxford-analytica-afghan-taliban-contain-islamic-states-regional-reach.pdf (accessed 24 February 2024).

Rzehak, Lutz (2018). Review of "Taliban Narratives: The Use and Power of Stories in the Afghanistan Conflict" by Thomas H. Johnson. *International Quarterly of Asian Studies* 49(1–2), 127–9.

Ṣābir, Muḥammad Shafī' (1986). *Tārīkh-i ṣūbah-yi sarḥadd*, Peshawar: Univarsitī buk ējansī.

(1990). *Tazkirah-yi sar'furūshān-i ṣūbah-i sarḥadd*, Peshawar: Univarsitī buk ējansī.

al-Ṣāfī, al-Duktūr Ḍiyā' al-Raḥmān ibn Jamīl al- Raḥmān (1441/2019). *Juhūd 'ulamā' al-ḥanafiyya fī'l-taḥdhīr al-bida' fī'l-'ibādāt*, 2 vols., al-Muḥammadiyya: Maktabat al-mīrāth al-nabawwī.

Ṣafiyallāh, Mullā (1305h). *Naẓm al-durar fī silk al-siyar*, ed. Muḥammad Mu'aẓẓam, Delhi: Maṭba'-i fārūqī.

Saharī, Dilāvar (1368sh/1989). *Jihād dar Kunar'hā*, Peshawar: Jaddūn prēss.

Ṣāḥib-i Islām (1421/2001). *Mughanim al-ḥuṣūl fī 'ilm al-uṣūl li-Ḥabīballāh ibn Fayẓallāh al-Qandahārī: dirāsatan wa-taḥqīqatan (min al-sunna 'ilá 'l-qiyās)*, unpublished PhD thesis, University of Peshawar.

Sahlins, Peter (1989). *Boundaries: The Making of France and Spain in the Pyrenees*, Berkeley, CA: University of California Press.

Salārzay, Abū 'Usmān (1436/2015). *Mawqif ḥarakat Ṭālibān al-bākistāniyya 'an khilāfat al-shaykh al-Baghdādī – ḥafiẓahu allāh – al-maz'ūma*, n.p.: Idārah 'Umar barā-yi nashr va ishā'at.

Saleh, Walid A. (2010). Ibn Taymiyya and the Rise of Radical Hermeneutics: An Analysis of An Introduction to the Foundations of Qur'ānic Exegesis. In *Ibn Taymiyya and his Times*, ed. Yossef Rapoport and Shahab Ahmed, Karachi: Oxford University Press, pp. 123–62.

(2020). The Place of the Medieval in Qur'an Commentary: A Survey of Recent Editions. In *Practices of Commentary*, ed. Christina Lechtermann and Markus Stock, Frankfurt am Main: Vittorio Klostermann, pp. 45–54.

Samī' al-Ḥaqq (n.d.). *Khuṭbāt-i ḥaqq*, ed. Mawlānā Muftī Mukhtārallāh Ḥaqqānī, Akōṛah Khaṫṫak: Mu'tamar al-muṣannifīn-i Dār al-'ulūm-i ḥaqqāniyyah.

ed. (2011a). *Mashāhīr bi-nām-i Shaykh al-Ḥadīs Mawlānā 'Abd al-Ḥaqq Ṣāḥib – raḥmatallāh 'alayh*, Akōṛah Khaṫṫak: Mu'tamar al-muṣannifīn-i Dār al-'ulūm-i ḥaqqāniyyah.

ed. (2011b). *Mashāhīr bi-nām-i Shaykh al-Ḥadīs Mawlānā Samī' al-Ḥaqq Ṣāḥib*, 6 vols., Akōṛah Khaṫṫak: Mu'tamar al-muṣannifīn-i Dār al-'ulūm-i ḥaqqāniyyah.

ed. (2015). *Khuṭbāt-i mashāhīr*, 11 vols., Akōṛah Khaṫṫak: Mu'tamar al-muṣannifīn-i Dār al-'ulūm-i ḥaqqāniyyah.

Sands, Chris, and Fazelminallah Qazizai (2019). *Night Letters: Gulbuddin Hekmatyar and the Afghan Islamists Who Changed the World*, London: Hurst.

Sanyal, Usha (1996). *Devotional Islam & Politics in British India: Ahmad Riza Khan Barelwi and His Movement, 1870–1920*, New Delhi: Oxford University Press.

"Sar'bāz-i Khalīfah" (1397sh/1439h). *Balah! Ṭālibān rā takfīr mīkunim bā dalīl va burhān az sharī'at-i rahmān*, n.p.: Maktabat al-muwaḥḥidīn.

Sarvānī, 'Abbās Khān (1964). *Tārīkh-i-Sher Shāhī* [sic], ed. Sayyid Muḥammad Imān al-Dīn, 2 vols., Dacca: University of Dacca.

Sayyāf, Ustād (ʿAbd Rabb al-Rasūl) (1366sh). *Də Kuvayt pah naṛəyvāl islāmī kanfrāns kē də ustād Sayyāf vīnā*, n.p.: Də Islāmī Ittiḥād maṭābiʿ.
Sayyāf, Ustād (ʿAbd Rabb al-Rasūl) (1370sh). *Majmūʿah-yi maqālāt-i ustād Sayyāf*, trans. ʿAbd al-Ḥaqq ʿAtīq, Kabul: Ittiḥād-i Islāmī-yi Afghānistān.
Sayyid Aḥmad (1395/1975). *Makātīb-i Sayyid Aḥmad-i shahīd*, ed. Sayyid Aḥmad-i shahīd akēḍimī, Lahore: Maktabah-yi rashīdiyyah.
Saʿīd, Ḥāfiẓ Muḥammad (1406/1986). Nifāẕ-i sharīʿat bill par Ahl-i Ḥadīs̱ kā mawqif jumlah-yi musalmān kē liʾē daʿvat-i ittiḥād. *Muḥāddis̱* 16(5), 2–6.
Schennach, Martin P. (2011). *Das Tiroler Landlibell von 1511: Zur Geschichte einer Urkunde*, Innsbruck: Wagner.
Schetter, Conrad (2002). The "Bazar Economy" of Afghanistan: A Comprehensive Approach. In *Afghanistan: A Country without a State?*, ed. Christine Noelle-Karimi, Conrad Schetter and Reinhard Schlagintweit, Frankfurt am Main: IKO-Verlag, pp. 109–27.
Schetter, Conrad, and Jörgen Klusmann, eds. (2011). *The Taliban-Komplex: Zwischen Aufstandsbewegung und Militäreinsatz*, Frankfurt am Main and New York: Campus.
Schimmel, Annemarie (1985). *And Muhammad Is His Messenger: The Veneration of the Prophet in Islamic Piety*, Chapel Hill, NC: The University of North Carolina Press.
Schmidt, Hans-Peter (1968). The Origins of *Ahiṃsā*. In *Mélanges d'indianisme: À la mémoire de Louis Renou*, Paris: Boccard, pp. 625–55.
Schober, Richard (1982). *Die Tiroler Frage auf der Friedenskonferenz von Saint Germain*, Innsbruck: Wagner.
Schulze, Reinhard (1981). *Der Aufstand der ägyptischen Fallahin 1919: Zum Konflikt zwischen der agrarisch-orientalischen Gesellschaft und dem kolonialen Staat in Ägypten 1820–1919*, Berlin: Baalbek.
(1990). *Islamischer Internationalismus im 20. Jahrhundert: Untersuchungen zur Geschichte der Islamischen Weltliga*, Leiden: Brill.
Schwartzberg, Joseph E., ed. (1992): *Historical Atlas of South Asia*, rev. ed., New York: Oxford University Press.
Scott, Richard B. (1980). *Tribal & Ethnic Groups in the Helmand Valley*. The Afghanistan Council Occasional Papers 21, New York: Afghanistan Council of The Asia Society.
Sedgwick, Mark (2004). In Search of a Counter-Reformation: Anti-Sufi Stereotypes and the Budshishiyya's Response. In *An Islamic Reformation?*, ed. Michaelle Browers and Charles Kurzman, Lanham, MD: Lexington Books, pp. 125–46.
(2015). Sufis as "Good Muslims": Sufism in the Battle against Jihadi Salafism. In *Sufis and Salafis in the Contemporary Age*, ed. Lloyd Ridgeon, London: Bloomsbury, pp. 105–17 and 249–53 (notes).
Sedition Committee (1918). *Report*, Calcutta: Superintendent Government Printing.
Semple, Michael (2014). *Rhetoric, Ideology, and Organizational Structure of the Taliban Movement*, Washington, D.C.: United States Institiute of Peace.

Senate of Pakistan (1988). *Decisions of the Chair (1985–1987)*, Islamabad: Parliament House.

(1991). *Directory of Members*, Islamabad: Parliament House.

al-Shāfiʿī, Muḥammad ibn Idrīs (1358/1939). *al-Risāla li'l-Imām al-muṭṭalibī*, ed. Aḥmad Muḥammad Shākir, Cairo: Maṭbaʿat al-maʿārif.

Shah, Gohar Ali (2013). Administration of Dir under Nawab Shah Jehan. *Pakistan Annual Research Journal* 49, 121–38.

Shah, Hassan (2019). *Voting Behaviour in Pakistan: An Analysis of Partisan and Floating Voters in [the] General Elections 2013 in Khyber Pakhtunkhwa*, unpublished PhD thesis, University of Peshawar.

Shāh'jahān Bēgam (1290h). *Tāj al-iqbāl yā tārīkh-i Bhōpal*, 3 vols., Kanpur: Maṭbaʿ-i niẓāmī.

Shāh Manṣūr, Muftī Abū Lubābah (1430–2/2009–11). *Dajjāl*, 3 vols., Karachi: al-Falāḥ.

Shah, Murad Ali (1983). *Maulana Ozair Gul: The Prisoner of Malta*, unpublished MA thesis, University of Peshawar.

Shah, Sayed Wiqar Ali (2015). *Ethnicity, Islam and Nationalism: Muslim Politics in the North-West Frontier Province (Khyber Pakhtunkhwa) 1937–1947*, Islamabad: National Institute of Historical and Cultural Research.

Shāhid, Sulaymān (2005). *Gumnām riyāsat: Dīr kē lākhōṇ maẓlūmōṇ kē nām*, Tīmargarah: Muḥammad Raḥmān bukḍīpō.

"Shāh'jī", Sayyid Muḥammad Yūsuf Shāh (1930). *Ḥalāt-i Mashvānī*, Lahore: Muḥammadī sṭīm prēss.

Shalmān, Faẕl-i Zamān (2016). *Mawlavī Faẕl Maḥmūd Makhfī*, Peshawar: ʿĀmir prinṭ ēnḍ pablisharz.

al-Shāmī, Abū Maysara (1438/2017). *Majmūʿ al-maqālāt Abī Maysara al-Shāmī – raḥmat allāh*, n.p.: Muʾassasat al-wafaʾ li-iʿlāmiyya.

Shāmzay, Muftī Niẓām al-Dīn (1424h). *Khuṭbāt-i Shāmzay*, ed. Mawlānā Quṭb al-Dīn "ʿĀbid", vol. ɪ, Karachi: Islāmī kutub'khānah.

(2000). *al-Itmām va 'l-akmāl fī ruʾyat al-hilāl*, Karachi: Majlis-i taʿāvun-i islāmī.

(1428/2007). *ʿAqīdah-yi ẓuhūr-i mahdī aḥādīs̱ kī rawshanī mēṇ*, Karachi: Maktabat Shāmzay.

(1433/2012). *Tuḥfah-yi dūlhā: izdavājī zindigī khūsh'gavār awr kāmiyāb banānē kē liʾē ēk bahtarīn kitāb*, Lahore: Bayt al-ʿilm ṭrasṭ.

Sharīʿatī, Shahīd ʿAlī (1356sh). *Khūd'sāzī-yi inqilābī*, Tehran: Ḥusayniyyah-yi irshād.

al-Shawkānī, Muḥammad ibn ʿAlī ibn Muḥammad (1408/1988). *Tuḥfat al-dhākirīn bi-ʿuddat al-ḥiṣn al-ḥaṣīn min kalām Sayyid al-murāsilīn*, Beirut: Muʾassasat al-kutub al-thaqāfiyya.

(1426/2005). *Nayl al-awṭār min asrār muntaqá al-akhbār*, ed. Abū Muʿādh Ṭāriq ibn ʿAwḍallāh, 7 vols., Riyadh: Dār Ibn Qayyim / Cairo: Dār Ibn ʿAffān.

(1428/2007). *Fatḥ al-qadīr: al-jāmiʿ bayna fannī al-riwāyat wa'l-dirrāya min ʿilm al-tafsīr*, ed. Yūsuf al-Ghūsh, Beirut: Dār al-maʿārifa.

al-Shaybānī, Muḥammad (2003). Afghānistān ... ḥaqīqat al-jihād wa-wāqiʿ al-irhāb. *Al-Riyāḍ* 30 December, 1.

Shiliwala, Wasim (2018). Constructing a Textual Tradition: Salafī Commentaries on *al-ʿAqīda al-ṭaḥāwiyya. Die Welt des Islams* 58(4), 461–503.

al-Shinqīṭī, Muḥammad Amīn ibn Muḥammad Mukhtār al-Janakī (1426 h). *Aḍwāʾ al-bayān fī īḍāḥ al-qurʾān biʾl-qurʾān*, ed. Bakr ibn ʿAbdallāh ibn Zayd, 8 vols., Mecca: Dār ʿilm al-fawāʾid.

Shinvārī, ʿAlī Muḥammad Mukhliṣ Kandahārī (1388sh/2009). *Ḥālʼnāmah-yi Miyā* [sic] *Rōx̌ān*, ed. Faẕl al-Raḥmān Fāẕil, Kabul: Vizārat-i iṭṭilāʿāt va farhang.

al-Shuʿaybī, Ḥamūd ibn ʿUqlāʾ(n.d.). *Sharḥ al-ʿAqīda al-ṭaḥāwiyya*, al-Raqqa: Maktabat al-raqīm.

SIGAR (Special Inspector General for Afghanistan Reconstruction) (2022). *Quarterly Report to the United States Congress*, January 30, Arlington, VA: SIGAR.

Sindhī, ʿUbaydallāh (1942). *Shāh Valiyallāh awr unkī siyāsī taḥrīk*, Lahore: Kitābʼkhānah-yi panjāb.

(1977). *Ilhām al-raḥmān fī tafsīr al-qurʾān*, ed. Muḥammad Muʿāviyah, Kabīrvālā: Idārah-yi bayt al-ḥikmah liʼl-imām Valiyallāh Dihlavī.

(2009). *Majmūʿah-yi tafāsīr-i Imām Sindhī*, ed. Bashīr Aḥmad Ludhiyānavī, Ghulām Muṣṭafá Qāsimī, Ghāzī Khudā Bakhsh and ʿAbdallāh Raḥīmābādī, Karachi: Ḥikmat-i qurʾān instiṭyūt.

Sirhindī, al-Shaykh Aḥmad (1397/1977). *Maktūbāt-i Imām-i rabbānī*, ed. Ḥusayn Ḥilmī ibn Saʿīd Istanbūlī, 3 vols., Istanbul: Işık Kitâbevi.

Sirrs, Owen L. (2017). *Pakistan's Inter-Services Intelligence Directorate: Covert Action and Internal Operations*, London and New York: Routledge.

Siyālkōṭī, Muḥammad Ibrāhīm Mīr (1995). *Tārīkh-i Ahl-i Ḥadīs̱*, reprint from 1932, New Delhi: al-Kitāb inṭarnēshnal.

Snider, L. Britt (2008). *The Agency and the Hill: CIA's Relationship with Congress, 1946–2004*, Washington, D.C.: Center for the Study of Intelligence at the CIA.

Spivak, Gayatri Cakravorty (1988). Can the Subaltern Speak? In *Marxism and the Interpretation of Culture*, ed. Cary Nelson and Lawrence Grossberg, Urbana, IL and Chicago, IL: University of Illinois Press, pp. 271–313.

Stanford, Edward (1897). *Stanford's Sketch Map of The North-Western Frontier of India*, London: Edward Stanford.

Steinberg, Guido (2002). *Religion und Staat in Saudi-Arabien: Die wahhabitischen Gelehrten, 1902–1953*, Würzburg: Ergon.

(2005). *Der nahe und der ferne Feind: Die Netzwerke des islamistischen Terrorismus*, Munich: Beck.

(2009). Jihadi-Salafism and the Shiʿis: Remarks about the Intellectual Roots of Anti-Shiʿism. In *Global Salafism: Islam's New Religious Movement*, ed. Roel Meijer, London: Hurst / New York: Columbia University Press, pp. 107–25.

Stenersen, Anne (2017). *Al-Qaida* [sic] *in Afghanistan*, Cambridge: Cambridge University Press.

Strand, Richard F. (2011). *The kom. Nûristan – Hidden Land of the Hindu-Kush.* URL: http://nuristan.info/Nuristani/Kamkata/Kom/kom.html (accessed 24 February 2024).

(2016). Nurestâni Languages. In *Encyclopædia Iranica: Online Edition*, ed. Ahmad Ashraf. URL: www.iranicaonline.org/articles/nurestani-languages (accessed 24 February 2024).

Strick van Linschoten, Alex, and Felix Kuehn, eds. (2012). *Poetry of the Taliban*, London: Hurst / New York: Columbia University Press / New Delhi: Hachette India / Karachi: Oxford University Press.

eds. (2018). *The Taliban Reader: War, Islam and Politics*, London: Hurst / New York: Oxford University Press.

Sultan-i-Rome (1994). The Sartōr Faqir: Life and Struggle against British Imperialism. *Journal of the Pakistan Historical Society* 42(1), 93–105.

(2008). *Swat State (1915–1969), from Genesis to Merger: An Analysis of Political, Administrative, Socio-Political, and Economic Developments*, Oxford: Oxford University Press.

(2012). Tahrik Nifaz-e-Shariat-e-Muhammadi and Democracy: TNSM's Critique of Democracy. *Pakistan Vision* 13(2), 109–44.

Sumbre, German, Y., Gutfreund, G. Fiorito, T. Flash, and B. Hochner (2001). Control of Octopus Arm Extension by a Peripheral Motor Program. *Science* 293, 1 845–48.

Sunarwoto (2016). Salafi *Dakwah* Radio: A Contest for Religious Authority. *Archipel* 91, 203–30.

(2020). Negotiating Salafī Islam and the State: The *Madkhaliyya* in Indonesia. *Die Welt des Islams* 60(2–3), 205–34.

al-Sūrī, Abū Muṣʿab (1419/1998). *Afghānistān wa'l-Ṭālibān wa-maʿrikat al-islām al-yawm*, Kabul: Markaz al-ghurabaʾ.

(1420/1999). *al-Muslimūn fī wasaṭ āsiyā wa-maʿrakat al-islām al-muqbila*, Kabul: Markaz al-ghurabāʾ.

(1436/2015). *al-Liqāʾ al-ṣawtī maʿa ṣaḥīfat al-Raʾī al-ʿāmm al-kuwaytiyya*, n.p.: Muʾassasat al-taḥāyā.

(1438/2018). *Daʿwat al-muqāwama al-islāmiyya al-ʿālamiyya: al-nuskha al-kāmila al-farīda al-munaqqaḥa al-muḥaqqaqa*, ed. Abū 'l-ʿAbbās al-Qalamūnī, n.p.: Maktabat al-jīl al-thālith.

Survey of Pakistan (1968). *D.I. Khān & Peshāwar Divisions, Amb, Chitrāl, Dīr and Swāt*, Rawalpindi: The Survey of Pākistān Offices.

Swami, Praveen (2001). Masood Azhar, in His Own Words. *Frontline* 18(21), 19.

"Syāl" Mōmand, M. J. (1365sh/1986). *Də Źīnō paxtanō qabīlō rivāyātī nasabī shajarē*, Peshawar: Yūnīvarsitī buk ējansī.

Syan, Hardip Singh (2013). *Sikh Militancy in the Seventeenth Century: Religious Violence in Mughal and Early Modern India*, London and New York: I.B. Tauris.

al-Ṭabarī, Abū Jaʿfar Muḥammad ibn Jarīr (1426/2005). *Taʾrīkh al-Ṭabarī: taʾrīkh al-umam wa'l-mulūk*, ed. Nawāf al-Jarrāḥ, 2nd ed., 6 vols., Beirut: Dār Ṣādir.

al-Tabrīzī, al-Khaṭīb (1399/1979). *Mishkāt al-maṣābīḥ*, ed. Nāṣir al-Dīn al-Albānī, 2nd ed., 3 vols., Beirut: Maktab al-islāmī.

Taeschner, Franz (1979). *Zünfte und Bruderschaften im Islam: Texte zur Geschichte der Futuwwa*, Zurich: Artemis.

al-Taftāzānī, Saʿd al-Dīn (1408/1988). *Sharḥ ʿaqāʾid al-nasafiyya*, ed. Dr Aḥmad Ḥijāzī Saqqā, Cairo: Maktabat al-kulliyāt al-azhariyya.

al-Ṭaḥāwī, Abū Jaʿfar Aḥmad ibn Muḥammad (1370h). *Mukhtaṣar al-Ṭaḥāwī*, ed. Abū Wafāʾ al-Afghānī, Hyderabad: Lajnat iḥyāʾ al-maʿārif al-nuʿmāniyya.

Ṭalāyī, ʿAbd al-Kabīr (1390sh). *Khāliṣ Bābā qadam pah qadam*, Islamabad: Də Iḥsān khparandōyah ṫōlanah.

Ṭālib al-Raḥmān (1995). *Tablīghī Jamāʿat kā islām*, Lahore: Idārah-yi iḥyā-yi sunnah-i Garjākh.

Tankel, Stephen (2013). *Storming the World Stage: The Story of Lashkar-e-Taiba* [sic], London: Hurst / New York: Oxford University Press.

Tapper, Nancy (1973). The Advent of Pashtūn *Māldārs* in North-Western Afghanistan. *Bulletin of the School of Oriental and African Studies* 36(1), 55–79.

(1991). *Bartered Brides: Politics, Gender and Marriage in an Afghan Tribal Society*, Cambridge: Cambridge University Press.

al-Ṭarṭūsī, Abū Baṣīr (1430/2009). al-Ḥiwār al-kāmil maʿa jarīdat "al-Sabīl" al-urduniyya al-shāmil lamā qad tamma ḥadhfihi min qibal al-jarīda. *al-Sabīl* 16(196) (18 Rajab / 11 July). URL: www.abubaseer.bizland.com/refutation/read/f95.doc (accessed 28 August 2023).

Tariq, Muhammad (2018). *Religio-political Movements in the North West* [sic] *Frontier Province: A Case Study of Jamiat-ul-Ulama-i-Sarhad* [sic] *(1920–1947)*, unpublished PhD thesis, University of Peshawar.

Tarzi, Amin (2017). *Tarikh-i Ahmad Shahi: The First History of "Afghanistan"*. In *Afghan History through Afghan Eyes*, ed. Nile Green, Karachi: Oxford University Press, pp. 79–96 and 281–7 (notes).

Tayob, Shaheed (2017). *Islam as a Lived Tradition: Ethical Constellations of Muslim Food Practices in Mumbai / Een verklaring van Islam als een levende traditie: Ethische constellaties van Moslim voedsel praktijken in Mumbai*, unpublished PhD thesis, University of Utrecht.

Ṭayyib, Mawlānā Qārī Muḥammad (1407/1988). *ʿUlamāʾ-i Dēoband kā dīnī ruḥ awr maslakī mizāj*, Lahore: Idārah-yi islāmiyyāt.

ter Haar, Johan G. J. (1992). *Follower and Heir of the Prophet: Shaykh Aḥmad Sirhindī (1564–1624) and His Followers*, Leiden: Het Oosters Instituut.

Thomä, Dieter (2016). *Puer robustus: Eine Philosophie des Störenfrieds*, Frankfurt am Main: Suhrkamp.

Torres-Soriano, Manuel R. (2012). Between the Pen and the Sword: The Global Islamic Media Front in the West. *Terrorism and Political Violence* 24(5), 769–86.

Trausch, Tilmann, ed. (2019). *Norm, Normabweichung und Praxis des Herrschaftsübergangs in transkultureller Perspektive*, Göttingen: V&R unipress.

Trefzer, Annette, Jeffrey T. Jackson, Kathryn McKee, and Kirsten Dellinger (2014). Introduction: The Global South and / in the Global North. Interdisciplinary Investigations. *The Global South* 8(2), 1–15.

Troll, Christian W., SJ (1978). *Sayyid Ahmad Khan: A Reinterpretation of Muslim Theology*, New Delhi: Vikas.

Trousdale, William B. (2021). *Kandahar in the Nineteenth Century*, Leiden and Boston, MA: Brill.

Turkmān, Iskandar Bayg (1382sh). *Tārīkh-i ʿālam'ārā-yi ʿabbāsī*, ed. Irāj Afshār, 2 vols., Tehran: Muʾassassah-yi intishārāt-i Amīr-i Kabīr.

Uddin, Layli (2016). *In The Land of Eternal Eid: Maulana Bhashani and the Political Mobilisation of Peasants and Lower-Class Urban Workers in East Pakistan, c. 1930s–1971*, unpublished PhD thesis, Royal Holloway, University of London.

Ünal, Yusuf (2016). Sayyid Quṭb in Iran: Translating the Islamist Ideologue in the Islamic Republic. *Journal of Islamic and Muslim Studies* 1(2), 35–60.

UNHCR, ed. (1989). *Background Report: Kunar Province*, Islamabad: UNHCR.

UNODC (1958). 1958/689(XXVI)H. Prohibition of Opium Production in Afghanistan. URL: www.unodc.org/unodc/en/Resolutions/resolution_1958-07-28_9.html (accessed 24 February 2024).

USCIA (United States Central Intelligence Agency) (1980). *Afghanistan*, Washington, D.C.: Central Intelligence Agency. URL: www.loc.gov/item/81692539 (accessed 24 February 2024).

(2010): *Afghanistan–Pakistan: Northern Border*, Washington, D.C.: Central Intelligence Agency. URL: www.loc.gov/item/2010594050 (accessed 24 February 2024).

ʿUs̱mān, Jamāl ʿAbdallāh, ed. (2014). *ʿAzīz-i jahāṇ: Qāẓī Ḥusayn Aḥmad – rḥ*, Islamabad: Idārah-yi fikr va ʿamal.

ʿUs̱mānī, Shabbīr Aḥmad (1428/2007). *Tafsīr-i ʿUs̱mānī maʿa iẓāfah-yi tafsīrī ʿanvānāt*, 3 vols., Karachi: Dār al-ishāʿat.

ʿUs̱mānī, Ẓafar Aḥmad, and ʿAbd al-Karīm Gamthalavī (1400h). *Imdād al-aḥkām: Imdād al-fatāvá kē takmilah jō sannah 1340 h kē baʿd kē taqrīban savā dō hazār fatāvá par mushtamil hē*, ed. Maḥmūd Ashraf ʿUs̱mānī and Rafīʿallāh ʿUs̱mānī, 4 vols., Sahāranpūr: Zakariyyā bukḍipō.

al-ʿUyayrī, Yūsuf ibn Ṣāliḥ (1422h). *al-Mīzān li-ḥarakat Ṭālibān*, n.p.: no publisher.

van Bruinessen, Martin (1992). *Agha, Shaikh and State: The Social and Political Structures of Kurdistan*, London: Zed Books.

van der Schriek, Daan (2005). Nuristan: Insurgent Hideout in Afghanistan. *Terrorism Monitor* 3(10). URL: http://jamestown.org/program/nuristan-insurgent-hideout-in-afghanistan (accessed 24 February 2024).

van Ess, Josef (1986). Kritisches zum *Fiqh akbar*. *Revue des Études Islamiques* 54, 327–38.

(2011). *Der Eine und das Andere: Beobachtungen an islamischen häresiographischen Texten*, 2 vols., Berlin and New York: de Gruyter.

Vazīr Khān, Navvāb Muḥammad (1428/2007). *Vaqā'i'-i aḥmadī*, ed. Sayyid Nafīs al-Ḥasanī, Lahore: Sayyid Aḥmad-i shahīd akēḋimī.

von Kügelgen, Anke (2002). *Die Legitimierung der mittelasiatischen Mangitendynastie in den Werken ihrer Historiker (18.–19. Jahrhundert)*, Istanbul and Würzburg: Ergon.

(2005). Ibn Tayīmyas Kritik an der aristotelischen Logik und sein Gegenentwurf. In *Logik und Theologie: Das Organon im arabischen und im lateinischen Mittelalter*, ed. Dominik Perler and Ulrich Rudolph, Leiden and Boston, MA: Brill, pp. 167–221.

von Moos, Iren (1996). *Nun hausen Schlangen in den Aprikosengärten: Eine Ethnologin berichtet aus Afghanistan*, ed. Jakob Tanner, Wuppertal: Hammer.

al-Wādi'ī, Abū 'Abd al-Raḥmān Muqbil (1421/2000). *Maqtal al-Shaykh Jamīl al-Raḥmān al-Afghānī wa-ma'ah (ḥawla kalamat al-wahhābī)*, 2nd ed., Ṣan'ā': Dār al-ashār.

Wagemakers, Joas (2009). The Transformation of a Radical Concept: *al-wala' wa-l-bara'* in the Ideology of Abu Muhammad al-Maqdisi. In *Global Salafism: Islam's New Religious Movement*, ed. Roel Meijer, London: Hurst / New York: Columbia University Press, pp. 81–106.

(2011). An Inquiry into Ignorance: A Jihādī–Salafī Debate on *jahl* as an Obstacle to *takfīr*. In *The Transmissions and Dynamics of the Textual Sources of Islam: Essays in Honour of Harald Motzki*, ed. Nicolet Boekhoff-van der Voort, Kees Versteegh and Joas Wagemakers, Leiden and Boston, MA: Brill, pp. 301–27.

(2012). *A Quietist Jihadi: The Ideology and Influence of Abu Muhammad al-Maqdisi*, Cambridge: Cambridge University Press.

(2015). The Concept of *bay'a* in the *Islamic State*'s Ideology. *Perspectives on Terrorism* 9(4), 98–106.

(2016). *Salafism in Jordan: Political Islam in a Quietist Community*, Cambridge: Cambridge University Press.

Waller, Altina L. (1988). *Feud: Hatfields, McCoys, and Social Change in Appalachia, 1860–1900*, Chapel Hill, NC and London: The University of North Carolina Press.

Warburton, Col. Robert (1900). *Eighteen Years in the Khyber, 1879–1898*, London: John Murray.

Wardak, Ali (2002). Jirga: Power and Traditional Conflict Resolution in Afghanistan. In *Law after Ground Zero*, ed. John Strawson, London: GlassHouse Press, pp. 187–204.

Warren, Alan (2000). *Waziristan, the Faqir of Ipi and the Indian Army: The North-West Frontier Revolt of 1936–37*, Oxford: Oxford University Press.

Weber, Eugen (1976). *Peasants into Frenchmen: The Modernization of Rural France, 1870–1914*, Stanford, CA: Stanford University Press.

Weber, Max (1950). *The Protestant Ethic and the Spirit of Capitalism* (1905), trans. Talcott Parsons, 3rd ed., New York: Charles Scribner's Sons / London: Allen & Unwin.

(1972). *Wirtschaft und Gesellschaft: Grundriß der verstehenden Soziologie*, ed. Johannes Winckelmann, 5th ed., Tübingen: Mohr.

Wieland-Karimi, Almut (1998). *Islamische Mystik in Afghanistan: Die strukturelle Einbindung der Sufik in die Gesellschaft*, Stuttgart: Steiner.

Wiktorowicz, Quintan (2006). Anatomy of the Salafi Movement. *Studies in Conflict & Terrorism* 29, 207–39.

Wirth, Louis (1938). Urbanism as a Way of Life. *American Journal of Sociology* 44(1), 1–24.

Wolfrum, Rüdiger, and Christiane E. Philipp (2002). The Status of the Taliban: Their Obligations and Rights under International Law. *Max Planck Yearbook of United Nations Law* 6, 559–601.

Wright, Lawrence (2006). *The Looming Tower: Al-Qaeda's Road to 9/11*, London: Allen Lane (Penguin).

Yaqubi, Himayatullah (2010). Conservative Sufism in the Pakhtun Borderland: Bayazid Ansari and [the] Roushaniya Movement. *Journal of South Asian and Middle Eastern Studies* 33(4), 61–86.

Yaʿqūb Khān, Muḥammad (2009). *Taḥrīk-i islāmī (ẓilaʿ Dīr) apnī kārkunōṇ kī naẓr mēṇ*, Tīmargarah: Ilyās prēss.

Yasmeen, Samina (2017). *Jihad and Dawah: Evolving Narratives of Lashkar-e-Taiba and Jamat ud Dawah* [sic], London: Hurst / New York: Oxford University Press.

Yekutiel, Yoram, German Sumbre, Tamar Flash, and Binyamin Hochner (2002). How to Move with No Rigid Skeleton? The Octopus Has the Answers? *Biologist* 49(6), 250–4.

Yousaf, Mohammad, and Mark Adkin (1992). *The Bear Trap: Afghanistan's Untold Story*, Lahore: Jang.

Yousafzai, Malala, with Christina Lamb (2013). *I Am Malala: The Girl Who Stood Up for Education and Was Shot by the Taliban*, London: Weidenfeld & Nicholson.

Youssef, Nancy A. (2013). Where's Pentagon "Terrorism Suspect"? Talking to Karzai. *McClatchy Newspapers* (7 July 2009, rev. 18 September). URL: www.mcclatchydc.com/news/politics-government/article24545041.html (accessed 24 February 2024).

Yü, Dan Smyer, and Jean Micheaud, eds. (2018). *Trans-Himalayan Borderlands: Livelihoods, Territorialities, Modernities*, Amsterdam: Amsterdam University Press.

Yūsufī, Allāhbakhsh (1960). *Yūsufzāʾī, yaʿnī tārīkh-i ʿilāqah-yi ẓilaʿ Mardān, Malākand, Svāt, Būnēr* [sic], *Dīr, Bājawṛ va ghayrah*, Karachi: Muḥammad ʿAlī ējūkeshnal sosāʾitī.

Yūsufzay, Jamīl (2012). Akhūnd Ćāllāk ćōk vu? *Paẍtō* 47(2), 221–30

Yunas, S. Fida (1998). *Afghanistan: Organization of the Peoples Democratic Party of Afghanistan/Watan Party, Governments and Biographical Sketches (1982–1998)*, 2 vols., Peshawar: self-published.

Zachariah, Benjamin (2005). *Developing India: A Social and Intellectual History, c. 1930–1950*, Delhi: Oxford University Press.

Zaeef, Abdul Salam (2010). *My Life with the Taliban*, ed. Alex Strick van Linschoten and Felix Kuehn, London: Hurst / New York: Columbia University Press.

Ẓafīr al-Dīn, Mawlānā Muḥammad, ed. (2002). *Fatāvá-yi Dār al-ʿulūm Dēoband*, 13 vols., Karachi: Dār al-ishāʿat.

Zahid, Farhat (2015). A Profile of Omar Khalid Khurasani: Emir of Jamaatal [*sic*] Ahrar. URL: www.researchgate.net/publication/294581560_A_Profile_of_Omar_Khalid_Khurasani_Emir_of_Jamaatal_Ahrar (accessed 24 February 2024).

al-Ẓāhirī, Abū Muḥammad ibn ʿAlī, a.k.a. Ibn Ḥazm (1416/1996). *al-Faṣl al-milal wa'l-ahwāʾ wa'l-niḥal*, ed. Dr Muḥammad Ibrāhīm Naṣr and Dr ʿAbd al-Raḥmān ʿAmayra, 3rd ed., Beirut: Dār al-jīl.

Ẓaʿīf, Mullā ʿAbd al-Salām (1390sh). *Də banstīzō stūnzō də ḥall larī*, Lahore: Mustaqbal khparandōyah ṫōlanah.

(1396sh/2018). *Ṭālibān lah Kandahārah tar Mazārah*, Kabul: Aksōs.

Zakharia, Katia (1999). Uways al-Qaranī, visages d'une légende. *Arabica* 46(2), 230–58.

Zalaf, Ahmed Abou El (2022). The Special Apparatus (al-Niẓām al-Khāṣṣ): The Rise of Nationalist Militancy in the Ranks of the Egyptian Muslim Brotherhood. *Religions* 13(1), 77. URL: www.mdpi.com/2077-1444/13/1/77/htm (accessed 24 February 2024).

Źalmay, Muḥammad Valī (1346sh). *Mujāhid afghān: Mawləynā Ḥājjī ʿAbd al-Rāziq*, Kabul: Maṭbaʿah dawlatī.

(1349sh). *Də Kandahār mashāhīr: ṣūfiyān, ʿārifān, mazārāt*, n.d.: no publisher.

(1368sh). *Zmūǵ ghāziyān*, Kabul: Də Afghānistān də ʿulūmō akādimī.

Zaman, Muhammad Qasim (1998). Sectarianism in Pakistan: The Radicalization of Shii and Sunni Identities. *Modern Asian Studies* 32(3), 689–716.

(2002). *The Ulama in Contemporary Islam: Custodians of Change*, Princeton, NJ: Princeton University Press.

(2007). *Ashraf ʿAli Thanawi: Islam in Modern South Asia*, Oxford: Oneworld.

(2012). *Modern Islamic Thought in a Radical Age: Religious Authority and Internal Criticism*, Cambridge: Cambridge University Press.

al-Zarqāwī, Abū Muṣʿab (1427/2006). *al-Arshīf al-jāmiʿ li-kalimāt wa-khuṭubāt asad al-islām al-shaykh Abū Muṣʿab al-Zarqāwī (raḥimahu allāh), ka-mā nushirat wa'l-tartīb al-zamanī*, n.p.: Shabakat al-burāq al-islāmiyya.

al-Ẓawāhirī, Ayman (1423/2002). *al-Walāʾ wa'l-barāʾ – ʿaqīda manqūla wa-wāqiʿ al-mafqūd*, n.p.: al-Saḥāb.

(1426/2005). *Ḥiṣād al-murr: al-Ikhwān al-Muslimūn fī sittīn ʿāman*, 2nd ed., n.p.: al-Saḥāb.

(1431/2010). *al-Fursān taḥta rāyat al-nabī – ṣallá 'llāh ʿalayhi wa-sallam*, 2nd ed., n.p.: al-Saḥāb.

(n.d.). *Risāla fī tabrīʾa ummat al-qalam wa'l-sayf min manqaṣat tuhmat al-khawar wa'l-ḍaʿf*, n.p.: al-Saḥāb.

Zaydan, Ahmad Muwaffaq (1999). *The Afghan Arabs Media at Jihad*, Islamabad: The Pakistan Futuristics Foundation & Institute.

al-Zayyāt, Muntaṣir (2005). *al-Jamāʿa al-Islāmiyya ruʾya min al-dākhil*, Cairo: Dār miṣr al-maḥrūsa.

Zelin, Aaron Y. (2013). *The State of Global Jihad Online: A Qualitative, Quantitative and Cross-Lingual Analysis*, Washington, D.C.: New America Foundation. URL: www.washingtoninstitute.org/media/3122 (accessed 24 February 2024).

Ziad, Waleed (2017). *Traversing the Indus and the Oxus: Trans-regional Islamic Revival in the Age of Political Fragmentation and the 'Great Game' 1747–1880*, unpublished PhD thesis, Yale University.

Periodicals

AFGHANews (Kabul)
Afghān Jihād (Islamabad; IIAA)
Ahl-i Ḥadīs̱ (Lahore)
Akhbār al-ʿĀlam al-Islāmī (Mecca; RAI)
Aligarh Institute Gazette (Aligarh; *Scientific Society of Aligarh*; 1866–97)
Amān-i Afghān (Kabul)
al-Balāgh (Karachi; *Dār al-ʿUlūm Kārāchī*)
al-Bunyān (Peshawar; IIAA)
al-Bunyān al-Marṣūṣ (Peshawar; IIAA)
Ćrak (Kabul, later online publication; IEA)
Dābiq (online publication; IS)
al-Daʿvah [Pashto] (Peshawar; JDQS)
Daʿvat [Pashto] (Peshawar; JDQS)
Daʿvat [Urdu] (Peshawar; JDQS)
al-Ḥaqq (Akōṛah Khaṫṫak; *Dār al-ʿUlūm-i Ḥaqqāniyyah*)
Ḥaqq Pāćūn (Peshawar; IIAA)
Ḥiṭṭīn (online publication; JQSQH)
Iḥyā-yi Khilāfat (online publication; TṬP)
al-Imāra al-Islāmiyya (Kandahar; ṬIT / IEA)
al-Jihād (Peshawar; MKh)
Khilāfat (Kandahar; ṬIT / IEA)
Khuddām al-Furqān (Peshawar and Tehran; ḤII, later ḤII[N])
Lashkar-i Khurāsān (online publication; IMU)
Maḥāẕ [Urdu] (Peshawar; MMIA)
Maḥāẕ [Pashto/Farsi] (Peshawar; MMIA)
Majallah-yi Taḥrīk-i Ṭālibān-i Pākistān (online publication; TṬP)
Majallat al-Mujāhidīn al-Tiqanī (online publication)
Manbaʿ al-Jihād [Pashto] (Peshawar; MʿUJM)
Manbaʿ al-Jihād [Arabic] (Peshawar; MʿUJM)
Mīs̱āq-i Khūn (Peshawar; JIA)

Mōrchal (Kabul, later online publication; IEA)
Muḥaddis̱ (Lahore)
al-Mujāhid (Peshawar; JDQS)
al-Murābiṭūn (Peshawar; JIM)
al-Nabāʾ (online publication; IS)
Navā-yi Afghān Jihād (online publication, since April 2020 continued as *Navā-yi Ghazvah-yi Hind*; JQSQH)
Nuṣrat al-Jihād (Peshawar; MʿUJM)
Payām-i Ḥaqq (Kabul)
al-Quds al-ʿArabī (London)
Rasmī Jarīdah-yi Afghānistān (Kabul)
Ṣawt al-Umma (Cairo)
Shafaq (Peshawar; ḤiI-Ḥ)
Shahāmat (Kandahar, later online publication; IEA)
al-Sharq al-Awsaṭ (London)
al-Ṣumūd (Kandahar, later online publication; IEA)
Tōrah Bōṛah (Jalalabad, later online publication; TBJM)

INDEXES

(*Note*: The bracketed lower-case roman numerals that precede cross-references indicate the number of the respective index in which the cross-referenced entry is to be found.)

(i) Persons and Works

(ii) Organizations

(iii) Ideational Currents

(iv) Polities and Dynasties

(v) Institutions

(vi) Localities

(vii) Ethnic and Religious Communities

(viii) Subjects

www.ingramcontent.com/pod-product-compliance
Lightning Source LLC
LaVergne TN
LVHW011007250326
834688LV00004B/121
* 9 7 8 1 0 0 9 2 8 9 2 7 6 *